LAW FLIX

At the end of most chapters you can find a reference to a Hollywood film, one that could be used to study and understand the concepts presented in the chapter. For example, what better film for understanding insurance law than Billy Wilder's *Double Indemnity*? And you can find a clip on insurable interest in West's Digital Video Library (**http://wdvl.westbuslaw.com**). Or you can assign the students the enviable task of watching the movie and determining the insurance law issues. Or, for contract formation you can watch another clip from *Midnight Run* and witness the great Robert DeNiro playing a bounty hunter who is trying to negotiate a binding contract with a bailbondsman. There is offer, counteroffer, statute of frauds, and good fun all in a short clip to get the students involved and thinking.

(LAWFLIX)

Midnight Run (1988) (R)

Is the contract Robert DeNiro has for bringing in Charles Grodin, an embezzler, legal? Discuss the issues of consideration and ethics as the bail bondsman puts another bounty hunter on the case and DeNiro flees from law enforcement agents in order to collect his fee. And finally, discuss the legality of DeNiro's acceptance of money from Grodin and his release of Grodin at the end of the movie.

For movie clips that illustrate business law concepts, see LawFlix at **http://wdvl.westbuslaw.com.**

ANDERSON'S
BUSINESS LAW

[*And The Legal Environment*]

STANDARD VOLUME

20e

ANDERSON'S
BUSINESS LAW
[*And The Legal Environment*]

STANDARD VOLUME

20 e

DAVID P. TWOMEY

Professor of Law
Carroll School of Management
Boston College
Member of the Massachusetts and Florida Bars

MARIANNE MOODY JENNINGS

Professor of Legal and Ethical Studies
W. P. Carey School of Business
Arizona State University
Member of the Arizona Bar

THOMSON

WEST

Australia · Brazil · Canada · Mexico · Singapore · Spain · United Kingdom · United States

Anderson's Business Law and the Legal Environment, Standard Volume, 20e
David P. Twomey, Marianne Moody Jennings

VP/Editorial Director:
Jack W. Calhoun

Publisher:
Rob Dewey

Acquisitions Editor:
Steven H. Silverstein, Esq.

Senior Developmental Editor:
Bob Sandman

Executive Marketing Manager:
Lisa L. Lysne

Content Project Manager:
Colleen A. Farmer

Technology Project Manager:
Pam Wallace

Manufacturing Coordinator:
Charlene Taylor

Production House:
LEAP Publishing Services, Inc.

Compositor:
ICC Macmillan Inc.

Printer:
Quebecor World
Versailles, KY

Art Director:
Michelle Kunkler

Internal Designer:
Design Matters
Nick and Diane Gliebe

Cover Designer:
Design Matters
Nick and Diane Gliebe

Cover Images:
© Jeremy Walker/The Image
Bank/Getty Images

Part Opener Image:
© DC Productions/Getty Images, Inc.

Chapter Opener Image:
© Akira Kaede/Getty Images, Inc.

Library of Congress Control Number:
2006940535

For more information about our
product, contact us at:

Thomson Learning
Academic Resource Center
1-800-423-0563

Thomson Higher Education
5191 Natorp Boulevard
Mason, Ohio 45040
USA

In memory of our dear friend,

Ivan Fox

Professor of Law

Pace University

BRIEF CONTENTS

CONTENTS

PART 2

CONTRACTS

PART 4

NEGOTIABLE INSTRUMENTS

PART 5

DEBTOR-CREDITOR RELATIONSHIPS

PREFACE

Regardless of the day of the week, newspapers and magazines constantly carry stories about law and business together. The chairwoman of the Hewlett-Packard (HP) board admitted that the board hired private investigators to obtain the phone records of HP board members because she felt there was a "snitch" among them. The private investigators used "pretexting," the act of pretending to be the directors themselves to get the records. HP is under state and federal investigation, executives were subpoenaed by Congress, and some were indicted. BP, the international energy company, is dealing with a burst pipeline and the damage to Alaska, an accident that followed years of warning about corrosion in BP pipes near Prudhoe Bay, Alaska. Fannie Mae, the federal mortgage company, was forced to remove its CEO and make a $7 billion restatement on its financials after auditors uncovered earnings manipulation. And all of these events are years after we witnessed the financial collapses of Enron, WorldCom, HealthSouth, and too many others.

Why, we even lost Martha Stewart to a five-month prison sentence for her lies to prosecutors about how she managed to sell her shares of ImClone stock just before the company announced some problems with its new key drug. Martha Stewart has done much for our homes and cooking, but her case can teach us much more, about obstruction of justice, regulatory consent decrees, jury *voir dire* and selection, appellate courts, and reversible error. Martha Stewart's legal difficulties presented a richness of legal issues each step of the way. What happened when she sold those shares? Did she indeed violate the law? Was it insider trading? What are the shareholders' rights? What about the creditors?

And there are so many other companies, here in the United States and around the world. Did Tyco, Adelphia, and Parmalat corporate officers intentionally overstate earnings? If so, are they criminally liable? And who is responsible for crimes committed by companies? As major corporations have continued to experience major criminal, legal, and ethical difficulties, we can see how important it is for business managers to understand the law and the foundations of ethics. When a manager has a void in knowledge on law and ethics, running a company can be tricky business. Microsoft Corporation learned the intricacies of federal antitrust laws while its charges of monopolization were tried in federal court. Wall Street analysts learned that internal e-mails are discoverable and admissible as evidence. And when those e-mails to co-workers and friends are inconsistent with public statements those analysts made about companies and the value of their stocks, the resulting embarrassment is the least of their worries. The analysts' companies learned the harsh (and pricey!) lesson about e-mails and the law: incurring nearly $1 billion in fines.

When an entrepreneur is struggling with the decision of whether to incorporate or create an LLC, or the shareholders of Disney are grappling with issues about their rights when their CEO makes a bad decision, the law is there. No business or manager can hope to succeed without an understanding of the laws and legal environment of business. Students in business must be equipped with both knowledge of the law and the skill of applying it in the business setting. We learn principles and application through interaction with examples and by working our way through dilemmas, issues, and problems. This edition of *Anderson's Business Law and the Legal Environment* enhances the learning process while still providing a detailed and rigorous case approach.

 ## FEATURES OF THE TEXT

The features of this text make the business and law connection easily understood and offer students clarity for grasping the often challenging complexities of law. The features are summarized in the following sections, which offer an overview of this edition.

SPORTS AND ENTERTAINMENT LAW—NEW!

New to this edition is a feature that is sure to engage students. Using pop culture, the book teaches students about law and ethics. Kate Moss lost an endorsement contract after a video surfaced in which she was shown to be using cocaine. Can contracts be terminated because of public behavior? Martha Stewart gave a highly recognizable face to the phrase "obstruction of justice." Was the clause in John Lennon's will, one that said anyone who contested the will lost his or her inheritance, valid? And what about baseball fans who lease space on rooftops to watch baseball games in stadiums across the way? And all without paying? What are their rights? What are the rights of the teams and stadium owners? And what happens when the yacht company that sold Tiger Woods his yacht uses Tiger's names in its ads and without his permission? Students have the chance to explore the law through these examples of sports figures' and entertainers' brushes with the law.

LAW FLIX—NEW!

At the end of most chapters you can find a reference to a Hollywood film, one that could be used to study and understand the concepts presented in the chapter. For example, what better film for understanding insurance law than Billy Wilder's *Double Indemnity*? And you can find a clip on insurable interest from that film in West's Digital Video Library (**http://wdvl.westbuslaw.com**). Or you can assign the students the enviable task of watching the movie and determining the insurance law issues. Or, for contract formation, you can watch another clip from *Midnight Run* and witness the great Robert DeNiro playing a bounty hunter who is trying to negotiate a binding contract with a bail-bondsman. There is offer, counteroffer, statute of frauds, and good fun all in a short clip to get the students involved and thinking.

CLARITY

The writing style has been evolving, and once again, we have changed those passages that fell victim to the passive voice. The writing is clear and lively. The examples are student-friendly, and the discussions of law are grounded in the book's strong connection to business. The principles of law are taught in the language and examples of business. Students can relate to the examples, which provide memorable illustrations of complex but critical legal concepts.

CPA HELPS

As always, the text provides coverage for all the legal topics covered on the CPA exam. This edition reflects the content changes to the law and business regulation portions of the recently revised CPA exam. For example, there is less detail on personal property and bailments and trusts. Business organizations, now a substantial portion of the exam, remain a focus of eight chapters with up-to-date coverage of Sarbanes-Oxley and its impact on business forms and disclosures. This edition continues to feature sample CPA exam questions at the end of those chapters that include legal areas covered on the exam. Answers for the odd-numbered CPA exam questions in each of the appropriate chapters are given in the Instructor's Manual along with explanations for the answers. This edition of the book also continues to use a CPA highlight icon to alert students to those areas that are particularly critical in preparing for the law portion of the CPA exam.

INNOVATIVE CHAPTERS

This text features, for example, a chapter on cyberlaw (Chapter 11). Updated for this edition, this chapter provides students with a look at how the Internet and new technology have resulted in new interpretations of existing laws as well as new laws to govern unique issues of commerce involving these new tools. Bloggers and spammers beware, for the law has caught up with you. This chapter has been shortened because so much of the cyberlaw material is now mainstream in other topic areas. But it provides a nice introductory tool for instructors who want to show how much the law affects this new generation of Internet-savvy students.

CASE SUMMARIES

Specially selected case summaries appear in abundance and are still at the core of this text. Most chapters include three to five case summaries, many of them with 2006 decision dates. Landmark decisions also appear. To highlight the charm and induce the student's recall of the principles of the cases, a one-line title appears above each case. These can be a humorous introduction, a play on words, or a simple memorable description of the parties or facts of the case. The one-line introduction is intriguing for students and makes the strong cases even more memorable.

E-COMMERCE AND CYBERLAW

Beyond the cyberlaw chapter (11), this feature covers e-mail privacy, Internet taxes, identity theft, contract formation on the Internet, e-commerce employment rules, electronic signatures, and more. Chapter 8, the criminal law chapter, also includes great detail on the new and evolving computer crimes. Chapter 10, the intellectual property chapter, features a section on Protection of Computer Software and Mask Works, covering copyright and patent protection of computer programs, restrictive licensing, semiconductor chip protection, and more.

THINKING THINGS THROUGH

This feature is designed to help students apply the law they have learned from the chapter and cases to a hypothetical or another case that varies slightly from the examples in the reading. With these problems built into the reading, students have the chance to really think through what they have just read and studied with regard to the law presented in that chapter. This feature can be used to promote classroom discussion or as an assignment for analysis. For example, in Chapter 11, students can walk through a series of examples on whether an Internet service provider must disclose a customer's name to the courts when the customer's posting on a blog or chat room has created potential legal liability.

MAJOR REGULATORY REFORMS: USA PATRIOT ACT AND SARBANES-OXLEY

Businesses have been affected dramatically not only by new laws at the federal level but also by complex and intricate new federal regulatory schemes. Sarbanes-Oxley affects everything from corporate governance to the Federal Sentencing Guidelines to accountants' liability. The USA Patriot Act has an impact on searches, funds transfers, and issues of citizenship for employers. These dramatic new pieces of legislation enjoy coverage throughout this edition.

ETHICAL FOCUS

In addition to Chapter 3, which is devoted exclusively to the current issues in business ethics, each chapter continues to provide students with an ethical dilemma related to that particular area of law. The Ethics & the Law feature presents problems in each area of law. Students will be able to analyze ethical issues and problems that are very real and very challenging for anyone in business. Examples include the issues involved in the Berkeley graduate school applicants who lied about their work experience in order to be admitted to the MBA program, the cast members of Friends and their salaries, the bankruptcies of musicians from TLC to George Michael, and the issues surrounding steroid use by professional baseball players.

WEEKLY UPDATES

Users of this text have the opportunity to catch up on new cases, business events, and changing laws and regulations with the weekly updates prepared by co-author Marianne Jennings. These updates carry information on law and business practice, which is often just days old and allows students to stay up to date. Instructors can use the cases, examples, and questions from the weekly updates for quizzes, class discussion, or exam questions. The weekly updates provide a never-ending resource for new and enhancing materials for lectures, discussions, assignments, and group work. Available to instructors and students, the weekly updates on the law are at **www.thomsonedu.com/westbuslaw/twomey.**

CRITICAL THINKING

This text addresses the mandate on critical thinking by the American Assembly of Collegiate Schools of Business (AACSB). The Thinking Things Through feature asks students to analyze a problem that requires application of the law and examination of slight changes in factual patterns from examples in the text and the cases. For example, in the negotiable instruments chapters, students can look at a sample instrument in one problem and apply the requirements for negotiability to determine whether the instrument is indeed negotiable. In the Ethics & the Law feature, students must connect ethical thought with law and public policy and walk through the logic of application and results. End-of-chapter problems are, for the most part, real cases that summarize fact patterns and ask the students to find the applicable laws in the chapter and determine applicability and results. The fact patterns in the chapter problems are detailed and realistic and offer students the chance to test their mastery of the chapter concepts.

FOR ADDITIONAL HELP IN TEACHING AND LEARNING

For more detailed information about any of the following ancillaries, contact your local Thomson Learning/West Legal Studies sales representative or visit the Anderson's Business Law and the Legal Environment Web site at **www.thomsonedu.com/ westbuslaw/twomey.**

STUDENT STUDY GUIDE (ISBN: 0-324-63986-4) Students may purchase a study guide that includes chapter outlines, general rules, study hints, and review and application exercises. Solutions to all study guide case problems are also included.

INSTRUCTOR'S RESOURCE CD (IRCD) (ISBN: 0-324-63819-1) The IRCD contains the Instructor's Manual in Microsoft Word files. This manual provides instructor insights, chapter outlines, and teaching strategies for each chapter. Discussion points are provided for Thinking Things Through and Ethics & the Law vignettes. Also included are answers to CPA questions. The Instructor's Manual is prepared by Marianne Jennings, one of the textbook authors. In addition, the IRCD includes the ExamView testing software files, the test bank in Microsoft Word files, and the Microsoft PowerPoint lecture slides.

EXAMVIEW TESTING SOFTWARE—COMPUTERIZED TESTING SOFTWARE This testing software contains all of the questions in the printed test bank. This program is an easy-to-use test creation software compatible with Microsoft Windows. Instructors can add or edit questions, instructions, and answers; they can select questions by previewing them on the screen, selecting them randomly, or selecting them by number. Instructors can also create and administer quizzes online, whether over the Internet, a local area network (LAN), or a wide area network (WAN). The ExamView testing software is available on the Instructor's Resource CD.

TEST BANK (ISBN: 0-324-63984-8) Thousands of true/false, multiple-choice, and case questions are available. The test bank may be obtained in hard copy or in electronic format.

MICROSOFT POWERPOINT® LECTURE REVIEW SLIDES PowerPoint slides are available for use by instructors for enhancing their lectures. Download these slides at **www.thomsonedu.com/westbuslaw/twomey**. The PowerPoint slides are also available on the IRCD.

WEST'S DIGITAL VIDEO LIBRARY Featuring 60+ segments on the most important topics in Business Law, West's Digital Video Library helps students make the connection between their textbook and the business world. Access to West's Digital Video Library is free when bundled with a new text. New to this edition are LawFlix, twelve scenes from Hollywood movies with instructor materials for each film clip. The accompanying instructor materials were written by co-author Marianne Jennings and include elements such as goals for the clips, questions for students (with answers for the instructor), background on the film and the scene, and fascinating trivia about the film, its actors, and its history. For more information about West's Digital Video Library, visit **http://digitalvideolibrary.westbuslaw.com**

WEST LEGAL STUDIES IN BUSINESS RESOURCE CENTER This Web site offers a unique, rich, and robust online resource for instructors and students. The address **http://www. thomsonedu.com/westbuslaw** provides customer service and product information, links to all text-supporting Web sites, and other cutting-edge resources such as **NewsEdge** and **Court Case Updates**.

THOMSON CUSTOM SOLUTIONS Whether you need print, digital, or hybrid course materials, Thomson Custom Solutions can help you create your perfect learning solution. Draw from Thomson's extensive library of texts and collections, add or create your own original work, and create customized media and technology to match your learning and course objectives. Our editorial team will work with you through each step, allowing you to concentrate on the most important thing—your students. Learn more about all our services at **www.thomsoncustom.com**.

CASENET CaseNet is Thomson's legal and business case collection featuring selections from the West Legal Studies in Business case database and other prestigious partners. Using TextChoice you can search, preview, arrange cases, and add your original material or legal cases from your state to create the perfect case resource for your course. To start building your casebook, visit CaseNet at **www.textchoice.com/casenet** or contact your local Thomson Learning/West Legal Studies sales representative.

ACKNOWLEDGMENTS

The development and revision of a textbook represent teamwork in its highest form. We thank the innumerable instructors, students, attorneys, and managers who have added to the quality of this textbook through its many editions. In particular, we thank the following reviewers who provided their honest and valuable commentary to this text:

Robert A. Arnold
Thomas More College

Todd Barnet
Pace University

Marie F. Benjamin
Valencia Community College

Kenneth V. Bevan
Valencia Community College

David A. Clough
Naugatuck Valley Community College

Lawrence J. Danks
Camden County College

Edward J. Gac
University of Colorado

Teresa R. Gillespie
Northwest University

Heidi Helgren
Delta College

Lawrence A. Joel
Bergen Community College

Neal Orkin
Drexel University

William B. Read
Huffon College

Richard J. Riley
Samford University

Samuel L. Schrager
University of Connecticut

Mike Teel
Samford University

We also thank the instructors who have reviewed previous editions of this text:

Dean Alexander
Miami-Dade Community College

John T. Ballantine
University of Colorado

Robert Boeke
Delta College

Greg Cermigiano
Widener University

Anne Cohen
University of Massachusetts

Thomas S. Collins
Loras College

Darrell Dies
Illinois State University

De Vee E. Dykstra
University of South Dakota

Adam Epstein
University of Tennessee

Phillip Evans
Kutztown University of Pennsylvania

Deborah Lynn Bundy Ferry
Marquette University

Darrel Ford
University of Central Oklahoma

David Grigg
Pfeiffer University

Ronald Groeber
Ball State University

Florence Elliot Howard
Stephen F. Austin University

Richard Hurley
Francis Marion University

Michael A. Katz
Delaware State University

Thomas E. Knothe
Viterbo University

Ruth Kraft
Audrey Cohen College

Claire La Roche
Longwood College

Susan D. Looney
Mohave Community College

Roy J. Millender, Jr.
Westmont College

Steven Murray
Community College of Rhode Island

Ann Olazábal
University of Miami

Ronald Picker
St. Mary's of the Woods College

Francis Polk
Ocean County College

Robert Prentice
University of Texas at Austin

Linda Reppert
Marymount University

Gary Sambol
Rutgers University School of Business

Lester Smith
Eastern New Mexico University

Michael Sugameli
Oakland University

Cathy L. Taylor
Park University and Webster University

Bob Vicars
Bluefield State University

James Welch
Kentucky Wesleyan College

We extend our thanks to our families for their support and patience as we work our long hours to ensure that each edition is better than the last.

ABOUT THE AUTHORS

David P. Twomey graduated from Boston College, earned his MBA at the University of Massachusetts at Amherst, and after two years of business experience, entered Boston College Law School, where he earned his Juris Doctor degree.

While a law student, he began his teaching career serving as a Lecturer in Finance and Marketing at Simmons College in Boston. He joined the faculty of the Boston College Carroll School of Management in 1968 as an assistant professor and was promoted to the rank of professor in 1978. Professor Twomey has received numerous teaching and service awards at Boston College. He has written 31 editions of books and numerous articles on labor, employment, and business law topics. He has a special interest in curriculum development, having served four terms as chairman of his school's Education Policy Committee. As chairman of the Business Law Department for over a decade, he serves as a spokesperson for a strong legal and ethical component in both the undergraduate and graduate curriculum.

Professor Twomey is a nationally known labor arbitrator, having been selected by the parties as arbitrator in numerous disputes throughout the country in the private and public sectors. In the context of impending nationwide railroad and airline strikes, his service includes appointments by Presidents Reagan, George Bush, Clinton, and George W. Bush to eight Presidential Emergency Boards, whose recommendations served as the basis for the resolution of these labor disputes. Professor Twomey is a member of the National Academy of Arbitrators. He is also a member of the Massachusetts, Florida, and federal Bars.

Marianne Jennings is a member of the Department of Management in the W.P. Carey School of Business at Arizona State University and is a professor of legal and ethical studies in business. She served as director of the Joan and David Lincoln Center for Applied Ethics from 1995 to 1999. In 2006, she was appointed faculty director for the W.P. Carey Executive MBA Program. She has done consulting work for law firms, businesses and professional groups including AES, AICPA, Boeing, Dial Corporation, Edward Jones, Mattel, Motorola, CFA Institute, Southern California Edison, the Institute of Internal Auditors, AIMR, DuPont, Blue Cross Blue Shield, Hy-Vee Foods, IBM, Bell Helicopter, Amgen, Raytheon, and VIAD.

The fifth edition of her textbook *Case Studies in Business Ethics* was published in February 2005. The eighth edition of her textbook *Business: Its Legal, Ethical, and Global Environment* is in production for 2007 release. Her book *A Business Tale: A Story of Ethics, Choices, Success, and a Very Large Rabbit*, a fable about business ethics, was chosen by Library Journal in 2004 as its business book of the year. *A Business Tale* was also a finalist for two other literary awards for 2004. In 2000, her book on corporate governance was published by the New York Times MBA Pocket

Series. Her book on long-term success, *Building a Business Through Good Times and Bad: Lessons from Fifteen Companies, Each With a Century of Dividends*, was published in October 2002 and has been used by Booz, Allen, Hamilton for its work on business longevity. Her latest book, *The Seven Signs of Ethical Collapse*, was published by St. Martin's Press in July 2006 and was named one of the best business books for 2006 by *Library Journal*.

Her weekly columns are syndicated around the country, and her work has appeared in the *Wall Street Journal, The Chicago Tribune, The New York Times, Washington Post*, and *Reader's Digest*. A collection of her essays, *Nobody Fixes Real Carrot Sticks Anymore*, first published in 1994, is still being published. She has been a commentator on business issues on *All Things Considered* for National Public Radio.

She has served on four boards of directors, including Arizona Public Service (1987–2000), Zealous Capital Corporation, and the Center for Children with Chronic Illness and Disability at the University of Minnesota. She was appointed to the board of advisors for the Institute of Nuclear Power Operators in 2004 and has served on the board of trustees for Think Arizona, a public policy think tank. She has appeared on CNBC, CBS This Morning, the Today Show, and CBS Evening News.

THE LEGAL AND SOCIAL

ENVIRONMENT OF BUSINESS

NATURE OF LAW AND LEGAL RIGHTS
1. **LEGAL RIGHTS**
2. **INDIVIDUAL RIGHTS**
3. **THE RIGHT OF PRIVACY**
4. **PRIVACY AND TECHNOLOGY**

B SOURCES OF LAW

C UNIFORM STATE LAWS

D CLASSIFICATIONS OF LAW

LEARNING OBJECTIVES

After studying this chapter, you should be able to

LO.1 Discuss the nature of law

LO.2 Define legal rights and give examples

LO.3 Explain how rights and duties relate

LO.4 Discuss the right to privacy and the protections it provides, including issues in Internet use

LO.5 List the sources of law and give examples from each level

LO.6 Describe uniform laws and their purposes

LO.7 Give the classifications of law

law the order or pattern of rules that society establishes to govern the conduct of individuals and the relationships among them.

Why have law? If you have ever been stuck in a traffic jam or jostled in a crowd leaving a stadium, you have observed the need for order to keep those involved moving in an efficient and safe manner. The interruptions and damages from Internet viruses demonstrate the need for rules and order in this era of new technology. When our interactions are not orderly, whether at our concerts or through our e-mail, all of us and our rights are affected. The order or pattern of rules that society uses to govern the conduct of individuals and their relationships is called **law**. Law keeps society running smoothly and efficiently.

 ## NATURE OF LAW AND LEGAL RIGHTS

Law consists of the body of principles that govern conduct and that can be enforced in courts or by administrative agencies. The law could also be described as a collection or bundle of rights.

1. LEGAL RIGHTS

right legal capacity to require another person to perform or refrain from an action.

duty an obligation of law imposed on a person to perform or refrain from performing a certain act.

A **right** is a legal capacity to require another person to perform or refrain from performing an act. Our rights flow from the U.S. Constitution, state constitutions, federal and state statutes, and ordinances at the local levels, including cities, counties, and boroughs. Within these sources of rights are also duties. A **duty** is an obligation of law imposed on a person to perform or refrain from performing a certain act.

Duties and rights coexist. No right exists in one person without a corresponding duty resting on some other person or persons. For example, if the terms of a lease provide that the premises will remain in a condition of good repair so that the tenant can live there comfortably, the landlord has a corresponding duty to provide a dwelling that has hot and cold running water.

2. INDIVIDUAL RIGHTS

The U.S. Constitution gives individuals certain rights. Those rights include the right to freedom of speech, the right to due process or the right to have a hearing before any freedom is taken away, and the right to vote. There are also duties that accompany individual rights, such as the duty to speak in a way that does not cause harm to others. For example, individuals are free to express their opinions about the government or its officials, but they would not be permitted to yell "Fire!" in a crowded theater and cause unnecessary harm to others. The rights given in the U.S. Constitution are rights that cannot be taken away or violated by any statutes, ordinances, or court decisions. These rights provide a framework for the structure of government and other laws.

3. THE RIGHT OF PRIVACY

right of privacy the right to be free from unreasonable intrusion by others.

One very important individual legal right is the right of privacy, which has has two components. The first is the right to be secure against unreasonable searches and seizures by the government. The Fourth Amendment of the U.S. Constitution guarantees this portion of the **right of privacy**. A police officer, for example, may not search your home unless the officer has a reasonable suspicion (which is generally established through a warrant) that your home contains evidence of a crime, such as illegal drugs. If your home or business is searched unlawfully, any items obtained

CASE SUMMARY

When Warrants Are Involved, No Brief Photographs

FACTS: In early 1992, the Attorney General of the United States approved Operation Gunsmoke, a special national fugitive apprehension program in which U.S. marshals worked with state and local police to apprehend dangerous criminals.

In the early morning hours of April 16, 1992, a Gunsmoke team of Deputy U.S. marshals and Montgomery County Maryland police officers executed warrants that had been issued against Dominic Wilson, who was wanted for robbery, theft, and assault and who had a "use caution" warning posted on law enforcement files and records. The team was accompanied by a reporter and a photographer from the *Washington Post*, who had been invited by the marshals to accompany them as part of a Marshals Service ride-along policy.

At around 6:45 A.M., the officers, with media representatives in tow, entered the dwelling noted in the warrant. They were unaware that the residence in the warrant and the one that they entered was actually the home of Dominic's parents, Charles and Geraldine Wilson. Charles and Geraldine were still in bed when they heard the officers enter the home. Charles Wilson, dressed only in a pair of briefs, ran into the living room to investigate. Discovering at least five men in street clothes with guns in his living room, he angrily demanded that they state their business and repeatedly cursed the officers. Geraldine Wilson next entered the living room to investigate, wearing only a nightgown. She observed her husband being restrained by the armed officers. The officers learned that Dominic Wilson was not in the house, and they departed. During the time that the officers were in the home, the *Washington Post* photographer took numerous pictures. The reporter was also apparently in the living room observing the confrontation between the police and Charles Wilson. The reporters were not involved in the execution of the arrest warrant. The *Washington Post* never published its photographs of the incident.

The Wilsons filed suit against the officers for invasion of their privacy and violation of their Fourth Amendment rights. The district court found that the officers could be held liable. The Court of Appeals reversed and found that the officers had immunity despite the presence of the photographer because the law on reporters and warrants was not clear at the time these officers used reporters. The U.S. Supreme Court granted *certiorari* because of several conflicting circuit decisions on the issue of cameras and reporters present during arrests and warrant executions.

DECISION: The court held that although there were reasons for having the reporters and cameras, such as public relations, safety for officers, and assistance, those reasons were not sufficient enough to disregard the Fourth Amendment rights of the homeowners. Citing "a man's home is his castle," the court noted the longstanding history of protecting individual actions in their homes. The court held that having reporters and photographers along in the execution of a warrant is a violation of the Fourth Amendment rights of the party who is subjected to the search. The finding also means that officers can be subject to some liability for their failure to honor the privacy protections. [**Wilson v. Layne, 526 U.S. 603 (1999)**]

during that unlawful search could be excluded as evidence in a criminal trial because of the Fourth Amendment's exclusionary rule. **For Example,** in the murder trial of O.J. Simpson, Judge Lance Ito excluded some of the evidence the police had obtained from inside Mr. Simpson's Ford Bronco, which was parked on the street outside his home. Judge Ito ruled that the officers should have first obtained a warrant for the locked vehicle, which was not going to be taken anywhere because Mr. Simpson was out of town at that time.

SPORTS & ENTERTAINMENT LAW

On March 17, 2005, former and current major league baseball players, Commissioner Bud Selig, and the parents of young baseball players who had taken their own lives after taking steroids testified before the U.S. House of Representatives Government Reform Committee. The House held the hearings to determine whether government regulation of baseball is necessary.

The committee issued subpoenas to seven current or former major league players: Jose Canseco, Jason Giambi, Mark McGwire, Rafael Palmeiro, Curt Schilling, Sammy Sosa, and Frank Thomas. Subpoenas were also issued to four baseball officials. Only Jose Canseco, Don Fehr, and Rob Manfred had already agreed to appear voluntarily, according to a release by the committee chair.*

Committee Chair Tom Davis made an opening statement with the following excerpts:

Fourteen years ago, anabolic steroids were added to the Controlled Substance Act as a Schedule III drug, making it illegal to possess or sell them without a valid prescription. Today, however, evidence strongly suggests that steroid use among teenagers–especially aspiring athletes–is a large and growing problem.

The Centers for Disease Control and Prevention tells us that more than 500,000 high school students have tried steroids, nearly triple the number just ten years ago. A second national survey, conducted in 2004 by the National Institute on Drug Abuse and the University of Michigan, found that over 40 percent of 12th graders described steroids as "fairly easy" or "very easy" to get, and the perception among high school students that steroids are harmful has dropped from 71 percent in 1992 to 56 percent in 2004.

This is but a snapshot of the startling data we face. Today we take the committee's first steps toward understanding how we got here, and how we begin turning those numbers around. Down the road, we need to look at whether and how Congress should exercise its legislative powers to further restrict the use and distribution of these substances.

Our specific purpose today is to consider MLB's recently negotiated drug policy; how the testing policy will be implemented; how it will effectively address the use of prohibited drugs by players; and, most importantly, the larger societal and public health ramifications of steroid use.

In February of this year, former MLB All-Star Jose Canseco released a book that not only alleges steroid use by well known MLB players, but also discusses the prevalence of steroids in baseball during his 17-year career. After hearing Commissioner Bud Selig's public statements that MLB would not launch an investigation into Mr. Canseco's allegations, my Ranking Member Henry Waxman wrote me asking for a Committee hearing to, quote, "find out what really happened and to get to the bottom of this growing scandal." End quote. Furthermore, today's hearing will not be the end of our inquiry. Far from it. Nor will Major League Baseball be our sole or even primary focus. We're in the first inning of what could be an extra inning ballgame.

Ultimately, it is MLB, the union, and team executives that will determine the strength of the game's testing policy. Ultimately, it is MLB and the union that will or will not determine accountability and punishment. Ultimately, it is MLB and the union that can remove the cloud over baseball, and maybe save some lives in the process.

---

* http://www.commondreams.org/news2005/0309-22.htm.

SPORTS & ENTERTAINMENT LAW

continued

Oh, somewhere in this favored land the sun is shining bright;
The band is playing somewhere, and somewhere hearts are light;
And somewhere men are laughing, and somewhere children shout;
But there is no joy in Mudville—until the truth comes out.**

Following are excerpts from the players' and former players' testimony:

Jose Canseco, whose book alleges that he, Sammy Sosa, and Mark McGwire, all used steroids, testified:

It was as acceptable in the late '80s and the mid-'90s as a cup of coffee.***

Mark McGwire, now retired, and a record holder, stated during the hearings:

Asking me, or any other player, to answer questions about who took steroids in front of television cameras, will not solve this problem. If a player answers 'no,' he simply will not be believed. If he answers 'yes,' he risks public scorn and endless government investigations. My lawyers have advised me that I cannot answer these questions without jeopardizing my friends, my family, or myself. I intend to follow their advice.†

Give a list of all the laws, rights, and duties you can find in this information.

** **http://reform.house.gov/GovReform/Hearings/EventSingle.aspx?EventID=1637**.
*** **http://reform.house.gov/GovReform/Hearings/EventSingle.aspx?EventID=1637**.
† **http://reform.house.gov/GovReform/Hearings/EventSingle.aspx?EventID=1637**. Click on Mark McGwire.

A second aspect of the right of privacy protects individuals against intrusions by others. Your private life is not subject to public scrutiny when you are a private citizen. This right is provided in many state constitutions and exists through interpretation at the federal level in the landmark case of *Roe v Wade*,[1] in which the U.S. Supreme Court established a right of privacy that gives women the right to choose whether to have an abortion.

These two components of the right to privacy have many interpretations. These interpretations are often found in statutes that afford privacy rights with respect to certain types of conduct. **For Example,** a federal statute provides a right of privacy to bank customers that prevents their banks from giving out information about their accounts except to law enforcement agencies conducting investigations. Some laws protect the rights of students. **For Example,** the Family Educational Rights and Privacy Act of 1974 (FERPA, also known as the *Buckley Amendment*) prevents colleges and universities from disclosing students' grades to third parties without the students' permission. From your credit information to your Social Security number, you have great privacy protections.

4. PRIVACY AND TECHNOLOGY

Technology creates new situations that may require the application of new rules of law. Technology has changed the way we interact with each other, and new rules of

---

[1] 410 US 113 (1973).

law have developed to protect our rights. Today, business is conducted by computers, wire transfers of funds, e-mail, electronic data interchange (EDI) order placements, and the Internet. We still expect that our communication is private. However, technology also affords others the ability to eavesdrop on conversations and intercept electronic messages. The law has stepped in to reestablish that the right of privacy still exists even in these technologically nonprivate circumstances. Some laws now make it a crime and a breach of privacy to engage in such interceptions of communications.[2] (See Chapter 11.)

 SOURCES OF LAW

constitution a body of principles that establishes the structure of a government and the relationship of the government to the people who are governed.

Several layers of law are enacted at different levels of government to provide the framework for business and personal rights and duties. At the base of this framework of laws is constitutional law. Constitutional law is the branch of law that is based on the constitution for a particular level of government. A **constitution** is a body of principles that establishes the structure of a government and the relationship of that government to the people who are governed. A constitution is generally a combination of the written document and the practices and customs that develop with the passage of time and the emergence of new problems. In each state, two constitutions are in force: the state constitution and the federal Constitution.

statutory law legislative acts declaring, commanding, or prohibiting something.

Statutory law includes legislative acts. Both Congress and the state legislatures enact statutory law. Examples of congressional legislative enactments include the Securities Act of 1933 (Chapter 46), the Sherman Antitrust Act (Chapter 5), the bankruptcy laws (Chapter 35), and consumer credit protection provisions (Chapter 33). At the state level, statutes govern the creation of corporations, probate of wills, and the transfer of title to property. In addition to the state legislatures and the U.S. Congress, all cities, counties, and other governmental subdivisions have some power to adopt ordinances within their sphere of operation. Examples of the types of laws found at this level of government include traffic laws, zoning laws, and pet and bicycle licensing laws.

administrative regulations rules made by state and federal administrative agencies.

Administrative regulations are rules promulgated by state and federal administrative agencies, such as the Securities and Exchange Commission and the National Labor Relations Board. These regulations generally have the force of statutes.

private law the rules and regulations parties agree to as part of their contractual relationships.

Even individuals and businesses create their own laws, or **private law**. Private law consists of the rules and regulations parties agree to as part of their contractual relationships. **For Example,** landlords develop rules for tenants on everything from parking to laundry room use. Employers develop rules for employees on everything from proper computer use to posting pictures and information on bulletin boards located within the company walls. Homeowner associations have rules on everything from your landscaping to the color of your house paint.

case law law that includes principles that are expressed for the first time in court decisions.

Law also includes principles that are expressed for the first time in court decisions. This form of law is called **case law**. When a court decides a new question or problem, its decision becomes a **precedent**, which stands as the law in future cases that involve that particular problem.

precedent a decision of a court that stands as the law for a particular problem in the future.

stare decisis "let the decision stand"; the principle that the decision of a court should serve as a guide or precedent and control the decision of a similar case in the future.

Using precedent and following decisions in similar cases is the doctrine of **stare decisis**. However, the rule of *stare decisis* is not cast in stone. Judges have some

---

[2] *State v Christensen*, 79 P3d 12 (CA Wash 2003).

flexibility. When a court finds an earlier decision to be incorrect, it overrules that decision. **For Example,** in 1954, the U.S. Supreme Court departed from the rule of *stare decisis* in *Brown v Board of Education*.[3] In that case, the Court decided that it was incorrect in 1896 when it held in *Plessy v Ferguson*[4] that separate facilities for blacks were equal to facilities for whites.

Court decisions do not always deal with new problems or make new rules. In many cases, courts apply rules as they have been for many years, even centuries. These time-honored rules of the community are called the **common law.** Statutes sometimes repeal or redeclare the common law rules. Many statutes depend on the common law for definitions of the terms in the statutes.

Law also includes treaties made by the United States and proclamations and executive orders of the president of the United States or of other public officials.

common law the body of unwritten principles originally based upon the usages and customs of the community that were recognized and enforced by the courts.

 ## UNIFORM STATE LAWS

To facilitate the national nature of business and transactions, the National Conference of Commissioners on Uniform State Laws (NCCUSL), composed of representatives from every state, has drafted statutes on various subjects for adoption by the states. The best example of such laws is the Uniform Commercial Code (UCC).[5] (See Chapters 23–31, 34.) The UCC regulates the sale and leasing of goods; commercial paper, such as checks; funds transfers; secured transactions in personal property; banking; and letters of credit. Having the same principles of law on contracts for the sale of goods and other commercial transactions in most of the 50 states makes doing business easier and less expensive. Other examples of uniform laws across the states include the Model Business Corporations Act (Chapter 44), the Uniform Partnership Act (Chapter 42), and the Uniform Residential Landlord Tenant Act (Chapter 51). The Uniform Computer Information Transactions Act (UCITA) as well as the Uniform Electronic Transactions Act (UETA) are new technology statutes that have been adopted or are under consideration for passage by the states. These two uniform laws and versions of them take contract law from the traditional paper era to the paperless computer age.

 ## CLASSIFICATIONS OF LAW

substantive law the law that defines rights and liabilities.

procedural law the law that must be followed in enforcing rights and liabilities.

Law is classified in many ways. **Substantive law** creates, defines, and regulates rights and liabilities. **Procedural law** specifies the steps that must be followed in enforcing those rights and liabilities. For example, the laws that grant employees protection against discrimination are substantive laws. The regulations of the Equal Employment Opportunity Commission (EEOC) for bringing suits against or investigations of employers for discrimination charges are procedural laws.

---

[3] 349 US 294 (1954).

[4] 163 US 537 (1895).

[5] The UCC has been adopted in every state, except that Louisiana has not adopted Article 2, Sales. Guam, the Virgin Islands, and the District of Columbia have also adopted the UCC. The NCCUSL has adopted amendments to Article 8, Investment Securities (1977 and 1994), and Article 9, Secured Transactions (1999, and as amended 2001). There have been new articles of the UCC: Article 2A, Leases, and Article 4A, Funds Transfers. The United Nations Convention on Contracts for the International Sale of Goods (CISG) has been adopted as the means for achieving uniformity in sale-of-goods contracts on an international level. Provisions of CISG were strongly influenced by Article 2 of the UCC.

ETHICS & THE LAW

Warning Customers Not to Take Your Medications

Johnson & Johnson has adopted a new policy on direct-to-consumer advertisements for prescription drugs as well as for its over-the-counter drugs. The new policy will have doctors disclose all of the risks to patients who are interested in taking the medication. For example, in an ad for J&J's Ortho Evra birth control patch, the doctor explains that the patch does contain hormones and that smokers have higher risks for strokes and blood clots if they choose to use it. In another ad, the company's director of marketing warns customers about the dangers of taking too much Tylenol and concludes by saying she would rather customers not take Tylenol at all than take too much Tylenol.

Johnson & Johnson CEO William Weldon announced the new policy in the following way:

> If our industry is to retain the important right to talk directly to consumers, each of our companies in its own way must work to make DTC [direct to consumer] what it very definitely can be—a way to educate and counsel consumers in improving their health.

Spending on DTC ads increased by 27 percent in 2004, for a total of $4.44 billion. Some in the industry say consumers will be frightened away. However, a J&J spokesperson said, "If a woman sees the Evra ad and she is a smoker (the ad discloses a higher risk of the drug for smokers), then quite frankly, she should be scared away. We're better off when they're not on the product." DTC advertising is under review by regulators following the withdrawal of popular DTC products such as Celebrex, Vioxx, and others from the market following consumer deaths and illnesses attributed to use of the drug when other conditions (such as heart problems) cautioned against their use.

Who regulates advertising? What types of laws cover advertising? Why would a company voluntarily disclose more information in ads than the government requires? What do you think of the statement by the J&J spokesperson who says everyone is better off if some consumers are frightened away by the ads? Why would a company deliberately advertise so as to keep consumers away from its products?

Source: Scott Hensley, "In Switch, J&J Gives Straight Talk on Drug Risks in New Ads," *Wall Street Journal,* March 21, 2005, B1, B6.

The laws that prohibit computer theft are substantive laws. The prosecution of someone for computer theft follows procedural laws. Law may also be classified in terms of its origin from Roman (or civil) law, from English common law based on customs and usages of the community,[6] or from the law merchant. Law may be classified according to subject matter, such as the law of contracts, the law of real estate, or the law of wills.

---

[6] For example, in *Welsh v Boy Scouts of America,* 510 US 1012 (1993), the Court relied on the age-old maxim, "A man's home is his castle," in its decision, and in *BMW of North America, Inc. v. Gore,* 517 US 559 (1996), Justice Antonin Scalia, in his dissenting opinion, wrote, "One expects the court to conclude, 'To thine own self be true.'"

E-COMMERCE AND CYBERLAW

Employers, E-mail, and Privacy

Courts have taken the position that e-mail accounts of employees that are created through their employers are not private and that any messages and information in the employees' e-mail are the property of the employer and can be reviewed. Courts also permit, during the course of litigation, discovery of employee e-mail messages when the employer is named in a lawsuit. All e-mail messages can be retrieved and read for information relevant to the litigation. A recent survey revealed that 50 percent of executive-level managers review their employees' e-mail. Two Nissan Motor Corporation employees were fired after their managers warned them not to use company e-mail for personal messages. The managers were monitoring all of their employees' e-mails.

The Principal Financial Group has the following policy in its employee handbook:

The corporation's electronic mail system is business property and is to be used for business purposes. The corporation reserves the right to monitor all electronic messages.

Michelle Murphy, a former customer service representative at Principal, was fired when her supervisor discovered she had used the company e-mail system to forward jokes, such as "A Few Good Reasons Cookie Dough Is Better Than Men" and "Top 10 Reasons Why Trick-or-Treating Is Better Than Sex."

Would you have fired Ms. Murphy? Why or why not? Should employees have any workplace protections for their e-mail? What problems would be created if the employer were denied the right to review employees' e-mail? What problems arise when managers are given access to employee e-mail?

---

equity the body of principles that originally developed because of the inadequacy of the rules then applied by the common law courts of England.

Law is at times classified in terms of principles of law and principles of equity. The early English courts were very limited as to the kinds of cases they could handle. Persons who could not obtain relief in those courts would petition the king to grant them special relief according to principles of **equity** and justice. In the course of time, these special cases developed certain rules that are called *principles of equity*. In general, the rules of equity apply when the remedies provided at law cannot provide adequate relief in the form of monetary damages. At one time, the United States had separate law courts and equity courts. Except in a few states, these courts have been combined so that one court applies principles of both law and equity. A party may ask for both legal and equitable remedies in a single court.[7] **For Example,** suppose a homeowner contracts to sell his home to a buyer. If the homeowner then refuses to go through with the contract, the buyer has the legal remedy of recovering damages. The rules of equity go further, when appropriate, and could require the owner to actually transfer the ownership of the house to the buyer. Such remedies require a court order for specific conduct, known as *specific performance*. Equitable remedies may also be available in certain contract breaches (see Chapters 2 and 20).

---

[7] *Actuant Corp. v Huffman*, 2005 WL 39661 (D Or).

LAWFLIX

And Justice for All (1979) (R)

An excellent film that gives an overview of the judicial system in Maryland. Rights, precedent, and the role of lawyers are all topics for satire and analysis in the movie. For movie clips that illustrate business law concepts, see LawFlix at **http://wdvl.westbuslaw.com.**

SUMMARY

Law consists of the pattern of rules established by society to govern conduct and relationships. These rules can be expressed as constitutional provisions, statutes, administrative regulations, and case decisions. Law can be classified as substantive or procedural, and it can be described in terms of its historical origins, by the subject to which it relates, or in terms of law or equity.

Law provides rights and imposes duties. One such right is the right of privacy, which affords protection against unreasonable searches of our property and intrusion into or disclosure of our private affairs.

The sources of law include constitutions, federal and state statutes, administrative regulations, ordinances, and uniform laws generally codified by the states in their statutes. The courts are also a source of law through their adherence to case precedent under the doctrine of *stare decisis* and through their development of time-honored principles called the common law.

QUESTIONS AND CASE PROBLEMS

1. Give an example of how law protects privacy.
2. The Family Educational Rights and Privacy Act (FERPA) protects students' rights to keep their academic records private. What duties are imposed and upon whom because of this protection of rights? Discuss the relationship between rights and duties.
3. List the sources of law.
4. What is the difference between common law and statutory law?
5. Classify the following laws as substantive or procedural:
   a. A law that requires public schools to hold a hearing before a student is expelled
   b. A law that establishes a maximum interest rate for credit transactions of 24 percent
   c. A law that provides employee leave for the birth or adoption of a child for up to 12 weeks
   d. A law that requires the county assessor to send four notices of taxes due and owing before a lien can be filed (attached) to the property

6. What do uniform laws accomplish? Why do states adopt them? Give an example of a uniform law.
7. Cindy Nathan is a student at West University. While she was at her 9:00 A.M. anthropology class, campus security entered her dorm room and searched all areas, including her closet and drawers. When Cindy returned to her room and discovered what had happened, she complained to the dorm's senior resident. The senior resident said that this was the university's property and that Cindy had no right of privacy. Do you agree with the senior resident's statement? Is there a right of privacy in a dorm room?
8. Professor Lucas Phelps sent the following e-mail to Professor Marlin Jones: "I recently read the opinion piece you wrote for the *Sacramento Bee* on affirmative action. Your opinion is incorrect, your reasoning and analysis are poor, and I am embarrassed that you are a member of the faculty here at Cal State Yolinda." Professor Jones forwarded the note from Professor Phelps to the

provost of the university and asked that Professor Phelps be disciplined for using the university e-mail system for harassment purposes. Professor Phelps objected when the provost contacted him: "He had no right to send that e-mail to you. That was private correspondence. And you have no right of access to my e-mail. I have privacy rights." Do you agree with Professor Phelps? Was there a breach of privacy?

9. Under what circumstances would a court disregard precedent?

10. What is the difference between a statute and an administrative regulation?

11. What is the difference between a remedy in equity and other forms of judicial remedies?

12. Give examples of the areas covered by federal laws. Give examples of areas covered by city ordinances. What are the limitations on these two sources of laws? What could the laws at these two levels not do?

13. What is the principle of *stare decisis?*

14. List some purposes of law that you were able to spot in reading this chapter.

15. During the 2001 baseball season, San Francisco Giants player Barry Bonds hit 73 home runs, a new record that broke the one set by Mark McGwire in 2000 (72 home runs). When Mr. Bonds hit his record-breaking home run, the ball went into the so-called cheap seats. Alex Popov was sitting in those seats and had brought along his baseball glove for purposes of catching any hits that might come into the stands. Everyone sitting in the area agreed that Mr. Popov's glove touched Bonds's home-run ball. Videotape also shows Mr. Popov's glove on the ball. However, the ball dropped and, following a melee among the cheap-seat fans, Patrick Hayashi ended up with Bonds's home-run ball. Mr. Popov filed suit for the ball, claiming it is his property. Such baseballs can be very valuable. The baseball from Mr. McGwire's record-breaking home run in 2000 sold for $3 million. List those areas of law that will apply as the case is tried and the owner of the baseball is determined.

THE COURT SYSTEM AND

DISPUTE RESOLUTION

LEARNING OBJECTIVES

After studying this chapter, you should be able to

LO.1 Explain the federal and state court systems

LO.2 Define the types of jurisdiction courts can have and how these are different

LO.3 Give the names of the parties and persons involved in a lawsuit

LO.4 List the initial steps in a lawsuit and explain how pleadings are used

LO.5 Describe the actual steps in a trial

LO.6 Explain how a party who prevails in court collects the judgment

LO.7 List the forms of alternative dispute resolution and distinguish among them

Despite carefully negotiated and well-written contracts and high safety standards in the workplace or in product design and production, businesses can still encounter disputes that may result in a lawsuit. **For Example,** you could hire the brightest and most expensive lawyer in town to prepare a contract with another party and believe the final agreement is "bulletproof." However, even a bulletproof contract does not guarantee performance by the other party, and a lawsuit for damages may be necessary.

Parties in a dispute either go to court to seek resolution or resolve the situation through alternative means. This chapter covers the structure of the court system and the litigation process as well as alternative means used to resolve disputes outside the court system.

THE COURT SYSTEM

court a tribunal established by government to hear and decide matters properly brought to it.

A **court** is a tribunal established by government to hear and decide matters brought before it, provide remedies when a wrong has been committed, and prevent possible wrongs from happening. A court could award to a business party money damages for a breach of contract following a trial, but it could also issue an injunction to halt patent infringement. **For Example,** in 2006, a court threatened to issue an injunction to shut down operation of the Blackberry wireless e-mail device system unless and until Research in Motion, Ltd. (RIM), the Blackberry service provider, compensated NTP, Inc., the company that had won its patent infringement case against RIM for the technology in the Blackberry device.[1]

1. THE TYPES OF COURTS

jurisdiction the power of a court to hear and determine a given class of cases; the power to act over a particular defendant.

Every type of court is given the authority to decide certain types or classes of cases. The power to hear cases is called **jurisdiction**. One form of jurisdiction, **subject matter jurisdiction**, covers the type of proceedings that the court holds. A court with **original jurisdiction** is the trial court or the court with the authority to conduct the first proceedings in the case. **For Example,** a court of original jurisdiction would be one where the witnesses actually testify, the documents are admitted into evidence, and the jury, in the case of a jury trial, is present to hear all the evidence and to make a decision.

subject matter jurisdiction judicial authority to hear a particular type of case.

original jurisdiction the authority to hear a controversy when it is first brought to court.

Other types of subject matter jurisdiction are applicable to courts. A court with **general jurisdiction** has broad authority over different types of cases. The authority of a court with general jurisdiction can extend to both general civil and criminal cases. When a general jurisdiction trial court hears criminal cases, it conducts the trials of those charged with crimes. When a general trial court exercises its civil jurisdiction, it uses its authority to hear civil disputes, such as breach of contract cases and disputes about leases between landlords and tenants.

general jurisdiction the power to hear and decide most controversies involving legal rights and duties.

limited (special) jurisdiction the authority to hear only particular kinds of cases.

A court with **limited** or **special jurisdiction** has the authority to hear only particular kinds of cases. **For Example,** many states have courts that can hear only disputes in which the damages are $10,000 or less. Many types of courts have special jurisdiction, including juvenile courts, probate courts, and domestic relations courts. States vary in the names they give these courts, but all are courts of special or limited jurisdiction because they have very narrow authority for their subject matter

---

[1] RIM eventually settled the suit with NTP by agreeing to pay $612.5 million.

appellate jurisdiction the power of a court to hear and decide a given class of cases on appeal from another court or administrative agency.

appeal taking a case to a reviewing court to determine whether the judgment of the lower court or administrative agency was correct. (Parties–appellant, appellee.)

reversible error an error or defect in court proceedings of so serious a nature that on appeal the appellate court will set aside the proceedings of the lower court.

jurisdiction. In the federal system, courts with limited or special jurisdiction include bankruptcy courts and the U.S. Tax Court.

A court with **appellate jurisdiction** reviews the work of a lower court. **For Example,** a trial court may issue a judgment that a defendant in a breach of contract suit should pay $500,000 in damages. That defendant could appeal the decision to an appellate court and seek review of the decision itself or even the amount of the damages.[2] An **appeal** is a review of the trial and decision of the lower court. An appellate court does not hear witnesses or take testimony. An appellate court, usually a panel of three judges, simply reviews the transcript and evidence from the lower court and determines whether there has been **reversible error**. A reversible error is a mistake in applying the law or a mistake in admitting evidence that affected the outcome of the

CASE SUMMARY

Law and Order on TV and in the Court

FACTS: Andrea Yates was charged with capital murder in the drowning deaths of her five young children. Mrs. Yates had been in and out of treatment facilities, had been taking antidepressants, and was under the care of several experts for her depression. She was also experiencing postpartum depression when she drowned each of her five children in the bathtub at their family home. She then called her husband to ask him to come home because the children were hurt. She also called 9-1-1 and told the operator that she needed a police officer to come to her home.

She entered a "not guilty by reason of insanity" plea, and 10 psychiatrists and two psychologists testified at the trial about Mrs. Yates's mental condition before, during, and after the deaths of the children.

Dr. Parke Dietz, the psychiatrist for the prosecution, testified that he believed Mrs. Yates knew right from wrong and that she was not insane at the time of the drownings. Dr. Dietz also served as a consultant for the television series *Law and Order* and testified as follows about one of the shows in the series:

As a matter of fact, there was a show of a woman with postpartum depression who drowned her children in the bathtub and was found insane and it was aired shortly before the crime occurred.

The prosecution used this information about the television show to cross-examine witnesses for Mrs. Yates and also raised its airing in its closing argument to the jury.

The jury found Mrs. Yates guilty. The defense lawyers later discovered that Dr. Dietz was mistaken and that there had been no such *Law and Order* show on postpartum depression. They appealed on the grounds that the evidence was material, prejudiced the jury, and required a new trial.

DECISION: The court held that because Dr. Dietz had testified about the show, that his testimony and the subject matter of the show were a part of the prosecution's examination of defense witnesses, that the prosecution raised the airing of the show in closing arguments, and that the defense had to respond by talking about it meant that the testimony was material. Inasmuch as it was false, there was a reversible error and a retrial was required without the untrue and highly prejudicial evidence. [*Yates v State* 171 S.W. 3d 215 (Tex. App. 2005)][3]

---

[2] A case that is sent back for a redetermination of damages is remanded for what is known as *remittur*.

[3] Mrs. Yates was found to be criminally insane in her 2006 retrial and is now institutionalized.

affirm action taken by an appellate court that approves the decision of the court below.

reverse the term used when the appellate court sets aside the verdict or judgment of a lower court.

remand term used when an appellate court sends a case back to trial court for additional hearings or a new trial.

federal district court a general trial court of the federal system.

case. An appellate court can **affirm** or **reverse** a lower court decision or **remand** that decision for another trial or additional hearings.

2. THE FEDERAL COURT SYSTEM

The federal court system consists of three levels of courts. Figure 2-1 illustrates federal court structure.

(a) FEDERAL DISTRICT COURTS   The **federal district courts** are the general trial courts of the federal system. They are courts of original jurisdiction that hear both civil and criminal matters. Criminal cases in federal district courts are those in which the defendant is charged with a violation of federal law (the U.S. Code). In addition to the criminal cases, the types of civil cases that can be brought in federal district courts include (1) civil suits in which the United States is a party, (2) cases between citizens of different states that involve damages of $75,000 or more, and (3) cases that arise under the U.S. Constitution or federal laws and treaties.

Federal district courts are organized within each of the states. There are 94 federal districts (each state has at least one federal district and there are 89 federal districts in the United States with the remaining courts found in Puerto Rico, Guam, etc.) Judges and courtrooms are assigned according to the caseload in that geographic area of the state.[4]

| FIGURE 2-1 | *The Federal Court System* |

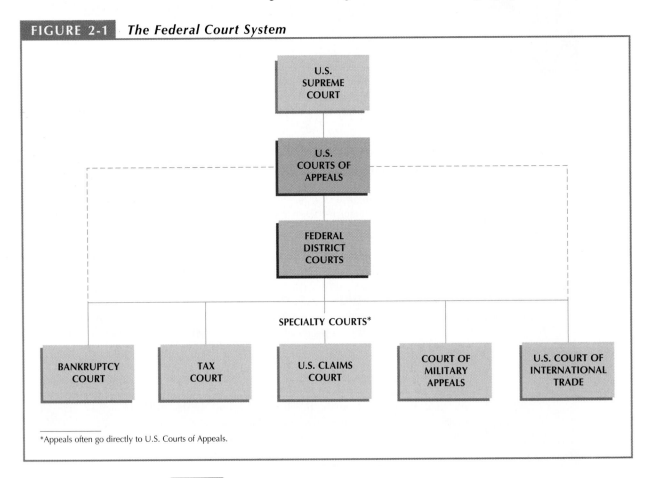

*Appeals often go directly to U.S. Courts of Appeals.

---

[4] For complete information about the courts and the number of judgeships, go to 28 USC §§ 81-144 and 28 USC §133.

Some states, such as New York and California, have several federal districts because of the population base and the resulting caseload. Figure 2-2 shows the geographic structure of the federal court system, including the appellate circuits.

The federal system has additional trial courts with limited jurisdiction, differing from the general jurisdiction of the federal district courts. These courts include, for example, the federal bankruptcy courts, Indian tribal courts, Tax Court, Court of Federal Claims, Court of Veterans Appeals, and the Court of International Trade.

(b) U.S. Courts of Appeals   The final decision in a federal district court is not necessarily the end of a case because it is a court of original jurisdiction, and its decisions can be appealed to a court with appellate jurisdiction. In the federal court system, the federal districts are grouped together geographically into 12 judicial circuits, including one for the District of Columbia. Additionally, a thirteenth federal circuit, called the *Federal Circuit,* hears certain types of appeals from all of the circuits, including specialty cases such as patent appeals. Each circuit has an appellate court called the U.S. Court of Appeals, and the judges for these courts review the decisions of the federal district courts. Generally, a panel of three judges reviews the cases. However, some decisions, called **en banc** decisions, are made by

en banc the term used when the full panel of judges on the appellate court hears a case.

FIGURE 2-2   *The Thirteen Federal Judicial Circuits*

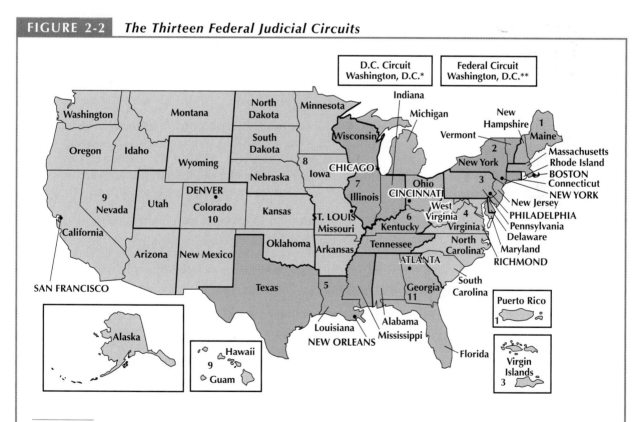

*A sizable portion of the caseload of the D.C. Circuit comes from the federal administrative agencies and offices located in Washington, D.C., such as the Securities and Exchange Commission, the National Labor Relations Board, the Federal Trade Commission, the Secretary of the Treasury, and the Labor Department, as well as appeals from the U.S. District Court of the District of Columbia.

**Rather than being defined by geography like the regional courts of appeals, the Federal Circuit is defined by subject matter, having jurisdiction over such matters as patent infringement cases, appeals from the Court of Federal Claims and the Court of International Trade, and appeals from administrative rulings regarding subject matter such as unfair import practices and tariff schedule disputes.

the circuit's full panel of judges. **For Example,** in 2003, the Ninth Circuit heard an appeal on a father's right to challenge the requirement that his daughter recite the Pledge of Allegiance in the public school she attended. The contentious case had so many issues that the Ninth Circuit issued three opinions and on the third opinion the case was heard *en banc.*[5]

(c) U.S. Supreme Court   The final court in the federal system is the U.S. Supreme Court. The U.S. Supreme Court has appellate jurisdiction over cases that are appealed from the federal courts of appeals as well as from state supreme courts when a constitutional issue is involved in the case or a state court has reversed a federal court ruling. The U.S. Supreme Court does not hear all cases from the federal courts of appeals but has a process called granting a **writ of *certiorari,*** which is a preliminary review of those cases appealed to decide whether a case will be heard or allowed to stand as ruled on by the lower courts.[6]

writ of *certiorari* order by the U.S. Supreme Court granting a right of review by the court of a lower court decision.

The U.S. Supreme Court is the only court expressly created in the U.S. Constitution. All other courts in the federal system were created by Congress pursuant to the Constitution's language allowing such a system if Congress found it necessary. The Constitution also makes the U.S. Supreme Court a court of original jurisdiction. The U.S. Supreme Court serves as the trial court for cases involving ambassadors, public ministers, or consuls and for cases in which two states are involved in a lawsuit. **For Example,** the U.S. Supreme Court has served for a number of years as the trial court for a Colorado River water rights case in which California, Nevada, and Arizona are parties.

3. STATE COURT SYSTEMS

(a) General Trial Courts   Most states have trial courts of general jurisdiction that may be called superior courts, circuit courts, or county courts. These courts of general and original jurisdiction usually hear both criminal and civil cases. Cases that do not meet the jurisdictional requirements for the federal district courts would be tried in these courts. Figure 2-3 illustrates a sample state court system.

(b) Specialty Courts   Most states also have courts with limited jurisdiction, sometimes referred to as *specialty courts.* **For Example,** most states have juvenile courts, or courts with limited jurisdiction over criminal matters that involve defendants who are under the age of 18. Other specialty courts or lesser courts in state systems are probate and family law courts.

(c) City, Municipal, and Justice Courts   Cities and counties may also have lesser courts with limited jurisdiction, which may be referred to as *municipal courts* or *justice courts.* These courts generally handle civil matters in which the claim made in the suit is an amount below a certain level, such as $5,000 or $10,000. These courts may also handle misdemeanor types of offenses, such as traffic violations or violations of noise ordinances, and the trials for them.

---

[5] *Newdow v. U.S. Congress,* 292 F.3d 597, 602 (CA9 2002) (*Newdow I*); *Newdow v. U.S. Congress,* 313 F3d 500, 502 (CA9 2002) (*Newdow II*); and *Newdow v. U.S. Congress,* 328 F.3d 466, 468 (CA9 2003) (*Newdow III*). The U.S. Supreme Court eventually heard the case. *Elkgrove Unified School District v. Newdow,* 542 US 1 (2004). Another *en banc* hearing occurred at the Ninth Circuit over the issues in the California gubernatorial recall election. The three-judge panel held that the voting methods in California violated the rights of voters and therefore placed a stay on the election. However, the Ninth Circuit then heard the case *en banc* and reversed the decision of the original three-judge panel. The recall election then proceeded.

[6] For example, the Supreme Court refused to grant *certiorari* in a Fifth Circuit case on law school admissions at the University of Texas. However, it granted *certiorari* in a later case involving law school admissions at the University of Michigan. *Gratz v Bollinger,* 539 US 244 (2003).

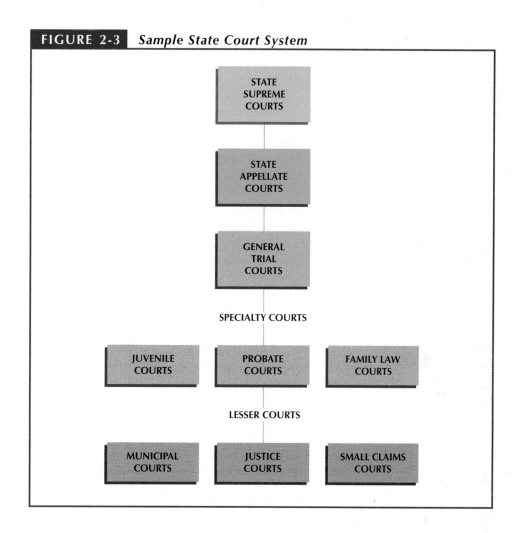

FIGURE 2-3   *Sample State Court System*

(Figure content: STATE SUPREME COURTS → STATE APPELLATE COURTS → GENERAL TRIAL COURTS; SPECIALTY COURTS: JUVENILE COURTS, PROBATE COURTS, FAMILY LAW COURTS; LESSER COURTS: MUNICIPAL COURTS, JUSTICE COURTS, SMALL CLAIMS COURTS)

small claims courts courts that resolve disputes between parties when those disputes do not exceed a minimal level; no lawyers are permitted; the parties represent themselves.

(d) SMALL CLAIMS COURTS   Most states also have **small claims courts** at the county or city level. These are courts of limited jurisdiction where parties with small amounts in dispute may come to have a third party, such as a justice of the peace or city judge, review their disputes and determine how they should be resolved. A true small claims court is one in which the parties are not permitted to be represented by counsel. Rather, the parties present their cases to the judge in an informal manner without the strict procedural rules that apply in courts of general jurisdiction. Small claims courts provide a faster and inexpensive means for resolving a dispute that does not involve a large amount of claimed damages.

(e) STATE APPELLATE COURTS   Most states also have intermediate-level courts similar to the federal courts of appeals. They are courts with appellate jurisdiction that review the decisions of lower courts in that state. Decisions of the general trial courts in a state would be appealed to these courts.

(f) STATE SUPREME COURTS   The highest court in most states is generally known as the *state supreme court,* but a few states, such as New York, may call their highest court the *court of appeals;* Maine and Massachusetts, for example, call their highest court the *supreme judicial court.* State supreme courts primarily have appellate jurisdiction, but some states' courts do have original jurisdiction, such as in Arizona, where counties in litigation have their trial at the supreme court level. Most state supreme courts do not hear all cases appealed. These courts also have a screening process. They are required to hear some cases, such as criminal cases in which the defendant has received the death penalty. A decision of a state supreme court is final except in those circumstances in which a federal law or treaty or the U.S. Constitution is involved. Cases with these federal subject matter issues can then be appealed to the U.S. Supreme Court.

 ## COURT PROCEDURE

Once a party decides to use the court system for resolution of a dispute, that party enters a world with specific rules, procedures, and terms that must be used to have a case proceed.

4. PARTICIPANTS IN THE COURT SYSTEM

The **plaintiff** is the party that initiates the proceedings in a court of original jurisdiction. In a criminal case in which charges are brought, the party initiating the proceedings would be called the **prosecutor**. The party against whom the civil or criminal proceedings are brought is the **defendant**. A **judge** is the primary officer of the court and is either an elected or an appointed official who presides over the matters brought before the court. Attorneys or lawyers are trained individuals selected by the plaintiff and the defendant as their representatives in the matter for purposes of presenting their cases.

A **jury** is a body of citizens sworn by a court to reach a verdict on the basis of the case presented to them. Jurors are chosen for service based on lists compiled from voter registration and driver's license records.

> **plaintiff** the party who initiates a lawsuit.
>
> **prosecutor** party who originates a criminal proceeding.
>
> **defendant** party charged with a violation of civil or criminal law in a proceeding.
>
> **judge** primary officer of the court.
>
> **jury** a body of citizens sworn by a court to determine by verdict the issues of fact submitted to them.

5. WHICH LAW APPLIES—CONFLICTS OF LAW

When a lawsuit is brought, there is not just the question of where a case will be tried but also of what law will be applied in determining the rights of the parties. The principle that determines when a court applies the law of its own state—the law of the forum—or some foreign law is called *conflict of laws*. Because there are 50 state court systems and a federal court system, as well as a high degree of interstate activity, conflicts of law questions arise frequently.

Some general rules apply. For example, the law of the state in which the court is located governs the case on procedural issues and rules of evidence. In contract litigation, the court applies the law of the state in which the contract was made for determining issues of formation. Matters relating to the performance of the contract, excuse or liability for nonperformance, and the measure of damages for nonperformance are generally governed by the law of the state where the contract is to be performed. Similar considerations apply to the interpretation of international contracts. **For Example,** a California court will apply Swiss law to a contract made in Switzerland that is to be performed in that country.

However, it is becoming more common in cases of contracts with interstate aspects for the parties to specify their choice of law in their contract. In the absence of a law-selecting provision in the contract, there is a growing acceptance of the rule that a contract should be governed by the law of the state that has the most significant contacts with the transaction.

For Example, assume the buyer's place of business and the seller's plant are located in Nebraska, and the buyer is purchasing goods from the seller to resell to Nebraska customers. Many courts will hold that this is a contract governed by the law of Nebraska in all respects. In determining which state has the most significant contacts, the court considers the place of contracting, negotiating, and performing; the location of the subject matter of the contract; and the domicile (residence), states of incorporation, and principal place of business of the parties.

6. INITIAL STEPS IN A LAWSUIT

The following steps in a lawsuit generally apply in cases brought in courts of original jurisdiction. Not every step applies in every case, but understanding the terminology of litigation is important for businesspeople.

complaint the initial pleading filed by the plaintiff in many actions, which in many states may be served as original process to acquire jurisdiction over the defendant.

(a) COMMENCEMENT OF A LAWSUIT   A lawsuit begins with the filing of a **complaint.** The complaint generally contains a description of the conduct complained of by the plaintiff and a request for damages, such as a monetary amount. **For Example,** a plaintiff in a contract suit would describe the contract, when it was entered into, and when the defendant stopped performance on the contract. A copy of the contract would be attached to the complaint.

process paperwork served personally on a defendant in a civil case.

(b) SERVICE OF PROCESS   Once the plaintiff has filed the complaint with the clerk of the court that has jurisdiction over the case, the plaintiff has the responsibility of notifying the defendant that the lawsuit has been filed. The defendant must be served with **process.** Process, often called a *writ, notice,* or *summons,* is delivered to the defendant and includes a copy of the complaint and notification that the defendant must appear and respond to the allegations in the complaint.

answer what a defendant must file to admit or deny facts asserted by the plaintiff.

motion to dismiss a pleading that may be filed to attack the adverse party's pleading as not stating a cause of action or a defense.

demurrer a pleading to dismiss the adverse party's pleading for not stating a cause of action or a defense.

(c) THE DEFENDANT'S RESPONSE AND THE PLEADINGS   After the defendant is served with process in the case, the defendant is required to make some response or to **answer** the complaint within the time provided under the court's rules. In answering the plaintiff's complaint, the defendant has several options. For example, the defendant could make a **motion to dismiss**, which is a request to the court to dismiss the lawsuit on the grounds that, even if everything the plaintiff said in the complaint were true, there is still no right of recovery. A motion to dismiss is also called a **demurrer**.

counterclaim a claim that the defendant in an action may make against the plaintiff.

A defendant could also respond and deny the allegations. **For Example,** in a contract lawsuit, the defendant-seller could say he did not breach the contract but stopped shipment of the goods because the plaintiff-buyer did not pay for the goods in advance as the contract required. A defendant could also **counterclaim** in the answer, which is asking the court for damages as a result of the underlying dispute. **For Example,** the defendant-seller in the contract lawsuit might ask for damages for the plaintiff-buyer's failure to pay as the contract required.

pleadings the papers filed by the parties in an action in order to set forth the facts and frame the issues to be tried, although, under some systems, the pleadings merely give notice or a general indication of the nature of the issues.

All documents filed in this initial phase of the case are referred to as the **pleadings**. The pleadings, when accepted following the defendant's objections and the plaintiff's corrections, are a statement of the case and the basis for recovery if all the facts alleged can be proved.

discovery procedures for ascertaining facts prior to the time of trial in order to eliminate the element of surprise in litigation.

(d) DISCOVERY   The Federal Rules of Civil Procedure and similar rules in all states permit one party to obtain from the adverse party information about all witnesses, documents, and any other items relevant to the case. **Discovery** requires each side to name its potential witnesses and to provide each side the chance to question those witnesses in advance of the trial. Each party also has the opportunity to examine, inspect, and photograph books, records, buildings, and machines. Even examining the physical or mental condition of a party is part of discovery when it has relevance in the case. The scope of discovery is extremely broad because the rules permit any questions that are likely to lead to admissible evidence.

deposition the testimony of a witness taken out of court before a person authorized to administer oaths.

impeach using prior inconsistent evidence to challenge the credibility of a witness.

(1) Deposition.   A **deposition** is the testimony of a witness taken under oath outside the courtroom; it is transcribed by a court reporter. Each party is permitted to question the witness. If a party or a witness gives testimony at the trial that is inconsistent with her deposition testimony, the prior inconsistent testimony can be used to **impeach** the witness's credibility at trial

Depositions can be taken either for discovery purposes or to preserve the testimony of a witness who will not be available during the trial. Some states now permit depositions to be videotaped. A videotape is a more effective way of presenting deposition testimony than reading that testimony at trial from a reporter's transcript because jurors can see the witness and the witness's demeanor and hear the words as they were spoken, complete with inflection.[7]

interrogatories written questions used as a discovery tool that must be answered under oath.

request for production of documents discovery tool for uncovering paper evidence in a case.

(2) Other Forms of Discovery.   Other forms of discovery include written **interrogatories** (questions) and written **requests for production of documents**. These discovery requests can be very time consuming to the answering party and often lead to pretrial legal disputes between the parties and their attorneys as a result of the legal expenses involved.

motion for summary judgment request that the court decide a case on basis of law only because there are no material issues disputed by the parties.

(e) MOTION FOR SUMMARY JUDGMENT   If no issue of material fact in the case is disputed, either party can file a **motion for summary judgment**. Using affidavits or deposition testimony obtained in discovery, the party can establish that there are no factual issues and that the case can be decided as an issue of law by a judge. For example, suppose that the parties can agree that they entered into a life insurance contract but dispute whether the policy applies when there is a suicide. The facts are not in dispute; the law on payment of insurance proceeds in the event that a suicide is in dispute. Such a case is one that is appropriate for summary judgment.

expert witness one who has acquired special knowledge in a particular field as through practical experience or study, or both, whose opinion is admissible as an aid to the trier of fact.

(f) DESIGNATION OF EXPERT WITNESSES   In some cases, such as those involving medical malpractice, the parties may want to designate an expert witness. An **expert witness** is a witness who has some special expertise, such as an economist who gives expert opinion on the value of future lost income or a physician who testifies whether a doctor followed protocol in treating a patient. There are rules for naming expert witnesses as well as for admitting into evidence any studies or documents of the expert.[8] The purpose of these rules is to avoid the problem of what

---

[7] At the civil trial of O. J. Simpson for the wrongful death of Nicole Brown Simpson and Ronald Goldman, Daniel Petrocelli used a videotape of Mr. Simpson's deposition very effectively in impeaching Mr. Simpson's testimony at trial. Daniel Petrocelli, *Triumph of Justice: The Final Judgment on the Simpson Saga* (New York: Crown, 1998).

[8] *Daubert v Merrell Dow Pharmaceuticals, Inc.*, 509 US 579 (1993).

has been called *junk science,* or the admission of experts' testimony and research that has not been properly conducted or reviewed by peers.

7. THE TRIAL

(a) Selecting a Jury   Jurors drawn for service are questioned by the judge and lawyers to determine whether they are biased or have any preformed judgments about the parties in the case. Jury selection is called ***voir dire*** examination. **For Example,** in the trial of Martha Stewart, the multimedia home and garden diva, it took a great deal of time for the lawyers to question the potential jurors about their prior knowledge concerning the case, which had received nationwide attention and much media coverage. Lawyers have the opportunity to remove jurors who know parties in the case or who indicate they have already formed opinions about guilt or innocence. The attorneys question the potential jurors to determine if a juror should be *challenged for cause* (e.g., when the prospective juror states he is employed by the plaintiff's company). Challenges for cause are unlimited, but each side can also exercise six to eight peremptory challenges.[9] A peremptory challenge is an arbitrary challenge that may be used to strike (remove) a juror except for racial reasons.

(b) Opening Statements   After the jury is called, the opposing attorneys make their **opening statements** to the jury. An opening statement, as one lawyer has explained, makes a puzzle frame for the case so jurors can follow the witnesses and place the pieces of the case—the various forms of evidence—within the frame.

(c) The Presentation of Evidence   Following the opening statements, the plaintiff then begins to present his case with witnesses and other evidence. A judge rules on the **admissibility** of evidence. Evidence can consist of documents, testimony, and even physical evidence.

In the case of testimony, the attorney for the plaintiff conducts **direct examination** of his witnesses during his case, and the defense attorney then **cross-examines** the plaintiff's witnesses. The plaintiff's attorney can then ask questions again of his witnesses in what is called **redirect examination.** Finally, the defendant may question the plaintiff's witnesses again in **recross-examination.** This procedure is followed with all of the plaintiff's witnesses, and then the defendant presents her case after the plaintiff's case concludes. During the defendant's case, the lawyer for the defendant conducts direct examination of the defendant's witnesses, and the plaintiff's lawyer can then cross-examine the defendant's witnesses.

(d) Motion for a Directed Verdict   A motion for a **directed verdict** asks the court to grant a verdict because even if all the evidence that has been presented by each side were true, there is either no basis for recovery or no defense to recovery. For example, in some states, the defendant can make a motion for a directed verdict after the plaintiff's case is concluded. The defendant's motion argues that even if the plaintiff's case were 100 percent true, there is no basis in law for recovery. It is also possible for either side to move for a directed verdict after both sides have presented their cases. The defendant is arguing the same position as stated earlier, that there is no basis for recovery even assuming all facts to be true.

---

voir dire **examination** the preliminary examination of a juror or a witness to ascertain fitness to act as such.

opening statements statements by opposing attorneys that tell the jury what their cases will prove.

admissibility the quality of the evidence in a case that allows it to be presented to the jury.

direct examination examination of a witness by his or her attorney.

cross-examination the examination made of a witness by the attorney for the adverse party.

redirect examination questioning after cross-examination, in which the attorney for the witness testifying may ask the same witness other questions to overcome effects of the cross-examination.

recross-examination an examination by the other side's attorney that follows the redirect examination.

directed verdict a direction by the trial judge to the jury to return a verdict in favor of a specified party to the action.

---

[9] The number of peremptory challenges varies from state to state and may also vary within a particular state depending on the type of case. For example, in Arizona, peremptory challenges are unlimited in capital cases.

ETHICS & THE LAW

On July 9, 1999, a Los Angeles jury awarded Patricia Anderson, her four children, and her friend Jo Tigner $107 million in actual damages and $4.8 billion in punitive damages from General Motors (GM) in a lawsuit the five brought against GM because they were trapped and burned in their Chevrolet Malibu when it exploded on impact following a rear-end collision.

Jury foreman Coleman Thorton, explaining the magnitude of the jury verdict, said, "GM has no regard for the people in their cars, and they should be held responsible for it." Richard Shapiro, an attorney for GM, said, "We're very disappointed. This was a very sympathetic case. The people who were injured were innocent in this matter. They were the victims of a drunk driver."

The accident, which occurred on Christmas Eve 1993, was the result of a drunk driver's striking the Anderson's Malibu at 70 mph. The driver's blood alcohol level was 0.20, but the defense lawyers noted they were not permitted to disclose to the jury that the driver of the auto that struck the Malibu was drunk.

During the discovery process, lawyers for the Andersons uncovered a 1973 internal "value analysis" memo written by a low-level engineer, Edward C. Ivey, analyzing the potential cost to GM of "post-collision fuel-tank fires." Mr. Ivey used a figure of $200,000 for the cost of a fatality and noted that there are 500 fatalities per year in GM auto fuel fire accidents. The memo also stated that his analysis must be read in the context of "it is really impossible to put a value on human life."* Mr. Ivey wrote that the cost of these explosions to GM would be $2.40 per car.

Lawyers uncovered another memo related to the Ivey memo. An in-house lawyer discovered the Ivey memo in 1981 and wrote:

Obviously, Ivey is not an individual whom we would ever, in any conceivable situation, want identified to the plaintiffs in a post-collision fuel-fed fire case, and the documents he generated are undoubtedly some of the potentially most harmful and most damaging were they ever to be produced.**

In the initial cases brought against GM, the company's defense was that the engineer's thinking was his own and did not reflect company policy. However, when the 1981 lawyer's commentary was found as part of discovery in a Florida case in 1998, GM lost that line of defense. In the Florida case in which a 13-year-old boy was burned to death in a 1983 Oldsmobile Cutlass station wagon, the jury awarded his family $33 million.

The two documents have become the center of each case. Judge Ernest G. Williams of Los Angeles Superior Court, who upheld the verdict in the $4.8 billion Los Angeles case but reduced the damages, wrote in his opinion:

The court finds that clear and convincing evidence demonstrated that defendants' fuel tank was placed behind the axle of the automobiles of the make and model here in order to maximize profits to the disregard of public safety.

On appeal, the California appellate court reduced the verdict amount to $1.2 billion.***

Discuss the ethical issues involved with Mr. Ivey's memo and the lawyer's conduct in 1981.

---

* Milo Geyelin, "How an Internal Memo Written 26 Years Ago Is Costing GM Dearly," *Wall Street Journal,* September 29, 1999, A1.

** Id. at A6.

*** Id.

(THINKING THINGS THROUGH)

Why Do We Require Sworn Testimony?

There is a difference between what people say in conversation and even what company executives say in speeches and reports and what they are willing to say under oath. The taking of the oath often means that different information and recollections will emerge. The oath is symbolic and carries the penalty of criminal prosecution for perjury if the testimony given is false.

The *Wall Street Journal* has reported that the testimony of executives in the Microsoft antitrust trial and their statements regarding their business relationships outside the courtroom are quite different. For example, the following quotations indicate some discrepancies. Eric Benhamou, the CEO of Palm, Inc., said:

We believe that the handheld opportunity remains wide open. . . . Unlike the PC industry, there is no monopoly of silicon, there is no monopoly of software.

However, at the Microsoft trial, another officer of Palm, Michael Mace, offered the following testimony:

We believe that there is a very substantial risk that Microsoft could manipulate its products and its standards in order to exclude Palm from the marketplace in the future.

Likewise, Microsoft has taken different positions inside and outside the courtroom. For example, an attorney for Microsoft, in grilling a witness for a competitor, stated that Microsoft had ''zero deployments of its interactive TV middleware products connected to cable systems in the United States; isn't that correct, sir?'' However, Microsoft's marketing materials provide as follows:

Microsoft's multiple deployments around the world now including Charter-show Microsoft TV is ready to deploy now and set the standard for what TV can be.*

For more information on the Microsoft antitrust cases, go to **http://www.usdoj.gov** or **http://www.microsoft.com**.

* Rebecca Buckman and Nicholas Kulish, ''*Microsoft Trial Prompts an Outbreak of Doublespeak*,'' Wall Street Journal, April 15, 2002, B1, B3.

---

summation the attorney address that follows all the evidence presented in court and sums up a case and recommends a particular verdict be returned by the jury.

mistrial a court's declaration that terminates a trial and postpones it to a later date; commonly entered when evidence has been of a highly prejudicial character or when a juror has been guilty of misconduct.

instruction summary of the law given to jurors by the judge before deliberation begins.

The plaintiff is arguing that even if everything the defendant presented was 100 percent true, there was nothing in the defense case that challenged the plaintiff's right to recovery.

(e) SUMMATION   After the witnesses for both parties have been examined and all the evidence has been presented, each attorney makes another address to the jury. These statements are called **summations** or *closing arguments;* they summarize the case and suggest that a particular verdict be returned by the jury.

(f) MOTION FOR MISTRIAL   During the course of a trial, when necessary to avoid great injustice, the trial court may declare that there has been a **mistrial**. The declaration of a mistrial terminates the trial and requires that it start over with a new jury. A mistrial can be declared for jury or attorney misconduct. **For Example,** if a juror were caught fraternizing with one of the lawyers in the case, objectivity would be compromised and the court would most likely declare a mistrial.

(g) JURY INSTRUCTIONS AND VERDICT   After the summation by the attorneys, the court gives the jurors **instructions** on the appropriate law to apply to the facts they find to be true or untrue. The jury then deliberates and renders its verdict. After the jury renders a verdict, the court enters a judgment conforming to the verdict. If the jury is deadlocked and unable to reach a verdict, the case is reset for a new trial at some future date.

(h) MOTION FOR NEW TRIAL; MOTION FOR JUDGMENT N.O.V.   A court may grant a judgment *non obstante veredicto* or a **judgment n.o.v.** (notwithstanding the verdict) if the verdict is clearly wrong as a matter of law. The court can set aside the verdict and enter a judgment in favor of the other party. Perhaps one of the most famous judgments n.o.v. occurred in Boston in 1997 when a judge reversed the murder conviction of nanny Louise Woodward, who was charged with the murder of one of her young charges.

judgment n.o.v., or *non obstante veredicto* (notwithstanding the verdict), a judgment entered after verdict upon the motion of the losing party on the ground that the verdict is so wrong that a judgment should be entered the opposite of the verdict.

8. POSTTRIAL PROCEDURES

(a) RECOVERY OF COSTS/ATTORNEY FEES   Generally, the prevailing party is awarded costs. Costs include filing fees, service-of-process fees, witness fees, deposition transcript costs, and jury fees. Costs do not include compensation spent by a party for preparing the case or being present at trial, including the time lost from work because of the case and the fee paid to the attorney, although lost wages from an injury are generally part of damages.

Attorney fees may be recovered by a party who prevails if a statute permits the recovery of attorney fees or if the complaint involves a claim for breach of contract and the contract contains a clause providing for recovery of attorney fees.

(b) EXECUTION OF JUDGMENT   After a judgment for the amount of damages plus costs has been entered or all appeals or appeal rights have ended, the losing party should comply with the judgment of the court. If not, the winning party may then take steps to execute, or carry out, the judgment. The **execution** is accomplished by the seizure and sale of the losing party's assets by the sheriff according to a writ of execution or a writ of possession.

execution the carrying out of a judgment of a court, generally directing that property owned by the defendant be sold and the proceeds first be used to pay the execution or judgment creditor.

garnishment the name given in some states to attachment proceedings.

Garnishment is a common method of satisfying a judgment. When the judgment debtor is an employee, the appropriate judicial authority in the state garnishes (by written notice to the employer) a portion of the employee's wages on a regular basis until the judgment is paid.

ALTERNATIVE DISPUTE RESOLUTION (ADR)

Parties can use means other than litigation to resolve disagreements or disputes. The discussion of the details of litigation shows its time and money costs and should encourage those with disputes to pursue alternative methods for resolving them. Those methods, which include arbitration, mediation, and several other forms of resolution, are enjoying increasing popularity. Figure 2-4 provides an overall view of dispute resolution procedures.

9. ARBITRATION

arbitration the settlement of disputed questions, whether of law or fact, by one or more arbitrators by whose decision the parties agree to be bound.

In **arbitration**, a dispute is settled by one or more arbitrators (disinterested persons selected by the parties to the dispute). Arbitration enables the parties to present the facts before trained experts familiar with the industry practices that may affect the nature and outcome of the dispute. Arbitration first reached extensive use in the field

FIGURE 2-4	*Dispute Resolution Procedures*

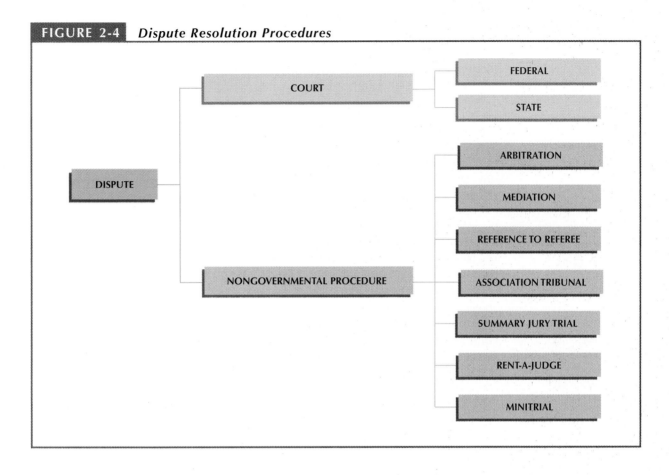

of commercial contracts and is encouraged as a means of avoiding expensive litigation and easing the workload of courts.[10]

A number of states have adopted the Uniform Arbitration Act.[11] Under this act and similar statutes, the parties to a contract may agree in advance that all disputes arising under it will be submitted to arbitration. In some instances, the contract will name the arbitrators for the duration of the contract. The uniform act requires a written agreement to arbitrate.[12]

The Federal Arbitration Act[13] provides that an arbitration clause in a contract relating to an interstate transaction is valid, irrevocable, and enforceable. When a contract subject to the Federal Arbitration Act provides for the arbitration of disputes, the parties are bound to arbitrate in accordance with the federal statute even if the agreement to arbitrate would not be binding under state law.

---

[10] *Hart v. McChristian,* 42 S.W.2d 552 (Ark 2001). Arbitration has existed in the United States since 1920 when New York passed an arbitration statute. For a look at the history of arbitration, see Charles L. Knapp, "Taking Contracts Private: The Quiet Revolution in Contract Law," 71 Fordham L. Rev. 761 (2002).

[11] On August 3, 2000, the National Conference of Commissioners on Uniform State Laws unanimously passed major revisions to the Uniform Arbitration Act (UAA). These revisions were the first major changes in 45 years to the UAA, which is the basis of arbitration law in 49 states, although not all states have adopted it in its entirety. Thirty-five states and the District of Columbia have adopted the 1955 version. Only 8 states have adopted the UAA 2000 revisions. Christopher Benne, *et al., State Legislative Update,* 2 Journal of Dispute Resolution 4A (2005).

[12] *Anderson v Federated Mutual Ins. Co.,* 465 NW2d 68 (Minn App 1991).

[13] 9 USC § 114 *et. seq.*

(a) MANDATORY ARBITRATION   In contrast with statutes that merely regulate arbitration when it is selected voluntarily by the parties, some statutes require that certain kinds of disputes be submitted to arbitration. In some states, by rule or statute, the arbitration of small claims is required.

(b) SCOPE OF ARBITRATION   When arbitration is required by statute, the terms of the statute will define the scope of the arbitration. When the parties have voluntarily agreed to arbitrate, their agreement will control the scope of the dispute. In such a case, questions may arise as to what disputes are covered. Because arbitration is now favored, any doubt as to its scope will be decided in favor of arbitration by the arbitrator.[14]

(c) FINALITY OF ARBITRATION   Most parties provide, within their arbitration agreements, that the decision of the arbitrator will be final. Such a clause is binding on the parties, even when the decision seems to be wrong, and can be set aside only if there is clear proof of fraud, arbitrary conduct, or a significant procedural error.[15]

In contrast, when arbitration is mandatory under statute or rule, it is generally provided that the losing party may appeal from such arbitration to a court.[16] The appeal proceeds just as though there had never been any prior arbitration. This new court proceeding is called a **trial *de novo*** and is necessary to preserve the constitutional right to a jury trial. As a practical matter, however, relatively few appeals are taken from arbitration decisions.

trial *de novo* a trial required to preserve the constitutional right to a jury trial by allowing an appeal to proceed as though there never had been any prior hearing or decision.

10. MEDIATION

In **mediation**, a neutral person acts as a messenger between opposing sides of a dispute, carrying to each side the latest settlement offer made by the other. The mediator has no authority to make a decision, although in some cases the mediator may make suggestions that might ultimately be accepted by the disputing parties.

The use of mediation has the advantage of keeping discussions going when the disputing parties have developed such fixed attitudes or personal animosity that direct discussion between them has become impossible.

mediation the settlement of a dispute through the use of a messenger who carries to each side of the dispute the issues and offers in the case.

11. MEDARB

In this new form of alternative dispute resolution (ADR), the arbitrator is also empowered to act as a mediator. Beyond just hearing a case, the arbitrator acts as a messenger for the parties on unresolved issues.

12. REFERENCE TO A THIRD PERSON

Many types of transactions provide for **reference to a third person**, in which a third person or a committee makes an out-of-court determination of the rights of persons. **For Example,** employees and an employer may have agreed as a term of the employment contract that claims of employees under retirement plans will be decided by a

reference to a third person settlement that allows a nonparty to resolve the dispute.

---

[14] *First Options v Kaplan,* 514 US 938 (1995). See also *Engel v Refco, Inc.,* 746 NYS 2d 826 (2002), in which the court noted that parties can agree to an arbitration clause through conduct.

[15] *Trans Chemical Ltd. v China Nat. Machinery Import & Export,* 161 F3d 314 (5th Cir 1998); *Crim v Pepperidge Farm, Inc.,* 32 F Supp 2d 326 (D Md 1999).

[16] *Porreco v Red Top RV Center,* 216 Cal App 3d 113, 264 Cal Rptr 609 (1989). See *Business Law Today* 8 (March/April 1999), which is an entire issue devoted to ADR issues and advantages.

(────── **E-COMMERCE AND CYBERLAW** ──────)

Speed of Light Injunctions: Remedies and the Internet

Because e-commerce moves quickly, legal wrongs in cyberspace can very rapidly cause irreparable damage. For example, suppose that a Web site is selling gray market goods. The trademark holder who relies on courts and an injunction will find the goods sold over the Internet before the court can rule. As a result, many judges, when facing a petition for an injunction for a cyberspace company, encourage the parties to discuss and resolve the issue because just a hearing for a preliminary injunction will take too much time. As one court notes, "technology can outdistance" us very quickly.*

_____

Sun Microsystems, Inc. v Microsoft Corp., 188 F3d 1115 (9th Cir 1999).

designated board or committee. In a sales contract, the seller and buyer can select a third person to determine the price to be paid for goods. Construction contracts often include a provision that any disputes shall be referred to the architect in charge of the construction and that the architect's decision will be final.

Ordinarily, with these types of clauses, the parties agree that the decision of such a third person or board is final and there will be no judicial appeal or review. These referrals often eliminate the disputes or pursuit of remedies. **For Example,** fire insurance policies commonly provide that if the parties cannot agree on the amount of the loss, each will appoint an appraiser, the two appraisers will appoint a third appraiser, and the three will determine the amount of the loss the insurer is required to pay. These appraisers must be independent and impartial.

13. ASSOCIATION TRIBUNALS

association tribunal a court created by a trade association or group for the resolution of disputes among its members.

Many disputes never reach the courts because both parties to a dispute belong to a group or an association, and the **association tribunal** created by the group or association disposes of the matter. A dispute between members of a labor union, a stockbrokers' exchange, or a church may be heard by some board or committee within the association or group. Courts review the actions of such tribunals to determine that a fair and proper procedure was followed, but generally they go no further. Courts do not examine the facts of the case to see if the association tribunal reached the same conclusion that the court could have reached.

Trade associations commonly require their members to employ out-of-court methods of dispute settlement. **For Example,** the National Association of Home Builders requires its member builders to employ arbitration. The National Automobile Dealers Association provides for panels to determine warranty claims of customers. The decision of such panels is final as to the builder or dealer, but the consumer can still bring a regular lawsuit after losing before the panel. Members of an association must use the association tribunal, which means they cannot bypass the association tribunal and go directly to a law court.[17]

_____

[17] *Canady v Meharry Medical College,* 811 SW2d 902 (Tenn App 1991).

14. SUMMARY JURY TRIAL

summary jury trial a mock or dry-run trial for parties to get a feel for how their cases will play to a jury.

A **summary jury trial** is, in effect, a dry run or mock trial in which the lawyers present their claims before a jury of six persons. The object is to get the reaction of a sample jury. No evidence is presented before this jury, and it bases its opinion solely on what the lawyers state. The determination of the jury has no binding effect, but it has value in that it gives the lawyers some idea of what a jury might think if there were an actual trial. This type of ADR has special value when the heart of a case is whether something is reasonable under all circumstances. When the lawyers and their clients see how the sample jury reacts, they may moderate their positions and reach a settlement.

15. RENT-A-JUDGE

rent-a-judge plan dispute resolution through private courts with judges paid to be referees for the cases.

Under the **rent-a-judge plan**, the parties hire a judge to hear the case. In many states, the parties voluntarily choose the judge as a "referee," and the judge acts under a statute authorizing the appointment of referees. Under such a statute, the referee hears all evidence just as though there were a regular trial, and the rented judge's determination is binding on the parties unless reversed on appeal if such an appeal (like a court trial) is permitted under the parties' agreement. In some jurisdictions, special provision is made for the parties to agree that the decision of the judge selected as referee will be final.

16. MINITRIAL

When only part of a case is disputed, the parties may stay within the framework of a lawsuit but agree that only the disputed issues will be taken to trial and submitted to a jury. When there is no real dispute over the liability of the defendant but the parties disagree as to the damages, the issue of damages alone may be submitted to the jury. This shortened trial is often called a **minitrial**.

minitrial a trial held on portions of the case or certain issues in the case.

A minitrial may also consist of the parties agreeing to submit their case to a particular person, frequently a retired judge, to listen to the evidence on just the disputed issues and decide the case. The agreement of the parties for the minitrial may specify whether this decision will be binding on the parties. As a practical matter, the evaluation of a case by a neutral person often brings the opposing parties together to reach a settlement.

17. JUDICIAL TRIAGE

judicial triage court management tool used by judges to expedite certain cases in which time is of the essence, such as asbestos cases in which the plaintiffs are gravely ill.

The court systems, experiencing heavy caseloads, now practice **judicial triage**. Judges examine cases from a timeliness perspective. For example, in asbestos cases, judges are now evaluating plaintiffs on the basis of "how sick they are" and expediting trials for those plaintiffs who are the most ill from the alleged effects of asbestos that are the subject of their suits. The trials of those who do not have medical documentation of current illness are postponed and placed on the inactive docket until the court can get to them or until the plaintiffs become sick. Using triage, one judge has been able to bring to trial 40 percent of all asbestos cases brought since 1992.[18]

---

[18] Susan Warren, "Swamped Courts Practice Plaintiff Triage," *Wall Street Journal*, January 27, 2003, B1, B3.

LAWFLIX

Class Action (1991) (R)

Here is a good movie to illustrate discovery and the ethics of withholding documents in production of evidence/paperwork.

For movie clips that illustrate business law concepts, see LawFlix at **http://wdvl.westbuslaw.com.**

18. CONTRACT PROVISIONS

The parties' contract may pave the way for the settlement of future disputes by containing clauses requiring the parties to use one of the procedures already described. In addition, contracts may provide that no action may be taken until after the expiration of a specified cooling-off period. Contracts may also specify that the parties should continue in the performance of their contract even though a dispute between them still exists.

19. DISPOSITION OF COMPLAINTS AND OMBUDSMEN

In contrast with the traditional and alternative procedures for resolving disputes are the procedures aimed at removing the grounds for a complaint before it develops into a dispute that requires resolution. **For Example,** the complaint department in a department store is often be able to iron out a difficulty before the customer and the store are locked in an adversarial position that could end in a lawsuit. Grievance committee procedures are often effective in bringing about an adjustment or resolution. A statute may designate a government official to examine complaints. Such an official is often called an **ombudsman.** The few federal statutes that have required such an officer have not given the ombudsman any judicial power. Typically, the ombudsman is limited to receiving complaints, supervising the administration of the system, and making recommendations for improvements.

ombudsman a government official designated by a statute to examine citizen complaints.

SUMMARY

Courts have been created to hear and resolve legal disputes. A court's specific power is defined by its jurisdiction. Courts of original jurisdiction are trial courts, and courts that review the decisions of trial courts are appellate courts. Trial courts may have general jurisdiction to hear a wide range of civil and criminal matters, or they may be courts of limited jurisdiction—such as a probate court or the Tax Court—with the subject matter of their cases restricted to certain areas.

The courts in the United States are organized into two different systems: the state and federal court systems. There are three levels of courts, for the most part, in each system, with trial courts, appellate courts, and a

supreme court in each. The federal courts are federal district courts, federal courts of appeals, and the U.S. Supreme Court. In the states, there may be specialized courts, such as municipal, justice, and small claims courts, for trial courts. Within the courts of original jurisdiction, there are rules for procedures in all matters brought before them. A civil case begins with the filing of a complaint by a plaintiff, which is then answered by a defendant. The parties may be represented by their attorneys. Discovery is the pretrial process used by the parties to find out the evidence in the case. The parties can use depositions, interrogatories, and document requests to uncover relevant information.

The case is managed by a judge and may be tried to a jury selected through the process of *voir dire,* with the parties permitted to challenge jurors on the basis of cause or through the use of their peremptory challenges. The trial begins following discovery and involves opening statements and the presentation of evidence, including the direct examination and cross-examination of witnesses. Once a judgment is entered, the party who has won can collect the judgment through garnishment and a writ of execution.

Alternatives to litigation for dispute resolution are available, including arbitration, mediation, MedArb, reference to a third party, association tribunals, summary jury trials, rent-a-judge plans, minitrials, and the use of ombudsmen. Court dockets are relieved and cases consolidated using judicial triage, a process in which courts hear the cases involving the most serious medical issues and health conditions first. Triage is a blending of the judicial and alternative dispute resolution mechanisms.

► QUESTIONS AND CASE PROBLEMS

1. List the steps in a lawsuit. Begin with the filing of the complaint, and explain the points at which there can be a final determination of the parties' rights in the case.

2. Distinguish between mandatory and voluntary arbitration.

3. What is the difference between mediation and arbitration?

4. Ralph Dewey has been charged with a violation of the Electronic Espionage Act, a federal statute that prohibits the transfer, by computer or disk or other electronic means, of a company's proprietary data and information. Ralph is curious. What type of court has jurisdiction? Can you determine which court?

5. Jerry Lewinsky was called for jury duty. When *voir dire* began, Jerry realized that the case involved his supervisor at work. Can Jerry remain as a juror on the case? Why or why not?

6. Carolyn, Elwood, and Isabella are involved in a real estate development. The development is a failure, and Carolyn, Elwood, and Isabella want to have their rights determined. They could bring a lawsuit, but they are afraid the case is so complicated that a judge and jury not familiar with the problems of real estate development would not reach a proper result. What can they do?

7. Larketta Randolph purchased a mobile home from Better Cents Home Builders, Inc., in Opelika, Alabama. She financed her purchase through Green Tree Financial Corporation. Ms. Randolph signed a standard form Manufactured Home Retail Installment Contract and Security Agreement that required her to buy Vendor's Single Interest insurance, which protects the seller against the costs of repossession in the event of default. The agreement also provided that all disputes arising from, or relating to, the contract, whether arising under case law or statutory law, would be resolved by binding arbitration. Larketta has a dispute with Green Tree over an additional $15 in finance charges she claims were not disclosed in the contract. She and other Green Tree customers file a class action suit to recover the fees. Green Tree has moved to dismiss the suit because Larketta had not submitted the issue to arbitration. Larketta protests, "But I want the right to go to court!" Does she have that right? What are the rights of parties under a contract with an arbitration clause? [*Green Tree Financial Corp. v Randolph,* 531 US 79]

8. Esmeralda sued Adolphus. She lost the lawsuit because the judge made a wrong decision. What can Esmeralda do now? Explain her options.

9. Indicate whether the following courts are courts of original, general, limited, or appellate jurisdiction:

   a. Small claims court
   b. Federal bankruptcy court
   c. Federal district court
   d. U.S. Supreme Court
   e. Municipal court
   f. Probate court
   g. Federal court of appeals

10. John purchased a computer from Gateway, Inc. He noted upon starting it up that he had to agree to a number of provisions in the contract of purchase in order to continue his initial installation. The program indicated that if he did not

wish to agree to the terms, he could return the computer to Gateway at Gateway's expense. One of the provisions requires that any disputes arising under the agreement be submitted to binding arbitration. John wonders if such a clause is valid. "What if I have statutory rights and protections in court?" Advise John on his rights under the Gateway agreement.

11. Mostek Corp., a Texas corporation, made a contract to sell computer-related products to North American Foreign Trading Corp., a New York corporation. North American used its own purchase order form, on which appeared the statement that any dispute arising out of an order would be submitted to arbitration, as provided in the terms set forth on the back of the order. Acting on the purchase order, Mostek delivered almost all of the goods but failed to deliver the final installment. North American then demanded that the matter be arbitrated. Mostek refused to do so. Was arbitration required? [*Application of Mostek Corp.,* 120 App Div 2d 383, 502 NYS2d 181]

12. Ceasar Wright was a longshoreman in Charleston, South Carolina, and a member of the International Longshoremen's Association (AFL-CIO). Wright used the union hiring hall. The collective bargaining agreement (CBA) of Wright's union provides for arbitration of all grievances. Another clause of the CBA states: "It is the intention and purpose of all parties hereto that no provision or part of this Agreement shall be violative of any Federal or State Law."

    On February 18, 1992, while Wright was working for Stevens Shipping and Terminal Company (Stevens), he injured his right heel and back. He sought permanent compensation from Stevens and settled his claims for $250,000 and another $10,000 in attorney fees. Wright was also awarded Social Security disability benefits.

    In January 1995, Wright, whose doctor had approved his return to work, returned to the hiring hall and asked to be referred for work. Wright did work between January 2 and January 11, 1995, but when the companies realized Wright had been certified as permanently

disabled, they deemed him not qualified for longshore work under the CBA and refused to allow him to work for them.

Wright did not file a grievance under the union agreement but instead hired a lawyer and proceeded with a claim under the Americans with Disabilities Act. The district court dismissed the case because Wright had failed to pursue the grievance procedure provided by the CBA. Must Wright pursue the dispute procedure first, or can he go right to court based on his federal rights under the Americans with Disabilities Act? [*Wright v Universal Maritime Service Corp.,* 525 US 70]

13. Winona Ryder was arrested for shoplifting from Saks Fifth Avenue in California. One of the members of the jury panel for her trial was Peter Guber, a Hollywood executive in charge of the production of three films in which Ms. Ryder starred, including *Bram Stoker's Dracula, The Age of Innocence,* and *Little Women.* If you were the prosecuting attorney in the case, how could you discover such information about this potential juror, and what are your options for excluding him from selection? [Rick Lyman, "For the Ryder Trial, a Hollywood Script," *New York Times,* November 3, 2002, SL-1]

14. What is the difference between the role of a trial court and the role of an appellate court? What functions do they perform, and how do they perform them?

15. Martha Simms is the plaintiff in a contract suit she has brought against Floral Supply, Inc., for its failure to deliver the green sponge Martha needed in building the floral designs she sells to exclusive home decorators. Martha had to obtain the sponge from another supplier and was late on seven deliveries. One of Martha's customers has been called by Martha's lawyer as a witness and is now on the witness stand, testifying about Martha's late performance and the penalty she charged. The lawyer for Floral Supply knows that Martha's customer frequently waives penalties for good suppliers. How can Floral Supply's lawyer get that information before the jury?

BUSINESS ETHICS,

SOCIAL FORCES,

AND THE LAW

LEARNING OBJECTIVES

After studying this chapter, you should be able to

LO.1 Describe the role of ethics in business and law

LO.2 List the methods for recognizing ethical dilemmas

LO.3 Explain the questions to address in resolving ethical dilemmas

LO.4 Understand the importance of ethics in e-commerce

Each day businesspeople work together on contracts and projects. Their completion of the work is partially the result of the laws that protect contract rights. Much of what businesspeople do, however, is simply a matter of their word. Executives arrive at a 9:00 A.M. meeting because they promised they would be there. An employee meets a deadline for an ad display board because she said she would. Business transactions are completed through a combination of the values of the parties and the laws that reflect those values and the importance of one's word in business. Over time, the rules that govern business, from written laws to unwritten expressions of value, have evolved to provide a framework of operation that ensures good faith in our dealings with each other.

This chapter takes you behind the rules of law to examine the objectives in establishing rules for business conduct. Both social forces and business needs contribute to the standards that govern businesses and their operations.

 ## WHAT IS BUSINESS ETHICS?

ethics a branch of philosophy dealing with values that relate to the nature of human conduct and values associated with that conduct.

Some people have said that the term *business ethics* is an oxymoron, that the word *business* and the word *ethics* contradict each other. **Ethics** is a branch of philosophy dealing with values that relate to the nature of human conduct and values associated with that conduct. Conduct and values in business operations become more complex because individuals are working together to maximize profit. Balancing the goal of profits with the values of individuals and society is the focus of **business ethics**. Some economists make the point that insider trading on the stock market is an efficient way to run that market. To an economist, inside information allows those with the best information to make the most money. This quantitative view ignores the issues of fairness: What about those who trade stock who do not have access to that information? Is the philosophy fair to them? What will happen to the stock market if investors perceive there is not a level playing field? In the U.S. Supreme Court decision *United States v O'Hagan*[1] on insider trading, Justice Ruth Ginsburg noted, "Investors likely wouldn't invest in a market where trading based on misappropriated nonpublic information is unchecked." The field of business ethics deals with the balance between society's values and the need for businesses to remain profitable.

business ethics balancing the goal of profits with values of individuals and society.

1. THE LAW AS THE STANDARD FOR BUSINESS ETHICS

positive law law enacted and codified by governmental authority.

Moral standards come from different sources. Philosophers debate the origin of moral standards as well as which of those standards should be applied. One set of moral standards is simply what codified or **positive law** requires. The test of whether an act is legal is a common moral standard used frequently in business. Codified law, or law created by governmental authority, is used as the standard for ethical behavior. Absent illegality, all behavior is ethical under this simple standard. The phrase "AS IS," when communicated conspicuously on a contract or electronic message (see Chapter 25 for further discussion), means by law that there are no warranties for the goods being sold. **For Example,** if a buyer purchases a used car and the phrase "AS IS" is in the contract, the seller has no legal obligation, in most states, if the transmission falls apart the day after the buyer's purchase. Following a positive law standard, the seller who refuses to

---

[1] 521 US 657 (1997).

repair the transmission has acted ethically. However, the issue of fairness still arises. We know there was no legal obligation to fix the transmission, but was it fair that the car fell apart the day after it was purchased?

---

2. THE NOTION OF UNIVERSAL STANDARDS FOR BUSINESS ETHICS

natural law a system of principles to guide human conduct independent of, and sometimes contrary to, enacted law and discovered by man's rational intelligence.

civil disobedience the term used when natural law proponents violate positive law.

Another view of ethics holds that standards exist universally and cannot be changed or modified by law. In many cases, individuals believe the universal standards stem from religious beliefs. In some countries today, the standards for business are still determined by religious tenets. Proponents of **natural law** maintain that higher standards of behavior than those required by positive law must be followed even if those higher standards run contrary to codified law. In the early nineteenth century when slavery was legally permissible in the United States, a positive law standard would sanction such ownership as legal. However, such deprivation of a person's rights violates the natural law principle of individual freedom and would be unethical. Accordingly, **civil disobedience** occurs when natural law proponents violate positive law.

Former Supreme Court Justice Sandra Day O'Connor, who was second in her class at Stanford Law School (the late Chief Justice William Rehnquist was first), was offered a job as a receptionist for a law firm while her male classmates were hired as attorneys. At that time, no law prohibited discrimination against women, so law firms' hiring practices, using only a positive law standard, were ethical. However, if the natural law standard of equality is applied, the refusal to hire Sandra O'Connor as a lawyer, a position for which she was qualified, was discriminatory conduct and unethical.

---

3. THE STANDARD OF SITUATIONAL BUSINESS ETHICS OR MORAL RELATIVISM

situational ethics a flexible standard of ethics that permits an examination of circumstances and motivation before attaching the label of right or wrong to conduct.

moral relativism takes into account motivation and circumstance to determine whether an act was ethical.

Situational ethics or **moral relativism** is a flexible standard of ethics that permits an examination of circumstances and motivation before attaching the label of right or wrong to conduct. The classic example of moral relativism: Would it be unethical to steal a loaf of bread to feed a starving child? A question a Florida court faced was whether to go forward with the prosecution for arson of a man who set fire to an abandoned property in his neighborhood that was used as a crack-cocaine house. In both cases, the law has been broken. The first crime is theft, and the second crime is arson. Neither person, either the bread thief or the arsonist, denied committing the crime. The issue in both cases is not whether the crime was committed but whether the motivation and circumstances excuse the actions and eliminate the punishment. An employee embezzles money from her employer because she is a single parent trying to make ends meet. Was her conduct unethical? The conduct is illegal, but moral relativism would consider the employee's personal circumstances in determining whether it is ethical.

Businesses use moral relativism standards frequently in their international operations. Bribery is illegal in the United States, but, as many businesses argue, it is an accepted method of doing business in other countries.[2] The standard of moral relativism is used to allow behavior in international business transactions that would

---

[2] The United States, Mexico, Korea, and most of the countries in the European Union have joined together and signed a resolution denouncing bribery, specifically noting that its practice is neither legally nor culturally accepted in their nations.

THINKING THINGS THROUGH

Corrupt Climates: Good or Bad for Business?

As you examine the following list of countries, those in the column labeled "Least Corrupt" (countries in which government officials are least likely to accept bribes) and those in the column marked "Most Corrupt" (countries in which government officials are most likely to accept bribes), can you comment on the business climates in them?

Least Corrupt (Least Likely to Accept Bribes)		Most Corrupt (Most Likely to Accept Bribes)	
Iceland	Luxembourg	Chad	Sudan
Finland	Canada	Bangladesh	Somalia
New Zealand	Hong Kong	Turkmenistan	Paraguay
Denmark	Germany	Myanmar	Pakistan
Singapore	USA	Haiti	Kenya
Sweden	France	Nigeria	Congo
Switzerland	Belgium	Equatorial Guinea	Uzbekistan
Norway	Ireland	Cote 'd Ivoire	Liberia
Australia	Chile	Angola	Iraq
Austria	Japan	Tajikistan	
Netherlands	Spain		
United Kingdom			

*From 2005 Transparency International annual survey, **http://www.transparency.org**.

be a violation of the law in the United States. For example, Google and other Internet service providers have agreed to do business in China despite the restrictions the Chinese government places on the use of the Internet and the content of search engines. Such restrictions in the United States would be an unconstitutional violation of our First Amendment. In China, however, government control of information is legal. Google and others testified before Congress that some entry, however restricted, was better for the Chinese people than no access at all. Their decision weighed the conflicting values and concluded that they would use the standard of honoring the law of China despite the censorship.

4. THE BUSINESS STAKEHOLDER STANDARD OF BEHAVIOR

Businesses have different constituencies, referred to as **stakeholders**, often with conflicting goals for the business. Shareholders, for example, may share economists' view that earnings, and hence dividends, should be maximized. Members of the community where a business is located are also stakeholders in the business and have an interest in preserving jobs. The employees of the business itself are stakeholders and certainly wish to retain their jobs. A **downsizing**, or reduction in workforce, would offer the shareholders of the company a boost in earnings and share price. That same reduction, however, would affect the local economy and community in a negative way. Balancing the interests of these stakeholders is a standard used in resolving ethical

stakeholders those who have a stake, or interest, in the activities of a corporation; stakeholders include employees, members of the community in which the corporation operates, vendors, customers, and any others who are affected by the actions and decisions of the corporation.

downsizing a reduction in workforce.

| FIGURE 3-1 | *Guidelines for Analyzing a Contemplated Action* |

1. **DEFINE THE PROBLEM FROM THE DECISION MAKER'S POINT OF VIEW.**
2. **IDENTIFY WHO COULD BE INJURED BY THE CONTEMPLATED ACTION.**
3. **DEFINE THE PROBLEM FROM THE OPPOSING POINT OF VIEW.**
4. **WOULD YOU (AS THE DECISION MAKER) BE WILLING TO TELL YOUR FAMILY, YOUR SUPERVISOR, YOUR CEO, AND THE BOARD OF DIRECTORS ABOUT THE PLANNED ACTION?**
5. **WOULD YOU BE WILLING TO GO BEFORE A COMMUNITY MEETING, A CONGRESSIONAL HEARING, OR A PUBLIC FORUM TO DESCRIBE THE ACTION?**
6. **WITH FULL CONSIDERATION OF THE FACTS AND ALTERNATIVES, REACH A DECISION ABOUT WHETHER THE CONTEMPLATED ACTION SHOULD BE TAKEN.**

dilemmas in business. Figure 3-1 lists the areas of concern that should be examined as businesses analyze an ethical dilemma.

As Figure 3-1 indicates, stakeholder analysis requires the decision maker to view a problem from different perspectives in the light of day. **Stakeholder analysis** requires measurement of the impact of a decision on various groups but also requires that public disclosure of that decision be defensible. The questions are helpful and provide insight in a variety of situations and ethical dilemmas. The employee who is about to leave the office for half a day without taking vacation time could ask: Could I tell my family or my supervisor that I have done this? A company faced with the temptation of price fixing: Could I describe before a congressional committee what I am about to do?

In other situations, a business is not facing questions of dishonesty or unfair competition. In many ethical dilemmas, a business faces the question of taking voluntary action or simply complying with the law. Some experts maintain that the shareholders' interest is paramount in resolving these conflicts among stakeholders. Others maintain that a business must assume some responsibility for social issues and their resolution. Economist Milton Friedman expresses his views on resolving the conflicts among stakeholders as follows:

> *A corporate executive's responsibility is to make as much money for the shareholders as possible, as long as he operates within the rules of the game. When an executive decides to take action for reasons of social responsibility, he is taking money from someone else—from the stockholders, in the form of lower dividends; from the employees, in the form of lower wages; or from the consumer, in the form of higher prices. The responsibility of the corporate executive is to fulfill the terms of his contract. If he can't do that in good conscience, then he should quit his job and find another way to do good. He has the right to promote what he regards as desirable moral objectives only with his own money.*[3]

In direct opposition to the Friedman view is the social responsibility view of Anita Roddick, CEO of Body Shop International. She has stated that she does not care about earning money because the sole reason for a business to exist is to solve social problems. In between these two views are compromise positions in which businesses exist primarily to benefit the shareholders but do take opportunities to solve social problems. Many businesses today have created flextime, job sharing, and

stakeholder analysis the term used when a decision maker views a problem from different perspectives and measures the impact of a decision on various groups.

---

[3] "Interview: Milton Friedman," *Playboy*, February 1973. © 1973 *Playboy*.

(**ETHICS & THE LAW**)

Ethics and Social Responsibility

Ben & Jerry's Homemade, Inc., is a Vermont-based ice-cream company founded by Ben Cohen and Jerry Greenfield, who began the company with the goal of social contribution. A portion of all proceeds from the sale of their ice cream is donated to charity.* The company issues strong position statements on social issues.

Following some slowing in market growth and reduction in profits, Cohen and Greenfield retired as officers of the company (although they remained majority share-holders and, therefore, in control of the board)** and hired Robert Holland as CEO. After Holland had been CEO for a year, a Japanese supplier approached him and offered to distribute Ben & Jerry's ice cream in Japan. Holland turned down the offer because the Japanese company had no history of involvement in social issues and explained, "The only clear reason to take the opportunity was to make money."

Do you agree with Holland's decision? What approach do Ben & Jerry's and Holland take with respect to their stakeholders? Is it troublesome that the company had not turned around financially when the offer was declined? Holland added that the only growth opportunities are in international markets. Is Ben & Jerry's passing up business? Is this a good or bad practice for a company? Holland left the company shortly after the decision on the Japanese opportunity had been made. How do you view Holland's position on business ethics and social responsibility? Is it best to find a company with values consistent with your own? How would you be able to tell the values of a company?

---

*Ben & Jerry's gave 7.5 percent of its pretax income to charity.

**Ben & Jerry's Homemade, Inc., has been sold and is now part of an international conglomerate, Unilever, Inc.

---

telecommuting as work options for their employees to accommodate family needs. These options are a response to larger societal issues surrounding children and their care but may also serve as a way to retain a quality workforce that is more productive without the worry of poor child care arrangements. The law currently does not require businesses to furnish such options, but the businesses offer the programs voluntarily as a means of addressing a social issue.

Between the Friedman and Roddick views on business ethics and social responsibility are businesses with varying views on the role of business in society. Among these businesses are very profitable firms that are also involved in their communities through employees' volunteer work and companies' charitable donations. For example, Bill Gates, the CEO of Microsoft who is ranked as the richest man in the United States, in 2003 pledged $3 billion for fighting AIDS and providing childhood vaccine programs around the world. He has also used his foundation to provide scholarships for minorities. One different view on the social responsibility of business comes from Warren Buffett, the second richest man in the United States, according to the *Forbes* ranking, and the CEO of Berkshire Hathaway, a company with shares selling for more than $60,000 each. Mr. Buffett's view is that Berkshire Hathaway should not try to determine the best charitable or social causes. The shareholders, not he, should make decisions about corporate profits and their use and do so on an

(ETHICS & THE LAW)

The "Bawdy" Magazines at Wal-Mart

Wal-Mart stores have banned three men's magazines—*Maxim, Stuff,* and *FHM*—from sales in its stores. The magazines feature scantily clothed women and "bawdy humor."

The banned products are parts of an ongoing series of decisions Wal-Mart has made about carrying products. Wal-Mart has long banned the sales of certain CDs in its stores. Last year it banned the sales of certain video games as well. Because it is the largest seller of CDs and DVDs, producers offer sanitized versions of these materials for sale at Wal-Mart.*

Why do you think Wal-Mart makes the voluntary decision to not sell certain products? Some argue that the First Amendment is violated with these bans on sales. Refer to Chapter 4 and evaluate whether they have a point.

_____
*David Carr and Constance L. Hays, "3 Racy Men's Magazine Are Banned by Wal-Mart," *New York Times,* May 6, 2003, C1, C3.

individual, not company, level. Mr. Buffett pledged his personal wealth to the Gates Foundation in 2006. In 2004, the average amount for corporate charitable giving was 1.3 percent of pretax income or an average of $31.79 million per Fortune 100 company. In addition, 81 percent of these companies have volunteer programs that provide help from employees to their communities.

(B) WHY IS BUSINESS ETHICS IMPORTANT?

Regardless of a firm's views on social responsibility issues, the notions of compliance with the law and fairness in business transactions and operations are universal concerns. Values represent an important part of business success. Business ethics is important for more than the simple justification that "it's the right thing to do." This section covers the significance of ethics in business success.

5. THE IMPORTANCE OF TRUST

Capitalism succeeds because of trust. Investors provide capital for a business because they believe the business will use it and return it with earnings. Customers are willing to purchase products and services from businesses because they believe the businesses will honor their commitments to deliver quality and then stand behind their product or service. Businesses are willing to purchase equipment and hire employees on the assumption that investors will continue to honor their commitment to furnish the necessary funds and will not withdraw their promises or funds. Business investment, growth, and sales are a circle of trust. Although courts provide remedies for breaches of agreements, no economy could grow if it were based solely on positive law and court-mandated performance. It is the reliance on promises, not the reliance on litigation, that produces good business relationships. In economics, the concept of rational expectations of investors and consumers plays a role in economic growth and performance. The assumption every investor makes is that her initial investment will earn a return. An assumption that employees make

Using Technology to Change the Ethical Culture of a Company

Companies are using technology to help them with the requirements of new ethics programs that must be part of their operations since the SOX legislation (the post-Enron changes on corporate governance and operations; see Chapters 8, 46, and 47). In addition to codes of ethics, companies must have the programs and technology for making sure that employees are complying with their codes and for reporting any violations they witness.

For example, Columbia HCA paid one of the largest fines in government history for Medicare fraud. To prevent such activity in the future and to comply with SOX requirements, HCA has now implemented the following for its 430 firms and 2.5 million employees:

- An anonymous hotline that now receives 100,000 calls every year
- A response to every call within 24 hours
- Documentation of what is found within the 24 hours
- Procedures by which callers can check on the status of their report and issue (even those who do not give their names can follow up with an identification number they are given for their complaint; about 30 percent report anonymously)
- A hotline staff who check employees' computers and e-mails for information and cull them to investigate charges and issues reported over the hotline*

---

*"Cops, Inc," *Forbes*, March 17, 2003, p. 68.

---

is that, absent problems with their performance, their employment will continue. Those assumptions encourage investment by investors and spending by employees. Their assumptions demonstrate trust in the relationship and in the underlying economic system.

As economists have had the opportunity to watch nations with new forms of government enter the international markets, they have documented distinctions in growth rates. In those countries where government officials control market access through individual payments to them, the business climate is stalled, and growth lags behind that found in free-market nations.

Following the financial collapse of many companies during the period from 2001 through 2002, Congress passed legislation known as *Sarbanes-Oxley* (covered in more detail in Chapters 8 and 46). SOX, as it is known, however, includes many provisions that apply to companies' ethics programs. For example, all publicly traded companies must have some form of anonymous method for employees to report issues with protection from retaliation. In carrying out the intent of SOX, publicly traded companies now have ethics officers and ethics programs to set the right tone and atmosphere for an ethical culture.

6. BUSINESS ETHICS AND FINANCIAL PERFORMANCE

Studies centering on a business's commitment to values and its financial performance suggest that those with the strongest value systems survive and do so successfully.

According to the book *Built to Last* by James C. Collins and Jerry I. Porras,[4] an in-depth look at companies with long-term growth and profits produced a common thread: the companies' commitment to values. All firms studied had focused on high standards for product quality, employee welfare, and customer service.

A study of companies that had paid dividends for 100 years without interruption revealed the same pattern of values.[5] Companies that had survived two world wars and a depression without missing a dividend remained committed to their customers and employees with standards of fairness and honesty. Recent studies in finance and accounting indicate that if investors want the greatest return on their investments over a 30-year period then they should invest in those companies that are the most candid in their disclosures about where the company stands and the risks it faces. For example, a company that indicates in its annual report that a major contract is at risk is being forthright and will perform over a 30-year period because it is facing its problems and coming up with strategies for coping. A company that boasts that it has met earnings to the penny for 47 quarters in a row, as HealthSouth did in the last year before it collapsed financially and many of its executives entered guilty pleas to fraud, is one to avoid.[6]

An examination of companies involved in an ethical breach demonstrates the impact of poor value choices on financial performance. A study of the impact of breaches of the law by companies showed that for five years after their regulatory or legal misstep, these companies were still struggling to recover the financial performances they had achieved prior to their legal difficulties.[7]

After Enron announced that it would restate its income because it had been spinning off its debt obligations into off-the-book-entities, its price per share dropped from $83 on January 14, 2001, to $0.67 on January 14, 2002.[8] By the time former Enron CEO Jeffrey Skilling and its former chairman, Kenneth Lay, were convicted of multiple federal felonies, Enron stock was trading at $0.15 per share, a figure that was up four cents from the pre-verdict value of $0.11. After WorldCom revealed that it had capitalized ordinary expenses, it had to reduce its earnings by $11 billion. The chief financial officer at WorldCom, Scott Sullivan, entered a guilty plea and testified against his boss, former CEO Bernie Ebbers. Mr. Ebbers was convicted of multiple federal felonies and sentenced to 25 years in prison, and other employees of both companies have been indicted, with many resulting guilty pleas and convictions. The accounting firm for both companies, Arthur Andersen, was convicted of obstruction of justice, a conviction that was later reversed but still destroyed the firm's reputation and resulted in its physical liquidation. Columbia Health Care's share price dropped 58 percent and it experienced a 93 percent drop in earnings after it was charged with overbilling for Medicare reimbursements. Its share price dropped from $40 to $18. The nation's largest hospital chain has had to spin off 100 hospitals and has paid record fines to settle the charges.[9]

---

[4] *Harper Business* (1994).

[5] Louis Grossman and Marianne Jennings, *Building and Growing a Business: The Story of 15 Extraordinary Companies Each with 100 Years of Consistent Dividends* (Greenwood, 2003).

[6] Stephen Taub, "Link Found Between Candor, Share Prices," *CFO.com*, June 24, 2004.

[7] Melinda S. Baucus and David A. Baucus, "Paying the Piper: An Empirical Examination of Longer-Term Financial Consequences of Illegal Corporate Behavior," 40 *Academic Management Journal* 129 (1997).

[8] From stock price chart, **http://www.enron.com**.

[9] Lucette Lagnado, "Columbia/HCA Warns of Profit Decline," *Wall Street Journal*, September 10, 1987, A3.

ETHICS & THE LAW

Ethics in Government Employment

The state of Arizona mandates emissions testing for cars before drivers can obtain updated registrations. The state hires a contractor to conduct the emissions tests in the various emissions-testing facilities around the state. In October 1999, the Arizona attorney general announced the arrest of 13 workers at one of the emissions-testing facilities for allegedly taking payoffs of between $50 to $200 from car owners to pass their cars on the emissions tests when those cars fell below emissions standards and would not have been registered. Nearly half of the staff at the emissions facility were arrested.

Why is it a crime for someone working in a government-sponsored facility to accept a payment for a desired outcome? Do the payoffs to the workers really harm anyone?

Insurance broker Marsh & McLennan paid $850 million to former clients to settle price-fixing charges brought by New York Attorney General Eliot Spitzer. The 134-year-old company saw a drop in both its earnings (64 percent) and its share price (40 percent).[10] The financial crunch resulted in 3,000 employees losing their jobs. AIG, the insurance giant, paid $1.64 billion, the largest penalty ever by a U.S. company, to settle charges that it smoothed its earnings over time. The fine came after the company was forced to reduce its reported earnings by $1.3 billion.[11] The company also issued an apology as part of the settlement, "Providing incorrect information to the investing public and regulators was wrong and is against the values of our current leadership and employees."[12] Its $73 share price dropped to $50 before the financial reporting allegations were settled.

Asbestos liability bankrupted Johns-Manville when documentation showed that the company's executives knew about the lethal effect of asbestos on the lungs but took no action to warn buyers and users of the product. Bausch & Lomb, Fannie Mae, Krispy Kreme, Leslie Fay, Nortel, Phar-Mor, Cendant, Refco, Sunbeam, Xerox, and even General Electric all experienced financial fallout after accounting irregularities carried out by company officers assisted by many employees resulted in earnings restatements when proper accounting rules were applied. Martha Stewart, once a billionaire, was convicted of federal crimes, including obstruction of justice, related to her conduct after she sold her ImClone stock one day prior to the company's announcement that the FDA was not yet approving the company's drug for the market. ImClone is a bio-tech company that was headed by Ms. Stewart's friend, former CEO Sam Waksal, who entered a plea regarding his activities related to the sales of his shares in advance of the FDA announcement and is now serving time in prison. As a result, Ms. Stewart's own company, Omnimedia, International, which was not involved in the ImClone share trading and did not face any charges of earnings misstatements, still experienced a dramatic drop in earnings and stock prices

---

[10] Ian McDonald, "After Spitzer Probe, Marsh CEO Tries Corporate Triage," *Wall Street Journal*, A1, A5.

[11] Ian McDonald and Liam Pleven, "AIG Reaches Accord with Regulators, Stock Rises But May Still Be a Bargain," *Wall Street Journal*, February 10, 2006, C1, C4.

[12] Gretchen Morgenson, "AIG Apologizes and Agrees to $1.64 Billion Settlement," *New York Times*, February 10, 2006, C1, C5.

because of the concerns about Ms. Stewart and shareholder concerns about their ability to trust her. Bankruptcy and/or free falls in the worth of shares are the fates that await firms that make poor ethical choices.

7. THE IMPORTANCE OF A GOOD REPUTATION

Richard Teerlink, the CEO of Harley-Davidson, once said, "A reputation, good or bad, is tough to shake.[13] A breach of ethics is costly to a firm not only in the financial sense of drops in earnings and possible fines. A breach of ethics also often carries with it a lasting memory that affects the business and its sales for years to come. **For Example,** following Sears, Roebuck's settlement with the California Consumer Affairs Department of fraud charges involving the operation of its auto centers, Montgomery Ward Auto Centers enjoyed an increase in business.[14] Customers were concerned about taking their cars to Sears because of the scandal surrounding the nationally reported charges of unnecessary repairs. Because business declined, Sears was forced to close some of its auto centers.

When an ethical breach occurs, businesses lose that component of trust important to customers' decisions to buy and invest. **For Example,** Beech-Nut, the baby food company, has an outstanding product line and offers quality at a good price. Yet it has not regained its former market share as a result of the federal charges it faced in 1986.[15] Its apple juice tasted good, but it was a chemical concoction containing no apple juice despite advertising claims to the contrary. Even though no one was harmed, the customers' view of Beech-Nut changed. Trust disappeared, and so did a good portion of the company's market share. Two decades later, the company continues to struggle to overcome that one-time breach in ethics.

8. BUSINESS ETHICS AND BUSINESS REGULATION: PUBLIC POLICY, LAW, AND ETHICS

When business behavior results in complaints from employees, investors, or customers, laws or regulations are often used to change the behavior. **For Example,** the bankruptcy of Orange County and the large losses experienced by Procter & Gamble and Gibson Greetings resulting from their heavy investments in high-risk financial instruments[16] motivated the Securities and Exchange Commission (SEC) (see Chapter 46) to promulgate regulations about disclosures in financial statements on high-risk investments known as *derivatives.* The collapse of Refco and other hedge funds now has the attention of regulators focused on these financial instruments and the relatively regulation-free environment in which they are run. The Federal Reserve stepped in to regulate virtually all aspects of credit transactions, focusing on the disclosure of the actual costs of credit to ensure full information for borrowers.

Confusion among consumers about car leasing and its true costs and the fees applicable at the end of the lease terms caused the Federal Reserve to expand its

---

[13] David K. Wright, *The Harley-Davidson Motor Co.: An Official Ninety-Year History* (Motorbook International, 1993).

[14] "Sears Fires Head of Its Auto Unit," *Wall Street Journal,* December 21, 1992, B6.

[15] Chris Welles, "What Led Beech-Nut Down the Road to Disgrace," *Business Week,* February 22, 1988, 128.

[16] Susan Antilla, "P & G Sees Charge on Derivatives," *New York Times,* April 13, 1994, C1, C16; Matt Murray and Paulette Thomas, "After the Fall: Fingers Point and Heads Roll," *Wall Street Journal,* December 23, 1994, B1, B4; Del Jones, "County Seeks Bankruptcy Protection," *USA Today,* December 7, 1994, IC, 2C.

ETHICS & THE LAW

Ethics & Social Responsibility

Aaron Feuerstein is the owner of Malden Mills, a textile plant in Methuen, Massachusetts. Feuerstein's grandfather founded the company in 1906 as a swimsuit and sweater manufacturer. Feuerstein changed the direction of traditional garment manufacturing when he switched the factory to produce Polartec, a revolutionary fabric made from recycled plastic bottles. The fabric is used in skiing and hiking clothing because of its unique qualities: warm, lightweight, and easy to dry and dye. L.L. Bean, Patagonia, and Eddie Bauer are all on Malden Mills' customer list, which has generated $425 million in sales each year.

On December 11, 1995, the Malden Mills factory was almost completely destroyed by a fire started by a boiler that exploded. Feuerstein held a meeting with his employees several days later and guaranteed their pay for 30 days and their health benefits for 90 days. Malden Mills had 3,000 employees and an annual payroll of $65 million.

Feuerstein gave all of his employees three months' pay and had all but 20 percent working full-time again by March 1996. By midsummer 1996, Malden Mills was back at full production. One employee said, "Another person would have taken the insurance money and walked away. I might have done that."* Feuerstein described his role as follows:

*The fundamental difference is that I consider our workers an asset, not an expense. I have a responsibility to the worker, both blue-collar and white-collar. I have an equal responsibility to the community. It would have been unconscionable to put 3,000 people on the streets and deliver a death blow to the cities of Lawrence and Methuen. Maybe on paper our company is worth less to Wall Street, but I can tell you it's worth more. We're doing fine.***

Was it right for Feuerstein to keep his promise to employees? Did he really have a promise to keep? Does it matter that Malden Mills was not a publicly held company? In 2002, Malden Mills entered Chapter 11 bankruptcy. It emerged from bankruptcy under new ownership with Feuerstein asked to stay on as CEO. He has been working to raise the money to buy his company back. Do you think Feuerstein behaved too ethically to be financially successful?

---

* Steve Wulf, "The Glow from a Fire," *Time*, January 8, 1996, 49.
** *Id.*

regulation of credit to car leases. Figure 3-2 depicts the relationships among ethics, the social forces of customers and investors, and the laws that are passed to remedy the problems raised as part of the social forces movement.

From the nutrition facts that appear on food packages to the type of pump at the gas station, government regulation of business activity is evident. Congress begins its legislative role and administrative agencies begin their process of regulation (see Chapter 6) when congressional hearings and studies reveal abuses and problems within an industry or throughout business. Legislation and regulation are responses

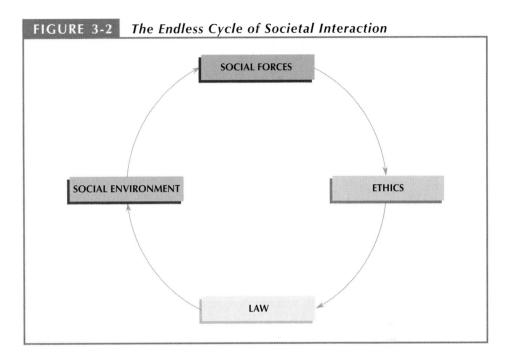

FIGURE 3-2   *The Endless Cycle of Societal Interaction*

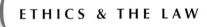

ETHICS & THE LAW

Ethics, Trust, and Analysts

The cover of *Fortune* magazine from May 14, 2001, featured a picture of Wall Street financial analyst Mary Meeker and the words, "Can we ever trust again?"* The inside story focused on the relationship of underwriters, analysts, and brokerage houses with the companies whose stocks they were touting and selling. They had continued to pump the virtues of stock shares they knew had overinflated prices. When the market bubble burst, the losses to shareholders were catastrophic. The analysts, underwriters, and brokers had not violated the law. Those in the financial markets had too much at stake to be honest with investors.

During 2002, new stories about analysts emerged, such as that of Jack Grubman, the analyst for Salomon Smith Barney (SSB) who continued to tout WorldCom stock even as it was headed downward and into financial ruin.** The father of twins, Jack Grubman wanted to see them admitted to one of Manhattan's most prestigious preschools—the 92nd Street Y. Mr. Grubman wrote a memo to Sanford Weill, the chairman of Citigroup, that contained the following language:

On another matter, as I alluded to you the other day, we are going through the ridiculous but necessary process of pre-school applications in Manhattan. For someone who grew up in a household with a father making $8,000 a year and for someone who attended public schools, I do find this process a bit strange, but there are no bounds for what you do for your children.

---

* "Can We Ever Trust Again?" *Fortune*, May 14, 2000 (cover).
** Charles Gasparino, "Ghosts of E-Mails Continue to Haunt Wall Street," *Wall Street Journal*, November 18, 2002, C1, C13.

ETHICS & THE LAW

continued

Anything, anything you could do Sandy would be greatly appreciated. As I mentioned, I will keep you posted on the progress with AT&T which I think is going well.

Thank you.

Citigroup pledged $1 million to the school at about the same time Grubman's children were admitted. Mr. Weill, Mr. Grubman's CEO at SSB, asked Mr. Grubman to "take a fresh look" at AT&T, a major corporate client of Citigroup. Mr. Weill served on the board of AT&T, and AT&T's CEO, C. Michael Armstrong, served as a Citigroup director. Mr. Weill was courting Armstrong's vote for the ouster of his co-chairman at Citigroup, John Reed. A follow-up e-mail from Mr. Grubman to Carol Cutler, another New York analyst, connected the dots:

I used Sandy to get my kids in the 92nd Street Y pre-school (which is harder than Harvard) and Sandy needed Armstrong's vote on our board to nuke Reed in showdown. Once the coast was clear for both of us (ie Sandy clear victor and my kids confirmed) I went back to my normal self on AT&T.

At the same time as all the other movements, Mr. Grubman upgraded AT&T from a "hold" to a "strong buy." After Mr. Reed was ousted, Mr. Grubman downgraded AT&T again. Mr. Grubman said that he sent the e-mail "in an effort to inflate my professional importance." In another e-mail, Mr. Grubman wrote, "I have always viewed [AT&T] as a business deal between me and Sandy."

The *Fortune* headline on June 10, 2002, read, "In search of THE LAST HONEST ANALYST."***

Were there conflicts of interest in this situation? Do you think any laws were violated? How do you think such problems in the market will be fixed? What types of rules do you think will result? Why?

***"In search of THE LAST HONEST ANALYST," *Fortune*, June 10, 2002 (cover).

to activities of businesses that are perfectly legal but raise questions of fairness that cause customer and investor protests.

Antidiscrimination laws were passed when evidence established that many companies had policies that required, for example, pregnant employees to stop working. Hotels at one time had policies that permitted minorities to work in kitchens and perform housekeeping tasks but did not permit them to hold "guest-contact" positions. These policies did not violate any laws at the time. However, employees justifiably raised concerns about the fairness or the ethics of such policies, and legislation was passed, in large part because of the unwillingness of business to change its practices to remedy employees' concerns. Businesses that act voluntarily on the basis of value choices often avoid the costs and the sometimes arbitrariness of legislation and regulation. Voluntary change by businesses is less costly and is considered less intrusive. Regulation costs are substantial, and regulation is extensive.

Businesses that respond to social forces and the movements of the cycle of societal interaction gain a competitive advantage. Businesses that act irresponsibly and disregard society's views and desire for change speed the transition from value choice to enforceable law. Businesses should watch the cycle of social forces and follow trends there to understand the values attached to certain activities and responses. These values motivate change either in the form of voluntary business activity or legislation. All values that precipitate change have one of several basic underlying goals. These underlying goals, discussed in the following sections, offer signals about the pattern of social change.

(a) PROTECTION OF THE STATE   A number of laws exist today because of the underlying goal or value of protection of the state. Laws that condemn treason are examples of laws passed to preserve the government of the state. Another less dramatic set of laws offering protection to the state are the tax codes, which provide authority for collecting taxes for the operation of government facilities and enforcement agencies. The U.S Patriot Act and airport security regulations are also examples of government programs and regulations created with the protection and security of the state as the goal.

(b) PROTECTION OF THE PERSON   A second social force is protection of the person. From the earliest times, laws have been developed to protect the individual from being injured or killed. Criminal laws are devoted to protection of individuals and their properties. In addition, civil suits permit private remedies for wrongful acts toward people and their property. Over time, the protection of personal rights has expanded to include the rights of privacy and the protection of individuals from defamation. Contract rights are protected from interference by others. Laws continue to evolve to protect the reputations, privacy, and mental and physical well-being of individuals.

Individual rights have been the values at the core of legislation and regulation relating to governmental assistance programs, public schools, service on a jury, and access to public facilities. The antidiscrimination laws that affect nearly all businesses are grounded in the value of protection of the individual. Labor laws and regulations exist to protect the individual rights of workers.

(c) PROTECTION OF PUBLIC HEALTH, SAFETY, AND MORALS   Food-labeling regulations are an example of laws grounded in the value of protecting the safety and health of individuals. Food and restaurant inspections, mandatory inoculation, speed limits on roadways, mandatory smoke detectors and sprinkler systems in hotels, and prohibitions on the sale of alcohol to minors are all examples of laws based on the value of safety for the public. Zoning laws that prohibit the operation of adult bookstores and movie theaters near schools and churches are examples of laws based on moral values.

(d) PROTECTION OF PROPERTY: ITS USE AND TITLE   Someone who steals another's automobile is a thief and is punished by law with fines and/or imprisonment. A zoning law that prohibits the operation of a steel mill in a residential area also provides protection for property. A civil suit brought to recover royalties lost because of another's infringement of one's copyrighted materials is based on federal laws that afford protection for property rights in nontangible or intellectual property (see Chapter 10). Laws afford protection of title for all forms of property. The deed recorded in the land record is the legal mechanism for protecting the owner's title. The copyright on a software program or a song protects the creator's rights in that intellectual property. The title documents issued by a department of motor vehicles afford protection of title for the owner of a vehicle.

Those who have title to property are generally free to use the property in any manner they see fit. However, even ownership has restrictions imposed by law. A landowner cannot engage in activities on his property that damage another's land or interfere with another's use of land. A business may operate a factory on its real property, but if the factory creates a great deal of noise, adjoining landowners may successfully establish it as a nuisance (see Chapter 49) that interferes with their use and enjoyment of their land. The law affords remedies for such a nuisance that might include an injunction, or court order, limiting the hours of the factory's operation so that neighbors have the opportunity to sleep.

If that factory releases chemicals into the river flowing nearby, others' rights and use of their land are affected. Environmental laws (see Chapter 50) have been passed that regulate the use of property. Those environmental laws evolved through social activism after landowners and residents located near factories and other operations with harmful emissions became concerned about the impact on the value of their properties as well as the impact on their health and safety. Environmental laws thus emerged as regulation of land use in response to concerns about legal, but harmful, emissions by companies.

(e) PROTECTION OF PERSONAL RIGHTS   The desire for individual freedom to practice religion and freedom from political domination gave rise to the colonization of the United States and, eventually, the American Revolution. The desire for freedom from economic domination resulted in the free enterprise philosophy that exists in the United States today. Individual freedoms and personal rights continue as a focus of value discussions followed by legislation if those individual rights are violated.

Economic freedoms and the free enterprise system were in jeopardy at the end of the nineteenth century as large conglomerates began to dominate certain markets and inhibit the ability of individuals to compete. Repressive activities in the marketplace by some companies led to federal regulation in the form of antitrust laws. These laws were passed in response to social concerns about economic freedom and individual opportunities within the economy (see Chapter 5). For example, Microsoft's 90 percent domination of the operating systems market led to extensive antitrust litigation against the company that was eventually settled.

(f) ENFORCEMENT OF INDIVIDUAL INTENT   When someone has voluntarily entered into a transaction, that person has a responsibility to carry forward the promises made. Principles of honesty and honoring commitments are the ethical values at the heart of the parties' conduct in carrying out contracts. If, however, the parties do not keep their promises, the law does enforce transactions through sets of rules governing requirements for them. **For Example,** if a person provides by will for the distribution of property at death, the law will generally allow the property to pass to the persons intended by the deceased owner. The law will also carry out the intentions of the parties to a business transaction.

Laws exist to honor the intent of parties because not all commitments are fulfilled voluntarily. The law may impose requirements that a transaction or agreement be in writing to ensure that the intent of the parties is adequately documented and fulfilled (see Chapter 17). The law may also place restrictions on honoring intentions. A contract to commit a murder may be evidenced by intent and fully documented in writing. However, the intent of the parties will not be honored because of the social values manifested in the protection of individuals and individuals' rights and safety.

(g) PROTECTION FROM EXPLOITATION, FRAUD, AND OPPRESSION   Many laws have evolved because businesses took advantage of another group. The law has given some groups or individuals protection because of excesses by businesses in dealing with them. Minors, or persons under legal age (see Chapter 14), are given special protections under contract laws that permit them to disaffirm their contracts so they are not disadvantaged by excessive commitments without the benefit of the wisdom of age and with the oppressive presence of an adult party.

The federal laws on disclosure with respect to the sales of securities and shareholder relations (see Chapters 45 and 46) were developed following the 1929 stock market crash when many investors lost all they had because of the lack of candor and information by the businesses in which they were investing.

Food manufacturers have exclusive control over the canning and processing of their products. The opportunity for taking advantage of customers who do not generally have access to the factories and plants is great. The contents of canned products are not visible to consumers before they make their purchases. Because of excesses and exploitations by food processors, there are both federal and state regulations of food processing and food labeling. Adulterating or poisoning food products carries criminal penalties. Misrepresenting the contents in food packages may constitute a federal felony.

(h) FURTHERANCE OF TRADE   Some laws are the result of social forces seeking to simplify business and trade. Installment sales and credit transactions, and their accompanying laws and regulations, have made additional capital available for businesses and provided consumers with alternatives to cash purchases. The laws on checks, drafts, and notes have created instruments used to facilitate trade. The Board of Governors of the Federal Reserve System's oversight of federal banks and interest rates has mitigated the harmful effects of alternating economic periods of depression and inflation.

(i) PROTECTION OF CREDITORS AND REHABILITATION OF DEBTORS   Society seeks to protect the rights of creditors and to protect them from dishonest or fraudulent acts of debtors. Initially, the laws that make contracts binding and enforceable protect creditors. Statutes that make it a fraud for a debtor to conceal property from a creditor also protect creditors. To meet the social demands for facilitation of trade, credit transactions were authorized. With that authorization, however, came the demand for the creditor's assurance of repayment by the debtor. Mortgages, security interests, and surety relationships (see Chapters 32, 34, and 49) are mechanisms created by law to provide creditors the legal mechanisms for collecting their obligations.

When collection techniques became excessive and exploitative, new laws on debtors' rights were enacted. Debtors' prisons were abolished. Congress mandated disclosure requirements for credit contracts. The Fair Debt Collections Practices Act (see Chapter 33) limited collection techniques. The remedy of bankruptcy was

ETHICS & THE LAW

Ethics and Lying to Get Ahead

A study by an executive search firm revealed that 25 percent of all the résumés they reviewed contained inaccurate information about the individual's educational background or past employment. The types of inaccuracies included listing attendance at and the receipt of a degree from a university that the applicant never attended and misrepresenting responsibilities at previous jobs (e.g., a sales manager referring to himself on his résumé as "director of marketing").*

Another study by Rutgers University concluded, based on surveys conducted of students, that 75 percent of all students in master of business administration (MBA) programs lied or cheated to get into their graduate programs. Examples of their misconduct included cheating in undergraduate school, falsifying letters of reference, and having someone else take the Graduate Management Admission Test (GMAT) for them.**

Ronald L. Zarrella, the CEO of Bausch & Lomb, admitted that he had included false information in his résumé, which stated that he had an MBA from New York University (NYU). He had attended NYU and taken graduate courses in business at night while he was working for Bristol-Myers, but he never completed the degree program. The information from the résumé had been included in Bausch & Lomb press releases since 1982. In addition, Credit Suisse First Boston released a statement indicating that information on Mr. Zarrella regarding his serving on its subsidiary's board, First USA, was inaccurate. He had instead served on the board of US First, a nonprofit organization that supported students entering the sciences and engineering fields.

The news about this false information resulted in a drop of $1.01 in the price of Bausch & Lomb's shares from $31.48. Mr. Zarrella said he would not resign, and the Board issued a statement expressing confidence in him. Mr. Zarrella had been hired as CEO just 11 months before this incident. Bausch & Lomb had hired Heidrick & Struggles to conduct its CEO search at that time, and the company had not checked Mr. Zarrella's background because he came in as a candidate through a board member's recommendation, not through the search firm.***

Why do people lie about their backgrounds and qualifications? Is anyone really hurt by this individual misconduct? Why is it important that the information on résumés and applications for graduate school be accurate?

---

*Dan Barry, "Cheating Hearts and Lying Resumes," *New York Times*, December 14, 1997, WK1, WK4.

**Carol Innerst, "Colleges Are Stepping Up the War Against Cheaters," *Washington Times*, November 6–12, 1995, 25.

***Leslie Wayne, "Bausch & Lomb Executive Admits to Falsified Resume," *New York Times*, October 20, 2002, C1; William M. Bulkeley, "Bausch & Lomb Now Says CEO Has No M.B.A.," *Wall Street Journal*, October 21, 2002, A10.

afforded debtors under federal law to provide them an opportunity to begin a new economic life when their existing debts reached an excessive level and could no longer be paid in a timely fashion (see Chapter 35).

(j) STABILITY AND FLEXIBILITY   Stability is particularly important in business transactions. When you buy a house, for example, you want to know not only what the exact meaning of the transaction is under today's law but also that the transaction will have the same meaning in the future.

Because of the desire for stability, courts will ordinarily follow former decisions unless there is a strong reason to depart from them. Similarly, when no former case bears on the point involved, a court will try to reach a decision that is a logical extension of some former decision or that follows a former decision by analogy rather than strike out on a new path to reach a decision unrelated to the past.

If stability were always required, the cause of justice would often be defeated. The reason that originally existed for a rule of law may have ceased to exist. Also, a rule may later appear unjust because it reflects a concept of justice that is outmoded or obsolete. The policies surrounding adoption of children and the rights of natural versus adoptive parents have continued to evolve because of changing attitudes about these relationships and new technology that permits laboratory creation and insemination.

The typical modern statute, particularly in the area of business regulation, often contains an escape clause by which a person can "escape" from the operation of the statute under certain circumstances. **For Example,** a rent control law may impose a rent ceiling, that is, a maximum rent a landlord can charge a tenant. The same law may also authorize a higher charge when special circumstances make it just and fair to allow such an exception. For example, the landlord may have made expensive repairs to the property or taxes on the property may have increased substantially.

Protection of the person is frequently the controlling factor in determining whether a court should adhere to the common law, thereby furthering stability, or whether it should change the law, thereby furthering flexibility.

 ## HOW TO RECOGNIZE AND RESOLVE ETHICAL DILEMMAS

Business managers find themselves in circumstances in which they are unclear about right and wrong and are confused about how to resolve the dilemmas they face. A recent survey showed that 98 percent of all Fortune 500 companies have codes of ethics designed to help their employees recognize and resolve ethical dilemmas. Nearly 75 percent of those firms provide their employees some form of training in ethics.[17] Almost 80 percent of companies now have an ethics officer. These codes of ethics provide employees information about categories of behavior that constitute ethical breaches. Regardless of the industry, the type of business, or the size of the company, certain universal categories can help managers recognize ethical dilemmas. Figure 3-3 provides a list of those categories.

9. CATEGORIES OF ETHICAL BEHAVIOR

(a) Integrity and Truthfulness   Mark Twain once wrote, "Always tell the truth. That way you don't have to remember anything." As discussed earlier, trust is a key component of business relationships and of the free enterprise system. Trust begins with the belief that honesty is at the heart of relationships. Many contract remedies in law are based on the failure of the parties to be truthful with each other. If you purchase a home that has been certified as termite free but you discover termites in the home shortly after you move in, someone has not been truthful. If you also discover that two termite inspections were conducted and that the first one, which revealed there were termites, was concealed from you, your trust in both the sellers and their exterminators is diminished.

---

[17] Survey of the Society for Human Resource Management and Ethics Resource Center (2005).

FIGURE 3-3	*Categories of Ethical Behavior*

1. **INTEGRITY AND TRUTHFULNESS**
2. **PROMISE KEEPING**
3. **LOYALTY—AVOIDING CONFLICTS OF INTEREST**
4. **FAIRNESS**
5. **DOING NO HARM**
6. **MAINTAINING CONFIDENTIALITY**

SPORTS & ENTERTAINMENT LAW

Hiring Prosecutors to Police Corporate Ethics

Ethics officers at companies now have unprecedented power. They have full access to speak to all employees and direct lines to boards and CEOs. For example, Patrick J. Gnazzo is the new ethics officer at Computer Associates (CA), a company whose former CEO has entered a guilty plea to federal fraud charges for cooking the books. At a speech at the company retreat in Las Vegas, Gnazzo told the 1,200 staff members there, "What happens at CA World can make us great. Don't lie, don't cheat, don't steal."*

To avoid criminal prosecution, the CA board agreed to accept Gnazzo, the former chief trial attorney for the U.S. Navy, as its chief compliance officer. Former prosecutors are now becoming ethics officers at companies that have experienced legal or ethical difficulties:

- Richard C. Breeden, former SEC chairman, is outside monitor at KPMG and at Hollinger.
- Eric R. Dinallo, formerly with Eliot Spitzer at the NY Attorney general's office, is chief compliance officer at Morgan Stanley.
- Beth L. Golden, also from Spitzer's office, is chief compliance officer at Bear Stearns.
- Mari B. Maloney, formerly with NASD and the Manhattan district attorney's office, is chief compliance officer at AIG.
- Frederick B. Lacey, former federal judge, will serve as independent monitor at Bristol-Myers Squibb.

The new ethics officer differs from those in the past who tended to come from human resources and public relations. They have direct access to boards and CEOs and also have an edge in knowing how to question employees to obtain information that will lead to halting unacceptable activities.

*Joseph Weber, "The New Ethics Enforcers," *Business Week*, February 13, 2006, 76–77.

(ETHICS & THE LAW)

Lying to Get into a Top School

The University of California at Berkeley has implemented a new step in its admission process. The Haas School of Business has begun running background checks on students who have applied to determine whether the information in their applications is correct. The Wharton School implemented a similar procedure and charges applicants a $35 fee for these background checks.

Of the 100 students admitted to Berkeley in the fall of 2003, 5 students were found to have offered false information on their admissions applications. The most common type of false information was the job titles they held, and the second most common type was their number of years of work experience. Haas admissions officers indicated that had the students not lied, they otherwise met the GMAT score and GPA standards for admission to Haas.

What risk do the students take in lying on their applications? What are the long-term consequences?

Source: "Cheaters Don't Make the Grade at Berkeley Business School," **http://www.azcentral.com**, March 14, 2003, AP wire reports.

An assurance that a seller has the expertise to handle your project is important in building that relationship. If you discover later that the seller lacks the expertise, you are harmed by the delay and possible poor work that has been done. When the prospectus for a stock offering fails to provide full information about the company's obsolete inventory, investors are not given the full truth and are harmed when they invest without complete disclosure. Investors become skeptical when offerings do not carry with them a very basic level of honesty in their disclosures. Honesty is necessary for the wheels of commerce to turn.

integrity the adherence to one's values and principles despite the costs and consequences.

Integrity is the adherence to one's values and principles despite the costs and consequences. **For Example,** an executive contracted with a variety of companies to sell his hard-to-find computer components. When he was approached by one of his largest customers to break a contract with a small customer, the executive refused. The customer assured the executive it would be his last order with the company if he did not get more components. Despite facing the threat of losing a multimillion-dollar customer, the executive fulfilled his promises to the small purchasers. The executive kept his word on all of his contracts and demonstrated integrity.

(b) PROMISE KEEPING   If we examine the types of things we do in a day, we would find that most of them are based on promises. We promise to deliver goods either with or without a contract. We promise to pay the dentist for our dental work. We promise to provide someone with a ride. Keeping those promises, regardless of whether there is a legal obligation to do so, is a key component of being an ethical person and practicing ethical business. Keeping promises is also evidence of integrity.

The issue of employee downsizing is debated with the underlying question of whether the downsized employees had a promise from their company of continued employment. As stakeholder analysis is reviewed, the ethical issue surrounding the question is whether there are promises to others who are at risk. Weren't shareholders

SPORTS & ENTERTAINMENT LAW

Oprah Was Duped

Oprah Winfrey named James Frey's autobiographical book, *A Million Little Pieces,* to her television book club. The impact of the book's inclusion in the Oprah Book Club was the sale of 10 million copies, making it the fastest-selling book in the club's history. The book allegedly addressed Mr. Frey's addictions and recovery. However, on January 8, 2006, the Web site The Smoking Gun found significant and multiple discrepancies between Frey's accounts of his life experiences in the book and what really happened. For example, Frey wrote that he spent 87 days in prison. In reality, he spent 3 hours. When the discrepancies initially emerged, Ms. Winfrey defended Mr. Frey, saying the book was the "essential truth" about his life. She also called the controversy "much ado about nothing."

The public reaction was different, and Ms. Winfrey had Mr. Frey on her show, or, as some critics labeled it, "had him into the woodshed." Ms. Winfrey told Mr. Frey, "I feel really duped. You betrayed millions of readers. Why would you lie?"

In the week following his Oprah appearance, Mr. Frey sold 50,000 copies of *A Million Little Pieces,* but the publisher for his next book canceled his contract. Was there truthfulness? Mr. Frey said the book was a "creative novel memoir" that had not been intended to be autobiographical. Does this clarification help? Were Mr. Frey's actions ethical? Evaluate Ms. Winfrey's initial response.

Source: Carol Memmot, "Oprah grills 'Pieces' author, apologizes," *USA Today,* January 26, 2006, p. 1D.

promised a return on their investment? Weren't suppliers promised payment? In many circumstances, the question is not *whether* a promise will be kept but rather *which* promise will be kept. The strategic issue is whether businesses should make commitments and promises in circumstances that create a very thin margin of profit and perhaps even thinner margin for error. Over the long term, the importance of a company's keeping its promises to all stakeholders translates into its reputation.

(c) Loyalty—Avoiding Conflicts of Interest An employee who works for a company owes allegiance to that company. Conduct that compromises that loyalty is a **conflict of interest. For Example,** suppose that your sister operates her own catering business. Your company is seeking a caterer for its monthly management meetings. You are responsible for these meetings and could hire your sister to furnish the lunches for the meetings. Your sister would have a substantial contract, and your problems with meal logistics would be solved. Nearly all companies have a provision in their codes of ethics covering this situation. An employee cannot hire a relative, friend, or even her own company without special permission because it is a conflict of interest. Your loyalty to your sister conflicts with the loyalty to your employer, which requires you to make the best decision at the best price.

A conflict of interest arises when a purchasing agent accepts gifts from suppliers, vendors, or manufacturers' representatives. The purchasing agent has introduced into the buy-sell relationship an element of *quid pro quo,* or the supplier's expectation that the gift will bring about a return from the agent in the form of a contract. Some companies have zero tolerance for conflicts and establish a complete prohibition on employees accepting

conflict of interest conduct that compromises an employee's allegiance to that company.

(ETHICS & THE LAW)

Conflicts and Combat

Richard N. Perle served as chairman of the Defense Policy Board, a position appointed by the Secretary of Defense, Donald H. Rumsfield. Mr. Perle was hired by Global Crossing, a telecommunications company in Chapter 11 bankruptcy, to work with the Defense Department because the Department opposed the sale of Global Crossing to Hutchison Whampoa and Singapore Technology, two foreign companies. Mr. Perle earned $725,000 for his work, $600,000 of which depended on the Defense Department's approval of the sale. The Defense Department opposed the sale because it used the Global Crossing fiber-optics network for its telecommunications needs and the sale would put that network under Chinese control.

Mr. Perle filed an affidavit in the review process for the FBI and Defense Department (whose approvals were required) that contained the following language:

*As the chairman of the Defense Policy Board, I have a unique perspective on and intimate knowledge of the national defense and security issues that will be raised by the CFUIS review process that is not and could not be available to the other CFIUS professionals.**

When asked about his dual role, Mr. Perle said,

*I've abided by the rules. The question, I think, is have I recommended anything to the secretary or discussed this with the secretary, and I haven't. The alternative is if you are on the board, you can't have any action before the Defense Department. That isn't the rule. If that were the rule, I'd have to make a choice between being on an unpaid advisory board and my business.***

What ethical issue exists in Mr. Perle's conduct?

---

* CFUIS is the Committee on Foreign Investment in the United States and consists of representatives from the Defense Department and other agencies. CFUIS has the authority to block foreign acquisitions.

** Stephen Labaton, "Pentagon Adviser Is Also Advising Global Crossing," *New York Times*, March 21, 2003, C1, C2.

---

any gifts from suppliers and manufacturers. **For Example,** Wal-Mart buyers are not permitted to accept even a cup of coffee from potential merchandise suppliers, and Amgen's buyers can go out to dinner with a supplier only if Amgen pays.

(d) FAIRNESS   In business transactions in which the buyer was not told about the crack in the engine block or the dry well on the property, a typical response is, "That's not fair. I wouldn't have bought it if I'd known." A question often posed to the buyer in response is "Wouldn't you have done the same thing?" We feel differently about such situations, depending on whether we are the victims of unfairness or whether we hold the superior knowledge in the transaction. The ethical standard of fairness requires both sides to ask these questions: "How would I want to be treated? Would this information make a difference to me?" Imposing our own standards and expectations on our own behavior in business transactions produces fairness in business.

(e) DOING NO HARM   Imagine selling a product that your company's internal research shows presents significant health dangers to its users. Selling the product

ETHICS & THE LAW

Ethics and Incendiary Devices

Dateline NBC, a television news magazine program that airs several nights a week, presented a segment on General Motors (GM) and the safety of GM's trucks with side-saddle gas tanks. *Dateline* producers staged and taped an accident with a GM truck that showed a gas tank explosion and subsequent fire that engulfed the pickup truck. The tape was shown on *Dateline.* Disclosures of several crew members later revealed that explosive devices had been used to create the scene for the cameras, but the use of those devices was not disclosed during the *Dateline* piece.*

Was it fair to use the explosive devices? Was it fair to use the explosive devices and not disclose that to the audience? Was the program fair to GM?

Note: *Dateline* later read an on-air apology for using the tape.

---

*Elizabeth Jensen, "Some Journalists Join GM in Criticizing NBC's Treatment of Truck Crash Story," *Wall Street Journal,* February 10, 1993, B1, B8.

---

without disclosure of the information is unfair. There is the additional ethical breach of physical harm to your customers and users. Ford designed and sold its Pinto with a fundamental flaw in the placement of the car's gas tank. Rear-end collisions in which a Pinto was involved resulted, even at very low speeds, in fires that engulfed the car so quickly that occupants could not always escape from it. An internal memo from engineers at Ford revealed that employees had considered doing an analysis of the risk of the tanks versus the cost of redesign but never did. The late Peter Drucker's advice on ethics for businesses is ***primum non nocere,*** or "above all, do no harm." Such a rule might have helped Ford.

primum non nocere above all do no harm.

(f) MAINTAINING CONFIDENTIALITY Often the success of a business depends on the information or technology that it holds. If the competitive edge that comes from the business's peculiar niche or knowledge is lost through disclosure, so are its profits. Employees not only owe a duty of loyalty to their employers, but they also owe an obligation of confidentiality. Employees should not use, either personally or through a competitor, information they have obtained through their employer's work or research. Providing customer lists or leads is a breach of employees' obligation of confidentiality.

In addition, managers have responsibilities regarding their employees' privacy. Performance evaluations of individual employees are private and should never be disclosed or revealed, even in one-on-one conversations outside the lines of authority and the workplace.

---

10. RESOLVING ETHICAL DILEMMAS

Recognizing an ethical dilemma is perhaps the easiest part of business ethics. Resolution of that dilemma is more difficult. The earlier section on stakeholders offers one model for resolution of ethical dilemmas (see Figure 3-1). Other models have been

E-COMMERCE AND CYBERLAW

Piggybacking on Wireless Networks

A new issue that has evolved because of technology could require legal steps to stop it. People are "piggybacking" or tapping onto their neighbors' wireless Internet connection. The original subscriber pays a monthly fee for the service, but without security, people located in the area are able to tap into the wireless network, which bogs down the speed of the service. Once limited to geeks and hackers, the practice is now common among the ordinary folk who just want free Internet service.

One college student said, "I don't think it's stealing. I always find people out there who aren't protecting their connection, so I just feel free to go ahead and use it."* According to a recent survey, only about 30 percent of the 4,500 wireless networks onto which the surveyors logged were encrypted.

An apartment dweller said she leaves her connection wide open because "I'm sticking it to the man. I open up my network, leave it wide open for anyone to jump on." One of the users of another's wireless network said, "I feel sort of bad about it, but I do it anyway. It just seems harmless." She said that if she gets caught, "I'm a grandmother. They're not going to yell at an old lady. I'll just play the dumb card."

Some neighbors offer to pay those with wireless service in exchange for their occasional use rather than paying a wireless company for full-blown service. However, the original subscribers do not really want to run their own Internet service.

Do you think we need new legislation to cover this activity? What do you think of the users' statements? Is their conduct legal? Is it ethical?

---

*Michael Marriott, "Hey Neighbor, Stop Piggybacking on My Wireless," *New York Times*, March 5, 2006, A1, A23.

---

developed to provide managers analytical methods for resolving dilemmas in a timely fashion.

(a) BLANCHARD AND PEALE THREE-PART TEST Dr. Kenneth Blanchard, author of books on the *One-Minute Manager,* and the late Dr. Norman Vincent Peale developed a model for evaluating ethical breaches that is widely used among Fortune 500 companies.[18] To evaluate situations, ask the following three questions: Is it legal? Is it balanced? How does it make me feel?

In answering the questions on legality, a manager should look to positive law both within and outside the company. If the proposed conduct would violate antitrust laws, the manager's analysis can stop there. If the proposed conduct would violate company policy, the manager's analysis can stop. In the field of business ethics, there is little room for civil disobedience. Compliance with the law is a critical component of a successful ethics policy in any company.

The second question on balance forces the manager to examine the ethical value of fairness. Perhaps the decision to downsize must be made, but couldn't the company offer the employees a severance package and outplacement assistance to ease the transition?

---

[18] Kenneth Blanchard and Norman Vincent Peale, *The Power of Ethical Management* (New York: William Morrow, 1986).

ETHICS & THE LAW

Bribery, Ethics, and Olympics

Salt Lake City, Utah, had been a contender as a potential site for the Winter Olympics for 30 years when the choice to locate the 2002 games was being made. Each time, the city, famous for its extensive ski resorts and powder snow, lost to other cities around the world. When city and state officials and representatives from business made their bid for Salt Lake for the 2002 Winter Olympics, they were determined to win. During the course of the International Olympic Committee's decision-making process, some members of the Salt Lake City Olympic Committee gave benefits to members of the International Olympic Committee. Those benefits included everything from entertainment to medical care and college educations for family members of International Olympic Committee members.

When all of the perks were revealed, members of the International Olympic Committee, as well as the Salt Lake City Olympic Committee, resigned. Some Olympic sponsors withdrew.*

How could the Blanchard and Peale test have helped those involved in courting the International Olympic Committee? Does it matter that those types of benefits and perks are expected in the cultures of some of the International Olympic Committee members?

---

*Ira Berkow, "Greed Knows Few Bounds in Olympics," *New York Times*, February 10, 1999, C23.

The final question of the Blanchard and Peale model is conscience based. Although some managers may employ any tactics to maximize profits, this final question forces a manager to examine the physical impact of a decision: Does it cause sleeplessness or appetite changes? Personalizing business choices often helps managers to see the potential harm that comes from poor ethical choices.

(b) The Front-Page-of-the-Newspaper Test   This simple but effective model for ethical evaluation helps a manager visualize the public disclosure of proposed conduct. When he temporarily took over as the leader of Salomon Brothers after its bond-trading controversy, Warren Buffett described the newspaper test as follows:

Contemplating any business act, an employee should ask himself whether he would be willing to see it immediately described by an informed and critical reporter on the front page of his local paper, there to be read by his spouse, children, and friends. At Salomon, we simply want no part of any activities that pass legal tests but that we, as citizens, would find offensive.[19]

(c) Laura Nash Model   In her work, business ethicist Laura Nash has developed a series of questions to help businesspeople reach the right decision in ethical dilemmas. These are her questions: Have you defined the problem accurately? How would you define the problem if you stood on the other side of the fence? How did this situation occur in the first place? What is your intention in making this decision? How does the intention compare with the probable results? Whom could your decision or action injure? Can you discuss your decision with the affected

---

[19] Janet Lowe, *Warren Buffett Speaks: Wit and Wisdom from the World's Greatest Investor* (New York: Wiley, 1997).

(ETHICS & THE LAW)

Burger King, Coke, and Numbers

Coca-Cola has admitted that it paid a consultant $10,000 to drive up the demand for its Frozen Coke beverage being test-marketed in Burger Kings in the Richmond, Virginia, area. The consultant used the money to make donations to Boys and Girls Clubs. The clubs then provided meal coupons to the children in exchange for them doing their homework. The impressive demand that resulted from the Richmond area test market led Burger King to invest $65 million to put the machines in restaurants around the country, However, the demand was not what it had been falsely alleged to be, and the result is that, following a six-week investigation by a law firm hired by the Coca-Cola board, Coca-Cola admitted that the marketing studies were inflated.

The board investigation followed an allegation in a lawsuit filed by a former employee, Matthew Whitley. Whitley was terminated following his questioning of an expense claim by the consultant and his resulting investigation that produced an internal memo describing the consultant's work on driving up the demand. Coca-Cola also issued an earnings restatement of $9 million based on an investigation of those allegations. The *Wall Street Journal* was following the Whitley lawsuit when the underlying issues emerged, and it reported the marketing scheme.* Coca-Cola settled with Burger King by paying $21 million.

Was this conduct ethical? Was it fraud? What does Mr. Whitley's termination say about the company? Does he have protection? Why do you think the marketing managers decided to involve the consultant and report the false demand? What effect does this incident have on Burger King's relationship with Coke? How do you think the story played on the front page of the *Wall Street Journal?***

---

* Chad Terhune, "Coke Employees Acted Improperly in Marketing Test," *Wall Street Journal,* June 18, 2003, A3, A6; Sherri Day, "Coke Confirms Product Test Was Rigged," *New York Times,* June 18, 2003, C1, C10.

** Marianne Jennings, one of the authors of this text, has done consulting work for Coca-Cola since this incident. Why is this disclosure important?

---

parties? Are you confident that your position will be as valid over a long period of time as it seems now? Could you discuss your decision with your supervisor, coworkers, officers, board, friends, and family?

The Nash model requires an examination of the dilemma from all perspectives. Defining the problem and how the problem arose provides the business assistance in avoiding the dilemma again. **For Example,** suppose that a supervisor is asked to provide a reference for a friend who works for her. The supervisor is hesitant because the friend has not been a very good employee. The ethical dilemma the manager believes she faces is whether to lie or tell the truth about the employee. The real ethical dilemma is why the supervisor never provided evaluation or feedback indicating the friend's poor performance. Avoiding the problem in the future is possible through candid evaluations. Resolving the problem requires that the supervisor talk to her friend now about the issue of performance and the problem with serving as a reference.

One final aspect of the Nash model that businesspeople find helpful is a question that asks for a perspective on an issue from family and friends. The problem of groupthink in business situations is very real. As businesspeople sit together in a room and discuss an ethical dilemma, they can persuade each other to think the same way. The power of consensus can overwhelm each person's concerns and values. There is a certain fear in bringing up a different point of view in a business meeting. Proper perspective is often lost as the discussion centers around numbers. Therefore, bringing in the views of an outsider is often helpful. For example, when McNeil, the manufacturer of Tylenol, faced the cyanide poisonings from contaminated capsules sold in the Chicago area, it had to make a decision about the existing Tylenol inventory. It was clear to both insiders and outsiders that the poison had not been put in the capsules at McNeil but after delivery to the stores. Despite the huge numbers involved in the recall and the destruction of inventory, the McNeil managers made the decision easily because they viewed the risk to their own families, that is, from the outside. From this standpoint, the issue became a question of human life, not of numbers.[20]

(d) *Wall Street Journal* Model   The *Wall Street Journal* presented a simple, three-prong test for resolving ethical dilemmas known as the three-C model: (1) Will this conduct be in compliance with the law? (2) What contribution does this decision make to the shareholders? To the community? To the employees? (3) What are the consequences of this decision? This model requires an examination of the impact of a choice, which then produces a different perspective on a course of conduct. **For Example,** Sears paid $475 million in fines and penalties for its unauthorized collection of debts from debtors who were in bankruptcy or had debts discharged in bankruptcy. Such collection beyond what the law allows did not comply with the law.[21] The contribution to the company was more collections and hence more cash, but the consequences were the large fine and the damage to Sears' reputation for putting its interests above the law and above the interests of other creditors who conducted themselves within the limits of the bankruptcy law. Sears may have resented the fact that debtors had not paid, but the company was not justified in taking the law into its own hands or profiting at the expense of other creditors.

(LAWFLIX)

Breaking Away (1979) (PG)

In this story about "cutters" (a nickname for natives of Bloomington, Indiana), a recent high school graduate trains to be a first-class bike rider. He idolizes the Italian world racing team and enters an Indiana race to have the opportunity to compete with them. He does well in the race and manages to catch up and keep pace with the Italian team. As he rides alongside his idols, one of the members of the Italian team places a tire pump in his spoke. His bike crashes, he loses the race and is injured. He becomes disillusioned. Is this experience like business? Do unethical tactics get you ahead? Do nice guys finish last? Are there sanctions for unethical conduct?

For movie clips that illustrate business law concepts, see LawFlix at **http://wdvl.westbuslaw.com.**

---

[20] "Brief History of Johnson & Johnson" (company pamphlet, 1992).

[21] Leslie Kaufman, "Sears Settles Suit on Raising of Its Credit Card Rates," *New York Times*, March 11, 1999, C2.

SUMMARY

Business ethics is the application of values and standards to business conduct and decisions. These values originate in various sources from positive (codified) law to natural law to stakeholder values. Business ethics is important because trust is a critical component of good business relationships and free enterprise. A business with values will enjoy the additional competitive advantage of a good reputation and, over the long term, better earnings. When businesses make decisions that violate basic ethical standards, they set into motion social forces and cause the area of abuse to be regulated, resulting in additional costs and restrictions for business. Voluntary value choices by businesses position them for a competitive advantage.

The categories of ethical values in business are truthfulness and integrity, promise keeping, loyalty and avoiding conflicts of interest, fairness, doing no harm, and maintaining confidentiality.

Resolution of ethical dilemmas is possible through the use of various models that require a businessperson to examine the impact of a decision before it is made. These models include stakeholder analysis, the Blanchard and Peale test, the front-page-of-the-newspaper test, the Laura Nash model, and the *Wall Street Journal* model.

QUESTIONS AND CASE PROBLEMS

1. Marty Mankamyer, the president of the United States Olympic Committee (USOC), resigned in early February 2003 following reports in *The Denver Post* that indicated she had demanded a commission from a fellow real estate broker in the Colorado Springs area, the home of the USOC, who had sold property to Lloyd Ward, the CEO of the USOC. Mr. Ward had purchased a 1.3-acre lot in Colorado Springs for $475,000 and had paid the listing broker, Brigette Ruskin, a commission. Ms. Mankamyer allegedly demanded a portion of the commission from Ms. Ruskin, and Ms. Ruskin sent her a check. Ms. Mankamyer had shown Mr. Ward and his wife properties in the area when they were being considered for the job and when he was considering taking the job. However, Mrs. Ward indicated that Ms. Mankamyer did not identify herself as a real estate agent and that she assumed that Ms. Mankamyer was showing the properties as a "goodwill gesture."[22] What conflicts of interest do you see here?

2. Ann Elkin, who works for Brill Co., has been sent out to conduct two customer evaluations, which have gone much more quickly than Ann anticipated. Her supervisor does not expect Ann back until after lunch. It is now 10:30 A.M., and Ann would like to run some personal errands and then go to lunch before returning to work at 1:00 P.M. Should Ann take the time? Would you? Why or why not? Be sure to consider the categories of ethical values and apply one or two models before reaching your conclusion.

3. Fred Sanguine is a New York City produce broker. Ned Santini is a 19-year-old college student who works for Sanguine from 4:00 A.M. until 7:00 A.M. each weekday before he attends classes at Pace University. Fred has instructed Ned on the proper packing of produce as follows: "Look, put the bad and small cherries at the bottom. Do the same with the strawberries and blueberries. Put the best fruit on top and hide the bad stuff at the bottom. This way I get top dollar on all that I sell." Ned is uncomfortable about the instructions, but, as he explains to his roommate, "It's not me doing it. I'm just following orders. Besides, I need the job." Should Ned just follow instructions? Is the manner in which the fruit is packed unethical? Would you do it? Why or why not? Is anyone really harmed by the practice?

4. Alan Gellen is the facilities manager for the city of Milwaukee and makes all final decisions on purchasing items such as chairs, lights, and other supplies and materials. Alan also makes the final decisions for the award of contracts to food vendors at event sites. Grand Beef Franks has submitted a bid to be one of the city's vendors. Alan went to school with Grand Beef's owner, Steve Grand, who phones Alan and explains that Grand Beef owns a condominium in Maui that

[22] Richard Sandomir, "U.S. Olympic Chief Resigns in a Furor Over Ethics Issues," *New York Times*, February 5, 2003, A1, C17; Bill Briggs, "*Realtor Waving Red Flag,*" **http://www.denverpost.com**, February 4, 2003.

Alan could use. Steve's offer to Alan is: "All it would cost you for a vacation is your airfare. The condo is fully stocked with food. Just let me know." Should Alan take the offer? Would you? Be sure to determine which category of ethical values this situation involves and to apply several models as you resolve the question of whether Alan should accept the invitation.

5. Television network CNBC and other television networks have been working to develop policies for their business correspondents and guests on their business shows because of a practice known as *pump-and-dump,* the practice of a Wall Street professional or network business correspondent appearing on television to tout a particular stock as being a good buy. Often, unbeknown to the viewing audience, the guest or correspondent promoting the stock has a large holding in it and, after the television show runs and the stock price creeps up, sells his or her interest at a higher price than would have been possible before the show on which the person raved about the stock. What category of ethical issue exists here? If you were a network executive, what would you do to remedy the problem? Could the government regulate such practices? What kind of regulation could it impose?

6. Adam Smith wrote the following in *The Theory of Moral Sentiments:*

   In the practice of the other virtues, our conduct should rather be directed by a certain idea of propriety, by a certain taste for a particular tenor of conduct, than by any regard to a precise maxim or rule; and we should consider the end and foundation of the rule, more than the rule itself.[23]

   Do you think Adam Smith adhered to positive law as his ethical standard? Was he a moral relativist? Does his quote match stakeholder analysis? What would his ethical posture be on violating the law?

7. A new phenomenon for admissions to MBA programs is hiring consultants to help applicants hone their applications. About 20 percent of those who apply to the top MBA programs have hired consultants at a cost of $150 to $200 per

hour to help them say and do the right things to be admitted. The total cost for most who use a consultant is $5,000. The consultants help with personal essays and applications. One admissions officer points out that one function of the consultant is to draw out and emphasize skills that the applicant may not see as important. For example, playing the piano is looked upon favorably because it shows discipline and focus. However, admissions committees are becoming adept at spotting the applications via consultant because, as the faculty describe it, these essays and applications have a certain "sameness" to them. The Fuqua School at North Carolina suggests that students simply call the admissions office and get comparable advice for free. Is it ethical to use an admissions consultant? When would you cross a line in using the consultant on the essay?

8. Marv Albert, the longtime NBC sportscaster famous for his "Yes!" commentary, was charged with violations of several Virginia statutes, including criminal assault, battery, and sodomy, for his alleged conduct with a woman in a hotel room. Initially, Albert went to trial on the case and denied that the charges were true. During the trial, another woman testified that Albert had engaged in similar behavior with her. Following plea negotiations, Albert entered a guilty plea the next day. NBC then fired him under a provision in his contract that prohibited employees from making false statements. Albert had assured his superiors at NBC that the charges were baseless. Do you agree with NBC's decision to fire Albert? Was his personal behavior relevant for his job performance? Do you agree that lying to your employer should result in automatic termination? Albert is back as a network commentator. Does his reinstatement mean that moral issues and private conduct are irrelevant in business decisions?

9. In 1997, the Federal Trade Commission (FTC) issued a cease-and-desist order against Toys "R" Us. The order required Toys "R" Us to stop what the FTC calls its "blacklisting" practices. The FTC ruled that Toys "R" Us had forced large toy manufacturers, such as Mattel and Hasbro, to withhold their products from such discount warehouse stores as Sam's Club and Costco. Toys "R" Us allegedly threatened not to carry these companies' products if they were also sold at the

---

[23] Adam Smith, *The Theory of Moral Sentiments* (Arlington House, 1969; originally published in 1769).

discount warehouse chains. Mattel's Barbie doll is one toy that Toys "R" Us carried that the discount warehouses were not permitted to carry. Costco CEO James Sinegal said, "You could fill Madison Square Garden with the people who don't want to sell to us." Are these types of sales agreements ethical? Is it fair for Toys "R" Us to insist on these arrangements? How do you think these arrangements would affect price?

10. The president and athletic director at the University of California at Los Angeles (UCLA) fired the school's basketball coach because an expense form he had submitted for reimbursement had the names of two students he said had joined him for a recruiting dinner. The students had not been to the dinner. The coach was stunned because he had been at UCLA for eight years and had established a winning program. He said, "And to throw it all away on a meal?" Do you agree with the coach's assessment? Was it too harsh to fire him for one inaccurate expense form? Did the coach commit an ethical breach?

11. A new trend is emerging in health insurance: premium increases based on claims. It is common practice in the auto insurance industry, for example, for insurers to revisit your premium each year and adjust it based on factors such as your driving record or number of accidents. However, health insurers have generally evaluated their insured's health only once, at the outset, when issuing a policy. The reevaluation of health and premiums was a practice that ended in the 1950s because the insurers feared regulators would impose limitations on premiums. At least one health insurer, however, has begun to evaluate the health of its insureds annually and to adjust policy premiums accordingly. Even without examination of insureds, some insurers have increased the insureds' premiums based simply on the nature of their claims for the year and the possibility that more claims will arise. Those who are healthy are in favor of this annual review. Perceiving themselves as the equivalent of good drivers, they want to pay less when they stay healthy. The health discount is, in their minds, the equivalent of the safe driver discount. However, those who are less healthy argue that people buy insurance so it will be there when they need it, and the coverage should apply without regard to claims. Consider the ethical issues in this type of pricing for health insurance.

12. David A. Vise, a Putlitzer Prize winner and a reporter for the *Washington Post,* wrote the book *The Bureau and the Mole.* When the book hit the market, Mr. Vise purchased 20,000 copies via Barnes & Noble.com, taking advantage of both free shipping offered by the publisher and a discounted initial price. Mr. Vise's book had already hit the *New York Times'* bestseller list in the week before the purchases. He used the books he purchased to conduct online sales of autographed copies of the books, and then returned 17,500 books and asked for his money back. However, that return of 17,500 books represented more books than a publisher generally runs for a book. Mr. Vise said that he did not intend to manipulate the market or profit from the transactions. He said his only intent was to "increase awareness of *The Bureau and the Mole.*" Mr. Vise's editor offered to pay Barnes & Noble for any expenses it incurred. Was it ethical to do what Mr. Vise did? Was he within his rights to return the books? What are his remedies? Does Barnes & Noble have any rights?

13. Suzy Wetlaufer, editor of the *Harvard Business Review,* interviewed former General Electric CEO Jack Welch for a piece in the business magazine. In December 2001, she asked that the piece be withdrawn because her objectivity might have been compromised. Those at the magazine did another interview and published that interview in the February issue of the magazine. Editorial director of the magazine, Walter Kiechel, who supervised Ms. Wetlaufer, acknowledged as true a report in the *Wall Street Journal* about an alleged affair between Ms. Wetlaufer and Mr. Welch and that Mr. Welch's wife had called to protest the article's objectivity. Mr. Welch refused to confirm or deny an affair with Ms. Wetlaufer, who was divorced. Some staff members asked that Ms. Wetlaufer resign from her $277,000-per-year job, but she refused. Their objections were that she compromised her journalistic integrity. Mr. Kiechel, on the other hand, noted that she did "the right thing in raising her concerns."[24]

---

[24] Del Jones, "Editor Linked with Welch Finds Job at Risk," *USA Today,* March 5, 2002, 3B.

About six weeks later, Ms. Wetlaufer did resign from her position as editor, announcing that she would be spending time with her four children. Do you think there was a conflict of interest because of the affair between Welch and Wetlaufer?[25] Note: Mr. Welch and Ms. Wetlaufer have married and have written a book together. They now write a semiweekly column for *Busienss Week* magazine.

14. Piper High School in Piper, Kansas, a town located about 20 miles west of Kansas City, experienced national attention because of questions about students and their term papers for a botany class. Christine Pelton, a high school science teacher, had warned students in her sophomore class not to use papers posted on the Internet for their projects. When their projects were turned in, Ms. Pelton noticed that the writing in some of the papers was well above the students' usual quality and ability. She found that 28 of her 118 students had taken substantial portions of their papers from the Internet. She gave these students a zero grade on their term paper projects with the result that many of the students were going to fail the course for that semester. The students' parents protested, and the school board ordered Ms. Pelton to raise the grades. She resigned in protest. She received a substantial number of job offers from around the country following her resignation. Nearly half of the high school faculty as well as its principal announced their plans to resign at the end of the year. Several of the parents pointed to the fact that there was no explanation in the Piper High School handbook on plagiarism. They also said that the students were unclear about what could be used, when they had to reword, and when quotations marks were necessary. The annual Rutgers University survey on academic cheating has revealed that 15 percent of college papers turned in for grades are completely copied from the Internet. Do you think such copying is unethical? Why do we worry about such conduct? Isn't this conduct just a function of the Internet? Isn't it accepted behavior?

15. Pharmaceutical companies, faced with the uphill battle of getting doctors to take a look at their new products, have created complex systems and programs for enticing doctors to come, sit, and absorb information about the new products.

Following is a list of the various type of benefits and gifts that drug companies have given doctors over the past few years to entice them to consider prescribing their new offerings:

- An event called "Why Cook?" in which doctors were given the chance to review drug studies and product information at a restaurant as their meals were being prepared—they could leave as soon as their meals were ready, and they were treated to appetizers and drinks as they waited
- Events at Christmas tree lots where doctors can come and review materials and pick up a free Christmas tree
- Flowers sent to doctors' offices on Valentine's Day with materials attached
- Manicures as they study materials on new drugs
- Pedicures as they study materials on new drugs
- Free car washes during which they study materials
- Free books with materials enclosed
- Free CDs with materials attached
- Bottles of wine with materials attached
- Events at Barnes & Noble where doctors can browse and pick out a book for themselves for free as long as they also take some materials on a new drug

Some doctors say that they can enjoy dinner on a drug company as often as five times per week. The American Medical Association (AMA) frowns on the "dine-and-dash" format because its rules provide that dinners are acceptable only as long as the doctors sit and learn something from a featured speaker. The AMA also limits gifts to those of a "minimal value" that should be related to their patients, such as note pads and pens with the new drug's name imprinted on them. The chairman of the AMA Committee on Ethics says the following about gifts, "There are doctors who say, 'I always do what's best for my patients, and these gifts and dinners and trips do not influence me.' They are wrong."[26] In which category of ethical issues do these gifts fall? Do you think doctors act ethically in accepting gifts, meals, and favors? The Food and Drug Administration recently issued rules about such favors and perks. Why?

---

[25] Ms. Wetlaufer and Mr. Welch were engaged to be married after Mr. Welch divorced Jane Welch.

[26] Chris Adams, "Doctors on the Run Can 'Dine 'n' Dash' in Style in New Orleans," *Wall Street Journal*, May 14, 2001, A1, A6.

THE CONSTITUTION AS THE FOUNDATION OF THE LEGAL ENVIRONMENT

LEARNING OBJECTIVES

After studying this chapter, you should be able to

LO.1 Describe the system of government created by the U.S. Constitution

LO.2 List the branches and levels of government and describe their relationship to each other

LO.3 Explain how the U.S. Constitution adapts to change

LO.4 List and describe three significant federal powers

LO.5 Discuss two significant constitutional limitations on governmental power

This chapter introduces you to the powers of government and to the protections that you have for your rights. The Constitution of the United States sets forth not only the structure and powers of government but also the limitations on those powers. This Constitution, together with the constitutions of each of the states, forms the foundation of our legal environment.

THE U.S. CONSTITUTION AND THE FEDERAL SYSTEM

federal system the system of government in which a central government is given power to administer to national concerns while individual states retain the power to administer to local concerns.

By establishing a central government to coexist with the governments of the individual states, the U.S. Constitution created a federal system. In a **federal system,** a central government has power to address national concerns, while the individual states retain the power to handle local concerns.

1. WHAT A CONSTITUTION IS

constitution a body of principles that establishes the structure of a government and the relationship of the government to the people who are governed.

A **constitution** is the written document that establishes the structure of the government and its relationship to the people. The U.S. Constitution was adopted in 1789 by the 13 colonies that had won their independence from King George.[1]

2. THE BRANCHES OF GOVERNMENT

tripartite three-part division (of government).

legislative branch the branch of government (e.g., Congress) formed to make the laws.

executive branch the branch of government (e.g., the president) formed to execute the laws.

The U.S. Constitution establishes a **tripartite** (three-part) government: a **legislative branch** (Congress) to make the laws, an **executive branch** (the president) to execute or enforce the laws, and a **judicial branch** (courts) to interpret the laws. The national legislature or Congress is a **bicameral** (two-house) body consisting of the Senate and the House of Representatives. Members of the Senate are popularly elected for a term of six years. Members of the House of Representatives are popularly elected for a term of two years. The president is elected by an electoral college whose membership is popularly elected. The president serves for a term of four years and is eligible for reelection for a second term. Judges of the United States are appointed by the president with the approval of the Senate and serve for life, subject to removal only by impeachment because of misconduct. (See Chapter 2 for a discussion of the federal court system.)

THE U.S. CONSTITUTION AND THE STATES

judicial branch the branch of government (courts) formed to interpret the laws.

bicameral a two-house form of the legislative branch of government.

The Constitution created certain powers within the national government that would have been exercised by the individual states, which are given their powers by the people of the state. Figure 4-1 illustrates the delegation of powers. Likewise, the states, as the power-granting authorities, reserved certain powers for themselves.

3. DELEGATED AND SHARED POWERS

delegated powers powers expressly granted the national government by the Constitution.

(a) DELEGATED POWERS The powers given by the states to the national government are described as *delegated powers.* Some of these **delegated powers** are given exclusively to the national government. For example, the national government alone may declare war or establish a currency.

---

[1] To examine the U.S. Constitution, go to **http://www.constitution.org** and click on "Founding Documents," or refer to Appendix 2.

FIGURE 4-1   *Governments of the United States*

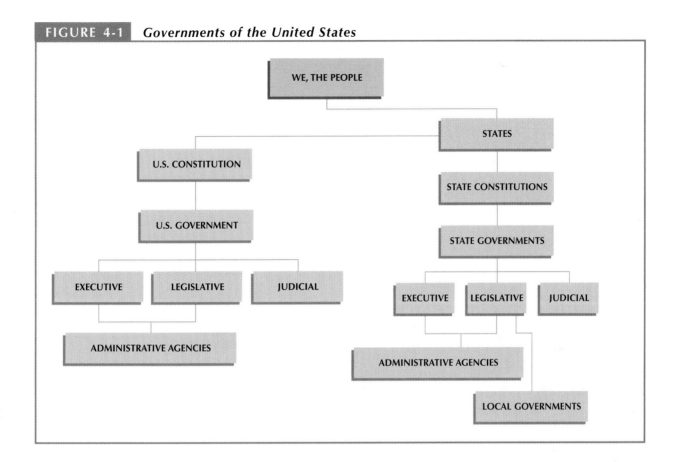

---

shared powers powers that are held by both state and national governments.

(b) Shared Powers   The powers delegated to the national government that may still be exercised by the states are **shared powers. For Example,** the grant of power to the national government to impose taxes did not destroy the state power to tax. Some of the shared powers may be exercised by the states only so long as there is no federal exercise.

For Example, a state's law on appliance safety may apply until Congress adopts a federal appliance safety law. In other cases, a state may provide regulation along with, but subject to the supremacy of, federal law. **For Example,** regulation of the use of navigable waterways within a state is an example of joint state and federal regulation.

police power the power to govern; the power to adopt laws for the protection of the public health, welfare, safety, and morals.

ex post facto law a law making criminal an act that was lawful when done or that increases the penalty when done. Such laws are generally prohibited by constitutional provisions.

4. OTHER POWERS

(a) State Police Power   The states possess the power to adopt laws to protect the general welfare, health, safety, and morals of the people. This authority is called the **police power. For Example,** states may require that businesses be licensed with state agencies to protect persons dealing with the business. State exercise of the police power may not unreasonably interfere with federal powers.

(b) Prohibited Powers   The Constitution also prohibits both states and the federal government from doing certain things. **For Example,** neither states nor the national government may adopt ***ex post facto*** laws, which make criminal an act that has already been committed but was not criminal when it was committed. Laws that increase the penalty for an act already committed above the penalty in force when the act was committed are also *ex post facto* laws.

5. FEDERAL SUPREMACY

Federal law bars or preempts conflicting state regulation when a federal law regulates that particular subject. Federal law also preempts state action when congressional intent to regulate exclusively can be inferred from the details of congressional regulation. **Preemption** means that the federal regulatory scheme is controlling.

preemption the federal government's superior regulatory position over state laws on the same subject area.

(a) EXPRESS FEDERAL REGULATION The Constitution and statutes passed by Congress are the supreme law of the land. They cancel out any conflicting state law.[2] When a direct conflict exists between federal and state statutes, it is clear that federal law prevails.

In some cases, however, no obvious conflict occurs because the federal statute covers only part of the subject matter. In such cases, the question becomes whether a

CASE SUMMARY

Truck Bingo: A Constitutional Issue

FACTS: Federal law requires most interstate truckers to obtain a permit that reflects compliance with certain federal requirements. The 1965 version of the law authorized states to require proof that a truck operator had such a permit. By 1991, 39 states had demanded such proof, requiring a $10 per truck registration fee and giving each trucker a stamp to affix to a multistate "bingo card" carried in the vehicle. Finding this scheme inefficient and burdensome, Congress created the current Single State Registration System (SSRS), which allows a trucking company to fill out one set of forms in one state, thereby registering in every participating state through which its trucks travel.

A subsection of Michigan's Motor Carrier Act imposes truck companies operating in interstate commerce an annual fee of $100 for each self-propelled motor vehicle operated by or on behalf of the motor carrier. The American Truckers Association (ATA) and others challenged the $100 fee as preempted by the extensive federal regulation of interstate trucking and trucking companies. The ATA and others argued that the federal government had preempted such registration requirements with SSRS. The trial court granted the state of Michigan summary judgment, and the appellate court affirmed. The ATA and others appealed to the U.S. Supreme Court.

DECISION: The U.S. Supreme Court held that the $100 fee charged interstate trucking companies by Michigan was not preempted by the SSRS. Congress did not specifically prohibit such a system and indicated that the SSRS may well be only a temporary system. The SSRS covers only those areas of registration including proof of insurance and the name of an agent for process. The SSRS did not address regulations such as this on specific items and conduct of truck deliveries. The court held that additional regulation did not return us to the so-called "bingo card system" of licensing and registration. [**Mid-Con Freight Systems, Inc., et al. *v* Michigan Public Service Commission, 545 US 440 (2005)**]

---

[2] U.S. Const., Art VI, cl 2. *Michigan Canners and Freezers' Ass'n, Inc. v Agricultural Marketing and Bargaining Board,* 467 US 461 (1984).

state law can regulate the areas not regulated by Congress or whether the partial regulation made by Congress preempts, or takes over, the field so as to preclude state legislation.

(b) Sɪʟᴇɴᴄᴇ ᴏꜰ Cᴏɴɢʀᴇss   In some situations, the silence of Congress in failing to cover a particular subject area indicates that Congress does not want any law on the matter. However, when national uniformity is essential, the silence of Congress generally means that the subject has been preempted for practical reasons by Congress and that no state law on the subject may be adopted.

(c) Eꜰꜰᴇᴄᴛ ᴏꜰ Fᴇᴅᴇʀᴀʟ Dᴇʀᴇɢᴜʟᴀᴛɪᴏɴ   The fact that the federal government removes the regulations from a regulated industry does not automatically give the states the power to regulate that industry. If under the silence-of-Congress doctrine the states cannot regulate, they are still barred from regulating after deregulation. **For Example,** deregulation cannot be considered authorization for state regulation.[3]

 ## INTERPRETING AND AMENDING THE CONSTITUTION

The Constitution as it is interpreted today has changed greatly from the Constitution as originally written. The change has been brought about by interpretation, amendment, and practice.

6. CONFLICTING THEORIES

Shortly after the Constitution was adopted, conflict arose over whether it was to be interpreted strictly, so as to give the federal government the least power possible, or broadly, so as to give the federal government the greatest power that the words would permit. These two views may be called the *bedrock view* and the *living-document view*, respectively.

bedrock view a strict constructionist interpretation of a constitution.

living-document view the term used when a constitution is interpreted according to changes in conditions.

In the **bedrock view,** or strict constuctionist or originalist view, the purpose of a constitution is to state certain fundamental principles for all time. In the **living-document view,** a constitution is merely a statement of goals and objectives and is intended to grow and change with time.

Whether the Constitution is to be liberally interpreted under the living-document view or narrowly interpreted under the bedrock view has a direct effect on the Constitution. For the last century, the Supreme Court has followed the living-document view. This view has resulted in strengthening the power of the federal government, permitting the rise of administrative agencies, and expanding the protection of human rights.

One view is not selected to the exclusion of the other. As contradictory as these two views sound, the Constitution remains durable. We do not want a set of New Year's resolutions that will soon be forgotten. At the same time, we know that the world changes, and therefore, we do not want a constitution that will hold us tied in a straitjacket of the past.

In terms of social forces that make the law, we are torn between our desire for stability and our desire for flexibility. We want a constitution that is stable. At the same time, we want one that is flexible.

---

[3] *New York v Trans World Airlines,* 556 NYS2d 803 (1990).

FIGURE 4-2 *Amending the U.S. Constitution*

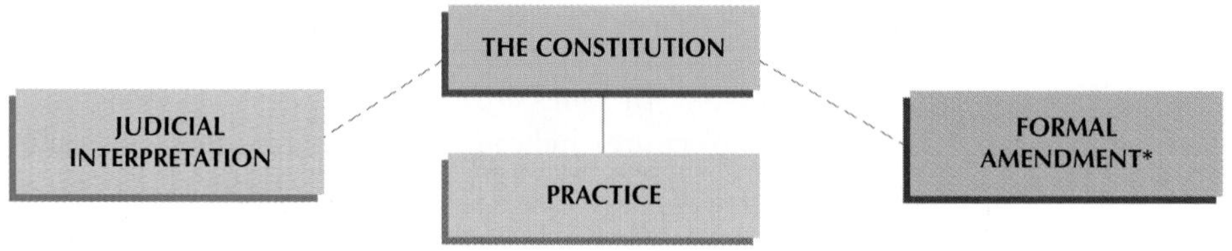

* Article V of the U.S. Constitution specifies the procedure for adopting amendments.

7. AMENDING THE CONSTITUTION

The U.S. Constitution has been amended in three ways: (1) expressly, (2) by interpretation, and (3) by practice. Figure 4-2 illustrates these three methods of amendment.

(a) CONSTITUTIONAL METHOD OF AMENDING Article V of the Constitution gives the procedure to be followed for amending the Constitution. Relatively few changes have been made to the Constitution by this formal process, although thousands of proposals have been made. Since the time of its adoption, there have been only 27 amendments to the Constitution.

(b) AMENDMENT BY JUDICIAL INTERPRETATION The U.S. Supreme Court has made the greatest changes to the written Constitution by interpreting it. Generally, interpretation is used to apply the Constitution to a new situation that could not have been foreseen when the written Constitution was adopted.

(c) AMENDMENT BY PRACTICE In practice, the letter of the Constitution is not always followed. Departure from the written Constitution began as early as 1793 when George Washington refused to make treaties as required by the Constitution, by and with the consent of the Senate. Washington began the practice of the president's negotiating a treaty with a foreign country and then submitting it to the Senate for approval. This practice has been followed since that time. Similarly, the electoral college was originally intended to exercise independent judgment in selecting the president, but it now automatically elects the official candidate of the party that elected the majority of the members of the electoral college.

8. THE LIVING CONSTITUTION

The Constitution that has developed in the manner described in the preceding section is radically different from the Constitution that was written on paper. The living Constitution has the following characteristics.

(a) STRONG GOVERNMENT One of the characteristics of the new Constitution is strong government. Business enterprises can now be regulated and the economy controlled.

(b) STRONG PRESIDENT Instead of being merely an officer who carries out the laws, the president has become the political leader of a party, exerting a strong influence on the lawmaking process. If the president's political party is in control of both houses of Congress, the president acts as the leader of the lawmaking process.

(c) ECLIPSE OF THE STATES   Under constitutional interpretations, all levels of government have powers that they never possessed before, but the center of gravity has shifted from the states to the nation. When the Constitution was adopted in 1789, the federal government was to have only the very limited powers specified in Article I, Section 8, of the Constitution. Whatever regulation of business was permissible was to be imposed by the states. Today, the great bulk of the regulation of business is adopted by the federal government through Congress or its administrative agencies. As the U.S. economy moved from the local community stage to the nationwide stage, the individual states were unable to provide effective regulation of business. It was inevitable that regulation would migrate to the central government.

(d) ADMINISTRATIVE AGENCIES   These units of government were virtually unheard of in 1789, and the Constitution made no mention of them. The vast powers of the new Constitution are exercised to a very large degree by administrative agencies. They are in effect a fourth branch of the government, not provided for in the written Constitution. More importantly, the administrative agencies are the ones that come in contact with the majority of businesspersons and citizens. The agencies are the government for most people.

In other words, the legislatures, the courts, or the executive officers do not directly exercise the vast power of government to regulate business. Rather, agencies exercise this power. The members and heads of the agencies, boards, or commissions are not elected by the voters (see Chapter 6). They are appointed by the president and, at certain levels of appointment in the agency, must be approved by Congress.

 ## D   FEDERAL POWERS

The federal government possesses powers necessary to administer matters of national concern.

9. THE POWER TO REGULATE COMMERCE

The desire to protect commerce from restrictions and barriers set up by the individual states was a prime factor leading to the adoption of the Constitution of 1789. To protect commerce, Congress was given Article I, Section 8, Clause 3—now known as the **commerce clause**—the power "[t]o regulate commerce with foreign nations, and among the several states, and with the Indian tribes."[4]

> **commerce clause** that section of the U.S. Constitution allocating business regulation.

Until 1937, the Supreme Court held that this provision gave Congress the power to control or regulate only that commerce crossing a state line, such as an interstate railway train or an interstate telegraph message.

(a) THE COMMERCE POWER BECOMES A GENERAL WELFARE POWER   In 1937, the Supreme Court began expanding the concept of interstate commerce. By 1946, the power to regulate interstate commerce had become very broad. By that year, the power had expanded to the point that it gave authority to Congress to adopt regulatory laws that were "as broad as the economic needs of the nation."[5] By virtue of this broad interpretation, Congress can regulate manufacturing, agriculture, mining, stock exchanges, insurance, loan sharking, monopolies, and conspiracies in restraint of

---

[4] For more details on the actual language in the U.S. Constitution, go to **http://www.constitution.org** and click on "Founding Documents" or refer to Appendix 2.

[5] *American Power & Light Co. v Securities and Exchange Commission*, 329 US 90 (1946).

trade. The far reach of the interstate commerce power is seen in the Freedom of Access to Clinic Entrances Act,[6] which prohibits obstruction of entrances to clinics.[7]

The case that was the beginning point in the transition of the commerce clause was *NLRB v Jones & Laughlin Steel,* 301 US 1 (1937). The "affectation" doctrine expanded the authority of the federal government under the commerce clause. At that time, the Court concluded, "If it is interstate commerce that feels the pinch, it does not matter how local the squeeze."

(b) THE COMMERCE CLAUSE TODAY   Today, judicial review of the commerce clause typically finds some connection between the legislation and congressional authority. However, in the past five years, the U.S. Supreme Court has found some areas Congress may not regulate and has placed some limitations on the commerce clause. These constraints on the commerce clause focus on the nature of the underlying activity being regulated. So long as the federal regulation relates to economic/commercial activity, it is constitutional. If, however, the underlying activity is not economic and has only an economic impact, the Supreme Court has imposed restrictions on congressional authority under the commerce clause.

(c) THE COMMERCE POWER AS A LIMITATION ON STATES   The federal power to regulate commerce not only gives Congress the power to act but also prevents states from acting in any way that interferes with federal regulation or burdens interstate commerce. **For Example,** if the federal government establishes safety device regulations for interstate carriers, a state cannot require different devices.

States may not use their tax power for the purpose of discriminating against interstate commerce, because such commerce is within the protection of the national government. **For Example,** a state cannot impose a higher tax on goods imported from another state than it imposes on the same kind of goods produced in its own territory.

CASE SUMMARY

The Commerce Clause Meets Violence

FACTS: Christy Brzonkala filed a suit under the federal Violence Against Women Act (VAWA) after she was raped by two of her fellow students at the Virginia Polytechnic Institute. The VAWA gives women who are the victims of violence a civil rights action against their assailants. The district court dismissed the suit because it found Congress lacked authority under the commerce clause for the VAWA. The court of appeals reversed. Because a lower court invalidated a federal statute, the Supreme Court granted *certiorari.*

DECISION: Congress does not have authority under the commerce clause for the VAWA. The Court held that neither the activity regulated by the VAWA nor the settings in which violence against women occur constitute interstate commerce. The VAWA did not regulate either the channels or instrumentalities of interstate commerce and must therefore rely on aggregating activities to show a substantial effect on interstate commerce. Because the commerce clause requires the aggregating of economic activities for substantial effect cases, the VAWA's underlying conduct of violence was insufficient to survive constitutional scrutiny. [**United States v Morrison, 529 US 598 (2000)**]

---

[6] 18 USC § 248.

[7] The act is constitutional. *United States v Wilson,* 73 F3d 675 (7th Cir 1995), *cert denied,* 519 US 806 (1996).

CASE SUMMARY

School, Guns, and Commerce: The Three Collide

FACTS: Alfonso Lopez, Jr., a 12th-grade student at Edison High School in San Antonio, Texas, arrived at school on March 10, 1992, carrying a concealed .38-caliber handgun and five bullets. School officials, acting on an anonymous tip, confronted Lopez. Lopez admitted that he had the gun. He was arrested and charged with a violation of the Texas Penal Code that prohibits possession of a firearm on school premises.

The following day the state charges were dropped after federal officials charged Lopez with violation of federal law, the Gun-Free School Zones Act of 1990. A federal grand jury indicted Lopez for knowing possession of a firearm in a school zone. Lopez moved to dismiss his indictment on the grounds that the provision of the Gun-Free School Zones Act with which he was charged is unconstitutional and beyond the power of Congress to legislate controls over public schools. The district court found the statute to be a constitutional exercise of congressional authority.

After Lopez waived a jury trial, there was a trial to the bench. Lopez was found guilty and sentenced to six months' imprisonment and two years' supervised release. Lopez appealed and challenged his conviction on the basis of the commerce clause and the lack of congressional authority to regulate public schools. The Fifth Circuit Court of Appeals agreed with Lopez, found the Gun-Free School Zones Act an unconstitutional exercise of congressional authority, and reversed the conviction. The U.S. Attorney appealed.

DECISION: Congress can regulate three areas under the commerce clause: (1) the channels of interstate commerce; (2) the instrumentalities of interstate commerce; and (3) activities having a substantial effect on interstate commerce. Although education and schools' sheer purchasing power have an impact on interstate commerce, the conduct attempted to be regulated here was a student activity and the possession of a weapon at school, a noneconomic activity. That school violence is costly still does not change the nature of the local conduct of a teen bringing a gun to school or an activity that is noneconomic. Congress did not have authority under the commerce clause for the Gun-Free School Zones Act. [**United States v Lopez, 514 US 549 (1995)**]

State regulations designed to advance local interests may conflict with the commerce clause. Such regulations are invalid. A state cannot refuse to allow an interstate waste collector to conduct business within the state on the ground that the state already has enough waste collectors.

10. THE FINANCIAL POWERS

The financial powers of the federal government include the powers to tax and to borrow, spend, and coin money.

(a) THE TAXING POWER   The federal Constitution provides that "Congress shall have power [t]o lay and collect taxes, duties, imposts and excises, to pay the debts and provide for the common defence and general welfare of the United States."[8] Subject to the express and implied limitations arising from the Constitution, the states may impose such taxes as they desire and as their own individual constitutions and statutes permit. In addition to express constitutional limitations, both national and

---

[8] U.S. Const., Art 1, § 8, cl 1. To read more of the U.S. Constitution, refer to Appendix 2 or go to **http://www.constitution.org** and click on "Founding Documents."

CASE SUMMARY

Whining about Wine

FACTS: Michigan and New York regulate the sale and importation of alcoholic beverages, including wine, through a three-tier distribution system. Separate licenses are required for producers, wholesalers, and retailers. Both New York and Michigan prohibit out-of-state wine producers from selling their wines directly to consumers there. In-state wineries can sell directly to consumers. The impact of the prohibition on the out-of-state wine producers is that they are required to pay wholesaler fees and thus cannot compete with in-state wine producers on direct-to-consumer sales. The direct-to-consumer sales avenue has been a means for small wineries to compete. Also, technological improvements, in particular the ability of wineries to sell wine over the Internet, have helped make direct shipments an attractive sales channel.

The wine producers challenging the New York and Michigan statutes are small wineries that rely on direct consumer sales as an important part of their businesses. Domaine Alfred, a winery located in San Luis Obispo, California, has received requests for its wine from Michigan consumers but cannot fill the orders because of the state's direct-shipment ban. Even if the winery could find a Michigan wholesaler to distribute its wine, the wholesaler's markup would render shipment economically infeasible.

Juanita Swedenburg and David Lucas operate small wineries in Virginia and California. Some of their customers are tourists from other states, who purchase wine while visiting the wineries. Swedenburg and Lucas are unable to fill orders from New York, the nation's second-largest wine market, because of the statutory restrictions.

The district court granted summary judgment for the state of Michigan. The Sixth Circuit Court of Appeals reversed on the grounds that the out-of-state restrictions violated the commerce clause. The state of Michigan appealed. In the New York case, the district court found that the out-of-state restrictions violated the commerce clause, and the Second Circuit Court of Appeals reversed and upheld the New York statute as constitutional. The out-of-state wine producers appealed.

DECISION: State laws violate the commerce clause if they treat in-state and out-of-state economic interests differently with the result that one benefits and the other is burdened. The mere fact that a wine producer is not a resident of the state should not foreclose access to markets there. The Michigan statutes prohibiting out-of-state wineries from shipping wine directly to in-state consumers, but permitting in-state wineries to do so if licensed, discriminated against interstate commerce. New York statutes imposing additional burdens on out-of-state wineries seeking to ship wine directly to New York consumers discriminated against interstate commerce. The effect of both statutes was to favor in-state wine producers and create the economic Balkanization that the commerce clause was intended to prevent. Both statutes violated the commerce clause. [**Granholm v Heald**, 544 U.S. 460 (2005)]

local taxes are subject to the unwritten limitation that they be imposed for a public purpose. Taxes must also be apportioned. A business cannot be taxed for all of its revenues in all 50 states. There must be apportionment of taxes, and there must be sufficient connection with the state.

(b) THE SPENDING POWER   The federal government may use tax money and borrowed money "to pay the debts and provide for the common defence and general welfare of the United States."[9]

---

[9] U.S. Const., Art 1, § 8, cl 1. See **http://www.constitution.org** or Appendix 2.

THINKING THINGS THROUGH

The $100 Michigan trucking fee noted earlier in the *American Trucking Association* case had an additional constitutional issue that was litigated at the same time as the question on preemption. This fee applied only to vehicles that engage in **intrastate** commercial operations—that is, on trucks that undertake point-to-point hauls between Michigan cities. The American Truckers Association (ATA) and others challenged the fee as an undue burden on interstate commerce. The trial court found for the state of Michigan, the court of appeals affirmed, and the Michigan Supreme Court refused to hear an appeal. The ATA and others appealed to the U.S. Supreme Court. What do you think the U.S. Supreme Court did with this commerce clause issue? Is the Michigan fee an unconstitutional burden on interstate commerce? [AMERICAN TRUCKING ASSOCIATION, INC. AND USF HOLLAND, INC. V MICHIGAN PUBLIC SERVICE COMMISSION 545 US 249 (2005)]

CASE SUMMARY

A Quill in Your State Means Taxes in the Coffer

FACTS: Quill is a Delaware corporation with offices and warehouses in Illinois, California, and Georgia. None of its employees works or lives in North Dakota, and Quill owns no property in North Dakota.

Quill sells office equipment and supplies; it solicits business through catalogs and flyers, advertisements in national periodicals, and telephone calls. Its annual national sales exceed $200 million, of which almost $1 million are made to about 3,000 customers in North Dakota. The sixth largest vendor of office supplies in the state, it delivers all of its merchandise to its North Dakota customers by mail or common carriers from out-of-state locations.

North Dakota requires every "retailer maintaining a place of business in" the state to collect the tax from the consumer and remit it to the state. In 1987, North Dakota amended its statutory definition of the term "retailer" to include "every person who engages in regular or systematic solicitation of a consumer market in th[e] state." State regulations in turn define "regular or systematic solicitation" to mean three or more advertisements within a 12-month period.

Quill has taken the position that North Dakota does not have the power to compel it to collect a use tax from its North Dakota customers. Consequently, the state, through its tax commissioner, filed this action to require Quill to pay taxes (as well as interest and penalties) on all such sales made after July 1, 1987. The trial court ruled in Quill's favor.

The North Dakota Supreme Court reversed, and Quill appealed.

DECISION: The issue is one of whether the taxation of a company with no contacts or property within the state other than catalogs sent to residents of the state is constitutional or a violation of the due process clause of the Fourteenth Amendment. The Court held that the issue is one of whether the company has intentionally placed itself within a state. Whether it does so with offices and salespeople or deluges the citizens with catalogs is irrelevant. So long as the company has voluntarily placed itself within the state, the taxation is neither unfair nor unconstitutional. [**Quill v North Dakota, 504 US 298 (1992)**]

E-COMMERCE AND CYBERLAW

Internet and Interstate

Collection of sales tax from Internet stores has been a stickler of an issue for businesses, state revenue officials, and the U.S. Supreme Court. All three were grappling with how to collect, what to collect, and whether anybody had any authority to collect. Internet sales represent a large, untapped source of revenue. A study from the Center for Business and Economic Research at the University of Tennessee estimates the lost tax revenue from untaxed Internet sales as $21 billion by 2008.

The merchants involved fell into several different legal groups in terms of their theories on whether tax was owed and if they paid it:

1. Those stores with physical presences in states (Wal-Mart and J.C. Penney) that just collected sales tax as if they were collecting it in a store in that state where the Internet purchaser was located.
2. Those stores without a physical presence (Amazon) that did collect taxes, particularly in those states known for taking a hard-line approach.
3. Those stores without a physical presence that do not collect taxes and maintain that it is unconstitutional to do so. Indeed, the U.S. Supreme Court held in 1992 that any tax rate with so many permutations that it becomes difficult for the retailer to administer is an undue burden on interstate commerce.
4. Those stores with or without a physical presence that have collected taxes but held them until everyone could figure out the legal status of the companies.

Wal-Mart, Target, and Office Depot settled an Internet sales tax case with Illinois for $2.4 million in sales taxes for 2003.

However, representatives from 18 states have formed the Architects of the Streamlined Sales Tax Project with the goal of finding a uniform and simple means for taxing Internet sales. The states involved in the initiative are:

- Indiana
- Iowa
- Kansas
- Kentucky
- Michigan
- Minnesota
- Nebraska
- New Jersey
- North Carolina
- North Dakota
- Oklahoma
- South Dakota
- West Virginia

Arkansas, Ohio, Tennessee, Utah, and Wyoming are in the process of obtaining the state approval necessary to join. Some states are reluctant to join because this group proposes giving the sales tax revenue to the state and local body where the purchaser is, not where the sale originates. Some of the states, such as Nevada, would lose a substantial amount

E-COMMERCE AND CYBERLAW

continued

of revenue if sales tax did not apply at the point of origin of the sale (e.g., the warehouse; Nevada, for example, is loaded with warehouses because of its no-inventory-tax policy).

As of October 1, 2006, eighteen states implemented a computer program that determines the average tax for the state and its localities and adds that on to the Internet purchase. The officials in the states are offering amnesty to merchants who sign up for the program. That is, if they owe taxes for past transactions, they are not liable if they go with the new program. Internet merchants have one year to sign up for the new rates and the amnesty. In addition to this incentive, Internet retailers who use the program are also immune from penalties for mistakes and miscalculations.

What are the constitutional issues in this taxation question?

Robery Guy Matthews, "Some States Push to Collect Sales Tax from Internet Stores," *Wall Street Journal*, Sept. 30, 2005, B1–B4.

(c) THE BANKING POWER   The federal Constitution is liberally interpreted to authorize the U.S. government to create banks and to regulate banks created under state laws. The Federal Reserve System is responsible for this regulatory oversight of banks.

 CONSTITUTIONAL LIMITATIONS ON GOVERNMENT

The constitutional limitations discussed in the following sections afford protections of rights for both persons and businesses.

11. DUE PROCESS

The power of government is limited by both the Fifth and Fourteenth Amendments to the Constitution. Those amendments respectively prohibit the national government and state governments from depriving any person "of life, liberty, or property without due process of law."[10]

(a) WHEN DUE PROCESS RIGHTS ARISE   As a result of liberal interpretation of the Constitution, the **due process clause** now provides a guarantee of protection against the loss of property or rights without the chance to be heard. These amendments also guarantee that all citizens are given the same protections. **For Example,** the Supreme Court has extended the due process clause to protect the record or standing of a student.[11] A student cannot lose credit in a course or be suspended or expelled without some form of a hearing.

Due process of law does not bar the regulation of business because any regulation that would have sufficient support to pass a legislature or Congress would have sufficient claim to validity to be debatable. The fact that many would deem a law unsound, unwise, hazardous, or un-American does not in itself make the law invalid

due process clause in the Fifth and Fourteenth Amendments, a guarantee of protection from unreasonable procedures and unreasonable laws.

---

[10] For more information on the language of the Fifth and Fourteenth Amendments, see the U.S. Constitution in Appendix 2 or go to **http://www.constitution.org**.

[11] That is, a student cannot be expelled without a chance to have his or her side of the story reviewed.

under the due process clause. There is, however, a remedy through legislative change, not individual accommodation. The laws apply to all equally, and the chance to be heard is during the legislative process.

Because the due process concept is a limitation on governmental action, it does not apply to transactions between private persons or to private employment or other nonpublic situations. In some cases, however, statutes, such as the federal Civil Rights Act and those addressing consumer protection, apply due process concepts to private transactions.

quasi-judicial proceedings forms of hearings in which the rules of evidence and procedure are more relaxed but each side still has a chance to be heard.

Speeding up due process has required the use of **quasi-judicial proceedings.** In these types of proceedings, the parties need not go through the complex, lengthy, and formal procedures of a trial (described in Chapter 2). Rather, these proceedings have a hearing officer or administrative law judge (see Chapter 6) who conducts an informal hearing in which the rules of evidence and procedure are relaxed.

For Example, a student taking a grade grievance beyond a faculty member's decision will generally have his case heard by a panel of faculty and students as established by college or university rules. An employer appealing its unemployment tax rate will have the appeal heard by an administrative law judge.

(b) What Constitutes Due Process?   Due process does not require a trial on every issue of rights. Shortcut procedures, such as grade grievance panels, have resulted as a compromise for providing the right to be heard along with a legitimate desire to be expeditious in resolving these issues.

12. EQUAL PROTECTION OF THE LAW

The Constitution prohibits the states and the national government from denying any person the equal protection of the law.[12] This guarantee prohibits a government from treating one person differently from another when there is no reasonable ground for classifying them differently.

(a) Reasonable Classification   Whether a classification is reasonable depends on whether the nature of the classification bears a reasonable relation to the wrong to be remedied or to the object to be attained by the law. In determining the constitutionality of classifications, the courts have been guided generally by historical treatment and logic. The judicial trend is to permit the classification to stand as long as there is a rational basis for the distinction made.[13] Whether a rational basis exists is determined by answering whether the lawmaking body has been arbitrary or capricious.

The equal protection clause provides broad protections and is the basis of many of the U.S. Supreme Court's most complicated decisions. **For Example,** during the 2000 presidential election, the U.S. Supreme Court faced an issue of equal protection with regard to the challenge then-vice president and presidential candidate Al Gore made to the undervotes in Florida's ballots. However, then-presidential candidate George W. Bush argued that counting the undervotes in some counties and not in others and applying different standards for counting or not counting the infamous dimpled chads, hanging chads, and other undervotes was unconstitutional because

---

[12] U.S. Constitution, Fourteenth Amendment as to the states; modern interpretation of due process clause of the Fifth Amendment as to national government. Congress adopted the Civil Rights Act to implement the concept of equal protection.

[13] *Urton v Hudson*, 101 Or App 147, 790 P2d 12 (1990).

it deprived other Florida voters of equal protection because each vote is intended to count equally and the recounts occuring in only some counties and using varying standards resulted in those counties being given greater weight in Florida's presidential election. The U.S. Supreme Court agreed in a 7–2 decision that the recounts were unconstitutional on equal protection grounds.[14] However, the ultimate decision in the case was based on a 5–4 vote because the justices could not agree on a remedy for the unconstitutional recounts.

(b) IMPROPER CLASSIFICATION   Laws that make distinctions in the regulation of business, the right to work, and the right to use or enjoy property on the basis of race, national origin, or religion are invalid. Also invalid are laws that impose restrictions on some, but not all, persons without any justification for the distinction.[15] A state statute taxing out-of-state insurance companies at a higher rate than in-state insurance companies violates the equal protection clause.[16]

13. PRIVILEGES AND IMMUNITIES

The federal Constitution declares that "[t]he citizens of each state shall be entitled to all privileges and immunities of citizens in the several states."[17] The so-called **privileges and immunities clause** means that a person going into another state is entitled to make contracts, own property, and engage in business to the same extent as the citizens of that state. **For Example,** a state cannot bar someone who comes from another state from engaging in local business or from obtaining a hunting or fishing license merely because the person is not a resident of that state. Likewise, a law that requires an attorney to be a resident of the state in order to practice is unconstitutional as a violation of this provision.[18]

privileges and immunities clause a clause that entitles a person going into another state to make contracts, own property, and engage in business to the same extent as citizens of that state.

14. PROTECTION OF THE PERSON

The Constitution does not contain any express provision protecting "persons" from governmental action. Persons are expressly protected by the Constitution with respect to particular matters, such as freedom of speech, ownership of property, right to a jury trial, and so on. There is, however, no general provision declaring that the government shall not impair rights of persons. The Constitution does not mention the phrase "unalienable right" that was part of the Declaration of Independence.[19]

The Bill of Rights, the first 10 amendments to the Constitution, do provide protections for freedom of speech, jury trials, and freedom of religion and association. It is within the Bill of Rights that the protections against unlawful searches and seizures as well as due process are found.

---

[14] *Bush v Gore*, 531 US 98 (2000).

[15] *Associated Industries of Missouri v Lohman*, 511 US 641 (1994).

[16] *Metropolitan Life Ins. Co. v Ward*, 470 US 869 (1985).

[17] U.S. Const., Art IV, § 2, cl 1. See **http://www.constitution.org** and click on "Founding Documents" to access more language of the Constitution, or see Appendix 2.

[18] *Barnard v Thorstenn*, 489 US 546 (1989).

[19] The term *unalienable right* is employed in reference to natural right, fundamental right, or basic right. Apart from the question of scope of coverage, the adjective *unalienable* emphasizes the fact that the people still possess the right rather than having surrendered or subordinated it to the will of society. The word *alien* is the term of the old common law for transferring title or ownership. Today, we would say *transfer* and, instead of saying unalienable rights, would say *nontransferable* rights. Unalienable rights of the people were therefore rights that the people not only possessed but also could not give up even if they wanted to. Thus, these rights are still owned by everyone. It is important to note that the Declaration of Independence actually uses the word "unalienable" when describing the rights eventually placed in the Constitution as Amendments I–X, the Bill of Rights, not "inalienable."

In addition, during the last six decades, the Supreme Court has been interpreting the rights in these amendments and has been finding constitutional protection for a wide array of rights of the person that are not expressly protected by the Constitution. Examples are the right of privacy, the right to marry the person one chooses,[20] protection from unreasonable zoning, protection of parental control, protection from discrimination because of poverty, and protection from gender discrimination.[21]

15. THE BILL OF RIGHTS AND BUSINESSES AS PERSONS

The first 10 amendments to the U.S. Constitution (the Bill of Rights) provide protections for both individuals and corporations. **For Example,** the Fourth Amendment (see Chapter 8) provides protections against unreasonable searches. Individuals enjoy that protection in their homes, and corporations enjoy that protection with their files, offices, and business records.

CASE SUMMARY

Banks Are People Too: First Amendment Political Speech

FACTS: Massachusetts had passed a statute that prohibited businesses and banks from making contributions or expenditures for the purpose of influencing or affecting the vote on any question submitted to the voters other than one materially affecting any of the property, business, or assets of the corporation. The statute also provided that no question submitted to the voters solely concerning the taxation of the income, property, or transactions of individuals would be deemed materially to affect the property, business, or assets of the corporation. The statute carried a fine of up to $50,000 for the corporation and $10,000 and/or one-year imprisonment for corporate officers.

First National Bank and other banks and corporations (appellants) wanted to spend money to publicize their views on an upcoming ballot proposition that would give the legislature the right to impose a graduated tax on individual income. Frances X. Bellotti, the attorney general for Massachusetts (appellee), told First National and the others that he intended to enforce the statute against them. First National and the others brought suit to have the statute declared unconstitutional, and First National appealed.

DECISION: The worth of speech is not determined by the source. The First Amendment provides protection to all forms of speech. Further, neither the Court nor the Constitution is in a position to restrict the speech of corporations on the grounds that the speech is not about business. That corporate advertising on ballot issues may be influential is not grounds for restricting the ability to advertise on political issues and social concerns. Further, the regulation was selective in that it would limit corporate participation on ballot initiatives but place no controls on lobbying for legislation. The purpose of the regulation was not compelling nor sufficiently narrowly drawn to justify its constitutionality. [**First National Bank of Boston v Bellotti, 435 US 765 (1978)**]

---

[20] *Akron v Akron Center for Reproductive Health, Inc.,* 462 US 416 (1983); but see *Colorado v Hill,* cert granted, 527 US 1068 (2000). For more on commercial speech and expression, see *Greater New Orleans Broadcasting Association, Inc., v U.S.* 527 US 173 (1999).

[21] In some cases, the courts have given the due process and equal protection clauses a liberal interpretation in order to find a protection of the person, thereby making up for the fact that there is no express constitutional guarantee of protection of the person. *Davis v Passman* 442 US 228 (1979) (due process); *Orr v Orr,* 440 US 268 (1979) (equal protection).

THINKING THINGS THROUGH

Sweating It Out on Free Speech

A third form of commercial speech has emerged through *Nike v Kasky*. In 1996, Nike was inundated with allegations about its labor practices in shoe factories around the world. Nike responded to the negative reports and allegations with a series of releases, advertisements, and op-ed pieces in newspapers around the country. In addition, Nike commissioned a report from a former Atlanta mayor and U.S. ambassador, Andrew Young, on the condition of its factories around the world. Young issued a report in 1997 that reflected favorably on Nike and its labor practices.

New York Times columnist Bob Herbert wrote two columns that were sharply critical of Nike's conditions in plants throughout Asia. The columns compared CEO Philip Knight's compensation with the $2.20 per day wages of Nike workers in Indonesia.

After the columns appeared, CEO Knight wrote a letter to the editor in response to them. In that letter, he wrote, "Nike has paid, on average, double the minimum wage as defined in countries where its products are produced under contract. History shows that the best way out of poverty for such countries is through exports of light manufactured goods that provide the base for more skilled production."[*]

Marc Kasky filed suit against Nike in California, alleging that the op-ed pieces and letters in response to negative op-ed pieces about Nike violated the False Advertising Act of California. The act permits state agencies to take action to fine corporate violators of the act as well as to obtain remedies such as injunctions to halt the ads.

Nike challenged the suit on the grounds that such an interpretation and application of the advertising regulation violated its rights of free speech. The lower court agreed with Kasky and held that the advertising statute applied to Nike's defense of its labor practices, even on the op-ed pages of newspapers. The California Supreme Court, 45 P.3d 243 (Cal. 2002), ruled that Nike could be subject to regulatory sanctions for false advertising. Nike appealed to the U.S. Supreme Court.

The Supreme Court did not reach the heart of the case—the commercial speech and First Amendment issues. Rather, the Court held that the case was not ripe for resolution because no action had been taken against Nike and because there had been no factual determinations with regard to the content of Nike's responses. There was, according to the Court, no final judgment in the case, and so it was not ripe for decision. The case was, therefore, remanded.

There is no substantive ruling from the case on commercial speech, but the Court's decision still constitutes precedent for appellate cases. An appellate court does not decide an issue in a case until the lower courts have made their factual determinations and a final decision. However, following the U.S. Supreme Court remand, Nike settled the case so that another similar case will be required before we have a definitive resolution to the questions surrounding this third form of commercial speech.

Read the Nike v Kasky opinion at **http://www.supremecourtus.gov/opinions/02pdf/02-575.pdf.** The opinion, however, is only one sentence: "The writ of certiorari is dismissed as improvidently granted." 539 US 654 (2003).

---

[*] Roger Parloff "Can We Talk?" *Fortune*, September 2, 2002, 102–110.

Businesses also enjoy freedom of speech protections under the First Amendment. The First Amendment provides that "Congress shall make no law . . . abridging the freedom of speech . . ."[22]

The U.S. Supreme Court has clarified the free speech rights of business through classification of the types of business speech. One form of business or commercial speech is advertising. This form of speech in which businesses tout their products is subject to regulation and restriction on form, content, and placement, and such regulation has been deemed constitutional. (See Chapter 25 and 33 for more information on the regulation of advertising.) However, there are other forms of commercial speech. Businesses do have the right to participate in political processes such as creating political action committees and supporting or opposing ballot initiatives. Businesses often take positions and launch campaigns on ballot initiatives that will affect the taxes they will be required to pay.

LAWFLIX

The Candidate (1972) (PG)

The movie depicts an idealist running for office who finds himself caught in the political process of fundraising, image-building, and winning. A number of scenes with speeches, fundraising, and principles in conflict provide excellent discussion issues with respect to government structure, the First Amendment, and campaign contributions.

For movie clips that illustrate business law concepts, see LawFlix at **http://wdvl.westbuslaw.com.**

---

[22] To read the full language of the First Amendment, go to Appendix 2 or **http://www.constitution.org** and click on "Founding Documents."

 SUMMARY

The U.S. Constitution created the structure of our national government and gave it certain powers. It also placed limitations on those powers. It created a federal system with a tripartite division of government and a bicameral national legislature.

The national government possesses some governmental powers exclusively, while both the states and the federal government share other powers. In areas of conflict, federal law is supreme.

The U.S. Constitution is not a detailed document. It takes its meaning from the way it is interpreted. In recent years, liberal interpretation has expanded the powers of the federal government. Among the powers of the federal government that directly affect business are the power to regulate commerce; the power to tax and to borrow, spend, and coin money; and the power

to own and operate businesses. Among the limitations on government that are most important to business are the requirement of due process and the requirement of equal protection of the law.

The due process requirement stipulates that no person shall be deprived of life, liberty, or property without due process of law. This requirement applies to both the federal government and the state governments but does not apply to private transactions.

The equal protection concept of the U.S. Constitution prohibits both the federal government and the state governments from treating one person differently from another unless there is a legitimate reason for doing so and unless the basis of classification is reasonable.

QUESTIONS AND CASE PROBLEMS

1. J.C. Penney, a retail merchandiser, has its principal place of business in Plano, Texas. It operates retail stores in all 50 states, including 10 stores in Massachusetts, and a direct mail catalog business. In connection with its catalog business, each year Penney issued three major seasonal catalogs, as well as various small sale or specialty catalogs, that described and illustrated merchandise available for purchase by mail order. The planning, artwork, design, and layout for these catalogs were completed and paid for outside of Massachusetts, primarily in Texas, and Penney contracted with independent printing companies located outside Massachusetts to produce the catalogs. The three major catalogs were generally printed in Indiana, while the specialty catalogs were printed in South Carolina and Wisconsin. Penney supplied the printers with paper, shipping wrappers, and address labels for the catalogs; the printers supplied the ink, binding materials, and labor. None of these materials was purchased in Massachusetts. Printed catalogs, with address labels and postage affixed, were transported by a common carrier from the printer to a U.S. Postal Service office located outside Massachusetts, where they were sent to Massachusetts addressees via third- or fourth-class mail. Any undeliverable catalogs were returned to Penney's distribution center in Connecticut.

   The catalogs advertised a broader range of merchandise than was available for purchase in Penney's retail stores. The purpose for mailing these catalogs, free of charge, to residents of, among other places, Massachusetts, was to solicit mail-order purchases from current and potential customers. Purchases of catalog merchandise were made by telephoning or returning an order form to Penney at a location outside Massachusetts, and the merchandise was shipped to customers from a Connecticut distribution center. The Massachusetts Department of Revenue audited Penney's in 1995 and assessed a use tax, penalty, and interest on the catalogs that had been shipped into Massachusetts. The use tax is imposed in those circumstances "in which tangible personal property is sold inside or outside the Commonwealth for storage, use, or other consumption within the Commonwealth."

   The position of the department was that there was a tax due of $314,674.62 on the catalogs that were used by Penney's Massachusetts customers. Penney said such a tax was unconstitutional in that it had no control or contact with the catalogs in the state. Can the state impose the tax? [*Commissioner of Revenue v J.C. Penney Co., Inc.,* 730 NE2d 266 (Mass)]

2. Wolens and others are participants in American Airlines' frequent flyer program, AAdvantage. AAdvantage members earn mileage credits when they fly on American. The members can exchange those credits for flight tickets or class-of-service upgrades. Wolens complained that AAdvantage program modifications, instituted by American in 1988, devalued credits that AAdvantage members had already earned. The examples Wolens gave were American's imposition of capacity controls (limiting the number of seats per flight available to AAdvantage members) and blackout dates (restrictions on dates AAdvantage members could use their credits). Wolens brought suit alleging that these changes and cutbacks violated the Illinois Consumer Fraud and Deceptive Business Practices Act. American Airlines challenged the suit on the grounds that the regulation of airlines was preempted by the Airline Deregulation Act (ADA) of 1978, which deregulated domestic air transportation but also included the following clause on preemption: "[N]o State . . . shall enact or enforce any law, rule, regulation, standard, or other provision having the force and effect of law relating to rates, routes, or services of any air carrier . . ." [49 USC App § 1305(a)] The Illinois Supreme Court found that the rules on the frequent flyer program were only tangentially related to rates, routes, and services and required American Airlines to defend the suit. American Airlines appealed. Is American Airlines correct? Is state regulation preempted here? [*American Airlines, Inc. v Wolens,* 513 US 219]

3. The state of Arizona passed a regulation that required that cantaloupes grown within the state be packed in in-state facilities before shipment. California companies with Arizona farms were thus required to build packing facilities in Arizona in order to ship their harvest. Is the

Arizona law constitutional? [*Pike v Bruce Church, Inc.,* 397 US 137]

4. The University of Wisconsin requires all of its students to pay, as part of their tuition, a student activity fee. Those fees are used to support campus clubs and activities. Some students who objected to the philosophies and activities of some of the student clubs filed suit to have the fees halted. What constitutional basis do you think they could use for the suit? [*Board of Regents of Wisconsin System v Southworth,* 529 US 217]

5. The Crafts' home was supplied with gas by the city gas company. Because of some misunderstanding, the gas company believed that the Crafts were delinquent in paying their gas bill. The gas company had an informal complaint procedure for discussing such matters, but the Crafts had never been informed that such a procedure was available. The gas company notified the Crafts that they were delinquent and that the company was shutting off the gas. The Crafts brought an action to enjoin the gas company from doing so on the theory that a termination without any hearing was a denial of due process. The lower courts held that the interest of the Crafts in receiving gas was not a property interest protected by the due process clause and that the procedures the gas company followed satisfied the requirements of due process. The Crafts appealed. Were they correct in contending that they had been denied due process of law]? Why or why not? [*Memphis Light, Gas and Water Division v Craft,* 436 US 1]

6. Alexis Geier was injured in an accident while driving a 1987 Honda Accord that did not have passive safety restraints. When her Honda Accord was manufactured, the U.S. Department of Transportation required passive safety restraints on some, but not all, vehicles. Geier and her parents filed suit against Honda for its negligence in not equipping the Honda Accord with a driver's side airbag. Geier alleged that because Honda knew of the safety standard but did not voluntarily comply with it (it was not required to do so under the federal regulations), it was negligent under state negligence standards for liability and should be held liable. The district court granted Honda summary judgment based on Honda's argument that safety requirements for cars were set exclusively by the federal government. The court of appeals affirmed, and Geier appealed. What would be the effect of a decision that requires a car company to comply with state-by-state standards of negligence? Would a state court finding of negligence be a constitutional exercise of state power? Should the U.S. Supreme Court affirm or reverse the summary judgment for Honda? [*Geier v American Honda Motor Co.,* 529 US 1913]

7. Montana imposed a severance tax on every ton of coal mined within the state. The tax varied depending on the value of the coal and the cost of production. It could be as high as 30 percent of the price at which the coal was sold. Montana mine operators and some out-of-state customers claimed that this tax was unconstitutional as an improper burden on interstate commerce. Decide. [*Commonwealth Edison Co. v Montana,* 453 US 609]

8. Ollie's Barbecue is a family-owned restaurant in Birmingham, Alabama, specializing in barbecued meats and homemade pies, with a seating capacity of 220 customers. It is located on a state highway 11 blocks from an interstate highway and a somewhat greater distance from railroad and bus stations. The restaurant caters to a family and white-collar trade, with a take-out service for "Negroes." (Note: This term is used by the Court in its opinion in the case.) In the 12 months preceding the passage of the Civil Rights Act, the restaurant purchased locally approximately $150,000 worth of food, $69,683 or 46 percent of which was meat that it bought from a local supplier who had procured it from outside the state. Ollie's has refused to serve Negroes in its dining accommodations since opening in 1927, and since July 2, 1964, it has been operating in violation of the Civil Rights Act. A lower court concluded that if it were required to serve Negroes, it would lose a substantial amount of business. The lower court found that the Civil Rights Act did not apply because Ollie's was not involved in "interstate commerce." Will the commerce clause permit application of the Civil Rights Act to Ollie's? [*Katzenbach v McClung,* 379 US 294]

9. Heald was the executor of the estate of a deceased person who had lived in Washington, D.C. Heald

refused to pay federal tax owed by the estate on the ground that the tax had been imposed by an act of Congress, and because residents of the District of Columbia had no vote in Congress, the tax law was adopted without their representation. Not only did District residents have no voice in the adoption of the tax laws, but also the proceeds from taxes collected in the District were paid into the general treasury of the United States and were not maintained as a separate District of Columbia fund. Heald objected that the tax law was void as contrary to the Constitution because it amounted to taxation without representation. Evaluate Heald's argument. [*Heald v District of Columbia,* 259 US 114]

10. Ellis was employed by the city of Lakewood. By the terms of his contract, he could be discharged only for cause. After working for six years, he was told that he was going to be discharged because of his inability to generate safety and self-insurance programs, because of his failure to win the confidence of employees, and because of his poor attendance. He was not informed of the facts in support of these conclusions and was given the option to resign. He claimed that he was entitled to a hearing. Is he entitled to one? Why or why not? [*Ellis v City of Lakewood,* 789 P2d 449 (Colo App)]

11. The Federal Food Stamp Act provided for the distribution of food stamps to needy households. In 1971, section 3(e) of the statute was amended to define households as limited to groups whose members were all related to each other. This was done because of congressional dislike for the lifestyles of unrelated hippies who were living together in hippie communes. Moreno and others applied for food stamps but were refused them because the relationship requirement was not satisfied. An action was brought to have the relationship requirement declared unconstitutional. Is it constitutional? Discuss why or why not. [*USDA v Moreno,* 413 US 528]

12. New Hampshire adopted a tax law that in effect taxed the income of nonresidents working in New Hampshire only. Austin, a nonresident who worked in New Hampshire, claimed that the tax law was invalid. Was he correct? Explain. [*Austin v New Hampshire,* 420 US 656]

13. Arkansas is primarily a rural state, and in many areas there, it is not feasible to employ cable

television. Arkansas imposes a tax on sales and services, and cable television service was added to the list of taxed enterprises. No tax, however, was imposed on satellite television service. The cable companies claimed there was a denial of equal protection by taxing them but not satellite transmission of television. Are they correct? Why or why not? [*Medlock v Leathers,* 842 SW2d 428 (Ark)]

14. Following a boom in cruise ship construction, the ships are now looking for ports at which they can dock in order to begin voyages, most of which begin in the United States. With so many new ships, the companies are trying to establish connections with cities that are not ordinarily considered cruise ship docks. The companies pursue these alternatives because the traditional docking cities of New York, Seattle, Miami, Los Angeles, and Houston have become crowded with cruise ship traffic. The following issues have arisen:

- Some ports are just not large enough for the larger cruise ships.
- Without proper scheduling and departures, cruise ships often end up waiting in the harbor for three to eight hours; as a result, ports such as Tampa, a nontraditional cruise ship port, are experiencing traffic jams of ships waiting to dock.
- The presence of the large boats and the resulting number of tourists cause overwhelming flooding of the often-quaint alternative ports such as Charleston, South Carolina. Charleston residents worry that tourists from the cruise ships flooding their city will result in irreversible destruction of the town's preserved landmarks and quaint looks.
- Rising water levels in ports such as New Orleans mean that the tall ships cannot clear power lines and have to be redirected to ports nearby that are not prepared, as when New Orleans had to redirect a 2,974-passenger cruise ship to Gulfport, Mississippi.
- The ships do bring passengers with tourist dollars to spend and additional work for harbor pilots and service industries.
- The port facilities are not adequate to handle all of the boats, the passengers, and even the ships' fueling needs.

Most cruise ship lines are incorporated outside of the United States, and they do not pay federal income taxes and are certainly not subject to state income taxes even though the bulk of their passengers comes from the United States.[23]

Can the ships be taxed to cover the harbor expenses? Can they be required by states and cities to pay docking fees, or are they internationally exempt companies?

15. A federal statute prohibited granting federal funds to libraries that did not control access to pornographic Internet sites on library computers so that children did not gain access and were not exposed to such sites as they used the public facilities. The American Library Association challenged the prohibition as a violation of First Amendment rights.

Are free speech rights violated with the funding regulation? [**www.supremecourtus.gov/ opinions/02pdf/02-361.pdf**, slip op. l; *U.S. v American Library Association,* 539 US 194; lower court decision at 201 F Supp 2d 401]

---

[23] Nicole Harris "Big Cruise Ships Cause Traffic Jams in Ports," *Wall Street Journal,* August 20, 2003, B1–B6.

GOVERNMENT REGULATION
OF COMPETITION AND PRICES

LEARNING OBJECTIVES

After studying this chapter, you should be able to

LO.1 State the extent to which government can regulate business

LO.2 Explain what laws protect free enterprise from unfair competition and from unfair restraints

LO.3 Define *price discrimination* and explain when it is prohibited

LO.4 Discuss the Sherman Antitrust Act, what it prohibits, and when it applies

The government can regulate not just businesses but also business competition and prices. Antitrust legislation and a regulatory scheme help to ensure that businesses compete fairly.

 ## POWER TO REGULATE BUSINESS

The federal government may regulate any phase of business that is necessary to advance the nation's economic needs.[1] Under the police power, states may regulate all aspects of business so long as they do not impose an unreasonable burden on interstate commerce or any activity of the federal government. (See Chapter 4 for a discussion of the protections and limits of the commerce clause.) Local governments may also exercise this power to the extent each state permits.

1. REGULATION, FREE ENTERPRISE, AND DEREGULATION

Milton Friedman, the Nobel economist, has written that government regulation of business interferes with the free enterprise system. Under a true free enterprise system, there would not be any regulation of airline safety, safety of food and drugs for human consumption, prices, and so on, for the free market would put those protections in place through demand. Sometimes, however, the demand response, or market reaction, to problems or services is not rapid enough to prevent harm, and government regulation steps in to stop abuses. For example, the FTC stepped in to curb the tactics and practices of telemarketers when the number of consumer complaints increased dramatically without any industry self-regulation.

There has been some deregulation in certain industries. For many years, for example, the banking and savings industry was heavily regulated, but beginning in 1978, various acts were adopted to deregulate this industry.[2] The deregulation did not proceed as well as anticipated, and the 1980s witnessed the collapse of major financial institutions attributed to lax oversight. As a result, Congress adopted bank-regulating laws and reforms toward the end of the 1980s. The broadest regulation was the Financial Institutions Reform, Recovery, and Enforcement Act of 1989 (FIRREA),[3] which regulates savings and loan associations and similar organizations to ensure their financial stability.

More recently, the collapse of companies such as Enron, WorldCom, Health-South, Adelphia, and others revealed that more oversight was necessary with regard to audit practice by CPAs as well as financial reporting by publicly traded companies. As a result, Congress passed extensive and detailed legislation regulating both accountants and financial reporting with the Sarbanes-Oxley Act and the mandated Securities and Exchange (SEC) regulations that implement its provisions. (See Chapters 8 and 47 for more details on Sarbanes-Oxley.)

2. REGULATION OF PRODUCTION, DISTRIBUTION, AND FINANCING

To protect the public from harm, government may prohibit false advertising and labeling, and establish health and purity standards for cosmetics, foods, and drugs. Licenses may be required to be able to deal in certain goods, and these licenses may be

---

[1] *American Power & Light Co. v SEC,* 329 US 90 (1946).

[2] See, for example, the Depository Institutions Deregulation and Monetary Control Act of 1980, 12 USC § 1735. *Sweeney v Savings First Mortgage, LLC,* 878 A2d 1037 (CA Md 2006).

[3] Act of October 9, 1989, PL 101-73, 103 Stat 183, codified at various sections of titles 12 and 15 of USC.

revoked for improper conduct or violations of statutes and regulations.[4] The government may also regulate markets themselves: the quantity of a product that may be produced or grown and the price at which the finished product may be sold. For example, agricultural products markets and commodities have significant government constraints. Government may also engage in competition with private enterprises or own and operate an industry. **For Example,** the U.S. Postal Service competes directly with UPS and FedEx for the delivery of packages as well as for overnight delivery services.

The financing of business is directly affected by the national government, which creates a national currency and maintains the Federal Reserve banking system. State and other national laws may also affect financing by regulating financing contracts and documents, such as bills of lading and commercial paper.

3. REGULATION OF UNFAIR COMPETITION

Each of the states and the federal government have statutes and regulations that prohibit unfair methods of competition. Unfair competition is controlled by both statutes and administrative agencies and regulations.

Congress has enacted the Federal Trade Commission Act,[5] which made all "unfair methods of competition . . . and unfair or deceptive acts or practices"[6] unlawful and created the Federal Trade Commission (FTC) to administer the act. The FTC has taken enforcement steps against refusals to sell, boycotts, market restrictions, disparagment of competitors' products, and unlawful methods of billing and collection. The FTC regulates false and misleading advertising and controls even the statements on packaged foods to ensure that the nutritional content of the food described on the label is accurate **For Example,** Beech-Nut Baby Food Company paid significant fines in the late 1980s for representing its baby apple juice to actually contain apple juice. The product was made from a very good-tasting chemical concoction, but it had no apple juice. Such misrepresentation on the label was a violation of Section 5 of the Federal Trade Commission Act that prohibits unfair methods of competition. Business missteps, from false advertising to boycotts, constitute unfair methods of competition prohibited under the FTC Act.[7]

 REGULATION OF MARKETS AND COMPETITION

4. REGULATION OF PRICES

Governments, both national and state, may regulate prices. Price regulation may be delegated to an administrative officer or agency. Prices in various forms are regulated, including not only what a buyer pays for goods purchased from a store (through controls on price fixing—see discussion that follows) but also through limits on interest rates and rent controls.

(a) PROHIBITION ON PRICE FIXING   Agreements among competitors, as well as "every contract, combination . . . or conspiracy," to fix prices violate Section 1 of the

---

[4] *Ganter v Dept. of Insurance,* 620 So 2d 202 (CA Fla 1993).

[5] 15 USC § 41 *et seq.*

[6] To review the Federal Trade Commission Act, go to **http://www.ftc.gov**.

[7] In many states, such a seller would also be guilty of committing a deceptive trade practice or violating a consumer protection statute.

Sherman Act.[8] Known as *horizontal price-fixing,* any agreements to charge an agreed-upon price or to set maximum or minimum prices between or among competitors are *per se*—in, through, or by themselves—a violation of the Sherman Act. An agreement among real estate brokers to never charge below a 6 percent commission is price-fixing.[9] **For Example,** in 2001, Christie's and Sotheby's auction houses settled an antitrust lawsuit for charging the same commissions for many years.[10]

Clayton Act a federal law that prohibits price discrimination.

Robinson-Patman Act a federal statute designed to eliminate price discrimination in interstate commerce.

price discrimination the charging practice by a seller of different prices to different buyers for commodities of similar grade and quality, resulting in reduced competition or a tendency to create a monopoly.

(b) PROHIBITED PRICE DISCRIMINATION   The **Clayton Act** and the **Robinson-Patman Act** prohibit price discrimination.[11] **Price discrimination** occurs when a seller charges different prices to different buyers for "commodities of like grade and quality," with the result being reduced competition or a tendency to create a monopoly.[12]

Price discrimination prohibits charging different prices to buyers as related to marginal costs. That is, volume discounts are permissible because the marginal costs are different on the larger volume of goods. However, the Robinson-Patman Act makes it illegal to charge different prices to buyers when the marginal costs of the seller for those goods are the same. Any added incentives or bonuses are also considered part of price.

For Example, offering one buyer free advertising while not offering it to another as an incentive to buy would be a violation of the Robinson-Patman Act. The Clayton Act makes both the giving and the receiving of any illegal price discrimination a crime.

State statutes frequently prohibit favoring one competitor by giving a secret discount when the effect is to harm the competition.[13] A state may prohibit either selling below cost to harm competitors or selling to one customer at a secret price that is lower than the price charged other customers when there is no economic justification for the lower price. Some state statutes specifically permit sellers to set prices so that they can match competitive prices, but not to undercut a competitor's prices.[14] The issue of state antitrust regulation and wide variations in state laws and decisions prompted the creation of the Antitrust Modernization Commission, a group likely to recommend changes in laws and judicial review standards at both the state and federal levels.[15]

(c) PERMITTED PRICE DISCRIMINATION   Price discrimination is expressly permitted when it can be justified on the basis of (1) a difference in grade, quality, or quantity; (2) the cost of transportation involved in performing the contract; (3) a good-faith effort to meet competition; (4) differences in methods or quantities; (5) deterioration of goods; or (6) a close-out sale of a particular line of goods. The Robinson-Patman Act[16] reaffirms the right of a seller to select customers and refuse to deal with anyone. The refusal, however, must be in good faith, not for the purpose of restraining trade.

---

[8] To view the full language of Section 1 of the Sherman Act, see 15 USC § 1.

[9] *McClain v Real Estate Board of New Orleans, Inc.,* 441 US 942 (1980).

[10] Carol Vogel and Ralph Blumenthall, "Ex-Chairman of Sotheby's Gets a Year and a Day for Price-Fixing," *New York Times,* April 12, 2002, A26.

[11] 15 USC §§ 1, 2, 3, 7, 8.

[12] 15 USC § 13a. To read the full Clayton Act, go to **http://www.usdoj.gov** or **http://www.justice.gov** and plug in "Clayton Act" in a site search.

[13] *Eddins v Redstone,* 35 Cal Rptr 3d 863 (2006).

[14] *Home Oil Company, Inc. v Sams East, Inc.* 252 F Supp 1302 (MD Ala 2003).

[15] 21st Century Department of Justice Appropriations Authorization Act, Pub. L. No. 107-273, 116 Stat. 1758 (2002), available at **http://amc.gov/pdf/statute/amc_act.pdf.**

[16] 15 USC §§ 13, 21.

CASE SUMMARY

Getting a Piece of the Pie Market

FACTS: Utah Pie Company is a Utah corporation that for 30 years has been baking pies in its plant in Salt Lake City and selling them in Utah and surrounding states. It entered the frozen pie business in 1957 and was immediately successful with its new line of frozen dessert pies— apple, cherry, boysenberry, peach, pumpkin, and mince.

Continental Baking Company, Pet Milk, and Carnation, all based in California, entered the pie market in Utah. When these companies entered the Utah market, a price war began. In 1958 Utah Pie was selling pies for $4.15 per dozen. By 1961, as all the pie companies competed, it was selling the same pies for $2.75 per dozen. Continental's price went from $5.00 per dozen in 1958 to $2.85 in 1961. Pet's prices went from $4.92 per dozen to $3.46, and Carnation's from $4.82 per dozen to $3.30.

Utah Pie filed suit charging price discrimination. The district court found for Utah Pie. The court of appeals reversed, and Utah Pie appealed.

DECISION: There was price discrimination. Pet was selling its pies in Utah through Safeway at prices that were lower than its prices in other markets and also much lower than its own brand pie in the Salt Lake City market. Pet also introduced a 20-ounce economy pie under the Swiss Miss label and began selling the new pie in the Salt Lake market in August 1960 at prices ranging from $3.25 to $3.30 for the remainder of the period. This pie was at times sold at a lower price in the Salt Lake City market than it was sold in other markets. For 7 of the 44 months in question for price discrimination, Pet's prices in Salt Lake were lower than prices charged in the California markets. This was true even though selling in Salt Lake involved a 30- to 35-cent freight cost.

Also, Pet had predatory intent to injure Utah Pie. Pet admitted that it sent into Utah Pie's plant an industrial spy to seek information. Pet suffered substantial losses on its frozen pie sales during the greater part of time involved in this suit. Pet had engaged in predatory tactics in waging competitive warfare in the Salt Lake City market. Coupled with the price discrimination, Pet's behavior lessened competition and violated Robinson-Patman. [**Utah Pie Co. v Continental Baking Co., 386 US 685 (1967)**]

5. PREVENTION OF MONOPOLIES AND COMBINATIONS

Monopolies and combinations that restrain trade are prohibited under the federal antitrust laws.

Sherman Antitrust Act a federal statute prohibiting combinations and contracts in restraint of interstate trade, now generally inapplicable to labor union activity.

(a) THE SHERMAN ACT   The **Sherman Antitrust Act** includes two very short sections that control anticompetitive behavior. They provide:

[§ 1] Every contract, combination in the form of trust or otherwise, or conspiracy, in restraint of trade or commerce among the several states, or with foreign nations, is declared to be illegal.

[§ 2] Every person who shall monopolize or attempt to monopolize, or combine or conspire with any other person or persons to monopolize any part of the trade or commerce among the several states, or with foreign nations, shall be deemed guilty of a felony.[17]

---

[17] 15 USC § 1. Read the full Sherman Antitrust Act at **http://www.usdoj.gov** or **http://www.justice.gov**. Plug in "Sherman Act" in a site search and you will be directed to all of the federal antitrust statutes. Free competition has been advanced by the Omnibus Trade and Competitiveness Act of 1988, 19 USC § 2901 *et seq.*

The Sherman Act applies not only to buying and selling activities but also to manufacturing and production activities. Section 1 of the Sherman Act applies to agreements, conduct, or conspiracies to restrain trade, which can consist of price-fixing, tying, and monopolization. Section 2 prohibits monopolizing or attempting to monopolize by companies or individuals.

market power the ability to control price and exclude competitors.

(b) MONOPOLIZATION   To determine whether a firm has engaged in monopolization or attempts to monopolize, the courts determine whether the firm has **market power,** which is the ability to control price and exclude competitors. Market power is defined by looking at both the geographic and product markets. **For Example,** a cereal manufacturer may have 65 percent of the nationwide market for its Crispy Clowns cereal (the product market), but it may have only 10 percent of the Albany, New York, market because of a local competitor, Crunchy Characters. Crispy Clowns may have market power nationally, but in Albany, it would not reach monopoly levels.

Having a large percentage of a market is not necessarily a monopoly. The Sherman Act requires that the monopoly position be gained because of a superior product or consumer preference, not because the company has engaged in purposeful conduct to exclude competitors by other means, such as preventing a competitor from purchasing a factory.

CASE SUMMARY

Performing an Illegal Operation

FACTS: Microsoft Corporation, a company based in the state of Washington and doing business in all 50 states and around the world, is the leading supplier of operating systems for personal computers (PCs). Although Microsoft licenses its software programs directly to consumers, the largest part of its sales consists of licensing the products to manufacturers of personal computers.

Microsoft was concerned about its strategic position with respect to the Internet, a global electronic network consisting of smaller interconnected networks, that allows millions of computers to exchange information over telephone wires, dedicated data cables, and wireless links.

The U.S. Justice Department had an ongoing inquiry into the market shares and practices of Microsoft. The concerns of the Justice Department included these:

1. Microsoft's position in the market as a monopolist (90 percent market share for operating systems).
2. Microsoft's barriers to entry for other operating systems and Web browsers. Microsoft has refused to sell its software operating system to computer companies that installed Microsoft's competitive browser, Netscape, which was gaining popularity as Microsoft's Explorer struggled.
3. Microsoft's efforts to inhibit the efforts of Netscape with its browser by first trying to acquire Netscape and then working to "cut off [its] air supply" by retarding Sun Corporation's development and implementation of the Java program. When Microsoft altered the portions of Sun's Java program that allowed it to work without Windows, Sun notified Microsoft that such was a violation of its licensing agreement. Microsoft's response was, "Sue us." Sun sued Microsoft one week before the Justice Department brought its suit against Microsoft. Sun's suit then ran parallel with the Justice Department's.

CASE SUMMARY

continued

In issuing a three-part opinion, Judge Thomas Penfield Jackson of the district court found that Microsoft had violated the antitrust laws and ordered the remedy to break up the company. Microsoft appealed the decision.

DECISION: The court found that Microsoft had monopoly power with its 95 percent market share. The court defined the market to be the PC market, not, as Microsoft had proposed, a much broader-scope market that included non-PC devices. It also found that the company's position and control of the market presented substantial barriers to entry for potential competitors.

The court also held that Microsoft had gained and retained its market position through anticompetitive behavior such as prohibiting original equipment manufacturers (OEMs, or the producers of the computer hardware) from removing any folders or icons from the Windows "Start" menu, altering the boot sequence, or changing the appearance of the Windows system. Those OEMs that did not comply risked losing Microsoft programs, and it was not practical to install two operating systems.

The court also found anticompetitive behavior in that Microsoft offered its Windows Explorer, an Internet Access Provider (IAP), to exile the competitive IAP, Navigator.

Finally, the court found that Microsoft had worked deals with software vendors for programs that worked only with Windows as the underlying operating system.

The conclusion of the court was that Microsoft's market dominance was not due to a superior product but was the result of anticompetitive behavior. It did, however, remand the case for a new determination of remedies, having determined that Judge Jackson had indicated some bias against Microsoft and had refused to allow evidence from the company in the remedies stage. [**United States v Microsoft, 253 F3d 34 (CA DC 2001)**]

THINKING THINGS THROUGH

Microsoft Settles Up

A federal district court* approved the Justice Department's settlement of the Microsoft antitrust litigation following the decision by the appellate court that had found a violation of the Sherman Act. The terms of the settlement are as follows:

- Microsoft can add any type of capabilities to its Windows operating system.
- Microsoft cannot impose restrictions on PC manufacturers that limit their ability to install non-Microsoft software on their computers.

- Microsoft cannot retaliate against PC manufacturers for installing non-Microsoft software on their computers.
- Microsoft must offer the same sale terms for Windows to all PC manufacturers, and those terms and conditions must be posted on a Web site for easy access.
- Microsoft must provide the information software rivals need in order to have their programs work successfully with Windows.

---

* "Ruling Stings but Doesn't Really Hurt Microsoft," *New York Times*, November 2, 2002, B5.

THINKING THINGS THROUGH

continued

- Microsoft cannot punish or retaliate against software manufacturers that develop competing software.
- Microsoft will appoint an internal compliance officer.
- All Microsoft officers and the board must sign off that they have read the provisions of the settlement.

- These conditions are in effect for five years.

Explain how these requirements help eliminate the antitrust violations discussed in the case and how each will work to restore competition.

(C) PRICE-FIXING The Sherman Act prohibits, as discussed previously, competitors agreeing to set prices. Price-fixing can involve competitors: agreeing to not sell below a certain price, agreeing on commission rates, agreeing on credit terms, or exchanging cost information. Price is treated as a sensitive element of competition, and discussion among competitors has also been deemed to be an attempt to monopolize.

CASE SUMMARY

Fill It Up: The Price Is Right and Fixed

FACTS: Barkat U. Khan and his corporation entered into an agreement with State Oil to lease and operate a gas station and convenience store owned by State Oil. The agreement provided that Khan would obtain the gasoline supply for the station from State Oil at a price equal to a suggested retail price set by State Oil, less a margin of $3.25 per gallon. Khan could charge any price he wanted, but if he charged more than State Oil's suggested retail price, the excess went to State Oil. Khan could sell the gasoline for less than State Oil's suggested retail price, but the difference would come out of his allowed margin.

After a year, Khan fell behind on his lease payments, and State Oil gave notice of, and began, eviction proceedings. The court had Khan removed and appointed a receiver to operate the station. The receiver did so without the price constraints and received an overall profit margin above the $3.25 imposed on Khan.

Khan filed suit, alleging that the State Oil agreement was a violation of Section 1 of the Sherman Act because State Oil was controlling price. The district court held that there was no *per se* violation and that Khan had failed to demonstrate antitrust injury. The court of appeals reversed, and State Oil appealed.

DECISION: In what was a reversal of prior decisions, the Court held that vertical maximum prices (as in this case in which a retailer was prohibited from charging above a certain amount) are not a *per se* violation of the Sherman Act. The Court noted that benefits can come from retailers' not being able to charge above a certain amount. At a minimum, such controls on maximum prices were not an automatic violation of the Sherman Act and need to be examined in light of what happens to competition. In determining whether such prices might affect competition, the Court noted that maximum prices might have an impact on the survival of inefficient dealers, as was the case here. However, encouraging inefficiency is not the purpose of either the market or the laws on anticompetitive behavior. [**State Oil v Khan, 522 US 3 (1997)**]

E-COMMERCE AND CYBERLAW

E-mail's Revelations

E-mail is redefining the way cases are tried. In the U.S. Justice Department's case against Microsoft, a lawyer commented, "The Government does not need to put Mr. Gates on the stand because we have his e-mail and memoranda."

The lawyer's comment reflects the tendency of e-mail to speak for itself. Witnesses can shrug and assert they cannot remember, but an e-mail from them is always available for recollection purposes as well as admission as evidence. At Microsoft, e-mail supplanted the telephone as the primary means of communication, and the government was able to tap into the entire e-mail system. There were 30 million pages of e-mail used as evidence in the Microsoft trial.

E-mail provides what is known as a *contemporaneous record of events* and has the added bonus that, for whatever psychological reason, those communicating with e-mail tend to be more frank and informal than they would be in a memo. E-mail can also contradict a witness's testimony and serve to undermine credibility. For example, when asked whether he recalled discussions with a subordinate about whether Microsoft should offer to invest in Netscape, Mr. Gates responded in his deposition, "I didn't see that as something that made sense." But Mr. Gates's e-mail included an urging to his subordinates to consider a Netscape alliance: "We could even pay them money as part of the deal, buying a piece of them or something."

E-mail is discoverable, admissible as evidence, and definitely not private. Employees should follow the admonition of one executive whose e-mail was used to fuel a million-dollar settlement by his company with a former employee, "If you wouldn't want anyone to read it, don't send it in e-mail."

The impact of e-mail in the Microsoft antitrust case on companies and their e-mail policies was widespread. For example, Amazon.com launched a companywide program called "Sweep and Keep," under which employees were instructed to purge e-mail messages no longer needed for conducting business. Amazon.com offered employees who purged their e-mail immediately free lattes in the company cafeteria. The company had a two-part program. The first portion included instructions on document retention and deletion. The second part of the program was on document creation and included the following warning for employees: "Quite simply put, there are some communications that should not be expressed in written form. Sorry, no lattes this time."

The American Management Association has reported that a 5 percent increase occurred in the number of companies monitoring their employees' e-mail, from 15 percent to 20 percent, during 1998. In 2005, employees around the country reported that they are now holding back on their e-mail communications and being careful about their choice of words.

Source: Adapted from Marianne M. Jennings, *Business: Its Legal, Ethical and Global Environment*, 6th ed. (Cincinnati, OH: West Legal Studies in Business , 2003), ch. 17, 674.

ETHICS & THE LAW

Marsh McLennan

Marsh-McLennan (MMC) is best known as the world's largest insurance broker with 43,000 employees in its global operations.* In 2004, its revenues were $2 billion more than those of its closest competitor, Aon Corporation.** MMC was a market performer with revenues of $6.9 billion in 2003, up from $5.9 billion in 2002, and $5.2 billion in 2001.*** MMC had a different way of achieving growth.

As a broker of the company it represents, MMC should have been obtaining competing bids. However, MMC developed a "pay-to-play" format for obtaining bids that allowed the insurers and MMC to profit. MMC received not only its commissions but also payments from insurers in exchange for renewals, or bonuses paid to MMC when its corporate customers renewed their policies. To be sure (1) that the policies were renewed and (2) that the renewal bonus was a given, MMC had all of its insurers agree to roll over on renewals. For example, if Insurer A was up for renewal, Insurers B and C would submit fake and higher bids that MMC would then take to the corporate client and, of course, recommend renewal at the lower rate. In some cases, MMC did not even have official bids from the competing insurers. MMC sent bids forward that had not even been signed by the insurers who were playing along to receive the same treatment when their renewals came along. There was no competitive bidding and the payments inflated the prices. Once MCC implemented the "pay-to-play system," its insurance revenue became 67.1% of its revenue.[†] Commissions from these arrangements represented one-half of MMC's 2003 income of $1.5 billion.[††]

One of the companies to complain about MMC's practices was Munich RE. One of its e-mails to an MMC executive (whose name was blacked out) wrote, "I am not some Goody Two Shoes who believes that truth is absolute, but I do feel I have a pretty strict ethical code about being truthful and honest. This idea of 'throwing the quote' by quoting artificially high numbers in some predetermined arrangement for us to lose is repugnant to me, not so much because I hate to lose, but because it is basically dishonest. And I basically agree with the comments of others that it comes awfully close to collusion and price-fixing."

New York Attorney General Eliot Spitzer filed suit against MMC for antitrust violations.[‡] Without admitting or denying guilt, MMC settled the case with Mr. Spitzer by agreeing to drop the commission system and pay $850 million to its clients as a means of compensating for what might have been overcharges. MMC also agreed to hire a new CEO. The value of MMC's shares dropped almost 50 percent within 10 days following the mid-October Spitzer announcement of his suit against the company.[‡‡] About 3,000 jobs were cut in early November 2004.[‡‡‡]

---

*Monica Langley and Ianthe Jeanne Dugan, "How a Top Marsh Employee Turned the Tables on Insurers," *Wall Street Journal*, October 23, 2004, A1, A9. Some put the number of employees at 60,000. Gretchen Morgenson, "Who Loses the Most at Marsh? Its Workers," *New York Times*, October 24, 2004, 3–1 (Sunday Business 1) and 9.

**Monica Langley and Theo Francis, "Insurers Reel From Bust of a 'Cartel,'" *Wall Street Journal*, October 18, 2004, A1, A14.

***Id.

†Monica Langley and Ianthe Jeanne Dugan, "How a Top Marsh Employee Turned the Tables on Insurers," *Wall Street Journal*, October 23, 2004, A1, A9.

††Id.

‡Thor Valdmanis, "Marsh & McLennan lops off 3,000 jobs," *USA Today*, November 10, 2004, 1B.

‡‡"The Chatter," *New York Times*, November 14, 2004, BU2.

‡‡‡"The Chatter," *New York Times*, November 14, 2004, BU2.

ETHICS & THE LAW

continued

What antitrust violations are part of "cartel" behavior? MMC's new CEO fired several senior executives despite the fact that there was no evidence that they had broken the law. When asked why he would fire them, Michael G. Cherkasky, a former district attorney in New York, said, "Freedom from criminal culpability is not our standard for executive leadership."[#] Is he employing a standard of ethics for his executives? What standard is it? What do the loss-of-income figures teach us about shortcuts on making money?

[#]Ian McDonald, "After Spitzer Probe, Marsh CEO Tries Corporate Triage," *Wall Street Journal,* August 29, 2005, p. A1.

THINKING THINGS THROUGH

Antitrust Violations and Corporate Defendants

Alfred Taubman, the former chairman of Sotheby's Auction House, was sentenced to one year and one day in federal prison and fined $7.5 million for his role in a price-fixing scheme between Sotheby's and Christie's. The government case said that the scheme resulted in damages of $100 million to those who used the services of the auction houses. The sentence of one year and one day allowed Mr. Taubman to take advantage of the federal early release provisions for good behavior. Mr. Taubman was released from the medical facility federal prison two months early for good behavior and served the remainder of his sentence at a half-way house.

The two auction houses have settled class-action lawsuits brought by more than 100,000 customers for a total of $512 million. Mr. Taubman paid $156 million of Sotheby's share of the class-action suit. Sotheby's paid a $45 million fine. Mr. Taubman also paid $30 million as his portion of a stockholder suit brought against the company.

Judge George Daniels said that Mr. Taubman had "neither acknowledged responsibility nor shown any remorse" and that "[p]rice-fixing is a crime whether it's committed in the grocery story or the halls of a great auction house."[*] Diana D. Brooks, the former CEO of Sotheby's, was sentenced to six months of house arrest. She cooperated with the federal government in the prosecution of the case against her former boss. Her testimony indicated that she was simply following the directions of her boss. Of Ms. Brooks, Judge Daniels said, "You substituted shame for fame."[**]

Do you think the judge held the corporation responsible through fines? Does the imprisonment and house arrest of the chairman and CEO bring personal accountability and responsibility to the conduct of corporations?

---

[*]Carol Vogel and Ralph Blumenthall, "Ex-Chairman of Sotheby's Gets a Year and a Day for Price-Fixing," *New York Times,* April 23, 2002, A26.
[**]Id.

SPORTS & ENTERTAINMENT LAW

Celebrity Issues and Antitrust

Public Interest Corporation (PIC) owned and operated television station WTMV-TV in Lakeland, Florida. MCA Television Ltd. (MCA) owns and licenses syndicated television programs. In 1990, the two companies entered into a licensing contract for several first-run television shows. With respect to all but one of these shows, MCA exchanged the licenses on a "barter" basis for advertising time on WTMV. However, MCA conditioned this exchange on PIC's agreeing to license the remaining show, *Harry and the Hendersons,* for cash as well as for barter. *Harry and the Hendersons* was what some in the industry would call a "dog," a show that was not very good that attempted to capitalize on a hit movie. PIC agreed to this arrangement, although it did not want *Harry and the Hendersons.* The shows that PIC did want were *List of a Lifetime, List of a Lifetime II, Magnum P.I.,* and 17 other miscellaneous features.

The relationship between the parties was strained over nonpayment, poor ratings performance of *Harry,* and other issues. When litigation resulted, PIC alleged that it had been subjected to an illegal tying arrangement. PIC requested damages for MCA's violation of the Sherman Act. What violation do you think occurred?

Source: Adapted from *MCA Television Ltd. v. Public Interest Corp.,* 171 F. 3d 1265 (CA 11 1998).

---

tying the anticompetitive practice of requiring buyers to purchase one product in order to get another.

(d) TYING   It is a violation of the Sherman Act to force "tying" sales on buyers. **Tying** occurs when the seller makes a buyer who wants to purchase one product buy an additional product that he or she does not want.

The essential characteristic of a tying arrangement that violates Section 1 of the Sherman Act is the use of control over the tying product within the relevant market to compel the buyer to purchase the tied article that either is not wanted or could be purchased elsewhere on better terms. **For Example,** in the Microsoft antitrust case, Microsoft is accused of requiring the purchase and use of its browser as a condition for purchasing its software. The Sherman Act also prohibits professional persons, such as doctors, from using a peer review proceeding to pressure another professional who competes with them in private practice and refuses to become a member of a clinic formed by them.

divestiture order a court order to dispose of interests that could lead to a monopoly.

(e) BUSINESS COMBINATIONS   The Sherman Antitrust Act does not prohibit bigness. However, Section 7 of the Clayton Act provides that "no corporation . . . shall acquire the whole or any part of the assets of another corporation . . . where in any line of commerce in any section of the country, the effect of such acquisition may be substantially to lessen competition, or to tend to create a monopoly." If the Clayton Act is violated through ownership or control of competing enterprises, a court may order the violating defendant to dispose of such interests by issuing a decree called a **divestiture order.**[18]

---

[18] *California v American Stores Co.,* 492 US 1301 (1989).

(1) Premerger Notification.   When large-size enterprises plan to merge, they must give written notice to the FTC and to the head of the Antitrust Division of the Department of Justice. This advance notice gives the department the opportunity to block the merger and thus avoid the loss that would occur if the enterprises merged and were then required to separate.[19] **For Example,** Time Warner was required to notify the Justice Department and seek approval for its merger with AOL, which the Justice Department eventually gave. However, when WorldCom proposed its merger with Sprint, the Justice Department refused approval because it believed this would reduce competition in telecommunications too much.[20]

(2) Takeover Laws.   Antitrust laws usually focus on whether the combination or agreement is fair to society or to a particular class, such as consumers. Some legislation aims to protect the various parties directly involved in combining different enterprises. Concern arises that one enterprise may in effect be raiding another enterprise. Congress and four-fifths of the states have adopted **takeover laws,** which seek to guard against unfairness in such situations. State laws apply only to corporations chartered in their state.

takeover laws laws that guard against unfairness in corporate takeover situations.

POWER TO PROTECT BUSINESS

In addition to controlling business combinations, the federal government protects others. By statute or decision, associations of exporters, marine insurance associations, farmers' cooperatives, and labor unions are exempt from the Sherman Act with respect to agreements between their members. Certain pooling and revenue-dividing agreements between carriers are exempt from the antitrust law when approved by the appropriate federal agency. The Newspaper Preservation Act of 1970 grants an antitrust exemption to operating agreements entered into by newspapers to prevent financial collapse. The Soft Drink Interbrand Competition Act[21] grants the soft drink industry an exemption when it is shown that, in fact, substantial competition exists in spite of the agreements.

The general approach of the U.S. Supreme Court has been that these types of agreements should not be automatically, or *per se,* condemned as a restraint of interstate commerce merely because they create the power or potential to monopolize interstate commerce. It is only when the restraint imposed is unreasonable that the practice is unlawful. The court applies the rule of reason in certain cases because the practice may not always harm competition.

6. REMEDIES FOR ANTICOMPETITIVE BEHAVIOR

(a) Criminal Penalties   A violation of either section of the Sherman Act is punishable by fine or imprisonment or both at the discretion of the court. The maximum fine for a corporation is $10 million. A natural person can be fined a maximum of $350,000 or imprisoned for a maximum term of three years or both.

---

[19] Antitrust Improvement Act of 1976, PL 94-435, § 201, PL 94-435, 90 Stat 1383, 15 USC § 1311 *et seq.*

[20] Rebecca Blumenstein and Jared Sandberg, ''WorldCom CEO Quits Amid Probe of Firm's Finances,'' *Wall Street Journal,* April 30, 2002, A1, A9.

[21] Act of July 9, 1980, PL 96-308, 94 Stat 939, 15 USC § 3501 *et seq.*

(b) CIVIL REMEDIES In addition to these criminal penalties, the law provides for an injunction to stop the unlawful practices and permits suing the wrongdoers for damages.

(1) Individual Damage Suit. Any person or enterprise harmed may bring a separate action for **treble damages** (three times the damages actually sustained).

treble damages three times the damages actually sustained.

(2) Class-Action Damage Suit by State Attorney General. When the effect of an antitrust violation is to raise prices, the attorney general of a state may bring a class-action suit to recover damages on behalf of those who have paid the higher prices. This action is called a *parens patriae* action on the theory that the state is suing as the parent of its people.

LAWFLIX

Antitrust (2001) (R)

This movie is based on Bill Gates and Microsoft.
For movie clips that illustrate business law concepts, see LawFlix at
http://wdvl.westbuslaw.com.

> SUMMARY

Regulation by government has occurred primarily to protect one group from the improper conduct of another group. The police power is the basis for government regulation. Regulation is passed when the free enterprise system fails to control abuses as with the recent passage of SOX. Unfair methods of competition are prohibited.

Prices have been regulated both by prohibiting setting the exact price or a maximum price and discrimination in pricing. Price discrimination between buyers is prohibited when the effect of such discrimination could tend to create a monopoly or lessen competition. Price discrimination occurs when the prices charged different buyers are different despite the same marginal costs.

The Sherman Antitrust Act prohibits conspiracies in restraint of trade and the monopolization of trade. The Clayton Act prohibits mergers or the acquisition of the assets of another corporation when this conduct would tend to lessen competition or create a monopoly. The Justice Department requires premerger notification for proposed mergers. Violation of the federal antitrust statutes subjects the wrongdoer to criminal prosecution and possible civil liability that can include treble damages.

> QUESTIONS AND CASE PROBLEMS

1. American Crystal Sugar Co. was one of several refiners of beet sugar in northern California, and it distributed its product in interstate commerce. American Crystal and the other refiners had a monopoly on the seed supply and were the only practical market for the beets. In 1939, all of the refiners began using identical form contracts that computed the price paid to the sugar beet growers using a "factor" common to all the refiners. As a result, all refiners paid the same price for beets of the same quality. Though there was no hard evidence of an illegal agreement, the growers brought suit under the Sherman Act against the refiners, alleging that they conspired to fix a single uniform price among themselves to hold down the cost of the beets. The growers sued for the

treble damages available under the Sherman Act. Can they recover? [*Mandeville Island Farms v American Crystal Sugar Co.,* 334 US 219]

2. A Wisconsin statute prohibits "the secret payment or allowance of rebates, refunds, commissions, or unearned discounts" to some customers without allowing them to all customers on the same conditions when such practices injure or tend to injure competition or a competitor. Kolbe generally gave dealers a 50 percent discount, but it gave Stock Lumber Co. a discount of 54 percent. Other dealers were not informed of this or of the conditions that had to be satisfied to obtain the same discount. Kolbe gave Jauquet, another lumber dealer, only a 50 percent discount and, when asked, expressly stated that it did not give any other dealer a higher discount. When Jauquet learned of the higher discount given to Stock, it brought suit against Kolbe for violation of the Wisconsin statute. Did Kolbe violate the statute? [*Jauquet Lumber Co., Inc. v Kolbe & Kolbe Millwork, Inc.,* 476 NW2d 305 (Wis App)]

3. The major record companies settled an antitrust suit brought by 40 state attorneys general against them for alleged price-fixing in the sale of CDs. The record companies agreed to pay $67.4 million to consumers who purchased CDs during the period from 1995 to 2000. The consent decree stipulated that the record companies had required retailers that accepted subsidies from record companies for advertising CDs not to advertise CDs for sale at a price agreed upon in advance. The record companies said that the policy helped keep independent retailers in business because they could not afford to price at Wal-Mart levels. Wal-Mart always advertised CDs for sale at a price below the floor agreed to by the subsidized independent retailers and the record companies. The record companies did not admit any wrongdoing and, in addition to agreeing to the $67.4 million, also agreed to provide 5.5 million CDs to libraries, schools, and nonprofit organizations (worth $75.7 million).[22] What antitrust violation were the attorneys general alleging? Is a minimum price a violation of antitrust laws?

4. The Three Tenors (Luciano Pavarotti, Placido Domingo, and Jose Carreras) make a record of their live performances together once every four years. The first two CDs and videos in the series, made by Time Warner, sold millions, with both becoming two of the highest-volume opera recordings in history. However, by the third performance and CD and video, the public demand was not as great, and Time Warner believed the first two releases would cannibalize the sales for the third. As a result, all parties involved in the sales of these CDs and tapes had to agree not to discount the first two performance tapes so that the third would have an opportunity to sell. The Federal Trade Commission (FTC) stumbled across the information on the pricing program when its staff members located a memo on the marketing plan and advertising constraints as it was reviewing documents for the proposed Time Warner/EMI Music merger proposal, a merger that fell through after European officials balked at the idea. The FTC pursued the case, and Time Warner settled the charges by agreeing not to restrain competition or set prices in the future. Is establishing a minimum price a violation of the Sherman Act? Is restricting advertising a violation of the Sherman Act?

5. Hines Cosmetic Co. sold beauty preparations nationally to beauty shops at a standard or fixed-price schedule. Some of the shops were also supplied with a free demonstrator and free advertising materials. The shops that were not supplied with them claimed that giving the free services and materials constituted unlawful price discrimination. Hines replied that there was no price discrimination because it charged everyone the same. What it was giving free was merely a promotional campaign that was not intended to discriminate against those who were not given anything free. Was Hines guilty of unlawful price discrimination? Explain.

6. Moore ran a bakery in Santa Rosa, New Mexico. His business was wholly intrastate. Meads Fine Bread Co., his competitor, engaged in an interstate business. Meads cut the price of bread in half in Santa Rosa but made no price cut in any other place in New Mexico or in any other state. This price-cutting drove Moore out of business. Moore then sued Meads for damages for violating the

[22] Claudia Deutsch, "Suit Settled over Pricing of Recordings at Big Chains," *New York Times,* October 1, 2002, C1, C10; David Lieberman, "States Settle CD Price-fixing Case," *USA Today,* October 1, 2002, 3B.

Clayton and Robinson-Patman Acts. Meads claimed that the price-cutting was purely intrastate and, therefore, did not constitute a violation of federal statutes. Was Meads correct? Why or why not? [*Moore v Meads Fine Bread Co.,* 348 US 115]

7. A&P Grocery Stores decided to sell its own brand of canned milk (referred to as *private label* milk). A&P asked its longtime supplier, Borden, to submit an offer to produce the private label milk. Bowman Dairy also submitted a bid, which was lower than Borden's. A&P's Chicago buyer then contacted Borden and said, "I have a bid in my pocket. You people are so far out of line it is not even funny. You are not even in the ballpark." The Borden representative asked for more details but was told only that a $50,000 improvement in Borden's bid "would not be a drop in the bucket." A&P was one of Borden's largest customers in the Chicago area. Furthermore, Borden had just invested more than $5 million in a new dairy facility in Illinois. The loss of the A&P account would result in underutilization of the plant. Borden lowered its bid by more than $400,000. The Federal Trade Commission charged Borden with price discrimination, but Borden maintained it was simply meeting the competition. Did Borden violate the Robinson-Patman Act? Does it matter that the milk was a private label milk, not its normal trade name Borden milk? [*Great Atlantic & Pacific Tea Co., Inc. v FTC,* 440 US 69]

8. James Owen was the general manager of Obron Atlantic Corp., a manufacturer of powdered brass, which is finely flaked metal used in metallic paints, brakes, and explosives. Trained as a chemist, Owen earned his MBA at night school while he worked in Obron's labs during the day. In 1985, he was promoted from the lab to management. During a business trip in 1986, a fellow executive from Obron's German operations, Bruno Dachlauer, told Owen that a price increase for the company's products would be coming in the fall. Dachlauer added that details of the price increase would have to be worked out with Obron's two main competitors based in the United States. Owen reminded Dachlauer that such an agreement about price was against the law in the United States, to which Dachlauer allegedly responded, "There are laws against speeding, too." Owen complied with the fall price increases but admitted that he began "cheating" by lowering those prices to win customers. He was then threatened by competitors. Following the threats, Owen went to the Antitrust Division of the Justice Department and explained his situation. The FBI wired Owen for his meetings. One taped conversation between him and his supervisor, Carl Eckart, was used in a price-fixing case filed in Ohio. The conversation is as follows:

Owen: *Carl, can we go over this one more time?*
Eckart: *You (expletive) dummy. One more time. On fine powders, 30 cents. Coarse powders, 15 cents.*
Owen: *Are you sure Rink will go along with it?*
Eckart: *Of course.*

In the course of a year, Owen taped more than 100 conversations involving internal and external meetings for the FBI and the Justice Department. Owen's activities were not revealed until the Justice Department served Obron with a subpoena for its sales records. Officers and directors of Obron and its competitors were indicted, and some entered guilty pleas. Owen, whose marriage of 32 years ended in 1993, said that his undercover work took a tremendous toll on him and his family. He said of his conduct, "I could see people being hurt, customers being cheated. My concern shifted to protecting the customer. Maybe that's not the fiduciary role of the general manager." Was what Owen did in recording the conversations ethical? Was it honest? What do you think of Owen's view of focusing on the customers' rights? Is his duty to his company even when the conduct is illegal?

9. Dr. Edwin G. Hyde, a board-certified anesthesiologist, applied for permission to practice at East Jefferson Hospital in Louisiana. An approval was recommended for his hiring, but the hospital's board denied him employment on grounds that the hospital had a contract with Roux & Associates for Roux to provide all anesthesiological services required by the hospital's patients. Dr. Hyde filed suit for violation of antitrust laws. Had the hospital done anything illegal? [*Jefferson Parish Hosp. Dist. No. 2 v Hyde,* 466 US 2]

10. BRG of Georgia, Inc. (BRG), and Harcourt Brace Jovanovich Legal and Professional Publications (HJB) are the nation's two largest providers of bar review materials and lectures. HJB

began offering a Georgia bar review course on a limited basis in 1976 and was in direct, and often intense, competition with BRG from 1977 to 1979 when the companies were the two main providers of bar review courses in Georgia. In early 1980, they entered into an agreement that gave BRG an exclusive license to market HJB's materials in Georgia and to use its trade name "Bar/Bri." The parties agreed that HJB would not compete with BRG in Georgia and that BRG would not compete with HJB outside of Georgia. Under the agreement, HJB received $100 per student enrolled by BRG and 40 percent of all revenues over $350. Immediately after the 1980 agreement, the price of BRG's course was increased from $150 to more than $400. Is their conduct illegal under federal antitrust laws? [*Palmer v BRG of Georgia, Inc.,* 498 US 46 (1990)]

11. Favorite Foods Corp. sold its food to stores and distributors. It established a quantity discount scale that was publicly published and made available to all buyers. The top of the scale gave the highest discount to buyers purchasing more than 100 freight cars of food in a calendar year. Only two buyers, both national food chains, purchased in such quantities, and therefore, they alone received the greatest discount. Favorite Foods was prosecuted for price discrimination in violation of the Clayton Act. Was it guilty?

12. Run America, Inc., manufactures running shoes. Its shoe is consistently rated poorly by *Run Run Run* magazine in its annual shoe review. The number one shoe in *Run Run Run*'s review is the Cheetah, a shoe that Run America has learned is manufactured by the parent company of the magazine. Is this conduct a violation of the antitrust laws? Do you think it is ethical to run the shoe review without disclosing ownership?

13. The Quickie brand wheelchair is the most popular customized wheelchair on the market. Its market share is 90 percent. Other manufacturers produce special-use wheelchairs that fold, that are made of mesh and lighter frames, and that are easily transportable. These manufacturers do not compete with Quickie on customized chairs. One manufacturer of the alternative wheelchairs has stated, "Look, it's an expensive market to be in, that Quickie market. We prefer the alternative

chairs without the headaches of customizations." Another has said, "It is such a drain on cash flow in that market because insurers take so long to pay. We produce chairs that buyers purchase with their own money, not through insurers. Our sales are just like any other product." Quickie entered the market nearly 40 years ago and is known for its quality and attention to detail. Buying a Quickie custom chair, however, takes time, and the revenue stream from sales is slow but steady because of the time required to produce custom wheelchairs. Has Quickie violated the federal antitrust laws with its 90 percent market share? Discuss.

14. Gardner-Denver is the largest manufacturer of ratchet wrenches and their replacement parts in the United States. Gardner-Denver had two different lists of prices for its wrenches and parts. Its blue list had parts that, if purchased in quantities of five or more, were available for substantially less than its white list prices. Did Gardner-Denver engage in price discrimination with its two price lists? [*D. E. Rogers Assoc., Inc. v Gardner-Denver Co.,* 718 F2d 1431 (6th Cir)]

15. The Aspen ski area consisted of four mountain areas. Aspen Highlands, which owned three of those areas, and Aspen Skiing, which owned the fourth, had cooperated for years in issuing a joint, multiple-day, all-area ski ticket. After repeatedly and unsuccessfully demanding an increased share of the proceeds, Aspen Highlands canceled the joint ticket. Aspen Skiing, concerned that skiers would bypass its mountain without some joint offering, tried a variety of increasingly desperate measures to recreate the joint ticket, even to the point of in effect offering to buy Aspen Highland's tickets at retail price. Aspen Highlands refused even that. Aspen Skiing brought suit under the Sherman Act, alleging that the refusal to cooperate was a move by Aspen Highlands to eliminate all competition in the area by freezing it out of business. Is there an antitrust claim here in the refusal to cooperate? What statute and violation do you think Aspen Skiing alleged? What dangers do you see in finding the failure to cooperate to be an antitrust violation? [*Aspen Skiing Co. v Aspen Highlands Skiing Corp.,* 472 US 585 (1985)]

ADMINISTRATIVE AGENCIES

LEARNING OBJECTIVES

After studying this chapter, you should be able to

LO.1 Describe the nature and purpose of administrative agencies

LO.2 Discuss the rights of access to administrative agencies and their records and processes

LO.3 Explain the legislative or rule-making function of administrative agencies

LO.4 Discuss agencies' authority to obtain business records

LO.5 Explain when an administrative agency's decision may be reviewed and reversed by a court

LO.6 Describe the rule on exhaustion of administrative remedies

Late in the nineteenth century, a new type of governmental structure began to develop to meet the highly specialized needs of government regulation of business: the administrative agency. The administrative agency is now typically the instrument through which government makes and carries out its regulations.

 NATURE OF THE ADMINISTRATIVE AGENCY

administrative agency government body charged with administering and implementing legislation.

An **administrative agency** is a government body charged with administering and implementing legislation. An agency may be a department, independent establishment, commission, administration, authority, board, or bureau. Agencies exist on the federal and state levels. One example of a federal agency is the Federal Trade Commission (FTC), whose structure is shown in Figure 6-1.

1. PURPOSE OF ADMINISTRATIVE AGENCIES

Federal administrative agencies are created to carry out general policies specified by Congress. Federal agencies include the Securities Exchange Commission (SEC), the Consumer Product Safety Commission (CPSC), and the Food and Drug Administration (FDA). The law governing these agencies is known as **administrative law.**

administrative law law governing administrative agencies.

State administrative agencies also exist and may have jurisdiction over areas of law affecting business, such as workers' compensation claims, real estate licensing, and unemployment compensation.

2. UNIQUENESS OF ADMINISTRATIVE AGENCIES

The federal government and state governments alike are divided into three branches: executive, legislative, and judicial. Many offices in these branches are filled by persons who are elected. In contrast, members of administrative agencies are ordinarily appointed (in the case of federal agencies, by the president of the United States with the consent of the Senate).

FIGURE 6-1   *Structure of the Federal Trade Commission*

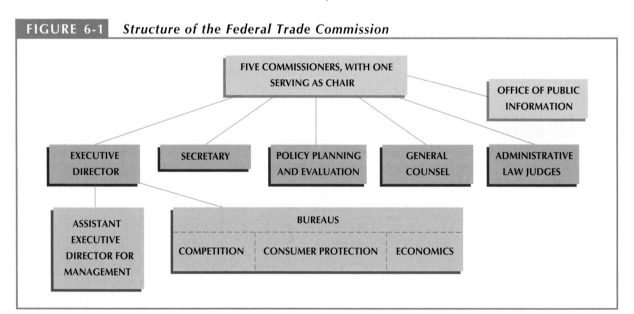

FIGURE 6-2   *The Administrative Chain of Command*

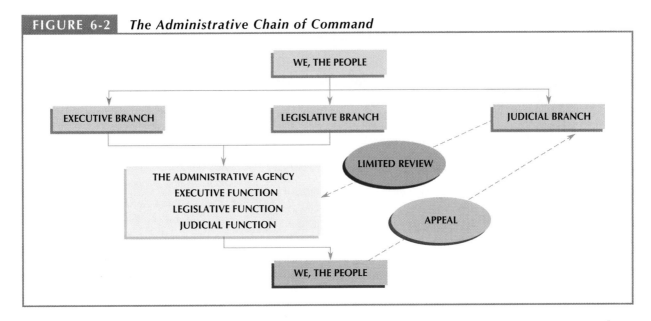

In the tripartite structure, the judicial branch reviews actions of the executive and legislative branches to ensure that they have not exceeded their constitutional powers. However, the major governmental agencies combine legislative, executive, and judicial powers (see Figure 6-2). These agencies make the rules, conduct inspections to see that the rules have been or are being obeyed, and sit in judgment to determine whether there have been violations of their rules. Because agencies have broad powers, they are subject to strict procedural rules as well as disclosure requirements (discussed in the following section).

3. OPEN OPERATION OF ADMINISTRATIVE AGENCIES

The public has ready access to the activity of administrative agencies. That access comes in three ways: (1) open records, (2) open meetings, and (3) public announcement of agency guidelines. The actions and activities of most federal agencies that are not otherwise regulated are controlled by the **Administrative Procedure Act** (APA).[1] Many states have adopted statutes with provisions similar to those of the APA.

(a) OPEN RECORDS   The **Freedom of Information Act**[2] (FOIA) provides that information contained in records of federal administrative agencies is available to citizens on proper request. The primary purpose of this statute is "to ensure that government activities be opened to the sharp eye of public scrutiny."[3] To ensure that members of the public understand how to obtain records, the FOIA provides, "Each agency shall ... publish in the *Federal Register* for the guidance of the public ... the methods whereby the public may obtain information, make submittals or requests, or obtain decisions.[4] There are exceptions to this right of public scrutiny. They prevent individuals and companies from obtaining information that

Administrative Procedure Act federal law that establishes the operating rules for administrative agencies.

Freedom of Information Act federal law permitting citizens to request documents and records from administrative agencies.

---

[1] Administrative Procedures Act 5 USC § 550 *et seq.*

[2] 5 USC § 552 *et seq.* The Electronic Freedom of Information Act Amendments of 1996 extend the public availability of information to electronically stored data.

[3] *Brady-Lunny v Massey*, 185 F Supp 2d 928 (CD Ill 2002).

[4] 5 USC § 552(a)(1)(a).

THINKING THINGS THROUGH

Allow Me to Make a Comment (Public)

The SEC began in May 2005 to publish its comments on companies' securities filings. Prior to this action, the SEC released the comments only in response to FOIA requests. The comments are very revealing, showing what the SEC accountants and staff members believe are important issues in company securities filings. For example, in a Brookstone, Inc., proxy statement filed in 2005 that included approval of a merger, the SEC issued a letter with 52 comments. One example was just a request for additional information:

19. *Please provide an organizational chart that shows how the ownership of Brookstone, Inc., will be structured after completion of the merger including the members of Brookstone management who will retain an indirect interest in Brookstone and the owners of Brookstone Holdings Corp.*

RESPONSE: Additional disclosure has been included in the Proxy Statement at page 11.

Brookstone added an organizational chart to its proxy.

Another request asked for more information on a possible delay in the meeting for the merger approval:

Adjournment or Postponement of the Annual Meeting (Proposal No. 2), page 102

52. *Please provide more details about the circumstances under which you would postpone the meeting and for how long.*

And the company offered the following response:

RESPONSE: The disclosure in the Proxy Statement has been revised in response to the Staff's comment. Please see page 109.

Not only will investors benefit from being able to read of the SEC's concerns, but also other companies will be able to make adjustments to their own decisions and reporting so that the SEC does not raise the same flags with each company. Many believe the comments will have the effect of developing a "case law" for financial reporting.

Explain how the release of these comments and the companies' responses will be helpful to businesses. Explain how they might cause some difficulties.

is not necessary to their legitimate interests and might harm the person or company whose information is being sought.[5] State statutes typically exempt from disclosure any information that would constitute an invasion of the privacy of others. However, freedom of information acts are broadly construed, and unless an exemption is clearly given, the information in question is subject to public inspection. Moreover, the person claiming that there is an exemption that prohibits disclosure has the burden of proving that the exemption applies to the particular request made. Exemptions include commercial or financial information not ordinarily made public by the person or company that supplies the information to the agency as part of the agency's enforcement role.[6]

---

[5] Additional protection is provided by the Privacy Act of 1974, 5 USC § 552a(b); *Pilon v U.S. Department of Justice,* 73 F3d 1111 (DC Cir 1996).

[6] *Sun-Sentinel Company v U.S. Dept. of Homeland Security,* 431 F Supp 2d 1258 (SD Fla 2006).

The FOIA 's primary purpose is to subject agency action to public scrutiny. Its provisions are liberally interpreted, and agencies must make good-faith efforts to comply with its terms.

open meeting law law that requires advance notice of agency meeting and public access.

(b) Open Meetings   Under the Sunshine Act of 1976,[7] called the **open meeting law,** the federal government requires most meetings of major administrative agencies to be open to the public. The Sunshine Act[8] applies to those meetings involving "deliberations" of the agency or those that "result in the joint conduct or disposition of official agency business." The object of this statute is to enable the public to know what actions agencies are taking and to prevent administrative misconduct by having open meetings and public scrutiny. Many states also have enacted sunshine laws.

(c) Public Announcement of Agency Guidelines   To inform the public of the way administrative agencies operate, the APA, with certain exceptions, requires that each federal agency publish the rules, principles, and procedures that it follows.[9]

 LEGISLATIVE POWER OF THE AGENCY

An administrative agency has the power to make laws and does so by promulgating regulations with public input.

4. AGENCY'S REGULATIONS AS LAW

An agency may adopt regulations within the scope of its authority. The power of an agency to carry out a congressional program "necessarily requires the formulation of policy and the making of rules to fill any gap left by Congress."[10] If the regulation is not authorized by the law creating the agency, anyone affected by it can challenge the regulation on the basis that the agency has exceeded its authority. [See Section 11(d), "Beyond the Jurisdiction of the Agency."]

An administrative agency cannot act beyond the scope of the authority in the statute that created it or assigned a responsibility to it.[11] However, the authority of an agency is not limited to the technology in existence at the time the agency was created or assigned jurisdiction for enforcement of laws. The sphere in which an agency may act expands with new scientific developments.[12]

When an agency's proposed regulation deals with a policy question that is not specifically addressed by statute, the agency that was created or given the discretion to administer the statute may establish new policies covering such issues. This power is granted regardless of whether the lawmaker intentionally left such matters to the agency's discretion or merely did not foresee the problem. In either case, the matter is one to be determined within the agency's discretion, and courts defer to agencies' policy decisions.[13] For example, the FCC has authority to deal with cell phones and

---

[7] The Government in the Sunshine Act can be found at 5 USC § 552b.

[8] 5 USC § 552b(a)(2).

[9] APA codified at 5 USC § 552. See Section 5(c) of this chapter for a description of the *Federal Register*, the publication in which these agency rules, principles, and procedures are printed.

[10] *Virginia v Browner*, 80 F3d 869 (4th Cir 1996).

[11] *Home Depot U.S.A. v Contractors' State License Board*, 49 Cal Rptr 302 (1996).

[12] *United States v Midwest Video Corp.*, 406 US 649 (1972) (sustaining a commission regulation that provided that "no CATV system having 3,500 or more subscribers shall carry the signal of any television broadcast station unless the system also operates to a significant extent as a local outlet by cablecasting and has available facilities for local production and presentation of programs other than automated services").

[13] *Chevron, U.S.A., Inc. v National Resources Defense Council, Inc.*, 467 US 837 (1984).

E-COMMERCE AND CYBERLAW

Complying with Regulations Online

Federal agencies have been adapting to online business. For example, the IRS offers electronic filing of income tax returns. The SEC permits electronic submission of various forms and reports due from companies. Corporations are using the Web to telecast their discussions with analysts to comply with SEC rules on uniform disclosure of all company information to all investors in the same time frame. All federal agencies are accepting e-mail comments on proposed rules as valid public comments during the public comment periods for proposed rules.

cell phone providers even though when the agency was created, there were only the traditional types of land-line telephones.

Today, regulations adopted by an agency may interpret or clarify the law. In effect, many regulations have the feel of legislation. Courts have come to recognize the authority of an agency even though the lawmaker creating the agency did nothing more than state the goal or objective to be attained by the agency. The modern approach is to regard the administrative agency as holding all powers necessary to effectively perform the duties entrusted to it. When the agency establishes a rational basis for its rule, courts accept the rule and do not substitute their own judgment.[14]

Legislatures have met the judicial standard for approval with various types of agencies created for different purposes such as licensing to protect the public, prohibiting unfair methods of competition, or administering the registration of autos and other vehicles. The purposes in these types of statutes include the typical public safety and welfare areas such as ensuring competence and integrity of professionals through the licensing process or ensuring that there are free markets that allow open competition.[15]

5. AGENCY ADOPTION OF REGULATIONS

(a) CONGRESSIONAL ENABLING ACT   Before an agency can begin rulemaking proceedings, it must be given jurisdiction by congressional enactment in the form of a statute. For example, Congress has enacted broad statutes governing discrimination in employment practices and has given authority to the Equal Employment Opportunity Commission (EEOC) to establish definitions, rules, and guidelines for compliance with those laws. Sometimes an existing agency is assigned the responsibility for new legislation implementation and enforcement. **For Example,** the Department of Labor has been assigned the responsibility to handle the whistle-blower protection provisions of Sarbanes-Oxley that provide protection against retaliation and/or termination to those who report financial chicanery at their companies. The Department of Labor has been in existence for almost a century, but it was assigned a new responsibility and given new jurisdiction by Congress.

---

[14] *Covad Communications Co. v FCC*, 430 F 3d 528 (DC Cir 2006).

[15] All of these are examples of the general legislative authority given to agencies. Agencies are given generic commands of law and then create the law's specifics.

ETHICS & THE LAW

Flush with Regulation: How Many Gallons and Where

The Energy Policy Act of 1992 requires that toilets installed after the act took effect (1994) use only 1.6 gallons of water rather than the nearly century-old standard of 3.5 gallons. As of 2000, about one-fourth of the nation's toilets were the 1.6-gallon types. The EPA mandated that permits be conditioned on the use of the 1.6-gallon toilets and that inspection approvals be denied if anything but a 1.6-gallon toilet had been installed.

As homeowners have remodeled and replaced older toilets, they have learned that the 3.5-gallon toilets are no longer sold in the United States. However, just across the U.S./Canadian border near Detroit, Canadian hardware stores are doing a land-office business selling 3.5-gallon tanks to U.S. citizens.

Those who are remodeling, and even some who are building new homes, provide for 1.6-gallon toilets in their plans and generally install $100 1.6-gallon toilets from Home Depot in order to pass inspection. They then purchase a standard fixture Canadian toilet for anywhere from $500 to $1,000 because of the high demand, and install it. Plumbing stores all over Canada report that sales are brisk. In a survey conducted in May 2000, the Canadian plumbing store owners said that they sell, on average, one toilet per day to U.S. citizens either via direct sale or shipment.

Do the citizens break any laws by what they do? Is what they do ethical? How could the regulation be challenged? What foundation in administrative law might be used?

(b) AGENCY RESEARCH OF THE PROBLEM   After jurisdiction is established, the agency has the responsibility to research the issues and various avenues of regulation for implementing the statutory framework. As the agency does so, it determines the cost and benefit of the problems, issues, and solutions. The study may be done by the agency itself, or it may be completed by someone hired by the agency. **For Example,** before red lights were required equipment in the rear windows of all cars, the Department of Transportation developed a study using taxicabs with the red lights in the rear windows and found that the accident rate for rear-end collisions with taxicabs was reduced dramatically. The study provided justification for the need for regulation as well as the type of regulation itself.

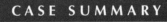

CASE SUMMARY

Seats Belts and Air Bags and Rules, Oh My!

FACTS: The U.S. Department of Transportation (DOT), charged with enforcing the National Traffic and Motor Vehicle Safety Act of 1966 and reducing auto accidents, passed Standard 208 in 1967, which required that all cars be equipped with seat belts. When another study showed the DOT that people did not use the belts, the department began a study of passive restraint systems which showed that these devices—automatic seat belts and air bags—could prevent approximately 12,000 deaths a year and over 100,000 serious injuries.

CASE SUMMARY

continued

In 1972, after many hearings and comments, the DOT passed a regulation requiring some type of passive restraint system on all vehicles manufactured after 1975. Because of changes in directors of the DOT and the unfavorable economic climate in the auto industry, the requirements for passive restraints were postponed. In 1981, the department proposed a rescission of the passive restraint rule. After receiving written comments and holding public hearings, the agency concluded there was no longer a basis for reliably predicting that passive restraints increased safety levels or decreased accidents. Furthermore, the agency found it would cost $1 billion to implement the rule, and it was unwilling to impose such substantial costs on auto manufacturers.

State Farm filed suit on the rescission of the rule on the basis that it was arbitrary and capricious. The court of appeals held that the rescission was, in fact, arbitrary and capricious. The auto manufacturers appealed.

DECISION: Just as an agency cannot pass regulations without studies, comments, and hearings, an agency cannot withdraw a regulation without going through the same process. In this case, the regulation was eliminated without any prior study of the issues and the impact of its elimination. The withdrawal of a regulation requires the same procedural steps as the promulgation of a rule. [**Motor Vehicles Manufacturers Ass'n v State Farm Mutual Ins. Co., 463 US 29 (1983)**]

Federal Register Act federal law requiring agencies to make public disclosure of proposed rules, passed rules, and activities.

Federal Register government publication issued five days a week that lists all administrative regulations, all presidential proclamations and executive orders, and other documents and classes of documents that the president or Congress direct to be published.

(c) PROPOSED REGULATIONS   Following a study, the agency proposes regulations, which must be published. To provide publicity for all regulations, the **Federal Register Act**[16] provides that proposed administrative regulation be published in the *Federal Register.* This is a government publication published five days a week that lists all administrative regulations, all presidential proclamations and executive orders, and other documents and classes of documents that the president or Congress directs to be published.

The Federal Register Act provides that printing an administrative regulation in the *Federal Register* is public notice of the contents of the regulation to persons subject to it or affected by it, but in addition, the Regulatory Flexibility Act,[17] passed during the Reagan administration, requires that all proposed rules be published in the trade journals of those trades that will be affected by the proposed rules. **For Example,** any changes in federal regulations on real property closings and escrows have to be published in real estate broker trade magazines. In addition to the public notice of the proposed rule, the agency must also include a "regulatory flexibility analysis" that "shall describe the impact of the proposed rule on small entities."[18] The goal of this portion of the APA was to be certain that small businesses were aware of proposed regulatory rules and their cost impact.

(d) PUBLIC COMMENT PERIOD   Following the publication of the proposed rules, the public has the opportunity to provide input on the proposed rules. Called the *public comment period,* this time must last at least 30 days (with certain emergency exceptions) and can consist simply of letters written by those affected

---

[16] 44 USC § 1505 *et seq.*
[17] 5 USC § 601 *et seq.*
[18] 5 USC § 603(a).

(**ETHICS & THE LAW**)

Ethics and Government Regulation

Rowena Fullinwider is the founder of Rowena's, Inc., which makes Rowena Fullinwider's Wonderful Almond Pound Cake and other products, such as lemon curd and carrot jam. The specialty gourmet food manufacturer specializes in high-calorie and, often, high-fat treats. When the Nutrition Labeling and Education Act requiring disclosure of food products' nutrients and contents went into effect in 1995, compliance with the new federal mandates for Rowena's 30 products cost $100,000 for redesigning the labels, testing the products for verification of ingredients, and printing and production.

Rowena's, like many other specialty food manufacturers, has very narrow profit margins, ranging from 0.5 percent to 5 percent. It employs 16 people and has $1 million in annual sales. At the top end of its profit margin, Rowena's has a net profit of $50,000.

Fullinwider expresses her concerns with the labeling act as follows: "I am not going to put new products out. In the gourmet industry, we are always improving our recipes. I want to make improvements, but I can't afford to if I'm all bound up by regulations."

Do you believe the federal food labeling act was necessary? Why or why not? Do you think Rowena's was guilty of deception in the sale of its products? Should food manufacturers voluntarily have disclosed the content of their products? Why would they resist? Is it possible that the label requirements will put some companies out of business? Is it desirable to have regulations that eliminate businesses? What could Rowena have done differently to change the content of the new regulations?

that are filed with the agency or of hearings conducted by the agency in Washington, D.C., or at specified locations around the country. An emergency exemption for the 30-day comment period was made when airport security measures and processes were changed following the September 11, 2001, attacks on the World Trade Center and the Pentagon that used domestic, commercial airliners.

(e) OPTIONS AFTER PUBLIC COMMENT After receiving the public input on the proposed rule, an agency can decide to pass, or promulgate, the rule. The agency can also decide to withdraw the rule. **For Example,** the EEOC had proposed rules on handling religious discrimination in the workplace. The proposed rules, which would have required employers to police those wearing a cross or other religious symbol, met with so much public and employer protest that they were withdrawn. Finally, the agency can decide to modify the rule based on comments and then promulgate or, if the modifications are extensive or material, modify and put the proposed rule back out for public comment again. A diagram of the rule-making process can be found in Figure 6-3.

| FIGURE 6-3 | *Steps in Agency Rulemaking* |

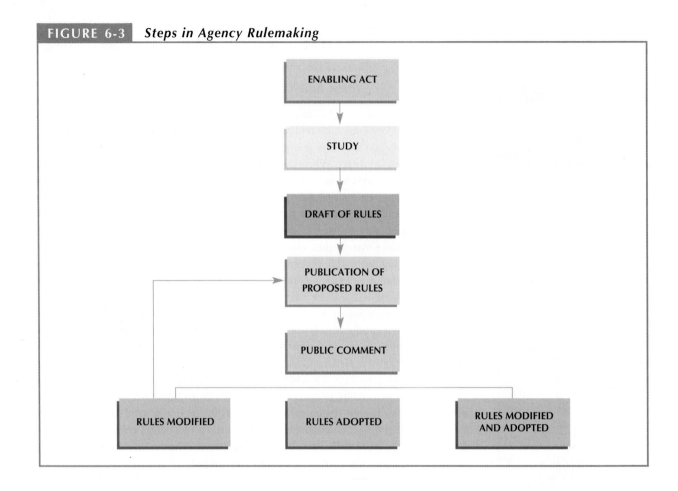

THINKING THINGS THROUGH

Cost-Benefit Analysis and Federal Regulation

Following a Supreme Court decision on the issue in 1983, the Department of Transportation (DOT) promulgated auto safety regulations that required automobile manufacturers to equip all vehicles with some form of passive restraint. The most popular was the air bag. The DOT had attempted to hold off on regulation until further information could be obtained about the efficacy and risks of air bags. General

Motors warned in 1979 that if an air bag were inflated while a child was sitting in the front passenger side of the vehicle, the effect would be severe injury or death. In 1984, Lee Iacocca, then CEO of Chrysler, wrote: "Air bags are one of those areas where the solution may actually be worse than the problem."* Insurers and consumer groups dismissed the claims as reflecting self-interest because of the costs mandatory

---

* James R. Heal and Jayne O'Donnell, "Deadly Air Bags," *USA Today*, July 8, 1996, 1B, 2B.

(THINKING THINGS THROUGH)

continued

passive restraints would impose on automobile manufacturers.

In 1996, the DOT revealed that 23 people had been killed by air bags; 22 were children between the ages of one week and nine years. A mother of one of those killed by an air bag said, "It's wrong for it to be in cars." In 1998, the DOT mandated disclosure stickers in all cars about the dangers of placing infants and children in passenger seats where there is an air bag:

WARNING: Children may be killed or injured by passenger air bag. The back seat is the safest place for children 12 and under.

Data released by the National Highway Traffic Safety Administration show that the complaints about airbags increased as more were installed in cars. So little was known about the technology and so many consumers were unfamiliar with them that the NHSTA began a decade of grappling with consumer complaints about the safety device. In 1990, only 200 air bag complaints were filed. In 2001, there were 3,000 with 2001 being the peak year. The NHSTA began changing the requirements and manufacturers made technological changes. By 2003, the number of complaints had dropped to just 800 and there was only one airbag death, down from a previous

high of 57. The types of complaints about the air bags were:

- Not being able to find the horn on the steering wheel because of the thickness the air bag brings
- Air bags inflating when there has not been a crash
- Air bags not inflating when there has been a crash
- Air bags' degree of inflation harming smaller passengers**

There have been 112 recalls of air bags in autos since 1990, and those recalls affected 6.2 million cars.

By 2003, air bags changed the dynamic of safety quite dramatically because at that point the bags carried sensors to determine the size of the individual and, therefore, how much to inflate. The air bags, however, remain at the standard of not inflating unless something hits the vehicle at a speed above 12 miles per hour.

Did the regulation move too quickly? What was the purpose of the regulation? Should more studies have been done before the airbags were mandated? Is cost-benefit analysis a good approach to making decisions on rules? You can visit the National Highway Traffic Safety Administration at **http://www.nhtsa.gov.**

**Jayne O'Donnell, "Air Bag Gripes Rise; New Rules May Complicate Matters," *USA Today,* April 9, 2002, 1B.

 ## EXECUTIVE POWER OF THE AGENCY

The modern administrative agency has the power to execute the law and to bring proceedings against violators.

6. ENFORCEMENT OR EXECUTION OF THE LAW

An agency has the power to investigate, to require persons to appear as witnesses, to require witnesses to produce relevant papers and records, and to bring proceedings against those who violate the law. In this connection, the phrase *the law* embraces regulations adopted by an agency as well as statutes and court decisions.

An agency may investigate to determine whether any violation of the law or of its rules generally has occurred. An agency may also investigate to determine whether additional rules need to be adopted, to ascertain the facts with respect to a particular suspected or alleged violation, and to see whether the defendant in a proceeding before it is complying with its final order. An agency may issue subpoenas to obtain information reasonably required by its investigation.[19]

7. CONSTITUTIONAL LIMITATIONS ON ADMINISTRATIVE INVESTIGATION

Although administrative agencies have broad enforcement authority, they remain subject to the constitutional protections afforded individuals and businesses.

(a) INSPECTION OF PREMISES   In general, a person has the same protection against unreasonable searches and seizures by an administrative officer as by a police officer. In contrast, when the danger of concealment is great, a warrantless search can be made of the premises of a highly regulated business, such as one selling liquor or firearms. Likewise, when violation of the law is dangerous to health and safety, the law may authorize inspection of the workplace without advance notice or a search warrant when such a requirement could defeat the purpose of the inspection.

(b) AERIAL INSPECTION   A search warrant is never required when the subject matter can be seen from a public place. **For Example,** when a police officer walking on a public sidewalk can look through an open window and see illegal weapons, a search warrant is not required to enter the premises and seize the weapons. Using airplanes and helicopters, law enforcement officers can see from the air; an agency, too, can gather information in this manner.[20]

(c) PRODUCTION OF PAPERS   For the most part, the constitutional guarantee against unreasonable searches and seizures does not afford much protection for papers and records being investigated by an agency. **For Example,** a subpoena to testify or to produce records cannot be opposed on the ground that it is a search and seizure. The constitutional protection is limited to cases of actual physical search and seizure rather than obtaining information by compulsion. Employers must turn over to the Occupational Health and Safety Administration (OSHA) their records on workplace injuries and lost workdays.

The protection afforded by the guarantee against self-incrimination is likewise narrow. It cannot be invoked when a corporate employee or officer in control of corporate records is compelled to produce those records even though he or she would be incriminated by them.[21] The privilege against self-incrimination cannot be invoked if records required to be kept by law are involved.

(d) COMPLIANCE VERIFICATION   To ensure that a particular person or business is obeying the law, including an agency's regulations and orders, the administrative agency may require proof of compliance. At times, the question of compliance may be directly determined by an agency investigation, involving an examination either

---

[19] *EEOC v Sidley, Austen, Brown and Wood,* 35 F 3d 696 (CA 7 2002).
[20] *Dow Chemical Co. v United States,* 476 US 1819 (1986).
[21] *Braswell v United States,* 487 US 99 (1988).

of a building or plant or of witnesses and documents. An agency may require the regulated person or enterprise to file reports in a specified form.[22]

 ## JUDICIAL POWER OF THE AGENCY

Once the investigation of an agency reveals a potential violation of the law, an agency assumes its third role of judicial arbiter to conduct hearings on violations.

8. THE AGENCY AS A SPECIALIZED COURT

An agency, although not a court by law, may be given power to sit as a court and to determine whether any violations of the law or of agency regulations have occurred. The National Labor Relations Board (NLRB) determines whether a prohibited labor practice has been committed. The Federal Trade Commission (FTC) acts as a court to determine whether someone has engaged in unfair competition.

(a) BEGINNING ENFORCEMENT—PRELIMINARY STEPS   Either a private individual or company or an agency may file a written complaint alleging some violation of law or regulation that is within the agency's jurisdiction. This complaint is then served on the company or individual named in the complaint, who then has the opportunity to file an answer to the allegations. There may be other phases of pleading between the parties and the agency, but eventually, the matter comes before the agency to be heard. After a hearing, the agency makes a decision and enters an order either dismissing the complaint or directing remedies or resolutions.

(b) THE ADMINISTRATIVE HEARING   To satisfy the requirements of due process, an agency handling a complaint must generally give notice and hold a hearing at which all persons affected may be present. A significant difference between an agency hearing and a court hearing is that there is no right of trial by jury before an agency. **For Example,** a workers' compensation board may decide a claim without any jury. Similarly, a case in which an employer protests the unemployment tax rate assigned to her company by a state agency has no right to a jury trial. The lack of a jury does not deny due process (see Chapter 4). An administrative law judge (ALJ) hears the complaint and has the authority to swear witnesses, take testimony, make evidentiary rulings, and make a decision to recommend to the agency heads for action.

An agency hearing is ordinarily not subject to the rules of evidence. Another difference between an administrative hearing and a judicial determination is that an agency may be authorized to make an initial determination without holding a hearing. If its conclusion is challenged, the agency then holds a hearing. A court, on the other hand, must have a trial before it makes a judgment. This difference has important practical consequences because the party objecting to the agency's initial determination has the burden of proof and the cost of going forward. The result is that fewer persons go to the trouble of seeking such a hearing, which reduces the number of hearings and the amount of litigation in which an agency becomes involved. The government saves money and time with this abbreviated process.

When an administrative action involves only the individuals directly affected rather than a class of persons or the community in general, the agency must have some form

---

[22] *United States v Morton Salt Co.,* 338 US 632 (1950).

ETHICS & THE LAW

The Other CIA

Corporate integrity agreements are forms of or parts of consent decrees entered into between federal agencies and corporations after charges have been settled. Corporate integrity agreements (CIAs) are common between health care providers, medical device manufacturers, and similar organizations and companies and the U.S. Department of Health and Human Services. CIAs generally require the company or organization to provide additional ethics training, enhance compliance program development, and step up audits to ensure that the same or similar problems do not arise again.

If the company or organization violates the CIA, which is a form of civil probation, the government can take additional steps. The usual step for a second violation during the CIA is to banish the company or organization from all federal programs, whether as a provider or a beneficiary of Medicare, Medicaid, and any Veteran's Administration program. The loss of such large customers can be devastating for the company or organization. These additional penalties are envisioned and discussed as part of the CIA.

However, the CIA has emerged as an issue in private litigation. For example, suppose that a pharmaceutical company is subject to a CIA for five years because it failed to alert the FDA to side effects of one of its drugs. The government could impose a fine and a CIA. What would happen if the company failed to notify the government of another side effect problem during the CIA's five-year period? What right would a patient who is harmed by the side effects have to use the CIA against the company to recover punitive damages?. The courts must determine how these government settlements and CIAs can be used in civil litigation.

Should the agencies cover all of these issues in the CIA or wait for the courts to determine the outcome? Should agency officials warn companies entering into CIAs of these potential minefields?

of hearing before it makes a decision. The Supreme Court has held that because a civil service employee may be removed only for cause, it is a denial of due process for a statute to authorize an agency to remove the employee without a hearing.[23] Just giving the employee the right to appeal such action is not sufficient. Because the employee has a significant interest in continued employment, there must be some form of hearing prior to removing the employee to determine that there were not errors in the administrative action.

informal settlements
negotiated disposition of a matter before an administrative agency, generally without public sanctions.

consent decrees informal settlements of enforcement actions brought by agencies.

(c) Streamlined Procedure: Consent Decrees Informal settlements or consent decrees are practical devices to cut across the procedures already outlined. In many instances, an alleged wrongdoer informally notified that a complaint has been made is willing to change. An agency's informing an alleged wrongdoer of the charge before filing any formal complaint is sound public relations, as well as expeditious policy. A matter that has already gone into the formal hearing stage may also be terminated by agreement, and a stipulation or consent decree may be

---

[23] *Cleveland Board of Education v Loudermill,* 470 US 532 (1985).

filed setting forth the terms of the agreement. The Administrative Dispute Resolution Act of 1990 encourages the streamlining of the regulatory process and authorizes federal agencies to use alternative means of dispute resolution.[24]

(d) Form of Administrative Decision   When an administrative agency makes a decision, it usually files an opinion that sets forth the findings of facts and reasons on which the decision is based. In some instances, a statute expressly requires this type of opinion, but an agency should always file one so that the parties and the court (in the event of an appeal) will understand the agency's action and reasoning.[25]

9. PUNISHMENT AND ENFORCEMENT POWERS OF AGENCIES

(a) Penalty   Within the last few decades, agencies have increasingly been given the power to impose a penalty and to issue orders that are binding on a regulated party unless an appeal is taken to a court, which reverses the administrative decision. As an illustration of the power to impose penalties, the Occupational Safety and Health Act of 1970 provides for the assessment of civil penalties against employers who fail to end dangerous working conditions when ordered to do so by the administrative agency created by that statute.[26]

cease-and-desist order order issued by a court or administrative agency to stop a practice that it decides is improper.

(b) Cease and Desist Order   Environmental protection statutes adopted by states commonly give a state agency the power to assess a penalty for violating environmental protection regulations. As an illustration of the issuance of binding orders, the FTC can issue a **cease-and-desist order** to stop a practice that it decides is improper. This order to stop is binding unless reversed on an appeal. **For Example,** the FTC can order a company to stop making claims in ads that have been determined by that agency to be deceptive.

10. EXHAUSTION OF ADMINISTRATIVE REMEDIES

All parties interacting with an agency must follow the procedure specified by the law. No appeal to a court is possible until the agency has acted on the party's matter before it. As a matter of policy, parties are required to exhaust administrative remedies before they may go into court or take an appeal.

As long as an agency is acting within the scope of its authority or jurisdiction, a party cannot appeal before the agency has made a final decision. The fact that the complaining party does not want the agency to decide the matter or is afraid that the agency will reach a wrong decision is not grounds for bypassing the agency by going to court before the agency has acted.

exhaustion of administrative remedies requirement that an agency make its final decision before the parties can go to court.

Exceptions to the **exhaustion-of-administrative-remedies** requirement are (1) available remedies that provide no genuine opportunity for adequate relief; (2) irreparable injury that could occur if immediate judicial relief is not provided; (3) an appeal to the administrative agency that would be useless; or (4) a substantial constitutional question that the plaintiff has raised.

---

[24] 5 USC § 571 *et. seq.*

[25] *Jordan v Civil Service Bd., Charlotte*, 570 SE 2d 912 (CA NC 2002).

[26] 29 USC § 651 *et seq.*

CASE SUMMARY

Get Off of My Cloud, er, Parachute

FACTS: San Diego Air Sports (SDAS) Center operates a sports parachuting business in Otay Mesa, California. SDAS offers training to beginning parachutists and facilitates recreational jumping for experienced parachutists. It indicates that the majority of SDAS jumps occur at altitudes in excess of 5,800 feet. The jump zone used by SDAS overlaps the San Diego Traffic Control Area (TCA). Although the aircraft carrying the parachutists normally operate outside the TCA, the parachutists themselves are dropped through it. Thus, the air traffic controllers must approve each jump.

In July 1987, an air traffic controller in San Diego filed an Unsatisfactory Condition Report with the Federal Aviation Administration (FAA), complaining of the strain that parachuting was putting on the controllers and raising safety concerns. The report led to a staff study of parachute jumping within the San Diego TCA. This was followed by a letter in March 1988 from the FAA to SDAS informing SDAS that "[e]ffective immediately parachute jumping within or into the San Diego TCA in the Otay Reservoir Jump Zone will not be authorized." The FAA stated that the letter was final and appealable.

SDAS challenged the letter in federal court on grounds that it constituted rulemaking without compliance with required Administrative Procedure Act (APA) procedures.

DECISION: The effect of the FAA letter was to promulgate a rule. Although the FAA characterized the ban on parachutes as simply a safety issue, it was a new rule for operation in the air space around San Diego, and SDAS had the right to participate and be heard in the process that led to the letter. No process was followed here at all in terms of the release of the findings or a public comment period. The FAA was required to follow the same steps for this new rule and could not circumvent that process by labeling a fundamental change in the rules as simply an interpretation. [**San Diego Air Sports Center, Inc. v FAA, 887 F2d 966 (9th Cir 1989)**]

11. APPEAL FROM ADMINISTRATIVE ACTION AND FINALITY OF ADMINISTRATIVE DETERMINATION

The statute creating the modern administrative agency generally provides that an appeal may be taken from the administrative decision to a particular court. The statute may provide the basis for an appeal. However, judicial precedent holds that courts may review administrative agency decisions on the bases covered in the following sections.

(a) PROCEDURAL ISSUES If the procedure that an agency is to follow is specified by law, a decision of the agency that was made without following that procedure will be set aside and the matter sent back to the agency to proceed according to the required law.[27] An agency's actions, whether enforcement or rule promulgation, can be set aside if the agency has not followed the procedures required for rulemaking or, in the case of enforcement, the due process rights of the charged business or individual.

(b) SUBSTANTIVE LAW OR FACT ISSUES When the question that an agency decides is a question of law, the court on appeal will reverse the agency if the court disagrees with the legal interpretation.[28] This concept is being eroded to some extent by

---

[27] *Tingler v State Board of Cosmetology,* 814 SW2d 683 (Mo App 1991).

[28] *In re Minnesota Joint Underwriting Ass'n,* 408 NW2d 599 (Minn App 1987).

technical aspects of regulation. Courts now accept an agency's interpretation of a statute that involves a technical matter. Courts now tend to accept the agency's interpretation so long as it was reasonable even though it was not the only interpretation that could have been made.

In contrast with an agency's decision on matters of law, a controversy may turn on a question of fact or a mixed question of law and fact. In such cases, a court accepts an agency's conclusion if it is supported by substantial evidence. This means that the court must examine the entire record of the proceedings before the administrative agency to determine if there was substantial evidence to support the administrative findings. So long as reasonable minds could have reached the same conclusion as the agency after considering all of the evidence as a whole, the court must sustain the agency's findings of fact.[29]

A court will not reverse an agency's decision merely because the court would have made a different decision based on the same facts.[30] Because most disputes before an agency are based on questions of fact, the net result is that the agency's decision will be final in most cases.

Courts must give administrative agencies the freedom to do the work delegated to them and should not intervene unless the agency action is clearly unreasonable or arbitrary (see below). The agency action is presumed proper, and a person seeking reversal of the agency action has the burden to prove a basis for reversal.[31]

(c) BEYOND THE JURISDICTION OF THE AGENCY   When the question is whether an administrative action is in harmony with the policy of the statute creating the agency, an appellate court will sustain the administrative action if substantial evidence supports it.

(d) ARBITRARY AND CAPRICIOUS   When an agency changes its prior decisions and customary actions, it must give its reasons. In the absence of such an explanation, a reviewing court cannot tell whether the agency changed its interpretation of the law for a valid reason or has made a mistake. The absence of an explanation condemns the agency action as arbitrary and requires reversal.[32]

The greatest limitation on court review of administrative action is the rule that a decision involving discretion will not be reversed in the absence of an error of law or a clear abuse of, or the arbitrary or capricious exercise of, discretion. The courts reason that because agency members were appointed on the basis of expert ability, it would be absurd for the court, which is unqualified technically to make a decision in the matter, to step in and determine whether the agency made the proper choice. Courts will not do so unless the agency has clearly acted wrongly, arbitrarily, or capriciously. As a practical matter, an agency's action is rarely found to be arbitrary or capricious. As long as an agency has followed proper procedure, the fact that the court disagrees with the agency's conclusion does not make that conclusion arbitrary or capricious. In areas in which economic or technical matters are involved, it is generally sufficient that the agency had a reasonable basis for its decision. A court will not attempt to second-guess the agency about complex criteria with which an administrative agency is intimately familiar. The judicial

---

[29] *Wilmer-Hutchins Independent School District v Brown,* 912 SW2d 848 (Tex App 1995).

[30] *In re Smith,* 121 P 3d 150 (Wyo 2005). An appellate court cannot review the evidence to determine the credibility of witnesses who testified before the administrative agency. *Hammann v City of Omaha,* 17 NW2d 323 (Neb 1987).

[31] *Reaux v Louisiana State Board of Medical Examiners,* 689 So 2d 718 (La App 1997).

[32] *Lorillard Tobacco Co. v Roth,* 786 NE 2d 7 (CA NY 2003).

CASE SUMMARY

I'll Call You—Maybe During Dinner: The FCC and the National Do-Not-Call List Regulation

FACTS: Many different organizations, including businesses, charities, religious groups, and political parties, generate revenue by calling individuals in their homes and soliciting sales and donations. This practice, known as *telemarketing,* has grown into an industry that generates $275 billion annually and employs roughly 5.4 million persons in the United States.

To protect consumers from this burgeoning industry, the FTC issued the rule for the do-not-call list under the authority of the Telephone Consumer Protection Act of 1991 (TCPA), which granted the FCC the authority to promulgate rules creating a procedure to protect telephone subscribers from receiving unwanted telemarketing calls. In 1994, Congress enacted the Telemarketing Act, which granted the FTC the authority to promulgate rules prohibiting "deceptive or abusive telemarketing practices." Congress specifically found that consumers were being increasingly victimized by telemarketing fraud and other abuses, and it required the FTC in promulgating its rules to (1) define "deceptive telemarketing acts or practices," (2) prohibit abusive patterns of unsolicited telephone calls, (3) restrict the hours of the day when telemarketing calls may be placed, and (4) require telemarketers to promptly disclose to call recipients the nature of their call.

In December 2002, the FTC issued amended rules that prohibit "deceptive or abusive telemarketing acts or practices."

Under the TCPA, the FCC announced its intention to adopt rules similar to the FTC's, enforcing the do-not-call list. On July 25, 2003, the FCC promulgated rules mirroring the FTC's amended rules and adding entities subject to the do-not-call restrictions to include those beyond the reach of the FTC's jurisdiction, such as banks, insurance companies, and common carriers.

Mainstream Marketing and TMG, independent telemarketing companies based in Colorado, brought suit challenging the FTC's authority to create a national do-not-call list that allows consumers to opt out, with certain exceptions, from receiving these telemarketing calls, alleging that the do-not-call list violates the First Amendment and the APA. The District Court for Colorado held that the FTC's do-not-call rules were unconstitutional on First Amendment grounds, and the District Court for the Western District of Oklahoma held that FTC lacked statutory authority to enact its do-not-call rules. The two appeals by the FCC and FTC were consolidated in the Tenth Circuit.

DECISION: The court held that Congress has granted clear authority under the statutes for both agencies to engage in the regulation of telemarketing. The enabling legislation gave the agencies the authority to create such a list as a means of controlling the telemarketing practices throughout the country. The court also held that the do-not-call registry did not violate the First Amendment because the government has a substantial interest in protecting the privacy of its citizens and the do-not-call list directly advances that governmental interest.

The FTC and the FCC regulations on the national "do-not-call" registry did not violate telemarketers' First Amendment free speech rights, even though the regulations did not apply to charitable and political callers. The regulations were enacted to protect the privacy of individuals in their homes and to protect consumers against the risk of fraudulent and abusive solicitation. The opt-in character of the list ensured that it did not inhibit any speech directed at the homes of willing listeners. The Congress, FTC, and FCC all determined that commercial calls affected by the registry were most to blame for the problems that the regulations remedied and the proposed alternative of company-specific approach had proven extremely burdensome to consumers. [**Mainstream Marketing Services, Inc. v F.T.C., 358 F.3d 1228 (10th Cir 2004);** *cert. denied* **543 US 812 (2004).**]

attitude is that for protection from laws and regulations that are unwise, improvident, or out of harmony with a particular school of thought, the people must resort to the ballot box, not to the court.

The fact that other agencies or trade associations disagree with the view of an agency does not make the latter's decision improper. There was much disagreement on the do-not-call list rules, but the court found that the FTC and FCC acted reasonably.[33]

Because of limited funding and staff, an agency must exercise discretion in deciding which cases it should handle. Ordinarily, a court will not reverse an agency's decision to do nothing about a particular complaint.[34] That is, the courts will not override an agency's decision to do nothing. Exceptions include acting arbitrarily in those enforcement actions as when an agency refuses to act in circumstances in which action is warranted and necessary.

12. LIABILITY OF THE AGENCY

The decision of an agency may cause substantial loss to a business by increasing its operating costs or by making a decision that later is shown to be harmful to the economy. An agency is not liable for such loss when it has acted in good faith in the exercise of discretionary powers. An administrator who wrongly denies a person the benefit of a government program is not personally liable to that person.

---

[33] *Mainstream Marketing Services, Inc. v FTC,* 358 F 3d 1228 (10th Cir 2004).

[34] *Heckler v Chaney,* 470 US 821 (1985).

 SUMMARY

The administrative agency is unique because it combines the three functions that are kept separate under our traditional governmental system: legislative, executive, and judicial. By virtue of legislative power, an agency adopts regulations that have the force of law, although agency members are not elected by those subject to the regulations. By virtue of the executive power, an agency carries out and enforces the regulations, makes investigations, and requires the production of documents. By virtue of the judicial power, an agency acts as a court to determine whether a violation of any regulation has occurred. To some extent, an agency is restricted by constitutional limitations in inspecting premises and requiring the production of papers. These limitations, however, have a very narrow application in agency actions. When an agency acts as a judge, a jury trial is not required, nor must ordinary courtroom procedures be followed. Typically, an agency gives notice to the person claimed to be acting improperly, and a hearing is then held before the agency. When the agency has determined that there has been a violation, it may order that the violation stop.

Under some statutes, the agency may go further and impose a penalty on the violator.

An appeal to a court may be taken from any decision of an agency by a person harmed by the decision. Only a person with a legally recognized interest can appeal from the agency ruling. No appeal can be made until every step available before the agency has been taken; that is, the administrative remedy must first be exhausted. An agency's actions can be reversed by a court if the agency exceeded its authority, the decision is not based in law or fact, the decision is arbitrary and capricious, or, finally, the agency violated procedural steps.

Protection from secret government is provided by Sunshine laws that afford the right to know what most administrative agency records contain; by the requirement that most agency meetings be open to the public; by the invitation to the public to take part in rulemaking; and by publicity given, through publication in the *Federal Register* and trade publications, to the guidelines followed by the agency and the regulations it has adopted.

> ## QUESTIONS AND CASE PROBLEMS

1. Following the events of September 11, 2001, in which four airplanes crashed as a result of the presence of terrorists on those flights, the FAA concluded that it needed to implement new procedures for airports and flights. The new procedures for security and flights took effect when the airports reopened five days later. Why did the FAA not need to go through the promulgation and public comment processes and time periods to have the new rules take effect?

2. Reserve Mining Co. obtained a permit from the Minnesota Pollution Control Agency to dump wastewater into the nearby Beaver River. The permit specified that no more than 1 million fibers per liter could be discharged in the company's wastewater. The agency did not make or file any explanation as to how or why that maximum was selected. Normally, the wastewater that the company generated was kept in a tailings dam with a discharge in the river necessary only in an emergency. Because of a sudden economic downturn, the company foresaw the need to dispose of wastewater in the river and discovered that the discharge it would have to make would likely be between 10 to 15 times the amount of fiber allowed by the permit. Reserve Mining appealed the maximum limitation imposed by the agency. How could Reserve Mining challenge the 1-million-fibers standard? [*Reserve Mining Co. v Minnesota Pollution Control Agency*, 364 NW2d 411 (Minn App)]

3. The Tacoma-Pierce County Health Department conducted an investigation into the quality of care provided by ambulance service providers in its jurisdiction. On the basis of that investigation, the department issued a set of temporary rules and regulations that established minimum requirements for equipment, drugs, and service availability for ambulance service providers in Pierce County. The *Tacoma News* wanted to publish an article on the matter and sought discovery of everything that had led to the adoption of the regulations, including all details of the investigation made by the health department. The health department objected to disclosing the names of the persons who had volunteered information on which the department had based its action and the names of the ambulance companies. Were the names subject to a Freedom of Information Act (FOIA) request? [*Tacoma News, Inc. v Tacoma-Pierce County Health Dept.*, 778 P2d 1066 (Wash App)]

4. Congress adopted a law to provide insurance to protect wheat farmers. The agency in charge of the program adopted regulations to govern applications for this insurance. These regulations were published in the *Federal Register*. Merrill applied for insurance, but his application did not comply with the regulations. He claimed that he was not bound by the regulations because he never knew they had been adopted. Is he bound by the regulations? [*Federal Crop Ins. Corp. v Merrill*, 332 US 380]

5. Santa Monica adopted a rent control ordinance authorizing the Rent Control Board to set the amount of rents that could be charged. At a hearing before it, the board determined that McHugh was charging his tenants a rent higher than the maximum allowed. McHugh claimed that the action of the board was improper because there was no jury trial. Is McHugh correct? Why or why not? [*McHugh v Santa Monica Rent Control Board*, 49 Cal 3d 348, 777 P2d 91]

6. New York City's charter authorized the New York City Board of Health to adopt a health code that it declared to have the force and effect of law. The board adopted a code that provided for the fluoridation of the public water supply. A suit was brought to enjoin the carrying out of this program on the grounds that it was unconstitutional and that money could not be spent to carry out such a program in the absence of a statute authorizing the expenditure. It was also claimed that the fluoridation program was unconstitutional because there were other means of reducing tooth decay; fluoridation was discriminatory by benefiting only children; it unlawfully imposed medication on children without their consent; and fluoridation was or may be dangerous to health. Was the code's provision valid? [*Paduano v City of New York*, 257 NYS2d 531]

7. What is the *Federal Register?* What role does it play in rulemaking?

8. The Consumer Product Safety Commission is reconsidering a rule it first proposed in 1997 that

would require child-resistant caps on household products, including cosmetics. When the rule was first proposed in 1997, it was resisted by the cosmetics industry and abandoned. However, in May 2001, a 16-month-old baby died after drinking baby oil from a bottle with a pull-tab cap.

The proposed rule would cover products such as baby oil and suntan lotion and any products containing hydrocarbons such as cleansers and spot removers. The danger, according to the commission, is simply the inhalation for children, not necessarily the actual ingestion of the products. Five children have died from inhaling such fumes since 1993, and 6,400 children under the age of 5 were brought into emergency rooms and/or hospitalized for treatment after breathing in hydrocarbons. There is no medical treatment for the inhalation of hydrocarbons.

Several companies in the suntan oil/lotion industry have supported the new regulations. The head of a consumer group has said, "We know these products cause death and injury. That is all we need to know."[35]

What process must the CPSC follow to promulgate the rules? What do you think of the consumer group head's statement? Will that statement alone justify the rulemaking?

9. The *Federal Register* contained the following provision from the Environmental Protection Agency on January 14, 2002:

> *We, the U.S. Fish and Wildlife Service (Service), announce the re-opening of the comment period on the proposed listing of* Lomatium cookii *(Cook's lomatium) and* Limnanthes floccosa ssp. grandiflora *(large-flowered wooly meadowfoam) as endangered species under the Endangered Species Act of 1973, as amended (Act). We are re-opening the comment period to provide the public an opportunity to review additional information on the status, abundance, and distribution of these plants, and to request additional information and comments from the public regarding the proposed rule. Comments previously submitted need not be resubmitted as they will be incorporated into the public record as part of this extended comment period; all comments will be fully considered in the final rule.*

DATES: We will accept public comments until March 15, 2002.

What was the EPA doing and why? What could those who had concerns do at that point?

10. Macon County Landfill Corp. applied for permission to expand the boundaries of its landfill. Tate and others opposed the application. After a number of hearings, the appropriate agency granted the requested permission to expand. Tate appealed and claimed that the agency had made a wrong decision on the basis of the evidence presented. Will the court determine whether the correct decision was made? [*Tate v Illinois Pollution Control Board*, 188 Ill App 3d 994, 544 NE2d 1176]

11. The planning commissioner and a real estate developer planned to meet to discuss rezoning certain land that would permit the real estate developer to construct certain buildings not allowed under the then-existing zoning law. A homeowners association claimed it had the right to be present at the meeting. This claim was objected to on the theory that the state's Open Meetings Act applied only to meetings of specified government units and did not extend to a meeting between one of them and an outsider. Was this objection valid?

12. The Michigan Freedom of Information Act declares that it is the state's policy to give all persons full information about the actions of the government and that "the people shall be informed so that they may participate in the democratic process." The union of clerical workers at Michigan State University requested the trustees of the university to give them the names and addresses of persons making monetary donations to the university. Michigan State objected because the disclosure of addresses was a violation of the right of privacy. Decide. [*Clerical-Technical Union of Michigan State University v Board of Trustees of Michigan State University*, 475 NW2d 373 (Mich)]

13. The Department of Health and Human Services has proposed new guidelines for the interpretation of federal statutes on gifts, incentives, and other benefits bestowed on physicians by pharmaceutical companies.

---

[35] Julian E. Barnes, "Safety Caps Are Considered for Cosmetics," *New York Times*, October 10, 2001, C1, C8.

The areas on which the interpretation focused follow:

- Paying doctors to act as consultants or market researchers for prescription drugs
- Paying pharmacies fees to switch patients to new drugs
- Providing grants, scholarships, and anything more than nominal gifts to physicians for time, information sessions, and so on, on new drugs[36]

The Office of Inspector General is handling the new rules interpretation and has established a public comment period of 60 days. Explain the purpose of the public comment period. What ethical issues do the regulations attempt to address?

14. A state law authorized the state's insurance commissioner to impose a fine and suspend the license of any insurance agent selling "unnecessary or excessive" insurance. The insurance commissioner fined Eloise, a licensed agent, $600 and suspended her license for three months for selling "unnecessary and excessive" insurance. She objected to this action on the ground that the statute under which the commissioner acted did not have any definitive meaning and the agency did not have the authority to define the term "unnecessary or excessive." Decide whether the agency had authority.

15. The Endangered Species Act (ESA) charges the National Marine Fisheries Service (a federal agency) with the duty to "ensure" that any proposed action by the Council does not "jeopardize" any threatened or endangered species. The Steller sea lion is on the list of endangered species. The agency developed a North Pacific marine fishery plan that permitted significant harvest of fish by commercial fisheries in the area. Greenpeace, an environmental group, challenged the agency on the grounds that the plan was not based on a sufficient number of biological studies on the impact of the allowed fishing on the Steller sea lion. Greenpeace's biologic opinion concluded that the fishery plan would reduce the level of food for the sea lions by about 40% to 60%, if the juvenile fish were not counted in that figure. Greenpeace's expert maintained that counting juvenile fish was misleading because they were not capable of reproducing and the government agency's figure was, as a result, much lower at 22%. What would Greenpeace need to show to be successful in challenging the agency's fishery plan? [*Greenpeace, American Oceans Campaign v National Marine Fisheries Service*, 237 F Supp 2d 1181 (W.D.Wash)]

---

[36] See 67 *Federal Register* 62057, October 3, 2002. Go to **http://www.oig.hhs.gov.** See also Robert Pear, "U.S. Warning to Drug Makers Over Payments," *New York Times,* October 1, 2002, A1, A23; Julie Appleby, "Feds Warn Drugmakers: Gifts to Doctors May Be Illegal," *USA Today,* October 2, 2002, 1A.

THE LEGAL ENVIRONMENT
OF INTERNATIONAL TRADE

CHAPTER

(7)

LEARNING OBJECTIVES

After studying this chapter, you should be able to

LO.1 Identify seven major international organizations, conferences, and treaties

LO.2 Describe the forms of business organizations that exist for doing business abroad

LO.3 Identify conduct outside the United States to which the U.S. antitrust laws will apply

LO.4 Differentiate between secrecy laws and blocking laws in regard to SEC enforcement of U.S. securities laws

LO.5 List and explain the laws that provide protection against unfair competition from foreign goods

LO.6 List and explain the laws that provide economic relief for those adversely affected by import competition

LO.7 List and explain the laws enacted to increase the foreign sales of U.S. firms

The success or failure of the U.S. firms doing business in foreign countries may well depend on accurate information about the laws and customs of the host countries. In their domestic operations, U.S. business firms compete against imports from other nations. Such imported goods include Canadian lumber, Mexican machinery, Japanese automobiles, German steel, French wine, Chinese textiles, and Chilean copper. To compete effectively, U.S. firms should learn about the business practices of foreign firms. They should be alert to unfair trade practices that will put U.S. firms at a disadvantage. Such practices may include the violation of U.S. antitrust and antidumping laws or violation of international trade agreements. Individuals from all over the world participate in the U.S. securities markets. Special problems exist in the regulation and enforcement of U.S. securities laws involving financial institutions of countries with secrecy laws.

 GENERAL PRINCIPLES

Nations enter into treaties and conferences to further international trade. The business world has developed certain forms of organizations for conducting that trade.

1. THE LEGAL BACKGROUND

Because of the complexity and ever-changing character of the legal environment of international trade, this section will focus on certain underlying elements.

(a) WHAT LAW APPLIES   When there is a sale of goods within the United States, one law typically applies to the transaction. Some variation may be introduced when the transaction is between parties in different states, but for the most part, the law governing the transaction is the U.S. law of contracts and the Uniform Commercial Code (UCC). In contrast, when an international contract is made, it is necessary to determine whether it is the law of the seller's country or the law of the importer's country that will govern. The parties to an international contract often resolve that question themselves as part of their contract, setting forth which country's law will govern should a dispute arise. Such a provision is called a **choice-of-law clause. For Example,** U.S. investors Irmgard and Mitchell Lipcon provided capital to underwriters at Lloyd's of London and signed choice-of-law clauses in their investment agreements binding them to proceed in England under English law should disputes arise. When the Lipcons realized that their investments were exposed to massive liabilities for asbestos and pollution insurance claims, they sued in U.S. district court in Florida for alleged U.S. securities acts violations. However, their complaints were dismissed based on the choice-of-law clauses in their contracts. The U.S. court of appeals stated that the Lipcons must "honor their bargains" and attempt to vindicate their claims in English courts under English law.[1]

The major trading countries of the world have entered into a number of treaties. When their citizens deal with each other and their respective rights are not controlled in their contract, their rights and liabilities are determined by looking at the treaty. These treaties are discussed in Section 7 of this chapter, including the United Nations Convention on Contracts for the International Sale of Goods (CISG), which deals with certain aspects of the formation and performance of international commercial contracts for the sale of goods.

choice-of-law clause clause in an agreement that specifies which law will govern should a dispute arise.

---

[1] *Lipcon v Underwriters at Lloyd's, London,* 148 F2d 1285, 1299 (11th Cir 1998).

(b) The Arbitration Alternative   Traditional litigation may be considered too time consuming, expensive, and divisive to the relationships of the parties to an international venture. The parties, therefore, may agree to arbitrate any contractual disputes that may arise according to dispute resolution procedures set forth in the contract.

Pitfalls exist for U.S. companies arbitrating disputes in foreign lands. **For Example,** were a U.S. company to agree to arbitrate a contractual dispute with a Chinese organization in China, it would find that the arbitrator must be Chinese. Also, under Chinese law, only Chinese lawyers can present an arbitration case, even if one party is a U.S. company. Because of situations like this, it is common for parties to international ventures to agree to arbitrate their disputes in neutral countries.

An arbitration agreement gives the parties more control over the decision-making process. The parties can require that the arbitrator have the technical, language, and legal qualifications to best understand their dispute. While procedures exist for the prearbitration exchange of documents, full "discovery" is ordinarily not allowed. The decision of the arbitrator is final and binding on the parties with very limited judicial review possible.

(c) Conflicting Ideologies   Law, for all people and at all times, is the result of the desire of the lawmaker to achieve certain goals. These are the social forces that make the law. In the eyes of the lawmaker, the attainment of these goals is proper and therefore ethical. This does not mean that we all can agree on what the international law should be because different people have different ideas as to what is right. This affects our views as to ownership, trade, and dealings with foreign merchants. **For Example,** a very large part of the world does not share the U.S. dislike of trusts. Other countries do not have our antitrust laws; therefore, their merchants can form a trust to create greater bargaining power in dealing with U.S. and other foreign merchants.

(d) Financing International Trade   There is no international currency. This creates problems as to what currency to use and how to make payment in international transactions. Centuries ago, buyers used precious metals, jewels, or furs in payment. Today, the parties to an international transaction agree in their sales contract on the currency to be used to pay for the goods. They commonly require that the buyer furnish the seller a **letter of credit,** which is a commercial device used to guarantee payment to a seller in an international transaction. By this, an issuer, typically a bank, agrees to pay the drafts drawn against the buyer for the purchase price. In trading with merchants in some countries, the foreign country itself will promise that the seller will be paid.

letter of credit commercial device used to guarantee payment to a seller, primarily in an international business transaction.

2. INTERNATIONAL TRADE ORGANIZATIONS, CONFERENCES, AND TREATIES

A large number of organizations exist that affect the multinational markets for goods, services, and investments. A survey of major international organizations, conferences, and treaties follows.

(a) GATT and WTO   The *General Agreement on Tariffs and Trade* 1994 (GATT 1994) is a multilateral treaty subscribed to by 126 member governments, including the United States.[2] It consists of the original 1947 GATT, numerous multilateral agreements negotiated since 1947, the Uruguay Round Agreements, and the agreement establishing the *World Trade Organization* (WTO). On January 1, 1995, the WTO took over responsibility for policing the objectives of the former GATT organization. Since 1947 and the end of the World War II era, the goal of the GATT has been to liberalize world trade and make it secure for furthering economic growth and human development. The current round of WTO negotiations began in Doha, Qatar, in 2001. As the talks continued in Cancun in 2003, the developed countries and developing countries divided on key issues such as agricultural subsidies. The Doha Round continues in an effort to meet the WTO's objectives of liberalizing world trade.

The GATT is based on the fundamental principles of (1) trade without discrimination and (2) protection through tariffs. The principle of trade without discrimination is embodied in its **most-favored-nation clause.** In treaties between countries, a most-favored-nation clause is one whereby any privilege subsequently granted to a third country in relation to a given treaty subject is extended to the other party to the treaty. In the application and administration of import and export duties and charges under the GATT most-favored-nation clause, all member countries grant each other equal treatment. Thus, no country gives special trading advantages to another. All member countries are equal and share the benefits of any moves toward lower trade barriers. Exceptions to this basic rule are allowed in certain special circumstances involving regional trading arrangements, such as the European Union (EU) and the North American Free Trade Agreement (NAFTA). Special preferences are also granted to developing countries. The second basic principle is protection for domestic industry, which should be extended essentially through a tariff, not through other commercial measures. The aim of this rule is to make the extent of protection clear and to make competition possible.

The WTO provides a **Dispute Settlement Body (DSB)** to enable member countries to resolve trade disputes rather than engage in unilateral trade sanctions or a trade war. The DSB appoints panels to hear disputes concerning allegations of GATT agreement violations, and it adopts (or rejects) the panels' decisions. If a GATT agreement violation is found and not removed by the offending country, trade sanctions authorized by a panel may be imposed on that country in an amount equal to the economic injury caused by the violation.

(b) CISG   The *United Nations Convention on Contracts for the International Sale of Goods* (CISG or convention) sets forth uniform rules to govern international sales contracts. National law, however, is sometimes required to fill gaps in areas not covered by the CISG. The CISG became effective on January 1, 1988, between the United States and the 60 other nations that had approved it.[3] The provisions of the CISG have been strongly influenced by Article 2 of the UCC.

most-favored-nation clause clause in treaties between countries whereby any privilege subsequently granted to a third country in relation to a given treaty subject is extended to the other party to the treaty.

Dispute Settlement Body means, provided by the World Trade Organization, for member countries to resolve trade disputes rather than engage in unilateral trade sanctions or a trade war.

---

[2] Russia has applied to join the GATT and is in the final phase of accession to the World Trade Organization. However, to attain this goal, it is widely accepted that Russia will have to provide meaningful market access to member countries in goods and services and have a solid legal and administrative framework that will guarantee the implementation of contractual commitments.

[3] 52 Fed Reg 6262 (1987). As of October 2003, the contracting nations were Argentina, Australia, Austria, Belarus, Belgium, Bosnia and Herzegovina, Bulgaria, Byelorussian Republic, Canada, Chile, China, Cuba, Czech Republic, Denmark, Ecuador, Egypt, Estonia, Finland, France, Georgia, Germany, Greece, Guinea, Hungary, Iraq, Israel, Italy, Latavia, Lesotho, Lithuania, Luxembourg, Mexico, Moldavia, Mongolia, the Netherlands, New Zealand, Norway, Peru, Poland, Romania, Russian Federation, Singapore, Slovakia, Slovenia, Spain, Sweden, Switzerland, Syria, Uganda, Ukraine, United States, Uruguay, Uzbekistan, Venezuela, Yugoslavia, and Zambia. Ratification proceedings are presently under way in other countries.

However, as set forth in Chapter 23 on sales, several distinct differences exist between the convention and the UCC. Excluded from the coverage of the convention under Article 2 are the sale of goods for personal, family, or household uses and the sale of watercraft, aircraft, natural gas, or electricity; letters of credit; and auctions and securities.[4] The CISG is often viewed by foreign entities as a neutral body of law, the utilization of which can be a positive factor in successfully concluding negotiations of a contract. The parties to an international commercial contract may opt out of the convention. However, absent an express "opt-out provision," the CISG is controlling and preempts all state actions.

(c) UNCTAD   The *United Nations Conference on Trade and Development (UNCTAD)* represents the interests of the less developed countries. Its prime objective is the achievement of an international redistribution of income through trade. Through UNCTAD pressure, the developed countries agreed to a system of preferences, with quota limits, for manufactured imports from the developing countries.

(d) EU   The *European Economic Community* (EEC) was established in 1958 by the Treaty of Rome to remove trade and economic barriers between member countries and to unify their economic policies. It changed its name and became the *European Union* (EU) after the Treaty of Maastricht was ratified on November 1, 1993. The Treaty of Rome containing the governing principles of this regional trading group was signed by the original six nations of Belgium, France, West Germany, Italy, Luxembourg, and the Netherlands. Membership expanded by the entry of Denmark, Ireland, and Great Britain in 1973; Greece in 1981; Spain and Portugal in 1986; and Austria, Sweden, and Finland in 1995. Ten countries joined the EU in 2004: Cyprus, the Czech Republic, Estonia, Hungary, Latvia, Lithuania, Malta, Poland, Slovakia, and Slovenia. Bulgaria, Romania, Croatia, and Turkey expect to join in the coming years.

Four main institutions make up the formal structure of the EU. The first, the European Council, consists of the heads of state of the member countries. The council sets broad policy guidelines for the EU. The second, the European Commission, implements decisions of the council and initiates actions against individuals, companies, or member states that violate EU law. The third, the European Parliament, has an advisory legislative role with limited veto powers. The fourth, the European Court of Justice (ECJ) and the lower Court of First Instance make up the judicial arm of the EU. The courts of member states may refer cases involving questions on the EU treaty to these courts.

The Single European Act eliminated internal barriers to the free movement of goods, persons, services, and capital between EU countries. The Treaty on European Union, signed in Maastricht, Netherlands (the Maastricht Treaty), amended the Treaty of Rome with a focus on monetary and political union. It set goals for the EU of (1) single monetary and fiscal policies, (2) common foreign and security policies, and (3) cooperation in justice and home affairs.

(e) NAFTA   The *North American Free Trade Agreement* (NAFTA) is an agreement between Mexico, Canada, and the United States, effective January 1, 1994, that included Mexico in the arrangements previously initiated under the United States–Canada Free Trade Agreement of 1989. NAFTA eliminates all tariffs among the

---

[4] CISG art. 2(a)–(f).

E-COMMERCE AND CYBERLAW

Global Facilitation of Electronic Contracts and Transactions

Under the Electronic Signatures in Global and National Commerce Act of 2000 (E-Sign), the Secretary of Commerce is directed to promote the use of electronic signatures on an international basis by (1) removing paper-based obstacles to electronic transactions by adopting relevant principles from the Model Law on Electronic Commerce adopted in 1996 by the UN Commission on International Trade Law; (2) permitting parties to a transaction to choose their own appropriate authentication technologies; and (3) permitting these parties to prove in court or other proceedings that their authentication approaches and their transactions are valid.

three countries over a 15-year period. Side agreements exist to prevent the exploitation of Mexico's lower environmental and labor standards.

Products are qualified for NAFTA tariff preferences only if they originate in one or more of the three member countries.

CASE SUMMARY

A Reason to Assemble Cars in Mexico

FACTS: DaimlerChrysler assembles trucks in Mexico utilizing sheet metal components manufactured in the United States. The sheet metal is subject to painting in Mexico, consisting of primer coats followed by a color-treated coat and a clear coat, referred to as the top coats. After the assembly is completed, the trucks are shipped to and sold in the United States. The U.S. Customs Service believes the top coats are subject to duty payments. DaimlerChrysler asserts that the entire painting process is duty free. Subheading 9802.00.80 of the Harmonized Tariffs Schedule of the U.S. (HTSUS) provides duty-free treatment for:

> Articles . . . assembled abroad in whole or in part of fabricated components, the product of the United States, which (a) were exported in condition ready for assembly without further fabrication, (b) have not lost their physical identity in such articles by change in form, shape or otherwise, and (c) have not been advanced in value or improved in condition abroad except by being assembled and except by operations incidental to the assembly process such as cleaning, lubricating and *painting.* [emphasis added by the court]

From a judgment by the Court of International Trade in favor of the United States, DaimlerChrysler appealed.

DECISION: Judgment for DaimlerChrysler. Because subheading HTSUS 9802.00.80 unambiguously covers painting operations broadly, DaimlerChrysler's entire painting process, including the application of the top coats, qualifies for duty-free treatment. [**DaimlerChrysler Corp. v U.S., 361 F3d 1378 (Fed Cir 2004)**]

Documentation is required in a NAFTA *Certificate of Origin,* except for certain "low-value" items for which the statement of North American origin is recorded on an invoice. NAFTA ensures nondiscriminatory and open markets for a wide range of services and lowers barriers to U.S. investments in both Canada and Mexico.

Although NAFTA does not create a common labor market, as does the European Union, the agreement provides temporary access for businesspersons across borders.

(f) Regional Trading Groups of Developing Countries   In recent years, numerous trading arrangements between groups of developing countries have been established.

(g) IMF—World Bank   The *International Monetary Fund* (IMF) was created after World War II by a group of nations meeting in Bretton Woods, New Hampshire. The Articles of Agreement of the IMF state that its purpose is "to facilitate the expansion and balanced growth of international trade" and to "shorten the duration and lessen the disequilibrium in the international balance of payments of members." The IMF helps to achieve such purposes by administering a complex lending system. A country can borrow money from other IMF members or from the IMF by means of **special drawing rights (SDRs)** sufficient to permit that country to maintain the stability of its currency's relationship to other world currencies. The Bretton Woods conference also set up the *International Bank for Reconstruction and Development* (World Bank) to facilitate the lending of money by capital surplus countries—such as the United States—to countries needing economic help and wanting foreign investments after World War II.

(h) OPEC   The *Organization of Petroleum Exporting Countries* (OPEC) is a producer cartel or combination. One of its main goals was to raise the taxes and royalties earned from crude oil production. Another major goal was to take control over production and exploration from the major oil companies. Its early success in attaining these goals led other nations that export raw materials to form similar cartels. **For Example,** copper and bauxite-producing nations have formed cartels.

3. FORMS OF BUSINESS ORGANIZATIONS

The decision to participate in international business transactions and the extent of that participation depend on the financial position of the individual firm, production and marketing factors, and tax and legal considerations. There are a number of forms of business organizations for doing business abroad.

(a) Export Sales   A direct sale to customers in a foreign country is an **export sale**. A U.S. firm engaged in export selling is not present in the foreign country in such an arrangement. The export is subject to a tariff by the foreign country, but the exporting firm is not subject to local taxation by the importing country.

(b) Agency Requirements   A U.S. manufacturer may decide to make a limited entry into international business by appointing an agent to represent it in a foreign market. An **agent** is a person or firm with authority to make contracts on behalf of another—the **principal**. The agent will receive commission income for sales made on behalf of the U.S. principal. The appointment of a foreign agent commonly constitutes "doing business" in that country and subjects the U.S. firm to local taxation.

(c) Foreign Distributorships   A **distributor** takes title to goods and bears the financial and commercial risks for the subsequent sale. To avoid making a major financial investment, a U.S. firm may decide to appoint a foreign distributor.

---

special drawing rights (SDRs) rights that allow a country to borrow enough money from other International Money Fund (IMF) members to permit that country to maintain the stability of its currency's relationship to other world currencies.

export sale direct sale to customers in a foreign country.

agent person or firm who is authorized by the principal or by operation of law to make contracts with third persons on behalf of the principal.

principal person or firm who employs an agent; the person who, with respect to a surety, is primarily liable to the third person or creditor; property held in trust.

distributor entity that takes title to goods and bears the financial and commercial risks for the subsequent sale of the goods.

A U.S. firm may also appoint a foreign distributor to avoid managing a foreign operation with its complicated local business, legal, and labor conditions. Care is required in designing an exclusive distributorship for an EU country lest it would violate EU antitrust laws.

(d) Licensing U.S. firms may select licensing as a means of doing business in other countries. **Licensing** involves the transfer of technology rights in a product so that it may be produced by a different business organization in a foreign country in exchange for royalties and other payments as agreed. The technology being licensed may fall within the internationally recognized categories of patents, trademarks, and "know-how" (trade secrets and unpatented manufacturing processes outside the public domain). These intellectual property rights, which are legally protectable, may be licensed separately or incorporated into a single, comprehensive licensing contract. **Franchising,** which involves granting permission to use a trademark, trade name, or copyright under specified conditions, is a form of licensing that is now very common in international business.

licensing transfer of technology rights to a product so that it may be produced by a different business organization in a foreign country in exchange for royalties and other payments as agreed.

franchising granting of permission to use a trademark, trade name, or copyright under specified conditions; a form of licensing.

(e) Wholly Owned Subsidiaries A firm seeking to maintain control over its own operations, including the protection of its own technological expertise, may choose to do business abroad through a wholly owned subsidiary. In Europe the most common choice of foreign business organization, similar to the U.S. corporate form of business organization, is called the *société anonyme* (S.A.). In German-speaking countries, this form is called *Aktiengesellschaft* (A.G.). Small and medium-size companies in Europe now utilize a newly created form of business organization called the limited liability company (*Gesellschaft mit beschränkter Haftung,* or "GmbH" in Germany; *Società a responsabilità limitata,* or "S.r.l." in Spain). It is less complicated to form but is restrictive for accessing public capital markets.

A corporation doing business in more than one country poses many taxation problems for the governments in those countries where the firm does business. The United States has established tax treaties with many countries granting corporations relief from double taxation. Credit is normally given by the United States to U.S. corporations for taxes paid to foreign governments.

There is a potential for tax evasion by U.S. corporations from their selling goods to their overseas subsidiaries. Corporations could sell goods at less than the fair market value to avoid a U.S. tax on the full profit for such sales. By allowing the foreign subsidiaries located in countries with lower tax rates to make higher profits, a company as a whole would minimize its taxes. Section 482 of the Internal Revenue Code (IRC), however, allows the Internal Revenue Service (IRS) to reallocate the income between the parent and its foreign subsidiary. The parent corporation is insulated from such a reallocation if it can show, based on independent transactions with unrelated parties, that its charges were at arm's length.[5]

joint venture relationship in which two or more persons or firms combine their labor or property for a single undertaking and share profits and losses equally unless otherwise agreed.

(f) Joint Ventures A U.S. manufacturer and a foreign entity may form a **joint venture,** whereby the two firms agree to perform different functions for a common result. The responsibilities and liabilities of such operations are governed by contract. **For Example,** Hughes Aircraft Co. formed a joint venture with two Japanese firms, C. Itoh & Co. and Mitsui, and successfully bid on a telecommunications space satellite system for the Japanese government.

---

[5] *Bausch & Lomb Inc. v Commissioner*, 933 F2d 1084 (2d Cir 1991).

> ## CASE SUMMARY
>
> ### A Taxing Case
>
> **FACTS:** E. I. Du Pont de Nemours created a wholly owned Swiss marketing and sales subsidiary: Du Pont International S.A. (DISA). Most of the Du Pont chemical products marketed abroad were first sold to DISA, which then arranged for resale to the ultimate consumer through independent distributors. Du Pont's tax strategy was to sell the goods to DISA at prices below fair market value so that the greater part of the total corporate profit would be realized by DISA upon resale. DISA's profits would be taxed at a much lower level by Switzerland than Du Pont would be taxed in the United States. The IRS, however, under Section 482 of the IRC, reallocated a substantial part of DISA's income to Du Pont, increasing Du Pont's taxes by a considerable amount. Du Pont contended that the prices it charged DISA were valid under the IRC.
>
> **DECISION:** Judgment for the IRS. The reallocation of DISA's income to Du Pont was proper. Du Pont's prices to DISA were set wholly without regard to the factors that normally enter into the setting of intercorporate prices on an arm's-length basis. For example, there was no correlation of prices to cost. Du Pont set prices for the two years in question based solely on estimates of the greatest amount of profits that could be shifted without causing IRS intervention. [**E.I. Du Pont de Nemours & Co. v United States, 608 F 2d 445 (Ct Cl 1979)**]

China has two forms of joint ventures: a *contract joint venture,* which allows the parties to operate as separate entities governed by a contract, and an *equity joint venture* whereby each party owns a portion of the business. Such an arrangement is governed by the Chinese Foreign Equity Joint Venture Law. This law requires a Chinese limited liability company to be formed and requires the foreign participant to contribute at least 25 percent of the firm's capital.

GOVERNMENTAL REGULATION

Nations regulate trade to protect the economic interests of their citizens or to protect themselves in international relations and transactions.

4. EXPORT REGULATIONS

For reasons of national security, foreign policy, or short supply of certain domestic products, the United States controls the export of goods and technology. The Export Administration Act[6] imposes export controls on goods and technical data from the United States. Since April 2002, the Bureau of Industry and Security (BIS) of the Department of Commerce has issued Export Administration Regulations to enforce export controls.

Export Administration Regulations effective in 1996 simplify the process and enhance export trade by U.S. citizens.[7] The new regulations eliminate the former

---

[6] The Export Administration Act of 1979 expired in August 1994 and was extended by Executive Orders signed by Presidents Clinton and G. W. Bush. The EAA is now extended annually by presidential notice published in the *Federal Register.*

[7] Simplification of Export Regulations, 61 Fed Reg 12,714 (1996).

system of general and validated licenses under which every export required a license. Under the 1996 *Simplification Regulations,* no license is required unless the regulations affirmatively require a license. However, when no license is required, the exporter must fill out a Shipper's Export Declaration and attach it to the bill of lading for shipment with the goods being exported.

(a) Determining If a License Is Needed   To determine whether a product requires a BIS export license, the exporter should review the Commerce Control List (CCL) to see whether the product to be exported is listed. Listed products have Export Control Classification Numbers (ECCNs) that conform to those used by the EU. If a product is on the list, the ECCN code will provide the reason for control, such as national security, missile technology, nuclear nonproliferation, chemical and/or biological weapons, antiterrorism, crime control, short supply, or UN sanctions.[8] The exporter should then consult the Commerce Country Chart to *determine whether* a license is needed to send the product to its proposed destination. **For Example,** domestic crude petroleum products and western red cedar are on the Commerce Control List because of the "short supply" of these products. As a result, they are controlled to all destinations, and no reference to the Commerce Country Chart is necessary.

(b) Sanctions   Export licenses are required for the export of certain high-technology and military products. **For Example,** a company intending to ship "maraging 350 steel" to a user in Pakistan would find by checking the CCL and the ECCN code for the product that such steel is used in making high-technology products and has nuclear applications. Thus, an export license would be required. Because Pakistan is a nonsignatory nation of the Nuclear Non-Proliferation Treaty, the Department of Commerce would be expected to deny a license application for the use of this steel in a nuclear plant. However, a license to export this steel for the manufacture of high-speed turbines or compressors might be approved. The prospective purchaser must complete a "Statement of Ultimate Consignee and Purchaser" form with the application for an export license. The prospective purchaser must identify the "end use" for the steel and indicate where the purchaser is located and the location in Pakistan where a U.S. embassy official can make an on-site inspection of the product's use. Falsification of the information in the license application process is a criminal offense. Thus, if the exporter of maraging 350 steel asserted that it was to be used in manufacturing high-speed turbines when in fact the exporter knew it was being purchased for use in a nuclear facility, the exporter would be guilty of a criminal offense.[9]

Civil charges may also be brought against U.S. manufacturers who fail to obtain an export license for foreign sales of civilian items that contain any components that have military applications under the Arms Control Export Act. For example, between 2000 and 2003, Boeing Co. shipped overseas 94 commercial jets that carried a gyrochip used as a backup system in determining a plane's orientation in the air. This 2-ounce chip that cost less than $2,000 also has military applications

---

[8] *Id.*

[9] See *United States v Perez,* 871 F2d 310 (3d Cir 1989), on the criminal application of the Export Administration Regulations to an individual who stated a false end use for maraging 350 steel on his export application to ship this steel to Pakistan.

and can be used to stabilize and steer guided missiles. Boeing is asserted to have made false statements on shipping documents to get around the export restrictions. Boeing argued that the State Department is without legal authority to regulate its civilian rather than military items. However, Boeing agreed to pay a $15 million fine for the violations.[10]

freight forwarder one who contracts to have goods transported and, in turn, contracts with carriers for such transportation.

(c) Expert Assistance   The Department of Commerce's Exporter Assistance Staff provides assistance to exporters needing help in determining whether an export license is needed.[11] Licensed foreign-**freight forwarders** are in the business of handling the exporting of goods to foreign destinations. They are experts on U.S. Department of Commerce export license requirements. Licensed foreign-freight forwarders can attend to all of the essential arrangements required to transport a shipment of goods from the exporter's warehouse to the overseas buyer's specified port and inland destination. They are well versed in all aspects of ocean, air, and inland transportation as well as banking, marine insurance, and other services relating to exporting.

5. PROTECTION OF INTELLECTUAL PROPERTY RIGHTS

intellectual property rights trademark, copyright, and patent rights protected by law.

U.S. laws protect **intellectual property rights**, which consist of trademarks, copyrights, and patents.

(a) Counterfeit Goods   The importation of counterfeit compact discs, tapes, computer software, and movies into the United States violates U.S. copyright laws. Importing goods, such as athletic shoes, jeans, or watches, bearing counterfeits of U.S. companies' registered trademarks violates the Lanham Act. Importing machines or devices that infringe on U.S. patents violates U.S. patent laws. A full range of remedies is available to U.S. firms under U.S. laws. Possible remedies include injunctive relief, seizure and destruction of counterfeit goods that are found in the United States, damages, and attorney fees. U.S. firms injured by counterfeit trademarks may recover triple damages from the counterfeiters.[12]

Intellectual property rights are also protected by international treaties, such as the Berne Convention, which protects copyrights; the Patent Cooperation Treaty, and the Madrid System of International Registration of Marks (the Madrid Protocol), a treaty providing for the international registration of marks applicable to more than 60 signatory countries, including the United States as of November 2003.[13]

(b) Gray Market Goods   A U.S. trademark holder may license a foreign business to use its trademark overseas. If a third party imports these foreign-made goods into the United States to compete against the U.S. manufacturer's goods, the foreign-made goods are called **gray market goods**. The Tariff Act of 1930 prevents importation of foreign-made goods bearing a U.S. registered trademark owned by a

gray market goods foreign-made goods with U.S. trademarks brought into the United States by a third party without the consent of the trademark owners to compete with these owners.

---

[10] Associated Press, "Boeing to Pay $15 Million Fine for Export of Military Technology," *The Boston Globe*, April 10, 2006, E3.

[11] Exporter Assistance Staff, U.S. Department of Commerce, Washington, DC 20230.

[12] 15 USC § 1117(b); *Nintendo of America v NTDEC*, 822 F Supp 1462 (D Ariz 1993).

[13] The Agreement on Trade-Related Aspects of Intellectual Property (TRIPS) is a WTO agreement that requires WTO members to adhere to certain treaties and guidelines in respecting copyright, trademark, and patent rights. Enforcement of such rights, however, varies, depending on national law.

U.S. firm unless the U.S. trademark owner gives written consent.[14] The Lanham Act may also be used to exclude gray market goods.[15]

A gray market situation also arises when foreign products made by affiliates of U.S. companies have trademarks identical to U.S. trademarks but the foreign products are physically different from the U.S. products.

CASE SUMMARY

Barring Imported Soap!

FACTS: Lever Brothers (Lever U.S.) manufactures a soap under the trademark Shield and a dishwashing liquid under the trademark Sunlight for sale in the United States. A British affiliate, Lever U.K., also makes products using the marks Shield and Sunlight. Because of different tastes of U.S. and U.K. consumers, the products have physical differences. Third parties imported these U.K. products into the United States. The Lanham Act prohibits "copying or simulating a trademark." The U.S. Customs Service refused to bar these foreign products because a markholder cannot "copy or simulate" its own trademark. That is, Lever U.K. could not copy the marks of its affiliated company, Lever U.S. Lever U.S. sought an injunction against the U.S. Customs Service, requiring it to bar these foreign products.

DECISION: Judgment for Lever U.S. American consumers desiring to purchase Shield and Sunlight may end up with different products not suited to their tastes and needs if the U.K. products continue to be allowed into the United States. Because of the confusion and dissatisfaction, the importation of foreign goods that bear trademarks identical to valid U.S. trademarks but that are physically different, regardless of the affiliation of markholders, are prohibited from import under Section 42 of the Lanham Act. [**Lever Brothers Co. v United States, 796 F Supp 1 (DDC 1992)**]

6. ANTITRUST

Antitrust laws exist in the United States to protect the U.S. consumer by ensuring the benefits of competitive products from foreign competitors as well as domestic competitors. Competitors' agreements designed to raise the price of imports or to exclude imports from our domestic markets in exchange for not competing in other countries are restraints of trade in violation of our antitrust laws.[16]

The antitrust laws also exist to protect U.S. export and investment opportunities against privately imposed restrictions, whereby a group of competitors seeks to exclude another competitor from a particular foreign market. Antitrust laws exist in other countries where U.S. firms compete. These laws are usually directed not at breaking up cartels to further competition but at regulating the cartels in the national interest.

---

[14] 19 USC § 1526(1). The Copyright Act of 1976 may also apply to gray market goods. One provision of this act gives the copyright holder exclusive right to distribute copies of the copyrighted work. Still another section states that once a copyright owner sells an authorized copy of the work, subsequent owners may do what they like with it. The gray market issue occurs when U.S. manufacturers sell their products overseas at deep discounts, and other firms reimport the products back to the United States for resale. The Supreme Court held that a copyrighted label on the products would not protect a U.S. manufacturer's claim of unauthorized importation because the copyright owner's rights cease upon the original sale to the overseas buyer. *Quality King v L'Anza Research*, 118 S Ct 1125 (1998).

[15] *Bourdeau Bros. v International Trade Commission*, 444 F3d 1314 (Fed Cir 2006).

[16] *United States v Nippon Paper Industries Co. Ltd.*, 64 F Supp 2d 173 (1999).

effects doctrine doctrine that states that U.S. courts will assume jurisdiction and will apply antitrust laws to conduct outside of the United States when the activity of business firms has direct and substantial effect on U.S. commerce; the rule has been modified to require that the effect on U.S. commerce also be foreseeable.

jurisdictional rule of reason rule that balances the vital interests, including laws and policies, of the United States with those of a foreign country.

comity principle of international and national law that the laws of all nations and states deserve the respect legitimately demanded by equal participants.

act-of-state doctrine doctrine whereby every sovereign state is bound to respect the independence of every other sovereign state, and the courts of one country will not sit in judgment of another government's acts done within its own territory.

sovereign compliance doctrine doctrine that allows a defendant to raise as an affirmative defense to an antitrust action the fact that the defendant's actions were compelled by a foreign state.

sovereign immunity doctrine doctrine that states that a foreign sovereign generally cannot be sued unless an exception to the Foreign Sovereign Immunities Act of 1976 applies.

(a) JURISDICTION   In U.S. courts, the U.S. antitrust laws have a broad extraterritorial reach. Our antitrust laws must be reconciled with the rights of other interested countries as embodied in international law.

(1) The Effects Doctrine.   Judge Learned Hand's decision in *United States v Alcoa*[17] established the **effects doctrine**. Under this doctrine, U.S. courts assume jurisdiction and apply the antitrust laws to conduct outside of the United States where the activity of the business firms outside the United States has a direct and substantial effect on U.S. commerce. This basic rule has been modified to require that the effect on U.S. commerce also be foreseeable.

(2) The Jurisdictional Rule of Reason.   The jurisdictional rule of reason applies when conduct taking place outside the United States affects U.S. commerce but a foreign state also has a significant interest in regulating the conduct in question. The **jurisdictional rule of reason** balances the vital interests, including laws and policies, of the United States with those of the foreign country involved. This rule of reason is based on **comity,** a principle of international law, that means that the laws of all nations deserve the respect legitimately demanded by equal participants in international affairs.

(b) DEFENSES   Three defenses are commonly raised to the extraterritorial application of U.S. antitrust laws. These defenses are also commonly raised to attack jurisdiction in other legal actions involving international law.

(1) Act-of-State Doctrine.   By the **act-of-state doctrine**, every sovereign state is bound to respect the independence of every other sovereign state, and the courts of one country will not sit in judgment of another government's acts done within its own territory.[18] The act-of-state doctrine is based on the judiciary's concern over its possible interference with the conduct of foreign relations. Such matters are considered to be political, not judicial, questions.

(2) The Sovereign Compliance Doctrine.   The **sovereign compliance doctrine** allows a defendant to raise as an affirmative defense to an antitrust action the fact that the defendant's actions were compelled by a foreign state. To establish this defense, compulsion by the foreign government is required. The Japanese government uses informal and formal contacts within an industry to establish a consensus on a desired course of action. Such governmental action is not a defense for a U.S. firm, however, because the activity in question is not compulsory.

(3) The Sovereign Immunity Doctrine.   The **sovereign immunity doctrine** states that a foreign sovereign generally cannot be sued unless an exception to the Foreign Sovereign Immunities Act of 1976 applies.[19] The most important exception covers the commercial conduct of a foreign state.[20] **For Example,** receivers for various insurance companies brought suit against the Vatican City State, contending that the Vatican's conduct fell within the commercial activity exception

---

[17] 148 F2d 416 (2d Cir 1945).

[18] *Underhill v Hernandez,* 108 US 250, 252 (1897).

[19] See *Verlinden B.V. v Central Bank of Nigeria,* 461 US 574 (1983).

[20] See *Dole Food Co. v Patrickson,* 123 S Ct 1655 (2003), for a limited discussion of when a foreign state can assert a defense of sovereign immunity under the Foreign Sovereign Immunities Act of 1976 (FSIA). The FSIA allows certain foreign-state commercial entities not entitled to sovereign immunity to have the merits of a case heard in federal court. The U.S. Supreme Court held in the *Dole Food* case that a foreign state must itself own a majority of the shares of a corporation if the corporation is to be deemed an instrumentality of the state under the FSIA, and the instrumentality status is determined at the time of the filing of the complaint.

to the FSIA. Martin Frankel had engaged in a massive insurance fraud scheme, using front organizations to acquire and loot several insurance agencies. Masquerading as "David Rose," a philanthropist, he met Monsignor Emilio Cologiovani and convinced him to create a Vatican-affiliated entity, the St. Francis of Assisi Foundation (SFAF), which was used as part of Frankel's scam. The Court of Appeals held, however, that Cologiovani, acting with only apparent authority of the state, could not trigger the commercial activity doctrine.[21]

(c) LEGISLATION   In response to business uncertainty as to when the antitrust laws apply to international transactions, Congress passed the Foreign Trade Antitrust Improvements Act of 1982. This act, in essence, codified the effects doctrine. The act requires a direct, substantial, and reasonably foreseeable effect on U.S. domestic commerce or exports by U.S. residents before business conduct abroad may come within the purview of U.S. antitrust laws.[22]

(d) FOREIGN ANTITRUST LAWS   Attitudes in different countries vary toward cartels and business combinations. Because of this, antitrust laws vary in content and application. **For Example,** Japan has stressed consumer protection against such practices as price-fixing and false advertising. However, with regard to mergers, stock ownership, and agreements among companies to control production, Japanese law is much less restrictive than U.S. law.

Europe is a major market for U.S. products, services, and investments. U.S. firms doing business in Europe are subject to the competition laws of the EU.[23] The Treaty of Rome uses the term *competition* rather than *antitrust*. Articles 85 and 86 of the Treaty of Rome set forth the basic regulation on business behavior in the EU.[24] Article 85(1) expressly prohibits agreements and concerted practices that

1. even indirectly fix prices of purchases or sales or fix any other trading conditions;
2. limit or control production, markets, technical development, or investment;
3. share markets or sources of supply;
4. apply unequal terms to parties furnishing equivalent considerations, thereby placing one at a competitive disadvantage; or
5. make a contract's formation depend on the acceptance of certain additional obligations that, according to commercial usage, have no connection with the subject of such contracts.

Article 85(3) allows for an individual exemption if the agreement meets certain conditions, such as improving the production or distribution of goods, promoting technical or economic progress, and reserving to consumers a fair share of the resulting economic benefits.

Article 86 provides that it is unlawful for one or more enterprises having a dominant market position within at least a substantial part of the EU to take improper advantage of such a position if trade between the member states may be affected.

---

[21] *Dale v Cologiovani*, 443 F3d 425 (5th Cir 2006).

[22] PL 97-290, 96 Stat 1233, 15 USC § 6(a).

[23] The European Commission is the executive branch of the EU government and performs most of the EU's regulatory work. The Competition Commission oversees antitrust and mergers for the European Commission. New merger regulations took effect on May 1, 2004. The regulations require the Competition Commission to review proposed mergers and prohibit those mergers when the effects may "significantly impede effective competition" (called the *SIEC test*). The U.S. test prohibits mergers when the effect "may substantially lessen competition. . . ." 15 USC § 18 (2005). The wording of the EU and U.S. tests is relatively similar.

[24] See *Osakeyhtio v EEC Commission*, 1988 Common Mkt Rep (CCH) ¶ 14,491 for discussion of the extraterritorial reach of the European Commission.

7. SECURITIES REGULATION IN AN INTERNATIONAL ENVIRONMENT

Illegal conduct in the U.S. securities markets, whether this conduct is initiated in the United States or abroad, threatens the vital economic interests of the United States. Investigation and litigation concerning possible violations of the U.S. securities laws often have an extraterritorial effect. Conflicts with the laws of foreign countries may occur.

(a) JURISDICTION   U.S. district courts have jurisdiction over violations of the antifraud provisions of the Securities Exchange Act of 1934 when losses occur from sales to Americans living in the United States.[25] U.S. district courts also have jurisdiction when losses occur to Americans living abroad if the acts occurred in the United States. The antifraud provisions do not apply, however, to losses from sales of securities to foreigners outside the United States unless acts within the United States caused the losses.

secrecy laws confidentiality laws applied to home-country banks.

blocking laws laws that prohibit the disclosure, copying, inspection, or removal of documents located in the enacting country in compliance with orders from foreign authorities.

(b) IMPACT OF FOREIGN SECRECY LAWS IN SEC ENFORCEMENT   **Secrecy laws** are confidentiality laws applied to home-country banks. These laws prohibit the disclosure of business records or the identity of bank customers. **Blocking laws** prohibit the disclosure, copying, inspection, or removal of documents located in the enacting country in compliance with orders from foreign authorities. These laws impede, and sometimes foreclose, the SEC's ability to police its securities markets properly.

CASE SUMMARY

The Long Reach of the SEC

FACTS: Banca Della Suizzera Italiana (BSI), a Swiss bank with an office in the United States, purchased certain call options and common stock of St. Joe Minerals Corporation (St. Joe), a New York corporation, immediately prior to the announcement on March 11, 1981, of a cash tender offer by Joseph Seagram & Sons Inc. for all St. Joe common stock at $45 per share. On March 11, 1981, when BSI acted, the stock moved sharply higher in price. BSI instructed its broker to close out the purchases of the options and sell most of the shares of stock, resulting in an overnight profit of $2 million. The SEC noticed the undue activity in the options market and initiated suit against BSI. The SEC, through the Departments of State and Justice, and the Swiss government sought without success to learn the identity of BSI's customers involved in the transactions. The SEC believed that the customers had used inside information in violation of the Securities Exchange Act of 1934. The SEC brought a motion to compel disclosure. BSI objected on the ground that it might be subject to criminal liability under Swiss penal and banking laws if it disclosed the requested information.

DECISION: Judgment for the SEC. BSI made deliberate use of Swiss nondisclosure law to evade the strictures of U.S. securities law against insider trading. Whether acting solely as an agent or also as a principal (something that can be clarified only through disclosure of the requested information), BSI voluntarily engaged in transactions in U.S. securities markets and profited in some measure thereby. It cannot rely on Swiss nondisclosure law to shield this activity. [SEC v Banca Della Suizzera Italiana, 92 FRD 111 (SDNY 1981)]

---

[25] *Kauthar Sdn Bhd v Sternberg*, 149 F3d 659 (7th Cir 1998).

The SEC is not limited to litigation when a securities law enforcement investigation runs into secrecy or blocking laws. For example, the SEC may rely on the 1977 Treaty of Mutual Assistance in Criminal Matters between the United States and Switzerland.[26] Although this treaty has served to deter the use of Swiss secrecy laws to conceal fraud in the United States, its benefits for securities enforcement have been limited. It applies only where there is a dual criminality—that is, the conduct involved constitutes a criminal offense under the laws of both the United States and Switzerland.

---

8. BARRIERS TO TRADE

The most common barrier to the free movement of goods across borders is a tariff. A wide range of nontariff barriers also restricts the free movement of goods, services, and investments. Government export controls used as elements of foreign policy have proven to be a major barrier to trade with certain countries.

tariff (1) domestically—government-approved schedule of charges that may be made by a regulated business, such as a common carrier or warehouser; (2) internationally—tax imposed by a country on goods crossing its borders, without regard to whether the purpose is to raise revenue or to discourage the traffic in the taxed goods.

(a) Tariff Barriers   A **tariff** is an import or export duty or tax placed on goods as they move into or out of a country. It is the most common method used by countries to restrict foreign imports. The tariff raises the total cost, and thus the price, of an imported product in the domestic market. Thus, the price of a domestically produced product not subject to the tariff is more advantageous.

The U.S. Customs Service imposes tariffs on imported goods at the port of entry. The merchandise is classified under a tariff schedule, which lists each type of merchandise and the corresponding duty rate (or percentage). The Customs Service also determines the "computed value" of the imported goods under very precise statutory formulas.[27] The total amount of the duty is calculated by applying the duty percentage to the computed value figure.[28]

CASE SUMMARY

Customs Crunch!

FACTS: Frito-Lay, Inc., owns a Mexican affiliate, Sabritas, S.A. de C.V., and it imports taco shells and *Munchos* potato chips from Mexico to the United States. The U.S. Customs Service classified these products as "other bakers' wares" under Section 1905.90.90 of the Tariff Schedule subject to a 10 percent duty rate. Frito-Lay contends before the Court of International Trade that the import of taco shells is properly classified as "bread," which carries duty-free status. It also contends that *Munchos* are properly classified as potato chips and entitled to duty-free treatment.

DECISION: Classification disputes are resolved by (1) ascertaining the proper meaning of the specified terms in the tariff provision; and (2) determining whether the article comes within the meaning of the terms as properly construed. The term "bread" is not specifically defined in the tariff provision or in the legislative history. Customs' food expert,

---

[26] 27 UST 2021.

[27] See Tariff Act of 1930, as amended, 19 USC § 1401a(e).

[28] It is common for importers to utilize customs brokers who research the tariff schedules to see whether a product fits unambiguously under one of the Customs Service's classifications. A broker will also research the classifications given to similar products. It may find that a fax switch may be classified as "other telephonic switching apparatus" at a tariff rate of 8.5 percent or "other telegraphic switching apparatus" with a tariff of 4.7 percent. Obviously, the importer desires to pay the lower rate, and the broker with the assistance of counsel will make a recommendation to the Customs Service for the lower rate, and Customs will make a ruling. The decisions of the Customs Service are published in the *Customs Bulletin*, the official weekly publication of the Customs Service. See *Command Communications v Fritz Cos.*, 36 P3d 182 (Colo App 2001).

CASE SUMMARY

continued

Dr. Pintauro, explained the leavening, loaf forming, and baking process of dough in his definition of bread. Such a narrow definition, however, ignores the reality that flat, fried, usually ethnic breads exist in the U.S. market and are generally accepted forms of bread. Therefore, hard, corn-based taco shells are properly classified as bread under the tariff provisions and are duty-free. *Munchos,* however, are composed of cornmeal, dehydrated potato flakes, and potato starch, while potato chips are produced entirely from sliced raw whole potatoes. As such, Customs properly classified the plaintiffs' *Munchos.* **[Sabritas v United States, 998 F Supp 1123 (Ct Int'l Trade 1998)]**

(b) NONTARIFF BARRIERS   Nontariff barriers consist of a wide range of restrictions that inhibit the free movement of goods between countries. An import quota, such as a limitation on the number of automobiles that can be imported into one country from another, is such a barrier. More subtle nontariff barriers exist in all countries. **For Example,** Japan's complex customs procedures resulted in the restriction of the sale of U.S.-made aluminum baseball bats in Japan. The customs procedures required the individual uncrating and "destruction testing" of bats at the ports of entry. Government subsidies are also nontariff barriers to trade.

One U.S. law—the Turtle Law—prohibits the importation of shrimp from countries that allow the harvesting of shrimp with commercial fishing technology that could adversely affect endangered sea turtles. **For Example,** two U.S. importers sought an exemption from the embargo, representing that their Brazilian supply of shrimp was caught in the wild by vessels using turtle excluder devices (TEDs). Because Brazil had failed to comply with the U.S. Turtle Law by requiring TEDs on its commercial shrimp fleet, even though it had seven years to do so, the exemption was not granted.[29]

(c) EXPORT CONTROLS AS INSTRUMENTS OF FOREIGN POLICY   U.S. export controls have been used as instruments of foreign policy in recent years. **For Example,** the United States has sought to deny goods and technology of strategic or military importance to unfriendly nations. The United States has also denied goods such as grain, technology, and machine parts, to certain countries to protest or to punish activities considered violative of human rights or world peace.

9. RELIEF MECHANISMS FOR ECONOMIC INJURY CAUSED BY FOREIGN TRADE

Certain U.S. industries may suffer severe economic injury because of foreign competition. U.S. law provides protection against unfair competition from foreigners' goods and provides economic relief for U.S. industries, communities, firms, and workers adversely affected by import competition. U.S. law also provides certain indirect relief for U.S. exporters and producers who encounter unfair foreign import restrictions.

dumping selling goods in another country at less than their fair value.

(a) ANTIDUMPING LAWS AND EXPORT SUBSIDIES   Selling goods in another country at less than their fair value is called **dumping.** The dumping of foreign goods in the

---

[29] *Earth Island Institute v Christopher,* 948 F Supp 1062 (Ct Int'l Trade 1996). See *Turtle Island Restoration Network v Evans,* 284 F3d 1282 (Fed Cir 2002), on the continuing litigation on this topic and the clash between statutory enforcement and political and diplomatic considerations.

United States is prohibited under the Tariff Act of 1930, as amended including the antidumping laws contained in the Uraguay Round Agreement Act of 1994.[30] Proceedings in antidumping cases are conducted by two federal agencies, which separately examine two distinct components. The International Trade Administration (ITA) of the Department of Commerce investigates whether specified foreign goods are being sold in the United States at less than fair value (LTFV). The International Trade Commission (ITC) conducts proceedings to determine if there is an injury to a domestic industry as a result of such sales. Findings of both LTFV sales and injury must be present before remedial action is taken. Remedial action might include the addition of duties to reflect the difference between the fair value of the goods and the price being charged in the United States. ITA and ITC decisions may be appealed to the Court of International Trade. Decisions of this court are reviewable by the U.S. Court of Appeals for the Federal Circuit and then the U.S. Supreme Court.

A settlement of the matter may be reached through a suspension agreement, whereby prices are revised to eliminate any LTFV sales and other corrective measures are taken.

The 1979 act also applies to subsidy practices by foreign countries. If subsidized goods are sold in the United States at less than their fair value, the goods may be subject to a countervailing duty.

Canada and Mexico may appeal countervailing duty assessments by the United States to an arbitration panel established under NAFTA. The NAFTA panel, however, can determine only whether the U.S. determinations were made in accordance with U.S. law. An appeal can also be made by member states to the WTO Dispute Settlement Body, which can determine whether the United States breached its obligations under the WTO.

A dispute between the United States and Canada over government subsidies to the Canadian softwood lumber industry and the dumping of softwood lumber products on the U.S. market at less than fair value is outlined in Figure 7-1.

(b) RELIEF FROM IMPORT INJURIES   Title II of the Trade Act of 1974[31] provides relief for U.S. industries, communities, firms, and workers when any one or more of them are substantially adversely affected by import competition. The Department of Commerce, the secretary of labor, and the president have roles in determining eligibility. The relief provided may be temporary import relief through the imposition of a duty or quota on the foreign goods. Workers, if eligible, may obtain readjustment allowances, job training, job search allowances, or unemployment compensation.

For Example, trade adjustment assistance, including unemployment compensation and training and relocation allowances, was provided for former employees of Johnson Controls Battery Group plants in Garland, Texas; Bennington, Vermont; and Owosso, Michigan; because surveys of the customers of those plants by the Department of Labor indicated that increased imports of aftermarket batteries, the products produced at these closed plants, caused the shutdowns. Former workers of the closed Louisville battery plant were not provided assistance because this plant

---

[30] 19 USC § 1675b (2000). See *Allegheny Ludlum Corp. v United States,* 287 F3d 1365 (Fed Cir 2002).

[31] PL 93-618, 88 Stat 1978, 19 USC §§ 2251, 2298.

| FIGURE 7-1 | *Countervailing Duty and Antidumping Proceedings* |

Phase 1: International Trade Administration (ITA)

Date	Event
April 2, 2001	Following the expiration of a softwood lumber agreement in 2001, the U.S. lumber industry files a countervailing duty petition alleging Canadian government subsidies and an antidumping petition to the ITA.
April–July 2001	ITA investigates whether lumber exports from Canada are subsidized and whether they are being sold at less than fair value (LTFV).
August 9, 2001	ITA issues its preliminary determination that Canadian softwood lumber exports to the U.S. are subsidized at 19.31%.
April 25, 2002	ITA issues its final subsidy determinations in both the antidumping (AD) and countervailing duty (CVD) cases. The final subsidy rate is set at 18.79% and the average dumping rate is set at 8.43% for a combined CVD/AD rate of 27.22%.

Phase 2: International Trade Commission (ITC)

May 16, 2001	ITC issues preliminary determination that subsidies pose a threat to U.S. industry.
May 2, 2002	ITC determines that U.S. lumber firms are suffering injury due to dumping and subsidies.
May 22, 2002	U.S. Customs begins collecting duties on Canadian softwood lumber imports.

Phase 3: Dispute Settlement Procedures Progress through NAFTA, the WTO, and the U.S. Court of International Trade

August 13, 2003	NAFTA panel rules that Canadian lumber industry is subsidized but the 18.79% tariff is too high. It orders a review by U.S. Commerce Department (ITA).
January 10, 2005	Proceedings initiated in the U.S. Court of International Trade challenging the CVD/AD duties.
August 10, 2005	NAFTA panel dismisses U.S. claims that Canadian softwood exports are subsidized. U.S. disagrees.
March, 2006	A NAFTA panel again rules in Canada's favor. At this point, the total duties collected by the U.S. Customs Service is $5.2 billion.
April, 2006	A WTO appellate body rejects Canada's request to overturn the ITC's May 22, 2002, rulings.

Phase 4: Resolution by a Negotiated Agreement

April 26, 2006	The trade representatives for both the United States and Canada reach agreement on a seven-year pact to end the dispute. The United States will return 80% of the $5 billion in tariffs it has collected. Canada-sourced lumber will be kept at its current 34% share of the U.S. softwood market, and Canada will collect an export tax on softwood lumber if the price drops below $355 per a thousand board feet.

produced new car batteries, and the work was shifted to another Johnson Controls plant in the United States.[32]

(c) RETALIATION AND RELIEF AGAINST FOREIGN UNFAIR TRADE RESTRICTIONS   U.S. exporters of agricultural or manufactured goods or of services may encounter unreasonable, unjustifiable, or discriminatory foreign import restrictions. At the same time, producers from the foreign country involved may be benefiting from trade agreement concessions that allow producers from that country access to U.S. markets. Prior trade acts and the Omnibus Trade and Competitiveness Act of 1988[33] contain broad authority to retaliate against "unreasonable," "unjustifiable," or "discriminatory" acts by a foreign country. The authority to retaliate is commonly referred to as "Section 301 authority." The fear or actuality of the economic sting of Section 301 retaliation often leads offending foreign countries to open their markets to imports. Thus, indirect relief is provided to domestic producers and exporters adversely affected by foreign unfair trade practices.

Enforcement of the act is entrusted to the U.S. trade representative (USTR), who is appointed by the president. Under the 1988 act, mandatory retaliatory action is required if the USTR determines that (1) rights of the United States under a trade agreement are being denied or (2) actions or policies of a foreign country are unjustifiable and a burden or restrict U.S. commerce. The overall thrust of the trade provisions of the 1988 act is to open markets and liberalize trade.

10. EXPROPRIATION

A major concern of U.S. businesses that do business abroad is the risk of expropriation of assets by a host government. Firms involved in the extraction of natural resources, banking, communications, or defense-related industries are particularly susceptible to nationalization. Multinational corporations commonly have a staff of full-time political scientists and former Foreign Service officers studying the countries relevant to their operations to monitor and calculate risks of expropriation. Takeovers of U.S.-owned businesses by foreign countries may be motivated by a short-term domestic political advantage or the desire to demonstrate political clout in world politics. Takeovers may also be motivated by long-term considerations associated with planned development of the country's economy.

Treaty commitments, or provisions in other international agreements between the United States and the host country, may serve to narrow expropriation uncertainties. Treaties commonly contain provisions whereby property will not be expropriated except for public benefit and with the prompt payment of just compensation.

One practical way to mitigate the risk of investment loss as a result of foreign expropriation is to purchase insurance through private companies, such as Lloyd's of London. Commercial insurance is also available against such risks as host governments' arbitrary recall of letters of credit and commercial losses resulting from embargoes.

---

[32] 20 F Supp 2d 1288 (Ct Int'l Trade 1998). See also *Former Employees of Merrill Corp. v U.S.*, 387 F Supp2d 1336 (Ct Int'l Trade 2005).
[33] PL 100-418, 102 Stat 1346, 15 USC § 4727.

The Overseas Private Investment Corporation (OPIC) is a U.S. agency under the policy control of the secretary of state. OPIC supports private investments in less developed, friendly countries. OPIC also offers asset protection insurance against risk of loss to plant and equipment as well as loss of deposits in overseas bank accounts to companies that qualify on the basis of the involvement of a "substantial U.S. interest."

11. GOVERNMENT-ASSISTED EXPORT PROGRAMS

The U.S. government has taken legislative action to increase the foreign sales of U.S. firms.

(a) EXPORT TRADING COMPANY ACT   The Export Trading Company Act (ETCA) of 1982[34] is designed to stimulate and promote additional U.S. exports. The ETCA promotes the formation of U.S.-based export trading companies and allows banks to invest in these export trading companies. The ETCA also clarifies applicable antitrust restrictions and provides a limited exception from antitrust liability.

(b) FOREIGN SALES CORPORATIONS   The Foreign Sales Corporation Act of 1984, Title VIII of the Tax Reform Act of 1984,[35] provides export incentives for U.S. firms that form foreign sales corporations (FSCs). To qualify for the tax incentives provided under the 1984 act, an FSC subsidiary of a U.S. firm must be organized under the laws of a U.S. possession (such as the Virgin Islands or Guam, but not Puerto Rico) or under the laws of a foreign country with an income tax treaty with the United States containing an exchange-of-information program. The FSC must satisfy certain other organizational requirements to be eligible for the tax incentives provided by the law.

(c) UNITED STATES EXPORT-IMPORT BANK (EXIMBANK)   EXIMBANK is wholly owned by the U.S. government. Its primary purpose is to facilitate U.S. exports by making direct loans in the form of dollar credits to foreign importers for the purchase of U.S. goods and services. Payments are then made directly to the U.S. exporter of goods and services. Such loans are made when private financial sources are unwilling to assume the political and economic risks that exist in the country in question. Loans are also made by EXIMBANK to enable U.S. suppliers of goods and services to compete for major foreign contracts with foreign firms that have government-subsidized export financing.

(d) OTHER PROGRAMS   As stated previously, OPIC provides expropriation insurance for U.S. private investments in friendly, less developed countries. The Commodity Credit Corporation (CCC) provides financing for agricultural exports. In addition, the Small Business Administration has an export loan program.

12. THE FOREIGN CORRUPT PRACTICES ACT

There are restrictions on U.S. firms doing business abroad that disallow payments to foreign government officials for getting business from their governments. The Foreign Corrupt Practices Act of 1977 requires strict accounting standards and internal

---

[34] PL 97-290, 96 Stat 1233, 15 USC § 4001.
[35] Title VIII of the Tax Reform Act of 1984, PL 98-369, 98 Stat 678. See IRC §§ 921–927.

CASE SUMMARY

You Just Can't Do That!

FACTS: Harry Carpenter, CEO of Kirkpatrick Company, agreed to pay Nigerian government officials a "commission" equal to 20 percent of the contract price if Kirkpatrick obtained the contract to build an aeromedical center in Nigeria. Kirkpatrick was awarded the contract, and the "commission" was paid to the Nigerian officials. A competitor for the project, ETC, International (ETC), learned of the "20 percent commission" and informed U.S. officials. Kirkpatrick and Carpenter pleaded guilty to violations of the Foreign Corrupt Practices Act by paying bribes to get the Nigerian contract. ETC then brought this civil action against Kirkpatrick, Carpenter, and others for damages under the Racketeer Influenced and Corrupt Organizations Act (RICO) and the New Jersey Antiracketeering Act. The district court ruled the suit was barred by the act-of-state doctrine, the court of appeals reversed, and the U.S. Supreme Court granted certiorari.

DECISION: Judgment for ETC. The act-of-state doctrine does not establish an exception for cases that may embarrass foreign governments. The doctrine merely requires that, in the process of deciding cases, the acts of foreign governments, taken in their own jurisdictions, shall be deemed valid. The doctrine has no application to the present case: The validity of a foreign sovereign act is not at issue because the payment and receipt of bribes are prohibited by Nigerian law. [**Kirkpatrick v ETC, International, 493 US 400 (1990)**]

LAWFLIX

The In-Laws (1979) (PG)

Review the segment in the film in which money is paid by a dictator for the sale of U.S. currency plates. The dictator's plan is to create worldwide inflation. List the various laws and conventions Peter Falk and Alan Arkin violate through their sale of the plates.

For movie clips that illustrate business law concepts, see LawFlix at **http://wdvl.westbuslaw.com.**

control procedures to prevent the hiding of improper payments to foreign officials. The act prohibits any offers, payments, or gifts to foreign officials—or third parties who might have influence with foreign officials—to influence a decision on behalf of the firm making the payment. It provides for sanctions of up to $1 million against the company and fines and imprisonment for the employees involved. Moreover, the individuals involved may be responsible for damages as a result of civil actions brought by competitors under federal and state antiracketeering acts.[36]

The act does not apply to payments made to low-level officials for expediting the performance of routine government services.

---

[36] PL 95-213, 94 Stat 1494, 15 USC § 78a nt.

> SUMMARY

The General Agreement on Tariffs and Trade, a multilateral treaty subscribed to by the United States and most of the industrialized countries of the world, is based on the principle of trade without discrimination. The United Nations Convention on Contracts for the International Sale of Goods provides uniform rules for international sales contracts between parties in contracting nations. The European Union is a regional trading group that includes most of western Europe. The North American Free Trade Agreement involves Mexico, Canada, and the United States and eliminates all tariffs between the three countries over a 15-year period.

U.S. firms may choose to do business abroad by making export sales or contracting with a foreign distributor to take title to their goods and sell them abroad. U.S. firms may also license their technology or trademarks for foreign use. An agency arrangement or the organization of a foreign subsidiary may be required to participate effectively in foreign markets. This results in subjecting the U.S. firm to taxation in the host country.

However, tax treaties commonly eliminate double taxation. The Export Administration Act is the principal statute imposing export controls on goods and technical data.

In choosing the form for doing business abroad, U.S. firms must be careful not to violate the antitrust laws of host countries. Anticompetitive foreign transactions may have an adverse impact on competition in U.S. domestic markets. U.S. antitrust laws have a broad extraterritorial reach. U.S. courts apply a "jurisdictional rule of reason," weighing the interests of the United States against the interests of the foreign country involved in making a decision on whether to hear a case. Illegal conduct may occur in U.S. securities markets. U.S. enforcement efforts sometimes run into foreign countries' secrecy and blocking laws that hinder effective enforcement.

Antidumping laws offer relief for domestic firms threatened by unfair foreign competition. In addition, economic programs exist to assist industries, communities, and workers injured by import competition. Programs also exist to increase the foreign sales of U.S. firms.

> QUESTIONS AND CASE PROBLEMS

1. How does the most-favored-nation clause of the GATT work to foster the principle of trade without discrimination?

2. How does the selling of subsidized foreign goods in the United States adversely affect free trade?

3. PepsiCo has registered its PEPSI trademarks in the U.S. Patent and Trademark Office. PEPSI products are bottled and distributed in the United States by PepsiCo and by authorized bottlers pursuant to Exclusive Bottling Appointment agreements, which authorize local bottlers to bottle and distribute PEPSI products in their respective territories. Similarly, PepsiCo has appointed local bottlers to bottle and distribute PEPSI products in Mexico within particular territories. Pacific Produce, Ltd., has been engaged in the sale and distribution within the United States and Nevada of PEPSI products that were manufactured and bottled in Mexico and intended for sale in Mexico ("Mexican product"). The Mexican product sold by Pacific Products in the United States has certain material differences from domestic PEPSI products sold by PepsiCo: (1) it contains inferior paper labels that improperly report nutritional information; (2) it does not comply with the labeling standards followed by PepsiCo in the United States; (3) it is sold in channels of trade different from PepsiCo's authorized distribution channels without "drink by" notice dates on the Mexican product and monitoring on the Mexican product for proper shipment and storage conditions; and (4) it conflicts with the bottle return policies of PepsiCo. The Mexican product with its "Marca Reg" and Spanish language bottle caps is well received by consumers in Pacific Produce distribution channels. Classify the goods being sold by Pacific Produce. State the applicable law governing a dispute between PepsiCo and Pacific Produce. How would you decide this case? [*PepsiCo, Inc. v Pacific Produce, Ltd.,* 2001 US Dist LEXIS 12085]

4. Ronald Sadler, a California resident, owned a helicopter distribution company in West Germany, Delta Avia. This company distributed U.S.-made Hughes civilian helicopters in western Europe. Sadler's German firm purchased 85 helicopters from Hughes Aircraft Co. After export licenses were obtained in reliance on the purchaser's written assurance that the goods would not be disposed of contrary to the export license, the helicopters were exported to Germany for resale in western Europe. Thereafter, Delta Avia exported them to North Korea, which was a country subject to a trade embargo by the United States. The helicopters were converted to military use. Sadler was charged with violating the Export Administration Regulations. In Sadler's defense, it was contended that the U.S. regulations have no effect on what occurs in the resale of civilian helicopters in another sovereign country. Decide.

5. Mirage Investments Corp. (MIC) planned a tender offer for the shares of Gulf States International Corp. (GSIC). Archer, an officer of MIC, placed purchase orders for GSIC stock through the New York office of the Bahamian Bank (BB) prior to the announcement of the tender offer, making a $300,000 profit when the tender offer was made public. The Bahamas is a secrecy jurisdiction. The bank informed the SEC that under its law, it could not disclose the name of the person for whom it purchased the stock. What, if anything, may the SEC do to discover whether the federal securities laws have been violated?

6. United Overseas, Ltd. (UOL), is a U.K. firm that purchases and sells manufacturers' closeouts in Europe and the Middle East. UOL's representative, Jay Knox, used stationery listing a UOL office in New York to solicit business from Revlon, Inc., in New York. On April 1, 1992, UOL faxed a purchase order from its headquarters in England to Revlon's New York offices for the purchase of $4 million worth of shampoo. The purchase order on its face listed six conditions, none of which referred to a forum selection clause. When Revlon was not paid for the shampoo it shipped, it sued UOL in New York for breach of contract. UOL moved to dismiss the complaint because of a forum selection clause, which it stated was on the reverse side of the purchase order and provided that "the parties hereby agree to submit to the jurisdiction of the English Courts disputes arising out of the contract." The evidence did not show that the reverse side of the purchase order had been faxed with the April 1992 order. Should the court dismiss the complaint based on the "forum selection clause"? Read Chapter 32 on letters of credit and advise Revlon how to avoid similar litigation in the future. [*Revlon, Inc. v United Overseas, Ltd.,* 1994 WL 9657 (SDNY)]

7. Reebok manufactures and sells fashionable athletic shoes in the United States and abroad. It owns the federally registered Reebok trademark and has registered this trademark in Mexico as well. Nathan Betech is a Mexican citizen residing in San Diego, California, with business offices there. Reebok believed that Betech was in the business of selling counterfeit Reebok shoes in Mexican border towns, such as Tijuana, Mexico. It sought an injunction in a federal district court in California ordering Betech to cease his counterfeiting activity and to refrain from destroying certain documents. It also asked the court to freeze Betech's assets pending the outcome of a Lanham Act lawsuit. Betech contended that a U.S. district court has no jurisdiction or authority to enter the injunction for the activities allegedly occurring in Mexico. Decide. [*Reebok Int'l, Ltd. v Marnatech Enterprises, Inc.,* 970 F2d 552 (9th Cir)]

8. Assume that before the formation of the European Union, the lowest-cost source of supply for a certain product consumed in France was the United States. Explain the basis by which, after the EU was formed, higher-cost German producers could have replaced the U.S. producers as the source of supply.

9. A complaint was filed with the U.S. Commerce Department's ITA by U.S. telephone manufacturers AT&T, Comidial Corp., and Eagle Telephones, Inc., alleging that 12 Asian manufacturers of small business telephones, including the Japanese firms Hitachi, NEC, and Toshiba and the Taiwanese firm Sun Moon Star Corp., were dumping their small business phones in the U.S. market at prices that were from 6 percent to 283 percent less than those in their home

markets. The U.S. manufacturers showed that the domestic industry's market share had dropped from 54 percent in 1985 to 33 percent in 1989. They asserted that it was doubtful if the domestic industry could survive the dumping. Later, in a hearing before the ITC, the Japanese and Taiwanese respondents contended that their domestic industry was basically sound and that the U.S. firms simply had to become more efficient to meet worldwide competition. They contended that the United States was using the procedures before the ITA and ITC as a nontariff barrier to imports. How should the ITC decide the case? [*American Telephone and Telegraph Co. v Hitachi,* 6 ITC 1511]

10. Campbell Soup Co. imports tomato paste from a wholly owned Mexican subsidiary, Sinalopasta, S.A. de C.V. It deducted $416,324 from the computed value of goods shipped to the United States, which was the cost of transportation of the finished tomato paste from Sinalopasta's loading dock in Mexico to the U.S. border. The deduction thus lowered the computed value of the goods and the amount of duty to be paid the U.S. government by Campbell Soup Co. United States Customs questioned this treatment of freight costs. Tariff Act § 140a(e)(1)(B) requires that profits and general expenses be included in calculating the computed value of goods, which in part quantify the value of the merchandise in the country of production. Is Campbell's position correct? [*Campbell Soup Co., Inc. v United States,* 107 F3d 1556 (Fed Cir)]

11. Roland Staemphfli was employed as the chief financial officer of Honeywell Bull, S.A. (HB), a Swiss computer company operating exclusively in Switzerland. Staemphfli purportedly arranged financing for HB in Switzerland through the issuance of promissory notes. He had the assistance of Fidenas, a Bahamian company dealing in commercial paper. Unknown to Fidenas, the HB notes were fraudulent. The notes were prepared and forged by Staemphfli, who lost all of the proceeds in a speculative investment and was convicted of criminal fraud. HB denied responsibility for the fraudulently issued notes when they came due. Fidenas's business deteriorated because of its involvement with the HB notes. It sued HB and others in the United States

for violations of U.S. securities laws. HB defended, arguing that the U.S. court did not have jurisdiction over the transactions in question. Decide. [*Fidenas v Honeywell Bull, S.A.,* 606 F2d 5 (2d Cir)]

12. Marc Rich & Co., A.G., a Swiss commodities trading corporation, refused to comply with a grand jury subpoena requesting certain business records maintained in Switzerland and relating to crude oil transactions and possible violations of U.S. income tax laws. Marc Rich contended that a U.S. court has no authority to require a foreign corporation to deliver to a U.S. court documents located abroad. The court disagreed and imposed fines, froze assets, and threatened to close a Marc Rich wholly owned subsidiary that did business in the state of New York. The fines amounted to $50,000 for each day the company failed to comply with the court's order. Marc Rich appealed. Decide. [*Marc Rich v United States,* 707 F2d 633 (2d Cir)]

13. U.S. Steel Corp. formed Orinoco Mining Co., a wholly owned corporation, to mine large deposits of iron ore that U.S. Steel had discovered in Venezuela. Orinoco, which was incorporated in Delaware, was subject to Venezuela's maximum tax of 50 percent on net income. Orinoco was also subject to U.S. income tax, but the U.S. foreign tax credit offset this amount. U.S. Steel purchased the ore from Orinoco in Venezuela. U.S. Steel formed Navios, Inc., a wholly owned subsidiary, to transport the ore. Navios, a Liberian corporation, was subject to a 2.5 percent Venezuelan excise tax and was exempt from U.S. income tax. Although U.S. Steel was Navios's primary customer, it charged other customers the same price it charged U.S. Steel. U.S. Steel's investment in Navios was $50,000. In seven years, Navios accumulated nearly $80 million in cash but had not paid any dividends to U.S. Steel. The IRS used IRC § 482 to allocate $52 million of Navios's income to U.S. Steel. U.S. Steel challenged this action, contending Navios's charges to U.S. Steel were at arm's length and the same it charged other customers. Decide. [*United States Steel Corp. v Commissioner,* 617 F2d 942 (2d Cir)]

14. National Computers, Inc., a U.S. firm, entered into a joint venture with a Chinese computer

manufacturing organization, TEC. A dispute arose over payments due the U.S. firm under the joint venture agreement with TEC. The agreement called for disputes to be arbitrated in China, with the arbitrator being chosen from a panel of arbitrators maintained by the Beijing arbitration institution, Cietac. What advantages and disadvantages exist for the U.S. firm under this arbitration arrangement? Advise the U.S. firm on negotiating future arbitration agreements with Chinese businesses.

15. Sensor, a Netherlands business organization wholly owned by Geosource, Inc., of Houston, Texas, made a contract with C.E.P. to deliver 2,400 strings of geophones to Rotterdam by September 20, 1982. The ultimate destination was identified as the USSR. Thereafter, in June 1982, the president of the United States prohibited shipment to the USSR of equipment manufactured in foreign countries under license from U.S. firms. The president had a foreign policy objective of retaliating for the imposition of martial law in Poland, and he was acting under regulations issued under the Export Administration Act of 1979. Sensor, in July and August of 1982, notified C.E.P. that as a subsidiary of a U.S. corporation, it had to respect the president's embargo. C.E.P. filed suit in a district court of the Netherlands asking that Sensor be ordered to deliver the geophones. Decide. [*Compagnie Européenne des Pétroles v Sensor Nederland*, 22 ILM 66]

CRIMES

 GENERAL PRINCIPLES
1. NATURE AND CLASSIFICATION OF CRIMES
2. BASIS OF CRIMINAL LIABILITY
3. RESPONSIBILITY FOR CRIMINAL ACTS
4. INDEMNIFICATION OF CRIME VICTIMS

B WHITE-COLLAR CRIMES
5. CONSPIRACIES
6. CRIMES RELATED TO PRODUCTION, COMPETITION, AND MARKETING
7. MONEY LAUNDERING
8. RACKETEERING
9. BRIBERY
10. COMMERCIAL BRIBERY
11. EXTORTION AND BLACKMAIL
12. CORRUPT INFLUENCE
13. COUNTERFEITING
14. FORGERY
15. PERJURY
16. FALSE CLAIMS AND PRETENSES
17. BAD CHECKS
18. CREDIT CARD CRIMES
19. EMBEZZLEMENT
20. OBSTRUCTION OF JUSTICE: SARBANES-OXLEY
21. CORPORATE FRAUD: SARBANES-OXLEY
22. THE COMMON LAW CRIMES

 CRIMINAL LAW AND THE COMPUTER
23. WHAT IS A COMPUTER CRIME?
24. THE COMPUTER AS VICTIM
25. UNAUTHORIZED USE OF COMPUTERS
26. COMPUTER RAIDING

27. **DIVERTED DELIVERY BY COMPUTER**
28. **ECONOMIC ESPIONAGE BY COMPUTER**
29. **ELECTRONIC FUND TRANSFER CRIMES**
30. **CIRCUMVENTING COPYRIGHT PROTECTION DEVICES VIA COMPUTER**
31. **SPAMMING**

 D   CRIMINAL PROCEDURE RIGHTS FOR BUSINESSES

32. **FOURTH AMENDMENT RIGHTS FOR BUSINESSES**
33. **FIFTH AMENDMENT SELF-INCRIMINATION RIGHTS FOR BUSINESSES**
34. **DUE PROCESS RIGHTS FOR BUSINESSES**

LEARNING OBJECTIVES

After studying this chapter, you should be able to

LO.1 Discuss the nature and classification of crimes

LO.2 Describe the basis of criminal liability

LO.3 Identify who is responsible for criminal acts

LO.4 Explain the penalties for crimes and the sentencing for corporate crimes

LO.5 List examples of white-collar crimes and their elements

LO.6 Describe the common law crimes

LO.7 Discuss crimes related to computers

LO.8 Describe the rights of businesses charged with crimes and the constitutional protections afforded them

Society sets certain standards of conduct and punishes a breach of those standards as a crime. This chapter introduces the means by which government protects people and businesses from prohibited conduct.

 A   GENERAL PRINCIPLES

Detailed criminal codes and statutes define crimes and specify their punishment. These vary from state to state but still show the imprint of a common law background through similar elements and structure.

1. NATURE AND CLASSIFICATION OF CRIMES

crime violation of the law that is punished as an offense against the state or government.

misdemeanor criminal offense with a sentence of less than one year that is neither treason nor a felony.

felony criminal offense that is punishable by confinement in prison for more than one year or by death, or that is expressly stated by statute to be a felony.

A **crime** is conduct that is prohibited and punished by a government. Crimes are classified as *common law* or *statutory* according to their origin. Offenses punishable by less than one year in prison are called **misdemeanors.** More serious crimes are called **felonies,** including serious business crimes such as bribery and embezzlement, which are punishable by confinement in prison for more than one year. Misdemeanors include weighing goods with uninspected scales or operating without a sales tax license. An act may be a felony in one state and a misdemeanor in another.[1]

---

[1] Some states further define crimes by seriousness with different degrees of a crime, such as first-degree murder, second-degree murder, and so on. Misdemeanors may be differentiated by giving special names to minor misdemeanors.

2. BASIS OF CRIMINAL LIABILITY

A crime generally consists of two elements: (1) a mental state and (2) an act or omission. Harm may occur as a result of a crime, but harm is not an essential element of a crime.

(a) MENTAL STATE   Mental state does not require an awareness or knowledge of guilt. In most crimes, it is sufficient that the defendant voluntarily committed the act that is criminal regardless of motive or intent. An act may be a crime even though the actor has no knowledge that a law is being broken. Actions that are in themselves crimes are not made innocent by the claim that the defendant was exercising a constitutional right. **For Example,** freedom of speech does not give the right to send threatening letters.

(b) ACT OR OMISSION.   Specific statutes define the conduct that, when coupled with sufficient mental state, constitutes a crime. **For Example,** writing a check knowing you do not have the funds available is conduct that is a crime.

CASE SUMMARY

Oh, You Mean *Those* E-Mails! Who Knew?

FACTS: In 2000, former investment banker Frank Quattrone was head of the technology division of Credit Suisse First Boston Corporation (CSFB), earning about $120 million per year. Quattrone and members of the Tech Group did the underwriting of the Tech Group's initial public offerings (IPOs) for a great many of the dot-coms.

Because of questions about those IPOs and who was given the first crack at buying these hot stocks, the National Association of Securities Dealers (NASD), the Securities and Exchange Commission (SEC), and a New York grand jury conducted investigations of CSFB in the fall of 2000. While the investigations were pending, Quattrone and others, including CFSB's general counsel, circulated e-mails that discussed the investigations. On December 5, 2000, Quattrone sent the following e-mail "endorsement":

having been a key witness in a securities litigation case in south texas (miniscribe) i strongly advise you to follow these procedures.

Quattrone then placed a day-old e-mail from Richard Char, a banker in the Tech Group, below his endorsement. The Char e-mail read:

Subject: Time to clean up those files

. . .

With the recent tumble in stock prices, and many deals now trading below issue price, the securities litigation bar is expected to [sic] an all out assault on broken tech IPOs.

In the spirit of the end of the year (and the slow down in corporate finance work), we want to remind [ ] you of the CSFB document retention policy [the policy was reproduced here].

Note that if a lawsuit is instituted, our normal document retention policy is suspended and any cleaning of files is prohibited under the CSFB guidelines (since it constitutes the destruction of evidence). We strongly suggest that before you leave for the holidays, you should catch up on file cleanup.

CASE SUMMARY

continued

As a result of the Quattrone e-mail, at least some Tech Group bankers began or continued "cleaning" their files.

Quattrone was indicted for obstruction of justice and witness tampering in connection with the investigations.

Quattrone testified that although he was aware of the SEC and grand jury investigations, he believed that the investigations did not relate to his unit's operations. He also testified that he did not intend to obstruct any SEC or grand jury investigation and did not intend to influence others to destroy documents that had been called for by a grand jury or SEC subpoena. Rather than thinking about the investigations when he sent the "Endorsement Email," Quattrone testified that he was concerned about getting home to meet family commitments.

The jury was unable to reach a verdict in Quattrone's first trial. The second jury found him guilty on all counts. The district court imposed a sentence of 18 months' imprisonment and concurrent two-year terms of supervised release for each count and fines and assessments totaling $90,300. Quattrone appealed both the verdict and the sentence.

DECISION: The court reversed the conviction because it found that the jury had not been given proper instructions on the so-called nexus requirement. To find Quattrone guilty, the jury had to find that there was a connection between the documents being destroyed and Quattrone's knowledge about the investigations. The jury could conclude that he destroyed documents and evidence but would still not be guilty of obstruction unless he was aware of specifics of the subpoenas and investigations. Because that nexus was not made clear in the jury instructions, the conviction had to be reversed for retrial with the correct jury instructions on obstruction. [**U.S. v Quattrone, 443 F3d 153 (2nd Cir 2006)**]

Aftermath: The government decided not to retry Mr. Quattrone after the reversal. The Justice Department and Mr. Quattrone entered into a deferred prosecution agreement. If he has no brushes with the law for three years, all the charges will be dropped and he can remain a licensed securities broker.

3. RESPONSIBILITY FOR CRIMINAL ACTS

In some cases, persons who did not necessarily commit the criminal act itself are still held criminally responsible for acts committed by others.

(a) CORPORATE LIABILITY   Corporations are held responsible for the acts of their employees. A corporation may also be held liable for crimes based on the failure of its employees to act. In the past decade, some of the nation's largest corporations have paid fines for crimes based on employees' failure to take action or for the actions they did take. **For Example, AIG,** the world's largest insurer, paid the largest fine in corporate history in the United States, $1.6 billion, for its questionable accounting practices and alleged sham insurance contracts undertaken for the purpose of boosting its earnings.[2]

(b) OFFICERS AND AGENTS OF CORPORATIONS   One of the main differences between nonbusiness and business crimes is that more people in a company can be convicted for the same business crime. For nonbusiness crimes, only those who are actually involved in the act itself can be convicted of the crime. For business

---

[2] **www.sec.gov**.

crimes, however, managers of firms whose employees commit criminal acts can be held liable if the managers authorized the conduct of the employees or knew about their conduct and did nothing or failed to act reasonably in their supervisory positions to prevent the employees from engaging in criminal conduct.

(c) Penalty for Crime: Forfeiture   When a defendant is convicted of a crime, the court may also declare that the defendant's rights in any property used or gained from a crime (an instrument of that crime) be confiscated. Some types of instruments of the crime are automatically forfeited, such as the tools of a crime. **For Example,** engraved plates can be used only to make counterfeit money or are the subject of an illegal sale, so the government can confiscate them. Confiscation is, in effect, an increased penalty for the defendant's crime.

Forfeiture is not limited to property that can be used only for crime. An automobile that is used to carry illegal merchandise may itself be seized by the government even though it is obvious that the automobile could also be put to a lawful use.

(d) Penalties for Business and White-Collar Crimes   As they existed at common law, most criminal penalties were created with "natural" persons in mind, as opposed to "artificial" or corporate persons. A $100,000 fine may be significant to an individual but to a corporation with $3 billion in assets and hundreds of millions in income, such a fine could be viewed as simply a relatively minimal cost of doing business.

Over the years criminal penalties have been reformed to address this need to have corporate penalties act as deterrents. Rather than using fixed-amount fines, statutes and courts apply a percentage of revenue penalties. **For Example,** a bad decision on a product line would cost a company 10 percent to 20 percent of its earnings. A criminal penalty could be imposed in the same percentage fashion with the idea that the company simply made a bad legal decision that should be reflected in earnings. A company that fixed prices might face a criminal fine of 20 percent of the profits it made from the price-fixing.

CASE SUMMARY

Rats in the Warehouse and a CEO with a Fine

FACTS: Acme Markets, Inc., was a national food retail chain headquartered in Philadelphia. At the time of the government action, John R. Park was president of Acme, which employed 36,000 people and operated 16 warehouses.

In 1970, the Food and Drug Administration (FDA) forwarded a letter to Park describing, in detail, problems with rodent infestation in Acme's Philadelphia warehouse facility. In December 1971, the FDA found the same types of conditions in Acme's Baltimore warehouse facility. In January 1972, the FDA's chief of compliance for its Baltimore office wrote to Park about the inspection. The letter included the following language:

> *We note with much concern that the old and new warehouse areas used for food storage were actively and extensively inhabited by live rodents. Of even more concern was the observation that such reprehensible conditions obviously existed for a prolonged period of time without any detection, or were completely ignored.*
>
> *We trust this letter will serve to direct your attention to the seriousness of the problem and formally advise you of the urgent need to initiate whatever measures are necessary to prevent recurrence and ensure compliance with the law.*

CASE SUMMARY

continued

After Park received the letter, he met with the vice president for legal affairs for Acme and was assured that he was "investigating the situation immediately and would be taking corrective action."

When the FDA inspected the Baltimore warehouse in March 1972, there was some improvement in the facility, but there was still rodent infestation. Acme and Park were both charged with violations of the federal Food, Drug and Cosmetic Act. Acme pleaded guilty. Park was convicted and fined $500; he appealed.

DECISION: Officers of a corporation can be held criminally liable for the conduct of others within the company if it can be shown that the officers knew of the issue and failed to take the steps necessary to eliminate the criminal activity. In this case, Park had been warned and had been given several opportunities to remedy the problem. Part of his responsibility as an officer is following up to be certain that tasks he has assigned are completed. Failure to follow through can be a basis for criminal liability. [**United States v Park, 421 US 658 (1975)**]

Another change in penalties for business and white collar crimes has been the requirement for mandatory prison sentences for officers and directors who are convicted of crimes committed as they led their corporations. The human element of the corporation is then punished for the crimes that the business committed. The U.S. Sentencing Commission, established by Congress in 1984, has developed both federal sentencing guidelines and a carrot-and-stick approach to fighting business crime. If the managers of a company are involved and working to prevent criminal misconduct in the company and a crime occurs, the guidelines permit sentence reductions for the managers' efforts. If the managers do not adequately supervise conduct and do not encourage compliance with the law, the guidelines require judges to impose harsher sentences and fines. The guidelines, referred to as the **Federal Sentencing Guidelines or the U.S. Sentencing Guidelines,** apply to federal crimes such as securities fraud, antitrust violations, racketeering, theft (embezzlement), Medicare fraud, and other business crimes. The sentencing guidelines permit a judge to place a guilty company on probation, with the length of the probation controlled by whether the company had prevention programs in place.

Federal Sentencing Guidelines federal standards used by judges in determining mandatory sentence terms for those convicted of federal crimes.

Following the collapse of companies such as Enron, WorldCom, and Adelphia, the U.S. Sentencing Commission (USSC) piloted the passage of the 2001 Economic Crime Package: Consolidation, Clarification, and Certainty. The 2001 package amends the Sentencing Guidelines. The Economic Crime Package consists of several major parts, including (1) consolidation of fraud, theft, and other financial crimes into one table for purposes of sentencing and (2) a revised, common loss table to determine losses. In addition to the statutory clarification on the types of financial crimes, the amendments also required the USSC to reform its guidelines according to the legislation. The guidelines, amended in November 2003 to address the increased corporate and white-collar criminal penalties enacted under Sarbanes-Oxley (SOX), consider the seriousness of the offense, the company's history of violations, its cooperation in the investigation, the effectiveness of its compliance program (often called an *ethics program*), and the role of senior management in the

THINKING THINGS THROUGH

Employees Shredding—Employer Liable?

As the financial problems of the infamous energy company Enron grew, its audit firm, Arthur Andersen, became concerned that some of Enron's accounting and financial statements were doubtful. On October 16, 2001, Enron would not change the numbers in an earnings release in response to Andersen's concerns. Nancy Temple, legal counsel for Arthur Andersen, wrote an e-mail to David Duncan, the audit partner for the Enron account in Houston, about a release that Andersen was going to issue regarding Enron's accounting.

Later that same day, Temple also sent an e-mail to a member of Andersen's internal team of accounting experts and attached a copy of the company's document policy. On October 20, the Enron crisis-response team held a conference call, during which Temple instructed everyone to "[m]ake sure to follow the [document] policy." On October 23, 2001, Enron CEO Ken Lay declined to answer questions during a call with analysts because of "potential lawsuits, as well as the SEC inquiry." After the call, Duncan met with other Andersen partners on the Enron engagement team and told everyone to comply with the document policy. Following the meeting, Andersen employees began destroying documents related to Enron.

On October 30, 2001, the SEC opened a formal investigation and sent Enron a letter that requested accounting documents.

Throughout this time period, the document destruction continued despite reservations by some of Andersen's managers. On November 8, 2001, Enron announced that it would issue a comprehensive restatement of its earnings and assets. Also on November 8, the SEC served Enron and Andersen with subpoenas for records. On November 9, Duncan's secretary sent an e-mail that stated: "Per Dave—No more shredding. ... We have been officially served for our documents." Enron filed for bankruptcy less than a month later. Duncan was fired and later pleaded guilty to witness tampering.*

Applying the *Park* case, who is criminally liable for the document shredding? The employees who actually did it? The managers who ordered it to begin? The company itself? [ARTHUR ANDERSEN **LLP v U.S., 544 US 696 (2005)**]

---

*Duncan withdrew his plea following the appeal and U.S. Supreme Court ruling in this case.

White-Collar Crime Penalty Enhancement Act of 2002
federal reforms passed as a result of the collapses of companies such as Enron; provides for longer sentences and higher fines for both executives and companies.

wrongdoing. Corporate managers found to have masterminded any criminal activity must be sentenced to prison time.[3] Figure 8-1 is a summary of the current penalties for federal crimes.

(e) SARBANES-OXLEY REFORMS TO CRIMINAL PENALTIES   Part of SOX, passed by Congress following the collapses of Enron and WorldCom corporations, was the **White-Collar Crime Penalty Enhancement Act of 2002**.[4] This act increases penalties substantially. **For Example,** the penalties for mail and wire fraud are

---

[3] Mary Kreiner Ramirez, "Just in Crime: Guiding Economic Crime Reform after the Sarbanes-Oxley Act of 2002," 34 *Loyola University of Chicago Law Journal* 359, 387 (2003).

[4] 18 USC § 1314 *et seq.*

FIGURE 8-1	*Penalties for Federal Crimes*

Company/Person	Issue	Status
Andrew Fastow, former CFO of Enron (2004)	Multimillion-dollar earnings from serving as principal in SPEs of Enron created to keep debts off the company books; significant sales of shares during the time frame preceding company collapse	Resigned as CFO; appeared before Congress and took the Fifth Amendment; entered guilty plea to securities and wire fraud; sentence of 10 years
Bernie Ebbers (2005) Former CEO, WorldCom	Fraud	Convicted; sentenced to 25 years
Computer Associates (2004)	Criminal investigation pending on securities fraud and obstruction following $2.2 billion restatement in sales	Pending investigations; former CEO entered guilty plea to felony charges
Enron (2001)	Earnings overstated through mark-to-market accounting; off-the-book/special-purpose entities (SPEs) carried significant amounts of Enron debt not reflected in the financial statements; significant offshore SPEs (881 of 3,000 SPEs were offshore, primarily in Cayman Islands)	Company in bankruptcy (touted as the largest bankruptcy in U.S. history); shareholder litigation pending; Congressional hearings held; CFO Andrew Fastow and others entered guilty pleas; *see* Lea Fastow, Kenneth Lay, and Jeffrey Skilling
HealthSouth (2003)	$2.7 billion accounting fraud; overstatement of revenues	16 former executives indicted; 5 guilty please; *see* Richard Scrushy
KPMG (2006)	Tax shelter fraud	Settled by paying a penalty of $456 million fine in lieu of indictment; 16 former partners and employees under indictment
L. Dennis Kozlowski, former CEO of Tyco (2003)	Accused of improper use of company funds	Indicted in New York for failure to pay sales tax on transactions in fine art; hung jury on charges of looting Tyco; convicted on retrial with 25-year sentence
Marsh McLennan (2005)	Price-fixing	Paid $850 million in restitution to end investigation of its brokerage practices
Martha Stewart, CEO of Martha Stewart Living, Omnimedia, Inc., and close friend of Dr. Waksal (2003)	Sold 5,000 shares of ImClone one day before public announcement of negative FDA action on Erbitux	Indicted and convicted, along with her broker at Merrill Lynch, of making false statements and conspiracy; served sentence and currently on probation
Parmalat (based in Italy) (2004)	Accounting fraud–fake $5 billion account in Bank of America via forged documents	Company entered bankruptcy; top executives charged or entered guilty pleas; trials began in 2006
Xerox (2003)	Improper booking of revenues ($6.4 billion)	Had settled charges with SEC in April 2003 for $10 million; inquiry expanded to KPMG (settled)

increased from a maximum of five years to a maximum of 20 years. Penalties for violation of pension laws increased from one year to 10 years and the fines increased from $5,000 to $100,000.[5] The U.S. Sentencing Commission has amended its guidelines to reflect the higher penalties and, as noted earlier, to group all types of financial crimes into the same treatment and results in terms of the sentence required and the formulas for determination of the number of years and the fine.[6]

4. INDEMNIFICATION OF CRIME VICTIMS

Penalties are paid to the government. Typically, the victim of a crime does not benefit from the criminal prosecution and conviction of the wrongdoer, although courts can order that restitution be paid to victims.

Several states have adopted statutes providing a limited degree of indemnification to victims of crime to compensate them for the harm or loss sustained.[7] Under some criminal victim indemnification statutes, dependents of a deceased victim are entitled to recover the amount of support they were deprived of by the victim's death. The Victims of Crime Act of 1984 creates a federal Crime Victims Fund. Using the fines paid into the federal courts as well as other monies, the federal government makes grants to the states to assist them in financing programs to provide assistance for victims of crime.[8] The Victim and Witness Protection Act of 1982 authorizes the sentencing judge in a federal district court to order, in certain cases, that the defendant make restitution (restoration) to the victim or pay the victim the amount of medical expenses or loss of income caused by the crime.[9]

(a) ACTION FOR DAMAGES   The criminal prosecution of a wrongdoer is not undertaken primarily for the financial benefit of the victim of the crime, but the victim is typically entitled to bring a civil action for damages against the wrongdoer for the harm sustained. Statutes creating business crimes often give the victim the right to sue for damages. **For Example,** a company or individual violating federal antitrust laws is liable to the victim for three times the damages actually sustained.

(b) INDEMNIFICATION OF UNJUSTLY CONVICTED   If an innocent person is convicted of a crime, the state legislature typically pays the person damages to compensate for the wrong that has been done. In some states, this right to indemnity is expressly established by statute, as in the case of the New York Unjust Conviction and Imprisonment Act. The fact that a person has been imprisoned while awaiting trial and is then acquitted does not entitle that person to compensation under such a statute because an acquittal does not mean that the person was found innocent. It means only that the government was not able to prove guilt beyond a reasonable doubt.[10]

[5] 18 USC §§ 1341 and 1343; 29 USC § 1131.

[6] 18 USCA § 1348 (West Supp. 2003).

[7] A 1973 Uniform Crime Victims Reparations Act was adopted in Kansas, Louisiana, Montana, North Dakota, Ohio, and Utah. This act has been superseded by the Uniform Victims of Crime Act of 1992 adopted only in Montana, with variations.

[8] 18 USC § 1401 *et seq.*

[9] 18 USC § 3579, as amended by 18 USC § 18.18; see *Hughey v United States,* 495 US 411 (1990). Some states likewise provide for payment into a special fund. *Ex parte* Lewis, 556 So 2d 370 (Ala 1989). In 2002, Congress passed another victims' compensation statute, with this one providing relief and assistance to the victims of terrorist attacks in the United States. 42 USCA § 10603b.

[10] *People v Neff,* 731 NY S2d 269 (2001).

CASE SUMMARY

Crack in the Sentencing Hearing and a Glitch in the Proceedings

FACTS: Freddie J. Booker was convicted of possession of 50 grams of cocaine after a jury found that he had 92.5 grams in a duffel bag. That possession statute prescribes a minimum sentence of 10 years in prison and a maximum sentence of life for that offense.

Based upon Booker's criminal history and the quantity of drugs found by the jury, the Sentencing Guidelines required the judge to select a "base" sentence of not less than 210 nor more than 262 months in prison. The judge, however, held a post-trial sentencing proceeding and concluded by a preponderance of the evidence that Booker had possessed an additional 566 grams of crack and that he was guilty of obstructing justice. Those findings required that the judge select a sentence between 360 months and life imprisonment; the judge imposed a sentence at the low end of the range. Instead of the sentence of 21 years and 10 months that the judge could have imposed on the basis of the facts proved to the jury beyond a reasonable doubt (the 92.5 grams of crack), Booker received a 30-year sentence. Booker appealed his sentence. The court of appeals remanded the case for resentencing and the government appealed.

DECISION: The Supreme Court held that the federal sentencing guidelines are subject to jury trial requirements of the Sixth Amendment. A jury is required to determine beyond a reasonable doubt any additional facts or evidence that is used in handing down the sentence. Any facts beyond prior convictions that the judge uses in determining the level of sentence under the federal sentencing guidelines must be established by the trier of fact and proved beyond a reasonable doubt. The failure to do so in the sentencing hearing deprives the defendant of the Sixth Amendment right to a trial by a jury. The court of appeals decision was affirmed and the case was remanded for Booker to be resentenced following the new procedures for jury determinations of facts, such as his possession of additional drugs. [**U.S. v Booker, 543 US 220 (2005)**]

 ## B   WHITE-COLLAR CRIMES

white-collar crimes crimes that do not use nor threaten to use force or violence or do not cause injury to persons or property.

White-collar crime is generally considered business crime, the type committed without physical threats or acts.

5. CONSPIRACIES

conspiracy agreement between two or more persons to commit an unlawful act.

Prior to the commission of an intended crime, a person may engage in conduct that is itself a crime, such as a conspiracy. A **conspiracy** is an agreement between two or more persons to commit an unlawful act or to use unlawful means to achieve an otherwise lawful result. The crime is the agreement itself; generally, it is immaterial that nothing is done to carry out the agreement, although some conspiracy statutes do require that some act is done to carry out the agreement before the crime of conspiracy is committed.

6. CRIMES RELATED TO PRODUCTION, COMPETITION, AND MARKETING

(a) IMPROPER USE OF INTERSTATE COMMERCE The shipment of improper goods or the transmission of improper information in interstate commerce constitutes a crime under various federal statutes. It is a federal crime to use interstate commerce as part of a scheme to defraud, blackmail, or extort. Shipping adulterated or mislabeled foods, drugs, or cosmetics is also a federal crime.

The Communications Act of 1934, as amended, makes it a crime to manufacture or sell devices knowing their primary use is to unscramble satellite telecasts without having paid for the right to do so.[11]

(b) SECURITIES CRIMES To protect the investing public, both state and federal laws have regulated the issuance and public sale of stocks and bonds. Between 1933 and 1940, Congress adopted seven such regulatory statutes. These statutes and the crimes associated with sales of securities are covered in Chapter 46.

7. MONEY LAUNDERING

The federal government has adopted a Money Laundering Control Act (MLCA).[12] The act prohibits the knowing and willful participation in a financial transaction involving unlawful proceeds when the transaction is designed to conceal or disguise the source of the funds. The so-called *USA Patriot Act* that was passed on October 26, 2001, less than two months after the destruction of the World Trade Center and the damage to the Pentagon on September 11, 2001, includes a substantial number of changes and amendments to the Money Laundering Control Act and the Bank Secrecy Act (BSA).[13] Both statutes have been used as means to control bribery, tax evasion, and money laundering. Their changes and amendments were designed to curb the funding of terrorist activities in the United States.

Prior to the September 11, 2001 reforms, these two statutes applied only to financial institutions. The Patriot Act expands the coverage of the law to anyone involved in financial transactions, which includes securities brokers; travel agents; those who close real estate transactions; insurance companies; loan or finance companies; casinos; currency exchanges; check-cashing firms; auto, plane, and boat dealers; and branches and agencies of foreign banks located in the United States. The amendments make even small businesses subject to the requirements of disclosure under MLCA and BSA, such as reporting cash transactions in excess of $10,000.

In addition, the types of accounts covered have been expanded. The accounts covered are not only securities accounts but also money market accounts. Furthermore, banks must designate one person who will be responsible for following through on information furnished to the bank by law enforcement agencies on suspicious transactions and activities as well as individuals. Following the receipt of this information from the federal government, the bank's designated official is required to implement new policies to prevent the transactions noted or investigate internally for transactions of any individuals reported.

---

[11] 47 USC § 705(d)(1), (e)(4), 47 USC § 605 (d)(1), (e)(4); *United States v Harrell*, 983 F2d 36 (5th Cir 1993); but see *DIRECTV, Inc. v Robson*, 420 F3d 532 (5th Cir. 2005).

[12] 18 USC §§ 1956–1957 (2000). *U.S. v Prince*, 214 F3d 740 (6th Cir 2000).

[13] 31 USC § 531(h).

The Patriot Act also expands the scope of the more detailed regulations from large financial institutions to smaller ones. Prior to the changes, most small banks assumed that they were exempt from the more detailed reporting and record-keeping requirements. With the changes, no bank is exempt unless it applies for such an exemption from the U.S. Treasury Department.

The businesses subject to these laws have developed anti–money-laundering programs. To enjoy reduced sentencing benefits under the Federal Sentencing Guidelines, businesses must have such a program in place. These programs must include a "Know Your Customer" training segment that teaches employees how to spot suspicious customers and transactions.

8. RACKETEERING

Racketeer Influenced and Corrupt Organizations (RICO) Act federal law, initially targeting organized crime, that has expanded in scope and provides penalties and civil recovery for multiple criminal offenses, or a pattern of racketeering.

Congress passed the **Racketeer Influenced and Corrupt Organizations (RICO) Act**[14] in 1970 as part of the Organized Crime Control Act. The law was designed primarily to prevent individuals involved in organized crime from investing money obtained through racketeering in legitimate businesses. However, the broad language of the act, coupled with a provision that allows individuals and businesses to sue for treble damages, has resulted in an increasing number of lawsuits against ordinary businesspersons not associated with organized crime.

(a) Criminal and Civil Applications RICO authorizes criminal and civil actions against persons who use any income derived from racketeering activity to invest in, control, or conduct an enterprise through a pattern of *racketeering activity.*[15] In criminal and civil actions under RICO, a pattern of racketeering activity must be established by proving that at least two acts of racketeering activity—so-called *predicate acts*—have been committed within 10 years.[16] Conviction under RICO's criminal provisions may result in a $25,000 fine and up to 20 years' imprisonment as well as forfeiture of the property involved. A successful civil plaintiff may recover three times the actual damages suffered and attorney fees.[17]

(b) Expanding Usage Civil RICO actions have been successful against business entities, such as accounting firms, labor unions, insurance companies, commercial banks, and stock brokerage firms. However, under the Private Securities Litigation Reform Act of 1995, securities fraud is eliminated as a **predicate act,** or a qualifying underlying offense, for private RICO actions, absent a prior criminal conviction.[18]

predicate act qualifying underlying offense for RICO liability.

---

[14] 18 USC §§ 1961–1968.

[15] § 1961. Definitions

(1) "Racketeering activity" means any act or threat involving murder, kidnapping, gambling, arson, robbery, bribery, extortion, dealing in obscene matter, dealing in a controlled substance or listed chemical, or sports bribery; counterfeiting; theft from interstate shipment; embezzlement from pension and welfare funds; extortionate credit transactions; fraud; wire fraud; mail fraud; procurement of citizenship or nationalization unlawfully; reproduction of naturalization or citizenship papers; obstruction of justice; tampering with a witness, victim, or an informant; retaliating against a witness, victim, or an informant; false statement in application and use of passport; forgery or false use of passport; fraud and misuse of visas, permits and other documents; racketeering; unlawful welfare fund payments; laundering of monetary instruments; use of interstate commerce facilities in the commission of murder-for-hire; sexual exploitation of children; interstate transportation of stolen motor vehicles; interstate transportation of stolen property; trafficking in counterfeit labels of phonorecords, computer programs or computer program documentation, or packaging and copies of motion pictures or other audiovisual works; criminal infringement of a copyright; trafficking in contraband cigarettes; and white slave traffic.

[16] Brian Slocum, "RICO and the Legislative Supremacy Approach to Federal Criminal Lawmaking," 31 *Loyola Univ. Chicago Law Journal* 639 (2000).

[17] 18 U.S.C. § 1963.

[18] 15 USC § 78(a), (n)–(t).

9. BRIBERY

Bribery is the act of giving money, property, or any benefit to a particular person to influence that person's judgment in favor of the giver. At common law, the crime was limited to doing such acts to influence a public official.

The giving and the receiving of a bribe constitute separate crimes. In addition, the act of trying to obtain a bribe may be a crime of solicitation of bribery in some states, while in other states bribery is broadly defined to include solicitation of bribes.

10. COMMERCIAL BRIBERY

Commercial bribery is a form of bribery in which an agent for another is paid or given something of value in order to make a decision on behalf of his or her principal that benefits the party paying the agent. **For Example,** a napkin supplier who pays a restaurant agent $500 in exchange for that agent's decision to award the restaurant's napkin contract to that supplier has engaged in commercial bribery. Connecticut's commercial bribery statute is a good example. It provides:

> *A person is guilty of commercial bribery when he confers, or agrees to confer, any benefit upon any employee, agent or fiduciary without the consent of the latter's employer or principal, with intent to influence his conduct in relation to his employer's or principal's affairs.*[19]

11. EXTORTION AND BLACKMAIL

Extortion and *blackmail* are crimes in which money is exchanged for either specific actions or restraint in taking action.

(a) EXTORTION When a public officer, acting under the apparent authority of his or her office, makes an illegal demand, the officer has committed the crime of **extortion. For Example,** if a health inspector threatens to close down a restaurant on a false charge of violating the sanitation laws unless the restaurant pays the inspector a sum of money, the inspector has committed extortion. (If the restaurant voluntarily offers the inspector the money to prevent the restaurant from being shut down because of actual violations of the sanitation laws, the crime committed would be bribery.) Modern statutes tend to ignore the public officer aspect of the common law and expand extortion to include obtaining anything of value by threat, which might be, for example, loan sharking. In a number of states, statutes extend the extortion concept to include making terrorist threats.[20]

(b) BLACKMAIL In jurisdictions where extortion is limited to the conduct of public officials, a nonofficial commits **blackmail** by making demands that would be

extortion illegal demand by a public officer acting with apparent authority.

blackmail extortion demands made by a nonpublic official.

---

[19] CGSA § 53a-160 (2002). Other examples of commercial bribery statues can be found at Minn Stat Ann § 6-9.86 (Minnesota 2001); NH Rev Stat § 638:8 (New Hampshire 2001); Alaska Stat 11.45.670 (Alaska 2001); and Ala Code § 13A-11-120 (Alabama 2001). Mississippi prohibits commercial bribery as well as sports bribery, which is paying the agent of a sports team in order to influence the outcome of a sporting event. Miss Code Ann § 97-9-10 (2001).

[20] *Pennsylvania v Bunting,* 426 A2d 130 (Pa 1981).

extortion if made by a public official. Ordinarily, blackmail is the act of threatening someone with publicity about a matter that would damage the victim's personal or business reputation.

12. CORRUPT INFLUENCE

In harmony with changing concepts of right and wrong, society has increasingly outlawed certain practices on the ground that they exert a corrupting influence on business transactions.

(a) IMPROPER POLITICAL INFLUENCE   To protect against the improper influencing of political or governmental action, various acts have been classified as crimes. **For Example,** it is a crime for the holder of a government office to be financially interested in, or to receive money from, an enterprise that is seeking to do business with the government. Such conflicts of interest are likely to produce a result that is harmful to the public. Likewise, lobbyists and foreign agents must register in Washington, D.C.,[21] and must adhere to statutes regulating the giving and receiving of contributions for political campaigns. Violation of these regulatory statutes is a crime.

Foreign Corrupt Practices Act (FCPA) federal law that makes it a felony to influence decision makers in other countries for the purpose of obtaining business, such as contracts for sales and services; also imposes financial reporting requirements on certain U.S. corporations.

(b) FOREIGN CORRUPT PRACTICES ACT   The **Foreign Corrupt Practices Act (FCPA)** is a federal criminal statute that applies to businesses whose principal offices are in the United States; it is an antibribery and anticorruption statute covering these companies' international operations.[22] The FCPA prohibits making, authorizing, or promising payments or gifts of money or anything of value with the intent to corrupt. This prohibition applies to payments or gifts designed to influence official acts of foreign officials, parties, party officials, candidates for office, nongovernmental organizations (NGOs), or any person who transmits the gift or money to these types of persons.

grease payments
(facilitation payments) legal payments to speed up or ensure performance of normal government duties.

The FCPA does not prohibit **grease** or **facilitation payments.** These are payments made only to get officials to perform their normal duties or to perform them in a timely manner. Facilitation payments are those made to (1) secure a permit or a license, (2) obtain paper processing, (3) secure police protection, (4) provide phone, water, or power services, or (5) obtain any other similar action.

facilitation payments
(grease payments) legal payments to speed up or ensure performance of normal government duties.

13. COUNTERFEITING

Counterfeiting is making, with fraudulent intent, a document or coin that appears to be genuine but is not because the person making it did not have the authority to make it. It is a federal crime to make, to possess with intent to transfer, or to transfer counterfeit coins, bank notes, or obligations or other securities of the United States. Legislation has also been adopted to prohibit the passing of counterfeit foreign securities or counterfeit notes of foreign banks. Various states also have statutes prohibiting the making and passing of counterfeit coins and bank notes. These statutes often provide, as does the federal statute, a punishment for the mutilation of bank notes or the lightening (of the weight) or mutilation of coins.

---

[21] Foreign Agents Registration Act, 22 USC § 611 *et seq.*, as amended.
[22] 15 USC § 78dd-1 *et seq.*

ETHICS & THE LAW

Why Regulate Bribes?

In 1999, a scandal involving the International Olympic Committee (IOC) erupted when it was discovered that members of the Salt Lake City Olympic Committee had given extensive gifts to members of the IOC to win the 2002 Winter Olympics for Salt Lake City. The gifts included everything from college tuition to medical care to entertainment. The attitude at the time toward the Salt Lake City revelations was, "It's always been done this way," or "Everybody does this," or "It doesn't really hurt anyone."

Why should criminal indictments be brought against the U.S. citizens who bribed IOC members?* Why do we care?

---

*The criminal charges against two members of the Salt Lake City Olympic Committee were dismissed by the court but were reinstated by the Tenth Circuit. *U.S. v Welch,* 327 F3d 1081 (10th Cir. 2003). The federal charges were conspiracy to commit commercial bribery in violation of the Utah statute prohibiting such.

14. FORGERY

Forgery consists of the fraudulent making or material altering of an instrument, such as a check, that attempts to create or changes a legal liability of another person.[23] The instrument must have the appearance of legal efficacy to constitute forgery.

Ordinarily, **forgery** consists of signing another's name with intent to defraud, but it may also consist of making an entire instrument or altering an existing one. It may result from signing a fictitious name or the offender's own name with the intent to defraud. When the nonowner of a credit card signs the owner's name on a credit card invoice without the owner's permission, this act is a forgery.

The issuing or delivery of a forged instrument to another person constitutes the crime of **uttering** a forged instrument. The elements of the crime are (1) the offering of a forged instrument with a representation by words or acts that it is true and genuine, (2) the knowledge that it is false, forged, or counterfeit, and (3) the intent to defraud.[24] Any sending of a forged check through the channels of commerce or of bank collection constitutes an uttering of a forged instrument. The act of depositing a forged check into the forger's bank account by depositing it in an automatic teller machine constitutes uttering within the meaning of a forgery statute.[25]

forgery fraudulently making or altering an instrument that apparently creates or alters a legal liability of another.

uttering crime of issuing or delivering a forged instrument to another person.

15. PERJURY

Perjury consists of knowingly giving false testimony in a judicial proceeding after having been sworn to tell the truth. Knowingly making false answers on any form filed with a government typically constitutes perjury or is subjected to the same

---

[23] A bank withdrawal slip or a charge slip may be a forged written instrument. See *State v Daniels,* 23 P3d 1125 (CA Wash 2001).

[24] Id.

[25] *Wisconsin v Tolliver,* 440 NW2d 571 (Wis App 1989).

punishment as perjury. In some jurisdictions, the false answers given in a situation other than in court or the litigation process is called the crime of *false swearing*.

16. FALSE CLAIMS AND PRETENSES

Many statutes make it a crime to submit false claims or to obtain goods by false pretenses.

(a) FALSE CLAIMS   Some statutes provide that making a false claim to an insurance company, a government office, or a relief agency is a crime. The federal false statement statute makes it a crime to knowingly and willfully make a false material statement about any matter within the jurisdiction of any department or agency of the United States. It is a crime for a contractor to make a false claim against the United States for payment for work that was never performed. Other statutes indirectly regulate the matter by declaring that signing a false written claim constitutes perjury or is subject to the same punishment as perjury.[26]

(b) OBTAINING GOODS BY FALSE PRETENSES   Almost all states have statutes that forbid obtaining money or goods under false pretenses.[27] These statutes vary in detail and scope. Sometimes they are directed against a particular form of deception, such as using a bad check. An intent to defraud is an essential element of obtaining property by false pretenses.[28]

Examples of false pretense include delivering a check knowing that there is insufficient money in the bank account to cover the check.[29] False representations as to future profits in a business are also forms of false pretenses.

Failing to perform on a contract is not a false pretense crime unless the contract had been entered into with the intent of not performing it.[30]

(c) UNAUTHORIZED USE OF AUTOMATED TELLER MACHINE   Obtaining money from an automated teller machine (ATM) by the unauthorized use of the depositor's ATM card is a federal crime.

(d) FALSE INFORMATION SUBMITTED TO BANKS   Knowingly making false statements in a loan application to a federally insured bank is a federal crime.[31] It is also a crime for a landowner to put a false value on land transferred to a bank as security for a loan.[32]

17. BAD CHECKS

The use of a bad check is commonly made a crime by statute. In the absence of a bad check statute, the use of a bad check could generally be prosecuted under a false pretenses statute.

Under a bad check statute, it is a crime to use or pass a check with the intent to defraud with the knowledge that there are insufficient funds in the bank to pay the

---

[26] The Federal False Claims Act is violated only when the false claim is submitted with knowledge of its falsity. *See U.S. ex rel. Foundation Aiding the Elderly v Horizon West*, 265 F3d 1011 (9th Cir 2001).

[27] *Mass. v Cheromcka*, 850 NE2d 1088 (Mass App 2006).

[28] *State v Moore*, 97 Conn App 2006 WL 2370553 243, (Conn App).

[29] *U.S. v Tudeme*, 457 F3d 577 (Fed App 2006).

[30] *Jacobs v State*, 2006 WL 2069423 (Tex App).

[31] 18 USC § 1014. See *United States v Autorino*, 381 F3d 48 (2nd Cir 2004).

[32] *United States v Faulkner*, 17 F3d 745 (5th Cir 1994).

check when it is presented for payment. Knowledge that the bad check will not be paid when presented to the bank is an essential element of the crime. The bad check statutes typically provide that if the check is not made good within a specified number of days after payment by the bank is refused, it is presumed that the defendant acted with the intent to defraud.[33] For more information on checks, see Chapter 28.

18. CREDIT CARD CRIMES

It is a crime to steal a credit card and, in some states, to possess the credit card of another person without that person's consent. Using a credit card without the permission of the card owner is the crime of obtaining goods or services by false pretenses or with the intent to defraud. Likewise, a person who continues to use a credit card with the knowledge that it has been canceled is guilty of the crime of obtaining goods by false pretenses.

When, without permission, someone signs the name of the card owner for the credit card transaction, she has committed the crime of forgery.

The Credit Card Fraud Act of 1984[34] makes it a federal crime to obtain anything of value in excess of $1,000 in a year by means of a counterfeit credit card, to make or sell such cards, or to possess more than 15 counterfeit cards at one time.

19. EMBEZZLEMENT

embezzlement statutory offense consisting of the unlawful conversion of property entrusted to the wrongdoer.

Embezzlement is the fraudulent conversion of another's property or money by a person to whom it has been entrusted.[35] Employees who take their employer's property or funds for personal use have committed the crime of embezzlement. An agent employee commits embezzlement when he receives and keeps payments from third persons— payments the agent should have turned over to the principal. **For Example,** when an insured gives money to an insurance agent to pay the insurance company but the insurance agent uses the money to pay premiums on the policies of other persons, the agent is guilty of embezzlement. Generally, the fact that the defendant intends to return the property or money embezzled or does in fact do so is no defense.

Today, every jurisdiction has not only a general embezzlement statute but also various statutes applicable to particular situations. **For Example,** statutes cover embezzlement by government officials and employees.

20. OBSTRUCTION OF JUSTICE: SARBANES-OXLEY

Another of the provisions of the Sarbanes-Oxley Act of 2002 clarifies what constitutes obstruction of justice and increases the penalties for such an act. The new section makes it a felony for anyone, including company employees, auditors, attorneys, and consultants,

> to alter, destroy, mutilate, conceal, cover up, falsify or make a false entry with the "intent to impede, obstruct, or influence the investigation or proper administration of any matter within the jurisdiction of any department or agency of the United States."[36]

---

[33] *U.S. v Smith,* 2003 WL 2145660 (CA 10).

[34] 18 USC § 1029.

[35] *State v Weaver,* 607 SE2d 599 (NC 2005).

[36] 18 USC § 1519. The newly defined and expanded crime of obstruction carries an unspecified fine and a sentence of up to 20 years.

The statute goes on to address audit records specifically and requires auditors to retain their work papers related to a client's audit for at least five years. Any destruction of documents prior to that time constitutes a felony and carries a penalty of up to 10 years. The statute is a direct response to the reversed federal case brought against Arthur Andersen, the audit firm for the collapsed Enron Corporation.

21. CORPORATE FRAUD: SARBANES-OXLEY

SOX also created a new form of mail and wire fraud. Ordinary, mail or wire fraud consists of the use of the mail or telephones for purposes of defrauding someone of money and/or property. However, the SOX form of mail or wire fraud is based on new requirements imposed on corporate officers to certify their financial statements when they are issued. If a corporate officer fails to comply with all requirements for financial statement certification or certifies financial statements that contain false material information, the officer and company have committed corporate fraud with penalties that range from fines of $1,000,000 and/or 10 years to $5,000,000 and/or 20 years for willful violation of the certification requirements.

SPORTS & ENTERTAINMENT LAW

Martha Stewart and Obstruction

Martha Stewart, the legendary domestic doyenne, had purchased shares in ImClone, a company headed by her friend, Dr. Sam Waksal. In early December 2001, the Food and Drug Administration (FDA) indicated to scientists and others at ImClone that its approval to sell its promising anti-cancer drug, Erbitux, would not be forthcoming. The company did not release this negative information. Waksal and his family, however, spent most of the month of December selling their shares of ImClone to avoid the losses they would experience when the information about the lack of approval for Erbitux was released. He was later sentenced to seven years in prison for selling his shares and forging documents that were necessary for such extensive sales by a corporate insider.

Peter Bacanovic was a Merrill Lynch broker whose clients included Stewart and Waksal. During the last week of December 2001 and the first week of January 2002, Bacanovic was vacationing in Florida. Douglas Faneuil, a Merrill Lynch client associate in his mid-twenties who had been working as Bacanovic's assistant for about six months, was responsible for covering Bacanovic's desk when he was away. Between 9 and 10 A.M. on December 27, 2001, Faneuil received several phone calls on Bacanovic's line from Sam Waksal's daughters. They wanted to sell their ImClone shares.

Faneuil kept Bacanovic apprised of the details of the calls from the Waksal family by telephone. In the midst of one of their conversations, Faneuil heard Bacanovic say suddenly, "Oh, my God, get Martha [Stewart] on the phone."

Shortly thereafter, Stewart—who was en route to Mexico for a vacation with her friend Mariana Pasternak—called Bacanovic's office. Stewart asked Faneuil for a price quote and directed him to sell all of the ImClone shares that remained in her portfolio.

SPORTS & ENTERTAINMENT LAW

continued

Stewart's ImClone sell order was executed at an average price of $58.43 per share, yielding proceeds of approximately $230,000. Pursuant to Stewart's instructions, Faneuil sent an e-mail to her personal account confirming the trade. Ms. Stewart was able to avoid a $40,000 loss by selling on December 27 as opposed to December 28 when the information became public.

When SEC and Justice Department officials confronted Stewart about the timing of her sale of ImClone stock, which did not violate any securities or criminal laws because she sold the stock based on others' sale of their shares, she was not forthright.

- On January 31, 2002, Stewart asked Ann Armstrong (her assistant) to show her the messages, including the entry for the December 27 message from Bacanovic. Upon reading the message, Stewart took the computer mouse from Armstrong and deleted and typed over a portion of the text so that what had initially read, "Peter Bacanovic thinks Imclone is going to start trading downward" was revised to read, "Peter Bacanovic re imclone [sic]." Immediately thereafter, Stewart told Armstrong to restore the message to the original, and Armstrong did so.
- On February 4, 2002, Stewart met at the offices of the U.S. Attorney with two SEC enforcement attorneys, an Assistant United States Attorney and an FBI agent, all of whom were investigating the December 27 ImClone trading. She produced a log showing the notation of this decision (a stop-loss order), but the government was able to show through scientific lab analysis that the date on the log had been altered from its original to reflect her contention and limited date and sale.

The government also uncovered the following:

- Discussions between and among the three about the "story" they would tell
- Faneuil's receipt of New York Knicks tickets given in exchange for remaining on the same page with the story of Stewart and Baconovic

A jury convicted Stewart of obstruction of justice.

List the mistakes Martha Stewart made in handling the government inquiry about her ImClone stock sales. What types of conduct described here would constitute obstruction of justice? If there is no underlying crime, can someone be convicted of obstruction of justice? Discuss the ethical issues in the series of actions Ms. Stewart took. [**U.S. v Stewart, 443 F3d 273 (2nd Cir NY 2006)**]

22. THE COMMON LAW CRIMES

In contrast to white-collar crimes, *common law crimes* are crimes that involve the use of force or the threat of force or cause injury to persons or damage to property. The following sections discuss crimes of force and crimes against property that affect businesses.

(a) Larceny   *Larceny* is the wrongful or fraudulent taking of the personal property of another by any person with fraudulent intent. Shoplifting is a common form of larceny. In many states, shoplifting is made a separate crime.

Although the term *larceny* is broadly used in everyday speech, not every unlawful taking is a larceny. At common law, a defendant who took property of another with the intent to return it was not guilty of larceny. The common law has been changed in some states so that a person who borrows a car for a joyride is guilty of larceny, theft, or some other statutory offense. In some states, all forms of larceny and robbery are consolidated into a statutory crime of theft. At common law, there was no crime known as theft.

(b) Robbery   *Robbery* is the taking of personal property from the presence of the victim by use of force or fear. Most states have aggravated forms of robbery, such as robbery with a deadly weapon. Snatching a necklace from the neck of the victim involves sufficient force to constitute robbery. When the unlawful taking is not by force or fear, as when the victim does not know that the property is being taken, the offense is larceny, but it cannot be robbery.

Some statutes may be aimed at a particular kind of robbery. **For Example,** carjacking is a federal crime under the Anti-Car Theft Act of 1992.[37]

(c) Burglary   At common law, *burglary* was the breaking and entering during the night into the dwelling house of another with the intent to commit a felony. Inserting the automatic teller card of another, without their knowledge or permission, into an automatic teller machine set in the wall of the bank may constitute an entry into the bank for the purpose of committing burglary.[38] Some states word their burglary statutes, however, so that there is no burglary in this automatic teller case. This act would be covered by other criminal statutes.

Modern statutes have eliminated many of the elements of the common law definition so that under some statutes it is now immaterial when or whether there was an entry to commit a felony. The elements of breaking and entering are frequently omitted. Under some statutes, the offense is aggravated and the penalty is increased, depending on the place where the offense was committed, such as a bank building, freight car, or warehouse. Related statutory offenses, such as the crime of possessing burglars' tools, have been created.

(d) Arson   At common law, *arson* was the willful and malicious burning of another's dwelling. The law was originally designed to protect human life, although arson has been committed just with the burning of the building even if no one is actually hurt. In most states, arson is a felony, so if someone is killed in the resulting fire, the offense is considered a felony-murder. Under the felony-murder rule, homicide, however unintended, occurring in the commission of a felony is automatically classified as murder.

Virtually every state has created a special offense of burning to defraud an insurer. Such burning is not arson when an insured burns his own house in order to collect insurance money.

(e) Riots and Civil Disorders   Damage to property in the course of a riot or civil disorder is ordinarily covered by other types of crimes such as the crime of larceny

---

[37] 18 USC § 2119. See *United States v Hutchinson*, 75 F3d 626 (11th Cir 1996).
[38] *California v Ravenscroft*, 243 Cal Rptr 827 (Ct App 1988).

or arson. In addition, the act of assembling as a riotous mob and engaging in civil disorders is generally some form of crime in itself under either common law concepts of disturbing the peace or modern antiriot statutes, even without destruction or theft of property.

A statute may make it a crime to riot or to incite to riot. However, a statute relating to inciting must be carefully drawn to avoid infringing on constitutionally protected free speech.

CRIMINAL LAW AND THE COMPUTER

In some situations, ordinary crimes cover computer crimes situations. In other situations, new criminal law statutes are required.

23. WHAT IS A COMPUTER CRIME?

computer crimes wrongs committed using a computer or with knowledge of computers.

The term **computer crime** is frequently used even though it has no established definition. Generally, the phrase is used to refer to a crime that can be committed only by a person having some knowledge of the operation of a computer. Just as stealing an automobile requires knowledge of how to operate and drive a car, so the typical computer crime requires the knowledge of how the computer works.

Because the more serious and costly wrongs relating to computers do not fit into the ordinary definitions of crime, there are now computer-specific criminal statutes: Computer crimes can be committed against the computer, using the computer, or through the computer.

24. THE COMPUTER AS VICTIM

A traditional crime may be committed by stealing or intentionally damaging a computer.

(a) THEFT OF HARDWARE   When a computer itself is stolen, the ordinary law relating to theft crimes should apply. Theft of a computer is subject to the same law as the theft of a typewriter or a desk.

(b) THEFT OF SOFTWARE   When a thief takes software, whether in the form of a program written on paper or a program on a disk or tape, a situation that does not fit into the common law definition of larceny arises. Larceny at common law was confined to the taking of tangible property. At common law, the value of stolen software would be determined by the value of the tangible substance on which the program was recorded. Under a traditional concept of property, which would ignore the value of the intangible program, theft of software would be only petty larceny. Now, however, virtually every state has amended its definition of larceny or theft to make stealing software a crime. In some states, the unauthorized taking of information may constitute a crime under a trade secrets protection statute.

(c) INTENTIONAL DAMAGE   The computer may be the "victim" of a crime when it is intentionally destroyed or harmed. In the most elementary form of damage, the computer could be harmed if it was smashed with an ax or destroyed in an explosion or a fire. In such cases, the purpose of the intentional damage is to cause the computer's owner the financial loss of the computer and the destruction of the information that is stored in it.

Intentional damage can result from more subtle means. Gaining access to the computer and then erasing or altering the data is also the crime of intentional damage. Likewise, interfering with the air conditioning so that damage to the computer results or the computer malfunctions would also be covered under intentional damage statutes. The wrongdoer also may intentionally plant a bug or virus in the software, causing the program to malfunction or to give incorrect output. Such damage may be the work of an angry employee or a former employee, or it may be the work of a competitor.

In earlier years, the crime of malicious destruction of, or damage to, property was used to prosecute computer crimes.[39] Again, lawmakers have filled the gap between the technological environment and the law. Many states have adopted statutes that now make it a crime to damage software or computer-stored information.

25. UNAUTHORIZED USE OF COMPUTERS

In contrast to conduct intended to harm a computer or its rightful user or to acquire secret information, the least serious of the computer crimes is the unlawful use of a computer belonging to someone else. In some states, however, the unlawful use of a computer is not a crime. Recent statutes have widely regulated this computer crime.

26. COMPUTER RAIDING

Taking information from a computer without the consent of the owner of the information is a crime. Whether this is done by instructing the computer to make a printout of stored information or by tapping into its data bank by some electronic means is not important. In many instances, taking information from the computer constitutes the crime of stealing trade secrets. In some states, taking information is known as the crime of "computer trespass."[40]

Both Congress and state legislatures have adopted statutes that declare it a crime to make any unauthorized use of a computer or to gain unauthorized access to a computer or the information stored in its database in order to cause harm to the computer or its rightful user.[41]

27. DIVERTED DELIVERY BY COMPUTER

In many industries, a computer controls the delivery of goods. The person in charge of that computer or someone unlawfully gaining access to it may cause the computer to direct delivery to an improper place. That is, instead of shipping goods to the customers to whom they should go, the wrongdoer diverts the goods to a different place, where the wrongdoer or a confederate receives them.

In precomputer days, written orders were sent from the sales department to the shipping department. The shipping department then sent the ordered goods to the

---

[39] The crime of maliciously damaging or destroying property is ordinarily a misdemeanor and, as such, is subject only to a relatively small fine or short imprisonment.

[40] *Washington v Riley,* 846 P2d 1365 (Wash 1993).

[41] The Counterfeit Access Device and Computer Fraud Act of 1984, 18 USC § 1030 *et seq.;* Computer Fraud and Abuse Act of 1986, as amended in 1999, 18 USC § 1001; Electronic Communications Privacy Act of 1986, Act of 1986, 18 USC § 2510; Computer Fraud Act of 1987, 15 USC §§ 272, 278, 40 USC § 759; National Information Infrastructure Protection Act, 18 USC § 1030 (protecting confidentiality and integrity on the Internet).

E-COMMERCE AND CYBERLAW

They Took Me: Identity Theft

Identity theft is an increasing problem with the Internet. Criminals are invading e-commerce Web sites and acquiring personal information about customers. They then use these customers' credit and credit cards to make purchases. Such criminals have acquired, in some cases, as many as 70 credit cards using other people's names and identities.

In 1998, the total number of identity thefts was 11,000; in 1997, it was only 7,868. In 2002, the FBI broke up one identity theft ring that had stolen funds and credit card access from more than 30,000 Americans. In 2004, the FBI had 150,000 victims of identity theft.

Identity thieves begin by obtaining a person's name, address, date of birth, and Social Security number. They then use the information to get fake driver's licenses, which they use to obtain credit cards. With these tools, they can live someone else's life.

Do you think e-commerce sites should be held responsible for lack of sufficient security to prevent identity theft?

proper places. If the person in the sales department or the person in the shipping department was dishonest, either one could divert the goods from the proper destination. Today, instructing the computer to give false directions can cause this fraudulent diversion of goods. Basically, the crime has not changed. The computer is merely the new instrument by which the old crime is committed. This old crime has taken on a new social significance because of the amazingly large dollar value of the thefts. In one case, several hundred loaded freight cars disappeared. In another case, a loaded oil tanker was diverted to unload into a fleet of tank trucks operated by an accomplice of the computer operator.

The crime of diverted delivery is not limited to goods. Diverted delivery can involve transferring money from a proper account to a wrong account. Computers can divert millions of dollars in a single criminal act. Statutes or courts may impose more severe penalties in these cases because of the huge dollar values involved.

28. ECONOMIC ESPIONAGE BY COMPUTER

Economic Espionage Act (EEA) federal law that makes it a felony to copy, download, transmit, or in any way transfer proprietary files, documents, and information from a computer to an unauthorized person.

The **Economic Espionage Act (EEA)** is a federal law[42] passed in response to several cases in which high-level executives took downloaded proprietary information from their computers to their new employers. The EEA makes it a felony to steal, appropriate, or take a trade secret as well as to copy, duplicate, sketch, draw, photograph, download, upload, alter, destroy, replicate, transmit, deliver, send, mail, or communicate a trade secret. The penalties for EEA violations are up to $500,000 and 15 years in prison for individuals and $10 million for organizations. When employees take new positions with another company, their former employers are permitted to check the departing employees' computer e-mails and hard drives to determine whether the employees have engaged in computer espionage.

---

[42] 18 USC § 1831.

ETHICS & THE LAW

Ethics and Competition

In a long-running case that involved international competition, General Motors and Volkswagen AG battled in courts and in newspapers over the departure of several GM employees for Volkswagen and allegedly taking proprietary information about GM's supply chain management system in Europe.* The case resulted in the passage of the Economic Espionage Act (EEA) in the United States, which makes it a crime to download or in any way, electronically or otherwise, take proprietary information from one company to give or sell to another company.

Why is it an ethical issue for an employee to take information that she memorized about her former employer? What risks do you see in hiring someone who offers to bring proprietary information to you? What precautions could companies take to prevent employees from taking proprietary information to competitors?

---

* *"Judge Sets Michigan Venue for GM Suit against VW,"* Wall Street Journal, October 18, 1996, B5.

---

29. ELECTRONIC FUND TRANSFER CRIMES

The Electronic Fund Transfers Act (EFTA)[43] makes it a crime to use any counterfeit, stolen, or fraudulently obtained card, code, or other device to obtain money or goods in excess of a specified amount through an electronic fund transfer system. The EFTA also makes it a crime to ship in interstate commerce devices or goods so obtained or to knowingly receive goods that have been obtained by means of the fraudulent use of the transfer system.

30. CIRCUMVENTING COPYRIGHT PROTECTION DEVICES VIA COMPUTER

The Digital Millennium Copyright Act (DMCA)[44] makes it a federal offense to circumvent or create programs to circumvent encryption devices that copyright holders place on copyrighted material to prevent unauthorized copying. **For Example,** circumventing the encryption devices on software or CDs or DVDs is a violation of the DMCA.

Dmitry Sklyarov, a Russian computer programmer, was the first person to be charged with a violation of the DMCA. Mr. Sklyarov was arrested in early 2002 at a computer show after giving a speech in Las Vegas at the Defcon convention on his product that he developed to permit the circumvention of security devices on copyrighted materials. His program unlocks password-protected e-books and PDF files. He gave his speech and was returned to Russia in exchange for his agreement to testify in a case that will determine the constitutionality of DMCA.

---

[43] 15 USC § 1693(n).
[44] 17 USC § (1998).

31. SPAMMING

More states are addressing the use of computers to send unsolicited e-mails. Nevada was the first state to regulate spam and California, Washington, and Virginia followed shortly after. Criminal regulation began with very narrowly tailored statutes such as one in Washington that made it a crime to send an e-mail with a misleading title line.[45] The specific criminal statutes on spamming are evolving, and Virginia became the first state to pass a criminal anti-spamming law. The statute prohibits sending "unsolicited bulk electronic mail" or spam and makes the offense a felony based on the level of activity.[46] Spamming becomes a felony if the volume of spam exceeds 10,000 in 24 hours or 100,000 in 30 days or 1 million in one year. Thirty-six states now have some form of spamming regulation. The penalties range from fines to imprisonment.

 ## CRIMINAL PROCEDURE RIGHTS FOR BUSINESSES

Business criminals are treated the same procedurally as other criminals. They have the same rights under the criminal justice system. The U.S. Constitution guarantees the protection of individual rights within the criminal justice system.

32. FOURTH AMENDMENT RIGHTS FOR BUSINESSES

Fourth Amendment privacy protection in the U.S. Constitution; prohibits unauthorized searches and seizures.

search warrant judicial authorization for a search of property where there is the expectation of privacy.

(a) SEARCH AND SEIZURE: WARRANTS   The **Fourth Amendment** to the U.S. Constitution provides that "the right of the people to be secure in their persons, houses, papers, and effects, against unreasonable searches and seizures, shall not be violated." This amendment protects individual privacy by preventing unreasonable searches and seizures. Before a government agency can seize the property of individuals or businesses, it must obtain a valid **search warrant** issued by a judge or magistrate, based on probable cause, or an exception to this warrant requirement must apply. In other words, there must be good reason to believe that instruments or other evidence of a crime are present at the business location to be searched. The Fourth Amendment applies equally to individuals and corporations. In an unauthorized search, a corporation's property is given the same protection. If an improper search is conducted, evidence obtained during the course of that search may be inadmissible in the criminal proceedings for the resulting criminal charges.

(b) EXCEPTIONS TO THE WARRANT REQUIREMENT   Exceptions to the warrant requirement are emergencies, such as a burning building, and the "plain-view" exception, which allows law enforcement officials to take any property that anyone can see, for no privacy rights are violated when items and property are left in the open for members of the public to see. **For Example,** you have an expectation of privacy in the garbage in your garbage can when it is in your house. However, once you move that garbage can onto the public sidewalk for pickup, you no longer have the expectation of privacy because you have left your garbage out in plain view of the public.

Another exception allows officers to enter when they are needed to give aid because of an ongoing criminal act. For example, officers who are able to see a fight through the windows of a house and that some are injured can enter to render help. Another

---

[45] Saul Hansell, "Total Up the Bill for Spam," *New York Times*, July 28, 2003, C1, C4.
[46] Ibid.

CASE SUMMARY

Low-Flying Aircraft Bearing Federal Agents with Cameras

FACTS: Dow Chemical (petitioner) operates a 2,000-acre chemical plant at Midland, Michigan. The facility, with numerous buildings, conduits, and pipes, is visible from the air. Dow has maintained ground security at the facility and has investigated flyovers by other, unauthorized aircraft. However, none of the buildings or manufacturing equipment is concealed.

In 1978, the Environmental Protection Agency (EPA) conducted an inspection of Dow. The EPA requested a second inspection, but Dow denied the request. The EPA then employed a commercial aerial photographer to take photos of the plant from 12,000, 3,000, and 1,200 feet. The EPA had no warrant, but the plane was always within navigable air space when the photos were taken.

When Dow became aware of the EPA photographer, it brought suit in federal district court and challenged the action as a violation of its Fourth Amendment rights. The district court found that the EPA had violated Dow's rights and issued an injunction prohibiting further use of the aircraft. The court of appeals reversed and Dow appealed.

DECISION: The court ruled against Dow, finding that the EPA did not need explicit statutory provisions to use methods of observation commonly available to the public. There was no expectation of privacy in an area that was not covered. [**Dow Chemical Co. v United States, 476 US 1819 (1986)**]

---

exception would be that the person who lives in the property to be searched has given permission for the search.

(c) BUSINESS RECORDS AND SEARCHES. In many business crimes, the records that prove a crime was committed are not in the hands of the person who committed that crime. Accountants, attorneys, and other third parties may have the business records in their possession. In addition to the Fourth Amendment issues involved in seizing these records (a warrant is still required), there may be protections for the business defendants. The next section covers those protections.

(d) PROTECTIONS FOR PRIVILEGED RECORDS AND DOCUMENTS All states recognize an attorney-client privilege, which means that an individual's conversations with her lawyer and the notes of those conversations are not subject to seizure unless the privilege is waived. In many of the prosecutions of companies, the Justice Department has asked companies to waive the attorney/client privilege so that it can have access to information that is then used to find other companies that may have participated in criminal activity. Some states recognize an accountant-client privilege and other privileges, such as those between priest and parishioner or doctor and patient. A privileged relationship is one in which the records and notes resulting from the contact between individuals cannot be seized even with a warrant (with some exceptions).

Fifth Amendment
constitutional protection against self-incrimination; also guarantees due process.

33. FIFTH AMENDMENT SELF-INCRIMINATION RIGHTS FOR BUSINESSES

(a) SELF-INCRIMINATION The words "I take the Fifth" are used to invoke the constitutional protections against self-incrimination provided under the **Fifth Amendment**

CASE SUMMARY

A Man's Home Is His Castle, but His Wife Can Still Turn on Him

FACTS: Scott Randolph and his wife, Janet, separated in late May 2001, when she left their Americus, Georgia, home and went to stay with her parents in Canada, taking their son and some belongings. In July, she returned to the Americus house with the child. No one is sure whether she had returned to reconcile or whether she had come to gather her remaining possessions.

On July 6, 2001, Janet called police and told them that Scott had taken their son. She also shared that her husband was a cocaine user whose habit had caused financial troubles and that they had marital problems and said that she and their son had only recently returned. Shortly after the police arrived, Scott returned and explained that he had removed the child to a neighbor's house out of concern that his wife might take the boy out of the country again; he denied cocaine use and countered that it was in fact his wife who abused drugs and alcohol.

One of the officers, Sergeant Murray, went with Janet to reclaim the child, and when they returned, she volunteered that there were "items of drug evidence" in the house. Sergeant Murray asked Scott Randolph for permission to search the house, which he refused.

The sergeant turned to Janet for consent to search, which she readily gave. She led the officer upstairs to a bedroom that she identified as Scott's, where the sergeant noticed a section of a drinking straw with a powdery residue he suspected was cocaine. He then left the house to get an evidence bag from his car and to call the district attorney's office, which instructed him to stop the search and apply for a warrant. When Sergeant Murray returned to the house, Janet Randolph withdrew her consent. The police took the straw and the Randolphs to the police station. After getting a search warrant, they returned to the house and seized further evidence of drug use, which served as the basis of Scott's indictment for possession of cocaine.

Scott Randolph moved to suppress the evidence, as products of a warrantless search. The trial court denied the motion, ruling that Janet had common authority to consent to the search.

The Court of Appeals of Georgia reversed, and the Georgia Supreme Court sustained the reversal. The state of Georgia appealed, and the U.S. Supreme Court granted *certiorari.*

DECISION: The court held that "a man's home is his castle" and that when he objects to a search, his spouse could not overrule his decision. Co-ownership of property does not necessarily mean that individuals are willing to waive their rights of privacy for purposes for warrantless searches. The dissent argued that sharing necessarily means waiving privacy. The fact that they are betrayed by a spouse, roommate, or others does not affect the consent exception to the Fourth Amendment because underlying that protection is the right to privacy and that right has been waived through the shared ownership or living arrangement. **[Georgia v Randolph, 126 S.Ct. 1515 (2006)]**

that prevents compelling a person to be a witness against himself. **For Example,** Charles Keating, the former CEO of a California savings and loan who was tried for fraud and other business crimes, invoked the Fifth Amendment 80 times in his testimony before Congress on the failure of his Lincoln Savings and Loan.[47] Ken Lay, former CEO and chairman of Enron, took the Fifth Amendment before Congress

---

[47] Keating's convictions were reversed in 1999.

when asked to testify as did Bernie Ebbers, former CEO of WorldCom. Richard Grasso, the former chairman of the New York Stock Exchange took the Fifth Amendment when he was questioned about his compensation package while he headed the NYSE. However, both Lay and Ebbers took the witness stand in their own trials. They were not required to, but hoped to help their cases. The Fifth Amendment protection applies only to individuals; corporations are not given Fifth Amendment protection. A corporation cannot prevent the disclosure of its books and records on the grounds of self-incrimination. The officers and employees of a corporation can assert the Fifth Amendment, but the records of the corporation belong to the corporation, not to them, so they cannot use the Fifth Amendment to prevent the disclosure of the records.

Miranda **warnings** warnings required to prevent self-incrimination in a criminal matter.

(b) MIRANDA RIGHTS   The famous ***Miranda* warnings** come from a case interpreting the extent of Fifth Amendment rights. In *Miranda v Arizona,*[48] the U.S. Supreme Court ruled that certain warnings must be given to persons who face custodial interrogation for the purposes of possible criminal proceedings. The warnings consist of an explanation to individuals that they have the right to remain silent; that if they do speak, anything they say can be used against them; that they have the right to have an attorney present; and that if they cannot afford an attorney, one will be provided for them. Failure to give the *Miranda* warnings means that any statements, including a confession, obtained while the individual was being interrogated cannot be used as evidence against that individual. The prosecution will have to rely on evidence other than the statements made in violation of *Miranda,* if such evidence exists.

CASE SUMMARY

I Confess, but Without *Miranda* You Can't Use It Against Me

FACTS: Dickerson confessed to robbing a bank at a field office of the Federal Bureau of Investigation (FBI). At the time he confessed, he was not a suspect, was free to leave, and was not in custody. He was not, however, given his *Miranda* warnings before the FBI agents interrogated him about the robbery. Dickerson's lawyer moved to have his confession excluded from his trial because it was obtained in violation of *Miranda.* The federal district court suppressed the confession. The court of appeals reversed, noting that while the warnings had not been given, the confession was clearly voluntary. Dickerson appealed.

DECISION: The U.S. Supreme Court held that the confession could not be used because Dickerson had not been given his warnings. The judicial decision is complex because it focuses on the difference between questioning in custody and the need to give *Miranda* warnings even when there is no custody of the person. The majority of the court ruled that *Miranda* warnings must still be given as a way to prevent those being questioned from unknowingly waiving their rights. [**Dickerson v United States, 530 US 428 (2000)**]

---

[48] 384 US 436 (1966).

34. DUE PROCESS RIGHTS FOR BUSINESSES

due process the constitutional right to be heard, question witnesses, and present evidence.

Also included in the Fifth Amendment is the language of due process. **Due process** is the right to be heard, question witnesses, and present evidence before any criminal conviction can occur. Due process in criminal cases consists of an initial appearance at which the charges and the defendant's rights are outlined; a preliminary hearing or grand jury proceeding in which the evidence is determined to be sufficient to warrant a trial; an arraignment for entering a plea and setting a trial date when the defendant pleads innocent; a period of discovery for obtaining evidence; and a trial at which witnesses for the prosecution can be cross-examined and evidence presented to refute the charges. In addition to these procedural steps, the **Sixth Amendment** guarantees that the entire process will be completed in a timely fashion because this amendment guarantees a speedy trial.

Sixth Amendment the U.S. constitutional amendment that guarantees a speedy trial.

LAWFLIX

Twelve Angry Men (1957)(G)

This film offers a look at the jury process and whether the evidence is sufficient to label the conduct a crime.

For movie clips that illustrate business law concepts, see LawFlix at **http://wdvl.westbuslaw.com.**

SUMMARY

When a person does not live up to the standards set by law, society may regard this person's conduct as so dangerous to the government, to other people, or to property that society will prosecute the person for the misconduct. This punishable conduct, called *crime,* may be common law or statutory in origin. Crimes are classified as *felonies,* which generally carry greater sentences and more long-term consequences, and *misdemeanors.*

Employers and corporations may be criminally responsible for their acts and the acts of their employees. The federal sentencing guidelines impose mandatory sentences for federal crimes and allow judges to consider whether the fact that a business promotes compliance with the law is a reason to reduce a sentence.

White-collar crimes include those relating to financial fraud. Sarbanes-Oxley reforms increased the penalties for financial fraud and added fraudulent financial statement

certification as a crime. Other white-collar crimes include bribery, extortion, blackmail, and corrupt influence in politics and in business. Also included as white-collar crimes are counterfeiting, forgery, perjury, making false claims against the government, obtaining goods or money by false pretenses, using bad checks, false financial reporting, and embezzlement. The common law crimes include those that involve injury to person and/or property, such as arson and murder.

Statutes have expanded the area of criminal law to meet situations in which computers are involved. Both federal and state statutes make the unauthorized taking of information from a computer a crime. The diversion of deliveries of goods and the transfer of funds, the theft of software, and the raiding of computers are made crimes to some extent by the federal Computer Access Device and Computer Fraud and Abuse Act of 1984 and the Electronic Fund Transfers Act of 1978. Newer federal statutes that apply to computers are the Economic Espionage Act, which prohibits downloading or copying information via computer to give to a competitor, and the Digital Millennium Copyright Act that prohibits circumventing or designing programs to circumvent encryption devices.

Criminal procedure is dictated by the Fourth, Fifth, and Sixth amendments. The Fourth Amendment protects against unreasonable searches, the Fifth Amendment protects against self-incrimination and provides due process, and the Sixth Amendment guarantees a speedy trial.

> QUESTIONS AND CASE PROBLEMS

1. Bernard Flinn operated a business known as Harvey Investment Co., Inc./High Risk Loans. Flinn worked as a loan broker, matching those who came to him with lenders willing to loan them money given their credit history and the amount involved. From 1982 through 1985, Flinn found loans for five people. Indiana requires that persons engaged in the business of brokering loans obtain a license from the state. Flinn was prosecuted for brokering loans without having a license. He raised the defense that he did not know that a license was required and that, accordingly, he lacked the criminal intent to broker loans without having a license. Does Flinn have a good defense? [*Flinn v Indiana,* 563 NE2d 536 (Ind)]

2. H. J., Inc., and other customers of Northwestern Bell Corp. alleged that Northwestern Bell had furnished cash and tickets for air travel, plays, and sporting events and had offered employment to members of the Minnesota Public Utilities Commission in exchange for favorable treatment in rate cases before the commission. A Minnesota statute makes it a felony to bribe public officials. H. J. and other customers brought suit against Northwestern for violating the criminal bribery statute. Can the customers bring a criminal action? [*H. J., Inc. v Northwestern Bell Corp.,* 420 NW 2d 673 (Minn App)]

3. Baker and others entered a Wal-Mart store shortly after 3:00 A.M. by cutting through the metal door with an acetylene torch. They had moved some of the merchandise in the store to the rear door, but the police arrived before the merchandise could be taken from the store. Baker was prosecuted for larceny. He raised the defense that he was not guilty of larceny because no merchandise had ever left the store. Is there enough intent and action for a crime? [*Tennessee v Baker,* 751 SW2d 154 (Tenn App)]

4. Gail drove her automobile after having had dinner and several drinks. She fell asleep at the wheel and ran over and killed a pedestrian. Prosecuted for manslaughter, she raised the defense that she did not intend to hurt anyone and because of the drinks did not know what she was doing. Was this a valid defense?

5. Clarence Conrad Bolton was in his early 90s in December 1989 when conservatorship proceedings were commenced in which Joyce Van Buren sought to be appointed his guardian and conservator. While the proceedings were pending and before the appointment could be completed, Bolton gave Souter two checks totaling $2,200 in an attempt to hide money from others and to establish an emergency fund. Souter cashed both checks and deposited $2,200 in an account she had opened at a Hutchinson bank. A few days after entrusting the money to Souter, Bolton asked for $500 "to test her out to see if she was honest about it." Souter delivered $500 to Bolton as he requested. Later, at Bolton's request, Souter cashed another check for $300, which Bolton gave Souter to help with the purchase of a car. When Bolton asked Souter to return more of his money, Souter refused, contending she was not indebted to him. Souter said that she deposited only $1,000 of Bolton's money in the account and that the $1,200 deposit shown on the bank statement came from her separate funds. She claimed she gave $800 to Bolton, which left $200 she claimed Bolton gave to her to buy a car and car insurance.

   The bank's records indicate that between late December 1989 and June 1, 1990, Souter wrote checks on the account payable to her children, Reno County, State Farm, KPL Gas Service, and others. On June 2, 1990, Souter deposited $1,172 of her income tax return into the account, and by October 1990, the balance was under $10.

The account was closed in overdraft status in March 1991. The state prosecuted Souter for embezzlement. She says you cannot embezzle money that was given to you. Is she right? [*Bolton v Souter,* 872 P2d 758 (Kan)]

6. Dr. Doyle E. Campbell, an ophthalmologist, established his practice in southern Ohio in 1971. Many of Dr. Campbell's patients are elderly people who qualify for federal Medicare benefits and state Medicaid benefits. Under the existing financing system, a doctor who treats a Medicare patient is required to submit a "Medicare Health Insurance Claim Form" (HCFA Form 1500). The doctor is required to certify that "the services shown on this form were medically indicated and necessary for the health of the patient and were personally rendered by me or were rendered incident to my professional service by my employees." Claims Dr. Campbell submitted for his elderly patients ranged from $900 to $950, of which $530 to $680 were covered by the Medicare program. The government alleged that Dr. Campbell billed Medicare for several treatments that were either not performed or not necessary. Dr. Campbell was charged with fraud for the paperwork he submitted. Has he committed a crime? [*United States v Campbell,* 845 F2d 1374 (6th Cir)]

7. In the late 1980s, Life Energy Resources, Ltd. (LER), a New York corporation, was a multilevel marketing network. LER's marketing plan provided that members of the general public could purchase its products only through an official LER distributor or by becoming LER distributors themselves. Each potential distributor had to be sponsored by an existing distributor and was required to sign a distributorship agreement with LER stating that he or she would not make medical claims or use unofficial literature or marketing aids to promote LER products.

Ballistrea and his partner Michael Ricotta were at the top of the LER distribution network. Two products sold by LER were the REM SuperPro Frequency Generator (REM) and the Lifemax Miracle Cream (Miracle Cream). The REM, which sold for $1,350 to distributors, was a small box powered by electricity that ran currents through the feet and body of the user.

Ballistrea and Ricotta distributed literature and audiotapes to many potential downstream distributors and customers—some of whom were undercover government agents—touting the REM and the Miracle Cream. Other literature claimed that the Miracle Cream could alleviate the discomforts of premenstrual syndrome and reverse the effects of osteoporosis. The Food and Drug Administration charged Ballistrea and Ricotta with violating federal law for making medical claims concerning LER products. Their defense is that they never sold any of the products. They simply earned commissions as part of the marketing scheme and could not be held criminally liable on the charges. Are they correct? [*United States v Ballistrea,* 101 F3d 827 (2d Cir)]

8. Thomas Iverson was a founder of CH2O, Inc., and served as the company's president and chairman of the board. CH2O ships blended chemicals to its customers in drums. CH2O asked its customers to return the drums so that it could reuse them. Although customers returned the drums, they often did not clean them sufficiently, and the drums still contained chemical residue. Before CH2O could reuse the drums, it had to remove that residue. To do so, CH2O instituted a drum-cleaning operation, which in turn generated wastewater.

Beginning in about 1985, Iverson personally discharged the wastewater and ordered employees of CH2O to discharge the wastewater. In April 1992, Iverson bought a warehouse in Olympia. After the purchase, CH2O restarted its drum-cleaning operation at the warehouse and disposed of its wastewater through the sewer. CH2O obtained neither a permit nor permission to make these discharges. The drum-cleaning operation continued until the summer of 1995, when CH2O learned that it was under investigation for discharging pollutants into the sewer.

A few months before CH2O restarted its drum-cleaning operation, Iverson had announced his "official" retirement from CH2O. However, he continued to receive money from CH2O, to conduct business at the company's facilities, and to give orders to employees. CH2O continued to list him as the president in documents that it filed with the state, and the employee who was responsible for running the day-to-day aspects of the drum-cleaning operation testified that he reported to Iverson.

The federal government has charged CH2O and Iverson with criminal violations of the Clean Water Act. Iverson says he is not responsible because he had retired. Can he be held criminally liable for a violation of the Clean Water Act through the drum-cleaning operations? [*United States. v Iverson,* 162 F3d 1015 (9th Cir)]

9. James Durham runs an art gallery. He has several paintings from unknown artists that he has listed for sale. The paintings always sell at his weekly auction for $20,000 to $50,000 above what James believes them to be worth. James learns that the bidders at the auctions are employed by an olive distributor located near the shipping yards of the city. What concerns should Durham have about the art, the bidders and the large purchase prices?

10. Jennings operated a courier service to collect and deliver money. The contract with his customers allowed him a day or so to deliver the money that had been collected. Instead of holding collections until delivered, Jennings made short-term investments with the money. He always made deliveries to the customers on time, but because he kept the profit from the investments for himself, Jennings was prosecuted for embezzlement. Was he guilty? [*New York v Jennings,* 504 NE2d 1079 (NY)]

11. Chaussee sold franchises to a number of persons authorizing them to sell a product that did not exist. He was prosecuted under the Colorado Organized Crime Control Act on the ground that he was guilty of a pattern of racketeering. His defense was that there was no pattern because there was only one scheme. Was he guilty?

12. Grabert ran Beck's, an amusement center in Louisiana. He held a license for video gambling machines. Louisiana makes it illegal to allow a minor to play a video gambling machine. A mother came into Grabert's center carrying her 23-month-old baby in her arms. She sat at the video poker machine with her child on her lap and proceeded to play. State troopers witnessed the baby pushing the buttons on the machine at least three times. The Department of Public Safety and Corrections revoked Grabert's video gaming license because a minor had been allowed to play the machines, and Grabert sought judicial review. The trial court reversed, and the department appealed. Has Grabert committed the crime of allowing a minor to engage in gaming? Is this the crime of allowing a minor to gamble? [*Grabert v Department of Public Safety & Corrections,* 680 So 2d 764 (La App) *cert. denied; Grabert v State Through Dept. of Public Safety and Corrections,* 685 So 2d 126 (La)]

13. The Banco Central administered a humanitarian plan for the government of Ecuador. Fernando Banderas and his wife presented false claims that the bank paid. After the fraud was discovered, the bank sued Banderas and his wife for damages for fraud and treble damages under the Florida version of RICO. Banderas and his wife asserted that they were not liable for RICO damages because there was no proof that they were related to organized crime and because the wrong they had committed was merely ordinary fraud. They had not used any racketeering methods. Is involvement with organized crime a requirement for liability under RICO? [*Banderas v Banco Central del Ecuador,* 461 So 2d 265 (Fla App)]

14. Kravitz owned 100 percent of the stock of American Health Programs, Inc. (AHP). To obtain the Philadelphia Fraternal Order of Police as a customer for AHP, Kravitz paid money bribes to persons who he thought were officers of that organization but who in fact were federal undercover agents. He was prosecuted for violating RICO. He was convicted, and the court ordered the forfeiture of all of Kravitz's shares of AHP stock. Can a forfeiture be ordered? [*United States v Kravitz,* 738 F2d 102 (3d Cir)]

15. Howell made long-distance telephone calls through the telephone company's computer-controlled switching system to solicit funding for a nonexistent business enterprise. What crimes did Howell commit? [*New Mexico v Howell,* 895 P2d 232 (NM App)]

TORTS

LEARNING OBJECTIVES

After studying this chapter, you should be able to

LO.1 Define torts and distinguish them from crimes

LO.2 List the types of torts

LO.3 Provide examples of intentional torts and the elements of each

LO.4 Discuss the elements of negligence

LO.5 Explain the defenses to negligence

LO.6 Explain concerns about levels of tort liability and possible reforms

The law of torts permits individuals and companies to recover from other individuals and companies for wrongs committed against them. Tort law provides rights and remedies for conduct that meets the elements required to establish that a wrong has occurred.

 ## GENERAL PRINCIPLES

Civil, or noncriminal, wrongs that are not breaches of contract are governed by tort law. This chapter covers the types of civil wrongs that constitute torts and the remedies available for those wrongs.

1. WHAT IS A TORT?

tort civil wrong that interferes with one's property or person.

Tort comes from the Latin term *tortus,* which means "crooked, dubious, twisted." Torts are actions that are not straight but are crooked, or civil, wrongs. A tort is an interference with someone's person or property. **For Example,** entering someone's house without his or her permission is an interference and constitutes the tort of trespass. Causing someone's character to be questioned is a wrong against the person and is the tort of defamation. The law provides protection against these harms in the form of remedies awarded after the wrongs are committed. These remedies are civil remedies for the acts of interference by others.

2. TORT AND CRIME DISTINGUISHED

A *crime* is a wrong that arises from a violation of a public duty, whereas a *tort* is a wrong that arises from a violation of a private duty. A crime is a wrong of such a serious nature that the appropriate level of government steps in to prosecute and punish the wrongdoer to deter others from engaging in the same type of conduct. However, whenever the act that is committed as a crime causes harm to an identifiable person, that person may recover from the wrongdoer for monetary damages to compensate for the harm. For the person who experiences the direct harm, the act is called a *tort*; for the government, the same act is called a *crime.*

When the same act is both a crime and a tort, the government may prosecute the wrongdoer for a violation of criminal law, and the individual who experiences the direct harm may recover damages. **For Example,** O. J. Simpson was charged by the state of California with the murder of his ex-wife, Nicole Brown Simpson, and her friend Ron Goldman. A criminal trial was held in which O. J. Simpson was acquitted. Simpson was subsequently sued civilly by the families of Nicole Simpson and Ron Goldman for the tort of wrongful death. The jury in the civil case found Simpson civilly liable and the court ordered him to pay nearly $20 million in damages plus interest. Only $382,000 of this judgment has actually been paid to the families.

3. TYPES OF TORTS

intentional torts civil wrong that results from intentional conduct.

There are three types of torts: intentional torts, negligence, and strict liability. **Intentional torts** are those that occur when wrongdoers engage in intentional conduct. **For Example,** striking another person in a fight is an intentional act and would be the tort of battery and possibly also the crime of battery. Your arm striking another person's nose in a fast-moving crowd of people at a rock concert is not a tort or crime because your arm was pushed unintentionally by the force of the crowd. If you stretched out your arms in that crowd or began to swing your arms about and struck another person, you would be behaving carelessly in a crowd of people; and, although you may not have committed an intentional tort, it is possible that your careless conduct constitutes the tort of **negligence**. Careless actions, or actions taken without thinking through their consequences, constitute negligence. The harm to the other person's nose may not have been intended, but there is liability for these accidental harms under negligence. **For Example,** if you run a red light, hit another car, and injure its driver, you did not intend the result. However, your careless behavior of disregarding a traffic signal resulted in the injury, and you would have liability for your negligence to that driver.

Strict liability is another type of tort that imposes liability without regard to whether there was any intent to harm or any negligence occurred. Strict liability is imposed without regard to fault. Strict or absolute liability is imposed because the activity involved is so dangerous that there must be full accountability. Nonetheless, the activity is necessary and cannot be prohibited. The compromise is to allow the activity but ensure that its dangers and resulting damages are fully covered through the imposition of full liability for all injuries that result. **For Example,** contractors often need to use dynamite to take a roadway through a mountainside or demolish a building that has become a hazard. When the dynamite is used, noise, debris, and possibly dangerous pieces of earth and building will descend on others' land and possibly on people. In most states, contractors are held strictly liable for the resulting damage from the use of dynamite. The activity is necessary and not illegal, but those who use dynamite must be prepared to compensate those who are injured as a result.

Other areas in which there is strict liability for activity include the storage of flammable materials and crop dusting. The federal government and the states have pure food laws that impose absolute liability on manufacturers who fail to meet the statutory standards for their products. Another area of strict liability is *product liability,* which is covered in Chapter 25.

B   INTENTIONAL TORTS

4. ASSAULT

An *assault* is intentional conduct that threatens a person with a well-founded fear of imminent harm coupled with the present ability to carry out the threat of harm. **For Example,** the angry assertion "I'm going to kick your butt" along with aggressive movement in the direction of the victim with the intent to carry out the threat is an assault, even though a third person intervenes to stop the intended action. Mere words, however, although insulting, are ordinarily insufficient to constitute an assault.

5. BATTERY

A *battery* is the intentional, wrongful touching of another person without that person's consent. Thus, a threat to use force is an assault, and the actual use of force is the battery. The single action of striking an individual can be both a crime and a tort.

---

negligence failure to exercise due care under the circumstances in consequence of which harm is proximately caused to one to whom the defendant owed a duty to exercise due care.

strict liability civil wrong for which there is absolute liability because of the inherent danger in the underlying activity, for example, the use of explosives.

A lawsuit for the tort of battery provides a plaintiff with the opportunity to recover damages resulting from the battery. The plaintiff must prove damages, however.

CASE SUMMARY

An Exchange of Unpleasantries . . .

FACTS: Moore and Beye had an altercation after a public meeting regarding airport expansion. Moore owns a ranch near the airport and staunchly opposes expansion. Beye owns a flying service and avidly supports expansion. Moore and Beye exchanged unpleasantries while leaving the meeting. Beye then punched Moore on the left side of the jaw. Moore stumbled but caught himself before falling. He then exclaimed to the crowd, "You saw that. You are my witnesses. I've been assaulted. I want that man arrested." Ravalli County deputies took Beye into custody, and the state charged him with misdemeanor assault. Moore visited the hospital complaining of back and neck pain two days later and contended that he injured his back while reeling from Beye's punch. He filed a civil complaint against Beye for damages. Moore's evidence mostly concerned his alleged back injury. Beye did not contest that he punched Moore. His evidence countered that Moore's back problems existed before the altercation. The judge instructed the jury that Beye had committed a battery as a matter of law and directed that they answer the question, "Was Moore damaged as a result of the battery?" The jury voted 11 to 1 that the battery did not injure Moore, and Moore appealed.

DECISION: Judgment for Beye. Beye presented the testimony of several eyewitnesses and a medical expert that Moore sustained no damages. Although Moore presented considerable evidence to the contrary, it was not the court's function to agree or disagree with the verdict. Beye presented sufficient evidence to uphold the jury's verdict. [**Moore v Beye, 122 P3d 1212 (Mont 2005)**]

6. FALSE IMPRISONMENT

false imprisonment intentional detention of a person without that person's consent; called the *shopkeeper's tort* when shoplifters are unlawfully detained.

False imprisonment is the intentional detention of a person without that person's consent.[1] The detention need not be for any specified period of time, for any detention against one's will is false imprisonment. False imprisonment is often called the *shopkeeper's tort* because so much liability has been imposed on store owners for their unreasonable detention of customers suspected of shoplifting. Requiring a customer to sit in the manager's office or not allowing a customer to leave the store can constitute the tort of false imprisonment. Shop owners do, however, need the opportunity to investigate possible thefts in their stores. As a result, all states have some form of privilege or protection for store owners called a *shopkeeper's privilege*.

shopkeeper's privilege right of a store owner to detain a suspected shoplifter based on reasonable cause and for a reasonable time without resulting liability for false imprisonment.

The **shopkeeper's privilege** permits the store owner to detain a suspected shoplifter based on reasonable suspicion for a reasonable time without resulting liability for false imprisonment to the accused customer.[2] The privilege applies even if the store owner was wrong about the customer being a shoplifter, so long as the store owner acted based on reasonable suspicions and treated the accused shoplifter in a reasonable

---

[1] *Forgie-Buccioni v Hannaford Bros. Inc.*, 413 F3d 175 (1st Cir 2005).

[2] *Limited Stores, Inc. v Wilson-Robinson*, 876 SW2d 248 (Ark 1994); see also *Wal-Mart Stores, Inc. v Binns*, 15 SW3d 320 (Ark 2000).

manner. These privilege statutes do not protect the store owner from liability for unnecessary physical force or for invasion of privacy.

CASE SUMMARY

Officer Rivera Flagged for Unnecessary Roughness?

FACTS: Dillard Department Stores, Inc. (Dillard), detained hairstylist Lyndon Silva at its Houston, Texas, store. Silva testified that he was stopped by security guard Kevin Rivera, an off-duty Houston police officer who was in uniform with his "gun on his hip," and he was accused of theft of three shirts. Silva testified that Rivera placed him on the floor, handcuffed him, and emptied his shopping bag onto the floor. Silva testified people were around him when he was taken upstairs in handcuffs and when he was later escorted to the police car. He further stated that the officer and a woman made fun of him while he was being detained upstairs. Silva stated that when the city police came to take him into custody, Rivera again placed him on the floor with his knee in his back and exchanged handcuffs with the city police. He further testified that he asked Rivera many times to check his car for the receipt for the three shirts he was returning, but these requests were ignored, and that during the entire time he was detained, no one asked him for any explanation.

Officer Rivera's testimony was in direct conflict with Silva's, stating that Silva offered no excuse for not having a receipt for the shirts, and disputing that there were a lot of people watching, stating that the store was a "ghost town" at that time of day, 1:30 P.M. Silva later produced a receipt for three shirts. A jury returned a verdict for Silva for $13,121 in damages for physical pain, mental anguish, and attorney fees for false imprisonment and $50,000 in punitive damages. Dillard appealed, contending its employee had a shopkeeper's privilege to detain a customer to investigate the ownership of property.

DECISION: Judgment for Silva. The shopkeeper's privilege is applicable so long as (1) the employee has a reasonable belief that the customer is attempting to steal store merchandise (2) the detention is for a reasonable period of time, and (3) the detention is in a reasonable manner. In this case there was a reasonable belief by a store employee that items were being stolen. The detention for approximately an hour while store employees and Silva were questioned and the police department was called was a reasonable period of time. Regarding the third component, however, the jury found that Silva's story was more credible than Rivera's. It concluded that the detention was not in a reasonable manner and, accordingly, the shopkeeper's privilege did not apply. Since Silva's testimony supported the jury's finding, Dillard's appeal was denied. [**Dillard Department Stores, Inc. v Silva, 106 SW3d 789 (Tex App 2003)**]

7. INTENTIONAL INFLICTION OF EMOTIONAL DISTRESS

intentional infliction of emotional distress tort that produces mental anguish caused by conduct that exceeds all bounds of decency.

The **intentional infliction of emotional distress** is a tort involving conduct that goes beyond all bounds of decency and produces mental anguish in the harmed individual. This tort requires proof of outrageous conduct and resulting emotional distress in the victim. The types of conduct for which this tort is used for recovery include outrageous collection methods employed by debt collection agencies. **For Example,** if a collection agent constantly called a debtor while he was hospitalized following heart surgery, such conduct would rise to the level of outrageous conduct beyond all standards of decency. Such a collection effort would constitute the tort of intentional infliction of emotional distress.

CASE SUMMARY

Out of Bounds

FACTS: In the fall of 2001, shortly after the terrorist attacks on the World Trade Center and the Pentagon, someone mailed letters laced with anthrax to several news organizations and members of Congress. Five people died from contact with these letters. By May 2002, the FBI had not been able to identify and arrest the perpetrator(s). *New York Times* (the *Times*) columnist Nicholas Kristof wrote several columns asserting that the FBI had not moved aggressively enough against a man he called "Mr. Z." In August 2002, he identified Mr. Z as Dr. Steven Hatfill, a research scientist employed by the Department of Defense. Dr. Hatfill sued the *Times* and Mr. Kristof for defamation and intentional infliction of emotional distress. The district court dismissed Hatfill's complaint, concluding in part that "publishing news or commentary on matters of public concern" can never be sufficiently extreme or outrageous to support a claim for intentional infliction of emotional distress. Hatfill appealed.

DECISION: At this stage of the litigation, the court's sole concern was whether Hatfill's allegations, taken as true, describe intentional and outrageous misconduct. The court concluded that they do. Hatfill's complaint on the issue of intentional infliction of emotional distress alleges that "[a]s a result of defendants' defamation here at issue, Dr. Hatfill has suffered severe and ongoing loss of reputation and professional standing, loss of employment, past and ongoing financial injury, severe emotional distress and other injury." The complaint further alleges that publication of Kristof's columns inflicted "grievous emotional distress" upon Hatfill. These allegations are adequate to state a claim for intentional infliction of emotional distress. The decision of the district court on this claim and the claim of defamation is reversed and remanded. [**Hatfill v New York Times, 427 F3d 253 (4th Cir 2005)**]

8. INVASION OF PRIVACY

invasion of privacy tort of intentional intrusion into the private affairs of another.

The right of privacy is the right to be free of unreasonable intrusion into one's private affairs. The tort of **invasion of privacy** actually consists of three different torts: (1) intrusion into the plaintiff's private affairs (for example, planting a microphone in an office or home); (2) public disclosure of private facts (for example, disclosing private financial information, such as a business posting returned checks from customers near its cash register in a public display); and (3) appropriation of another's name, likeness, or image for commercial advantage. This form of invasion of privacy is generally referred to as the *right of publicity.* The elements of this tort are (1) appropriation of the plaintiff's name or likeness for the value associated with it, and not in an incidental manner or for a newsworthy purpose, (2) identification of the plaintiff in the publication, and (3) an advantage or benefit to the defendant. The right of publicity is designed to protect the commercial interest of celebrities in their identities. **For Example,** popular and critically acclaimed rock and roll musician Don Henley, the founder and member of the band The Eagles, successfully sued a department store chain that ran an international newspaper advertisement for its Henley shirt, which stated in large letters as the focus of the ad "This is Don's henley." The ad (1) used the value associated with the famous name Don Henley to get consumers to read it, (2) the plaintiff was identifiable in the ad, and (3) the ad was created with the belief that use of the words "Don's henley" would help sell the product.[3]

CASE SUMMARY

Cashing in on Catherine's Vacation

FACTS: Catherine Bosley worked as a television news anchor for WKBN, Channel 27, in Youngstown, Ohio. While on vacation with her husband in Florida, she participated in a "wet t-shirt" contest that was videotaped without her consent by DreamGirls, Inc., and licensed to Marvad Corp., which runs a Web site for adult entertainment through a subscription service on the Internet. Marvad used depictions of her in advertisements to promote the materials and services it markets. Web site searches related to Catherine Bosley in 2004 were the most popular search on the World Wide Web. Due to the publicity, she resigned from her position at WKBN and was prevented from seeking other employment. Bosley seeks an injunction under the right to publicity theory against the defendants from using her image in any manner that promotes the sale of their goods or services. The defendants contend that an injunction would violate their First Amendment rights.

DECISION: Judgment for Bosley. The First Amendment does not immunize defendants from damages for infringement of the right to publicity. No significant editorial comment or artistic expression involving First Amendment protections applies in this case. If any "speech" interest is involved, it is commercial speech. At its core, the defendants are selling Bosley's image for a profit without her consent. It is in violation of her right to publicity, which protects one's right to be free from the appropriation of one's persona. The injunction sought was granted. [**Bosley v Wildwett.com,** 310 F Supp 2d 914 (ND Ohio 2004)]

9. DEFAMATION

defamation untrue statement by one party about another to a third party.

slander defamation of character by spoken words or gestures.

libel written or visual defamation without legal justification.

Defamation is an untrue statement by one party about another to a third party. **Slander** is oral or spoken defamation, and **libel** is written (and in some cases broadcast) defamation. The elements for defamation are (1) a statement about a person's reputation, honesty, or integrity that is untrue; (2) publication (which is accomplished when a third party hears or reads the defamatory statement); (3) a statement that is directed at a particular person; and (4) damages that result from the statement.

For Example, a false statement by the owner of a business that the former manager was fired for stealing when he was not would be defamation, and the former manager's damages could be his inability to find another position because of the statement's impact on his reputation.

In cases in which the victim is a public figure, such as a Hollywood celebrity or a professional sports player, another element is required, the element of malice, which means that what was said or written was done with the knowledge that the information was false or with reckless disregard for whether it was true or false.

The defenses to defamation include the truth. If the statement is true, even if it is harmful to the victim, it is not the tort of defamation.

Some statements are privileged, and this privilege provides a full or partial defense to the tort of defamation. **For Example,** members of Congress enjoy an **absolute privilege** when they are speaking on the floor of the Senate or the House because

absolute privilege complete defense against the tort of defamation, as in the speeches of members of Congress on the floor and witnesses in a trial.

---
[3] *Henley v Dillard Department Stores,* 46 F Supp 2d 587 (ND Tex 1999).

CASE SUMMARY

Home Run Hitter Has Good Defense Too

FACTS: The *San Francisco Chronicle* published an article about doctors who hang autographed photos of sports figures in their waiting rooms as a marketing device, with money to be made by impressing prospective patients that the doctors treated the famous athletes, even if it is not entirely true. Baseball slugger Barry Bonds' statement to the reporter about a podiatrist, Andrew Carver, that "I don't like that man.... He's a liar" was included in the article. Carver sued the newspaper, the reporter, and Bonds for defamation. Bonds asserted that Carver had been less than truthful with him, giving the impression that he was giving him free orthotics and then billing him for them and threatening to lie about Bonds to the press, statements which Carver did not deny. Carver appealed the trial court's dismissal of the case.

DECISION: Judgment for Bonds. In view of the undisputed facts, Bonds was justified in calling the plaintiff a liar. The defense of substantial truth is permitted in defamation actions. **[Carver v Bonds, 37 Cal Rptr 3d 480 (Cal App 2005)]**

E-COMMERCE AND CYBERLAW

Many companies are working to resolve a defamation issue facilitated by the Internet. The defamation of a company occurs because a disgruntled employee posts false information in a chat room about a company's earnings or an investor who wishes to affect the value of a particular stock for exercising call and put options likewise posts negative information in a chat room. For example, Mark S. Jakob was dealing in call options in Emulex stock in mid-August. His prediction that Emulex stock would take a dive was wrong; the stock in fact increased in value with a resulting loss of $100,000 for Jacob. To cover his losses, the 23-year-old sent an e-mail press release to an Internet wire service. The fake press release indicated that the CEO of Emulex would resign because earnings had been overstated.* The news release was then distributed to various Web sites.

The overall loss to shareholders when the market opened in reaction to Jakob's fake news release was $2.5 billion as the share price plummeted. However, Jakob made $240,000 by selling short in the stock. He was arrested for securities fraud and wire fraud.

Visit some investor chat rooms:

http://www.vault.com

http://www.greedyassociates.com

In addition to securities issues (see Chapter 46), there is the issue of defamation and the resulting damage to the company because of false statements posted on the Internet. The Internet is a rapid source of information and misinformation.

Following the Emulex fiasco, the FBI and other law enforcement officials counseled investors to "Know thy source" and always question information posted on Internet chat rooms.

---

* Alex Berenson, "Man Charged in Stock Fraud Based on Fake News," *New York Times*, September 1, 2000, C1, C2.

public policy requires a free dialogue on the issues pending in a legislative body. The same absolute privilege applies to witnesses in court proceedings to encourage witnesses with information to come forward and testify.

The media enjoy a **qualified privilege** for stories that turn out to be false. Their qualified privilege is a defense to defamation so long as the information was released without malice and a retraction or correction is made when the matter is brought to their attention.

A *qualified privilege* to make a defamatory statement in the workplace exists when the statement is made to protect the interests of the private employer on a work-related matter, especially when reporting actual or suspected wrongdoing. **For Example,** Neda Lewis was fired from her job at Carson Oil Company for allegedly stealing toilet paper. The employee in charge of supplies noticed toilet paper was regularly missing from the ladies room, and one evening from a 3rd floor window overlooking the parking lot, she observed that the plaintiff's bag contained two rolls of toilet paper. She reported the matter to the executive secretary, who reported it to both the president and the CEO of the firm, who decided to fire her. Two other employees were also informed. The employer was able to successfully raise the defense of a qualified privilege to Ms. Lewis' defamation action for "false accusations of theft" since all of the employees involved were participants in the investigation and termination of the employee.[4]

A new statutory privilege has been evolving over the past few years with respect to letters of recommendation and references given by employers for employees who are applying for jobs at other companies. Most companies, because of concerns about liability for defamation, will only confirm that a former employee did work at their firm and will provide the time period during which the person was employed. However, many employees who had histories that should have been revealed for safety reasons have been hired because no negative information was released. About one-third of the states now have statutes that provide employers a qualified privilege with respect to references and recommendations. So long as the employer acts in good faith in providing information, there is no liability for defamation to the former employee as a result of the information provided.

qualified privilege media privilege to print inaccurate information without liability for defamation, so long as a retraction is printed and there was no malice.

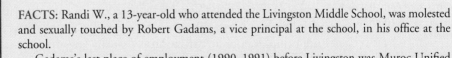

CASE SUMMARY

Putting In an Exaggerated Good Word

FACTS: Randi W., a 13-year-old who attended the Livingston Middle School, was molested and sexually touched by Robert Gadams, a vice principal at the school, in his office at the school.

Gadams's last place of employment (1990–1991) before Livingston was Muroc Unified School District, where disciplinary actions were taken against him for sexual harassment. When allegations of "sexual touching" of female students were made, Gadams was forced to resign from Muroc. Nonetheless, Gary Rice and David Malcolm, officials at Muroc, provided a letter of recommendation for Gadams that described him as "an upbeat, enthusiastic

---

[4] *Lewis v Carson Oil Co.*, 127 P3d 1207 (Or App 2006).

CASE SUMMARY

continued

administrator who relates well to the students" and who was responsible "in large part" for making Boron Junior High School (located in Muroc) "a safe, orderly and clean environment for students and staff." The letter concluded that they recommended Gadams "for an assistant principalship or equivalent position without reservation." Randi W. filed suit against the school districts, alleging that her injuries from Gadams's sexual touching were proximately caused by their failure to provide full and accurate information about Gadams to the placement service. The trial court dismissed the case, and the court of appeals reversed. The districts appealed.

DECISION: One of society's highest priorities is to protect children from sexual or physical abuse. On the other hand, a rule imposing liability in a case like this where a letter of recommendation fails to disclose material information could greatly inhibit the preparation and distribution of reference letters, to the general detriment of employers and employees alike. However, the balancing of these two competing policy issues simply requires that employers prepare recommendation letters stating all "material" facts, positive and negative, and simply decline to write a reference letter or, at most, merely confirm the former employee's position, salary, and dates of employment. Misleading letters of recommendation for potentially dangerous employees present foreseeable risks of harms to others, like the young person harmed here.

The judgment of the court of appeals is affirmed as to liability for negligent misrepresentation and fraud. [**Randi W. v Muroc Joint Unified School District**, 929 P2d 582 (Cal 1997)]

10. PRODUCT DISPARAGEMENT

slander of title malicious making of false statements as to a seller's title.

trade libel written defamation about a product or service.

product disparagement false statements made about a product or business.

Although the comparison of products and services is healthy for competition, false statements about another's products constitute a form of slander called **slander of title** or libel called **trade libel**; collectively, these are known as **product disparagement**, which occurs when someone makes false statements about another business, its products, or its abilities.[5] The elements of product disparagement are (1) a false statement about a particular business product or about its service in terms of honesty, reputation, ability, or integrity; (2) communication of the statement to a third party; and (3) damages.

11. WRONGFUL INTERFERENCE WITH CONTRACTS

contract interference tort in which a third party interferes with others' freedom to contract.

The tort of **contract interference** or (tortious interference with contracts) occurs when parties are not allowed the freedom to contract without interference from third parties. While the elements required to establish the tort of contract interference are complex, a basic definition is that the law affords a remedy when a third party intentionally causes another to break a contract already in existence. **For Example,** Nikke Finke, a newspaper reporter who had a contract with the *New York Post* to write stories about the entertainment industry for the *Post's* business section, wrote two articles about a lawsuit involving a literary agent and the Walt Disney Company over merchandising rights to the Winnie-the-Pooh characters. Finke reported that

---

[5] *Sannerud v Brantz*, 879 P2d 341 (Wyo 1994). See *Suzuki Motor Corp. v Consumers Union*, 230 F3d 1110 (9th Cir 2003), cert denied 2003 WL 22005685 (US), for an example of the complexity of a product disparagement action.

the trial court sanctioned Disney for engaging in "misuse of the discovery process" and acting in "bad faith" and ordered Disney to pay fees and costs of $90,000. Disney's president, Robert Iger, sent a letter to the *Post's* editor-in-chief, Col Allan, calling Finke's reporting an "absolute distortion" of the record and "absolutely false." Approximately two weeks after the Pooh articles were published, the *Post* fired Finke; her editor told her she was being fired for the Pooh articles. She sued Disney on numerous tort theories, including interference with her contract with the *Post*. Disney sought to have the complaint dismissed, which motion was denied by the court. The court of appeals concluded that Finke demonstrated a reasonable probability of proving that Iger's allegations that she made false statements in her article were themselves false; and it concluded that a jury could find Disney liable for intentional interference with contractual relations based on circumstantial evidence and negligent interference with contractual relations because it was reasonably foreseeable to Disney that the nature of its accusations against Finke would result in her termination from employment.[6]

12. TRESPASS

trespass unauthorized action with respect to person or property.

A **trespass** is an unauthorized action with respect to land or personal property. A *trespass to land* is any unpermitted entry below, on, across, or above the land of another. **For Example,** Joyce Ameral's home abuts the mid-way point of the 240-yard, par-4 ninth hole of the public Middlebrook Country Club. Balls sliced and hooked by golfers have damaged her windows and screens, dented her car, and made her deck too dangerous for daytime use. Her landscapers are forced to wear hard hats when cutting her lawn. In her lawsuit against the country club owner, the court ruled that the projection of golf balls onto Ameral's property constituted a continuing trespass and it enjoined the trespass.[7]

A *trespass to personal property* is the invasion of personal property without the permission of the owner. **For Example,** the use of someone's car without that person's permission is a trespass to personal property.

NEGLIGENCE

The widest range of tort liability today arises in the field of negligence. Accidents happen! Property is damaged, and/or injuries result. The fact that an individual suffers an injury does not necessarily mean that the individual will be able to recover damages for the injury. **For Example,** Rhonda Nichols was shopping in the outdoor garden center at a Lowe's Home Center when a "wild bird" flew into the back of her head, causing injuries. Her negligence lawsuit against Lowe's was dismissed because the owner did not have a duty to protect her from a wild bird attack because it was not reasonably foreseeable.[8] Jane Costa was passively watching a Boston Red Sox baseball game at Fenway Park when a foul ball struck her in the face, causing severe and permanent injuries. Her negligence lawsuit against the Boston Red Sox was unsuccessful because it was held that the owners had no duty to warn Ms. Costa of the obvious danger of foul balls being hit into the stands.[9] Although cases involving

[6] *Finke v The Walt Disney Co.,* 2 Cal Rptr 3d 436 (Cal App 2003).

[7] *Ameral v Pray,* 831 NE2d 915 (Mass App 2005).

[8] *Nichols v Lowe's Home Center, Inc.,* 407 F Supp 2d 979 (SD Ill 2006).

[9] *Costa v Boston Red Sox Baseball Club,* 809 NE2d 1090 (Mass App 2004).

injury to spectators at baseball games in other jurisdictions have turned on other tort doctrines, injured fans, like Ms. Costa, are left to bear the costs of their injuries. Only when an injured person can demonstrate the following four elements of negligence is a right to recover established: (1) a duty, (2) breach of duty, (3) causation, and (4) damages. Several defenses may be raised in a negligence lawsuit.

13. ELEMENTS OF NEGLIGENCE

(a) DUTY TO EXERCISE REASONABLE CARE   The first element of negligence is a *duty*. There is a general duty of care imposed to act as a reasonably prudent person would in similar circumstances. **For Example,** Gustavo Guzman worked for a sub-contractor as a chicken catcher at various poultry farms where a Tyson Foods employee, Brian Jones, operated a forklift and worked with the catchers setting up cages to collect birds for processing at a Tyson plant. Contrary to Tyson's instructions "never to allow catchers to move behind the forklift or otherwise out of sight," Brian moved his forklift and struck Guzman, who suffered a serious spinal injury. A general contractor, Tyson Foods, owes a duty to exercise reasonable care to a subcontractor's employee, Gustavo Guzman.[10]

malpractice when services are not properly rendered in accordance with commonly accepted standards; negligence by a professional in performing his or her skill.

Professionals have a duty to perform their jobs at the level of a reasonable professional. For a professional such as an accountant, doctor, lawyer, dentist, or architect to avoid liability for **malpractice,** the professional must perform his or her skill in the same manner as, and at the level of, other professionals in the same field.

Those who own real property have a duty of care to keep their property in a condition that does not create hazards for guests. Businesses have a duty to inspect and repair their property so that their customers are not injured by hazards, such as spills on the floor or uneven walking areas. When customer safety is a concern, businesses have a duty to provide adequate security, such as security patrols in mall parking lots.

(b) BREACH OF DUTY   The second element of negligence is the breach of duty imposed by statute or by the application of the reasonable person standard. The defendant's conduct is evaluated against what a reasonable person would have done under the circumstances. That is, when there is sufficient proof to raise a jury question, the jury decides whether the defendant breached the duty to the injured person from a reasonable person's perspective.[11] **For Example,** the jury in Guzman's lawsuit against Tyson Foods (the *Tyson* case), after weighing all of the facts and circumstances, determined that Tyson's employee's operation of the forklift constituted a breach of Tyson's duty of care to Guzman.

(c) CAUSATION   A third element of negligence is *causation*, the element that connects the duty and the breach of duty to the injuries to the plaintiff. **For Example,** in Guzman's lawsuit, the forklift operator's careless conduct was the cause in fact of this worker's injuries. A "but for" test for causation is used. *But for* Tyson employee Brian Jones' negligent conduct in moving the forklift under the circumstances surrounding the accident, Guzman would not have been injured.

---

[10] *Tyson Foods Inc. v Guzman*, 116 SW3d 233 (Tex App 2003).

[11] A breach of duty may be established by the very nature of the harm to the plaintiff. The doctrine of *res ipsa loquitur* ("the event speaks for itself") provides a rebuttable presumption that the defendant was negligent when a defendant owes a duty to the plaintiff, the nature of the harm caused the plaintiff is such that it ordinarily does not happen in the absence of negligence, and the instrument causing the injury was in the defendant's exclusive control. An example of the doctrine is a lawsuit against a surgeon after a surgical device is discovered in a former patient months after the surgery by another physician seeking the cause of the patient's continuing pain subsequent to the operation.

Once the cause in fact is established, the plaintiff must establish *proximate cause.* That is, it must establish that the harm suffered by the injured person was a foreseeable consequence of the defendant's negligent actions. Foreseeability requires only the general danger to be foreseeable. In the *Tyson* case, the court determined that while there was some evidence that a jury could possibly infer that Tyson could not foresee an accident similar to the one involving Guzman, the evidence was legally sufficient to support the jury's finding that Tyson's negligence was foreseeable and the cause in fact of Guzman's injuries.

The landmark *Palsgraf v Long Island Rail Road Co.* case established a limitation on liability for unforeseeable or unusual consequences following a negligent act.

CASE SUMMARY

The Scales Tipped on Causation

FACTS: Helen Palsgraf lived in Brooklyn. On a summer's day, she purchased tickets to travel to Rockaway Beach on the Long Island Rail Road (LIRR) with her two daughters. She was standing on a platform on the LIRR's East New York station when two men ran to catch another train. One of the men made it onto the train, but the other man, who was carrying a package, was unsteady as the train was about to pull out of the station. The LIRR conductor pulled him up, while the LIRR platform guard pushed him in the train, but in the process, he dropped the package. It contained fireworks and exploded! The concussion from the explosion caused the scales located next to Mrs. Palsgraf to fall over, striking and injuring her. Mrs. Palsgraf sued LIRR for the negligence of the two employees who had assisted the passenger with the package to board the train. A jury awarded her $6,000, which was upheld 3-2 by the Appellate Division. Thereafter the state's highest court considered the railroad's appeal.

DECISION: Recovery for negligence is not available unless there has been some violation of a right. Helen Palsgraf was too remote in distance from the accident for any invasion of rights. To reach a different decision would mean that there could be no end to those who might be harmed. By helping someone onto a moving train, the train employees can anticipate that the passenger himself might be injured, that other passengers might be injured, and that those around the immediate scene might be injured. But Mrs. Palsgraf was too remote for her injuries to be reasonably foreseeable as a consequence of the action of helping a passenger onto a moving train. She was 25 to 30 feet away from the scene, and the explosion cannot be called the proximate cause of her concussion and other injuries. [**Palsgraf v Long Island RR. Co., 162 NE 99 (NY 1928)**]

(d) DAMAGES   The plaintiff in a personal injury negligence lawsuit must establish the actual losses caused by the defendant's breach of duty of care and is entitled to be made whole for all losses. The successful plaintiff is entitled to compensation for (1) past and future pain and suffering (mental anguish), (2) past and future physical impairment, (3) past and future medical care, and (4) past and future loss of earning capacity. Life and work life expectancy are critical factors to consider in assessing damage involving permanent disabilities with loss of earning capacity. Expert witnesses are utilized at trial to present evidence based on worklife tables and present value tables to deal with these economic issues. The jury considers all of the evidence in the context of the elements necessary to prove negligence and all defenses raised, and it renders a verdict. **For Example,** in the *Tyson* case, the defendant presented evidence and argued that Gustavo Guzman was himself negligent regarding the accident. The jury found that both parties were negligent and attributed 80 percent of the fault to Tyson and 20 percent to Guzman (this is called *comparative negligence* and is discussed in the following section). The jury awarded Guzman $931,870.51 in damages ($425,000.00 for past physical pain and mental anguish, $150,000.00 for future physical pain and mental anguish, $10,000.00 for past physical impairment, $10,000.00 for future physical impairment, $51,870.51 for past medical care, $5,000.00 for future medical care, $70,000.00 for past lost earning capacity, and $210,000.00 for future lost earning capacity). After deducting 20 percent of the total jury award for Guzman's own negligence, the trial court's final judgment awarded Guzman $745,496.41.

In some situations, the independent actions of two defendants occur to cause harm. **For Example,** Penny Shipler was rendered a quadriplegic as a result of a Chevrolet S-10 Blazer rollover accident. She sued the driver Kenneth Long for negligence and General Motors for negligent design of the Blazer's roof. She was awarded $18.5 million in damages. Because two causes provided a single indivisible injury, the two defendants were held jointly and severally liable.[12] Under *joint and several liability,* each defendant may be held liable to pay the entire judgment. However, should one defendant pay the entire judgment, that party may sue the other for "contribution" for its proportionate share.

In some cases in which the breach of duty was shocking, plaintiffs may be awarded *punitive damages*. However, punitive (also called *exemplary*) damages are ordinarily applied when the defendant's tortious conduct is attended by circumstances of fraud, malice, or willful or wanton conduct.[13]

14. DEFENSES TO NEGLIGENCE

contributory negligence
negligence of the plaintiff that contributes to injury and at common law bars from recovery from the defendant although the defendant may have been more negligent than the plaintiff.

(a) Contributory Negligence   A plaintiff who is also negligent gives the defendant the opportunity to raise the defense of **contributory negligence**, which the defendant establishes by utilizing the elements of negligence previously discussed, including the plaintiff's duty to exercise reasonable care for his or her own safety, the breach of that duty, causation, and harm. Under common law, the defense of contributory negligence, if established, is a complete bar to recovery of damages from the defendant.

CASE SUMMARY

Keep Your Eye on the Ball in Sports: Keep Your Eye on the 300-Pound Boxes in Trucking

FACTS: Lawrence Hardesty is an over-the-road tractor-trailer truck driver who picked up a load of stadium seating equipment for the NFL stadium under construction in Baltimore. The equipment was packaged in large corrugated cardboard boxes weighing several hundred pounds. The shipper, American Seating Co., loaded the trailer while Hardesty remained in the cab of his truck doing "paperwork" and napping. Considerable open space existed

---

[12] *Shipler v General Motors Corp.,* 710 NW2d 807 (Neb 2006).

[13] See *Eden Electrical, Ltd. v Amana Co.,* 370 F3d 824 (8th Cir 2004); and *University of Colorado v American Cyanamid Co.,* 342 F3d 1298 (Fed Cir 2003).

CASE SUMMARY

continued

between the boxes and the rear door of the trailer. The evidence showed that Hardesty failed to properly examine the load bars used to secure the boxes from movement during transit. When Hardesty arrived at the Baltimore destination, he opened the rear trailer door and boxes at the end of the trailer fell out and injured him. Hardesty brought a personal injury negligence action against the shipper. American Seating Co. responded that Hardesty was contributorily negligent, thus barring his negligence claim.

DECISION: Judgment for American Seating Co. because the claim is barred by Hardesty's contributory negligence. His decision to ignore the loading process by remaining in his truck, oblivious to the manner and means of the loading of the trailer, coupled with his own failure to examine the load bars sufficiently to confirm that they would "adequately secure" the cargo, together with his decision, in the face of his prior omissions, to open the doors of the trailer upon his arrival in Baltimore while standing within the zone of danger created by the possibility (of which he negligently failed to inform himself) of injury from cargo falling out of the trailer, cohered to rise to the level of a cognizable breach of duty—contributory negligence. [**Hardesty v American Seating Co., 194 F Supp 2d 447 (D Md 2002)**]

The contributory negligence defense has given way to the defense of comparative negligence in most states.

(b) COMPARATIVE NEGLIGENCE Because contributory negligence produced harsh results with no recovery of damages for an injured plaintiff, most states have adopted a fairer approach to handling situations in which both the plaintiff and the defendant are negligent; it is called *comparative negligence*. Comparative negligence is a defense that permits a negligent plaintiff to recover some damages but only in proportion to the defendant's degree of fault.[14] **For Example,** in the *Tyson* case, both the defendant and the plaintiff were found to be negligent. The jury attributed 80 percent of the fault for the plaintiff's injury to Tyson and 20 percent of the fault to the plaintiff, Guzman. While Guzman's total damages were $931,870, they were reduced by 20 percent, and the final judgment awarded Guzman was $745,496.

Some comparative negligence states refuse to allow the plaintiff to recover damages if the plaintiff's fault was more than 50 percent of the cause of the harm.[15]

(c) ASSUMPTION OF THE RISK The assumption of the risk defense has two categories. *Express assumption of the risk* involves a written exculpatory agreement under which a plaintiff acknowledges the risks involved in certain activities and releases the defendant from prospective liability for personal injuries sustained as a result of the defendant's negligent conduct. Examples include ski lift tickets, white water rafting contracts, permission for high school cheerleading activities, and parking lot claim checks. In most jurisdictions these agreements are enforceable as written. However, in some jurisdictions they may be considered unenforceable because they violate public policy. **For Example,** Gregory Hanks sued the Powder Ridge Ski Resort for negligence regarding serious injuries he sustained while snowtubing at the

---

[14] *City of Chicago v M/V Morgan*, 375 F3d 563 (7th Cir 2004).

[15] *Davenport v Cotton Hope Plantation*, 482 SE2d 569 (SC App 1997).

defendant's facility. He had signed a release which explicitly provided that the snowtuber: *["fully] assume[s] all risks associated with [s]nowtubing*, even if due to the NEGLIGENCE" of the defendants [emphasis in original]. The Supreme Court of Connecticut found that the release was unenforceable because it violated the public policy by shifting the risk of negligence to the weaker bargainer.[16]

Implied primary assumption of the risk arises when a plaintiff has impliedly consented, often in advance of any negligence by the defendant, to relieve a defendant of a duty to the plaintiff regarding specific known and appreciated risks. It is a subjective standard, one specific to the plaintiff and his or her situation. **For Example,** baseball mom Delinda Taylor took her two boys to a Seattle Mariners baseball game and was injured during the pregame warm-up when a ball thrown by José Mesa got past Freddie Garcia, striking Taylor in the face and causing serious injuries. The defendant baseball team successfully raised the affirmative defense of implied primary assumption of the risk by showing that Mrs. Taylor had full subjective understanding of the specific risk of getting hit by a thrown baseball, and she voluntarily chose to encounter that risk.[17]

A number of states have either abolished the defense of assumption of the risk, reclassifying the defense as comparative negligence so as not to completely bar a plaintiff's recovery of damages, or have eliminated the use of the assumption of the risk terminology and handle cases under the duty, breach of duty, causation, and harm elements of negligence previously discussed.[18]

(d) IMMUNITY   Governments are generally immune from tort liability.[19] This rule has been eroded by decisions and in some instances by statutes, such as the Federal Tort Claims Act. Subject to certain exceptions, this act permits the recovery of damages from the United States for property damage, personal injury, or death action claims arising from the negligent act or omission of any employee of the United States under such circumstances that the United States, if a private person,

SPORTS & ENTERTAINMENT LAW

Charles "Booby" Clark played football for the Cincinnati Bengals as a running back on offense. Dale Hackbart played defensive free safety for the Denver Broncos. As a consequence of an interception by the Broncos, Hackbart became an offensive player, threw a block, and was watching the play with one knee on the ground when Clark "acting out of anger and frustration, but without a specific intent to injure," stepped forward and struck a blow to the back of Hackbart's head and neck, causing a serious neck fracture. Is relief precluded for injuries occurring during a professional football game? The answer is no. While proof of mere negligence is insufficient to establish liability during such an

---

[16] *Hanks v Powder Ridge*, 885 A2d 734 (Conn 2005).

[17] *Taylor v Baseball Club of Seattle*, 130 P3d 835 (Wash App 2006).

[18] See, for example, *Costa v The Boston Red Sox Baseball Club*, 809 NE2d 1090 (Mass App 2004), where the court cites state precedent that " ... the abolition of assumption of the risk as an affirmative defense did not alter the plaintiff's burden ... to prove the defendant owed [the plaintiff] a duty of care ... and thus left intact the open and obvious damages rule, which operates to negate the existence of a duty to care."

[19] *Kirby v Macon County*, 892 SW2d 403 (Tenn 1994).

SPORTS & ENTERTAINMENT LAW

continued

athletic contest, liability must instead be premised on heightened proof of reckless or intentional conduct on the part of the defendant. In the *Hackbart* case, the court determined that if the evidence established that the injury was the result of acts of Clark that were in reckless disregard of Hackbart's safety, Hackbart is entitled to damages.* Why didn't Hackbart pursue recovery under negligence law, contending that Clark had a general duty of care to act as a reasonably prudent person would in similar circumstances? Because football and other contact sports contain within the rules of the games inherent *unreasonable* risks of harm, a negligence theory is not applicable. What contact sports do you believe qualify under this "sports exception" doctrine for which proof of negligence is insufficient to establish liability for injuries sustained during the athletic contest?

PGA golfer Walter Mallin sued PGA golfer John Paesani for injuries that Mallin sustained while competing in a PGA golf tournament when Paesani drove a golf ball that struck Mallin in the head on his right temple. Paesani contends that the "sports exception" doctrine applies and the negligence case must be dismissed. How would you decide this case?**

---

* *Hackbart v Cincinnati Bengals, Inc.*, 601 F2d 516 (10th Cir 1979).

** *Mallin v Paesani*, 892 A2d 1043 (Conn Super, 2005).

would be liable to the claimant in accordance with the law of the place where the act or omission occurred. A rapidly growing number of states have abolished governmental immunity, although many still recognize it.

Until the early 1900s, charities were immune from tort liability, and children and parents and spouses could not sue each other. These immunities are fast disappearing. **For Example,** if a father's negligent driving of his car causes injuries to his minor child passenger, the child may recover from the father for his injuries.[20]

D   STRICT LIABILITY

The final form of tort liability is known as *strict liability*. When the standards of strict liability apply, very few defenses are available. Strict liability was developed to provide guaranteed protection for those who are injured by conduct the law deems both serious and inexcusable.

15. WHAT IS STRICT LIABILITY?

Strict liability is an absolute standard of liability imposed by the law in circumstances the courts or legislatures have determined require a high degree of protection. When strict liability is imposed, the result is that the company or person who has caused injury or damages by the conduct will be required to compensate for those damages in an absolute sense. Few, if any, defenses apply in a situation in which the law imposes a strict liability standard. **For Example,** as noted earlier in the chapter, engaging in

---

[20] *Cates v Cates*, 588 NE2d 330 (Ill App 1992); see also *Doe v McKay*, 700 NE2d 1018 (Ill 1998).

THINKING THINGS THROUGH

Torts and Public Policy

Over a decade ago, a jury awarded 81-year-old Stella Liebeck nearly $3 million because she was burned after she spilled a cup of McDonald's coffee on her lap. Based on these limited facts, a national discussion ensued about a need for tort reform, and to this day "Stella Awards" are given on Web sites for apparently frivolous or excessive lawsuits. Consider the following additional facts and the actual damages awarded Stella Liebeck. Decide whether her recovery was just.

- McDonald's coffee was brewed at 195 to 205 degrees.
- McDonald's quality assurance manager "was aware of the risk [of burns] ... and had no plans to turn down the heat."
- Mrs. Liebeck spent seven days in the hospital with third degree burns and had skin grafts. Gruesome photos of burns of the inner thighs, groin, and buttocks were entered as evidence.
- Compensatory damages were $200,000, which were reduced to $160,000 because Mrs. Liebeck was determined to be 20 percent at fault.
- The jury awarded $2.7 million in punitive damages. The trial court judge reduced this amount to $480,000.
- The total recovery at the trial court for Mrs. Liebeck was $640,000. Both parties appealed, and a settlement was reached at what is believed to be close to the $640,000 figure.

Tort remedies have evolved because of public policy incentives for the protection of individuals from physical, mental, and economic damage. Tort remedies provide economic motivation for individuals and businesses to avoid conduct that could harm others.

The amount of the compensation and the circumstances in which compensation for torts should be paid are issues that courts, juries, and legislatures review. Many legislatures have examined and continue to review the standards for tort liability and damages.

The U.S. Supreme Court devoted three decisions over a recent seven-year period dealing with excessive punitive damages in civil litigation, and it has set "guideposts" to be used by courts in assessing punitive damages.[*] In *State Farm Mutual Automobile Insurance Co. v Campbell*, compensatory damages for the plaintiffs at the trial court level were $1 million, and punitive damages, based in part on evidence that State Farm's nationwide policy was to underpay claims regardless of merit to enhance profits, were assessed at $145 million. The Supreme Court concluded that the facts of *Campbell* would likely justify a punitive damages award only at or near the amount of compensatory damages. Thus, even those who act very badly as State Farm Insurance did have a constitutionally protected right under the Due Process Clause of the Fourteenth Amendment to have civil law damages assessed in accordance with the Supreme Court's guideposts.

---

[*] *BMW of North America v Gore,* 517 US 559 (1996); *Cooper Industries v Leatherman Tool Group, Inc.,* 532 US 424 (2001); and *State Farm Insurance v Campbell,* 538 US 408 (2003).

---

ultrahazardous activities, such as using dynamite to excavate a site for new construction, results in strict liability for the contractor performing the demolition. Any damages resulting from the explosion are the responsibility of that contractor, so the contractor is strictly liable.

16. IMPOSING STRICT LIABILITY

Strict liability arises in a number of different circumstances, but the most common are in those situations in which a statutory duty is imposed and in product liability. For example at both the state and federal levels, there are requirements for the use, transportation, and sale of radioactive materials, as well as the disposal of biomedical materials and tools. Any violation of these rules and regulations would result in strict liability for the company or person in violation.

Product liability, while more fully covered in Chapter 25, is another example of strict liability. A product that is defective through its design, manufacture, or instructions and that injures someone results in strict liability for the manufacturer.

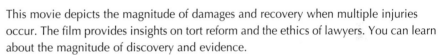

LAWFLIX

Class Action (1991) (R)

This movie depicts the magnitude of damages and recovery when multiple injuries occur. The film provides insights on tort reform and the ethics of lawyers. You can learn about the magnitude of discovery and evidence.

For movie clips that illustrate business law concepts, see LawFlix at **http://wdvl.westbuslaw.com.**

 SUMMARY

A *tort* is a civil wrong that affords recovery for damages that result. The three forms of torts are intentional torts, negligence, and strict liability. A tort differs from a crime in the nature of its remedy. Fines and imprisonment result from criminal violations, whereas money damages are paid to those who are damaged by conduct that constitutes a tort. An action may be both a crime and a tort, but the tort remedy is civil in nature.

Selected intentional torts are false imprisonment, defamation, product disparagement, contract interference or tortious interference, and trespass. False imprisonment is the detention of another without his or her permission. False imprisonment is often called the *shopkeeper's tort* because store owners detain suspected shoplifters. Many states provide a privilege to store owners if they detain shoplifting suspects based on reasonable cause and in a reasonable manner. Defamation is slander (oral) or libel (written) and consists of false statements about another that damage the person's reputation or integrity. Truth is an

absolute defense to defamation, and there are some privileges that protect against defamation, such as those for witnesses at trial and for members of Congress during debates on the floor. There is a developing privilege for employers when they give references for former employees. Invasion of privacy is intrusion into private affairs; public disclosure of private facts; or appropriation of someone's name, image, or likeness for commercial purposes.

To establish the tort of negligence, one must show that there has been a breach of duty in the form of a violation of a statute or professional competency standards or of behavior that does not rise to the level of that of a reasonable person. That breach of duty must have caused the foreseeable injuries to the plaintiff, and the plaintiff must be able to quantify the damages that resulted. Possible defenses to negligence include contributory negligence, comparative negligence, and assumption of risk.

Strict liability is absolute liability with few defenses.

QUESTIONS AND CASE PROBLEMS

1. Christensen Shipyards built a 155-foot yacht for Tiger Woods at its Vancouver, Washington, facilities. It used Tiger's name and photographs relating to the building of the yacht in promotional materials for the shipyard without seeking his permission. Was this a right to publicity tort because Tiger could assert that his name and photos were used to attract attention to the shipyard to obtain commercial advantage? Did the shipyard have a First Amendment right to present the truthful facts regarding their building of the yacht and the owner's identity as promotional materials? Does the fact that the yacht was named *Privacy* have an impact on this case? Would it make a difference as to the outcome of this case if the contract for building the yacht had a clause prohibiting the use of Tiger's name or photo without his permission?

2. ESPN held its Action Sports and Music Awards ceremony in April, at which celebrities in the fields of extreme sports and popular music such as rap and heavy metal converged. Well-known musicians Ben Harper and James Hetfield were there, as were popular rappers Busta Rhymes and LL Cool J. Famed motorcycle stuntman Evel Knievel, who is commonly thought of as the "father of extreme sports," and his wife Krystal were photographed. The photograph depicted Evel, who was wearing a motorcycle jacket and rose-tinted sunglasses, with his right arm around Krystal and his left arm around another young woman. ESPN published the photograph on its "extreme sports" Web site with a caption that read "Evel Knievel proves that you're never too old to be a pimp." The Knievels brought suit against ESPN, contending that the photograph and caption were defamatory because they accused Evel of soliciting prostitution and implied that Krystal was a prostitute. ESPN contends that the caption was a figurative and slang usage and was not defamatory as a matter of law. Decide. [*Knievel v ESPN*, 393 F3d 1068 (9th Cir)]

3. While snowboarding down a slope at Mammoth Mountain Ski Area (Mammoth), 17-year-old David Graham was engaged in a snowball fight with his 14-year-old brother. As he was "preparing to throw a snowball" at his brother, David slammed into Liam Madigan, who was working as a ski school instructor for Mammoth, and injured him. Madigan sued Graham for damages for reckless and dangerous behavior. The defense contended that the claim was barred under the doctrine of assumption of the risk, applicable in the state, arising from the risk inherent in the sport that allows for vigorous participation and frees a participant from a legal duty to act with due care. Decide. [*Mammoth Mountain Ski Area v Graham*, 38 Cal Rptr 3d 422 (Cal App)]

4. James Lee Boyter, a cement truck driver for Concrete Specialties of America, collided head-on with Robin Langley as she drove on a curved portion of a two-lane road. Langley testified that Boyter hit her head-on as he came around the curve because he was in her lane and hence driving on the wrong side of the road. A witness testified that Langley was driving at an excessive rate of speed before Boyter's truck struck her car between the left front fender and the door. Langley filed suit against Boyter and Concrete Specialties. They defended on the grounds that Langley was contributorily negligent. What happens if there is contributory negligence on the part of Langley? Do you think she was contributorily negligent? [*Langley v Boyter*, 325 SE2d 550 (SC)]

5. JoKatherine Page and her 14-year-old son Jason were robbed at their bank's ATM at 9:30 P.M. one evening by a group of four thugs. The thieves took $300, struck Mrs. Page in the face with a gun, and ran. Mrs. Page and her son filed suit against the bank for its failure to provide adequate security. Should the bank be held liable? [*Page v American National Bank & Trust Co.*, 850 SW2d 133 (Tenn)]

6. A Barberton Glass Co. truck was transporting large sheets of glass down the highway. Elliot Schultz was driving his automobile some distance behind the truck. Because of the negligent way that the sheets of glass were fastened in the truck, a large sheet fell off the truck, shattered on hitting the highway, and then bounced up and broke the windshield of Schultz's car. He was not injured but suffered great emotional shock. He sued Barberton to recover damages for this shock.

Barberton denied liability on the ground that Schultz had not sustained any physical injury at the time or as the result of the shock. Should he be able to recover? [*Schultz v Barberton Glass Co.,* 447 NE2d 109 (Ohio)]

7. Mallinckrodt produces nuclear and radioactive medical pharmaceuticals and supplies. Maryland Heights Leasing, an adjoining business owner, claimed that low-level radiation emissions from Mallinckrodt damaged its property and caused a loss in earnings. What remedy should Maryland Heights have? What torts are involved here? [*Maryland Heights Leasing, Inc. v Mallinckrodt, Inc.,* 706 SW2d 218 (Mo App)]

8. An owner abandoned his van in an alley in Chicago. In spite of repeated complaints to the police, the van was allowed to remain in the alley. After several months, it was stripped of most of the parts that could be removed. Jamin Ortiz, age 11, was walking down the alley when the van's gas tank exploded. The flames from the explosion set fire to Jamin's clothing, and he was severely burned. Jamin and his family brought suit brought against the city of Chicago to recover damages for his injuries. Could the city be held responsible for injuries caused by property owned by someone else? Why or why not? [*Ortiz v Chicago,* 398 NE2d 1007 (Ill App)]

9. Carrigan, a district manager of Simples Time Recorder Co., was investigating complaints of mismanagement of the company's Jackson office. He called at the home of Hooks, the secretary of that office, who expressed the opinion that part of the trouble was caused by the theft of parts and equipment by McCall, another employee. McCall was later discharged and sued Hooks for slander. Was she liable? [*Hooks v McCall,* 272 So 2d 925 (Miss)]

10. Defendant no. 1 parked his truck in the street near the bottom of a ditch on a dark, foggy night. Iron pipes carried in the truck projected nine feet beyond the truck in back. Neither the truck nor the pipes carried any warning light or flag, in violation of both a city ordinance and a state statute. Defendant no. 2 was a taxicab owner whose taxicab was negligently driven at an excessive speed. Defendant no. 2 ran into the pipes, thereby killing the passenger in the taxicab. The plaintiff brought an action for the passenger's death against both defendants. Defendant no. 1 claimed he was not liable because it was Defendant no. 2's negligence that had caused the harm. Was this defense valid? [*Bumbardner v Allison,* 78 SE2d 752 (NC)]

11. A customer was shopping at the handbag counter of the defendant's store. She did not make any purchase and left the store. When she was a few feet away from the store, a store employee tapped her lightly on the shoulder to attract her attention and asked her if she had made any purchases. When she inquired why, he asked, "What about that bag in your hand?" The customer said that it belonged to her, and she opened it to show by its contents that it was not a new bag. The employee gave the customer a "real dirty look" and went back into the store without saying a word. The customer then sued the store for false imprisonment. Was the store liable? [*Abner v W.T. Grant Co.,* 139 SE2d 408 (Ga App)]

12. Hegyes was driving her car when it was negligently struck by a Unjian Enterprises truck. She was injured, and an implant was placed in her body to counteract the injuries. She sued Unjian, and the case was settled. Two years later Hegyes became pregnant. The growing fetus pressed against the implant, making it necessary for her doctor to deliver the child 51 days prematurely by Cesarean section. Because of its premature birth, the child had a breathing handicap. Suit was brought against Unjian Enterprises for the harm sustained by the child. Was the defendant liable? [*Hegyes v Unjian Enterprises, Inc.,* 286 Cal Rptr 85 (Cal App)]

13. Kendra Knight took part in a friendly game of touch football. She had played before and was familiar with football. Michael Jewett was on her team. In the course of play, Michael bumped into Kendra and knocked her to the ground. He stepped on her hand, causing injury to a little finger that later required its amputation. She sued Michael for damages. He defended on the ground that she had assumed the risk. Kendra claimed that assumption of risk could not be raised as a defense because the state legislature had adopted the standard of comparative negligence. What happens if contributory negligence applies? What

happens if the defense of comparative negligence applies?

14. A passenger on a cruise ship was injured by a rope thrown while the ship was docking. The passenger was sitting on a lounge chair on the third deck when she was struck by the weighted end of a rope thrown by an employee of Port Everglades, where the boat was docking. These ropes, or heaving lines, were being thrown from the dock to the second deck, and the passenger was injured by a line that was thrown too high.

   The trial court granted the cruise line's motion for directed verdict on the ground there was no evidence that the cruise line knew or should have known of the danger. The cruise line contended that it had no notice that this "freak accident" could occur. What is the duty of a cruise ship line to its passengers? Is there liability here? Does it

matter that an employee of the port city, not the cruise lines, caused the injury? Should the passenger be able to recover? Why or why not? [*Kalendareva v Discovery Cruise Line Partnership*, 798 So 2d 804 (Fla App)]

15. Blaylock was a voluntary psychiatric outpatient treated by Dr. Burglass, who became aware that Blaylock was violence prone. Blaylock told Dr. Burglass that he intended to do serious harm to Wayne Boynton, Jr., and shortly thereafter he killed Wayne. Wayne's parents then sued Dr. Burglass on grounds that he was liable for the death of their son because he failed to give warning or to notify the police of Blaylock's threat and nature. Was a duty breached here? Should Dr. Burglass be held liable? [*Boynton v Burglass*, 590 So 2d 446 (Fla App)]

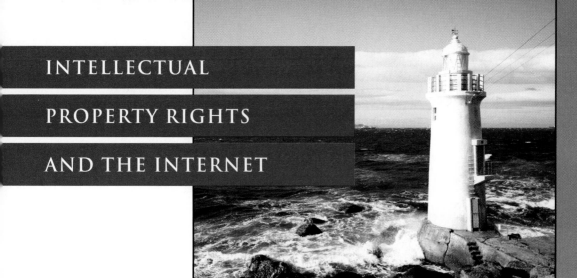

INTELLECTUAL PROPERTY RIGHTS AND THE INTERNET

CHAPTER (10)

PROTECTION OF COMPUTER SOFTWARE
AND MASK WORKS
25. COPYRIGHT PROTECTION OF COMPUTER PROGRAMS
26. PATENT PROTECTION OF PROGRAMS
27. TRADE SECRETS
28. RESTRICTIVE LICENSING
29. SEMICONDUCTOR CHIP PROTECTION

LEARNING OBJECTIVES

After studying this chapter, you should be able to

LO.1 Explain how to obtain a copyright, a patent, and a trademark

LO.2 Identify the rights obtained by owners of copyrights, patents, and trademarks

LO.3 State the duration of the protection afforded owners of copyrights, trademarks, and patents

LO.4 Set forth the remedies available to owners for infringement of intellectual property rights

LO.5 List and explain the extent of protection provided by federal laws for owners of software and mask works

Intellectual property comes in many forms: the writing by an author or the software developed by an employee, the new product or process developed by an inventor, the company name Hewlett-Packard, and the secret formula used to make Coca-Cola. Federal law provides rights to owners of these works, products, company names, and secret formulas that are called *copyrights, patents, trademarks,* and *trade secrets.* State laws provide protection for trade secrets. These basic legal principles are also applicable in an Internet and e-commerce context. This chapter discusses the federal and state laws governing intellectual property rights and their Internet context.

A   TRADEMARKS AND SERVICE MARKS

The Lanham Act, a federal law, grants a producer the exclusive right to register a trademark and prevent competitors from using that mark. This law helps assure a producer that it, not an imitating competitor, will reap the financial, reputation-related rewards of a desirable product.

1. INTRODUCTION

trademark mark that identifies a product.

service mark mark that identifies a service.

A mark is any word, name, symbol, device, or combination of these used to identify a product or service.[1] If the mark identifies a product, such as an automobile or soap, it is called a **trademark.** If it identifies a service, such as a restaurant or dry cleaner, it is called a **service mark.**

---

[1] 15 USC § 1127.

The owner of a mark may obtain protection from others using it by registering the mark in accordance with federal law.[2] To be registered, a mark must distinguish the goods or services of the applicant from those of others. Under the federal statute, a register, called the Principal Register, is maintained for recording such marks. Inclusion on the Principal Register grants the registrant the exclusive right to use the mark. Challenges may be made to the registrant's right within five years of registration, but after five years, the right of the registrant is incontestable.

An advance registration of a mark may be made not more than three years before its actual use by filing an application certifying a bona fide "intent-to-use." Fees must be paid at six-month intervals from the filing of the application until actual use begins.

2. REGISTRABLE MARKS

Marks that are coined, completely fanciful, or arbitrary are capable of registration on the Principal Register. The mark Exxon, for example, was coined by the owner. The name Kodak is also a creation of the owner of this trademark and has no other meaning in English, but it serves to distinguish the goods of its owner from all others.

A suggestive term may also be registered. Such a term suggests rather than describes some characteristics of the goods to which it applies and requires the consumer to exercise some imagination to reach a conclusion about the nature of the goods. **For Example,** as a trademark for refrigerators, Penguin would be suggestive of the product's superior cooling and freezing features. As a trademark for paperback books, however, Penguin is arbitrary and fanciful.

Ordinarily, descriptive terms, surnames, and geographic terms are not registrable on the Principal Register.[3] A descriptive term identifies a characteristic or quality of an article or service, such as color, odor, function, or use. **For Example,** America Online, Inc (AOL) sued its Internet competitor AT&T for trademark infringement over the use of the words "You Have Mail!" by AT&T, relating to e-mail service. AOL's displaying the words "You Have Mail" and playing a recording "You've got mail" when a subscriber in fact has e-mail are words used in their common meaning and are thus a functional use and may not be appropriated as exclusive trademark property.[4] Boston Beer was denied trademark protection because it was a geographic term.[5]

An exception is made, however, when a descriptive or geographic term or a surname has acquired a *secondary meaning;* such a mark is registrable. A term or terms that have a primary meaning of their own acquire a secondary meaning when, through long use in connection with a particular product, they have come to be known by the public as identifying the particular product and its origin. **For Example,** the geographic term *Philadelphia* has acquired a secondary meaning when applied to cream cheese. It is widely accepted by the public as denoting a particular brand rather

---

[2] Lanham Act, 15 USC §§ 1050–1127.

[3] A Supplemental Register exists for recording such marks. This recording does not give the registrant any protection, but it provides a source to which other persons designing a mark can go to make sure they are not duplicating an existing mark.

[4] *America Online, Inc. v AT&T Corporation,* 243 F3d 812 (4th Cir 2001).

[5] *Boston Beer Co. v Slesar Bros. Brewing Co.,* 9 F3d 125 (1st Cir 1994).

than any cream cheese made in Philadelphia. Factors considered by a court in determining whether a trademark has acquired secondary meaning are the amount and manner of advertising, volume of sales, length and manner of use, direct consumer testimony, and consumer surveys.

With a limited number of colors available for use by competitors, along with possible shade confusion, courts had held for some 90 years that color alone could not function as a trademark. The U.S. Supreme Court has overturned this legal rule, and now if a color serves as a symbol that distinguishes a firm's goods and identifies their source without serving any other significant function, it may, sometimes at least, meet the basic legal requirements for use as a trademark.[6] **For Example,** Owens-Corning Fiberglass Corp. has been allowed to register the color pink as a trademark for its fiberglass insulation products.

Generic terms—that is, terms that designate a kind or class of goods, such as *soap, shirts, cola* or *rosé wine*—are never registrable.

CASE SUMMARY

No Hogging Generic Terms

FACTS: Beginning in the late 1960s and thereafter, the word *hog* was used by motorcycle enthusiasts to refer to large motorcycles. Into the early 1980s, motorcyclists came to use the word *hog* when referring to Harley-Davidson (Harley) motorcycles. In 1981, Harley itself began using *hog* in connection with its merchandise. In 1983, it formed Harley Owners Group, used the acronym H.O.G., and registered the acronym in conjunction with various logos in 1987. Since 1909, Harley has used variations of its bar-and-shield logo. Ronald Grottanelli opened a motorcycle repair shop under the name The Hog Farm in 1969. At some point after 1981, he sold products such as Hog Wash engine degreaser and a Hog Trivia board game. Grottanelli had used variants of Harley's bar-and-shield logo since 1979 on signs and T-shirts, dropping the name Harley-Davidson from the bar of the logo in 1982 after receiving a letter of protest from the company. He continued to use the bar-and-shield, however, and featured a drawing of a pig wearing sunglasses and a banner with the words "Unauthorized Dealer." From a judgment for Harley for infringement of the bar-and-shield trademark and an injunction prohibiting the use of the word *hog* in reference to some of his products and services, Grottanelli appealed.

DECISION: *Hog* was a generic word in the language as applied to large motorcycles before segments of the public began using it to refer to Harley-Davidson motorcycles. Neither a manufacturer nor the public can withdraw from the language a generic term, already applicable to a category of products, and accord it trademark significance as long as the term retains some generic meaning. It was an error to prohibit Grottanelli from using the word *hog.* Harley must rely on a portion of its trademark to identify the brand of motorcycles, for example, Harley Hogs. Grottanelli was properly enjoined from using the bar-and-shield logo. Grottanelli's mark uses Harley's mark in a somewhat humorous manner to promote his own products, which is not a permitted trademark parody use. The use of the prefix "UN" before "AUTHORIZED DEALER" is no defense. The courts have ordinarily found the use of such disclaimers insufficient to avoid liability for infringement. [**Harley-Davidson v Grottanelli, 164 F3d 806 (2d Cir 1999)**]

[6] *Qualitex Co. v Jacobson Products Co., Inc.,* 514 US 159 (1995).

Generic terms also apply to service marks. **For Example,** Robert Donchez was the first licensed beer vendor hired by the Colorado Rockies baseball team for its inaugural season. He was referred to as "Bob the Beerman." He authored a book about his first season vending beer titled in part... "A Season with Bob the Beerman"; and he obtained a service mark for the "Bob the Beerman" character under state law. Coors Brewing Co. began an advertising campaign for its Coors Light product using many different actors and actresses portraying beer vendors interacting with the crowd in amusing ways. Some of the vendors called themselves "the beerman" or "Hey, beerman." Bob Donchez's lawsuit against Coors and the ad agency under the Lanham Act was unsuccessful because the word *beerman* is an unprotected generic term.

3. INTERNATIONAL REGISTRATION

Under the Madrid System of International Registration of Marks (the Madrid Protocol), the United States became a party to a treaty providing for the international registration of marks in November 2003. Now U.S. companies that sell products and provide services in foreign countries may register their marks and obtain protection for them in more than 60 signatory countries by filing a single application in English for each mark with the U.S. Patent and Trademark Office.[7] Before the mark can be the subject of an international application, it must have already been registered or applied for with the U.S. Patent and Trademark Office (PTO). A change in ownership of a mark can be accomplished by a single filing. Renewal is required every 10 years by paying a single renewal fee.

4. TRADE DRESS PROTECTION

Firms invest significant resources to develop and promote the appearance of their products and the packages in which these products are sold so that they are clearly recognizable by consumers.

trade dress product's total image including its overall packaging look.

Trade dress involves a product's total image and, in the case of consumer goods, includes the overall packaging look in which each product is sold.

When a competitor adopts a confusingly similar trade dress, it dilutes the first user's investment and goodwill and deceives consumers, hindering their ability to distinguish between competing brands. The law of trade dress protection was initially settled by the U.S. Supreme Court in 1992,[8] and courts have subsequently become more receptive to claims of trade dress infringement under Section 43(a) of the Lanham Act. To prevail, a plaintiff must prove that its trade dress is distinctive and nonfunctional and the defendant's trade dress is confusingly similar to the plaintiff's.[9] Thus, a competitor who copied the Marlboro cigarettes package for its Gunsmoke brand of cigarettes was found to have infringed the trade dress of the Marlboro brand.[10] Trade dress protection under the Lanham Act is the same as that provided a qualified unregistered trademark and does not provide all of the protection available to the holder of a registered trademark.

---

[7] Signatory countries include most U.S. trading partners with the exception of Canada and Mexico.

[8] *Two Pesos, Inc. v Taco Cabana, Inc.,* 505 US 763 (1992).

[9] *Clicks Billiards v Sixshooters, Inc.,* 251 F3d 1252 (9th Cir 2001); and *Woodland Furniture, LLC v Larsen,* 124 P3d, 1016 (Idaho 2005).

[10] *Philip Morris, Inc. v Star Tobacco Corp.,* 879 F Supp 379 (SDNY 1995).

5. LIMITED LANHAM ACT PROTECTION OF PRODUCT DESIGN

Trade dress originally included only the packaging and "dressing" of a product, but in recent years, federal courts of appeals' decisions have expanded trade dress to encompass the design of a product itself. Some manufacturers have been successful in asserting Section 43(a) Lanham Act protection against "knockoffs"—that is, copies of their furniture designs, sweater designs, and notebook designs. In this context, Samara Brothers, Inc., discovered that Wal-Mart Stores, Inc., had contacted a supplier to manufacture children's outfits based on photographs of Samara garments, and Wal-Mart was selling these so-called knockoffs. Samara sued Wal-Mart, claiming infringement of unregistered trade dress under Section 43(a) of the Lanham Act. The matter progressed to the U.S. Supreme Court, which considered whether a product's design can be distinctive and, therefore, protectable under Section 43(a) of the Lanham Act. The Court set aside the trial court's decision in favor of Samara Brothers and concluded that a product's design is not inherently distinctive and can meet only the "distinctiveness" element required in a Section 43(a) case by a showing of secondary meaning. That is, the manufacturer must show that the design has come to be known by the public as identifying the product in question and its origin. The matter was remanded for further proceeding consistent with the Court's decision.[11]

It is clear from the Supreme Court's *Wal-Mart Stores, Inc. v Samara Bros, Inc.* decision that ordinarily only famous designers whose works are widely recognized by the public by their designs alone, such as certain Tommy Hilfiger and Ralph Lauren garments, Dooney & Bourke handbags, and Movado watches, will be able to successfully pursue Section 43(a) trade dress protection for their designs against knockoff versions of their works sold under Wal-Mart or other private labels. Of course, if a manufacturer's design is copied along with the manufacturer's labels or logo, the makers and sellers of these counterfeit goods are always in clear violation of the Lanham Act. As discussed later, design patents also have limited applicability and protect new and nonobvious ornamental features of a product.

6. INJUNCTION AGAINST IMPROPER USE OF MARK

A person who has the right to use a mark may obtain a court order prohibiting a competitor from imitating or duplicating the mark. The basic question in such litigation is whether the general public is likely to be confused by the mark of the defendant and to believe wrongly that it identifies the plaintiff.[12] If there is this danger of confusion, the court will enjoin the defendant from using the particular mark.

In some cases, the fact that the products of the plaintiff and the defendant did not compete in the same market was held to entitle the defendant to use a mark that would have been prohibited as confusingly similar if the defendant manufactured the same product as the plaintiff. **For Example,** it has been held that Cadillac, as applied to boats, is not confusingly similar to Cadillac as applied to automobiles; therefore, its use cannot be enjoined.[13]

---

[11] *Wal-Mart Stores, Inc. v Samara Bros, Inc.*, 529 US 205 (2000).

[12] *Resource Lenders, Inc. v Source Solutions, Inc.*, 404 F Supp2d 1232 (ED Cal 2005).

[13] *General Motors Corp. v Cadillac Marine and Boat Co.*, 140 USPQ (BNA) 447 (1964). See also *Amstar Corp. v Domino's Pizza, Inc.*, 615 F2d 252 (5th Cir 1980), where the mark Domino as applied to pizza was held not to be confusingly similar to Domino as applied to sugar.

> ## CASE SUMMARY
>
> ### But... What's Wrong with Diverting Traffic?
>
> **FACTS:** ETS Inc. manufactures Australian Gold, Caribbean Gold, and Swedish Beauty indoor tanning products (ETS products), which are used in some 60 percent of the 25,000 tanning salons in the United States. ETS contracts with independent distributors to sell its products who in turn may only sell the products to tanning salons. Its contracts with the distributors prohibit them from selling products over the Internet or to the general public. The Hatfields used fictitious names to purchase products from ETS-authorized distributors and used up to seven Web sites to sell ETS products to the general public, using ETS's trademarks on their Web sites and in the metatags of the Web sites. The Hatfields thus used the goodwill associated with the ETS trademarks to divert traffic to their Web sites where consumers could be lured to buy lotions from ETS's competition. ETS sued for trademark infringement and other theories of relief. From a judgment for ETS for more than $3.7 million and injunctive relief, the Hatfields appealed.
>
> **DECISION:** Judgment for ETS Inc. "Initial interest confusion" results in trademark infringement when consumers seeking to find a particular trademark holder's products on the Internet are lured to the defendant's Web sites by unauthorized use of the plaintiff's trademarks on the defendant's Web sites and in its metatags. By diverting traffic to their Web sites, the Hatfields were able to lure consumers to purchase lotions from ETS's competition. This is a violation of the Lanham Act. [**Australian Gold, Inc. v Hatfield**, 436 F3d 1228 (10th Cir 2006)]

7. ABANDONMENT OF EXCLUSIVE RIGHT TO MARK

An owner who has an exclusive right to use a mark may lose that right. If other persons are permitted to use the mark, it loses its exclusive character and is said to pass into the English language and become generic. Examples of formerly enforceable marks that have made this transition into the general language are *aspirin, thermos, cellophane,* and *shredded wheat.* Nonuse for three consecutive years is prima facie evidence of abandonment.[14]

8. PREVENTION OF DILUTION OF FAMOUS MARKS

The Federal Trademark Dilution Act of 1995 (FTDA)[15] provides a cause of action against the "commercial use" of another's famous mark or trade name when it results in a "dilution of the distinctive quality of the mark." The act protects against discordant uses, such as Du Pont shoes, Buick aspirin, and Kodak pianos. Unlike an ordinary trademark infringement action, a dilution action applies in the absence of competition and likelihood of confusion. However, when the trademarks at issue in a trademark dilution case are not identical, the famous mark must show actual dilution—actual injury to the economic value of the famous mark—rather than a presumption of harm arising from a subjective "likelihood of dilution" standard, to obtain injunctive and other relief.

---

[14] *Doeblers' Pennsylvania Hybrids Inc. v Doebler,* 442 F3d 812 (3rd Cir 2006).
[15] PL 104-98, 109 Stat 985, 15 USC § 125(c)(1).

> ## CASE SUMMARY
>
> ### Keeping a Secret Untarnished
>
> **FACTS:** Victoria's Secret distributes 400 million copies of its catalog each year and operates more than 750 Victoria's Secret stores, two of which are in Louisville, Kentucky, a short drive from Elizabethtown, Kentucky, where Victor and Cathy Moseley owned and operated an adult-toy, gag gift, and lingerie shop named "Victor's Little Secret." They had no employees. An army colonel from nearby Fort Knox notified Victoria's Secret after seeing a "Victor's Secret" ad in a weekly newspaper distributed on the base. Counsel for Victoria's Secret requested immediate discontinuance of the name, and it was changed to "Victor's Little Secret." Because the change did not satisfy counsel, an action was filed in federal district court claiming "federal dilution" in violation of the FTDA. Evidence before the trial court showed the vast size of the business and enormous value of the "Victoria's Secret" mark. No witness expressed an opinion concerning the impact if any, of the Moseleys' use of the name "Victor's Little Secret" on that value. Summary judgment was granted for Victoria's Secret, and affirmed on appeal. The Moseleys' petition to the Supreme Court was granted.
>
> **DECISION:** Judgement for the Moseleys. The relevant text of the FTDA provides that "the owner of a famous mark" is entitled to injunctive relief against another person's commercial use of a mark if that use "*causes dilution* of the distinctive quality" of the famous mark (emphasis added). The text requires a showing of actual dilution rather than likelihood of dilution. When the marks are not identical, the mere fact that consumers mentally associate a user's mark with a famous mark is not sufficient to establish actionable dilution. Tarnishing is not a necessary consequence of mental association. The evidence before the trial court was not sufficient to support summary judgment for Victoria's Secret. [**Mosley v V Secret Catalogue, Inc.,** 123 S Ct 1115 (2003)]

The FTDA exempts "fair use" of a mark in comparative advertising as well as uses in news reporting and commentary.

9. INTERNET DOMAIN NAMES AND TRADEMARK RIGHTS

An *Internet domain name* is a unique address by which an Internet resource can be identified and found by a Web browser accessing the Internet. Examples of commercial Internet domain names are "Amazon.com," "Priceline.com," and the publisher of this book, "westbuslaw.com." These domain names match the names of their respective businesses, and these domain names are also trademarks.

Any unused domain name can be registered on a first-come, first-served basis for a rather modest fee, so long as the name differs from a previously registered name by at least one character. With such quick and inexpensive registration and with the addition of new registrars and new global suffixes such as ".biz," ".info," ".name," and ".pro" to relieve ".com" overcrowding, there exists an ever-increasing chance of intentional and unintentional trademark infringement.

cybersquatters term for those who register and set up domain names on the Internet for resale to the famous users of the names in question.

(a) CYBERSQUATTERS **Cybersquatters** are individuals who register and set up domain names on the Internet that are identical, or confusingly similar, to existing trademarks that belong to others or are the personal names of famous persons. The cybersquatter hopes to sell or "ransom" the domain name to the trademark owner or the famous individual. The Federal Trademark Dilution Act has been used against cybersquatters.

For Example, Toeppen registered the domain name "panavision.com" with Network Solutions, Inc. Toeppen demanded $13,000 from Panavision to discontinue use, and Panavision sued Toeppen under the Federal Trademark Dilution Act. The court held that Toeppen diluted Panavision's famous mark by preventing it from identifying and distinguishing its goods on the Internet.[16]

Because the extent of the legal remedies available to trademark owners or famous individuals who have been victims of cybersquatters have not always been certain, Congress passed the Federal Anticybersquatting Consumer Protection Act (ACPA)[17] in 1999 to prohibit the practice of cybersquatting and cyberpiracy and to provide clear and certain remedies. Remedies include (1) injunctive relief preventing the use of the name, (2) forfeiture of the domain name, and (3) attorney fees and costs. In addition, trademark owners may obtain damages and profits that cybersquatters made from the use of the name.

A safe harbor exists under the ACPA for defendants who both "believed and had reasonable grounds to believe that the use of the domain name was fair use or otherwise lawful."[18] A defendant who acts even partially in bad faith in registering a domain name is not entitled to the shelter of the safe harbor provision. **For Example,** Howard Goldberg, the president of Artco, is an operator of Web sites that sell women's lingerie and other merchandise. He registered a domain name http://www.victoriassecrets.net to divert consumers to his Web sites to try to sell them his goods. The court rejected his ACPA safe harbor defense that he intended in good faith to have customers compare his company's products with those of Victoria's Secret. The fact that Victoria's Secret is a distinctive or famous mark deserving of the highest degree of trademark protection, coupled with the fact that the defendant added a mere *s* to that mark and gave false contact information when he requested the domain name, indicates that he and his company acted in bad faith and intended to profit from the famous mark.[19]

(b) DISPUTE AVOIDANCE   To avoid the expense of trademark litigation, it is prudent to determine whether the Internet domain name selected for your new business is an existing registered trademark or an existing domain name owned by another. Commercial firms provide comprehensive trademark searches for less than $500. Determining whether a domain name is owned by another may be done online at http://www.internic.net/whois.html.

The Internet Corporation for Assigned Names and Numbers (ICANN) provides fast-track arbitration procedures to protect trademark owners from conflicting online domain names under the auspices of the World Intellectual Property Organization (WIPO). **For Example,** Victoria's Secret stores arbitrated the "victoriassecrets.net" domain name held by Howard Goldberg's company, and the arbitration panel transferred the ownership of the name to Victoria's Secret stores. Victoria's Secret

---

[16] *Panavision v Toeppen*, 945 F Supp 1296 (CD Cal 1996).

[17] Pub L 106, 113 Stat 1536, 15 USC § 1051.

[18] 15 USC § 1125(d)(1)(B)(ii).

[19] *Victoria's Secret Stores v Artco*, 194 F Supp2d 204 (SD Ohio 2002).

E-COMMERCE AND CYBERLAW

Metatags describe the contents of a Web site using keywords. Some search engines search metatags to identify Web sites related to a search. In *PLAYBOY ENTERPRISES, INC.* (PEI) v *WELLES*,* PEI sued "Playmate of the year 1981" Terri Welles for using that and other phrases involving PEI's trademarks on her Internet Web site metatags. Some search engines that use their own summaries of Web sites, or that search the entire text of sites, would be likely to identify Welles's site as relevant to a search for "Playboy" or "Playmate," thus allowing Welles to trade on PEI's marks, PEI asserted. Remembering that the purpose of a trademark is not to provide a windfall monopoly to the mark owner but to prevent confusion over the source of products or services, the court applied a three-factor test for normative use to this case: (1) the product or service must be one not readily identifiable without the use of the mark, (2) only so much of the mark may be used as reasonably necessary to identify the product or service, and (3) the user must not suggest sponsorship or endorsement by the trademark holder.

Welles had no practical way of describing herself without using the trademark terms. The court stated, "We can hardly expect someone searching for Welles's site. . . to describe Welles without referring to Playboy—as the nude model selected by Mr. Hefner's organization."

The court stated that there is no descriptive substitute for the trademarks used in Welles's metatags, and to preclude their use would inhibit the free flow of information on the Internet, which is not a goal of trademark law. Moreover, the metatag use was reasonable use to identify her products and services and did not suggest sponsorship, thus satisfying the second and third elements of the court's test.

PLAYBOY ENTERPRISES, INC. v WELLES, 279 F3d 796 (9th Cir 2002).

stores subsequently brought an action against Goldberg and Artco for damages and injunctive relief under trademark law and the ACPA.

Registrants who lose use of a domain name in a WIPO arbitration proceeding may bring suit in federal court under Article III of the ACPA to require return of the domain name.[20]

 ## COPYRIGHTS

copyright exclusive right given by federal statute to the creator of a literary or an artistic work to use, reproduce, and display the work.

A **copyright** is the exclusive right given by federal statute to the creator of a literary or an artistic work to use, reproduce, and display the work. Under the international treaty called the *Berne Convention,* copyright of the works of all U.S. authors is protected automatically in all Berne Convention nations that have agreed under the treaty to treat nationals of other member countries like their own nationals.

[20] *Sallen v Corinthians Licencimenos LTDA,* 273 F3d 14 (1st Cir 2001).

A copyright prevents not the copying of an idea but only the copying of the way the idea is expressed.[21] That is, the copyright is violated when there is a duplication of the words, pictures, or other form of expression of the creator but not when there is just use of the idea those words, pictures, or other formats express.

The Copyright Act does not apply extraterritorially. However, if the infringement is completed in the United States and the copied work is then disseminated overseas, there is liability under the act for the resulting extraterritorial damages. **For Example,** the Los Angeles News Service (LANS), an independent news organization, produced two copyrighted videotapes of the beating of Reginald Denny during the Los Angeles riots of April 1992, and LANS licensed them to NBC for use on the *Today Show* in New York. Visnews taped the works and transmitted them by satellite to Reuters in London, which provided copies to its overseas subscribers. The infringement by Visnews occurred in New York, and Visnews was liable for the extraterritorial damages that resulted from the overseas dissemination of the work.[22]

It is a violation of U.S. copyright law for satellite carriers to capture signals of network stations in the United States and transmit them abroad. For example Prime Time's satellite retransmission of copyrighted NFL football games to satellite dish owners in Canada was held to be a violation of U.S. copyright law, notwithstanding testimony of PrimeTime's CEO that a law firm in Washington, D.C., told him that U.S. law did not pertain to distributing product in Canada. The NFL was awarded $2,557,500 in statutory damages.[23]

10. DURATION OF COPYRIGHT

Article 1, Section 8, of the U.S. Constitution empowered Congress to

> *promote the Progress of Science and useful Arts, by securing for limited times to Authors and Inventors the exclusive Right to their respective Writings and Discoveries.*

The first U.S. copyright statute was enacted soon after in 1790 and provided protection for any "book, map or chart" for 14 years, with a privilege to renew for an additional 14 years. In 1831, the initial 14-year term was extended to 28 years, with a privilege for an additional 14 years. Under the 1909 Copyright Act, the protection period was for 28 years, with a right of renewal for an additional 28 years.

The Copyright Act of 1976 set the duration of a copyright at the life of the creator of the work plus 50 years. Under the Sonny Bono Copyright Term Extension Act of 1998, the duration has been extended to the life of the creator plus 70 years.[24] If a work is a "work made for hire"—that is, a business pays an individual to create the work—the business employing the creator registers the copyright. Under the 1998 Extension Act, such a copyright has been extended by 20 years and now runs for 120 years from creation or 95 years from publication of the work, whichever period is shorter. After a copyright has expired, the work is in the public domain and may be used by anyone without cost.[25]

---

[21] *Attia v New York Hospital,* 201 F3d 50 (2d Cir 2000).

[22] *Los Angeles News Service v Reuters,* 149 F3d 987 (9th Cir 1998).

[23] *National Football League v PrimeTime 24 Joint Venture,* 131 F Supp2d 458 (SDNY 2001).

[24] PL 105-298, 112 Stat 2827, 17 USC § 302(b).

[25] Without the Sonny Bono Extension Act of 1998, the copyright on Mickey Mouse, created by Walt Disney Co. in 1928, was set to expire in 2003 and enter the public domain. Pluto, Goofy, and Donald Duck would have followed soon after.

11. COPYRIGHT NOTICE

Prior to March 1, 1989, the author of an original work secured a copyright by placing a copyright notice on the work, consisting of the word *copyright* or the symbol ©, the year of first publication, and the name or pseudonym of the author. The author was also required to register the copyright with the Copyright Office. Under the Berne Convention Implementation Act of 1988,[26] a law that adjusts U.S. copyright law to conform to the Berne Convention, it is no longer mandatory that works published after March 1, 1989, contain a notice of copyright. However, placing a notice of copyright on published works is strongly recommended. This notice prevents an infringer from claiming innocent infringement of the work, which would reduce the amount of damages owed. To bring a copyright infringement suit for a work of U.S. origin, the owner must have submitted two copies of the work to the Copyright Office in Washington, D.C., for registration.

12. WHAT IS COPYRIGHTABLE?

Copyrights protect literary, musical, dramatic, and artistic work. Protected are books and periodicals; musical and dramatic compositions; choreographic works; maps; works of art, such as paintings, sculptures, and photographs; motion pictures and other audiovisual works; sound recordings; architectural works; and computer programs.

The work must be original, independently created by the author, and possess at least some minimal degree of creativity.[27] **For Example,** William Darden, a Web page designer, challenged the Copyright Office's denial of a copyright registration for a series of existing maps with some changes in the nature of shading, coloring, or font. A court found that the Copyright Office acted within its discretion when it denied Darden's registration with the finding by the examiner from the Visual Arts Section that the maps were "representations of the preexisting census maps in which the creative spark is utterly lacking or so trivial as to be virtually nonexistent."[28]

13. COPYRIGHT OWNERSHIP AND THE INTERNET

Businesses today commonly use offsite programming services to create copyrightable software, with the delivery of code over the Internet. As set forth previously, when a business pays an employee to create a copyrightable work, it is a "work for hire" and the business employing the creator owns and may register the copyright. On the other hand, if a freelancer is employed offsite to create software for a fixed fee without a contract setting forth the ownership of the work, the freelancer owns the work product and the company utilizing the freelancer has a license to use the work product but does not have ownership of it. To avoid disputes about ownership of custom software, a written contract that addresses these ownership and license questions is necessary.

14. RIGHTS OF COPYRIGHT HOLDERS

A copyright holder has the exclusive right to (1) reproduce the work; (2) prepare derivative works, such as a script from the original work; (3) distribute copies of recordings of the work; (4) publicly perform the work, in the case of plays and motion

---

[26] PL 100-568, 102 Stat 2854, 17 USC § 101 *et seq.*

[27] *Feist Publications Inc. v Rural Telephone Services Co.,* 499 US 340 (1991).

[28] *Darden v Peters,* 402 F Supp2d 638 (ED NC 2005).

pictures; and (5) publicly display the work, in the case of paintings, sculptures, and photographs.

The copyright owner may assign or license some of the rights listed and will receive royalty payments as part of the agreement. The copyright law also ensures royalty payments. **For Example,** Jessie Riviera is a songwriter whose songs are sung at public performances and are recorded by performers on records, tapes, and CDs. Jessie is entitled to royalties from the public performance of her works. Such royalties are collected by two performing rights societies, the American Society of Composers, Authors, and Publishers (ASCAP) and Broadcast Music, Inc. (BMI), who act on behalf of the copyright holders. Jessie is also entitled to so-called mechanical royalties that refer to the royalty stream derived from "mechanically" reproduced records, tapes, and CDs. The principal payers of mechanical royalties are record companies, and the rates are set by the Copyright Royalty Tribunal.[29]

In addition to rights under the copyright law and international treaties, federal and state laws prohibit record and tape piracy.

15. LIMITATION ON EXCLUSIVE CHARACTER OF COPYRIGHT

A limitation on the exclusive rights of copyright owners exists under the principle of *fair use,* which allows limited use of copyrighted material in connection with criticism, news reporting, teaching, and research. Four important factors to consider when judging whether the use made in a particular case is fair use include

1. the purpose and character of the use, including whether such use is of a commercial nature or is for nonprofit educational purposes[30];
2. the nature of the copyrighted work;
3. the amount and substantiality of the portion used in relation to the copyrighted work as a whole; and
4. the effect of the use on the potential market for or value of the copyrighted work.

CASE SUMMARY

Fair Use or Not Fair Use—That Is the Question

FACTS: The American Geophysical Union and 82 other publishers of scientific and technical journals brought a class-action lawsuit against Texaco, claiming that Texaco's unauthorized photocopying of articles from their journals constituted a copyright infringement. Texaco's defense was that the copying was fair use under Section 107 of the Copyright Act of 1976. To avoid extensive discovery, the parties agreed to focus on one randomly selected Texaco scientist, Dr Donald Chickering, who had photocopies of eight articles from the *Journal of Catalysis* in his files. The trial court judge held that the copying of the eight articles did not constitute fair use, and Texaco appealed.

---

[29] The statutory mechanical rates are 9.1 cents or 1.75 cents per minute, whichever is greater. See **http://www.copyright.gov/carp/m200a.html.**

[30] In *Princeton University Press v Michigan Document Services, Inc.,* 99 F3d 1381 (6th Cir 1996), a commercial copyshop reproduced "coursepacks" and sold them to students attending the University of Michigan. The court refused to consider the "use" as one for nonprofit educational purposes because the use challenged was that of the copyshop, a for-profit corporation that had decided to duplicate copyrighted material for sale to maximize its profits and give itself a competitive edge over other copyshops by declining to pay the royalties requested by the holders of the copyrights.

CASE SUMMARY

continued

DECISION: Judgment for the publishers. Applying the four statutory standards to determine whether Texaco's photocopying of the scientific journal articles was fair use, three of the four factors favor the publishers. The first factor, purpose and character of use, favors the publishers because the purpose of Texaco's use was to multiply the number of copies for the benefit of its scientists, which is the same purpose for which additional subscriptions are normally sold. The second factor, the nature of the copyrighted work, which in this case is scientific articles, favors Texaco. The third factor, the amount and substantiality of the portion used, favors the publishers because Texaco copied the entire works. The fourth factor, effect on the potential market or value of the work, favors the publishers because they have shown substantial harm due to lost licensing revenue and lost subscription revenue. The aggregate assessment is that the photocopying was not fair use. [**American Geophysical Union v Texaco Inc.**, 60 F3d 913 (2d Cir 1995)]

First Amendment privileges of freedom of speech and the press are preserved through the doctrine of *fair use,* which allows for use of portions of another's copyrighted work for matters such as comment and criticism. Parodies and caricatures are the most penetrating forms of criticism and are protected under the fair use doctrine. Moreover, while injunctive relief is appropriate in the vast majority of copyright infringement cases because the infringements are simply piracy, in the case of parodies and caricatures where there are reasonable contentions of fair use, preliminary injunctions to prevent publication are inappropriate. The copyright owner can be adequately protected by an award of damages should infringement be found. **For Example,** Suntrust Bank, the trustee of a trust that holds the copyright to Margaret Mitchell's *Gone with the Wind,* one of the all-time best-selling books in the world, obtained a preliminary injunction preventing Houghton Mifflin Co. from publishing Alice Randall's *The Wind Done Gone.* The Randall book is an irreverent parody that turns old ideas upside down. The Court of Appeals set aside the injunction of the federal district court because Houghton Mifflin had a viable fair use defense.[31]

16. SECONDARY LIABILITY FOR INFRINGEMENT

An entity that distributes a device with the object of promoting its use to infringe copyrights as shown by clear expression or other active steps taken to foster the resulting acts of infringement is liable for these acts of infringement by third parties, regardless of the device's lawful uses. **For Example,** Grokster, Ltd., and StreamCast Networks, Inc., distributed free software products that allow all computer users to share electronic files through peer-to-peer networks, so called because users' computers communicate directly with each other, not through central servers. When these firms distributed their free software, each clearly voiced the objective that the recipients use the software to download copyrighted works. These firms derived profits from selling advertising space and streaming ads to the software users. Liability for infringement was established under the secondary liability doctrines of contributory or vicarious infringement.[32]

---

[31] *Suntrust Bank v Houghton Mifflin Co.,* 268 F3d 1257 (11th Cir 2001).
[32] *Metro-Goldwyn-Mayer Studios, Inc. v Grokster, Ltd.,* 125 SCt 2764 (2005).

17. DIGITAL MILLENNIUM COPYRIGHT ACT

The Digital Millennium Copyright Act of 1998 (DMCA)[33] was enacted to curb the pirating of software and other copyrighted works, such as books, films, videos, and recordings, by creating civil and criminal penalties for anyone who circumvents encryption software. The law also prohibits the manufacture, import, sale, or distribution of circumvention devices.

Title II of the DMCA provides a "safe harbor" for Internet Service Providers (ISP) from liability for direct, vicarious, and contributory infringement of copyrights provided the ISP (1) does not have actual knowledge of the infringing activity or expeditiously removed access to the problematic material upon obtaining knowledge of infringing activity, (2) does not receive financial benefit directly attributable to the infringing activity, and (3) responded expeditiously upon notification of the claimed infringement.

 ## PATENTS

Under Article 1, Section 8, of the U.S. Constitution, the founding fathers of our country empowered Congress to promote the progress of science by securing for limited times to inventors the exclusive rights to their discoveries. Federal patent laws established under Article 1, Section 8, protect inventors just as authors are protected under copyright law authorized by the same section of the U.S. Constitution.

18. TYPES, DURATION, AND NOTICE

There are three types of patents, the rights to which may be obtained by proper filing with the Patent and Trademark Office (PTO) in Washington, D.C. The types and duration of patents are as follows.

(a) UTILITY PATENTS   *Utility* or *functional patents* grant inventors of any new and useful process, machine, manufacture, or composition of matter or any new and useful improvement of such devices the right to obtain a patent.[34] Prior to 1995, these utility patents had a life of 17 years from the date of grant. Under the Uruguay Round Trade Agreement Act, effective June 8, 1995, the duration of U.S. utility patents was changed from 17 years from the date of grant to 20 years from the date of filing to be consistent with the patent law of General Agreement on Tariffs and Trade (GATT) member states.

(b) DESIGN PATENTS   A second kind of patent exists under U.S. patent law that protects new and nonobvious ornamental features that appear in connection with an article of manufacture.[35] These patents are called *design patents* and have a duration of 14 years. Design patents have limited applicability, for they must not only be new and have nonobvious ornamental features but also be nonfunctional. Thus, when the "pillow shape" design of Nabisco Shredded Wheat was found to be functional, the design patent was held invalid, as the cereal's shape was not capable of design patent protection.[36]

---

[33] 17 USC § 1201.
[34] 35 USC § 101.
[35] 35 USC § 173.
[36] *Kellogg Co. v National Biscuit Co.*, 305 US 111 (1938).

(c) PLANT PATENTS   A third type of patent, called a *plant patent,* protects the inventors of asexually reproduced new varieties of plants. The duration is 20 years from the date of filing, the same duration applied to utility patents.

(d) NOTICE   The owner of a patent is required to mark the patented item or device using the word *patent* and must list the patent number on the device to recover damages from an infringer of the patent.

19. PATENTABILITY AND EXCLUSIVE RIGHTS

To be patentable, an invention must be something that is new and not obvious to a person of ordinary skill and knowledge in the art or technology to which the invention is related. Whether an invention is new and not obvious in its field may lead to highly technical proceedings before a patent examiner, the PTO's Board of Patent Appeals, or the U.S. Court of Appeals for the Federal Circuit (CAFC). **For Example,** Thomas Devel's application for a patent on complementary DNA (cDNA) molecules encoding proteins that stimulated cell division was rejected by a patent examiner as "obvious" and affirmed by the PTO's Board of Patent Appeals. However, after a full hearing before the CAFC, which focused on the state of research in the field as applied to the patent application, Devel's patent claims were determined to be "not invalid because of obviousness."[37]

Once approved by the Patent and Trademark Office, a patent is presumed valid. However, a defendant in a patent infringement lawsuit may assert a patent's invalidity as a defense to an infringement claim by showing the invention as a whole would have been obvious to a person of ordinary skill in the art when the invention was patented. This showing is called *prior art.* **For Example,** Ron Rogers invented and patented a tree-trimming device that is essentially a chain saw releasably mounted on the end of a telescoping pole. Rogers sued Desa International, Inc. (DIA), for patent infringement after DIA introduced the Remington Pole Saw, a chain saw releasably mounted on the end of a telescoping pole. DIA provided evidence of prior art, citing four preexisting patents dealing with "trimming tools on extension poles" that correlated with Rogers's patent. The court nullified Rogers's patent because it concluded the DIA had met its heavy burden of proof that releasably mounting a lightweight chain saw on the end of a telescoping pole assembly to trim trees would be obvious to a person of ordinary skill in the art.[38]

The invention itself is what is patented. Thus, new and useful ideas and scientific principles by themselves cannot be patented. There must be an actual physical implementation of the idea or principle in the form of a process, machine, composition of matter, or device.

Under the Supreme Court's "doctrine of equivalents," infringers may not avoid liability for patent infringement by substituting insubstantial differences for some of the elements of the patented product or process. The test for infringement requires an essential inquiry: Does the accused product or process contain elements identical or equivalent to each claimed element of the patented invention?[39]

---

[37] *In re Devel,* 51 F3d 1552 (Fed Cir 1995). See also *Rhenalu v Alcoa,* 224 F Supp2d 773 (D Del 2002).

[38] *Rogers v Desa International, Inc.,* 166 F Supp2d 1202 (ED Mich 2001).

[39] *Warner-Jenkinson Co. v Hilton-Davis Chemical Co.,* 117 S Ct 1040 (1997).

CASE SUMMARY

Crude Life Forms Can Be Patented

FACTS: Chakrabarty was a microbiologist. He found a way of creating a bacterium that would break down crude oil. This could not be done by any bacteria that exist naturally. His discovery had a great potential for cleaning up oil spills. When he applied for a patent for this process, the commissioner of patents refused to grant it because what he had done was not a "manufacture" or "composition of matter" within the meaning of the federal statute and because a patent could not be obtained on something that was living. Chakrabarty appealed.

DECISION: Judgment for Chakrabarty. Discovering a way to produce a living organism that is not found in nature is within the protection of the patent laws. The fact that this kind of invention was not known when the patent laws were first adopted has no effect on the decision. The patent laws are to be interpreted according to the facts existing when an application for a patent is made. [**Diamond v Chakrabarty, 447 US 303 (1980)**]

The patent owner has the exclusive right to make, use, sell, or import into the United States the product or process that uses the patented invention. It is a violation of U.S. patent law to make, use, sell, offer to sell, or import any patented invention within the United States without authority from the patent owner.

20. PATENTABLE BUSINESS METHODS

Business method patents are proper subjects for patents. A pure business method patent consists basically of a series of steps related to performing a business process. For example, Patent No. 6,846,131 sets forth a legitimate method of doing business setting forth steps for Producing Revenue from Gypsum-Based Refuse Sites. So-called junk patents have also been issued as business method patents. For example, Patent No. 4,022,227 Method of Concealing Baldness contains a series of steps for combing one's hair amounting to what is best known as a *comb-over*. Business methods are often in the form of software programs and encompass e-commerce applications.

Competitors of business method patent holders often challenge such patents by attempting to show prior art—that the process was clearly obvious to people in the industry in question. **For Example,** Barnesandnoble.com Inc., attempted to defend a patent infringement lawsuit brought by Amazon.com on the basis that Amazon.com's One Click method for placing a purchase order over the Internet was not new to a person of ordinary skill in this technology, arguing it was just like prior shopping cart models of online purchasing. While the trial court initially issued a preliminary injunction prohibiting Barnes & Noble from using the one-click process, the Federal Circuit Court of Appeals reversed the trial court, holding that a substantial question of patent validity existed.[40] Thereafter, the parties settled the case.

With ever-evolving advancements being developed in information technology and telecommunications, a small patented component needed for a new product

---

[40] *Amazon.com, Inc., v Barnesandnoble.com Inc.,* 239 F3d 1343, 1358-1359 (Fed Cir 2001).

that a manufacturer seeks to bring to market may lead the patent holder to seek an excessive licensing fee from the manufacturer. An industry has developed that exists not to produce and sell innovative patented products but to charge others for the use of the patented technology inventories owned.

Business method patents as a classification permit the owner under the Patent Act to exclude others "from making, using, offering for sale or selling the invention."[41]

In *MercExchange, LLC v eBay,* the U.S. Supreme Court dealt with the question of whether the patent holder had the right to obtain permanent injunctive relief stopping a business entity from "using" the patented technology in addition to obtaining damages for the patent violation. The threat of a court order is used to seek high and often unreasonable licensing fees. Major technology companies contended that trial courts should consider multiple factors in deciding whether to issue a permanent injunction.

CASE SUMMARY

"Squeeze Play" Averted

FACTS: eBay and its subsidiary half.com operate popular Internet Web sites that allow private sellers to list goods they wish to sell at either an auction or a fixed price (its "Buy It Now" feature). MercExchange, LLC sought to license its business method patent to eBay, but no agreement was reached. In MercExchange's subsequent patent infringement suit, a jury found that its patent was valid, eBay had infringed the patent, and $29.5 million in damages were appropriate. However, the District Court denied MercExchange's motion for permanent injunctions against patent infringement absent exceptional circumstances. MercExchange appealed. The Federal Circuit Court of Appeals reversed, and the U.S. Supreme Court granted certiorari.

DECISION: Judgment against MercExchange's position. The traditional four-factor test of equity applied by courts when considering whether to award permanent injunctive relief to a prevailing plaintiff applies to disputes arising under the Patent Act. That test requires a plaintiff to demonstrate that (1) it has suffered an irreparable injury, (2) remedies available at law are inadequate to compensate for that injury, (3) considering the balance of hardships between the plaintiff and defendant, a remedy in equity is warranted, and (4) the public interest would not be disserved by a permanent injunction. The decision to grant or deny such relief is an act of equitable discretion by the district court, reviewable on appeal for abuse of discretion. The Federal Circuit's ruling was vacated and remanded to the district court to apply the four-factor test. [A concurring opinion written by Justice Kennedy and joined by Justices Stevens, Souter, and Breyer stated that "an industry has developed in which firms use patents not as a basis for producing and selling goods but, instead, primarily for obtaining licensing fees. For these firms, an injunction, and the potentially serious sanctions arising from its violation, can be employed as a bargaining tool to charge exorbitant fees to companies that seek to buy licenses to practice the patent." Such may be considered under the four-factor test.] [**eBay Inc. v MercExchange, LLC, 126 SCt 1837 (2006)**]

---

[41] U.S.C. § 154(a)(1).

Believing that many business method patents are obvious to persons of ordinary skill in their respective fields and have a chilling effect on consumer and public interests, a number of organizations have filed multiple reexamination requests with the PTO to invalidate these patents.[42] For example, Merc Exchange's patent at issue in the *eBay* case is being challenged in proceedings before the PTO.

(D) SECRET BUSINESS INFORMATION

A business may have developed information that is not generally known but that cannot be protected under federal law, or a business may want to avoid the disclosure required to obtain a patent or copyright protection of computer software. As long as such information is kept secret, it will be protected under state law relating to trade secrets.[43]

21. TRADE SECRETS

trade secret any formula, device, or compilation of information that is used in one's business and is of such a nature that it provides an advantage over competitors who do not have the information.

A **trade secret** may consist of any formula, device, or compilation of information that is used in one's business and is of such a nature that it provides an advantage over competitors who do not have the information. It may be a formula for a chemical compound; a process of manufacturing, treating, or preserving materials; or, to a limited extent, certain confidential customer lists.[44]

Courts will not protect customer lists if customer identities are readily ascertainable from industry or public sources or if products or services are sold to a wide group of purchasers based on their individual needs.[45]

22. LOSS OF PROTECTION

When secret business information is made public, it loses the protection it had while secret. This loss of protection occurs when the information is made known without any restrictions. In contrast, there is no loss of protection when secret information is shared or communicated for a special purpose and the person receiving the information knows that it is not to be made known to others.

When a product or process is unprotected by a patent or a copyright and is sold in significant numbers to the public, whose members are free to resell to whomever they choose, competitors are free to reverse engineer (start with the known product and work backward to discover the process) or copy the article. **For Example,** Crosby Yacht Co., a boatbuilder on Cape Cod, developed a hull design that is not patented. Maine Boatbuilders, Inc. (MBI), purchased one of Crosby's boats and copied the hull by creating a mold from the boat it purchased. MBI is free to build and sell boats utilizing the copied hull.

---

[42] See Electronic Frontier Foundation, Patent Busting Project at **www.eff.org/patent/wanted** (June 1, 2006).

[43] The Uniform Trade Secrets Act was officially amended in 1985. It is now in force in Alabama, Alaska, Arizona, Arkansas, California, Colorado, Connecticut, Delaware, Florida, Georgia, Hawaii, Idaho, Illinois, Indiana, Iowa, Kansas, Kentucky, Louisiana, Maine, Minnesota, Mississippi, Montana, Nebraska, Nevada, New Hampshire, New Mexico, North Dakota, Ohio, Oklahoma, Oregon, Rhode Island, South Carolina, South Dakota, Utah, Vermont, Virginia, Washington, West Virginia, and Wisconsin. Trade secrets are protected in all states either under the uniform act or common law and under both criminal and civil statutes.

[44] Restatement (Second) of Torts § 757 cmt b. See *Home Pride Foods, Inc. v Johnson,* 634 NW2d 774 (Neb 2001).

[45] *Xpert Automation Systems Corp. v Vibromatic Co.,* 569 NE2d 351 (Ind App 1990).

23. DEFENSIVE MEASURES

Employers seek to avoid the expense of trade secret litigation by limiting disclosure of trade secrets to employees with a "need to know." Employers also have employees sign nondisclosure agreements, and they conduct exit interviews when employees with confidential information leave, reminding the employees of the employer's intent to enforce the nondisclosure agreement. In addition, employers have adopted industrial security plans to protect their unique knowledge from "outsiders," who may engage in theft, trespass, wiretapping, or other forms of commercial espionage.

24. CRIMINAL SANCTIONS

Under the Industrial Espionage Act of 1996,[46] knowingly stealing, soliciting, or obtaining trade secrets by copying, downloading, or uploading via electronic means or otherwise with the intention that it will benefit a foreign government or agent is a crime. This act also applies to the stealing or purchasing of trade secrets by U.S. companies or individuals who intend to convert trade secrets to the economic benefit of anyone other than the owner. The definition of trade secret is closely modeled on the Uniform Trade Secrets Act and includes all forms and types of financial, business, scientific, technical, economic, and engineering information. The law requires the owner to have taken "reasonable and proper" measures to keep the information secret. Offenders are subject to fines of up to $500,000 or twice the value of the proprietary information involved, whichever is greater, and imprisonment for up to 15 years.

Corporations may be fined up to $10,000,000 or twice the value of the secret involved, whichever is greater. In addition, the offender's property is subject to forfeiture to the U.S. government, and import-export sanctions may be imposed.

PROTECTION OF COMPUTER SOFTWARE AND MASK WORKS

Computer programs, chip designs, and mask works are protected from infringement with varying degrees of success by federal statutes, restrictive licensing, and trade secrecy.

25. COPYRIGHT PROTECTION OF COMPUTER PROGRAMS

Under the Computer Software Copyright Act of 1980,[47] a written program is given the same protection as any other copyrighted material regardless of whether the program is written in source code (ordinary language) or object code (machine language). **For Example,** Franklin Computer Corp. copied certain operating-system computer programs that had been copyrighted by Apple Computer, Inc. When Apple sued Franklin for copyright infringement, Franklin argued that the object code on which its programs had relied was an uncopyrightable "method of operation." The Third Circuit held that computer programs, whether in source code or in object code embedded on ROM chips, are protected under the act.[48]

---

[46] PL 104–294, 18 USC § 1831 *et seq.* (1996).

[47] Act of December 12, 1980, PL 96–517, 94 Stat 3015, 17 USC §§ 101, 117.

[48] *Apple Computer Inc. v Franklin Computer Corp.*, 714 F2d 1240 (3d Cir 1983).

In determining whether there is a copyright violation under the Computer Software Copyright Act, courts will examine the two programs in question to compare their structure, flow, sequence, and organization. Moreover, the courts in their infringement analysis look to see whether the most *significant* steps of the program are similar rather than whether most of the program's steps are similar. To illustrate a copyright violation, substantial similarity in the structure of two computer programs for dental laboratory record-keeping was found even though the programs were dissimilar in a number of respects because five particularly important subroutines within both programs performed almost identically."[49]

The protection afforded software by the copyright law is not entirely satisfactory to software developers because of the distinction made by the copyright law of protecting expressions but not ideas. Also, Section 102(b) of the 1980 Computer Software Copyright Act does not provide protection for "methods of operation." A court has allowed a competitor to copy the identical menu tree of a copyrighted spreadsheet program because it was a noncopyrightable method of operation.[50]

As set forth previously, the Digital Millennium Copyright Act of 1998 was enacted to curb the pirating of a wide range of works, including software.

26. PATENT PROTECTION OF PROGRAMS

Patents have been granted for computer programs; for example, a method of using a computer to carry out translations from one language to another has been held patentable.

The disadvantage of patenting a program is that the program is placed in the public records and may thus be examined by anyone. This practice poses a potential danger that the program will be copied. To detect patent violators and bring legal action is difficult and costly.[51]

27. TRADE SECRETS

While primary protection for computer software is found in the Computer Software Copyright Act, industry also uses trade secret law to protect computer programs. When software containing trade secrets is unlawfully appropriated by a former employee, the employee is guilty of trade secret theft.[52]

28. RESTRICTIVE LICENSING

To retain greater control over proprietary software, it is common for the creator of the software to license its use to others rather than selling it to them. Such licensing agreements typically include restrictions on the use of the software by the licensee

---

[49] *Whelen Associates v Jaslow Dental Laboratory,* 797 F2d 1222 (3d Cir 1986).

[50] *Lotus Development Corp. v Borland International Inc.,* 49 F3d 807 (1st Cir 1995), aff'd, 116 S Ct 804 (1996).

[51] The PTO has adopted guidelines for the examination of computer-related inventions, 61 CFR §§ 7478–7502.

[52] The National Conference of Commissioners on Uniform State Laws (NCCUSL) has promulgated a new uniform law, the Uniform Computer Information Transactions Act (UCITA), to govern contracts involving the sale, licensing, maintenance, and support of computer software and books in digital form. This uniform act had been identified as Article 2B and was part of the comprehensive revisions to Article 2 of the Uniform Commercial Code. The act is supported by software publishers and opposed by software developers and buyers. The act can be obtained from the NCCUSL at **http://www.nccusl.org.** Information for and against the UCITA can be found at **http://www.ucitaonline.com.** The act has been adopted by Maryland and Virginia.

| FIGURE 10-1 | *Summary Comparison of Intellectual Property Rights* |

TYPE OF INTELLECTUAL PROPERTY	TRADEMARKS	COPYRIGHTS	PATENTS	TRADE SECRETS
PROTECTION	WORDS, NAMES, SYMBOLS, OR DEVICES USED TO IDENTIFY A PRODUCT OR SERVICE	ORIGINAL CREATIVE WORKS OF AUTHORSHIP, SUCH AS WRITINGS, MOVIES, RECORDS, AND COMPUTER SOFTWARE	UTILITY, DESIGN, AND PLANT PATENTS	ADVANTAGEOUS FORMULAS, DEVICES, OR COMPILATION OF INFORMATION
APPLICABLE STANDARD	IDENTIFIES AND DISTINGUISHES A PRODUCT OR SERVICE	ORIGINAL CREATIVE WORKS IN WRITING OR IN ANOTHER FORMAT	NEW AND NONOBVIOUS, ADVANCED IN THE ART	NOT READILY ASCERTAINABLE, NOT DISCLOSED TO THE PUBLIC
WHERE TO APPLY	PATENT AND TRADEMARK OFFICE	REGISTER OF COPYRIGHTS	PATENT AND TRADEMARK OFFICE	NO PUBLIC REGISTRATION NECESSARY
DURATION	INDEFINITE SO LONG AS IT CONTINUES TO BE USED	LIFE OF AUTHOR PLUS 70 YEARS, OR 95 YEARS FROM PUBLICATION FOR ÒWORKS FOR HIREÓ	UTILITY AND PLANT PATENTS, 20 YEARS FROM DATE OF APPLICATION; DESIGN PATENTS, 14 YEARS	INDEFINITE SO LONG AS SECRET IS NOT DISCLOSED TO PUBLIC

and give the licensor greater protection than that provided by copyright law. These restrictions commonly prohibit the licensee from providing, in any manner whatsoever, the software to third persons or subjecting the software to reverse engineering.[53]

mask work specific form of expression embodied in a chip design, including the stencils used in manufacturing semiconductor chip products.

29. SEMICONDUCTOR CHIP PROTECTION

The Semiconductor Chip Protection Act (SCPA) of 1984[54] created a new form of industrial intellectual property by protecting mask works and the semiconductor chip products in which they are embodied against chip piracy. A **mask work** refers to the specific form of expression embodied in chip design, including the stencils

---

[53] See *Fonar Corp. v Domenick*, 105 F3d 99 (2d Cir 1997).
[54] PL 98-620, 98 Stat 3347, 17 USC § 901.

semiconductor chip product product placed on a piece of semiconductor material in accordance with a predetermined pattern that is intended to perform electronic circuitry functions.

used in manufacturing semiconductor chip products. A **semiconductor chip product** is a product placed on a piece of semiconductor material in accordance with a predetermined pattern that is intended to perform electronic circuitry functions. These chips operate microwave ovens, televisions, computers, robots, x-ray machines, and countless other devices. This definition of semiconductor chip products includes such products as analog chips, logic function chips like microprocessors, and memory chips like RAMS and ROMs.

(a) DURATION AND QUALIFICATIONS FOR PROTECTION   The SCPA provides the owner of a mask work fixed in semiconductor chip products the exclusive right for 10 years to reproduce and distribute the products in the United States and to import them into the United States. These rights fully apply to works first commercially exploited after November 8, 1984, the date of the law's enactment. However, the protection of the act applies only to those works that, when considered as a whole, are not commonplace, staple, or familiar in the semiconductor industry.

(b) APPLICATION PROCEDURE   The owner of a mask work subject to protection under the SCPA must file an application for a certificate of registration with the Register of Copyrights within two years of the date of the work's first commercial exploitation. Failure to do so within this period will result in forfeiture of all rights under the act. Questions concerning the validity of the work are to be resolved through litigation or arbitration.

(c) LIMITATION ON EXCLUSIVE RIGHTS   Under the SCPA's reverse engineering exemption, competitors may not only study mask works but may also use the results of that study to design their own semiconductor chip products embodying their own original masks even if the masks are substantially similar (but not substantially identical) so long as their products are the result of substantial study and analysis, not merely the result of plagiarism.

Innocent infringers are not liable for infringements occurring before notice of protection is given them and are liable for reasonable royalties on each unit distributed after notice has been given them. However, the continued purchasing of infringing semiconductors after notice has been given can result in penalties of up to $250,000.

(d) REMEDIES   The SCPA provides that an infringer will be liable for actual damages and will forfeit its profits to the owner. As an alternative, the owner may elect to receive statutory damages of up to $250,000 as determined by a court. The court may also order destruction or other disposition of the products and equipment used to make the products. **For Example,** Altera Corporation manufactures programmable logic devices. It was successful in the lawsuit against its competitor Clear Logic, Inc., which works from a different business model. Altera was successful in its lawsuit against Clear Logic under the SCPA, asserting that Clear Logic had copied the layout design of its registered mask works. It also was successful in its claim that Clear Logic induced breach of software licenses with Altera customers. Damages were assessed at $36 million.[55]

---

[55] *Altera Corp. v Clear Logic Inc.,* 424 F3d 1079 (9th Cir 2005).

ETHICS & THE LAW

Not long ago, the dance song "Macarena" hit the pop music scene and charts in the United States. The line-type dance inspired by the song also is called the Macarena. At camps around the country, the song was played, and children were taught the dance.

The American Society of Composers, Authors, and Publishers (ASCAP) is the organization that serves as a clearinghouse for fee payments for use of copyrighted materials belonging to its members. ASCAP sent a letter to the directors of camps and nonprofit organizations sponsoring camps (Girl Scouts, Boy Scouts, Camp Fire Girls, American Cancer Association, and so forth) warning them that licensed songs should not be used without paying ASCAP the licensing fees and that violators would be pursued. ASCAP's prices for songs are, for example, $591 for the camp season for "Edelweiss" (from *The Sound of Music*) or "This Land Is Your Land."

Some of the nonprofit-sponsored camps charge only $44 per week per camper. The directors could not afford the fees, and the camps eliminated their oldies from their dances and dance classes. ASCAP declined to offer discounted licensing fees for the camps.

Why did ASCAP work so diligently to protect its rights? What ethical and social responsibility issues do you see with respect to the nonprofit camps? Some of these camps are summer retreats for children who suffer from cancer, AIDS, and other terminal illnesses. Does this information change your feelings about ASCAP's fees? What would you do if you were an ASCAP member and owned the rights to a song a camp wished to use?

LAWFLIX

The Jerk (1979) (R)

Steve Martin invents a special handle for eyeglasses that is mass marketed by a businessman who gives him a percentage of the royalties from sales. Should Martin be paid?

For movie clips that illustrate business law concepts, see LawFlix at **http://wdvl.westbuslaw.com.**

> SUMMARY

Property rights in trademarks, copyrights, and patents are acquired as provided primarily in federal statutes. A trademark or service mark is any word, symbol, design, or combination of these used to identify a product (in the case of a trademark) or a service (in the case of a service mark). Terms will fall into one of four categories: (1) generic, (2) descriptive, (3) suggestive, or (4) arbitrary or fanciful. Generic terms are never registrable. However, if a descriptive term has acquired a secondary meaning, it is registrable. Suggestive and arbitrary marks are registrable as well. If there is likelihood of confusion, a court will enjoin the second user from using a particular registered mark.

A copyright is the exclusive right given by federal statute to the creator of a literary or an artistic work to use, reproduce, or display the work for the life of the creator and 70 years after the creator's death.

A patent gives the inventor an exclusive right for 20 years from the date of application to make, use, and sell an invention that is new and useful but not obvious to those in the business to which the invention is related. Trade secrets that give an owner an advantage over competitors are protected under state law for an unlimited period so long as they are not made public.

Protection of computer programs and the design of computer chips and mask works is commonly obtained, subject to certain limitations, by complying with federal statutes, by using the law of trade secrets, and by requiring restrictive licensing agreements. Many software developers pursue all of these means to protect their proprietary interests in their programs.

> QUESTIONS AND CASE PROBLEMS

1. China is a signatory country to the Madrid Protocol on the international registration of trademarks. Starbucks opened its first café in China in 1999 and has added outlets in numerous locations including Shanghai and at the Great Wall and the imperial palace in Beijing. Xingbake Café Corp. Ltd. has imitated the designs of Starbuck's cafés in its business coffee café locations in Shanghai. *Xing* (pronounced "Shing") means star, and *bake*, or "bak kuh" is pronounced like "bucks." Does the Seattle, Washington, Starbucks Corporation have standing to bring suit in China against Xingbake Café Corp. Ltd? If so, on what theory? Decide. (*Boston Globe*, January 3, 2006, 1)

2. Cable News Network with its principal place of business in Atlanta, Georgia, is the owner of the trademark CNN in connection with providing news and information services to people worldwide through cable and satellite television networks, Web sites, and news services. Its services are also available worldwide on the Internet at the domain name CNN.com. Maya Online Broadband Network (Maya HK) is a Chinese company. It registered the domain name CNNEWS.com with Network Solutions, Inc. The CNNews.com Web site was designed to provide news and information to Chinese-speaking individuals worldwide, making significant use of the terms *CNNews* and *CNNews.com* as brand names and logos that the Atlanta company contends resembles its logos. Maya HK has admitted that CNNews in fact stands for China Network News abbreviated as CNN. The Atlanta company notified Maya HK of its legal rights in the CNN mark before the Chinese company registered the CNNews.com domain name. Does the federal Anticybersquatting Consumer Protection Act apply to this case? If so, does a "safe harbor" exist under the ACPA for Maya HK in that most people who access its Web site in China have never heard of CNN? Decide. [*Cable News Network v CNN News.com*, 177 F Supp 2d 506 (ED Va)]

3. Banion manufacturers semiconductor chips. He wants to obtain protection for his mask works under federal law, particularly so that competitors will be prohibited from reverse engineering these works. Advise Banion of his legal options, if any, to accomplish his objective.

4. Jim and Eric work for Audio Visual Services (AVS) at Cramer University in Casper, Wyoming. For "expenses" of $5 and the provision of a blank tape, Jim and Eric used AVS facilities after hours to make tapes of Pearl Jam's CD *Vitology* for 25 friends or friends of friends from school. When Mrs. Mullen, who is in charge of AVS, discovered this and confronted them, Jim, a classics major, defended their actions, telling her, "It's *de minimus* . . . I mean, who cares?" Explain to Jim and Eric the legal and ethical ramifications of their actions.

5. Sullivan sold t-shirts with the name *Boston Marathon* and the year of the race imprinted on them. The Boston Athletic Association (BAA) sponsors and administers the Boston Marathon and has used the name *Boston Marathon* since 1917. The BAA registered the name *Boston Marathon* on the Principal Register. In 1986, the BAA entered into an exclusive license with Image, Inc., to use its service mark on shirts and other apparel. Thereafter, when Sullivan continued to

sell shirts imprinted with the name *Boston Marathon,* the BAA sought an injunction. Sullivan's defense was that the general public was not being misled into thinking that his shirts were officially sponsored by the BAA. Without this confusion of source, he contended, no injunction should be issued. Decide. [*Boston Athletic Ass'n v Sullivan,* 867 F2d 22 (1st Cir)]

6. The University of Georgia Athletic Association (UGAA) brought suit against beer wholesaler Bill Laite for marketing Battlin' Bulldog Beer. The UGAA claimed that the cans infringed its symbol for its athletic teams. The symbol, which depicted an English Bulldog wearing a sweater with a G and the word BULLDOGS on it, had been registered as a service mark. Soon after the beer appeared on the market, the university received telephone calls from friends of the university who were concerned that Battlin' Bulldog Beer was not the sort of product that should in any way be related to the University of Georgia. The university's suit was based on the theory of false designation of origin in violation of the Lanham Act. Laite contended that there was no likelihood of confusion because his bulldog was different from the university's and his cans bore the disclaimer "Not associated with the University of Georgia." Decide. [*University of Georgia Athletic Ass'n v Laite,* 756 F2d 1535 (11th Cir)]

7. Twentieth Century Fox (Fox) owned and distributed the successful motion picture *The Commitments.* The film tells the story of a group of young Irish men and women who form a soul music band. In the film, the leader of the band, Jimmy, tries to teach the band members what it takes to be successful soul music performers. Toward that end, Jimmy shows the band members a videotape of James Brown's energetic performance of the song "Please, Please, Please." This performance came from Brown's appearance in 1965 on a television program called the *TAMI Show.* Portions of the 1965 performance are shown in *The Commitments* in seven separate "cuts" for a total of 27 seconds. Sometimes the cuts are in the background of a scene, and sometimes they occupy the entire screen. Brown's name is not mentioned at all during these relatively brief cuts. His name is mentioned only once later in the film, when Jimmy urges the band members to abandon their current musical interests and tune in to the great soul performers, including James Brown: "Listen, from now on I don't want you listening to Guns & Roses and The Soup Dragons. I want you on a strict diet of soul. James Brown for the growls, Otis Redding for the moans, Smokey Robinson for the whines, and Aretha for the whole lot put together." Would it be fair use under U.S. copyright law for Fox to use just 27 seconds of James Brown cuts in the film without formally obtaining permission to use the cuts? Advise Fox as to what, if anything, would be necessary to protect it from a lawsuit. [See *Brown v Twentieth Century Fox Film Corp.,* 799 F Supp 166 (DDC)]

8. Sony Corporation manufactures videocassette recorders (VCRs) to tape television shows for later home viewing (time-shifting). Sony sold them under the trade name Betamax through retail establishments throughout the country. Universal City Studios and Walt Disney Productions owned the copyrights on some of the television programs that were broadcast on public airwaves. Universal and Disney brought an action against Sony and certain large retailers, contending that VCR consumers had recorded some of their copyrighted works that had been shown on commercially sponsored television and thereby infringed the copyrights. These plaintiffs sought damages and an injunction against the manufacture and marketing of VCRs. Sony contended that the noncommercial, home-use recording of material broadcast over public airwaves for later viewing was a fair use of copyrighted works. Decide. [*Sony Corp. v Universal Studios,* 464 US 417]

9. The menu commands on the Lotus 1-2-3 spreadsheet program enable users to perform accounting functions by using such commands as "Copy," "Print," and "Quit." Borland International, Inc., released its Quattro spreadsheet, a program superior to Lotus 1-2-3 that did, however, use an identical copy of the entire Lotus 1-2-3 menu tree but did not copy any of Lotus's computer code. Lotus believed that its copyright in Lotus 1-2-3 had been violated. Borland insisted that the Lotus menu command

was not copyrightable because it is a method of operation foreclosed from protection under Section 102(b) of the Copyright Act of 1976. Decide. [*Lotus Development Corp. v Borland International, Inc.,* 49 F3d 807 (1st Cir), aff'd, 116 S Ct 904]

10. Diehr devised a computerized process for curing rubber that was based on a well-known mathematical formula related to the cure time, and he devised numerous other steps in his synthetic rubber-curing process. The patent examiner determined that because abstract ideas, the laws of nature, and mathematical formulas are not patentable subject matter, the process in this case (based on a known mathematical formula) was also not patentable. Diehr contended that all of the steps in his rubber-curing process were new and not obvious to the art of rubber curing. He contended also that he did not seek an exclusive patent on the mathematical formula, except for its use in the rubber-curing process. Decide. [*Diamond v Diehr,* 450 US 175]

11. Aries Information Systems, Inc., develops and markets computer software specifically designed to meet the financial accounting and reporting requirements of such public bodies as school districts and county governments. One of Aries's principal products is the POBAS III accounting program. Pacific Management Systems Corporation was organized by Scott Dahmer, John Laugan, and Roman Rowan for marketing a financial accounting and budgeting system known as FAMIS. Dahmer, Laugan, and Rowan were Aries employees before, during, and shortly after they organized Pacific. As employees, they each gained access to Aries's software materials (including the POBAS III system) and had information about Aries's existing and prospective clients. Proprietary notices appeared on every client contract, source code list, and magnetic tape. Dahmer, Laugan, and Rowan signed an Employee Confidential Information Agreement after beginning employment with Aries. While still employees of Aries, they submitted a bid on behalf of Pacific to Rock County and were awarded the contract. Pacific's FAMIS software system is substantially identical to Aries's proprietary POBAS III system. Aries sued Pacific to

recover damages for misappropriation of its trade secrets. Pacific's defense was that no "secrets" were misappropriated because many employees knew the information in question. Decide. [*Aries Information Systems, Inc. v Pacific Management Systems Corp.,* 366 NW2d 366 (Minn App)]

12. The plaintiff, Herbert Rosenthal Jewelry Corporation, and the defendant, Kalpakian, manufactured jewelry. The plaintiff obtained a copyright registration of a jeweled pin in the shape of a bee. Kalpakian made a similar pin. Rosenthal sued Kalpakian for infringement of copyright registration. Kalpakian raised the defense that he was only copying the idea, not the way the idea was expressed. Was he liable for infringement of the plaintiff's copyright? [*Herbert Rosenthal Jewelry Corp. v Kalpakian,* 446 F2d 738 (9th Cir)]

13. Mineral Deposits, Ltd. (MD, Ltd.), an Australian company, manufactures the Reichert Spiral, a device used for recovering gold particles from sand and gravel. The spiral was patented in Australia, and MD, Ltd., had applied for a patent in the United States. Theodore Zigan contacted MD, Ltd., stating he was interested in purchasing up to 200 devices for use in his gravel pit. MD, Ltd., agreed to lend Zigan a spiral for testing its efficiency. Zigan made molds of the spiral's components and proceeded to manufacture 170 copies of the device. When MD, Ltd., found out that copies were being made, it demanded the return of the spiral. MD, Ltd., also sought lost profits for the 170 spirals manufactured by Zigan. Recovery was sought on a theory of misappropriation of trade secrets. Zigan offered to pay for the spiral lent him by MD, Ltd. He argued that trade secret protection was lost by the public sale of the spiral. What ethical values are involved? Was Zigan's conduct a violation of trade secret law? [*Mineral Deposits, Ltd. v Zigan,* 773 P2d 609 (Colo App)]

14. Village Voice Media, owners of the famous *Village Voice* newspaper in New York City, sent a letter to *The Cape Cod Voice,* a year-old publication located in Orleans, Massachusetts, objecting to the use of the word *Voice* in the title of its publication. It warned that the Cape Cod publication could cause "confusion as to the source affiliation with the famous Village

Voice marks." The publisher of *The Cape Cod Voice* responded that "small places have a right to their own voices." The use of the word *Voice* is thus in dispute between these parties. Would you classify it as generic, descriptive, suggestive, arbitrary, or fanciful? How would you resolve this controversy? [*Cape Cod Times* Business Section, Amy Zipkin, *The New York Times,* October 16, 2004, G-1].

> CPA QUESTIONS

1. Multicomp Company wishes to protect software it has developed. It is concerned about others copying this software and taking away some of its profits. Which of the following is true concerning the current state of the law?

   a. Computer software is generally copyrightable.
   b. To receive protection, the software must have a conspicuous copyright notice.
   c. Software in human readable source code is copyrightable but machine language object code is not.
   d. Software can be copyrighted for a period not to exceed 20 years.

2. Which of the following is not correct concerning computer software purchased by Gultch Company from Softtouch Company? Softtouch originally created this software.

   a. Gultch can make backup copies in case of machine failure.
   b. Softtouch can typically copyright its software for at least 75 years.
   c. If the software consists of compiled computer databases, it cannot be copyrighted.
   d. Computer programs are generally copyrightable.

3. Using his computer, Professor Bell makes 15 copies to distribute to his accounting class of a database in some software he has purchased for his personal research. The creator of this software is claiming copyright. Which of the following is correct?

   a. This is an infringement of copyright, since he bought the software for personal use.
   b. This is not an infringement of copyright, since databases cannot be copyrighted.
   c. This is not an infringement of copyright because the copies were made using a computer.
   d. This is not an infringement of copyright because of the fair use doctrine.

4. Intellectual property rights included in software may be protected under which of the following?

   a. Patent law
   b. Copyright law
   c. Both of the above
   d. None of the above

CYBERLAW

LEARNING OBJECTIVES

After studying this chapter, you should be able to

LO.1 Identify the legal and ethical issues of the new technologies in business

LO.2 Discuss the various areas of law that apply to business issues in cyberspace and the use of the new technologies

LO.3 Explain how the flexibility of the law allows for the resolution of new issues and problems in business

Ⓐ INTRODUCTION TO CYBERLAW

1. WHAT IS CYBERLAW?

Figures from 2005 conclude that 331,473,276 people in North America use the Internet on a regular basis, a whopping 68.1 percent of the population. In Europe, the number of regular users is 807,289,020 or 35.9 percent of the population.[1] About 80 percent of managers and professionals use a computer at work each day. About 55 percent of all U.S. workers use a computer at work, with two of every five (40 percent) workers using e-mail daily.[2] They also use their computers for communicating, contracting, and doing research. The World Wide Web has enabled businesses to move goods and services through commerce at lightning speed. In many ways, the changes in technology and resulting changes in business practices have occurred at speeds that have not permitted the law to keep pace with them. As a result, this new world of business has caused some distress among managers, law professors, and students as they wonder, "Are there laws that cover this new way of doing business?"

The answer to the question is both yes and no. Although certainly some new laws govern aspects of using and operating systems in the new economy and cyberspace, a body of law and precedent—the same body of law and precedent that has seen businesses through many economic and technological revolutions—remains. This same body of law and its characteristics are again a resource for resolving the new economy's legal issues. Examining how the law applies to the new technology provides further evidence of the law's stability, innovation, and flexibility. (See Chapter 1 for more discussion of the characteristics of law.) The rise of the Internet and its pervasive use in business is not the first time the law has had to change to keep pace with technological revolutions. For example, the new clarity of satellite pictures and observation techniques such as thermal scanning have raised new issues concerning searches and the requirements for warrants. The law adjusts and survives through a balancing of the interests at stake as issues arise from the use of new technologies.

cyberlaw laws and precedent applicable to Internet transactions and communications.

Even though the law that is applied to resolve the problems of the new technologies and the new economy is often referred to as **cyberlaw,** you need not fear that you will be required to learn a whole new body of law. There have been and will continue to be changes in the law to accommodate new ways of doing business, but there has also been and will continue to be reliance on the fundamental principles that underlie our laws and the rights they protect. This chapter simply examines the issues and concerns in cyberspace and covers their resolution through a brief overview of new and existing laws. Although other chapters provide more details on these rights and protections, this chapter provides a framework for both the challenges of legal issues in **cyberspace** as well as discussion of the valuable nature of a legal system that can adjust to and absorb the changes business brings about.

cyberspace World Wide Web and Internet communication.

2. WHAT ARE THE ISSUES IN CYBERLAW?

While no new body of law called *cyberlaw* exists, there are new issues in the use of cyberspace in business that require resolution by new statutes, by judicial decisions, or by reliance on existing laws and case precedent. The legal issues of cyberspace can be

---

[1] See **www.internetworldstats.com**, with additional data from Nielsen and the International Telecommunications Union.
[2] "Internet Use at Work," Bureau of Labor Statistics, **www.bls.gov**.

tort civil wrong that interferes with one's property or person.

broken down into six areas: **tort** issues, contract issues, intellectual property issues, criminal law issues, constitutional restraints and protections, and securities law issues. Within each of these six areas of existing law are a number of new legal issues that have arisen because of the nature of cyberspace and the conduct of business there. That various cyberlaw issues can be grouped into traditional areas of law demonstrates the not-so-new nature of cyberlaw in the new economy. The following sections in this chapter include discussions of these six main areas and the new issues that technology has raised for resolution.

 ## TORT ISSUES IN CYBERSPACE

The tort issues in cyberlaw are privacy, appropriation, and defamation.

3. PRIVACY ISSUES IN CYBERLAW

(a) E-Mail and Privacy   E-mail use in the workplace is a nearly universal practice. Employees use e-mails for contract, customer, supplier, and shareholder communications. However, studies show that 86 percent of employees use their company e-mail systems to communicate with their families, and 38 percent of employees indicate that they have used company e-mail systems to send messages that served political purposes. Finally, 30 percent of employees indicate that they have used e-mail to send racist, pornographic, sexist, or otherwise discriminatory messages.[3]

Courts are forced to balance interests when they deal with questions of privacy of such e-mail communication. For example, employers are held responsible for the content of e-mail that serves to create an atmosphere of harassment. (See Chapter 40 for more information on sexual harassment.) If employers are held accountable for the content of e-mail, as they are in cases of harassment and in other forms of discrimination, some means of controlling the content of those e-mails is important. In some cases, employees' e-mails have resulted in convictions or settlements. For example, in 2004, New York's attorney general and federal regulators reached a settlement with the major Wall Street investment houses for the inconsistent stock evaluations of their employees that were found in their e-mails. The employees offered favorable evaluations of companies in their public statements but referred to the companies as "dogs" in their e-mail communications with each other and colleagues. In 2005, Marsh & McLennan, an international insurance broker, settled its price-fixing case with New York's attorney general after e-mails that showed employees were concerned about possible antitrust violations emerged. Monitoring the content of employee e-mails is important for keeping companies out of legal difficulties. However, employees may believe they have an expectation of privacy in their e-mails, even when those e-mails are sent from work.

There were some efforts initially to apply existing law to ensure e-mail privacy. The Electronic Communications Privacy Act of 1986 (ECPA) prohibits the interception

---

[3] W. Michael Hoffman, Laura P. Hartman, and Mark Rowe, "You've Got Mail . . . And the Boss Knows: A Survey by the Center for Business Ethics of Companies' Email and Internet Monitoring," 108 *Business and Society* 285 (2003). See also **http://www.elronsoftware.com** for more information on employee use of e-mail.

CASE SUMMARY

The Joke's on the Employee: E-Mail Content Can Get You Fired

FACTS: Nancy Garrity ("Mrs. Garrity") and Joanne Clark ("Ms. Clark") were employees of John Hancock Mutual Life Insurance Company ("Hancock") for 12 and 2 years, respectively. Mrs. Garrity and Ms. Clark received, on their office computers, sexually explicit e-mails from Internet joke sites and other third parties, including Mrs. Garrity's husband, Arthur Garrity, which they then sent to coworkers. Examples included "The Top Ten Reasons Cookie Dough Is Better Than Men."

A fellow employee complained after receiving one such e-mail. Hancock investigated Mrs. Garrity's and Ms. Clark's e-mail folders, as well as the folders of those with whom they e-mailed on a regular basis. Based on the information gleaned from this investigation, Hancock determined that Mrs. Garrity and Ms. Clark had violated its e-mail policy, which stated:

> *Messages that are defamatory, abusive, obscene, profane, sexually oriented, threatening or racially offensive are prohibited.*
>
> *The inappropriate use of E-mail is in violation of company policy and may be subject* [sic] *to disciplinary action, up to and including termination of employment.*
>
> *All information stored, transmitted, received, or contained in the company's E-mail systems is the property of John Hancock. It is not company policy to intentionally inspect E-mail usage. However, there may be business or legal situations that necessitate company review of E-mail messages and other documents.*
>
> *[C]ompany management reserves the right to access all E-mail files.*

Hancock periodically sent reminders, but it also provided information on how to keep e-mails private through password usage for the files.

Hancock fired both women, and the women filed suit for invasion of privacy as well as wrongful termination.

DECISION: No invasion of privacy occurred because Hancock had warned employees about the lack of privacy. Furthermore, the women, even if they had kept the e-mails under passwords, waived their right to privacy when they sent the e-mails to coworkers. Employees using the company e-mail system to send offensive e-mails to other employees can have no expectation of privacy. The court granted summary judgment for Hancock. [**Garrity v John Hancock Mut. Life Ins. Co., 2002 WL 974676 (D Mass 2002) (memorandum opinion)**]

---

of "live" communications, as when someone uses a listening device to intercept a telephone conversation. However, e-mail is stored information, and the question of this act's application for resolving the privacy issue is doubtful.[4]

invasion of privacy tort of intentional intrusion into the private affairs of another.

The tort of **invasion of privacy**, or intrusion into private affairs, has application to this cyberspace communication. The tort of intrusion into private affairs or public disclosure of private facts requires not just the act of revelation of private information but that the information revealed is presumed to be private and entitled to privacy protection.

(b) WEB SITE INFORMATION AND PRIVACY   A second privacy issue in cyberlaw is the use of information that Web sites have gleaned from their users. **For Example,** if

---

[4] "Every circuit court to have considered the matter has held that an 'intercept' under the ECPA must occur contemporaneously with transmission." See *Fraser v Nationwide Mut. Ins. Co.,* 352 F3d 107, 113 (3d Cir 2003).

THINKING THINGS THROUGH

The Boss Is Watching and Reading Your E-Mails

Discuss whether employees would have the right of privacy in the following e-mail situations:

1. E-mail sent in a company in which there is no warning given about the lack of privacy in e-mails. SMYTH V PILLSBURY, 914 F Supp 97 (ED Pa 1996).
2. An e-mail sent to coworkers from home using the employee's AOL account.
3. An e-mail sent from a laptop while the employee is traveling for the company.
4. An e-mail sent to a coworker over a company Internet system in a company in which the employer has promised privacy in e-mail. COMMONWEALTH V PROETTO, 771 A2d 823 (Pa Super Ct 2001).
5. Employer monitoring of the e-mails of any employee when those e-mails were stored in a file folder marked "Personal." MCLAREN V MICROSOFT CORP., 1999 WL 339015 (Tex App–Dallas 1999).
6. Employees using company e-mail for union organization purposes. PRATT & WHITNEY, NLRB GEN. COUNS. AD V. MEM. Cases 12-CA-18446, 12-CA-18722, 12-CS-18863 (February 23, 1998).

you use an airline's Web site to book your travel arrangements, that Web site has a profile of your travel habits. The airline knows how frequently you travel and where you travel. That type of targeted customer information is something other Web sites and retailers are willing to pay dearly for because they know their product is being considered by those most likely to purchase it. If you use Amazon.com to buy books, that Web site has relevant information about the types of books you read, your interests, and even some indications about your income level based on your spending habits. When you log on to a Web site, do you expect that private information about you will be gathered and sold to others for purposes of marketing goods and services to you?

Even though this issue of privacy may seem new and peculiar to cyberspace, it is, in fact, a rather old issue that has long been a concern of credit card companies. These companies' use and sale of information about their customers are restricted. Customers must be given the right to refuse such use of their names and other information for sale as part of lists for target marketing. Some state attorneys general are utilizing these credit card privacy rights to enforce privacy rights against Web site owners who sell information about their users. The Federal Trade Commission (FTC) has begun to take positions that are identical to its stances on other types of commerce issues. **For Example,** if catalog companies are required to provide notice to customers about delays in shipment of goods to customers, Internet companies must comply with the same notification rules.

In 2002 the FTC reached a settlement with Microsoft over its practice of collecting data through its Passport Service.[5] The FTC found that the payment system Microsoft had consumers use that assured them of privacy was actually

---

[5] *In re Microsoft Corp.,* FTC No. 012 3240, Complaint at 1-2 (2002) [hereinafter Passport Complaint], available at **http://www.ftc.gov/**

ETHICS & THE LAW

Employer Tips on Monitoring Employees

Because the law on Internet and e-mail privacy is evolving, taking the initiative not only can avoid future legal problems but also can help employees feel comfortable about company policies and their own e-mail and Internet use. A lawyer for businesses interested in solving the issues of technology, the workplace, and cyberspace provided the following tips.

Ten Commandments for Avoiding Workplace Exposure

1. Publish policies regarding employee use of e-mail, the Internet, and any employer-issued hardware or software.
2. Have employees sign off on the policy each year.
3. Tell employees that the company will monitor e-mail, Internet use, and any other use of employer-issued computers. Be sure to cover all new technology, such as Palm Pilots, Blackberries, and two-way text messaging systems.
4. Create a style guide for writing business e-mails.
5. Train all employees on how to write appropriate business e-mails.
6. Develop a document/e-mail retention policy.
7. Tell employees you will cooperate with law enforcement officials and turn over any evidence of illegal activities.
8. Enforce all policies in an even-handed manner.
9. Keep current on new technology in the marketplace and how it can be used and monitored.
10. Reevaluate all technology-related policies annually.*

About 88 percent of employers tell their employees about the privacy limitations of using the company e-mail system, and about 92 percent of companies engage in monitoring of employees' e-mails.** However, the lack of notice does not mean that the employee has an expectation of privacy. If the employee is using the employer's e-mail system, any messages sent or received on that system are subject to employer review.

Many corporations have monitoring firms that keep track of employee use of Web sites, and the reports of these electronic consultants are then used to confront employees about everything from breach of company rules to efficient use of time at work. Recent surveys indicate that 92 percent of companies monitor their employees' Web site access.*** Of these companies, 91 percent disclose to their employees that they are monitoring their Web site use. Disclosure is again key in allowing employer monitoring of employee Web site use.

---

* Frank C. Morris, Jr., "The Electronic Platform: Email and Other Privacy Issues in the Workplace," 20 *Computer & Internet Law* (no. 8) 1–20.

** "2001 Survey on Privacy, Technology and Internet Use in the Workplace," **http://www.marketingpower.com.**

*** Hoffman, Hartman, and Rowe, "You've Got Mail . . . And the Boss Knows." See also **http:// www.elronsoftware.com** for more information on employee use of e-mail.

being used by the company for data gathering on the consumers. As part of the settlement, Microsoft must submit to 20 years of annual privacy audits.[6]

---

[6] However, see *In re DoubleClick, Inc., Privacy Litig.*, 154 F Supp 2d 497, 500 (SDNY 2001), in which the court dismissed a similar privacy suit that gathered information from consumer Web browsing.

(c) Freedom of Speech, Screen Names, and Privacy   Another privacy issue that has arisen is whether plaintiffs in suits for defamation can successfully subpoena Internet Service Providers (ISPs) to obtain the identity of individuals who post statements in chat rooms and across the Internet. The issue has been in litigation a number of times in various states with different results. Music companies' actions against individuals who download music but do not pay for their songs requires the discovery of the identity of those who are doing the downloading. Can the music companies require the ISPs to disclose the names of their customers for purposes of preventing copyright infringement? There are now clear standards for determining disclosure of identity.

(d) Cookies and Privacy   Technology has permitted companies to plant "cookies" on the computers of those who are using certain Internet sites. With those "cookies" in place, the Web site owner has a way to track the computer owner's activity. At least one court has held that a Web site operator's placing cookies on a

CASE SUMMARY

The Ratfink ISP: Telling Who's Doing the Downloading

FACTS: Sony and others own the copyrights and exclusive licenses to their various sound recordings. Without permission, 40 unidentified individuals (called Does) used "Fast Track," an online media distribution system—or "peer to peer" ("P2P") file-copying network—to download hundreds or thousands of copyrighted sound recordings. Sony was able to identify Cablevision as the Internet service provider (ISP) to which the Does subscribed. Sony did so by using a publicly available database to trace the Internet Protocol (IP) address for each Doe.

As a condition of providing its Internet service, Cablevision requires its subscribers to agree to its "Terms of Service" under which "[t]ransmission or distribution of any material in violation of any applicable law or regulation is prohibited. This includes, without limitation, material protected by copyright, trademark, trade secret or other intellectual property right used without proper authorization."

On January 26, 2004, the court issued an order granting Sony the right to serve a subpoena upon Cablevision to obtain the identity of each Doe by requesting the name, address, telephone number, e-mail address, and Media Access Control address for each defendant.

On February 23, 2004, Cablevision complied with the subpoena and provided relevant identifying information for 36 Does, who filed a motion to quash the subpoena.

DECISION: The court held for Sony, finding that there are five relevant factors when weighing privacy and First Amendment rights with the issue of copyright infringement. These factors include (1) the concrete showing of a prima facie claim of actionable harm, (2) the specificity of the discovery request, (3) the absence of alternative means to obtain the subpoenaed information, (4) a central need for the subpoenaed information to advance the claim, and (5) the party's expectation of privacy. The court found that the infringement was a substantial harm to Sony, that Sony had narrowed its request specifically based on the public information about who was doing the downloading, that the request for identification was specific, that there was no other source for the information and identity and that Sony had done as much as it could to determine the identities, and that the right to privacy was clearly waived by the customer's agreement not to be involved in copyright infringement. [**Sony Music Entertainment Inc. v Does 1– 40, 326 F Supp 2d 556 (SDNY 2004)**]

E-COMMERCE AND CYBERLAW

Blogging, Ethics, and Cyber Law

By the end of 2005, there were approximately 27 million U.S. adults who had created a blog or web-based diary.* That means 6% of the U.S. population are bloggers. Employers have begun using Google for more than the ego trip. Rather than plugging their own names into the search engine to see the number of hits and what is said about them, they are plugging in the names of job applicants as a way to uncover information that the job interview and other sources cannot reveal. Employers realize that they have online access as a way to obtain information for job screening and hiring decisions. For example, MySpace.com has proven to be a gold mine for employers in learning more about job applicants.

Employers are also using Google and other internet sources to track employee work excuses. One company's human resources official was on the phone with the company employment lawyer seeking to determine what action could be taken against an employee who was absent frequently but who claimed he was absent to care for his ill grandmother. While they were talking, the lawyer Googled the employee's name and found that he was being arraigned in federal court.

Schools, employment counselors, and lawyers are offering the following warnings about the dangers of Google:

1. Nothing is private on the Internet. People can see everything.
2. Be careful what you blog.
3. Protect your identity when in chat rooms.
4. Assume that everything you write and post will be seen.
5. You can clean up your name on Google using several services, but having no hits at all can lead to suspicions.
6. Think before you write, blog, post, or do anything on the Internet.

---

*Rainie, "The State of Blogging," Pew Internet and American Life Project Nov. 2005, available at **http://www.pewinternet.org/pdfs/PIP_blogging_data.pdf.** and **www.technorati.com.**

Source: Michelle Conlin, "You Are What You Post," *Business Week*, March 27, 2006, 52–53.

---

user's computer is a violation of an unauthorized access statute that would provide the computer owner a right of action for that breach of the statute and privacy (see discussion of criminal law in Section 8 for more information on unauthorized access).[7]

(e) STATUTORY PROTECTIONS FOR PRIVACY IN CYBERSPACE   Several federal laws and some state laws provide privacy protections, although somewhat limited, for Internet users. The Privacy Act of 1974 controls the use of information gathered about consumers, but it applies only to government-collected data such as information gathered by the Social Security Administration or the Internal Revenue Service. Furthermore, there are exceptions for the agencies for "routine use."[8] Some

---

[7] *In re Intuit Privacy Litigation,* 138 F Supp 2d 1272 (CD Cal 2001); see also *In re Toys R Us, Inc., Privacy Litig.,* 2001 WL 34517252 (ND Cal), in which the court reached a different conclusion.

[8] 5 USC § 552a (2000).

(ETHICS & THE LAW)

The following are Web sites that post information about the performance of companies:

> **http://www.lfilmpro.com**
> **http://www.vault.com**
> **http://www.greedyassociates.com**

Are those who sponsor these Web sites and those who post information there responsible for the postings? If the information is incorrect, are they liable for defamation? What if there is a disclaimer about the information they have posted there?

segments of the Computer Fraud and Abuse Act (CFAA) and the ECPA provide privacy protection for certain types of communications, such as financial information and its use and transfer.[9] These privacy laws are not general protections but address specific issues. For example, the Children's Online Privacy Protection Act (COPPA) targets online informational privacy but applies only to Web sites that collect information from children.[10]

Numerous state laws on privacy exist; the problem comes in enforcing those laws against Web site sponsors who have no presence in the state. (See the discussion of long-arm jurisdiction over these Internet players in Section 12, Due Process Issues in Cyberspace.)

4. APPROPRIATION IN CYBERSPACE

appropriation taking of an image, likeness, or name for commercial advantage.

The tort of **appropriation** involves taking an image, likeness, or name for purposes of commercial advantage. A business cannot use someone's name or likeness for advertising or endorsement without permission. The use of that name or image in cyberspace does not change the nature of the protection that this form of the privacy tort provides. **For Example,** a screen saver program that uses a likeness of Richard, the million-dollar winner on the CBS television program *Survivor,* without his permission has violated his privacy rights. The use of his likeness for the Conniver screen saver program with the *Survivor* logo was appropriation. The method of appropriation may be different, but the elements are the same. Appropriation in cyberspace is still the tort of appropriation.

5. DEFAMATION IN CYBERSPACE

defamation untrue statement by one party about another to a third party.

The elements of **defamation** remain the same in cyberspace. (See Chapter 9 for more details.) You must show that someone said or wrote something false that portrayed you in a bad light and that the statement, written or oral, was published, heard, or read by others. That the defamation occurs in a chat room does not change the application of tort law. However, the pervasive nature of the Internet could increase the damages for defamation because of the large number of people who obtain the

---

[9] 18 USC § 1030 and 18 USC §§ 2510–2520, 2701 (1997).
[10] 15 USC §§ 6501–6506.

information quickly, and damage can be done rapidly. **For Example,** Mark S. Jakob, a securities trader who had lost $100,000 in August 2000 with poor trades in Emulex, Inc., stock options, decided to correct his declining earnings trend by posting a false press release on the Internet that Emulex's earnings were overstated and that its CEO would resign. The news release was distributed to various Web sites. The overall loss in the value of Emulex stock was $2.5 billion before trading was stopped and the false nature of the press release revealed. As a result of this action, Jakob made $240,000 through a short position.[11] The tort of defamation would permit the investors to recover their losses.

 ## CONTRACT ISSUES IN CYBERSPACE

6. FORMATION OF CONTRACTS IN CYBERSPACE

contract binding agreement based upon the genuine assent of the parties, made for a lawful object, between competent parties, in the form required by law, and generally supported by consideration.

Formation of a **contract** in cyberspace is simply the result of the desire for speed and better communication in business. If you wanted to form a contract with a New York seller 20 years ago and you were in Los Angeles, you drafted a proposal and mailed it to the seller. The back-and-forth negotiations took time through the mail. Then overnight delivery service arrived to speed up your cross-country negotiations. Next came faxes and their instantaneous exchanges of terms and negotiations. When there was speed, however, businesses wanted to reduce the amount of paperwork involved in transactions. They also recognized the flaws in the paper system: Had the letter arrived? Did the fax get through? Was it legible? Paperless contracts were born with the availability of electronic digital interchange (EDI), and companies using EDI have set and followed contract formation guidelines for almost 20 years. EDI is simply the electronic exchange of business forms. Contracts are formed using purchase orders and invoices submitted via computer.[12]

Even EDI had its flaws, however, in requiring the comparison of forms and numbers and verification of the interchange. With the Internet, e-mail, and the ability to attach documents, cyberspace has provided business yet another method for forming contracts.

Despite this new way of doing business with the instantaneous response to new term proposals, basic contract issues exist in cyberspace contracts that are no different from the contract issues that existed when the law merchant first began to work at finding uniform ways of doing business. Contract issues that continue to dominate discussions in cyberlaw are these: When is a contract formed? What are the contract terms?

The same laws that apply when contracts are formed in a business office govern the formation of contracts in cyberspace. Was there an offer and acceptance, and when did those two requirements come together? Some issues that arise in contract formation in the new economy are, for example, whether a contract is formed when someone downloads a program from the Internet. The person may have paid for the program by credit card and simply downloaded it on the computer. Does the click of the mouse accepting the program mean that all terms of the contract have been accepted? How does the seller of the program make sure that the buyer is aware of all terms in the contract that governs the sale of the program? Can the click of the mouse constitute a signature for the purposes of contracting?

---

[11] Alex Berenson, "Man Charged in Stock Fraud Based on Fake News," *New York Times*, September 1, 2000, C1, C2.
[12] L. J. Kutten, Bernard D. Reams, and Allen E. Strehler, *Electronic Contracting Law* (Clark Boardman, 1991).

Several new laws currently govern the formation of contracts. (See Chapters 12–17 for more information on the formation of contracts in cyberspace.) The Electronic Signatures in Global and National Commerce Act (called **E-sign**) is a federal law that recognizes digital signatures as authentic for purposes of contract formation. Even though E-sign recognizes the validity of electronic signatures, states are responsible for passing laws regulating the authenticity and security of signatures.

E-sign signature over the Internet.

States have responded to the need for legislation on contract formation and authentication with the Uniform Electronic Transactions Act (UETA) and the Uniform Computer Information Transaction Act (UCITA). UETA is a uniform law that 46 states plus the District of Columbia have adopted;[13] two states have adopted UCITA.[14] (See also Chapter 23 for more information on the formation of sales contracts in cyberspace.)

7. MISREPRESENTATION AND FRAUD IN CYBERSPACE

fraud making a false statement of a past or existing fact, with knowledge of its falsity or with reckless indifference as to its truth, with the intent to cause another to rely thereon, and such person does rely thereon and is harmed thereby.

The FBI reported in 2000 that its number one source of **fraud** complaints is the Internet. Its Internet Fraud Computer Center receives 1,000 complaints per day, and the FBI has forwarded 4,000 cases to local authorities for prosecution. The average loss per fraud complaint is $800.[15] In 2005, the FBI received 228,400 complaints of Internet fraud. One of the Internet fraud cases sent forward for prosecution was the sale of kidneys for transplantation. The amount spent on computer security is expected to go from $13.5 billion in 2003 to $20 billion in 2004.[16]

misrepresentation false statement of fact, although made innocently without any intent to deceive.

The types of **misrepresentation** and fraud on the Internet range from promises of delivery not fulfilled to promises of performance not met. The majority of the fraud complaints relate to Internet auctions. These issues are not new legal issues; only the form of misrepresentation or fraud has changed. **For Example,** seven retailers signed a consent decree with the FTC, which requires them to pay fines totaling $1.5 million to settle a complaint against them for late delivery of Christmas merchandise ordered over the Web. Macys.com, Toysrus.com, and CDNOW all signed the consent decree that was based on the FTC mail-and-telephone rule requiring retailers to let customers know when they do not have a product or that there will be a delay in the shipment. The existing notification rule was simply applied to Internet transactions.

search engine Internet service used to locate Web sites.

In marketing **search engines,** some companies have misrepresented the capabilities of their products or have failed to disclose the methods they use to give preference to certain links and their order of listing when the search engine is used. The remedy for such misrepresentations and fraud on the Internet is the same as the remedy in situations with paper contracts. Misrepresentation and fraud are defenses to formation and entitle the party who was misled or defrauded to rescind the agreement and/or collect money damages.

In addition to contract remedies available for misrepresenting the nature of the search engine product and capabilities, a small group of search engine companies has proposed a code of ethics for search engine firms. Headed by Mike Adams, founder and owner of WebSeed.com, the rules are called "Search Engine Promotion Code of

---

[13] Forty-six jurisdictions have adopted UETA. The states that have not adopted it are: Georgia, Illinois, New York, and Washington.

[14] Maryland Commercial Law §§ 22-101 to 22-816, and Virginia Code §§ 59.1-501.1 to 59.1-509.2. Both laws can be found online: **http://www.uetaonline.com** and **http://www.ucitaonline.com**.

[15] Noelle Know, "Online Auctions Top List of Internet Fraud," *USA Today,* August 29, 2000, 1A.

[16] Arleene Weintraub and Jim Kerstetter, "Cyber Alert: Portrait of an Ex-Hacker," *Business Week,* June 9, 2003, 118.

Ethics." Adams says that his industry needs reform and gave the following example of Dotsubmit.com, a former company that claimed it would submit its clients' Web sites to 10,000 search engines. Other problems include the lack of limitations on the number of pages from any domain, which means there is so much space used that consumers have difficulty finding what they are looking for.

Key provisions of the search engine code of ethics include the following:

- Search engine optimization services shall not impose undue bandwidth burdens on search engines.

- Services shall abide by each search engine's page-submission guidelines and will not attempt to subvert them.

- No service shall say it can submit pages to more search engines than actually exist.

- No service shall engage in keyword repetition, page repetition, invisible hypertext markup language tags, or the use of robot pages.

 ## INTELLECTUAL PROPERTY ISSUES IN CYBERSPACE

intellectual property rights
trademark, copyright, and patent rights protected by law.

Intellectual property rights have not changed simply because the Internet has facilitated the ability to copy everything from trademarks to songs with great ease. As noted in Chapter 10, intellectual property rights are protected for the sake of innovation. As in the other areas of law discussed to this point, the Internet simply presents new challenges for interpretation of copyright law. The ease of posting items to the internet and the ability to copy them quickly does not change the rights of copyright ownership. As with all other reproductions of work, permission to reproduce copyrighted work, either using a copy machine or the Internet, is required.[17]

Perhaps no case has brought to a head the discussion of intellectual property rights and their application to cyberspace than that of Napster. Shawn Fanning and Sean Parker, two college students who were then 19 and 20 years old, respectively, founded this company. Napster developed a software program that enabled users to download music files over the Internet at no cost.

The Napster litigation, as with that of other similar companies and programs, such as Grokster, has been either settled or fully litigated with arrangements for music companies to charge fees for access to music and then paying those fees to the copyright holders.

The Recording Industry Association of America (RIAA) has undertaken an aggressive litigation strategy against music downloaders. The first wave of lawsuits consisted of suits against 261 people who were considered the most active "file sharers" of music files. The lawsuits were accompanied by an offer of amnesty for downloaders who turned themselves in prior to having a suit filed against them.

Penalties for copyright infringement range from $750 to $150,000 per incident. In the past, the RIAA has settled the suits for an average of $3,000. However, four university students operating campus-wide file-sharing operations paid between $12,000 and $17,500 in July 2003.

---

[17] See *Lowry's Reports, Inc. v Legg Mason, Inc.,* 271 F Supp 2d 737 (D Md 2003) in which the employer was found liable for copyright infringement by its employees who posted subscription e-mail of financial newsletter on employer's intranet using employer's equipment and on company time, even though employees violated employer's policy not to do so.

The RIAA estimates that 11 million home computers actively share music files in one month. KaZaA is the most frequently used system, carrying 7.2 million computers. WinMX has 2.3 million homes, and the remaining systems all have fewer than 1 million users. A survey showed that 67 percent of downloaders did not care whether the music they were downloading was copyrighted.[18]

The legal issue in the music cases, as with all other Internet infringement cases, is one that has existed since the copyright laws were first passed: What is fair use of another's intellectual property? Related to this same question is the new technology practice of linking Web sites. Is it **fair use** or **infringement** to provide a link on a Web site to another Web site for copyrighted materials there? The Digital Millennium Copyright Act (DMCA)[19] was enacted as an amendment to federal copyright laws and makes clear that linking to a copyrighted site can constitute an infringement. **For Example,** in *Sega Enterprises, Ltd v MAPHIA,* 857 F Supp 679 (ND Cal 1994), the court held that the creator of a bulletin board that permitted the free downloading of computer games was in violation of the federal copyright laws.

Even when Web sites are not linked, is it fair use to reproduce without permission an article printed on one Web site that is free on another Web site? The universal access of the Web raises interesting questions about fair use. However, existing laws on copyrights and infringement provide the foundation for resolving issues presented for the first time because of new technology. The DMCA[20] makes it a federal offense to circumvent or create programs to circumvent encryption devices placed in copyrighted material to prevent unauthorized copying. **For Example,** circumventing the encryption devices on software or DVDs violates the DMCA.

Another issue that has resulted because of the universal access and availability of the Internet is that of disputes over names for Internet sites. In October 1999, the Internet Corporation for Assigned Names and Numbers (ICANN) approved the Uniform Domain Name Dispute Resolution Policy (UDRP). Prior to this policy, Network Solutions Inc. (NSI) had followed a policy of allowing trademark holders to halt the use of trademarked names for Web sites until the issue of ownership was resolved.

Under UDRP, the parties go through arbitration, and the current user continues to use the name until the matter is resolved. The UDRP also does not require a registration for a complainant to bring proceedings—the party can bring the action without registration and can base a complaint on a Web site's name being deceptively similar.

The first decision under UDRP was issued in January 2000 and granted the rights to the domain name of worldwidewrestlingfederation.com to the Worldwide Wrestling Federation (WWF). Since then, 591 UDRP proceedings have commenced with 120 decisions.

In addition to the use of this international registration system, existing U.S. laws can help protect the identity and property of businesses. **For Example,** the Federal Trademark Dilution Act permits a company whose name is harmed or diluted through its use by another to bring suit for injunctions and damages. Also, the FTC's rules on trademark protection are equally applicable to the Internet.

fair use principle that allows the limited use of copyrighted material for teaching, research, and news reporting.

infringement violation of trademarks, patents, or copyrights by copying or using material without permission.

---

[18] Amy Harmon, "261 Lawsuits Filed on Music Sharing," *New York Times,* September 9, 2003, A1, C6; Nick Wingfield, "The High Cost of Sharing," *Wall Street Journal,* September 9, 2003, B1, B8.

[19] 17 USC § 1201 *et seq.*

[20] Id.

CRIMINAL LAW ISSUES IN CYBERSPACE

8. NATURE AND TYPES OF CYBERSPACE CRIMES

cybercrime crimes committed via the Internet.

The FBI has labeled **cybercrime** "epidemic."[21] More than 25 percent of the Fortune 500 companies have fallen victim to computer crime.[22] A summer 2006 computer virus affected web cams on computers. As one expert put it, computer viruses cost the United States more than the total cost of the war in Afghanistan. One virus, known as the "Love Letter" virus, cost U.S. businesses $10 billion.[23] In 1999, one man was able to perpetrate a fraud of $45 million by simply making credit card charges to various credit cards from around the world with information he had gleaned by searching Web sites with consumer information.[24]

Computer crime is simply a more conventional crime carried out through the use of a computer. In other words, using someone else's credit card is fraud, whether you steal the credit card and hand it to the clerk or you use the card number through a transaction on the Web. Some crimes, however, owe their existence to the Internet. **For Example,** rerouting users from the domain they were trying to access to a pornographic Web site does not fit the elements of any particular common law crime, but it is a wrongful use of a computer and its systems. Likewise, using a computer to ensure that your call to a radio station will be answered before other callers' calls is wrong and an unlawful trespass into the radio station's system, but no common law crime covers it. Special computer crime statutes must be developed to deal with the use of computers to carry out new forms of fraud and unfair advantage.[25] Computers can be tools of the crime (**identity theft**), targets of crime (hacking into a system of another), or incidental to a crime (as when they are used for money laundering). Several new crimes have arisen as technology has evolved that are variations of the theft statutes. *Phishing* refers to sending e-mails that appear to be from banks and other account sources to get consumers to respond with their private financial information. *Pharming* is the term for a new tool that redirects consumers to another Web site (even when they have correctly entered the right address) so the redirected site can obtain financial information from the consumers.

identity theft use of another's credit tools, social security number, or other IDs to obtain cash, goods, or credit without permission.

Finally, the *evil twins phenomenon* consists of wireless networks that lure consumers to the networks by appearing to be legitimate Wi-Fi networks available in locations such as Starbucks, airports, and hotels. The Wi-Fi networks seem to be original and legitimate. However, they are simply created by hackers as the evil twin of the good Wi-Fi sites. The evil twin manipulators/hackers are just seeking financial information and passwords. Evil twins have also been known to infect computers with viruses.

The Internet has been used to transport pornography across state lines and to children; to facilitate contacts with children by pedophiles; to harass employees via e-mail; to stalk victims; to make threats of harm or death; to commit fraud; to facilitate bets and other means of illegal gambling; to commit industrial and economic espionage; to extort money; to sell controlled substances without authorization; to

---

[21] http://www.emergency.com

[22] http://www.jaring.my

[23] http://www.computereconomics.com

[24] http://www.computerworld.com/news/1999/

[25] *United States v Peterson*, 98 F3d 502 (9th Cir 1996).

(THINKING THINGS THROUGH)

Free-Riders and Piggybacking

A new issue that has evolved because of technology could require legal steps. Neighbors are *piggybacking* or tapping into their neighbors' wireless Internet connection. The original subscriber pays a monthly fee for the service but, without security, people in the area are able to tap into the wireless network and bog down the speed of the service. Once limited to geeks and hackers, the practice is now common among ordinary folk who just want free Internet service.

One college student said, "I don't think it's stealing. I always find people out there who aren't protecting their connection, so I just feel free to go ahead and use it."* According to a recent survey, only about 30 percent of the 4,500 wireless networks onto which the surveyors logged were encrypted.

An apartment dweller said she leaves her connection wide open because, "I'm sticking it to the man. I open up my network, leave it wide open for anyone to jump on." One of the users of another's wireless network said, "I feel sort of bad about it, but I do it anyway. It just seems harmless." She said that if she gets caught, "I'm a grandmother. They're not going to yell at an old lady. I'll just play the dumb card."

Some neighbors offer to pay those with wireless service in exchange for their occasional use rather than paying a wireless company for full-blown service. However, the original subscribers do not really want to run their own Internet service.

What possible crimes could be committed here? Do you think we need new legislation to cover this activity? What do you think of the users' statements?

*Michael Marriott, "Hey Neighbor, Stop Piggybacking on My Wireless," *New York Times,* March 5, 2006, A1, A23.

pirate software; to vandalize, trespass, and steal; to shut down companies and services; and even to facilitate terrorism.

In all of these forms of conduct, either an underlying criminal statute addresses the conduct (such as prohibitions on bribery, money laundering, and gambling) or computer-specific statutes have been passed to place a criminal sanction on such computer use. The statutes covering criminal laws specifically applicable to computer crime were covered in Chapter 8 and include the Computer Fraud and Abuse Act[26] and the Economic Espionage Act (EEA).[27] Although the means of committing the crime can be different, the government is still required to prove that criminal intent existed and that the conduct committed using a computer meets the definition in the statute.

The same issue that has arisen with identifying music downloaders applies to criminal violations. Can the federal and state governments require ISPs and search engines to provide information to identify users or even to identify who is looking up what on the Internet? Google has objected to demands from the federal government that it release information about who is requesting what types of information, particularly when the information is related to child pornography. This question leads to issues related to the constitutional rights in criminal procedures for violations of laws related to Internet use and abuse.

---

[26] 18 USC § 1030 (2002).
[27] 18 USC § 1831 *et seq.* (2002).

THINKING THINGS THROUGH

College Campuses and Cyberspace

Colleges and universities continue to work to help students understand that what they post on the Web is not private information and can often have unintended consequences. The following examples resulted in student disciplinary proceedings:

- Several students at The Ohio State University boasted on Facebook (a networking/socializing site) that they had stormed the field after Ohio State beat Penn State and had taken part in what erupted into a riot. Law enforcement officials were able to trace the students through the university system, and 50 Ohio State students were referred to the office of judicial affairs.
- Students at the University of Mississippi stated on an open site that they wanted to have sex with a professor.
- A student at Fisher College threatened to take steps to silence a campus police officer.

Another problem with the open sites is that the students are posting personal information with which stalkers and others can access them. These nefarious individuals can then easily obtain students' cell phone numbers, addresses, whereabouts, and other information.

The most popular college site, Face-book, indicates that students spend an average of 17 minutes per day on the site. A great deal of information can be conveyed during that time period. Students do so without thinking through the possibility that outsiders with bad intentions could be seeking and using information about them that is posted there.

As a result of the increased activity levels on Web sites and related problems, many colleges and universities are offering sessions on Internet security and safety to their entering students. Helping students understand issues of privacy and risk is a critical part of orientation.

What legal and ethical issues do you see in the types of comments that students make on these sites and in the sites themselves? Why and how can the colleges and universities obtain information from these sites without a warrant?

Source: For more information, see Brock Read, "THINK Before You Share," *Chronicle of Higher Education,* January 20, 2006, A38–A40.

9. CRIMINAL PROCEDURE AND RIGHTS IN CYBERSPACE

warrant authorization via court order to search private property for tools or evidence of a crime.

Another issue that arises because of cyberspace relates to **warrants.** Can government law enforcement authorities obtain access to computer information for the purposes of investigating a crime? The Fourth Amendment applies not only to searches of offices and homes but also to searches of computers. Indeed, when a warrant specifies that the officers search computers and files, at least one court has ordered that the warrant be specific as to whether it includes home and/or office computers and files.[28] The protection against unlawful searches and seizures has not changed; only the objects being searched have become more sophisticated, and a warrant can include them as well, so long as it specifies the extent of the computer and file search. Just as in

---

[28] *United States v Hunter,* 13 F Supp 2d 574 (D Vt 1998).

the case of the employer access and the music downloaders, the question for the courts is whether Internet users who are identified only by their screen names have an expectation of privacy.

 ## CONSTITUTIONAL RESTRAINTS AND PROTECTIONS IN CYBERSPACE

The constitutional issues that have arisen as a result of the new technology cover everything from the First Amendment to the commerce clause and involve issues ranging from pornography to taxation to Fourth Amendment searches.

10. FIRST AMENDMENT RIGHTS IN CYBERSPACE

The Internet is a method of communication. Some speech on the Internet is commercial, but other forms of speech involve communications relating to voting and ballot initiatives. Speech on the Internet enjoys constitutional protection, but the Internet has also facilitated the transport of pornography with great ease because photos can be sent from computer to computer. The presence of pornography on the Internet and the ease of access that children have to that material have presented challenges for regulation. The Child Pornography Prevention Act[29] made it a crime to knowingly sell, possess, or distribute child pornography on the Web. However, the U.S. Supreme Court ruled that the statute was void for both vagueness and violating First Amendment rights.[30]

11. COMMERCE CLAUSE ISSUES IN CYBERSPACE

The commerce clause has also come into play with the Internet because of the desire of both the states and the federal government to tax the transactions taking place via the Internet. The U.S. Constitution requires that there be some "nexus" between the taxing authority and the business paying the tax (see Chapter 4 for more information on constitutional issues in taxation), and many questions arise about the constitutionality of taxing Internet sales because of the lack of "bricks and mortar" in these businesses. Some Internet retailers are located in one state and have no contact, physically, with any other states. Their only contact is through the computers of their customers, who may be located in all 50 states. Is it constitutional for Colorado to tax a New Jersey company operating out of a small office in Trenton? Although the nature of business has changed, the constitutional tests remain the same; and courts will simply apply the standards of fairness and allocation that they have relied on in other eras as businesses grew in reach even though their physical locations did not change.

The Internet Tax Freedom Act (ITFA)[31] has been renewed. The ITFA provides that states and local governments cannot tax Internet access. Contrary to popular belief, ITFA does not suspend sales taxes on transactions over the Internet. However, the same constitutional standards that apply to sales via catalog and phone to residents of other states also apply to the taxation of sales over the Internet. To tax such sales, the seller must have some physical presence in the state or a pattern of distribution and

---

[29] 18 USC § 2252 *et seq.* (2002).

[30] *United States v Hilton,* 167 F3d 61 (1st Cir 1999), *cert denied,* 528 US 844 (1999); *United States v Acheson,* 195 F3d 645 (11th Cir 1999); and *Free Speech Coalition v Reno,* 220 F3d 1113 (9th Cir 1999), *cert granted as Ashcroft v Free Speech Coalition,* 535 US 234 (2002).

[31] Pub. L. No. 105-277, originally enacted on October 21, 1998, and renewed on November 16, 2001.

doing business there. **For Example,** Nordstrom might not have stores located in a particular state, but it would be required to collect sales taxes from sales to residents of that state if it had warehouse facilities in that state. Refer to Chapter 3 for a full discussion of the Internet and sales tax.

12. DUE PROCESS ISSUES IN CYBERSPACE

Related to the nexus doctrine and taxation of Internet sales is the issue of whether an Internet business site with few physical facilities and no real presence in other states can be required to travel to the states where its customers are to litigate cases brought by those customers. The notion of long-arm jurisdiction (see Chapter 4) becomes even more critical because of the Internet. When does a company have a sufficient presence in a state that requires it to defend a lawsuit in that state? The answer is the same as the answer for the presence of a "bricks and mortar" business. Is requiring the Internet retailer to come to a state to defend a lawsuit fair, or does it offend notions of justice and fair play? Is reaching out to customers in a state through the Internet sufficient to require the Internet company to come to that state and defend lawsuits brought by those customers, or should the customers be required to travel to the state where the Internet company is located?

 SECURITIES LAW ISSUES IN CYBERSPACE

The Internet has facilitated access to the capital markets. The existence of computers have led to *day traders,* investors who have online second-by-second financial information about companies as well as the ability to track trades in order to buy and sell stock. However, this universal access means an increase in the players in the market, and those players have often used tactics not entirely within the boundaries of the existing legal framework or the level playing field so important in the stock markets.

pump-and-dump self-touting a stock to drive its price up and then selling it.

One practice that has begun is **pump-and-dump** through which a trader buys a certain stock and then posts information on the Web to increase interest in it, which drives up its price. When the price has climbed to a sufficiently high level, the trader sells it and walks away with the profits earned by the hype she created on the Web. The tactic is new and the response time faster, but the practice of pump-and-dump is nothing more than securities fraud. The trader is spreading false information and then trading on that information to personal advantage.

So pervasive is the practice of pump-and-dump that 15-year-old Jonathan Lebed successfully employed it to turn his $8,000 in savings into $800,000 in stock gains. He became the first minor ever prosecuted by the Securities and Exchange Commission (SEC) for securities fraud. His penalty was to repay the gains that he made.[32]

Existing securities laws also cover other issues that have emerged with cyberspace companies. **For Example,** America Online entered into a consent decree with the SEC for its accounting practices in which the company predicted sales on the basis of advertising expenses. The SEC found the model for predicting sales untested and misleading. The advertising methods and the company and its technology were all new, but the same securities principles and laws applied: The financial projections must be based on adequate information.[33]

---

[32] Gretchen Morgenson, "S.E.C. Says Teenager Had After-School Hobby: Online Stock Fraud," *New York Times,* September 21, 2000, A1, C10.

[33] Floyd Norris, "AOL Pays a Fine to Settle a Charge That It Inflated Profits," *New York Times,* May 16, 2000, C6.

> SUMMARY

The term *cyberlaw* seems to indicate a new body of law that exists or is being created to manage all of the legal issues of the cybereconomy, cyberspace, and cyber-technology. Even though some new criminal statutes have been enacted to address specific types of computer crimes, the law, with its great flexibility, has been able to easily adapt to address many of the legal issues that affect the new economy in cyberspace.

Six existing areas of law apply to cyberspace: tort issues, contract issues, intellectual property issues, criminal violations, constitutional restraints and protections, and securities law issues.

In tort law, the issues that arise on the Internet relate to privacy and defamation. In contracts, the issues center around formation and signatures, as well as the need for diligence in handling fraud and misrepresentation in the course of formation of contracts. Infringement and fair use are the key topics of intellectual property law that arise through the Internet. Although some peculiar issues such as linking Web sites and copyrighted materials or the types of domain names that may be used exist, the laws to address these new ways of possible infringement of others' intellectual property rights are in place. Criminal violations remain centered around the crimes of trespass and theft. Computers are either used to commit crimes or become the object of crimes, and both old criminal statutes and new ones protect property from harm, even on the Internet. The Constitution still applies to questions of jurisdiction and taxation. The standards of fairness still apply, and courts simply face the issue of whether a company is present because the Internet is available in every state and country. Finally, securities fraud is securities fraud whether committed face-to-face, by paper, by phone, or by chat room.

> QUESTIONS AND CASE PROBLEMS

1. In the midst of the litigation surrounding its program for downloading music, Napster, Inc., discovered that a company was selling t-shirts with its logo on them. Can Napster do anything to prevent the use of its logo? Is the use of the logo for t-shirts any different from the use of songs for purposes of downloading for individual listening?

2. The *New York Times* discovered that 24 of the employees in its payroll processing center were sending "inappropriate and offensive e-mail in violation of corporate policy." Do the employees have any right to privacy with regard to the jokes they send over their e-mail accounts at work? Applying what you have learned about the nature of cyberlaw, determine whether, under existing sexual harassment laws, a company could be held liable for harassment via e-mails.

3. Daniel Dagesse suffered serious injuries when he slipped and fell in his hotel room at the Aruba Marriott Resort (the Plant Hotel). He sued Plant Hotel N.V., the limited liability company that owns the resort; Oranjestad Property Management N.V., Plant Hotel's parent company; Marriott Aruba N.V., the company that manages the resort; and Marriott International, Inc., a corporation that was the agent and management company for Plant Hotel and Oranjestad. Elaine Dagesse, Daniel's wife, also filed suit against the same companies alleging loss of consortium. The Dagesses filed suit in federal district court in New Hampshire, seeking to have the companies come and defend the lawsuit there. The companies filed a motion to dismiss on the grounds that they had no physical presence in the state of New Hampshire. The Dagesses contended that all of the companies operated an interactive Web site to which they went and through which they made their reservations as they sat in their home in New Hampshire, and that this Web site resulted in New Hampshire's jurisdiction over the companies. Were they correct? [*Dagesse v Plant Hotel N.V.,* 113 F Supp 2d 211 (D NH)]

4. List the areas of law that apply in cyberspace and explain why they are still applicable even though the nature of commerce has changed.

5. On July 24, 2002, the Recording Industry Association of America (RIAA) served its first subpoena to obtain the identity of a Verizon subscriber alleged to have made more than 600 copyrighted songs available for downloading over

the Internet through peer-to-peer file transfer software provided by KaZaA. Verizon claimed that because RIAA's subpoena related to material transmitted over Verizon's network—rather than stored on it—it fell outside the scope of the subpoena power. Should the subpoena be quashed as Verizon requests, or should it be honored? [*In re Verizon Internet Services, Inc.,* 257 F Supp 2d 244 (DDC)]

6. Glenayre Electronics announced to its employees that it could inspect the laptops it furnished for its employees to use. An employee challenged the inspection of his laptop as a violation of his privacy. Could the company search the laptops? [*Muick v Glenayre Electronics,* 280 F3d 741 (7th Cir)]

7. A state university provided a written notice to employees that their computers could be monitored and added a splash screen with the same notice that appears on the computers each time employees start their computers. Has the university done enough to allow monitoring without invading employee privacy? Would it make any difference if the employees had a password for their e-mail access and computer access? What about state public records law? Would employee e-mails be subject to public disclosure because the e-mails would be considered public record? [*U.S. v Angevine,* 281 F3d 1130 (10th Cir)]

8. APTC, a publicly traded corporation, filed a complaint, captioned "*Anonymous Publicly Traded Company v John Does 1 through 5,*" asserting that the John Doe defendants, whose identities and residences were unknown, "made defamatory and disparaging material misrepresentations" about APTC in Internet chat rooms. APTC asserted its belief that the John Doe defendants were current and/or former employees who breached their fiduciary duties and contractual obligations by publishing "confidential material insider information" about APTC on the Internet. Although it did not specify what harm would be incurred by identifying itself, APTC contended that it had to proceed anonymously "because disclosure of its true company name will cause it irreparable harm." APTC wanted the court to issue subpoenas to the ISP to determine the identity of the John Does. How do you think the court will decide on the issue of the John Does' identity? [*America Online, Inc. v Anonymous Publicly Traded Co.,* 542 SE2d 377 (Va)]

9. In response to legal cases in which companies have had their internal e-mails used to their disadvantage, several companies have developed programs that automatically destroy e-mails once they have been opened and read on the other end. Is it legal and ethical to destroy e-mails on a regular basis such as this? To visit an e-mail destruction site, go to **http://www.authentica. com** or **http://www.qvtech.com.**

10. Scott McNealy, the founder of Sun Micro-Systems, made the following statement in response to questions about privacy and the Internet: "You have zero privacy, anyway. . . . Get over it."[34] Evaluate his statement and its implications for cyberlaw and ethics in cyberspace transactions.

11. Immunomedics, Inc., has discovered sensitive information about its technology posted on various Web sites and chat rooms. The information is so proprietary that it could have come only from company employees, all of whom have signed agreements not to disclose such information. Those who posted the information used screen names, and Immunomedics has asked the court to issue a subpoena to the ISP so that it can determine the identity of those posting the information and recover for breach of contract and trade secret infringement. Should the court issue the subpoena? [*Immunomedics, Inc. v Does 1–10,* 2001 WL 770389 (NJ Super)]

12. Jane Doe filed a complaint against Richard Lee Russell and America Online (AOL) to recover for alleged emotional injuries suffered by her son, John Doe. Doe claimed that in 1994, Russell lured John Doe, who was then 11 years old, and two other minor males to engage in sexual activity with each other and with Russell. She asserted that Russell photographed and videotaped these acts and used AOL's chat rooms to market the photographs and videotapes and to sell a videotape. Doe did not allege that Russell transmitted photographs or images of her son via the AOL

---

34 Polly Sprenger, "Sun on Privacy: 'Get Over It,'" *Wired News,* January 26, 1999, at **http://www.wired.com/news/politics/0,1283,17538,00.html.**

service. In her six-count complaint, Doe claimed that AOL violated criminal statutes and that AOL was negligent *per se* in distributing an advertisement offering "a visual depiction of sexual conduct involving [John Doe]" and by allowing Russell to sell or arrange to sell child pornography, thus aiding in the sale and distribution of child pornography, including obscene images of John Doe. Does Mrs. Doe have a cause of action? What laws discussed in this chapter apply? [*Doe v America Online, Inc.,* 783 So 2d 1010 (Fla)]

13. Customers of a chat room are using the chat room, Maphia, for access to each other and to transfer Sega games to each other. They are able to avoid paying the $19 to $60 the games cost for purchase in the stores. The users say they are simply transferring files and that there is no crime. The chat room says it cannot stop customers from interacting. Do you think there are any civil or criminal law violations in their conduct? [*Sega Enterprises, Ltd. v Maphia,* 857 F Supp 679 (ND Cal)]

14. The police intercepted a telephone call that one of its informants placed from the police station where he was working with officers. All of the informant's phone calls were being monitored with his consent. The informant called the defendant at his home. Based on the content of that conversation, officers were able to obtain a warrant that permitted them to search the luggage of the defendant who was arriving in Miami from an overseas trip. The defendant's luggage contained cocaine. When the defendant was charged with possession of drugs, he challenged the warrant because it was based on an invasion of privacy of his phone conversation with the informant. The informant did not realize that this particular conversation was being monitored. Is there an expectation of privacy in phone conversations at the police station? Is there an expectation of privacy by the defendant for phone calls in his home? The police argue they were allowed to intercept the calls because the technology was available and because one side had consented. Was the warrant valid? [*Commonwealth v Rekasie,* 778 A2d 624 (Pa)]

15. On October 21, 1999, Amazon.com (Amazon) brought suit against Barnesandnoble.com (BN) alleging infringement of its patent for its one-click order system. Amazon's patent is directed to a method and system for "single-action" ordering of items in a client/server environment such as the Internet. The patent describes a method and system in which a consumer can complete a purchase order for an item via an electronic network using only a "single action," such as the click of a computer mouse button on the client computer system. Amazon developed the patent to cope with what it considered to be frustrations presented by what is known as the "shopping cart model" purchase system for electronic commerce. BN alleges that there is nothing unique about the system that warrants a patent and that its ordering system and that of other dot.com retailers is simply a convenience, not a patentable idea. What laws will the courts apply to this intellectual property dispute for Internet merchants? Are the laws the same for patents on devices and products? [*Amazon.com, Inc. v Barnesandnoble.com,* 239 F3d 1343 (Fed Cir)]

CONTRACTS

NATURE AND CLASSES OF CONTRACTS: CONTRACTING ON THE INTERNET

 A NATURE OF CONTRACTS
1. DEFINITION OF A CONTRACT
2. ELEMENTS OF A CONTRACT
3. SUBJECT MATTER OF CONTRACTS
4. PARTIES TO A CONTRACT
5. HOW A CONTRACT ARISES
6. INTENT TO MAKE A BINDING AGREEMENT
7. FREEDOM OF CONTRACT

 B CLASSES OF CONTRACTS
8. FORMAL AND INFORMAL CONTRACTS
9. EXPRESS AND IMPLIED CONTRACTS
10. VALID AND VOIDABLE CONTRACTS AND VOID AGREEMENTS
11. EXECUTED AND EXECUTORY CONTRACTS
12. BILATERAL AND UNILATERAL CONTRACTS
13. QUASI CONTRACTS

 C CONTRACTING ON THE INTERNET

LEARNING OBJECTIVES

After studying this chapter, you should be able to

LO.1 List the essential elements of a contract

LO.2 Describe the way in which a contract arises

LO.3 State how contracts are classified

LO.4 Differentiate contracts from agreements that are not contracts

LO.5 Differentiate formal contracts from simple contracts

LO.6 Differentiate express contracts from implied contracts

LO.7 Differentiate contractual liability from quasi-contractual liability

Practically every business transaction affecting people involves a contract.

 NATURE OF CONTRACTS

This introductory chapter will familiarize you with the terminology needed to work with contract law. In addition, the chapter introduces quasi contracts, which are not true contracts but obligations imposed by law.

1. DEFINITION OF A CONTRACT

contract a binding agreement based on the genuine assent of the parties, made for a lawful object, between competent parties, in the form required by law, and generally supported by consideration.

A **contract** is a legally binding agreement.[1] By one definition, "a contract is a promise or a set of promises for the breach of which the law gives a remedy, or the performance of which the law in some way recognizes as a duty."[2] Contracts arise out of agreements, so a contract may be defined as an agreement creating an obligation.

The substance of the definition of a contract is that by mutual agreement or assent, the parties create enforceable duties or obligations. That is, each party is legally bound to do or to refrain from doing certain acts.

2. ELEMENTS OF A CONTRACT

The elements of a contract are (1) an agreement (2) between competent parties (3) based on the genuine assent of the parties that is (4) supported by consideration, (5) made for a lawful objective, and (6) in the form required by law, if any. These elements will be considered in the chapters that follow.

3. SUBJECT MATTER OF CONTRACTS

promisor person who makes a promise.

promisee person to whom a promise is made.

obligor promisor.

obligee promisee who can claim the benefit of the obligation.

privity succession or chain of relationship to the same thing or right, such as privity of contract, privity of estate, privity of possession.

privity of contract relationship between a promisor and the promisee.

The subject matter of a contract may relate to the performance of personal services, such as contracts of employment to work developing computer software or to play professional football. A contract may provide for the transfer of ownership of property, such as a house (real property) or an automobile (personal property), from one person to another.

4. PARTIES TO A CONTRACT

The person who makes a promise is the **promisor,** and the person to whom the promise is made is the **promisee.** If the promise is binding, it imposes on the promisor a duty or obligation, and the promisor may be called the **obligor.** The promisee who can claim the benefit of the obligation is called the **obligee.** The parties to a contract are said to stand in **privity** with each other, and the relationship between them is termed **privity of contract. For Example,** when the state of North Carolina and the architectural firm of O'Brien/Atkins Associates executed a contract for the construction of a new building at the University of North Carolina, Chapel Hill, these parties were in privity of contract. However, a building contractor, RPR & Associates, who worked on the project did not have standing to

---

[1] The Uniform Commercial Code defines *contract* as "the total legal obligation which results from the parties' agreement as affected by [the UCC] and any other applicable rules of law." UCC § 1–201(11).

[2] Restatement (Second) of Contracts § 1.

sue on the contract between the architect and the state because the contractor was not in privity of contract.[3]

In written contracts, parties may be referred to by name. More often, however, they are given special names that better identify each party. For example, consider a contract by which one person agrees that another may occupy a house upon the payment of money. The parties to this contract are called *landlord* and *tenant,* or *lessor* and *lessee,* and the contract between them is known as a *lease.* Parties to other types of contracts also have distinctive names, such as *vendor* and *vendee* for the parties to a sales contract, *shipper* and *carrier* for the parties to a transportation contract, and *insurer* and *insured* for the parties to an insurance policy.

A party to a contract may be an individual, a partnership, a limited liability company, a corporation, or a government.[4] One or more persons may be on each side of a contract. Some contracts are three-sided, as in a credit card transaction, which involves the company issuing the card, the holder of the card, and the business furnishing goods and services on the basis of the credit card.

If a contract is written, the persons who are the parties and who are bound by it can ordinarily be determined by reading what the document says and seeing how it is signed. A contract binds only the parties to the contract. It cannot impose a duty on a person who is not a party to it. Ordinarily, only a party to a contract has any rights against another party to the contract.[5] In some cases, third persons have rights on a contract as third-party beneficiaries or assignees. A person cannot be bound, however, by the terms of a contract to which that person is not a party.[6]

CPA

5. HOW A CONTRACT ARISES

offeror person who makes an offer.

A contract is based on an agreement. An agreement arises when one person, the **offeror,** makes an offer and the person to whom the offer is made, the **offeree,** accepts. There must be both an offer and an acceptance. If either is lacking, there is no contract.

offeree person to whom an offer is made.

6. INTENT TO MAKE A BINDING AGREEMENT

Because a contract is based on the consent of the parties and is a legally binding agreement, it follows that the parties must have an intent to enter into an agreement that is binding. Sometimes the parties are in agreement, but their agreement does not produce a contract. Sometimes there is merely a preliminary agreement, but the parties never actually make a contract, or there is merely an agreement as to future plans or intentions without any contractual obligation to carry out those plans or intentions.

---

[3] *RPR & Associates v O'Brien/Atkins Associates, P.A.,* 24 F Supp 2d 515 (MDNC 1998). See also *Roof Techs Int. Inc. v State,* 57 P3d 538 (Kan App 2002), where a layer of litigation was avoided regarding lawsuits involving the renovation of the Farrell Library at Kansas State University. The state was the only party in privity of contract with the architectural firm and would thus have to bring claims against the architectural firm on behalf of all of the contractors. Two subcontractors, the general contractor, and the owner of the library, the state of Kansas, used a settlement and liquidation agreement assigning all of the state's claims against the architect to the general contractor.

[4] See *Purina Mills, LLC v Less,* 295 F Supp 2d 1017 (ND Iowa 2003) in which the pig-seller plaintiff, which converted from a corporation to a limited liability company (LLC) while the contract was in effect, was a proper party in interest and could maintain a contract action against defendant buyers.

[5] *Hooper v Yakima County,* 904 P2d 1193 (Wash App 1995).

[6] *Walsh v Telesector Resources Group, Inc.,* 662 NE2d 1043 (Mass App 1996).

7. FREEDOM OF CONTRACT

In the absence of some ground for declaring a contract void or voidable, parties may make such contracts as they choose. The law does not require parties to be fair, or kind, or reasonable, or to share gains or losses equitably.

 ## CLASSES OF CONTRACTS

Contracts may be classified according to their form, the way in which they were created, their binding character, and the extent to which they have been performed.

8. FORMAL AND INFORMAL CONTRACTS

Contracts can be classified as formal or informal.

formal contracts written contracts or agreements whose formality signifies the parties' intention to abide by the terms.

(a) FORMAL CONTRACTS   **Formal contracts** are enforced because the formality with which they are executed is considered sufficient to signify that the parties intend to be bound by their terms. Formal contracts include (1) **contracts under seal** where a person's signature or a corporation's name is followed by a scroll, the word *seal,* or the letters *L.S.;*[7] (2) contracts of record, which are obligations that have been entered before a court of record, sometimes called a **recognizance;** and (3) negotiable instruments.

contract under seal contract executed by affixing a seal or making an impression on the paper or on some adhering substance such as wax attached to the document.

(b) INFORMAL CONTRACTS   All contracts other than formal contracts are called **informal** (or simple) **contracts** without regard to whether they are oral or written. These contracts are enforceable, not because of the form of the transaction but because they represent agreement of the parties.

recognizance obligation entered into before a court to do some act, such as to appear at a later date for a hearing. Also called a *contract of record.*

9. EXPRESS AND IMPLIED CONTRACTS

Simple contracts may be classified as express *contracts* or *implied contracts* according to the way they are created.

informal contract simple oral or written contract.

(a) EXPRESS CONTRACTS   An **express contract** is one in which the terms of the agreement of the parties are manifested by their words, whether spoken or written.

express contract agreement of the parties manifested by their words, whether spoken or written.

implied contract contract expressed by conduct or implied or deduced from the facts.

(b) IMPLIED CONTRACTS   An **implied contract** (or, as sometimes stated, a *contract implied in fact*) is one in which the agreement is shown not by words, written or spoken, but by the acts and conduct of the parties.[8] Such a contract arises when (1) a person renders services under circumstances indicating that payment for them is expected and (2) the other person, knowing such circumstances, accepts the benefit of those services. **For Example,** when a building owner requests a professional roofer to make emergency repairs to the roof of a building, an obligation arises to pay the reasonable value of such services, although no agreement has been made about compensation.

An implied contract cannot arise when there is an existing express contract on the same subject.[9] However, the existence of a written contract does not bar recovery on an implied contract for extra work that was not covered by the contract.

---

[7] Some authorities explain *L.S.* as an abbreviation for *locus sigilium* (place for the seal).

[8] *Janusauskas v Fichman,* 793 A2d 1109 (Conn App 2002).

[9] *Pepsi-Cola Bottling Co. of Pittsburgh, Inc., v PepsiCo, Inc.,* 431 F3d 1241 (10th Cir 2000)

FIGURE 12-1 *Contractual Liability*

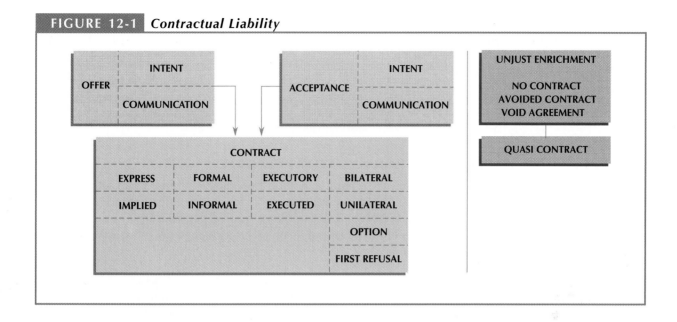

CPA

10. VALID AND VOIDABLE CONTRACTS AND VOID AGREEMENTS

Contracts may be classified in terms of enforceability or validity.

valid contract agreement that is binding and enforceable.

(a) VALID CONTRACTS   A **valid contract** is an agreement that is binding and enforceable.

voidable contract agreement that is otherwise binding and enforceable but may be rejected at the option of one of the parties as the result of specific circumstances.

(b) VOIDABLE CONTRACTS   A **voidable contract** is an agreement that is otherwise binding and enforceable, but because of the circumstances surrounding its execution or the lack of capacity of one of the parties, it may be rejected at the option of one of the parties. **For Example,** a person who has been forced to sign an agreement that that person would not have voluntarily signed may, in some instances, avoid the contract.

void agreement agreement that cannot be enforced.

(c) VOID AGREEMENTS   A **void agreement** is without legal effect. An agreement that contemplates the performance of an act prohibited by law is usually incapable of enforcement; hence it is void. Likewise, it cannot be made binding by later approval or ratification.

11. EXECUTED AND EXECUTORY CONTRACTS

Contracts may be classified as *executed contracts* and *executory contracts* according to the extent to which they have been performed.

executed contract agreement that has been completely performed.

(a) EXECUTED CONTRACTS   An **executed contract** is one that has been completely performed. In other words, an executed contract is one under which nothing remains to be done by either party.[10] A contract may be executed immediately, as in the case of a cash sale, or it may be executed or performed in the future.

---

[10] *Marsh v Rheinecker*, 641 NE2d 1256 (Ill App 1994).

executory contract
agreement by which
something remains to be
done by one or both parties.

(b) Executory Contracts In an **executory contract,** something remains to be done by one or both parties.[11] **For Example,** on July 10, Mark agreed to sell to Chris his Pearl drum set for $600, the terms being $200 upon delivery on July 14, with $200 to be paid on July 21, and the final $200 being due July 28. Prior to the July 14 delivery of the drums to Chris, the contract was entirely executory. After the delivery by Mark, the contract was executed as to Mark and executory as to Chris until the final payment was received on July 28.

12. BILATERAL AND UNILATERAL CONTRACTS

In making an offer, the offeror is in effect extending a promise to do something, such as pay a sum of money, if the offeree will do what the offeror requests. Contracts are classified as *bilateral* or *unilateral*. Some bilateral contracts look ahead to the making of a later contract. Depending on their terms, these are called *option contracts* or *first-refusal contracts*.

CPA

bilateral contract agreement
under which one promise is
given in exchange for
another.

(a) Bilateral Contract If the offeror extends a promise and asks for a promise in return and if the offeree accepts the offer by making the promise, the contract is called a **bilateral contract.** One promise is given in exchange for another, and each party is bound by the obligation. **For Example,** when the house painter offers to paint the owner's house for $3,700 and the owner promises to pay $3,700 for the job, there is an exchange of promises, and the agreement gives rise to a bilateral contract.

unilateral contract contract
under which only one party
makes a promise.

(b) Unilateral Contract In contrast with a bilateral contract, the offeror may promise to do something or to pay a certain amount of money only when the offeree does an act.[12] **For Example,** suppose the Tyler family posts notices throughout the community offering to pay a $100 reward for the safe return of their lost golden retriever puppy, Henry. A contract is formed when the finder, Billy Sullivan, returns the puppy to the Tylers. It is a **unilateral contract** because only one party, the Tylers, made a promise, and the Tylers were obligated to perform only when the contract was formed by Billy's action of returning the puppy.

option contract contract to
hold an offer to make a
contract open for a fixed
period of time.

(c) Option and First-Refusal Contracts The parties may make a contract that gives a right to one of them to enter into a second contract at a later date. If one party has an absolute right to enter into the later contract, the initial contract is called an **option contract.** Thus, a bilateral contract may be made today giving one of the parties the right to buy the other party's house for a specified amount. This is an option contract because the party with the privilege has the freedom of choice, or option, to buy or not buy. If the option is exercised, the other party to the contract must follow the terms of the option and enter into the second contract. If the option is never exercised, no second contract ever arises, and the offer protected by the option contract merely expires.

right of first refusal right of a
party to meet the terms of a
proposed contract before it
is executed, such as a real
estate purchase agreement.

In contrast with an option contract, a contract may merely give a **right of first refusal.** This imposes only the duty to make the first offer to the party having the right of first refusal.

---

[11] *DiGeneraro v Rubbermaid, Inc.,* 214 F Supp 2d 1354 (SO Fla 2002).

[12] See *Young v Virginia Birth-Related Neurological Injury Compensation Program,* 620 SE2d 131 (Va App 2005).

FIGURE 12-2 *Contract*

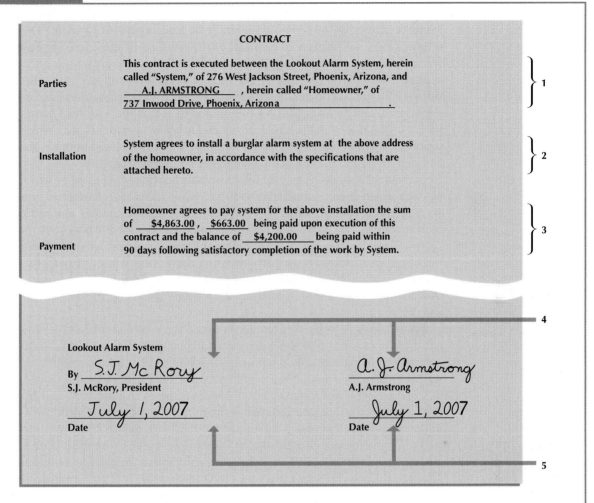

CONTRACT

Parties

This contract is executed between the Lookout Alarm System, herein called "System," of 276 West Jackson Street, Phoenix, Arizona, and ___A.J. ARMSTRONG___ , herein called "Homeowner," of 737 Inwood Drive, Phoenix, Arizona   .

} 1

Installation

System agrees to install a burglar alarm system at the above address of the homeowner, in accordance with the specifications that are attached hereto.

} 2

Payment

Homeowner agrees to pay system for the above installation the sum of ___$4,863.00___ , ___$663.00___ being paid upon execution of this contract and the balance of ___$4,200.00___ being paid within 90 days following satisfactory completion of the work by System.

} 3

4

Lookout Alarm System

By ___S.J. Mc Rory___
S.J. McRory, President
___July 1, 2007___
Date

___A. J. Armstrong___
A.J. Armstrong
___July 1, 2007___
Date

5

Note that this contract includes the following important information: (1) the name and address of each party, (2) the promise or consideration of the seller, (3) the promise or consideration of the buyer, (4) the signature of the two parties, and (5) the date.

13. QUASI CONTRACTS

quasi contract court-imposed obligation to prevent unjust enrichment in the absence of a contract.

In some cases, a court will impose an obligation even though there is no contract.[13] Such an obligation is called a **quasi contract**, which is an obligation imposed by law.

(a) Prevention of Unjust Enrichment   A quasi contract is not a true contract reflecting all of the elements of a contract set forth previously in this chapter. The court is not seeking to enforce the intentions of the parties contained in an agreement. Rather, when a person or enterprise receives a benefit from another, even in the absence of a promise to pay for the benefit, a court may impose an obligation to pay for the reasonable value of that benefit, to avoid *unjust enrichment.*

[13] *Thayer v Dial Industrial Sales, Inc.,* 85 F Supp 2d 263 (SDNY 2000).

A successful claim for unjust enrichment usually requires (1) a benefit conferred on the defendant, (2) the defendant's knowledge of the benefit, and (3) a finding that it would be unjust for the defendant to retain the benefit without payment. The burden of proof is on the plaintiff to prove all of the elements of the claim. **For Example,** Hiram College sued Nicholas Courtad for $6,000 plus interest for tuition and other expenses. Because no evidence of a written contract was produced, the court considered it an unjust enrichment claim by the college. Courtad had attended classes for a few weeks and had not paid his tuition due to a problem with his financial aid package. Because he did not receive any credit hours toward a degree, which is the ultimate benefit of attending college, the court found that he did not receive a benefit and that a finding of unjust enrichment was not appropriate.[14]

Sometimes a contract may be unenforceable because of a failure to set forth the contract in writing in compliance with the statute of frauds. In other circumstances, no enforceable contract exists because of a lack of definite and certain terms. Yet in both situations, one party may have performed services for the benefit of the other party and the court will require payment of the reasonable value of services to avoid the unjust enrichment of the party receiving the services without paying for them. These damages are sometimes referred to as *restitution damages*. Some courts refer to this situation as an action or recovery in *quantum meruit* (as much as he or she deserved).

quantum meruit as much as deserved; an action brought for the value of the services rendered the defendant when there was no express contract as to the purchase price.

For Example, Arya Group, Inc. (Arya), sued the entertainer Cher for unjust enrichment. In June 1996, Cher negotiated an oral agreement with Arya to design and construct a house on her Malibu property for $4,217,529. The parties' oral agreement was set forth in a written contract with an August 1997 date and was delivered to Cher in October 1997. She never signed it. However, between June 1996 and November 1997, Arya performed and received payment for a number of services discharged under the unsigned contract. In August 1997, Cher requested Arya to meet with a home designer named Bussell who had previously worked with Cher on a Florida project, and Arya showed Bussell the plans and designs for the Malibu property and introduced her to his subcontractors. In November 1997, Cher terminated her agreement with Arya without paying the balance then due, as asserted by Arya, of $415,169.41. Arya claims that Cher and Bussell misappropriated the plans and designs Arya had prepared. Cher and the other defendants demurred to Arya's unjust enrichment complaint, pointing out that construction contracts must be evidenced in a writing signed by both parties under state law in order to be enforceable in a court of law. The appeals court determined that Arya's noncompliance with the state law requiring a signed written contract did not absolutely foreclose Arya from seeking damages for unjust enrichment if he could prove the assertions in the complaint that Cher was a sophisticated homeowner with previous involvement in residential construction, who had legal representation in negotiating the agreement with Arya, and Cher would be unjustly enriched if she were not required to compensate Arya for the reasonable value of the work already performed.[15]

A situation may arise over the mistaken conference of a benefit. **For Example,** Nantucket Island has a few approved colors for houses in its historic district. Using the approved gray color, Martin Kane and his crew began painting Sheldon Adams's house in the historic district as the result of a mistaken address. Adams observed the initiation

---

[14] *Hiram College v Courtad,* 834 NE2d 432 (Ohio App 2005).

[15] *Arya Group, Inc. v Cher,* 91 Cal Rptr 2d 815 (Cal App 2d 2000). See also *Fischer v Flax,* 816 A2d 1 (2003).

CASE SUMMARY

No Free Rides

FACTS: PIC Realty leased farmland to Southfield Farms. After Southfield harvested its crop, it cultivated the land in preparation for the planting in the following year. However, its lease expired, so it did not plant that crop. It then sued PIC for reimbursement for the reasonable value of the services and materials used in preparing the land because this was a benefit to PIC. There was evidence that it was customary for landlords to compensate tenants for such work.

DECISION: Southfield was entitled to recover the reasonable value of the benefit conferred upon PIC. This was necessary in order to prevent the unjust enrichment of PIC. [**PIC Realty Corp. v Southfield Farms, Inc., 832 SW2d 610 (Tex App 1992)**]

of the work from his office across the street but did nothing to stop the painters. At the end of the day when the work was done, Adams refused to pay for the work, saying, "I signed no contract and never approved this work." The law deems it inequitable that Adams should have received the benefit of this work, having observed the benefit being conferred and knowing that the painters expected payment. Adams would be unjustly enriched if he were allowed to retain the benefit without payment for the reasonable value of the work. If Adams did not have knowledge that the work was being done and thus that payment was expected, quasi-contractual liability would not be imposed.

The mistake that benefits the defendant may be the mistake of a third party.

CASE SUMMARY

Who Pays the Piper?

FACTS: When improvements or buildings are added to real estate, the real estate tax assessment is usually increased to reflect the increased value of the property. Frank Partipilo and Elmer Hallman owned neighboring tracts of land. In 1977 Hallman made improvements to his land, constructing a new building and driveway on the tract. The tax assessor made a mistake about the location of the boundary line between Partipilo's and Hallman's land and thought the improvements were made on Partipilo's property. Instead of increasing the taxes on Hallman's land, the assessor wrongly increased the taxes on Partipilo's land. Partipilo paid the increased taxes for three years. When he learned why his taxes had been increased, he sued Hallman for the amount of the increase that Partipilo had been paying. Hallman raised the defense that he had not done anything wrong and that the mistake had been the fault of the tax assessor.

DECISION: Judgment for Partipilo. Because the improvements were made to Hallman's land, Hallman should be the one to pay the tax increase. When Partipilo paid it, Hallman received a benefit to which he was not entitled. This was an unjust enrichment. Therefore, Partipilo could recover the amount of the increased taxes without regard to the fact that Hallman was free of any fault and that the only fault in the case was the fault of the tax assessor. [**Partipilo v Hallman, 510 NE2d 8 (Ill App 1987)**]

THINKING THINGS THROUGH

Twelve Years of Litigation

Brown University accepted the bid of Marshall Contractors, Inc. (Marshall), to build the Pizzitola Sports Facility on its Providence, Rhode Island, campus. The parties intended to execute a formal written contract. Brown decided to pay $7,157,051 for the project, but Marshall sought additional payment for items it deemed extras and not contemplated in its bid. Because the parties were unable to agree on the scope of the project as compared to the price Brown was willing to pay, they never executed the formal written contract. Nevertheless, in the context of this disagreement over terms and price, construction began in May 1987. When the parties could not resolve their disagreements as the project neared completion in January 1989, Marshall sued Brown University, seeking to recover the costs for what it deemed "changes." Brown asserted that an implied-in-fact contract existed for all work at the $7,157,051 figure because the contractor went ahead with the project knowing the money Brown would pay. The litigation ended up in the Supreme Court of Rhode Island, and in 1997, the court concluded that no express or implied-in-fact contract had ever been reached by the parties concerning the scope of the project and what costs were to be included in the price stipulated by Brown. The case was remanded to the trial court for a new trial. After a trial on the theories of *quantum meruit* and unjust enrichment, a jury awarded Marshall $1.2 million dollars, which was some $3.1 million less than Marshall sought. Brown University appealed, and on November 21, 2001, the Supreme Court of Rhode Island affirmed the jury verdict for the contractor, determining that the proper measure of damages on unjust enrichment and *quantum meruit* theories was "the reasonable value of the work done."*

In May 1987 when the parties could not reach agreement enabling the execution of a formal written contract, THINKING THINGS THROUGH at that point in time should have exposed the potential for significant economic uncertainties to both parties in actually starting the building process under such circumstances. In the spring of 1987 when all parties were unable to reach agreement, mediation or expedited arbitration by construction experts may well have resolved the controversy and yielded an amicable written contract with little or no delay to the project. Instead, the unsettled cost issues during the building process could have had an adverse impact on the "job chemistry" between the contractor and the owner, which may have adversely affected the progress and quality of the job. The 12 years of litigation that, with its economic and human resource costs, yielded just $1.2 million for the contractor was a no-win result for both sides. A primary rule for all managers in projects of this scope is to make sure the written contracts are executed before performance begins! Relying on "implied-in-fact" or quasi-contract legal theories is simply a poor management practice.

---

* *ADP Marshall, Inc. v Brown University*, 784 A2d 309 (RI 2001).

(b) Extent of Recovery   When recovery is allowed in quasi contract, the plaintiff recovers the reasonable value of the benefit conferred on the defendant,[16] or the fair and reasonable[17] value of the work performed, depending on the jurisdiction. Thus,

---

[16] *Ramsey v Ellis*, 484 NW2d 331 (Wis 1992).

[17] *ADP Marshall, Inc. v Brown University*, 784 A2d 309 (RI 2001).

the plaintiff cannot recover lost profits or other kinds of damages that would be recovered in a suit for breach of a contract.

For Example, Peabody New England, Inc., is in the business of constructing waste system facilities for cities and towns. A facility that Peabody contracted to build for the town of Marshfield was not completed on time. The project's completion date was delayed in part by the contractor's mismanagement. The town also contributed to the delays. The court refused to allow Peabody to recover under the terms of the contract because Peabody did not live up to the contract's terms. However, the court did allow limited damages to Peabody for the reasonable value of the services rendered, an amount that was less than the contract price and did not include lost profits and "overhead" expenses.[18]

C   CONTRACTING ON THE INTERNET

Doing business online for consumers is very similar to doing business through a catalog purchase or by phone. Before placing an order, a buyer is commonly concerned about the reputation of the seller. The basic purchasing principle of *caveat emptor* still applies: buyer beware! The Internet provides valuable tools to allow a buyer to research the reputation of the seller and its products. Online evaluations of companies and their products can be found at Web sites, such as Consumer Reports (**http:// www.consumerreports.org**), Consumer Digest (**http://www.consumersdigest.com**), or the Better Business Bureau (**http://www.bbb.org**). E-consumers may have access to categorized histories of comments by other e-consumers, such as Planet Feedback ratings at **http://planetfeedback.com.**

The intellectual property principles set forth in Chapter 10—as well as the contractual principles, the law of sales, and privacy laws you are about to study—all apply to e-commerce transactions. When you are purchasing an item online, you must carefully read all of the terms and conditions set forth on the seller's Web site when assessing whether to make a contemplated purchase. The proposed terms may require that any disputes be litigated in a distant state or be resolved through arbitration with restricted remedies, or there may be an unsatisfactory return policy, warranty limitations, or limitation of liability. Generally, the Web site terms become the contract of the parties and are legally enforceable.

The laws you have studied that prevent deceptive advertising by brick and mortar businesses also apply to Internet sites.[19] If an in-state site is engaging in false advertising, you may be able to exercise consumer protection rights through your state's attorney general's office, or you may find some therapeutic relief by reporting the misconduct to the Internet Scambusters site (**http://www.scambusters.com**).

From a seller's perspective, it is exceedingly helpful to have as much information as possible on your potential customers' buying habits. Federal law prohibits the collection of personal information from children without parental consent, and some states restrict the unauthorized collection of personal information. European Union countries have strict laws protecting the privacy of consumers. Sellers intending to collect personal information should obtain the consent of their customers, make

[18] *Peabody New England, Inc. v Town of Marshfield,* 689 NE2d 774 (Mass 1998).

[19] See *MADCAP I, LLC v McNamee,* 702 NW2d 16 (Wis App 2005) in which the court found genuine issues of material fact as to whether a business Web site falsely represented the size and nature of its business to induce the public to purchase products and services described on its Web site in violation of the state's fraudulent representations statute.

certain that children are excluded, and make sure that the information is stored in a secure environment.

Advanced encryption technology has made the use of credit card payments through the Internet very safe. No computer system connected to the Internet is totally secure however. In the worst case scenario, credit card issuers will not charge a user for more that the first $50 of unauthorized activity.

As opposed to business-to-consumer and consumer-to-consumer e-commerce, B2B is business-to-business e-commerce.

At the turn of the century, B2B online commerce was perceived as a potentially enormous marketplace that would enable businesses to better manage inventories, save costs, and create new revenue streams. However, the efficiencies and profit margins did not materialize as many venture capitalists and dot-com investors had expected. E-marketplaces tended to oversimplify inherently complex interactions. With pricing, delivery, and payment issues to be resolved, "clicking" often turned out to be less flexible than phoning. Today, ChemConnect is an example of a successful Internet-based exchange for chemicals and plastics. It has succeeded in simulating a physical marketplace, having created online "trading rooms" where buyers and sellers can negotiate in private. B2B online commerce today also consists of manufacturers and various suppliers entering into Trading Partner Agreements setting forth the terms, conditions, and methods for the conducting of business electronically.

State and local governments and the federal government provide a large market for the procurement of goods, services, and information. B2G is business-to-government e-commerce.

Internet contracts involve the same types of issues that are addressed in contracts offline but with certain technology-related nuances. The parties to the e-contracts must still negotiate their obligations in clear and unambiguous language, including such terms as quantity, quality, and price as well as warranties, indemnification responsibilities, limitations on liability, and termination procedures. The federal Electronic Signatures in Global and National Commerce Act (E-Sign) and the Uniform Electronic Transactions Act (UETA) mandate parity between paper and electronic contracts. The basic legal rules that govern contracts offline are the very same rules that govern online contracts. Boxes identifying special Internet e-commerce topics are strategically placed throughout these chapters.

LAWFLIX

Paper Moon (1973) (PG)

In this movie for which Tatum O'Neal was given an Oscar, the ongoing issue between Annie and her alleged father is her recoupment of the money she says he promised. Discuss the contract issues (voidable [minor], formation, unilateral vs. bilateral, express, informal, etc.).

For movie clips that illustrate business law concepts, see LawFlix at **http://wdvl.westbuslaw.com**.

> SUMMARY

A contract is a binding agreement between two or more parties. A contract arises when an offer is accepted with contractual intent (the intent to make a binding agreement).

Contracts may be classified in a number of ways according to form, the way in which they were created, validity, and obligations. With respect to form, a contract may be either informal or formal, such as those under seal or those appearing on the records of courts. Contracts may be classified by the way they were created as those that are expressed by words—written or oral—and those that are implied or deduced from conduct. The question of validity requires distinguishing between contracts that are valid, those that are voidable, and those that are not contracts at all but are merely void agreements. Contracts can be distinguished on the basis of the obligations created as executed contracts, in which everything has been performed, and executory contracts, in which something

remains to be done. The bilateral contract is formed by exchanging a promise for a promise, so each party has the obligation of thereafter rendering the promised performance. In the unilateral contract, which is the doing of an act in exchange for a promise, no further performance is required of the offeree who performed the act.

In certain situations, the law regards it as unjust for a person to receive a benefit and not pay for it. In such a case, the law of quasi contracts allows the performing person to recover the reasonable value of the benefit conferred on the benefited person even though no contract between them requires any payment. Unjust enrichment, which a quasi contract is designed to prevent, sometimes arises when there was never any contract between the persons involved or when there was a contract, but for some reason it was avoided or held to be merely a void agreement.

> QUESTIONS AND CASE PROBLEMS

1. What is a contract?
2. Fourteen applicants for a city of Providence, Rhode Island, police academy training class each received from the city a letter stating that it was a "conditional offer of employment" subject to successful completion of medical and psychological exams. The fourteen applicants passed the medical and psychological exams. However, these applicants were replaced by others after the city changed the selection criteria. Can you identify an offer and acceptance in this case? Can you make out a bilateral or unilateral contract? [*Ardito et al. v City of Providence,* 213 F Supp 2d 358 (D RI)]
3. Compare an implied contract with a quasi contract.
4. The Jordan Keys law firm represented the Greater Southeast Community Hospital of Washington, D.C., in a medical malpractice suit against the hospital. The hospital was self-insured for the first $1,000,000 of liability and the St. Paul Insurance Co. provided excess coverage up to $4,000,000. The law firm was owed $67,000 for its work on the malpractice suit when the hospital went into bankruptcy. The bankruptcy court ordered the

law firm to release its files on the case to St. Paul to defend under the excess coverage insurance, and the Jordan Keys firm sued St. Paul for its legal fees of $67,000 expended prior to the bankruptcy under an "implied-in-fact contract" because the insurance company would have the benefit of all of its work. Decide. [*Jordan Keys v St. Paul Fire,* 870 A2d 58 (DC)]

5. Beck was the general manager of Chilkoot Lumber Co. Haines sold fuel to the company. To persuade Haines to sell on credit, Beck signed a paper by which he promised to pay any debt the lumber company owed Haines. He signed this paper with his name followed by "general manager." Haines later sued Beck on this promise, and Beck raised the defense that the addition of "general manager" showed that Beck, who was signing on behalf of Chilkoot, was not personally liable and did not intend to be bound by the paper. Was Beck liable on the paper? [*Beck v Haines Terminal and Highway Co.,* 843 P2d 1229 (Alaska)]

6. *A* made a contract to construct a house for *B.* Subsequently, *B* sued *A* for breach of contract. *A* raised the defense that the contract was not

binding because it was not sealed. Is this a valid defense? [*Cooper v G. E. Construction Co.,* 158 SE2d 305 (Ga App)]

7. Edward Johnson III, the CEO and principal owner of the world's largest mutual fund company, Fidelity Investments, Inc., was a longtime tennis buddy of Richard Larson. In 1995, Johnson asked Larson, who had construction experience, to supervise the construction of a house on Long Pond, Mount Desert Island, Maine. Although they had no written contract, Larson agreed to take on the project for $6,700 per month plus lodging. At the end of the project in 1997, Johnson made a $175,000 cash payment to Larson, and he made arrangements for Larson to live rent-free on another Johnson property in the area called Pray's Meadow in exchange for looking after Johnson's extensive property interests in Maine. In the late summer of 1999, Johnson initiated a new project on the Long Pond property. Johnson had discussions with Larson about doing this project, but Larson asked to be paid his former rate, and Johnson balked because he had already hired a project manager. According to Johnson, at a later date he again asked Larson to take on the "shop project" as a favor and in consideration of continued rent-free use of the Pray's Meadow home. Johnson stated that Larson agreed to do the job "pro bono" in exchange for the use of the house, and Johnson acknowledged that he told Larson he would "take care" of Larson at the end of the project, which could mean as much or as little as Johnson determined. Larson stated that Johnson told him that he would "take care of" Larson if he would do the project and told him to "trust the Great Oracle" (meaning Johnson, the highly successful businessperson). Larson sought payment in March 2000 and asked Johnson for "something on account" in April. Johnson offered Larson a loan. In August during a tennis match, Larson again asked Johnson to pay him. Johnson became incensed, and through an employee, he ended Larson's participation in the project and asked him to vacate Pray's Meadow. Larson complied and filed suit for payment for work performed at the rate of $6,700 per month. Did Larson have an express contract with Johnson? What legal theory or theories could Larson utilize in his lawsuit?

How would you decide this case if you believed Larson's version of the facts? How would you decide the case if you believed Johnson's version of the facts? [*Larson v Johnson,* 2002 U.S. Dist. LEXIS 1953. See *Bangor Daily News,* March 8, 2002, 1]

8. While Clara Novak was sick, her daughter Janie helped her in many ways. Clara died, and Janie then claimed that she was entitled to be paid for the services she had rendered her mother. This claim was opposed by three brothers and sisters who also rendered services to the mother. They claimed that Janie was barred because of the presumption that services rendered between family members are gratuitous. Janie claimed that this presumption was not applicable because she had not lived with her mother but had her own house. Was Janie correct? [*In re Estate of Novak,* 398 NW2d 653 (Minn App)]

9. Dozier and his wife, daughter, and grandson lived in the house Dozier owned. At the request of the daughter and grandson, Paschall made some improvements to the house. Dozier did not authorize these, but he knew that the improvements were being made and did not object to them. Paschall sued Dozier for the reasonable value of the improvements, but Dozier argued that he had not made any contract for such improvements. Was he obligated to pay for such improvements?

10. When Harriet went away for the summer, Landry, a house painter, painted her house. He had a contract to paint a neighbor's house but painted Harriet's house by mistake. When Harriet returned from vacation, Landry billed her for $3,100, which was a fair price for the work. She refused to pay. Landry claimed that she had a quasi-contractual liability for that amount. Was he correct?

11. Margrethe and Charles Pyeatte, a married couple, agreed that she would work so that he could go to law school and that when he finished, she would go back to school for her master's degree. After Charles was admitted to the bar and before Margrethe went back to school, the two were divorced. She sued Charles, claiming that she was entitled to quasi-contractual recovery of the money that she had paid for Charles's support and law school tuition. He denied liability. Was

she entitled to recover for the money she spent for Charles's maintenance and law school tuition? [*Pyeatte v Pyeatte,* 661 P2d 196 (Ariz App)]

12. Carriage Way was a real estate development of approximately 80 houses and 132 apartments. The property owners were members of the Carriage Way Property Owners Association. Each year, the association would take care of certain open neighboring areas, including a nearby lake, that were used by the property owners. The board of directors of the association would make an assessment or charge against the property owners to cover the cost of this work. The property owners paid these assessments for a number of years and then refused to pay any more. In spite of this refusal, the association continued to take care of the areas in question. The association then sued the property owners and claimed that they were liable for the benefit that had been conferred on them. Were the owners liable? [*Board of Directors of Carriage Way Property Owners Ass'n v Western National Bank,* 487 NE2d 974 (Ill App)]

13. Lombard insured his car, and when it was damaged, the insurer sent the car to General Auto Service for repairs. The insurance company went bankrupt and did not pay the repair bill. General Auto Service then sued Lombard for the bill because he had benefited from the repair work. Was he liable?

14. When a college student complained about a particular course, the vice president of the college asked the teacher to prepare a detailed report about the course. The teacher did and then demanded additional compensation for the time spent in preparing the report. He claimed that the college was liable to provide compensation on an implied contract. Was he correct? [*Zadrozny v City Colleges of Chicago,* 581 NE2d 44 (Ill App)]

15. Smith made a contract to sell automatic rifles to a foreign country. Because the sale of such weapons to that country was illegal under an act of Congress, the U.S. government prosecuted Smith for making the contract. He raised the defense that because the contract was illegal, it was void and there is no binding obligation when a contract is void; therefore, no contract for which he could be prosecuted existed. Was he correct?

CPA QUESTIONS

1. Kay, an art collector, promised Hammer, an art student, that if Hammer could obtain certain rare artifacts within two weeks, Kay would pay for Hammer's postgraduate education. At considerable effort and expense, Hammer obtained the specified artifacts within the two-week period. When Hammer requested payment, Kay refused. Kay claimed that there was no consideration for the promise. Hammer would prevail against Kay based on

    a. Unilateral contract
    b. Unjust enrichment
    c. Public policy
    d. Quasi contract

FORMATION OF CONTRACTS: OFFER AND ACCEPTANCE

CHAPTER (13)

LEARNING OBJECTIVES

After studying this chapter, you should be able to

LO.1 Decide whether a statement is an offer or an invitation to negotiate

LO.2 Decide whether an agreement is too indefinite to be enforced

LO.3 Describe the exceptions that the law makes to the requirement of definiteness

LO.4 List all of the ways an offer is terminated

LO.5 Compare offers, firm offers, and option contracts

LO.6 Define what constitutes the acceptance of an offer

A *contract* consists of enforceable obligations that have been voluntarily assumed. Thus, one of the essential elements of a contract is an agreement. This chapter explains how the basic agreement arises, when there is a contract, and how there can be merely unsuccessful negotiations without a resulting contract.

 ## REQUIREMENTS OF AN OFFER

offer expression of an offeror's willingness to enter into a contractual agreement.

An **offer** expresses the willingness of the offeror to enter into a contractual agreement regarding a particular subject. It is a promise that is conditional upon an act, a forbearance (a refraining from doing something one has a legal right to do), or a return promise.

CPA

1. CONTRACTUAL INTENTION

To make an offer, the offeror must appear to intend to create a binding obligation. Whether this intent exists is determined by objective standards.[1] This intent may be shown by conduct.

For Example, when one party signs a written contract and sends it to the other party, such action is an offer to enter into a contract on the terms of the writing.

There is no contract when a social invitation is made or when an offer is made in obvious jest or excitement. A reasonable person would not regard such an offer as indicating a willingness to enter into a binding agreement.

(a) Invitation to Negotiate   The first statement made by one of two persons is not necessarily an offer. In many instances, there may be a preliminary discussion or an invitation by one party to the other to negotiate or to make an offer. Thus, an inquiry by a school as to whether a teacher wished to continue the following year was merely a survey or invitation to negotiate and was not an offer that could be accepted. Therefore, the teacher's affirmative response did not create a contract.

Ordinarily, a seller sending out circulars or catalogs listing prices is not regarded as making an offer to sell at those prices. The seller is merely indicating a willingness to consider an offer made by a buyer on those terms. The reason for this rule is, in part, the practical consideration that because a seller does not have an unlimited supply of any commodity, the seller cannot possibly intend to make a contract with everyone who sees the circular. The same principle is applied to merchandise that is displayed with price tags in stores or store windows and to most advertisements. An advertisement in a newspaper is ordinarily considered an invitation to negotiate and is not an offer that can be accepted by a reader of the paper.[2] However, some court decisions have construed advertisements as offers that called for an act on the part of the customer thereby forming a unilateral contract, such as the advertisement of a reward for the return of lost property.

Quotations of prices, even when sent on request, are likewise not offers unless the parties have had previous dealings or unless a trade custom exists that would give the recipient of the quotation reason to believe that an offer was being made. Whether a price quotation is to be treated as an offer or merely an invitation to negotiate is a question of the intent of the party giving the quotation.[3]

---

[1] *Glass Service Co. v State Farm Mutual Automobile Ins. Co.,* 530 NW2d 867 (Minn App 1995).

[2] *Pico v Cutter Dodge, Inc.,* 98 Hawaii 309 (2002).

[3] Statutes prohibiting false or misleading advertising may require adherence to advertised prices.

(b) AGREEMENT TO MAKE A CONTRACT AT A FUTURE DATE   No contract arises when the parties merely agree that at a future date they will consider making a contract or will make a contract on terms to be agreed on at that time.[4] In such a case, neither party is under any obligation until the future contract is made. No binding contract to renew a contract when it expires is created by a provision in the original contract that, when it expires, the parties intend to "negotiate in good faith to renew this agreement for an additional year upon terms and conditions to be negotiated."

2. DEFINITENESS

An offer, and the resulting contract, must be definite and certain.[5] If an offer is indefinite or vague or if an essential provision is lacking,[6] no contract arises from an attempt to accept it. The reason is that courts cannot tell what the parties are to do. Thus, an offer to conduct a business for as long as it is profitable is too vague to be a valid offer. The acceptance of such an offer does not result in a contract that can be enforced. Statements by a bank that it was "with" the debtors and would "support" them in their proposed business venture were too vague to be regarded as a promise by the bank to make necessary loans to the debtors.

CASE SUMMARY

What Is the Meaning of an Agreement for a "Damn Good Job"?

FACTS: Larry Browneller made an oral contract with Hubert Plankenhorn to restore a 1963 Chevrolet Impala convertible. The car was not in good condition. Hubert advised the owner that his work would not yield a car of "show" quality because of the condition of the body, and he accordingly believed that the owner merely wanted a presentable car. Larry, on the other hand, having told Hubert that he wanted a "damn good job," thought this statement would yield a car that would be competitive at the small amateur car shows he attended. When the finished car had what Larry asserted were "waves" in the paint as a result of an uneven surface on the body, Larry brought suit against Hubert for breach of the oral contract.

DECISION: There was clearly a misunderstanding between the parties over the quality of work that could and would be obtained. *Quality* was a material term of the oral contract between the parties, on which there was no shared understanding. Accordingly, a court will not find an individual in breach of a term of the contract where the term did not exist. [**In re Hubert Plankenhorn 228 BR 638 (ND Ohio 1998)**]

The fact that minor, ministerial, and nonessential terms are left for future determination does not make an agreement too vague to be a contract.[7]

---

[4] *Ellis v Taylor*, 49 SE2d 487 (SC 1994).

[5] *Graziano v Grant*, 744 A2d 156 (NJ Super AD 1999).

[6] *Peace v Doming Holdings Inc.*, 554 SE2d 314 (Ga App 2001).

[7] *Hsu v Vet-A-Mix, Inc.*, 479 NW2d 336 (Iowa App 1991). But see *Ocean Atlantic Development Corp v Aurora Christian Schools, Inc.*, 322 F3d 983 (7th Cir 2003), where letter offers to purchase (OTP) real estate were signed by both parties, but the offers conditioned the purchase and sale of each property upon the subsequent execution of a purchase and sale agreement. The court held that the parties thus left themselves room to walk away from the deal under Illinois law, and the OTPs were not enforced.

CASE SUMMARY

Offer to Purchase Is Controlling Legal Document

FACTS: John McCarthy executed an offer to purchase (OTP) real estate on a preprinted form generated by the Greater Boston Real Estate Board. The OTP contained a description of the property, the price to be paid, deposit requirements, limited title requirements, and the time and place for closing. The OTP required the parties to execute the applicable Standard Form Purchase and Sale Agreement recommended by the Greater Boston Real Estate Board that, when executed, was to be the agreement between the parties. An unnumbered paragraph immediately above the signature line stated: "NOTICE: This is a legal document that creates binding obligations. If not understood, consult an attorney." The seller, Ann Tobin, signed the OTP. While lawyers for the parties exchanged drafts of a purchase and sale agreement (PSA), a much higher offer for the property was made to Tobin by the Diminicos. Because she had not yet signed the purchase and sale agreement, Tobin accepted the Diminicos's offer and executed a purchase and sales agreement with them. Before that deal closed, McCarthy filed an action for specific performance of the OTP. McCarthy contended he and Tobin intended to be bound by the OTP and that the execution of a PSA was merely a formality. Tobin contended the OTP language contemplated the execution of a final written document, thus clearly indicating that the parties had not agreed to all material aspects of the transaction, and thus the parties did not intend to be bound until the PSA was signed. From a judgment for Tobin and the Diminicos, McCarthy appealed.

DECISION: Judgment for McCarthy. Although the provisions of the purchase and sale agreement can be the subject of negotiation, norms exist for their customary resolution. The inference that the OTP was legally binding is bolstered by the notice printed on the form. McCarthy and Tobin were alerted to the fact that the OTP "creates binding obligations." The OTP employed familiar contractual language. It stated that McCarthy "hereby offers to buy" the property, and Tobin's signature indicates that "this Offer is hereby accepted." The OTP also details the amount to be paid and when, describes the property bought, and specifies for how long the offer was open. This was a firm offer, the acceptance of which bound Tobin to sell and McCarthy to buy the subject property. [**McCarthy v Tobin, 706 NE2d 629 (Mass 1999)**]

The law does not favor the destruction of contracts because that would go against the social force of carrying out the intent of the parties.[8] Consequently, when it is claimed that a contract is too indefinite to be enforced, a court will do its best to find the intent of the parties and thereby reach the conclusion that the contract is not too indefinite. **For Example,** boxing promoter Don King had both a Promotional Agreement and a Bout Agreement with boxer Miguel Angel Gonzalez. The Bout Agreement for a boxing match held on March 7, 1998, with Julio Cesar Chavez gave King the option to promote the next four of Gonzalez's matches. The contract made clear that if Gonzalez won the Chavez match, he would receive at least $75,000 for the next fight unless the parties agreed otherwise, and if he lost, he would receive at least $25,000 for the subsequent fight unless otherwise agreed. The agreement did not explicitly state the purse for the subsequent match in the event of a draw. The Chavez match ended in a draw, and Gonzalez contended that this omission rendered the contract so indefinite that it was unenforceable. The court disagreed, stating that striking down a contract as indefinite and in essence meaningless is at best a last resort.

---

[8] *Mears v Nationwide Mut, Inc. Co.*, 91 F3d 1118 (8th Cir 1996).

THINKING THINGS THROUGH

The Rules of Negotiations

Business agreements are often reached after much discussion, study, and posturing by both sides. Many statements may be made by both sides about the price or value placed on the subject of the transaction. Withholding information or presenting selective, self-serving information may be perceived by a party to the negotiations as protective self-interest. Does the law of contracts apply a duty of good faith and fair dealing in the negotiation of contracts? Does the Uniform Commercial Code provide for a general duty of good faith in the negotiation of contracts? Are lawyers under an ethical obligation to inform opposing counsel of relevant facts? The answer to all of these questions is no.

The Restatement (Second) of Contracts applies the duty of good faith and fair dealing to the performance and enforcement of contracts, not their negotiation*; so also does the UCC.** The American Bar Association's Model Rules of Professional Conduct, Rule 4.1 Comment 1 requires a lawyer to be "truthful" when dealing with others on a client's behalf, but it also states that generally a lawyer has "no affirmative duty to inform an opposing party of relevant facts."*** Comment 2 to Rule 4.1 contains an example of a "nonmaterial" statement of a lawyer as "estimates of price or value placed on the subject of a transaction."

The legal rules of negotiations state that—in the absence of fraud, special relationships, or statutory or contractual duties—negotiators are not obligated to divulge pertinent information to the other party to the negotiations. The parties to negotiations themselves must demand and analyze pertinent information and ultimately assess the fairness of the proposed transaction. Should a party conclude that the elements of a final proposal or offer are excessive or dishonest, that party's legal option is to walk away from the deal. Generally, the party has no basis to bring a lawsuit for lack of good faith and fair dealing in negotiations.

However, THINKING THINGS THROUGH, the ethical standards for negotiations set forth in Chapter 2 indicate that establishing a reputation for trustworthiness, candor, and reliability oftens lead to commercial success for a company's continuing negotiations with its customers, suppliers, distributors, lenders, unions, and employees.

_____

* Restatement (Second) of Contracts § 105, comment (c).
** Uniform Commercial Code § 1-203.
*** American Bar Association Model Rule of Professional Conduct 4.1(a) Comment 1.

The court held that although the contract was poorly drafted, the Promotional Agreement contained explicit price terms for which a minimum purse for fights following a draw may be inferred.[9] A court may not rewrite the agreement of the parties in order to make it definite.

(a) Definite by Incorporation   An offer and the resulting contract that by themselves may appear "too indefinite" may be made definite by reference to another writing. **For Example,** a lease agreement that was too vague by itself was made definite because the parties agreed that the lease should follow the standard form with

_____

[9] *Gonzalez v Don King Productions, Inc.,* 17 F Supp 2d 313 (SDNY 1998); see also *Echols v Pelullo,* 377 F3d 272 (3rd Cir 2004).

| FIGURE 13-1 | *Offer and Acceptance* |

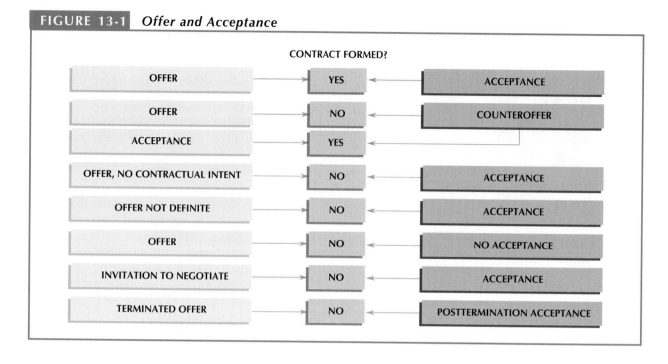

(b) IMPLIED TERMS Although an offer must be definite and certain, not all of its terms need to be expressed. Some omitted terms may be implied by law. **For Example,** an offer "to pay $400" for a certain Movado timepiece does not state the terms of payment. A court, however, would not condemn this provision as too vague but would hold that it required that cash be paid and that the payment be made on delivery of the watch. Likewise, terms may be implied from conduct. As an illustration, when borrowed money was given to the borrower by a check on which the word *loan* was written, the act of the borrower in endorsing the check constituted an agreement to repay the amount of the check.

(c) "BEST EFFORTS" CLAUSES While decades ago it was generally accepted that a duty defined only in terms of "best efforts" was too indefinite to be enforced, such a view is no longer widely held. **For Example,** Thomas Hinc, an inventor, executed a contract with Lime-O-Sol Company (LOS) for LOS to produce and distribute Hinc's secret ingredient Stain Remover. Under the contract, Hinc was to receive $10 per gallon sold. The contract contained a clause obligating both parties to use their "best efforts" to market the product "in a manner that seems appropriate." Ultimately, LOS never produced, marketed, or sold Stain Remover for the duration of the contract. The court rejected the defense that the "best efforts" provision was vague and unenforceable stating "[b]est efforts, as commonly understood, means, at the very least *some* effort. It certainly does not mean *zero* effort—the construction LOS urges here to escape any obligation under its contract."[10]

---

[10] *Hinc v Lime-O-Sol Company,* 382 F3d 716 (7th Cir 2004).

(d) Divisible Contracts   When the agreement consists of two or more parts and calls for corresponding performances of each part by the parties, the agreement is a **divisible contract**. Thus, in a promise to buy several separate articles at different prices at the same time, the agreement may be regarded as separate or divisible promises for the articles. When a contract contains a number of provisions or performances to be rendered, the question arises as to whether the parties intended merely a group of separate, divisible contracts or whether it was to be a package deal so that complete performance by each party was essential.

divisible contract agreement consisting of two or more parts, each calling for corresponding performances of each part by the parties.

CASE SUMMARY

Just Throw the Bad Part Away

FACTS: Kazem Moini's company, West Candies, Inc., manufactured candy that it sold to Maureen Hewes's candy store. Hewes made a contract with Moini in which she agreed (1) to purchase all of her candy from Moini, (2) to keep her showcase adequately stocked at all times, and (3) to maintain an inventory equal to or greater than that specified in Exhibit A. In fact, there never was an Exhibit A. Hewes did not pay for some of the candy delivered to her. Moini sued her and then Hewes claimed that the contract was not binding because it was too indefinite, as there was no Exhibit A defining the required inventory amount.

DECISION: Judgment for Moini. The promise to maintain inventory or stock as specified in Exhibit A was too indefinite to be binding because there was no Exhibit A. That, however, did not establish that there was no contract, because the two other promises made by Hewes could be enforced. They were sufficiently definite in themselves and were not in any way related to the promise regarding inventory maintenance. There was nothing in the contract manifesting any intent that it was necessary that all three promises be binding before any of them could be binding. The contract was therefore divisible. As a result, it failed only as to the inventory promise but was binding as to the other promises. Therefore, Hewes was required to pay at the contract rate for the candy received. [**Moini v Hewes, 763 P2d 414 (Or App 1988)**]

(e) Exceptions to Definiteness   The law has come to recognize certain situations in which the practical necessity of doing business makes it desirable to have a contract, yet the situation is such that it is either impossible or undesirable to adopt definite terms in advance. In these cases, the indefinite term is often tied to the concept of good-faith performance or to some independent factor that will be definitely ascertainable at some time in the future. The indefinite term might be tied to market price, cost to complete, production, or sales requirements. Thus, the law recognizes binding contracts in the case of a **requirements contract**—that is, a contract to buy all requirements of the buyer from the seller.[11] **For Example,** an agreement between Honeywell International Inc. and Air Products and Chemicals Inc. whereby Air Products would purchase its total requirements of wet process chemicals from Honeywell was held to be an enforceable requirements contract.[12] The law also recognizes as binding an **output contract**—that is, the contract of a producer to sell the entire production or output to a given buyer. These are binding contracts even though they do not state the exact quantity of goods that are to be bought or sold.

requirements contract contract to buy all requirements of the buyer from the seller.

output contract contract of a producer to sell its entire production or output to a given buyer.

---

[11] *Simcala v American Coal Trade, Inc.,* 2001 WL 139 1992 (Nov 9, 2001).
[12] *Honeywell International Inc. v Air Products and Chemicals, Inc.,* 872 A2d 944 (Sup Ct Del 2005).

3. COMMUNICATION OF OFFER TO OFFEREE

An offer must be communicated to the offeree. Otherwise, the offeree cannot accept even though knowledge of the offer has been indirectly acquired. Internal management communications of an enterprise that are not intended for outsiders or employees do not constitute offers and cannot be accepted by them. Sometimes, particularly in the case of unilateral contracts, the offeree performs the act called for by the offeror without knowing of the offer's existence. Such performance does not constitute an acceptance. Thus, without knowing that a reward is offered for information leading to the arrest of a particular criminal, a person may provide information that leads to the arrest of the criminal. In most states, if that person subsequently learns of the reward, the reward cannot be recovered.[13]

Not only must the offer be communicated but also it must be communicated by the offeror or at the offeror's direction.

 B   TERMINATION OF OFFER

An offeree cannot accept a terminated offer. Offers may be terminated by revocation, counteroffer, rejection, lapse of time, death or disability of a party, or subsequent illegality.

4. REVOCATION OF OFFER BY OFFEROR

Ordinarily, an offeror can revoke the offer before it is accepted. If this is done, the offeree cannot create a contract by accepting the revoked offer. Thus, the bidder at an auction sale may withdraw (revoke) a bid (offer) before it is accepted, and the auctioneer cannot accept that bid later.

An ordinary offer may be revoked at any time before it is accepted even though the offeror has expressly promised that the offer will be good for a stated period and that period has not yet expired. It may also be revoked even though the offeror has expressly promised to the offeree that the offer would not be revoked before a specified later date.

The fact that the offeror expressly promised to keep the offer open has no effect when no consideration was given for that promise.

(a) WHAT CONSTITUTES A REVOCATION?   No particular form or words are required to constitute a revocation. Any words indicating the offeror's termination of the offer are sufficient. A notice sent to the offeree that the property that is the subject of the offer has been sold to a third person is a revocation of the offer. A customer's order for goods, which is an offer to purchase at certain prices, is revoked by a notice to the seller of the cancellation of the order, provided that such notice is communicated before the order is accepted.

(b) COMMUNICATION OF REVOCATION   A revocation of an offer is ordinarily effective only when it is made known to the offeree.[14] Until it is communicated to the offeree, directly or indirectly, the offeree has reason to believe that there is still an offer that may be accepted, and the offeree may rely on this belief. A letter revoking

---

[13] With respect to the offeror, it should not make any difference, as a practical matter, whether the services were rendered with or without knowledge of the existence of the offer. Only a small number of states have adopted this view, however.

[14] *MD Drilling and Blasting, Inc. v MLS Construction, LLC,* 889 A2d 850 (Conn App 2006).

an offer made to a particular offeree is not effective until the offeree receives it. It is not a revocation when the offeror writes it or even when it is mailed or dispatched. A written revocation is effective, however, when it is delivered to the offeree's agent or to the offeree's residence or place of business under such circumstances that the offeree may be reasonably expected to be aware of its receipt.

It is ordinarily held that there is a sufficient communication of the revocation when the offeree learns indirectly of the offeror's revocation. This is particularly true in a land sale when the seller-offeror, after making an offer to sell the land to the offeree, sells the land to a third person and the offeree indirectly learns of such sale. The offeree necessarily realizes that the seller cannot perform the original offer and therefore must be considered to have revoked it.

If the offeree accepts an offer before it is effectively revoked, a valid contract is created.

(c) Option Contracts   An *option contract* is a binding promise to keep an offer open for a stated period of time or until a specified date. An option contract requires that the promisor receive consideration—that is, something, such as a sum of money—as the price for the promise to keep the offer open. In other words, the option is a contract to refrain from revoking an offer.

(d) Firm Offers   As another exception to the rule that an offer can be revoked at any time before acceptance, statutes in some states provide that an offeror cannot revoke an offer prior to its expiration when the offeror makes a firm offer. A **firm offer** is an offer that states that it is to be irrevocable, or irrevocable for a stated period of time. Under the Uniform Commercial Code, this doctrine of firm offers applies to a merchant's signed, written offer to buy or sell goods but with a maximum of three months on its period of irrevocability.[15]

firm offer offer stated to be held open for a specified time, which must be so held in some states even in the absence of an option contract, or under the UCC, with respect to merchants.

5. COUNTEROFFER BY OFFEREE

The offeree rejects the offer when she ignores the original offer and replies with a different offer.[16] If the offeree purports to accept an offer but in so doing makes any change to the terms of the offer, such action is a **counteroffer** that rejects the original offer. An "acceptance" that changes the terms of the offer or adds new terms is a rejection of the original offer and constitutes a counteroffer.[17]

counteroffer proposal by an offeree to the offeror that changes the terms of, and thus rejects, the original offer.

Ordinarily, if *A* makes an offer, such as to sell a used automobile to *B* for $3,000, and *B* in reply makes an offer to buy at $2,500, the original offer is terminated. *B* is in effect indicating refusal of the original offer and in its place is making a different offer. Such an offer by the offeree is known as a *counteroffer*. No contract arises unless the original offeror accepts the counteroffer.

Counteroffers are not limited to offers that directly contradict the original offers. Any departure from or addition to the original offer is a counteroffer even though the original offer was silent on the point added by the counteroffer.

6. REJECTION OF OFFER BY OFFEREE

If the offeree rejects the offer and communicates this rejection to the offeror, the offer is terminated. Communication of a rejection terminates an offer even though the

---

[15] UCC § 2-205.

[16] *Bourque v FDIC*, 42 F3d 704 (1st Cir 1994).

[17] *McLaughlin v Heikkila*, 697 NW2d 731 (Minn App 2005).

period for which the offeror agreed to keep the offer open has not yet expired. It may be that the offeror is willing to renew the offer, but unless this is done, there is no longer any offer for the offeree to accept.

7. LAPSE OF TIME

When the offer states that it is open until a particular date, the offer terminates on that date if it has not yet been accepted. This is particularly so when the offeror declares that the offer shall be void after the expiration of the specified time. Such limitations are strictly construed.

If the offer contains a time limitation for acceptance, an attempted acceptance after the expiration of that time has no effect and does not give rise to a contract.[18] When a specified time limitation is imposed on an option, the option cannot be exercised after the expiration of that time, regardless of whether the option was exercised within what would have been held a reasonable time if no time period had been specified.

If the offer does not specify a time, it will terminate after the lapse of a reasonable time. What constitutes a reasonable time depends on the circumstances of each case— that is, on the nature of the subject matter, the nature of the market in which it is sold, the time of year, and other factors of supply and demand. If a commodity is perishable or fluctuates greatly in value, the reasonable time will be much shorter than if the subject matter is of a stable value. An offer to sell a harvested crop of tomatoes would expire within a very short time. When a seller purports to accept an offer after it has lapsed by the expiration of time, the seller's acceptance is merely a counteroffer and does not create a contract unless the buyer accepts that counteroffer.

8. DEATH OR DISABILITY OF EITHER PARTY

If either the offeror or offeree dies or becomes mentally incompetent before the offer is accepted, the offer is automatically terminated. **For Example,** Chet Wilson offers to sell his ranch to Interport, Inc., for $2.5 million. Five days later, Chet is killed in an aviation accident. Interport, Inc., subsequently writes to Chet Wilson Jr., an adult, that his father's offer is accepted. No contract is formed because the offer made by Chet died with him.

9. SUBSEQUENT ILLEGALITY

If the performance of the contract becomes illegal after the offer is made, the offer is terminated. **For Example,** if an offer is made to sell six semiautomatic handguns to a commercial firing range for $550 per weapon but a new law prohibiting such sales is enacted before the offer is accepted, the offer is terminated.

ACCEPTANCE OF OFFER

acceptance unqualified assent to the act or proposal of another; as the acceptance of a draft (bill of exchange), of an offer to make a contract, of goods delivered by the seller, or of a gift or deed.

An **acceptance** is the assent of the offeree to the terms of the offer. Objective standards determine whether there has been an agreement of the parties.

---

[18] *Century 21 Pinetree Properties, Inc. v Cason,* 469 SE2d 458 (Ga App 1996).

10. WHAT CONSTITUTES AN ACCEPTANCE?

No particular form of words or mode of expression is required, but there must be a clear expression that the offeree agrees to be bound by the terms of the offer. If the offeree reserves the right to reject the offer, such action is not an acceptance.[19]

11. PRIVILEGE OF OFFEREE

Ordinarily, the offeree may refuse to accept an offer. If there is no acceptance, by definition there is no contract. The fact that there had been a series of contracts between the parties and that one party's offer had always been accepted before by the other does not create any legal obligation to continue to accept subsequent offers.

12. EFFECT OF ACCEPTANCE

The acceptance of an offer creates a binding agreement or contract,[20] assuming that all of the other elements of a contract are present. Neither party can subsequently withdraw from or cancel the contract without the consent of the other party.

13. NATURE OF ACCEPTANCE

An *acceptance* is the offeree's manifestation of intent to enter into a binding agreement on the terms stated in the offer. Whether there is an acceptance depends on whether the offeree has manifested an intent to accept. It is the objective or outward appearance that is controlling rather than the subjective or unexpressed intent of the offeree.[21]

In the absence of a contrary requirement in the offer, an acceptance may be indicated by an informal "okay," by a mere affirmative nod of the head, or in the case of an offer of a unilateral contract, by performance of the act called for.

The acceptance must be absolute and unconditional. It must accept just what is offered.[22] If the offeree changes any terms of the offer or adds any new term, there is no acceptance because the offeree does not agree to what was offered.

When the offeree does not accept the offer exactly as made, the addition of any qualification converts the "acceptance" into a counteroffer, and no contract arises unless the original offeror accepts such a counteroffer.

14. WHO MAY ACCEPT?

Only the person to whom an offer is directed may accept it. If anyone else attempts to accept it, no agreement or contract with that person arises.

If the offer is directed to a particular class rather than a specified individual, anyone within that class may accept it. If the offer is made to the public at large, any member of the public at large having knowledge of the existence of the offer may accept it.

When a person to whom an offer was not made attempts to accept it, the attempted acceptance has the effect of an offer. If the original offeror is willing to

[19] *Pantano v McGowan*, 530 NW2d 912 (Neb 1995).
[20] *Ochoa v Ford*, 641 NE2d 1042 (Ind App 1994).
[21] *Cowan v Mervin Mewes, Inc.*, 546 NW2d 104 (SD 1996).
[22] *Jones v Frickey*, 618 SE2d 29 (Ga App 2005).

accept this offer, a binding contract arises. If the original offeror does not accept the new offer, there is no contract.

CASE SUMMARY

There's No Turning Back

FACTS: As a lease was about to expire, the landlord, CRA Development, wrote the tenant, Keryakos Textiles, setting forth the square footage and the rate terms on which the lease would be renewed. Keryakos sent a reply stating that it was willing to pay the proposed rate but wanted different cancellation and option terms in the renewal contract. CRA rejected Keryakos's terms, and on learning this, Keryakos notified CRA that it accepted the terms of its original letter. CRA sought to evict Keryakos from the property, claiming that no lease contract existed between it and Keryakos.

DECISION: The lease contract is governed by ordinary contract law. When the tenant offered other terms in place of those made by the landlord's offer, the tenant made a counteroffer. This had the effect of rejecting or terminating the landlord's offer. The tenant could not then accept the rejected offer after the tenant's counteroffer was rejected. Therefore, there was no contract. [**Keryakos Textiles, Inc. v CRA Development, Inc. 563 NYS2d 308 (App Div 1990)**]

CPA

15. MANNER AND TIME OF ACCEPTANCE

The offeror may specify the manner and time for accepting the offer. When the offeror specifies that there must be a written acceptance, no contract arises when the offeree makes an oral acceptance. If the offeror calls for acceptance by a specified time and date, a late acceptance has no legal effect, and a contract is not formed. Where no time is specified in the offer, the offeree has a reasonable period of time to accept the offer. After the time specified in the offer or a reasonable period of time expires (when no time is specified in the offer), the offeree's power to make a contract by accepting the offer "lapses."

When the offeror calls for the performance of an act or of certain conduct, the performance thereof is an acceptance of the offer and creates a unilateral contract.

When the offeror has specified a particular manner and time of acceptance, generally, the offeree cannot accept in any other way. The basic rule applied by the courts is that the offeror is the master of the offer![23]

CPA

(a) SILENCE AS ACCEPTANCE In most cases, the offeree's silence and failure to act cannot be regarded as an acceptance. Ordinarily, the offeror is not permitted to frame an offer in such a way as to make the silence and inaction of the offeree operate as an acceptance. Nor can a party to an existing contract effect a modification of that agreement without the other party's actual acceptance or approval.
For Example, H. H. Taylor made a contract with Andy Stricker, a civil engineer, to design a small hotel. The parties agreed on an hourly rate with "total price not to exceed $7,200," and required that additional charges be presented to Taylor prior to proceeding with any changes. Andy was required to dedicate more hours to the

---

[23] See *1-800 Contacts, Inc v Weigner*, 127 P3d 1241 (Utah App 2005).

E-COMMERCE AND CYBERLAW

Contract Formation on the Internet

It is not possible for an online service provider or seller to individually bargain with each person who visits its Web site. The Web site owner, therefore, as offeror, places its proposed terms on its Web site and requires visitors to assent to these terms in order to access the site, download software, or purchase a product or service.

In a written contract, the parties sign a paper document indicating their intention to be bound by the terms of the contract. Online, however, an agreement may be accomplished by the visitor-offeree simply typing the words "I Accept" in an onscreen box and then clicking a "send" or similar button that indicates acceptance. Or the individual clicks an "I Agree" or "I Accept" icon or checkbox. Access to the site is commonly denied those who do not agree to the terms.

Such agreements have come to be called *clickon, clickthrough, or clickwrap* agreements. The agreements contain fee schedules and other financial terms and may contain terms such as a notice of the proprietary nature of the material contained on the site and of any limitations on the use of the site and the downloading of software. Moreover, the clickon agreements may contain limitations on liability, including losses associated with the use of downloaded software or products or services purchased from the site.

The use of clickon agreements has become standard practice for the sale of certain products and services online and the distribution of software. Although case law is scarce, where the agreements are not contrary to the basic principles of contract law, the contracts are legally enforceable.*

In Caspi v Microsoft Network,** the Superior Court of New Jersey Appellate Division upheld the enforcement of certain terms of Microsoft Network's (MSN) clickon membership agreement and dismissed a suit brought by subscribers on the basis of a forum selection clause contained in the membership agreement. The plaintiff-subscribers had argued in part that the forum selection clause did not apply to them because they did not receive adequate notice of the clause. The agreement formation process was explained by the trial court as follows:

> Before becoming an MSN member, a prospective subscriber is prompted by MSN software to view multiple computer screens of information, including a membership agreement which contains the above clause. MSN's membership agreement appears on the computer screen in a scrollable window next to blocks providing the choices "I Agree" and "I Don't Agree." Prospective members assent to the terms of the agreement by clicking on "I Agree" using a computer mouse.

The court stated that the plaintiffs were free to scroll through the various computer screens that presented the terms of their contracts before clicking their agreement. The court found that in any sense that matters, there is no significant distinction between the electronic form of this contract and a contract in printed form. Accordingly, the plaintiffs were forced to comply with the forum selection clause and bring their lawsuit challenging MSN's billing practices in the state of Washington rather than New Jersey.

In contrast, the U.S. Court of Appeals for the Second Circuit declined to enforce a clickthrough agreement in Specht v Netscape Communications Corp.*** in connection with Netscape's SmartDownload software. Users were able to download the program from

E·COMMERCE AND CYBERLAW

continued

Netscape's site simply by clicking a download icon. At the bottom of the download page, the text invited the user to review a licensing agreement before downloading and using the software, but the agreement itself was not available on the page. The court concluded that "a consumer's clicking on a download button does not communicate assent to contractual terms if the offer did not make clear to the consumer that clicking on the download button would signify assent to those terms."

---

* As will be seen in Chapter 23, Article Two of the Uniform Commercial Code deals with the sale of goods. It was adopted by most states in the 1960s, well before the contemplation and existence of the Internet and electronic contracting issues. The Uniform Computer Information Transactions Act (UCITA), a uniform law promulgated in July 1999 by the National Conference of Commissioners on Uniform State Laws, governs contracts involving the sale, licensing, maintenance, and support of computer software. The UCITA has been adopted by just two states, Virginia and Maryland. However, successful producers of software or financial institutions that license software to their customers may choose to locate or open an office in one of the UCITA states in order to obtain the coverage of UCITA rules. Choice-of-law rules under Section 109(b)(1) of the UCITA provide that the law of the UCITA state will govern each transaction as long as the software is delivered over the Internet. The UCITA is clear that clickon agreements allowing a user to convey consent through an onscreen click are legally enforceable as long as there has been an opportunity to review the terms before assenting. See UCITA § 112, Reporter Notes No. 5, Illustration 1. The UCITA is not applicable to electronically conducted transactions for the sale of goods that contain no embedded software.

** 732 A2d 528 (NJ Super 1999).

*** 306 F3d 17, 29-30 (2d Cir 2002).

---

project than anticipated but could not present the additional charges to Taylor because Taylor would not return his phone calls. He billed Taylor $9,035 for his services. Taylor's failure to act in not returning phone calls is not a substitute for the assent needed to modify a contract. Stricker is thus only entitled to $7,200.[24]

(b) Unordered Goods and Tickets   Sometimes a seller writes to a person with whom the seller has not had any prior dealings, stating that unless notified to the contrary, the seller will send specified merchandise and the recipient is obligated to pay for it at stated prices. There is no acceptance if the recipient of the letter ignores the offer and does nothing. The silence of the person receiving the letter is not an acceptance, and the sender, as a reasonable person, should recognize that none was intended.

This rule applies to all kinds of goods, books, magazines, and tickets sent through the mail when they have not been ordered. The fact that the items are not returned does not mean that they have been accepted; that is, the offeree is required neither to pay for nor to return the items. If desired, the recipient of the unordered goods may write "Return to Sender" on the unopened package and put the package back into the mail without any additional postage. The Postal Reorganization Act provides that the person who receives unordered mailed merchandise from a commercial sender has the right "to retain, use, discard, or dispose of it in any manner the recipient sees fit without any obligation whatsoever to the sender."[25] It provides further that any

---

[24] *Stricker v Taylor,* 975 P2d 930 (Or App 1999).

[25] Federal Postal Reorganization Act § 3009.

unordered merchandise that is mailed must have attached to it a clear and conspicuous statement of the recipient's right to treat the goods in this manner.

CPA **16. COMMUNICATION OF ACCEPTANCE**

Acceptance by the offeree is the last step in the formation of a bilateral contract. Intuitively, the offeror's receipt of the acceptance should be the point in time when the contract is formed and its terms apply. When the parties are involved in face-to-face negotiations, a contract is formed upon the offeror's receipt of the acceptance. When the offeror hears the offeree's words of acceptance, the parties may then shake hands, signifying their understanding that the contract has been formed.

CPA **(a) The Mailbox Rule**   When the parties are negotiating at a distance from each other, special rules have developed as to when the acceptance takes effect based on the commercial expediency of creating a contract at the earliest period of time and the protection of the offeree. Under the so-called *mailbox rule,* a properly addressed, postage-paid mailed acceptance takes effect when the acceptance is placed into the control of the U.S. Postal Service[26] or, by judicial extension, is placed in the control of a private third-party carrier such as Federal Express or United Parcel Service. That is, the acceptance is effective upon dispatch even before it is received by the offeror.

CASE SUMMARY

When the Mailbox Bangs Shut

FACTS: The Thoelkes owned land. The Morrisons mailed an offer to the Thoelkes to buy their land. The Thoelkes agreed to this offer and mailed back a contract signed by them. While this letter was in transit, the Thoelkes notified the Morrisons that their acceptance was revoked. Were the Thoelkes bound by a contract?

DECISION: The acceptance was effective when mailed, and the subsequent revocation of the acceptance had no effect. [**Morrison v Thoelke, 155 So 2d 889 (Fla App 1963)**]

The offeror may avoid the application of this rule by stating in the offer that acceptance shall take effect upon receipt by the offeror.

CPA **(b) Determining the Applicable Means of Communication**   The modern rule on the selection of the appropriate medium of communication of acceptance is that unless otherwise unambiguously indicated in the offer, it shall be construed as inviting acceptance in any manner and by any medium reasonable under the circumstances.[27] A medium of communication is normally reasonable if it is one used by the offeror or if it is customary in similar transactions at the time and place the offer is received. Thus, if the offeror uses the mail to extend an offer, the offeree may accept by using the mail. Indeed, acceptance by mail is ordinarily reasonable when the parties are negotiating at a distance even if the offer is not made by mail.

---

[26] See *Adams v Lindsell,* 106 Eng Rep 250 (KB 1818). Common law jurisdictions have unanimously adopted the mailbox rule, as has the Restatement (Second) of Contracts § 63, and the UCC [see UCC § 1-201(26),(38)].

[27] Restatement (Second) of Contracts § 30; UCC § 2-206(1)(a).

CASE SUMMARY

Just Be Reasonable

FACTS: Maria Cantu was a special education teacher under a one-year contract with the San Benito School District for the 1990–1991 school year. On Saturday, August 18, just weeks before fall-term classes were to begin, she hand delivered a letter of resignation to her supervisor. Late Monday afternoon the superintendent put in the mail a properly stamped and addressed letter to Cantu accepting her offer of resignation. The next morning at 8:00, before the superintendent's letter reached her, Cantu hand delivered a letter withdrawing her resignation. The superintendent refused to recognize the attempted rescission of the resignation.

DECISION: Cantu was wrong. The resignation became binding when the acceptance of the resignation was mailed. The fact that the offer to resign had been delivered by hand did not require that the offer be accepted by a hand delivery of the acceptance. The use of mail was reasonable under the circumstances, and therefore the mailing of the acceptance made it effective. [**Cantu v Central Education Agency, 884 SW2d 563 (Tex App 1994)**]

CPA **(c) TELEPHONE AND ELECTRONIC COMMUNICATION OF ACCEPTANCE**   Although telephonic communication is very similar to face-to-face communication, most U.S. courts, nevertheless, have applied the mailbox rule, holding that telephoned acceptances are effective where and when dispatched.

The courts have yet to address the applicability of the mailbox rule to e-mail. However, when the offeree's server is under the control of an independent entity, such as an online service provider, and the offeree cannot withdraw the message, it is anticipated that the courts will apply the mailbox rule, and acceptance will take effect on proper dispatch. In the case of companies that operate their own servers, the acceptance will take effect when the message is passed onto the Internet.

Facsimile transmissions are substantially instantaneous and could be treated as face-to-face communications. However, it is anticipated that U.S. courts, when called upon to deal with this issue, will apply the mailbox acceptance-upon-dispatch rule as they do with telephoned acceptances.

(d) EFFECTS OF THE MAILBOX RULE   If an offer requires that acceptance be communicated by a specific date and the acceptance is properly dispatched by the offeree on the final date, the acceptance is timely and the contract is formed, even though the offeror actually receives the acceptance by well after the specified date has passed.

A situation may occur when a revocation and acceptance cross in the mail. As set forth previously, a revocation is effective only on the offeree's receipt. If an offeree dispatches an acceptance after the offeror has dispatched a revocation but before the revocation arrives, a contract is formed.

17. AUCTION SALES

At an auction sale, the statements made by the auctioneer to draw forth bids are merely invitations to negotiate. Each bid is an offer, which is not accepted until the

ETHICS & THE LAW

PepsiCo ran an ad and promotional campaign in 1996 called the "Drink Pepsi Get Stuff" campaign. The enormously successful campaign allowed customers to claim prizes in exchange for points on PepsiCo beverage containers, and the points could be combined with cash payments to obtain the prizes. The campaign was so successful that the second round of ads and promotions was not run because the prizes were nearly exhausted.

In one television ad, PepsiCo pictured a Harrier jet as a satirical spoof on the prizes available under the campaign. The jet was offered in the ad for 7 million beverage points. Harrier jets are made only for the Marine Corps and are not sold in the open market. They cost $33.8 million each and can be produced at a rate of only one dozen at a time.

John Leonard, a 21-year-old business student, called PepsiCo and was told he would need to drink 16.8 million cans of Pepsi in order to obtain the required points. He was also told that he had the option of buying PepsiCo points for 10¢ each. Leonard developed a pool of investors (Pepsi drinkers) and delivered 15 PepsiCo points and a check for $700,008.50 for the remaining 6,999,985 points plus shipping and handling.

PepsiCo refused to provide a Harrier jet to Leonard because it said the ad was not an offer but a joke. Leonard filed suit on August 6, 1996, but PepsiCo had already filed a preemptive suit on July 18, asking that Leonard's suit be dismissed and declared frivolous and that PepsiCo be reimbursed for its legal expenses.

Did PepsiCo make an offer? Did Leonard accept? What is the significance of Leonard's phone call and the verification of the PepsiCo points needed? Is there a contract? If you were a PepsiCo executive, what would you do? If there is a misunderstanding about the ad, is there an ethical obligation on the part of PepsiCo? Was Leonard taken advantage of, or is he taking advantage of PepsiCo? [*Leonard v PepsiCo, Inc.,* 210 F3d 88 (2d Cir 2000)]

auctioneer indicates that a particular offer or bid is accepted. Usually, this is done by the fall of the auctioneer's hammer, indicating that the highest bid made has been accepted.[28] Because a bid is merely an offer, the bidder may withdraw the bid at any time before it is accepted by the auctioneer.

Ordinarily, the auctioneer who is not satisfied with the amounts of the bids that are being made may withdraw any article or all of the property from the sale. Once a bid is accepted, however, the auctioneer cannot cancel the sale. In addition, if it had been announced that the sale was to be made "without reserve," the property must be sold to the person making the highest bid regardless of how low that bid may be.

In an auction "with reserve," the auctioneer takes bids as agent for the seller with the understanding that no contract is formed until the seller accepts the transaction.[29]

---

[28] *Dry Creek Cattle Co. v Harriet Bros. Limited Partnership,* 908 P2d 399 (Wyo 1995).

[29] *Marten v Staab,* 543 NW2d 436 (Neb 1996). Statutes regulate auctions and auctioneers in all states. For example, state of Maine law prohibits an auctioneer from conducting an auction without first having a written contract with the consignor of any property to be sold, including (1) whether the auction is with reserve or without reserve, (2) the commission rate, and (3) a description of all items to be sold. See *Street v Board of Licensing of Auctioneers,* 889 A2d 319 ([Me] 2006).

> SUMMARY

Because a contract arises when an offer is accepted, it is necessary to find that there was an offer and that it was accepted. If either element is missing, there is no contract.

An offer does not exist unless the offeror has contractual intent. This intent is lacking if the statement of the person is merely an invitation to negotiate, a statement of intention, or an agreement to agree at a later date. Newspaper ads, price quotations, and catalog prices are ordinarily merely invitations to negotiate and cannot be accepted.

An offer must be definite. If an offer is indefinite, its acceptance will not create a contract because it will be held that the resulting agreement is too vague to enforce. In some cases, an offer that is by itself too indefinite is made definite because some writing or standard is incorporated by reference and made part of the offer. In some cases, the offer is made definite by implying terms that were not stated. In other cases, the indefinite part of the offer is ignored when that part can be divided or separated from the balance of the offer. In other cases, the requirement of definiteness is ignored either because the matter that is not definite is unimportant or because there is an exception to the rule requiring definiteness.

Assuming that there is in fact an offer that is made with contractual intent and that it is sufficiently definite, it still does not have the legal effect of an offer unless it is communicated to the offeree by or at the direction of the offeror.

In some cases, no contract arises because there is no offer that satisfies the requirements just stated. In other cases, there was an offer, but it was terminated before it was accepted. By definition, an attempted acceptance made after the offer has been terminated has no effect. The offeror may revoke the ordinary offer at any time. All that is required is the showing of intent to revoke and the communication of that intent to the offeree. The offeror's power to revoke is barred by the existence of an option contract under common law or a firm offer under the Uniform Commercial Code or local non-Code statute and by the application of the doctrine of detrimental reliance by the offeree. An offer is also terminated by the express rejection of the offer or by the making of a counteroffer, by the lapse of the time stated in the offer or of a reasonable time when none is stated, by the death or disability of either party, or by a change of law that makes illegal a contract based on the particular offer.

When the offer is accepted, a contract arises. Only the offeree can accept an offer, and the acceptance must be of the offer exactly as made without any qualification or change. Ordinarily, the offeree may accept or reject as the offeree chooses. Limitations on this freedom of action have been imposed by antidiscrimination and consumer protection laws.

The acceptance is any manifestation of intent to agree to the terms of the offer. Ordinarily, silence or failure to act does not constitute acceptance. The recipient of unordered goods and tickets may dispose of the goods or use the goods without such action constituting an acceptance. An acceptance does not exist until the words or conduct demonstrating assent to the offer is communicated to the offeror. Acceptance by mail takes effect at the time and place when and where the letter is mailed or the fax is transmitted. A telephoned acceptance is effective when and where dispatched.

In an auction sale, the auctioneer asking for bids makes an invitation to negotiate. A person making a bid is making an offer, and the acceptance of the highest bid by the auctioneer is an acceptance of that offer and gives rise to a contract. When the auction sale is without reserve, the auctioneer must accept the highest bid. If the auction is not expressly without reserve, the auctioner may refuse to accept any of the bids.

> QUESTIONS AND CASE PROBLEMS

1. Bernie and Phil's Great American Surplus store placed an ad in the *Sunday Times* stating, "Next Saturday at 8:00 A.M. sharp, 3 brand new mink coats worth $5,000 each will be sold for $500 each! First come, First served." Marsha Lufklin was first in line when the store opened and went directly to the coat department, but the coats identified in the ad were not available for sale. She identified herself to the manager and pointed out that she was first in line in conformity with the store's advertised offer and that she was ready to pay the $500 price set forth in the store's offer. The manager responded that a newspaper ad is just an invitation to negotiate and that the store decided to withdraw "the mink coat promotion." Review the text on unilateral contracts in Section 12(b) of Chapter 12. Decide.

2. Brown made an offer to purchase Overman's house on a standard printed form. Underneath Brown's signature was the statement: "ACCEPTANCE ON REVERSE SIDE." Overman did not sign the offer on the back but sent Brown a letter accepting the offer. Later, Brown refused to perform the contract, and Overman sued him for breach of contract. Brown claimed there was no contract because the offer had not been accepted in the manner specified by the offer. Decide. [*Overman v Brown*, 372 NW2d 102 (Neb)]

3. Katherine mailed Paul an offer stating that it was good for 10 days. Two days later, she mailed Paul another letter stating that the original offer was revoked. That evening Paul phoned Katherine to say he accepted the offer. She said that he could not because she had mailed him a letter of revocation that he would undoubtedly receive in the next morning's mail. Was the offer revoked by Katherine?

4. Nelson wanted to sell his home. Baker sent him a written offer to purchase the home. Nelson made some changes to Baker's offer and wrote him that he, Nelson, was accepting the offer as amended. Baker notified Nelson that he was dropping out of the transaction. Nelson sued Baker for breach of contract. Decide. What social forces and ethical values are involved? [*Nelson v Baker,* 776 SW2d 52 (Mo App)]

5. Lessack Auctioneers advertised an auction sale that was open to the public and was to be conducted with reserve. Gordon attended the auction and bid $100 for a work of art that was worth much more. No higher bid, however, was made. Lessack refused to sell the item for $100 and withdrew the item from the sale. Gordon claimed that because he was the highest bidder, Lessack was required to sell the item to him. Was he correct?

6. Willis Music Co. advertised a television set at $22.50 in the Sunday newspaper. Ehrlich ordered a set, but the company refused to deliver it on the grounds that the price in the newspaper ad was a mistake. Ehrlich sued the company. Was it liable? Why or why not? [*Ehrlich v Willis Music Co.,* 113 NE2d 252 (Ohio App)]

7. When a movement was organized to build Charles City College, Hauser and others signed pledges to contribute to the college. At the time of signing, Hauser inquired what would happen if he should die or be unable to pay. The representative of the college stated that the pledge would then not be binding and that it was merely a statement of intent. The college failed financially, and Pappas was appointed receiver to collect and liquidate the assets of the college corporation. He sued Hauser for the amount due

on his pledge. Hauser raised the defense that the pledge was not a binding contract. Decide. What ethical values are involved? [*Pappas v Hauser,* 197 NW2d 607 (Iowa)]

8. *A* signed a contract agreeing to sell land he owned but reserved the right to take the hay from the land until the following October. He gave the contract form to *B*, a broker. *C*, a prospective buyer, agreed to buy the land and signed the contract but crossed out the provision regarding the hay crop. Was there a binding contract between *A* and *C* ?

9. A. H. Zehmer discussed selling a farm to Lucy. After a 40-minute discussion of the first draft of a contract, Zehmer and his wife, Ida, signed a second draft stating: "We hereby agree to sell to W. O. Lucy the Ferguson farm complete for $50,000 title satisfactory to buyer." Lucy agreed to purchase the farm on these terms. Thereafter, the Zehmers refused to transfer title to Lucy and claimed they had made the contract for sale as a joke. Lucy brought an action to compel performance of the contract. The Zehmers claimed there was no contract. Were they correct? [*Lucy v Zehmer,* 84 SE2d 516 (Va App)]

10. Wheeler operated an automobile service station, which he leased from W. C. Cornitius, Inc. The lease ran for three years. Although the lease did not contain any provision for renewal, it was in fact renewed six times for successive three-year terms. The landlord refused to renew the lease for a seventh time. Wheeler brought suit to compel the landlord to accept his offer to renew the lease. Decide. [*William C. Cornitius, Inc. v Wheeler,* 556 P2d 666 (Or)]

11. Buster Cogdill, a real estate developer, made an offer to the Bank of Benton to have the bank provide construction financing for the development of an outlet mall, with funds to be provided at prime rate plus two percentage points. The bank's president Julio Plunkett thanked Buster for the proposal and said, "I will start the paperwork." Did Cogdill have a contract with the Bank of Benton? [*Bank of Benton v Cogdill,* 454 NE2d 1120 (Ill App)]

12. Ackerley Media Group, Inc., claimed to have a three-season advertising Team Sponsorship Agreement (TSA) with Sharp Electronics Corporation to promote Sharp products at all Seattle Supersonics NBA basketball home games. Sharp contended that a valid agreement did not exist for the third season (2000–2001) because a material price term was missing, thus resulting in an unenforceable "agreement to agree." The terms of the TSA for the 2000–2001 third season called for a base payment of $144,200 and an annual increase "not to exceed 6% . . . [and] to be mutually agreed upon by the parties." No "mutually agreed" increase was negotiated by the parties. Ackerley seeks payment for the base price of $144,200 only. Sharp contends that since no mutually agreed price was agreed upon for the season, the entire TSA is unenforceable, and it is not obligated to pay for the 2000–2001 season. Is Sharp correct? [*Ackerley Media Group, Inc. v Sharp Electronics Corp.,* 170 F Supp 2d 445 (SDNY)]

13. Calvin and Audrey Bones listed their ranch for sale with their real estate agent, Loren Johnson. On July 17, 1997, Dean Keller submitted an offer to buy the ranch for $490,000, with a deposit of $49,000 payable to the agent. The terms of the offer stated that it would be withdrawn if not accepted by July 21 at 5:00 P.M. At 4:53 P.M. on July 21, the Boneses faxed a signed copy of the offer to their agent. Paragraph 15 of the offer stated in part that "upon execution by seller this agreement shall become a binding contract." Loren Johnson, the sellers' real estate agent, did not telephone the buyer Keller to inform him of the acceptance until 5:12 P.M. on July 21, and then did so by leaving a message on Keller's answering machine. On July 22, the sellers had a change of heart and decided to sell to the current tenants of the ranch. Ms. Johnson called Keller to ask if he would be willing to allow the sellers to back out of the deal. Keller refused and brought suit to enforce "the contract." The Boneses contend that no valid contract was formed because the sellers' acceptance was not communicated to the buyer until after the deadline set forth in the offer had expired. Keller contends that as offeror he is the master of the offer, and the offer was silent with respect to the manner and time of acceptance. Thus, the manner and the time of acceptance must be rendered in a reasonable time and manner, where

none is specified. The seller's agent left a message on the buyer's answering machine only 19 minutes after the seller signed the acceptance and 12 minutes after the 5:00 P.M. signing deadline, which according to Keller is a reasonable time and manner. Decide. [*Keller v Bones,* 615 NW2d 883 (Neb)]

14. On August 15, 2003, Wilbert Heikkila signed an agreement with Kangas Realty to sell eight parcels of Heikkila's property. On September 8, 2003, David McLaughlin met with a Kangas agent who drafted McLaughlin's offer to purchase three of the parcels. McLaughlin signed the offer and gave the agent checks for each parcel. On September 9 and 10, 2003, the agent for Heikkila prepared three printed purchase agreements, one for each parcel. On September 14, 2003, David's wife, Joanne McLaughlin, met with the agent and signed the agreements. On September 16, 2003,

Heikkila met with his real estate agent. Writing on the printed agreements, Heikkila changed the price of one parcel from $145,000 to $150,000, the price of another parcel from $32,000 to $45,000, and the price of the third parcel from $175,000 to $179,000. Neither of the McLaughlins signed an acceptance of Heikkila's changes to the printed agreements before Heikkila withdrew his offer to sell. The McLaughlins learned that Heikkila had withdrawn his offer on January 1, 2004, when the real estate agent returned the checks to them. Totally shocked at Heikkila's conduct, the McLaughlins brought action to compel specific performance of the purchase agreement signed by Joanne McLaughlin on their behalf. Decide. [*McLaughlin v Heikkila,* 697 NW2d 231 (Minn App)]

> CPA QUESTIONS

1. Able Sofa, Inc., sent Noll a letter offering to sell Noll a custom-made sofa for $5,000. Noll immediately sent a telegram to Able purporting to accept the offer. However, the telegraph company erroneously delivered the telegram to Abel Soda, Inc. Three days later, Able mailed a letter of revocation to Noll, which was received by Noll. Able refused to sell Noll the sofa. Noll sued Able for breach of contract. Able

    a. Would have been liable under the deposited acceptance rule only if Noll had accepted by mail
    b. Will avoid liability since it revoked its offer prior to receiving Noll's acceptance
    c. Will be liable for breach of contract
    d. Will avoid liability due to the telegraph company's error (Law, #2, 9911)

2. On September 27, Summers sent Fox a letter offering to sell Fox a vacation home for $150,000. On October 2, Fox replied by mail agreeing to buy the home for $145,000. Summers did not reply to Fox. Do Fox and Summers have a binding contract?

    a. No, because Fox failed to sign and return Summers's letter

    b. No, because Fox's letter was a counteroffer
    c. Yes, because Summers's offer was validly accepted
    d. Yes, because Summers's silence is an implied acceptance of Fox's letter (Law, #2, 0462)

3. On June 15, Peters orally offered to sell a used lawn mower to Mason for $125. Peters specified that Mason had until June 20 to accept the offer. On June 16, Peters received an offer to purchase the lawn mower for $150 from Bronson, Mason's neighbor. Peters accepted Bronson's offer. On June 17, Mason saw Bronson using the lawn mower and was told the mower had been sold to Bronson. Mason immediately wrote to Peters to accept the June 15 offer. Which of the following statements is correct?

    a. Mason's acceptance would be effective when received by Peters.
    b. Mason's acceptance would be effective when mailed.
    c. Peters's offer had been revoked and Mason's acceptance was ineffective.
    d. Peters was obligated to keep the June 15 offer open until June 20. (Law, #13, 3095)

CAPACITY AND GENUINE ASSENT

LEARNING OBJECTIVES

After studying this chapter, you should be able to

LO.1 Define *contractual capacity*

LO.2 State the extent and effect of avoidance of a contract by a minor

LO.3 Classify unilateral and bilateral mistakes

LO.4 Distinguish between innocent misrepresentation, fraud, and nondisclosure

LO.5 List those classes of persons who lack contractual capacity

LO.6 Distinguish between undue influence and duress

A *contract* is a binding agreement. This agreement must be made between parties who have the capacity to do so. They must also truly agree so that all parties have really consented to the contract. This chapter explores the elements of contractual capacity of the parties and the genuineness of their assent.

CONTRACTUAL CAPACITY

Some persons lack contractual capacity, a lack that embraces both those who have a status incapacity, such as minors, and those who have a factual incapacity, such as persons who are insane.

1. CONTRACTUAL CAPACITY DEFINED

contractual capacity ability to understand that a contract is being made and to understand its general meaning.

Contractual capacity is the ability to understand that a contract is being made and to understand its general meaning. However, the fact that a person does not understand the full legal meaning of a contract does not mean that contractual capacity is lacking. Everyone is presumed to have capacity unless it is proven that capacity is lacking or there is status incapacity.[1] **For Example,** Jacqueline, aged 22, entered into a contract with Sunrise Storage Co. but later claimed it was not binding because she did not understand several clauses in the printed contract. The contract was binding. No evidence supported her claim that she lacked capacity to contract or to understand its subject. Contractual capacity can exist even though a party does not understand every provision of the contract.

(a) STATUS INCAPACITY   Over the centuries, the law has declared that some classes of persons lack contractual capacity. The purpose is to protect these classes by giving them the power to get out of unwise contracts. Of these classes, the most important today is the class identified as minors.

Until recent times, some other classes were held to lack contractual capacity in order to discriminate against them. Examples are married women and aliens. Still

> ## CASE SUMMARY
>
> ### We Really Mean Equal Rights
>
> FACTS: An Alabama statute provided that a married woman could not sell her land without the consent of her husband. Montgomery made a contract to sell land she owned to Peddy. Montgomery's husband did not consent to the sale. Montgomery did not perform the contract and Peddy sued her. The defense was raised that the contract was void and could not be enforced because of the statute. Peddy claimed that the statute was unconstitutional.
>
> DECISION: The statute was unconstitutional. Constitutions, both federal and state, guarantee all persons the equal protection of the law. Married women are denied this equal protection when they are treated differently than married men and unmarried women. The fact that such unequal treatment had once been regarded as proper does not justify its modern continuation. [**Peddy v Montgomery, 345 So 2d 631 (Ala 1977)**]

---

[1] *In re Adoption of Smith*, 578 So 2d 988 (La App 1991).

other classes, such as persons convicted of and sentenced for a felony, were held to lack contractual capacity in order to punish them. Today, these discriminatory and punitive incapacities have largely disappeared. Married women have the same contractual capacity as unmarried persons.[2]

By virtue of international treaties, the discrimination against aliens has been removed.

(b) Factual Incapacity   A *factual incapacity* contrasts with incapacity imposed because of the class or group to which a person belongs. A factual incapacity may exist when, because of a mental condition caused by medication, drugs, alcohol, illness, or age, a person does not understand that a contract is being made or understand its general nature. However, mere mental weakness does not incapacitate a person from contracting. It is sufficient if the individual has enough mental capacity to understand, to a reasonable extent, the nature and effect of what he is doing.[3]

---

2. MINORS

Minors may make contracts.[4] To protect them, however, the law has always treated minors as a class lacking contractual capacity.

(a) Who Is a Minor?   At common law, any person, male or female, under 21 years of age was a minor. At common law, minority ended the day before the twenty-first birthday. The "day before the birthday" rule is still followed, but the age of majority has been reduced from 21 years to 18 years.

`CPA`   **(b) Minor's Power to Avoid Contracts**   With exceptions that will be noted later, a contract made by a minor is voidable at the election of the minor. The minor may affirm or ratify the contract on attaining majority by performing the contract, by expressly approving the contract, or by allowing a reasonable time to lapse without avoiding the contract.

`CPA`   *(1) What Constitutes Avoidance?*   A minor may avoid or *disaffirm* a contract by any expression of an intention to repudiate the contract. Any act inconsistent with the continuing validity of the contract is also an avoidance.

`CPA`   *(2) Time for Avoidance.*   A minor can disaffirm a contract only during minority and for a reasonable time after attaining majority. After the lapse of a reasonable time, the contract is deemed ratified and cannot be avoided by the minor.

`CPA`   *(3) Minor's Misrepresentation of Age.*   Generally, the fact that the minor has misrepresented her age does not affect the minor's power to disaffirm the contract. Some states hold that such fraud of a minor bars contract avoidance. Some states permit the minor to disaffirm the contract in such a case but require the minor to pay for any damage to the property received under the contract.

In any case, the other party to the contract may disaffirm it because of the minor's fraud.

---

[2] A few states have a limitation that a married woman cannot make a binding contract to pay the debt of her husband if he fails to.

[3] *Fisher v Schefers,* 656 NW2d 591 (Minn App 2003).

[4] *Buffington v State Automobile Mut. Ins. Co.,* 384 SE2d 873 (Ga App 1989).

status quo ante original positions of the parties.

CPA **(c) Restitution by Minor after Avoidance** When a minor disaffirms a contract, the question arises as to what the minor must return to the other contracting party.

(1) Original Consideration Intact. When a minor still has what was received from the other party, the minor, on avoiding the contract, must return it to the other party or offer to do so. That is, the minor must put things back to the original position or, as it is called, restore the **status quo ante**.

(2) Original Consideration Damaged or Destroyed. What happens if the minor cannot return what has been received because it has been spent, used, damaged, or destroyed? The minor's right to disaffirm the contract is not affected. The minor can still disaffirm the contract and is required to return only what remains. The fact that nothing remains or that what remains is damaged does not bar the right to disaffirm the contract. In states that follow the common law rule, minors can thus refuse to pay for what has been received under a contract or can get back what had been paid or given even though they do not have anything to return or return property in a damaged condition. There is, however, a trend to limit this rule.

(d) Recovery of Property by Minor on Avoidance When a minor disaffirms a contract, the other contracting party must return the money received. Any property received from the minor must also be returned. If the property has been sold to a third person who did not know of the original seller's minority, the minor cannot get the property back. In such cases, however, the minor is entitled to recover the property's monetary value or the money received by the other contracting party.

CPA **(e) Contracts for Necessaries** A minor can disaffirm a contract for necessaries but must pay the reasonable value for furnished necessaries.

necessaries things indispensable or absolutely necessary for the sustenance of human life.

(1) What Constitutes Necessaries? Originally, **necessaries** were limited to those things absolutely necessary for the sustenance and shelter of the minor. Thus limited, the term would extend only to food, clothing, and lodging. In the course of time, the rule was relaxed to extend generally to things relating to the health, education, and comfort of the minor. Thus, the rental of a house used by a married minor is a necessary.

(2) Liability of Parent or Guardian. When a third person supplies the parents or guardian of a minor with goods or services that the minor needs, the minor is not liable for these necessaries because the third person's contract is with the parent or guardian, not with the minor.

When necessary medical care is provided a minor, a parent is liable at common law for the medical expenses provided the minor child. However, at common law, the child can be held contractually liable for her necessary medical expenses when the parent is unable or unwilling to pay.

CPA **(f) Ratification of Former Minor's Voidable Contract** A former minor cannot disaffirm a contract that has been ratified after reaching majority.[5]

---

[5] *Fletcher v Marshall*, 632 NE2d 1105 (Ill App 1994).

CASE SUMMARY

The Concussion and Legal Repercussions

FACTS: Sixteen-year-old Michelle Schmidt was injured in an automobile accident and taken to Prince George's Hospital. Although the identities of Michelle and her parents were originally unknown, the hospital provided her emergency medical care for a brain concussion and an open scalp wound. She incurred hospital expenses of $1,756.24. Ms. Schmidt was insured through her father's insurance company. It issued a check to be used to cover medical expenses. However, the funds were used to purchase a car for Ms. Schmidt. Since she was a minor when the services were rendered, she believed that she had no legal obligation to pay. After Ms. Schmidt attained her eighteenth birthday and failed to pay the hospital, it brought suit against her.

DECISION: Judgment for the hospital. The prevailing modern rule is that minors' contracts are voidable except for necessaries. The doctrine of necessaries states that a minor may be held liable for necessaries, including medical necessaries when parents are unwilling to pay. The court concluded that Ms. Schmidt's father demonstrated a clear unwillingness to pay by using the insurance money to purchase a car rather than pay the hospital. The policy behind the necessaries exception is for the benefit of minors because the procurement of such is essential to their existence, and if they were not permitted to bind themselves, they might not be able to obtain the necessaries. [**Schmidt v Prince George's Hospital, 784 A2d 1112 (Md 2001)**]

CPA *(1) What Constitutes Ratification?*   Ratification consists of any words or conduct of the former minor manifesting an intent to be bound by the terms of a contract made while a minor.

CPA *(2) Form of Ratification.*   Generally, no special form is required for ratification of a minor's voidable contract, although in some states a written ratification or declaration of intention is required.

CPA *(3) Time for Ratification.*   A person can disaffirm a contract any time during minority and for a reasonable time after that but, of necessity, can ratify a contract only after attaining majority. The minor must have attained majority, or the ratification would itself be regarded as voidable.

(g) Contracts That Minors Cannot Avoid   Statutes in many states deprive a minor of the right to avoid an educational loan[6]; a contract for medical care; a contract made while running a business; a contract approved by a court; a contract made in performance of a legal duty; and a contract relating to bank accounts, insurance policies, or corporate stock.

(h) Liability of Third Person for a Minor's Contract   The question arises as to whether parents are bound by the contract of their minor child. The question of

---

[6] A Model Student Capacity to Borrow Act makes educational loans binding on minors in Arizona, Mississippi, New Mexico, North Dakota, Oklahoma, and Washington. This act was reclassified from a uniform act to a model act by the Commissioners on Uniform State Law, indicating that uniformity was viewed as unimportant and that the matter was primarily local in character.

whether a person cosigning a minor's contract is bound if the contract is avoided also arises.

(1) Liability of Parent.   Ordinarily, a parent is not liable on a contract made by a minor child. The parent may be liable, however, if the child is acting as the agent of the parent in making the contract. Also, the parent is liable to a seller for the reasonable value of necessaries supplied by the seller to the child if the parent had deserted the child.

(2) Liability of Cosigner.   When the minor makes a contract, another person, such as a parent or a friend, may sign along with the minor to make the contract more acceptable to the third person.

With respect to the other contracting party, the cosigner is bound independently of the minor. Consequently, if the minor disaffirms the contract, the cosigner remains bound by it. When the debt to the creditor is actually paid, the obligation of the cosigner is discharged.

If the minor disaffirms a sales contract but does not return the goods, the cosigner remains liable for the purchase price.

---

3. MENTALLY INCOMPETENT PERSONS

A person with a mental disorder may be so disabled as to lack capacity to make a contract. If the person is so mentally incompetent as to be unable to understand that a contract is being made or the general nature of the contract, the person lacks contractual capacity.

(a) EFFECT OF INCOMPETENCY   An incompetent person may ordinarily avoid a contract in the same manner as a minor. Upon the removal of the disability (that is, upon becoming competent), the formerly incompetent person can either ratify or disaffirm the contract.

CASE SUMMARY

Friends Should Tell Friends About Medical Leaves

FACTS: Wilcox Manufacturing Group, Inc., did business under the name of Superior Automation Co., and Howard Wilcox served as Superior's president. As part of a loan "lease agreement" of $50,000 executed on December 5, 2000, Superior was to repay Marketing Services of Indiana (MSI) $67,213.80 over the course of 60 months. Wilcox gave a personal guarantee for full and prompt payment. Wilcox had been a patient of psychiatrist Dr. Shaun Wood since May 21, 1999, and was diagnosed as suffering from bipolar disorder during the period from June 2000 to January 2001. On June 9, 2000, Wilcox told Dr. Wood he was having problems functioning at work, and Dr. Wood determined that Wilcox was experiencing lithium toxicity, which lasted for 10 months, during which time he suffered from impaired cognitive functions that limited his capacity to understand the nature and quality of his actions and judgments. Superior made monthly payments though to October 28, 2003, and the balance owed at that time was $33,031.37. MSI sued Wilcox personally and the corporation for

CASE SUMMARY

continued

breach of contract. The defendants raise the defense of lack of capacity and contend that they are not liable on the loan signed by the corporate president when he was incapacitated.

DECISION: Judgment for MSI. The acts or deeds of a person of unsound mind whose condition has not been judicially ascertained and who is not under guardianship are voidable and not absolutely void. The acts are subject to ratification or disaffirmance on removal of the disability. The latest Wilcox could have been experiencing the effects of lithium toxicity was October 2001. Wilcox thus regained his capacity by that date. No attempt was made to disaffirm the contract. Rather, monthly payments continued to be made for a year and one-half before the payments ceased. The contract was thus ratified by the conduct of the president of Superior after he recovered his ability to understand the nature of the contract. [**Wilcox Manufacturing, Inc. v Marketing Services of Indiana, Inc., 832 NE2d 559 (Ind App 2005)**]

A mentally incompetent person or his estate is liable for the reasonable value of all necessaries furnished that individual.

A current trend in the law is to treat an incompetent person's contract as binding when its terms and the surrounding circumstances are reasonable and the person is unable to restore the other contracting party to the status quo ante.

(b) APPOINTMENT OF GUARDIAN If a court appoints a guardian for the incompetent person, a contract made by that person before the appointment may be ratified or, in some cases, disaffirmed by the guardian. If the incompetent person makes a contract after a guardian has been appointed, the contract is void and not merely voidable.

4. INTOXICATED PERSONS

The capacity of a party to contract and the validity of the contract are not affected by the party's being impaired by alcohol at the time of making the contract so long as the party knew that a contract was being made.

If the degree of intoxication is such that a person does not know that a contract is being made, the contract is voidable by that person. The situation is the same as though the person were insane at the time and did not know what he or she was doing. On becoming sober, the individual may avoid or rescind the contract. However, an unreasonable delay in taking steps to set aside a known contract entered into while intoxicated may bar the intoxicated person from asserting this right.[7]

For Example, Edward made a contract while intoxicated. When he sobered up, he immediately disaffirmed the contract for lack of capacity as the result of his intoxication. The other contracting party claimed that voluntary intoxication cannot void a contract, but Edward could disaffirm the contract because he lacked the legal capacity to enter a contract.

The courts treat impairment caused by the use of drugs the same as impairment caused by the excessive use of alcohol.

---

[7] *Diedrich v Diedrich*, 424 NW2d 580 (Minn App 1988).

ETHICS & THE LAW

Globe Life Insurance Company has undertaken a new sales program that targets neighborhoods in Los Angeles where drive-by shootings were a nightly occurrence. In two such shootings, children were killed as they sat in their living rooms.

Globe salespeople were instructed to "hit" the houses surrounding those where children were victims. They were also told to contact the parents of those children to sell policies for their other children.

Tom Raskin, an experienced Globe salesman, read of a drive-by shooting at Nancy Leonard's home, in which Leonard's five-year-old son was killed. The *Los Angeles Times* reported that Leonard was a single parent with four other children.

Raskin traveled to Leonard's home and described the benefits of a Globe policy for her other children. He offered her the $10,000 term life policy for each of the children for a total cost of $21 per month. Leonard was in the process of making funeral arrangements for her son, and Raskin noted, "See how much it costs for a funeral."

Leonard had been given several tranquilizers the night before by a physician at the hospital's emergency room. The physician had also given her 15 more tranquilizers to help her through the following week. She had taken one additional tranquilizer an hour before Raskin arrived, using a Coors Lite beer to take the pill.

Leonard signed the contract for the policy. After her son's funeral, she received the first month's bill for it and exclaimed, "I didn't buy any life insurance! Where did this come from?"

After you discuss Leonard's legal standing, discuss the ethical issues involved in Globe's sales program. Discuss the legal issues involved in Raskin's decision to target Leonard the day after her son's death.

MISTAKE

The validity of a contract may be affected by the fact that one or both of the parties made a mistake. In some cases, the mistake may be caused by the misconduct of one of the parties.

5. UNILATERAL MISTAKE

A *unilateral mistake*—that is, a mistake by only one of the parties—as to a fact does not affect the contract when the mistake is unknown to the other contracting party.[8] When a contract is made on the basis of a quoted price, the validity of the contract is not affected by the fact that the party furnishing the quotation made a mathematical mistake in computing the price if there was no reason for the other party to recognize that there had been a mistake.[9] The party making the mistake may avoid the contract if the other contracting party knew or should have known of the mistake.

---

[8] *Truck South Inc. v Patel*, 528 SE2d 424 (SC 2000).

[9] *Procan Construction Co. v Oceanside Development Corp.*, 539 NYS2d 437 (App Div 2d 1989).

CASE SUMMARY

Bumper Sticker: "Mistakes Happen!"

FACTS: Lipton-U City, LLC (Lipton), and Shurgard Storage Centers discussed the sale of a self-storage facility for approximately $7 million. Lipton became concerned about an existing environmental condition and as a result, the parties agreed to a lease with an option to buy rather than an outright sale. The contract specified a 10-year lease with an annual rent starting at $636,000 based on a property valuation of $7 million. Section 2.4 of the contract contained the purchase option. Shurgard representatives circulated an e-mail with a copy to Lipton representatives that a purchase option price would be based on six months of *annualized* net operating income. When the lease was submitted to Lipton, inexplicably any language regarding multiplying by 2 or annualizing the net income was omitted. Donn Lipton announced to his attorneys that the lease reflected his successful negotiation of a purchase option based on six months of *unannualized* net operating income. Eight months after signing the lease, Lipton sought to exercise the purchase option under Section 2.4 and stated a price of $2,918,103. Shurgard rejected the offer and filed suit for rescission, citing the misunderstanding about the price terms.

DECISION: Judgment for Shurgard. Under state law, if a material mistake made by one party is known to the other party or is of such a character or circumstances that the other party should know of it, the mistaken party has a right to rescission. Lipton knew or should have known of the mistake of the lessor (Shurgard) in believing that the purchase price would be based on a full year of net operating income rather than six months of net operating income. Lipton was notified by e-mail that the six-month figure was to be annualized and knew that the property was valued at approximately $7 million. [**Shurgard Storage Centers v Lipton-U City, LLC, 394 F3d 1041 (8th Cir 2005)**]

FIGURE 14-1   *Avoidance of Contract*

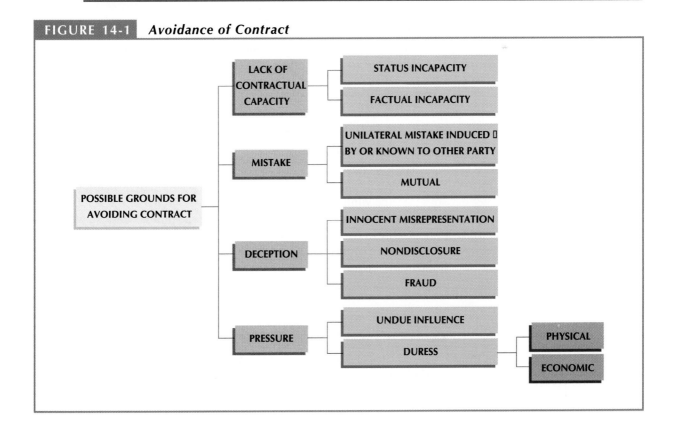

6. MUTUAL MISTAKE

When both parties enter into a contract under a mutually mistaken understanding concerning a basic assumption of fact or law on which the contract is made, the contract is voidable by the adversely affected party if the mistake has a material effect on the agreed exchange.[10]

CASE SUMMARY

Ignorance of the Law Is an Excuse in This Case

FACTS: Barbara Mattson is the sister of Jerry Rachetto. When Jerry finished law school, he went to work for Barbara's husband, Jon Mattson. When Jerry later expressed a desire to build a house on Tract A of the Mattson Ranch, the Mattsons deeded Tract A to Jerry and Joan Rachetto and sought no payment for the land. In 1984, the Rachettos approached the Mattsons about buying Tract C, an 18-acre portion of the Mattson Ranch, to ensure no future development adjacent to the Rachetto house. The Mattsons were willing to sell Tract C but not without a specific agricultural leaseback provision that allowed the Mattson Ranch to cultivate hay and graze livestock for their lifetime. Jon Mattson and Jerry Rachetto drafted the necessary documents, including the agricultural lease, and the documents were executed in 1984. In 1996, it was discovered that under state law, an agricultural lease for a period longer than 20 years is invalid. The Mattsons then sought to rescind the entire transaction because of the mistaken belief of all parties to the transaction. The Rachettos claim that the Mattsons want the land back because of its significant increase in value. From a judgment for the Mattsons, the Rachettos appealed.

DECISION: State law provides that a mistake of law in relation to consent to contract constitutes a mistake resulting in voidable consent only when it arises from a misapprehension of the law by all parties, all supposing that they knew and understood it, and all making substantially the same mistake as to the law. This provision is a statutorily recognized exception to the old axiom "ignorance of the law is no excuse." The trial court properly restored the parties to where they were before they made the contractual mistake, rescinding the 1984 contract and requiring the Mattsons to repay the purchase price and interest. [**Mattson v Rachetto, 591 NW2d 814 (SD 1999)**]

A contract based on *a mutual mistake in judgment* is not voidable by the adversely affected party. **For Example,** if both parties believe that a colt is not fast enough to develop into a competitive race horse and effect a sale accordingly, when the animal later develops into the winner of the Preakness as a three-year-old, the seller cannot rescind the contract based on mutual mistake because the mutual mistake was a mistake in judgment. In contrast, when two parties to a contract believe a cow to be barren at the time they contract for its sale, but before delivery of the animal to the buyer, it is discovered that the assumption was mistaken, such is a mutual mistake of fact making the contract void.[11]

7. MISTAKE IN THE TRANSCRIPTION OR PRINTING OF THE CONTRACT: REFORMATION

In some instances, the parties make an oral agreement, and in the process of committing it to writing or printing it from a manuscript, a phrase, term, or segment is

---

[10] See *Browning v Howerton*, 966 P2d 367 (Wash App 1998).
[11] See *Sherwood v Walker*, 66 Mich 568 (1887).

inadvertently left out of the final, signed document. The aggrieved party may petition the court to **reform** the contract to reflect the actual agreement of the parties. However, the burden of proof is heightened to clear and convincing evidence that such a mistake was made. **For Example,** the Printers International Union reached agreement for a new three-year contract with a large regional printing company. As was their practice, the union negotiators then met with Sullivan Brothers Printers, Inc., a small specialty shop employing 10 union printers, and Sullivan Brothers and the union agreed to follow the contractual pattern set by the union and the large printer. That is, Sullivan Brothers agreed to give its workers all of the benefits negotiated for the employees of the large printing company. When the contract was typed, a new benefit of 75 percent employer-paid coverage for a dental plan was inadvertently omitted from the final contract that the parties signed. The mistake was not discovered until later, and Sullivan Brothers, Inc., is now reluctant to assume the additional expense. Based on the clear and convincing evidence of a practice of following the contractual pattern set by the large printer and Sullivan's assent to again follow the pattern, a court or arbitrator will reform the contract.

reformation remedy by which a written instrument is corrected when it fails to express the actual intent of both parties because of fraud, accident, or mistake.

 ## DECEPTION

One of the parties may have been misled by a fraudulent statement. In such situations, there is no true or genuine assent to the contract, and it is voidable at the innocent party's option.

8. INTENTIONAL MISREPRESENTATION

Fraud is a generic term embracing all multifarious means that human ingenuity can devise and that are resorted to by one individual to get advantage over another. It is classified in the law as a *tort*. However, where a party is induced into making a contract by a material misrepresentation of fact, this form of fraudulent activity adversely affects the genuineness of the assent of the innocent party, and this type of fraud is the focus of our discussion in the chapters on contracts.

9. FRAUD

fraud making of a false statement of a past or existing fact, with knowledge of its falsity or with reckless indifference as to its truth, with the intent to cause another to rely thereon, and such person does rely thereon and is harmed thereby.

Fraud is the making of a material misrepresentation (or false statement) of fact with (1) knowledge of its falsity or reckless indifference to its truth, (2) the intent that the listener rely on it, (3) the result that the listener does so rely, and (4) the consequence that the listener is harmed.[12]

To prove fraud, there must be a material misrepresentation of fact. Such a misrepresentation is one that is likely to induce a reasonable person to assent to a contract. **For Example,** if a used car salesman says, "This Buick had but one owner, a retired teacher who kept it in mint condition," when in fact the auto had several owners, the last of which was an auto salvage company that rebuilt the car after a serious accident, the salesman's statement is a material misrepresentation of fact.

(a) STATEMENT OF OPINION OR VALUE Ordinarily, matters of opinion of value or opinions about future events are not regarded as fraudulent. Thus, statements that a building was "very good," it "required only normal maintenance," and the "deal was excellent" were merely matters of opinion. Therefore, a court considered the

12 *Maack v Resource Design & Construction, Inc.,* 875 P2d 570 (Utah 1994); *Bortz v Noon,* 729 A2d 555 (Pa 1999).

CASE SUMMARY

Watch Out! Some People Have a Lot of Nerve

FACTS: German citizens Klaus and Gerda Tschira brought suit against Corim, Inc., a U.S. real estate investment firm and its president, Ben Willingham Jr., for fraudulent misrepresentation during a real estate transaction between the Tschiras and Corim. Klaus attended a meeting in Walldorf, Germany, in which Willingham, who speaks fluent German, made a presentation. Willingham explained that Corim proposed to obtain buildings for investors to purchase at a "fair market price"; Corim then intended to enter into management contracts with the new owners. By the terms of the management contracts, Corim and Willingham would lease the buildings from the investors and, in return, would then pay the investors a contractually established rent. The Tschiras subsequently purchased a Nashville, Tennessee, commercial property on December 14, 1990, for $1,985,000. The Tschiras did not visit the property, secure independent counsel, or obtain an appraisal. They later discovered that two closings occurred on December 14, 1990. In the first, One Church Street, Inc., a shell corporation owned by Corim and Willingham, purchased the property from its owner, First Atlanta Services Corporation. The selling price in this deal was $774,000. In the second transaction, One Church Street, Inc., sold the building to the Tschiras for $1,985,000. The title insurance policy Willingham forwarded to the Tschiras indicated that the Ticor Title Insurance Company had provided protection up to $1,985,000. In actuality, Lisa Wilson, the branch manager of Ticor, testified that the policy the company extended for the property was for only $774,000. Willingham and Corim contended that any representations were not material because they "guaranteed" a return on the investment. From a judgment for the Tschiras in the amount of $1,420,000 in compensatory damages and $1,750,000 in punitive damages, Corim and Willingham appealed.

DECISION: Judgment for the Tschiras. Willingham and Corim argue that there was no fraudulent misrepresentation because the representations made were not material because they provided a "guaranteed" return on the Tschiras' investment through the rental income. However, the jury could have reasonably found otherwise. The Tschiras believed they were paying "fair market price" for the purchase of the property in addition to receiving a guaranteed return on their investment. The Tschiras believed, and the jury could have reasonably concluded, that the Tschiras actually paid $1,211,000 over the fair market price of the property and therefore lost that amount on their investment at the time of purchase. The Tschiras reasonably relied on the representations and suffered the damages as a result of that reliance. [**Tschiras v Willingham, 133 F3d 1077 (6th Cir 1998)**]

sophistication and expertise of the parties and the commercial setting of the transaction and enforced the contract "as is." The theory is that the person hearing the statement recognizes or should recognize that it is merely the speaker's personal opinion, not a statement of fact. A statement that is mere sales talk cannot be the basis of fraud liability. **For Example,** CEO Bernard Ellis sent a memo to shareholders of his Internet-related services business some four days before the expiration of a lockup period during which these shareholders had agreed not to sell their stock. In the memo, he urged shareholders not to sell their stock on the release date because in the event of a massive sell-off "our stock could plummet." He also stated, "I think our share price will start to stabilize and then rise as our company's strong performance continues." Based on Ellis's "strong performance" statement, a major corporate shareholder did not sell. The price of the stock fell from $40 a share to

29 cents a share over the subsequent nine-month period. The shareholder sued Ellis for fraud, seeking $27 million in damages. The court held that the first half of the sentence in question was framed as a mere opinion as to future events and thus was nonactionable; and as to the characterization of the company's performance as "strong," such a self-congratulatory comment constituted mere puffery on which no reasonable investor would rely.[13]

A statement of opinion may be fraudulent when the speaker knows of past or present facts that make the opinion false. **For Example,** Biff Williams, the sales manager of Abrasives International (AI), sold an exclusive dealership selling AI products to Fred Farkas for $100,000 down and a 3 percent royalty on all gross proceeds. Williams told Farkas, "You have the potential to earn $300,000 to $400,000 a year in this territory." He later added, "We have four dealerships making that kind of money today." Farkas was thus persuaded by the business potential of the territory and executed the purchase contract. He later found out AI had a total of just four distributorships at that time, and the actual earnings of the highest producer was $43,000. Assertions of opinions about the future profit potential alone may not amount to fraud, but the assertion of present fact—that four dealerships were presently earning $300,000 to $400,000 a year—was a material misstatement of fact that made the forecast sales potential for Farkas's territory a material misstatement of fact as well. Because there were reliance and damages, Farkas can rescind the contract based on fraud and recover all damages resulting from it.[14]

(b) Reliance on Statement   A fraudulent statement made by one party has no importance unless the other party relies on the statement's truth. **For Example,** after making thorough tests of Nagel Company's pump, Allstate Services Company ordered 100 pumps. It later sued Nagel on the ground that advertising statements made about the pumps were false. Allstate Services cannot impose fraud liability on Nagel for the advertisements, even if they were false, because it had not relied on them in making the purchase but had acted on the basis of its own tests.

If the alleged victim of the fraud knew that the statements were false because the truth was commonly known, the victim cannot rely on the false statements. When the statements of a seller are so "indefinite and extravagant" that reasonable persons would not rely on them, the statements cannot be the basis of a claim of fraud.[15]

(c) Proof of Harm   For an individual to recover damages for fraud, proof of harm to that individual is required. The injured party may recover the actual losses suffered as a result of the fraud as well as punitive damages when the fraud is gross or oppressive. The injured party has the right to have the court order the rescission or cancellation of the contract that has been induced by fraud.[16]

10. NEGLIGENT MISREPRESENTATION

While fraud requires the critical element of a known or recklessly made falsity, a claim of negligent misrepresentation contains similar elements except that it is predicated on a negligently made false statement. That is, the speaker failed to exercise due care

---

[13] *Next Century Communications v Ellis,* 318 F3d 1023 (11th Cir 2003).

[14] The Federal Trade Commission and state agencies have franchise disclosure rules that will penalize the franchisor in this case. See Chapter 41.

[15] *Eckert v Flair Agency, Inc.,* 909 P2d 1201 (Okla App 1995) (seller's statement that house would never be flooded again).

[16] *Paden v Murray,* 523 SE2d 75 (Ga App 2000).

regarding material information communicated to the listener but did not intend to deceive. When the negligent misrepresentation of a material fact that the listener relies on results in harm to the listener, the contract is voidable at the option of the injured party. If fraud is proven, as opposed to misrepresentation, recovery of punitive damages in addition to actual damages can occur. Because it may be difficult to prove the intentional falsity required for fraud, it is common for a lawsuit to allege both a claim of fraud and a claim of negligent misrepresentation. **For Example,** Marshall Armstrong worked for Fred Collins, the owner of Collins Entertainment, Inc., a conglomerate that owns and operates video games. Collins Entertainment's core product video poker was hurt by a court ruling that prohibited cash payouts, which adversely affected its business and resulted in a debt of $13 to $20 million to SouthTrust bank. Chief operating officer Armstrong, on his own time, came up with the idea of modifying bingo machines as a new venture. To exploit this idea, Collins agreed to form a corporation called Skillpins Inc., that was unencumbered by the SouthTrust debt and to give Armstrong a 10 percent ownership interest. After a period of time, with some 300 Skillpins machines producing income, Armstrong discovered the revenues from the new venture on the debt-laden Collins Entertainment profit and loss statement, not that of Skillpins, Inc. Armstrong's suit for both fraud and intentional misrepresentation was successful. In addition to actual damages, he received $1.8 million in punitive damages for fraud.[17]

11. NONDISCLOSURE

Under certain circumstances, nondisclosure serves to make a contract voidable, especially when the nondisclosure consists of active concealment.

(a) GENERAL RULE OF NONLIABILITY   Ordinarily, a party to a contract has no duty to volunteer information to the other party. **For Example,** if Fox does not ask Tehan any questions, Tehan is not under any duty to make a full statement of material facts. Consequently, the nondisclosure of information that is not asked for does not impose fraud liability or impair the validity of a contract.

CASE SUMMARY

Welcome to the Seesaw: Buyer versus Seller

FACTS: Dalarna Management Corporation owned a building constructed on a pier on a lake. There were repeated difficulties with rainwater leaking into the building, and water damage was visible in the interior of the building. Dalarna made a contract to sell the building to Curran. Curran made several inspections of the building and had the building inspected twice by a licensed engineer. The engineer reported there were signs of water leaks. Curran assigned his contract to Puget Sound Service Corporation, which then purchased the building from Dalarna. Puget Sound spent approximately $118,000 attempting to stop the leaks. Puget Sound then sued Dalarna for damages, claiming that Dalarna's failure to disclose the extent of the water leakage problem constituted fraud.

---

[17] 621 SE2d 368 (SC App 2005).

CASE SUMMARY

continued

DECISION: Judgment for Dalarna. Curran was aware there was a water leakage problem, and therefore the burden was on the buyer to ask questions to determine the extent of the problem. There was no duty on the seller to volunteer the extent of the water damage merely because it had been a continuing problem that was more than just a simple leak. The court reached this conclusion because the law "balances the harshness of the former rule of caveat emptor [let the buyer beware] with the equally undesirable alternative of courts standing in loco parentis [in the place of a parent] to parties transacting business." [**Puget Sound Service Corp. v Dalarna Management Corp., 752 P2d 1353 (Wash App 1988)**]

(b) Exceptions   The following exceptions to the general rule of nonliability for nondisclosure exist.

(1) Unknown Defect or Condition.   A duty may exist in some states for a seller who knows of a serious defect or condition to disclose that information to the other party where the defect or condition is unknown to the other person and is of such a nature that it is unlikely that the other person would discover it. However, a defendant who had no knowledge of the defect cannot be held liable for failure to disclose it.[18]

confidential relationship
relationship in which, because of the legal status of the parties or their respective physical or mental conditions or knowledge, one party places full confidence and trust in the other.

(2) Confidential Relationship.   If parties stand in a **confidential relationship**, failure to disclose information may be regarded as fraudulent. For example, in an attorney-client relationship,[19] the attorney has a duty to reveal anything that is material to the client's interest when dealing with the client. The attorney's silence has the same legal consequence as a knowingly made false statement that there was no material fact to be told the client.

(3) Active Concealment.   Nondisclosure may be more than the passive failure to volunteer information. It may consist of a positive act of hiding information from the other party by physical concealment, or it may consist of knowingly or recklessly furnishing the wrong information. Such conduct constitutes fraud. **For Example,** when Nigel wanted to sell his house, he covered the wooden cellar beams with plywood to hide extensive termite damage. He sold the house to Kuehne, who sued Nigel for damages on later discovering the termite damage. Nigel claimed he had no duty to volunteer information about the termites, but by covering the damage with plywood, he committed active fraud as if he had made a false statement that there were no termites.

D   PRESSURE

What appears to be an agreement may not in fact be voluntary because one of the parties entered into it as the result of undue influence or physical or economic duress.

    12. UNDUE INFLUENCE

An aged parent may entrust all business affairs to a trusted child; a disabled person may rely on a nurse; a client may follow implicitly whatever an attorney recommends.

---

[18] *Nesbitt v Dunn,* 672 So 2d 226 (La App 1996).
[19] *In re Boss Trust,* 487 NW2d 256 (Minn App 1992).

The relationship may be such that for practical purposes, one person is helpless in the hands of the other. When such a confidential relationship exists, it is apparent that the parent, the disabled person, or the client is not exercising free will in making a contract suggested by the child, nurse, or attorney but is merely following the will of the other person. Because of the great possibility of unfair advantage, the law presumes that the dominating person exerts **undue influence** on the other person whenever the dominating person obtains any benefit from a contract made with the dominated person. The contract is then voidable. It may be set aside by the dominated person unless the dominating person can prove that, at the time the contract was made, no unfair advantage had been taken.

> **undue influence** influence that is asserted upon another person by one who dominates that person.

The class of confidential relationships is not well defined. It ordinarily includes the relationships of parent and child, guardian and ward, physician and patient, and attorney and client, and any other relationship of trust and confidence in which one party exercises a control or influence over another.

Whether undue influence exists is a difficult question for courts (ordinarily juries) to determine. The law does not regard every influence as undue.

> **physical duress** threat of physical harm to person or property.
>
> **economic duress** threat of financial loss.

An essential element of undue influence is that the person making the contract does not exercise free will. In the absence of a recognized type of confidential relationship, such as that between parent and child, courts are likely to take the attitude that the person who claims to have been dominated was merely persuaded and there was therefore no undue influence.

CASE SUMMARY

Cards and Small Talk Sometimes Make the Sale

FACTS: John Lentner owned the farm adjacent to the Schefers. He moved off the farm to a nursing home in 1999. In the fall of 2000, Kristine Schefers visited Lentner at the nursing home some 15 times, engaging in small talk and watching him play cards. In the spring of 2001, Lentner agreed to sell his farm to Kristine and her husband Thomas for $50,000 plus $10,000 for machinery and tools. Kristine drove Lentner to the bank to get the deed from his safe deposit box. She also took him to the abstractor who drafted the transfer documents. Soon after the sale, Earl Fisher was appointed special conservator of Lentner. Fisher sought to set aside the transaction, asserting that Kristine's repeated visits to the nursing home and her failure to involve Lentner's other family members in the transaction unduly influenced Lentner.

DECISION: Judgment for Thomas and Kristine Schefers. Undue influence is shown when the person making the contract ceased to act of his own free volition and became a mere puppet of the wielder of that influence. Mere speculation alone that Lentner was a "puppet" acting according to the wishes of Schefers is insufficient to set aside the sale. Undue influence was not established. [**Fisher v Schefers, 656 NW2d 592 (Minn App 2003)**]

CPA

13. DURESS

> **duress** conduct that deprives the victim of free will and that generally gives the victim the right to set aside any transaction entered into under such circumstances.

A party may enter into a contract to avoid a threatened danger. The danger threatened may be a physical harm to person or property, called **physical duress**, or it may be a threat of financial loss, called **economic duress**.

(a) PHYSICAL DURESS A person makes a contract under **duress** when there is such violence or threat of violence that the person is deprived of free will and makes the contract to avoid harm. The threatened harm may be directed either at a near relative of the contracting party or against the contracting party. If a contract is made under duress, the resulting agreement is voidable at the victim's election.

Agreements made to bring an end to mass disorder or violence are ordinarily not binding contracts because they were obtained by duress.

One may not void a contract on grounds of duress merely because it was entered into with great reluctance and proves to be very disadvantageous to that individual.[20]

(b) Economic Duress   Economic duress is a condition in which one is induced by a wrongful act or threat of another to make a contract under circumstances that deprive one of the exercise of his own free will.[21] **For Example,** Richard Case, an importer of parts used to manufacture high-quality mountain bicycles, had a contractual duty to supply Katahdin Manufacturing Company's needs for specifically manufactured stainless steel brakes for the 2007 season. Katahdin's president, Bill Read, was in constant contact with Case about the delay in delivery of the parts and the adverse consequences it was having on Katahdin's relationship with its retailers. Near the absolute deadline for meeting orders for the 2007 season, Case called Read and said, "I've got the parts in, but I'm not sure I'll be able to send them to you because I'm working on next year's contracts, and you haven't signed yours yet." Case's 2008 contract increased the cost of parts by 38 percent. Read signed the contract to obtain the delivery but later found a new supplier and gave notice to Case of this action. The defense of economic duress would apply in a breach of contract suit brought by Case on the 2008 contract because Case implicitly threatened to commit the wrongful act of not delivering parts due under the prior contract, and Katahdin Company had no means available to obtain parts elsewhere to prevent the economic loss that would occur if it did not receive those parts.

(**LAWFLIX**)

Jerry Maguire (1996) (R)

Consider the marriage proposal, its validity, and Dorothy's later statement, "I did this. I made this happen. And the thing is, I can do something about it." What was Maguire's state of mind at the time of the proposal? Consider its possible hypothetical nature and the issues of whether it was a joke and the possible presence of undue influence (the young boy).

For movie clips that illustrate business law concepts, see LawFlix at **http://wdvl.westbuslaw.com.**

---

[20] *Miller v Calhoun Johnson Co.,* 497 SE2d 397 (Ga App 1998).
[21] *Hurd v Wildman, Harrold, Allen, and Dixon,* 707 NE2d 609 (Ill App 1999).

▶ SUMMARY

An agreement that otherwise appears to be a contract may not be binding because one of the parties lacks contractual capacity. In such a case, the contract is ordinarily voidable at the election of the party who lacks contractual capacity. In some cases, the contract is void. Ordinarily, contractual incapacity is the inability, for mental or physical reasons, to understand that a contract is being made and to understand its general terms and nature. This is typically the case when it is claimed that incapacity exists because of insanity, intoxication, or drug use. The incapacity of minors arises because society discriminates in favor of that class to protect them from unwise contracts.

The age of majority is 18. Minors can disaffirm most contracts. If a minor received anything from the other party, the minor, on avoiding the contract, must return what had been received from the other party if the minor still has it.

When a minor disaffirms a contract for a necessary, the minor must pay the reasonable value of any benefit received.

Minors only are liable for their contracts. Parents of a minor are not liable on the minor's contracts merely because they are the parents. Frequently, an adult enters into the contract as a coparty of the minor and is then liable without regard to whether the minor has avoided the contract.

The contract of an insane person is voidable to much the same extent as the contract of a minor. An important distinction is that if a guardian has been appointed for the insane person, a contract made by the insane person is void, not merely voidable.

An intoxicated person lacks contractual capacity if the intoxication is such that the person does not understand that a contract is being made.

The consent of a party to an agreement is not genuine or voluntary in certain cases of mistake, deception, or pressure. When this occurs, what appears to be a contract can be avoided by the victim of such circumstances or conduct.

As to mistake, it is necessary to distinguish between unilateral mistakes that are unknown to the other contracting party and those that are known. Mistakes that are unknown to the other party usually do not affect the binding character of the agreement. A unilateral mistake of which the other contracting party has knowledge or has reason to know makes the contract avoidable by the victim of the mistake.

The deception situation may be one of innocent misrepresentation, nondisclosure, or fraud. A few courts allow recovery of damages. When one party to the contract knows of a fact that has a bearing on the transaction, the failure to volunteer information about that fact to the other contracting party is called *nondisclosure*. The law ordinarily does not attach any significance to nondisclosure. Contrary to this rule, there is a duty to volunteer information when a confidential relationship exists between the possessor of the knowledge and the other contracting party.

When concealment goes beyond mere silence and consists of actively taking steps to hide the truth, the conduct may be classified as fraud. A statement of opinion or value cannot ordinarily be the basis for fraud liability.

The free will of a person, essential to the voluntary character of a contract, may be lacking because the agreement had been obtained by pressure. This may range from undue influence through the array of threats of extreme economic loss (called *economic duress*) to the threat of physical force that would cause serious personal injury or damage to property (called *physical duress*).

When the voluntary character of an agreement has been destroyed by mistake, deception, or pressure, the victim may avoid or rescind the contract or may obtain money damages from the wrongdoer. When the mistake consists of an error in putting an oral contract in writing, either party may ask the court to reform the writing so that it states the parties' actual agreement.

> ## QUESTIONS AND CASE PROBLEMS

1. Lester purchased a used automobile from MacKintosh Motors. He asked the seller if the car had ever been in a wreck. The MacKintosh salesperson had never seen the car before that morning and knew nothing of its history but quickly answered Lester's question by stating: "No. It has never been in a wreck." In fact, the auto had been seriously damaged in a wreck and, although repaired, was worth much less than the value it would have had if there had been no wreck. When Lester learned the truth, he sued MacKintosh Motors and the salesperson for damages for fraud. They raised the defense that the salesperson did not know the statement was false and had not intended to deceive Lester. Did the conduct of the salesperson constitute fraud?

2. Helen, age 17, wanted to buy a Harley-Davidson "Sportster" motorcycle. She did not have the funds to pay cash but persuaded the dealer to

sell the cycle to her on credit. The dealer did so partly because Helen said that she was 22 and showed the dealer an identification card that falsely stated her age as 22. Helen drove the motorcycle away. A few days later, she damaged it and then returned it to the dealer and stated that she disaffirmed the contract because she was a minor. The dealer said that she could not because (1) she had misrepresented her age and (2) the motorcycle was damaged. Can she avoid the contract?

3. Paden signed an agreement dated May 28 to purchase the Murrays' home. The Murrays accepted Paden's offer the following day, and the sale closed on June 27. Paden and his family moved into the home on July 14, 1997. Paden had the home inspected prior to closing. The report listed four minor repairs needed by the home, the cost of which was less than $500. Although these repairs had not been completed at the time of closing, Paden decided to go through with the purchase. After moving into the home, Paden discovered a number of allegedly new defects, including a wooden foundation, electrical problems, and bat infestation. The sales agreement allowed extensive rights to inspect the property. The agreement provided:

> *Buyer . . . shall have the right to enter the property at Buyer's expense and at reasonable times . . . to thoroughly inspect, examine, test, and survey the Property. . . . Buyer shall have the right to request that Seller repair defects in the Property by providing Seller within 12 days from Binding Agreement Date with a copy of inspection report(s) and a written amendment to this agreement setting forth the defects in the report which Buyer requests to be repaired and/or replaced. . . . If Buyer does not timely present the written amendment and inspection report, Buyer shall be deemed to have accepted the Property "as is."*

Paden sued the Murrays for fraudulent concealment and breach of the sales agreement. If Mr. Murray told Paden on May 26 that the house had a concrete foundation, would this be fraud? Decide. [*Paden v Murray,* 523 SE2d 75 (Ga App)]

4. High-Tech Collieries borrowed money from Holland. High-Tech later refused to be bound by the loan contract, claiming the contract was not binding because it had been obtained by duress. The evidence showed that the offer to make the loan was made on a take-it-or-leave-it basis. Was the defense of duress valid? [*Holland v High-Tech Collieries, Inc.,* 911 F Supp 1021 (DC WA)]

5. Thomas Bell, a minor, went to work in the Pittsburgh beauty parlor of Sam Pankas and agreed that when he left the employment, he would not work in or run a beauty parlor business within a 10-mile radius of downtown Pittsburgh for a period of two years. Contrary to this provision, Bell and another employee of Pankas's opened a beauty shop three blocks from Pankas's shop and advertised themselves as Pankas's former employees. Pankas sued Bell to stop the breach of the noncompetition, or restrictive, covenant. Bell claimed that he was not bound because he was a minor when he had agreed to the covenant. Was he bound by the covenant? [*Pankas v Bell,* 198 A2d 312 (Pa)]

6. Aldrich and Co. sold goods to Donovan on credit. The amount owed grew steadily, and finally Aldrich refused to sell any more to Donovan unless Donovan signed a promissory note for the amount due. Donovan did not want to but signed the note because he had no money and needed more goods. When Aldrich brought an action to enforce the note, Donovan claimed that the note was not binding because it had been obtained by economic duress. Was he correct? [*Aldrich & Co. v Donovan,* 778 P2d 397 (Mont)]

7. James Fitl purchased a 1952 Mickey Mantle Topps baseball card from baseball card dealer Mark Strek for $17,750 and placed it in a safe deposit box. Two years later, he had the card appraised, and he was told that the card had been refinished and trimmed, which rendered it valueless. Fitl sued Strek and testified that he had relied on Strek's position as a sports card dealer and on his representations that the baseball card was authentic. Strek contends that Fitl waited too long to give him notice of the defects that would have enabled Strek to contact the person who sold him the card and obtain relief.

Strek asserts that he therefore is not liable. Advise Fitl concerning possible legal theories that apply to his case. How would you decide the case? [See *Fitl v. Strek,* 690 NW2d 605 (Neb)]

8. An agent of Thor Food Service Corp. was seeking to sell Makofske a combination refrigerator-freezer and food purchase plan. Makofske was married and had three children. After being informed of the eating habits of Makofske and his family, the agent stated that the cost of the freezer and food would be about $95 to $100 a month. Makofske carefully examined the agent's itemized estimate and made some changes to it. Makofske then signed the contract and purchased the refrigerator-freezer. The cost proved to be more than the estimated $95 to $100 a month, and Makofske claimed that the contract had been obtained by fraud. Decide. [*Thor Food Service Corp. v Makofske,* 218 NYS2d 93]

9. Blubaugh was a district manager of Schlumberger Well Services. Turner was an executive employee of Schlumberger. Blubaugh was told that he would be fired unless he chose to resign. He was also told that if he would resign and release the company and its employees from all claims for wrongful discharge, he would receive about $5,000 in addition to his regular severance pay of approximately $25,000 and would be given job-relocation counseling. He resigned, signed the release, and received about $40,000 and job counseling. Some time thereafter, he brought an action claiming that he had been wrongfully discharged. He claimed that the release did not protect the defendants because the release had been obtained by economic duress. Were the defendants protected by the release? [*Blubaugh v Turner,* 842 P2d 1072 (Wyo)]

10. Sippy was thinking of buying Christich's house. He noticed watermarks on the ceiling, but the agent showing the house stated that the roof had been repaired and was in good condition. Sippy was not told that the roof still leaked and that the repairs had not been able to stop the leaking. Sippy bought the house. Some time later, heavy rains caused water to leak into the house, and Sippy claimed that Christich was liable for damages. What theory would he rely on? Decide. [*Sippy v Christich,* 609 P2d 204 (Kan App)]

11. Pileggi owed Young money. Young threatened to bring suit against Pileggi for the amount due. Pileggi feared the embarrassment of being sued and the possibility that he might be thrown into bankruptcy. To avoid being sued, Pileggi executed a promissory note to pay Young the amount due. He later asserted that the note was not binding because he had executed it under duress. Is this defense valid? [*Young v Pileggi,* 455 A2d 1228 (Pa Super)]

12. Office Supply Outlet, Inc., a single-store office equipment and supply retailer, ordered 100 model RVX-414 computers from Compuserve, Inc. A new staff member made a clerical error on the order form and ordered a quantity that was far in excess of what Office Supply could sell in a year. Office Supply realized the mistake when the delivery trucks arrived at its warehouse. Its manager called Compuserve and explained that it had intended to order just 10 computers. Compuserve declined to accept the return of the extra machines. Is the contract enforceable? What additional facts would allow the store to avoid the contract for the additional machines?

13. C&J Publishing Co. told a computer salesman that it wanted a computer system that would operate its printing presses. C&J specified that it wanted only new equipment and no used equipment would be acceptable. The seller delivered a system to C&J that was a combination of new and secondhand parts because it did not have sufficient new parts to fill the order. When C&J later learned what had happened, it sued the seller for fraud. The seller contended that no statement or warranty had been made that all parts of the system were new and that it would not therefore be liable for fraud. Decide.

14. The city of Salinas entered into a contract with Souza & McCue Construction Co. to construct a sewer. City officials knew unusual subsoil conditions (including extensive quicksand) existed that would make performance of the contract unusually difficult. This information was not disclosed when city officials advertised for bids. The advertisement for bids directed bidders to examine carefully the site of the work and declared that the submission of a bid would constitute evidence that the bidder had made an

examination. Souza & McCue was awarded the contract, but because of the subsoil conditions, it could not complete on time and was sued by Salinas for breach of contract. Souza & McCue counterclaimed on the basis that the city had not revealed its information on the subsoil conditions and was thus liable for the loss. Was the city liable? [*City of Salinas v Souza & McCue Construction Co.,* 424 P2d 921 (Cal App 3d)]

15. Vern Westby inherited a "ticket" from Anna Sjoblom, a survivor of the sinking of the *Titanic,* which had been pinned to the inside of her coat. He also inherited an album of postcards, some of which related to the *Titanic.* The ticket was a one-of-a-kind item in good condition. Westby needed cash and went to the biggest antique dealer in Tacoma, operated by Alan Gorsuch and his family, doing business as Sanford and Sons, and asked about the value of these items. Westby testified that after Alan Gorsuch examined the ticket, he said, "It's not worth nothing." Westby then inquired about the value of the postcard album, and Gorsuch advised him to come back

later. On Westby's return, Gorsuch told Westby, "It ain't worth nothing." Gorsuch added that he "couldn't fetch $500 for the ticket." Since he needed money, Westby asked if Gorsuch would give him $1,000 for both the ticket and the album, and Gorsuch did so.

Six months later, Gorsuch sold the ticket at a nationally advertised auction for $110,000 and sold most of the postcards for $1,200. Westby sued Gorsuch for fraud. Testimony showed that Gorsuch was a major buyer in antiques and collectibles in the Puget Sound area and that he would have had an understanding of the value of the ticket. Gorsuch contends that all elements of fraud are not present since there was no evidence that Gorsuch intended that Westby rely on the alleged representations, nor did Westby rely on such. Rather, Gorsuch asserts, it was an arm's-length transaction and Westby had access to the same information as Gorsuch. Decide. [*Westby v Gorsuch,* 112 Wash App 558 (2002)]

> CPA QUESTIONS

1. A building subcontractor submitted a bid for construction of a portion of a high-rise office building. The bid contained material computational errors. The general contractor accepted the bid with knowledge of the errors. Which of the following statements best represents the subcontractor's liability?

   a. Not liable, because the contractor knew of the errors
   b. Not liable, because the errors were a result of gross negligence
   c. Liable, because the errors were unilateral
   d. Liable, because the errors were material
      (5/95, Law, #17, 5351)

2. Egan, a minor, contracted with Baker to purchase Baker's used computer for $400. The computer was purchased for Egan's personal use. The

agreement provided that Egan would pay $200 down on delivery and $200 thirty days later. Egan took delivery and paid the $200 down payment. Twenty days later, the computer was damaged seriously as a result of Egan's negligence. Five days after the damage occurred and one day after Egan reached the age of majority, Egan attempted to disaffirm the contract with Baker. Egan will

   a. Be able to disaffirm despite the fact that Egan was *not* a minor at the time of disaffirmance
   b. Be able to disaffirm only if Egan does so in writing
   c. Not be able to disaffirm because Egan had failed to pay the balance of the purchase price
   d. Not be able to disaffirm because the computer was damaged as a result of Egan's negligence
      (11/93, Law, #21, 4318)

CONSIDERATION

A GENERAL PRINCIPLES
1. CONSIDERATION DEFINED AND EXPLAINED
2. GIFTS
3. ADEQUACY OF CONSIDERATION
4. FORBEARANCE AS CONSIDERATION
5. ILLUSORY PROMISES
6. THIRD PARTIES

B SPECIAL SITUATIONS
7. PREEXISTING LEGAL OBLIGATION
8. PAST CONSIDERATION
9. MORAL OBLIGATION

C EXCEPTIONS TO THE LAWS OF CONSIDERATION
10. EXCEPTIONS TO CONSIDERATION

LEARNING OBJECTIVES

After studying this chapter, you should be able to

LO.1 Explain what constitutes consideration

LO.2 State the effect of the absence of consideration

LO.3 Identify promises that can serve as consideration

LO.4 Distinguish between present consideration and past consideration

LO.5 State when forbearance can be consideration

LO.6 Recognize situations in which adequacy of consideration has significance

LO.7 List the exceptions to the requirement of consideration

Will the law enforce every promise? Generally, a promise will not be enforced unless something is given or received for the promise.

 ## GENERAL PRINCIPLES

As a general rule, one of the elements needed to make an agreement binding is consideration.

1. CONSIDERATION DEFINED AND EXPLAINED

consideration promise or performance that the promisor demands as the price of the promise.

Consideration is what each party to a contract gives up to the other in making their agreement.

(a) BARGAINED-FOR EXCHANGE   *Consideration* is the bargained-for exchange between the parties to a contract. In order for consideration to exist, something of value must be given or promised in return for the performance or promise of performance of the other.[1] The value given or promised can be money, services, property, or the forbearance of a legal right.

For Example, Beth offers to pay Kerry $100 for her used skis, and Kerry accepts. Beth has promised something of value, $100, as consideration for Kerry's promise to sell the skis, and Kerry has promised Beth something of value, the skis, as consideration for the $100. If Kerry offered to *give* Beth the used skis and Beth accepted, these parties would have an agreement but not an enforceable contract because Beth did not provide any consideration in exchange for Kerry's promise of the skis. There was no *bargained-for exchange* because Kerry was not promised anything of value from Beth.

(b) BENEFIT-DETRIMENT APPROACH   Some jurisdictions analyze consideration from the point of view of a *benefit-detriment approach,* defining *consideration* as a benefit received by the promisor or a detriment incurred by the promisee.

As an example of a unilateral contract analyzed from a benefit-detriment approach to consideration, Mr. Scully, a longtime summer resident of Falmouth, states to George Corfu, a college senior, "I will pay you $3,000 if you paint my summer home." George in fact paints the house. The work of painting the house by George, the promisee, was a legal detriment to him. Also, the painting of the house was a legal benefit to Scully, the promisor. There was consideration in this case, and the agreement is enforceable.

2. GIFTS

Promises to make a gift are unenforceable promises under the law of contracts because of lack of consideration, as illustrated previously in the scenario of Kerry promising to give her used skis to Beth without charge. There was no bargained-for exchange because Kerry was not promised anything of value from Beth. A completed gift, however, cannot be rescinded for lack of consideration.[2]

Charitable subscriptions by which individuals make pledges to finance the construction of a college building, a church, or another structure for charitable purposes are binding to the extent that the donor (promisor) should have reasonably realized

[1] *Brooksbank v Anderson,* 586 NW2d 789 (Minn App 1998).
[2] *Homes v O'Bryant,* 741 So 2d 366 (Miss App 1999).

that the charity was relying on the promise in undertaking the building program. Some states require proof that the charity has relied on the subscription.[3]

CASE SUMMARY

You Can't Back Out Now

FACTS: Salsbury was attempting to establish a new college, Charles City College. Salsbury obtained a pledge from Northwestern Bell Telephone Company to contribute to the college. When the company did not pay, Salsbury sued the company. The company raised the defense that there was no consideration for its promise and that nothing had been done by the college in reliance on the promise.

DECISION: Judgment for Salsbury. As a matter of public policy, a promise of a charitable contribution is binding even though there is no consideration for the promise and without regard for whether the charity had done any acts in reliance on the promise. The company was therefore liable on its promise to contribute. [**Salsbury v Northwestern Bell Telephone Co., 221 NW2d 609 (Iowa 1974)**]

3. ADEQUACY OF CONSIDERATION

Ordinarily, courts do not consider the adequacy of the consideration given for a promise. The fact that the consideration supplied by one party is slight when compared with the burden undertaken by the other party is immaterial. It is a matter for the parties to decide when they make their contract whether each is getting a fair return. In the absence of fraud or other misconduct, courts usually will not interfere to make sure that each side is getting a fair return.

CASE SUMMARY

Who's to Say?

FACTS: On the death of their aunt, a brother and sister became the owners of shares of stock of several corporations. They made an agreement to divide these shares equally between them, although the sister's shares had a value approximately seven times those of the brother. The brother died before the shares were divided. The sister then claimed that the agreement to divide was not binding because the consideration for her promise was not adequate.

DECISION: The value of stock cannot be determined precisely. It may change with time. In addition, the value that one person may see can be different than that seen by another. The court therefore will not make a comparison of the value that each party was to receive under the agreement. It was sufficient that a promise was exchanged for a promise. The adequacy of the consideration would not be examined. This sister was therefore bound by her promise to divide the shares. [**Emberson v Hartley 762 P2d 364 (Wash App 1988)**]

Because the adequacy of consideration is ignored, it is immaterial that consideration is so slight that the transaction is in part a "gift." However, the Internal Revenue

---

[3] *King v Trustees of Boston University*, 647 NE2d 1176 (Ma 1995).

Service may view a given transaction as part consideration, part gift, and assess a gift tax as appropriate.

The fact that the consideration turns out to be disappointing does not affect the binding character of the contract. Thus, the fact that a business purchased by a group of investors proves unprofitable does not constitute a failure of consideration that releases the buyers from their obligation to the seller.

CASE SUMMARY

Expectations versus Consideration

FACTS: Aqua Drilling Company made a contract to drill a well for the Atlas Construction Company. It was expected that this would supply water for a home being constructed by Atlas. Aqua did not make any guarantee or warranty that water would be produced. Aqua drilled the well exactly as required by the contract, but no water was produced. Atlas refused to pay. It asserted that the contract was not binding on the theory that there had been a failure of consideration because the well did not produce water.

DECISION: The contract was binding. Atlas obtained the exact performance required by the contract. While Atlas had expected that water would be obtained, Aqua did not make any guarantee or warranty that this would be so. Hence, there was no failure of consideration. [Atlas Construction Co., Inc. v Aqua Drilling Co., 559 P2d 39 (Wyo 1977)]

4. FORBEARANCE AS CONSIDERATION

forbearance refraining from doing an act.

In most cases, consideration consists of the performance of an act such as providing a service, or the making of a promise to provide a service or goods, or paying money.[4] Consideration may also consist of **forbearance**, which is refraining from doing an act that an individual has a legal right to do, or it may consist of a promise of forbearance. In other words, the promisor may desire to buy the inaction or a promise of inaction of the other party.

The giving up of any legal right can be consideration for the promise of the other party to a contract. Thus, the relinquishment of a right to sue for damages will support a promise for the payment of money given in return for the promise to relinquish the right, if such is the agreement of the parties.

The promise of a creditor to forbear collecting a debt is consideration for the promise of the debtor to modify the terms of the transaction.

5. ILLUSORY PROMISES

illusory promise promise that in fact does not impose any obligation on the promisor.

In a bilateral contract, each party makes a promise to the other. For a bilateral contract to be enforceable, there must be *mutuality of obligation*. That is, both parties must have created obligations to the other in their respective promises. If one party's promise contains either no obligation or only an apparent obligation to the other, this promise is an **illusory promise**. The party making such a promise is not bound because he or she has made no real promise. The effect is that the other party, who has

---

[4] *Prenger v Baumhoer*, 914 SW2d 413 (Mo App 1996).

made a real promise, is also not bound because he or she has received no consideration. It is said that the contract fails for lack of mutuality.

For Example, Mountain Coal Company promises to sell Midwest Power Company all the coal it may order for $48 per ton for the year 2006, and Midwest Power agrees to pay $48 for any coal it orders from Mountain Coal. Mountain Coal in its promise to Midwest Power has obligated itself to supply all coal ordered at a stated price. However, Midwest Power's promise did not obligate it to buy any coal whatsoever from Mountain Coal (note that it was not a requirements contract). Because Midwest has no obligation to Mountain Coal under its promise, there is no mutuality of obligation, and Midwest cannot enforce Mountain Coal's promise when the market price of coal goes to $55 a ton in the winter of 2006 as the result of severe weather conditions.

Consider as well the example of the Jacksonville Fire soccer team's contract with Brazilian soccer star Edmundo. Edmundo signed a contract to play for the Jacksonville franchise of the new International Soccer League for five years at $25 million. The extensive document signed by Edmundo set forth the details of the team's financial commitment and the details of Edmundo's obligations to the team and its fans. On page 4 of the document, the team inserted a clause reserving the right "to terminate the contract and team obligations at any time in its sole discretion." During the season, Edmundo received a $40 million five-year offer to play for Manchester United of the English Premier League, which he accepted. Because Jacksonville had a free way out of its obligation by the unrestricted cancellation provision in the contract, it thus made its promises to Edmundo illusory. Edmundo was not bound by the Jacksonville contract as a result of a lack of mutuality and was free to sign with Manchester United.

(a) Cancellation Provisions Although a promise must impose a binding obligation, it may authorize a party to cancel the agreement under certain circumstances on giving notice by a certain date. Such a provision does not make this party's promise illusory, for the party does not have a free way out and is limited to living up to the terms of the **cancellation provision. For Example,** actress Zsa Zsa Gabor made a contract with Hollywood Fantasy Corporation to appear at a fantasy vacation in San Antonio, Texas, on May 2–4, for a $10,000 appearance fee plus itemized (extravagant) expenses. The last paragraph of the agreement stated: "It is agreed that if a significant acting opportunity in a film comes up, Ms. Gabor will have the right to cancel her appearance in San Antonio by advising Hollywood Fantasy in writing by April 15, 1991." Ms. Gabor sent a telegram on April 15, 1991, canceling her appearance. During the May 2 through 4 period, Ms. Gabor's only acting activity was a 14-second cameo role during the opening credits of *Naked Gun 2½*. In a lawsuit for breach of contract that followed, the jury saw this portion of the movie and concluded that Ms. Gabor had not canceled her obligation on the basis of a "significant acting opportunity," and she was held liable for breach of contract.[5]

(b) Conditional Promises A *conditional promise* is a promise that depends on the occurrence of a specified condition in order for the promise to be binding. **For Example,** Mary Sparks, in contemplation of her signing a lease to take over a restaurant at Marina Bay, wanted to make certain that she had a highly qualified

cancellation provision
crossing out of a part of an instrument or a destruction of all legal effect of the instrument, whether by act of party, upon breach by the other party, or pursuant to agreement or decree of court.

---

5 *Hollywood Fantasy Corp. v Gabor*, 151 F2d 203 (5th Cir 1998).

chef to run the restaurant's food service. She made a contract with John "Grumpy" White to serve as executive chef for a one-year period at a salary of $150,000. The contract set forth White's responsibilities and was conditioned on the successful negotiation of the restaurant lease with Marina Bay Management. Both parties signed it. Although the happening of the condition was within Mary's control because she could avoid the contract with Grumpy White by not acquiring the restaurant lease, she limited her future options by the contract with White. Her promise to White was not illusory because after signing the contract with him, if she acquired the restaurant lease, she was bound to hire White as her executive chef. Before signing the contract with White, she was free to sign any chef for the position. The contract was enforceable.

6. THIRD PARTIES

Because consideration is the price paid for each promise in a bilateral contract, it is unimportant who pays the price as long as it has been agreed that it should be paid in that manner. When a creditor releases a third person in consideration of the promise of another person to pay the debt of the released person, the fact that the promisor did not receive a direct benefit is immaterial. The obtaining of the release of the third person as desired was consideration for the promise to pay the debt.[6]

 ## SPECIAL SITUATIONS

The following sections analyze certain common situations in which a lawsuit turns on whether the promisor received consideration for the promise sued on.

7. PREEXISTING LEGAL OBLIGATION

Ordinarily, doing or promising to do what one is already under a legal obligation to do is not consideration.[7] Similarly, a promise to refrain from doing what one has no legal right to do is not consideration. This preexisting duty or legal obligation can be based on statute, on general principles of law, on responsibilities of an office held, or on a preexisting contract.

For Example, Officer Mary Rodgers is an undercover police officer in the city of Pasadena, California. Officer Rodgers promised Elwood Farnsworth that she would diligently patrol the area of the Farnsworth estate on weekends to keep down the noise and drinking of rowdy young persons who gathered in this area, and Mr. Farnsworth promised to provide a $500 per month gratuity for this extra service. Farnsworth's promise is unenforceable because Officer Rodgers has a preexisting official duty as a police officer to protect citizens and enforce the antinoise and public drinking ordinances.

 (a) COMPLETION OF CONTRACT Suppose that a contractor refuses to complete a building unless the owner promises a payment or bonus in addition to the sum specified in the original contract, and the owner promises to make that payment. The question then arises as to whether the owner's promise is binding. Most courts hold that the second promise of the owner is without consideration.

---

[6] *First Union Bank of Georgia v Gurley*, 431 SE2d 379 (Ga App 1993).
[7] *Gardiner, Kamya & Associates v Jackson*, 369 F3d 1318 (Fed Cir 2004).

CASE SUMMARY

You're Already Under Contract

FACTS: Crookham & Vessels had a contract to build an extension of a railroad for the Little Rock Port Authority. It made a contract with Larry Moyer Trucking to dig drainage ditches. The ditch walls collapsed because water would not drain off. This required that the ditches be dug over again. Larry Moyer refused to do this unless extra money was paid. Crookham & Vessels agreed to pay the additional compensation, but after the work was done, it refused to pay. Larry Moyer sued for the extra compensation promised.

DECISION: Judgment against Moyer. Moyer was bound by its contract to dig the drainage ditches. Its promise to perform that obligation was not consideration for the promise of Crookham & Vessels to pay additional compensation. Performance of an obligation is not consideration for a promise by a party entitled to that performance. The fact that performance of the contract proved more difficult or costly than originally contemplated does not justify making an exception to this rule. [**Crookham & Vessels, Inc. v Larry Moyer Trucking, Inc., 699 SW2d 414 (Ark App 1985)**]

If the promise of the contractor is to do something that is not part of the first contract, then the promise of the other party is binding. **For Example,** if a bonus of $5,000 is promised in return for the promise of a contractor to complete the building at a date earlier than that specified in the original agreement, the promise to pay the bonus is binding.

CPA   *(1) Good-Faith Adjustment.*   A current trend is to enforce a second promise to pay a contractor a higher amount for the performance of the original contract when there are extraordinary circumstances caused by unforeseeable difficulties and when the additional amount promised the contractor is reasonable under the circumstances.

(2) Contract for Sale of Goods.   When the contract is for the sale of goods, any modification made in good faith by the parties to the contract is binding without regard to the existence of consideration for the modification.

CPA   **(b) Compromise and Release of Claims**   The rule that doing or promising to do what one is already legally bound to do is not consideration applies to a part payment made in satisfaction of an admitted or *liquidated debt.* Thus, a promise to pay part of an amount that is admittedly owed is not consideration for a promise to discharge the balance. It will not prevent the creditor from demanding the remainder later. **For Example,** John owes Mark $100,000, which was due on March 1, 2006. On March 15, John offers to pay back $80,000 if Mark will agree to accept this amount as the discharge of the full amount owed. Mark agrees to this proposal, and it is set forth in writing signed by the parties. However, Mark later sues for the $20,000 balance. Mark will be successful in the lawsuit because John's payment of the $80,000 is not consideration for Mark's promise to discharge the full amount owed because John was doing only what he had a preexisting legal duty to do.

If the debtor pays the part payment before the debt is due, there is consideration because, on the day when the payment was made, the creditor was not entitled to demand any payment. Likewise, if the creditor accepts some article (even of slight value) in addition to the part payment, consideration exists.

A debtor and creditor may have a bona fide dispute over the amount owed or whether any amount is owed. Such is called an *unliquidated debt*. In this case, payment by the debtor of less than the amount claimed by the creditor is consideration for the latter's agreement to release or settle the claim. It is generally regarded as sufficient if the claimant believes in the merit of the claim.[8]

(c) PART-PAYMENT CHECKS When there is a good-faith dispute about the amount of a debt and the debtor tenders a check that states on its face "paid in full" and references the transaction in dispute, but the amount of the check is less than the full amount the creditor asserts is owed, the cashing of the check by the creditor discharges the entire debt.

composition of creditors
agreement among creditors that each shall accept a part payment as full payment in consideration of the other creditors doing the same.

(d) COMPOSITION OF CREDITORS In a **composition of creditors**, the various creditors of one debtor mutually agree to accept a fractional part of their claims in full satisfaction of the claims. Such agreements are binding and are supported by consideration. When creditors agree to extend the due date of their debts, the promise of each creditor to forbear is likewise consideration for the promise of other creditors to forbear.

8. PAST CONSIDERATION

past consideration
something that has been performed in the past and which, therefore, cannot be consideration for a promise made in the present.

A promise based on a party's past performance lacks consideration.[9] It is said that **past consideration** is no consideration. **For Example,** Fred O'Neal came up with the idea for the formation of the new community bank of Villa Rica and was active in its formation. Just prior to the execution of the documents creating the bank, the organizers discussed that once the bank was formed, it would hire O'Neal, giving him a three-year contract at $65,000 the first year, $67,000 the second year, and $70,000 the third. In a lawsuit against the bank for breach of contract, O'Neal testified that the consideration he gave in exchange for the three-year contract was his past effort to organize the bank. The court stated that past consideration generally will not support a subsequent promise and that the purported consideration was not rendered to the bank, which had not yet been established when his promotion and organization work took place.[10] The presence of a bargained-for exchange is not present when a promise is made in exchange for a past benefit.

9. MORAL OBLIGATION

In most states, promises made to another based on "moral obligation" lack consideration and are not enforceable.[11] They are considered gratuitous promises and unenforceable. **For Example,** while on a fishing trip, Tom Snyder, a person of moderate means, met an elderly couple living in near-destitute conditions in a rural area of Texas. He returned to the area often, and he regularly purchased groceries for the couple and paid for their medical needs. Some two years later, the couple's son,

---

[8] *F. H. Prince & Co. v Towers Financial Corp.,* 656 NE2d 142 (Ill App 1995).

[9] *Smith v Locklear,* 906 So2d 1273 (Fla App 2005).

[10] *O'Neal v Home Town Bank of Villa Rica,* 514 SE2d 669 (Ga App 1999).

[11] *Production Credit Ass'n of Manaan v Rub,* 475 NW2d 532 (ND 1991). As to the Louisiana rule of moral consideration, see *Thomas v Bryant,* 596 So 2d 1065 (La App 1992).

ETHICS & THE LAW

Alan Fulkins, who owns a construction company that specializes in single-family residences, is constructing a small subdivision with 23 homes. Tretorn Plumbing, owned by Jason Tretorn, was awarded the contract for the plumbing work on the homes at a price of $4,300 per home.

Plumbing contractors complete their residential projects in three phases. Phase one consists of digging the lines for the plumbing and installing the pipes that are placed in the foundation of the house. Phase two consists of installing the pipes within the walls of the home, and phase three is installing of the surface plumbing, such as sinks and tubs. However, industry practice dictates that the plumbing contractor receive one-half of the contract amount after completion of phase one.

Tretorn completed the digs of phase one for Fulkins and received payment of $2,150. Tretorn then went to Fulkins and demanded an additional $600 per house to complete the work. Fulkins said, "But you already have a contract for $4,300!" Tretorn responded, "I know, but the costs are killing me. I need the additional $600."

Fulkins explained the hardship of the demand, "Look, I've already paid you half. If I hire someone else, I'll have to pay them two-thirds for the work not done. It'll cost me $5,000 per house."

Tretorn responded, "Exactly. I'm a bargain because the additional $600 I want only puts you at $4,900. If you don't pay it, I'll just lien the houses and then you'll be stuck without a way to close the sales. I've got the contract all drawn up. Just sign it and everything goes smoothly."

Should Fulkins sign the agreement? Does Tretorn have the right to the additional $600? Was it ethical for Tretorn to demand the $600? Is there any legal advice you can offer Fulkins?

David, discovered what Tom had been doing and promised to reimburse Snyder for what he had furnished his parents. This promise, based on a moral obligation, is unenforceable. A "past consideration" analysis also renders David's promise as unenforceable.

 ## EXCEPTIONS TO THE LAWS OF CONSIDERATION

The ever-changing character of law clearly appears in the area of consideration as part of the developing law of contracts.

10. EXCEPTIONS TO CONSIDERATION

By statute or decision, traditional consideration is not required in the following situations.

(a) CHARITABLE SUBSCRIPTIONS   Where individuals made pledges to finance the construction of buildings for charitable purposes, consideration is lacking according to

FIGURE 15-1   *Consideration and Promises*

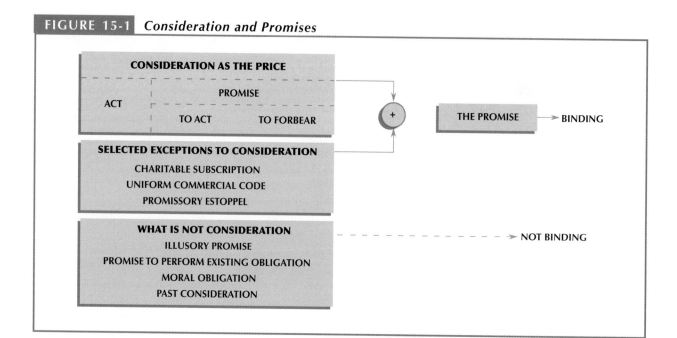

technical standards applied in ordinary contract cases. For public policy reasons, the reliance of the charity on the pledge in undertaking the project is deemed a substitute for consideration.

(b) Uniform Commercial Code   In a number of situations, the Uniform Commercial Code abolishes the requirement of consideration. **For Example,** under the Code, consideration is not required for (1) a merchant's written, firm offer for goods stated to be irrevocable, (2) a written discharge of a claim for an alleged breach of a commercial contract, or (3) an agreement to modify a contract for the sale of goods.[12]

promissory estoppel
doctrine that a promise will
be enforced although it is
not supported by
consideration when the
promisor should have
reasonably expected that the
promise would induce
action or forbearance of a
definite and substantial
character on the part of the
promised and injustice can
be avoided only by
enforcement of the promise.

(c) Promissory Estoppel   Under the doctrine of **promissory estoppel**, a promisor may be prevented from asserting that her promise is unenforceable because the promisee gave no consideration for the promise. This doctrine, sometimes called the *doctrine of detrimental reliance,* is applicable when (1) the promisor makes a promise that lacks consideration, (2) the promisor intends or should reasonably expect that the promisee will rely on the promise, (3) the promisee in fact relies on the promise in some definite and substantial manner, and (4) enforcement of the promise is the only way to avoid injustice.[13]

Legal difficulties often arise because parties take certain things for granted. Frequently, they will be sure that they have agreed to everything and that they have a valid contract. Sometimes, however, they do not. The courts are then faced with the problem of leaving them with their broken dreams or coming to their rescue when promissory estoppel can be established.

---

[12] UCC § 2-209(1).

[13] *Neuhoff v Marvin Lumber and Cedar Co.,* 370 F3d 197 (1st Cir 2004).

CASE SUMMARY

Brits Rescued by Promissory Estoppel

FACTS: Portman Lamborghini, Ltd. (Portman), was owned by Chaplake Holdings, Ltd., a United Kingdom company, which was owned by David Jolliffe and David Lakeman as equal shareholders. Between 1984 and 1987, Portman sold approximately 30 new Lamborghinis each year through its exclusive concession contract with the car maker. It was then the largest Lamborghini dealer in the world since Lamborghini's production was just 250 cars per year. These cars sold at a retail price between $200,000 and $300,000. In 1987, Chrysler Corporation bought Lamborghini, and its chairman, Lee Iacocca, presented a plan to escalate production to 5,000 units within five years. The plan included the introduction of a new model, the P140, with a retail price of $70,000. Between 1987 and 1991, *all* of the Chrysler/Lamborghini top executives with whom Jolliffe and Lakeman and their top advisors came in contact provided the same message to them: Chrysler was committed to the Expansion Plan, and in order for Portman to retain its exclusive U.K. market, it must expand its operational capacity from 35 cars in 1987 to 400 cars by 1992. Accordingly, Portman acquired additional financing, staff, and facilities and built a new distribution center. An economic downturn in the United States and major development and production problems at Lamborghini led Chrysler to reduce its expansion investment by two-thirds. Factory production delays eroded Portman's profitability and success, and it entered into receivership in April 1992. Suit was brought on behalf of the Portman and Chaplake entities on a promissory estoppel theory against Chrysler, a Delaware corporation.

DECISION: Judgment for Portman and Chaplake on the promissory estoppel theory. (1) A promise was made by Chrysler that the Lamborghini line would expand tenfold and that Portman would retain its exclusivity deal *only* if it expanded its operational capacity. (2) The promisor, Chrysler, should have reasonably expected that Portman would rely on this promise. (3) Lakeman and Jolliffe were given the same message and promise by *all* of the top executives involved, and it was therefore not unreasonable for them to rely upon the promises made by these executives and to undertake the detriment of major expansion activity that would have been unnecessary but for the Expansion Plan and the role they were promised. (4) The prevention of injustice is the "fundamental idea" underlying the doctrine of promissory estoppel, and injustice can be avoided in this case only by the enforcement of Chrysler's promise. Portman is entitled to £ 569,321 for its costs to implement its Expansion Plan, and Chaplake is entitled to £ 462,686 for its investment in Portman's expansion. **[Chrysler Corp. v Chaplake Holdings, Ltd., 822 A2d 1024 (Del 2003)]**

LAWFLIX

Baby Boom (1987) (PG)

Review the scene near the end of the movie when Diane Keaton is presented with an offer for the purchase of her company, Country Baby. List the elements of consideration that Food Giant is paying for the company. Explain what Ms. Keaton's consideration is in exchange.

For movie clips that illustrate business law concepts, see LawFlix at **http://wdvl.westbuslaw.com.**

> SUMMARY

A promise is not binding if there is no consideration for the promise. Consideration is what the promisor requires as the price for his promise. That price may be doing an act, refraining from the doing of an act, or merely promising to do or to refrain. In a bilateral contract, it is necessary to find that the promise of each party is supported by consideration. If either promise is not so supported, it is not binding, and the agreement of the parties is not a contract. Consequently, the agreement cannot be enforced. When a promise is the consideration, it must be a binding promise. The binding character of a promise is not affected by the circumstance that there is a condition precedent to the performance promised. Likewise, the binding character of the promise and of the contract is not affected by a provision in the contract for its cancellation by either one or both of the parties. A promise to do what one is already obligated to do is not consideration, although some exceptions are made. Such exceptions include the rendering of a partial performance or a modified performance accepted as a good-faith adjustment to a changed situation, a compromise and release of claims, a part-payment check, and a compromise of creditors. Because consideration is the price that is given to obtain the promise, past benefits conferred on the promisor cannot be consideration. In the case of a complex transaction, however, the past benefit and the subsequent transaction relating to the promise may have been intended by the parties as one transaction. In such a case, the earlier benefit is not past consideration but is the consideration contemplated by the promisor as the price for the promise subsequently made.

A promise to refrain from doing an act can be consideration. A promise to refrain from suing or asserting a particular claim can be consideration. Generally, the promise to forbear must be for a specified time, as distinguished from agreeing to forbear at will. When consideration is forbearance to assert a claim, it is immaterial whether the claim is valid as long as the claim has been asserted in the good-faith belief that it was valid.

When the promisor obtains the consideration specified for the promise, the law is not ordinarily concerned with the value or adequacy of that consideration. Exceptions are sometimes made in the case of fraud or unconscionability and under consumer protection statutes.

When the promisor does not actually receive the price promised for the promise, there is a failure of consideration, which constitutes a breach of the contract.

> QUESTIONS AND CASE PROBLEMS

1. Sarah's house caught on fire. Through the prompt assistance of her neighbor Odessa, the fire was quickly extinguished. In gratitude, Sarah promised to pay Odessa $1,000. Can Odessa enforce this promise?

2. William E. Story agreed to pay his nephew, William E. Story II, a large sum of money (roughly equivalent to $50,000 in 2007 dollars) "if he would refrain from drinking liquor, using tobacco, swearing, and playing cards or billiards for money until he should come to be 21 years of age." William II had been using tobacco and occasionally drank liquor but refrained from using these stimulants over several years until he was 21 and also lived up to the other requirements of his uncle's offer. Just after William II's 21st birthday, Story acknowledged that William II had fulfilled his part of the bargain and advised that the money would be invested for him with interest. Story died, and his executor, Sidway, refused to pay William II because he believed the contract between Story and William II was without consideration. Sidway asserted that Story received no benefit from William II's performance and William II suffered no detriment (in fact, by his refraining from the use of liquor and tobacco, William II was not harmed but benefited, Sidway asserted). Is there any theory of consideration that William II can rely on? How would you decide this case? [*Hamer v Sidway*, 124 NY 538]

3. Dale Dyer, who was employed by National By-Products, Inc., was seriously injured at work as the result of a job-related accident. He agreed to give up his right to sue the employer for

damages in consideration of the employer's giving him a lifetime job. The employer later claimed that this agreement was not binding because Dyer's promise not to sue could not be consideration for the promise to employ on the ground that Dyer in fact had no right to sue. Dyer's only remedy was to make a claim under workers' compensation. Was the agreement binding? [*Dyer v National By-Products, Inc.,* 380 NW2d 732 (Iowa)]

4. Charles Sanarwari retained Stan Gissel to prepare his income tax return for the year 2006. The parties agreed on a fee of $400. Charles had done a rough estimate based on last year's return and believed he would owe the IRS approximately $2,000. When Stan's work was completed, it turned out that Charles would receive a $2,321 tax refund. Stan explained how certain legitimate advantages were used to reduce Charles's tax obligation. Charles paid for Stan's services and was so pleased with the work that he promised to pay Stan an additional $400 for the excellent job on the tax return when he received his tax refund. Thereafter, Stan and Charles had a falling out over a golf tournament where Charles was late for his tee time and Stan started without him, causing Charles to lose an opportunity to win the club championship. Stan was not paid the $400 promised for doing an excellent job on the tax return, and he sued Charles as a matter of principle. Decide.

5. Koedding hired West Roofers to put a roof on her house. She later claimed that the roofing job was defective, and she threatened to sue West. Both parties discussed the matter in good faith. Finally, West guaranteed that the roof would be free from leaks for 20 years in return for the guarantee by Koedding not to sue West for damages. The roof leaked the next year, and Koedding sued West on the guarantee. West claimed that the guarantee was not binding because there was no consideration for it. According to West, Koedding's promise not to sue had no value because Koedding did not have any valid claim against West; therefore, she was not entitled to sue. Was this defense valid?

6. Fedun rented a building to Gomer, who did business under the name of Mike's Cafe. Later,

Gomer was about to sell the business to Brown and requested Fedun to release him from his liability under the lease. Fedun agreed to do so. Brown sold the business shortly thereafter. The balance of the rent due by Gomer under the original lease agreement was not paid, and Fedun sued Gomer on the rent claim. Could he collect after having released Gomer? [*Fedun v Mike's Cafe,* 204 A2d 776 (Pa Super)]

7. Alexander Proudfoot Co. was in the business of devising efficiency systems for industry. It told Sanitary Linen Service Co. that it could provide an improved system for Sanitary Linen that would save Sanitary Linen money. It made a contract with Sanitary Linen to provide a money-saving system. The system was put into operation, and Proudfoot was paid the amount due under the contract. The system failed to work and did not save money. Sanitary Linen sued to get the money back. Was it entitled to do so? [*Sanitary Linen Service Co. v Alexander Proudfoot Co.,* 435 F2d 292 (5th Cir)]

8. Sears, Roebuck and Co. promised to give Forrer permanent employment. Forrer sold his farm at a loss to take the job. Shortly after beginning work, he was discharged by Sears, which claimed that the contract could be terminated at will. Forrer claimed that promissory estoppel prevented Sears from terminating the contract. Was he correct? [*Forrer v Sears, Roebuck & Co.,* 153 NW2d 587 (Wis)]

9. Kemp leased a gas filling station from Baehr. Kemp, who was heavily indebted to Penn-O-Tex Oil Corp., transferred to it his right to receive payments on all claims. When Baehr complained that the rent was not paid, he was assured by the corporation that the rent would be paid to him. Baehr did not sue Kemp for the overdue rent but later sued the corporation. The defense was raised that there was no consideration for the promise of the corporation. Decide. [*Baehr v Penn-O-Tex Corp.,* 104 NW2d 661 (Minn)]

10. Bogart owed several debts to Security Bank & Trust Co. and applied to the bank for a loan to pay the debts. The bank's employee stated that he would take the application for the loan to the loan committee and "within two or three days, we ought to have something here, ready for you

to go with." The loan was not made. The bank sued Bogart for his debts. He filed a counterclaim on the theory that the bank had broken its contract to make a loan to him and that promissory estoppel prevented the bank from going back on what the employee had said. Was this counterclaim valid?

11. Kelsoe worked for International Wood Products, Inc., for a number of years. One day Hernandez, a director and major stockholder of the company, promised Kelsoe that the corporation would give her 5 percent of the company's stock. This promise was never kept, and Kelsoe sued International for breach of contract. Had the company broken its contract? [*Kelsoe v International Wood Products, Inc.,* 588 So 2d 877 (Ala)]

12. Kathy left her classic 1978 Volkswagen convertible at Freddie's Service Station, requesting a "tune-up." When she returned that evening, Freddie's bill was $374. Kathy stated that Firestone and Sears advertise tune-ups for $70, and she asked Freddie, "How can you justify this bill?" Freddie responded, "Carburetor work." Kathy refused to pay the bill and left. That evening, when the station closed, she took her other set of keys and removed her car, after placing a check in the station's mail slot. The check was made out to Freddie's Service Station for $200 and stated on its face: "This check is in full payment of my account with you regarding the tune-up today on my 1978 Volkswagen convertible." Freddie cashed the check in order to meet his business expenses and then sued Kathy for the difference owed. What result?

13. On the death of their mother, the children of Jane Smith gave their interests in their mother's estate to their father in consideration of his payment of $1 to each of them and his promise to leave them the property on his death. The father died without leaving them the property. The children sued their father's second wife to obtain the property in accordance with the agreement. The second wife claimed that the agreement was not a binding contract because the amount of $1 and future gifts given for the children's interests were so trivial and uncertain. Decide.

14. Radio Station KSCS broadcast a popular music program. It announced that it would pay $25,000 to any listener who detected that it did not play three consecutive songs. Steve Jennings listened to and heard a program in which two songs were followed by a commercial program. He claimed the $25,000. The station refused to pay on the ground that there was no consideration for its promise to pay that amount. Was the station liable? [*Jennings v Radio Station KSCS,* 708 SW2d 60 (Tex App)]

15. Hoffman wanted to acquire a franchise for a Red Owl grocery store. (Red Owl was a corporation that maintained a system of chain stores.) An agent of Red Owl informed Hoffman and his wife that if they would sell their bakery in Wautoma, acquire a certain tract of land in Chilton (another Wisconsin city), and put up $6,000, they would be given a franchise. In reliance on the agent's promise, Hoffman sold his business and acquired the land in Chilton, but he was never granted a franchise. He and his wife sued Red Owl. Red Owl raised the defense that there had been only an assurance that Hoffman would receive a franchise, but because there was no promise supported by consideration, there was no binding contract to give him a franchise. Decide. [*Hoffman v Red Owl Stores, Inc.,* 133 NW2d 267 (Wis)]

LEGALITY AND
PUBLIC POLICY

CHAPTER
(16)

(A) GENERAL PRINCIPLES
1. EFFECT OF ILLEGALITY
2. EXCEPTIONS TO EFFECT OF ILLEGALITY
3. PARTIAL ILLEGALITY
4. CRIMES AND CIVIL WRONGS
5. GOOD FAITH AND FAIRNESS
6. UNCONSCIONABLE CLAUSES

(B) AGREEMENTS AFFECTING PUBLIC WELFARE
7. AGREEMENTS CONTRARY TO PUBLIC POLICY
8. GAMBLING, WAGERS, AND LOTTERIES

(C) REGULATION OF BUSINESS
9. EFFECT OF VIOLATION
10. STATUTORY REGULATION OF CONTRACTS
11. LICENSED CALLINGS OR DEALINGS
12. CONTRACTS IN RESTRAINT OF TRADE
13. AGREEMENTS NOT TO COMPETE
14. USURIOUS AGREEMENTS

LEARNING OBJECTIVES

After studying this chapter, you should be able to

LO.1 State the effect of illegality on a contract

LO.2 Compare illegality and unconscionability

LO.3 Distinguish between illegality in performing a legal contract and the illegality of a contract

LO.4 Recognize when a contract is invalid because it obstructs legal processes

LO.5 State the elements of a lottery

LO.6 State the extent to which agreements not to compete are lawful

A court will not enforce a contract if it is illegal, contrary to public policy, or unconscionable.

 ## A GENERAL PRINCIPLES

An agreement is illegal either when its formation or performance is a crime or a tort or when it is contrary to public policy or unconscionable.

1. EFFECT OF ILLEGALITY

Ordinarily, an illegal agreement is void. When an agreement is illegal, the parties are usually not entitled to the aid of the courts. Examples of illegal contracts where the courts have left the parties where they found them include a liquor store owner not being allowed to bring suit for money owed for goods (liquor) sold and delivered on credit in violation of statute and an unlicensed home improvement contractor not being allowed to enforce his contract for progress payments due him. If the illegal agreement has not been performed, neither party can sue the other to obtain performance or damages. If the agreement has been performed, neither party can sue the other to obtain damages or to set the agreement aside.[1]

CASE SUMMARY

The Illegal Paralegal

FACTS: Brian Neiman was involved in the illegal practice of law for over seven years. Having been found guilty of illegally practicing law, he sought to collect disability benefits under his disability insurance policy with Provident Life due to an alleged bipolar disorder, the onset of which occurred during the pendency of criminal and bar proceedings against him. Neiman contends that his bipolar disorder prevents him from working as a paralegal. Provident contends that Neiman should not be indemnified for the loss of income generated from his illegal practice of law.

DECISION: Because all of Neiman's income was derived from the unlawful practice of law in the seven years preceding his claim, as a matter of public policy, a court will not enforce a disability benefits policy that compensates him for his loss of income he was not entitled to earn. Neiman's own wrongdoing caused the contract to be void. Accordingly, Neiman was *in pari delicto* [equally guilty], if not more at fault than the insurance company, in causing the contract to be void and will recover neither benefits nor the premiums he paid. The court must leave the parties where it found them. [**Neiman v Provident Life & Accident Insurance Co., 217 F Supp 2d 1281 (SD Fla 2002)**]

Even if a contract appears to be legal on its face, it may be unenforceable if it was entered into for an illegal purpose. **For Example,** if zoning regulations in the special-purpose district of Washington, D.C., require that only a professional can lease space in a given building, and the rental agent suggests that two nonprofessionals take out the lease in their attorney's name, but all parties realize that the premises will be used only by the nonprofessionals, then the lease in question is illegal and unenforceable.[2]

---

[1] *Sabia v Mattituck Inlet Marina, Inc.,* 805 NYS2d 346 (AD 2005).
[2] *McMahon v A, H, & B,* 728 A2d 656 (DC 1999).

2. EXCEPTIONS TO EFFECT OF ILLEGALITY

To avoid hardship, exceptions are made to the rules stated in Section 1.

(a) PROTECTION OF ONE PARTY   When the law that the agreement violates is intended to protect one of the parties, that party may seek relief. **For Example,** when, in order to protect the public, the law forbids the issuance of securities by certain classes of corporations, a person who has purchased them may recover the money paid.

(b) UNEQUAL GUILT   When the parties are not ***in pari delicto***—equally guilty—the least guilty party is granted relief when public interest is advanced by doing so. **For Example,** when a statute is adopted to protect one of the parties to a transaction, such as a usury law adopted to protect borrowers, the person to be protected will not be deemed to be *in pari delicto* with the wrongdoer when entering into a transaction that the statute prohibits.

in pari delicto equally guilty; used in reference to a transaction as to which relief will not be granted to either party because both are equally guilty of wrongdoing.

3. PARTIAL ILLEGALITY

An agreement may involve the performance of several promises, some of which are illegal and some legal. The legal parts of the agreement may be enforced provided that they can be separated from the parts that are illegal.

When the illegal provision of a contract may be ignored without defeating the contract's basic purpose, a court will merely ignore the illegal provision and enforce the balance of the contract. Consequently, when a provision for the payment of an attorney's fee in a car rental agreement was illegal because a local statute prohibited it, the court would merely ignore the fee provision and enforce the balance of the contract.[3]

If a contract is susceptible to two interpretations, one legal and the other illegal, the court will assume that the legal meaning was intended unless the contrary is clearly indicated.

4. CRIMES AND CIVIL WRONGS

An agreement is illegal, and therefore void, when it calls for the commission of any act that constitutes a crime. To illustrate, one cannot enforce an agreement by which the other party is to commit an assault, steal property, burn a house, or kill a person. A contract to obtain equipment for committing a crime is illegal and cannot be enforced. Thus, a contract to manufacture and sell illegal slot machines is void.

An agreement that calls for the commission of a civil wrong is also illegal and void. Examples are agreements to slander a third person; defraud another; infringe another's patent, trademark, or copyright; or fix prices.

5. GOOD FAITH AND FAIRNESS

Every contract has an implied obligation that neither party shall do anything that will have the effect of destroying or injuring the right of the other party to receive the fruits of the contract. This means that in every contract there exists an implied covenant of **good faith** and fair dealing. Thus, an owner of a large parcel of land

good faith absence of knowledge of any defects or problems.

---

[3] *Harbour v Arelco, Inc.,* 678 NE2d 381 (Ind 1997).

on the Boston waterfront having the right under a contract with a real estate developer to approve or reject the plans submitted by the developer was guilty of a breach of the duty to act in good faith when it was shown that the owner refused to approve the developer's plans, not because the plans were "disapproved," but because the owner was trying to get more money from the developer.

6. UNCONSCIONABLE CLAUSES

Ordinarily, a court will not consider whether a contract is fair or unfair, is wise or foolish, or operates unequally between the parties. **For Example,** the Kramper Family Farm sold 17.59 acres of land to Dakota Industrial Development, Inc. (DID), for $35,000 per acre if the buyer constructed a paved road along the property by December 31. The contract also provided that if the road was not completed by the date set forth in the contract, the price per acre would be $45,000. When the road was not completed by the December 31 date, Family Farm sued DID for the additional $10,000 per acre. DID defended that to apply the contract according to its plain language would create an unconscionable result and was an unenforceable penalty provision contrary to public policy. The court refused to allow DID to escape its contractual obligations on the pretext of unconscionability and public policy arguments. The parties are at liberty to contract as they see fit, the court concluded, and generally, a court will not inquire into the adequacy of consideration inasmuch as the value of property is a matter of personal judgment by the parties to the contract. In this case, the price consisted of either $45,000 per acre, or $35,000 per acre with the road by a certain date.[4]

However, in certain unusual situations, the law may hold a contract provision unenforceable because it is too harsh or oppressive to one of the parties. This principle may be applied to invalidate a clause providing for the payment by one party of an excessive penalty on the breaking of a contract or a provision inserted by the dominant party that it shall not be liable for the consequences of intentional torts, fraud, or gross negligence. This principle is extended in connection with the sale of goods to provide that "if the court . . . finds the contract or any clause of the contract to have been unconscionable at the time it was made, the court may refuse to enforce the contract, or it may enforce the remainder of the contract without the unconscionable clause, or it may so limit the application of any unconscionable clause as to avoid any unconscionable result."[5]

(a) WHAT CONSTITUTES UNCONSCIONABILITY? A provision in a contract that gives what the court believes is too much of an advantage over a buyer may be held void as unconscionable.

(b) DETERMINATION OF UNCONSCIONABILITY Some jurisdictions analyze unconscionability as having two separate elements: procedural and substantive. Both elements must be present for a court to refuse to enforce a contract provision. Other jurisdictions analyze unconscionability by considering the doctrine of adhesion and whether the clause in question is unduly oppressive.

Procedural unconscionability has to do with matters of freedom of assent resulting from inequality of bargaining power and the absence of real negotiations and meaningful choice or a surprise resulting from hiding a disputed term in an unduly long

---

[4] *Kramper Family Farm v Dakota Industrial Development, Inc.,* 603 NW2d 463 (Neb App 1999).
[5] UCC § 2-302(1).

contract of adhesion
contract offered by a dominant party to a party with inferior bargaining power on a take-it-or-leave-it basis.

document or fine print. Companywide standardized form contracts imposed on a take-it-or-leave-it basis by a party with superior bargaining strength are called **contracts of adhesion,** and they may sometimes be deemed procedurally unconscionable.

Substantive unconscionability focuses on the actual terms of the contract itself. Such unconscionability is indicated when the contract terms are so one-sided as to shock the conscience or are so extreme as to appear unconscionable according to the mores and business practices of the time and place.

The U.S. Supreme Court has made clear that arbitration is an acceptable forum for the resolution of employment disputes between employees and their employers, including employment-related claims based on federal and state statutes.[6] The controlling arbitration agreement language is commonly devised and implemented by the employer. Under the Federal Arbitration Act (FAA), the employer can obtain a court order to stay court proceedings and compel arbitration according to the terms of the controlling arbitration agreement. The Supreme Court also made clear that in agreeing to arbitration of a statutory claim, a party does not forgo substantive rights afforded by the statute. In a growing number of court decisions, in effect employers are finding that courts will not enforce arbitration agreements in which the employer has devised an arbitration agreement that functions as a thumb on the employer's side of the scale.[7]

CASE SUMMARY

Arbitration Agreement Short-Circuited

FACTS: Saint Clair Adams completed an application to work as a salesperson at Circuit City. As part of the application, Adams signed the "Circuit City Dispute Resolution Agreement" (DRA). The DRA requires employees to submit all claims and disputes to binding arbitration. Incorporated into the DRA is a set of "Dispute Resolution Rules and Procedures" that defines the claims subject to arbitration, discovery rules, allocation of fees, and available remedies. Under these rules, the amount of damages is restricted: Back pay is limited to one year, front pay to two years, and punitive damages to the higher of the amount of front and back pay awarded or $5,000. In addition, the employee is required to split the cost of the arbitration, including the daily fees of the arbitrator, the cost of a reporter to transcribe the proceedings, and the expense of renting the room in which the arbitration is held, unless the employee prevails and the arbitrator decides to order Circuit City to pay the employee's share of the costs. Circuit City is not required under the agreement to arbitrate any claims against the employee. An employee cannot work at Circuit City without signing the DRA.

Adams filed a state court lawsuit against Circuit City and three coworkers alleging sexual harassment, retaliation, constructive discharge, and intentional infliction of emotional distress under the California Fair Employment and Housing Act (FEHA). Adams sought compensatory, punitive, and emotional distress damages for alleged repeated harassment during his entire term of employment. Circuit City responded by filing a petition in federal district court to compel arbitration pursuant to the FAA. The petition was granted by the trial court, reversed by the Ninth Circuit Court of Appeals, which court was reversed by the U.S. Supreme Court (*Circuit City 1*) and the case remanded to the Ninth Circuit Court of Appeals.

---

[6] *Gilmer v Interstate/Johnson Lane Corp.,* 500 US 20 (1991); *Circuit City Stores, Inc. v Adams,* 121 S Ct 1301 (2001).
[7] See *Vassi/Kouska v Woodfield Nissan Inc.,* 830 NE2d 619 (Ill App 2005).

CASE SUMMARY

continued

DECISION: Judgment for Adams. The arbitration provision is unenforceable. General contract defenses such as fraud, duress, or unconscionability can operate to invalidate arbitration agreements. The DRA is procedurally unconscionable because it is a contract of adhesion drafted by the party with superior bargaining power, which relegates to the other party the option of either adhering to its terms without modification or rejecting the contract entirely.

The DRA is substantively unconscionable because employees must arbitrate "any and all employment-related claims" while Circuit City is not obligated to arbitrate their claims against employees and may bring lawsuits against employees, thus depriving the DRA of any modicum of bilaterality. Moreover, the remedies are limited under the DRA, including a one-year back pay limit and a two-year front pay limit, with a cap on punitive damages of an amount up to the higher of the amount of back pay and front pay awarded or $5,000. By contrast, in a civil lawsuit under state law, a plaintiff is entitled to all forms of relief. Further, the DRA requires that the employee split the cost of the arbitrator's fees with the employer while an individual would not be required to split the cost of a judge. [**Circuit City Stores, Inc. v Adams (Circuit City II), 279 F3d 889 (9th Cir 2002)**]

B AGREEMENTS AFFECTING PUBLIC WELFARE

Agreements that may harm the public welfare are condemned as contrary to public policy and are not binding. Agreements that interfere with public service or the duties of public officials, obstruct legal process, or discriminate against classifications of individuals may be considered detrimental to public welfare and, as such, are not enforceable.

7. AGREEMENTS CONTRARY TO PUBLIC POLICY

A given agreement may not violate any statute but may still be so offensive to society that the courts feel that enforcing the contract would be contrary to public policy.

public policy certain objectives relating to health, morals, and integrity of government that the law seeks to advance by declaring invalid any contract that conflicts with those objectives even though there is no statute expressly declaring such a contract illegal.

Public policy cannot be defined precisely but is loosely described as protection from that which tends to be injurious to the public or contrary to the public good or which violates any established interest of society. Contracts that may be unenforceable as contrary to public policy frequently relate to the protection of the public welfare, health, or safety; to the protection of the person; and to the protection of recognized social institutions. **For Example,** a woman entered into a services contract with a male in exchange for financial support. The record disclosed, however, that the association between the parties was one founded upon the exchange of money for sex. The court determined that the agreement for financial support in exchange for illicit sexual relations was violative of public policy and thus was unenforceable.[8] Courts are cautious in invalidating a contract on the ground that it is contrary to public policy because courts recognize that, on the one hand, they are applying a very vague standard and, on the other hand, they are restricting the freedom of the contracting parties to contract freely as they choose.[9]

---

[8] *Anonymous v Anonymous*, 740 NYS2d 341 (App Div 2002).

[9] *Beacon Hill Civic Ass'n v Ristorante Toscano, Inc.*, 662 NE2d 1015 (Mass 1996).

THINKING THINGS THROUGH

Fair Arbitration Agreements

An arbitration agreement that is fundamentally unfair will be subject to challenge by attorneys seeking to avoid arbitration. In cases when the arbitration agreement and employer actions "indicate a systematic effort to impose arbitration on an employee . . . as an inferior forum that works to the employer's advantage," the employer may well find that it will be unable to enforce the agreement to arbitrate under the FAA in federal court. Contrary to the perception that business may be attempting to "stack the deck" against claimant-employees, in reality most corporate boards and company executives devote significant human and economic resources to make sure that their companies are in full compliance with federal and state employment laws.

THINKING THINGS THROUGH, a fair arbitration agreement will better serve the needs of employers than an unbalanced arbitration agreement that is unenforceable in court under the FAA. The advantages to arbitration for both the employer and employees are that the matters at issue are resolved in an expeditious, timely, and just manner, before an expert on employment law, with lower overall costs and in a shorter period of time than litigation. The decision is final and binding on the parties, with a very limited review of the decision under Section 10 of the FAA. Should the employee be successful and the actions of the employer's agents be found to be contrary to employment law, the employer is informed of the decision much sooner than in litigation, and the employer can take appropriate corrective action in a more expeditious fashion. The remedies for the employee are the same as provided in a court, and the process is a private one, not a source of adverse publicity with loss of goodwill. Should the employee be unsuccessful in her claims, the controversy is resolved in a shorter time than litigation, and the individual can move forward with her life, avoiding years of prolonged litigation.

CASE SUMMARY

Horseplay Prohibited

FACTS: Robert Bovard contracted to sell American Horse Enterprises, Inc., to James Ralph. When Ralph did not make payments when due, Bovard brought suit against him. The trial judge raised the question whether the contract was void for illegality. American Horse Enterprises was predominantly engaged in manufacturing devices for smoking marijuana and tobacco, and to a lesser degree in manufacturing jewelry. When the contract was made, there was no statute prohibiting the manufacture of any of these items, but there was a statute making it illegal to possess, use, or transfer marijuana.

DECISION: Although the question of illegality had not been raised by the parties, the trial judge had the duty to question the validity of the contract when it appeared that the contract might be illegal. Although there was no statute expressly making the contract illegal, the statute prohibiting the possession and sale of marijuana manifested a public policy against anything that would further the use of marijuana. It was therefore against public policy to make the devices used in smoking marijuana or to sell a business that engaged in such manufacture. The sales contract was therefore contrary to public policy and void and could not be enforced. [**Bovard v American Horse Enterprises, Inc.**, 247 Cal Rptr 340 (Cal App 1988)]

8. GAMBLING, WAGERS, AND LOTTERIES

lottery any plan by which a consideration is given for a chance to win a prize; it consists of three elements: (1) there must be a payment of money or something of value for an opportunity to win, (2) a prize must be available, and (3) the prize must be offered by lot or chance.

Gambling contracts are illegal. Largely as a result of the adoption of antigambling statutes, wagers or bets are generally illegal. Private **lotteries** involving the three elements of prize, chance, and consideration (or similar affairs of chance) are also generally held illegal. In many states, public lotteries (lotteries run by a state government) have been legalized by statute. Raffles are usually regarded as lotteries. In some states, bingo games, lotteries, and raffles are legalized by statute when the funds raised are used for a charitable purpose.

Sales promotion schemes calling for the distribution of property according to chance among the purchasers of goods are held illegal as lotteries without regard to whether the scheme is called a *guessing contest,* a *raffle,* or a *gift.*

Giveaway plans and games are lawful so long as it is not necessary to buy anything or give anything of value to participate. If participation is free, the element of consideration is lacking, and there is no lottery.

An activity is not gambling when the result is solely or predominantly a matter of skill. In contrast, it is gambling when the result is solely a matter of luck. Rarely is any activity 100 percent skill or 100 percent luck.

 REGULATION OF BUSINESS

Local, state, and national laws regulate a wide variety of business activities and practices.

9. EFFECT OF VIOLATION

Whether an agreement made in connection with business conducted in violation of the law is binding or void depends on how strongly opposed the public policy is to the prohibited act. Some courts take the view that the agreement is not void unless the statute expressly specifies this. In some instances, a statute expressly preserves the validity of the contract. **For Example,** if someone fails to register a fictitious name under which a business is conducted, the violator, after registering the name as required by statute, is permitted to sue on a contract made while illegally conducting business.

10. STATUTORY REGULATION OF CONTRACTS

To establish uniformity or to protect one of the parties to a contract, statutes frequently provide that contracts of a given class must follow a statutory model or must contain specified provisions. **For Example,** statutes commonly specify that particular clauses must be included in insurance policies to protect the persons insured and their beneficiaries. Other statutes require that contracts executed in connection with credit buying and loans contain particular provisions designed to protect the debtor.

Consumer protection legislation gives the consumer the right to rescind the contract in certain situations. Laws relating to truth in lending, installment sales, and home improvement contracts commonly require that an installment-sale contract specify the cash price, the down payment, the trade-in value (if any), the cash balance, the insurance costs, and the interest and finance charges.

CPA   ## 11. LICENSED CALLINGS OR DEALINGS

Statutes frequently require that a person obtain a license, certificate, or diploma before practicing certain professions, such as law and medicine. A license may also be required before carrying on a particular business or trade, such as that of a real estate broker, stockbroker, hotel keeper, or pawnbroker.

If a license is required to protect the public from unqualified persons, a contract made by an unlicensed person is unenforceable.[10] **For Example,** a corporation that does not hold a required real estate broker's license cannot sue to recover fees for services as a broker. An unlicensed insurance broker who cannot recover a fee because of the absence of a license cannot evade the statutory requirement by having a friend who is a licensed broker bill for the services and collect the payment for him.

CASE SUMMARY

How Much for a Brokerage License? How Much Commission Was Lost?

FACTS: Thompson Halbach & Associates, Inc., an Arizona corporation, entered into an agreement with Meteor Motors, Inc., the owner of Palm Beach Acura, to find a buyer for the dealership, and Meteor agreed to pay a 5 percent commission based on the closing price of the sale. Working out of Scottsdale, Arizona, Thompson solicited potential Florida purchasers for the Florida business by phone, fax, and e-mail. Among those contacted was Craig Zinn Automotive Group, which ultimately purchased Palm Beach Acura from Meteor Motors for $5,000,000. Thompson was not paid its $250,000 commission and brought suit against Meteor for breach of contract. Meteor defended that Thompson was an unlicensed broker and that a state statute declares a contract for a commission with an unlicensed broker to be invalid. Thompson responded that the Florida state statue did not apply because it worked out of Scottsdale.

DECISION: Judgment for Meteor. The Florida statute clearly applies to a foreign broker who provides brokerage activities in Florida. Thompson solicited potential Florida purchasers for the Florida business and that purchaser was a Florida corporation. [**Meteor Motors v Thompson Halbach & Associates, 914 So2d 479 (Fla App 2005)**]

CPA   ## 12. CONTRACTS IN RESTRAINT OF TRADE

An agreement that unreasonably restrains trade is illegal and void on the ground that it is contrary to public policy. Such agreements take many forms, such as a combination to create a monopoly or to obtain a corner on the market or an association of merchants to increase prices. In addition to the illegality of the agreement based on general principles of law, statutes frequently declare monopolies illegal and subject the parties to various civil and criminal penalties.[11]

CPA   ## 13. AGREEMENTS NOT TO COMPETE

In the absence of a valid restrictive covenant, the seller of a business may compete with the buyer, or an ex-employee may solicit customers of the former employer.

---

[10] *Hancock Gannon Joint Venture II v McNuly*, 800 So 2d 294 (Fla App 2000).

[11] Sherman Antitrust Act, 15 USC §§ 1–7; Clayton Act, 15 USC §§ 12–27; Federal Trade Commission Act, 15 USC §§ 41–58.

A noncompetition covenant may be held invalid because of vagueness concerning the duration and geographic area of the restriction.[12] Moreover, if the agreement not to compete is not properly executed in accordance with state law, it will not be enforced. **For Example,** Holly Martinez worked for Avis Rent-A-Car at the New Bern, North Carolina, airport. When hired, she printed her name on the top of the form containing an agreement not to compete but did not sign it. On December 17, she resigned her position to return to school, saying that she planned to get a part-time job. The next day, she began working for Hertz Rent-A-Car at the counter adjacent to the Avis counter. Avis was unsuccessful in obtaining a restraining order to prevent Holly from working for its competitor because the agreement was not signed as required by state law.[13]

CPA **(a) Sale of Business** When a going business is sold, it is commonly stated in the contract that the seller shall not go into the same or a similar business again within a certain geographic area or for a certain period of time, or both. In early times, such agreements were held void because they deprived the public of the service of the person who agreed not to compete, impaired the latter's means of earning a livelihood, reduced competition, and exposed the public to monopoly. To modern courts, the question is whether, under the circumstances, the restriction imposed on one party is reasonably necessary to protect the other party. If the restriction is reasonable, it is valid.

On the ground of reasonableness, a restriction has been sustained by which a business owner selling the business to a new owner agreed not to open a competing business within a 50-mile radius (where the business has a territorial range up to 100 miles) for five years.[14]

(b) Employment Contract Restrictions to prevent competition by a former employee are held valid when reasonable and necessary to protect the interest of the former employer. **For Example,** a noncompete covenant executed by Dr. Samuel Keeley that prohibited his "establishing a competing cardiovascular surgery practice within a 75-mile radius of Albany, Georgia, for a period of two years following the date of termination" was upheld in court and did not include more territory than necessary to protect the professional corporation's business interests.[15]

Public policy requires that noncompetition covenants be strictly construed in favor of freedom of action of the employee.[16] A restrictive covenant is not binding when it places a restriction on the employee that is broader than reasonably necessary to protect the employer. **For Example,** Illinois manufacturer Arcor's noncompetition covenant, which had a restricted area of "the United States and Canada" precluding competition by a former employee for a one-year period, was found to be unenforceable as an industrywide ban that constituted a "blanket prohibition on competition."[17] In determining the validity of a restrictive covenant binding an

---

[12] *Vukovich v Coleman,* 2003 WL 21290639 (Ind App).

[13] *New Hanover Rent-A-Car, Inc. v Martinez,* 525 SE2d 487 (NC App 2000).

[14] *Hicks v Doors By Mike, Inc.,* 579 SE2d 833 (Ga App 2003).

[15] *Keeley v CSA, P.C.,* 510 SE2d 880 (Ga App 1999).

[16] Noncompetition covenants are not valid in California. However, confidentiality agreements protecting trade secrets are enforceable in that state.

[17] *Arcor, Inc. v Haas,* 842 NE2d 265 (Ill App 2005).

E-COMMERCE AND CYBERLAW

Special Rules for Internet E-Commerce Employees?

Traditional noncompetition clauses are enforceable against former employees when the restrictions are reasonable and necessary to protect the interests of the employer who contracted for this protection. A one-year noncompetition clause is ordinarily a reasonable duration for such a restrictive covenant. However, a federal court has refused to issue a preliminary injunction against an Internet publishing business executive, Mark Schlack, who had signed a one-year noncompetition clause as part of his employment contract with EarthWeb, Inc., and thereafter left this company to start a competing Web site, **http://www.ITWorld.com,** for International Data Group, Inc. The court reasoned in part that "a one-year hiatus from the [Internet information technology] workforce is several generations, if not an eternity." The court ruled that EarthWeb's restrictive covenant "is too long . . . given the dynamic nature of this industry [and] its lack of geographical borders." This ruling may be the foundation on which special rules develop for Internet-related employment contracts.*

*EARTHWEB, INC, V SCHLACK, 71 F Supp 2d 299 (1999), aff'd in part, 205 F3d 1322 (2000).

employee, the court balances the aim of protecting the legitimate interests of the employer with the right of the employee to follow gainful employment and provide services required by the public and other employers.

(c) EFFECT OF INVALIDITY   When a restriction of competition agreed to by the parties is invalid because its scope as to time or geographic area is too great, how does this affect the contract? Some courts trim the restrictive covenant down to a scope they deem reasonable and require the parties to abide by that revision.[18] This rule is nicknamed the "blue-pencil rule." By applying this rule, one court has held that a covenant not to compete for three years was void because it was excessive but that it would be enforced for one year. In the *Arcor* case, the court refused to "blue pencil" the covenant because to render the clause reasonable, the court would in effect be writing a new agreement, which is inappropriate.[19]

Other courts refuse to apply the blue-pencil rule and hold that the restrictive covenant is void or that the entire contract is void.[20] There is also authority that a court should refuse to apply the blue-pencil rule when the restrictive covenant is manifestly unfair and would virtually keep the employee from earning a living.

[18] *Unisource Worldwide, Inc. v Valenti,* 196 F Supp 2d 269 (EDNY 2002).

[19] *Arcor Inc.,* 847 NE2d at 374.

[20] *SWAT 24 v Bond,* 759 So 2d 1047 (La App 2000). Under California law, any "contract by which anyone is restrained from engaging in a lawful profession, trade or business is to that extent void." Cal B&P Code § 16600. A noncompete provision is permitted, however, when "necessary to protect the employer's trade secrets." See *Lotona v Aetna U.S. Healthcare Inc.,* 82 F Supp 2d 1089 (CD Cal 1999), where Aetna was liable for wrongful termination when it fired a California employee for refusing to sign a noncompete agreement.

ETHICS & THE LAW

William Stern and his wife were unable to have children because the wife suffered from multiple sclerosis and pregnancy posed a substantial health risk. Stern's family had been killed in the Holocaust, and he had a strong desire to continue his bloodline.

The Sterns entered into a surrogacy contract with Mary Beth Whitehead through the Infertility Center of New York (ICNY). William Stern and the Whiteheads (husband and wife) signed a contract for Mary Beth to be artificially inseminated and carry Stern's child to term, for which Stern was to pay Mary Beth $10,000 and ICNY $7,500.

Mary Beth was successfully artificially inseminated in 1985, and Baby M was born on March 27, 1986. To avoid publicity, the parents of Baby M were listed as "Mr. and Mrs. Whitehead," and the baby was called Sara Elizabeth Whitehead. On March 30, 1986, Mary Beth turned Baby M over to the Sterns at their home. They renamed the little girl Melissa.

Mary Beth became emotionally distraught and was unable to eat or sleep. The Sterns were so frightened by her behavior that they allowed her to take Baby M for one week to help her adjust. The Whiteheads took the baby and traveled throughout the East, staying in 20 different hotels and motels. Florida authorities found Baby M with Mary Beth's parents and returned her to the Sterns.

Mary Beth said the contract was one to buy a baby and was against public policy and therefore void. She also argued that the contract violated state laws on adoption and the severance of parental rights. The Sterns brought an action to have the contract declared valid and custody awarded to them.

Should the contract be valid or void? What types of behavior would be encouraged if the contract were declared valid? Is it ethical to "rent a womb"? Is it ethical to sell a child? See *In re Baby M,* 537 A2d 15 (NJ 1988).

14. USURIOUS AGREEMENTS

usury lending money at an interest rate that is higher than the maximum rate allowed by law.

Usury is committed when money is loaned at a higher rate of interest than the law allows. Most states prohibit by statute charging more than a stated amount of interest. These statutes provide a maximum annual contract rate of interest that can be exacted under the law of a given state. In many states, the usury law does not apply to loans made to corporations.

When a lender incurs expenses in making a loan, such as the cost of appraising property or making a credit investigation of the borrower, the lender will require the borrower to pay the amount of such expenses. Any fee charged by a lender that goes beyond the reasonable expense of making the loan constitutes "interest" for the purposes of determining whether the transaction is usurious.[21]

---

[21] *Lentimo v Cullen Center Bank and Trust Co.,* 919 SW2d 743 (Tex App 1996).

THINKING THINGS THROUGH

Legality and Public Policy

Karl Llewellyn, the principal drafter of the law that governs nearly all sales of goods in the United States—the Uniform Commercial Code (UCC)—once wrote, "Covert tools are never reliable tools." He was referring to unfairness in a contract or between the contracting parties.

The original intent of declaring certain types of contracts void because of issues of imbalance was based in equity. Courts stepped in to help parties who found themselves bound under agreements that were not fair and open in both their written terms and the communications between the parties. One contracts scholar wrote that the original intent could be described as courts stepping in to help "presumptive sillies like sailors and heirs . . ." and others who, if not crazy, are "pretty peculiar."

However, as the sophistication of contracts and commercial transactions increased, the importance of accuracy, honesty, and fairness increased. Unconscionability is a contracts defense that permits courts to intervene where contracts, if enforced, would "affront the sense of decency." UNCONSCIONABILITY is a term of ethics or moral philosophy used by courts to prevent exploitation and fraud.

Penalites for violating usury laws vary from state to state, with a number of states restricting the lender to the recovery of the loan but no interest whatsoever; other states allow recovery of the loan principal and interest up to the maximum contract rate. Some states also impose a penalty on the lender such as the payment of double the interest paid on a usurious loan.

CASE SUMMARY

Would You Recommend Karen Canzoneri as an Investment Advisor?

FACTS: Karen Canzoneri entered into two agreements with Howard Pinchuck. Under the first agreement, Canzoneri advanced $50,000 to be repaid at 12 percent per month for 12 consecutive months "as an investment profit." The second agreement required "$36,000 to be repaid on or before 6/1/01 with an investment profit of $36,000, total being $72,000." The annualized rate of return for the first transaction was 144 percent and for the second transaction was 608 percent. The civil penalty for violating the state's maximum interest rate of 25 percent per annum is forfeiture of the entire principal amount. Canzoneri contends that the transactions were investments not subject to the usury law.

DECISION: Judgment for Pinchuck. The four elements of a usurious transaction are present: (1) the transaction was a loan, (2) the money loaned required that it be returned, (3) an interest rate higher than allowed by law was required, and (4) a corrupt intention to take more than the legal rate for the use of the money loaned exists. Even though the terms called for "profit," not "interest," the courts looked to the substance, not the form of the transaction. [**Pinchuck v Canzoneri, 920 So2nd 713 (Fla App 4 Dist, 2006)**]

LAWFLIX

Midnight Run (1988) (R)

Is the contract Robert DeNiro has for bringing in Charles Grodin, an embezzler, legal? Discuss the issues of consideration and ethics as the bail bondsman puts another bounty hunter on the case and DeNiro flees from law enforcement agents in order to collect his fee. And finally, discuss the legality of DeNiro's acceptance of money from Grodin and his release of Grodin at the end of the movie.

For movie clips that illustrate business law concepts, see LawFlix at **http://wdvl.westbuslaw.com.**

> SUMMARY

When an agreement is illegal, it is ordinarily void and no contract arises from it. Courts will not allow one party to an illegal agreement to bring suit against the other party. There are some exceptions to this, such as when the parties are not equally guilty or when the law's purpose in making the agreement illegal is to protect the person who is bringing suit. When possible, an agreement will be interpreted as being lawful. Even when a particular provision is held unlawful, the balance of the agreement will generally be saved so that the net result is a contract minus the clause that was held illegal.

The term *illegality* embraces situations in unconscionable contract clauses in which the courts hold that contract provisions are unenforceable because they are too harsh or oppressive to one of the parties to a transaction. If the clause is part of a standard form contract drafted by the party having superior bargaining power and is presented on a take-it-or-leave-it basis (a contract of adhesion) and the substantive terms of the clause itself are unduly oppressive, the clause will be found to be unconscionable and not enforced.

Whether a contract is contrary to public policy may be difficult to determine because public policy is not precisely defined. That which is harmful to the public welfare or general good is contrary to public policy. Contracts condemned as contrary to public policy include those designed to deprive the weaker party of a benefit that the lawmaker desired to provide, agreements injuring public service, and wagers and private lotteries. Statutes commonly make the wager illegal as a form of gambling. The lottery is any plan under which, for a consideration, a person has a chance to win a prize.

Illegality may consist of the violation of a statute or administrative regulation adopted to regulate business. An agreement not to compete is illegal as a restraint of trade except when reasonable in its terms and when it is incidental to the sale of a business or to a contract of employment.

The charging by a lender of a higher rate of interest than allowed by law is usury. Courts must examine transactions carefully to see whether a usurious loan is disguised as a legitimate transaction.

> QUESTIONS AND CASE PROBLEMS

1. When are the parties to an illegal agreement *in pari delicto?*

2. John Iwen sued U.S. West Direct because of a negligently constructed yellow pages advertisement. U.S. West Direct moved to stay litigation and compel arbitration under the yellow pages order form, which required advertisers to resolve all controversies through arbitration, but allowed U.S. West (the publisher) to pursue judicial remedies to collect amounts due it. Under the

arbitration provision, Iwen's sole remedy was a pro rata reduction or refund of the cost of the advertisement. The order form language was drafted by U.S. West Direct on a take-it-or-leave-it basis and stated in part:

> *Any controversy or claim arising out of or relating to this Agreement, or breach thereof, other than an action by Publisher for the collection of amounts due under this Agreement, shall be settled by final, binding arbitration in accordance with the Commercial Arbitration rules of the American Arbitration Association.*

If forced to arbitration, Iwen would be unable to recover damages for the negligently constructed yellow pages ad, nor could he recover damages for infliction of emotional distress and punitive damages related to his many efforts to adjust the matter with the company, which were ignored or rejected. Must Iwen have his case resolved through arbitration rather than a court of law? [*Iwen v U.S. West Direct,* 977 P2d 989 (Mont)]

3. Alman made a contract to purchase an automobile from Crockett Motors on credit but failed to make payments on time. When Crockett sued to enforce the contract, Alman raised the defense that the price of the car had been increased because she was buying on credit and this increase was unconscionable. Crockett proved that the automobile was exactly what it was represented to be and that no fraud had been committed in selling the car to Alman. Does Crockett's evidence constitute a defense to Alman's claim of unconscionability?

4. The Civic Association of Plaineville raffled an automobile to raise funds to build a hospital. Lyons won the automobile, but the association refused to deliver it to her. She sued the association for the automobile. Can Lyons enforce the contract?

5. Ewing was employed by Presto-X-Co., a pest exterminator. His contract of employment specified that he would not solicit or attempt to solicit customers of Presto-X for two years after the termination of his employment. After working several years, his employment was terminated. Ewing then sent a letter to customers of Presto-X stating that he no longer worked for Presto-X and that he was still certified by the state. Ewing set forth his home address and phone number, which the customers did not previously have. The letter ended with the statement, "I thank you for your business throughout the past years." Presto-X brought an action to enjoin Ewing from sending such letters. He raised the defense that he was prohibited only from soliciting and there was nothing in the letters that constituted a seeking of customers. Decide. What ethical values are involved? [*Presto-X-Co. v Ewing,* 442 NW2d 85 (Iowa)]

6. The Minnesota adoption statute requires that any agency placing a child for adoption make a thorough investigation and not give a child to an applicant unless the placement is in the best interests of the child. Tibbetts applied to Crossroads, Inc., a private adoption agency, for a child to adopt. He later sued the agency for breach of contract, claiming that the agency was obligated by contract to supply a child for adoption. The agency claimed that it was required only to use its best efforts to locate a child and was not required to supply a child to Tibbetts unless it found him to be a suitable parent. Decide. [*Tibbetts v Crossroads, Inc.,* 411 NW2d 535 (Minn App)]

7. Siddle purchased a quantity of fireworks from Red Devil Fireworks Co. The sale was illegal, however, because Siddle did not have a license to make the purchase, which the seller knew because it had been so informed by the attorney general of the state. Siddle did not pay for the fireworks, and Red Devil sued him. He defended on the ground that the contract could not be enforced because it was illegal. Was the defense valid? [*Red Devil Fireworks Co. v Siddle,* 648 P2d 468 (Wash App)]

8. Onderdonk entered a retirement home operated by Presbyterian Homes. The contract between Onderdonk and the home required Onderdonk to make a specified monthly payment that could be increased by the home as the cost of operations increased. The contract and the payment plan were thoroughly explained to Onderdonk. As the cost of operations rose, the home continually raised the monthly payments to cover these costs. Onderdonk objected to the increases on the

ground that the increases were far more than had been anticipated and that the contract was therefore unconscionable. Was his objection valid?

9. Smith was employed as a salesman for Borden, Inc., which sold food products in 63 counties in Arkansas, 2 counties in Missouri, 2 counties in Oklahoma, and 1 county in Texas. Smith's employment contract prohibited him from competing with Borden after leaving its employ. Smith left Borden and went to work for a competitor, Lady Baltimore Foods. Working for this second employer, Smith sold in 3 counties of Arkansas. He had sold in 2 of these counties while he worked for Borden. Borden brought an injunction action against Smith and Lady Baltimore to enforce the noncompete covenant in Smith's former contract. Was Borden entitled to the injunction? [*Borden, Inc. v Smith,* 478 SW2d 744 (Ark)]

10. Central Water Works Supply, a corporation, had a contract with its shareholders that they would not compete with it. There were only four shareholders, of whom William Fisher was one, but he was not an employee of the corporation. When he sold his shares in the corporation and began to compete with it, the corporation went to court to obtain an injunction to stop such competition. Fisher claimed that the corporation was not entitled to an injunction because he had not obtained any confidential information or made customer contacts. The corporation claimed that such matters were relevant only when an employee had agreed not to compete but were not applicable when there was a noncompetitive covenant in the sale of a business and that the sale-of-a-business rule should be applied to a shareholder. Who was correct?

11. Vodra was employed as a salesperson and contracting agent for American Security Services. As part of his contract of employment, Vodra signed an agreement that for three years after leaving this employment, he would not solicit any customer of American. Vodra had no experience in the security field when he went to work for American. To the extent that he became known to American's customers, it was because of being American's representative rather than because of his own reputation in the security field. After

some years, Vodra left American and organized a competing company that solicited American's customers. American sued him to enforce the restrictive covenant. Vodra claimed that the restrictive covenant was illegal and not binding. Was he correct? [*American Security Services, Inc. v Vodra,* 385 NW2d 73 (Neb)]

12. Potomac Leasing Co. leased an automatic telephone system to Vitality Centers. Claudene Cato signed the lease as guarantor of payments. When the rental was not paid, Potomac Leasing brought suit against Vitality and Cato. They raised the defense that the rented equipment was to be used for an illegal purpose—namely, the random sales solicitation by means of an automatic telephone in violation of state statute; that this purpose was known to Potomac Leasing; and that Potomac Leasing could therefore not enforce the lease. Was this defense valid? [*Potomac Leasing Co. v Vitality Centers, Inc.,* 718 SW2d 928 (Ark)]

13. The English publisher of a book called *Cambridge* gave a New York publisher permission to sell that book any place in the world except in England. The New York publisher made several bulk sales of the book to buyers who sold the book throughout the world, including England. The English publisher sued the New York publisher and its customers for breach of the restriction prohibiting sales in England. Decide.

14. A state law required builders of homes to be licensed and declared that an unlicensed contractor could not recover compensation under a contract made for the construction of a residence. Although Annex Construction, Inc., did not have a license, it built a home for French. When he failed to pay what was owed, Annex sued him. He raised the defense that the unlicensed contractor could not recover for the contract price. Annex claimed that the lack of a license was not a bar because the president of the corporation was a licensed builder and the only shareholder of the corporation, and the construction had been properly performed. Was Annex entitled to recover?

15. Yarde Metals, Inc., owned six season tickets to New England Patriots football games. Gillette Stadium, where the games are played, had

insufficient men's restrooms in use for football games at that time, which was the subject of numerous newspaper columns. On October 13, 2002, a guest of Yarde Metals, Mikel LaCroix, along with others, used available women's restrooms to answer the call of nature. As LaCroix left the restroom, however, he was arrested and charged with disorderly conduct. The Patriots organization terminated all six of Yarde's season ticket privileges, incorrectly giving as a reason that LaCroix was ejected "for throwing bottles in the seating section." Yarde sued, contending that "by terminating the plaintiff's season tickets for 2002 and for the future arbitrarily, without cause and based on false information," the Patriots had violated the implicit covenant of good faith and fair dealing of the season tickets contract. The back of each Patriots ticket states:

> *This ticket and all season tickets are revocable licenses. The Patriots reserve the right to revoke such licenses, in their sole discretion, at any time and for any reason.*

How would you decide this case? [*Yarde Metals, Inc. v New England Patriots Ltd.,* 834 NE2d 1233 (Mass App Ct)]

> CPA QUESTIONS

1. West, an Indiana real estate broker, misrepresented to Zimmer that West was licensed in Kansas under the Kansas statute that regulates real estate brokers and requires all brokers to be licensed. Zimmer signed a contract agreeing to pay West a 5 percent commission for selling Zimmer's home in Kansas. West did not sign the contract. West sold Zimmer's home. If West sued Zimmer for nonpayment of commission, Zimmer would be

   a. Liable to West only for the value of services rendered
   b. Liable to West for the full commission
   c. Not liable to West for any amount because West did not sign the contract
   d. Not liable to West for any amount because West violated the Kansas licensing requirements (5/92, Law, #25)

2. Blue purchased a travel agency business from Drye. The purchase price included payment for Drye's goodwill. The agreement contained a covenant prohibiting Drye from competing with Blue in the travel agency business. Which of the following statements regarding the covenant is *not* correct?

   a. The restraint must be *no* more extensive than is reasonably necessary to protect the goodwill purchased by Blue.
   b. The geographic area to which it applies must be reasonable.
   c. The time period for which it is to be effective must be reasonable.
   d. The value to be assigned to it is the excess of the price paid over the seller's cost of all tangible assets. (11/87, Law, #2)

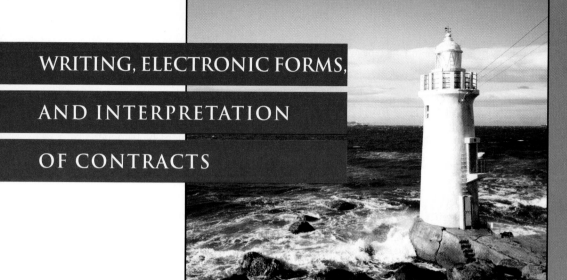

WRITING, ELECTRONIC FORMS, AND INTERPRETATION OF CONTRACTS

CHAPTER (17)

LEARNING OBJECTIVES

After studying this chapter, you should be able to

LO.1 State when a contract must be evidenced by a writing

LO.2 List the requirements of a writing that evidence a paper or electronic contract

LO.3 State the effects of the absence of a sufficient writing when a contract must be evidenced by a writing

LO.4 List the exceptions that have been made by the courts to the laws requiring written evidence of contracts

LO.5 Compare statute of frauds requirements with the parol evidence rule

LO.6 List exceptions to the parol evidence rule

LO.7 Compare the effects of objective and subjective intent of the parties to a contract

LO.8 State the rules for interpreting ambiguous terms in a contract

LO.9 State the effect of contradictory terms

When must a contract be written? What is the effect of a written contract? These questions lead to the statute of frauds and the parol evidence rule.

 STATUTE OF FRAUDS

A *contract* is a legally binding agreement. Must the agreement be evidenced by a writing?

1. VALIDITY OF ORAL CONTRACTS

In the absence of a statute requiring a writing, a contract may be oral or written. Managers and professionals should be more fully aware that their oral communications, including telephone conversations and dinner or breakfast discussions, may be deemed legally enforceable contracts. **For Example,** suppose that Mark Wahlberg, after reviewing a script tentatively entitled *The Bulger Boys*, meets with Steven Spielberg to discuss Mark's playing mobster James "Whitey" Bulger in the film. Steven states, "You *are* 'Whitey,' Marky! The nuns at Gate of Heaven Grammar School in South Boston—or maybe it was St. Augustine's—they don't send for the Boston Police when they are troubled about drug use in the schools; they send for you to talk to the kids. Nobody messes with you, and the kids know it. This is true stuff, I think, and this fugitive's brother Bill comes out of the Southie projects to be president of U Mass." Mark likes the script. Steven and Mark block out two months of time for shooting the film this fall. They agree on Mark's usual fee and a "piece of the action" based on a set percentage of the net income from the film. Thereafter, Mark's agent does not like the deal. He believes there are better scripts for Mark. Incredibly brutal things are coming out about "Whitey" that could severely tarnish the film. And with Hollywood accounting, a percentage of the "net" take is usually of little value. However, all of the essential terms of a contract have been agreed on, and such an oral agreement would be legally enforceable. As set forth in the following text, no writing is required for a services contract that can be performed within one year after the date of the agreement.

Certain contracts, on the other hand, must be evidenced by a writing to be legally enforceable. These contracts are covered by the **statute of frauds.**[1]

Because many oral contracts are legally enforceable, it is a good business practice in the preliminary stages of discussions to stipulate that no binding agreement is intended to be formed until a written contract is prepared and signed by the parties.

statute of frauds statute that, in order to prevent fraud through the use of perjured testimony, requires that certain kinds of transactions be evidenced in writing in order to be binding or enforceable.

2. CONTRACTS THAT MUST BE EVIDENCED BY A WRITING

The statute of frauds requires that certain kinds of contracts be evidenced by a writing or they cannot be enforced. This means that either the contract itself must be in writing and signed by both parties or there must be a sufficient written memorandum of the oral contract signed by the person being sued for breach of contract. A *part*

---

[1] The name is derived from the original English Statute of Frauds and Perjuries, which was adopted in 1677 and became the pattern for similar legislation in America. The 17th section of that statute governed the sale of goods, and its modern counterpart is § 2-201 of the UCC. The 4th section of the English statute provided the pattern for U.S. legislation with respect to contracts other than for the sale of goods described in this section of the chapter. The English statute was repealed in 1954 except as to land sale and guarantee contracts. The U.S. statutes remain in force, but the liberalization by UCC § 2-201 of the pre-Code requirements with respect to contracts for the sale of goods lessens the applicability of the writing requirement. Additional movement away from the writing requirement is seen in the 1994 Revision of Article 8, Securities, which abolishes the statute of frauds provision of the original UCC § 8-319 and goes beyond by declaring that the one-year performance provision of the statute of frauds is not applicable to contracts for securities. UCC § 8-113 [1994 Revision].

performance doctrine or exception to the statute of frauds may exist when the plaintiff's part performance is "unequivocally referable" to the oral agreement.[2]

(a) Agreement That Cannot Be Performed within One Year after the Contract Is Made   A writing is required when the contract, by its terms or subject matter, cannot be performed within one year after the date of the agreement. An oral agreement to supply a line of credit for two years cannot be enforced because of the statute of frauds. Likewise, a joint venture agreement to construct a condominium complex was subject to the one-year provision of the statute of frauds when the contract could not reasonably have been performed within one year. The plans of the parties projected a development over the course of three years.

The year runs from the time the oral contract is made rather than from the date when performance is to begin. In computing the year, the day on which the contract was made is excluded.

No *part performance* exception exists to validate an oral agreement not performable within one year. **For Example,** Babyback's Foods negotiated a multiyear oral agreement to comarket its barbecue meat products with the Coca-Cola Co. nationwide and arranged to have several coolers installed at area grocery stores in Louisville under the agreement. Babyback's faxed to Coca-Cola a contract that summarized the oral agreement but Coca-Cola never signed it. Because Coca-Cola did not sign and no part performance exception exists for an oral agreement not performable within one year, Babyback's lawsuit was unsuccessful.[3]

When no time for performance is specified by the oral contract and complete performance could "conceivably occur" within one year, the statute of frauds is not applicable to the oral contract.[4]

When a contract may be terminated at will by either party, the statute of frauds is not applicable because the contract may be terminated within a year. **For Example,** David Ehrlich was hired as manager of Gravediggaz pursuant to an oral management agreement that was terminable at will by either Ehrlich or the group. He was entitled to receive 15 percent of the gross earnings of the group and each of its members, including rap artist Robert Diggs, professionally known as RZA, for all engagements entered into while he was manager under this oral agreement. Such an at-will contract is not barred by the statute of frauds.[5]

(1) Oral Extension of a Contract.   A contract in writing, but not required to be so by the statute of frauds because it is terminable at will, may be varied by a new oral contract, even if the original written contract provided that it should not be varied except by writing. However, the burden of proof on the party asserting the oral modification is a heavy one. The modification must be shown by "clear, unequivocal and convincing evidence, direct or implied." **For Example,** John Boyle is the sole shareholder of numerous entertainment-related companies called the Cellar Door Companies, valued at some $106,000,000. Through these companies, he controls much of the large concert business at outdoor amphitheaters in Virginia and North

---

[2] *Carey & Associates v Ernst*, 802 NYS2d 160 (AD 2005).

[3] *Coca-Cola Co. v Babyback's International Inc.*, 841 NE2d 557 (Ind 2006).

[4] *El Paso Healthcare System v Piping Rock Corp.*, 939 SW2d 695 (Tex App 1997).

[5] See *Ehrlich v Diggs*, 169 F Supp 2d 124 (EDNY 2001). See also *Sterling v Sterling*, 800 NYS2d 463 (AD 2005), in which the statute of frauds was no bar to an oral partnership agreement, deemed to be at will, that continued for an indefinite period of time.

FIGURE 17-1   *Hurdles in the Path of a Contract*

WRITING REQUIRED	
STATUTE OF FRAUDS	**EXCEPTIONS**
MORE THAN ONE YEAR TO PERFORM SALE OF LAND ANSWER FOR ANOTHERÕS DEBT OR DEFAULT PERSONAL REPRESENTATIVE TO PAY DEBT OF DECEDENT FROM PERSONAL FUNDS PROMISE IN CONSIDERATION OF MARRIAGE SALE OF GOODS FOR $500 OR MORE MISCELLANEOUS	PART PERFORMANCE PROMISOR BENEFIT DETRIMENTAL RELIANCE
PAROL EVIDENCE RULE	**EXCEPTIONS**
EVERY COMPLETE, FINAL WRITTEN CONTRACT	INCOMPLETE CONTRACT AMBIGUOUS TERMS FRAUD, ACCIDENT, OR MISTAKE TO PROVE EXISTENCE OR NONBINDING CHARACTER OF CONTRACT MODIFICATION OF CONTRACT ILLEGALITY

Carolina. Bill Reid worked for Boyle beginning in 1983 as president of one of Boyle's companies. Boyle conducted financial affairs with an "air of informality." Reid proposed to Boyle the need for an amphitheater in Virginia Beach, and Boyle promised him a "33 percent interest" "if he pulled it off." As a result of Reid's efforts, the 20,000-seat Virginia Beach Amphitheater opened in 1996. The Supreme Court of Virginia determined that clear and convincing evidence did support the oral modification of Reid's written contract, including the following excerpt from the Court's opinion:

> *Thomas J. Lyons, Jr., Boyle's friend for over 35 years, testified on behalf of Reid. Lyons and his wife attended a concert in July 1996 at the newly constructed Virginia Beach Amphitheater as guests of Boyle and his wife. Lyons complimented Boyle for the excellent work and effort that Reid had undertaken in making the amphitheater a reality. According to Lyons, Boyle stated: "Well that's why he's my partner . . . that's why he owns 35 percent in this—in the Amphitheater or this project." After Lyons finished his testimony, the chancellor remarked on the record that Boyle stood up from his seat and "hugged" Lyons, even though Lyons had just provided testimony detrimental to Boyle.*

Reid was thus entitled to a judgment equivalent to the value of his interest in the project, $3,566,343.[6]

(b) Agreement to Sell or a Sale of an Interest in Land All contracts to sell land, buildings, or interests in land, such as mortgages, must be evidenced by a writing. Leases are also interests in land and must be in writing, except in some states where leases for one year or less do not have to be in writing.[7] **For Example,** if Mrs. O'Toole orally agrees to sell her house to the Gillespies for $250,000 and, thereafter, her children convince her that she could obtain $280,000 for the property if she is patient, Mrs. O'Toole can raise the defense of the statute of frauds should she be sued for breach of the oral agreement. Under the *part performance doctrine,* an exception exists by which an oral contract for the sale of land will be enforced by a court of equity in a suit for specific performance if the buyer has taken possession of the land under an oral contract and has made substantial improvements, the value of which cannot easily be ascertained, or has taken possession and paid part of the purchase price.

(c) Promise to Answer for the Debt or Default of Another If an individual *I* promises a creditor *C* to pay the debt of *D* if *D* does not do so, *I* is promising to answer for the debt of another. Such a promise is sometimes called a **suretyship** contract, and it must be in writing to be enforceable. *I,* the promisor, is obligated to pay only if *D* does not pay. *I*'s promise is a *collateral* or *secondary* promise, and such promises must be in writing under the statute of frauds.[8]

suretyship undertaking to pay the debt or be liable for the default of another.

(1) Main Purpose of Exception. When the main purpose of the promisor's promise to pay the debt of another is to benefit the promisor, the statute of frauds is not applicable, and the oral promise to pay the debt is binding.

For Example, an individual *I* hires a contractor *C* to repair *I*'s building, and the supplier *S* is unwilling to extend credit to *C*. In an oral promise by *I* to pay *S* what is owed for the supplies in question if *C* does not pay, *I* is promising to pay for the debt of another, *C*. However, the *main purpose* of *I*'s promise was not to aid *C* but to get his own house repaired. This promise is not within the statute of frauds.

CASE SUMMARY

"I Personally Guarantee" Doesn't Mean I'm Personally Liable, Does It?

FACTS: Joel Burgower owned Material Partnerships Inc. (MPI), which supplied Sacos Tubulares del Centro, S.A. de C.V. (Sacos), a Mexican bag manufacturer, essential materials

---

[6] *Reid v Boyle,* 527 SE2d 137 (Va 2000).

[7] See, however, *BBQ Blues Texas, Ltd. v Affiliated Business,* 183 SW3d 543 (Tex App 2006), in which Eddie Calagero of Affiliated Business and the owners of BBQ Blues Texas, Ltd. entered an oral commission agreement to pay a 10 percent commission if he found a buyer for the restaurant, and he did so. The oral agreement was held to be outside the statute of frauds because this activity of finding a willing buyer did not involve the transfer of real estate. The second contract between the buyer and seller of the restaurant, which involved the transfer of a lease agreement, was a separate and distinct agreement over which Calagero had no control.

[8] See *Martin Printing, Inc. v Sone,* 873 A2d 232 (Conn App 2005), in which James Kuhe in writing personally guaranteed Martin Printing, Inc, to pay for printing expenses of *Pub Links Golfer Magazine,* if his corporation, Abbey Inc., failed to do so. When Abbey, Inc., failed to pay, the court enforced Kuhe's promise to pay.

CASE SUMMARY

continued

to make its products. When MPI was not paid for shipments, it insisted that Jorge Lopez, Sacos's general manager, personally guarantee all past and future obligations to MPI. In a letter to Burgower dated September 25, 1998, Lopez wrote:

> *I . . . want to certify you [sic] that I, personally, guaranty all outstanding [sic] and liabilities of Sacos Tubulares with Material Partnerships as well as future shipments.*

Lopez drafted the letter himself and signed it over the designation "Jorge Lopez Venture, General Manager."

After receiving the September 25th letter, MPI resumed shipping product to Sacos, sending additional shipments valued at approximately $200,000. MPI subsequently received one payment of approximately $60,000 from Sacos. When Sacos did not pay for the additional shipments, MPI stopped shipping to it. The Sacos plant closed, and MPI brought suit in a Texas court against Lopez, claiming he was individually liable for the corporate debt of more than $900,000 under the terms of the personal guarantee. Lopez contended that he signed the letter in his capacity as general manager of Sacos as a corporate guarantee and that it was not an enforceable personal guarantee. MPI contended that the letter was a clear personal guarantee.

DECISION: The essential terms of a guarantee agreement required by the statute of frauds were present in this case. Lopez stated in his September 25th letter that "I, personally, guaranty," manifesting an intent to guarantee, and described the obligation being guaranteed as "all outstandings and liabilities of Sacos," as well as "future shipments." Lopez's signature over his corporate office does not render the document ambiguous because the clear intent was expressed in the word "personally." [**MPI v Jorge Lopez Ventura, 102 SW2d 252 (Tex App 2003)**]

(d) PROMISE BY THE EXECUTOR OR ADMINISTRATOR OF A DECEDENT'S ESTATE TO PAY A CLAIM AGAINST THE ESTATE FROM PERSONAL FUNDS   The **personal representative** (**executor** or **administrator**) has the duty of handling the affairs of a deceased person, paying the debts from the proceeds of the estate and distributing any balance remaining. The executor or administrator is not personally liable for the claims against the estate of the **decedent.** If the personal representative promises to pay the decedent's debts with his or her own money, the promise cannot be enforced unless it is evidenced by a writing.

If the personal representative makes a contract on behalf of the estate in the course of administering the estate, a writing is not required. The representative is then contracting on behalf of the estate. Thus, if the personal representative employs an attorney to settle the estate or makes a burial contract with an undertaker, no writing is required.

(e) PROMISES MADE IN CONSIDERATION OF MARRIAGE   Promises to pay a sum of money or give property to another in consideration of marriage must be in writing under the statute of frauds.

For Example, if Mr. John Bradley orally promises to provide Karl Radford $20,000 on Karl's marriage to Mr. Bradley's daughter Michelle and Karl and Michelle marry, the agreement is not enforceable under the statute of frauds because it was not in writing.

Prenuptial or *antenuptial* agreements are entered into by the parties before their marriage. After full disclosure of each party's assets and liabilities, and in some states,

---

personal representative administrator or executor who represents decedents under UPC.

executor, executrix person (man, woman) named in a will to administer the estate of the decedent.

administrator, administratrix person (man, woman) appointed to wind up and settle the estate of a person who has died without a will.

decedent person whose estate is being administered.

income,[9] the parties set forth the rights of each partner regarding the property and, among other things, set forth rights and obligations should the marriage end in a separation or divorce. Such a contract must be in writing.

For Example, when Susan DeMatteo married her husband M. J. DeMatteo in 1990, she had a 1977 Nova and $5,000 in the bank. M. Joseph DeMatteo was worth as much as $112 million at that time, and he insisted that she sign a prenuptial agreement before their marriage. After full disclosure of each party's assets, the prenuptial agreement was signed and videotaped some five days before their marriage ceremony. The agreement gave Susan $35,000 a year plus cost-of-living increases, as well as a car and a house, should the marriage dissolve. After the couple divorced, Susan argued before the state's highest court that the agreement was not "fair or reasonable" because it gave her less than 1 percent of her former husband's wealth. The court upheld the agreement, however, pointing out that Susan was fully informed about her fiancé's net worth and was represented by counsel.[10] When there is full disclosure and representation, prenuptial agreements, like other contracts, cannot be set aside unless they are unconscionable, which in a domestic relations setting means leaving a former spouse unable to support herself or himself.

(f) Sale of Goods   As will be developed in Chapter 23, Nature and Form of Sales, contracts for the sale of goods priced at $500 or more must ordinarily be in writing under UCC § 2-201.[11]

3. NOTE OR MEMORANDUM

The statute of frauds requires a writing to evidence those contracts that come within its scope. This writing may be a note or memorandum as distinguished from a contract.[12] The statutory requirement is, of course, satisfied if there is a complete written contract signed by both parties.

(a) Signing   The note or memorandum must be signed by the party sought to be bound by the contract. **For Example,** in the previous scenario involving Mark Wahlberg and Steven Spielberg, suppose the parties agreed to do the film according to the same terms but agreed to begin shooting the film a year from next April, and Mark wrote the essential terms on a napkin, dated it, and had Steven sign it "to make sure I got it right." Mark then placed the napkin in his wallet for his records. Because the contract could not be performed within one year after the date of the agreement, a writing would be required. If Steven thereafter decided not to pursue the film because of new murder indictments against Whitey Bulger, Mark could enforce the contract against him because the napkin-note had been signed by the party to be bound or "sought to be charged," Steven. However, if Mark later decided not to appear in the film, the agreement to do the film could not be enforced against Mark because no writing existed signed by Mark, the party sought to be charged.

Some states require that the authorization of an agent to execute a contract coming within the statute of frauds must also be in writing. In the case of an auction, it is usual practice for the auctioneer to be the agent of both parties for the purpose of signing the memorandum.

---

[9] See FLA, STAT § 732 · 702 (2).

[10] *DeMatteo v DeMatteo*, 762 NE2d 797 (Mass 2002). See also *Waton v Waton*, 887 So2d 419 (Fla App 2004).

[11] As will be presented in Chapter 23, under Revised Article 2, § 2-201, the $500 amount is increased to $5,000. This revision has not yet been adopted by any states.

[12] *McLinden v Coco*, 765 NE2d 606 (Ind App 2002).

E-COMMERCE AND CYBERLAW

Electronic Signatures in the Internet Age

A SIGNATURE authenticates a writing by identifying the signers through their distinctive marks. The act of signing a document calls to the attention of the signing parties the legal significance of their act and expresses authorization and assent to the body of the signed writing. An ELECTRONIC SIGNATURE, including technology having digital or wireless capabilities, means any electronic sound, symbol, or process attached to, or logically associated with, a contract or other electronic record and executed with the intent to sign the record. An ELECTRONIC RECORD means any contract or other record created or stored in an electronic medium and retrievable in a perceivable form.

Conducting business electronically over the Internet has many advantages for consumers, businesses, and governments by allowing the instant purchase of goods, information, and services, and the reduction of sales, administrative, and overhead expenses. To facilitate the expansion of electronic commerce and place electronic signatures and electronic contracts on an equal footing with written signatures and paper contracts, Congress enacted a federal electronic signatures law.

Under the Electronic Signatures in Global and National Commerce Act (E-Sign),* electronically signed contracts cannot be denied legal effect because the signatures are in electronic form, nor can they be denied legal effect because they are delivered electronically. Contracts or documents requiring a notarized signature can be satisfied by the electronic signatures of the notaries coupled with the enclosure of all other required information as part of the record.

One of the goals of E-Sign is to spur states to enact the Uniform Electronic Transactions Act (UETA). Under E-Sign, a state may "modify, limit or supersede" the provisions of the federal act by enacting UETA "as approved and recommended for enactment in all the states" by the National Conference of Commissioners on Uniform State Laws or enacting a law that is consistent with E-Sign.** Thus, if a state enacts the official version of UETA or one consistent with E-Sign, the federal law is superceded by the state law. UETA is similar to E-Sign. It specifies that e-signatures and e-records can be used in contract formation, in audits, and as evidence. Selective differences between E-Sign and UETA are identified below. **For Example,** inventor Stewart Lamle sued toy maker Mattel, Inc., for breach of contract. The U.S. Court of Appeals for the Federal Circuit remanded the case for trial after resolving the motions before it. The facts reveal that after a June 11, 1997, meeting of the parties, Mattel employee Mike Bucher sent an e-mail dated June 26 to Lamle, which set forth the terms agreed to in principle at the meeting with the salutation "Best regards, Mike Bucher" appearing at the end of the e-mail. The court resolved the issue of whether an e-mail is a writing "subscribed by the party to be charged or the party's agent" in Lamle's favor. The court stated that under the UETA, the e-signature satisfies the state's (California's) Statute of Frauds. Because the e-mail was sent in 1997 prior to the effective date on the UETA, January 1, 2000, an evaluation of state common law was necessary. The court stated that it could see no meaningful difference between a

---

*Pub L 106-229, 114 Stat 464, 15 USC § 7001.

** § 102(a) and 102(a)(2). Forty-eight states and the District of Columbia have enacted the UETA in some form.

E-COMMERCE AND CYBERLAW

continued

typewritten signature on a telegram, which is sufficient to be a signature under state law, and the typed signature on the June 26 e-mail. It concluded that the e-mail satisfies the Statute of Frauds, assuming that there was a binding oral agreement on June 11.***

(a) General Rule of Parity. E-Sign provides for parity of electronic and paper signatures, contracts, and records. Electronic signatures and contracts satisfy the statute of frauds to the same extent they would if embodied as paper contracts with handwritten signatures. Internet contracts are neither more nor less valid, legal, and binding than are offline paper contracts. The rules are the same! The UETA is comparable to E-Sign in that it treats e-signatures and e-records as if they were handwritten.†

(b) Identity Verification. Neither E-Sign nor UETA is a digital signature law in that neither requires security procedures or a certification authority for the verification of electronic signatures. The parties themselves determine how they will verify each other's identity. Some options are a credit card, a password or PIN, public-key cryptographic exchange of digital signatures, or biometric signatures.

(c) Exceptions. The E-Sign Act exempts documents and records on trust and estate law so that it does not cover wills, codicils, and testamentary trusts or commercial law matters such as checks, negotiable instruments, and letters of credit. The act also does not cover court documents and cancellation of health and life insurance. Generally, the UETA also does not apply to these documents and records set forth previously.

(d) Consumer Protection and Notice and Consent Requirements. Consumer protection laws remain intact under E-Sign. Protections exist for consumers to consent to receiving electronic contracts, records, and documents; and businesses must tell consumers of their right to receive hard-copy documents.

Consumers must consent to receiving documents electronically or confirm consent electronically. For example, a consumer and a business may have negotiated terms of a contract by telephone and agreed to execute their agreement by e-mail. The consumer is then sent an e-mail that contains a consent disclosure, which contains a hypertext markup language (HTML) link the consumer can use to test her ability to view the contract in HTML. The consumer then returns the e-mail message to the business, thereby confirming electronically her consent to use this electronic means.

The UETA, like E-Sign, defers to existing substantive law regarding consumer protection.

(e) Time and Place of Sending and Receipt. E-Sign does not contain a provision addressing basic contract requirements such as sending and delivery, leaving such matters to existing contract law. However, the UETA provides that an electronic record is sent when it (1) is properly directed to an information processing system designated or used by the recipient to receive such records and from which the recipient may recover that record; (2) is in a form that the recipient's system is able to process; and (3) enters an information processing system that is in the control of the recipient but outside the control

---

*** *Lamle v Mattel, Inc.*, 394 F3d 1355 (Fed Cir 2005).
† UETA § 7(a) and 7(b).

E-COMMERCE AND CYBERLAW

continued

of the sender. An electronic record is received when (1) it enters an information processing system designated or used by the recipient to receive such records and from which the recipient is able to obtain the record and (2) it is in a form that the recipient's system can process.[††]

(f) Errors. Unlike E-Sign, which leaves matters relating to errors to be resolved by existing state contract law, UETA creates a system for dealing with errors. For example, when Marv Hale clicks on "buy" to make an online purchase of 12 bottles of Napa Valley Supreme Chardonnay at $9.90 per bottle, the computer will produce the equivalent of an invoice that includes the product's name, description, quantity, and price to enable Marv to avoid possible error when forming the electronic contract. This procedure gives the buyer an opportunity to identify and immediately correct an error. When such a procedure is not in effect and an error is later discovered, prompt notice to the other party can cure the error under Section 10 of the UETA.[†††]

[††] UETA § 15.
[†††] UETA § 10(2)(A)-(C).

The signature may be an ordinary one or any symbol that is adopted by the party as a signature. It may consist of initials, figures, or a mark. In the absence of a local statute that provides otherwise, a signature may be made by pencil, pen, typewriter, print, or stamp. As will be discussed, electronic signatures have parity with on-paper signatures.

(b) CONTENT The note or memorandum must contain all of the essential terms of the contract so the court can determine just what was agreed. If any essential term is missing, the writing is not sufficient. A writing evidencing a sale of land that does not describe the land or identify the buyer does not satisfy the statute of frauds. The subject matter must be identified either within the writing itself or in other writings to which it refers. A deposit check given by the buyer to the seller does not take an oral land sales contract out of the statute of frauds. This is so because the check does not set forth the terms of the sale.

The note or memorandum may consist of one writing or of separate papers, such as letters, or a combination of such papers. Separate writings cannot be considered together unless they are linked. Linkage may be express reference in each writing to the other or by the fact that each writing clearly deals with the same subject matter.

---

4. EFFECT OF NONCOMPLIANCE

The majority of states hold that a contract that does not comply with the statute of frauds is not enforceable.[13] If an action is brought to enforce the contract, the

---

[13] The UCC creates several statutes of frauds of limited applicability, in which it uses the phrase "not enforceable": § 1-206 (sale of intangible personal property); § 2-201 (sale of goods); and § 8-319 (sale of securities).

defendant can raise the defense that the alleged contract is not enforceable because it is not evidenced by a writing, as required by the statute of frauds.

(a) Recovery of Value Conferred   In most instances, a person who is prevented from enforcing a contract because of the statute of frauds is nevertheless entitled to recover from the other party the value of any services or property furnished or money given under the oral contract. Recovery is not based on the terms of the contract but on a quasi-contractual obligation. The other party is to restore to the plaintiff what was received in order to prevent unjust enrichment at the plaintiff's expense. **For Example,** when an oral contract for services cannot be enforced because of the statute of frauds, the person performing the work may recover the reasonable value of the services rendered.

CASE SUMMARY

Limited Effect of Oral Contract under Statute of Frauds

FACTS: Richard Golden orally agreed to sell his land to Earl Golden, who paid a deposit of $3,000. The transaction was never completed, and Earl sued for the return of his deposit. Richard claimed that the statute of frauds prevented Earl from proving that there ever was an oral contract under which a deposit of money had been paid.

DECISION: Judgment for Earl. The statute of frauds bars enforcement of an oral contract for the sale of land. It does not prevent proof of the contract for the purpose of showing that the seller has received a benefit that would unjustly enrich him if he retained it. Earl could therefore prove the existence of the unperformed oral contract to show that Richard had received a deposit that should be returned. [**Golden v Golden**, 541 P2d 1397 (Or 1975)]

(b) Who May Raise the Defense of Noncompliance?   Only a party to the oral contract may raise a defense that it is not binding because there is no writing that satisfies the statute of frauds. Third persons, such as an insurance company or the Internal Revenue Service, cannot claim that a contract is void because the statute of frauds was not satisfied.

 B ## PAROL EVIDENCE RULE

When the contract is evidenced by a writing, may the contract terms be changed by the testimony of witnesses?

5. EXCLUSION OF PAROL EVIDENCE

The general rule is that parol or extrinsic evidence will not be allowed into evidence to add to, modify, or contradict the terms of a written contract that is fully integrated or complete on its face.[14] Evidence of an alleged earlier oral or written agreement within the scope of the fully integrated written contract or evidence of an alleged contemporaneous oral agreement within the scope of the fully integrated written contract is inadmissible as *parol evidence.*

---

[14] *Speed v Muhana*, 619 SE2d 324 (Ga App 2005).

CASE SUMMARY

Closing the Door on Different Terms

FACTS: Airline Construction, Inc., made a contract with William Barr to build a hotel within 240 calendar days. Barr completed the work 57 days late. Airline Construction sued for damages for delay, and the contractor raised the defense that he had been induced to enter into the contract because it had been agreed that he would have additional time in which to complete the work. Airline Construction objected to the admission of evidence of this agreement.

DECISION: Parol evidence could not be admitted to show that there was a prior oral agreement that was inconsistent with the terms of the written contract. It was immaterial that the contractor had been "induced" to make the contract because of the alleged agreement. The fact remained that the written contract signed by him specified the time for performance and the parol evidence rule barred proof of any prior inconsistent oral agreement. [**Airline Construction, Inc. v Barr, 807 SW2d 247 (Tenn App 1990)**]

parol evidence rule rule that prohibits the introduction into evidence of oral or written statements made prior to or contemporaneously with the execution of a complete written contract, deed, or instrument, in the absence of clear proof of fraud, accident, or mistake causing the omission of the statement in question.

Parol evidence is admissible, however, to show fraud, duress, or mistake and under certain other circumstances to be discussed in the following paragraphs.

The **parol evidence rule** is based on the theory that either there never was an oral agreement or, if there was, the parties abandoned it when they reached the stage in negotiations of executing their written contract. The social objective of the parol evidence rule is to give stability to contracts and to prevent the assertion of terms that did not exist or did not survive the bargaining of the parties so as to reach inclusion in the final written contract.

For Example, *L* (landlord), the owner of a new development containing a five-store mall, discusses leasing one of the stores to *T* (tenant), who is viewing the property with his sister *S*, a highly credible poverty worker on leave from her duties in Central America. *L*, in the presence of *S*, agrees to give *T* the exclusive right to sell coffee and soft drinks in the five-store mall. Soon *L* and *T* execute a detailed written lease for the store, which makes no provision for *T*'s exclusive right to sell soft drinks and coffee in the mall. Subsequently, when two of the mall's new tenants begin to sell soft drinks and coffee, *T* brings suit against *L* for the breach of the oral promise granting him exclusive rights to sell soft drinks and coffee. *T* calls *S* as his first witness to prove the existence of the oral promise. *L*, through his attorney, will object to the admission of any evidence of a prior oral agreement that would add to or amend the fully integrated written lease, which set forth all restrictions on the landlord and tenant as to uses of the premises. After study of the matter, the court, based on the parol evidence rule, will not hear testimony from either *S* or *T* about the oral promise *L* made to *T*. In order to preserve his exclusive right to sell the drinks in question, *T* should have made certain that this promise was made part of the lease. His lawsuit will not be successful.

6. WHEN THE PAROL EVIDENCE RULE DOES NOT APPLY

The parol evidence rule will not apply in certain cases. The most common of these are discussed in the following paragraphs.

ambiguous having more than one reasonable interpretation.

(a) AMBIGUITY   If a written contract is **ambiguous** or may have two or more different meanings, parol evidence may generally be admitted to clarify the meaning.[15]

Parol evidence may also be admitted to show that a word used in a contract has a special trade meaning or a meaning in the particular locality that differs from the common meaning of that word.

(b) FRAUD, DURESS, OR MISTAKE   A contract apparently complete on its face may have omitted a provision that should have been included. Parol evidence may be admitted to show that a provision was omitted as the result of fraud, duress, or mistake and to further show what that provision stated. Parol evidence is admissible to show that a provision of the written contract was a mutual mistake even though the written provision is unambiguous.[16] When one party claims to have been fraudulently induced by the other to enter into a contract, the parol evidence rule does not bar proof that there was a fraud. **For Example,** the parol evidence rule does not bar proof that the seller of land intentionally misrepresented that the land was zoned to permit use as an industrial park. Such evidence does not contradict the terms of the contract but shows that the agreement is unenforceable.[17]

(c) MODIFICATION OF CONTRACT   The parol evidence rule prohibits only the contradiction of a complete written contract. It does not prohibit proof that the contract was thereafter modified or terminated.

CASE SUMMARY

All Sail and No Anchor

FACTS: On April 2, 1990, Christian Bourg hired Bristol Boat Co., Inc., and Bristol Marine Co. (defendants) to construct and deliver a yacht on July 1, 1990. However, the defendants did not live up to their promises and the contract was breached. On October 22, 1990, the defendants executed a written settlement agreement whereby Bourg agreed to pay an additional sum of $135,000 for the delivery of the yacht and to provide the defendants a loan of $80,000 to complete the construction of the vessel. Referencing the settlement agreement, the defendants at the same time executed a promissory note obliging them to repay the $80,000 loan plus interest in annual installments due on November 1 of each year, with the final payment due on November 1, 1994. The court stated in presenting the facts: "However, like the yacht itself, the settlement agreement soon proved to be just another hole in the water into which the plaintiff threw his money." Bourg sued the defendants after they failed to make certain payments on the note, and the court granted a motion for summary judgment in favor of Bourg for $59,081. The defendants appealed.

---

[15] *Berg v Hudesman,* 801 P2d 222 (Wash 1990). This is also the view followed by UCC § 2-202(a), which permits terms in a contract for the sale of goods to be "explained or supplemented by a course of dealing or usage of trade . . . or by course of performance." Such evidence is admissible not because there is an ambiguity but "in order that the true understanding of the parties as to the agreement may be reached." Official Code Comment to § 2-202.

[16] *Thompson v First Citizens Bank & Trust Co,* 151 NC App 704 (2002).

[17] *Edwards v Centrex Real Estate Corp.,* 61 Cal Rptr 518 (Cal App 1997).

{ **CASE SUMMARY** }

continued

DECISION: Judgment for Bourg. Because the defendants' affidavit recites that an alleged oral side agreement was entered into at the same time as the settlement agreement and promissory note—the oral side agreement allegedly stated "that the note would be paid for by services rendered by the defendants"—the oral side agreement would have constituted a contemporaneous modification that would merge into the integrated promissory note and settlement agreement and thus be barred from admission into evidence under the parol evidence rule. Although parties to an integrated written contract can modify their understanding by a subsequent oral pact, to be legally effective, there must be evidence of mutual assent to the essential terms of the modification and adequate consideration. Here the defendants adduced no competent evidence of either mutual assent to particular terms or a specific consideration that would be sufficiently definite to constitute an enforceable subsequent oral modification to the parties' earlier written agreements. Thus, legally this alleged oral agreement was all sail and no anchor. [**Bourg v Bristol Boat Co., 705 A2d 969 (RI 1998)**]

 RULES OF CONSTRUCTION AND INTERPRETATION

In interpreting contracts, courts are aided by certain rules.

7. INTENTION OF THE PARTIES

When persons enter into an agreement, it is to be presumed that they intend for their agreement to have some effect. A court will strive to determine the intent of the parties and to give effect to it. A contract, therefore, is to be enforced according to its terms.[18] A court cannot remake or rewrite the contract of the parties under the pretense of interpreting.[19]

No particular form of words is required, and any words manifesting the intent of the parties are sufficient. In the absence of proof that a word has a peculiar meaning or that it was employed by the parties with a particular meaning, a common word is given its ordinary meaning.

(a) MEANING OF WORDS Ordinary words are to be interpreted according to their ordinary meaning.[20] **For Example,** when a contract requires the gasoline dealer to pay the supplier for "gallons" supplied, the term *gallons* is unambiguous and does not require that an adjustment of the gallonage be made for the temperature.[21] When a contract calls for a businessperson to pay a builder for the builder's "costs," the term *costs* is unambiguous, meaning actual costs, not a lesser amount based on the builder's bid.[22]

If there is a common meaning to a term, that meaning will be followed even though the dictionary may contain additional meanings. If technical or trade terms are used in a contract, they are to be interpreted according to the area of technical knowledge or trade from which the terms are taken.

---

[18] See *Greenwald v Kersh*, 621 SE2d 463 (Ga App 2005).

[19] *Abbot v Schnader, Harrison, Segal & Lewis, LLP*, 805 A2d 547 (Pa Super 2002).

[20] *Thorton v D.F.W. Christian Television, Inc.*, 925 SW2d 17 (Tex App 1995).

[21] *Hopkins v BP Oil, Inc.*, 81 F3d 1070 (11th Cir 1996).

[22] *Batzer Construction, Inc. v Boyer*, 125 P3d 773 (Or App 2006).

(ETHICS & THE LAW)

Marvin Windows Cases

Marvin Windows and Doors Company of Minnesota (Marvin Windows) is the largest custom window manufacturer in the world. The president of this privately held company, Bill Marvin, and his son Jake, the company's chief operating officer, met with PPG Industries' Bob Ponchot on Jake's front lawn on a summer morning in 1984 and listened to Ponchot sell PPG's new wood preservative PILT. Panchot allegedly said that products treated with PILT would last longer than the windows on Jake Marvin's home, which had been treated by a competitor's product "Penta" and had already lasted 26 years. Relying on Ponchot's promises made on behalf of PPG, Bill Marvin made a handshake deal to use the new product. The product was used by the company for four years and soon thereafter Marvin Windows started receiving complaints about premature wood rot from customers. Marvin Windows' study of the problem concluded that PILT was the culprit. PPG's analysis found PILT blameless, and it refused to help Marvin Windows cover the cost of replacing the defective windows. In 1994, Marvin Windows sued PPG for, *inter alia,* breach of contract, and four years of discovery ensued. Bill Marvin stated that promises were made on Jake's lawn that summer morning, and he had a right to rely on them. "We never had a written contract, and I don't think that's naïve. They reneged on a handshake deal, and simply speaking, that's not right." PPG defended that there was no written agreement obliging PPG to pay for a portion of the cost of replacing the defective windows. PPG's attorney asserted that "Marvin Windows likes to tell you about a family-run business from a small town in Minnesota that does business on a handshake. . .but they are a $100 million international corporation with a long history of litigation." He further asserted that "experienced merchants ought to be smart enough to write a contract outlining who is responsible for what if the product they are buying doesn't work properly." Is Bill Marvin or PPG correct? Is it good business practice to have a written contract in effect for all company purchases, specifying the responsibilities of the parties if each product purchased does not work properly, or will this lead to a "battle of the forms" and increased expenses for both parties? Based on the assertions made by both Bill and Jake Marvin about the promises made by PPG, is it unethical for PPG to renege on the promises?

Assume that Marvin Windows prevails, asserting a warranty of future performance based on Panchot's statements. Acceptance of this theory allowed Marvin Windows to get around the statute of limitations issue raised by PPG and to obtain in excess of $100 million in damages, based in part on the position that it was incurring costs related to customer claims arising from the leaky and rotten windows. In *Kelleher v Marvin Lumber and Cedar Co.,* [*] however, a homeowner who had purchased Marvin windows treated with PILT in 1986, discovered window rot problems in 17 of his windows in 1998. Litigation ensued, and Marvin Windows, seeking to avoid financial responsibility for the defective windows, produced a one-year limited warranty effective in 1986, which accompanied the windows that were delivered to the plaintiff. Marvin appealed a judgment for Kelleher, asserting the position that the one-year warranty applied, which position was directly contrary to the position it took in its litigation with PPG. Was it ethical for Marvin to take such a contradictory position in the lawsuit against it by the homeowner, after collecting more than $100 million in its successful lawsuit with PPG, in an attempt to avoid its liability for the homeowner's claim?

---

[*] 891 A.2d 477 (NH 2005); See *Marvin Lumber and Cedar Co. v PPG Industries,* 223 F3d 873 (8th Cir 2000).

(b) INCORPORATION BY REFERENCE   The contract may not cover all of the agreed terms. The missing terms may be found in another document. Frequently, the parties executing the contract for storage will simply state that a storage contract is entered into and that the contract applies to the goods listed in the schedule attached to and made part of the contract. Likewise, a contract for the construction of a building may involve plans and specifications on file in a named city office. The contract will simply state that the building is to be constructed according to those plans and specifications that are "incorporated herein and made part of this contract." When there is such an **incorporation by reference,** the contract consists of both the original document and the detailed statement that is incorporated in it.

incorporation by reference contract consisting of both the original or skeleton document and the detailed statement that is incorporated in it.

When a contract refers to another document, however, the contract must sufficiently describe the document or so much of it as is to be interpreted as part of the contract.

CASE SUMMARY

Specificity Required

FACTS: Consolidated Credit Counseling Services, Inc. (Consolidated), sued Affinity Internet, Inc., doing business as SkyNet WEB (Affinity) for breach of its contract to provide computer and Web-hosting services. Affinity moved to compel arbitration, and Consolidated argued that the contract between the parties did not contain an arbitration clause. The contract between the parties stated in part: "This contract is subject to all of SkyNet WEB's terms, conditions, user and acceptable use policies located at http://www.skynetweb.com/company/legal/legal.php." By going to the Web site and clicking to paragraph 17 of the User Agreement, an arbitration provision can be found. The contract itself, however, makes no reference to an agreement to arbitrate, nor was paragraph 17 expressly referred to or described in the contract. Nor was a hard copy of the information on the Web site either signed by or furnished to Consolidated.

DECISION: Judgment for Consolidated. Mere reference to another document is not sufficient to incorporate that document into the contract absent specificity describing the portion of the writing to apply to the contract. [**Affinity Internet v Consolidated Credit, 920 So2d 1286 (Fla App 2006)**]

---

8. WHOLE CONTRACT

The provisions of a contract must be construed as a whole in such a way that every part is given effect.

Every word of a contract is to be given effect if reasonably possible. The contract is to be construed as a whole, and if the plain language of the contract thus viewed solves the dispute, the court is to make no further analysis.

---

9. CONTRADICTORY AND AMBIGUOUS TERMS

One term in a contract may conflict with another term, or one term may have two different meanings. It is then necessary for the court to determine whether there is a contract and, if so, what the contract really means.

CASE SUMMARY

Who Pays the Piper?

FACTS: Olander Contracting Co., developer Gail Wachter, and the City of Bismarck, North Dakota, entered into a water and sewer construction contract including, among other things, connecting a 10-inch sewer line from Wachter's housing development to the city's existing 36-inch concrete sewer main and installing a manhole at the connection, to be paid for by Wachter. Olander installed the manhole, but it collapsed within a few days. Olander installed a second manhole, with a large base supported by pilings, but it too failed a few days after it was installed. Olander then placed a rock bedding under the city's sewer main, replaced 78 feet of the existing concrete pipe with PVC pipe, and installed a manhole a third time on a larger base. Olander sued Wachter and the City of Bismarck for damages of $456,536.25 for extra work it claims it was required to perform to complete its contract. Both defendants denied they were responsible for the amount sued under the contract. The jury returned a special verdict, finding that Olander performed "extra work/unforeseen work . . . for which it is entitled to be compensated in excess of the contract price" in the amount of $220,849.67, to be paid by the City of Bismarck. Appeals were taken.

DECISION: Judgment for Olander. The trial judge properly made the initial determination that the contract language was ambiguous. That is, the language used by the parties could support good arguments for the positions of both parties. This resolved a question of law. Once this determination had been made, the judge allowed extrinsic evidence from all parties as to what they meant when they negotiated the contract. This evidence related to the questions of fact, which were left to the jury. Testimony was taken from the parties who negotiated the contract, and testimony was also heard about the role of each of the parties in the actual construction of the manhole, the cause for the collapses, and why the contractor had to replace the city's existing concrete pipe with PVC pipe and the city's role in making this determination. The jury then fulfilled its role answering the question whether or not Olander had performed extra work in the affirmative, concluding that the city was required to pay for it. [**Olander Contracting v Wachter, 643 NW2d 29 (2002)**]

In some instances, apparent conflict between the terms of a contract is eliminated by the introduction of parol evidence or by the application of an appropriate rule of construction.[23]

(a) NATURE OF WRITING   When a contract is partly a printed form or partly type-written and partly handwritten and the written part conflicts with the printed or typewritten part, the written part prevails. When there is a conflict between a printed part and a typewritten part, the latter prevails. Consequently, when a clause typewritten on a printed form conflicts with what is stated by the print, the conflicting print is ignored and the typewritten clause controls. This rule is based on the belief that the parties had given greater thought to what they typed or wrote for the particular contract as contrasted with printed words already in a form designed to cover many transactions. Thus, a typewritten provision to pay 90 cents per unit overrode a preprinted provision setting the price as 45 cents per unit.

When there is a conflict between an amount or quantity expressed both in words and figures, as on a check, the amount or quantity expressed in words prevails. Words control because there is less danger that a word will be wrong than a number.

---

[23] *Lennox Lewis v Don King Productions,* 94 F Supp 2d 430 (SDNY 2000).

(b) Ambiguity   A contract is *ambiguous* when the intent of the parties is uncertain and the contract is capable of more than one reasonable interpretation.[24] The background from which the contract and the dispute arose may help in determining the intention of the parties. **For Example,** when suit was brought in Minnesota on a Canadian insurance policy, the question arose whether the dollar limit of the policy referred to Canadian or U.S. dollars. The court concluded that Canadian dollars were intended. Both the insurer and the insured were Canadian corporations; the original policy, endorsements to the policy, and policy renewals were written in Canada; over the years, premiums had been paid in Canadian dollars; and a prior claim on the policy had been settled by the payment of an amount computed on the basis of Canadian dollars.

(c) Strict Construction against Drafting Party   An ambiguous contract is interpreted strictly against the party who drafted it.[25] **For Example,** an insurance policy containing ambiguous language regarding coverage or exclusions is interpreted against the insurer and in favor of the insured when two interpretations are reasonably possible. This rule is a secondary rule that may be invoked only after all of the ordinary interpretive guides have been exhausted. The rule basically assigns the risk of an unresolvable ambiguity to the party creating it.[26]

10. IMPLIED TERMS

In some cases, a court will imply a term to cover a situation for which the parties failed to provide or, when needed, to give the contract a construction or meaning that is reasonable.

The court often implies details of the performance of a contract not expressly stated in the contract. In a contract to perform work, there is an implied promise to use such skill as is necessary to properly perform the work. When a contract does not specify the time for performance, a reasonable time is implied.

In every contract, there is an implied obligation that neither party shall do anything that will have the effect of destroying or injuring the right of the other party to receive the fruits of the contract. This means that in every contract there exists an implied covenant of **good faith** and fair dealing. When a contract may reasonably be interpreted in different ways, a court should make the interpretation that is in harmony with good faith and fair dealing. **For Example,** when a contract is made subject to the condition that one of the parties obtain financing, that party must make reasonable, good-faith efforts to obtain financing. The party is not permitted to do nothing and then claim that the contract is not binding because the condition has not been satisfied. Likewise, when a contract requires a party to obtain government approval, the party must use all reasonable means to obtain it.[27]

The Uniform Commercial Code imposes an obligation of good faith in the performance or enforcement of every contract.[28]

good faith absence of knowledge of any defects or problems.

11. CONDUCT AND CUSTOM

The conduct of the parties and the customs and usages of a particular trade may give meaning to the words of the parties and thus aid in the interpretation of their contract.

---

[24] *Kaufman & Stewart v Weinbrenner Shoe Co.,* 589 NW2d 499 (Minn App 1999).

[25] *Idaho Migrant Council, Inc. v Warila,* 89 P2d 39 (Wyo 1995).

[26] *Premier Title Co. v Donahue,* 765 NE2d 513 (Ill App 2002).

[27] *Kroboth v Brent,* 625 NYS2d 748 (App Div 1995).

[28] UCC §§ 1-201(19), 1-203.

(a) Conduct of the Parties   The conduct of the parties in carrying out the terms of a contract is the best guide to determine the parties' intent. When performance has been repeatedly tendered and accepted without protest, neither party will be permitted to claim that the contract was too indefinite to be binding. **For Example,** a travel agent made a contract with a hotel to arrange for trips to the hotel. After some 80 trips had already been arranged and paid for by the hotel at the contract price without any dispute about whether the contract obligation was satisfied, any claim by the travel agent that it could charge additional fees must be rejected.

usage of trade language and customs of an industry.

(b) Custom and Usage of Trade   The customs and **usages of trade** or commercial activity to which the contract relates may be used to interpret the terms of a contract.[29] **For Example,** when a contract for the construction of a building calls for a "turn-key construction," industry usage is admissible to show what this means: a construction in which all the owner needs to do is to turn the key in the lock to open the building for use and in which all construction risks are assumed by the contractor.[30]

Custom and usage, however, cannot override express provisions of a contract that are inconsistent with custom and usage.

12. AVOIDANCE OF HARDSHIP

As a general rule, a party is bound by a contract even though it proves to be a bad bargain. If possible, a court will interpret a contract to avoid hardship. Courts will, if possible, interpret a vague contact in a way to avoid any forfeiture of a party's interest.

When hardship arises because the contract makes no provision for the situation that has occurred, the court will sometimes imply a term to avoid the hardship.

CASE SUMMARY

Court Glides with Clyde

FACTS: Standard Oil Company made a nonexclusive jobbing or wholesale dealership contract with Perkins, which limited him to selling Standard's products and required Perkins to maintain certain minimum prices. Standard Oil had the right to approve or disapprove Perkins's customers. To be able to perform under his contract, Perkins had to make a substantial monetary investment, and his only income was from the commissions on the sales of Standard's products. Standard Oil made some sales directly to Perkins's customers. When Perkins protested, Standard Oil pointed out that the contract did not contain any provision making his rights exclusive. Perkins sued Standard Oil to compel it to stop dealing with his customers.

DECISION: Judgment for Perkins. In view of the expenditure required of Perkins to operate his business and to perform his part of the contract and because of his dependence on his customers, the interpretation should be made that Standard Oil would not solicit customers of Perkins. This is true even though the contract did not give Perkins an exclusive dealership within the given geographic area. [**Perkins v Standard Oil Co., 383 P2d 107 (Or 1963)**]

---

[29] *Affiliated FM Ins. Co. v Constitution Reinsurance Corp.,* 626 NE2d 878 (Mass 1994).
[30] *Blue v R.L. Glossen Contracting, Inc.,* 327 SE2d 582 (Ga App 1985).

LAWFLIX

The Santa Clause (1996) (PG)

When Scott Calvin (Tim Allen) tries on a Santa suit, he discovers that he has assumed all of Santa's responsibility. Calvin tries to challenge his acceptance of the terms of the agreement. Analyze the problems with offer, acceptance, and terms in very fine print (a magnifying glass is required). Do the terms of the suit contract apply when Calvin did not know them at the time he put on the suit?

For movie clips that illustrate business law concepts, see LawFlix at **http://wdvl.westbuslaw.com.**

> SUMMARY

An oral agreement may be a contract unless it is the intention of the parties that they should not be bound by the agreement without a writing executed by them. Certain contracts must be evidenced by a writing, however, or else they cannot be enforced. The statutes that declare this exception are called *statutes of frauds.* Statutes of frauds commonly require that a contract be evidenced by writing in the case of (1) an agreement that cannot be performed within one year after the contract is made, (2) an agreement to sell any interest in land, (3) a promise to answer for the debt or default of another, (4) a promise by the executor or administrator of a decedent's estate to pay a claim against the estate from personal funds, (5) a promise made in consideration of marriage, and (6) a contract for the sale of goods for a purchase price of $500 or more.

To evidence a contract to satisfy a statute of frauds, there must be a writing of all essential terms. The writing must be signed by the defendant against whom suit is brought for enforcement of the contract.

If the applicable statute of frauds is not satisfied, the oral contract cannot be enforced. To avoid unjust enrichment, a plaintiff barred from enforcing an oral contract may recover from the other contracting party the reasonable value of the benefits conferred by the plaintiff on the defendant.

When there is a written contract, the question arises whether that writing is the exclusive statement of the parties' agreement. If the writing is the complete and final statement of the contract, parol evidence as to matters agreed to before or at the time the writing was signed is not admissible to contradict the writing. This is called the *parol evidence rule.* In any case, the parol evidence rule does not bar parol evidence when (1) the writing is ambiguous, (2) the writing is not a true statement of the agreement of the parties because of fraud, duress, or mistake, or (3) the existence, modification, or illegality of a contract is in controversy.

Because a contract is based on the agreement of the parties, courts must determine the intent of the parties manifested in the contract. The intent that is to be enforced is the intent as it reasonably appears to a third person. This objective intent is followed.

In interpreting a contract, ordinary words are to be given their ordinary meanings. If trade or technical terms have been used, they are interpreted according to their technical meanings. The court must consider the whole contract and not read a particular part out of context. When different writings are executed as part of the same transaction, or one writing refers to or incorporates another, all of the writings are to be read together as the contract of the parties.

When provisions of a contract are contradictory, the court will try to reconcile or eliminate the conflict. If this cannot be done, the conclusion may be that there is no contract because the conflict makes the agreement indefinite as to a material matter. In some cases, conflict is solved by considering the form of conflicting terms. Handwriting prevails over typing and a printed form, and typing prevails over a printed form. Ambiguity will be eliminated in some cases by the admission of parol evidence or by interpreting the provision strictly against the party preparing the contract, particularly when that party has significantly greater bargaining power.

In most cases, the parties are held to their contract exactly as it has been written. The law implies that performance is to be made within a reasonable time and that details of performance are reasonable when the contract fails to be specific on these points. Also, the law implies an obligation to act in good faith.

> QUESTIONS AND CASE PROBLEMS

1. Kelly made a written contract to sell certain land to Brown and gave Brown a deed to the land. Thereafter, Kelly sued Brown to get back a 20-foot strip of the land. Kelly claimed that before making the written contract, it was agreed that Kelly would sell all of his land to Brown to make it easier for Brown to get a building permit, but after that was done, the 20-foot strip would be reconveyed to Kelly. Was Kelly entitled to the 20-foot strip? What ethical values are involved? [*Brown v Kelly,* 545 So 2d 518 (Fla App)]

2. Martin made an oral contract with Cresheim Garage to work as its manager for two years. Cresheim wrote Martin a letter stating that the oral contract had been made and setting forth all of its terms. Cresheim later refused to recognize the contract. Martin sued Cresheim for breach of the contract and offered Cresheim's letter in evidence as proof of the contract. Cresheim claimed that the oral contract was not binding because the contract was not in writing and the letter referring to the contract was not a contract but only a letter. Was the contract binding?

3. Lawrence loaned money to Moore, who died without repaying the loan. Lawrence claimed that when he mentioned the matter to Moore's widow, she promised to pay the debt. She did not pay it, and Lawrence sued her on her promise. Does she have any defense? [*Moore v Lawrence,* 480 SW2d 941 (Ark)]

4. Jackson signed an agreement to sell 79 acres of land to Devenyns. Jackson owned 80 acres and was apparently intending to keep for himself the acre on which his home was located. The written agreement also stated that "Devenyns shall have the option to buy on property _____," but nothing was stated in the blank space. Devenyns sued to enforce the agreement. Was it binding? [*In re Jackson's Estate,* 892 P2d 786 (Wyo)]

5. Boeing Airplane Co. contracted with Pittsburgh–Des Moines Steel Co. for the latter to construct a supersonic wind tunnel. R.H. Freitag Manufacturing Co. sold materials to York-Gillespie Co., which subcontracted to do part of the work. To persuade Freitag to keep supplying materials on credit, Boeing and the principal contractor both assured Freitag that he would be paid. When Freitag was not paid by the subcontractor, he sued Boeing and the contractor. They defended on the ground that the assurances given Freitag were not written. Decide. What ethical values are involved? [*R.H. Freitag Mfg. Co. v Boeing Airplane Co.,* 347 P2d 1074 (Wash)]

6. Louise Pulsifer owned a farm that she wanted to sell and ran an ad in the local newspaper. After Russell Gillespie agreed to purchase the farm, Pulsifer wrote him a letter stating that she would not sell it. He sued her to enforce the contract, and she raised the defense of the statute of frauds. The letter she had signed did not contain any of the terms of the sale. Gillespie, however, claimed that the newspaper ad could be combined with her letter to satisfy the statute of frauds. Was he correct? [*Gillespie v Pulsifer,* 655 SW2d 123 (Mo)]

7. In February or March, Corning Glass Works orally agreed to retain Hanan as management consultant from May 1 of that year to April 30 of the next year for a present value fee of $200,000. Was this agreement binding? Is this decision ethical? [*Hanan v Corning Glass Works,* 314 NYS2d 804 (App Div)]

8. In letters between the two, Rita Borelli contracted to sell "my car" to Viola Smith for $2,000. It was later shown that Borelli owned two cars. She refused to deliver either car to Smith, and Smith sued Borelli for breach of contract. Borelli raised the defense that the contract was too indefinite to be enforced because it could not be determined from the writing which car was the subject matter

of the contract. Is the contract too indefinite to be enforced?

9. Panasonic Industrial Co. (PIC) created a contract making Manchester Equipment Co., Inc. (MECI), a nonexclusive wholesale distributor of its products. The contract stated that PIC reserved the unrestricted right to solicit and make direct sales of the products to anyone, anywhere. The contract also stated that it contained the entire agreement of the parties and that any prior agreement or statement was superseded by the contract. PIC subsequently began to make direct sales to two of MECI's established customers. MECI claimed that this was a breach of the distribution contract and sued PIC for damages. Decide. What ethical values are involved? [*Manchester Equipment Co. Inc. v Panasonic Industrial Co.*, 529 NYS2d 532 (App Div)]

10. A contract made for the sale of a farm stated that the buyer's deposit would be returned "if for any reason the farm cannot be sold." The seller later stated that she had changed her mind and would not sell, and she offered to return the deposit. The buyer refused to take the deposit back and brought suit to enforce the contract. The seller contended that the "any reason" provision extended to anything, including the seller's changing her mind. Was the buyer entitled to recover? [*Phillips v Rogers*, 200 SE2d 676 (W Va)]

11. Integrated, Inc., entered into a contract with the state of California to construct a building. It then subcontracted the electrical work to Alec Fergusson Electrical Contractors. The subcontract was a printed form with blanks filled in by typewriting. The printed payment clause required Integrated to pay Fergusson on the 15th day of the month following the submission of invoices by Fergusson. The typewritten part of the contract required Integrated to pay Fergusson "immediately following payment" (by the state) to the general contractor. When was payment required? [*Integrated, Inc. v Alec Fergusson Electrical Contractors*, 58 Cal Rptr 503 (Cal App)]

12. Norwest Bank had been lending money to Tresch to run a dairy farm. The balance due the bank after several years was $147,000. The loan agreement stated that Tresch would not buy any new equipment in excess of $500 without the express consent of the bank. Some time later, Tresch applied to the bank for a loan of $3,100 to purchase some equipment. The bank refused to make the loan because it did not believe the new equipment would correct the condition for which it would be bought and would not result in significant additional income. Tresch then sued the bank, claiming that its refusal to make the loan was a breach of the implied covenant of good faith and fair dealing. Decide. [*Tresch v Norwest Bank of Lewistown*, 778 P2d 874 (Mont)]

13. Physicians Mutual Insurance Co. issued a policy covering Brown's life. The policy declared that it did not cover any deaths resulting from "mental disorder, alcoholism, or drug addiction." Brown was killed when she fell while intoxicated. The insurance company refused to pay because of the quoted provision. Her executor, Savage, sued the insurance company. Did the insurance company have a defense? [*Physicians Mutual Ins. Co. v Savage*, 296 NE2d 165 (Ind App)]

14. The Dickinson Elks Club conducted an annual Labor Day golf tournament. Charbonneau Buick-Pontiac offered to give a new car as a prize to anyone making "a hole in one on hole no. 8." The golf course of the club was only nine holes. To play 18 holes, the players would go around the course twice, although they would play from different tees or locations for the second nine holes. On the second time around, what was originally the eighth hole became the seventeenth hole. Grove was a contestant in the tournament. He scored 3 on the no. 8 hole, but on approaching it for the second time as the seventeenth hole, he made a hole in one. He claimed the prize car from Charbonneau. The latter claimed that Grove had not won the prize because he did not make the hole in one on the eighth hole. Decide. [*Grove v Charbonneau Buick-Pontiac, Inc.*, 240 NW2d 8533 (ND)]

15. Beck and Co., a brewery, gave Gianelli Distributing Co. a franchise to distribute Beck's Beer. The franchise agreement specified that it would continue "unless and until terminated at any time by 30 days' written notice by either party to the other." Some time thereafter, Beck notified Gianelli that the franchise was terminated. Gianelli claimed that the franchise could be

terminated only upon proof of reasonable cause. He offered evidence of trade usage to show that common practice required cause for termination and further claimed that such usage would be read into the franchise agreement with Beck. Is this evidence admissible?

> CPA QUESTIONS

1. Which of the following statements is true with regard to the statute of frauds?

   a. All contracts involving consideration of more than $500 must be in writing.
   b. The written contract must be signed by all parties.
   c. The statute of frauds applies to contracts that can be fully performed within one year from the date they are made.
   d. The contract terms may be stated in more than one document.

2. With regard to an agreement for the sale of real estate, the statute of frauds

   a. Requires that the entire agreement be in a single writing
   b. Requires that the purchase price be fair and adequate in relation to the value of the real estate
   c. Does *not* require that the agreement be signed by all parties
   d. Does *not* apply if the value of the real estate is less than $500

3. In negotiations with Andrews for the lease of Kemp's warehouse, Kemp orally agreed to pay one-half of the cost of the utilities. The written lease, later prepared by Kemp's attorney, provided that Andrews pay all of the utilities. Andrews failed to carefully read the lease and signed it. When Kemp demanded that Andrews pay all of the utilities, Andrews refused, claiming that the lease did not accurately reflect the oral agreement. Andrews also learned that Kemp intentionally misrepresented the condition of the structure of the warehouse during the negotiations between the parties. Andrews sued to rescind the lease and intends to introduce evidence of the parties' oral agreement about sharing the utilities and the fraudulent statements made by Kemp. Will the parol evidence rule prevent the admission of evidence concerning each of the following?

	Oral agreement regarding who pays the utilities	*Fraudulent statements by Kemp*
a.	Yes	Yes
b.	No	Yes
c.	Yes	No
d.	No	No

THIRD PERSONS
AND CONTRACTS

 THIRD-PARTY BENEFICIARY CONTRACTS

1. DEFINITION
2. MODIFICATION OR TERMINATION OF INTENDED THIRD-PARTY BENEFICIARY CONTRACT
3. LIMITATIONS ON INTENDED THIRD-PARTY BENEFICIARY
4. INCIDENTAL BENEFICIARIES

 ASSIGNMENTS

5. DEFINITIONS
6. FORM OF ASSIGNMENT
7. NOTICE OF ASSIGNMENT
8. ASSIGNMENT OF RIGHT TO MONEY
9. NONASSIGNABLE RIGHTS
10. RIGHTS OF ASSIGNEE
11. CONTINUING LIABILITY OF ASSIGNOR
12. LIABILITY OF ASSIGNEE
13. WARRANTIES OF ASSIGNOR
14. DELEGATION OF DUTIES

LEARNING OBJECTIVES

After studying this chapter, you should be able to

LO.1 Distinguish between a third-party beneficiary and an incidental beneficiary

LO.2 Define an assignment of contract rights

LO.3 State the limitations on assignability and right to performance

LO.4 Describe what constitutes a delegation of duties

LO.5 State the liability of the parties after a proper delegation of duties has been made

LO.6 Describe the status of an assignee with respect to defenses and setoffs available against the assignor

LO.7 State the significance of a notice of assignment

LO.8 State the liability of an assignor to an assignee

THIRD-PARTY BENEFICIARY CONTRACTS

Generally, only the parties to a contract may sue on it. However, in some cases a third person who is not a party to the contract may sue on the contract.

1. DEFINITION

intended beneficiary third person of a contract whom the contract is intended to benefit.

third-party beneficiary third person whom the parties to a contract intend to benefit by the making of the contract and to confer upon such person the right to sue for breach of contract.

When a contract is intended to benefit a third person, such a person is an **intended beneficiary** and may bring suit on and enforce the contract. In some states, the right of the intended **third-party beneficiary** to sue on the contract is declared by statute. **For Example,** Ibberson Co., the general contractor hired by AgGrow Oils, LLC to design and build an oilseed processing plant, contracted with subcontractor Anderson International Corp. to supply critical seed processing equipment for the project. Anderson's formal proposal to Ibberson identified the AgGrow Oils Project, and the proposal included drawings of the planned AgGrow plant. Under state law, this contract made between the contractor and subcontractor for the express benefit of the third party AgGrow Oils could be enforced by the intended third party beneficiary AgGrow Oils. The project was a failure. AgGrow was successful in the lawsuit against Anderson under the Anderson-Ibberson contract, having the standing to sue as an intended third-party beneficiary of that contract.[1]

(a) CREDITOR BENEFICIARY   The intended beneficiary is sometimes classified as a *creditor beneficiary* when the promisee's primary intent is to discharge a duty owed to the third party.[2] **For Example,** when Max Giordano sold his business, Sameway Laundry, to Harry Phinn, he had three years of payments totaling $14,500 owing to Davco, Inc., on a commercial Davco shirt drying and pressing machine purchased in 2006. Max (the promisee) made a contract with Harry to sell the business for a stipulated sum. A provision in this contract selling the business called for Harry (the promisor) to make the Davco machine payments when due over the next three years. Should Harry fail to make payments, Davco, Inc., as an intended creditor beneficiary under the contract between Max and Harry, would have standing to sue Harry for breach of the payment provision in the contract.

(b) DONEE BENEFICIARY   The second type of intended beneficiary is a *donee beneficiary* to whom the promisee's primary intent in contracting is to give a benefit. A life insurance contract is such an intended third-party beneficiary contract. The promisee-insured pays premiums to the insurer under the contract of insurance so that, upon the death of the insured, the promisor-insurer would pay the sum designated in the contract to the beneficiary. The beneficiary's rights vest upon the insured's death, and the beneficiary can sue the insurance company upon the insured's death even though the insurance company never made any agreement directly with the beneficiary.

(c) NECESSITY OF INTENT   A third person does not have the status of an intended third-party beneficiary unless it is clear at the time the contract was formed that the parties intended to impose a direct obligation with respect to the third person.[3]

[1] *AgGrow Oils, LLC v National Union Fire Ins.*, 420 F3d 751 (8th Cir 2005).

[2] The Restatement (Second) of Contracts § 302 substitutes "intended beneficiary" for the terms "creditor" and "donee" beneficiary. However, some courts continue to use the classifications of creditor and donee third-party beneficiaries. Regardless of the terminology, the law continues to be the same. See *Stein v Stewart*, 80 SW2d 586 (Tex 2002).

[3] *American United Logistics, Inc. v Catellus*, 319 F3d 921 (7th Cir 2003).

In determining whether there is intent to benefit a third party, the surrounding circumstances as well as the contract may be examined.[4] There is a strong presumption that the parties to a contract intend to benefit only themselves.[5]

CASE SUMMARY

The Pest Control Case

FACTS: Admiral Pest Control had a standing contract with Lodging Enterprises to spray its motel every month to exterminate pests. Copeland, a guest in the motel, was bitten by a spider. She sued Admiral on the ground that she was a third-party beneficiary of the extermination contract.

DECISION: Judgment against Copeland. There was no intent manifested in the contract that guests of the motel were beneficiaries of the contract. The contract was made by the motel to protect itself. The guests were incidental beneficiaries of that contract and therefore could not sue for its breach. [**Copeland v Admiral Pest Control Co., 933 P2d 937 (Okla App 1996)**]

(d) DESCRIPTION   It is not necessary that the intended third-party beneficiary be identified by name. The beneficiary may be identified by class, with the result that any member of that class is a third-party beneficiary. **For Example,** a contract between the promoter of an automobile stock car race and the owner of the racetrack contains a promise by the owner to pay specified sums of money to each driver racing a car in certain races. A person driving in one of the designated races is a third-party beneficiary and can sue the owner on the contract for the promised compensation.

2. MODIFICATION OR TERMINATION OF INTENDED THIRD-PARTY BENEFICIARY CONTRACT

Can the parties to the contract modify or terminate it so as to destroy the right of the intended third-party beneficiary? If the contract contains an express provision allowing a change of beneficiary or cancellation of the contract without the consent of the intended third-party beneficiary, the parties to the contract may destroy the rights of the intended beneficiary by acting in accordance with that contract provision.[6]

For Example, Roy obtained a life insurance policy from Phoenix Insurance Company that provided the beneficiary could be changed by the insured. Roy named his son, Harry, as the beneficiary. Later, Roy had a falling out with Harry and removed him as beneficiary. Roy could do this because the right to change the beneficiary was expressly reserved by the contract that created the status of the intended third-party beneficiary.

---

[4] *Gilliana v Paniaguas,* 708 NE2d 895 (Ind App 1999).

[5] *Barney v Unity Paving, Inc.,* 639 NE2d 592 (Ill App 1994).

[6] A common form of reservation is the life insurance policy provision by which the insured reserves the right to change the beneficiary. Section 142 of the Restatement (Second) of Contracts provides that the promisor and the promisee may modify their contract and affect the right of the third-party beneficiary thereby unless the agreement expressly prohibits this or the third-party beneficiary has changed position in reliance on the promise or has manifested assent to it.

In addition, the rights of an intended third-party beneficiary are destroyed if the contract is discharged or ended by operation of law, for example, through bankruptcy proceedings.

3. LIMITATIONS ON INTENDED THIRD-PARTY BENEFICIARY

Although the intended third-party beneficiary rule gives the third person the right to enforce the contract, it obviously gives no more rights than the contract provides. That is, the intended third-party beneficiary must take the contract as it is. If there is a time limitation or any other restriction in the contract, the intended beneficiary cannot ignore it but is bound by it.

If the contract is not binding for any reason, that defense may be raised against the intended third-party beneficiary suing on the contract.[7]

CPA 4. INCIDENTAL BENEFICIARIES

Not everyone who benefits from the performance of a contract between other persons is entitled to sue as a third-party beneficiary.[8] If the benefit was intended, the third person is an intended beneficiary with the rights described in the preceding sections. If the benefit was not intended, the third person is an *incidental beneficiary*.

Whether or not a third party is an *intended* or *incidental* beneficiary, therefore, comes down to determining whether or not a reasonable person would believe that the promisee intended to confer on the beneficiary an enforceable benefit under the contract in question. The intent must be clear and definite or expressed in the contract itself or in the circumstances surrounding the contract's execution.

CASE SUMMARY

Third-Party Must Be Identified in the Four Corners of the Contract

FACTS: Novus International, Inc., manufactures a poultry-feed supplement named Alimet at its plant in Chocolate Bayou, Texas. A key component of Alimet is the chemical MMP. Novus contracted with Union Carbide to secure MMP from Carbide's plant in Taft, Louisiana. Sometime later, Carbide entered into a major rail-transportation contract with the Union Pacific Railroad (UP). The rail contract consisted of nearly 100 pages. Exhibit 2 of the contract delineated inbound and outbound shipments to and from all of Carbide's Texas and Louisiana facilities. Among the hundreds of shipments listed in Exhibit 2 were three outbound MMP shipments from Taft, Louisiana, to Chocolate Bayou, Texas. These shipments were described as "Taft outbound liquid chemicals." Due to difficulties that arose from its merger with the Southern Pacific Railroad, UP experienced severe disruptions in its rail service over parts of two years and was unable to transport sufficient MMP to Chocolate Bayou. As a result, Novus had to utilize more expensive methods of transportation to obtain Alimet. It sued UP to recover the increased costs of premium freight resulting from UP's breach of its rail contract with Carbide. UP asserts that Novus did not have standing to sue; and Novus contends that it had standing to sue as an intended third-party beneficiary.

---

[7] *XL Disposal Corp. v John Sexton Contractors Co.,* 659 NE2d 1312 (Ill App 1995).
[8] *Jahannes v Mitchell,* 469 SE2d 255 (Ga App 1996).

CASE SUMMARY

continued

DECISION: Judgment for UP. Third-party beneficiary claims succeed or fail according to the provisions of the contact upon which suit is brought. The intention to confer a direct benefit on a third party must be clearly and fully spelled out in the four corners of the contract. Otherwise, enforcement of the contract by a third party must be denied. After reviewing the rail contract, no intent to confer a direct benefit on Novus is evident. Novus is never named in the contract, and all obligations flow between UP and Carbide. Nor is it stated anywhere in the contract that the parties are contracting for the benefit of Carbide's customers. Novus, thus, is an incidental beneficiary without standing to sue. [**Union Pacific Railroad v Novus International, Inc., 2003 WL 21101421 (Tex Civ App)**]

ETHICS & THE LAW

Ruth Bullis, 37, is a waitress at Stanford's Restaurant & Bar in Lake Oswego, Oregon. One evening, Bullis served a lumber broker who ordered a gin and tonic for $3.95. Before leaving, he put the tab for his drink on his American Express card and added a $1,000 tip for Bullis. Bullis verified with him that his intent was to give her the tip. Several other servers verified the tip and the fact that the lumber broker was not tipsy or addled.

After Bullis had spent the $1,000, American Express contacted Stanford's to reclaim the $1,000 because the customer had notified American Express that the tip was a mistake.

After you evaluate the legal positions of the four parties (Bullis, Stanford's, American Express, and the lumber broker), consider the ethical issues of giving a tip and then revoking it.

B ## ASSIGNMENTS

right legal capacity to require another person to perform or refrain from an action.

duty obligation of law imposed on a person to perform or refrain from performing a certain act.

assignment transfer of a right; generally used in connection with personal property rights, as rights under a contract, commercial paper, an insurance policy, a mortgage, or a lease. (Parties–assignor, assignee.)

The parties to a contract have both rights and duties. Can rights be transferred or sold to another person or entity? Can duties be transferred to another person?

5. DEFINITIONS

Contracts create **rights** and **duties** between the parties to the contract. An **assignment** is a transfer of contractual rights to a third party. The party owing a duty or debt under the contract is the **obligor** or **debtor**, and the party to whom the obligation is owed is the **obligee**. The party making the assignment is the **assignor**. The third party to whom the assignment is made is the **assignee**. **For Example,** Randy Marshall and Marilee Menendez own Huntington Beach Board (HBB) Company, LLC, a five-employee start-up company making top-of-the line surfboards. Marilee was able to sell 100 Duke Kahanamoku–inspired "longboards" to Watersports, Inc., a large retail sporting goods chain, for $140 per board. However, the best payment terms she could obtain were payment in full in 90 days. A contract containing these terms was

FIGURE 18-1 *Surfboard Transaction Diagram*

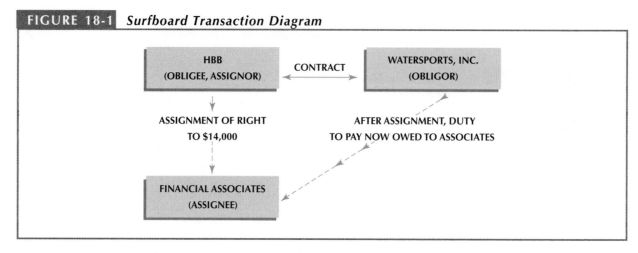

obligor promisor.

debtor buyer on credit (i.e., a borrower).

obligee promisee who can claim the benefit of the obligation.

assignor party who assigns contract rights to a third party.

assignee third party to whom contract benefits are transferred.

executed, and the goods were delivered. To meet internal cash flow needs, HBB assigned its right to receive the $14,000 payment from the buyer to West Coast Financial Associates (Associates) and received $12,800 cash from Associates on execution of the assignment documents. Notice was given at that time to Watersports, Inc., of the assignment. The right to receive the payment due in 90 days under the sales contract has thus been transferred by the seller HBB (assignor) to the third party, Associates (the assignee), to whom the buyer, Watersports, Inc. (obligor), now owes the duty of payment. Under the law of assignments, Associates, the assignee, now has direct rights against the obligor, Watersports, Inc. (See Figure 18-1.)

6. FORM OF ASSIGNMENT

Generally, an assignment may be in any form. Statutes, however, may require that certain kinds of assignments be in writing or be executed in a particular form. Any words, whether written or spoken, that show an intention to transfer or assign will be given the effect of an assignment.[9]

7. NOTICE OF ASSIGNMENT

An assignment, if otherwise valid, takes effect the moment it is made. The assignee should give immediate notice of the assignment to the obligor, setting forth the obligor's duty to the assignee, in order to prevent improper payment.[10]

CASE SUMMARY

When You Find Yourself in a Hole, NationsBank, Stop Digging

FACTS: L & S General Contractors, LLC (L & S), purchased a book-entry certificate of deposit (CD 005) in the principal amount of $100,000 from NationsBank, N.A. L & S later

---

[9] *Lone Mountain Production Co. v Natural Gas Pipeline Co. of America,* 984 F2d 1551 (10th Cir 1992).

[10] In some cases, an assignee will give notice of the assignment to the obligor in order to obtain priority over other persons who claim the same right or in order to limit the defenses that the obligor may raise against the assignee. UCC § 9-318.

CASE SUMMARY

continued

assigned CD 005 to Credit General Insurance Company (Credit General) as collateral security for performance and payment bonds on a Howard Johnson construction project. Credit General forwarded to NationsBank a written notice of the assignment that stated, "Please hold this account as assigned to use until demanded or released by us." NationsBank recorded the assignment and executed a written acknowledgment. When CD 005 matured, L & S rolled over the proceeds into a short-term certificate of deposit (CD 058) and, upon maturity, rolled over the proceeds of CD 058 into another short-term certificate of deposit (CD 072).

The bank book entries of CD 058 and CD 072 recorded L & S as the only principal/payee and did not reflect Credit General's assignment interest. NationsBank admitted its failure to show Credit General as assignee on the rollover book entries for CD 058 and CD 072 was a mistake.

Upon maturity, L & S withdrew the proceeds of CD 072 without the knowledge or consent of Credit General. Later Credit General made written demand on NationsBank for the proceeds of CD 005, and NationsBank informed Credit General that CD 005 had been redeemed and refused payment. Credit General sued NationsBank for wrongful payment of proceeds. NationsBank argues that the assignment was limited in time to the completion of the Howard Johnson project.

DECISION: Judgment for the assignee, Credit General. Upon notice and acknowledgment of the assignment, NationsBank incurred a legal duty to pay the account proceeds only to the assignee, Credit General, in whom the account was vested by the terms of the assignment. The assignment was absolute and unambiguous on its face and clearly was not limited as NationsBank proposes. The assignment language controls. [**Credit General Insurance Co. v NationsBank, 299 F3d 943 (8th Cir 2002)**]

If the obligor is notified in any manner that there has been an assignment and that any money due must be paid to the assignee, the obligor's obligation can be discharged only by making payment to the assignee.

If the obligor is not notified that there has been an assignment and that the money due must be paid to the assignee, any payment made by the obligor to the assignor reduces or cancels that portion of the debt. The only remedy for the assignee is to sue the assignor to recover the payments that were made by the obligor.

The Uniform Consumer Credit Code (UCCC) protects consumer-debtors making payments to an assignor without knowledge of the assignment[11] and imposes a penalty for using a contract term that would destroy this protection of consumers.[12]

8. ASSIGNMENT OF RIGHT TO MONEY

Assignments of contracts are generally made to raise money. **For Example,** an automobile dealer assigns a customer's credit contract to a finance company and receives cash for it. Sometimes assignments are made when an enterprise closes and transfers its business to a new owner.

---

[11] UCCC § 2.412.
[12] UCCC § 5.202.

claim right to payment.

cause of action right to damages or other judicial relief when a legally protected right of the plaintiff is violated by an unlawful act of the defendant.

A person entitled to receive money, such as payment for goods sold to a buyer or for work done under a contract, may generally assign that right to another person.[13] A **claim** or **cause of action** against another person may be assigned. Isaac Hayes, an Academy Award®–winning composer, producer, and the voice of Chef in the television series South Park, assigned his copyright interests in several musical works in exchange for royalties from Stax Records.[14] A contractor entitled to receive payment from a building's owner can assign that right to a bank as security for a loan or can assign it to anyone else.

For Example, Celeste owed Roscoe Painters $5,000 for painting her house. Roscoe assigned this claim to the Main Street Bank. Celeste later refused to pay the bank because she had never consented to the assignment. The fact that Celeste had not consented is irrelevant. Roscoe was the owner of the claim and could transfer it to the bank. Celeste, therefore, is obligated to pay the assignee, Main Street Bank.

(a) FUTURE RIGHTS By the modern rule, future and expected rights to money may be assigned. Thus, prior to the start of a building, a building contractor may assign its rights to money not yet due under an existing contract's payment on completion-phase schedule.

(b) PURPOSE OF ASSIGNMENT The assignment of the right to money may be a complete transfer of the right that gives the assignee the right to collect and keep the money. In contrast, the assignment may be held for security. In this case, the assignee may hold the money only as a security for some specified obligation.

(c) PROHIBITION OF ASSIGNMENT OF RIGHTS A clear and specific contractual prohibition against the assignment of rights is enforceable at common law. However, the UCC favors the assignment of contracts, and express contractual prohibitions on assignments are ineffective against (1) the assignment of rights to payment for goods or services, including accounts receivable,[15] and (2) the assignment of the rights to damages for breach of sales contracts.[16]

9. NONASSIGNABLE RIGHTS

If the transfer of a right would materially affect or alter a duty or the rights of the obligor, an assignment is not permitted.[17]

(a) ASSIGNMENT INCREASING BURDEN OF PERFORMANCE When the assignment of a right would increase the burden of the obligor in performing, an assignment is ordinarily not permitted. To illustrate, if the assignor has the right to buy a certain quantity of a stated article and to take such property from the seller's warehouse, this right can be assigned. However, if the sales contract stipulates that the seller should deliver to the buyer's premises and the assignee's premises are a substantial distance from the assignor's place of business, the assignment would not be given effect. In this case, the seller would be required to give a different performance by providing greater transportation if the assignment were permitted.

---

[13] *Pravin Banker Associates v Banco Popular del Peru,* 109 F3d 850 (2d Cir 1997).

[14] *Hayes v Carlin America, Inc.,* 168 F Supp 2d 154 (SDNY 2001).

[15] UCC § 9-318(4). This section of the UCC is applicable to most commercial assignments.

[16] UCC § 2-210(2).

[17] *Aslakson v Home Savings Ass'n,* 416 NW2d 786 (Minn App 1987) (increase of credit risk).

FIGURE 18-2	*Limitations on Transfer of Rights and Duties*

ASSIGNMENT OF RIGHT TO MONEY	ASSIGNMENT OF RIGHT TO PERFORMANCE	DELEGATION OF DUTIES
GENERALLY NO LIMITATION	INCREASE OF BURDEN PERSONAL SERVICES CREDIT TRANSACTION	PERSONAL OR NONSTANDARDIZED PERFORMANCE

(b) PERSONAL SERVICES   Contracts for personal services are generally not assignable. **For Example,** were golf instructor David Ledbetter to sign a one-year contract to provide instruction for professional golfer Davis Love III, David Ledbetter could not assign his first assistant to provide the instruction, nor could Davis Love assign a protégé to receive instruction from Ledbetter. Professional athletes and their agents commonly deal with assignment or trading rights of the athletes in their contracts with professional sports franchises.

There is a split among jurisdictions regarding whether employee noncompetition covenants are assignable to the new owner of a business absent employee consent. That is, some courts permit a successor employer to enforce an employee's non-competition agreement as an assignee of the original employer. However, a majority of states that have considered this issue have concluded that restrictive covenants are personal in nature and not assignable. **For Example,** in September 2000, Philip Burkhardt signed a noncompetition agreement with his employer, NES Trench Shoring. On June 30, 2002, United Rentals Purchased NES with all contracts being assigned to United Rentals. Burkhardt stayed on with the new owner for five weeks and thereafter went to work for Traffic Control Services, a direct competitor of United. United was unsuccessful in its action to enforce the noncompetition covenant Burkhardt had signed with NES. Burkhardt's covenant with NES did not contain a clause allowing the covenant to be assigned to a new owner, and the court refused to enforce it, absent an express clause permitting assignment.[18]

(c) CREDIT TRANSACTION   When a transaction is based on extending credit, the person to whom credit is extended cannot assign any rights under the contract to another. **For Example,** Jack Aldrich contracted to sell his summer camp on Lake Sunapee to Pat Norton for $200,000, with $100,000 in cash due at the closing and the balance due on an installment basis secured by a mortgage on the property to be executed by Norton. Several days later, Norton found a more desirable property, and her sister Meg was very pleased to take over the Sunapee contract. Pat assigned her rights to Meg. Jack Aldrich, having received a better offer after contracting with Pat, refused to consent to the assignment. In this situation, the assignment to Meg is prohibited because the assignee, Meg, is a different credit risk even though the property to serve as security remained unchanged.

---

[18] *Traffic Control Sources, Inc. v United Rentals Northwest, Inc.,* 87 P3d 1054 (Nov 2004).

10. RIGHTS OF ASSIGNEE

Unless restricted by the terms of the assignment or applicable law, the assignee acquires all the rights of the assignor.[19]

An assignee stands exactly in the position of the assignor. The assignee's rights are no more or less than those of the assignor. If the assigned right to payment is subject to a condition precedent, that same condition exists for the assignee. **For Example,** when a contractor is not entitled to receive the balance of money due under the contract until all bills of suppliers of materials have been paid, the assignee to whom the contractor assigns the balance due under the contract is subject to the same condition. As set forth previously, in some states the assignee of a business purchasing all of the assets and rights of the business has the right to enforce a confidentiality and noncompetition agreement against a former employee of the assignor, just as though it were the assignor.[20]

11. CONTINUING LIABILITY OF ASSIGNOR

The making of an assignment does not relieve the assignor of any obligation of the contract. In the absence of a contrary agreement, an assignor continues to be bound by the obligations of the original contract. Thus, the fact that a buyer assigns the rights to goods under a contract does not terminate the buyer's liability to make payment to the seller. Similarly, when an independent contractor is hired to perform a party's obligations under a contract, that party is liable if the independent contractor does not properly perform the contract.

When a lease is assigned, the assignee becomes the principal obligor for rent payments, and the leasee becomes a surety toward the lessor for the assignee's performance. **For Example,** Tri-State Chiropractic (TSC) held a five-year lease on premises at 6010 East Main Street in Columbus, Ohio. Without the leasor's consent, TSC assigned that lease to Dr. T. Wilson and Buckeye Chiropractic, LLC, prior to the expiration of the lease. TSC continues to be liable for rent as surety during the term of the lease, even if the leasor (owner) had consented to the assignment or accepted payment from the assignee.[21] In order to avoid liability as a surety, TSC would have to obtain a discharge of the lease by **novation**, in which all three parties agree that the original contract (the lease) would be discharged and a new lease between Dr. Wilson and the owner would take effect. A novation allows for the discharge of a contractual obligation by the substitution of a new contract involving a new party.

novation substitution for an old contract with a new one that either replaces an existing obligation with a new obligation or replaces an original party with a new party.

12. LIABILITY OF ASSIGNEE

It is necessary to distinguish between the question of whether the obligor can assert a particular defense against the assignee and the question of whether any person can sue the assignee. Ordinarily, the assignee is not subject to suit by virtue of the fact that the assignment has been made.

(a) Consumer Protection Liability of Assignee   The assignee of the right to money may have no direct relationship to the original debtor except with respect to

---

[19] *Puget Sound National Bank v Washington Department of Revenue*, 868 P2d 127 (Wash 1994).

[20] *Artromick International, Inc. v Koch*, 759 NE2d 385 (Ohio App 2001).

[21] *Schottenstein Trustees v Carano*, 2000 Ohio App LEXIS 4493.

receiving payments. Consumer protection laws in most states, however, may subject the assignee to some liability for the assignor's misconduct.

CASE SUMMARY

The Pool and the Agreement Will Not Hold Any Water

FACTS: Homeowner Michael Jackson entered into a contract with James DeWitt for the construction of an in-ground lap pool. The contract provided for a 12 ft. × 60 ft. pool at an estimated cost of $21,000. At the time the contract was signed, Jackson paid DeWitt $11,400 in cash and financed $7,500 through a Retail Installment Security Agreement (RISA). Associates Financial Services Company (Associates) provided DeWitt with all of the forms necessary to document the financing of the home improvements. Consumer requests for financing were subject to Associates's approval, which was given for Jackson's lap pool. When the RISA was completed, DeWitt assigned it to Associates. Jackson made two monthly payments of $202.90 and a final payment of $7,094.20 while the lap pool was still under construction. When the pool was filled, it failed to hold water and Jackson had the pool and deck removed. Jackson sued DeWitt for breach of contract. He asserted that all valid claims and defenses he had against DeWitt were also valid against the assignee, Associates. Jackson sought the return of the $7,500 he had financed from Associates. The trial court held that because Jackson had paid the entire balance of the loan before Associates knew of Jackson's claim, he could not obtain relief from Associates under the consumer protection law, section ATCP 110.06 of the Wisconsin Administrative Code. Jackson appealed this decision.

DECISION: Judgment for Jackson. As one commentator has noted, "ch. ATCP 110 deals with virtually a laundry list of unfair or deceptive home improvement practices that have resulted from substantial financial losses to home owners over the years. Jeffries, 57 MARQ. L. REV at 578." Associates is an assignee of a "home improvement contract" that is governed by section ATCP 110.06. The regulation provides that "[e]very assignee of a home improvement contract takes subject to all claims and defenses of the buyer or successors in interest." Therefore, as the assignee of the RISA, Associates is subject to any claims without regard to the negotiability of the contract. [**Jackson v DeWitt, 592 NW2d 262 (Wis App 1999)**]

(b) DEFENSES AND SETOFFS   The assignee's rights are no greater than those of the assignor.[22] If the obligor could successfully defend against a suit brought by the assignor, the obligor will also prevail against the assignee.

The fact that the assignee has given value for the assignment does not give the assignee any immunity from defenses that the other party, the obligor, could have asserted against the assignor. The rights acquired by the assignee remain subject to any limitations imposed by the contract.

13. WARRANTIES OF ASSIGNOR

implied warranty warranty that was not made but is implied by law.

When the assignment is made for a consideration, the assignor is regarded as providing an **implied warranty** that the right assigned is valid. The assignor also warrants that the assignor is the owner of the claim or right assigned and that the assignor will not interfere with the assignee's enforcement of the obligation.

---

[22] *Shoreline Communications, Inc. v Norwich Taxi, LCC,* 70 Conn App 60 (2002).

FIGURE 18-3   *Can a Third Person Sue on a Contract?*

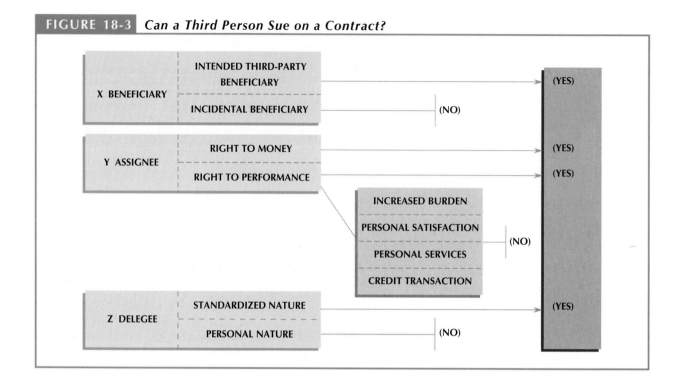

14. DELEGATION OF DUTIES

delegation of duties transfer of duties by a contracting party to another person who is to perform them.

delegation transfer to another of the right and power to do an act.

A **delegation of duties** is a transfer of duties by a contracting party to another person who is to perform them. Under certain circumstances, a contracting party may obtain someone else to do the work. When the performance is standardized and nonpersonal, so that it is not material who performs, the law will permit the **delegation** of the performance of the contract. In such cases, however, the contracting party remains liable in the case of default of the person doing the work just as though no delegation had been made.[23]

A contract may prohibit a party owing a duty of performance under a contract from delegating that duty to another. **For Example,** Tom Joyce of Patriot Plumbing Co. contracts to install a new heating system for Mrs. Lawton. A notation on the sales contract that Tom Joyce will do the installation prohibits Patriot Plumbing from delegating the installation to another equally skilled plumber or to another company if a backlog of work occurs at Patriot Plumbing.

If the performance of a party to a contract involves personal skill, talents, judgment, or trust, the delegation of duties is barred unless consented to by the person entitled to the performance. Examples include performance by professionals such as physicians, dentists, lawyers, consultants, celebrities, artists, and craftpersons with unusual skills.

(a) INTENTION TO DELEGATE DUTIES   An assignment of rights does not in itself delegate the performance of duties to the assignee. In the absence of clear language in the assignment stating that duties are or are not delegated, all circumstances

[23] *Orange Bowl Corp. v Warren*, 386 SE2d 293 (SC App 1989).

must be examined to determine whether there is a delegation. When the total picture is viewed, it may become clear what was intended. The fact that an assignment is made for security of the assignee is a strong indication there was no intent to delegate to the assignee the performance of any duty resting on the assignor.[24]

CASE SUMMARY

Duties Were Delegated Too, Dude

FACTS: Smith, who owned the Avalon Apartments, a condominium, sold individual apartments under contracts that required each purchaser to pay $15 a month extra for hot and cold water, heat, refrigeration, taxes, and fire insurance. Smith assigned his interest in the apartment house under various contracts to Roberts. When Roberts failed to pay the taxes on the building, the purchasers of the individual apartments sued to compel Roberts to do so.

DECISION: Judgment against Roberts. In the absence of a contrary indication, it is presumed that an assignment of a contract delegates the performance of the duties as well as transfers the rights. Here, there was no indication that a package transfer was not intended, and the assignee was therefore obligated to perform in accordance with the contract terms. [*Radley v Smith and Roberts*, 313 P2d 465 (Utah 1957)]

(b) DELEGATION OF DUTIES UNDER THE UCC   With respect to contracts for the sale of goods, "an assignment of 'the contract' or of 'all my rights under the contract' or an assignment in similar general terms is an assignment of rights and, unless the language or the circumstances (as in an assignment for security) indicate the contrary, it is a delegation of performance of the duties of the assignor, and its acceptance by the assignee constitutes a promise . . . to perform those duties. This promise is enforceable by either the assignor or the other party to the original contract."[25]

LAWFLIX

It Could Happen to You (1996) (PG)

Discuss the legal, ethical and contract issues involved in the first portion of the film in which a police officer (Nicholas Cage) promises to split a lottery ticket with a coffee shop waitress (Bridget Fonda) as her tip because he does not have enough money. The lottery ticket (purchased by Cage and his wife, Rosie Perez) is a winner, and Cage wrestles with his obligation to tell Fonda. You could discuss whether there was an assignment or whether Fonda was added as a third party beneficiary after the fact.

For movie clips that illustrate business law concepts, see LawFlix at **http://wdvl.westbuslaw.com.**

24 *City National Bank of Fort Smith v First National Bank and Trust Co. of Rogers*, 732 SW2d 489 (Ark App 1987).
25 UCC § 2-210(4).

> SUMMARY

Ordinarily, only the parties to contracts have rights and duties with respect to such contracts. Exceptions are made in the case of third-party beneficiary contracts and assignments.

When a contract shows a clear intent to benefit a third person or class of persons, those persons are called *intended third-party beneficiaries*, and they may sue for breach of the contract. A third-party beneficiary is subject to any limitation or restriction found in the contract. A third-party beneficiary loses all rights when the original contract is terminated by operation of law or if the contract reserves the right to change the beneficiary and such a change is made.

In contrast, an incidental beneficiary benefits from the performance of a contract, but the conferring of this benefit was not intended by the contracting parties. An incidental beneficiary cannot sue on the contract.

An assignment is a transfer of a right; the assignor transfers a right to the assignee. In the absence of a local statute, there are no formal requirements for an assignment. Any words manifesting the intent to transfer are sufficient to constitute an assignment. No consideration is required. Any right to money may be assigned, whether the assignor is entitled to the money at the time of the assignment or will be entitled or expects to be entitled at some time in the future.

A right to a performance may be assigned except when (1) it would increase the burden of performance, (2) the contract involves the performance of personal services, or (3) the transaction is based on extending credit.

When a valid assignment is made, the assignee has the same rights—and only the same rights—as the assignor. The assignee is also subject to the same defenses and setoffs as the assignor had been.

The performance of duties under a contract may be delegated to another person except when a personal element of skill or judgment of the original contracting party is involved. The intent to delegate duties may be expressly stated. The intent may also be found in an "assignment" of "the contract" unless the circumstances make it clear that only the right to money was intended to be transferred. The fact that there has been a delegation of duties does not release the assignor from responsibility for performance. The assignor is liable for breach of the contract if the assignee does not properly perform the delegated duties. In the absence of an effective delegation or the formation of a third-party beneficiary contract, an assignee of rights is not liable to the obligee of the contract for its performance by the assignor.

Notice is not required to effect an assignment. When notice of the assignment is given to the obligor together with a demand that future payments be made to the assignee, the obligor cannot discharge liability by payment to the assignor.

When an assignment is made for a consideration, the assignor makes implied warranties that the right assigned is valid and that the assignor owns that right and will not interfere with its enforcement by the assignee. The assignor does not warrant that the obligor on the assigned right will perform the obligation of the contract.

> QUESTIONS AND CASE PROBLEMS

1. Give an example of a third-party beneficiary contract.
2. A court order required John Baldassari to make specified payments for the support of his wife and child. His wife needed more money and applied for Pennsylvania welfare payments. In accordance with the law, she assigned to Pennsylvania her right to the support payments from her husband. Pennsylvania then increased her payments. Pennsylvania obtained a court order directing John, in accordance with the terms of the assignment from his wife, to make the support-order payments directly to the Pennsylvania Department of Public Welfare. John refused to pay on the ground that he had not been notified of the assignment or the hearing directing him to make payment to the assignee. Was he correct? *Pennsylvania v Baldassari*, 421 A2d 306 (Pa Super)
3. Lee contracts to paint Sally's two-story house for $1,000. Sally realizes that she will not have sufficient money, so she transfers her rights under

this agreement to her neighbor Karen, who has a three-story house. Karen notifies Lee that Sally's contract has been assigned to her and demands that Lee paint Karen's house for $1,000. Is Lee required to do so?

4. Assume that Lee agrees to the assignment of the house-painting contract to Karen as stated in question 3. Thereafter, Lee fails to perform the contract to paint Karen's house. Karen sues Sally for damages. Is Sally liable?

5. Jessie borrows $1,000 from Thomas and agrees to repay the money in 30 days. Thomas assigns the right to the $1,000 to Douglas Finance Co. Douglas sues Jessie. Jessie argues that she had agreed to pay the money only to Thomas and that when she and Thomas had entered into the transaction, there was no intention to benefit Douglas Finance Co. Are these objections valid?

6. Washington purchased an automobile from Smithville Motors. The contract called for payment of the purchase price in installments and contained the defense preservation notice required by the Federal Trade Commission regulation. Smithville assigned the contract to Rustic Finance Co. The car was always in need of repairs, and by the time it was half paid for, it would no longer run. Washington canceled the contract. Meanwhile, Smithville had gone out of business. Washington sued Rustic for the amount she had paid Smithville. Rustic refused to pay on the grounds that it had not been at fault. Decide.

7. Helen obtained an insurance policy insuring her life and naming her niece Julie as beneficiary. Helen died, and about a year later the policy was found in her house. When Julie claimed the insurance money, the insurer refused to pay on the ground that the policy required that notice of death be given to it promptly following the death. Julie claimed that she was not bound by the time limitation because she had never agreed to it, as she was not a party to the insurance contract. Is Julie entitled to recover?

8. Lone Star Life Insurance Co. agreed to make a long-term loan to Five Forty Three Land, Inc., whenever that corporation requested one. Five Forty Three wanted this loan to pay off its short-term debts. The loan was never made, as it was never requested by Five Forty Three, which owed the Exchange Bank & Trust Co. on a short-term debt. Exchange Bank then sued Lone Star for breach of its promise on the theory that the Exchange Bank was a third-party beneficiary of the contract to make the loan. Was the Exchange Bank correct? [*Exchange Bank & Trust Co. v Lone Star Life Ins. Co.,* 546 SW2d 948 (Tex App)]

9. The New Rochelle Humane Society made a contract with the city of New Rochelle to capture and impound all dogs running at large. Spiegler, a minor, was bitten by some dogs while in her schoolyard. She sued the school district of New Rochelle and the Humane Society. With respect to the Humane Society, she claimed that she was a third-party beneficiary of the contract that the Humane Society had made with the city. She claimed that she could therefore sue the Humane Society for its failure to capture the dogs that had bitten her. Was she entitled to recover? [*Spiegler v School District of the City of New Rochelle,* 242 NYS2d 430]

10. Zoya operated a store in premises rented from Peerless. The lease required Zoya to maintain liability insurance to protect Zoya and Peerless. Caswell entered the store, fell through a trap door, and was injured. She then sued Zoya and Peerless on the theory that she was a third-party beneficiary of the lease requirement to maintain liability insurance. Was she correct? [*Caswell v Zoya Int'l,* 654 NE2d 552 (Ill App)]

11. Henry was owed $10,000 by Jones Corp. In consideration of the many odd jobs performed for him over the years by his nephew, Henry assigned the $10,000 claim to his nephew Charles. Henry died, and his widow claimed that the assignment was ineffective so that the claim was part of Henry's estate. She based her assertion on the ground that the past performance rendered by the nephew was not consideration. Was the assignment effective?

12. Industrial Construction Co. wanted to raise money to construct a canning factory in Wisconsin. Various persons promised to subscribe the needed amount, which they agreed to pay when the construction was completed.

The construction company assigned its rights and delegated its duties under the agreement to Johnson, who then built the cannery. Vickers, one of the subscribers, refused to pay the amount that he had subscribed on the ground that the contract could not be assigned. Was he correct?

13. The Ohio Department of Public Welfare made a contract with an accountant to audit the accounts of health care providers who were receiving funds under the Medicaid program. Windsor House, which operated six nursing homes, claimed that it was a third-party beneficiary of that contract and could sue for its breach. Was it correct? [*Thornton v Windsor House, Inc.,* 566 NE2d 1220 (Ohio)]

> CPA QUESTIONS

1. On August 1, Neptune Fisheries contracted in writing with West Markets to deliver to West 3,000 pounds of lobster at $4.00 a pound. Delivery of the lobsters was due October 1, with payment due November 1. On August 4, Neptune entered into a contract with Deep Sea Lobster Farms that provided as follows: "Neptune Fisheries assigns all the rights under the contract with West Markets dated August 1 to Deep Sea Lobster Farms." The best interpretation of the August 4 contract would be that it was

   a. only an assignment of rights by Neptune.
   b. only a delegation of duties by Neptune.
   c. an assignment of rights and a delegation of duties by Neptune.
   d. an unenforceable third-party beneficiary contract.

2. Graham contracted with the city of Harris to train and employ high school dropouts residing in Harris. Graham breached the contract. Long, a resident of Harris and a high school dropout, sued Graham for damages. Under the circumstances, Long will

   a. win, because Long is a third-party beneficiary entitled to enforce the contract.
   b. win, because the intent of the contract was to confer a benefit on all high school dropouts residing in Harris.
   c. lose, because Long is merely an incidental beneficiary of the contract.
   d. lose, because Harris did not assign its contract rights to Long.

3. Union Bank lent $200,000 to Wagner. Union required Wagner to obtain a life insurance policy naming Union as beneficiary. While the loan was outstanding, Wagner stopped paying the premiums on the policy. Union paid the premiums, adding the amounts paid to Wagner's loan. Wagner died, and the insurance company refused to pay the policy proceeds to Union. Union may

   a. recover the policy proceeds because it is a creditor beneficiary.
   b. not recover the policy proceeds because it is a donee beneficiary.
   c. not recover the policy proceeds because it is not in privity of contract with the insurance company.
   d. not recover the policy proceeds because it is only an incidental beneficiary.

DISCHARGE OF
CONTRACTS

(A) CONDITIONS RELATING TO PERFORMANCE
   1. CLASSIFICATIONS OF CONDITIONS

(B) DISCHARGE BY PERFORMANCE
   2. NORMAL DISCHARGE OF CONTRACTS
   3. NATURE OF PERFORMANCE
   4. TIME OF PERFORMANCE
   5. ADEQUACY OF PERFORMANCE

(C) DISCHARGE BY ACTION OF PARTIES
   6. DISCHARGE BY UNILATERAL ACTION
   7. DISCHARGE BY AGREEMENT

(D) DISCHARGE BY EXTERNAL CAUSES
   8. DISCHARGE BY IMPOSSIBILITY
   9. DEVELOPING DOCTRINES
   10. TEMPORARY IMPOSSIBILITY
   11. DISCHARGE BY OPERATION OF LAW

LEARNING OBJECTIVES

After studying this chapter, you should be able to

LO.1 List the ways in which a contract can be discharged

LO.2 Distinguish between the effect of a rejected tender of payment and a rejected tender of performance

LO.3 Define when time is of the essence

LO.4 Compare performance to the satisfaction of the other contracting parties, performance to the satisfaction of a reasonable person, and substantial performance

LO.5 State when the consumer may rescind a consumer contract

LO.6 Compare the discharge of a contract by rescission, cancellation, substitution, and novation

LO.7 State the effect on a contract of the death or disability of one of the contracting parties

LO.8 Define the concept of *economic frustration*

In the preceding chapters, you studied how a contract is formed, what a contract means, and who has rights under a contract. In this chapter, attention is turned to how a contract is ended or discharged. In other words, what puts an end to the rights and duties created by a contract?

 ## A   CONDITIONS RELATING TO PERFORMANCE

As developed in the body of this chapter, the ordinary method of discharging obligations under a contract is by performance. Certain promises may be less than absolute and instead come into effect only upon the occurrence of a specified event, or an existing obligation may be extinguished when an event happens. These are conditional promises.

1. CLASSIFICATIONS OF CONDITIONS

condition stipulation or prerequisite in a contract, will, or other instrument.

When the occurrence or nonoccurrence of an event, as expressed in a contract, affects the duty of a party to the contract to perform, the event is called a **condition**. Terms such as *if, provided that, when, after, as soon as, subject to,* and *on the condition that* indicate the creation of a condition.[1] Conditions are classified as *conditions precedent, conditions subsequent,* and *concurrent conditions.*

condition precedent event that if unsatisfied would mean that no rights would arise under a contract.

(a) CONDITION PRECEDENT   A **condition precedent** is a condition that must occur before a party to a contract has an obligation to perform under the contract. **For Example,** a condition precedent to a contractor's (MasTec's) obligation to pay a subcontractor (MidAmerica) under a "pay-if-paid" by the owner (PathNet) clause in their subcontract agreement is the receipt of payment by MasTec from PathNet. The condition precedent—payment by the owner—did not occur due to bankruptcy, and therefore MasTec did not have an obligation to pay MidAmerica.[2]

> ## CASE SUMMARY
>
> ### A Blitz on Offense?
>
> **FACTS:** Richard Blitz owns a piece of commercial property at 4 Old Middle Street. On February 2, 1998, Arthur Subklew entered into a lease with Blitz to rent the rear portion of the property. Subklew intended to operate an auto sales and repair business. Paragraph C of the lease was a zoning contingency clause that stated, "Landlord [plaintiff] will use Landlord's best efforts to obtain a written verification that Tenant can operate [an] Auto Sales and Repair Business at the demised premises. If Landlord is unable to obtain such commitment from the municipality, then this agreement shall be deemed null and void and Landlord shall immediately return deposit monies to Tenant." The zoning board approved the location only as a general repair business. When Subklew refused to occupy the premises, Blitz sued him for breach of contract.
>
> **DECISION:** Judgment for Subklew. A condition precedent is a fact or event that the parties intend must exist before there is right to a performance. If the condition is not fulfilled, the right to enforce the contract does not come into existence. Blitz's obligation to obtain written approval of a used car business was a condition precedent to the leasing agreement. Since it was not obtained, Blitz cannot enforce the leasing agreement. [**Blitz v Subklew 74 Conn App 183 (2002)**]

---

[1] *Harmon Cable Communications v Scope Cable Television, Inc.*, 468 NW2d 350 (Neb 1990).

[2] *MidAmerica Construction Management, Inc. v MasTec North America, Inc.*, 436 F3d 1257 (10th Cir 2006).

(b) CONDITION SUBSEQUENT   The parties to a contract may agree that a party is obligated to perform a certain act or pay a certain sum of money, but the contract contains a provision that relieves the obligation on the occurrence of a certain event. That is, on the happening of a **condition subsequent**, such an event extinguishes the duty to thereafter perform. **For Example,** Chad Newly served as the weekend anchor on *Channel 5 News* for several years. The station manager, Tom O'Brien, on reviewing tapes in connection with Newly's contract renewal, believed that Newly's speech on occasion was slightly slurred, and he suspected that it was from alcohol use. In the parties' contract discussions, O'Brien expressed his concerns about an alcohol problem and offered help. Newly denied there was a problem. O'Brien agreed to a new two-year contract with Newly at $167,000 for the first year and $175,000 for the second year with other benefits subject to "the condition" that the station reserved the right to make four unannounced drug-alcohol tests during the contract term; and should Newly test positive for drugs or alcohol under measurements set forth in the contract, then all of Channel 5's obligations to Newly under the contract would cease. When Newly subsequently failed a urinalysis test three months into the new contract, the happening of this event extinguished the station's obligation to employ and pay him under the contract.

condition subsequent event whose occurrence or lack thereof terminates a contract.

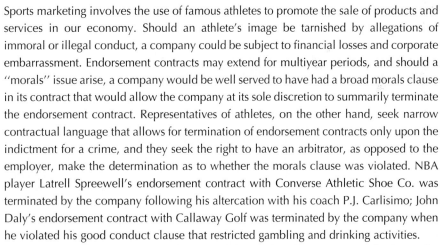

SPORTS & ENTERTAINMENT LAW

Endorsement Contracts

Sports marketing involves the use of famous athletes to promote the sale of products and services in our economy. Should an athlete's image be tarnished by allegations of immoral or illegal conduct, a company could be subject to financial losses and corporate embarrassment. Endorsement contracts may extend for multiyear periods, and should a "morals" issue arise, a company would be well served to have had a broad morals clause in its contract that would allow the company at its sole discretion to summarily terminate the endorsement contract. Representatives of athletes, on the other hand, seek narrow contractual language that allows for termination of endorsement contracts only upon the indictment for a crime, and they seek the right to have an arbitrator, as opposed to the employer, make the determination as to whether the morals clause was violated. NBA player Latrell Spreewell's endorsement contract with Converse Athletic Shoe Co. was terminated by the company following his altercation with his coach P.J. Carlisimo; John Daly's endorsement contract with Callaway Golf was terminated by the company when he violated his good conduct clause that restricted gambling and drinking activities.

Corporate sponsorship of the Olympics was recently subject to a "morals clause" by John Hancock Financial Services Co. in its sponsorship contract, allowing it the right to terminate its financial commitment to the International Olympic Committee (IOC) if the IOC became involved in improprieties. The Houston Astros did not have a morals clause in its $100 million, 30-year naming rights contract for its baseball stadium with the sponsoring Enron Corporation. When Enron refused to allow its name to be removed from the stadium, the Astros bought out the rights for $2.1 million.

Can the courts be utilized to resolve controversies over whether a "morals clause" has been violated? If so, is the occurrence of a morals clause violation a condition precedent or a condition subsequent?

(c) CONCURRENT CONDITION   In most bilateral contracts, the performances of the parties are *concurrent conditions*. That is, their mutual duties of performance under the contract are to take place simultaneously. **For Example,** concerning a contract for the sale and delivery of certain goods, the buyer must tender to the seller a certified check at the time of delivery as set forth in the contract, and the seller must tender the goods to the buyer at the same time.

 DISCHARGE BY PERFORMANCE

When it is claimed that a contract is discharged by performance, questions arise as to the nature, time, and sufficiency of the performance.

2. NORMAL DISCHARGE OF CONTRACTS

A contract is usually discharged by the performance of the terms of the agreement. In most cases, the parties perform their promises and the contract ceases to exist or is thereby discharged. A contract is also discharged by the expiration of the time period specified in the contract.[3]

3. NATURE OF PERFORMANCE

Performance may be the doing of an act or the making of payment.

tender goods have arrived, are available for pickup and buyer is notified.

(a) TENDER   An offer to perform is known as a **tender**. If performance of the contract requires the doing of an act, the refusal of a tender discharges the party offering to perform and is a basis for that party to bring a lawsuit.

A valid tender of payment consists of an unconditional offer of the exact amount due on the date when due. A tender of payment is not just an expression of willingness to pay; it must be an actual offer to perform by making payment of the amount owed.

(b) PAYMENT   When the contract requires payment, performance consists of the payment of money.

(1) Application of Payments.   If a debtor owes more than one debt to the creditor and pays money, a question may arise as to which debt has been paid. If the debtor specifies the debt to which the payment is to be applied and the creditor accepts the money, the creditor is bound to apply the money as specified.[4] Thus, if the debtor specifies that a payment is to be made for a current purchase, the creditor may not apply the payment to an older balance.

(2) Payment by Check.   Payment by commercial paper, such as a check, is ordinarily a conditional payment. A check merely suspends the debt until the check is presented for payment. If payment is then made, the debt is discharged; if not paid, the suspension terminates, and suit may be brought on either the debt or the check. Frequently, payment must be made by a specified date. It is generally held that the payment is made on time if it is mailed on or before the final date for payment.

---

[3] *Washington National Ins. Co. v Sherwood Associates,* 795 P2d 665 (Utah App 1990).
[4] *Oakes Logging, Inc. v Green Crow, Inc.,* 832 P2d 894 (Wash App 1992).

CASE SUMMARY

The Mailed-Check Payment

FACTS: Thomas Cooper was purchasing land from Peter and Ella Birznieks. Cooper was already in possession of the land but was required to pay the amount owed by January 30; otherwise, he would have to vacate the property. The attorney handling the transaction for the Birznieks told Cooper that he could mail the payment to him. On January 30, Cooper mailed to the attorney a personal check drawn on an out-of-state bank for the amount due. The check arrived at the Birznieks' attorney's office on February 1. The Birznieks refused to accept the check on the grounds that it was not a timely payment and moved to evict Cooper from the property.

DECISION: Because of the general custom to regard a check mailed to a creditor as paying the bill that is owed, payment was made by Cooper on January 30 when he mailed the check. Payment was therefore made within the required time even though received after the expiration of the required time. [**Birznieks v Cooper 275 NW2d 221 (Mich 1979)**]

E-COMMERCE AND CYBERLAW

Cyberspace Payments

The use of credit cards is the dominant form of payment for Internet transactions between businesses and consumers. Many businesses use Secure Sockets Layer (SSL) protocol to provide security for the transmission of customers' credit card information. SSL provides authentication of the merchant's server to the purchaser and encrypts the messages sent between the purchaser and the merchant. **For Example,** Amazon.com uses SSL.

New credit cards with built-in microprocessor chips plus hardware allowing cards to be read by home computers are now in use. Advantages include the ability to store account numbers and scramble them for safe e-mailing.

Credit cards offer consumers protection from losses from unauthorized transactions, international acceptance, and the ability to buy now and pay later.

4. TIME OF PERFORMANCE

When the date or period of time for performance is specified in the contract, performance should be made on that date or within that time period.

(a) No Time Specified   When the time for performance is not specified in the contract, an obligation to perform within a reasonable time is implied.[5] The fact that no time is specified neither impairs the contract on the ground that it is indefinite nor allows an endless time in which to perform. What constitutes a

---

[5] *First National Bank v Clark,* 447 SE2d 558 (W Va 1994).

reasonable time is determined by the nature of the subject matter of the contract and the facts and circumstances surrounding the making of the contract.

(b) WHEN TIME IS ESSENTIAL   If performance of the contract on or within the exact time specified is vital, it is said that "time is of the essence." Time is of the essence when the contract relates to property that is perishable or that is fluctuating rapidly in value. When a contract fixes by unambiguous language a time for performance and where there is no evidence showing that the parties did not intend that time should be of the essence, failure to perform within the specified time is a breach of contract entitling the innocent party to damages. **For Example,** Dixon and Gandhi agreed that Gandhi would close on the purchase of a motel as follows: "Closing Date. The closing shall be held . . . on the date which is within twenty (20) days after the closing of Nomura Financing." Gandhi did not close within the time period specified, and Dixon was allowed to retain $100,000 in prepaid closing costs and fees as liquidated damages for Gandhi's breach of contract.[6]

(c) WHEN TIME IS NOT ESSENTIAL   Unless a contract so provides, time is ordinarily not of the essence, and performance within a reasonable time is sufficient. In the case of the sale of property, time is not regarded as of the essence when there has not been any appreciable change in the market value or condition of the property and when the person who delayed does not appear to have done so for the purpose of speculating on a change in market price.

(d) WAIVER OF ESSENCE OF TIME LIMITATION   A provision that time is of the essence may be waived. It is waived when the specified time has expired but the party who could complain requests the delaying party to take steps necessary to perform the contract.

5. ADEQUACY OF PERFORMANCE

When a party renders exactly the performance called for by the contract, no question arises as to whether the contract has been performed. In other cases, there may not have been a perfect performance, or a question arises as to whether the performance satisfies the standard set by the contract.

CPA

substantial performance
equitable rule that if a good-faith attempt to perform does not precisely meet the terms of the agreement, the agreement will still be considered complete if the essential purpose of the contract is accomplished.

(a) SUBSTANTIAL PERFORMANCE   Perfect performance of a contract is not always possible when dealing with construction projects. A party who in good faith has provided **substantial performance** of the contract may sue to recover the payment specified in the contract. However, because the performance was not perfect, the performing party is subject to a counterclaim for the damages caused the other party. When a building contractor has substantially performed the contract to construct a building, the contractor is responsible for the cost of repairing or correcting the defects as an offset from the contract price.[7]

The measure of damages under these circumstances is known as "cost of completion" damages. If, however, the cost of completion would be unreasonably disproportionate to the importance of the defect, the measure of damages is the diminution in value of the building due to the defective performance.

---

[6] *Woodhull Corp. v Saibaba Corp.*, 507 SE2d 493 (Ga App 1998).

[7] Substantial performance is not a defense to a breach of contract claim, however. See *Bentley Systems Inc. v Intergraph Corp.*, 922 So2d 61 (Ala 2005).

FIGURE 19-1   *Causes of Contract Discharge*

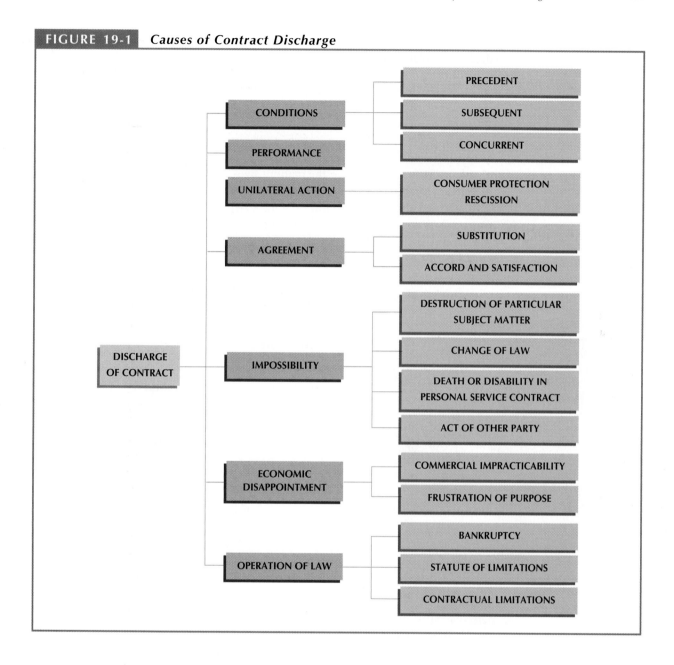

Whether there is substantial performance is a question of degree to be determined by all of the facts, including the particular type of structure involved, its intended purpose, and the nature and relative expense of repairs.

For Example, a certain building contractor (BC) and a certain owner (O) made a contract to construct a home overlooking Vineyard Sound on Martha's Vineyard according to plans and specifications that clearly called for the use of General Plumbing Blue Star piping. The contract price was $1,100,000. Upon inspecting the work before making the final $400,000 payment and accepting the building, O discovered that BC had used Republic piping throughout the house. O explained to BC that his family had made its money by investing in General Plumbing, and he, therefore, would not make the final payment until the breach of contract was remedied. BC explained that Republic pipes were of the same industrial grade and quality as the Blue Star pipes. Moreover, BC estimated that it would cost nearly $300,000 to replace all of the pipes because of the destruction of walls and fixtures necessary to accomplish such a task. BC may sue O for $400,000 for breach of contract, claiming he had substantially performed the contract, and O may counterclaim for $300,000, seeking an offset for the cost of remedying the breach. The court will find in favor of the contractor and will not allow the $300,000 offset but will allow a "nominal" offset of perhaps $100 to $1,000 for the amount by which the Republic pipes diminished the value of the building.[8]

In most jurisdictions, the willfulness of the departure from the specifications of the contract does not by itself preclude some recovery for the contractor on the "cost of completion" basis but rather is a factor in consideration of whether there was substantial performance by the contractor.[9]

CASE SUMMARY

When Perfection Is Not Required

FACTS: Beeson Company made a contract to construct a shopping center for Sartori. Before the work was fully completed, Sartori stopped making the payments to Beeson that the contract required. The contract provided for liquidated damages of $1,000 per day if Beeson failed to substantially complete the project within 300 days of the beginning of construction. The contract also provided for a bonus of $1,000 for each day Beeson completed the project ahead of schedule. Beeson then stopped working and sued Sartori for the balance due under the contract, just as though it had been fully performed. Sartori defended on the ground that Beeson had not substantially completed the work. Beeson proved that Sartori had been able to rent most of the stores in the center.

DECISION: The fact that the shopping center could be used for its intended purpose, that of renting stores to others, showed that there had been a substantial performance of the contract. The contractor therefore could recover the contract price less any amount required to complete the construction. [J.M. Beeson Co. v Sartori 553 So 2d 180 (Fla App 1989)]

(b) FAULT OF COMPLAINING PARTY A party cannot complain that a performance was defective when the performance follows the terms of the contract required by the complaining party. Thus, a homeowner who supplied the specifications for poured cement walls could not hold a contractor liable for damages when the walls that were poured in exact compliance with those specifications proved defective.

(c) PERFORMANCE TO THE SATISFACTION OF THE CONTRACTING PARTY OR A THIRD PARTY Sometimes an agreement requires performance to the satisfaction, taste, or judgment of the other party to the contract. When the contract specifically stipulates that the performance must satisfy the contracting party, the courts will ordinarily enforce the plain meaning of the language of the parties and the work

---

[8] See *Jacob & Youngs, Inc. v Kent*, 230 NY 239 (1921).

[9] But see *USX Corp. v M. DeMatteo Construction Co.*, 315 F3d 43 (1st Cir 2002), for application of a common law rule that prohibits a construction contractor guilty of a willful breach of contract from maintaining any suit on the contract against the other party.

must satisfy the contracting party—subject, of course, to the requirement that dissatisfaction be made in good faith. **For Example,** the Perrones' written contract to purchase
the Hills' residence contained a clause making performance subject to inspection to
the Perrones' satisfaction. During the house inspection, the inspector found a piece of
wood in a crawl space that appeared to have been damaged by termites and had possibly been treated some 18 years before with chlordane. At the end of the inspection
Mr. Perrone indicated that he would perform on the contract. Thereafter, he went on
the Internet and found that chlordane is a highly toxic pesticide now banned from
use as a termite treatment. As a result, the Perrones rescinded the contract under the
buyer satisfaction clause. The Hills sued, believing that speculation about a pesticide
treatment 18 years ago was absurd. They contended that the Perrones had breached
the contract without a valid reason. The court decided for the Perrones, since they
exercised the "satisfaction clause" in good faith.[10] Good-faith personal satisfaction is
generally required when the subject matter of the contract is personal, such as interior
design work, tailoring, or the painting of a portrait.

With respect to things mechanical or routine performances, courts require that the
performance be such as would satisfy a reasonable person under the circumstances.

When work is to be done subject to the approval of an architect, engineer, or
another expert, most courts apply the reasonable person test of satisfaction.

 ## DISCHARGE BY ACTION OF PARTIES

Contracts may be discharged by the joint action of both contracting parties or, in
some cases, by the action of one party alone.

6. DISCHARGE BY UNILATERAL ACTION

Ordinarily, a contract cannot be discharged by the action of either party alone. In
some cases, however, the contract gives one of either party the right to cancel the
contract by unilateral action, such as by notice to the other party. Insurance policies
covering loss commonly provide that the insurer may cancel the policy upon giving a
specified number of days' notice.

(a) CONSUMER PROTECTION RESCISSION   A basic principle of contract law is that once
made, a contract between competent persons is a binding obligation. Consumer
protection legislation introduces into the law a contrary concept—that of giving
the consumer a chance to think things over and to rescind the contract. Thus, the
federal Consumer Credit Protection Act (CCPA) gives the debtor the right to
rescind a credit transaction within three business days when the transaction would
impose a lien on the debtor's home. **For Example,** a homeowner who mortgages
his or her home to obtain a loan may cancel the transaction for any reason by
notifying the lender before midnight of the third full business day after the loan
is made.[11]

A Federal Trade Commission regulation gives the buyer three business days in
which to cancel a home-solicited sale of goods or services costing more than $25.[12]

---

[10] *Hill v Perrones*, 42 P3d 210 (Kan App 2002).

[11] If the owner is not informed of this right to cancel, the three-day period does not begin until that information is given.
Consumer Credit Protection Act § 125, 15 USC § 1635(a), (e), (f).

[12] CFR § 429.1. This displaces state laws making similar provisions for rescission, such as UCCC § 2.502.

7. DISCHARGE BY AGREEMENT

rescission action of one party to a contract to set the contract aside when the other party is guilty of a breach of the contract.

A contract may be discharged by the operation of one of its provisions or by a subsequent agreement. Thus, there may be a discharge by (1) the terms of the original contract, such as a provision that the contract should end on a specified date; (2) a mutual cancellation, in which the parties agree to end their contract; (3) a mutual **rescission**, in which the parties agree to annul the contract and return both parties to their original positions before the contract had been made; (4) the **substitution** of a new contract between the same parties; (5) a novation or substitution of a new contract involving a new party;[13] (6) an **accord and satisfaction**; (7) a release; or (8) a **waiver**.

substitution substitution of a new contract between the same parties.

(a) SUBSTITUTION   The parties may decide that their contract is not the one they want. They may then replace it with another contract. If they do, the original contract is discharged by substitution.[14]

accord and satisfaction agreement to substitute for an existing debt some alternative form of discharging that debt, coupled with the actual discharge of the debt by the substituted performance.

(b) ACCORD AND SATISFACTION   When the parties have differing views as to the performance required by the terms of a contract, they may agree to a different performance. Such an agreement is called an *accord*. When the accord is performed or executed, there is an accord and satisfaction, which discharges the original obligation. To constitute an accord and satisfaction, there must be a bona fide dispute, a proposal to settle the dispute, and performance of the agreement.

waiver release or relinquishment of a known right or objection.

CASE SUMMARY

A Full Court Press to No Avail

FACTS: In September 2002, La Crosse Litho Supply, LLC (La Crosse) entered into a distribution agreement with MKL Pre-Press Electronics (MKL) for the distribution of a printing system. La Crosse purchased a 7000 System unit from MKL for its end user Printing Plus. MKL technicians were to provide service and training for the unit. The 7000 System at Printing Plus failed on three occasions, and ultimately repairs were unsuccessful. On September 30, 2003, La Crosse cancelled the distribution agreement. On October 2, 2003, La Crosse sent a letter to MKL's sales vice president Bill Landwer setting forth an itemized accounting of what it owed MKL Pre-Press with deductions for the purchase price of the failed 7000 System and other offsets. MKL sent a subsequent bill for repairs and services, to which La Crosse objected and stated that it would not pay. MKL's attorney sent a demand letter for $26,453.31. La Crosse's president, Randall Peters, responded by letter dated December 30, 2003, explaining that with an offset for training and warranty work it had performed, "we are sending you the final payment in the amount of $1,696.47." He added, "[w]ith this correspondence, we consider all open issues between La Crosse Litho Supply and MKL Pre-Press closed." Enclosed with the letter was a check for $1,696.47 payable to MKL Pre-Press. In the remittance portion of the check, under the heading "Ref," was typed "FINAL PAYM." The check was endorsed and deposited on either January 26 or 27, 2004.

---

[13] *Eagle Industries, Inc. v Thompson*, 900 P2d 475 (Or 1995). In a few jurisdictions, the term *novation* is used to embrace the substitution of any new contract, whether between the original parties or not.

[14] *Shawnee Hospital Authority v Dow Construction, Inc.*, 812 P2d 1351 (Okla 1990).

CASE SUMMARY

continued

MKL sued La Crosse for $24,756.84. La Crosse defended that the tender and subsequent deposit of the check for $1,696.47 constituted an accord and satisfaction. Jill Fleming, MKL's office manager, stated that it was her duty to process checks and that she did not read Peters' letter. From a judgment for La Crosse, MKL appealed.

DECISION: Judgment for La Crosse. There was an honest dispute as to the amount owed, as evident from the exchange of letters. La Crosse tendered an amount with the explicit understanding that it was the "final payment" of all demands, and the creditor MKL's acceptance and negotiation of a check for that amount constitutes an accord and satisfaction. Ms. Fleming had the authority to endorse checks and deposit them, and her doing so can and should be imputed to her employer, thereby constituting an accord and satisfaction. [**MKL Pre-Press Electronics v La Crosse Litho Supply, LLC, 840 NE2d 687 (Ill App 2005)**]

(D) DISCHARGE BY EXTERNAL CAUSES

Circumstances beyond the control of the contracting parties may discharge the contract.

8. DISCHARGE BY IMPOSSIBILITY

Impossibility of performance refers to external or extrinsic conditions. This is contrasted with an individual's personal inability to perform.[15] **For Example,** Pollard Excavating, Inc., made a contract with Comprehensive Builders, Inc., to install sewer piping from the foundation of a new home to the sewer main but withdrew from the job asserting impossibility because of problems arising from subsurface soil conditions and the fact that the sewer main was farther underground than the builder had stated. Pollard was held liable for "cost of completion" damages. The subsoil conditions and the location of the sewer main were discussed prior to making the contract and were not unanticipated events that made performance objectively impossible.[16]

Shortages of materials and similar factors, even though external, ordinarily do not excuse performance under a contract. However, a seller's duty may be excused by a failure of a particular source of supply that was specified by the parties to the contract. **For Example,** if a contractor's usual gravel source cannot be used (and it is necessary to transport gravel from a more distant source, making performance more costly), this by itself does not discharge the contractor from the obligation to construct a road. If there is nothing in the contract requiring that the gravel be obtained from the unavailable source, no question of impossibility of performance exists. A contract is not discharged merely because performance proves to be more burdensome or costly than was originally contemplated. However, if the parties specified the source of supply in their contract, that would constitute an impossibility that would excuse performance.

---

[15] *Haessly v Safeco Title Ins. Co.*, 825 P2d 1119 (Idaho 1992).
[16] *Comprehensive Bldg. v Pollard Excavating*, 674 NYS2d 869 (App Div 1998).

(a) DESTRUCTION OF PARTICULAR SUBJECT MATTER   When parties contract expressly for, or with reference to, a particular subject matter, the contract is discharged if the subject matter is destroyed through no fault of either party. When a contract calls for the sale of a wheat crop growing on a specific parcel of land, the contract is discharged if that crop is destroyed by blight.

On the other hand, if there is merely a contract to sell a given quantity of a specified grade of wheat, the seller is not discharged when the seller's crop is destroyed by blight. The seller had made an unqualified undertaking to deliver wheat of a specified grade. No restrictions or qualifications were imposed as to the source. If the seller does not deliver the goods called for by the contract, the contract is broken, and the seller is liable for damages.

The parties may, by their contract, allocate the risk of loss. Thus, a contract for the sale of a building and land may specify that the seller should bear any loss from damage to the building.

(b) CHANGE OF LAW   A contract is discharged when its performance is made illegal by a subsequent change in the law. Thus, a contract to construct a nonfireproof building at a particular place is discharged by the adoption of a zoning law prohibiting such a building within that area. Mere inconvenience or temporary delay caused by the new law, however, does not excuse performance.

(c) DEATH OR DISABILITY   When the contract obligates a party to render or receive personal services requiring peculiar skill, the death, incapacity, or illness of the party that was either to render or receive the personal services excuses both sides from a duty to perform. It is sometimes said that "the death of either party is the death of the contract."

The rule does not apply, however, when the acts called for by the contract are of such a character that (1) the acts may be as well performed by others, such as the promisor's personal representatives, or (2) the contract's terms contemplate continuance of the obligations after the death of one of the parties. **For Example,** Lynn Jones was under contract to investor Ed Jenkins to operate certain Subway sandwich shops and to acquire new franchises with funding provided by Jenkins. After Jenkins's death, Jones claimed he was no longer bound under the contract and was free to pursue franchise opportunities on his own. The contract between Jones and Jenkins expressed that it was binding on the parties' "heirs and assigns" and that the contract embodied property rights that passed to Jenkins's widow. The agreement's provisions thus established that the agreement survived the death of Jenkins, and Jones was therefore obligated to remit profits from the franchise he acquired for himself after Jenkins's death.[17]

(d) ACT OF OTHER PARTY   Every contract contains "an implied covenant of good faith and fair dealing." As a result of this covenant, a promisee is under an obligation to do nothing that would interfere with the promisor's performance. When the promisee prevents performance or otherwise makes performance impossible, the promisor is discharged from the contract. Thus, a subcontractor is discharged from any obligation when it is unable to do the work because the principal contractor refuses to deliver the material, equipment, or money required by the subcontract. When the default of the other party consists of failing to supply

---

[17] *Jenkins Subway, Inc. v Jones*, 990 SW2d 713 (Tenn App 1998).

goods or services, the duty may rest on the party claiming a discharge of the contract to show that substitute goods or services could not be obtained elsewhere.

9. DEVELOPING DOCTRINES

Commercial impracticability and frustration of purpose may excuse performance.

(a) COMMERCIAL IMPRACTICABILITY   The doctrine of *commercial impracticability* (as opposed to *impossibility*) was developed to deal with the harsh rule that a party must perform its contracts unless it is absolutely impossible. However, not every type of impracticability is an excuse for nonperformance. **For Example,** I. Patel was bound by his franchise agreement with Days Inn, Inc., to maintain his 60-room inn on old Route 66 in Lincoln, Illinois, to at least minimum quality assurance standards. His inn failed five consecutive quality inspections over two years, with the inspector noting damaged guest rooms, burns in the bedding, and severely stained carpets. Patel's defense when his franchise was cancelled after the fifth failed inspection was that bridge repairs on the road leading from I-55 to his inn had adversely affected his business and made it commercially impractical to live up to the franchise agreement. The court rejected his defense, determining that while the bridge work might have affected patronage, it had no effect on his duty to comply with the quality assurance standards of his franchise agreement.[18] Commercial impracticability is available only when the performance is made impractical by the subsequent occurrence of an event whose nonoccurrence was a basic assumption on which the contract was made.[19]

CASE SUMMARY

A Bolt Out of the Blue

FACTS: CIT, a major equipment leasing company, entered into a sale/leaseback contract with Condere Tire Corporation for 11 tire presses at Condere's tire plant in Natchez, Mississippi. Condere ceased making payments on these presses owned by CIT, and Condere filed for Chapter 11 bankruptcy. CIT thereafter contracted to sell the presses to Specialty Tires, Inc., for $250,000. When the contract was made, CIT, Condere, and Specialty Tires believed that CIT was the owner of the presses and was entitled to immediate possession. When CIT attempted to gain access to the presses to have them shipped, Condere changed its position and refused to allow the equipment to be removed from the plant. When the presses were not delivered, Specialty sued CIT for damages for nondelivery of the presses to date, and CIT asserted the defense of impracticability.

DECISION: Summary judgment for CIT. The delivery of the presses to Specialty Tires Company was made impracticable by the actions of Condere in refusing to give up the presses. Condere's change of its position and refusal to give up the presses was "a bolt out of the blue" for both CIT and Specialty. It was not a risk that CIT should have expected to either bear or contract against. CIT is excused by the doctrine of impracticability from damages for nondelivery of the presses to date. The impracticability relieves the obligation for only so long as the impracticability lasts. CIT asserts it will perform when it receives possession of the presses. [**Specialty Tires, Inc. v CIT, 82 F Supp 2d 434 (WD Pa 2000)**]

---

[18] *Days Inn of America, Inc. v Patel*, 88 F Supp 2d 928 (CD Ill 2000).
[19] See Restatement (Second) of Contracts § 261; UCC § 2-615.

If a subsequent event occurs involving a severe shortage of raw materials or supplies that results in a marked increase in the cost of the materials or supplies and this event was foreseeable, the defense of commercial impracticability is not available.

(b) FRUSTRATION OF PURPOSE DOCTRINE   Because of a change in circumstances, the purpose of the contract may have no value to the party entitled to receive performance. In such a case, performance may be excused if both parties were aware of the purpose and the event that frustrated the purpose was unforeseeable.[20]

For Example, National Southern Bank rents a home near Willowbend Country Club on the southeastern shore of North Carolina for $75,000 a week to entertain business guests at the Ryder Cup matches scheduled for the week in question. Storm damage from Hurricane David the week before the event caused the closing of the course and the transfer of the tournament to another venue in a different state. The bank's duty to pay for the house may be excused by the doctrine of *frustration of purpose,* because the transfer of the tournament fully destroyed the value of the home rental, both parties were aware of the purpose of the rental, and the cancellation of the golf tournament was unforeseeable.

CASE SUMMARY

Relief for Broken Dreams

FACTS: John J. Paonessa Company made a contract with the state of Massachusetts to reconstruct a portion of highway. Paonessa then made a contract with Chase Precast Corporation to obtain concrete median barriers for use in the highway. Thereafter, the state highway department decided that such barriers would not be used. Paonessa therefore had no reason to go through with the contract to purchase the barriers from Chase because it could not use them and could not get paid for them by the state. Chase sued Paonessa for the profit Chase would have made on the contract for the barriers.

DECISION: Judgment for Paonessa. The change to the highway construction plan made by the State Department of Highways made the barriers worthless. There was accordingly a frustration of the purpose for which the contract had been made to purchase the barriers. Therefore, the contract for the median barriers was discharged by such frustration of purpose and did not bind Paonessa. [**Chase Precast Corp. v John J. Paonessa Co., Inc. 566 NE2d 603 (Mass 1991)**]

(c) COMPARISON TO COMMON LAW RULE   The traditional common law rule refuses to recognize commercial impracticability or frustration of purpose. By the common law rule, the losses and disappointments against which commercial impracticability and frustration of purpose give protection are merely the risks that one takes in

---

[20] The defense of frustration of purpose, or commercial frustration, is very difficult to invoke because the courts are extremely reluctant to allow parties to avoid obligations to which they have agreed. See *Wal-Mart Stores, Inc. v AIG Life Insurance Co.,* 872 A2d 611 (Del Ch 2005), denying application of the commercial frustration doctrine when the supervening event, the invalidation of hundreds of millions in tax deductions by the IRS, was reasonably foreseeable and could have been provided for in the contract.

entering into a contract. Moreover, the situations could have been guarded against by including an appropriate condition subsequent in the contract. A condition subsequent declares that the contract will be void if a specified event occurs.[21] The contract also could have provided for a readjustment of compensation if there was a basic change of circumstances. The common law approach also rejects these developing concepts because they weaken the stability of a contract.

An indication of a wider recognition of the concept that "extreme" changes of circumstances can discharge a contract is found in the Uniform Commercial Code. The UCC provides for the discharge of a contract for the sale of goods when a condition that the parties assumed existed, or would continue, ceases to exist.[22]

---

10. TEMPORARY IMPOSSIBILITY

Ordinarily, a temporary impossibility suspends the duty to perform. If the obligation to perform is suspended, it is revived on the termination of the impossibility. If, however, performance at that later date would impose a substantially greater burden on the party obligated to perform, some courts discharge the obligor from the contract.

After the September 11, 2001, terrorist attack on the World Trade Center, New York City courts followed wartime precedents that had developed the law of temporary impossibility. Such impossibility, when of brief duration, excuses performance until it subsequently becomes possible to perform rather than excusing performance altogether. Thus, an individual who was unable to communicate her cancellation of travel 60 days prior to her scheduled travel as required by her contract, which needed to occur on or before September 14, 2001, could expect relief from a cancellation penalty provision in the contract based on credible testimony of attempted phone calls to the travel agent on and after September 12, 2001, even though the calls did not get through due to communication problems in New York City.[23]

(a) WEATHER   Acts of God, such as tornadoes, lightning, and floods, usually do not terminate a contract even though they make performance difficult. Thus, weather conditions constitute a risk that is assumed by a contracting party in the absence of a contrary agreement. Consequently, extra expense sustained by a contractor because of weather conditions is a risk that the contractor assumes in the absence of an express provision for additional compensation in such a case. **For Example,** Danielo Contractors made a contract to construct a shopping mall for the Rubicon Center, with construction to begin November 1. Because of abnormal cold and blizzard conditions, Danielo was not able to begin work until April 1 and was five months late in completing the construction of the project. Rubicon sued Danielo for breach of contract by failing to perform on schedule. Danielo is liable. Because the contract included no provision covering delay caused by weather, Danielo bore the risk of the delay and resulting loss.

Modern contracts commonly contain a "weather clause" and reflect the parties' agreement on this matter. When the parties take the time to discuss weather issues, purchasing insurance coverage is a common resolution.

---

[21] *Wermer v ABI*, 10 SW3d 575 (Mo App 2000).

[22] UCC § 2-615.

[23] See *Bugh v Protravel International, Inc.*, 746 NYS2d 290 (Civ Ct NYC 2002).

11. DISCHARGE BY OPERATION OF LAW

operation of law attaching of certain consequences to certain facts because of legal principles that operate automatically as contrasted with consequences that arise because of the voluntary action of a party designed to create those consequences.

A contract is discharged by **operation of law** by (1) an alteration or a material change made by a party, (2) the destruction of the written contract with intent to discharge it, (3) bankruptcy, (4) the operation of a statute of limitations, or (5) a contractual limitation.

(a) BANKRUPTCY   As set forth in the chapter on bankruptcy, even though all creditors have not been paid in full, a discharge in **bankruptcy** eliminates ordinary contract claims against the debtor.

bankruptcy procedure by which one unable to pay debts may surrender all assets in excess of any exemption claim to the court for administration and distribution to creditors, and the debtor is given a discharge that releases him from the unpaid balance due on most debts.

(b) STATUTE OF LIMITATIONS   A **statute of limitations** provides that after a certain number of years have passed, a contract claim is barred. The time limitation provided by state statutes of limitations varies widely. The time period for bringing actions for breach of an oral contract is two to three years. The period may differ with the type of contract—ranging from a relatively short time for open accounts (ordinary customers' charge accounts) to four years for sales of goods.[24] A somewhat longer period exists for bringing actions for breach of written contracts (usually four to ten years). **For Example,** Prate Installations, Inc., sued homeowners Richard and Rebecca Thomas for failure to pay for a new roof installed by Prate. Prate had sent numerous invoices to the Thomases over a four-year period seeking payment to no avail. The Thomases moved to dismiss the case under a four-year limitation period. However, the court concluded that the state's ten-year limitations period on written contracts applied.[25] The maximum period for judgments of record is usually 10 to 20 years.

statute of limitations statute that restricts the period of time within which an action may be brought.

(c) CONTRACTUAL LIMITATIONS   Some contracts, particularly insurance contracts, contain a time limitation within which suit must be brought. This is in effect a private statute of limitations created by the agreement of the parties.

A contract may also require that notice of any claim be given within a specified time. A party who fails to give notice within the time specified by the contract is barred from suing on the contract.

A contract provision requiring that suit be brought within one year does not violate public policy, although the statute of limitations would allow two years in the absence of such a contract limitation.[26]

(**LAWFLIX**)

Uncle Buck (1989) (PG-13)

John Candy plays ne'er-do-well Uncle Buck who promises to go to work at his girlfriend's tire store and marry her. When his brother calls in the middle of the night seeking help with his children, Buck tells his girlfriend (Chenise) that he can no longer honor his promise because he must go to the suburbs to care for his brother's children

---

[24] UCC § 2-725(1).

[25] *Prate Installations, Inc. v Thomas*, 842 NE2d 1205 (Ill App 2006).

[26] *Keiting v Skauge*, 543 NW2d 565 (Wis App 1995).

LAWFLIX

continued

while his brother and sister-in-law travel to Indiana to be with his sister-in-law's very ill father.

Discuss Buck's excuse. Is it impossibility? Does the change in circumstances excuse Buck?

For movie clips that illustrate business law concepts, see LawFlix at **http://wdvl.westbuslaw.com.**

> SUMMARY

A party's duty to perform under a contract can be affected by a condition precedent, which must occur before a party has an obligation to perform; a condition subsequent, that is, a condition or event that relieves the duty to thereafter perform; and concurrent conditions, which require mutual and often simultaneous performance.

Most contracts are discharged by performance. An offer to perform is called a *tender of performance.* If a tender of performance is wrongfully refused, the duty of the tenderer to perform is terminated. When the performance called for by the contract is the payment of money, it must be legal tender that is offered. In actual practice, it is common to pay and to accept payment by checks or other commercial paper.

When the debtor owes the creditor on several accounts and makes a payment, the debtor may specify which account is to be credited with the payment. If the debtor fails to specify, the creditor may choose which account to credit.

When a contract does not state when it is to be performed, it must be performed within a reasonable time. If time for performance is stated in the contract, the contract must be performed at the time specified if such time is essential (is of the essence). Performance within a reasonable time is sufficient if the specified time is not essential. Ordinarily, a contract must be performed exactly in the manner specified by the contract. A less-than-perfect performance is allowed if it is a substantial performance and if damages are allowed the other party. The other contracting party or

a third person may guarantee a perfect performance. Such a guarantor is then liable if the performance is less than perfect.

A contract cannot be discharged by unilateral action unless authorized by the contract itself or by statute, as in the case of consumer protection rescission.

Because a contract arises from an agreement, it may also be terminated by an agreement. A contract may also be discharged by the substitution of a new contract for the original contract; by a novation, or making a new contract with a new party; by accord and satisfaction; by release; or by waiver.

A contract is discharged when it is impossible to perform. Impossibility may result from the destruction of the subject matter of the contract, the adoption of a new law that prohibits performance, the death or disability of a party whose personal action was required for performance of the contract, or the act of the other party to the contract. Some courts will also hold that a contract is discharged when its performance is commercially impracticable or there is frustration of purpose. Temporary impossibility, such as a labor strike or bad weather, has no effect on a contract. It is common, though, to include protective clauses that excuse delay caused by temporary impossibility.

A contract may be discharged by operation of law. This occurs when (1) the liability arising from the contract is discharged by bankruptcy, (2) suit on the contract is barred by the applicable statute of limitations, or (3) a time limitation stated in the contract is exceeded.

> QUESTIONS AND CASE PROBLEMS

1. McMullen Contractors made a contract with Richardson to build an apartment house for a specific price. A number of serious apartment house fires broke out in the city, and the city council adopted an ordinance increasing the fire precautions that had to be taken in the construction of a new building. Compliance with these new requirements would make the construction of the apartment house for Richardson more expensive than McMullen had originally contemplated. Is McMullen discharged from the contract to build the apartment house?

2. Lymon Mitchell operated a Badcock Home Furnishings dealership, under which as dealer he was paid a commission on sales and Badcock retained title to merchandise on display. Mitchell sold his dealership to another and to facilitate the sale, Badcock prepared a summary of commissions owed with certain itemized offsets it claimed that Mitchell owed Badcock. Mitchell disagreed with the calculations, but he accepted them and signed the transfer documents closing the sale on the basis of the terms set forth in the summary and was paid accordingly. After pondering the offsets taken by Badcock and verifying the correctness of his position, he brought suit for the additional funds owed. What defense would you expect Badcock to raise? How would you decide the case? Explain fully. [*Mitchell v Badcock Corp.*, 496 SE2d 502 (Ga App)]

3. American Bank loaned Koplik $50,000 to buy equipment for a restaurant about to be opened by Casual Citchen Corp. The loan was not repaid, and Fast Foods, Inc., bought out the interest of Casual Citchen. As part of the transaction, Fast Foods agreed to pay the debt owed to American Bank, and the parties agreed to a new schedule of payments to be made by Fast Foods. Fast Foods did not make the payments, and American Bank sued Koplik. He contended that his obligation to repay $50,000 had been discharged by the execution of the agreement providing for the payment of the debt by Fast Foods. Was this defense valid? [*American Bank & Trust Co. v Koplik*, 451 NYS2d 426 (App Div)]

4. Metalcrafters made a contract to design a new earth-moving vehicle for Lamar Highway Construction Co. Metalcrafters was depending on the genius of Samet, the head of its research department, to design a new product. Shortly after the contract was made between Metalcrafters and Lamar, Samet was killed in an automobile accident. Metalcrafters was not able to design the product without Samet. Lamar sued Metalcrafters for damages for breach of the contract. Metalcrafters claimed that the contract was discharged by Samet's death. Is it correct?

5. The Tinchers signed a contract to sell land to Creasy. The contract specified that the sales transaction was to be completed in 90 days. At the end of the 90 days, Creasy requested an extension of time. The Tinchers refused to grant an extension and stated that the contract was terminated. Creasy claimed that the 90-day clause was not binding because the contract did not state that time was of the essence. Was the contract terminated? [*Creasy v Tincher*, 173 SE2d 332 (W Va)]

6. Christopher Bloom received a medical school scholarship created by the U.S. Department of Health and Human Services to increase the number of doctors serving rural areas. In return for this assistance, Bloom agreed to practice four years in a region identified as being underserved by medical professionals. After some problem with his postgraduation assignment, Bloom requested a repayment schedule from the agency. Although no terms were offered, Bloom tendered to the agency two checks totaling $15,500 and marked "Final Payment." Neither check was cashed, and the government sued Bloom for $480,000, the value of the assistance provided. Bloom claimed that by tendering the checks to the agency, his liability had been discharged by an accord and satisfaction. Decide. [*United States v Bloom*, 112 F3d 200 (7th Cir)]

7. Dickson contracted to build a house for Moran. When it was approximately 25 percent to 40 percent completed, Moran would not let Dickson work any more because he was not following the building plans and specifications and there were many defects. Moran hired

another contractor to correct the defects and finish the building. Dickson sued Moran for breach of contract, claiming that he had substantially performed the contract up to the point where he had been discharged. Was Dickson correct? [*Dickson v Moran*, 344 So 2d 102 (La App)]

8. A lessor leased a trailer park to a tenant. At the time, sewage was disposed of by a septic tank system that was not connected with the public sewage system. The tenant knew this, and the lease declared that the tenant had examined the premises and that the landlord made no representation or guarantee as to the condition of the premises. Some time thereafter, the septic tank system stopped working properly, and the county health department notified the tenant that he was required to connect the septic tank system with the public sewage system or else the department would close the trailer park. The tenant did not want to pay the additional cost involved in connecting with the public system. The tenant claimed that he was released from the lease and was entitled to a refund of the deposit that he had made. Was he correct? [*Glen R. Sewell Street Metal v Loverde*, 451 P2d 721 (Cal App)]

9. Oneal was a teacher employed by the Colton Consolidated School District. Because of a diabetic condition, his eyesight deteriorated so much that he offered to resign if he would be given pay for a specified number of "sick leave" days. The school district refused to do this and discharged Oneal for nonperformance of his contract. He appealed to remove the discharge from his record. Decide. What ethical values are involved? [*Oneal v Colton Consolidated School District*, 557 P2d 11 (Wash App)]

10. Northwest Construction, Inc., made a contract with the state of Washington for highway construction. Part of the work was turned over under a subcontract to Yakima Asphalt Paving Co. The contract required that any claim be asserted within 180 days. Yakima brought an action for damages after the expiration of 180 days. The defense was that the claim was too late. Yakima replied that the action was brought within the time allowed by the statute of limitations and that the contractual limitation of 180 days was therefore not binding. Was Yakima correct?

11. The Metropolitan Park District of Tacoma gave Griffith a concession to run the district's parks. The agreement gave the right to occupy the parks and use any improvements found therein. The district later wished to set this agreement aside because it was not making sufficient money from the transaction. While it was seeking to set the agreement aside, a boathouse and a gift shop in one of the parks were destroyed by fire. The district then claimed that the concession contract with Griffith was discharged by impossibility of performance. Was it correct? [*Metropolitan Park District of Tacoma v Griffith*, 723 P2d 1093 (Wash)]

12. Suburban Power Piping Corp., under contract to construct a building for LTV Steel Corp., made a subcontract with Power & Pollution Services, Inc., to do some of the work. The subcontract provided that the subcontractor would be paid when the owner (LTV) paid the contractor. LTV went into bankruptcy before making the full payment to the contractor, who then refused to pay the subcontractor on the ground that the "pay-when-paid" provision of the subcontract made payment by the owner a condition precedent to the obligation of the contractor to pay the subcontractor. Was the contractor correct? [*Power & Pollution Services, Inc. v Suburban Power Piping Corp.*, 598 NE2d 69 (Ohio App)]

13. Ellen borrowed money from Farmers' Bank. As evidence of the loan, she signed a promissory note by which she promised to pay to the bank in installments the amount of the loan together with interest and administrative costs. She was unable to make the payments on the scheduled dates. She and the bank then executed a new agreement that gave her a longer period of time for making the payments. However, after two months, she was unable to pay on this new schedule. The bank then brought suit against her under the terms of the original agreement. She raised the defense that the original agreement had been discharged by the execution of the second agreement and could not be sued on. Decide.

14. Acme Hydraulic Press Co. manufactured large presses and sold them throughout the United States. The agreement-of-sale contract that Acme executed with its customers specified that they could make no claim for breach of contract unless

notice of the breach was given within 10 days after the delivery of a press in question to the buyer and that no lawsuit could thereafter be brought if notice had not been given. Was this time limitation valid?

15. New Beginnings provides rehabilitation services for alcohol and drug abuse to both adults and adolescents. New Beginnings entered into negotiation with Adbar for the lease of a building in the city of St. Louis, and subsequently entered into a three-year lease. The total rent due for the three-year term was $273,000. After the lease was executed, the city denied an occupancy permit because Alderman Bosley and residents testified at a hearing in vigorous opposition to the presence of New Beginnings in the neighborhood. A court ordered the permit issued. Alderman Bosley thereafter contacted the chair of the state's appointment committee and asked her to pull the agency's funding. He received no commitment from her on this matter. After a meeting with the state director of Alcohol and Drug Abuse where it was asserted that the director said the funding would be pulled if New Beginnings moved into the Adbar location, New Beginnings's board decided not to occupy the building. Adbar brought suit for breach of the lease, and New Beginnings asserted it was excused from performance because of commercial impracticability and frustration of purpose. Do you believe the doctrine of commercial impracticability should be limited in its application so as to preserve the certainty of contracts? What rule of law applies to this case? Decide. [*Adbar v New Beginnings,* 103 SW2d 799 (Mo App 2003)]

> CPA QUESTIONS

1. Parc hired Glaze to remodel and furnish an office suite. Glaze submitted plans that Parc approved. After completing all the necessary construction and painting, Glaze purchased minor accessories that Parc rejected because they did not conform to the plans. Parc refused to allow Glaze to complete the project and refused to pay Glaze any part of the contract price. Glaze sued for the value of the work performed. Which of the following statements is correct?

   a. Glaze will lose because Glaze breached the contract by not completing performance.
   b. Glaze will win because Glaze substantially performed and Parc prevented complete performance.
   c. Glaze will lose because Glaze materially breached the contract by buying the accessories.
   d. Glaze will win because Parc committed anticipatory breach.

2. Ordinarily, in an action for breach of a construction contract, the statute of limitations time period would be computed from the date the:

   a. contract is negotiated.
   b. contract is breached.
   c. contract is begun.
   d. contract is signed.

3. Which of the following will release all original parties to a contract but will maintain a contractual relationship?

	Novation	*Substituted contract*
a.	Yes	Yes
b.	Yes	No
c.	No	Yes
d.	No	No

BREACH OF CONTRACT
AND REMEDIES

LEARNING OBJECTIVES

After studying this chapter, you should be able to

LO.1 List and define the kinds of damages that may be recovered when a contract is broken

LO.2 Describe the requirement of mitigation of damages

LO.3 State when liquidated damages clauses are valid

LO.4 State when liability-limiting clauses are valid

LO.5 State when a breach of contract is waived

LO.6 List the steps that may be used to prevent a waiver of breach of contract

What can be done when a contract is broken?

 A WHAT CONSTITUTES A BREACH OF CONTRACT?

The question of remedies does not become important until it is first determined that a contract has been violated or breached.

1. DEFINITION OF BREACH

breach failure to act or perform in the manner called for in a contract.

A **breach** is the failure to act or perform in the manner called for by the contract. When the contract calls for performance, such as painting an owner's home, the failure to paint or to paint properly is a *breach of contract*. If the contract calls for a creditor's forbearance, the creditor's action in bringing a lawsuit is a breach of the contract.

2. ANTICIPATORY BREACH

When the contract calls for performance, a party may make it clear before the time for performance arrives that the contract will not be performed. This is referred to as an **anticipatory breach**.

anticipatory breach promisor's repudiation of the contract prior to the time that performance is required when such repudiation is accepted by the promisee as a breach of the contract.

anticipatory repudiation repudiation made in advance of the time for performance of the contract obligations.

(a) ANTICIPATORY REPUDIATION   When a party expressly declares that performance will not be made when required, this declaration is called an **anticipatory repudiation** of the contract. To constitute such a repudiation, there must be a clear, absolute, unequivocal refusal to perform the contract according to its terms. **For Example,** Procter & Gamble (P&G) sought payment on four letters of credit issued by a Serbian bank, Investbanka. P&G presented two letters by June 8, prior to their expiration dates, with the necessary documentation for payment to Beogradska Bank New York, Investbanka's New York agent. A June 11 letter from Beogradska Bank broadly and unequivocally stated that the bank would not pay the letters of credit. Two additional letters of credit totaling $20,000 issued by Investbanka that expired by June 30 were not thereafter submitted to the New York agent bank by P&G. However, a court found that the bank had anticipatorily breached its obligations under those letters of credit by its broad renouncements in the June 11 letter, and judgments were rendered in favor of P&G.[1]

> ## CASE SUMMARY
>
> ### Splitting Tips—Contract Price Less Cost of Completion
>
> FACTS: Hartland Developers, Inc., agreed to build an airplane hangar for Robert Tips of San Antonio for $300,000, payable in three installments of $100,000, with the final payment due upon the completion of the building and the issuance of a certificate of completion by the engineer representing Tips. The evidence shows that Tips's representative, Mr. Lavelle, instructed Hartland to cease work on the building because Tips could no longer afford to make payments. Hartland ceased work as instructed before the final completion of the

[1] *Procter & Gamble v Investbanka*, 2000 US Dist LEXIS 5636 (SDNY 2000).

CASE SUMMARY

continued

building, having been paid $200,000 at the time. He sued Tips for breach of contract. On May 6, 1996, the trial court allowed Hartland the amount owing on the contract, $100,000, less the cost of completing the building according to the contract, $65,000, plus attorney fees and prejudgment interest. Tips appealed, pointing out, among other assertions, that he was required to spend $23,000 to provide electrical outlets for the hangar, which were contemplated in the contract.

DECISION: Judgment for Tips, subject to offsets. The trial judge based his damages assessment on anticipatory repudiation of contract. The evidence that Tips's representative, Lavelle, instructed Hartland to cease work on the project because Tips no longer could afford to make payments was sufficient to support this finding. However, Tips is entitled to an offset for electrical connections of $23,000 under a breach of contract theory. [**Tips v Hartland Developers, Inc., 961 SW2d 618 (Tex App 1998)**]

A refusal to perform a contract that is made before performance is required unless the other party to the contract does an act or makes a concession that is not required by the contract, is an anticipatory repudiation of the contract.[2]

SPORTS & ENTERTAINMENT LAW

Get It While You Can?

In 2000, the cast of *Friends*, one of the hottest shows on television, demanded a pay increase. The demand was made with a valid contract in place and near the time NBC was to announce its fall lineup. The six stars demanded $1,000,000 each per episode. NBC settled for $750,000 per star, up from the stars' $150,000 per episode figure renegotiated in 1998.

When stars seek to renegotiate contracts before their expiration, the network can replace them if they fail to live up to their contracts, and it can enforce the standard contractual clause, which prohibits them from doing other television work until the expiration of their contracts. Recasting six stars for a highly successful show would not be feasible. To offset the stars' bargaining power, NBC prepared a television promotion that would relabel the last show for that season as the "series finale" and announce "See how it all ends on *Friends*." The cast were informed of NBC's threat to end the series in this manner. Renegotiations quickly ensued and led to the $750,000 agreement. Two years later the six stars obtained their goal of $1 million per episode paychecks. Was it ethical for the stars to threaten to strike just before the fall lineup announcements? When Jay Leno was asked about the tactics of the *Friends* stars, he responded, "You have to get what you can while you can in this business." Is Mr. Leno right? Is such an attitude ethical? When the new agreement was reached, was there a mutual rescission of the existing contract and the substitution of a new contract, or did the new contract fail for lack of consideration?

---

[2] *Chamberlain v Puckett Construction*, 921 P2d 1237 (Mont 1996).

A party making an anticipatory repudiation may retract or take back the repudiation if the other party has not changed position in reliance on the repudiation. However, if the other party has changed position, the party making the anticipatory repudiation cannot retract it. **For Example,** if a buyer makes another purchase when the seller declares that the seller will not perform the contract, the buyer has acted in reliance on the seller's repudiation. The seller will therefore not be allowed to retract the repudiation.

(b) ANTICIPATORY REPUDIATION BY CONDUCT   The anticipatory repudiation may be expressed by conduct that makes it impossible for the repudiating party to perform subsequently. To illustrate, there is a repudiation by conduct if a farmer makes a contract to sell an identified quantity of potatoes nearly equivalent to his entire crop and then sells and delivers them to another buyer before the date specified for the delivery to the first buyer.

 WAIVER OF BREACH

The breach of a contract may have no importance because the other party to the contract waives the breach.

3. CURE OF BREACH BY WAIVER

waiver release or relinquishment of a known right or objection.

The fact that one party has broken a contract does not necessarily mean that there will be a lawsuit or a forfeiture of the contract. For practical business reasons, one party may be willing to ignore or waive the breach. When it is established that there has been a **waiver** of a breach, the party waiving the breach cannot take any action on the theory that the contract was broken. The waiver, in effect, erases the past breach. The contract continues as though the breach had not existed.

The waiver may be express or it may be implied from the continued recognition of the existence of the contract by the aggrieved party.[3] When the conduct of a party shows an intent to give up a right, it waives that right.[4]

4. EXISTENCE AND SCOPE OF WAIVER

It is a question of fact whether there has been a waiver.

CASE SUMMARY

Have You Driven a Ford Lately, Jennifer?

FACTS: In 1995, Northland Ford Dealers, an association of dealerships, offered to sponsor a "hole in one" contest at Moccasin Creek Country Club. A banner announced that a hole in one would win a car but gave no other details, and the local dealer parked a Ford Explorer near the banner. Northland paid a $4,602 premium to Continental Hole-In-One, Inc., to

---

[3] *Huger v Morrison*, 2000 La App LEXIS 241.
[4] *Stronghaven Inc. v Ingram*, 555 SE2d 49 (Ga App 2001).

CASE SUMMARY

continued

ensure the award of the contest prize. The insurance application stated in capital letters that "ALL AMATEUR MEN AND WOMEN WILL UTILIZE THE SAME TEE." And Continental established the men/women yardage for the hole to be 170 yards, but did not make this known to the participants. Jennifer Harms registered for the tournament and paid her entrance fee. At the contest hole, she teed off from the amateur women's red marker, which was a much shorter distance to the pin than the 170 yards from the men's marker—and she made a hole in one. When she inquired about the prize, she was told that because of insurance requirements, all amateurs had to tee off from the amateur men's tee box, and because she had not done so, she was disqualified. Harms, a collegiate golfer at Concordia College, returned there to complete her last year of athletic eligibility and on graduation sued Northland for breach of contract. Northland contends that under NCAA rules, accepting a prize or agreeing to accept a prize would have disqualified Harms from NCAA competition. It also asserts that her continuation of her NCAA competition evinced intent to waive acceptance of the car.

DECISION: Judgment for Harms. Northland must abide by the rules it announced, not by the ones it left unannounced that disqualified all amateur women from the contest. This was a vintage unilateral contract with performance by the offeree as acceptance. Harms earned the prize when she sank her winning shot. Waiver is a volitional relinquishment, by act or word, of a known existing right conferred in law or contract. Harms could not disclaim the prize; it was not hers to refuse. She was told her shot from the wrong tee disqualified her. One can hardly relinquish what was never conferred. Northland's waiver defense is devoid of merit. [*Harms v Northland Ford Dealers*, 602 NW2d 58 (SD 1999)]

(a) EXISTENCE OF WAIVER A party may express or declare that the breach of a contract is waived. A waiver of a breach is more often the result of an express forgiving of a breach. Thus, a party allowing the other party to continue performance without objecting that the performance is not satisfactory waives the right to raise that objection when sued for payment by the performing party.

For Example, a contract promising to sell back a parcel of commercial property to Jackson required Jackson to make a $500 payment to Massey's attorney on the first of the month for five months, December through April. It was clearly understood that the payments would be "on time without fail." Jackson made the December payment on time. New Year's Day, a holiday, fell on a Friday, and Jackson made the second payment on January 4. He made $500 payments on February 1, March 1, and March 31, respectively, and the payments were accepted and a receipt issued on each occasion. However, Massey refused to convey title back to Jackson because "the January 4 payment was untimely and the parties' agreement had been breached." The court held that the doctrine of waiver applied due to Massey's acceptance of the late payment and the three subsequent payments without objection, and the court declared that Jackson was entitled to possession of the land.[5]

(b) SCOPE OF WAIVER The waiver of a breach of contract extends only to the matter waived. It does not show any intent to ignore other provisions of the contract.

---

[5] *Massey v Jackson*, 726 So 2d 656 (Ala Civ App 1998).

(c) ANTIMODIFICATION CLAUSE   Modern contracts commonly specify that the terms of a contract shall not be deemed modified by waiver as to any breaches. This means that the original contract remains as agreed to. Either party may therefore return to, and insist on, compliance with the original contract.

In the example involving Jackson and Massey's contract, the trial court reviewed the contract to see whether the court was restricted by the contract from applying the waiver. It concluded: "In this case, the parties' contract did not contain any terms that could prevent the application of the doctrine of waiver to the acceptance of late payments."[6]

5. RESERVATION OF RIGHTS

reservation of rights
assertion by a party to a contract that even though a tendered performance (e.g., a defective product) is accepted, the right to damages for nonconformity to the contract is reserved.

It may be that a party is willing to accept a defective performance but does not wish to surrender any claim for damages for the breach. **For Example,** Midwest Utilities, Inc., accepted 20 carloads of Powder River Basin coal (sometimes called *Western coal*) from its supplier, Maney Enterprises, because its power plants were in short supply of coal. Midwest's requirements contract with Maney called for Appalachian coal, a low-sulfur, highly efficient fuel, which is sold at a premium price per ton. Midwest, in accepting the tendered performance with a **reservation of rights**, gave notice to Maney that it reserved all rights to pursue damages for the tender of a nonconforming shipment.

C   REMEDIES FOR BREACH OF CONTRACT

remedy action or procedure that is followed in order to enforce a right or to obtain damages for injury to a right.

One or more **remedies** may be available to the innocent party in the case of a breach of contract. There is also the possibility that arbitration or a streamlined out-of-court alternative dispute resolution procedure is available or required for determining the rights of the parties.

6. REMEDIES UPON ANTICIPATORY REPUDIATION

When an anticipatory repudiation of a contract occurs, the aggrieved person has several options. He may (1) do nothing beyond stating that performance at the proper time will be required, (2) regard the contract as having been definitively broken and bring a lawsuit against the repudiating party without waiting to see whether there will be proper performance when the performance date arrives, or (3) regard the repudiation as an offer to cancel the contract. This offer can be accepted or rejected. If accepted, there is a discharge of the original contract by the subsequent cancellation agreement of the parties.

7. REMEDIES IN GENERAL AND THE MEASURE OF DAMAGES

Courts provide a *quasi-contractual* or *restitution* remedy in which a contract is unenforceable because it lacked definite and certain terms or was not in compliance with the statute of frauds, yet one of the parties performed services for the other. The measure of damages in these and other quasi-contract cases is the reasonable value of the services performed, not an amount derived from the defective contract.

---

[6] Id., at 659.

FIGURE 20-1   *What Follows the Breach*

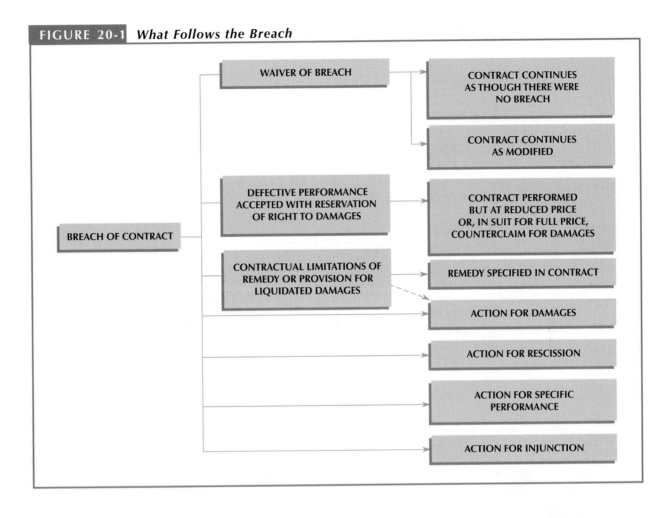

In cases when a person retains money or when a contemplated contract is not properly formed and no work is performed, the party retaining the benefit is obligated to make restitution to the person conferring the benefit. **For Example,** Kramer Associates, Inc. (KAI), a Washington D.C., consulting firm, accepted $75,000 from a Ghana-based corporation, Ikam, Ltd., to secure financing for a Ghana development project. No contract was ever executed, and KAI did virtually nothing to secure financing for the project. Restitution of the $75,000 was required.[7]

When there is a breach of contract, the regular remedy is an award of *monetary damages*. In unusual circumstances, when monetary damages are inadequate, the injured party may obtain **specific performance**, whereby the court will order that the contract terms be carried out.

The measure of monetary damages when there has been a breach of contract is the sum of money that will place the injured party in the same position that would have been attained if the contract had been performed.[8] That is, the injured party will be given the *benefit of the bargain* by the court. As seen in the *Tips v Hartland Developers* case, the nonbreaching party, Hartland, was awarded the contract price

specific performance action brought to compel the adverse party to perform a contract on the theory that merely suing for damages for its breach will not be an adequate remedy.

---

[7] *Kramer Associates, Inc. v IKAM, Ltd.,* 888 A2d 247 (DC 2005).
[8] *Leingang v City of Mandan Weed Board,* 468 NW2d 397 (ND 1991).

compensatory damages sum of money that will compensate an injured plaintiff for actual loss.

nominal damages nominal sum awarded the plaintiff in order to establish that legal rights have been violated although the plaintiff in fact has not sustained any actual loss or damages.

punitive damages damages, in excess of those required to compensate the plaintiff for the wrong done, that are imposed in order to punish the defendant because of the particularly wanton or willful character of wrongdoing; also called *exemplary damages.*

direct damages losses that are caused by breach of a contract.

less the cost of completion of the project, which had the effect of giving the builder the benefit of the bargain.

8. MONETARY DAMAGES

Monetary damages are commonly classified as compensatory damages, nominal damages, and punitive damages. **Compensatory damages** compensate the injured party for the damages incurred as a result of the breach of contract. Compensatory damages have two branches, *direct damages* and *consequential* (or *special*) *damages.*

Injured parties that do not sustain an actual loss because of a breach of contract are entitled to a judgment of a small sum of money such as $1; these damages are called **nominal damages**.

Damages in excess of actual loss, imposed for the purpose of punishing or making an example of the defendant, are known as **punitive damages** or *exemplary damages.* In contract actions, punitive damages are not ordinarily awarded.[9]

(a) DIRECT AND CONSEQUENTIAL DAMAGES **Direct damages** (sometimes called *general damages*) are those that naturally flow from the given type of breach of contract involved and include *incidental damages*, which are extra expenditures made by the injured party to rectify the breach or mitigate damages. **Consequential damages** (sometimes called *special damages*) are those that do not necessarily flow from the type of breach of contract involved but happen to do so in a particular case as a result of the injured party's particular circumstances.

CASE SUMMARY

Who Pays the Expenses?

FACTS: Jerry Birkel was a grain farmer. Hassebrook Farm Service, Inc., made a contract with Jerry to sell to him and install a grain storage and drying bin. Jerry traded in his old dryer to the seller. The new equipment did not work properly, and Jerry had to pay other persons for drying and storing his grain. Jerry sued Hassebrook for damages and claimed the right to be repaid what he had paid to others for drying and storage.

DECISION: Jerry was entitled to recover what he had paid others for drying and storage. Because Jerry had traded in his old dryer to the seller, it was obvious to the seller that if the new equipment did not work properly, Jerry would be forced to pay for alternative drying and storage to prevent the total loss of his crops. The cost of such an alternative was therefore within the seller's contemplation when the contract was made, and so the buyer could recover this cost as an element of damages for the seller's breach of contract. [**Birkel v Hassebrook Farm Service, Inc.**, 363 NW2d 148 (Neb 1985)]

consequential damages damages the buyer experiences as a result of the seller's breach with respect to a third party, also called *special damages.*

Consequential damages may be recovered only if it was reasonably foreseeable to the defendant that the kind of loss in question could be sustained by the nonbreaching party if the contract were broken.

---

[9] A party who is not awarded actual damages but wins nominal damages can be considered a "prevailing party" for the purposes of a contractual attorney fee-shifting provision. *Brock v King,* 629 SE2d 829 (Ga App 2006).

For Example, in early August, Spencer Adams ordered a four-wheel-drive GMC truck with a rear-end hydraulic lift for use on his Aroostook County, Maine, potato farm. The contract price was $58,500. He told Brad Jones, the owner of the dealership, that he had to have the truck by Labor Day so he could use it to bring in his crop from the fields before the first frost, and Brad nodded that he understood. The truck did not arrive by Labor Day as promised in the written contract. After a two-week period of gradually escalating recriminations with the dealership, Adams obtained the same model GMC truck at a dealership 40 minutes away in Houlton but at the cost of $60,500. He was also able to rent a similar truck from the Houlton dealer for $250 for the day while the new truck was being prepared. Farmhands had used other means of harvesting, but because of the lack of the truck, their work was set back by five days. As a result of the delays, 30 percent of the crop was still in the fields when the first frost came, causing damages expertly estimated at $320,000. The *direct damages* for the breach of contract in this case would be the difference between the contract price for the truck of $58,500 and the market price of $60,500, or $2,000. These direct damages naturally flow from the breach of contract for the purchase of a truck. Also, the *incidental damages* of $250 for the truck rental are recoverable direct damages. The $320,000 loss of the potato crop was a consequence of not having the truck, and this sum is arguably recoverable by Spencer Adams as *consequential or special damages*. Adams notified Brad Jones of the reason he needed to have the truck by Labor Day, and it should have been reasonably foreseeable to Jones that loss of a portion of the crop could occur if the truck contract was breached. However, because of Spencer Adams's obligation to mitigate damages (as discussed below), it is unlikely that Adams will recover the full consequential damages. Truck rental availability or the lack of availability within the rural area, alternative tractor usage, and the actual harvesting methods used by Adams all relate to the mitigation issue to be resolved by the jury.

(b) Mitigation of Damages   The injured party is under the duty to mitigate damages if reasonably possible.[10] In other words, damages must not be permitted to increase if an increase can be prevented by reasonable efforts. This means that the injured party must generally stop any performance under the contract to avoid running up a larger bill. The duty to mitigate damages may require an injured party to buy or rent elsewhere the goods that the wrongdoer was obligated to deliver under the contract. In the case of breach of an employment contract by the employer, the employee is required to seek other similar employment. The wages earned from other employment must be deducted from the damages claimed. The discharged employee, however, is not required to take employment of less-than-comparable work.

(1) Effect of Failure to Mitigate Damages.   The effect of the requirement of mitigating damages is to limit recovery by the nonbreaching party to the damages that would have been sustained had this party mitigated the damages where it was possible to do so. **For Example,** self-described "sports nut" Gary Baker signed up for a three-year club-seat "package" that entitled him and a companion to tickets for 41 Boston Bruins hockey games and 41 Boston Celtics basketball games at the New Boston Garden Corporation's Fleet Center for approximately $18,000 per year. After one year, Baker stopped paying for the tickets, thinking that he would

---

10 *West Pinal Family Health Center, Inc. v McBride*, 785 P2d 66 (Ariz 1989).

simply lose his $5,000 security deposit. Baker, a CPA, tried to work out a compromise settlement to no avail. New Boston sued Baker for breach of contract, seeking the balance due on the tickets of $34,866. At trial, Baker argued to the jury that although he had breached his contract, New Boston had an obligation to mitigate damages, for example, by treating his empty seats and those of others in the same situation as "rush seats" shortly before game time and selling them at a discount. New Boston argued that just as a used luxury car cannot be returned for a refund, a season ticket cannot be canceled without consequences. The jury accepted Baker's position on mitigation and reduced the amount owed New Boston by $21,176 to $13,690.[11]

9. RESCISSION

When one party commits a material breach of the contract, the other party may rescind the contract; if the party in default objects, the aggrieved party may bring an action for rescission. A breach is *material* when it is so substantial that it defeats the object of the parties in making the contract.[12]

An injured party who rescinds a contract after having performed services may recover the reasonable value of the performance rendered under restitutionary or quasi-contractual damages. Money paid by the injured party may also be recovered. The purpose is to restore the injured party to the position occupied before the contract was made. However, the party seeking restitutionary damages must also return what this party has received from the party in default.

For Example, Pedro Morena purchased real estate from Jason Alexander after Alexander had assured him that the property did not have a flooding problem. In fact, the property regularly flooded after ordinary rainstorms. Morena was entitled to the return of the purchase price and payment for the reasonable value of the improvements he made to the property. Alexander was entitled to a setoff for the reasonable rental value of the property during the time Morena was in possession of this property.

10. ACTION FOR SPECIFIC PERFORMANCE

Under special circumstances, an injured party may obtain the equitable remedy of specific performance, which compels the other party to carry out the terms of a contract. Specific performance is ordinarily granted only if the subject matter of the contract is "unique," thereby making an award of money damages an inadequate remedy. Contracts for the purchase of land will be specifically enforced.[13]

Specific performance of a contract to sell personal property can be obtained only if the article is of unusual age, beauty, unique history, or other distinction. **For Example,** Maurice owned a rare Revolutionary War musket that he agreed to sell to Herb. Maurice then changed his mind because of the uniqueness of the musket. Herb can sue and win, requesting the remedy of specific performance of the contract because of the unique nature of the goods.

---

[11] Sacha Pfeiffer, "Disenchanted Fan Scores Win in Ticket Fight," *Boston Globe*, August 28, 1999, B-4.
[12] *Greentree Properties, Inc. v Kissee*, 92 SW3d 289 (Mo App 2003).
[13] *English v Muller*, 514 SE2d 195 (Ga 1999).

When the damages sustained by the plaintiff can be measured in monetary terms, specific performance will be refused. Consequently, a contract to sell a television station will not be specifically enforced when the buyer had made a contract to resell the station to a third person; the damages caused by the breach of the first contract would be the loss sustained by being unable to make the resale, and such damages would be adequate compensation to the original buyer.[14]

Ordinarily, contracts for the performance of personal services are not specifically ordered. This is because of the difficulty of supervision by the court and the restriction of the U.S. Constitution's Thirteenth Amendment prohibiting involuntary servitude except as criminal punishment.

11. ACTION FOR AN INJUNCTION

injunction order of a court of equity to refrain from doing (negative injunction) or to do (affirmative or mandatory injunction) a specified act. Statute use in labor disputes has been greatly restricted.

When a breach of contract consists of doing an act prohibited by the contract, a possible remedy is an **injunction** against doing the act. **For Example,** when the obligation in an employee's contract is to refrain from competing after resigning from the company and the obligation is broken by competing, a court may order or enjoin the former employee to stop competing. Similarly, when a vocalist breaks a contract to record exclusively for a particular label, she may be enjoined from recording for any other company. This may have the indirect effect of compelling the vocalist to record for the plaintiff.

12. REFORMATION OF CONTRACT BY A COURT

At times, a written contract does not correctly state the agreement already made by the parties. When this occurs, either party may seek to have the court reform or correct the writing to state the agreement actually made.

A party seeking reformation of a contract must clearly prove both the grounds for reformation and what the agreement actually was. This burden is particularly great when the contract to be reformed is written. This is so because the general rule is that parties are presumed to have read their written contracts and to have intended to be bound by them when they signed the contracts.

When a unilateral mistake is made and it is of such consequence that enforcing the contract according to its terms would be unreasonable, a court may reform the contract to correct the mistake.

CASE SUMMARY

Will a Court Correct a Huge Mistake?

FACTS: New York Packaging Corp. (NYPC) manufactured plastic sheets used by Owens Corning (OC) at its asphalt plants throughout the country as dividers to separate asphalt

---

[14] *Miller v LeSea Broadcasting, Inc.*, 87 F3d 224 (7th Cir 1996).

CASE SUMMARY

continued

containers and prevent them from sticking to one another. Janet Berry, a customer service representative at OC, called and received a price from NYPC of "$172.50 per box," with a box containing 200 plastic sheets. Ms. Berry put the information into OC's computer systems, which in turn generated a purchase order. She mistakenly believed that the unit of measurement designated as "EA" on the purchase order was per box when it in fact was per sheet. As a result, the purchase orders likewise reflected a price of $172.50 per sheet rather than per box. The computer automatically calculated the total price of the purchase order and faxed it to NYPC as $1,078,195, without Ms. Berry seeing the huge total price. NYPC filled the order, which included overrun sheets, and billed OC $1,414,605.60. NYPC sought payment at the contract price of $172.50 per sheet. It points out that the purchase order contained a "no oral modification" clause and, by its terms, the order was binding when NYPC accepted. The buyer contends that NYPC is attempting to take advantage of this huge and obvious mistake and that the contract should be reformed.

DECISION: Ms. Berry made a unilateral mistake that was, or should have been, known by NYPC. OC used the sheets after its offer to return them to NYPC was refused. Therefore, the contract could not be rescinded. The drafting error in this case was so huge that to enforce the written contract would be unconscionable. Accordingly, the unit of measurement is amended to read "per box" rather than "EA"; the "Order Qty" is amended to read "41 boxes of 200 sheets per box"; and the overall price is modified to read $7,072.50, not $1,078,195. [**In re Owens Corning et al., Debtors in Possession, 91 BR 329 (2003)**]

(D) CONTRACT PROVISIONS AFFECTING REMEDIES AND DAMAGES

The contract of the parties may contain provisions that affect the remedies available or the recovery of damages.

13. LIMITATION OF REMEDIES

The contract of the parties may limit the remedies of the aggrieved parties. **For Example,** the contract may give one party the right to repair or replace a defective item sold or to refund the contract price. The contract may require both parties to submit any dispute to arbitration or another streamlined out-of-court dispute resolution procedure.

liquidated damages
provision stipulating the amount of damages to be paid in the event of default or breach of contract.

valid legal.

liquidated damages clause
specification of exact compensation in case of a breach of contract.

14. LIQUIDATED DAMAGES

The parties may stipulate in their contract that a certain amount should be paid in case of a breach. This amount is known as liquidated damages and may be variously measured by the parties. When delay is possible, **liquidated damages** may be a fixed sum, such as $1,000 for each day of delay. When there is a total default, damages may be a percentage of the contract price or the amount of the down payment.

(a) VALIDITY To be **valid,** a **liquidated damages clause** must satisfy two requirements: (1) The situation must be one in which it is difficult or impossible to determine the actual damages and (2) the amount specified must not be excessive when compared with the probable damages that would be sustained.[15] The validity of a liquidated damages clause is determined on the basis of the facts existing when the clause was agreed to.

CASE SUMMARY

Can We Freeze the Damages?

FACTS: Manny Fakhimi agreed to buy an apartment complex for $697,000 at an auction from David Mason. Fakhimi was obligated to put up 10 percent of the agreed-to price at the auction as a deposit. The agreement signed by Fakhimi allowed Mason to keep this deposit should Fakhimi fail to come up with the remaining 90 percent of the auction price as liquidated damages for the default. Shortly after the auction, Fakhimi heard a rumor that the military base located near the apartment complex might be closing. Fakhimi immediately stopped payment on the check and defaulted on the agreement. Mason sued Fakhimi for the liquidated damages specified in the sales contract.

DECISION: Because of the difficulty of forecasting the loss that might be caused by the breach of a real estate purchase contract, it is held that a liquidated damage clause of 10 percent of the sale price is valid and is not a penalty. The fact that the damages sustained thereafter were less than 10 percent does not convert the 10 percent into an unreasonable forecast. The 10 percent clause remained valid as it would have remained had the damages on resale been more than 10 percent. [**Mason v Fakhimi, 865 P2d 333 (Neb 1993)**]

(b) Effect When a liquidated damages clause is held valid, the injured party cannot collect more than the amount specified by the clause. The defaulting party is bound to pay such damages once the fact is established that there has been a default. The injured party is not required to make any proof as to damages sustained, and the defendant is not permitted to show that the damages were not as great as the liquidated sum.

(c) Invalid Clauses If the liquidated damages clause calls for the payment of a sum that is clearly unreasonably large and unrelated to the possible actual damages that might be sustained, the clause will be held to be void as a penalty.
For Example, a settlement agreement between 27 plaintiffs seeking recovery for injuries resulting from faulty breast implants and the implants' manufacturer, Dow Corning Corp., called for seven $200,000 payments to each plaintiff. The agreement also called for a $100 per day payment to each plaintiff for any time when the payments were late as "liquidated damages." The court held that the $100 per day figure was not a reasonable estimate of anticipated damages. Rather, it was an unenforceable "penalty" provision.[16]

When a liquidated damages clause is held invalid, the effect is merely to erase the clause from the contract, and the injured party may proceed to recover damages for breach of the contract. Instead of recovering the liquidated damages amount, the injured party will recover whatever actual damages he can prove. **For Example,** JRC

---

[15] *Southeast Alaska Construction Co. v Alaska*, 791 P2d 339 (Alaska 1990).
[16] *Bear Stearns v Dow Corning Corp.*, 419 F3d 543 (6th Cir 2005).

CASE SUMMARY

Could We Make It Any Clearer?

FACTS: Woodside Homes made a contract to build a house for Russ. He and his wife later visited the construction site, where his wife slipped and fell into a hole in the driveway in front of the house. The fall caused a blood clot to form, which caused the wife's death. Russ sued Woodside for damages for his wife's death, claiming that she had been harmed because of Woodside's negligence. There was no evidence of negligence. Woodside raised the defense that the construction contract stated that "the construction site is a dangerous place to visit" and that Woodside would not be liable for any accident, injury, or death resulting from a visit to the jobsite.

DECISION: Judgment for Woodside. The contractor gave adequate warning of the danger, and the wife assumed the risk in visiting the site. The exculpation clause therefore shielded the contractor from liability. [**Russ v Woodside Homes, Inc., 905 P2d 901 (Utah App 1995)**]

Trading Corp (JRC) bought computer software and hardware from Progressive Data Systems (PDS) for $167,935, which it paid in full, to track the movement of its trucks with inventory and to process transactions. The purchase agreement also called for a $7,500 per year licensing fee for an 18-year period, and it stated that in the event of default, PDS could "accelerate and declare all obligations of Customer as a liquidated sum." A dispute arose between the parties, and when the case was litigated, the only actual contract charges owed PDS were license fees of $7,500 for two years. The application of the liquidated damages clause would yield an additional $120,000 cash for PDS for the future fees for 16 years without any reduction for expenses or the present cash value for the not-yet-earned fees. Actual damages were clearly ascertainable and not difficult to determine, and the amount sought was excessive. The court deemed the liquidated damages clause an unenforceable penalty and PDS was relegated to recovering its actual contractual damages.[17]

15. LIMITATION OF LIABILITY CLAUSES

exculpatory clause provision in a contract stating that one of the parties shall not be liable for damages in case of breach; also called a *limitation-of-liability clause.*

limitation-of-liability clause provision in a contract stating that one of the parties shall not be liable for damages in case of breach; also called an *exculpatory clause.*

A contract may contain a provision stating that one of the parties shall not be liable for damages in case of breach. Such a provision is called an **exculpatory clause,** or when a monetary limit to damages for breach of contract is set forth in the contract, it may be referred to as a **limitation-of-liability clause.**

(a) CONTENT AND CONSTRUCTION If an exculpatory clause or a limitation-of-liability clause limits liability for damages caused only by negligent conduct, liability is neither excluded nor limited if the conduct alleged is found to be grossly negligent, willful, or wanton. **For Example,** Security Guards Inc. (SGI) provided services to Dana Corporation, a truck frame manufacturer under a contract that contained a limitation-of-liability clause capping losses at $50,000 per occurrence for damages "caused solely by the negligence" of SGI or its employees. When a critical alarm was activated by a fire in the paint shop at 5:39 P.M., the SGI guard on duty did not follow appropriate procedures, which delayed notification to the fire

---

[17] *Jefferson Randolf Corporation v PDS,* 553 SE2d 304 (Ga App 2001).

department for 15 minutes. Royal Indemnity Co., Dana's insurer, paid Dana $16,535,882 for the fire loss and sued SGI for $7 million, contending that the SGI guard's actions were grossly negligent and caused the plant to suffer increased damages. The court held that if SGI were to be found grossly negligent, the liability would not be limited to $50,000, and a jury could find damages far exceeding that amount.[18]

(b) Validity   As a general rule, experienced businesspersons are free to allocate liability in their contracts as they see fit. They have freedom to contract—even to make bad bargains or relinquish fundamental rights. However, courts in most states will not enforce a contract provision that *completely exonerates* a party from gross negligence or intentional acts.

(c) Releases   Release forms signed by participants in athletic and sporting events declaring that the sponsor, proprietor, or operator of the event shall not be liable for injuries sustained by participants because of its negligence are binding. **For Example,** when Merav Sharon sued the city of Newton for negligence as a result of an injury received while participating in a high school cheerleading practice, the city successfully raised a signed exculpatory release as a defense.[19] So also the exculpatory contract Nathan Henderson signed releasing a white-water rafting expedition operator from liability for its negligence barred Henderson's negligence claim against the operator for an injury suffered disembarking from the operator's bus.[20]

(LAWFLIX)

The Goodbye Girl (1977) (PG)

Richard Dreyfuss plays Elliott Garfield, a struggling Shakespearean actor who lands in New York with a sublease on an apartment still occupied by divorcee Marsha Mason and her daughter. The two work out living arrangements, split rent and food, and deal with the issue of whether Mason has any rights. Review all aspects of contracts as the characters discuss subleases, rent payment, living arrangements, and food costs.

For movie clips that illustrate business law concepts, see LawFlix at **http://wdvl.westbuslaw.com.**

---

[18] *Royal Indemnity Co. v Security Guards, Inc.*, 255 F Supp 2d 497 (ED Pa 2003).

[19] *Sharon v City of Newton*, 437 Mass 99 (2002).

[20] *Henderson v Quest Expeditions, Inc.*, 174 SW3d 730 (Tenn App 2005).

> SUMMARY

When a party fails to perform a contract or performs improperly, the other contracting party may sue for damages caused by the breach. What may be recovered by the aggrieved person is stated in terms of being direct or consequential damages. Direct damages are those that ordinarily will result from the breach. Direct damages may be recovered on proof of causation and amount. Consequential damages can be recovered only if, in addition to proving causation and amount, it is shown that they were reasonably within the contemplation of the contracting parties as a probable result of a breach of the contract. The right to recover consequential damages is lost if the aggrieved party could reasonably have taken steps to avoid such damages. In other words, the aggrieved person has a duty to mitigate or reduce damages by reasonable means.

In any case, the damages recoverable for breach of contract may be limited to a specific amount by a liquidated damages clause. Damages may be canceled completely by a limitation-of-liability clause.

In a limited number of situations, an aggrieved party may bring an action for specific performance to compel the other contracting party to perform the acts called for by the contract. Specific performance by the seller is always obtainable for the breach of a contract to sell land or real estate on the theory that such property has a unique value. With respect to other contracts, specific performance will not be ordered

unless it is shown that there was some unique element present so that the aggrieved person would suffer a damage that could not be compensated for by the payment of money damages.

The aggrieved person also has the option of rescinding the contract if (1) the breach has been made concerning a material term and (2) the aggrieved party returns everything to the way it was before the contract was made.

Although there has been a breach of the contract, the effect of this breach is nullified if the aggrieved person by word or conduct waives the right to object to the breach. Conversely, an aggrieved party may accept a defective performance without thereby waiving a claim for breach if the party makes a reservation of rights. A reservation of rights can be made by stating that the defective performance is accepted "without prejudice," "under protest," or "with reservation of rights."

> QUESTIONS AND CASE PROBLEMS

1. The Forsyth School District contracted with Textor Construction, Inc., to build certain additions and alter school facilities, including the grading of a future softball field. Under the contract, the work was to be completed by August 1. Various delays occurred at the outset of the project attributable to the school district, and the architect's representative on the job, Mr. Hamilton, told Textor's vice president, William Textor, not to be concerned about a clause in the contract of $250 per day liquidated damages for failure to complete the job by August 1. Textor sued the school district for breach of contract regarding payment for the grading of the softball field, and the District counterclaimed for liquidated damages for 84 days at $250 per day for failure to complete the project by the August 1 date. What legal basis exists for Textor to defend against the counterclaim for failure to complete the job on time? Was it ethical for the school district to bring this counterclaim based on the facts before you? [*Textor Construction, Inc. v Forsyth R-III School District*, 60 SW3d 692 (Mo App)]

2. Anthony makes a contract to sell a rare painting to Laura for $100,000. The written contract

specifies that if Anthony should fail to perform the contract, he will pay Laura $5,000 as liquidated damages. Anthony fails to deliver the painting and is sued by Laura for $5,000. Can she recover this amount?

3. Rogers made a contract with Salisbury Brick Corp. that allowed it to remove earth and sand from land he owned. The contract ran for four years with provision to renew it for additional four-year terms up to a total of 96 years. The contract provided for compensation to Rogers based on the amount of earth and sand removed. By an unintentional mistake, Salisbury underpaid Rogers the amount of $863 for the months of November and December 1986. Salisbury offered this amount to Rogers, but he refused to accept it and claimed that he had been underpaid in other months. Rogers claimed that he was entitled to rescind the contract. Was he correct? [*Rogers v Salisbury Brick Corp.*, 882 SE2d 915 (SC)]

4. A contractor departed from the specifications at a number of points in a contract to build a house. The cost to put the house in the condition called for by the contract was approximately $14,000. The contractor was sued for $50,000 for breach

of contract and emotional disturbance caused by the breach. Decide.

5. Protein Blenders, Inc., made a contract with Gingerich to buy from him the shares of stock of a small corporation. When the buyer refused to take and pay for the stock, Gingerich sued for specific performance of the contract on the ground that the value of the stock was unknown and could not be readily ascertained because it was not sold on the general market. Was he entitled to specific performance? [*Gingerich v Protein Blenders, Inc.*, 95 NW2d 522 (Iowa)]

6. The buyer of real estate made a down payment. The contract stated that the buyer would be liable for damages in an amount equal to the down payment if the buyer broke the contract. The buyer refused to go through with the contract and demanded his down payment back. The seller refused to return it and claimed that he was entitled to additional damages from the buyer because the damages that he had suffered were more than the amount of the down payment. Decide. [*Waters v Key Colony East, Inc.*, 345 So 2d 367 (Fla App)]

7. Kuznicki made a contract for the installation of a fire detection system by Security Safety Corp. for $498. The contract was made one night and canceled at 9:00 the next morning. Security then claimed one-third of the purchase price from Kuznicki by virtue of a provision in the contract that "in the event of cancellation of this agreement . . . the owner agrees to pay 33⅓ percent of the contract price, as liquidated damages." Was Security Safety entitled to recover the amount claimed? [*Security Safety Corp. v Kuznicki*, 213 NE2d 866 (Mass)]

8. Health United Family Care, Inc., and its principals Maldonado, Romero, and Benitez entered into a five-year lease of office space with GFIC Management, Inc., to operate a medical facility. Rent was set at $4,041 per month. As part of the lease, GFIC agreed to expend $17,000 of its funds to renovate the leased space for use as a medical facility, to be finished by October 28 so that the medical facility could open on November 1. The parties agreed in the lease that if the construction was not finished on time, no rent would be due until actual possession. On October 26, Benitez called GFIC President Moses Grad and told him to stop construction. Grad met with Benitez and Romero soon thereafter, and they explained their problem as follows:

Grad: What happened?

Benitez and Romero [B+R]: The medical board came down hard on us O.K. The problem is that we have one doctor, one doctor, and he is covering (mumble) right now he is under investigation. As a matter of fact, they did investigate us, and right now they are coming down hard on us, and we are under a lawsuit. O.K., and he is ready to lose his license, and they will not give you another building to open O.K. I wish we could put this on hold, and right now if we get into this we cannot open.

[B+R]: We cannot open; we have no license to open.

Grad: What's the problem with getting another doctor? . . .

[B+R]: Right now no doctors want to touch us; we are under investigation.

Grad: I see.

[B+R]: Nobody wants to touch us at all, . . . but right now our attorney has instructed us to get out of it. You know he needs to get into it, but we don't want him because it's going to cost us more money, O.K. We would get some kind of agreement with you to see how we get out of it.

Grad: Is there anything I can do as the landlord of the premises to make you stay in the building?

[B+R]: No, because they won't give us permission to open.

Grad: Is there anything I can do for you? The only solution at this time that you see is to cancel the contract, this is the only. . . .

[B+R]: I think that's what our attorney instructed us to do, is to get out of it because right now our name is not the most popular name out there with the medical board, they will nail us, they are out to get us. . . . I think we should put a hold on the construction right now; that's what we should do.

Grad stopped the construction after this discourse on October 28. Subsequently, Ernesto Maldonado talked with Grad about settling obligations under the lease and stated that if the construction were completed by Grad, he would attempt to find a doctor. At that point, Grad was seeking one year's rent as damages for breach of the lease. Brad never restarted the construction, and Health United never took possession of the premises. GFIC sued Health United for breach of the lease contract. Health United denies the breach of the lease, contending that GFIC failed to perform a condition precedent by not completing the construction necessary to occupy the space. What legal theory would you rely on to respond to Health United's position that GFIC failed to perform the condition precedent? Do you believe Benitez and Romero were prudent in not utilizing their attorney to facilitate an amicable settlement of the contractual obligations? How would you decide this case? [*Health United Family Care, Inc. v GFIC Management, Inc.*, 2001 TexApp LEXIS]

9. Melodee Lane Lingerie Co. was a tenant in a building that was protected against fire by a sprinkler and alarm system maintained by the American District Telegraph Co. (ADT). Because of the latter's fault, the controls on the system were defective and allowed the discharge of water into the building, which damaged Melodee's property. When Melodee sued ADT, its defense was that its service contract limited its liability to 10 percent of the annual service charge made to the customer. Was this limitation valid? [*Melodee Lane Lingerie Co. v American District Telegraph Co.*, 218 NE2d 661 (NY)]

10. In May, a homeowner made a contract with a roofer to make repairs to her house by July 1. The roofer never came to repair the roof, and heavy rains in the fall damaged the interior of the house. The homeowner sued the roofer for breach of contract and claimed damages for the harm done to the interior of the house. Is the homeowner entitled to recover such damages?

11. Ken Sulejmanagic, aged 19, signed up for a course in scuba diving taught by Madison at the YMCA. Before the instruction began, Ken was required to sign a form releasing Madison and the YMCA from liability for any harm that might occur. At the end of the course, Madison, Ken, and another student went into deep water. After Ken made the final dive required by the course program, Madison left him alone in the water while he took the other student for a dive. When Madison returned, Ken could not be found, and it was later determined that he had drowned. Ken's parents sued Madison and the YMCA for negligence in the performance of the teaching contract. The defendants raised the defense that the release Ken signed shielded them from liability. The plaintiffs claimed that the release was invalid. Who was correct? [*Madison v Superior Court*, 250 Cal Rptr 299 (Cal App)]

12. Wassenaar worked for Panos under a three-year contract stating that if the contract were terminated wrongfully by Panos before the end of the three years, he would pay as damages the salary for the remaining time that the contract had to run. After three months, Panos terminated the contract, and Wassenaar sued him for pay for the balance of the contract term. Panos claimed that this amount could not be recovered because the contract provision for the payment was a void penalty. Was this provision valid? [*Wassenaar v Panos*, 331 NW2d 357 (Wis)]

13. Soden, a contractor, made a contract to build a house for Clevert. The sales contract stated that "if either party defaults in the performance of this contract," that party would be liable to the other for attorney fees incurred in suing the defaulter. Soden was 61 days late in completing the contract, and some of the work was defective. In a suit by the buyer against the contractor, the contractor claimed that he was not liable for the buyer's attorney fees because he had made only a defective performance and because "default" in the phrase quoted meant "nonperformance of the contract." Was the contractor liable for the attorney fees? [*Clevert v Soden*, 400 SE2d 181 (Va)]

14. Protection Alarm Co. made a contract to provide burglar alarm security for Fretwell's home. The contract stated that the maximum liability of the alarm company was the actual loss sustained or $50, whichever was the lesser, and that this provision was agreed to "as liquidated damages and not as a penalty." When Fretwell's home was burglarized, he sued for the loss of approximately $12,000, claiming that the alarm company had been negligent. The alarm company asserted that

its maximum liability was $50. Fretwell claimed that this was invalid because it bore no relationship to the loss that could have been foreseen when the contract was made or that in fact "had been sustained." Decide.

15. Shepherd-Will made a contract to sell Emma Cousar:

    5 acres of land adjoining property owned by the purchaser and this being formerly land of Shepherd-Will, Inc., located on north side of Highway 223.

    This 5 acres to be surveyed at earliest time possible at which time plat will be attached and serve as further description on property.

    Shepherd-Will owned only one 100-acre tract of land that adjoined Emma's property. This tract had a common boundary with her property of 1,140 feet. Shepherd-Will failed to perform this contract. Emma sued for specific performance of the contract. Decide. [*Cousar v Shepherd-Will, Inc.*, 387 SE2d 723 (SC App)]

> CPA QUESTIONS

1. Master Mfg., Inc., contracted with Accur Computer Repair Corp. to maintain Master's computer system. Master's manufacturing process depends on its computer system operating properly at all times. A liquidated damages clause in the contract provided that Accur pay $1,000 to Master for each day that Accur was late responding to a service request. On January 12, Accur was notified that Master's computer system had failed. Accur did not respond to Master's service request until January 15. If Master sues Accur under the liquidated damages provision of the contract, Master will

   a. win, unless the liquidated damage provision is determined to be a penalty.
   b. win, because under all circumstances liquidated damages provisions are enforceable.
   c. lose, because Accur's breach was *not* material.
   d. lose, because liquidated damage provisions violate public policy. (5/93, Law, #25)

2. Jones, CPA, entered into a signed contract with Foster Corp. to perform accounting and review services. If Jones repudiates the contract prior to the date performance is due to begin, which of the following is *not* correct?

   a. Foster could successfully maintain an action for breach of contract after the date performance was due to begin.
   b. Foster can obtain a judgment ordering Jones to perform.
   c. Foster could successfully maintain an action for breach of contract prior to the date performance is due to begin.
   d. Foster can obtain a judgment for the monetary damages it incurred as a result of the repudiation. (5/89, Law, #35)

3. Which of the following concepts affect(s) the amount of monetary damages recoverable by the nonbreaching party when a contract is breached?

	Forseeability of damages	Mitigation of damages
a.	Yes	Yes
b.	Yes	No
c.	No	Yes
d.	No	No

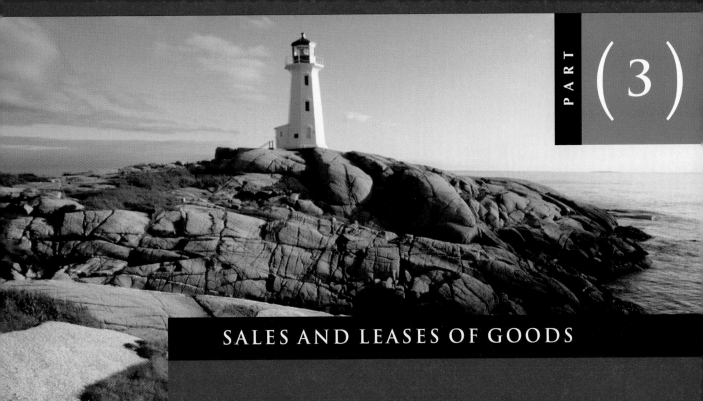

SALES AND LEASES OF GOODS

CHAPTER 21

PERSONAL PROPERTY

AND BAILMENTS

CHAPTER

$\left(21\right)$

 PERSONAL PROPERTY

1. **PERSONAL PROPERTY IN CONTEXT**
2. **TITLE TO PERSONAL PROPERTY**
3. **GIFTS**
4. **FINDING OF LOST PROPERTY**
5. **OCCUPATION OF PERSONAL PROPERTY**
6. **ESCHEAT**
7. **MULTIPLE OWNERSHIP OF PERSONAL PROPERTY**
8. **COMMUNITY PROPERTY**

 BAILMENTS

9. **DEFINITION**
10. **ELEMENTS OF BAILMENT**
11. **NATURE OF THE PARTIES' INTERESTS**
12. **CLASSIFICATION OF ORDINARY BAILMENTS**
13. **RENTING OF SPACE DISTINGUISHED**
14. **DUTIES AND RIGHTS OF THE BAILEE**
15. **BREACH OF DUTY OF CARE: BURDEN OF PROOF**
16. **LIABILITY FOR DEFECTS IN BAILED PROPERTY**
17. **CONTRACT MODIFICATION OF LIABILITY**

LEARNING OBJECTIVES

After studying this chapter, you should be able to

LO.1 Write a definition of personal property

LO.2 List and explain various types of gifts

LO.3 Identify the public policy reasons behind the law of escheat

LO.4 Identify the four forms of multiple ownership of personal property

LO.5 Describe how a bailment is created

LO.6 List and distinguish the various classifications of bailments

LO.7 Contrast the renting of space with the creation of a bailment

LO.8 Explain the standard of care a bailee is required to exercise over bailed property

LO.9 State the burden of proof when a bailor sues a bailee for damages to bailed property

What is personal property? Who owns it? How is it acquired? Think of personal property as all things of value other than real estate. Many instances arise in which the owner of personal property entrusts it to another—a person checks a coat at a restaurant or leaves a watch with a jeweler for repairs; or a company rents a car to a tourist for a weekend. The delivery of personal property to another under such circumstances is a bailment.

 PERSONAL PROPERTY

1. PERSONAL PROPERTY IN CONTEXT

In common usage, the term *property* refers to a piece of land or a thing or an object. As a legal concept, however, property also refers to the rights that an individual may possess in the piece of land or that thing or that object.[1] Property includes the rights of any person to possess, use, enjoy, and dispose of a thing or object of value. A right in a thing is property, without regard to whether this right is absolute or conditional, perfect or imperfect, legal or equitable.

real property land and all rights in land.

personal property property that is movable or intangible, or rights in such things.

Real property means land and things embedded in the land, such as oil tanks. It also includes things attached to the earth, such as buildings or trees, and rights in any of these things. **Personal property** is property that is movable or intangible, or rights in such things. As described in Chapter 10, rights in intellectual property, such as writings, computer programs, inventions, and trademarks, are valuable business properties that are protected by federal statutes.

chose in action intangible personal property in the nature of claims against another, such as a claim for accounts receivable or wages.

Personal property then consists of (1) whole or fractional rights in things that are tangible and movable, such as furniture and books; (2) claims and debts, which are called **choses in action**; and (3) intangible property rights, such as trademarks, copyrights, and patents.

2. TITLE TO PERSONAL PROPERTY

Title to personal property may be acquired in different ways. For example, property is commonly purchased. The purchase and sale of goods is governed by the law of sales. In this chapter, the following methods of acquiring personal property will be discussed: gift, finding lost property, occupation, and escheat.

No title is acquired by theft. The thief acquires possession only, and if the thief makes a sale or gift of the property to another, the latter acquires only possession of the property. The true owner may reclaim the property from the thief or a thief's transferee. **For Example,** through a response to a classified ad, Ray purchased a Mongoose bicycle for his son from Kevin for $200, a favorable but fair price for this used bicycle. To protect himself, he obtained from Kevin a handwritten bill of sale that was notarized by a notary public. In fact, Kevin had stolen the bicycle. Its true owner, Juan, can reclaim the bike from Ray, even though Ray has a notarized bill of sale. Ray does not have legal title to the bicycle.

---

[1] *Presley Memorial Foundation v Crowell*, 733 SW2d 89 (Tenn App 1987).

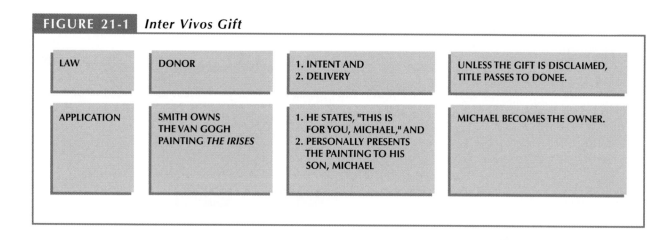

FIGURE 21-1 *Inter Vivos Gift*

| LAW | DONOR | 1. INTENT AND
2. DELIVERY | UNLESS THE GIFT IS DISCLAIMED, TITLE PASSES TO DONEE. |
| APPLICATION | SMITH OWNS THE VAN GOGH PAINTING *THE IRISES* | 1. HE STATES, "THIS IS FOR YOU, MICHAEL," AND
2. PERSONALLY PRESENTS THE PAINTING TO HIS SON, MICHAEL | MICHAEL BECOMES THE OWNER. |

CPA

3. GIFTS

gift title to an owner's personal property voluntarily transferred by a party not receiving anything in exchange.

donor person making a gift.

donee recipient of a gift.

inter vivos gift any transaction that takes place between living persons and creates rights prior to the death of any of them.

Title to personal property may be transferred by the voluntary act of the owner without receiving anything in exchange—that is, by **gift.** The person making the gift, the **donor,** may do so because of things that the recipient of the gift, the **donee,** has done in the past or is expected to do in the future. However, such things are not deemed consideration and thus do not alter the "free" character of the gift. Five types of gifts are discussed below.

(a) INTER VIVOS GIFTS   The ordinary gift that is made between two living persons is an **inter vivos gift.** For practical purposes, such a gift takes effect when the donor (1) expresses an intent to transfer title and (2) makes delivery, subject to the right of the donee to disclaim the gift within a reasonable time after learning that it has been made.[2] Because there is no consideration for a gift, there is no enforceable contract, and an intended donee cannot sue for breach of contract if the donor fails to complete the gift.[3]

(1) Intent.   The intent to make a gift requires an intent to transfer title at that time. **For Example,** former ballet star Rudolf Nureyev made a valid gift when he extended deeds of gift granting ownership of his New York City apartment and its $5 million artwork collection to a nonprofit dance foundation even though he retained the right to visit the apartment and pay for its maintenance. He gave up the right to live in the apartment and executed all documents necessary to divest his domain over it.[4] In contrast, an intent to confer a benefit at a future date is not a sufficient intent to create any right in the intended donee.

A delivery of property without the intent to make a gift does not transfer title. **For Example,** Mrs. Simpson's $80,000 check to her daughter and son-in-law, Shari and Karl Goodman, to help them buy a house was not a gift if the transaction was structured as a loan, notwithstanding Shari and Karl's assertion that it was structured as a loan simply to avoid gift taxes. The legal documents setting up the loan transaction indicated that no gift was intended.[5]

---

[2] *Bishop v Bishop,* 961 SW2d 770 (Ark 1998).

[3] *Dellagrotta v Dellagrotta,* 873 A2d 101 (RI 2005).

[4] *Rudolf Nureyev Dance Foundation v Noureeva-Francois,* 7 F Supp 2d 402 (SDNY 1998).

[5] *Simpson v Goodman,* 727 So 2d 555 (La App 1998). See also *Wright v Mallet,* 894 A2d 1016 (Conn App 2006) in which the evidence showed that a transfer in an interest in land was not intended to be a gift.

CPA

symbolic delivery delivery of goods by delivery of the means of control, such as a key or a relevant document of title, such as a negotiable bill of lading; also called constructive delivery.

constructive delivery see "symbolic delivery."

(2) Delivery.   Ordinarily, the delivery required to make a gift will be an actual handing over to the donee of the thing that is given.

The delivery of a gift may also be made by a **symbolic** or **constructive delivery**, such as by the delivery of means of control of property. Such means of control might be keys to a lock or keys to a garden tractor or papers that are essential to or closely associated with the ownership of the property, such as documents of title or a ship's papers.

CASE SUMMARY

But You Gave It to Me in Front of All Those People?

FACTS: On March 6, 1999, Colt Manufacturing Co., a handgun manufacturer, sponsored a farewell dinner for one of its officers, Marc Fontane. At the dinner, two Colt officials presented Fontane with a single-action, .45-caliber Colt revolver. After the presentation, an agent of Colt's took possession of the revolver for the purpose of improving it by installing ivory grips and adding engraving. Fontane inquired over a period of months as to when he would receive the revolver and was ultimately told "the gun has been sold and there will be no replacement." Fontane sued Colt for the conversion of the gift, with the promised improvements.

DECISION: Judgment for Fontane. When actual delivery has not occurred, the resolution of whether the donor has made a constructive or symbolic delivery depends on the circumstances of each case. The donor must do that which under the circumstances will in reason be equivalent to actual delivery. The public presentation of the revolver to the departing employee at his retirement dinner constituted a constructive form of delivery. Thus, Fontane is entitled to the value of the revolver with improvements. [**Fontane v Colt Manufacturing Co., 814 A2d 433 (Conn App 2003)**]

Failure to meet the "delivery" requirement will result in an ineffective gift. **For Example,** Walter Brownlee signed a bill of sale and attached a list of valuable construction equipment to it and left it with his attorney with instructions that it be passed to his son Randy after Walter's death. By leaving the bill of sale with his attorney, Walter retained control over the property, and therefore it was never effectively delivered to Randy, resulting in an ineffective gift.[6]

CPA

(3) Donor's Death.   If the donor dies before doing what is needed to make an effective gift, the gift fails.[7] An agent or the executor or administrator of the estate cannot thereafter perform the missing step on behalf of the decedent.

For Example, Mary Manning, who was in poor health, wanted to give her college-age granddaughter, Phyllis, her antique 1966 Ford Mustang convertible. She sent her daughter, Nel, to obtain the car's title from a file in the basement but was too tired to sign it on Nel's return. Mary passed away the next day without signing the document. Nel, the executrix under Mary's will, cannot complete the delivery of the gift by signing the title because it is beyond the authority of an executrix. Even though donative intent existed, no evidence of transfer of ownership and delivery to Phyllis occurred prior to Mary's death. Therefore, no valid gift was made.

---

[6] *In re Estate of Walter Brownlee, Sr.*, 654 NW2d (SD 2002).

[7] *Laverman v Destocki*, 622 NE2d 1122 (Ohio App 1994).

gift causa mortis gift, made by the donor in the belief that death was immediate and impending, that is revoked or is revocable under certain circumstances.

(b) Gifts Causa Mortis   A **gift causa mortis** is made when the donor, contemplating imminent and impending death, delivers personal property to the donee with the intent that the donee shall own it if the donor dies. This is a conditional gift, and the donor is entitled to take the property back if (1) the donor does not die, (2) the donor revokes the gift before dying, or (3) the donee dies before the donor.

(c) Gifts and Transfers to Minors   Uniform acts provide for transferring property to a custodian to hold for the benefit of a minor.[8] When a custodian holds property for the benefit of a minor under one of the uniform acts, the custodian has discretionary power to use the property "for the support, maintenance, education, and benefit" of the minor, but the custodian may not use the custodial property for the custodian's own personal benefit. The gift is final and irrevocable for tax and all other purposes on complying with the procedures of the acts.

Under the uniform acts, custodianships terminate and the property is distributed when the minor reaches age 21.

CASE SUMMARY

Ignorance Is No Defense

FACTS: In 1980, Larry Heath received $10,000 from his father. With interest, these funds grew to $13,381 by 1983, and in March he used this money to establish two custodian bank accounts for his minor children under the Uniform Gifts to Minors Act (UGMA). Larry was listed as custodian on each account. In August 1984, Larry closed both accounts and returned the proceeds to his mother while his father was then in Europe. The children's mother, Pamela, brought suit to recover the funds on behalf of the children, contending that the deposits were irrevocable gifts. Larry contended that the money was his father's and was never intended as a gift. Larry testified that he was a mere factory worker and was ignorant of the legal effect of his signing the signature cards for the custodian accounts.

DECISION: Judgment for Pamela on behalf of the children. To find that an inter vivos gift has been made, there must be donative intent and delivery. The UGMA expressly deals with "delivery" and provides that this element of a gift is satisfied by documentary compliance with the procedures of the statute. The issue of "donative intent" is not conclusively resolved by making a determination that there was documentary compliance with the statute. However, documentary compliance with the procedures set forth by the UGMA is highly probative on the issue of intent. Larry's testimony that he was ignorant of the legal effect of his signing the signature cards was unworthy of belief and insufficient to rebut the strong documentary showing that he had created irrevocable gifts. [**Heath v Heath, 493 NE2d 97 (Ill App 1986)**]

(d) Conditional Gifts   A gift may be made subject to a condition, such as "This car is yours when you graduate" or "This car is yours unless you drop out of school." In the first example, the gift is subject to a condition precedent—graduation. A condition precedent must be satisfied before any gift or transfer takes place. In the

---

[8] The Uniform Gifts to Minors Act (UGMA) was originally proposed in 1956. It was revised in 1965 and again in 1966. One of these versions is in effect in the following states: Delaware, New York, South Carolina, and Vermont. It has been adopted for the U.S. Virgin Islands.

The Uniform Transfers to Minors Act, which expands the type of property that can be made the subject of a gift, was originally proposed in 1983. It has been adopted, often with minor variations, in all states and the District of Columbia except South Carolina and Vermont.

second example, the gift is subject to a condition subsequent—dropping out of school.

Absent a finding of an intent to create a trust, a donative transaction will be analyzed as a gift subject to conditions. **For Example,** the gift by the Tennessee United Daughters of the Confederacy (UDC) to a building fund for Peabody College expressly reserved the right to recall the gift if the college failed to comply with the conditions of placing an inscription on the 1935 building naming it Confederate Memorial Hall. Peabody College for Teachers was merged into Vanderbilt University in 1979. In 2002, Vanderbilt decided to rename Confederate Memorial Hall. The Tennessee UDC's suit for the return of its gift was successful; the court decided it was not at liberty to relieve a party from its contractual obligations.[9]

Most courts regard an engagement ring as a conditional gift subject to the condition subsequent of a failure to marry. The inherent symbolism of the gift itself is deemed to foreclose the need to establish an express condition that there be a marriage.

Some jurisdictions require return of engagement rings only if the donor has not unjustifiably broken off the engagement. Most states now reject considerations of "fault" in the breaking of an engagement and always require the return of the ring to the donor when an engagement is broken. This "modern trend" is based on the theory that, in most cases, "fault" is impossible to determine.

CASE SUMMARY

Your Honor, Marriages Are Not Made in Heaven, You Say?

FACTS: Dr. Barry Meyer and Robyn Mitnick became engaged on August 9, 1996, at which time Barry gave Robyn a custom-designed engagement ring that he purchased for $19,500. On November 8, 1996, Barry asked Robyn to sign a prenuptial agreement and Robyn refused. The engagement was broken during that meeting, with both Barry and Robyn contending the other party caused the breakup. Robyn did not return the ring, and Barry sued for its return. Robyn filed a countercomplaint, alleging that the ring was an unconditional gift and that because Barry broke the engagement, she was entitled to keep the ring.

DECISION: Judgment for Barry Meyer. Following the "modern trend," the court decided that an engagement ring given in contemplation of marriage is an impliedly conditional gift that is completed only upon marriage. If the engagement is called off, regardless of fault, the gift is not complete and must be returned to the donor. The court rejected the "older view" of returning the gift to the donor only when the engagement is unjustifiably broken off by the donee, or by mutual agreement. As stated by the court in *Aronow v Silver*, 223 NJ Super 344 (1987):

> *What fact justifies the breaking of an engagement? The absence of a sense of humor? Differing musical tastes? Differing political views? The painfully-learned fact is that marriages are made on earth, not in heaven. They must be approached with intelligent care and should not happen without a decent assurance of success. When either party lacks that assurance, for whatever reason, the engagement should be broken. No justification is needed. Either party may act. Fault, impossible to fix, does not count.* [**Meyer v. Mitnick, 625 NW2d 136 (Mich App 2001)***]

---

*Texas courts apply the fault-based conditional gift rule when a donee breaks the engagement. When the giver of the ring violates his promise to marry, it would seem to Texas courts that a similar result should follow; that is, he should lose, not gain, rights to the ring. [See *Curtis v Anderson*, 2003 WL 1832257 (Tex App)]

---

[9] *Tennessee UDC v Vanderbilt University*, 174 SW3d 98 (Tenn Ct App 2005).

(e) ANATOMICAL GIFTS   Persons may make gifts of parts of their bodies, as in the case of kidney transplants. Persons may also make postdeath gifts. The Uniform Anatomical Gift Act[10] permits persons 18 years or older to make gifts of their bodies or any parts thereof. The gift takes effect on the death of the donor. The gift may be made to a school, a hospital, an organ bank, or a named patient. Such a gift may also be made, subject to certain restrictions, by the spouse, adult child, parent, adult brother or sister, or guardian of a deceased person. If a hospital misleads family members into consenting to tissue or organ donations that exceed their express wishes, such misconduct is sufficiently outrageous to support a claim for intentional infliction of emotional distress.[11]

CPA

4. FINDING OF LOST PROPERTY

Personal property is lost when the owner does not know where it is located but intends to retain title to or ownership of it. The person finding lost property does not acquire title but only possession. Ordinarily, the finder of lost property is required to surrender the property to the true owner when the latter establishes ownership. Meanwhile, the finder is entitled to retain possession as against everyone else.

Without a contract with the owner or a statute so providing, the finder of lost property usually is not entitled to a reward or to compensation for finding or caring for the property.

(a) FINDING IN PUBLIC PLACE   If the lost property is found in a public place, such as a hotel, under such circumstances that to a reasonable person it would appear the property had been intentionally placed there by the owner and the owner would be likely to recall where the property had been left and to return for it, the finder is not entitled to possession of the property. The finder must give it to the proprietor or manager of the public place to keep it for the owner. This exception does not apply if it appears that the property was not intentionally placed where it was found. In that case, it is not likely that the owner will recall having left it there.

(b) STATUTORY CHANGE   Some states have adopted statutes permitting the finder to sell the property or keep it if the owner does not appear within a stated period of time. In this case, the finder is required to give notice—for example, by newspaper publication—to attempt to reach the owner.

5. OCCUPATION OF PERSONAL PROPERTY

In some cases, title to personal property may be acquired by occupation—that is, by taking and retaining possession of the property.

(a) WILD ANIMALS   Wild animals, living in a state of nature, are not owned by any individual. In the absence of restrictions imposed by game laws, the person who acquires dominion or control over a wild animal becomes its owner. What constitutes sufficient dominion or control varies with the nature of the animal and the surrounding circumstances. If the animal is killed, tied, imprisoned, or otherwise prevented from going at its will, the hunter exercises sufficient dominion or control

---

[10] This act has been adopted in every state.
[11] See *Perry v Saint Francis Hospital*, 886 F Supp 1551 (D Kan 1995).

over the animal and becomes its owner. If the wild animal, subsequent to its capture, should escape and return to its natural state, it resumes the status of a wild animal.

As a qualification to the ordinary rule, the following exception developed. If an animal is killed or captured on the land of another while the hunter is on the land without permission of the landowner, the animal, when killed or captured, belongs not to the hunter but to the landowner.

(b) ABANDONED PERSONAL PROPERTY   Personal property is deemed abandoned when the owner relinquishes possession of it with the intention to disclaim title to it. Yesterday's newspaper that is thrown out in the trash is abandoned personal property. Title to abandoned property may be acquired by the first person who obtains possession and control of it. A person becomes the owner at the moment of taking possession of the abandoned personal property. If, however, the owner of property flees in the face of an approaching peril, property left behind is not abandoned. An abandonment occurs only when the owner voluntarily leaves the property.

CASE SUMMARY

Not an Ordinary Bank

FACTS: Charles and Rosa Nelson owned a home in Selma, Iowa, for over one-half a century. After their death, the property was abandoned because of the substantial unpaid real estate taxes. The Selma United Methodist Church purchased the property at a tax sale. When the church razed the dwelling, it found $24,547 in cash and coins that had been buried in the ground in glass jars by Charles many years before. The heirs of the Nelson family claimed the money. The church claimed that because the real estate was abandoned by the estate, the church was now the true owner of the money.

DECISION: Judgment for the heirs. Although the real estate was abandoned, the money found by the church had not been abandoned by its owner, Charles Nelson. The fact that it was buried in glass jars indicates that the owner was trying to preserve it. Therefore, the money had not been abandoned and was owned by Nelson's heirs. [**Ritz v Selma United Methodist Church, 467 NW2d 266 (Iowa 1991)**]

(c) CONVERSION   The tort of conversion has its origins in the ancient common law writ of trover, created "as a remedy against the finder of lost goods who refused to return them."[12] Because of that origin, the tort of conversion was limited to property that could be lost and found (i.e., tangible personalty as opposed to real property). As the nature of personal property evolved to the point that tangible documents represented highly valuable rights, such as promissory notes, stock certificates, insurance policies, and bank books, common law courts expanded the tort of conversion to include such documents within its definitional scope despite their intangible aspects, which, invariably, are primary components of the document's value. The concept of conversion today, which is the wrongful exclusionary retention of an owner's physical property, applies to an electronic record as much as it does to a paper record such as valuable stock certificates and bank books. For example, a

---

[12] Restatement, Second of Torts § 242, comment d.

computerized client/investor list created by a real estate agent is "property" protected by the law of conversion.[13]

6. ESCHEAT

Who owns unclaimed property? In the case of personal property, the practical answer is that the property will probably "disappear" after a period of time, or if in the possession of a carrier, hotel, or warehouse, it may be sold for unpaid storage charges. A growing problem arises with respect to unclaimed corporate dividends, bank deposits, insurance payments, and refunds. Most states have a statute providing for the transfer of such unclaimed property to the state government. This transfer to the government is often called by its feudal name of **escheat**. **For Example,** when James Canel's 280 shares of stock in Patrick Industries were turned over to the state treasurer's office by Harris Bank because his account at the bank had been inactive for more than five years, the property was presumed to be abandoned. Once Canel claimed the property, however, he was entitled to the return of the stock and the past dividends. The state was not entitled to retain the dividends under the court's reading of the state's Unclaimed Property Act.[14] Funds held by stores for layaway items for customers who fail to complete the layaway purchases are subject to escheat to the state. To provide for unclaimed property, many states have adopted the Uniform Unclaimed Property Act (UUPA),[15] formerly called the Uniform Disposition of Unclaimed Property Act.

> **escheat** transfer to the state of the title to a decedent's property when the owner of the property dies intestate and is not survived by anyone capable of taking the property as heir.

CASE SUMMARY

The King Is Dead! Who Gets the Unrefunded Ticket Proceeds?

FACTS: Elvis Presley contracted with the Mid-South Coliseum Board (City of Memphis) for the rental of the Coliseum and for personnel to sell tickets for concerts on August 27 and 28, 1977. Subsequently, $325,000 worth of tickets were sold. On August 16, 1977, Elvis Presley died. Refunds were given to those who returned their tickets to the coliseum board. Ten years after his death, however, $152,279 worth of ticket proceeds remained unclaimed in the custody of the board. This fund had earned $223,760 in interest. Priscilla Presley and the coexecutors of the estate of Elvis Presley brought an action claiming the unrefunded ticket proceeds for the canceled concerts. The state of Tennessee claimed that it was entitled to the proceeds under the Uniform Disposition of Unclaimed Property Act (UDUPA).

DECISION: Judgment for the state. Elvis Presley's estate has no legal claim to the ticket proceeds because his death discharged the contract represented by each ticket sold. Ticket holders would have claimed the refunds if it had not been for Presley's legendary status, and they chose to keep the tickets as memorabilia. The drafters of the UDUPA intended that windfalls such as the unrefunded proceeds in this case benefit the public rather than individuals. [**Presley v City of Memphis, 769 SW2d 221 (Tenn App 1988)**]

---

[13] *Shmueli v Corcoran Group*, 802 NYS2d 871 (2005).

[14] *Canel v Topinka*, 818 NE2d 311 (Ill 2004).

[15] The 1981 or 1995 version of the Act has been adopted in Alaska, Arizona, Arkansas, Colorado, Florida, Hawaii, Idaho, Illinois, Indiana, Kansas, Louisiana, Maine, Michigan, Montana, Nevada, New Hampshire, New Jersey, New Mexico, North Carolina, North Dakota, Oklahoma, Oregon, Rhode Island, South Carolina, South Dakota, U.S. Virgin Islands, Utah, Virginia, Washington, West Virginia, Wisconsin, and Wyoming.

CPA

severalty ownership of property by one person.

cotenancy when two or more persons hold concurrent rights and interests in the same property.

tenancy in common relationship that exists when two or more persons own undivided interests in property.

CPA

joint tenancy estate held jointly by two or more with the right of survivorship as between them, unless modified by statute.

7. MULTIPLE OWNERSHIP OF PERSONAL PROPERTY

When all rights in a particular object of property are held by one person, that property is held in **severalty**. However, two or more persons may hold concurrent rights and interests in the same property. In that case, the property is said to be held in **cotenancy**. The various forms of cotenancy include (1) tenancy in common, (2) joint tenancy, (3) tenancy by entirety, and (4) community property.

(a) Tenancy in Common   A **tenancy in common** is a form of ownership by two or more persons. The interest of a tenant in common may be transferred or inherited, in which case the taker becomes a tenant in common with the others. **For Example,** Brandt and Vincent restored an 18-foot 1940 mahogany-hulled Chris Craft runabout and own it as tenants in common. If Brandt sold his interest in the boat to Andrea, then Vincent and Andrea would be co-owners as tenants in common. If Brandt died before Vincent, a one-half interest in the boat would become the property of Brandt's heirs.

(b) Joint Tenancy   A **joint tenancy** is another form of ownership by two or more persons, but a joint tenancy has a *right of survivorship*.[16] On the death of a joint tenant, the remaining tenants take the share of the deceased tenant. The last surviving joint tenant takes the property as a holder in severalty. **For Example,** in Brandt and Vincent's Chris Craft case, if the boat were owned as joint tenants with a right of survivorship, Vincent would own the boat outright upon Brandt's death, and Brandt's heirs would obtain no interest in it.

A joint tenant's interest may be transferred to a third person, but this destroys the joint tenancy. If the interest of one of two joint tenants is transferred to a third person, the remaining joint tenant becomes a tenant in common with the third person. **For Example,** if Brandt sold his interest to Andrea, Vincent and Andrea would be co-owners as tenants in common.

Statutes in many states have modified the common law by adding a formal requirement to the creation of a joint tenancy with survivorship. At common law, such an estate would be created by a transfer of property to "*A* and *B* as joint tenants."[17] Under these statutes, however, it is necessary to add the words "with right of survivorship" or other similar words if a right of survivorship is desired.

CASE SUMMARY

Honor Thy Mother's Wishes?

FACTS: Rachel Auffert purchased a $10,000 certificate of deposit on January 7, 1981, creating a joint tenancy in this bank deposit payable to herself or either of two children, Leo

---

[16] *Estate of Munier v Jacquemin*, 899 SW2d 114 (Mo App 1995).

[17] Some states have modified the common law by creating a condition that whenever two or more persons are listed as owners of a bank account or certificate of deposit, a presumption of joint tenancy with right of survivorship arises unless expressly negated by the signature card or another instrument or by extrinsic proof. Thus, when Herbert H. Herring had his bank change the designated owners of a certificate of deposit to read, "Herbert H. Herring or [his grandson] Robert J. Herring," and no words indicating survivorship upon the death of either were on the certificate, nevertheless under a 1992 Florida statute creating a presumption of survivorship, which presumption was not rebutted, grandson Robert was declared the owner of the certificate. *In re Estate of H. H. Herring*, 670 So 2d 145 (Fla App 1996).

continued

or Mary Ellen, "either or the survivor." When Rachel died, a note dated January 7, 1981, written in Rachel's handwriting and signed by her, was found with the certificate of deposit. The note stated:

> Leo: If I die this goes to Sr. Mary Ellen,
> Wanted another name on it.
> S/Rachel Auffert
> Jan 7 1981

Mary Ellen cashed the certificate of deposit and retained the proceeds. Leo sued to recover one-half the value of the certificate.

DECISION: Judgment for Leo. There was statutory compliance when the certificate of deposit was purchased, and thus a statutory joint tenancy was created. The only means available to Rachel to alter the joint tenants' proportionate interests was to change the names on the account during her lifetime. Because Rachel failed to do so, the law presumes that Leo and Mary Ellen equally owned the certificate of deposit. [**Auffert v Auffert, 829 SW2d 95 (Mo App 1992)**]

If no words of survivorship are used, the transfer of property to two or more persons will be construed as creating a tenancy in common. Under such a statute, a certificate of deposit issued only in the name of "*A* or *B*" does not create a joint tenancy because it does not contain words of survivorship.

tenancy by entirety or **tenancy by the entireties**
transfer of property to both husband and wife.

(C) TENANCY BY ENTIRETY At common law, a **tenancy by entirety** or **tenancy by the entireties** was created when property was transferred to both husband and wife. It differs from joint tenancy in that it exists only when the transfer is to husband and wife. Also, the right of survivorship cannot be extinguished, and one spouse's interest cannot be transferred to a third person. However, in some jurisdictions, a spouse's right to share the possession and the profits may be transferred. This form of property holding is popular in common law jurisdictions because creditors of only one of the spouses cannot reach the property while both are living. Only a creditor of both the husband and the wife under the same obligation can obtain execution against the property.

For Example, a husband and wife, Rui and Carla Canseco, purchased a 2007 Lexus LS 430 for cash. It was titled in the names of "Rui J. *and* Carla T. Canseco." Later that year, State National Bank obtained a money judgment against Rui for $200,000, and the bank claimed entitlement to half the value of the Cansecos' car, which it asserted was Rui's share as a joint tenant. A tenancy by entirety had been created, however, so the bank could not levy against the auto. If the car had been titled "Rui *or* Carla T. Canseco," in most states the use of the word "or" would indicate that the vehicle was held in joint tenancy even if the co-owners are husband and wife. As such, Rui's half interest could be reached by the bank.

The tenancy by entirety is, in effect, a substitute for a will because the surviving spouse acquires the complete property interest on the death of the other. There are usually other reasons, however, why each spouse should make a will.

In many states, the granting of an absolute divorce converts a tenancy by the entireties into a tenancy in common.

8. COMMUNITY PROPERTY

In some states, property acquired during the period of marriage is the **community property** of the husband and wife. Some statutes provide for the right of survivorship; others provide that half of the property of the deceased husband or wife shall go to the heirs of that spouse or permit such half to be disposed of by will. It is commonly provided that property acquired by either spouse during the marriage is **prima facie** community property, even though title is taken in the spouse's individual name, unless it can be shown that it was obtained with property possessed by the spouse prior to the marriage.

Ⓑ BAILMENTS

9. DEFINITION

A **bailment** is the relationship that arises when one person delivers possession of personal property to another under an agreement, express or implied, by which the latter is under a duty to return the property or to deliver it or dispose of it as agreed. The person who turns over the possession of the property is the **bailor**. The person who accepts is the **bailee**. **For Example,** Arthur Grace, a world renowned photojournalist, had an agreement with Sygma-Paris and Sygma-New York whereby Grace turned over his photographs to Sygma, and Sygma agreed to act as Grace's agent to license the images and administer the fee-setting process and delivery and return of the images. The *bailor,* Grace, terminated its agreement with the *bailee,* Sygma, in 2001, and the *bailee* was unable to return all of the photographs to Grace as obligated under the agreement. Sygma's system of keeping track of images was "completely inadequate"; hence, it was liable for $472,000 in damages to the *bailor* for the failure to return some 40,000 images.[18]

10. ELEMENTS OF BAILMENT

A bailment is created when the following elements are present.

(a) AGREEMENT   The bailment is based on an *agreement*. This agreement may be express or implied. Generally, it contains all of the elements of a contract. The bailment transaction in fact consists of (1) a contract to bail and (2) the actual bailing of the property. Ordinarily, there is no requirement that the contract of bailment be in writing. The subject of a bailment may be any personal property of which possession may be given.[19] Real property cannot be bailed.

(b) DELIVERY AND ACCEPTANCE   The bailment arises when, pursuant to the agreement of the parties, the property is delivered to the bailee and accepted by the bailee as subject to the bailment agreement.

In the absence of a prior agreement to the contrary, a valid delivery and acceptance generally require that the bailee be aware that goods have been placed within the bailee's exclusive possession or control. **For Example,** photography equipment belonging to Bill Bergey, the photographer of Roosevelt University's student

---

[18] *Grace v Corbis Sygma*, 403 F Supp2d 337 (SDNY 2005).
[19] *Stone v CDI Corp.*, 9 SW3d 699 (Mo App 1999).

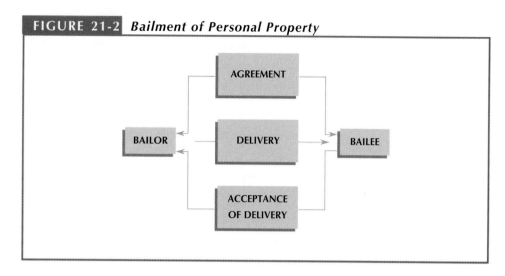

FIGURE 21-2 *Bailment of Personal Property*

newspaper, was stolen from the newspaper's campus office. Bergey believes that the university breached its duty as bailee because records showed that no campus police officer checked the building on the night of the theft. Bergey's case against the university on this bailment theory will fail, however, because the university did not know the equipment was left in the office. Without this knowledge, there was neither a bailment agreement nor acceptance of delivery by the university as a bailee.

11. NATURE OF THE PARTIES' INTERESTS

The bailor and bailee have different legal interests in the bailed property.

(a) Bailor's Interest   The bailor is usually the owner, but ownership by the bailor is not required. It is sufficient that the bailor have physical possession. **For Example,** Crella Magee delivered a blue fox jacket for summer storage to Walbro, Inc. When it was not returned, she sued Walbro for the replacement cost of the jacket, $3,400. Walbro's defense that Magee was not entitled to recover the replacement cost of the lost jacket because she did not prove ownership was rejected as irrelevant by the court, and the case was decided in favor of Magee.[20]

(b) Bailee's Interest   The bailee has possession of the property only. Title to the property does not pass to the bailee, and the bailee cannot sell the property to a third person. If the bailee attempts to sell the property, such sale transfers only possession, and the owner may recover the property from the buyer.

12. CLASSIFICATION OF ORDINARY BAILMENTS

bailment for mutual benefit
bailment in which the bailor and bailee derive a benefit from the bailment.

gratuitous bailment
bailment in which the bailee does not receive any compensation or advantage.

Ordinary bailments are generally classified as being for (1) the sole benefit of the bailor, (2) the sole benefit of the bailee, or (3) the mutual benefit of both.

Bailments may or may not provide for compensation to the bailee. On the basis of compensation, bailments may be classified as (1) **bailments for mutual benefit** in which one party takes the personal property of another into her care or custody in exchange for payment or other benefit and (2) **gratuitous bailments** in which the

[20] *Magee v Walbro, Inc.,* 525 NE2d 975 (Ill App 1988).

transfer of possession and use of the bailed property is without compensation. Bailments for the sole benefit of the bailor or for the sole benefit of the bailee are sometimes described as gratuitous. The fact that no charge is made by the bailor does not necessarily make the transaction a gratuitous bailment. If the bailment is made to further a business interest of the bailor, as when something is loaned free to a customer, the bailment is not gratuitous.

constructive bailment
bailment imposed by law as opposed to one created by contract, whereby the bailee must preserve the property and redeliver it to the owner.

A **constructive bailment** arises when one person has lawfully acquired possession of another's personal property other than by virtue of a bailment contract and holds it under such circumstances that the law imposes on the recipient of the property the obligation to keep it safely and redeliver it to the owner. **For Example,** the City of Chicago is the constructive bailee of an automobile impounded by Chicago police at the time of a driver's arrest for drunk driving. It has a duty to keep the automobile safely and turn it over to the owner upon payment of towing and storage fees. When this duty is delegated to a private contractor to tow and store, a constructive bailment for the mutual benefit of the contractor and the owner exists.

13. RENTING OF SPACE DISTINGUISHED

When a person rents space in a locker or building under an agreement that gives the renter the exclusive right to use that space, the placing of goods by the renter in that space does not create a bailment, for it does not constitute a delivery of goods into the possession of the owner of the space. **For Example,** Winston Hutton entered into a rental agreement for a storage space at Public Storage Management's self-storage facility in New York City, and his stored property was stolen from the space. Hutton had procured his own lock for the storage space, and the rental agreement provided that management would not have a key. Hutton's lawsuit was unsuccessful because the defendant did not take possession of the property. The legal relationship was not a bailment.[21]

14. DUTIES AND RIGHTS OF THE BAILEE

The bailee has certain duties concerning performance, care, and return of the bailed property. The bailee must perform his part of a contract and is liable for ordinary contract damages for failure to perform the contract.

The bailee is under a duty to care for the bailed property, and the duty of care owed differs according to classification, based in terms of "benefit." A bailment may be for the sole benefit of the bailor. **For Example,** when Fred allows Mary, a college classmate from out of state, to store her books and furniture in his basement over the summer, Fred, the bailee, is liable only for gross negligence relating to damage to these stored belongings. A bailment may be for the sole benefit of the bailee, as when Mary allows Fred to borrow her Les Paul Gibson guitar. Fred, the bailee, is liable even for slight negligence in the case of any damage to the guitar. Most bailments, however, are mutual benefit bailments. **For Example,** when Harry rents for a fee a trailer from U-Haul, Inc., to transport his son's belongings to college, Harry, the bailee, is responsible for using reasonable or ordinary care under the circumstances while possessing and using the trailer. U-Haul, the bailor, has a duty to warn Harry of any known defects or defects that could be discovered on reasonable inspection.

bailee's lien specific, possessory lien of the bailee upon the goods for work done to them. Commonly extended by statute to any bailee's claim for compensation, eliminating the necessity of retention of possession.

A bailee has a right to receive payment for charges due for storage or repairs. A **bailee's lien** gives the bailee the right to keep possession of the bailed property until

---

[21] *Hutton v Public Storage Management, Inc.,* 676 NYS2d 887 (NY City Civ Ct 1998).

charges are paid. A bailee who is authorized by statute to sell the bailed property to enforce a charge or claim against the bailor must give such notice as is required by the statute. A bailee who sells without giving the required notice is liable for conversion of the property.

15. BREACH OF DUTY OF CARE: BURDEN OF PROOF

Although a bailment is contractual in nature, an action for breach of duty of care by a bailee "sounds in tort." That is, the true nature of the liability is not contractual at all but based on tort principles.

When the bailor sues the bailee for damages to the bailed property, the bailor has the burden of proving that the bailee was at fault and that such fault was the proximate cause of the loss. A prima facie right of the bailor to recover is established, however, by proof that the bailor delivered the property to the bailee in good condition and subsequently could not be returned by the bailee or was returned in a damaged condition. When this is done, the bailee has the burden of proving that the loss or damage was not caused by the bailee's failure to exercise the care required by law, which in the case of a mutual benefit bailment is that of an ordinary or due care, under all of the circumstances.

CASE SUMMARY

Towed into Court

FACTS: Mark Hadfield, a medical student in Charleston, South Carolina, went to retrieve his 1988 Lincoln Continental from a parking space on private property near the medical school where his wife had parked the car earlier that day without permission. The property owner had called Gilchrist Towing Co., and the auto had been removed. When Hadfield discovered that the car had been towed, he telephoned Gilchrist Towing and was told that he would have to wait until the next morning to retrieve the car after paying towing and storage fees. The next morning, after paying the charges, he went to the storage lot and found that his car had been extensively vandalized along with a number of other vehicles. The owner of the company, S.S. Gilchrist, refused to pay the estimated cost of repairs, $4,021.43. Hadfield brought suit, contending that a constructive bailment for the mutual benefit of Hadfield and Gilchrist had been created, and that Gilchrist breached his duty of care to Hadfield. Gilchrist contended that he towed the vehicle pursuant to Charleston Municipal Ordinances, which are for the sole benefit of the vehicle owners, intended to preserve their property. As such, the relationship created was a gratuitous bailment, which limited his duty of care. Gilchrist contended he was not liable for damages caused by unknown vandals.

DECISION: Judgment for Hadfield. Where a city ordinance is utilized as the legal justification for taking possession of a vehicle on private property, the person or entity lawfully acquiring possession of the property under the ordinance becomes a constructive bailee as a matter of law. A constructive bailment, for the mutual benefit of Hadfield and Gilchrist, was created. The burden of proof in a constructive bailment case rests upon a bailor to prove a prima facie case, and once so proven, the burden shifts to the bailee to show the use of ordinary care in the storage and safekeeping of the property. The fact that a guard was not on duty at the impound lot and the only other security for the vehicles was a chain-link fence, a reasonable basis existed to conclude that Gilchrist failed to exercise ordinary care. [**Hadfield v Gilchrist, 343 SC 88 (SC App 2000)**]

16. LIABILITY FOR DEFECTS IN BAILED PROPERTY

In the case of a mutual benefit bailment, the bailor must not only inform the bailee of known defects but also make a reasonable investigation to discover defects. The bailor is liable for harm resulting from any such defects. If the bailment is for the sole benefit of the bailee, the bailor must inform the bailee of known defects.

In bailments for hire where the bailor is in the business of renting vehicles, machines, or equipment for use by bailees, such as Hertz or Avis car rental companies, Article 2A of the Uniform Commercial Code provides an implied warranty of merchantability and fitness for a particular purpose for the protection of bailee customers.[22]

17. CONTRACT MODIFICATION OF LIABILITY

An ordinary bailee may limit liability (except for willful misconduct) by agreement or contract. If the bailee seeks to limit liability for its own negligence, the wording of the contract must clearly express this intention so that the other party will know what is being contracted away.[23] In some states, statutes prohibit certain kinds of paid bailees, such as automobile parking garages, from limiting their liability for negligence. Statutes in some states declare that a party cannot bar liability for negligent violations of common law standards of care where a public interest is involved. **For Example,** Bruce Gardner left his Porsche 911 automobile to be repaired at Downtown Porsche Auto, signing a repair order standardized adhesion contract that stated Downtown was "not responsible for loss of cars . . . in case of . . . theft." The car was stolen while in the garage for repairs due to Downtown's negligence. The California appeals court determined that because automobile repair contracts "affect the public interest," Down-town's exculpatory clause was invalid as to public policy.[24]

When a bailee attempts to limit liability by printing such a limitation on a claim check, the limitation must be called to the attention of the bailor in some reasonable fashion, such as a sign at the point of purchase, before it may become part of the bailment contract. **For Example,** a claim check for a coat that purports to limit liability is ineffective without a reasonably placed sign notifying customers of the limitation.

LAWFLIX

The Goonies (1985)(PG)

This story is about children finding a lost treasure they wish to claim as theirs and use to stop the condemnation of their parents' properties by developers. The issue of who owns the treasure is a fascinating one for discussion.

For movie clips that illustrate business law concepts, see LawFlix at **http://wdvl.westbuslaw.com.**

---

[22] UCC §§ 2A-212, 2A-213.

[23] *Hertz v Klein Mfg., Inc.*, 636 So 2d 189 (Fla App 1994).

[24] *Gardner v Downtown Porsche Auto*, 225 Cal Rptr 757 (1986).

> SUMMARY

Personal property consists of whole or fractional ownership rights in things that are tangible and movable, as well as rights in things that are intangible.

Personal property may be acquired by purchase. Personal property may also be acquired by gift when the donor has present intent to make a gift and delivers possession to the donee or makes a constructive delivery. Personal property may be acquired by occupation and under some statutes may be acquired by finding. The state may acquire property by escheat.

All rights in a particular object of property can be held by one individual, in which case it is said to be held *in severalty*. Ownership rights may be held concurrently by two or more individuals, in which case it is said to be held in cotenancy. The major forms of cotenancy are (1) tenancy in common, (2) joint tenancy, (3) tenancy by entirety, and (4) community property.

A bailment is the relationship that exists when tangible personal property is delivered by the bailor into the possession of the bailee under an agreement, express or implied, that the identical property will be returned or delivered in accordance with the agreement. No title is transferred by a bailment. The bailee has the right of possession. When a person comes into the possession of the personal property of another without the owner's consent, the law classifies the relationship as a constructive bailment.

Bailments may be classified in terms of benefit—that is, for the (1) sole benefit of the bailor, (2) sole benefit of the bailee, or (3) benefit of both parties (mutual benefit bailment). Some courts state the standard of care required of a bailee in terms of the class of bailment. Thus, if the bailment is for the sole benefit of the bailor, the bailee is required to exercise only slight care and is liable for gross negligence only. When the bailment is for the sole benefit of the bailee, the bailee is liable for the slightest negligence. When the bailment is for the mutual benefit of the parties, as in a commercial bailment, the bailee is liable for ordinary negligence. An ordinary bailee may limit liability except for willful misconduct or where prohibited by law.

A bailee must perform the bailee's part of the contract. The bailee has a lien on the bailed property until they have paid for storage or repair charges.

In a mutual benefit bailment, the bailor is under a duty to furnish goods reasonably fit for the purposes contemplated by the parties. The bailor may be held liable for damages or injury caused by the defective condition of the bailed property.

> QUESTIONS AND CASE PROBLEMS

1. Can a creditor of both the husband and wife under the same obligation obtain an execution against a Winnebago mobile home owned by the husband and wife in tenancy by entirety?

2. Joe obtained a box of antique Lenox china dishes that had been left at the Mashpee town dump. He supplemented the sizable but incomplete set of dishes with other Lenox pieces found at antique dealers. At dinner parties, he proudly told of the origin of his china. When Marlene discovered that Joe had taken her dishes from the dump, she hired an attorney to obtain their return. What result?

3. Joyce Clifford gave a check for $5,000 to her nephew Carl to help with living expenses for his last year of college. The face of the check stated, "As a loan." Years later, Carl wrote to his aunt asking what he should do about the loan. She responded on her Christmas card simply, "On money—keep it—no return." After Joyce's death, her administrator sued Carl after discovering the "As a loan" canceled check. Decide.

4. Ruth and Stella were sisters. They owned a house as joint tenants with right of survivorship. Ruth sold her half interest to Roy. Thereafter, Stella died, and Roy claimed the entire property by survivorship. Was he entitled to it?

5. Mona found a wallet on the floor of an elevator in the office building where she worked. She posted several notices in the building about finding the wallet, but no one appeared to claim it. She waited for six months and then spent the money in the wallet in the belief that she owned it. Jason, the person who lost the wallet, subsequently brought suit to recover the money. Mona's defense was that the money was hers because

Jason did not claim it within a reasonable time after she posted the notices. Is she correct? (Assume that the common law applies.)

6. In 1971, Harry Gordon turned over $40,000 to his son, Murray Gordon. Murray opened two $20,000 custodial bank accounts under the Uniform Gifts to Minors Act for his minor children, Eden and Alexander. Murray was listed as the custodian of both accounts. On January 9, 1976, both accounts were closed, and a single bank check representing the principal of the accounts was drawn to the order of Harry Gordon. In April 1976, Murray and his wife, Joan, entered into a separation agreement and were later divorced. Thereafter, Joan, on behalf of her children, Eden and Alexander, brought suit against Murray to recover the funds withdrawn in January 1976, contending that the deposits in both accounts were irrevocable gifts. Murray contended that the money was his father's and that it was never intended as a gift but was merely a means of avoiding taxes. Decide. [*Gordon v Gordon*, 419 NYS2d 684 (App Div)]

7. New York's banking law provides that a presumption arises that a joint tenancy has been created when a bank account is opened in the names of two persons "payable to either or the survivor." While he was still single, Richard Coddington opened a savings account with his mother, Amelia. The signature card they signed stated that the account was owned by them as joint tenants with the right of survivorship. No statement as to survivorship was made on the passbook. Richard later married Margaret. On Richard's death, Margaret claimed a share of the account on the ground that it was not held in joint tenancy because the passbook did not contain words of survivorship and because the statutory presumption of a joint tenancy was overcome by the fact that Richard had withdrawn substantial sums from the account during his life. Decide. [*Coddington v Coddington*, 391 NYS2d 760 (Sup Ct App Div)]

8. Martin Acampora purchased a shotgun at a garage sale years ago, never used the weapon, and did not know of any defects in it. His 31-year-old son Marty borrowed the shotgun to go duck hunting. As Marty attempted to engage the safety mechanism, the shotgun fired. The force of the shotgun's firing caused it to fall to the ground and to discharge another shot, which struck Marty in the hand. Classify the bailment in this case. What duty of care was owed by the bailor in this case? Is Martin liable to his son for the injury?

9. Baena Brothers agreed to reupholster and reduce the size of the arms of Welge's sofa and chair. The work was not done according to the contract, and the furniture when finished had no value to Welge and was not accepted by him. Baena sued him for the contract price. Welge counterclaimed for the value of the furniture. Decide. [*Baena Brothers v Welge*, 3 Conn Cir 67, 207 A2d 749]

10. Schroeder parked his car in a parking lot operated by Allright, Inc. On the parking stub given him was printed in large, heavy type that the lot closed at 6:00 P.M. Under this information, printed in smaller, lighter type, was a provision limiting the liability of Allright for theft or loss. A large sign at the lot stated that after 6:00 P.M. patrons could obtain their car keys at another location. Schroeder's car was stolen from the lot sometime after the 6:00 P.M. closing, and he sued Allright for damages. Allright defended on the basis of the limitation-of-liability provision contained in the parking stub and the notice given Schroeder that the lot closed at 6:00 P.M. Decide. [*Allright, Inc. v Schroeder*, 551 SW2d 745 (Tex Civ App)]

11. John Hayes and Lynn Magosian, auditors for a public accounting firm, went to lunch at the Bay View Restaurant in San Francisco. John left his raincoat with a coatroom attendant, but Lynn took her new raincoat with her to the dining room, where she hung it on a coat hook near her booth. When leaving the restaurant, Lynn discovered that someone had taken her raincoat. When John sought to claim his raincoat at the coatroom, it could not be found. The attendant advised that it might have been taken while he was on his break. John and Lynn sued the restaurant, claiming that the restaurant was a bailee of the raincoats and had a duty to return them. Are both John and Lynn correct?

12. Rhodes parked his car in the self-service park-and-lock lot of Pioneer Parking Lot, Inc. The ticket that he received from the ticket meter stated the following: "NOTICE. THIS

CONTRACT LIMITS OUR LIABILITY. READ IT. WE RENT SPACE ONLY. NO BAILMENT IS CREATED." Rhodes parked the car himself and kept the keys. There was no attendant at the lot. The car was stolen from the lot. Rhodes sued the parking lot on the theory that it had breached its duty as a bailee. Was there a bailment? [*Rhodes v Pioneer Parking Lot, Inc.*, 501 SW2d 569 (Tenn)]

13. Newman underwent physical therapy at Physical Therapy Associates of Rome, Inc. (PTAR), in Rome, Georgia, for injuries sustained in an auto accident. At a therapy session on February 6, it was necessary for Newman to take off two necklaces. She placed one of the necklaces on a peg on the wall in the therapy room, and the therapist placed the other necklace on another peg. After the session, Newman forgot to retrieve her jewelry from the wall pegs. When she called the next day for the forgotten jewelry, it could not be found. She sued PTAR for the value of the jewelry on a bailment theory. PTAR raised the defense that there was no bailment because Newman retained the right to remove the jewelry from the wall pegs. Decide. [*Newman v Physical Therapy Associates of Rome, Inc.*, 375 SE2d 253 (Ga App)]

14. Contract Packers rented a truck from Hertz Truck Leasing. The brakes of the truck did not function properly. This resulted in injuring Packers' employee Cintrone while he was riding in the truck as it was driven by his helper. Cintrone sued Hertz for breach of the implied warranty that the truck was fit for normal use on public highways. Hertz contended that implied warranties apply only to sales, not to bailments for hire. Decide. [*Cintrone v Hertz Truck Leasing & Rental Service*, 212 A2d 769 (NJ)]

15. Charter Apparel, Inc., supplied fabric to Marco Apparel, Inc., in December to manufacture finished articles of clothing at its Walnut Grove, Mississippi, facilities. The fabric arrived just before the Christmas holiday shutdown and was stacked on cutting tables in the old building, which was known to have a roof that leaked. The evidence showed that no precautions were taken to cover the fabric and no guard was posted at the plant during the shutdown. Severe weather and freezing rain occurred during the shutdown, and it was discovered that the rain had leaked through the roof and destroyed more than $400,000 worth of the fabric. Marco denied that it was negligent and argued that it exercised ordinary care. It offered no evidence to rebut Charter's prima facie case or to rebut Charter's evidence of negligence. It asserted, however, that as a bailee it was not an insurer of goods against severe weather conditions. Decide. [*California Union Ins. v City of Walnut Grove*, 857 F Supp 515 (SD Miss)]

> CPA QUESTIONS

1. Which of the following requirements must be met to create a bailment?

   I. Delivery of personal property to the intended bailee

   II. Possession by the intended bailee

   III. An absolute duty on the intended bailee to return or dispose of the property according to the bailor's directions

   a. I and II only

   b. I and III only

   c. II and III only

   d. I, II, and III.

LEGAL ASPECTS OF SUPPLY CHAIN MANAGEMENT

LEARNING OBJECTIVES

After studying this chapter, you should be able to

LO.1 Differentiate between negotiable and nonnegotiable warehouse receipts

LO.2 List the three types of carriers of goods

LO.3 State the common carrier's liability for loss or damage to goods

LO.4 Explain the effect of a sale on a consignment

LO.5 Describe a hotelkeeper's liability for loss of a guest's property

All bailments are not created equal. Because of the circumstances under which possession of the bailed property is transferred, the law imposes special duties in some cases on warehouses, common carriers, factors, and hotelkeepers. Documents of title facilitate the transportation, storage, and financing of goods in commerce.

 # WAREHOUSES

The storage of goods in a warehouse is a special bailment.

1. DEFINITIONS

warehouse entity engaged in the business of storing the goods of others for compensation.

A **warehouse** is an entity engaged in the business of storing the goods of others for compensation. **Public warehouses** hold themselves out to serve the public generally, without discrimination.

A building is not essential to warehousing. Thus, an enterprise that stores boats outdoors on land is engaged in warehousing, for it is engaged in the business of storing goods for hire.

2. RIGHTS AND DUTIES OF WAREHOUSES

public warehouses entities that serve the public generally without discrimination.

The rights and duties of a warehouse are for the most part the same as those of a bailee under a mutual benefit bailment.[1] A warehouse is not an insurer of goods. A warehouse is liable for loss or damage to goods stored in its warehouse when the warehouse is negligent.

(a) STATUTORY REGULATION   The rights and duties of warehouses are regulated by the UCC, Article 7. Article 7 was revised in 2003 and 16 states have adopted the revised version.[2] The purpose of revision was to provide a framework for the future development of electronic documents of title and to update the article for modern times in light of state, federal, and international developments, including the need for medium and gender neutrality. For example, the term utilized to designate a person engaged in storing goods for hire under Article 7 is *warehouseman*.[3] The revised act uses the term *warehouse*.[4] In addition, most states have passed warehouse acts defining the rights and duties of warehouses and imposing regulations. Regulations govern charges and liens, bonds for the protection of patrons, maintenance of storage facilities in a suitable and safe condition, inspections, and general methods of transacting business.

specific lien right of a creditor to hold particular property or assert a lien on particular property of the debtor because of the creditor's having done work on or having some other association with the property, as distinguished from having a lien generally against the assets of the debtor merely because the debtor is indebted to the lien holder.

(b) LIEN OF WAREHOUSE   The public warehouse has a lien against the goods for reasonable storage charges.[5] It is a **specific lien** in that it attaches only to the property on which the charges arose and cannot be asserted against any other property of the same owner in the possession of the warehouse. However, the warehouse may make a lien carry over to other goods by noting on the receipt for

---

[1] UCC § 7-204.

[2] Revised Article 7 (2003) has been adopted by Alabama, Connecticut, Delaware, Hawaii, Idaho, Maryland, Minnesota, Montana, Nebraska, Nevada, New Jersey, New Mexico, North Dakota, Oklahoma, Texas, and Virginia. For more modern statutory drafting, the revised edition converts subparagraph designations from numbers to letters. For example, UCC § 7-307(1) is designated as Rev. UCC § 7-307(a).

[3] UCC § 7-102(1)(h).

[4] Rev. UCC § 7-102(a)(13).

[5] UCC § 7-209(1). The warehouse's lien provision of the UCC is constitutional as a continuation of the common law lien.

one lot of goods that a lien is also claimed for charges on the other goods. The warehouse's lien for storage charges may be enforced by sale after due notice has been given to all persons who claim any interest in the stored property.

3. WAREHOUSE RECEIPTS

warehouse receipt receipt issued by the warehouse for stored goods. Regulated by the UCC, which clothes the receipt with some degree of negotiability.

A **warehouse receipt** is a written acknowledgment or record of an acknowledgment by a warehouse (bailee) that certain property has been received for storage from a named person called a **depositor** (bailor). The warehouse receipt is a memorandum of the contract between the **issuer**, the warehouse that prepares the receipt, and the depositor. No particular form is required, but usually the receipt (record) will provide:

depositor person, or bailor, who gives property for storage.

(1) the location of the warehouse where the goods are stored, (2) the date of issuance of the receipt, (3) the consecutive number of the receipt, (4) information on the negotiability of the receipt, (5) the rate of storage and handling charges, (6) a description of the goods or the packages containing them, and (7) a statement of any liabilities incurred for which the warehouse claims a lien or security interest.[6]

issuer warehouse that prepares a receipt of goods received for storage.

document of title document treated as evidence that a person is entitled to receive, hold, and dispose of the document and the goods it covers.

A warehouse receipt (as well as a bill of lading, discussed at a later point in this chapter) is considered a **document of title**—that is, a document that in the regular course of business or financing is treated as evidence that a person is entitled to receive, hold, and dispose of the document and the goods it covers.[7] Under Revised Article 7 of the UCC, the term *record* is used in the definition of document of title, reflecting the present commercial reality of the use of electronic records as documents of title, in addition to traditional "written" documents of title inscribed on a tangible medium.[8] The person holding a warehouse receipt or the person specified in the receipt is entitled to the goods represented by the receipt. A warehouse receipt as a document of title can be bought or sold and can be used as security for a loan.

4. RIGHTS OF HOLDERS OF WAREHOUSE RECEIPTS

The rights of the holders of warehouse receipts differ depending on whether the receipts are nonnegotiable or negotiable.

CPA

nonnegotiable warehouse receipt receipt that states the covered goods received will be delivered to a specific person.

(a) NONNEGOTIABLE WAREHOUSE RECEIPTS   A warehouse receipt in which it is stated that the goods received will be delivered to a specified person is a **nonnegotiable warehouse receipt.** A transferee of a nonnegotiable receipt acquires only the title and rights that the transferor had actual authority to transfer. Therefore, the transferee's rights may be defeated by a good-faith purchaser of the goods from the transferor of the receipt.

negotiable warehouse receipt receipt that states the covered goods will be delivered "to the bearer" or "to the order of."

(b) NEGOTIABLE WAREHOUSE RECEIPTS   A warehouse receipt stating that the goods will be delivered "to the bearer" or "to the order of" any named person is a **negotiable warehouse receipt.**

---

[6] UCC § 7-202(2)(a)–(i).

[7] UCC § 1-201(15).

[8] Rev. 1-201(b)(16). An "electronic" document of title is evidenced by a record consisting of information stored in an electronic medium. A "tangible" document of title is evidenced by a record consisting of information that is inscribed on a tangible medium.

(1) Negotiation. If the receipt provides for the delivery of the goods "to the bearer," the receipt may be negotiated by transfer of the document. If the receipt provides for delivery of the goods "to the order of" a named individual, the document must be indorsed[9] and delivered by that person in order for the document to be negotiated.

(2) Due Negotiation. If a receipt is duly negotiated, the person to whom it is negotiated may acquire rights superior to those of the transferor. A warehouse receipt is "duly negotiated" when the holder purchases the document in good faith without notice of any defense to it, for value, in an ordinary transaction in which nothing appears improper or irregular.[10] The holder of a duly negotiated document acquires title to the document and title to the goods.[11] The holder also acquires the direct obligation of the issuer to hold or deliver the goods according to the terms of the warehouse receipt. The rights of a holder of a duly negotiated document cannot be defeated by the surrender of the goods by the warehouse to the depositor.[12]

It is the duty of the warehouse to deliver the goods only to the holder of the negotiable receipt and to cancel this receipt on surrendering the goods.[13]

The rights of a purchaser of a warehouse receipt by due negotiation are not cut off by the fact that (1) an original owner was deprived of the receipt in "bearer" form by misrepresentation, fraud, mistake, loss, theft, or conversion or (2) a bona fide purchaser bought the goods from the warehouse.

A purchaser of a warehouse receipt who takes by due negotiation does not cut off all prior rights. If the person who deposited the goods with the warehouse did not own the goods or did not have power to transfer title to them, the purchaser of the receipt is subject to the title of the true owner. Accordingly, when goods are stolen and delivered to a warehouse and a warehouse receipt is issued for them, the owner of the goods prevails over the due-negotiation purchaser of the warehouse receipt.

---

[9] The spelling *endorse* is commonly used in business. The spelling *indorse* is used in the UCC.

[10] UCC § 7-501(4).

[11] UCC § 7-502(1).

[12] For electronic documents of title, Revised Article 7, Section 7-106, includes a list of how a party becomes a holder, and the result is that Article 7 creates a new concept of "control." That is, a holder who has control of a document of title (as evidenced by a record that may be electronic) has all the rights of a holder. The Revised Article states:

(a) A person has control of an electronic document of title if a system employed for evidencing the transfer of interests in the electronic document reliably establishes that person as the person to which the electronic document was issued or transferred,

(b) A system satisfies subsection (a) and a person is deemed to have control of an electronic document of title, if the electronic document is created, stored, and assigned in such a manner that:

(1) a single authoritative copy of the document exists which is unique, identifiable, and, except as otherwise provided in paragraphs (4), (5), and (6), unalterable.

(2) the authoritative copy identifies the person asserting control as:

(A) the person to which the document was issued; or

(B) if the authoritative copy indicates that the document has been transferred, the person to which the document was most recently transferred;

(3) the authoritative copy is communicated to and maintained by the person asserting control or its designated custodian;

(4) copies or amendments that add or change an identified assignee of the authoritative copy can be made only with the consent of the person asserting control;

(5) each copy of the authoritative copy and any copy of a copy is readily identifiable as a copy that is not the authoritative copy; and

(6) any amendment of the authoritative copy is readily identifiable as authorized or unauthorized.

[13] UCC § 7-403(3).

FIGURE 22-1 *Negotiable Warehouse Receipt*

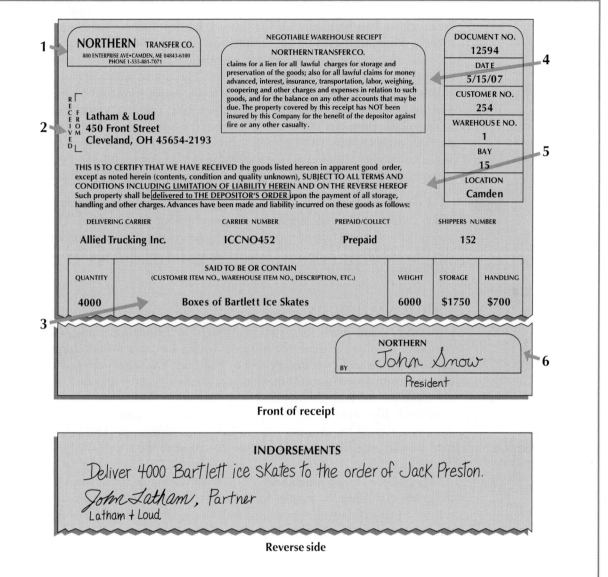

(1) Warehouse, (2) depositor, (3) goods, (4) warehouse's lien, (5) negotiable delivery terms, (6) warehouse's authorized agent. A negotiable warehouse receipt contains a promise to deliver the goods to the bearer or to the order of the depositor, unlike a nonnegotiable warehouse receipt, which promises only to deliver them to the depositor.

Study Figure 22-1, and note all of the features of a negotiable warehouse receipt in the context of the following. **For Example,** Latham and Loud (L&L) sporting goods manufacturers' representatives in Cleveland, Ohio, hijacked a truckload of ice skates from Bartlett Shoe and Skate Company of Bangor, Maine. L&L warehoused the skates at the Northern Transfer Company warehouse, and received a negotiable warehouse receipt. Jack Preston, a large sporting goods retailer who had had previous business dealings with L&L and believed it to be operated by honest individuals, made a bona fide purchase of the receipt. Bartlett, the true owner, discovered that the skates were at Northern's warehouse and informed Northern of the hijacking. Northern delivered the skates to Bartlett; Latham and Loud had fled the country. Preston believed he was entitled to delivery of the skates because he acquired the negotiable receipt by due negotiation and informed Northern of his status before delivery of the skates to Bartlett. He contemplated legal action against Northern. Preston, however, is not entitled to the skates. Ordinarily, a purchaser of a warehouse receipt obtained by due negotiation takes title to the document and title to the goods. However, an exception exists in the case of theft. Thus, because of the theft by L&L, Preston's rights have been cut off by the true owner in this case. When conflicting claims exist, the warehouse can protect itself by instituting proceedings under UCC § 7-603 to ascertain the validity of the conflicting claims.

CPA   **(c) Warranties**   The transferor of a negotiable or nonnegotiable warehouse receipt makes certain implied warranties for the protection of the transferee. These warranties are that (1) the receipt is genuine, (2) its transfer is rightful and effective, and (3) the transferor has no knowledge of any facts that impair the validity or worth of the receipt.[14]

5. FIELD WAREHOUSING

Ordinarily, stored goods are placed in a warehouse belonging to the warehouse company. In other instances, the owner of goods, such as a manufacturer, keeps the goods in the owner's own storage area or building. The warehouse may then take exclusive control over the area in which the goods are stored and issue a receipt for the goods just as though they were in the warehouse. Such a transaction has the same legal effect with respect to other persons and purchasers of the warehouse receipts as though the property were in fact in the warehouse. This practice is called **field warehousing** because the goods are not taken to the warehouse but remain "in the field."

field warehousing stored goods under the exclusive control of a warehouse but kept on the owner's premises rather than in a warehouse.

The purpose of field warehousing is to create warehouse receipts that the owner of the goods may pledge as security for loans. The owner could, of course, have done this by actually placing the goods in a warehouse, but this would have involved the expense of transportation and storage.

CPA   ## 6. LIMITATION OF LIABILITY OF WAREHOUSES

A warehouse may limit liability by a provision in the warehouse receipt specifying the maximum amount for which the warehouse can be held liable. This privilege is subject to two qualifications. First, the customer must be given the choice of storing the goods without such limitation if the customer pays a higher storage rate, and, second, the limitation must be stated for each item or for each unit of weight.[15] **For Example,** a limitation is proper when it states that the maximum liability for a piano is $5,000 or that the maximum liability per bushel of wheat is a stated amount.

---

[14] UCC § 7-507. These warranties are in addition to any that may arise between the parties by virtue of the fact that the transferor is selling the goods represented by the receipt to the transferee. See Chapter 25 for a discussion of seller's warranties.

[15] UCC § 7-204(2); *Lobel v Samson Moving & Storage, Inc.*, 737 NYS2d 24 (App Div 2002).

Conversely, there cannot be a blanket limitation of liability, such as "maximum liability $100," when the receipt covers more than one item.

General contract law determines whether a limitation clause is a part of the contract between the warehouse and the customer. **For Example,** warehouse Eastern Warehousing, Inc., and customer Delavau, Inc., executed a comprehensive contract for storage of a nutritional supplement after extensive negotiations between Eastern's chief operating officer and Delavau's president. The goods were damaged due to a leaking warehouse roof. Eastern was unsuccessful in its argument that the contract was formed when the goods were subsequently delivered to the warehouse and a preprinted warehouse receipt containing a limitation-of-liability provision was given to the customer's driver. The court ruled that the terms of the receipt were not part of the contract of the parties, and awarded Delavau $1,358,601 in damages.[16]

B COMMON CARRIERS

The purpose of a bailment may be transportation. In this case, the bailee may be a common carrier.

7. DEFINITIONS

A **carrier** of goods is an individual or organization undertaking the transportation of goods regardless of the method of transportation or the distance covered. The **consignor** or shipper is the person who delivers goods to the carrier for shipment. The **consignee** is the person to whom the goods are shipped and to whom the carrier should deliver the goods.

A carrier may be classified as a common carrier, a contract carrier, or a private carrier. A **common carrier** holds itself out as willing to furnish transportation for compensation without discrimination to all members of the public who apply, assuming that the goods to be carried are proper and facilities of the carrier are available. A **contract carrier** transports goods under individual contracts, and a **private carrier** is owned and operated by the shipper. **For Example,** a truck fleet owned and operated by an industrial firm is a private carrier. Common carrier law or special bailment law applies to common carriers, ordinary bailment law to contract carriers, and the law of employment to private carriers.

The Federal Motor Carrier Safety Administration is the successor agency to the Interstate Commerce Commission and was created under the Interstate Commerce Commission Termination Act (ICCTA).[17] Under the ICCTA, Congress merged the separate classifications of common and contract carrier into one classification termed

carrier individual or organization undertaking the transportation of goods.

consignor (1) person who delivers goods to the carrier for shipment, (2) party with title who turns goods over to another for sale.

consignee (1) person to whom goods are shipped, (2) dealer who sells goods for others.

common carrier carrier that holds out its facilities to serve the general public for compensation without discrimination.

contract carrier carrier that transports on the basis of individual contracts that it makes with each shipper.

private carrier carrier owned by the shipper, such as a company's own fleet of trucks.

CASE SUMMARY

The Distinction Continues

FACTS: M. Fortunoff of Westbury operates a chain of department stores in New York and New Jersey. In March of 1997, the company entered into a contract with Frederickson Motor

---

[16] *Delavau v Eastern American Trading & Warehousing, Inc.,* 810 A2d 672 (Pa Super 2002).
[17] 49 USC § 13906 (a)(3) (2000) (amended 2005).

CASE SUMMARY

continued

Express, whereby the carrier agreed "as contract carrier and independent contractor . . . to transfer shipments . . . as authorized in Carrier's contract carrier permit . . . issued by the ICC." The contract further provided: "Although carrier is authorized to operate . . . as a common carrier, each and every shipment tendered to carrier by shipper . . . shall be deemed to be a tender to carrier as a motor contract carrier. . . ." Fortunoff's goods were damaged in transit, prompting it to make a claim against Frederickson. When the carrier went out of business, Fortunoff asserted the same claim against the carrier's insurer, Peerless Insurance Co., for $13,249.42 under the BMC-32 endorsement (the mandatory attachment to all common carrier insurance policies), which was part of Frederickson's insurance policy. From a judgment for Fortunoff, on the ground that the ICCTA mandated the extension of BMC-32 endorsements to all motor carriers, Peerless appealed.

DECISION: Judgment against the shipper, Fortunoff. Historically, many trucking companies obtained both a common carrier certificate and a contract carrier permit, meaning they were authorized to operate as either type of carrier. If the carrier agreed to transport a shipper's goods according to standard terms and at a fixed rate (i.e. without an individually negotiated contract) on a nonrecurring basis, the transportation was conducted under the carrier's common carrier certificate. Accordingly, common carrier rules, including the cargo liability insurance and the BMC-32 endorsement requirement, applied. If the carrier and the shipper wished to negotiate a bilateral contract for an ongoing course of shipping services, the carrier was required to operate under its contract carrier permit, and no cargo insurance was necessary.

Requiring cargo liability insurance for common carriage but not contract carriage is not an arbitrary distinction. Instead, it makes economic sense because of the different types of services performed and the customers served by common carriage. Although the ICCTA abolished the licensing distinction between common and contract carriers, it did so in large part because most carriers had a common carrier certificate and a contract carrier permit and provided both types of service anyway. But the functional distinction between the two types of carriage survives and is still highly relevant to deciding which motor carriers must have cargo liability insurance. The administrative agency's decision to require BMC-32 cargo insurance only when performing common carriage service is consistent with the ICCTA. The district court's ruling is reversed. [**M. Fortunoff of Westbury Corp. v Peerless Ins., 432 F3d 127 (2nd Cir 2005)**]

"motor carrier." However, as will be seen in the *Fortunoff* case, the fundamental distinction between the types of carriage remains explicit in the act.

---

8. BILLS OF LADING

bill of lading document issued by a carrier reciting the receipt of goods and the terms of the contract of transportation. Regulated by the Federal Bills of Lading Act or the UCC.

airbill document of title issued to a shipper whose goods are being sent via air.

When the carrier accepts goods for shipment or forwarding, the carrier ordinarily issues to the shipper a **bill of lading** in the case of land or water transportation or an **airbill** for air transportation. This instrument is a document of title and provides rights similar to those provided by a warehouse receipt. A bill of lading is both a receipt for the goods and a memorandum of a contract stating the terms of carriage. Title to the goods may be transferred by a transfer of the bill of lading made with that intention.

Bills of lading for intrastate shipments are governed by the Uniform Commercial Code. For interstate shipments, bills of lading are regulated by the Federal Bills of Lading Act (FBLA).[18]

---

[18] 49 USC § 81 *et seq.*

CPA   **(a) Contents of Bill of Lading**   The form of the bill of lading is regulated in varying degrees by administrative agencies. Prior to the revisions to Article 7, negotiable bills of lading were printed on yellow paper, and nonnegotiable or straight bills of lading were printed on white paper. This color-coding may continue as commercial practice for those documents reduced to written form, but new commercial practices will evolve regarding the use of "records.[19]

As against the good faith transferee of the bill of lading, a carrier is bound by the recitals in the bill as to the contents, quantity, or weight of goods.[20] This means that the carrier must produce the goods that are described or pay damages for failing to do so. This rule is not applied if facts appear on the face of the bill that should keep the transferee from relying on the recital.

negotiable bill of lading document of title that by its terms calls for goods to be delivered "to the bearer" or "to the order of" a named person.

(b) Negotiation   A bill of lading is a **negotiable bill of lading** when by its terms the goods are to be delivered "to the bearer" or "to the order of" a named person.[21] Any other bill of lading, such as one that consigns the goods to a named person, is a **nonnegotiable** or **straight bill of lading**. Like transferees of warehouse receipts who take by due negotiation, holders of bills of lading who take by due negotiation ordinarily also acquire title to the bills and title to the goods represented by them.

nonnegotiable bill of lading see *straight bill of lading.*

straight (or nonnegotiable) bill of lading document of title that consigns transported goods to a named person.

Rights of a transferee are defeated by the true owner, however, when a thief delivers the goods to the carrier and then negotiates the bill of lading. The thief had no title to the goods at any time.

CASE SUMMARY

International Intrigue

FACTS: Banque de Depots, a Swiss bank, sued Bozel, a Brazilian corporation, for money owed the bank. Banque obtained a writ of attachment from the court against goods being shipped by Bozel from Rio de Janeiro through the port of New Orleans for transit to purchasers located in three states. Bozel claimed that the writ of attachment must be dissolved because the cargo was shipped under negotiable bearer bills of lading and the bills of lading had been sent to U.S. banks for collection from the purchasers.

DECISION: Judgment for Bozel. The writ of attachment must be dissolved. Goods shipped pursuant to a negotiable bill of lading cannot be seized unless the bill of lading is surrendered to the carrier or impounded by a court. On the day of the seizure of the cargo under the writ, the negotiable bills of lading were outstanding. The bills of lading were not in the hands of the carrier, and their negotiation had not been enjoined by the court. The law protects holders of duly negotiated bills of lading from purchasing such bills and then finding out that the goods have been seized by judicial process. The holder of a duly negotiated bill of lading acquires title to the document and title to the goods described in the document. [**Banque de Depots v Bozel, 569 So 2d 40 (La App 1990)**]

---

[19] The UCC contains no provision regulating the form of the bill of lading and the use of records, including electronic tracking, now covered under Revised Article 7. This means that new commercial practices will evolve.

[20] UCC § 7-301(1).

[21] UCC § 7-104(1)(a).

(c) WARRANTIES   By transferring for value a bill of lading, whether negotiable or nonnegotiable, the transferor makes certain implied warranties to the transferee. The transferor impliedly warrants that (1) the bill of lading is genuine, (2) its transfer is rightful and is effective to transfer the goods represented by it, and (3) the transferor has no knowledge of facts that would impair the validity or worth of the bill of lading.[22]

9. RIGHTS OF COMMON CARRIER

A common carrier of goods has the right to make reasonable and necessary rules for the conduct of its business. It has the right to charge such rates for its services to yield it a fair return on the property devoted to the business of transportation.

As security for unpaid transportation and service charges, a common carrier has a lien on goods that it transports. The carrier's lien also secures demurrage, the costs of preservation of the goods, and the costs of sale to enforce the lien.[23]

10. DUTIES OF COMMON CARRIER

A common carrier is required (1) to receive and carry proper and lawful goods of all persons who offer them for shipment as long as the carrier has space, (2) to furnish facilities that are adequate for the transportation of freight in the usual course of business and to furnish proper storage facilities for goods awaiting shipment or awaiting delivery after shipment, (3) to follow the directions given by the shipper, (4) to load and unload goods delivered to it for shipment (in less-than-carload lots in the case of railroads), but the shipper or consignee may assume this duty by contract or custom, and (5) to deliver the goods in accordance with the shipment contract.

Goods must be delivered at the usual place of delivery at the specified destination. When goods are shipped under a negotiable bill of lading, the carrier must not deliver the goods without obtaining possession of the bill, properly indorsed. When goods are shipped under a straight bill of lading, the carrier may deliver the goods to the consignee or the consignee's agent without receiving the bill of lading unless notified by the shipper to deliver the goods to someone else. If the carrier delivers the goods to the wrong person, the carrier is liable for breach of contract and for the tort of conversion.

CASE SUMMARY

Miami Ice

FACTS: Bottoms & Tops International Inc. shipped a package containing jewelry by United Parcel Service (UPS) to its salesman Ed Dwek at the Marco Polo Hotel in Miami Beach, Florida. The package was delivered to the hotel and signed for by the bell captain, who placed it in the package room and alerted Dwek by illuminating the call light in his room to contact

---

[22] UCC § 7-507; FBLA, 49 USC §§ 114, 116. When the transfer of the bill of lading is part of a transaction by which the transferor sells the goods represented thereby to the transferee, there will also arise the warranties that are found in other sales of goods.

[23] UCC § 7-307(1); FBLA, 49 USC § 105.

CASE SUMMARY

continued

the front desk. The bell captain released the package to an individual bearing a key to Dwek's room. Dwek did not receive the package, and Bottoms & Tops sued UPS for failure to deliver the package to the consignee Dwek.

DECISION: Judgment for UPS. In the circumstances of delivering packages to hotel guests, delivery persons are generally not permitted access to guest rooms. When the terms of the bill of lading do not mandate delivery only to a named individual, delivery of a package by a common carrier to a bell captain terminates the carrier's duty owed to the shipper. [**Bottoms & Tops Int'l Inc. v UPS, 610 NYS2d 439 (NY City Civ Ct 1994)**]

CPA

11. LIABILITIES OF COMMON CARRIER

When goods are delivered to a common carrier for immediate shipment and while they are in transit, the carrier is absolutely liable for any loss or damage to the goods unless it can prove that the loss or damage was due solely to one or more of the following excepted causes: (1) an act of God, meaning a natural phenomenon that is not reasonably foreseeable, (2) an act of a public enemy, such as the military forces of an opposing government, as distinguished from ordinary robbers, (3) an act of a public authority, such as a health officer removing goods from the carrier, (4) an act of the shipper, such as fraudulent labeling or defective packing, or (5) the inherent nature of the goods, such as those naturally tending to spoil or deteriorate.

CASE SUMMARY

Landstar Learns the Hard Way

FACTS: Tempel Steel Corporation shipped a large machine press from Minster, Ohio, to Monterrey, Mexico, by Landstar Inway, Inc., a common carrier. Landstar issued Tempel a through bill of lading for this service. It then hauled the press to the U.S. border, where it hired a customs broker who utilized a local carrier, Teresa de Jesus Ortiz Obregon, to move the cargo through U.S. and Mexican customs to interchange with a Mexican carrier. It was determined that Obregon failed to secure the press properly and drove too fast, causing $300,000 damage to the press. Tempel sued Landstar to recover for this damage. Landstar defended that it was not responsible for causalities in Mexico and that the loss was the fault of Obregon.

DECISION: Landstar is financially responsible for the entire movement by having entered a competitive bid to transport goods from Ohio through to Mexico and having issued a through bill of lading. Tempel is thus entitled to hold Landstar liable for the damage, and Landstar then bears the responsibility for seeking compensation from the carrier actually responsible for the loss. Although Landstar had every legal right to issue a bill of lading that stopped at the U.S. border, it did not do so. Landstar must accept the legal consequences of the issuance of the through bill of lading without limitation of liability for losses. [**Temple Steel Corp. v Landstar Inway, Inc., 211 F 3d 1029 (2000)**]

(a) CARRIER'S LIABILITY FOR DELAY A carrier is liable for losses caused by its failure to deliver goods within a reasonable time. **For Example,** J.B. Hunt Transport, Inc., "lost" a shipment of boxed Christmas cards specially packaged for Target Stores, Inc., by the shipper, Paper Magic, Inc. The goods were shipped on October 16, 1998, and the invoice valued them at $130,080.48. Hunt located the shipment on February 5, 1999, and Target refused the goods because it was well after Christmas and the goods were worthless to Target. The cards were worthless to Paper Magic because they were packaged with Target's private label. The court found that awarding the shipper the invoice value was a permissible award under the Carmack Amendment to the Interstate Commerce Act.[24]

The carrier, however, is not liable for every delay. The shipper assumes the risk of ordinary delays incidental to transporting goods.

(b) LIMITATION OF LIABILITY OF CARRIER In the absence of a constitutional or statutory prohibition, a common carrier generally has the right to limit its liability by contract.

Common carriers operating interstate may limit their liability for the negligent loss of consigned items to a stated dollar amount, such as $100 per package. Shippers, however, must be given a reasonable opportunity to select excess liability coverage for the higher value of their shipment, with payment of higher freight charges.[25]

The Carmack Amendment to the Interstate Commerce Act governs the liability of carriers for loss or damage in the interstate shipment of goods.[26] Shippers displeased with liability limitations permitted carriers under the Carmack

---

CASE SUMMARY

Did the Shipper Miss the Class on Limitation of Liability by Carriers?

FACTS: Richard Trujillo, a jeweler, sent a commercial package valued at $123,490 on American Airlines, Inc., from Los Angeles to Dallas. An American employee prepared a waybill, which limited the carrier's cargo liability to $50 for the package plus the shipping cost, which was $76.50. The package was lost, and Trujillo sued American for breach of contract. American contends that it offered a choice of paying a higher rate for greater protection but that Trujillo left the declared value box on the waybill blank. This was Trujillo's first time using American, and he was confused about its procedures. He denied that he was made aware of the limitation of liability.

DECISION: Judgment for American. The carrier properly limited its liability in the waybill, and the shipper Trujillo is bound by the terms stated in the waybill even though he complained he was not aware of the limitation. Trujillo was entitled to only $126.50 for the lost package ($50 plus the amount paid to the air carrier by the shipper). [**Trujillo v American Airlines, Inc., 938 F Supp 389 (ND Tex 1995)**]

---

[24] *The Paper Magic Group, Inc. v J.B. Hunt Transport, Inc.,* 318 F3d 458 (3d Cir 2003). See also *National Hispanic Circus, Inc. v Rex Trucking,* 414 F3d 546 (5th Cir 2005).

[25] In *Sassy Doll Creations Inc. v Watkins Motor Lines Inc.,* 331 F3d 834 (11th Cir 2003), the carrier was held liable for the full value of a lost shipment of perfume, $28,273.60, rather than $10,000.00, the carrier's established limitation of its liability. The bill of lading prepared by the carrier contained a declared value box, which the shipper filled in. However, the document did not contain any space for requesting excess liability coverage and thus did not give the shipper a reasonable opportunity to select a higher level of coverage as required by the Carmack Amendment to the Interstate Commerce Act.

[26] 49 USC § 11707.

ETHICS & THE LAW

The life of the long-haul trucker is grueling. Shippers impose deadlines that require round-the-clock time behind the wheel. The U.S. Department of Commerce regulates the maximum number of hours a trucker can log behind the wheel before a break is required. Enforcement of those maximums is difficult because the truckers themselves maintain the logs.

The investigation of an accident involving a semitrailer truck and several autos, in which there were fatalities, revealed that the driver of the truck had driven for 47 hours without sleep. The driver's logs showed that he was in compliance with U.S. mandates for breaks and sleep. A fellow trucker commented, "It's not us. To make a living, you have to meet their deadlines. They screw up and get behind on shipment dates and we're supposed to make up the time."

Who is responsible for violations of the break-and-sleep requirements? Is it just drivers, or do those paying for shipments share some responsibility? Do you think shippers should assume some responsibility for supervision of their drivers? Is it ethical for shippers to ask their drivers to make up the time they themselves have lost in fulfilling an order?

Amendment may not sue a carrier under any state statute if the statute in any way enlarges the responsibility of a carrier for loss or damage to the goods.[27] The Carmack Amendment provides the exclusive remedy for loss or damage, and its purpose is to provide uniformity in the disposition of claims brought under a bill of lading or waybill.

(c) Notice of Claim   The bill of lading and applicable government regulations may require that a carrier be given notice of any claim for damages or loss of goods within a specified time, generally within nine months.

(d) COD Shipment   A common carrier transporting goods under a COD (cash on delivery) shipment may not make delivery of the goods without first receiving payment. If it does, it is liable to the shipper for any resulting loss. Thus, if a FedEx or UPS driver were to accept a bad check from a consignee on a COD shipment, the carrier would be liable to the shipper for the amount owed.

There are two forms of COD payments in addition to cash—certified and cashier's checks.

CASE SUMMARY

Cashier's Check Is King

FACTS: ABF Freight Systems, Inc., accepted a certified check for a COD fee owed upon delivery of 511 cartons of shoes to the location designated in the bill of lading. It turned out that the bank certification stamped on the face of the check was a forgery. The bill of lading

---

[27] *Dugan v FedEx Corp.,* 2002 WL 31305208 (CD Cal).

CASE SUMMARY

continued

included the specification that delivery be "COD Cashier's Check" and that ABF collect payment on behalf of Imports, Ltd. Imports sued ABF for $53,180.90, the full value of the COD payment. From a judgment for Imports for the full amount plus interest, ABF appealed.

DECISION: Judgment for Imports, Ltd. The primary difference between a bank certified check and a cashier's check is in the ease with which one can create a fraudulent instrument. To forge a cashier's check, one would need to replicate all of the other features of the bank's form. To forge a bank check, on the other hand, one need only have a writing on the check indicating that the check is "certified." Imports had a right to believe that a cashier's check is a better form of payment than a certified check. The agreement that ABF would accept only a cashier's check reflected this belief. ABF broke its contract with Imports by accepting a bank certified check rather than a cashier's check for the COD payment. [**Imports, Ltd., v ABF Freight Systems, Inc., 162 F3d 528 (8th Cir 1998)**]

(e) REJECTED SHIPMENTS When a common carrier tenders delivery of consigned goods to a consignee that refuses to accept the delivery, the carrier is no longer a common carrier but becomes a warehouser. When the carrier-turned-warehouser receives new shipping instructions from the owner, its status again changes to that of a common carrier.

 ## FACTORS AND CONSIGNMENTS

factor bailee to whom goods are consigned for sale.

A **factor** is a special type of bailee who sells consigned goods as though the factor were the owner of those goods.

12. DEFINITIONS

selling on consignment entrusting a person with possession of property for the purpose of sale.

commission merchant bailee to whom goods are consigned for sale.

commission or **factorage** consignee's compensation.

Entrusting a person with the possession of property for the purpose of sale is commonly called **selling on consignment**.[28] The owner who consigns the goods for sale is the *consignor*. The person or agent to whom they are consigned is the factor or *consignee*; this individual may also be known as a **commission merchant**. A consignee's compensation is known as a **commission** or **factorage**. **For Example,** *consignor* Rolly Tasker Sails Co., Ltd. (RTS) would ship sails from Thailand to the *consignee*, Bacon & Associates of Annapolis, Maryland, with a bill of lading and an "invoice price" for each sail. Mrs. Bacon would then set her "retail fair market value price." Once a set of sails was sold, Mrs. Bacon would deposit a check to the consignor's account at Alex Brown Co. at the invoice price. Her *commission* was the difference between the retail price and the invoice price. This arrangement began in 1971, but began to unravel 27 years later. RTS was successful in its breach of *consignment agreement* lawsuit against Bacon for $345,327 in damages and $78,660 in interest.[29]

---

[28] *Amoco Oil Co. v DZ Enterprises, Inc.,* 607 F Supp 595 (SDNY 1985).
[29] *Bacon & Associates, Inc. v Rolly Tasker Sails Co. Ltd. (Thailand),* 841 A2d 53 (Md App 2004).

13. EFFECT OF FACTOR TRANSACTION

In a sale on consignment, the property remains the property of the owner-consignor, and the consignee acts as the agent of the owner to pass the owner's title to the buyer. A consignment sale is treated as a sale or return under Article 2 of the Uniform Commercial Code (UCC), and the factor-consignee has full authority to sell the goods for the consignor and can pass title to those goods. For this reason, creditors of the consignee can obtain possession of the goods and have a superior right to them over the consignor. If, however, the owner-consignor complies with the security interest and perfection provisions of Article 9 of the UCC (Chapter 34), there is public notice of the consignment, and the goods will be subject to the claims of the owner's creditors, but not to those of the factor-consignee.[30]

conversion act of taking personal property by a person not entitled to it and keeping it from its true owner or prior possessor without consent.

If the consignor is not the owner, as when a thief delivers stolen goods to the factor, a sale by the factor passes no title and is an unlawful **conversion**.

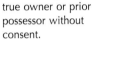 **HOTELKEEPERS**

A hotelkeeper has a bailee's liability with respect to property specifically entrusted to the hotelkeeper's care. In addition, the hotelkeeper has special duties with respect to a guest's property brought into the hotel. The rules governing the special relationship between a hotelkeeper and a guest arose because of the special needs of travelers.

14. DEFINITIONS

The definitions of *hotelkeeper* and *guest* exclude lodging of a more permanent character, such as that provided by boardinghouse keepers to boarders.

hotelkeeper one regularly engaged in the business of offering living accommodations to all transient persons.

(a) HOTELKEEPER   A **hotelkeeper** is an operator of a hotel, motel, or tourist home or anyone who is regularly engaged in the business of offering living accommodations to transient persons. In the early law, the hotelkeeper was called an *innkeeper* or a *tavernkeeper*.

guest transient who contracts for a room or site at a hotel.

(b) GUEST   A **guest** is a transient. The guest need not be a traveler or come from a distance. A person living within a short distance of a hotel who engages a room at the hotel and remains there overnight is a guest.

In contrast, a person who enters a hotel at the invitation of a guest or attends a dance or a banquet given at the hotel is not a guest. Similarly, the guest of a registered occupant of a motel room who shares the room with the occupant without the

---

[30] Revised Article 2 (1999) modifies the rules on consignments slightly in that all transactions are treated as sales or return or sales on approval unless steps are taken to identify a transaction as a consignment and to comply with state laws on consignment. The new UCC § 2-326(a), (b), and (c) provides as follows:

  The provisions of this subsection are applicable even though an agreement purports to reserve title to the person making delivery until payment or resale or uses such words as "on consignment" or "on memorandum."
  However, this subsection is not applicable if the person making delivery
  (a) complies with an applicable law providing for a consignor's interest or the like to be evidenced by a sign, or
  (b) establishes that the person conducting the business is generally known by his creditors to be substantially engaged in selling the goods of others, or
  (c) complies with the filing provisions of the Article on Second Transactions (Article 9).

knowledge or consent of the management is not a guest of the motel because there is no relationship between that person and the motel.

15. DURATION OF GUEST RELATIONSHIP

The relationship of guest and hotelkeeper does not begin until a person is received as a guest by the hotelkeeper. The guest–hotelkeeper relationship does not automatically end when the hotel bill is paid.[31]

The relationship terminates when the guest leaves or ceases to be a transient, as when the guest arranges for a more or less permanent residence at the hotel. The transition from the status of guest to the status of boarder or lodger must be clearly indicated. It is not established by the mere fact that one remains at the hotel for a long period, even though it runs into months.

Circumstances arise when a hotel assumes an obligation to deliver packages to a guest from a person who is not a guest of the hotel. The hotelkeeper has a bailee's liability for the care of such packages. **For Example,** Richard St. Angelo, vice president of sales for jewelry manufacturer Don-Linn Inc., left two boxes of jewelry prototypes at the front desk of the Westin Hotel with instructions to deliver the boxes to the hotel's guest from Dillard's Inc., a national department store. This delivery took place. Thereafter, a Dillard's representative notified St. Angelo that Dillard's review of the products was complete and he could pick up the boxes at the hotel but specified no location. St. Angelo and the Westin staff later searched for the boxes, but they were never found. The manufacturer's lawsuit against the Westin asserting a breach of bailment was not successful. St. Angelo was not a guest at the Westin, thus the obligation assumed for the care of the packages initially left at the Westin was not as a hotelkeeper but a bailee. When the Westin surrendered the packages to Dillard's group, it completed its bailment agreement. No bailment or any other legal obligation between Don-Linn and the Westin was shown to exist with regard to the return of the jewelry prototypes.[32]

16. HOTELKEEPER'S LIABILITY FOR GUEST'S PROPERTY

With respect to property expressly entrusted to the hotelkeeper's care, the hotelkeeper has a bailee's liability. At common law, the hotelkeeper was absolutely liable for damage to, or loss of, a guest's property unless the hotelkeeper could show that the damage or loss was caused solely by an act of God, a public enemy, an act of a public authority, the inherent nature of the property, or the fault of the guest.[33]

In most states, statutes limit or provide a method of limiting the common law liability of a hotelkeeper. The statutes may limit the extent of liability, reduce the liability of a hotelkeeper to that of an ordinary bailee, or permit the hotelkeeper to limit liability by contract or by posting a notice of the limitation. Some statutes relieve the hotelkeeper from liability when the guest has not complied with directions for

[31] *Garrett v Impac Hotels, LLC,* 87 SW3d 870 (Mo App 2002).

[32] *Don-Linn Jewelry Co. v The Westin Hotel Co.,* 877 A2d 621 (RI 2005).

[33] *Cook v Columbia Sussex Corp.,* 807 SW2d 567 (Tenn App 1991).

depositing valuables with the hotelkeeper.[34] A hotelkeeper must substantially comply with such statutes in order to obtain their protection.

CASE SUMMARY

Problems of the Rich and Famous at a Five-Star Hotel

FACTS: Thelma Paraskevaides and others were guests at the Four Seasons Hotel in Washington, D.C. Upon arrival, they placed and locked their valuables in their room safe and left the room for the day. Upon their return, they found the room ransacked and the safe opened, and their valuables worth $1.2 million missing. Thelma theorized that the hotel's master key to the hotel's room safes had been missing, and she believed she should have been informed of this by the hotel. The hotel contends that it satisfied the conditions for the statutory bar to strict liability for the loss under District of Columbia law.

DECISION: Judgment for the hotel. Under the common law rule, an innkeeper is statutorily liable for loss or damage to a guest's property. In D.C. and many other jurisdictions, however, the common law rule has been modified. Section 34-101 of the D.C. Code frees hotels of liability when the host hotel conspicuously posts a copy or summary of § 34-101 and information that safety deposit boxes are maintained at the front desk. The plaintiffs admitted the hotel did post a summary of § 34-101 next to the room safe; and this was sufficient to place the plaintiffs on notice. The hotel is not liable for the plaintiffs' property loss. [**Paraskevaides v Four Seasons Washington, 148 F Supp 2d 20 (D DC 2002)**]

17. HOTELKEEPER'S LIEN

The hotelkeeper has a lien on the baggage of guests for the agreed charges or, if no express agreement was made, for the reasonable value of the accommodations furnished. Statutes permit the hotelkeeper to enforce this lien by selling the goods of the guests at a public sale. The lien of the hotelkeeper is terminated by (1) the guest's payment of the hotel charges, (2) any conversion of the guest's goods by the hotelkeeper, or (3) final return of the goods to the guest.

18. BOARDERS OR LODGERS

The hotelkeeper owes only the duty of an ordinary bailee of personal property under a mutual benefit bailment to those persons who are permanent boarders or lodgers rather than transient guests.

A hotelkeeper has no lien on property of boarders or lodgers, as distinguished from guests, in the absence of an express agreement creating such a lien. A number of states, however, have adopted legislation giving a lien to keepers of boardinghouses or lodging houses.

---

[34] *Chappone v First Florence Corp.*, 504 SE2d 761 (Ga App 1998). But see *World Diamond Inc. v Hyatt Corp.*, 699 NE2d 980 (Ohio App 1997), where the court held that when special arrangements have been made between the innkeeper and the guest, the innkeeper is liable for the loss of any property so received when the loss is caused by the innkeeper's negligence.

LAWFLIX

Nine to Five (1980) (PG)

At the heart of the twists and turns in this boss/secretary caper are the warehouse receipts an executive is using to embezzle from his company. Analyze what the executive was doing with the documents.

For movie clips that illustrate business law concepts, see LawFlix at **http://wdvl.westbuslaw.com**.

> SUMMARY

A warehouse stores the goods of others for compensation and has the rights and duties of a bailee in an ordinary mutual benefit bailment. A warehouse issues a warehouse receipt to the depositor of the goods. This receipt is a document of title that ordinarily entitles the person in possession of the receipt to receive the goods. The warehouse receipt can be bought, sold, or used as security to obtain a loan. A nonnegotiable warehouse receipt states that the goods received will be delivered to a specified person. A negotiable warehouse receipt states that the goods will be delivered "to the bearer" or "to the order of" a named person. If a negotiable warehouse receipt is duly negotiated, the transferee may acquire rights superior to those of the transferor. A warehouse may limit its liability for loss or damage to goods resulting from its own negligence to an agreed valuation of the property stated in the warehouse receipt, provided the depositor is given the right to store the goods without the limitation at a higher storage rate.

A common carrier of goods is in the business of transporting goods received from the general public.

It issues to the shipper a bill of lading or an airbill. Both of these are documents of title and provide rights similar to those provided by a warehouse receipt. A common carrier is absolutely liable for any loss or damage to the goods unless the carrier can show that the loss was caused solely by an act of God, an act of a public enemy, an act of a public authority, an act of the shipper, or the inherent nature of the goods. The carrier may limit its liability in the same manner as a warehouse.

A factor is a special type of bailee who has possession of the owner's property for the purpose of sale. The factor, or consignee, receives a commission on the sale.

A hotelkeeper is in the business of providing living accommodations to transient persons called guests. Subject to exceptions, at common law, hotelkeepers were absolutely liable for loss or damage to their guests' property. Most states, however, provide a method of limiting this liability. A hotelkeeper has a lien on the property of the guest for the agreed charges.

> QUESTIONS AND CASE PROBLEMS

1. What social forces are involved in the rule of law governing the liability of a common carrier for loss of freight?
2. American Cyanamid shipped 7,000 vials of DPT—a vaccine for immunization of infants and children against diphtheria, pertussis, and tetanus—from its Pearl River, New York, facility to the U.S. Defense Department depot in Mechanicsburg, Pennsylvania, by New Penn Motor Express, a common carrier. Cyanamid's bill of lading included a "release value," which stated the value of the property was declared as not exceeding $1.65 per pound. Cyanamid's shipment weighed 1,260 pounds. The bill of lading accepted by New Penn on picking up the DPT vaccine on February 6 also clearly stated that the shipment contained drugs and clearly warned to "protect from freezing." The bill

further recited "rush . . . must be delivered by February 8, 1989." New Penn permitted the vaccine to sit in an unheated uninsulated trailer while it gathered enough other merchandise to justify sending a truck to Mechanicsburg. The DPT vaccine was delivered on February 10 in worthless condition, having been destroyed by the cold. New Penn admitted it owed $2,079 in damages pursuant to the bill of lading ($1.65 × 1,260 lbs.). Cyanamid claimed that the actual loss was much greater, $53,936.75. It stated that because New Penn breached its contract with Cyanamid, it could not invoke the benefits of that same contract, namely, the release value clause.

Was it ethical for New Penn to hold the vaccine while waiting for enough merchandise to justify the trip? How would you decide the case? [*American Cyanamid Co. v New Penn Motor Express, Inc.,* 979 F2d 301 (3d Cir)]

3. Compare the liens of carriers, warehouses, and hotels in terms of being specific.

4. Compare the limitations of the liability of a warehouse and of a hotelkeeper.

5. Compare warehouse receipts and bills of lading as to negotiability.

6. Doyle Harms applied to his state's Public Utilities Commission for a Class B permit authorizing performance as a common carrier. Doyle testified that it was not his intention to haul in a different direction than he was already going, stating in part:

No way, that's not what I'm asking for. I've got enough business of my own, it's just the times when you get done with a sale at the end of the day and you've got a half load and somebody else has a half load, then you'd be able to help each other out. It's kind of the name of the game in my mind.

He also testified that the application was so he could haul cattle for his own customers. State law defines a common carrier as "a motor carrier which holds itself out to the general public as engaged in the business of transporting persons or property in intrastate commerce which it is accustomed to and is capable of transporting from place to place in this state, for hire." Its property is "devoted to the public service."

Should Doyle Harms be issued a common carrier permit? [*In re Harms,* 491 NW2d 760 (SD)]

7. Welch Brothers Trucking, Inc., a common carrier, made an agreement with B&L Export and Import Co. of San Francisco to transport a shipment of freshly harvested bluefin tuna from Calais, Maine, to the Japan Air Lines freight terminal at New York's Kennedy Airport. The bluefin tuna had been packed in ice and were to be shipped by Japan Air Lines to Tokyo. Fresh bluefin are used in the traditional Japanese raw fish dish sashimi and command very high prices. When transportation charges were not paid by B&L's representative in New York, Welch Brothers refused to release the shipment to Japan Air Lines. B&L's representative in New York explained that he had no check-writing authority but assured Welch that it would be paid and pleaded for the release of the cargo because of its perishable nature. Transportation charges were not paid in the next 12-hour period because the principals of B&L were on a business trip to the Far East and could not be contacted. After waiting the 12-hour period, Welch sent a telegram to B&L's offices in San Francisco, stating the amount due and that it intended to auction the cargo in 24 hours if transportation charges were not paid. Welch also sent telegrams seeking bidders to all fish wholesalers listed in the New York City Yellow Pages. In the telegrams, Welch advised that the cargo would be sold at auction in 24 hours if the charges were not paid. Welch sold the shipment to the highest bidder at the appointed time for an amount just in excess of the transportation charges plus a demurrage charge for the 36-hour waiting period. When the principals of B&L were later informed of what happened, they sued Welch for the profits they would have earned if the cargo had been shipped and sold in Japan. Decide.

8. Richard Schewe and others placed personal property in a building occupied by Winnebago County Fair Association, Inc. Prior to placing their property in the building, they signed a "Storage Rental Agreement" prepared by the County Fair Association, which stated: "No liability exists for damage or loss to the stored equipment from the perils of fire. . . ." The

property was destroyed by fire. Suit was brought against the County Fair Association to recover damages for the losses on the theory of negligence of a warehouse. The County Fair Association claimed that the language in the storage agreement relieved it of all liability. [*Allstate Ins. Co. v Winnebago County Fair Ass'n, Inc.,* 475 NE2d 230 (Ill App)]

9. Buffett sent a violin to Strotokowsky by International Parcel Service (IPS), a common carrier. Buffett declared the value of the parcel at $500 on the pick-up receipt given him by the IPS driver. The receipt also stated: "Unless a greater value is declared in writing on this receipt, the shipper hereby declares and agrees that the released value of each package covered by this receipt is $100.00, which is a reasonable value under the circumstance surrounding the transportation." When Strotokowsky did not receive the parcel, Buffett sued IPS for the full retail value of the violin—$2,000. IPS's defense was that it was liable for just $100. Decide.

10. Glen Smith contracted with Dave Watson, a common carrier, to transport 720 hives of live bees along with associated equipment from Idabel, Oklahoma, to Mandan, North Dakota. At 9:00 A.M. on May 24, 1984, while en route, Watson's truck skidded off the road and tipped over, severely damaging the cargo. Watson notified Smith what had happened, and Smith immediately set out for the scene of the accident. He arrived at 6:00 P.M. with two bee experts and a Bobcat loader. They were hindered by the turned-over truck on top of the cargo, and they determined that they could not safely salvage the cargo that evening. The next day, an insurance adjuster determined that the cargo was a total loss. The adjuster directed a bee expert, Dr. Moffat, to conduct the cleanup; Moffat was allowed to keep the salvageable cargo, valued at $12,326, as compensation. Smith sued Watson for damages. Watson denied liability and further contended that Smith failed to mitigate damages. Decide. [*Smith v Watson,* 406 NW2d 685 (ND)]

11. A guest in a motel opened the bedroom window at night and went to sleep. During the night, a prowler pried open the screen, entered the room, and stole property of the guest. The guest sued the motel. The motel asserted that it was not responsible for property in the possession of the guest and that the guest had been contributorily negligent in opening the window. Could the guest recover damages? [*Buck v Hankin,* 269 A2d 344 (Pa Super)]

12. On March 30, Emery Air Freight Corp. picked up a shipment of furs from Hopper Furs, Inc. Hopper's chief of security filled in certain items in the airbill. In the box entitled ZIP Code, he mistakenly placed the figure "61,045," which was the value of the furs. The ZIP Code box was immediately above the Declared Value box. The airbill contained a clause limiting liability to $10 per pound of cargo lost or damaged unless the shipper makes a declaration of value in excess of the amount and pays a higher fee. A higher fee was not charged in this case, and Gerald Doane signed the airbill for the carrier and took possession of the furs. The furs were lost in transit by Emery, and Hopper sued for the value of the furs, $61,045. Emery's offer to pay $2,150, the $10-per-pound rate set forth in the airbill, was rejected. Hopper claimed that the amount of $61,045, which was mistakenly placed in the ZIP Code box, was in fact part of the contract set forth in the airbill and that Emery, on reviewing the contract, must have realized a mistake was made. Decide. [*Hopper Furs, Inc., v Emery Air Freight Corp.,* 749 F2d 1261 (8th Cir)]

13. When de Lema, a Brazilian resident, arrived in New York City, his luggage consisted of three suitcases, an attaché case, and a cylindrical bag. The attaché case and the cylindrical bag contained jewels valued at $300,000. De Lema went from JFK Airport to the Waldorf Astoria Hotel, where he gave the three suitcases to hotel staff in the garage, and then he went to the lobby to register. The assistant manager, Baez, summoned room clerk Tamburino to assist him. De Lema stated, "The room clerk asked me if I had a reservation. I said, 'Yes. The name is José Berga de Lema.' And I said, 'I want a safety deposit box.' He said, 'Please fill out your registration.'" While de Lema was filling out the registration form, paying $300 in cash as an advance, and Tamburino was filling out a receipt for that

amount, de Lema had placed the attaché case and the cylindrical bag on the floor. A woman jostled de Lema, apparently creating a diversion, and when he next looked down, he discovered that the attaché case was gone. De Lema brought suit against the hotel for the value of the jewels stolen in the hotel's lobby. The hotel maintained a safe for valuables and posted notices in the lobby, garage, and rooms as required by the New York law that modifies a hotelkeeper's common law liability. The notices stated in part that the hotel was not liable for the loss of valuables that a guest neglected to deliver to the hotel for safekeeping. The hotel's defense was that de Lema neglected to inform it of the presence of the jewels and to deliver the jewels to the hotel. Is the hotel liable for the value of the stolen jewels? [*De Lema v Waldorf Astoria Hotel, Inc.*, 588 F Supp 19 (SDNY)]

14. Frosty Land Foods shipped a load of beef from its plant in Montgomery, Alabama, to Scott Meat Co. in Los Angeles via Refrigerated Transport Co. (RTC), a common carrier. Early Wednesday morning, December 7, at 12:55 A.M., two of RTC's drivers left the Frosty Land plant with the load of beef. The bill of lading called for delivery at Scott Meat on Friday, December 9, at 6:00 A.M. The RTC drivers arrived in Los Angeles at approximately 3:30 P.M. on Friday, December 9. Scott notified the drivers that it could not process the meat at that time. The drivers checked into a motel for the weekend, and the load was delivered to Scott on Monday, December 12. After inspecting 65 of the 308 carcasses, Scott determined that the meat was in off condition and refused the shipment. On Tuesday, December 13, Frosty Land sold the meat, after extensive trimming, at a loss of $13,529. Frosty Land brought suit against RTC for its loss. Decide. [*Frosty Land Foods v Refrigerated Transport Co.*, 613 F2d 1344 (5th Cir)]

15. Tate hired Action-Mayflower Moving & Storage to ship his belongings. Action prepared a detailed inventory of Tate's belongings, loaded them on its truck, and received the belongings at its warehouse, where they would be stored until Tate asked that they be moved. Months later, a dispute arose, and Tate asked Action to release his property to a different mover. Tate had prepaid more than enough to cover all charges to this point. Action refused to release the goods and held them in storage. After allowing storage charges to build up for 15 months, Action sold Tate's property under the warehouser's public sale law. Tate sued Action for damages. Decide. [*Tate v Action-Mayflower Moving & Storage, Inc.*, 383 SE2d 229 (NC App)]

CPA QUESTIONS

1. A common carrier bailee generally would avoid liability for loss of goods entrusted to its care if the goods are

   a. Stolen by an unknown person
   b. Negligently destroyed by an employee
   c. Destroyed by the derailment of the train carrying them due to railroad employee negligence
   d. Improperly packed by the party shipping them

2. Under a nonnegotiable bill of lading, a carrier who accepts goods for shipment must deliver the goods to

   a. Any holder of the bill of lading
   b. Any party subsequently named by the seller
   c. The seller who was issued the bill of lading
   d. The consignee of the bill of lading

3. Under the UCC, a warehouse receipt

   a. Is negotiable if, by its terms, the goods are to be delivered to bearer or to the order of a named person
   b. Will not be negotiable if it contains a contractual limitation on the warehouse's liability

c. May qualify as both a negotiable warehouse receipt and negotiable commercial paper if the instrument is payable either in cash or by the delivery of goods

d. May be issued only by a bonded and licensed warehouser

4. Under the Documents of Title Article of the UCC, which of the following acts may limit a common carrier's liability for damages to the goods in transit?

a. Vandalism

b. Power outage

c. Willful acts of third person

d. Providing for a contractual dollar liability limitation

NATURE AND FORM
OF SALES

After studying this chapter, you should be able to

LO.1 Define a sale of goods and explain when UCC Article 2 applies to contracts

LO.2 Distinguish between an actual sale of goods and other types of transactions in goods

LO.3 Describe how contracts are formed under Article 2, and list the differences in formation standards between the UCC and common law

LO.4 Explain when a contract for the sale of goods must be in writing

LO.5 List and explain the exceptions to the requirement that certain contracts be in writing

LO.6 Discuss the purpose of the United Nations Convention on Contracts for the International Sale of Goods

LO.7 Discuss the distinguishing features of a consumer lease and a finance lease

---

Article 2 section of Uniform Commercial Code that governs contracts for the sale of goods.

Chapters 12 through 20 examined the common law of contracts. That source of contract law applies to contracts whose subject matter is land or services. However, there is another source of contract law, **Article 2** of the Uniform Commercial Code (UCC).

Article 2 was revised substantially by the National Conference of Commissioners on Uniform State Laws (NCCUSL) and the American Law Institute (ALI) in August 2003. As of June 2006, Revised Article 2 had not been adopted in any states.[1] The changes to Article 2 that have been adopted but not yet fully legislated are covered in this chapter and Chapters 24–27.

Article 2 governs the sale of everything from boats to televisions to compact discs. The UCC is a source of contract law derived from the law merchant, a body of contract law that began in common law England to facilitate transactions in goods. Today's UCC Article 2, which applies to contracts for the sale of goods, exists as a result of the work of businesspeople, commercial transactions lawyers, and legal experts who together have developed a body of contract law suitable for the fast pace of business. Article 2 continues to be refined and modified to ensure seamless laws for transactions in goods across the country.[2]

 NATURE AND LEGALITY

A *sale of goods* is defined under Article 2 as transfer of title to tangible personal property for a price.[3] This price may be a payment of money, an exchange of other property, or the performance of services.

---

[1] Kansas had introduced Article 2 for passage in 2005 but did not adopt it. The reluctance of states to adopt the revised version may have its roots in the disagreement that existed during the revision process.

[2] The UCC Article 2 (prior to the 2003 revisions) has been adopted in 49 states plus the Virgin Islands and the District of Columbia. Louisiana adopted only Article 1; 1990 Revision of Article 3; 1990 Amendments to Article 4; Article 4A (Funds Transfers); 1995 Revision of Articles 5 and 7; 1994 Revision of Article 8; and 2000 Revision of Article 9. The newest revisions of Article 2 were reconciled in July, 2003. The changes in Revised Article 2 are noted throughout this chapter and Chapters 24–27.

[3] UCC § 2-105(1).

The parties to a sale are the person who owns the goods, the seller or vendor, and the person to whom the title is transferred, the buyer or vendee.

1. SUBJECT MATTER OF SALES

goods anything movable at the time it is identified as the subject of a transaction.

Goods, as defined under the UCC, consist of all forms of tangible personal property, including specially manufactured goods—everything from a fan to a painting to a yacht.[4] Not covered under Article 2 are (1) investment securities, such as stocks and bonds, the sale of which is regulated by Article 8 of the UCC; (2) insurance policies, commercial paper, such as checks, and promissory notes because they are regulated under Articles 3 and 4 of the UCC; and (3) real estate, such as houses, factories, farms, and land itself.

(a) NATURE OF GOODS   Article 2 applies not only to contracts for the sale of familiar items of personal property, such as automobiles or chairs, but also to the transfer of commodities, such as oil, gasoline, milk, and grain.[5]

existing goods goods that physically exist and are owned by the seller at the time of a transaction.

future goods goods that exist physically but are not owned by the seller and goods that have not yet been produced.

(b) EXISTING AND FUTURE GOODS   Goods that are already manufactured or crops already grown and owned by the seller at the time of the transaction are called **existing goods.** All other goods are called **future goods,** which include both goods that physically exist but are not owned by the seller and goods that have not yet been produced, as when a buyer contracts to purchase custom-made office furniture.

2. SALE DISTINGUISHED FROM OTHER TRANSACTIONS

Other types of transactions in goods are not covered by Article 2 because they are not transfers of title to the goods.

bailment relationship that exists when personal property is delivered into the possession of another under an agreement, express or implied, that the identical property will be returned or will be delivered in accordance with the agreement. (Parties—bailor, bailee)

(a) BAILMENT   A **bailment** is not a sale because only possession is transferred to a **bailee.** Title to the property is not transferred. (For more information on bailments, their nature, and the rights of the parties, see Chapter 21.) A lease of goods, such as an automobile, is governed by Article 2A of the UCC, which is covered later in Section D of this chapter.

bailee person who accepts possession of a property.

(b) GIFT   A **gift** is a gratuitous (free) transfer of the title to property. The Article 2 definition of a sale requires that the transfer of title be made for a price. Gifts are not covered under Article 2.

gift title to an owner's personal property voluntarily transferred by a party not receiving anything in exchange.

(c) CONTRACT FOR SERVICES   A contract for services, such as a contract for painting a home, is not a sale of goods and is not covered under Article 2 of the UCC. Contracts for services are governed by common law principles.

---

[4] *State v Cardwell*, 718 A2d 594 (Conn 1998) (concert tickets are goods); *Leal v Holtvogh*, 702 NE2d 1246 (Ohio App 1998) (transfer of part interest in a horse is a good); *Bergeron v Aero Sales*, 134 P3d 964 (Or App 2006) (jet fuel is a good); *Rite Aid Corp. v Levy-Gray*, 894A 2d 563 (Md 2006) (prescription drug is a good); *Willis Mining v Noggle*, 509 SE2d 731 (Ga App 1998) (granite blocks are goods); *Sterling Power Partners, L.P. v Niagra Mohawk Power Corp.*, 657 NYS2d 407 (1997) (electricity is a good); *Gladhart v Oregon Vineyard Supply Co.*, 994 P2d 134 (Or App 1999) (grape plants bought from nursery are goods); *Dantzler v S.P. Parks, Inc.*, 1988 WL 131428 (ED Pa 1988) (purchase of ticket to amusement ride is not transaction in goods); *Rossetti v Busch Entm't Corp.*, 87 F Supp 2d 415 (ED Pa 2000) (computer software programs are goods); and *Saxton v Pets Warehouse, Inc.*, 691 NYS2d 872 (1999) (dog is goods).

[5] UCC § 2-105(1)–(2). Goods include minerals, some fixtures (or personal property attached to the land), growing crops, the unborn young of animals, and building materials to be removed by the seller. UCC § 2-105 (1990); *Koch Oil Co. v Wilber*, 895 SW2d 85 (Tex App 1995).

CASE SUMMARY

The Decaying Relationship between the Dentist and His Patient: When the Dentures Do Not Fit, Does the UCC Apply?

FACTS: Mrs. Downing was fitted for dentures by a dentist, Dr. Cook. After she received her dentures, Mrs. Downing began experiencing mouth pain that she attributed to Dr. Cook's manufacture of dentures that did not fit her properly. Mrs. Downing filed suit against Dr. Cook for breach of warranty under Article 2 of the UCC. Dr. Cook defended on the grounds that his denture work was a service and therefore not covered under Article 2 warranties. The trial court found for Mrs. Downing, and Dr. Cook appealed.

DECISION: A dentist is not a merchant and the UCC does not apply to the making and sale of these dentures. A dentist could be sued for breach of contract or for tort. Mrs. Downing erroneously based her cause of action on the UCC rather than negligence. There is no remedy under the UCC, and the case should be dismissed with judgment in favor of the dentist. [**Cook v Downing, 891 P2d 611 (Okla App 1995)**]

(d) CONTRACT FOR GOODS AND SERVICES   If a contract calls for both rendering services and supplying materials to be used in performing the services, the contract is classified according to its dominant element. **For Example,** a homeowner may purchase a security system. The homeowner is paying for the equipment that is used in the system as well as for the seller's expertise and installation of that system. Is the homeowner's contract governed by Article 2, or is it a contract for services and covered under the common law of contracts?

If the service element dominates, the contract is a service contract and is governed by common law rather than Article 2. If the goods make up the dominant element of the contract, then the parties' rights are determined under Article 2. In the home security system contract example, the question requires comparing the costs of the system's parts versus the costs of its installation. In some contracts, the equipment costs are minimal, and installation is key for the customer. In more sophisticated security systems, the installation is a small portion of the overall contract price, and the contract would be governed by the UCC.[6]

One of the critical issues under Article 2 that has resulted from the new high-tech environment is whether Article 2 covers computer software included with the sale of a computer, thus subjecting software manufacturers to warranty liability and the damage provisions of the UCC.[7] Whether software would be covered under Article 2 was the most spirited debate in the 2003 revision process.[8] Under the final draft, Article 2 does not cover "information," but information is not defined. Comments on this issue (comments are insights into the UCC sections, but they are not part of the code) indicate that Article 2 does not cover the sale of "information"

---

[6] *TK Power, Inc. v Textron, Inc.,* 433 F Supp 2d 1058 (ND Cal 2006); see also *J. O. Hooker's Sons v Roberts Cabinet,* 683 So 2d 396 (Miss 1996), in which a subcontractor's agreement to dispose of cabinets it removed from a public housing redevelopment project was held to be a service contract not governed by the UCC.

[7] *Multi-Tech Systems, Inc. v Floreat, Inc.,* 47 UCC Rep Serv 2d 924 (D Minn 2002).

[8] Section 2-103(1)(k) of Revised Article 2 defines goods as follows:
all things movable at the time of identification to a contract for sale. The term includes future goods, specially manufactured goods, the unborn young of animals, growing crops, and other identified things attached to realty as described in § 2-107. The term does not include information, the money in which the price is to be paid, investment securities under Article 8, the subject matter of foreign exchange transactions and choses in action.

not associated with goods. If this interpretation in the comment is applied, courts will be required to apply the test of whether a contract is primarily for the goods or the "information."[9]

3. FORMATION OF SALES CONTRACTS

(a) Necessary Detail for Formation   To streamline business transactions, Article 2 of the UCC does not have standards as rigid as the formation standards of common law contracts.

Under the UCC, the formation of a contract can be recognized even though one or more terms are left open so long as the parties clearly intend to contract.[10] The minimum terms required for formation of an agreement under the UCC are the subject matter and quantity (if there is more than one).[11] **For Example,** an agreement that described "the sale of my white Ford Taurus" would be sufficient, but an agreement to purchase "some Ford Tauruses" would require a quantity in order to qualify for formation.[12] Other provisions under Article 2 can cover any missing terms so long as the parties are clear on their intent to contract. Article 2 contains provisions covering price, delivery, time for performance, payment, and other details of performance in the event the parties agree to a sale but have not discussed or reduced to writing their desires in these areas.[13]

(b) The Merchant versus Nonmerchant Parties   Because Article 2 applies to all transactions in goods, it is applicable to sales by both **merchants** and nonmerchants,[14] including consumers. In most instances, the UCC treats all buyers and sellers alike. However, some sections in Article 2 are applicable only to merchants, and as a result, there are circumstances in which merchants are subject to different standards and rules. Generally, these areas of different treatment constitute the UCC's recognition that merchants are experienced, have special knowledge of the relevant commercial practices, and often need to have greater flexibility and speed in their transactions. The sections that have different rules for merchants and nonmerchants are noted throughout Chapters 24–27.

merchant seller who deals in specific goods classified by the UCC.

(c) Offer   Just as in common law, the **offer** is the first step in formation of a sales contract under Article 2.[15] The common law contract rules on offers are generally applicable in sales contract formation with the exception of the **firm offer**[16]

offer expression of an offeror's willingness to enter into a contractual agreement.

firm offer offer stated to be held open for a specified time, under the UCC, with respect to merchants.

---

[9] Section 2-102(4)–(5) provides:
  (4) A transaction in a product consisting of computer information and goods that are solely the medium containing the computer information is not a transaction in goods, but a court is not precluded from applying provisions in this article to a dispute concerning whether the goods conform to the contract.
  (5) Nothing in this article alters, creates, or diminishes rights in intellectual property.

[10] 5 UCC § 2-204(3); *Cargill v Jorgenson Farms,* 719 NW 2d 226 (Minn App 2006). This provision on formation assumes that the agreement the parties do have provides "a reasonably certain basis for giving an appropriate remedy." Revised § 2-204 provides for electronic communication.

[11] Although, see *A. M. Capern's Co. Inc. v American Trading & Production Corp.,* 973 F Supp 247 (DPR 1997), in which the court held that the absence of quantity was not fatal to the formation of a contract.

[12] *Syrovy v Alpine Resources, Inc.,* 859 P2d 51 (Wash 1993).

[13] For information on terms, see UCC §§ 2-305 (price), 2-307 to 2-308 (delivery), 2-310 (payment), and 2-311 (performance).

[14] *Merchant* is defined in UCC § 2-104(1). An operator of a turkey farm is not a merchant with regard to heaters used on turkey farms, only for the turkeys themselves. *Jennie-O-Foods, Inc. v Safe-Glo Prods. Corp.,* 582 NW2d 576 (Minn App 1998).

[15] A purchase order is generally considered an offer, but it must have enough information to meet the minimum standards for an offer. *Biotech Pharmacal, Inc. v International Business Connections,* LLC184 SW3d 447, 53 UCC Rep Serv 2d 476 (Ark Ct App 2004).

[16] Firm offers are found in UCC § 2-205.

provision, which is a special rule on offers applicable only to merchants: An offer by a merchant cannot be revoked if the offer (1) expresses an intention that it will be kept open, (2) is in a writing, and (3) is signed by the merchant.[17]

The period of irrevocability in a merchant's offer cannot exceed three months. If no specific time is given in the merchant's firm offer for its duration, it remains irrevocable only for a reasonable time. A firm offer for the three months' maximum time is effective regardless of whether the merchant received any consideration to keep the offer open. **For Example,** a rain check given by a store on advertised merchandise is a merchant's firm offer. The rain check guarantees that you will be able to purchase two bottles of Windex at $1.99 each for a period specified in the rain check.

For nonmerchants and contracts in which the parties want periods in excess of three months, there must be consideration because to be enforceable, there must be an option contract just like those used in common law contracts (see Chapters 12 and 13).

(d) ACCEPTANCE—MANNER Unlike the common law rules on acceptance, which control with great detail the method of **acceptance,** the UCC rules on acceptance are much more flexible. Under Article 2, an acceptance of an offer may be in any manner and by any medium that is reasonable under the circumstances.[18] Acceptance can occur through written communication or through performance as when a seller accepts an offer for prompt shipment of goods by simply shipping the goods.[19] However, just as under common law, Article 2 requires that if the offer specifies the manner or medium of acceptance, the offer can be accepted only in that manner.

acceptance unqualified assent to the act or proposal of another; as the acceptance of an offer to make a contract.

CPA

(e) ACCEPTANCE—TIMING The timing rules of the common law for determining when a contract has been formed are used to determine the formation of a contract under Article 2 with one slight modification. The **mailbox rule** applies under the UCC not just for the use of the same method of communication as that used by the offeror, but so long as the acceptance is communicated using any reasonable method of communication. Under the common law, the same method of communication used by the offeror had to be used by the offeree in order to have the mailbox rule of acceptance be effective upon mailing or dispatch. A UCC offeree can use a reasonable method and still obtain the priority timing so that his acceptance is effective when it is sent. For example, suppose that Feather-Light Brownies sent a letter offer to Cane Sugar Suppliers offering to buy 500 pounds of confectioner's sugar at $1 per pound. Cane Sugar Suppliers faxes back an acceptance of the letter offer. Cane Sugar Suppliers' acceptance is effective when it sends the fax.

mailbox rule timing for acceptance tied to proper acceptance.

CPA

mirror image rule common law contract rule on acceptance that requires language to be absolutely the same as the offer, unequivocal and unconditional.

(f) ACCEPTANCE—LANGUAGE Under the common law, the **mirror image rule** applies to acceptances. To be valid acceptances under common law, the language of the acceptance must be absolute, unconditional, and unequivocal; that is, the

---

[17] A *quotation* is a firm offer. *Rich Products Corp. v Kemutec, Inc.,* 66 F Supp 2d 937 (ED Wis 1999).

[18] UCC § 2-206(1). UCC § 2-206 governs acceptance methods and provides:
> (1) Unless otherwise unambiguously indicated by the language or circumstances (a) an offer to make a contract shall be construed as inviting acceptance in any manner and by any medium reasonable in the circumstances; (b) an order or other offer to buy goods for prompt or current shipment shall be construed as inviting acceptance either by a prompt promise to ship or by the prompt . . . shipment of . . . [goods].

See *Gulf States Utilities Co. v NEI Peebles Elec. Products, Inc.,* 819 F Supp 538 (MD La 1993).

[19] UCC § 2-206(1)(b). Shipment of coal in response to an offer is acceptance. *Central Illinois Public Service Co. v Atlas Minerals, Inc.,* 146 F3d 448 (7th Cir 1998).

acceptance under common law must be the mirror image of the offer in order for a contract to be formed. However, the UCC has liberalized this rigid rule and permits formation even in circumstances when the acceptance includes terms that vary from the offer. The following sections explain the old UCC rules on differing terms in acceptances. These rules for additional terms in acceptance will be eliminated under Revised Article 2 (discussed later).

(1) Additional Terms in Acceptance—Nonmerchants.   Under Article 2, unless an offer expressly specifies that an offer to buy or sell goods must be accepted exactly as made, the offeree may accept an offer and at the same time propose an additional term or terms. The additional term or terms in the acceptance does not result in a rejection as it would under common law. A contract is formed with the terms of the original offer. The additional terms are proposals for addition to the contract and may or may not be accepted by the other party.[20] **For Example,** Joe tells Susan, "I'll sell you my X-box for $150," and Susan responds, "I'll take it. The Halo game is included." Susan has added an additional term in her acceptance. At this point, Joe and Susan have a contract for the sale of the X-box for $150. Whether the Halo game is included is up to Joe; Joe is free to accept Susan's proposal or reject it, but his decision does not control whether he has a contract. There is a contract because Susan has made a definite statement of acceptance. To avoid being bound by a contract before she is clear on the terms, Susan should make an inquiry before using the language of acceptance, such as "Would you include the Halo game as part of the sale?" Susan's inquiry is not an acceptance and leaves the original offer still outstanding, which she is free to accept or reject.

(2) Additional Terms in Acceptance—Merchants.   Under Article 2, the use of additional terms in acceptances by merchants is treated slightly differently. The different treatment of merchants in acceptances is the result of a commercial practice known as the **battle of the forms**, which results because a buyer sends a seller a purchase order for the purchase of goods. The seller sends back an invoice to the buyer. Although the buyer and seller may agree on the front of their documents that the subject matter of their contracts is 500 treadmills, the backs of their forms have details on the contracts, often called *boilerplate language,* that will never match. Suppose, for example, that the seller's invoice adds a payment term of "10 days same as cash." Is the payment term now a part of the parties' agreement? The parties have a meeting of the minds on the subject matter of the contract but now have a slight difference in performance terms.

battle of the forms
merchants' exchanges of invoices and purchase orders with differing boilerplate terms.

Under Article 2, in a transaction between merchants, the additional term or terms sent back in an acceptance become part of the contract if the additional term or terms do not materially alter the offer and the offeror does not object in a timely fashion.[21] **For Example,** returning to the Joe and Susan example, suppose that they are both now secondary market video game merchants negotiating for the sale and purchase of a used X-box. They would have a contract, and the Halo game would be included as part of the sale. Joe could, however, avoid the problem by adding a limitation to his offer, such as "This offer is limited to these terms." With that limitation, Susan would have a contract, but the contract would not include the

[20] Revised Article 2 provides protections for consumers on terms they would not expect, that were not negotiated, or of which they had no knowledge. Rev UCC § 2-206.
[21] UCC § 2-207(2).

Halo game. Joe could also object immediately to Susan's proposal for the Halo game and still have a contract without this additional term.[22]

If the proposed additional term in the acceptance is material, a contract is formed, but the material additional term does not become a part of the contract.[23] **For Example,** if Susan added to her acceptance the statement, "Game system carries one-year warranty," she has probably added a material term because the one-year warranty for a used game system would be unusual in the secondary market and costly for Joe.[24] Again, Joe can avoid this problem by limiting his offer so as to strike any additional terms, whether material or immaterial.

The most significant changes under Revised Article 2 deal with § 2-207. Because there were so many confusing circumstances with additional terms, the effect of the new § 2-207 is to leave the issues of what is or is not included in a contract to the courts. The courts will determine, on a case-by-case basis, what is included as part of the contract, in some cases regardless of what the "record" provides. Revised § 2-207 applies to merchants and nonmerchants alike and regardless of whether the parties use forms.

Figure 23-1 is a graphic picture of the rules on acceptance and contract terms under current Article 2 when additional terms are proposed. Figure 23-2 provides a diagram of Revised § 2-207.

Even without all the UCC provisions on contract terms, an offeror may expressly or by conduct agree to a term added by the offeree to its acceptance of the offer.

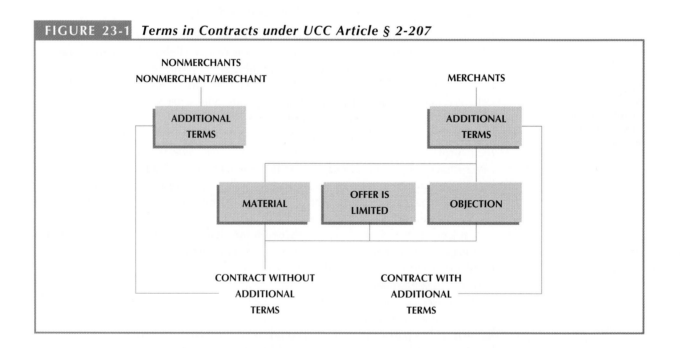

FIGURE 23-1 *Terms in Contracts under UCC Article § 2-207*

---

[22] *Transwestern Pipeline Co. v Monsanto Co.,* 53 Cal Rptr 2d 887 (Ct App 1996). Revised UCC Article 2 makes changes in the way these additional terms operate. When there is a record of an agreement, with no objection, the terms in the record are the terms of the contract.

[23] Damage limitations clauses are considered material. *Jom, Inc. v Adell Plastics, Inc.,* 193 F3d 47 (1st Cir 1999).

[24] A statute of limitations of one year added to the acceptance of an offer is considered a material change because it limits so severely the amount of time for bringing suit on the contract. *American Tempering, Inc. v Craft Architectural Metals Corp.,* 483 NYS2d 304 (1985).

FIGURE 23-2   *Terms in Contracts under UCC Revised Article § 2-207*

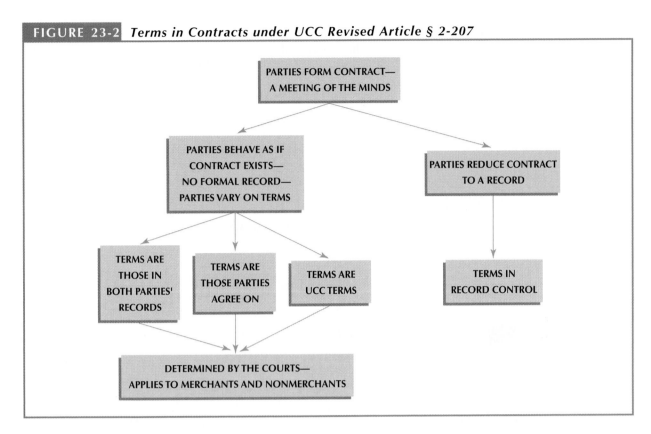

The offeror may agree orally or in writing to the additional term. There can be acceptance by conduct of the additional term if the parties just perform their obligations under the contract with knowledge that the term has been added by the offeree.[25]

(3) Conflicting Terms in Acceptance.   In some situations, the offeree has not added a different term from the original offer but has instead proposed terms that contradict the terms of the offer. **For Example,** a buyer's purchase order may require the seller to offer full warranty protection, whereas the seller's invoice may include a disclaimer of all warranties. The buyer's purchase order may include a clause that provides "payment in 30 days same as cash," whereas the seller's invoice may include a term that has "10 days same as cash." Once again, it is clear that the parties intended to enter into a contract, and the subject matter is also clear. The task for Article 2 becomes one of establishing the rules that determine the terms of a contract when both sides have used different forms. However, if there are conflicting terms on the basic requirements (such as price) for formation, the courts may conclude that the parties have not met minds.[26]

When a term of an acceptance conflicts with a term of an offer but it is clear that the parties intended to be bound by a contract, the UCC still recognizes the

---

[25] Revised UCC §2-207 provides: (3) Conduct by both parties which recognizes the existence of a contract is sufficient to establish a contract for sale although the writings of the parties do not otherwise establish a contract. In such case the terms of the particular contract consist of those terms on which the writings of the parties agree, together with any supplementary terms incorporated under any other provisions of this Act.

[26] *Howard Const. Co. v Jeff-Cole Quarries, Inc.,* App, 669 SW2d 221(1984), where the acceptance changed the price there was not an acceptance but a counteroffer.

formation of a contract. The terms that are conflicting cancel each other and are ignored. The contract then consists of the terms of the offer and acceptance that agree. **For Example,** if one party's contract form provided for full warranty protection and the other party's form provided for no warranty protection, the terms cancel each other out, and the parties' contract includes only those warranties provided under Article 2 (see Chapter 25 for a discussion of those warranties).

(g) DEFENSES TO FORMATION Article 2 incorporates the common law defenses to formation of contracts by reference to the common law defenses in § 1-103 (see Chapter 14 for a full discussion of those defenses). **For Example,** a party to a contract who can establish that the other party engaged in fraud to get the contract formed may cancel the contract and recover for losses that result from any damages for goods already delivered or payment already made.

CASE SUMMARY

Cuts Like a Knife and More Than Once

FACTS: U.S. Surgical manufactures medical surgical instruments and markets the instruments to hospitals. U.S. Surgical registered trademarks on its own name and its products' names and registered patents on its products. The packaging for U.S. Surgical's disposable medical instruments is labeled "for single use only." As an example, one label contains the following language: "Unless opened or damaged, contents of package are sterile. DO NOT RESTERILIZE. For multiple use during a SINGLE surgical procedure. DISCARD AFTER USE." The instruction booklets contain similar language in the "Cautions" section: "These devices are provided STERILE and are intended for use during a SINGLE procedure only. DISCARD AFTER USE. DO NOT RESTERILIZE."

Orris provides a service to the hospitals that purchase U.S. Surgical's disposable instruments. After the hospitals use or open the instruments, Orris cleans, resterilizes, and/or resharpens the instruments for future use and returns them to the hospitals from which they came. U.S. Surgical admits that Orris may resterilize opened but unused instruments notwithstanding the "do not resterilize" language. The Food and Drug Administration requires the "single use only" or similar language on the labels of instruments that U.S. Surgical designates as disposable. The same or similar "single use only" language is also used on U.S. Surgical's nonpatented disposable instruments. The only significant difference between U.S. Surgical's labels for its patented and nonpatented instruments is that the labels for the patented instruments contain the U.S. patent number. U.S. Surgical filed suit asserting that reprocessing, repackaging, and reuse of its disposable instruments constituted a violation of its patent and trademark rights.

DECISION: The sale of medical instruments is governed by Article 2 of the UCC. Even if the product label is considered a written confirmation of the order under UCC § 2-207, the "single use only" term is not binding on the customer if the additional term materially alters the agreement and the customer does not confirm the seller's expressly conditional acceptance requiring the additional term or otherwise expressly assent to the additional term. The single-use terms on the package were a material change that the hospitals were free to reject and that they did not accept by use. The warning on the package did not make the use of the instruments the acceptance of the package terms. [**U.S. Surgical Corp. v Orris, Inc.,** 5 F Supp 2d 1201 (D Kan 1998); Affirmed 185 F3d 885 (10th Cir. 1999) and 230 F3d 1382 (Fed Cir 2000)]

(1) *Unconscionability.* The UCC includes an additional contract defense for parties to a sale contract called *unconscionability.*[27] This section permits a court to refuse to enforce a sales contract that it finds to be **unconscionable,** which is generally defined as grossly unfair.[28] A court may also find a clause or portions of a contract to be unconscionable and refuse to enforce those clauses or sections.[29]

unconscionable
unreasonable, not guided or restrained by conscience and often referring to a contract grossly unfair to one party because of the superior bargaining powers of the other party.

(2) *Illegality.* At common law, a contract is void if its subject matter itself is illegal, such as a contract for hire to murder someone. Under the UCC, a contract for the sale of heroin would be void. Likewise, a contract for the sale of a recalled or banned toy would be void.

(3) *The Effect of Illegal Sale.* An illegal sale or contract to sell cannot be enforced. As a general rule, courts will not aid either party in recovering money or property transferred under an illegal agreement.

4. TERMS IN THE FORMED CONTRACT

As noted earlier, contracts can be formed under Article 2 with terms of performance still missing or open. A contract is formed with just the quantity agreed on, but there are issues that must be resolved if the contract is to be completed. Article 2 has provisions for such missing terms.

CPA

(a) Price If the price for the goods is not expressly fixed by the contract, the price may be an open term, whereby the parties merely indicate how the price should be determined at a later time. In the absence of any reference to price, the price will be a reasonable price at the time of the delivery of the goods, which is generally the market price.[30]

Parties often use formulas for determining price in sales of goods. The price itself is missing from the contract until the formula is applied at some future time. The so-called **cost plus** formula for determining price has been used a great deal, particularly in commercial contracts. Under this formula, the buyer pays the seller the seller's costs for manufacture or obtaining the goods plus a specified percentage as profit.

cost plus method of determining the purchase price or contract price equal to the seller's or contractor's costs plus a stated percentage as the profit.

The UCC allows contracts that expressly provide that one of the parties may determine the price. In such a case, that party must act in good faith, another requirement under the UCC that applies to merchants and nonmerchants in the formation and performance of their contracts.[31]

CPA

(b) Output and Requirements Contracts The **output contract** and the **requirements contract**[32] do not specify the quantity to be sold or purchased. Instead, the contract amount is what the seller produces or the buyer requires. **For Example,** a homeowner may contract to purchase propane fuel for her winter heating needs.

output contract contract of a producer to sell its entire production or output to a buyer.

requirements contract contract in which the buyer buys its needs (requirements) from the seller.

---

[27] UCC § 2-302. *El Paso Natural Gas Co. v Minco Oil & Gas Co., Inc.,* 8 SW3d 309 (Tex 1999).

[28] Disparity in bargaining power is an issue but is not controlling. In *Intrastate Piping & Controls, Inc. v Robert-James Sales, Inc.,* 39 UCC Rep Serv 2d 347 (Ill Cir Ct 1999), a clause limiting remedies to replacement of defective pipe with no additional damages was upheld because while the seller was a large, national business and the buyer a small, local business, the contract merely incorporated industry practice in terms of remedies.

[29] An example would be voiding exorbitant interest charges but enforcing the underlying sale.

[30] UCC § 2-305(1) provides, "the price is a reasonable price at the time for delivery."

[31] Good faith requires that the party act honestly and, in the case of a merchant, also requires that the party follow reasonable commercial standards of fair dealing that are recognized in the trade. UCC §§ 1-201(1)(a), 2-103(1)(b); *Uptown Heights Associates, Ltd., Partnership v Seafirst Corp.,* 891 P2d 693 (Or 1995).

[32] UCC § 2-306; *Lenape Resources Corp. v Tennessee Gas Pipeline Co.,* 925 SW2d 565 (Tex 1996).

The propane company agrees to sell her the amount of propane she needs, which will vary from year to year according to the winter weather, her time at home, and other factors. Although the open quantity in contracts such as these introduces an element of uncertainty, such sales contracts are valid but subject to two limitations: (1) The parties must act in good faith and (2) the quantity offered or demanded must not be unreasonably disproportionate to prior output or requirements or to a stated estimate. With these restrictions, the homeowner will obtain all of the propane she needs for heating but could not use her particularly beneficial price under her open-quantity contract to purchase additional propane to sell to others.

(c) Indefinite Duration Term   When the sales contract is a continuing contract, such as one calling for periodic delivery of coal, but no time is set for the life of the contract, the contract runs for a reasonable time. It may be terminated by notice from either party to the other party.

CPA

(d) Changes in Terms: Modification of Contract   An agreement to modify a contract for the sale of goods is binding even though the modification is not supported by consideration.[33] The modification is valid so long as the agreement is voluntary. **For Example,** suppose that Chester's Drug Store has agreed to purchase 300 bottles of vitamins from Pro-Life, Inc., at a price of $3.71 per bottle. Pro-Life has experienced substantial cost increases from its suppliers and asks Chester to pay $3.74 per bottle. Chester is not required to agree to such a price increase because it has a valid contract for the lower price. If Chester agrees to the price increase, however, the agreement for the higher price is valid despite the lack of additional consideration on the part of Pro-Life. Chester may agree to the higher price because Pro-Life's price is still much lower than its competitors and Chester has a longstanding relationship with Pro-Life and values its customer service. However, Pro-Life could not threaten to cut off Chester's supply in order to obtain the price increase because that would be a breach of contract and would also be duress that would invalidate Chester's consent to the higher price. (See Chapter 14 for a discussion of duress.)

CPA

parol evidence rule rule that prohibits the introduction in evidence of oral or written statements made prior to or contemporaneously with the execution of a complete written contract, deed, or instrument, in the absence of fraud, accident, or mistake.

(e) Contradicting Terms: Parol Evidence Rule   The **parol evidence rule** (see Chapter 17 for a complete discussion) applies to the sale of goods, with the slight modification that a writing is not presumed to represent the entire contract of the parties unless the court specifically decides that it does.[34] If the court so decides, parol evidence is not admissible to add to or contradict the terms of the writing. **For Example,** suppose that Ralph Rhodes and Tana Preuss negotiate the sale of Ralph's 1965 Mustang to Tana. During their discussions, Ralph agrees to pay for an inspection and for new upholstery for the car. However, Tana and Ralph sign a simple sales contract that includes only a description of the Mustang and the price. Tana cannot enforce the two provisions because she failed to have them written into their final agreement. The parol evidence rule requires the parties to be certain that everything they want is in their agreement before they sign. The courts cannot referee disputes over collateral agreements the parties fail to put in writing.

---

[33] UCC § 2-209(1); *Horbach v Kacz Marek,* 934 F Supp 981 (ND Ill 1996), aff'd, 388 F3d 969 (7th Cir 2002).
[34] UCC § 2-202.

If the court decides that the writing was not intended to represent the entire contract, the writing may be supplemented by additional extrinsic evidence, including the proof of additional terms as long as these terms are not inconsistent with the written terms. Parol evidence may also be admitted to interpret contract terms or show what the parties meant by their words. The parol evidence rule also does not prohibit the proof of fraud, misrepresentation, and any other defenses in formation.

(f) INTERPRETING CONTRACT TERMS: COURSE OF DEALING AND USAGE OF TRADE   The patterns of doing business the parties develop through their prior contractual transactions, or **course of dealing,** become part of their contract.[35] These patterns may be used to find what was intended by the express provisions in their contract and to supply otherwise missing terms. **For Example,** if the parties had 10 previous agreements and payment was always made on the 30th day following delivery, that conduct could be used to interpret the meaning of a clause "payment due in 30 days" when the start of the 30 days is not specifically agreed to in the contract.

In addition, the customs of the industry, or **usage of trade,** are adopted by courts in their interpretation of contract terms. **For Example,** suppose that a contract provides for the sale of mohair. There are two types of mohair: adult and kid. Because adult mohair is cheaper and easier to find, industry custom provides that unless the parties specifically place the term *kid* with the term *mohair* in the contract, the contract is one for the sale of adult mohair. Under Article 2, the court need not find that a contract is ambiguous or incomplete in order to examine the parties' pattern of previous conduct as well as industry custom.[36]

> **course of dealing** pattern of performance between two parties to a contract.

> **usage of trade** language and customs of an industry.

ETHICS & THE LAW

Triple Crown America, Inc., said that it had been involved in extensive discussions with Biosynth AG, a German company, to be Biosynth's exclusive distributor for melotonin to the U.S. "natural food" market. The companies, in fact, began performance of a distribution contract with Biosynth sending melotonin to Triple Crown. Triple Crown, however, said that the amount sent was insufficient for national distribution. Biosynth was, in fact, sending melotonin to other distributors and not honoring what Triple Crown maintained was an exclusive sales arrangement. In addition, an article in the *Chemical Marketing Reporter* quoted a "spokeswoman" for Biosynth as saying that it had an exclusive distributorship arrangement with Triple Crown.

Biosynth said that it never formalized its arrangements with Triple Crown and was free to deal with others. Should Biosynth be held to its publicly reported statements, or should it be able to rely on contract formation issues and the lack of specifics as a defense to the agreement? Do you think the article is an admission of the contract?*

---

* Triple Crown America, Inc. v Biosynth AG, 38 UCC Rep Serv 2d 746 (1999).

---

[35] UCC § 2-208. Under Revised Article 2, § 2-208 is eliminated for those states that have adopted Revised Article 1 because Revised Article 1 contains the definition for course of performance.

[36] Revised § 2-202 provides different rules for the use of extrinsic evidence but still includes "course of performance, course of dealing, or usage of trade" as sources for interpretation of contract terms.

5. BULK TRANSFERS

Bulk transfer law, Article 6 of the UCC, was created to deal with situations in which sellers of businesses fail to pay the creditors of the business and instead use the proceeds of the sale for their own use.

In 1989, the NCCUSL recommended that UCC Article 6 be repealed because it was obsolete and had little value in the modern business world. At the same time, the commissioners adopted a revised version of Article 6 (Alternative B) for adoption by those states that desired to retain the concept for bulk sales. Rather than relying on the bulk sales law, the trend is for suppliers to use UCC Article 9, Secured Transactions, for protection (See Chapter 34).

 B   FORM OF SALES CONTRACT

A contract for the sale of goods may be oral or written. However, under the UCC, certain types of contracts must be in writing or they cannot be enforced in court.

CASE SUMMARY

It's Elementary: A Crayon-Scrawled Contract Is Good Enough for the Statute of Frauds

FACTS: Michelle Rosenfeld, an art dealer, alleges she contracted with artist Jean-Michel Basquiat to buy three of his paintings. The works that she claims she contracted to buy were entitled *Separation of the K, Atlas,* and *Untitled Head.* Rosenfeld went to Basquiat's apartment on October 25, 1982; while she was there, Basquiat agreed to sell her three paintings for $4,000 each, and she picked out three. Basquiat asked for a cash deposit of 10 percent; Rosenfeld left the loft but returned later with $1,000 in cash, which she paid to Basquiat. When she asked for a receipt, he insisted on drawing up a contract and got down on the floor and wrote it out in crayon on a large piece of paper, remarking that someday this contract would be worth money. The handwritten document listed the three paintings, bore Rosenfeld's signature and Basquiat's signature and stated: "$12,000—$1,000 DEPOSIT = Oct 25 82." Rosenfeld later returned to Basquiat's loft to discuss delivery, but Basquiat convinced her to wait for at least two years so that he could show the paintings at exhibitions. After Basquiat's death, the estate argued that there was no contract because the statute of frauds made the agreement unenforceable. The estate contended that a written contract for the sale of goods must include the date of delivery. From a judgment in favor of the estate, Rosenfeld appealed.

DECISION: The contract for the sale of three paintings is governed by the UCC, and its statute of frauds applies to "transactions in goods for $500 which must be in writing or they are unenforceable. All that is required for a writing is that it provide some basis for believing that there is a real transaction." The writing supplied in this case indicated the price, the date, the specific paintings involved, and that Rosenfeld paid a deposit. It also bore the signatures of the buyer and seller and satisfied the requirements of UCC § 2-201. Because the writing, scrawled in crayon by Jean-Michel Basquiat on a large piece of paper, easily satisfied the requirements of § 2-201 of the UCC, the alleged contract is valid. [**Rosenfeld v Basquiat, 78 F3d 84 (2d Cir 1996)**]

CPA

6. AMOUNT

Whenever the sales price of goods is $500 or more, the sales contract must be in writing to be enforceable. Under Revised Article 2, this amount has been increased to $5,000.[37] The section of the UCC that establishes this requirement is known as the **statute of frauds.** (For more detail on the statute of frauds and its role in common law contracts, see Chapter 17.)

statute of frauds statute that, to prevent fraud through the use of perjured testimony, requires that certain kinds of contracts be in writing to be binding or enforceable.

7. NATURE OF THE WRITING REQUIRED

The requirement for a written contract may be satisfied by a complete written contract signed by both parties. Under Article 2, so that the state laws will be consistent with federal laws on electronic signatures (see Chapter 11), the requirement of a writing has been changed to the requirement of a "record." Under Article 2, two merchants can reduce their agreement to a record in much simpler fashion because the detail required under common law is not required to satisfy the UCC standards.

(a) TERMS   To satisfy the UCC statute of frauds, the record must indicate that there has been a completed transaction covering certain goods. Specifically, the record must (1) indicate that a sale or contract to sell has been made and (2) state the quantity of goods involved.[38] Any other missing terms may be supplied by reference to Code sections (discussed earlier) or shown by parol evidence.

CPA

(b) SIGNATURE   The record must be signed or authenticated by the person who is being held to the contract or by the authorized agent of that person. Whatever form of authentication is being used must be put in place in the record with the intention of authenticating the record. The authentication may consist of initials or may be a printed, stamped, electronic, or typewritten signature placed with the intent to authenticate.[39] **For Example,** when you enter into a contract as part of an online transaction, you are generally asked to check a box that states that you understand you are entering into a contract. Once you check that box, a pop-up appears that explains that you are about to charge your credit card or account and that you have agreed to the purchase. These steps are used to authenticate your electronic version of a signature.

The UCC statute of frauds does provide an important exception to the signature requirement for merchants that enables merchants to expedite their transactions. This exception allows merchants to create a confirmation memorandum of their oral agreement as evidence of an agreement. A merchant's *confirmation memorandum* is a letter, memo, or electronic document signed or authenticated by one of the two merchant parties to an oral agreement.[40] This memorandum can be used by either party to enforce the contract. **For Example,** suppose that Ralph has orally agreed to purchase 1,000 pounds of T-bone steak from Jane for $5.79 per pound. Jane sends

---

[37] Under Revised Article 2, the new amount of $5,000 is found at UCC Rev. Art. 2, § 2-201.

[38] *Kelly-Stehney & Assoc., Inc. v McDonald's Indus. Products, Inc.,* 893 NW2d 394 (Mich 2005).

[39] UCC §§ 1-201(39), 2-201; *Nebraska Builders Products Co. v Industrial Erectors, Inc.,* 478 NW2d 257 (Neb 1992). Revised Article 2 permits electronic forms and signature and "record" includes e-mail, EDI transmissions, faxes, and printouts of screen pages reflecting transactions.

[40] *GPL Treatment, Ltd. v Louisiana-Pacific Corp.,* 914 P2d 682 (Ore 1996). A farmer was held not to be a merchant because of his lack of experience in selling his crops and a confirmation memo could not be used to enforce a contract against him. *Harvest State Co-op v Anderson,* 577 NW2d 381 (Wis App 1998), review denied, 584 NW2d 124 (Wis 1998).

Ralph a signed memo that reads, "This is to confirm our telephone conversation earlier today. I will sell you 1,000 pounds of T-bone @ $5.79 per pound." Either Ralph or Jane can use the memo to enforce the contract.

A confirming memo, in various forms of communication, sent by one merchant to another results in a binding and enforceable contract that satisfies the statute of frauds. Such a confirmation binds the nonsigning or nonauthenticating merchant, just as if he had signed the letter or a contract. A merchant can object when he receives

CASE SUMMARY

A Real Basket Case

FACTS: The Greenbrier Basket Company (GBC), a goods distributor, entered into a business relationship in October 2003 to sell woven baskets to The Pampered Chef (TPC). On October 28, 2003, an executive sales agreement was drafted but never signed by the parties.

The ordering process would begin with TPC e-mailing GBC an offer to fill an order. GBC would then go to TPC's Web site and fill out the purchase order using TPC's purchase order management system and would click on the Accept P.O. button at the end of the terms and conditions field.

TPC sent Mark Beal (a GBC employee) an e-mail with an attachment showing him how to use TPC's purchase order management system, including the following:

Clicking on the Accept P.O. button will cause the terms and conditions of the purchase order to pop-up. The user should review these terms and conditions and click the Accept P.O. button at the bottom of the pop-up screen. . . . If the purchase order is not acceptable in it's [sic] current form, the user may click on the Reject and Request Changes button. This causes a pop-up window to appear where the user may enter a free-form text describing the reason for rejecting the purchase order and request changes that would make the purchase order acceptable.

Clause 17 of the Terms and Conditions in TPC's purchase management order system states:

This Purchase Order shall be deemed to have been made in Addison, Illinois USA and shall be governed by and construed in accordance with the laws of State of Illinois [sic]. The sole and exclusive jurisdiction for the purpose of resolving any dispute shall be the United States District Court, Northern District of Illinois, Eastern Division.

When disputes over orders and payments arose, GBC filed suit against TPC in Kansas for breach of contract. TPC moved to dismiss the suit for improper venue.

DECISION: TPC's e-mails containing purchase order information constituted an offer to buy baskets. The e-mails consisted of information about the quantity of baskets to be bought, price, shipment information, and delivery dates. They also provided that to accept the P.O., GBC should go via Internet to TPC's Web site.

GBC was under a duty to read and understand the terms and conditions prior to clicking the Accept P.O. button because this was the formal acceptance required by TPC's offer to purchase baskets. Failure to read or understand the terms and conditions is not a valid reason to set those provisions aside.

A meeting of the minds requirement is proved when the minds of the parties met on the same matter and agreed up on the terms of the contract. GBC agreed upon these terms and conditions published on TPC's Web site by clicking the Accept P.O. button.

The case was dismissed in Kansas and transferred to Illinois. [**Home Basket Co., LLC v Pampered Chef, Ltd. 55 UCC Rep Serv 2d 792 (D Kan 2005)**]

the confirmation memo, but he must do so immediately because the confirming memo takes effect in 10 days if there is no objection.[41] This confirmation procedure makes it necessary for merchants to watch their communications and all forms of correspondence and to act within 10 days of receiving a confirmation.

(c) Purpose of Execution   A writing or record can satisfy a statute of frauds even though it was not made for that purpose. For example, if a buyer writes to the seller to complain that the goods have not been delivered, there is proof of the contract because the buyer's complaint indicates that there was some kind of understanding or an acknowledgment that there was a sale of those goods.

(d) Particular Writings   Formal contracts, bills of sale, letters, and telegrams are common forms of writings that satisfy the recorder writing requirement.[42] E-mails, faxes, EDI communications, and verifications through screen printouts will generally satisfy the requirement as to record and authentication so long as they meet minimum formation standards and comply with the requirement of the UCC to specify any quantity. Two or more writings grouped together may constitute a record that will be sufficient to satisfy the UCC statute of frauds.[43]

8. EFFECT OF NONCOMPLIANCE

A sales agreement that does not satisfy the statute of frauds cannot be enforced. However, the oral contract itself is not unlawful and may be voluntarily performed by the parties.

9. EXCEPTIONS TO REQUIREMENT OF A WRITING

The absence of a writing does not always mean that a sales contract is unenforceable. Article 2 provides some exceptions for the enforceability of certain oral contracts.

CPA   **(a) Specially Manufactured Goods**   No writing is required when the goods are specially made for the buyer and are of such an unusual nature that they are not suitable for sale in the ordinary course of the seller's business. **For Example,** a manufacturer who builds a stair lift for a two-story home cannot resell the $8,000 device to someone else because it is specially built for the stairs in the buyer's home. The manufacturer could enforce the oral contract against the buyer despite the price being in excess of $500 ($5,000 under Revised Article 2).

For this nonresellable goods exception to apply, the seller must have made a substantial beginning in manufacturing the goods or, if a distributor is the seller, in procuring them before the buyer indicates she will not honor the oral contract.[44] The stair lift manufacturer, for example, must have progressed to a point beyond

---

[41] A confirmation memo is not effective when there is no underlying agreement or the parties did not agree on the terms. *Precise-Marketing Corp. v Simpson Paper Co.,* 38 UCC Rep Serv 2d 717, 1999 WL 259518 (SDNY 1999).

[42] Contract terms can be pieced together from invoices sent over the period of the agreement and that the buyer paid. *Fleming Companies, Inc. v. Krist Oil Co.,* 324 F Supp 933, 54 UCC Rep Serv 2d 120 (WD Wi 2004).

[43] *American Dredging Co. v Plaza Petroleum, Inc.,* 799 F Supp 1335 (EDNY 1993), vacated in part on issues related to negligence and seaworthiness, 845 F Supp 91 (EDNY 1993). Letters grouped together satisfy UCC § 2-201. *Pepsi-Cola Co. v Steak 'N Shake, Inc.,* 981 F Supp 1149 (SD Ind 1997). Letters and faxes also satisfy the writing requirement. *Den Norske Stats Oljeselskap,* 992 F Supp 913 (SD Tex 1998), aff'd, 161 F3d 8 (5th Cir 1998).

[44] *Golden State Porcelain Inc. v Swid Powell Design Inc.,* 37 UCC Rep Serv 2d 928 (NY 1999). Where manufacture has not begun, this exception to the statute of frauds does not apply. *EMSG Sys. Div., Inc. v Miltope Corp.,* 37 UCC Rep Serv 2d 39 (EDNC 1998).

simply ordering materials for construction of the lift because those materials could be used for any lift.

CPA **(b) Receipt and Acceptance**   An oral sales contract may be enforced if it can be shown that the goods were delivered by the seller and were both received and accepted by the buyer even if the amount involved is over $500 ($5,000 Revised) and there is no writing. The receipt and acceptance of the goods by the buyer makes the contract enforceable despite the statute of frauds issue. Both receipt and acceptance of the goods by the buyer must be shown. If only part of the goods have been received and accepted, the contract may be enforced only insofar as it relates to those goods received and accepted.[45] **For Example,** suppose that Wayne ordered 700 baseball jackets at a price of $72 each from Pamela. The order was taken over the telephone, and Wayne emphasized urgency. Pamela immediately

---

THINKING THINGS THROUGH

Stop the Presses! Or At Least Stop Printing!

Clinton Press of Tolland operated a printing press and, for several decades, provided written materials, including books and pamphlets for Adelma G. Simmons, a woman who operated a farm known as Caprilands Herb Farm, an attraction for tourists. The books and pamphlets contained informational articles as well as collections of recipes. They were clearly identified as Caprilands Herb Farm materials.

Due to limited storage space at Caprilands, Clinton and Simmons agreed that the written materials would remain stored at the print shop until Simmons decided that delivery was necessary. The materials were delivered either routinely, based on Simmons' ordinary need for materials, or upon her request for a special delivery. After each delivery, Clinton sent an invoice requesting payment by Simmons, who honored these invoices.

In 1991, the town of Tolland acquired the land on which Simmons resided. In early 1997, Simmons was notified that she would have to leave the property by the end of the year. She closed Caprilands Herb Farm as a result. Clinton and Simmons agreed that the materials printed for Caprilands and stored at the print shop would be delivered on an accelerated basis. Simmons directed an employee, Jack Lee, to begin to transport the stored materials to Caprilands, and he made occasional trips to the print shop to do so.

On December 3, 1997, after several months of deterioration of her physical health, Simmons died. Simmons' will was admitted to probate, and Mr. Edward Cook was appointed executor of her estate. Clinton submitted a claim against the estate for $24,599.38 for unpaid deliveries to Caprilands. These deliveries took place from February 12, 1997, to December 11, 1997, with the last two deliveries occurring after Simmons' death. The court denied the claim.*

Why would the court deny the claim? Think through the UCC Article 2 issues you see in the situation. Should the decision be reversed?

---
* *Kalas v Cook,* 800 A2d 553 (Conn. 2002).

---

[45] *Allied Grape Growers v Bronco Wine Co.,* 249 Cal Rptr 872 (Ct App 1988).

shipped the 320 jackets she had on hand and assured Wayne the remainder would be finished during the next two weeks. Wayne received the 320 jackets and sold them to a golf tournament sponsor. Wayne refused to pay Pamela because the contract was oral. Wayne must pay for the 320 jackets, but Pamela will not be able to recover for the remaining 380 jackets she manufactured.

CPA

(c) Payment An oral contract may be enforced if the buyer has made full payment. In the case of partial payment for divisible units of goods, a contract may be enforced only with respect to the goods for which payment has been made and accepted. In the Pamela and Wayne example, if the circumstances were changed so that Pamela agreed to ship only if Wayne sent payment, then Pamela, upon accepting the payment, would be required to perform the contract for the amount of payment received. If partial payment is made for indivisible goods, such as an automobile, a partial payment avoids the statute of frauds and is sufficient proof to permit enforcement of the entire oral contract.

(d) Admission An oral contract may be enforced against a party if that party admits in pleadings, testimony, or otherwise in court that a contract for sale was made. The contract, however, is not enforceable beyond the quantity of goods admitted.[46]

10. NONCODE REQUIREMENTS

In addition to the UCC requirements for contracts that must be evidenced by a record, other statutes may impose requirements. **For Example,** state consumer protection legislation commonly requires that there be a detailed contract and that a copy of it be given to the consumer.

11. BILL OF SALE

bill of sale writing signed by the seller reciting that the personal property therein described has been sold to the buyer.

Regardless of the requirement of the statute of frauds, the parties may wish to execute a writing as evidence or proof of the sale. Through custom, this writing has become known as a **bill of sale,** but it is neither a bill nor a contract. It is merely a receipt or writing signed by the seller reciting the transfer to the buyer of the title to the described property. A bill of sale can be used as proof of an otherwise oral agreement.

UNIFORM LAW FOR INTERNATIONAL SALES

Contracts for the International Sale of Goods (CISG) uniform international contract code contracts for international sale of goods.

The United Nations Convention on **Contracts for the International Sale of Goods (CISG)** applies to contracts between parties in the United States and parties in the other nations that have ratified the convention.[47] The provisions of this convention or international agreement have been strongly influenced by Article 2 of the UCC. The international rules of the convention automatically apply to contracts for the sale of goods if the buyer and seller have places of business in different countries that have ratified the convention. The parties may, however, choose to exclude the convention provisions in their sales contract.

---

[46] *Harvey v McKinney,* 581 NE2d 786 (Ill App 1991).

[47] 52 Fed Reg 6262 (1987). While the list of adopting countries is always increasing, those countries involved in NAFTA, GATT, and the European Union (EU) (see Chapter 7) have adopted the CISG. For complete text, commentary, and case law on CISG, go to **http://www.cisg.law.pace.edu.**

12. SCOPE OF THE CISG

The CISG does not govern all contracts between parties in the countries that have ratified it. The CISG does not apply to goods bought for personal, family, or household use. The CISG also does not apply to contracts in which the predominant part of the obligations of the party who furnishes the goods consists of the supply of labor or other services. In addition, the CISG does not apply the seller's liability to any person for death or personal injury caused by the goods.

The CISG governs the formation of the contract of sale and the rights and obligations of the seller and the buyer arising from such a contract. The CISG provides a basis for answering questions and settling issues the parties failed to cover in their contract. The CISG has five chapters and 101 articles, and the articles have no titles to them. There is a limited body of case law interpreting the CISG because so many of the decisions under the CISG come through arbitration and other forms of dispute resolution, typical of international commercial arrangements.

13. IRREVOCABLE OFFERS

An offer under the CISG is irrevocable if it states that it is irrevocable or if the offeree reasonably relies on it as being irrevocable. Such a CISG offer is irrevocable even if there is no writing and no consideration. This provision differs from the common law, which requires consideration for an offer to be irrevocable, and from the UCC's merchant's firm offer, which must be in writing to be irrevocable.

14. STATUTE OF FRAUDS

Under the CISG, a contract for the sale of goods need not be in any particular form and can be proven by any means. The convention, by this provision, has abolished the statute of frauds' requirement of a writing. Article 11 of the CISG provides, "A contract of sale need not be concluded in or evidenced by writing and is not subject to any other requirement as to form. It may be proved by any means, including witnesses." Countries may, however, retain the UCC requirements of the statute of frauds by requiring certain contracts to be in writing.

15. THE MIRROR-IMAGE RULE RETURNS UNDER CISG

Under Article 19 of the CISG, the rules of common law acceptance with regard to additional terms in acceptance are the dominating theme for acceptance. The UCC provisions on additional terms are recognized in part, but the parties cannot vary certain aspects of the offer if they wish to form a contract. If one party objects or the provision is material, then such additional terms and provisions are eliminated from the parties' agreement.

LEASES OF GOODS

Leases of goods represent a significant part of both contract law and the economy. There are more than $240 billion worth of lease transactions in the United States

CASE SUMMARY

No Stomach for Fitness Equipment

FACTS: On August 5, 1993, Reeder bought a premier family membership with Bally's. Shortly after purchasing the membership, Reeder, accompanied by her husband, attended two orientation sessions at Bally's Chesapeake Club.

On August 19, 1993, the Reeders made their third visit and first nonorientation visit to the club. Both Reeders exercised on various pieces of exercise equipment. Ms. Reeder experienced no difficulty until she tried to use a Pyramid Stomach Curl Machine, designed to strengthen the abdominal muscles. The stomach curl machine can be adjusted to provide greater or lesser resistance by selecting weights of appropriate denomination. She set the machine's weight at 20 or 30 pounds, a weight she had comfortably used on other exercise machines; she looked for a seat belt but did not see one. After reading approximately two lines of written instructions attached to the machine explaining its use, she attempted to perform the exercise but fell forward and struck her head on something near the base of the machine and passed out. Ms. Reeder, who suffers from continuing neurological difficulties, sued for breach of express and implied warranties or lease agreement and for negligence. Bally moved for summary judgment.

DECISION: Reeder did not purchase equipment. She purchased the right to use equipment that could be removed and replaced by Bally's. The membership is not a bailment or lease of any individual item of equipment under the UCC. Reeder was simply a business invitee on the defendant's premises.

Even if the membership agreement could be construed as creating a bailment or lease, there was no evidence that Bally's granted any express warranties or that it breached any implied warranties applicable to bailments or leases. Plaintiff presented no evidence that the exercise machine she used was defective when she was injured, nor was there any evidence that the machine was inherently dangerous. [**Reeder v Bally's Total Fitness Corp., 963 F Supp 530 (ED Va 1996)**]

CASE SUMMARY

I'm Just the Lender; I Never Drove the Car

FACTS: Judith J. Oliveira (Oliveira) suffered severe injuries in a 1998 automobile accident when a car that Chase Manhattan Automotive Finance Corporation owned—and leased to Salvatore Lombardi—collided with the rear end of Oliveira's vehicle. Lessee Lombardi's son, Steven Lombardi, was driving the car when the accident occurred. Oliveira filed suit against both Lombardis as well as Chase. The trial court dismissed the action against Chase on summary judgment. Oliveira appealed.

DECISION: The court held that Chase—as the lessor, legal titleholder, and registered owner of the vehicle in question—was the "owner" of the vehicle under the Rhode Island statute that imposes liability on bailors for injuries and liabilities resulting from the use of their property. In a landmark decision, the court imposed vicarious liability on auto lessors for the torts of their lessees occurring as they drive the leased vehicles. [**Oliveira v Lombardi, 794 A2d 453 (RI 2002)**]

each year, an amount equal to roughly one-third of all capital investment each year in the United States.[48] One-fourth of all vehicles in the United States are leased. Article 2A of the UCC codifies the law of leases for tangible movable goods. Article 2A applies to any transaction, regardless of form, that creates a lease of personal property or fixtures. Many of the provisions of Article 2 were carried over but changed to reflect differences in style, leasing terminology, or leasing practices.[49] As a practical matter, leases will be of durable goods, such as equipment and vehicles of any kind, computers, boats, airplanes, and household goods and appliances. A **lease** is "a transfer of the right to possession and use of goods for a term in return for consideration."[50]

lease agreement between the owner of property and a tenant by which the former agrees to give possession of the property to the latter for payment of rent. (Parties–landlord or lessor, tenant or lessee)

16. TYPES OF LEASES

Article 2A regulates consumer leases, commercial leases, finance leases, nonfinance leases, and subleases. These categories may overlap in some cases, such as when there is a commercial finance lease.

(a) Consumer Lease   A **consumer lease** is made by a merchant lessor regularly engaged in the business of leasing or selling the kinds of goods involved. A consumer lease is made to a natural person (not a corporation) who takes possession of the goods primarily for personal, family, or household use. Each state places a cap on the amount that will be considered a consumer lease. Section 2A-103(f) simply provides that the state should place its own amount in this section with the admonition to place the cap at a level that ensures that vehicle leases will be covered under the law.

consumer lease lease of goods by a natural person for personal, family, or household use.

(b) Commercial Lease   When a lease does not satisfy the definition of a consumer lease, it may be called a **nonconsumer** or a **commercial lease.** **For Example,** a contractor's one-year rental of a truck to haul building materials is a commercial lease.

nonconsumer lease lease that does not satisfy the definition of a consumer lease; also known as a *commercial lease.*

commercial lease any nonconsumer lease.

(c) Finance Lease   A **finance lease** is a three-party transaction involving a lessor, a lessee, and a supplier. Instead of going directly to a supplier for goods, the customer goes to a financier and tells the financier where to obtain the goods and what to obtain. The financier then acquires the goods and either leases or subleases the goods to its customer. The financier-lessor is in effect a paper channel, or conduit, between the supplier and the customer-lessee. The customer-lessee must approve the terms of the transaction between the supplier and the financier-lessor.[51]

finance lease three-party lease agreement in which there is a lessor, a lessee, and a financier.

---

[48] U.S. Department of Commerce, Bureau of Economic Analysis, International Trade Administration and Equipment Leasing Association of America, Trends and Forecasts for Equipment Leasing in the United States (2002).

[49] Forty-nine states (Louisiana has not adopted Article 2A), the District of Columbia, and the Virgin Islands have adopted all or some portions of Article 2A. Not all states have adopted the 1997 version of Article 2A, and some have adopted only selected portions of the 1997 version.

[50] UCC § 2A-103(1)(j). The definition of what constitutes a lease is the subject of continuing examination by the UCC Article 2A drafters and the American Law Institute. The questions being examined are installment contracts, rent-to-own contracts, and other such arrangements to determine whether these are leases, secured transactions, or sales of goods.

[51] UCC § 2A-103(1)(g). One of the evolving issues in lease financing is the relationship of the parties, the use of liens, and the role of Article 9 security interests (see Chapter 34). The NCCUSL has appointed a drafting committee to create a new uniform state Certificate of Title Act (COTA) so that the interrelationships of lien laws, Article 2, and Article 9 are clear.

17. FORM OF LEASE CONTRACT

The lease must be evidenced by a record if the total of the payments under the lease will be $1,000 or more. The record must be authenticated by the party against whom enforcement is sought. The record must describe the leased goods, state the term of the lease, and indicate that a lease contract has been made between the parties.[52]

18. WARRANTIES

Under Article 2A, the lessor, except in the case of finance leases, makes all usual warranties that are made by a seller in a sale of goods. In a finance lease, however, the real parties in interest are the supplier, who supplies the lessor with the goods, and the lessee, who leases the goods. The supplier and the lessee stand in a position similar to that of seller and buyer. The lessee looks to the supplier of the goods for warranties. Any warranties, express or implied, made by the supplier to the lessor are passed on to the lessee, who has a direct cause of action on them against the supplier regardless of the lack of privity.[53] **For Example,** if a consumer leased an auto and the auto had a defective steering mechanism that resulted in injury to the consumer, the consumer would have a cause of action against the auto manufacturer. The financier-lessor does not make any implied warranty, but does have liability for any express warranties it makes.

One area of lessor liability that has been evolving is that of the liability of the lessor to those who are injured by the lessee. In New York alone, there were almost $7 billion in vicarious liability claims against automobile lessors in 2004. Vicarious liability suits result, for example, when the lessee of an auto is in an accident. A third party is injured as a result of the lessee's accident. The injured party can recover from the lessee, but increasingly, third parties have been turning to the lessor for recovery.[54] Twenty-one states have vicarious liability statutes. Other states have no statutes, and some states have vicarious liability by case law.[55] Congress has legislation pending to limit the vicarious liability of lessors to third parties for injuries caused by the lessees.[56] Many financing companies and leasing firms have stopped doing business in states in which they have exposure for the injuries caused by their lessees.[57]

19. IRREVOCABLE PROMISES: COMMERCIAL FINANCE LEASES

Under ordinary contract law, the obligations of the lessee and lessor are mutually dependent. In contrast, upon a commercial finance lessee's acceptance of the goods,

---

[52] UCC § 2-201(b).

[53] UCC § 2A-209.

[54] *Andreozzi v Brownell* Not Reported in A2d, 2004 WL 1542228 (RI Super)

[55] Alabama, Alaska, District of Columbia, Georgia, Idaho, Iowa, Kansas, Kentucky, Louisiana, Michigan, Minnesota, Mississippi, Montana, Nebraska, Nevada, New Mexico, North Dakota, Ohio, Oregon, South Dakota, and Utah. The 17 states with no vicarious liability and no vicarious liability statutes or case law include Arizona, Arkansas, Colorado, Hawaii, Indiana, Missouri, New Hampshire, North Carolina, Pennsylvania, South Carolina, Tennessee, Texas, Vermont, Virginia, Washington, West Virginia, and Wyoming.

[56] The Small Business Liability Reform Act of 2001, H.R. 1805, S. 865, 107th Cong. § 204(c)(2) (2001).

[57] In New York, Connecticut, Rhode Island, Maine, and the District of Columbia, a vehicle owner/lessor's vicarious liability is potentially unlimited; in California, Florida, Idaho, Michigan, and Minnesota, a vehicle owner/lessor's vicarious liability is "capped" at the statutory minimum for mandatory auto insurance. Treatise on Leasing, UCC Transaction Guide § 11:17; Equipment Leasing-Leveraged Leasing § 10:5.1 (2001). Prosser & Keeton, *On the Law of Torts* §§ 69–73 (W. Page Keeton ed., 5th ed. 1984). In some states, banks will no longer finance auto loans due to liability as owners.

E-COMMERCE AND CYBERLAW

LOL at Wax Seals: The Electronic Contract

The federal Electronic Signatures in Global and National Commerce Act (E-Sign) took effect October 1, 2000. The NATIONAL LAW JOURNAL stated: "Not since notarized written signatures replaced wax and signet rings has history seen such a fundamental change in contract law."*

The states can now use the Uniform Electronic Transactions Act (UETA) for meeting the new federal mandates on E-sign. The UETA was passed as a uniform law in July 1999, and 43 states plus the District of Columbia and the Virgin Islands have adopted it in some form.**

Issues that remain unresolved in this new era of electronic contracting are security and verification. Businesses must be able to verify that the electronic signatures are authentic and that orders from their stated origins are authentic. Furthermore, companies must be able to provide some form of record for auditors to verify transactions.

Consumer signatures will remain a different issue because the problems of security and authenticity are exacerbated when there are not ongoing relationships as there are in business-to-business transactions.

---

*Mark Ballard, "E-Sign a Nudge, Not a Revolution," *NATIONAL LAW JOURNAL*, September 25, 2000, B1, B4.

**UETA states are Alabama, Arizona, Arkansas, California, Colorado, Connecticut, Delaware, District of Columbia, Florida, Hawaii, Idaho, Indiana, Iowa, Kansas, Kentucky, Louisiana, Maine, Maryland, Massachusetts, Michigan, Minnesota, Mississippi, Montana, Nebraska, Nevada, New Hampshire, New Jersey, New Mexico, North Carolina, North Dakota, Ohio, Oklahoma, Oregon, Pennsylvania, Rhode Island, South Carolina, South Dakota, Tennessee, Texas, Utah, Virginia, West Virginia, Wisconsin, and Wyoming. State legislatures will continue to consider passage of both of UETA and other uniform acts such as the Uniform Computer Information Transactions Act (UCITA).

---

the lessee's promises to the lessor become irrevocable and independent from the obligations of the lessor. This irrevocability and independence require the lessee to perform even if the lessor's performance after the lessee's acceptance is not in accordance with the lease contract. The lessee must make payment to the lessor no matter how badly the leased goods perform. This is known as a **"hell or high water" clause**. It does not apply to consumer leases.[58] In some cases, the lessor assigns the lease contract to a third party, and that third party collects payment from the lessee. Some courts are requiring that the assignee of the lease contract take the lease assignment in good faith and without knowledge of problems with the lease or leased goods.

In a finance lease, the only remedy of the lessee for nonconformity of the goods is from the supplier. That is, the lessee can recover from the lessor only if the lease is not a finance lease or if the lessor has made an express warranty or promise.

"hell or high water" clause lease agreement clause that requires the lessee to continue paying regardless of any problems with the lease.

20. DEFAULT

The lease agreement and provisions of Article 2A determine whether the lessor or lessee is in default. If either the lessor or the lessee is in default under the lease contract, the party seeking enforcement may obtain a judgment or otherwise enforce the lease

---

[58] UCC § 2A-407; *Wells Fargo Bank Northwest, N.A. v TACA International Airlines, S.A.*, 247 F Supp 2d 352 (SDNY 2002).

contract by any available judicial or nonjudicial procedure. Neither the lessor nor the lessee is entitled to notice of default or notice of enforcement from the other party. Both the lessor and the lessee have rights and remedies similar to those given to a seller in a sales contract.[59] If the lessee defaults, the lessor is entitled to recover any rent due, future rent, and incidental damages.[60](See Chapter 27 for more information on remedies.)

---

[59] UCC §§ 2A-501, 2A-503; *Torres v Banc One Leasing Corp,* 226 F Supp 2d 1345 (ND Ga 2002).
[60] UCC § 2A-529.

> SUMMARY

Contracts for services and real estate are governed by the common law. Contracts for the sale of goods are governed by Article 2 of the UCC. *Goods* are defined as anything movable at the time they are identified as the subject of the transaction. Goods physically existing and owned by the seller at the time of the transaction are *existing goods.*

A *sale of goods* is the transfer of title to tangible personal property for a price. A *bailment* is a transfer of possession but not title and is therefore not a sale. A *gift* is not a sale because no price is paid for the gift. A contract for services is an ordinary contract and is not governed by the UCC. If a contract calls for both the rendering of services and the supplying of goods, the contract is classified according to its dominant element.

The common law contract rules for intent to contract apply to the formation of contracts under the UCC. However, several formation rules under the UCC differ from common law contract rules. A merchant's firm offer is irrevocable without the payment of consideration. The UCC rules on additional terms in an acceptance permit the formation of a contract despite the changes. These proposals for new terms are not considered counteroffers under the UCC. The terms that are included are determined by detailed rules under both the current and Revised UCC. If the transaction is between nonmerchants, a contract is formed without the additional terms, which the original offeror is free to accept or reject. If the transaction is between merchants, the additional terms become part of the contract if those terms do not materially alter the offer and no objection is made to them. Under Revised Article 2, terms that are in both parties' records, that the parties agree on, that are part of the Code terms or that are part of their ongoing

performance become part of the contract. There is no distinction between merchant and nonmerchant for additional terms under Revised Article 2.

The same defenses available to formation under common law are incorporated in Article 2. In addition, the UCC recognizes unconscionability as a defense to formation.

The UCC does not require the parties to agree on every aspect of contract performance for the contract to be valid. Provisions in Article 2 will govern the parties' relationship in the event their agreement does not cover all terms. The price term may be expressly fixed by the parties. The parties may make no provision as to price, or they may indicate how the price should be determined later. In output or requirements contracts, the quantity that is to be sold or purchased is not specified, but such contracts are nevertheless valid. A contract relating to a sale of goods may be modified even though the modification is not supported by consideration. The parol evidence rule applies to a sale of goods in much the same manner as to ordinary contracts. However, the UCC permits the introduction of course of dealing and usage of trade as evidence for clarification of contract terms and performance.

The UCC's statute of frauds provides that a sales contract for $500 (now $5,000 under Revised Article 2) or more must be evidenced by a writing (Revised Article 2 requires only a "record" in order to allow for e-commerce transactions). The UCC's merchant's confirmation memorandum allows two merchants to be bound to an otherwise oral agreement by a memo or letter signed by only one party that stands without objection for 10 days. Several exceptions to the UCC statute of frauds exist: when the goods are specially made or procured for the buyer and are nonresellable in the seller's ordinary market; when the buyer has received and accepted the goods; when the buyer has made either full or partial payment; and when the party against whom enforcement is sought admits in court pleadings or testimony that a contract for sale was made.

Uniform rules for international sales are applicable to contracts for sales between parties in countries that have ratified the CISG. Under the CISG, a contract for the sale of goods need not be in any particular form and can be proven by any means.

Article 2A of the UCC regulates consumer leases, commercial leases, finance leases, nonfinance leases, and subleases of tangible movable goods. A lease subject to Article 2A must be in writing if the lease payments will total $1,000 or more.

> QUESTIONS AND CASE PROBLEMS

1. Triple H Construction Co. contracted with Hunter's Run Stables, Inc., to erect a horse barn and riding arena on Hunter's Run's property in Big Flats, New York. Hunter's Run got a guarantee in its contract with Triple H that "such design with the span so shown will support its weight and will withstand natural forces including but not limited to snow load and wind." Hunter's Run also got the following guarantee from Rigidply, the manufacturer of the rafters: "Rigidply . . . hereby guarantees that the design to be used for the construction of a horse barn by Triple H . . . will support the weight of such barn and to snow load and wind as per drawings." The barn was completed in 1983 and collapsed under the weight of snow in 1994. Hunter's Run has sued Triple H for UCC Article 2 remedies. Does Article 2 apply? [*Hunter's Run Stables, Inc. v Triple H, Inc.,* 938 F Supp 166 (WDNY)]

2. R-P Packaging manufactured cellophane wrapping material that was used by Kern's Bakery in packaging its product. Kern's decided to change its system for packaging cookies from a tied bread bag to a tray covered with printed cellophane wrapping. R-P took measurements to determine the appropriate size for the cellophane wrapping and designed the artwork to be printed on the wrapping. After agreeing that the artwork was satisfactory, Kern placed a verbal order for the cellophane at a total cost of $13,000. When the printed wrapping material was received, Kern complained that it was too short for the trays and the artwork was not centered. The material, however, conformed exactly to the order placed by Kern. Kern returned the material to R-P by overnight express. R-P sued Kern. Kern claimed that because there was no written contract, the suit was barred by the statute of frauds. What resulted? [*Flowers Baking Co. v R-P Packaging, Inc.,* 329 SE2d 462 (Va)]

3. Smythe wrote to Lasco Dealers inquiring about the price of a certain freezer. Lasco wrote her a letter, signed by its credit manager, stating that Smythe could purchase the freezer in question during the next 30 days for $400. Smythe wrote back the next day ordering a freezer at that price. Lasco received Smythe's letter the following day, but Lasco wrote a response letter stating that it had changed the price to $450. Smythe claims that Lasco could not change its price. Is she correct?

4. Would silicone breast implants be covered by the UCC Article 2 warranties? Does implantation of silicone gel implants constitute a sale of goods by the surgeon? [*In re Breast Implant Product Liability Litigation,* 503 SE2d 445 (SC)]

5. Meyers was under contract with Henderson to install overhead doors in a factory that Henderson was building. Meyers obtained the disassembled doors from the manufacturer. His contract with Henderson required Meyers to furnish all labor, materials, tools, and equipment to satisfactorily complete the installation of all overhead doors. Henderson felt the doors were not installed properly and paid less than one-half of the contract price after subtracting his costs for correcting the installation. Because of a business sale and other complications, Meyers did not sue Henderson for the difference in payment until five years later. Henderson raised the defense that because the contract was for the sale of goods, it was barred by the Code's four-year statute of limitations. Meyers claimed that it was a contract for services

and that suit could be brought within six years. Decide. [*Meyers v Henderson Construction Co.,* 370 A2d 547 (NJ Super)]

6. Valley Trout Farms ordered fish food from Rangen. Both parties were merchants. The invoice that was sent with the order stated that a specified charge—a percentage common in the industry—would be added to any unpaid bills. Valley Trout Farms did not pay for the food and did not make any objection to the late charge stated in the invoice. When sued by Rangen, Valley Trout Farms claimed that it had never agreed to the late charge and therefore was not required to pay it. Is Valley Trout Farms correct? [*Rangen, Inc. v Valley Trout Farms, Inc.,* 658 P2d 955 (Idaho)]

7. On August 14, 1998, Justin Wyman was driving a vehicle leased by his mother (Maureen Wyman) with her permission. While Justin was driving the car in Cranston, Rhode Island, the vehicle left the roadway and struck a tree, injuring Michael Regan, who was a passenger in the car. Michael Regan filed suit against both Wymans and the leasing company, Nissan North America, Inc. Regan alleges that Wyman was either vicariously liable for the negligence of her son or was negligent in entrusting her vehicle to her son. Regan alleges that Nissan is liable to him for his injuries because it is the owner of property that caused physical injury and damages. Is Regan correct? [*Regan v Nissan North America, Inc.,* 810 A2d 255 (RI)]

8. LTV Aerospace Corp. manufactured all-terrain vehicles for use in Southeast Asia. LTV made an oral contract with Bateman under which Bateman would supply the packing cases needed for the vehicles' overseas shipment. Bateman made substantial beginnings in the production of packing cases following LTV's specifications. LTV thereafter stopped production of its vehicles and refused to take delivery of any cases. When Bateman sued for breach of contract, LTV argued that the contract could not be enforced because there was no writing that satisfied the statute of frauds. Was this a valid defense? [*LTV Aerospace Corp. v Bateman,* 492 SW2d 703 (Tex App)]

9. Syrovy and Alpine Resources, Inc., entered into a "Timber Purchase Agreement." Syrovy agreed to sell and Alpine agreed to buy all of the timber produced during a two-year period. The timber to be sold, purchased, and delivered was to be produced by Alpine from timber on Syrovy's land. Alpine continued harvesting for one year and then stopped after making an initial payment. Syrovy sued Alpine. Alpine alleged there was no contract because the writing to satisfy the statute of frauds must contain a quantity term. Decide. [*Syrovy v Alpine Resources, Inc.,* 841 P2d 1279 (Wash App)]

10. Ray Thomaier placed an order with Hoffman Chevrolet, Inc., for a specifically optioned 1978 Limited Edition Corvette Coupe. The order form described the automobile and the options Mr. Thomaier wanted, included the purchase price, and provided for delivery to the purchaser "A.S.A.P." Thomaier signed the order form in the place designated for his signature and gave the dealer a $1,000 check as a deposit. This check was deposited into the account of Hoffman Chevrolet and cleared. On the same day that Thomaier gave Hoffman the check, Hoffman placed a written order with defendant General Motors Corporation, Chevrolet Motor Division, for the 1978 Limited Edition Corvette Coupe. The order was placed on a form supplied by General Motors, was signed by the dealer and listed Thomaier as the "customer." About a month later, Hoffman sent Thomaier a letter that explained that "market conditions" had made his "offer" unacceptable and that his deposit of $1,000 was being refunded. The vehicle was ultimately manufactured by Chevrolet and delivered to Hoffman. Hoffman sold this specific vehicle to a third party.

Thomaier filed suit, but Hoffman responded that because it had never signed the order, it was not binding. Hoffman argues there was no acceptance and therefore no binding contract. Is Hoffman correct? [*Thomaier v. Hoffman Chevrolet, Inc.,* 410 NYS2d 645 (Supreme Court NY)]

11. Fastener Corp. sent a letter to Renzo Box Co. that was signed by Ronald Lee, Fastener's sales manager, and read as follows: "We hereby offer you 200 type #14 Fastener bolts at $5 per bolt. This offer will be irrevocable for ten days." On the fifth day, Fastener informed Renzo it was

revoking the offer, alleging that there was no consideration for the offer. Could Fastener revoke? Explain.

12. Richard, a retailer of video equipment, telephoned Craft Appliances and ordered a $1,000 videotape recorder for his business. Craft accepted Richard's order and sent him a copy of the purchase memorandum that stated the price, quantity, and model ordered and that was stamped "order accepted by Craft." Richard, however, did not sign or return the purchase memorandum and refused to accept delivery of the recorder when Craft delivered it to him three weeks later. Craft sued Richard, who raised the statute of frauds as a defense. Will Richard prevail? Why or why not?

13. REMC furnished electricity to Helvey's home. The voltage furnished was in excess of 135 volts and caused extensive damage to his 110-volt household appliances. Helvey sued REMC for breach of warranty. Helvey argued that providing electrical energy is not a transaction in goods but a furnishing of services, so that he had six years to sue REMC rather than the UCC's four-year statute of limitations, which had expired. Was it a sale of goods or a sale of services? Identify the ethical principles involved in this case. [*Helvey v Wabash County REMC,* 278 NE2d 608 (Ind App)]

14. Curtis Moeller is a crop and dairy farmer. Huntting Elevator Company sells and applies herbicides and fertilizers in addition to its other grain and crop-related businesses. In the spring of 1995, Moeller met with Huntting's manager, Paul Steier, who suggested fertilizers and herbicides that Moeller should use on his fields. Moeller agreed to notify the elevator when his fields were ready to be sprayed with herbicide. Between May 5 and May 18, 1995, Moeller planted corn. On May 20, 1995, he told the secretary at Huntting that he had finished planting and that his fields were ready for spraying. After waiting 10 days for the sprayers,

Moeller returned to Huntting and again notified the company that his fields were ready for spraying.

On June 13, 1995, after considerable complaining from Moeller about the height of the foxtail and other weeds in his field, Huntting's staff sprayed 119 acres of Moeller's fields and, three days later, sprayed the remaining 34 acres.

The spray was not as effective as promised, and Moeller, who lost substantial portions of his crops, filed suit under UCC Article 2 for breach of express warranty, warranty for a particular purpose, and the warranty of merchantability. Huntting maintains the contract is not covered under the UCC and that Moeller's only remedy must be to show that Huntting was somehow negligent in its work. Who is correct? Is the contract governed by UCC or common law? [*Moeller v Huntting Elevator Co.,* 1999 WL 387320 (Minn App 1999)]

15. Flora Hall went to Rent-A-Center in Milwaukee and signed an agreement to make monthly payments of $77.96 for 19 months in exchange for Rent-A-Center's allowing her to have a Rent-A-Center washer and dryer in her home. In addition, the agreement required Hall to pay tax and a liability waiver fee on the washer and dryer. The total amount she would pay under the agreement was $1,643.15. The agreement provided that Hall would return the washer and dryer at the end of the 19 months, or she could, at that time, pay $161.91 and own the washer and dryer as her own. Is this a sales contract? Is this a consumer lease? At the time Hall leased her washer and dryer, she could have purchased a set for about $600. What do you think about the cost of her agreement with Rent-A-Center? Is it unconscionable? Refer to Chapter 33, and determine whether any other consumer laws apply. Must this contract be in writing? [*Rent-A-Center, Inc. v Hall,* 510 NW2d 789 (Wis)]

CPA QUESTIONS

1. Webstar Corp. orally agreed to sell Northco, Inc., a computer for $20,000. Northco sent a signed purchase order to Webstar confirming the agreement. Webstar received the purchase order and did not respond. Webstar refused to deliver the computer to Northco, claiming that the purchase order did not satisfy the UCC statute of frauds because it was not signed by Webstar. Northco sells computers to the general public, and Webstar is a computer wholesaler. Under the UCC Sales Article, Webstar's position is:

   a. Incorrect, because it failed to object to Northco's purchase order

   b. Incorrect, because only the buyer in a sale-of-goods transaction must sign the contract

   c. Correct, because it was the party against whom enforcement of the contract is being sought

   d. Correct, because the purchase price of the computer exceeded $500

2. On May 2, Lace Corp., an appliance wholesaler, offered to sell appliances worth $3,000 to Parco, Inc., a household appliances retailer. The offer was signed by Lace's president and provided that it would not be withdrawn before June 1. It also included the shipping terms: "F.O.B.—Parco's warehouse." On May 29, Parco mailed an acceptance of Lace's offer. Lace received the acceptance June 2. Which of the following is correct if Lace sent Parco a telegram revoking its offer and Parco received the telegram on May 25?

   a. A contract was formed on May 2.

   b. Lace's revocation effectively terminated its offer on May 25.

   c. Lace's revocation was ineffective because the offer could not be revoked before June 1.

   d. No contract was formed because Lace received Parco's acceptance after June 1.

3. Bond and Spear orally agreed that Bond would buy a car from Spear for $475. Bond paid Spear a $100 deposit. The next day, Spear received an offer of $575, the car's fair market value. Spear immediately notified Bond that Spear would not sell the car to Bond and returned Bond's $100. If Bond sues Spear and Spear defends on the basis of the statute of frauds, Bond will probably:

   a. Lose, because the agreement was for less than the fair market value of the car

   b. Win, because the agreement was for less than $500

   c. Lose, because the agreement was not in writing and signed by Spear

   d. Win, because Bond paid a deposit

4. Cookie Co. offered to sell Distrib Markets 20,000 pounds of cookies at $1.00 per pound, subject to certain specified terms for delivery. Distrib replied in writing as follows: "We accept your offer for 20,000 pounds of cookies at $1.00 per pound, weighing scale to have valid city certificate." Under the UCC:

   a. A contract was formed between the parties.

   b. A contract will be formed only if Cookie agrees to the weighing scale requirement.

   c. No contract was formed because Distrib included the weighing scale requirement in its reply.

   d. No contract was formed because Distrib's reply was a counteroffer.

TITLE AND RISK OF LOSS

LEARNING OBJECTIVES

After studying this chapter, you should be able to

LO.1 Explain when title and risk of loss pass with respect to goods

LO.2 Determine who bears the risk of loss when goods are damaged or destroyed

LO.3 Discuss carrier liability and risk of loss

LO.4 Explain why it is important to know when risk of loss and title pass in transactions for the sale of goods

LO.5 Describe the passage of title and risk in special situations, such as a sale or return or a sale on approval

LO.6 Classify the various circumstances in which title can be passed to a bona fide purchaser

LO.7 Discuss risk of loss and title in special situations, such as bailments, consignments, factors, sales on approval, and sales or returns

In most sales, the buyer receives the proper goods and makes payment, and the transaction is completed. However, problems may arise during performance that can result in issues of liability. For example, what if the goods are lost in transit? Must the buyer still pay for those lost goods? Can the seller's creditors take goods from the seller's warehouse when they are packed for shipment to buyers? The parties can include provisions in their contract to address these types of problems. If their contract does not cover these types of problems, however, then specific rules under Uniform Commercial Code (UCC) Article 2 apply. These rules are covered in this chapter.

In businesses today, the management of issues of risk and title as goods flow through commerce is called *supply chain management.* Effective managers know the law and the rules of risk of loss and title so that they can negotiate risk-reducing contracts and be certain that they have all necessary arrangements and paperwork to move goods through streams of commerce.

 IDENTIFYING TYPES OF POTENTIAL PROBLEMS AND TRANSACTIONS

The types of problems that can arise in supply chain management include damage to the goods in transit, claims by creditors of buyers and sellers while the goods are in transit, and questions relating to whose insurance will cover what damage and when such coverage applies.

1. DAMAGE TO GOODS

One potential problem occurs if the goods are damaged or totally destroyed without any fault of either the buyer or the seller. With no goods and a contract performance still required, the parties have questions: Must the seller bear the loss and supply new goods to the buyer? Or is it the buyer's loss so that the buyer must pay the seller the purchase price even though the goods are damaged or destroyed?[1] What liability does a carrier have when goods in its possession are damaged? The fact that there may be insurance does not avoid this question because the questions of whose insurer is liable and the extent of liability still remain.

2. CREDITORS' CLAIMS

Another potential problem that can arise affecting the buyer's and seller's rights occurs when creditors of the seller or buyer seize the goods under the belief that their debtor has title. The buyer's creditors may seize them because they believe them to be the buyer's. The seller's creditors may step in and take goods because they believe the goods still belong to the seller, and the buyer is left with the dilemma of whether it can get the goods back from the creditors. The question of title or ownership is also important in connection with a resale of the goods by the buyer and in determining the parties' liability for, or the computation of, inventory or personal property taxes.

3. INSURANCE

insurable interest the right to hold a valid insurance policy on a person or property.

Until the buyer has received the goods and the seller has been paid, both the seller and the buyer have an economic interest in the sales transaction. A question that can arise is whether either or both have enough of an interest in the goods to allow them to insure them, in other words, do they have an **insurable interest?** There are certain steps that must take place and timing requirements that must be met before that insurable interest can arise. Once buyers have an insurable interest in goods that are the subject matter of their contracts, they have the right to obtain insurance and can submit claims for losses on the goods.

DETERMINING RIGHTS: IDENTIFICATION OF GOODS

identification point in the transaction when the buyer acquires an interest in the goods subject to the contract.

The **identification** of the goods to the contract is a necessary step to provide the buyer an insurable interest. How goods that are the subject matter of a contract are identified depends on the nature of both the contract and the goods themselves.[2]

4. EXISTING GOODS

existing goods goods that physically exist and are owned by the seller at the time of a transaction.

identified term applied to particular goods selected by either the buyer or the seller as the goods called for by the sales contract.

Existing goods are goods physically in existence at the time of the contract and owned by the seller. When particular goods have been selected by either the buyer or the seller, or both, as being the goods called for by the sales contract, the goods are **identified. For Example,** when you go into a store, point to a particular item, and tell the clerk, "I'll take that one," your sales transaction relates to existing goods that are now identified by you. This step of identification provides you with certain rights in those goods because of your contract as well as Article 2 protections for buyers when goods are identified.

5. FUTURE GOODS

future goods goods that exist physically but are not owned by the seller as well as goods that have not yet been produced.

Future goods are those not yet owned by the seller or not yet in existence. **For Example,** suppose that your company is sponsoring a 10-K run and will furnish the

---

[1] UCC § 2-509 provides for the allocation of the risk of loss in those situations where the goods are destroyed and neither party has breached the contract.

[2] UCC § 2-501(1)(a).

t-shirts for the 10,000 runners expected to participate in the race. You have contacted Sporting Tees, Inc., to produce the t-shirts with the name of the race and your company logo on the shirts. The shirts are future goods because you are contracting for goods that will be produced.

Future goods are identified when they are shipped, marked, or otherwise designated by the seller as goods to which the contract refers.[3] The t-shirts cannot be identified until Sporting Tees has manufactured them and designated them for your company. The earliest that the shirts can be identified is when they come off the production line and are designated for your company. Prior to identification of these goods, the buyer has only a future interest at the time of the contract and has few rights with respect to them.[4]

CPA

6. FUNGIBLE GOODS

fungible goods
homogeneous goods of which any unit is the equivalent of any other unit.

Fungible goods are goods that, when mixed together, are indistinguishable. **For Example,** crops such as soybeans and dairy products such as milk are fungible goods. A seller who has 10,000 cases of cling peaches has fungible, unidentified goods. Like future goods, these fungible goods are identified when they are shipped, marked, or otherwise designated for the buyer.[5] The seller's act of tagging, marking, labeling, or in some way indicating to those responsible for shipping the goods that certain goods are associated with a particular contract or order means that identification has occurred.

CPA

7. EFFECT OF IDENTIFICATION

Once goods that are the subject matter of a contract have been identified, the buyer holds an *insurable interest* in them. Once the buyer's economic interest in and the identity of the goods are clear, the buyer's insurance company has an obligation to provide coverage for any mishaps that could occur until the contract is performed completely.

Identification is also significant because the questions surrounding passage of title and risk of loss cannot be resolved until the goods have been identified. Identification is the first step in resolving questions about liability for damaged goods and rights of the parties and third parties, including creditors, in the goods. UCC § 2-401(1) provides, "Title to goods cannot pass under a contract for sale prior to their identification to the contract."

 ## DETERMINING RIGHTS: PASSAGE OF TITLE

When title to goods passes to the buyer (following identification) depends on whether there is a document of title, whether the seller is required to ship the goods, and what the terms of that shipping agreement are. In the absence of an agreement by the parties as to when title will pass, several Article 2 rules govern the timing for passage of title.

---

[3] UCC § 2-501(1)(b). Specially manufactured goods are fully identified when the goods are made. *Colonel's Inc. v Cincinnati Milacron Marketing Co.,* 149 F3d 1182 (6th Cir 1998).

[4] *In re Quality Processing, Inc.,* 9 F3d 1360 (8th Cir 1993).

[5] Farm products, such as corn, are fungible goods. However, contracts for future crops are not contracts for the sale of goods because there are no goods identified as yet for such contracts. *Top of Iowa Co-Op v Sime Farms, Inc.,* 608 NW2d 454 (Iowa 2000).

8. PASSAGE OF TITLE USING DOCUMENTS OF TITLE

document of title document treated as evidence that a person is entitled to receive, hold, and dispose of the document and the goods it covers.

A **document of title** is a means whereby the parties can faciliate the transfer of title to the goods without actually moving them or provide a means for a creditor to take an interest in the goods. The use of a document of title also provides a simple answer to the question of when title to the goods passes from seller to buyer in a sales transaction. Title to the goods passes when the document of title is transferred from the seller to the buyer.[6]

Documents of title are governed under Article 7 of the UCC, the final section of the UCC to undergo major revisions in the last decade of the 20th century. The purpose of the 2003 revisions to Article 7 was to address the issues that have arisen because of electronic filing of documents of title. Article 7 adoptions have just begun with seven states passing the new Article 7 by 2006.[7]

bill of lading document issued by a carrier acknowledging the receipt of goods and the terms of the contract of transportation.

Article 7 now addresses the commercial reality of electronic tracking and the use of electronic records as documents of title. Under Article 7, the definition of a document of title now includes electronic documents of title.

warehouse receipt receipt issued by the warehouser for stored goods; regulated by the UCC, which clothes the receipt with some degree of negotiability.

The discussion of documents of title here is limited to commercial transactions, transport, and storage. Many forms of documents of title are not covered under Article 7. For example, all states have some form of title system required for the transfer of title to motor vehicles.[8] Those systems govern title passage for automobiles. The two primary forms of documents of title under Article 7 used to pass title to goods are **bills of lading** (issued by a carrier) and **warehouse receipts**.[9] Details on these documents and the rights of the parties are found in Chapter 22.

9. PASSAGE OF TITLE IN NONSHIPMENT CONTRACTS

Unless the parties to the contract agree otherwise, UCC Article 2 does not require that the seller deliver the contracted-for goods to the buyer. In the absence of a provision in the contract, the place of delivery is the seller's place of business or the seller's residence if the seller is not a merchant. When there is no specific agreement for shipment or delivery of the goods and there is no document of title and the goods to the contract have been identified, title passes to the buyer at the time the contract is entered into by the buyer and seller.

10. PASSAGE OF TITLE IN WAREHOUSE ARRANGEMENTS

When the goods to a contract are in a warehouse or the possession of a third party (not the seller), the title to the goods passes from the seller to the buyer when the buyer receives the document of title or, if there is no document of title, any other paperwork required for the third party or warehouse to turn over the goods and the goods are available for the buyer to take. When goods are in the possession of a warehouse,

---

[6] UCC § 2-401(3).

[7] The revisions to Article 7 and their history can be found at **http://www.nccusl.org.** The seven states that had adopted Revised Article 7 as of July 2006 were New Hampshire, Utah, West Virginia, Mississippi, Colorado, Arizona, and Rhode Island. States where Article 7 is under legislative review are Massachusetts, California, and North Carolina.

[8] Other types of transportation, such as a boat, may not require a title document to be transferred, and title passes at the time of contracting. However, where there are title statutes, they preempt UCC provisions. *Ladd v NBD Bank,* 550 NW2d 826 (Mich App 1996). See also *Pierce v First Nat'l Bank,* 899 SW2d 365 (Tex App 1995).

[9] UCC § 7-202(1) provides, ''A warehouse receipt need not be in any particular form. Under Revised Article 7, it can be in electronic form.''

the parties have certain duties and rights. Those rights and duties were covered in Chapter 22.

11. PASSAGE OF TITLE IN BAILMENTS AND OTHER FORMS OF POSSESSION

As a general rule, a seller can sell only what the seller owns. However, some issues of passage of title can arise in specific circumstances. Those circumstances are covered in the following sections.

CPA

(a) Stolen Property   Neither those who find stolen property nor thieves can pass title to goods. A thief simply cannot pass good title to even a good-faith purchaser. Anyone who has purchased stolen goods must surrender them to the true owner. The fact that the negligence of the owner made the theft possible or contributed to losing the goods does not bar the owner from recovering the goods or money damages from the thief, the finder, or a good-faith purchaser. It does not matter that the thief may have passed the goods along through several purchasers. Title cannot be cleansed by distance between the thief and the good-faith purchaser. The good-faith purchaser always takes the goods subject to the claim by the owner. The public policy reason for this protection of true owners is to deter theft. Knowing there is no way to sell the goods should deter those who steal and caution those who buy goods to check title and sources.

estoppel principle by which a person is barred from pursuing a certain course of action or of disputing the truth of certain matters.

(b) Estoppel   If an owner has acted in a way that misleads others, the owner of personal property may be prevented, or **estopped,** from asserting ownership. The owner would be barred from denying the right of another person to sell the property. **For Example,** a minor buys a car and puts it in his father's name so that

CASE SUMMARY

The Downside of Buying a Lexus Curbside

FACTS: John C. Clark, using the alias Thomas Pecora, rented a 1994 Lexus from Alamo Rent-A-Car on December 21, 1994. Clark did not return the car and, using falsified signatures, obtained a California so-called quick title. Clark advertised the car for sale in the *Las Vegas Review Journal.* Terry and Vyonne Mendenhall called the phone number in the ad and reached Clark. He told them that he lived at a country club and could not have people coming to his house to look at the car. He instead drove the car to their house for their inspection the next morning. The car title was in the name of J. C. Clark Enterprises. The Mendenhalls bought the car for $34,000 in cash. They made some improvements on the car and registered it in Utah. On February 24, 1995, Alamo reported the car stolen. On March 21, 1995, the Nevada Department of Motor Vehicles seized the car from the Mendenhalls. The car was returned to Alamo and the Mendenhalls filed suit. The lower court found for the Mendenhalls, and Alamo appealed.

DECISION: Although the Mendenhalls might have been bona fide purchasers, Clark did not have voidable title. He was a thief, and a thief can never pass good title to stolen property. Even in the case of good-faith purchasers for value, void title can never be turned into good title. The car belongs to Alamo, and the Mendenhalls' only remedy is against Clark. [**Alamo Rent-A-Car v Mendenhall, 937 P2D 69 (Nev 1997)**]

he can obtain lower insurance rates. If the father then sells the car to a good-faith purchaser, the son would be estopped from claiming ownership.

(c) Authorization   In certain circumstances, persons who just possess someone else's property may sell the property and pass title. Lienholders can sell property if there is a default on the money owed to them. **For Example,** if you store your personal property in a storage locker and fail to pay rent, the owner of the storage locker holds a lien on your personal property and could sell it to pay the rent due on your storage unit. Good title passes to the buyer from such a sale. All states have some form of statute giving those who find property the authority to sell the property after certain time periods have passed or when the owner cannot be found.

voidable title title of goods that carries with it the contingency of an underlying problem.

(d) Voidable Title   If the buyer has a **voidable title**—for example, when the goods were obtained by fraud—the seller can rescind the sale. However, if the buyer resells the property to a good-faith purchaser before the seller has rescinded the transaction, the subsequent purchaser acquires valid title. It is immaterial whether the buyer with the voidable title had obtained title by criminal fraud.[10]

THINKING THINGS THROUGH

Even the Best Jeweler in Orange County Can't Always Spot a Phony

Scott Wayne Simmons purchased a 15.05-carat heart-shaped diamond from Angel Archer Estate Jewelers. Simmons gave a check for $70,000 for the diamond and was given a certificate of authenticity from the European Gemological Laboratory (EGL). Simmons then sold the diamond to Glenn Verdult, d/b/a Winston's Newport Jewelers, a jewelry store named the best in Orange County with an impeccable reputation. Verdult paid $40,000 for the diamond and the certificate from EGL. The Simmons check was fictitious; there was no money in the account. Simmons was charged with writing a fictitious check by Riverside County, and the Riverside County Sheriff's Office took the diamond back to Angel Archer as its rightful owner. Verdult filed suit, claiming that he was the rightful owner of the diamond. What could Verdult argue to convince the court that he is entitled to the diamond? People v Simmons, 2003 WL 21350737 (Cal App 4 Dist, unpublished opinion)

(e) Bailments or Sale by an Entrustee   A bailee can pass good title to a good-faith purchaser even when the sale was not authorized by the owner and the bailee has no title to the goods but is in the business of selling those particular types of goods.[11] **For Example,** if Gunnell's Jewelry sells and repairs watches and Julie has left her watch with Gunnell's for repair, she has created a bailment. If Gunnell's Jewelry sells Julie's watch by mistake because it is both a new and old watch dealer

---

[10] "Criminal fraud" is the language of Revised Article 2, adopted to increase the scope of the original term *larceny* and intended to encompass all forms of criminal activity that might lead to the possession or entrustment of goods. Revised Article 2 also covers all conduct punishable under criminal law.

[11] *Beall Transport Equipment Co. v Southern Pacific Transportation,* 13 P3d 130 (Or App 2000), affirmed, 60 P2d 530 (Or 2002), with decision clarified, 68 P3d 259 (Or App 2003); see also *Abrams v General Start Indemnity,* 67 P3d 931 (Or 2003).

to David, a good-faith purchaser, David has valid title to the watch. Julie will have a cause of action against Gunnell's for conversion, and in some states, if Gunnell's sold the watch knowing that it belonged to Julie, the sale could constitute a crime, such as larceny. However, all of these legal proceedings will involve Gunnell's, Julie, and possibly a government prosecution, but not David who will take good title to the watch.

In the case of an entrustee who is not a merchant, such as a prospective customer trying out an automobile, there is no transfer of title to the buyer from the entrustee. Similarly, there is no transfer of title when a mere bailee, such as a repairer who is not a seller of goods of that kind, sells the property of a customer.

---

12. DELIVERY AND SHIPMENT TERMS

If delivery is required under the terms of the parties' agreement, the seller is normally required only to make shipment, and the seller's part of the contract is completed by placing the goods in the possession of a carrier for shipment. However, the parties may agree to various shipping provisions that do affect the passage of title under Article 2.[12] With the 2003 changes to Article 2, the statutory definitions of terms such as *FOB, FAS, CF,* and *CIF* were eliminated. The elimination occurred because the nature of contracts and shipping has changed substantially and continues to do so at such a rapid pace that it is difficult to have any generic and statutory definitions that will have universal application.[13] The parties can still use such terms, but Article 2 no longer controls their intent and interpretation. Because the terms are still used, Figure 24-1 summarizes the shipping terms the parties can use in their sales contracts and the liabilities and responsibilities under each.

FIGURE 24-1 *Delivery and Shipping Terms*

COD	CASH ON DELIVERY (PAYMENT TERM, NOT SHIPMENT TERM)
CF	COST PLUS FREIGHT LUMP SUM; PRICE INCLUDES COST AND FREIGHT
	RISK: BUYER ON DELIVERY TO CARRIER
	TITLE: BUYER ON DELIVERY TO CARRIER
	COST, INSURANCE AND FREIGHT EXPENSES: SELLER PAYS; INCLUDES COST OF FREIGHT IN CONTRACT PRICE
CIF	LUMP SUM; PRICE INCLUDES COST, INSURANCE, AND FREIGHT
	RISK: BUYER ON DELIVERY TO CARRIER
	TITLE: BUYER ON DELIVERY TO CARRIER
	EXPENSES: INCLUDED IN CONTRACT PRICE (SELLER BUYS INSURANCE IN BUYER'S NAME AND PAYS FREIGHT)
FOB	FREE ON BOARD
FAS	FREE ALONGSIDE SHIP (FOB FOR BOATS)

---

[12] UCC § 2-401(2). When a seller simply ships goods in response to a telephone order and there is no paperwork to indicate shipping terms, the contract is one of shipment (FOB place of shipment). *California State Electronics Ass'n v Zeos Int'l Ltd.,* 49 Cal Rptr 2d 127 (1996).

[13] Under Revised Article 2, §§ 2-319 through 2-324 are deleted. The comment to the section indicates that Article 2 will no longer contain "terms that amount to commercial shorthand."

FOB place of shipment
"ship to" contract.

(a) FOB Place of Shipment   *FOB* is a shipping term that is an acronym for free on board.[14] If a contract contains a delivery term of **FOB place of shipment,** then the seller's obligation under the contract is to deliver the goods to a carrier for shipment. **For Example,** if the contract between a New York buyer and a Los Angeles seller provides for delivery as FOB Los Angeles, then the seller's responsibility is to place the goods in the possession of a Los Angeles carrier and enter into a contract to have the goods shipped to New York.

CPA

FOB place of destination
general commercial
language for delivery to the
buyer.

(b) FOB Place of Destination   If a contract contains a delivery term of **FOB place of destination,** then the seller's responsibility is to get the goods to the buyer. **For Example,** if the contract between the New York buyer and the Los Angeles seller is FOB New York, then the seller is responsible for getting the goods to New York. An FOB destination contract holds the seller accountable throughout the journey of the goods across the country.

CPA

FAS free alongside the
named vessel.

(c) FAS   **FAS** is a shipping term that means free alongside ship; it is the equivalent of FOB for boat transportation.[15] **For Example,** a contract between a London buyer and a Norfolk, Virginia, seller that is FAS Norfolk requires only that the seller deliver the goods to a ship in Norfolk.

CPA

CF cost and freight.

CIF cost, insurance, and
freight.

(d) CF, CIF, and COD   **CF** is an acronym for cost and freight, and **CIF** is an acronym for cost, insurance, and freight.[16] Under a CF contract, the seller gets the goods to a carrier, and the cost of shipping the goods is included in the contract price. Under a CIF contract, the seller must get the goods to a carrier and buy an insurance policy in the buyer's name to cover the goods while in transit. The costs of the freight and the insurance policy are included in the contract price.

COD cash on delivery.

Often contracts for the sale of goods provide for **COD.** The acronym stands for cash on delivery. Even though the term includes the word *delivery,* COD is not a shipping term but a payment term that requires the buyer to pay in order to gain physical possession of the goods.

13. PASSAGE OF TITLE IN SHIPMENT CONTRACTS

When the parties have shipment and delivery terms in their contract, the type of shipment contract the parties have agreed to controls when title to the goods has passed and, as a result, the rights of creditors of the buyer and seller in those goods.

Revised Article 2 provides for the same results on passage of title in shipment contracts as under Article 2, but the FOB terms are not specifically delineated under the Revised Article 2. (See Figure 24-2.) Revised Article 2 simply uses the generic language of shipment contracts and those shipment contracts in which the seller is required to get the goods to a particular destination.

CPA

(a) Passage of Title in a Shipment only Contract (FOB Shipment)   Title to the goods passes from the seller to the buyer in an FOB shipment contract or under a shipment contract for Revised Article 2 when the seller delivers the goods to the

---

[14] UCC § 2-319.
[15] UCC § 2-319.
[16] UCC §§ 2-320 and 2-321.

FIGURE 24-2 *Passage of Title under Article 2 and Revised Article 2*

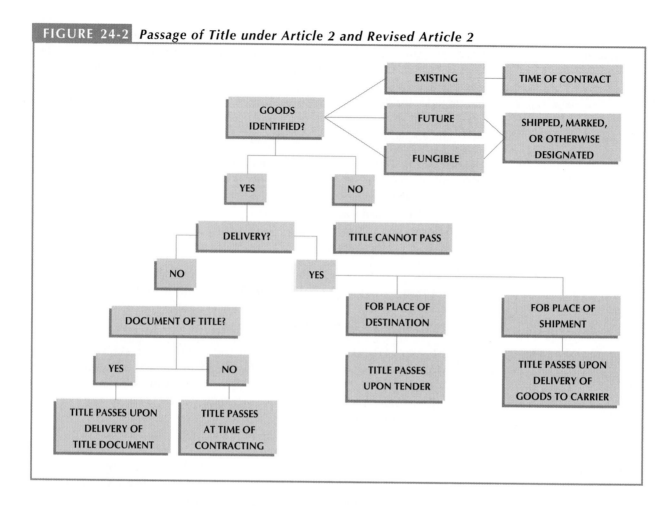

carrier.[17] The title to the goods no longer rests with the Los Angeles seller once the goods are delivered to the carrier if the contract is just a shipment contract only (an FOB Los Angeles contract). **For Example,** if the Internal Revenue Service received authorization to collect taxes by seizing the seller's property, it could not take those goods once they were delivered to the carrier. Under a shipment contract (an FOB shipment contract), the buyer owns the goods once they are in the hands of the carrier.

CPA

(b) Passage of Title in a Destination Contract (FOB Place of Destination)   Title to the goods passes from the seller to the buyer in an FOB destination contract when the goods are tendered to the buyer at the destination. **Tender** occurs when the goods have arrived and are available for the buyer to pick up and the buyer has been notified of their availability. **For Example,** when the contract contains an FOB destination provision requiring the seller to deliver to New York, title to the goods passes to the New York buyer when the goods have arrived in New York, they are available for pickup, and the buyer has been notified of their arrival. Thus, the IRS could seize the goods during shipment if the contract is FOB New York because title remains with the seller until actual tender. In the preceding example, the

tender goods have arrived, are available for pickup, and buyer is notified.

---

[17] UCC § 2-401(2).

CASE SUMMARY

The Taiwan Burlington Express

FACTS: Burlington Express issued a negotiable bill of lading to the seller of goods (Lite-On) being shipped from Taiwan to the United States. Under the contractual terms of the bill of lading, Burlington Express was not to deliver the goods to the buyer (consignee) until the buyer presented the negotiable bill of lading. Burlington Express delivered the goods to the buyer without having the buyer turn over the negotiable bill of lading.

Burlington Express maintained that the shipping contract was FOB Taiwan, which meant that title passed to the buyer upon loading in Taiwan, making the bill of lading irrelevant. The court entered summary judgment for Lite-On for the full value of the goods that Burlington had turned over to the nonpaying buyer, a value of $101,602.80. Burlington appealed.

DECISION: The court ruled that Burlington was bound by its bill of lading contractual terms and that the bill of lading controlled any passing of title to the buyer and for the risk of loss passing at the point of loading. The appellate court affirmed the holding for the judgment for Lite-On. Sadly, however, by the time the appellate process concluded, the Lite-On buyer had entered bankruptcy, and Lite-On was able to recover very little of its judgment. [**Lite-On Peripherals, Inc. v Burlington Air Express, Inc.,** 255 F3d 1189 (9th Cir 2001)]

seller's obligation is complete when the goods are at the rail station in New York and the buyer has been notified that she may pick them up at any time during working hours.

D   DETERMINING RIGHTS: RISK OF LOSS

risk of loss in contract performance, the cost of damage or injury to the goods contracted for.

Identification determines insurability, and title determines rights of such third parties as creditors. **Risk of loss** determines who must pay under a contract in the event the goods that are the subject of the contract are damaged or destroyed during the course of performance.

E-COMMERCE AND CYBERLAW

Supply Chain and Risk Management

In today's sophisticated supplier and transportation relationships, buyers, sellers, and carriers can pinpoint exactly where goods are and when they have been delivered, and all parties have access to that information online. In many contracts, the parties can avert problems or breaches by monitoring closely the progress of the shipment. The computer interconnection of the supply chain permits faster and better communication among the parties when problems under the contract or in shipment arise. The shipment can be tracked from the time of delivery to the carrier through its route to final signature upon its arrival.

14. RISK OF LOSS IN NONSHIPMENT CONTRACTS

As noted earlier, Article 2 has no provision for delivery in the absence of an agreement. The rules for passage of risk of loss from the seller to the buyer in a nonshipment contract make a distinction between a merchant seller and a nonmerchant seller. If the seller is a merchant, the risk of loss passes to the buyer on actual receipt of the

FIGURE 24-3   *Risk of Loss*

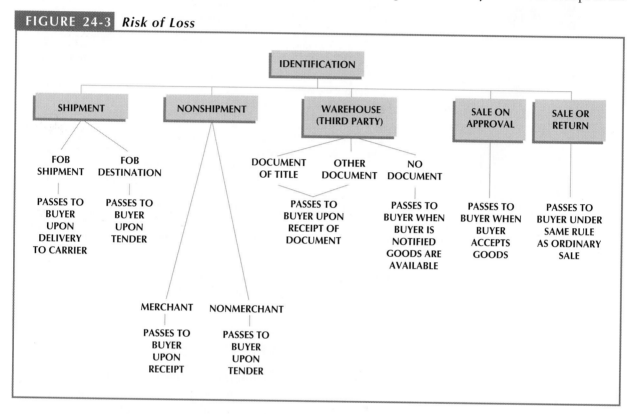

FIGURE 24-4   *Risk of Loss—Revised Article 2*

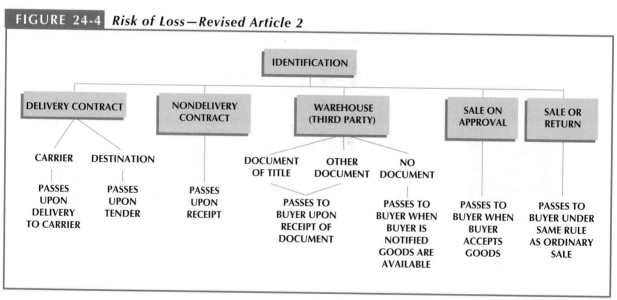

goods from the merchant.[18] If the seller is a nonmerchant, the risk of loss passes when the seller makes the goods available to the buyer or upon tender.

The highly technical aspect of the nonshipment rule was modified under Revised Article 2, which has a uniform rule on nonshipment contracts with the risk of loss passing upon receipt of the goods, whether a merchant or nonmerchant seller is involved.[19] **For Example,** if John buys a refrigerator at Kelvinator Appliances or at his neighbor's garage sale and then leaves it there while he goes to borrow a pickup truck, the risk of loss has not yet passed to John under Revised Article 2. He may have had title at the time he entered into the contract for the existing goods, and the goods are identified, but the risk of loss will not pass to John until he has actually receives the refrigerator. His receipt will not occur until the refrigerator is placed in the back of his pickup truck. John is fully protected if anything happens to the refrigerator until then.

15. RISK OF LOSS IN SHIPMENT CONTRACTS

If the parties have agreed to delivery or shipment terms as part of their contract, the rules for risk of loss are different.[20]

CPA **(a) CONTRACT FOR SHIPMENT TO BUYER (FOB PLACE OF SHIPMENT)** In a contract for shipment only, or FOB place of shipment, the risk of loss passes to the buyer at the same time as title does: when the goods are delivered to the carrier, that is, at the time and place of shipment. After the goods have been delivered to the carrier, the seller has no liability for, or insurable interest in, the goods unless the seller has reserved a security interest in them. **For Example,** if the Los Angeles seller has a shipment contract (an FOB Los Angeles contract), once the goods are in the hands of the carrier, the risk belongs to the buyer or the buyer's

---

CASE SUMMARY

Peeling Back the Layers in the Great Onion Contract Breach

FACTS: Bakker Brothers of Idaho agreed to buy Charles E. Graff's 1989 onion seed crop. The contract required that the onion seeds have an 85 percent germination rate. Despite careful testing and advice from experts, Bakker Brothers could not get a germination rate on the seed tested higher than 62 to 69 percent. Bakker Brothers rejected the seed, notified Graff, and awaited instructions. Graff gave no instructions and the seed spoiled. Graff sought to recover the contract price from Bakker Brothers because the risk of loss had passed. The trial court granted summary judgment for Bakker Brothers, and Graff appealed.

DECISION: The risk of loss never passed to Bakker Brothers because Graff did not ship goods in compliance with the terms of the contract. The seed did not meet the germination rate, and Bakker Brothers did not have the risk of loss when the seed was destroyed. [**Graff v Bakker Brothers of Idaho, Inc., 934 P2d 1228 (Wash App 1997)**]

---

[18] UCC § 2-509; *Charia v Cigarette Racing Tea, Inc.,* 583 F2d 184 (5th Cir 1978).

[19] UCC § 2-509(3).

[20] UCC § 2-509. Revised UCC § 2-612 retains the rules for risk of loss in shipment contracts. See Patricia A., Tauchert, "Symposium on Revised Article 1 and Proposed Revised Article 2 of the Uniform Commercial Code Article," 54 *Southern Methodist Law Review* 971 (2001).

insurer. If the goods are hijacked outside Kansas City, the New York buyer must still pay the Los Angeles seller for the goods according to the contract price and terms.

(b) CONTRACT FOR DELIVERY AT DESTINATION (FOB PLACE OF DESTINATION) When the contract requires the seller to deliver the contract goods at a particular destination (FOB place of destination), the risk of loss does not pass to the buyer until the carrier tenders the goods at the destination. **For Example,** if the contract is FOB New York and the goods are hijacked in Kansas City, the seller is required to find substitute goods and perform under the contract because the risk of loss does not pass to the buyer until the goods arrive in New York and are available to the notified buyer.

---

16. DAMAGE TO OR DESTRUCTION OF GOODS

In the absence of a contract provision, Article 2 provides for certain rights for the parties in the event of damage to or destruction of goods that are the subject matter in a contract.

(a) DAMAGE TO IDENTIFIED GOODS BEFORE RISK OF LOSS PASSES Goods that were identified at the time the contract was made may be damaged or destroyed without the fault of either party before the risk of loss has passed. If so, the UCC provides, "if the loss is total the contract is avoided."[21] The loss may be partial, or the goods may have so deteriorated that they do not conform to the contract. In this case, the buyer has the option, after inspecting the goods, to either avoid the contract or accept the goods subject to an allowance or a deduction from the contract price. There is no breach by the seller, so the purpose of the law is simply to eliminate the legal remedies, allow the buyer to choose to take the goods, and have the insurers involved cover the losses.[22]

(b) DAMAGE TO IDENTIFIED GOODS AFTER RISK OF LOSS PASSES If partial damage or total destruction occurs after the risk of loss has passed to the buyer, it is the buyer's loss. The buyer may be able to recover the amount of the damages from the carrier, an insurer, the person in possession of the goods (such as a warehouse), or any third person causing the loss.[23]

(c) DAMAGE TO UNIDENTIFIED GOODS As long as the goods are unidentified, no risk of loss passes to the buyer. If any goods are damaged or destroyed during this period, the loss is the seller's. The buyer is still entitled to receive the goods described by the contract. The seller is therefore liable for breach of contract if the proper goods are not delivered.

The only exceptions to these general rules on damage or destruction arise when the parties have expressly provided in the contract that the destruction of the seller's inventory, crop, or source of supply releases the seller from liability, or when it is clear that the parties contracted for the purchase and sale of part of the seller's supply to the exclusion of any other possible source of such goods. In these cases, destruction of, or damage to, the seller's supply is a condition subsequent that discharges the contract.

---

[21] UCC § 613(a).

[22] *Design Data Corp. v Maryland Casualty Co.,* 503 NW2d 552 (Neb 1993).

[23] For a discussion of parties' rights, see *Learning Links, Inc. v United Parcel Services of America, Inc.* 2006 WL 785274 (SDNY).

17. EFFECT OF SELLER'S BREACH IN RISK OF LOSS

When the seller breaches the contract by sending the buyer goods that do not conform to the contract and the buyer rejects them, the risk of loss does not pass to the buyer. If there has been a breach, the risk of loss remains with the seller even though the risk, according to the contract terms or the Article 2 rules discussed earlier, would ordinarily have passed to the buyer.

Figures 24-3 and 24-4 (page 520) provide a summary of all the risk provisions for parties in a sales transaction.

ETHICS & THE LAW

High-Falutin' Merchandise and High Charge Backs

Some vendors are going to court to challenge the deductions retailers take before paying their vendors' bills. In May 2005, Ben Elias Industries, a family-owned clothing manufacturer, located in the garment district of New York City, and that holds the license of making the Mary McFadden line of clothing, filed suit against Dillard's, the third-largest department store in the United States. In the suit, Elias offered the following information about the scope of the markdowns:

> *Dillard's took a 36.1% discount on $842,621 invoiced amount when the maximum discount the contract provided for was 10%. The discounts are taken for a variety of reasons that range from merchandise defects and quality to the inability to sell the line of clothing. Candie's filed suit against Saks for taking $176,016 in deductions on $200,000 in merchandise.*

No one is quite sure how this practice of charge backs became so entrenched. However, there was at least some reciprocity in the 1980s when the practice began. Manufacturers wanted their clothing lines in stores such as Saks, Bloomingdale's, and others. When a store agreed to sell a line, it would order, for example, $100,000 in inventory. The manufacturers would encourage the retailer to take $150,000 (pitching the idea that the retailer could sell more). The manufacturer agreed to take a discount or "markdown" on what actually sold so that the retailer would still have a profit on the $150,000 in merchandise. The retailers began deducting other amounts from invoices, and the phenomenon of charge backs began. Manufacturers were charged for goods that did not arrive on time, failure to sell, mislabeling, and mispackaging. Some retailers were so finely attuned to this process that they drafted unduly complex contracts for charge backs, right down to allow certain types of hangers to be used. The following have been the results of these systems:

- Increasingly complex and increasing amount of charge backs and markdowns
- Difficulties with accounting to reflect the practices

How would the risk of loss rules apply to these situations?

Source: Tracie Rozhon, "Stores and Vendors Take Their Haggling over Payments to Court," *New York Times,* May 17, 2005, C1, C3.

DETERMINING RIGHTS: SPECIAL SITUATIONS

18. RETURNABLE GOODS TRANSACTIONS

The parties may agree that the goods to be transferred under the contract can be returned to the seller. This type of arrangement in which goods may be returned is classified as one of the following: (1) a sale on approval, (2) a sale or return, or (3) a consignment sale. In the first two types of transactions, the buyer is allowed to return the goods as an added inducement to purchase. The consignment sale is used when the seller is actually the owner's agent for the purpose of selling goods.[24]

sale on approval term indicating that no sale takes place until the buyer approves or accepts the goods.

(a) SALE ON APPROVAL   In a **sale on approval,** no sale takes place (meaning there is no transfer of title) until the buyer approves, or accepts, the goods. Title and risk of loss remain with the seller until there is an approval. Because the buyer is not the "owner" of the goods before approval, the buyer's creditors cannot attach or take the goods before the buyer's approval of the goods.

The buyer's approval may be shown by (1) express words, (2) conduct, or (3) lapse of time. Trying out or testing the goods does not constitute approval or acceptance. Any use that goes beyond trying out or testing, such as repairing the goods or giving them away as a present, is inconsistent with the seller's continued ownership. These types of uses show approval by the buyer. **For Example,** a buyer may order a home gym through a television ad. The ad allows buyers to try the room full of equipment for 30 days and then promises, "If you are not completely satisfied, return the home gym and we'll refund your money." The offer is one for a sale on approval. If the buyer does not return the home gym equipment or contact the seller within 30 days, the sale is complete.

The contract may give the buyer a fixed number of days for approval. The expiration of that period of time, without any action by the buyer, constitutes an approval. Also during this time, the buyer's creditors cannot take the goods pursuant to a judgment or lien. If no time is stated in the contract, the lapse of a reasonable time without action by the buyer constitutes an approval. If the buyer gives the seller notice of disapproval, the lapse of time thereafter has no effect.

If the buyer does not approve the goods, the seller bears the risk of and expense for their return.

sale or return sale in which the title to the property passes to the buyer at the time of the transaction but the buyer is given the option of returning the property and restoring the title to the seller.

(b) SALE OR RETURN   A **sale or return** is a completed sale with an option for the buyer to return the goods. Revised Article 2 provides a new distinction between sale on approval and sale or return but with the same basic rules on title and risk of loss:

Unless otherwise agreed, if delivered goods may be returned by the buyer even though they conform to the contract, the transaction is:

(a) a "sale on approval" if the goods are delivered primarily for use, and
(b) a "sale or return" if the goods are delivered primarily for resale.[25]

In a sale or return transaction, title and risk of loss pass to the buyer as in the case of the ordinary or absolute sale. Until the actual return of the goods is made, title and risk of loss remain with the buyer. The buyer bears the expense for and risk of

---

[24] *In re Thomas,* 182 BR 347, 26 UCC2d 774 (Bankr SD Fla 1995).

[25] For a discussion of the distinctions between sale on approval and sale or return, see 1 Hawkland UCC Series § 2-326:2 (2006).

return of the goods. In a sale or return, so long as the goods remain in the buyer's possession, the buyer's creditors may treat the goods as belonging to the buyer.

19. CONSIGNMENTS AND FACTORS

consignment bailment made for the purpose of sale by the bailee. (Parties–consignor, consignee)

consignor (1) person who delivers goods to the carrier for shipment; (2) party with title who turns goods over to another for sale.

consignee (1) person to whom goods are shipped; (2) dealer who sells goods for others.

factor bailee to whom goods are consigned for sale.

Under a **consignment**, the owner of the goods entrusts them to a dealer for the purpose of selling them. The seller is the **consignor**, and the dealer is the **consignee**. The dealer-consignee is often referred to as a **factor**, a special type of bailee (see Chapter 22) who sells consigned goods just as if the goods were her own. The dealer-consignee is paid a fee for selling the goods on behalf of the seller-consignor. A consignment sale is treated as a sale or return under Article 2, and the dealer-consignee has full authority to sell the goods for the consignor and can pass title to those goods. While the goods are in the possession of the consignee, they are subject to the claims of the seller's creditors.[26]

20. SELF-SERVICE STORES

In the case of goods in a self-service store, the reasonable interpretation of the circumstances is that the store, by its act of putting the goods on display on its shelves, makes an offer to sell such goods for cash and confers on a prospective customer a license to carry the goods to the cashier to make payment. Most courts hold that there is no transfer of title until the buyer makes payment to the cashier. Under this view, the store does not have warranty liability until the buyer pays. For example, if a customer is injured because a light bulb in his cart explodes as he is shopping, the remedy is against the manufacturer, not the store, unless the shopper could show that the store was storing the bulbs in a manner that would cause their sudden explosion.

A contrary rule adopts the view that a contract to sell is formed when the customer accepts the seller's offer by taking the item from the shelf. In other words, a sale actually occurs when the buyer takes the item from the shelf. Title passes at that moment to the buyer even though the goods have not yet been paid for. Under this view, the buyer would have a right of recovery for injury resulting from goods in the cart.

21. AUCTION SALES

CPA

When goods are sold at an auction in separate lots, each lot is a separate transaction, and title to each passes independently of the other lots. Title to each lot passes when the auctioneer announces by the fall of the hammer or in any other customary manner that the lot in question has been sold to the bidder. Under Revised Article 2, a bid that is made while the auctioneer is in the process of accepting a bid can be honored or not honored at the discretion of the auctioneer. It is the auctioneer's choice whether to end the bidding or reopen the process to allow the new bid and any others that might follow.

"With reserve" auctions are those that give the auctioneer the right to withdraw the goods from the sale process if the bids are not high enough. If an auction is held "without reserve," the goods must be sold regardless of whether the auctioneer is satisfied with the levels of the bids.

---

[26] This clarification of creditors' rights in consignments came from Revised Article 9 (see Chapter 34). Revised Article 2 was changed to make the sale or return rights of creditors consistent with Revised Article 9. Prior to these changes, and under current Article 2, whether the seller's creditor could seize the goods depended upon the filing of an Article 9 security interest.

> SUMMARY

All along the supply chain of a business are issues of risk and title that are often complicated by additional questions about damage to goods in transit, the claims of creditors to goods that are in process under a contract, and insurance. Unless the parties specifically agree otherwise, the solution to these problems depends on the nature of the transaction between the seller and the buyer.

The first issue to be addressed in answering questions of risk, title, and loss is whether the goods are identified. Existing goods are identified at the time the contract is entered into. Future goods, or goods not yet owned by the seller or not yet in existence (as in goods to be manufactured by the seller), are identified when they are shipped, marked, or otherwise designated for the buyer. Without identification, title and risk of loss cannot pass from buyer to seller, nor can the buyer hold an insurable interest.

Once identification has occurred, the issue of title, and hence creditor's rights, can be addressed. If there are identified goods but there is no document of title associated with the goods, then title to the goods passes from the seller to the buyer at the time of the contract.

Sellers can have their goods covered by a document of title. The most common types of documents of title are bills of lading and warehouse receipts. These documents of title, if properly transferred, transfer title to both the document and the underlying goods.

While the seller has no obligation under UCC Article 2 to deliver the goods to the buyer, the parties can agree on delivery as part of their contract. Several common delivery terms are used in supply chain management. *FOB* is "free on board," and its meaning depends on the location that follows the term. *FOB place of shipment* requires the seller to deliver the goods to the carrier. In an FOB place of shipment contract, title to the goods passes from the seller to the buyer when the goods are delivered to the carrier. *FOB place of destination* requires the seller to get the goods to the buyer or a location specified by the buyer and tender the goods there. *FAS* is "free alongside ship," which means free on board for shipment by sea. *CF* is "cost and freight" and requires the seller to deliver the goods to the carrier and make a contract for their shipment. *CIF* is "cost, insurance, and freight" and requires

the seller to deliver the goods to the carrier, make a contract for shipment, and purchase insurance for the goods in transit. *COD* means "cash on delivery" and requires the buyer to pay for the goods before taking possession of them.

Revised Article 2 no longer uses these commercial shipping terms. It simply makes a distinction between those types of contracts in which the seller agrees to ship the goods only and those in which the seller agrees to deliver the goods to a particular destination. For delivery to a particular destination (FOB place of destination), the time for passage of risk of loss and title is upon tender. *Tender* means that the goods are available for the buyer to pick up, the buyer is aware that the goods are available, and the buyer has the necessary documentation to pick up the goods.

Ordinarily, sellers cannot pass any title greater than that which they possess. In some cases, however, the law permits a greater title to be transferred even though the transferor may hold voidable title or be in possession of the goods only as in a bailment. These exceptions protect good-faith purchasers.

Risk of loss is an issue for buyers, sellers, and insurers. When risk of loss passes from seller to buyer is controlled, again, by the terms of the contract. In a contract in which there is no agreement on delivery, the risk of loss passes to the buyer upon receipt of the goods if the seller is a merchant and upon tender if the seller is a nonmerchant. Under Revised Article 2, the risk of loss in nonshipment contracts always passes upon receipt, regardless of whether the contract involves a merchant or nonmerchant. If there is an agreement for delivery and the contract provides for shipment only, or FOB place of shipment, then risk of loss passes from seller to buyer when the goods are delivered to the carrier. If the contract provides for delivery to a particular location, or FOB place of destination, then the risk of loss passes from the seller to the buyer when the goods are tendered to the buyer.

Some types of arrangements, such as sales on approval, sales or returns, and consignments or factor arrangements, have specific rules for passage of title and risk of loss. Also, if there is a breach of the contract and the seller ships goods different from those ordered, the breach prevents the risk of loss from passing from the seller to the buyer.

QUESTIONS AND CASE PROBLEMS

1. Schock, the buyer, negotiated to purchase a mobile home that was owned by and located on the sellers' property. On April 15, 1985, Schock appeared at the Ronderos' (the sellers') home and paid them the agreed-on purchase price of $3,900. Shock received a bill of sale and an assurance from the Ronderos that the title certificate to the mobile home would be delivered soon. Also on April 15 and with the permission of the sellers, Schock prepared the mobile home for removal. His preparations included the removal of skirting around the mobile home's foundation, the tie-downs, and the foundation blocks, leaving the mobile home to rest on the wheels of its chassis. Schock intended to remove the mobile home from the Ronderos' property a week later, and the Ronderos had no objection to having the mobile home remain on their premises until that time. The Ronderos also promised to have the electricity and natural gas disconnected by that time. Two days later, the mobile home was destroyed by high winds as it sat on the Ronderos' property. Schock received a clear certificate of title to the mobile home in the mail. Thereafter, Schock sued the Ronderos for return of his money on the ground that when the mobile home was destroyed, the risk of loss remained with the Ronderos. Who should win the lawsuit? [*Schock v Ronderos,* 394 NW2d 697 (ND)]

2. In 1989, Michael Heinrich wanted to buy a particular model of a new Ford pickup truck. James Wilson represented himself to Heinrich as a dealer-broker who was licensed to buy and sell vehicles. Because he did not know that Wilson had lost his Washington vehicle dealer's license a year earlier, Heinrich retained Wilson to make the truck purchase but did not direct Wilson to any particular dealer.

   Wilson negotiated with Titus-Will Sales for a pickup truck with the options Heinrich had specified. Wilson had completed hundreds of transactions over the years with Titus-Will, which also was unaware that Wilson had lost his license. Heinrich made two initial payments to Wilson: an $1,800 down payment and a $3,000 payment when Titus-Will ordered the truck. Wilson gave Heinrich a receipt with his vehicle dealer's license number and then ordered the truck from Titus-Will, using his own check to provide a $7,000 down payment. Wilson told the Titus-Will salesman with whom he placed the order that he was buying the truck for resale.

   When the truck arrived, Titus-Will issued a dealer-to-dealer title to it after Heinrich had paid the remaining $15,549.55 due on the sale. However, Wilson's original check for $7,000 failed to clear, and Titus-Will refused to issue the title and took the truck back from Heinrich. Seeking to have his truck returned, Heinrich sued Titus-Will and Wilson. Can Heinrich get his truck back? [*Heinrich v Titus-Will Sales, Inc.,* 868 P2d 169 (Wash App)]

3. Felix DeWeldon is a well-known sculptor and art collector. He owned three paintings valued at $26,000 that he displayed in his home in Newport, Rhode Island. In 1991, he declared bankruptcy and DeWeldon, Ltd., purchased all of DeWeldon's personal property from the bankruptcy trustee. Nancy Wardell, the sole shareholder of DeWeldon, Ltd., sold her stock to Byron Preservation Trust, which then sold Felix an option to repurchase the paintings. At all times, the paintings were on display in DeWeldon's home.

   In 1994, DeWeldon's son Byron told Robert McKean that his father was interested in selling the paintings. After viewing them, McKean then purchased the paintings for $50,000. DeWeldon, Ltd., brought suit to have the paintings returned, claiming McKean did not have title because Byron did not have the authority to sell the paintings. Will McKean get the paintings? [*DeWeldon, Ltd. v McKean,* 125 F3d 24 (1st Cir)]

4. Helen Thomas contracted to purchase a pool heater from Sunkissed Pools. As part of the $4,000 contract, Sunkissed agreed to install the pool heater, which was delivered to Thomas's home and left in the driveway. The heater was too heavy for Thomas to lift, and she was forced to leave it in the driveway because no one from Sunkissed responded to her calls about its installation. Subsequently, the heater

disappeared from the driveway. Sunkissed maintained the risk of loss had passed to Thomas. Thomas maintained that the failure to install the heater as promised is a breach of contract. Who should bear the risk for the stolen pool heater? [*In re Thomas,* 182 BR 774 (Bankr SD Fla)]

5. Petrosol, a wholesale marketer and distributor of petroleum products, acts as an agent between gas line producers and gas distributors. Because it immediately resells the propane that it purchases, Petrosol does not have its own storage facilities. Commonwealth, also a marketer and distributor, does have such storage facilities and reserves much of the liquid propane gas it purchases for resale on a later date.

   On November 5, 1982, Cal Gas Corporation, a propane supplier, entered into a contract with Petrosol for the sale and delivery of 10,000 barrels of propane stored at Lake Underground Storage, a storage facility in Painesville, Ohio. Petrosol agreed to pay $0.57 per gallon for the propane. Petrosol entered into a contract with Commonwealth on the same day for the sale and delivery of 10,000 barrels of propane at a price of $0.58 per gallon. Commonwealth paid Petrosol for the propane two days later. Sales Acknowledgements indicated that the "delivery point" was "Painesville, Ohio" and that the stated price was "$0.58 USF/USG F.O.B. Lake Underground Storage." In addition, beside the "to be delivered in" caption on the front of the Sales Acknowledgments, there were five boxes indicating different types of delivery methods (buyer's tank trucks or cars, seller's tank trucks or cars, or pipeline PTO). None of these boxes was checked on either form.

   In February 1983, a wall in the cavern of Lake Underground collapsed. As a result, the propane was apparently either lost or destroyed before Commonwealth was able to remove it from the storage facility. Commonwealth subsequently sued both Petrosol and Cal Gas for the lack of sufficient propane to fill the agreements. Had the risk of loss passed to Commonwealth, or was Petrosol still responsible for the loss of the propane? [*Commonwealth Petroleum Co. v Petrosol Intern., Inc.,* 901 F2d 1314 (6th Cir)]

6. A thief stole a car and sold it to a good-faith purchaser for value. This person resold the car to another buyer, who also purchased in good faith and for value. The original owner of the car sued the second purchaser for the car. The defendant argued that he had purchased the car in good faith from a seller who had sold in good faith. Was this defense valid? [*Johnny Dell, Inc. v New York State Police,* 375 NYS2d 545 (Misc)]

7. Using a bad check, B purchased a used automobile from a dealer. B then took the automobile to an auction at which the automobile was sold to a party who had no knowledge of its history. When B's check was dishonored, the dealer brought suit against the party who purchased the automobile at the auction. Was the dealer entitled to reclaim the automobile? [*Greater Louisville Auto Auction, Inc. v Ogle Buick, Inc.,* 387 SW2d 17 (Ky)]

8. Coppola, who collected coins, joined a coin club, First Coinvestors, Inc. The club would send coins to its members, who were to pay for them or return them within 10 days. What was the nature of the transaction? [*First Coinvestors, Inc. v Coppola,* 388 NYS2d 833 (Misc)]

9. Would buying a car from a mechanic who works at a car dealership qualify as purchasing a car in the ordinary course of business? [*Steele v Ellis,* 961 F Supp 1458 (D Kan)]

10. Does a pawnbroker who purchases property in good faith acquire good title to that property? Can the pawnbroker pass good title? [*Fly v Cannon,* 813 SW2d 458 (Tenn App)]

11. Larsen Jewelers sold a necklace to Conway on a layaway plan. Conway paid a portion of the price and made additional payments from time to time. The necklace was to remain in the possession of Larsen until payment was fully made. The Larsen jewelry store was burglarized, and Conway's necklace and other items were taken. Larsen argued that Conway must bear the risk of loss. Conway sought recovery of the full value of the necklace. Decide. [*Conway v Larsen Jewelry,* 429 NYS2d 378 (Misc)]

12. Future Tech International, Inc., is a buyer and distributor of Samsung monitors and other computer products. In 1993, Future Tech

determined that brand loyalty was important to customers, and it sought to market its own brand of computer products. Future Tech, a Florida firm, developed its own brand name of MarkVision and entered into a contract in 1994 with Tae II Media, a Korean firm. The contract provided that Tae II Media would be the sole source and manufacturer for the MarkVision line of computer products.

The course of performance on the contract did not go well. Future Tech alleged that from the time the ink was dry on the contract, Tae II Media had no intention of honoring its commitment to supply computers and computer products to Future Tech. Future Tech alleged that Tae II Media entered into the contract with the purpose of limiting Future Tech's competitive ability because Tae II Media had its own Tech Media brand of computers and computer products.

Future Tech, through threats and demands, was able to have the first line of MarkVision products completed. Tae II Media delivered the computers to a boat but, while in transit, ordered the shipping line (Maersk Lines) to return the computers. The terms of their contract provided for delivery "FOB Pusan Korea." Future Tech filed suit, claiming that Tae II Media could not take the computer products because title had already passed to Future Tech. Is this interpretation of who has title correct? [*Future Tech Int'l, Inc. v Tae II Media, Ltd.,* 944 F Supp 1538 (SD Fla 1996)]

13. Smith operated a marina and sold and repaired boats. Gallagher rented a stall at the marina, where he kept his vessel, the *River Queen*. Without any authorization, Smith sold the vessel to Courtesy Ford. Gallagher sued Courtesy Ford for the vessel. What was the result? [*Gallagher v Unenrolled Motor Vessel River Queen,* 475 F2d 117 (5th Cir)]

14. Without permission, Grissom entered onto land owned by another and then proceeded to cut and sell the timber from the land. On learning that the timber had been sold, the owner of the land brought an action to recover the timber from the purchaser. The purchaser argued that he was a good-faith purchaser who had paid value and therefore was entitled to keep the timber. Decide. [*Baysprings Forest Products, Inc. v Wade,* 435 So 2d 690 (Miss)]

15. Brown Sales ordered goods from Eberhard Manufacturing Co. The contract contained no agreement about who would bear the risk of loss. There were no shipping terms. The seller placed the goods on board a common carrier with instructions to deliver the goods to Brown. While in transit, the goods were lost. Which party will bear the loss? Explain. [*Eberhard Manufacturing Co. v Brown,* 232 NW2d 378 (Mich App)]

> CPA QUESTIONS

1. Bond purchased a painting from Wool, who is not in the business of selling art. Wool tendered delivery of the painting after receiving payment in full from Bond. Bond informed Wool that Bond would be unable to take possession of the painting until later that day. Thieves stole the painting before Bond returned. The risk of loss

   a. Passed to Bond at Wool's tender of delivery
   b. Passed to Bond at the time the contract was formed and payment was made
   c. Remained with Wool, because the parties agreed on a later time of delivery
   d. Remained with Wool, because Bond had not yet received the painting

2. Which of the following statements applies to a sale on approval under the UCC Sales Article?

   a. Both the buyer and seller must be merchants.
   b. The buyer must be purchasing the goods for resale.
   c. Risk of loss for the goods passes to the buyer when the goods are accepted after the trial period.
   d. Title to the goods passes to the buyer on delivery of the goods to the buyer.

3. If goods have been delivered to a buyer pursuant to a sale or return contract, the

   a. Buyer may use the goods but not resell them
   b. Seller is liable for the expenses incurred by the buyer in returning the goods to the seller
   c. Title to the goods remains with the seller
   d. Risk of loss for the goods passed to the buyer

4. Cey Corp. entered into a contract to sell parts to Deck, Ltd. The contract provided that the goods would be shipped "FOB Cey's warehouse." Cey shipped parts different from those specified in the contract. Deck rejected the parts. A few hours after Deck informed Cey that the parts were rejected, they were destroyed by fire in Deck's warehouse. Cey believed that the parts were conforming to the contract. Which of the following statements is correct?

   a. Regardless of whether the parts were conforming, Deck will bear the loss because the contract was a shipment contract.
   b. If the parts were nonconforming, Deck had the right to reject them, but the risk of loss remains with Deck until Cey takes possession of the parts.
   c. If the parts were conforming, risk of loss does not pass to Deck until a reasonable period of time after they are delivered to Deck.
   d. If the parts were nonconforming, Cey will bear the risk of loss, even though the contract was a shipment contract.

5. Under the Sales Articles of the UCC, when a contract for the sale of goods stipulates that the seller ship the goods by common carrier "FOB purchaser's loading dock," which of the parties bears the risk of loss during shipment?

   a. The purchaser, because risk of loss passes when the goods are delivered to the carrier
   b. The purchaser, because title to the goods passes at the time of shipment
   c. The seller, because risk of loss passes only when the goods reach the purchaser's loading dock
   d. The seller, because risk of loss remains with the seller until the goods are accepted by the purchaser

PRODUCT LIABILITY:

WARRANTIES AND TORTS

CHAPTER

(25)

LEARNING OBJECTIVES

After studying this chapter, you should be able to

LO.1 List the theories of product liability

LO.2 Identify who may sue and who may be sued when a defective product causes harm

LO.3 List and define the implied warranties and distinguish them from express warranties

LO.4 Explain and distinguish between full warranties and limited warranties under federal law

LO.5 State what constitutes a breach of warranty

LO.6 Describe the extent and manner in which implied warranties may be disclaimed under the UCC and the CISG

What happens when goods do not work? Who can recover for injury caused by defective goods? What can you do when the goods are not as promised or pictured?

 ## A   GENERAL PRINCIPLES

When defective goods result in damages or injury to the buyer or other parties, the UCC and tort law provide remedies.

1. THEORIES OF LIABILITY

Two centuries ago, a buyer was limited to recovery from a seller for breach of an express guarantee or for negligence or fraud. After the onset of mass production and distribution, however, these remedies had little value. A guarantee was good, but in the ordinary sales transaction no one stopped to get a guarantee. Few customers remembered to ask the manager of the supermarket to give a guarantee that the loaf of bread purchased was fit to eat. Further, negligence and fraud have become difficult to prove in a mass production world. How can one prove there was a problem in the production process for a can of soup prepared months earlier?

warranty promise either express or implied about the nature, quality, or performance of the goods.

To give buyers protection from economic loss and personal injuries, the concept of warranty liability developed. **Warranties** are either express or implied and can be found in the UCC. As with other UCC areas, there have been changes in warranty liability under the Revised UCC, and those areas of change are discussed in the sections that follow. Many courts have decided that still broader protection beyond the UCC contract remedies is required and have created the additional concept of **strict tort liability** for defective goods.

strict tort liability product liability theory that imposes liability upon the manufacturer, seller, or distributor of goods for harm caused by defective goods.

There are five theories in law for what is often called *product liability*, or the protection of buyers for injury and economic loss: express warranty, implied warranty, negligence, fraud, and strict tort liability. Any statutory remedies under consumer law or employment law are additional means of recovery. The plaintiff does not have a choice of all theories in every case; the facts of the case dictate the choices the plaintiff has available for possible theories of recovery.

2. NATURE OF HARM

A defective product can cause harm to person, property, or economic interests. **For Example,** the buyer of a truck may be injured when, through a defect, the truck goes out of control and plunges down the side of a hill. Passengers in the truck, bystanders, or the driver of a car hit by the truck may also be injured. The defective truck may cause injury to a total stranger who seeks to rescue one of the victims. Property damage could occur if the buyer's truck careens off the road into a fence or even a house and causes damages. Another driver's car may be damaged. Commercial and economic interests of the buyer are affected by the fact that the truck is defective. Even if there is no physical harm, the defective truck is not as valuable as it would have been. The buyer who has paid for the truck on the basis of its value as it should have been has sustained an economic loss. If the buyer is required to rent a truck from someone else or loses an opportunity to haul freight for compensation, the fact that the truck was defective also causes economic or commercial loss.

3. WHO IS LIABLE IN PRODUCT LIABILITY

`CPA`

Until the early part of the 20th century, only the parties to a sales contract could recover from each other on product liability issues. A seller was liable to the buyer, but the seller was not liable to others because they were not in **privity of contract** with the seller or in a direct contract relationship with the seller.

privity of contract relationship between a promisor and the promisee.

This requirement of privity of contract has now been widely rejected.[1] The law has moved toward the notion that persons harmed because of a defective product may recover from anyone who is in any way responsible.

(a) WHO CAN RECOVER UNDER UCC WARRANTIES   Today, not only the buyer but also customers and employees of the buyer and even third persons or bystanders may recover because of harm caused by a defective product. Most states have abolished the requirement of **privity** when the person injured by a product is a member of the buyer's family or household or is a guest of the buyer and has sustained personal injury because of the product.[2] A few states require privity of contract, particularly when the plaintiff does not sustain personal injury or property damage and seeks to recover only economic loss.[3]

privity succession or chain of relationship to the same thing or right, such as privity of contract, privity of estate, privity of possession.

Revised section 2-318 provides alternatives for who can recover for breach of warranty (and these protections cannot be excluded or limited by the seller under Alternatives A and B and cannot be excluded or limited for personal injury under Alternative C). Revised section 2-318 now includes definitions of those covered by the

---

[1] UCC § 2-318, Alternative A. The Code gives the states the option of adopting the provision summarized in this chapter or of making a wide abolition of the requirement of privity by adopting Alternative B or C of § 2-318. As of March 2004, these states/areas had adopted the versions of § 2-318 (not Revised Article 2) as follows: Alternative A adopted in Alaska, Arizona, Arkansas, Connecticut, District of Columbia, Florida, Georgia, Idaho, Illinois, Indiana, Kentucky, Maryland, Michigan, Mississippi, Missouri, Montana, Nebraska, Nevada (has adopted Revised Article 2), New Jersey, New Mexico, North Carolina, Ohio, Oklahoma, Oregon, Pennsylvania, Tennessee, Virgin Islands, Washington, West Virginia, and Wisconsin. Alternative B adopted in Alabama, Colorado, Delaware, Kansas (has adopted Revised Article 2), New York, South Carolina, South Dakota, Vermont, and Wyoming. Alternative C adopted in Hawaii, Iowa, Minnesota, North Dakota, and Utah.

[2] Lack of privity is not a defense in a suit for breach of warranty. *Williams v Gradall Co.*, 990 F Supp 442 (D Va 1998). Revised Article 2 extends warranty protection (§§ 2-408 and 2-409) to immediate buyers, remote buyers, or transferees who use or are affected by the product.

[3] *Barnett v Leiserv, Inc.*, 137 F3d 1356 (11th Cir 1998).

warranties. Under Revised Article 2, the following alternatives are available for state adoption for determining who has rights of recovery:

- Alternative A extends warranty protection to "any natural person who is in the family or household . . . of the remote purchaser or who is a guest in the home [of the remote purchaser] . . . if it is reasonable to expect that the person may use, consume or be affected by the goods" and is "injured in person" by breach of remedial promise, warranty, or obligation.

- Alternative B extends warranty protection to "any natural person who may reasonably be expected to use, consume or be affected by the goods" and is "injured in person" by the breach of the remedial promise, warranty, or obligation.

- Alternative C extends warranty protection to "any person that may reasonably be expected to use, consume or be affected by the goods" and is injured by the breach of the remedial promise, warranty, or obligation.

(b) Who Is Liable under UCC Warranties   Someone who is injured by a defective product can recover from the seller, a remote seller, the manufacturer of the product, and generally even the manufacturer of the component part of the product that caused the harm.[4] **For Example,** when a person is struck by an automobile because the driver has lost control because of the car's defective brakes, the person who was struck and injured may seek recovery from the seller and the manufacturer of the car. The maker of the brake assembly or system that the car manufacturer installed in the car may also be liable. The concepts of remote purchasers and immediate buyers have been defined and incorporated into Revised Article 2 and are defined in a new subsection added to section 2-313.[5]

B   EXPRESS WARRANTIES

A warranty may be express or implied. Both express and implied warranties operate as though the defendant had made an express promise or statement of fact. Both express and implied warranties are governed primarily by the UCC.

4. DEFINITION OF EXPRESS WARRANTY

express warranty statement by the defendant relating to the goods, which statement is part of the basis of the bargain.

An **express warranty** is a statement by the defendant relating to the goods; the statement is part of the basis of the bargain.[6]

"Basis of the bargain" means that the buyer has purchased the goods because of what the seller has stated about those goods. A statement by the seller regarding the quality, capacity, or other characteristic of the goods is an express warranty. **For Example,** express warranties in sellers' statements are "This cloth is all wool," "This paint is for household woodwork," and "This engine can produce 50 horsepower."

---

[4] However, see *Barnett v Leiserv,* 968 F Supp 690 (ND Ga 1997), where the child of the person who bought coffee for a friend could not sue to recover for burns from coffee spilled on her by the friend. The court also noted that a child who spills coffee on himself could not recover either.

[5] Revised UCC § 2-313(1)(a) and (b).

[6] UCC § 2-313; *Valleyside Dairy Farms, Inc. v A. O. Smith Corp.,* 944 F Supp 612 (WD Mich 1995); *Smith v Bearfield,* 950 SW2d 39 (Tenn App 1997). In the UCC Revised Article 2, the "basis of the bargain" requirement is changed to "become part of the agreement." UCC § 2-313(1)(a). Also, § 2-404 is the new express warranty section.

A representation that an airplane is a 2007 model is an express warranty. "This computer monitor has a glare-proof screen" is another example of an express warranty.

The changes in Revised Article 2 in the express warranty section deal with promises made by parties in direct contract and the validity of those promises to "remote buyers"—that is, those buyers who purchase farther down the chain of distribution from the manufacturer who is selling to the wholesaler under a direct contract. The revisions to section 2-313 change the language to "the immediate buyer" when an express warranty is defined. Section 2-313 applies only in situations in which there is privity of contract between the parties. Section 2-313(1)(a) and (b) outlines the responsibilities of sellers to "remote purchasers"—that is, those who buy from the immediate buyer or others in the chain of distribution.[7] **For Example,** WorldWide Wholesalers could purchase Pop-Tarts from Kellogg's. Kellogg's makes warranties to WorldWide Wholesalers directly through their contract relationship, one of privity. WorldWide Wholesalers then sells those Pop-Tarts to grocery stores, convenience stores, and perhaps even to commercial food distributors who then sell them to cafeterias in schools and nursing homes. WorldWide's buyers are remote purchasers. Only WorldWide (and any other companies who buy from Kellogg's directly) is an immediate buyer.

Under Revised UCC, the seller's obligations and promises to remote buyers are the same as the seller's obligations and promises to immediate buyers if the seller "makes an affirmation of fact or promise that relates to the goods, provides a description that relates to the goods, or makes a remedial promise"; and that affirmation, promise, description, or remedial promise is "in a record packaged with or accompanying the goods"; and the seller "reasonably expects the record to be, and the record is, furnished to the remote purchaser."[8]

5. FORM OF EXPRESS WARRANTY

No particular group of words is necessary to constitute an express warranty. A seller need not state that a warranty is being made or that one is intended. It is sufficient that the seller asserts a fact that becomes a basis of the bargain or transaction between the parties. UCC § 2-313(2) provides, "It is not necessary to the creation of an express warranty that the seller use formal words such as 'warrant' or 'guarantee' or that the seller have a specific intention to make a warranty."[9]

An express warranty can be written or printed as well as oral. The words on the label of a can and in a newspaper ad for "boned chicken" constitute an express warranty that the can contains chicken that is free of bones.

Descriptions of goods, such as the illustrations in a seller's catalog, are express warranties. The express warranty given is that the goods will conform to the catalog illustrations.

6. TIME OF MAKING EXPRESS WARRANTY

It is immaterial whether the express warranty is made at the time of or after the sale. No separate consideration is required for the warranty when it is part of a sale. If a

---

[7] Revised UCC § 2-313(1)(a) and (b).
[8] Revised UCC § 2-313(2)(a).
[9] UCC § 2-313(2).

warranty is made after the sale, no consideration is required because it is regarded as a modification of the sales contract.

7. SELLER'S OPINION OR STATEMENT OF VALUE

A statement about the value of goods or the seller's opinion or commendation of the goods does not create a warranty.[10] Section 2-313(1)(b) provides, "an affirmation merely of the value of the goods or a statement purporting to be merely the seller's opinion or commendation of goods does not create a warranty."[11] A buyer cannot hold a seller liable for sales talk. **For Example,** sales talk or puffery by a seller that his cloth is "the best piece of cloth on the market" or that her glassware is "as good as anyone else's" is merely an opinion that the buyer cannot ordinarily treat as a warranty. Statements made by a cosmetics seller that its products are "the future of beauty" and are "just the product for [the plaintiff]" are sales talk arising in the ordinary course of merchandising. They do not constitute warranties.

The UCC does permit an exception to the sales talk liability exemption when the circumstances are such that a reasonable person would rely on such a statement. If the buyer has reason to believe that the seller has expert knowledge of the conditions of the market, and the buyer requests the seller's opinion as an expert, the buyer is entitled to accept as a fact the seller's statement of whether a particular good is the best obtainable. The opinion statement could be reasonably regarded as forming part of the basis of the bargain. A statement by a florist that bulbs are of first-grade quality may be a warranty.[12]

8. WARRANTY OF CONFORMITY TO DESCRIPTION, SAMPLE, OR MODEL

When the contract is based in part on the understanding that the seller will supply goods according to a particular description or that the goods will be the same as the sample or a model, the seller is bound by an express warranty that the goods conform to the description, sample, or model.[13] Section 2-313 of the UCC provides, "Any sample or model which is made part of the basis of the bargain creates an express warranty that the whole of the goods shall conform to the sample or model."[14] **For Example,** a blender sitting out in a store is a warranty that the blenders in the boxes below are the same. A model of a mobile home is an express warranty that the mobile home being sold contains the same features.

9. FEDERAL REGULATION OF EXPRESS WARRANTIES

A seller who makes a written express warranty for a consumer product costing more than $10 must conform to certain standards imposed by federal statute[15] and by regulations of the Federal Trade Commission (FTC).[16] The seller is not required to make any express warranty. However, if the seller does make an express warranty in a consumer sale, it must be stated in ordinary, understandable language and must

---

[10] Id.; *Jordan v Paccar, Inc.,* 37 F3d 1181 (6th Cir 1994).

[11] UCC § 2-313(1)(b).

[12] Likewise, a statement by an art gallery owner that a "painting is by Francis Bacon" is an express warranty. *Rogath v Siebenmann,* 129 F3d 902 (7th Cir 1997).

[13] *Poly Products Corp. v AT&T Nassau Metals, Inc.,* 839 F Supp 1238 (ED Tex 1993).

[14] UCC § 2-313(1)(c).

[15] The Magnuson-Moss Act, or Federal Consumer Product Warranty Law, can be found at 15 USC § 2301 *et seq.*

[16] 16 CFR § 700.1 *et seq.*

be made available for inspection before purchasing so that the consumer may comparison shop.[17]

(a) FULL WARRANTIES   If the seller or the label states that a full warranty is made, the seller is obligated to fix or replace a defective product within a reasonable time without cost to the buyer. If the product cannot be fixed or if a reasonable number of repair attempts are unsuccessful, the buyer has the choice of a cash refund or a free replacement. No unreasonable burden may be placed on a buyer seeking to obtain warranty service. **For Example,** a manufacturer offering a full warranty cannot require that the buyer pay the cost of sending the product to or from a warranty service point. A warrantor making a full warranty cannot require the buyer to return the product to a warranty service point if the product weighs over 35 pounds, to return a part for service unless it can be easily removed, or to fill out and return a warranty registration card shortly after purchase to make the warranty effective. If the manufacturer imposes any of these requirements, the warranty is not a "full warranty" under federal law and must be labeled a *limited warranty*. A **full warranty** runs with the product and lasts for its full term regardless of who owns the product.

> **full warranty** obligation of a seller to fix or replace a defective product within a reasonable time without cost to the buyer.
>
> **limited warranty** any warranty that does not provide the complete protection of a full warranty.

(b) LIMITED WARRANTIES   A **limited warranty** is any warranty that does not meet the requirements for a full warranty. **For Example,** a warranty is limited if the buyer must pay any cost for repair or replacement of a defective product, if only the first buyer is covered by the warranty, or if the warranty covers only part of the product. A limited warranty must be conspicuously described as such by the seller.[18]

10. EFFECT OF BREACH OF EXPRESS WARRANTY

If an express warranty is false, there is a breach of warranty. The warrantor is then liable. It is no defense that the seller or manufacturer who made the express warranty honestly believed that the warranty was true, had exercised due care in manufacturing or handling the product, or had no reason to believe that the warranty was false.[19]

IMPLIED WARRANTIES

Whenever a sale of goods is made, certain warranties are implied unless they are expressly excluded. Implied warranties differ depending on whether the seller is a merchant.

11. DEFINITION OF IMPLIED WARRANTY

> **implied warranty** warranty that was not made but is implied by law.

An **implied warranty** is one that was not expressly made by the seller but that is implied in certain circumstances by law. An implied warranty arises automatically from the fact that a sale has been made regardless of the seller's conduct.

Express warranties arise because they form part of the basis on which the sale has been made. Implied warranties can exist independent of express warranties. When

---

[17] Federal warranty language rules apply only in consumer sales, or sales for personal or home use, not in business purchases. *Weaver v Dan Jones Ford, Inc.,* 679 So 2d 1105 (Ala 1996).

[18] The federal regulations here do not preempt Article 2 warranty coverage. *Mitchell v Collagen Corp.,* 126 F3d 902 (7th Cir 1997).

[19] The failure to disclose, however, is not covered—that is, there is no warranty of omission. *Witherspoon v Philip Morris, Inc.,* 964 F Supp 455 (DDC 1997).

CASE SUMMARY

An Inflated Air Bag Warranty?

FACTS: On December 15, 1997, Hilda Forbes and her three grandchildren were traveling to Columbia, Mississippi, in her 1992 Oldsmobile Delta 88. Mrs. Forbes was driving behind a 1981 Chevrolet Chevette, which suddenly stopped and attempted to turn into a private driveway. Mrs. Forbes struck the Chevette from the rear. Both automobiles were damaged. The air bag in Mrs. Forbes' automobile did not inflate.

As a result of the impact, Mrs. Forbes was propelled forward into the windshield. She suffered a subdural hematoma. Dr. Howard Katz, a specialist in physical medicine, rehabilitation, and spinal cord injuries, testified by deposition that Mrs. Forbes suffered significant cognitive dysfunction and never completely recovered from the injury to her brain.

The air bag system and Mrs. Forbes' automobile were manufactured by GM. The owner's manual contains the following statement, "The 'air bag' part of the SIR [Supplemental Inflatable Restraint] system is in the middle of the steering wheel. The SIR system is only for crashes where the front area of your vehicle hits something. If the collision is hard enough, the 'air bag' inflates in a fraction of a second." Mr. Forbes asked the salesman about the air bag and was assured that the car had an effective one.

The Forbeses purchased their car from Mike Smith Motors, which subsequently was purchased by Mack Grubbs Motors, Inc. Angela Coleman was the driver of the 1981 Chevrolet Chevette.

On December 7, 2000, Hilda and Hoyt Forbes filed suit against Angela Coleman and later added GM as a defendant. Following their case, the Forbeses voluntarily dismissed Coleman from the suit. Mack Grubbs Motors, Inc., moved for a directed verdict, which was granted. GM moved for a directed verdict, which the judge also granted. The Forbeses appealed on the grounds that GM had breached an express warranty.

DECISION: To survive the directed verdict, the Forbeses must show that the car and its air bag either "breached an express warranty or failed to conform to other express factual representations" upon which they justifiably relied in electing to use the product. The questions to the salesman showed their reliance. There is both an express warranty, the promise of a functional driver's side air bag, and justifiable reliance, the fact that, but for the promise of the air bag, Forbes would not have purchased the vehicle. The statutory requirements are met and the case was remanded for trial on the issue of a breach of an express warranty. [**Forbes v General Motors Corp.,** 2006 WL 1431228 (Miss)]

both express and implied warranties exist, they are interpreted as consistent, if possible. If the warranties cannot be applied together, then the express warranty prevails over any implied warranty except that an implied warranty of fitness for a particular purpose prevails over an express warranty.

12. IMPLIED WARRANTIES OF SELLERS

Sellers give different types of implied warranties.

(a) WARRANTY OF TITLE Every seller, by the mere act of selling, makes an implied warranty that the seller's title to the goods is good and that the seller has the right to transfer title to the goods.[20]

---

[20] UCC § 2-312. The key change in the language in Revised Article 2 is that the seller warrants that the buyer will not be subjected to unreasonable litigation.

warranty of title implied warranty that title to the goods is good and transfer is proper.

The **warranty of title** may be disclaimed either by using the words, "There is no warranty of title," or by certain circumstances.[21] If a buyer has reason to know that the seller does not claim to hold the title or that the seller is limited in what can be promised, the warranty of title is disclaimed. **For Example,** no warranty of title arises when the seller makes the sale in a representative capacity, such as a sheriff, an auctioneer, or an administrator of a decedent's estate. Similarly, no warranty arises when the seller makes the sale as a creditor disposing of a debtor's collateral (security). The damages for warranty of title are often the purchase price because the buyer may have to surrender the goods to their rightful owner.[22]

warranty against encumbrances warranty that there are no liens or other encumbrances to goods except those noted by seller.

(b) WARRANTY AGAINST ENCUMBRANCES   Every seller makes an implied **warranty against encumbrances**, that is, that the goods will be delivered free from any security interest or any other lien or encumbrance of which the buyer at the time of the sales transaction had no knowledge. If the seller sells an automobile to the buyer and then delivers a car with an outstanding lien on it that was unknown to the buyer at the time of the sale, there is a breach of the warranty against encumbrances.

CPA

(c) WARRANTY OF FITNESS FOR A PARTICULAR PURPOSE[23]   A buyer may intend to use the goods for a particular or unusual purpose, as contrasted with the ordinary use for which they are customarily sold. If the seller states that the goods will be fit for the buyer's purpose with the buyer relying on the seller's skill or judgment to select or furnish suitable goods, and the seller, at the time of contracting, knows or has reason to know of both the buyer's particular purpose and the buyer's reliance on the seller's judgment, then the seller has created an implied warranty of fitness for a particular purpose.[24] **For Example,** when the seller represents to a buyer that the two hamsters being sold are of the same gender and can safely occupy the same cage with no offspring, an implied warranty of fitness has been given. When the buyer makes the purchase without relying on the seller's skill and judgment, no warranty of fitness for a particular purpose arises.[25]

13. ADDITIONAL IMPLIED WARRANTIES OF MERCHANT SELLERS

A seller who deals in goods of the kind in question is classified as a merchant by the UCC and is held to a higher degree of responsibility for the product than one who is merely making a casual sale.

(a) WARRANTY AGAINST INFRINGEMENT   Unless otherwise agreed, every merchant seller warrants that the goods will be delivered free of the rightful claim of any third person by way of patent, copyright, or trademark infringement.

For Example, if a buyer purchases videos from a seller who is later discovered to be a bootlegger of the films on the videos, the buyer has a cause of action against the seller

---

[21] *Quality Components Corp. v Kel-Keef Enterprises, Inc.,* 738 NE2d 524 (Ill App 2000).

[22] *Curran v Ciaramelli,* 37 UCC Rep Serv 2d 94 (NY 1998).

[23] UCC § 2-315. The warranty does not apply when the injury is not caused by any function represented for the product. For example, a buyer could not recover when she hit her head on a wall-mounted fire extinguisher, for the representations were that it would work for home fires, not about mounting it in the home. *Hayes v Larsen Mfg. Co., Inc.,* 871 F Supp 56 (D Me 1996).

[24] UCC § 2-315. This warranty applies to every seller, but ordinarily it is merchant sellers who have such skill and judgment that the UCC provision will apply.

[25] *Potomac Plaza Terraces, Inc. v QSC Products, Inc.,* 868 F Supp 346 (DDC 1994). Manufacturing to buyer's specifications precludes recovery for breach of the warranty of fitness for a particular purpose. *Saratoga Spa & Bath, Inc. v Beeche Systems Corp.,* 656 NYS2d 787 (1997).

for any damages he experiences for perhaps renting out the bootlegged videos. Under Revised Article 2, the seller can disclaim the warranty against infringement.

(b) Warranty of Merchantability or Fitness for Normal Use A merchant seller makes an **implied warranty of the merchantability** of the goods sold.[26] This warranty is a group of promises, the most important of which is that the goods are fit for the ordinary purposes for which they are sold. This warranty, unless disclaimed, is given in every sale of goods by a merchant. Section 2-314 provides, "Unless excluded or modified, a warranty that the goods shall be merchantable is implied in a contract for their sale if the seller is a merchant with respect to goods of that kind."[27]

implied warranty of merchantability group of promises made by the seller, the most important of which is that the goods are fit for the ordinary purposes for which they are sold.

CASE SUMMARY

The Snow Job on the Awnings

FACTS: On July 27, 2000, Sheldorado Aluminum Products, Inc., installed an aluminum awning on the back of Marie Villette's home for use as a carport. On January 11, 2001, the awning collapsed on top of Ms. Villette's new Mercedes automobile. Ms. Villette brought suit against Sheldorado seeking recovery of the $3,000 she had paid to them for the awning.

There was no formal written contract between the parties; the only writing is a one-page order/bill designated a "contract," dated July 11, 2000, and signed by Ms. Villette and apparently by Jack Finklestein, Sheldorado's salesman. No advertising or promotional material was presented by either party. Ms. Villette testified to no express warranty or representation on the transaction, and none appears in the writing. Sheldorado acknowledges that no instructions or warnings were given to Ms. Villette as to care, maintenance, or use of the awning.

Ms. Villette and Dr. Max Samuel (her husband) testified to a leak from the awning the day after it was installed. Sheldorado attempted to repair the leak without success three weeks later.

When the awning collapsed, Sheldorado took the position that the cause was an accumulation of snow and high winds and that it bore no responsibility for the loss. It did not inspect the collapsed awning, contending at trial it was intimidated by Dr. Samuel. Its only response to the incident was to refer Ms. Villette and Dr. Samuel to the insurer on their homeowner's policy.

DECISION: The ordinary purposes of an awning are to provide shade and other protection from the elements; an awning that leaks and then collapses is clearly not fit for those purposes.

Sheldorado had knowledge of how the carport had been installed, and what precautions should have been taken to prevent the defect that resulted. The foreseeability of the risk of the weight of snow operating upon a defective installation is something the seller understands. The purchaser was not given any warnings about the awning, the weather, and maintenance. Without such, the weather was foreseeable and the awning was not fit for use in a climate in which snow could accumulate and weigh down the awning. Villette recovered her $3,000. [*Villette v Sheldorado Aluminum Products, Inc.*, 2001 WL 881055 (NY Supp), 45 UCC Rep Serv 2d 470 (NY Civ Ct 2001)]

---

[26] UCC § 2-314; *Ford v Starr Fireworks, Inc.*, 874 P2d 230 (Wyo 1994); *Williams v Gradall Co.*, 990 F Supp 442 (ED Va 1998).

[27] UCC § 2-314. Revised Article 2 makes only one change as follows: "(c) are fit for the ordinary purposes for which [deleted word *such* here] goods [added following phrase] *of that description* are used. . . ." The comment explains the change: "The phrase 'goods of that description' rather than 'for which such goods are used' is used in subsection (2)(c). This emphasizes the importance of the agreed description in determining fitness for ordinary purposes."

E-COMMERCE AND CYBERLAW

The warranty against infringement has become a critical one because of issues relating to software as well as the downloading of copyrighted music from the Internet. Those who are selling software warrant that they have the rights to do so and would be liable for infringement themselves, as well as the costs their buyers incur in defending themselves against charges of infringement.

Even those who provide the servers for the downloading of music or films can be held liable for infringement if they are aware of the downloading of copyrighted music or copyrighted films and take no steps to stop or prevent it. In fact, those who operate servers must be able to show that they took appropriate precautions to prevent such downloading and warn users against doing it.

14. IMPLIED WARRANTIES IN PARTICULAR SALES

Particular types of sales may involve special considerations in terms of the seller's liability and the buyer's rights.

(a) SALE ON BUYER'S SPECIFICATIONS   When the buyer furnishes the seller with exact specifications for the preparation or manufacture of goods, the same warranties arise as in the case of any other sale of such goods by the particular seller. No warranty of fitness for a particular purpose can arise, however. It is clear that the buyer is purchasing on the basis of the buyer's own decision and is not relying on the seller's skill and judgment. Similarly, the manufacturer is not liable for loss caused by a design defect.[28]

(b) SALE OF SECONDHAND OR USED GOODS   Under the UCC, there is a warranty of merchantability in the sale of both new and used goods unless it is specifically disclaimed. However, with respect to used goods, what is considered "fit for normal use" under the warranty of merchantability will be a lower standard. Some courts still follow their pre-Code law under which no warranties of fitness arise in the sale of used goods.

CPA   **(c)** SALE OF FOOD OR DRINK   The implied warranty of merchantability also applies to the purchase of food in grocery stores and restaurants. The food sold must be of average quality and fit for its ordinary purpose, which is consumption by humans.[29] The types of restaurant and grocery store cases brought under the warranty of merchantability include those in which the buyer or customer finds foreign substances such as grasshoppers in a can of baked beans.[30]

The application of this warranty to food cases becomes more complex when it is not a nail in a can of crabmeat, but crab shell in a can of crabmeat, or a cherry pit in the cherries of a McDonald's cherry pie. Some courts refuse to impose warranty

---

[28] *Hallday v Sturm, Ruger, & Co., Inc.*, 792 A2d 1145 (CA MD 2002).

[29] *Goldman v Food Lion, Inc.*, 879 F Supp 33 (ED Va 1995).

[30] *Metty v Shurfine Central Corporation*, 736 SW2d 527 (Mo 1987).

liability if the thing in the food that caused the harm was naturally present, such as crab shell in crabmeat, prune stones in stewed prunes, or bones in canned fish. Other courts reject this foreign substance/natural substance liability test. They hold that there is liability if the seller does not deliver to the buyer goods of the character that the buyer reasonably expected. Under this view, there is a breach of the implied warranty of fitness for normal use if the buyer reasonably expected the food to be free of harm-causing natural things, such as shells and bones that could cause harm.[31]

CASE SUMMARY

Digging for Teeth among the Clams

FACTS: On April 11, 1996, Sandra Mitchell (appellant) was having dinner at T.G.I. Friday's restaurant (hereinafter "Friday's" or appellee). Ms. Mitchell was eating a fried clam strip when she bit into a hard substance that she believed to be a piece of a clam shell. She experienced immediate pain and later sought dental treatment. Some time later, the crown of a tooth came loose. It was determined that the crown could not be reattached, and the remaining root of the tooth was extracted.

Ms. Mitchell filed a product liability action against Friday's, which served the meal, and Pro Source Distributing, the supplier of the fried clams. Both Friday's and Pro Source filed motions for summary judgment, which the trial court granted without explanation. Ms. Mitchell appealed.

DECISION: Two tests can be used for determining whether there should be recovery. One is the "foreign-natural test"; in this case, a clam shell is a natural part of eating clams. The other test is the "reasonable expectation test," and the court ruled that someone eating clams, even fried clams, should reasonably expect that shells might be part of the experience.

The possible presence of a piece of oyster shell in or attached to an oyster is so well known to anyone who eats oysters that all should reasonably anticipate and guard against eating such a piece of shell. The court held that, as a matter of law, one who eats clams can reasonably anticipate and guard against eating a piece of shell. [**Mitchell v T.G.I. Friday's, 748 NE2d 89 (Ohio App 2000)**]

---

15. NECESSITY OF DEFECT

To impose liability for breach of the implied warranty of merchantability, it is ordinarily necessary to show that there was a defect in the product, that this defect made the product unfit for its normal use, and that this caused the buyer's harm. A product may be defective because there is (1) a manufacturing defect, (2) a design defect, (3) inadequate instruction on how to use the product, or (4) inadequate warning against dangers involved in using the product.

For Example, if the manufacturer's blueprint shows that there should be two bolts at a particular place and the factory puts in only one bolt, there is a manufacturing defect. If the two bolts are put in but the product breaks because four bolts are

---

[31] A new type of test for the food cases is called the "duty risk analysis" rule, in which the court examines the injury in light of the risk that comes from the failure to process the items out of the food and weighs that risk with the cost of the processing. *Porteous v St. Ann's Café & Deli,* 713 So 2d 454 (La 1998). Note that the case is from Louisiana, the nation's non-UCC state.

THINKING THINGS THROUGH

What's Foreign to You . . .

Based on the discussion and the *T. G. I. Friday's* case, decide which of the following would be considered a breach of the implied warranty of merchantability:

Customer suffered an injury to the throat as a result of a bone in a chicken sandwich getting stuck in his throat. Ruvolo v Homovich 778 NE2d 661 (Ohio App 2002).

Customer bit into a Baby Ruth candy bar, manufactured by Standard Brands, that contained a "snake bone (vertebrae)" and the customer experienced severe psychological difficulty. Gates v Standard Brands Inc., 719 P2d 130 (Wash App 1986).

Customer experienced tooth and jaw damage after she bit into a pistachio nut while eating an ice cream cone with pistachio nut ice cream. Lewis v Handel's Homemade Ice Cream and Yogurt 2003 WL 21509258 (Ohio App).

---

required to provide sufficient strength, there is no manufacturing defect, but there is a design defect. A product that is properly designed and properly manufactured may be dangerous because the user is not given sufficient instructions on how to use the product. Also, a product is defective if there is a danger that is not obvious and there is no warning at all or a warning that does not describe the full danger.[32]

Many courts impose liability when the goods are in fact not fit for their normal purpose. These courts allow the buyer to prove that the goods are not fit for their normal purpose with evidence that the goods do not function properly even though the buyer does not establish the specific defect.

In contrast with a breach of the implied warranty of merchantability, it is not necessary under the breach of the implied warranty of fitness for a particular purpose or of an express warranty or a guarantee to show that there was a defect that caused the breach. It is sufficient to show that the goods did not perform to meet the particular purpose or did not conform to the express warranty or to the guarantee. Why they did or did not so conform is immaterial.

CASE SUMMARY

Getting the Shaft on the Shingles

FACTS: In August 1989, GAF, a manufacturer of shingles, shipped 48 squares of its Timberline shingles to Mr. Antz for purposes of installation at his newly constructed home. The package in which the shingles were shipped contained a label stating the shingles were covered by a 30-year limited warranty, and a copy of the warranty was available from the distributor of the shingles or directly from GAF. No other language appeared on the label to clarify the express limited warranty, and no other warranty language was included with the shingles when they were delivered to Mr. Antz. The express limited warranty contained a

---

[32] *Red Hill Hosiery Mill, Inc. v Magnetek, Inc.* 582 SE2d 632 (NC Ct App 2003). Following government standards does not mean a product is without defect.

CASE SUMMARY

continued

disclaimer of the implied warranties of merchantability and fitness for a particular purpose. In addition, it contained language limiting replacement labor costs to within the first year following installation.

After approximately 48 months of use, the shingles showed signs of defects, and Mr. Antz made a claim to GAF pursuant to the 30-year warranty. After investigation, GAF determined the shingles contained manufacturing defects. GAF sent Mr. Antz a letter dated December 29, 1994, informing him that his claim was being approved for settlement. GAF thereafter sent Mr. Antz a roofing materials certificate for Timberline shingles. Mr. Antz refused to redeem the certificate and instead retained a roofer to install another brand of shingles on his house.

Mr. Antz filed suit against GAF asserting breaches of express warranty, warranty of merchantability, and warranty of fitness for a particular purpose. He sought to recover the labor costs involved in replacing the Timberline shingles and the value of the new shingles.

The trial court issued an opinion and order awarding Mr. Antz damages in the amount of $11,745.00 for replacement labor costs and the replacement shingles. GAF appealed.

DECISION: The limitation-of-remedies provisions were not provided to Mr. Antz at the time of purchase and delivery. The only information Mr. Antz was provided when the shingles were shipped was a label that included language stating "30-Year LIMITED WARRANTY only." The language explaining the terms and conditions of the limitations was not given to Mr. Antz.

The language limiting Mr. Antz's damages was well beyond merely inconspicuous. The provisions were not even in his possession but were in the possession of GAF. Because the terms were not given at the time of sale nor were they conspicuous, the limitations do not apply to Mr. Antz. [**Antz v GAF Materials Corp., 719 A2d 758 (Pa Super 1998) appeal denied 739 A2d 1054 (Pa 1999)**]

16. WARRANTIES IN THE INTERNATIONAL SALE OF GOODS

The warranties of both merchantability and fitness for a particular purpose exist under the Convention on Contracts for the International Sale of Goods (CISG). In most cases, the provisions are identical to those of the UCC. Sellers, however, can expressly disclaim the convention's warranties without mentioning merchantability or making the disclaimer conspicuous.

 ## DISCLAIMER OF WARRANTIES

The seller and the buyer may ordinarily agree that there will be no warranties. In some states, disclaimers of warranties are prohibited for reasons of public policy or consumer protection.

17. VALIDITY OF DISCLAIMER

Warranties may be disclaimed by agreement of the parties, subject to the limitation that such a provision must not be unconscionable, must be conspicuous, and in certain cases must use certain language.[33]

---

[33] UCC § 2-316; *Safadi v Thompson,* 487 SE2d 457 (Ga App 1997). The revised UCC section is now § 2-406.

(a) Conspicuousness   A disclaimer provision is made conspicuous when it appears in a record under a conspicuous heading that indicates there is an exclusion or modification of warranties. A heading cannot be relied on to make such a provision conspicuous when the heading is misleading and wrongfully gives the impression there is a warranty. **For Example,** the heading "Vehicle Warranty" is misleading if the provision that follows contains a limitation of warranties. A disclaimer that is hidden in a mass of materials or records handed to the buyer is not conspicuous and is not effective to exclude warranties. Similarly, an inconspicuous disclaimer of warranties under a posted notice of "Notice to Retail Buyers" has no effect.

When a disclaimer of warranties fails because it is not conspicuous, the implied warranties apply to the buyer.[34]

(b) Unconscionability and Public Policy   An exclusion of warranties made in the manner specified by the UCC is not unconscionable. In some states, warranty disclaimers are invalid because they are contrary to public policy or because they are prohibited by consumer protection laws.

When a breach of warranty is the result of negligence of the seller, a disclaimer of warranty liability and a limitation of remedies to a refund of the purchase price are not binding. Such limitations are unreasonable, unconscionable, and against public policy.

18. PARTICULAR LANGUAGE FOR DISCLAIMERS

The disclaimer requirements under Revised Article 2 have been changed in a way that makes disclaimers for consumer contracts different from disclaimers for contracts between merchants. The rules for disclaimer of warranties for merchants remain the same as they were under previous Article 2. Language such as "as is," "with all faults," "as they stand," or "There are no warranties that extend beyond the description on the face hereof," serve to exclude the implied warranty of merchantability as well as the implied warranty of fitness for a particular purpose. Such disclaimers are valid between merchants even if they are oral.

Under Revised Article 2, any warranty disclaimers for consumer buyers must be placed in a record (*record* includes written agreements but, as noted in Chapter 23, also includes e-mail and electronic exchanges), must be conspicuous, and must use statutory language now provided. To waive the warranty of merchantability, the record must contain the following language: "The seller undertakes no responsibility for the quality of the goods except as otherwise provided in this contract."[35] The required language for waiving the warranty of fitness for a particular purpose is as follows: "The seller assumes no responsibility that the goods will be fit for any particular purpose for which you may be buying these goods, except as otherwise provided in the contract."[36]

In consumer contracts, the use of terms such as "as is" can also disclaim the warranties, as it does for merchant transactions, but the disclaimers must be in the record and must be conspicuously set forth in that record.

---

[34] A warranty disclaimer written in all caps just below the signature line is conspicuous. *Gooch v E. I. DuPont de Nemours & Co.,* 40 F Supp 3d 863 (WD Ky 1999).

[35] Revised UCC § 2-316(2).

[36] *Id.*

FIGURE 25-1	*UCC Warranties*

NAME OF WARRANTY	CREATION	RESTRICTION	DISCLAIMER
EXPRESS	AFFIRMATION OF FACT, PROMISE OF PERFORMANCE (INCLUDES SAMPLES, MODELS, DESCRIPTIONS)	MUST BE PART OF THE BASIS OF THE BARGAIN	CANNOT MAKE A DISCLAIMER INCONSISTENT WITH AN EXPRESS WARRANTY
IMPLIED WARRANTY OF MERCHANTABILITY	GIVEN IN EVERY SALE OF GOODS BY A MERCHANT ("FIT FOR ORDINARY PURPOSES")	ONLY GIVEN BY MERCHANTS	MUST USE STATUTORY LANGUAGE DISCLAIMER OF "AS IS" OR "WITH ALL FAULTS"; MUST BE CONSPICUOUS IN THE RECORD
IMPLIED WARRANTY OF FITNESS FOR A PARTICULAR PURPOSE	SELLER KNOWS OF BUYER'S RELIANCE FOR A PARTICULAR USE (BUYER IS IGNORANT)	SELLER MUST HAVE KNOWLEDGE; BUYER MUST RELY ON SELLER	(1) MUST HAVE A RECORD (2) MUST BE CONSPICUOUS (3) ALSO DISCLAIMED WITH "AS IS" OR "WITH ALL FAULTS"
TITLE	GIVEN IN EVERY SALE	DOES NOT APPLY IN CIRCUMSTANCES WHERE APPARENT WARRANTY IS NOT GIVEN	MUST SAY "THERE IS NO WARRANTY OF TITLE"
MAGNUSON-MOSS (FEDERAL CONSUMER PRODUCT WARRANTY LAW)	ONLY CONSUMER PRODUCTS OF $10 OR MORE	MUST LABEL "FULL" OR "LIMITED"	

Figure 25-1 provides a summary of the warranties under Article 2 and the methods for making disclaimers.

19. EXCLUSION OF WARRANTIES BY EXAMINATION OF GOODS

Revised Article 2 modifies the requirements for inspections as a waiver of warranty. For an inspection of goods by the buyer to constitute a waiver, the seller must demand that the buyer inspect the goods as part of the contracting process. The seller may not use inspection as a defense to warranty issues if that demand was not made at the time the parties contracted.[37]

---

[37] Revised UCC § 2-316(3)(b).

20. POSTSALE DISCLAIMER

Frequently, a statement purporting to exclude or modify warranties appears for the first time in a written contract sent to confirm or memorialize an oral contract made earlier. The exclusion or modification may likewise appear in an invoice, a bill, or an instruction manual delivered to the buyer at or after the time the goods are received. Such postsale disclaimers have no effect on warranties that arose at the time of the sale.

 # OTHER THEORIES OF PRODUCT LIABILITY

In addition to recovery for breach of an express guarantee, an express warranty, or an implied warranty, a plaintiff in a given product liability case may be able to recover for negligence, fraud, or strict tort liability.

21. NEGLIGENCE

negligence failure to exercise due care under the circumstances that results in harm proximately caused to one owed a duty to exercise due care.

A person injured because of the defective condition of a product may be entitled to recover from the seller or manufacturer for the damages for **negligence**. The injured person must be able to show that the seller was negligent in the preparation or manufacture of the article or failed to provide proper instructions and warnings of dangers. An action for negligence rests on common law tort principles. Negligence does not require privity of contract.

22. FRAUD

The UCC expressly preserves the pre-Code law governing fraud. A person defrauded by a distributor's or manufacturer's false statements about a product generally will be able to recover damages for the harm sustained because of such misrepresentations. False statements are fraudulent if the party who made them did so with knowledge that they were false or with reckless indifference to their truthfulness.

 ## 23. STRICT TORT LIABILITY

Independently of the UCC, a manufacturer or distributor of a defective product is liable under strict tort liability to a person who is injured by the product. Strict tort liability exists without regard to whether the person injured is a purchaser, a consumer, or a third person, such as a bystander.[38] It is no defense that privity of contract does not exist between the injured party and the defendant. Likewise, it is no defense that the defect was found in a component part purchased from another manufacturer.[39] **For Example,** defective tires sold on a new car were probably purchased from a tire supplier by the auto manufacturer. However, the manufacturer is not excused from liability.

---

[38] The concept of strict tort liability was judicially declared in *Greenman v Yuba Power Products,* 377 P2d 897 (Cal 1963). This concept has been incorporated in the Restatement (Second) and (Third) of Torts as § 402A.

[39] *Guiffrida v Panasonic Industrial Co., Inc.,* 607 NYS2d 72 (Sup Ct App Div 1994); *Ford v Beam Radiator, Inc.,* 708 So 2d 1158 (La App 1998).

Strict tort liability requires that the defect in the product exist at the time it left the control of the manufacturer or distributor. The defective condition is defined in the same way as under negligence: defective by manufacturing error or oversight, defective by design, or defective by the failure to warn.[40] There is liability if the product is defective and unreasonably dangerous and has caused harm. It is immaterial whether the seller was negligent or whether the user was contributorily negligent. Knowledge of the defect is not a requirement for liability. Assumption of risk by the injured party, on the other hand, is a defense available to the seller.[41]

24. CUMULATIVE THEORIES OF LIABILITY

The theories of product liability are not mutually exclusive. A given set of facts may give rise to two or more theories of liability. **For Example,** suppose that a manufacturer advertises, "Coaches! Protect your players' eyes! Shatterproof sunglasses for baseball." If the glasses shattered and injured a player, an express warranty, implied warranty, implied warranty for a particular purpose, and strict tort liability could apply for recovery.

CASE SUMMARY

Shocking Warranty Issues

FACTS: Will-Burt builds steel masts used by the military, border control, firefighters, and the television broadcast industry. Will-Burt built one such mast in 1982 for use in the television broadcast industry on an electronic news-gathering van (ENG van). Will-Burt sold the mast in 1982 to Quality Coach of Elkhart, Indiana. In 1989, this mast resurfaced by reference in an invoice from a business called Alan W. Haines, Custom Construction (Haines). The invoice indicates that the mast had been "completely rebuilt." Mississippi Telecasting Company d/b/a WABG-TV purchased the mast from Haines along with several other component parts from Mobile Manufacturers and others who previously settled their cases with Barksdale Austin, a 24-year-old college graduate employed as a production manager by WABG-TV in Greenville, Mississippi. One of his duties at WABG was to set up the TV station's ENG van for remote broadcasts. This duty entailed operating the telescoping mast on the van. Austin received safety training that included checking for obstructions before raising the mast, to ensure that the ENG van was on level ground and, pursuant to station policy, keeping a clearance of at least 20 feet from any power line if the mast was to be raised.

On June 17, 1997, Austin was assigned to a live shot at Greenville City Hall, three blocks from the WABG-TV station and within the direct line of sight of the station's antenna. The van was parked underneath visible transformers and power lines by someone other than Austin. The Will-Burt mast, which was attached to the van, contacted an 8,000-volt power line while being raised. The voltage went down the mast and into the van, energizing the van and its extending cables. Austin walked to the van, touched it, and was electrically shocked to death.

---

[40] *Lewis v Ariens,* 751 NE 2d 862 (Mass 2001).

[41] *Clark v Mazda Motor Corp.,* 68 P3d 207 (OK 2003).

CASE SUMMARY

continued

The mast still had the following warnings on its base: "DANGER! PLEASE READ INSTRUCTIONS BEFORE RAISING!" and "DANGER. WATCH FOR WIRES. YOU CAN BE KILLED IF THIS PRODUCT COMES NEAR ELECTRICAL POWER LINES." The labels were located on the base of the mast inside the van in bright yellow with red and black lettering. The instructions in the product manual also warned operators to never to raise the mast under or near power lines and to check for obstructions within the proximity to the maximum height of the mast.

Austin's family filed suit for breach of warranty and negligence.

DECISION: The court held that no express warranty was breached because no one at WABG had relied on any statements from Will-Burt in purchasing the mast. The court held that while the mast was warranted for a particular purpose of use by an ENG van, that use carried sufficient limitations and warnings that put buyers and users on notice of its limitations for that use. The court did not find negligence because there was no evidence that Will-Burt was aware of any incidents with its masts. Further, the product liability claim was eliminated because of the warning, the fact that the mast had been sold so many times and had been in use for nearly 20 years, and indications that its conducting qualities may have been affected by the failure to keep it clean and maintained. The court granted summary judgment for Will-Burt on all product liability theories under both the UCC and tort law. [**Austin v Will-Burt Company, 232 F Supp 2d 682 (D Miss 2002)**] affirmed, 361 F3d 862 (5th Cir 2004)]

ETHICS & THE LAW

The Heart of the Merck Cases

The first of the Merck product liability cases for its drug Vioxx (now withdrawn from the market) began in late July 2005. The first case was brought by Carol Ernst, 59, the widow of Robert Ernst, a man who died of arrhythmia, an irregular interruption of the heart rhythm. Mr. Ernst was also 59 and was an accomplished triathlete. He was taking Vioxx at the time of his arrhythmia and resulting death. Mrs. Ernst alleged that Vioxx, an anti-arthritic drug manufactured by Merck, was placed on the market despite the company's knowledge of its risks and evidence of harm in patients with heart problems. The company estimates that 20 million people in the United States have taken Vioxx, and between 4,000 and 7,000 product liability suits are pending (there are differing reports on the total).

In his 2.5-hour opening statement, Mark Lanier, the lawyer for Mrs. Ernst, told the jury to be "detectives." "If we were going to put it into a TV show, this would be 'CSI Angleton.' "* The first witness in the case Mrs. Ernst's lawyer presented was Dr. Nancy Santanello, a physician employed by Merck as its head of epidemiology, and an adverse or hostile witness. Dr. Santanello's job at Merck is to study data results from tests involving Merck drugs. Dr. Santanello took Vioxx herself.

ETHICS & THE LAW

continued

Critical elements that came out during the trial:

- Merck had evidence from a study in 2000 that 14.6 percent of 4,000 Vioxx patients studied (590 people) had cardiovascular problems while taking the drug.
- In a letter to physicians once it had the 14.6 percent number, Merck said the percentage was 0.5, or a total of 20 people.
- The study showed that only 0.5 percent had heart attacks while on Vioxx. The 14.6 percent did indeed have less severe cardiovascular problems. The letter from Merck reads "the rate of cardiovascular events was 0.5 percent among patients taking VIOXX."
- Merck also sent the study along to the *New England Journal of Medicine* and suggested in the letter to doctors that they consult that report for more details on the study.
- A training document for sales representatives compared answering questions about Vioxx safety to a game of dodge ball.
- Dr. James F. Fries, a professor at Stanford University, criticized Vioxx and then sent a letter to Merck complaining that he was threatened by Dr. Louis Sherwood, a senior scientist at Merck. Dr. Fries wrote that Sherwood threatened to destroy his career.
- Merck did no follow-up studies after the 2000 study.
- Dr. Santanello removed the name of one of her subordinates from authorship on a research paper that reached negative conclusions about Vioxx. The study was published in *Circulation* and had been a joint study by Harvard Medical School and Merck.

List the possible theories that Mrs. Ernst could use for recovery.

---

*Barbara Martinez, "Merck Doctor Likely to Testify In Vioxx Trial," *Wall Street Journal*, July 18, 2005, B1, B6.

Sources: Alex Berenson, "Merck's Case Withstands First Week of Punches," *New York Times*, July 25, 2005, C1, C7; and Alex Berenson, "At Vioxx Trial, a Discrepancy Appears to Undercut Merck's Defense," *New York Times*, July 20, 2005, C1, C8.

LAWFLIX

The Incredible Shrinking Woman (1981) (PG)

Lily Tomlin's exposure to various combinations of products causes her to shrink. Which companies would be liable and how could one go about proving joint and several liability? Discuss privity of contract and whether the interaction with other products would be covered.

For movie clips that illustrate business law concepts, see LawFlix at **http://wdvl.westbuslaw.com.**

> SUMMARY

Five theories protect parties from loss caused by non-conforming goods: (1) express warranty, (2) implied warranty, (3) negligence, (4) fraud, and (5) strict tort liability.

Theories of product liability are not mutually exclusive. A given set of facts may give rise to liability under two or more theories.

The requirement of privity of contract (that is, the parties to the sales contract for warranty liability) has been widely rejected. The law is moving toward the conclusion that persons harmed because of an improper product may recover from anyone who is in any way responsible. The requirement of privity has been abolished by most states, and remote buyers as well as their families, members of their households, and guests are covered under the UCC warranties.

Warranties may be express or implied. The types of implied warranties are the warranty of title, the implied warranty of merchantability, and the implied warranty of fitness for a particular purpose. The warranty of title provides that the transfer is lawful, the title is good, and there are no infringement issues. Under Revised Article 2, the warranty of title also protects the buyer against unreasonable litigation. The warranty of merchantability is given by merchants and warrants that the goods are of average quality and will do what those types of goods commonly can do. The implied warranty of fitness for a particular purpose is given in those circumstances in which the buyer relies on the seller's expertise and the seller is aware of that reliance and offers a recommendation on the types of goods.

Express warranties arise from statements of fact and promises of performance made by the seller to the buyer that become a part of the basis for the buyer contracting. Express warranties arise from samples, models, and descriptions.

Warranties may be disclaimed by agreement of the parties provided the disclaimer is not unconscionable. Merchants can have oral disclaimers, but for consumers, warranty disclaimers must be in a record and must be conspicuous. Also for consumers, certain language must be used to disclaim each type of warranty. However, for both merchants and non-merchants, the use of terms such as "as is" or "with all faults" can disclaim both the warranty of merchantability and the implied warranty of fitness for a particular purpose (although for consumers, there must still be a record and the language must be conspicuous).

The warranties of merchantability and fitness exist under the CISG. However, disclaimers under the CISG need not mention merchantability, nor must such disclaimers be conspicuous.

The strict tort liability plaintiff must show that there was a defect in the product at the time it left the control of the defendant. No negligence need be established on the part of the defendant, nor is the plaintiff's contributory negligence a defense. If negligence is established, however, knowledge by the seller can result in punitive damages. The defendant may show that the injured party assumed the risk.

> QUESTIONS AND CASE PROBLEMS

1. Maria Gonzalez lived in a rental unit with her sons in Queens, New York. The hot water supplied to their apartment was heated by a Morflo water heater, which had a temperature control device on its exterior manufactured by Robertshaw and sold to Morflo. Maria Garcia, the owner of the Gonzalezes' apartment, had purchased and installed the water heater. The Morflo heater was located in the basement of the apartment house, which was locked and inaccessible to tenants.

    Extensive warnings were on the water heater itself and in the manual given to Garcia at the time of her purchase. The warning on the Robertshaw temperature device read: "CAUTION: Hotter water increases the risk of scald injury." The heater itself contained a picture of hot water coming from a faucet with the word "DANGER" printed above it. In addition, the water heater had a statement on it: "Water temperature over 120 degrees Fahrenheit can cause severe burns instantly or death from scalds. Children, disabled, and elderly are at highest risk of being scalded. Feel water before bathing or showering. Temperature limiting valves are available, see manual."

In the Morflo manual, the following warning appeared:

DANGER! The thermostat is adjusted to its lowest temperature position when shipped from the factory. Adjusting the thermostat past the 120 degree Fahrenheit bar on the temperature dial will increase the risk of scald injury. The normal position is approximately 120 degrees Fahrenheit.

DANGER: WARNING: Hot water can produce first degree burns in 3 seconds at 140 degrees Fahrenheit (60 degrees Celsius), in 20 seconds at 130 degrees Fahrenheit (54 degrees Celsius), in 8 minutes at 120 degrees Fahrenheit (49 degrees Celsius).

On October 1, 1992, 15-month-old Angel Gonzalez was being bathed by his 15-year-old brother, Daniel. When the telephone rang, Daniel left Angel alone in the bathtub. No one else was at home with the boys, and Daniel left the water running. Angel was scalded by the water that came from the tap. Angel and his mother brought suit against Morflo and Robertshaw, alleging defects in the design of the water heater and the failure to warn. Should they recover? [*Gonzalez v Marflo Industries, Inc.,* 931 F Supp 159 (EDNY)]

2. Paul Parrino purchased from Dave's Professional Wheelchair Service a wheelchair manufactured by 21st Century Scientific, Inc. The sales brochure from 21st Century Scientific stated that the wheelchair would "serve [the buyer] well for many years to come." Parrino had problems with the wheelchair within a few years and filed suit against Dave's and 21st Century for breach of express warranty. Both defended on the grounds that the statement on years of service was puffery, not an express warranty. Are they right? *Parrino v Sperling,* 648 NYS2d 702

3. Jane Jackson purchased a sealed can of Katydids, chocolate-covered pecan caramel candies manufactured by NestlT. Shortly after, Jackson bit into one of the candies and allegedly broke a tooth on a pecan shell embedded in the candy. She filed a complaint, asserting breach of implied warranty. How would you argue on behalf of the company? How would you argue on behalf of Jackson? In your answer, discuss both the reasonable

expectation test and the foreign substance/natural substance test. [*Jackson v NestlT-Beich, Inc.,* 589 NE2d 547 (Ill App)]

4. Webster ordered a bowl of fish chowder at the Blue Ship Tea Room. She was injured by a fish bone in the chowder, and she sued the tea room for breach of the implied warranty of merchantability. The evidence at trial showed that when chowder is made, the entire unboned fish is cooked. Should she recover? [*Webster v Blue Ship Tea Room,* 198 NE2d 309]

5. Andy's Sales (owned by Andy Adams) sold a well-built trampoline to Carl and Shirley Wickers. The Wickerses later sold the trampoline to Herbert Bryant. While using the trampoline, Herbert's 14-year-old nephew, Rex, sustained injuries that left him a quadriplegic. Rex's guardian filed suit for breach of express warranty and merchantability. The sales brochure for the round trampoline described it as "safe" because it had a "uniform bounce" and "natural tendency to work the jumper toward the center." The Wickerses had purchased an oval-shaped trampoline. Discuss Rex's ability to recover. Is privity an issue? [*Bryant v Adams,* 448 SE2d 832 (NC App)]

6. Advent purchased ink from Borden. On the labels of the ink drums delivered to Advent, Borden had imprinted in one-sixteenth-inch type in all caps:

SELLER MAKES NO WARRANTY, EXPRESS OR IMPLIED, CONCERNING THE PRODUCT OR THE MERCHANTABILITY OR FITNESS THEREOF FOR ANY PURPOSE CONCERNING THE ACCURACY OF ANY INFORMATION PROVIDED BY BORDEN.

This language was printed beneath the following:

BORDEN PRINTING INKS—"ZERO DEFECTS: THAT'S OUR GOAL"

All of the printing was in boldface type. The disclaimer was also printed on the sales invoice and on the reverse side of the Borden form, but there was nothing on the front to call attention to the critical nature of the terms on the back because there were simply capital letters reading "SEE REVERSE SIDE." All of the terms on the back were in boldface and although the disclaimer was the first of 19 paragraphs, nothing distinguished it from the other 18 paragraphs of detailed contract terms.

Advent said that Borden failed to age the black ink that it purchased with the result that the ink separated in Advent's printing machines. Advent refused to pay for the ink and wrote to Borden explaining that it would not tender payment because the ink was defective and demanding that Borden reimburse it for its lost profits from the downtime of printing machines. The trial court held that Borden had disclaimed any and all warranties on the ink and Advent appealed. What would you decide about the disclaimer and why? [*Borden, Inc. v Advent Ink Co.,* 701 A2d 255 (Pa Sup)]

7. Avery purchased a refrigerator from a retail store. The written contract stated that the refrigerator was sold "as is" and that the warranty of merchantability and all warranties of fitness were excluded. This was stated in large capital letters printed just above the line on which Avery signed her name. The refrigerator worked properly for a few weeks and then stopped. The store refused to do anything about it because of the exclusion of the warranties made by the contract. Avery claimed that this exclusion was not binding because it was unconscionable. Was Avery correct? [*Avery v Aladdin Products Div., Nat'l Service Industries, Inc.,* 196 SE2d 357 (Ga App)]

8. The 1143 East Jersey Avenue Associates, Inc., owned a 10-story building. The Associates hired Duall Building Restoration, Inc., to restore the surface of its building. The contract between the Associates and Duall specified that Duall would use Modac, a waterproof paint manufactured by Monsey Products, to cover the three brick sides of the building.

Shortly after the Modac paint was applied to the three sides of the building, it began to peel disastrously. One of the principals in the Associates described the situation as follows: "The entire building is peeling. It's . . . going wild. I mean . . . the surface is a whole bunch of spaghetti. Maybe noodles, I should say. It's curlicues of surface coming off all over the place." The Associates sued both Duall and Monsey Products. Monsey Products claimed that the

Associates were remote purchasers and it was not liable to the Associates because of lack of privity. It would cost $185,000 for a new paint job. Can there be recovery? As you answer, be sure to discuss which warranty theory you would use and whether the issue of privity prevents recovery. [*Duall Bldg. Restoration, Inc. v 1143 East Jersey Avenue Associates, Inc.,* 652 A2d 1225 (NJ Super)]

9. In April 1990, Herbert S. Garten went to Valley Motors to purchase a new 1990 Mercedes-Benz Model 300E. Robert Bell, a Mercedes salesman, told Garten that except for some cosmetic changes, the 1990 300E was "identical" to the 1986 300E.

On April 9, 1990, Garten brought in his 1986 car and asked Bell to describe the exact differences between the 1986 model and the new 1990 model of the 300E. Bell explained the changes as only cosmetic; he gave Garten a $17,500 trade-in allowance for his 1986 300E and sold him a 1990 300E for $42,500.

The following morning, Garten had trouble shifting from second to third gear in his new car and called to complain to Bell. Bell convinced him to wait until the 1,000-mile check to see if the problem worked itself out.

On May 3, 1990, Garten brought the 1990 300E to Valley Motors for the 1,000-mile checkup and presented a memorandum describing the problems he was having with the car, focusing on the automobile's delayed upshift from second to third gear. (The delayed upshift was the result of an emissions control system designed to bring the catalytic converter quickly to operating temperature from a cold start.) Garten returned the 1990 300E to Valley Motors on May 9, 1990, and on the same day, Garten delivered two letters to Valley Motors stating that the 1990 300E was defective and he was revoking his acceptance and rescinding the sale. Garten left the keys to the 1990 300E, requested the return of his 1986 300E, and asked Valley Motors how it could retransfer titles to the two cars. Finally, Garten informed Valley Motors that he would be renting a car until this matter was resolved.

The 1990 300E sat parked in the lot at Valley Motors for approximately seven months until December 1990, when Garten retrieved the car. He subsequently traded in the 1990 300E for a new 1991 300E that he purchased from another Mercedes-Benz dealer. The total purchase price of the 1991 300E was $43,123.50; he also traded in the 1990 300E for $31,500. Garten says the salesman's statement was an express warranty that he relied on in buying the car. Can he recover? [*Mercedes-Benz of North America, Inc. v Garten,* 618 A2d 233 (Md App)]

10. Zogarts manufactured and sold a practice device for beginning golfers. According to the statements on the package, the device was completely safe, and a player could never be struck by the device's golf ball. Hauter was hit by the ball while practicing with the device. He sued Zogarts, which denied liability on the ground that the statements were merely matters of opinion, so liability could not be based on them. Was this a valid defense? [*Hauter v Zogarts,* 534 P2d 377 (Cal)]

11. A buyer purchased an engine to operate an irrigation pump. The buyer selected the engine from a large number that were standing on the floor of the seller's stockroom. A label on the engine stated that it would produce 100 horsepower. The buyer needed an engine that would generate at least 80 horsepower. In actual use in the buyer's irrigation system, the engine generated only 60 horsepower. The buyer sued the seller for damages. The seller raised the defense that no warranty of fitness for the buyer's particular purpose of operating an irrigation pump had arisen because the seller did not know of the use to which the buyer intended to put the engine. Also, the buyer had not relied on the seller's skill and judgment in selecting the particular engine. Did the seller have any liability based on warranties? [*Potter v Tyndall,* 207 SE2d 762 (NC)]

12. After watching a male horse owned by Terry and Manita Darby perform at a horse show, Ashley Sheffield contacted the Darbys about buying him. The Darbys assured her that the horse had no problems and would make a good show horse for use in competition. In the presence of and in consultation with her father (who raised horses for a business), Sheffield rode the horse and decided to purchase him for $8,500. Within three weeks, Sheffield and her trainer discerned that the horse was lame. Sheffield sued the Darbys for fraud and

for breach of express and implied warranties, and the court entered summary judgment in favor of the Darbys on all claims. Sheffield appealed. Was the court correct in granting summary judgment? Was there a breach of an express warranty? [*Sheffield v Darby,* 535 SE2d 776 (Ga App)]

13. Drehman Paving & Flooring Co. installed a brick floor at Cumberland Farms that its salesman promised would be "just like" another floor Cumberland had installed several years earlier. The bricks in the new floor came loose because Drehman had failed to install expansion joints. Expansion joints were not included in the second floor contract but were part of the first. Can Cumberland recover? What theory? [*Cumberland Farms, Inc. v Drehman Paving & Flooring Co.,* 520 NE2d 1321 (Mass Ct App)]

14. Brian Felley went to the home of Tom and Cheryl Singleton on June 8 to look at a used car that the Singletons had advertised for sale in the local paper. The car was a 1991 Ford with 126,000 miles on it. Following a test drive and the Singletons' representation that the car was "in good mechanical condition," Felley purchased the car for $5,800. By June 18, 1997, Felley had the car in the shop and paid $942.76 to have its clutch fixed. By July 9, 1997, Felley also had paid $971.18 for a new brake job. By September 16, 1997, Felley had paid another $429.09 for further brake work.

Felley brought suit for breach of express warranty. An auto expert testified that the clutch and brakes were defective when Felley bought the car. Was an express warranty breached? Why or why not? [*Felley v Singleton,* 705 NE2d 930 (Ill App)]

15. Lewis and Sims, a contracting corporation, was installing a water and sewer system in the town of North Pole, Alaska. The order for the pipe stated the size and quantity and specified that the pipe had to be "coal tar enamel lined." The pipe could not withstand the intense cold, and before the pipelines could be constructed, the enamel lining had pulled away from the pipe. Lewis and Sims then sued the suppliers of the original pipe for damages for breach of warranty of fitness for a particular purpose. Can it recover? [*Lewis and Sims, Inc. v Key Industries, Inc.,* 557 P2d 1318]

CPA QUESTIONS

1. Under the UCC Sales Article, the warranty of title may be excluded by

   a. Merchants or nonmerchants, provided the exclusion is in writing
   b. Nonmerchant sellers only
   c. The seller's statement that it is selling only such right or title that it has
   d. Use of an "as is" disclaimer

2. Which of the following factors result(s) in an express warranty with respect to a sale of goods?

   I. The seller's description of the goods is part of the basis of the bargain.
   II. The seller selects goods knowing the buyer's intended use.

   a. I only
   b. II only
   c. Both I and II
   d. Neither I nor II

3. Morgan is suing the manufacturer, wholesaler, and retailer for bodily injuries caused by a power saw Morgan purchased. Which of the following statements is correct under the theory of strict liability?

   a. The manufacturer will avoid liability if it can show it followed the custom of the industry.
   b. Morgan may recover even if he cannot show any negligence was involved.

   c. Contributory negligence on Morgan's part will always be a bar to recovery.
   d. Privity will be a bar to recovery insofar as the wholesaler is concerned if the wholesaler did not have a reasonable opportunity to inspect.

4. On May 2, Handy Hardware sent Ram Industries a signed purchase order that stated, in part: "Ship for May 8 delivery 300 Model A-X socket sets at current dealer price. Terms 2/10/net 30." Ram received Handy's purchase order on May 4. On May 5, Ram discovered that it had only 200 Model A-X socket sets and 100 Model W-Z socket sets in stock. Ram shipped the Model A-X and Model W-Z sets to Handy without any explanation concerning the shipment. The socket sets were received by Handy on May 8. Assuming a contract exists between Handy and Ram, which of the following implied warranties would result?

   I. Implied warranty of merchantability
   II. Implied warranty of fitness for a particular purpose
   III. Implied warranty of title

   a. I only
   b. III only
   c. I and III only
   d. I, II, and III

OBLIGATIONS AND PERFORMANCE

CHAPTER

(26)

 GENERAL PRINCIPLES
1. **OBLIGATION OF GOOD FAITH**
2. **TIME REQUIREMENTS OF OBLIGATIONS**
3. **REPUDIATION OF THE CONTRACT**
4. **ADEQUATE ASSURANCE OF PERFORMANCE**

 DUTIES OF THE PARTIES
5. **SELLER'S DUTY TO DELIVER**
6. **BUYER'S DUTY UPON RECEIPT OF GOODS**
7. **BUYER'S DUTY TO ACCEPT GOODS**
8. **BUYER'S DUTY TO PAY**
9. **WHEN DUTIES ARE EXCUSED**

LEARNING OBJECTIVES

After studying this chapter, you should be able to

LO.1 Define the obligation of good faith as applied to merchants and nonmerchants

LO.2 List the steps that can be taken when a party to a sales contract feels insecure about the other party's performance

LO.3 Explain the obligations of the seller and the buyer in a sales contract

LO.4 Identify the types of actions and conduct that constitute acceptance

Contracts for the sale of goods impose both obligations and requirements for performance on the parties.

 GENERAL PRINCIPLES

Each party to a sales contract is bound to perform according to the terms of the contract. Each is likewise under a duty to exercise **good faith** in the contract's performance and to do nothing that would impair the other party's expectation that the contract will be performed.

good faith absence of knowledge of any defects or problems.

1. OBLIGATION OF GOOD FAITH

Every contract or duty within the Uniform Commercial Code (UCC) imposes an obligation of good faith in its performance or enforcement.[1] The UCC defines good faith as "honesty in fact in the conduct or transaction concerned."[2] In the case of a merchant seller or buyer of goods, the UCC carries the concept of good faith further. The UCC imposes the additional requirement that merchants observe "reasonable commercial standards of fair dealing in the trade."[3] Section 1-203 of the UCC provides, "Every contract or duty within this Act imposes an obligation of good faith in its performance or enforcement."[4]

2. TIME REQUIREMENTS OF OBLIGATIONS

In a cash sale that does not require delivery of the goods, the duties of the seller and buyer are concurrent. Each one has the right to demand that the other perform at the same time. That is, as the seller hands over the goods, the buyer hands over the purchase money. If either party refuses to act, the other party has the right to withhold performance. In self-service stores, the performance occurs simultaneously—the buyer pays as the items are bagged at checkout.

In other types of contracts, there may be blocks of time between when the parties enter into an agreement and when performance, either delivery or payment, is due. During those time periods, buyers may become concerned about the ability of a seller experiencing a labor strike to complete production of the goods ordered in the contract. A seller may feel that a buyer who is experiencing credit difficulties may not be able to pay for the goods. Article 2 covers these periods of time and the conduct of the parties after the contract is entered into but before performance is due.

3. REPUDIATION OF THE CONTRACT

repudiation result of a buyer or seller refusing to perform the contract as stated.

If the seller or the buyer refuses to perform the contract when the time for performance arises, a **repudiation** of the contract results. Often, before the time for performance arrives, a party to the contract may inform the other that she will not perform the terms of the contract. This repudiation made in advance of the time

---

[1] UCC § 1-203; *Potomac Plaza Terraces, Inc. v QSC Products, Inc.*, 868 F Supp 346 (DDC 1994).

[2] UCC § 1-201(19); *Kotis v Nowlin Jewelry, Inc.*, 844 SW2d 920 (Tex App 1992). Revised UCC adds "observance of reasonable commercial standards of fair dealing" as part of good faith.

[3] UCC § 2-103(1)(b); *Amoco Oil Co. v Ervin*, 908 P2d 493 (Colo 1995); *El Paso Natural Gas Co. v Minco Oil & Gas Co.*, 964 SW2d 54 (Tex App 1998); *General Electric Co. v Compagnie Euralair*, 945 F Supp 527 (SDNY 1996).

[4] UCC § 1-203.

anticipatory repudiation
repudiation made in advance of the time for performance of the contract obligations.

for performance is called an **anticipatory repudiation.**[5] Under Revised Article 2, repudiation occurs when the party furnishes a *record* (as noted in other chapters, a term that allows for e-mails) including "language that a reasonable party would interpret to mean that the other party will not or cannot make a performance still due under the contract" or when the party exhibits "voluntary, affirmative conduct that would appear to a reasonable party to make a future performance by the other party impossible."[6]

4. ADEQUATE ASSURANCE OF PERFORMANCE

This time between contracting and actual performance may see some developing events that cause the parties concern about the ability of each to perform.[7] **For Example,** if the seller's warehouse is destroyed by fire, the buyer might conclude that the seller might not be able to make a delivery scheduled for the following month. Whenever a party to a sales contract has reasonable grounds to be concerned about the future performance of the other party, a demand may be made in a record for *assurance* that the contract will be performed.[8] **For Example,** a seller who is concerned about a buyer's ability to pay for goods could demand an updated credit report, financial statement, or even additional security or payment.

(a) FORM OF ASSURANCE   The person on whom demand for assurance is made must give "such assurance of due performance as is adequate under the circumstances of the particular case."[9] The UCC does not specify the exact form of assurance. If the party on whom demand is made has an established reputation, a reaffirmation of the contract obligation and a statement that it will be performed may be sufficient to assure a reasonable person that it will be performed. In contrast, if the party's reputation or economic position at the time is such that mere words and promises would not give any real assurance, it may be necessary to have a third person (or an insurance company) guarantee performance or to put up property as security for performance.

(b) FAILURE TO GIVE ASSURANCE   If adequate assurance is not given within 30 days from the time of demand, the demanding party may treat the contract as repudiated. The party demanding assurances may then proceed as if there were a breach and may pursue damage remedies. The nonbreaching party also has the right to enter into a substitute contract with a third person to obtain goods contracted for under the now-broken contract.

 DUTIES OF THE PARTIES

The obligations of the parties to a sales contract include (1) the seller's duty to deliver the goods, (2) the buyer's duty to accept the goods, and (3) the buyer's duty to pay for the goods.

---

[5] UCC § 2-610; *Aero Consulting Corp. v Cessna Aircraft Co.,* 867 F Supp 1480 (D Kan 1994).

[6] Revised UCC § 2-610. This change incorporates the definition of repudiation from both the existing comments to § 2-610 as well as the language from the Restatement of Contracts § 250.

[7] UCC § 2-609.

[8] *S & S, Inc. v Meyer,* 478 NW2d 857 (Iowa App 1991).

[9] UCC § 2-609(4).

CASE SUMMARY

The Evaporating Lines of Credit for the Beverage Distributor

FACTS: Hornell Brewing Company is a supplier and marketer of alcoholic and nonalcoholic beverages, including the popular iced tea drink, Arizona. In 1992, Stephen A. Spry and Don Vultaggio, Hornell's chairman of the board, made an oral agreement for Spry to be the exclusive distributor of Arizona products in Canada. The initial arrangement was an oral agreement, and in response to Spry's request for a letter he needed to secure financing, Hornell provided a letter that confirmed the distributorship.

During 1993 and 1994, Hornell shipped beverages on 10-day credit terms, but between December 1993 and February 1994, Spry's credit balances grew from $20,000 to $100,000, and a $31,000 check from Spry was returned for insufficient funds.

In March 1994, Hornell demanded that Spry obtain a line and/or letter of credit to pay for the beverages to place their relationship on a more secure footing. An actual line of credit never came about. Hornell did receive a partial payment by a wire transfer on May 9, 1994. Spry ordered 30 trailer loads of "product" from Hornell at a total purchase price of $390,000 to $450,000. Hornell learned from several sources, including its regional sales manager Baumkel, that Spry's warehouse was empty; that he had no managerial, sales, or office staff; that he had no trucks; and that his operation was a sham.

On May 10, 1994, Hornell wrote to Spry, telling him that it would extend up to $300,000 of credit to him, net 14 days cash "based on your prior representation that you have secured a $1,500,000 U.S. line of credit." Spry did not respond to this letter. After some months of futile negotiations by counsel, Hornell filed suit.

DECISION: Because Hornell had reasonable grounds for doubting performance, it could demand adequate assurances for performance. If those assurances were not forthcoming, Hornell had the right to terminate the contract. The ability of Spry to perform under the contract was in doubt from the outset. Spry had no financing in place and had failed to set up the system necessary for distribution of the products. Furthermore, Spry had misled Hornell about the nature of his connections and business, and when that deception came to Hornell's attention, it was entitled to demand assurances. When no assurances were forthcoming from Spry, it had the right to end the relationship. Furthermore, its assurances of shipment for cash within 14 days were not unreasonable. [**Hornell Brewing Co., Inc. v Spry, 664 NYS2d 698 (Sup Ct 1997)**]

5. SELLER'S DUTY TO DELIVER

The seller has the duty to deliver the goods according to the terms of the contract.

(a) PLACE, TIME, AND MANNER OF DELIVERY   The terms of the contract determine whether the seller is to send the goods or the buyer is to call for them and whether the goods are to be transported from the seller to the buyer or the transaction is to be completed by the delivery of documents without the movement of the goods. In the absence of a provision in the contract or a contrary course of performance or usage of trade, the place of delivery is the seller's place of business if the seller has one; otherwise, it is the seller's residence. (See Chapter 24 for more details on delivery and shipping terms.)[10] However, if the subject matter of the contract consists of identified goods that are known by the parties to be in some other place,

---

[10] UCC § 2-308.

that place is the place of delivery. If no time for shipment or delivery is stated, delivery or shipment is required within a reasonable time.

When a method of transportation called for by the contract becomes unavailable or commercially unreasonable, the seller must make delivery by means of a commercially reasonable substitute if available.

(b) QUANTITY DELIVERED   The buyer has the right to insist that all the goods be delivered at one time. If the seller delivers a smaller or larger quantity than what is stipulated in the contract, the buyer may refuse to accept the goods.[11]

6. BUYER'S DUTY UPON RECEIPT OF GOODS

The buyer must accept goods that conform to the contract, and the refusal to do so is a breach of the contract. However, the buyer has certain rights prior to acceptance.

CPA

(a) RIGHT TO EXAMINE GOODS—THE BUYER'S RIGHT OF INSPECTION[12]   To determine whether the goods in fact conform to the contract, the buyer has the right to examine the goods when tendered by the seller. An exception to this rule occurs when goods are sent COD. In a COD shipment, the buyer has no right to examine the goods until payment is made.

The buyer's right of inspection includes the right to remove goods from cartons and to conduct tests. **For Example,** a buyer who is purchasing potatoes for use in making potato chips has the right to peel and test a portion of the potatoes to determine whether they are the appropriate type for "chipping."

(b) RIGHT TO REFUSE OR RETURN THE GOODS—THE BUYER'S RIGHT OF REJECTION[13]   If the goods the seller has tendered do not conform to the contract in any way, the buyer can *reject* the goods. **For Example,** the buyer may reject a mobile home when it does not contain an air conditioner with the capacity specified by the contract. The buyer may reject the goods if they are not perfect.[14] The standard for rejection does not require that the defect in the goods or the breach be material. **For Example,** a small pressure mark on an ottoman is not material; the ottoman will function just as well. However, the buyer still has the right to reject the ottoman because it has a defect.

The buyer has the right to reject the full shipment, accept the full shipment and seek damages for the goods' diminished value (see Chapter 27), or accept any commercial units and reject the remainder. Commercial units are defined by trade and industry according to the customary size of cartons or containers for the goods shipped. Envelopes come in **commercial units** of boxes of 500. Computer disks often come in packages of 20 or 50. Rejection by a buyer would be not of individual envelopes or disks but of boxes. **For Example,** if Donna purchased a package of 20 disks and 4 of the 20 disks were defective, Donna would return the box of 20 disks

commercial unit standard of the trade for shipment or packaging of a good.

---

[11] UCC § 2-307; Seller must not cause damage during delivery. *Kaghann's Korner, Inc. v Brown & Sons Fuel Co., Inc.,* 706 NE 2d 556 (Ind App 1999).

[12] UCC § 2-601.

[13] UCC § 2-602; *In re S.M. Acquisition Co.,* 319 BR 553 (ND Ill 2005)

[14] Revised UCC eliminates the word "rightful" from the title of § 2-601, clarifying a point the drafters thought important: A buyer has the right of rejection even if it is wrongful and a breach of contract. The title "Manner and Effect of Rightful Rejection" has now been changed to "Manner and Effect of Rejection." *Precision Mirror & Glass v Nelms,* 797 NYS 2d 720 (2005).

for a new box. Rejection and acceptance in commercial units prevent the problems created when a seller has to open other units and mix and match goods in each.

After rejecting the goods, the buyer may not exercise any right of ownership over the goods.

The buyer's rejection must be made within a reasonable time after the delivery or tender of the goods. The buyer must notify the seller of the rejection and, in transactions with merchants particularly, provide the seller with the reason for the rejection.[15]

CPA

right to cure second chance for a seller to make a proper tender of conforming goods.

(c) Cure of Defective Tender or Delivery   The reason for the notification of rejection to the seller by the buyer is that the UCC gives a right of cure to the seller if the seller tenders or delivers nonconforming goods. The buyer's rejection is not an end to the transaction. The seller is given a second chance, or a **right to cure,** to make a proper tender of conforming goods.[16]

seasonable timely.

This right of cure means that the buyer must give notice of rejection and the reason for that rejection, if the seller has the right, but not necessarily the intent, to cure. That is, the seller has the right to cure if the seller is able to make the cure within the time remaining under the contract. If the time for making delivery under the contract has not expired, the seller need only give the buyer **seasonable** (timely) notice of the intention to make a proper delivery within the time allowed by the contract. Under Revised Article 2, the seller also has the right of cure if the time for making the delivery has expired through the allowance of additional reasonable time in which to make a substitute conforming tender. Such additional time is allowed if (1) the seller so notifies the buyer and (2) the seller had acted reasonably in making the original tender, believing that it would be acceptable to the buyer.[17] Under Revised UCC, installment contracts are also governed under this rule.

CASE SUMMARY

Leaving the Sellers Hanging on a Painting: Brushing Off Rejection

FACTS: Mark Murray and Ian Peck are art dealers who own separate art galleries located in New York. Robert and Jean Weil reside in Montgomery, Alabama, and are art collectors. Murray and Sam Lehr, a business acquaintance of his, traveled to Montgomery to see the various paintings in the Weils' collection, including a painting by Edgar Degas titled *Aux Courses*, which Murray examined under ultraviolet light. Murray later telephoned Weil and told him that he had spoken with someone who might be interested in purchasing the Degas.

On November 3, 1997, the director of Murray's gallery, Stephanie Calman, traveled to the Weils' home in Alabama. Calman, on behalf of Murray, and Robert Weil executed an agreement that provided for consignment of the Degas to Murray's gallery "for a private inspection in New York for a period of a week" from November 3, "to be extended only with

---

[15] UCC § 2-602(1); *Loden v Drake*, 881 P2d 467 (Colo App 1994). Revised UCC makes significant changes for rejection and buyers' rights regarding notifying or the failure to notify the seller of the rejection and the reasons for that rejection. *Adams v Wacaster Oil Co., Inc.*, 98 SW 3d 832, 50 UCC Rep Serv 2d (West) 774 (Ark Ct App 2003).

[16] *Allied Semi-Conductors Int'l v Pulsar Components Int'l, Inc.*, 907 F Supp 618 (EDNY 1995). The seller's right to cure is expanded under Revised Article 2 (§ 2-709) in that the seller can cure whether there is acceptance or rejection by the buyer.

[17] This right to cure after the time for performance has expired exists in nonconsumer contracts only.

CASE SUMMARY

continued

the express permission of the consignor." Calman returned to New York with the painting the same day.

Murray then showed the Degas to Peck. Peck expressed an interest in purchasing the Degas after seeing it and the price of $1,125,000 was discussed.

On November 26, 1997, Murray signed an agreement drafted by Weil and retyped on Murray's letterhead. Weil signed the agreement on December 1, 1997.

Neither Murray nor anyone else ever paid Weil the $1 million. Nonetheless, Murray maintained possession of the Degas from November 3, 1997, through March 25, 1998, when Weil requested its return.

The Weils filed suit seeking the price for the painting via summary judgment.

DECISION: There was no proper rejection of goods and the Weils were entitled to collect the price of the painting. Not only did Murray have a reasonable time to inspect the goods, but also it is undisputed that he actually did inspect the Degas. There is no evidence that Murray found the painting to be unsatisfactory or nonconforming. Murray inspected the Degas on at least two occasions, signed the written agreement, and continued to retain possession of the Degas. The right of rejection was not exercised and Murray had exercised ownership over the painting. [**Weil v Murray, 161 F Supp 2d 250 (SDNY 2001)**]

E-COMMERCE AND CYBERLAW

Rejection in Cyberspace

Rejection of computers and software present novel issues for the UCC provisions on rejection because use of the goods is not so easily defined or distinguished by a bright line. With software, for example, the buyer can use the software as a means of conducting an inspection of the goods. However, fully loading the software constitutes acceptance, and the buyer would then step into the UCC provisions on revocation of acceptance, as opposed to rejection. If the software causes the buyer's computer to "crash" every 10 minutes, the buyer has grounds for either rejection or revocation of acceptance. The buyer could also agree to allow the seller to modify the software to prevent the "crashing" problems. Once the buyer decides to reject the software or revoke acceptance of it, he or she cannot continue to use the software, for such use is inconsistent with the claim that the goods (the software) fail to conform to the contract.[*]

A buyer is also permitted to test a computer for purposes of inspection and rejection. If, however, the buyer rejects the computer system, it cannot continue to use the system, and allowing third parties to make alterations to the system to help it function better constitutes acceptance.[**]

[*] *Cooperative Resources, Inc. v Dynasty Software, Inc.*, 39 UCC Rep Serv 2d 101 (NH Dist Ct 1998).

[**] *Softa Group, Inc. v Scarsdale Development*, 632 NE2d 13 (Ill App 1993) (using a computer the buyer claims was "defective from inception" is inconsistent with rejection and the required basis for a rejection). *Licitra v Gateway, Inc.*, 189 Misc2d 721, 734 NYS2d 389, 47 UCC Rep Serv 2d 59 (2001).

7. BUYER'S DUTY TO ACCEPT GOODS

Assuming that the buyer has no grounds to reject the goods after inspection, the next step in the performance of the contract is the buyer's **acceptance** of the goods.

acceptance unqualified assent to the act or proposal of another, such as the acceptance of a draft (bill of exchange), of an offer to make a contract, of goods delivered by the seller, or of a gift or deed.

(a) WHAT CONSTITUTES ACCEPTANCE OF GOODS[18] Acceptance of goods means that the buyer, pursuant to a contract, has, either expressly or by implication, taken the goods permanently. The buyer's statement of acceptance is an express acceptance. A buyer can accept goods by implication if there is no rejection after a reasonable opportunity to inspect them or within a reasonable time after the buyer has inspected them. Another form of acceptance by implication is conduct by the buyer that is inconsistent with rejection, as when a buyer uses or sells the delivered goods.[19]

A buyer accepts goods by making continued use of them and by not attempting to return them. A buyer also accepts goods by modifying them because such action is inconsistent with a rejection or with the continued ownership of the goods by the seller.[20]

(b) REVOCATION OF ACCEPTANCE Even after acceptance of the goods, the performance under the contract may not be finished if the buyer exercises the right to revoke acceptance of the goods.[21] The buyer may revoke acceptance of the goods when they do not conform to the contract, the defect is such that it substantially impairs the value of the contract to the buyer, and either the defect is such that the buyer could not discover the problem or the seller has promised to correct a problem the buyer was aware of and pointed out to the seller prior to acceptance.[22] **For Example,** a buyer who purchased an emergency electric power generator found that the generator produced only about 65 percent of the power called for by the contract. This amount of power was insufficient for the operation of the buyer's electrical equipment. The seller's repeated attempts to improve the generator's output failed. The buyer, despite having used the generator for three months, could revoke his acceptance of it because its value was substantially impaired and he continued to keep it and use it only because of the seller's assurances that it would be repaired.

substantial impairment material defect in a good.

Substantial impairment is a higher standard than the one of "fails to conform in any respect" for rejection. Substantial impairment requires proof of more than the mere fact that the goods do not conform to the contract. The buyer is not required to show that the goods are worthless but must prove that their use to the buyer is substantially different from what the contract promised.

A revocation of acceptance is not a cancellation of the contract with the seller. After revocation of acceptance, the buyer can choose from the remedies available for breach

---

[18] UCC § 2-606; *Stenzel v Dell, Inc.,* 870 A2d 133 (ME 2005).

[19] *Fabrica de Tejidos Imperial v Brandon Apparel Group, Inc.,* 218 F Supp 2d 974 (ND Ill 2002).

[20] Under Revised Article 2 (§ 2-706), the buyer is deemed to have accepted goods even if the buyer communicates acceptance to the seller before inspection. UCC § 2-606(1)(a), (b), and (c).

[21] UCC § 2-608; *Fode v Capital RV Center, Inc.,* 575 NW2d 682 (ND 1998).

[22] Repeated requests for service satisfy the requirement for notifying the seller. *Cliffstar Corp. v Elmar Industries, Inc.,* 678 NYS2d 222 (1998).

CASE SUMMARY

Jackson Hole Traders: The Retailer Looking for a Loophole

FACTS: Catherine Joseph, who does business as Metro Classics, sold clothing to Jackson Hole Traders, a corporation owned by David and Elizabeth Speaks. Jackson Hole Traders is located in Jackson, Wyoming, and sells clothing for men and women through a retail store and mail-order catalog business. The clothing Joseph sold was specially manufactured for Jackson Hole Traders and had a total contract price of $50,000 with net 30 terms.

When the clothing items were shipped between July and September 1994, approximately 900 items were sent. Elizabeth Speaks complained about the quality of some of the clothing items when they arrived and was given a credit of $1,096 for returned merchandise. However, Jackson Hole Traders did not pay $33,000 of the total Joseph bill despite its being well past the net 30-day period for payment. When Joseph demanded payment, Elizabeth Speaks boxed up approximately 350 items of the clothing and sent them back, demanding a credit for revocation of acceptance. Joseph filed suit for payment, alleging that it was too late for revocation of acceptance. The trial court found for Joseph, and the Speakses appealed.

DECISION: The Speakses breached the contract when they failed to pay for the garments that had been sent to them and that they had accepted for resale. They could not revoke acceptance after so much time had passed and they had offered the goods for sale. They sent the goods back not because they were defective but because they were unable to make the payments or sell the merchandise. [**Jackson Hole Traders, Inc. v Joseph, 931 P2d 244 (Wyo 1997)**]

of contract or demand that the seller deliver conforming goods. (See Chapter 27 for more information on remedies for breach.)

(c) NOTIFICATION OF REVOCATION OF ACCEPTANCE To revoke acceptance properly, the buyer must take certain steps. The buyer must give the seller notice of revocation. The revocation of acceptance is effective when the buyer notifies the seller. The buyer need not actually return the goods to make the notification or the revocation effective.

The notice of revocation of acceptance must be given within a reasonable time after the buyer discovers or should have discovered the problems with the goods. The right of revocation is not lost if the buyer gives the seller a longer period of time to correct the defects in the goods.[23] Even the lapse of a year will not cost the buyer the right of revocation of acceptance if the seller has been experimenting during that time trying to correct the problems with the goods.

(d) BUYER'S RESPONSIBILITIES UPON REVOCATION OF ACCEPTANCE After a revocation of acceptance, the buyer must hold the goods and await instructions from the seller. If the buyer revokes acceptance after having paid the seller in advance, the buyer may retain possession of the goods as security for the refund of the money that has been paid.

---

[23] A buyer who took her pop-up camper in for repairs but was then given a different camper without being told about it was entitled to revoke her acceptance. *Head v Phillips Camper Sales & Rental, Inc.*, 593 NW2d 595 (Mich Ct App 1999).

THINKING THINGS THROUGH

What To Do When You Wanted Flakes and Got Chunks Instead

Scotwood, a wholesaler, sells calcium chloride flake to suppliers, including Miller and Sons, for use in ice melt products. In 2004, Miller and Sons ordered from Scotwood a large number of bags of 74–75 percent calcium chloride flake. From July 19, 2004, until September 3, 2004, Scotwood delivered 37 shipments of calcium chloride flake to Miller and Sons' warehouse. Following each delivery, Scotwood forwarded to Miller and Sons an invoice listing numerous "Terms and Conditions," including paragraph 8(a), which limited the time for bringing any claims against Scotwood.

Although it paid 35 of the 37 invoices for the 37 shipments it received, Miller and Sons was not happy with the deliveries because the calcium chloride flake was substantially defective. The bags it was delivered in were ripped and the calcium chloride flake in the bags was chunked. Miller and Sons was forced to conduct the labor-intensive process of sorting the chunked calcium chloride from the usable flakes in the shipments it received from Scotwood.

What did they do that constituted rejection? What did they do that constituted acceptance? What should Miller and Sons have done? [SCOTWOOD INDUSTRIES, INC. V FRANK MILLER & SONS, INC., 453 F Supp 2d 1160 (D Kan 2006)].

ETHICS & THE LAW

At Saks Fifth Avenue, they call it the "return season." Return season occurs within the week following a major fund-raising formal dance. Women who have purchased formal evening wear return the dresses after the dance. The dresses have been worn, and the tags have been cut, but the women return the dresses with requests for a full refund. Neiman Marcus also experiences the same phenomenon of returns.

Some stores have implemented a policy that formal evening wear may not be returned if the tags are cut from it. Others require a return within a limited period of seven days. Others offer an exchange only after five days.

Are the women covered by a right of rejection under Article 2? What do you think of the conduct of the women? Is it simply revocation of acceptance? Is there good faith on the part of the women?

8. BUYER'S DUTY TO PAY

The buyer must pay the amount stated in the sales contract for accepted goods.

(a) TIME OF PAYMENT   The sales contract may require payment in advance or may give the buyer credit by postponing the time for payment.[24]

---
[24] UCC § 2-310.

(b) FORM OF PAYMENT   Unless otherwise agreed, payment by the buyer requires payment in cash. The seller may accept a check or a promissory note from the buyer. If the check is not paid by the bank, the purchase price remains unpaid. A promissory note payable at a future date gives the buyer credit by postponing the time for payment.

The seller can refuse to accept a check or a promissory note as payment for goods but must give the buyer reasonable time in which to obtain legal tender with which to make payment.

CPA

9. WHEN DUTIES ARE EXCUSED

commercial impracticability
situation that occurs when costs of performance rise suddenly and performance of a contract will result in a substantial loss.

Under Article 2, the doctrine of commercial impracticability is available as a defense to performance of a contract. The doctrine of **commercial impracticability** is the modern commercial law version of the common law doctrine of impossibility. If a party to a contract can establish that there has been an occurrence or a contingency not anticipated by the parties and not a basic assumption in their entering into a contract, the party can be excused from performance.

The standard for commercial impracticability is objective, not subjective. Additional cost alone is not grounds for application of commercial impracticability.[25]

For Example, if a farmer has contracted to sell 2 tons of peanuts to an airline and the crop fails, the farmer is not excused on the grounds of commercial impracticability. So long as peanuts are available for the farmer to buy, even at a higher price, and then sell to the buyer to satisfy their contract terms, the farmer is not excused. Commercial impracticability refers to those circumstances in which peanuts are not available anywhere because the entire peanut harvest was destroyed rather than just the individual farmer's crop.

CASE SUMMARY

When the Cartons Cannot Be Contained

FACTS: Leanin' Tree, a Colorado corporation, manufactures, distributes, and sells greeting cards. In 1995, Leanin' Tree entered into a written agreement with Thiele in late March or early April 1998 whereby Thiele agreed to design and manufacture a "cartoner" (i.e., an automated carton-packing machine). Thiele specializes in the design and manufacture of cartoning equipment and, at the time of the agreement, had considerable experience in designing and manufacturing equipment that utilized cardboard cartons but very little experience in designing and manufacturing equipment that utilized plastic cartons, such as those used by Leanin' Tree.

On September 11, 1998, Thiele wrote to Leanin' Tree setting forth various "specifications concerning the manufacture of [the] cartons."

---

[25] UCC § 2-615(a). The key change in Revised Article 2 for this section is that "delivery" is changed to "performance" because the issues may relate to other aspects of performance beyond just delivery of the goods.

CASE SUMMARY

continued

The parties revised their agreement on several occasions between late 1998 and May 1999 to allow for various design changes. According to the final revised agreement, the machine was to be completed and shipped to Leanin' Tree on June 30, 1999, at a total price of $468,682. Despite the agreed-upon shipping date, and its previous assurances to Leanin' Tree that it could design and produce a functioning machine, Thiele was unable to get the cartoner to operate properly.

In late November or early December 1999, Thiele decided to stop working on the cartoner even though the carton set-up portion of the machine was still not functioning properly. Thiele's costs in designing and producing the machine were in the neighborhood of $750,000, more than $250,000 above the contract price, and more than $350,000 above Thiele's anticipated costs of design and production. Thiele maintained performance was commercially impracticable.

After sending a representative to observe the cartoner at Thiele's facility (and confirming that the cartoner was not working properly), Leanin' Tree formally rejected the cartoner "based on its failure to conform to the [parties'] agreement." Leanin' Tree filed suit for breach of contract. The district court found in favor of Leanin' Tree on its breach of contract claim. The district court awarded Leanin' Tree (1) $283,669, an amount equal to the payments it had made to Thiele under the written agreement, plus prejudgment interest and (2) consequential damages in the amount of $146,508.22 (to cover costs incurred by Leanin' Tree on the cartoner project).

Thiele appealed.

DECISION: The court held that all of the problems Thiele encountered were ones that a manufacturer should know about and were not out of the ordinary. Thiele should have anticipated them when it entered into the contract for a design that was new. The additional cost does not control whether a performance has become impracticable where those costs are foreseeable and perhaps preventable with more research on the product line, issues, and needs. [**Leanin' Tree, Inc. v Thiele Technologies, Inc.**, 48 UCC Rep Serv 2d 991 (CA Colo 2002)]

> SUMMARY

Every sales contract imposes an obligation of good faith in its performance. Good faith means honesty in fact in the conduct or transaction concerned. For merchants, the UCC imposes the additional requirement of observing "reasonable commercial standards of fair dealing in the trade."

In the case of a cash sale where no transportation of the goods is required, both the buyer and the seller may demand concurrent performance.

A buyer's or a seller's refusal to perform a contract is called a *repudiation*. A repudiation made in advance of the time for performance is called an *anticipatory repudiation* and is a breach of the contract. If either party to a contract feels insecure about the performance of the other, that party may demand by a record adequate assurance of performance. If that assurance is not given, the demanding party may treat the contract as repudiated.

The seller has a duty to deliver the goods in accordance with the terms of the contract. This duty does not require physical transportation; it requires that the seller permit the transfer of possession of the goods to the buyer.

With the exception of COD contracts, the buyer has the right to inspect the goods upon tender or delivery. Inspection includes the right to open cartons and conduct tests. If the buyer's inspection reveals that the seller has tendered nonconforming goods, the buyer may reject them. Subject to certain limitations, the seller may then offer to replace the goods or cure the problems the buyer has noted.

The buyer has a duty to accept goods that conform to the contract, and refusal to do so is a breach of contract. The buyer is deemed to have accepted goods either expressly or by implication through conduct inconsistent with rejection or by lapse of time. The buyer must pay for accepted goods in accordance with the terms of the contract. The buyer can reject goods in commercial units, accept the goods and collect damages for their problems, or reject the full contract shipment. The buyer must give notice of rejection to the seller and cannot do anything with the goods that would be inconsistent with the seller's ownership rights. The buyer should await instructions from the seller on what to do with the goods.

Even following acceptance, the buyer may revoke that acceptance if the problems with the goods substantially impair their value and the problems were either not easily discoverable or the buyer kept the goods based on the seller's promises to repair them and make them whole. Upon revocation of acceptance, the buyer should await instructions from the seller on what steps to take.

Performance can be excused on the grounds of commercial impracticability, but the seller must show objective difficulties that have created more than cost increases.

❯ QUESTIONS AND CASE PROBLEMS

1. In 1992, Donna Smith telephoned Clark, the manager of Penbridge Farms, in response to an advertisement Clark had placed in the July issue of the *Emu Finder* about the availability for sale of proven breeder pairs. Clark told Smith he had a breeder pair available for purchase. Clark sold the pair to Smith for $16,500. Some months later, after Smith had had a chance to inspect the pair, she discovered that Clark had sold her two male emus. Smith immediately notified Clark and revoked her acceptance of the animals. Clark said the revocation was too late. Was it? [*Smith v Penbridge Associates, Inc.,* 655 A2d 1015 (Pa Super)]

2. On January 3, 1991, Central District Alarm (CDA) and Hal-Tuc entered into a written sales agreement providing that CDA would sell and install new security equipment described on an equipment list attached to the contract. This list included a Javelin VCR. When the system was installed, CDA installed a used JVC VCR instead of a new Javelin VCR. Hal-Tuc called CDA the day after the installation and complained that the equipment was not the Javelin brand, and that the VCR was a used JVC VCR. CDA told Hal-Tuc that the equipment was not used and that a JVC VCR was better than a Javelin. Hal-Tuc telephoned CDA personnel over a two-week period during which they denied that the equipment was used.

   After two weeks of calls, CDA's installation manager went to the store to see the equipment and admitted that it was used. No one from CDA advised Hal-Tuc in advance that it was installing used equipment temporarily until the right equipment arrived. CDA offered to replace it with a new Javelin VCR as soon as one arrived, which would take one or two months. Hal-Tuc asked CDA to return its deposit and take the equipment back, but CDA refused. Hal-Tuc put all the equipment in boxes and stored it. CDA filed a petition against Hal-Tuc for damages for breach of contract. Hal-Tuc filed a counterclaim, alleging fraud. CDA asserted it had the right to cure by tendering conforming goods after Hal-Tuc rejected the nonconforming goods. Was CDA correct? [*Central District Alarm, Inc. v Hal-Tuc, Inc.,* 866 SW2d 210 (Mo App)]

3. Bobby Murray Chevrolet, Inc., submitted a bid to the Alamance County Board of Education to supply 1,200 school bus chassis to the district. Bobby Murray was awarded the contract and contracted with General Motors (GM) to purchase the chassis for the school board.

Between the time of Bobby Murray's contract with GM and the delivery date, the Environmental Protection Agency (EPA) enacted new emission standards for diesel vehicles, such as school buses. Under the new law, the buses Bobby Murray ordered from GM would be out of compliance, as would the buses Bobby Murray specified in its bid to the school board.

GM asked for several extensions to manufacture the buses within the new EPA guidelines. The school board was patient and gave several extensions, but then, because of its need for buses, purchased them from another supplier after notifying Bobby Murray of its intent to do so. The school board had to pay an additional $150,152.94 for the buses from its alternative source and sued Bobby Murray for that amount. Bobby Murray claimed it was excused from performance on the grounds of commercial impracticability. Is Bobby Murray correct? Does the defense of commercial impracticability apply in this situation? Be sure to compare this case with other cases and examples in the chapter. [*Alamance County Board of Education v Bobby Murray Chevrolet, Inc.,* 465 SE2d 306 (NC App); rev. denied, 467 SE2d 899 (NC)]

4. The Home Shopping Club ordered 12,000 Care Bear lamps from Ohio International, Ltd. When the lamps arrived, they had poor painting and staining, certain elements were improperly glued and could come loose (a danger to the children likely to have the lamps in their rooms), and they overheated very easily (another danger for children as well as a fire hazard). Home Shopping Network notified International and gave it three months to remedy the problems and provide different lamps. After three months, Home Shopping Network returned all lamps and notified International that it was pulling out of the contract. Could they do so, or had too much time passed? [*Home Shopping Club, Inc. v Ohio International, Ltd.,* 27 UCC Rep Serv 2d 433 (Fla Cir Ct)]

5. Lafer Enterprises sold Christmas decorations to B. P. Development & Management Corp., the owners and operators of the Osceola Square Mall. The package of decorations was delivered to Osceola Square Mall prior to Thanksgiving 1986 for a total cost of $48,775, which B. P. would pay in three installments. Cathy Trivigno, a manager at B. P. who supervised the installation of the decorations, indicated that she and the Osceola Square Mall merchants were not satisfied with the quality of the decorations, but they needed to be in place for the day after Thanksgiving (the start of the holiday shopping season). B. P. complained to Lafer about the quality of the decorations but had the decorations installed. B. P. paid the first installment to Lafer but then stopped payment on the last two checks. B. P. claimed it had rejected the decorations. Lafer claimed breach for nonpayment because B. P. used the decorations. Did B. P. accept the decorations? [*B. P. Dev. & Management Corp. v Lafer Enterprises, Inc.,* 538 So 2d 1379 (Fla App)]

6. Westinghouse Electric Corporation entered into uranium supply contracts with 22 electric utilities during the late 1960s. The contract prices ranged from $7 to $10 per pound. The Arab oil embargo and other changes in energy resources caused the price of uranium to climb to between $45 and $75 per pound. Supply tightened because of increased demand.

In 1973, Westinghouse wrote to the utilities and explained that it was unable to perform on its uranium sales contracts. The utilities needed uranium. Westinghouse did not have sufficient funds to buy the uranium it had agreed to supply, assuming that it could find a supply. One utility executive commented, after totaling up all 22 supply contracts, that Westinghouse could not have supplied the uranium even under the original contract terms. He said, "Westinghouse oversubscribed itself on these contracts. They hoped that not all the utilities would take the full contract amount."

Westinghouse says it is impossible for it to perform. The utilities say they are owed damages because they must still find uranium somewhere. What damages would the law allow? What ethical issues do you see in the original contracts and in Westinghouse's refusal to deliver? Should we excuse parties from contracts because it is so expensive for them to perform? [*In re Westinghouse Uranium Litigation,* 436 F Supp 990 (ED Va)]

7. Steel Industries, Inc., ordered steel from Interlink Metals & Chemicals. The steel was to be delivered from a Russian mill. There were political and other issues in Russia, and the mill was shut down. Interlink did not deliver the steel to Steel Industries, claiming that it was excused from performance because it could not get the steel from the Russian mill. What would Interlink have to establish to show that it was excused from performing under the doctrine of commercial impracticability? [*Steel Industries, Inc. v Interlink Metals & Chemicals, Inc.,* 969 F Supp 1046 (ED Mich)]

8. Spaulding & Kimball Co. ordered from Aetna Chemical Co. 75 cartons of window washers. The buyer received them and sold about a third to its customers but later refused to pay for them, claiming that the quality was poor. The seller sued for the price. Would the seller be entitled to the contract price? Refer to the case in this chapter regarding the Degas painting for some insight. [*Aetna Chemical Co. v Spaulding & Kimball Co.,* 126 A 582 (Vt)]

9. A computer manufacturer promoted the sale of a digital computer as a "revolutionary break-through." The manufacturer made a contract to deliver one of these computers to a buyer. The seller failed to deliver the computer and explained that its failure was caused by unanticipated technological difficulties. Was this an excuse for nonperformance by the seller? [*United States v Wegematic Corp.,* 360 F2d 674 (2d Cir)]

10. Economy Forms Corp. sold concrete-forming equipment to Kandy. After using the equipment for more than six months, Kandy notified Economy that the equipment was inadequate.

Economy Forms alleged that Kandy had accepted the goods. Kandy denied liability. Was there an acceptance? Why or why not? [*Economy Forms Corp. v Kandy, Inc.,* 391 F Supp 944 (ND Ga)]

11. Michael Smyers operates his business, Engineered Specialty Products (ESP), in Olathe, Kansas. ESP manufactures and sells resistance welders and quartz crystal X-ray machines called *goniometers.* Quartz Works is a Massachusetts corporation in the business of purchasing welders, goniometers, and other related equipment and reselling the equipment as a package to businesses that wish to operate quartz crystal manufacturing facilities.

Quartz Works and ESP began negotiations for Quartz Works to purchase two welders from ESP, and they also explored the possibility of ESP manufacturing two goniometers for Quartz Works. On September 21, 1992, Quartz Works offered to purchase two welders from ESP at a total price of $88,825. At the time of its offer, Quartz Works also sent ESP a check for $66,618.75, representing a 75 percent down payment. Upon receiving Quartz Works' order, ESP sent back a counteroffer reflecting price adjustments for some of the related parts and a total purchase price of $89,125 for the welders. The invoice that ESP sent back to Quartz Works credited the payment Quartz Works had made and indicated that the total amount due was now $22,506.25. ESP began work on the goniometers, but after nine months, Quartz Works still owed money on the welders and had not paid 90 percent of what was due on the contract for the goniometers. ESP demanded full payment on the welders or it would not continue work on the goniometers. Quartz Works said that ESP could not demand assurances related to nonperformance on another contract. Was Quartz Works correct? Could ESP stop work on the goniometers if the welder contract was not performed? Why or why not? [*Smyers v Quartz Works Corp.,* 880 F Supp 1425 (D Kan)]

12. Rockland Industries is a Maryland corporation that manufactures drapery lining fabrics. Rockland uses approximately 500,000 pounds per year of antimony oxide, a fire retardant, on its

fabrics. Manley-Regan is a Pennsylvania chemical distribution company. Rockland usually purchased its antimony oxide from HoltraChem on an "as-needed" basis, where HoltraChem had quoted a price based on the understanding that Rockland required approximately 500,000 pounds per year of antimony oxide. HoltraChem charged about $0.86 per pound during its last year as Rockland's supplier.

Due to a serious worldwide crisis in the supply of this chemical in the spring of 1994, HoltraChem could no longer maintain its existing supply relationship with Rockland. Rockland, in exploring other suppliers, found that the antimony oxide market was extremely tight, with rising prices and no known recovery period.

Rockland contracted with Manley-Regan for delivery of antimony oxide (114,000 pounds total) at $1.80 per pound. That supply fell through because of the nature of the market and Rockville contracted with another supplier for 44,092 pounds of antimony oxide at $2.65 per pound and with still another supplier for 88,184 pounds at $2.54 per pound.

Rockland filed suit seeking as damages the difference between the price of $1.80 per pound and the various other prices it had paid. Manley-Regan used UCC § 2-615 as its defense claiming commercial impracticability. Does Manley-Regan have a good case using this defense? [*Rockland Industries, Inc. v E+E (US) Inc.,* 991 F Supp 468 (D Md)]

13. Trefalcon (a commercial arm of the government of Ghana) entered into a contract with Supply Commission as a purchaser of residual fuel oil (RFO). Supply Commission agreed, among other things, to supply Trefalcon with RFO at competitive prices as reserves permitted. Approximately six weeks into the agreement, on May 3, 1974, Supply Commission wrote a letter to Trefalcon proposing a method for pricing the refined fuel it would sell to Trefalcon.

A dispute arose six months later when Supply Commission first began to raise the price of RFO to account for escalations. In an effort to continue the contract, the parties orally agreed to a so-called Standstill Agreement, pursuant to which Ghana temporarily would forgo payment of escalations. By May 12, 1975, Trefalcon had paid only the base price for each of the 26 residual fuel cargoes it had received.

On May 26, 1975, J.V.L. Mensah, a representative of Supply Commission, sent a letter to Trefalcon demanding payment of $7,885,523.12 for escalation charges and declaring that no further oil would be sold until payment in full was made. After receiving the Mensah letter, Trefalcon tendered two payments to the Bank of Ghana—one in the amount of $1,617,682.29 (tendered June 10, 1975), and the other in the amount of $1,185,000 (tendered June 27, 1975).

With full payment still outstanding in July 1975, Supply Commission canceled the contract and sought damages for breach following the failure to provide assurances. Will Supply Commission recover? [*Reich v Republic of Ghana,* 2002 WL 142610 (SDNY 2002)]

14. Harry Ulmas made a contract to buy a new car from Acey Oldsmobile. He was allowed to keep his old car until the new car was delivered. The sales contract gave him a trade-in value of $650 on the old car but specified that the car would be reappraised when it was actually brought to the dealer. When Ulmas brought the trade-in to the dealer, an Acey employee took it for a test drive and said that the car was worth between $300 and $400. Acey offered Ulmas only $50 for his trade-in. Ulmas refused to buy from Acey and purchased from another dealer, who appraised the trade-in at $400. Ulmas sued for breach of contract on the grounds of violation of good faith. Was he right? [*Ulmas v Acey Oldsmobile, Inc.,* 310 NYS2d 147 (NY Civ)]

15. Cornelia and Ed Kornfeld contracted to sell a signed Picasso print to David Tunick, Inc. The print, entitled *Le Minotauromachie,* was signed "Pablo Picasso." The signature on the print was discovered to be a forgery, and the Kornfelds offered Tunick a substitute Picasso print. Tunick refused the Kornfelds' substituted performance and demanded a return of the contract price. The Kornfelds refused on the grounds that their cure had been refused. Was the substitute print an adequate cure? [*David Tunick, Inc. v Kornfeld,* 838 F Supp 848 (SDNY)]

CPA QUESTIONS

1. Under the sales article of the UCC, which of the following statements is correct?

   a. The obligations of the parties to the contract must be performed in good faith.
   b. Merchants and nonmerchants are treated alike.
   c. The contract must involve the sale of goods for a price of more than $500.
   d. None of the provisions of the UCC may be disclaimed by agreement.

2. Rowe Corp. purchased goods from Stair Co. that were shipped COD. Under the sales article of the UCC, which of the following rights does Rowe have?

   a. The right to inspect the goods before paying
   b. The right to possession of the goods before paying
   c. The right to reject nonconforming goods
   d. The right to delay payment for a reasonable period of time

3. Bibbeon Manufacturing shipped 300 designer navy blue blazers to Custom Clothing Emporium. The blazers arrived on Friday, earlier than Custom had anticipated and on an exceptionally busy day for its receiving department. They were perfunctorily examined and sent to a nearby warehouse for storage until needed. On Monday of the following week, upon closer examination, it was discovered that the quality of the blazer linings was inferior to that specified in the sales contract. Which of the following is correct insofar as Custom's rights are concerned?

   a. Custom can reject the blazers upon subsequent discovery of the defects.
   b. Custom must retain the blazers since it accepted them and had an opportunity to inspect them upon delivery.
   c. Custom's only course of action is rescission.
   d. Custom had no rights if the linings were merchantable quality.

4. Parker ordered 50 cartons of soap from Riddle Wholesale Company. Each carton contains 12 packages of soap. The terms were: $8.00 per carton 2/10, net/30, FOB buyer's delivery platform, delivery June 1. During transit approximately one-half the packages were damaged by the carrier. The delivery was made on May 28. Answer the following with "Yes" or "No."

   a. Riddle had the risk of loss during transit.
   b. If Parker elects to accept the undamaged part of the shipment, he will be deemed to have accepted the entire shipment.
   c. To validly reject the goods, Parker must give timely notice of rejection to Riddle within a reasonable time after delivery.
   d. If Riddle were notified of the rejection on May 28, Riddle could cure the defect by promptly notifying Parker of intention to do so and making a second delivery to Parker of conforming goods by June 1.
   e. The statute of frauds is inapplicable to the transaction in the facts given.

REMEDIES FOR BREACH OF SALES CONTRACTS

CHAPTER

(27)

24. **LIMITATION OF REMEDIES**
25. **WAIVER OF DEFENSES**
26. **PRESERVATION OF DEFENSES**

E REMEDIES IN THE INTERNATIONAL SALE
OF GOODS
27. **REMEDIES OF THE SELLER**
28. **REMEDIES OF THE BUYER**

**LEARNING
OBJECTIVES**

*After studying
this chapter,
you should be
able to*

LO.1 List the remedies of the seller when
the buyer breaches a sales contract

LO.2 List the remedies of the buyer when
the seller breaches a sales contract

LO.3 Determine the validity of clauses
limiting damages

LO.4 Discuss the waiver of and preservation
of defenses of a buyer

If one of the parties to a sale fails to perform the contract, the nonbreaching party has remedies under Article 2 of the Uniform Commercial Code (UCC). In addition, the parties may have included provisions on remedies in their contract.

STATUTE OF LIMITATIONS

Judicial remedies have time limitations. After the expiration of a particular period of time, the party seeking a remedy can no longer resort to the courts. The UCC **statute of limitations** applies to actions brought for remedies on the breach of a sales contract.[1] When a suit is brought on the basis of a tort theory, such as negligence, fraud, or strict tort liability, other general statutes of limitations apply.

statute of limitations statute that restricts the period of time within which an action may be brought.

1. TIME LIMITS FOR SUITS UNDER THE UCC

An action for breach of a sales contract must be commenced within four years after the time of the **breach**.[2] Revised UCC § 2-725(1) extends the statute of limitations to a maximum of five years to cover those cases in which the breach is discovered in year four.[3] The statute of limitations can be reduced as between merchants to as little as one year but cannot be reduced in consumer contracts.

When a cause of action arises depends on the nature of the breach. The previous UCC had three measurements for determining when a breach occurs. Revised Article 2 has eight accrual rules for the timing of a breach and the resulting statute of limitations. The basic rule is that the time begins to run when the breach occurs, but that rule has seven exceptions that include special timing rules for repudiation, infringement, breach of warranty, and future performance.

breach failure to act or perform in the manner called for in a contract.

---

[1] UCC § 2-703.

[2] The cause of action arises as soon as the breach occurs even if the party is unaware of the breach at that time. This unfairness is remedied under Revised Article 2 with a statute of limitations of the latter of four years after the breach or one year after the breach was or should have been discovered (no longer than five years total).

[3] Revised UCC § 2-725(1).

A buyer seeking damages because of a breach of the sales contract must give the seller notice of the breach within a reasonable time after the buyer discovers or should have discovered it.[4]

2. TIME LIMITS FOR OTHER SUITS

When a party seeks recovery on a non-Code theory, such as on the basis of strict tort liability, fraud, or negligence, the UCC statute of limitations does not apply. The action is subject to each state's tort statute of limitations. Tort statutes of limitations are found in individual state statutes, and the time limitations vary by state. However, the tort statutes of limitations tend to be shorter than the UCC statute of limitations.

REMEDIES OF THE SELLER

When the buyer breaches a sales contract, the seller has different remedies available that are designed to afford the seller compensation for the losses caused by the buyer's breach.[5] Revised Article 2 allows the remedies provided to be used together, and although the various remedies may be called out in separate sections, there is no requirement that a party elect only one of the remedies. In many cases of breach, only a combination of the various remedies can make the nonbreaching party whole again.

3. SELLER'S LIEN

In the absence of an agreement for the extension of credit to the buyer for the purchase of goods, and until the buyer pays for the goods or performs whatever actions the contract requires, the seller has the right to retain possession of the goods.[6]

4. SELLER'S REMEDY OF STOPPING SHIPMENT

When the buyer has breached the contract prior to the time the goods have arrived at their destination, the seller can stop the goods from coming into the buyer's possession. This remedy is important to sellers because it eliminates the need for sellers to try to recover goods from buyers who have indicated they cannot or will not pay.

A seller has the right to stop shipment if the buyer has received goods on credit and the seller learns that the buyer is insolvent, the buyer has not provided assurances as requested, or the seller has grounds to believe performance by the buyer will not occur.[7] Also, the right to retrieve the goods in the case of a credit buyer's insolvency continues for "a reasonable time after the buyer's receipt of the goods."

Revised UCC eliminates the time limit of 10 days after the buyer actually has received the goods. Revised UCC also eliminates the distinctions on sizes of shipments and rights because of the ease with which all types and sizes of shipments can now be tracked.[8]

---

[4] UCC § 2-607(3)(a).

[5] Under Revised Article 2 (§ 2-803), the overall policy change on remedies relates to the parties' expectations. The revision allows courts to deny a remedy if one party thereby benefits to more than a full performance position.

[6] UCC § 2-703.

[7] Revised UCC § 2-705. Under Revised UCC, the right of the seller has been broadened. Because shipments are tracked so easily now with technology, the seller can stop a shipment of any size for any of the reasons given, regardless of shipment size.

[8] Revised UCC § 2-705(1).

CPA

5. RESALE BY SELLER

When the buyer has breached the contract, the seller may resell any of the goods the seller still holds. After the resale, the seller is not liable to the original buyer on the contract and does not have to surrender any profit obtained on the resale. On the other hand, if the proceeds are less than the contract price, the seller may recover the loss from the original buyer.[9] Under Revised UCC, the failure of the seller to resell the goods does not mean the seller cannot recover under the other remedies available under Article 2.

The seller must give reasonable notice to the breaching buyer of the intention to resell the goods. Such notice need not be given if the goods are perishable or could decline rapidly in value. The seller must conduct any method of resale under standards of commercial reasonableness.[10] The formula for damages under resale is provided in Revised § 2-706(1) is substantially similar.[11]

6. CANCELLATION BY SELLER

When the buyer materially breaches the contract, the seller may cancel the contract. Such a cancellation ends the contract and discharges all unperformed obligations on both sides. Following cancellation, the seller has any remedy with respect to the breach by the buyer that is still available.

CPA

7. SELLER'S ACTION FOR DAMAGES UNDER THE MARKET PRICE FORMULA

When the buyer fails to pay for accepted goods, the seller may resell the goods, as discussed earlier, or bring a contract action to recover damages. One formula for a seller's damages is the difference between the market price at the time and place of the tender of the goods and the contract price.[12] Under Revised Article 2, in the case of an anticipatory repudiation, the measurement of damages is the difference between the contract price and the market price "at the expiration of a commercially reasonable time after the seller learned of the repudiation" but not later than the time of tender. Whether the seller chooses to resell or recover the difference between the contract price and the market price is the seller's decision. The flexibility in the remedies under the UCC is provided because certain goods have very high market fluctuations. **For Example,** suppose that Sears has agreed to purchase 10 refrigerators from Whirlpool at a price of $1,000 each, but then Sears notifies Whirlpool that it will not be buying the refrigerators after all. Whirlpool determines the market price at the time of tender to be $850 per refrigerator. The best Whirlpool can find from an alternate buyer after a search is $800. Whirlpool can select the resale remedy ($1,000 − $800, or $200 in damages) to adequately compensate for the change in the market price between the time of tender and the time damages are sought.

---

[9] Revised UCC § 2-706(1), (6); *Cook Composites, Inc. v Westlake Styrene Corp.,* 155 W3d 124 (CA Tex 2000).
[10] *Plano Lincoln Mercury, Inc. v Roberts,* 167 SW3d 616 (CA Tex 2005).
[11] Revised UCC § 2-706(1).
[12] Revised UCC § 2-708.

CPA   ## 8. SELLER'S ACTION FOR LOST PROFITS

If the market and resale price measures of damages do not place the seller in the same position in which the seller would have been had the buyer performed, the seller is permitted to recover lost profits.[13] The recovery of lost profits reimburses the seller for costs incurred in gearing up for contract performance.[14] **For Example,** suppose that a buyer has ordered 200 wooden rocking horses from a seller-manufacturer. Before production on the horses begins, the buyer breaches. The seller has nothing to resell, and the goods have not been identified to even permit a market value assessment. Nonetheless, the seller has geared up for production, counted on the contract, and perhaps bypassed other contracts in order to perform. An appropriate remedy for the seller of the rocking horses would be the profits it would have made had the buyer performed.

Some courts also follow the lost volume doctrine that allows sellers to recover for the profits they would have made if the buyer had completed the transaction.[15] For example, suppose that Maytag has a contract to sell 10 washing machines for $600 each to Lakewood Apartment Managers. Lakewood breaches the agreement and refuses to take or pay for the washing machines. Maytag is able to resell them to Suds 'n Duds Laundromat for $600 each. The price is the same, but, the theory of lost volume profits is that Maytag could have sold 20 washers, not just 10, if Lakewood had not breached. Maytag's profit on each machine is $200. Lost volume profits in this situation would be 10 times the $200, or $2,000.

incidental damages incurred by the nonbreaching party as part of the process of trying to cover (buy substitute   CPA   goods) or sell (selling subject matter of contract to another); includes storage fees, commissions, and the like.

9. OTHER TYPES OF DAMAGES

So far, the discussion of remedies has focused on the damages that result because the seller did not sell the goods. However, the seller may incur additional expenses because of the breach. Some of those expenses can be recovered as damages. UCC § 2-710 provides that the seller can also recover, as **incidental damages,**

THINKING THINGS THROUGH

In 1996, Collins Entertainment Corporation contracted to lease video poker machines to two bingo hall operations known as Ponderosa Bingo and Shipwatch Bingo. The six-year lease required that any purchaser of the premises assume the lease. In 1997, American Bingo and Gaming Corporation purchased the assets of the bingo parlors. American failed to assume the lease and removed Collins' machines from the premises. Collins had $1.5 million in profits remaining on the lease at the time its machines were removed. However, Collins was able to place the video poker machines in other casinos. Collins filed suit against American Bingo. American Bingo says that Collins has no damages because the machines were already earning money for it. Is American Bingo correct? [COLLINS ENTERTAINMENT CORP. v COATS AND COATS RENTAL AMUSEMENT, 629 SE2d 635 (SC 2006)]

---

[13] Note that this is a change under Revised Article 2. Prior to this change, the remedy of lost profits was available only under the market price remedy. Now it is available under market price and resale remedies.

[14] Revised UCC § 2-709.

[15] *Sunrich v Pacific Foods of Oregon,* 2004 WL 1124495 (D Or 2004)

any commercially reasonable charges, expenses, or commissions incurred[16] in recovering damages.[17] **For Example,** the seller may recover expenses for the transportation, care, and storage of the goods after the buyer's breach, as well as any costs incurred in the return or resale of the goods. Such damages are in addition to any others that may be recovered by the seller.

CPA

10. SELLER'S ACTION FOR THE PURCHASE PRICE

If goods are specially manufactured and the buyer refuses to take them, it is possible for the seller to recover as damages the full purchase price and keep the goods.[18] **For Example,** a printing company that has printed catalogs for a retail mail-order merchant will not be able to sell the catalogs to anyone else. The remedy for the seller is recovery of the purchase price.[19]

11. SELLER'S NONSALE REMEDIES

In addition to the seller's traditional sales remedies, many sellers enter into other transactions that provide protection from buyer breaches. One such protection is afforded when the seller obtains a security interest from the buyer under UCC Article 9. A **secured transaction** is a pledge of property by the buyer-debtor that enables the seller to take possession of the goods if the buyer fails to pay the amount owed. (See Chapter 34.)

secured transaction credit sale of goods or a secured loan that provides special protection for the creditor.

Figure 27-1 is a summary of the remedies available to the seller under Article 2.

FIGURE 27-1 *Seller's Remedies under Article 2*

REMEDY	STOP DELIVERY	RESALE PRICE	MARKET PRICE	ACTION FOR PRICE	LOST PROFIT
SECTION NUMBER	2–703	2–706 2–710	2–708 2–710	2–709 2–708	2–708(2)
WHEN AVAILABLE	Insolvency Advance breach by buyer	Buyer fails to take goods	Buyer fails to take goods	Specially manufactured goods	Anticipatory repudiation Breach
NATURE OF REMEDY	Stop delivery of any size shipment or recover goods if buyer insolvent (Revised UCC)	Contract price – Resale price + Incidental damages – Expenses saved + Consequential damages	Contract price – Market price + Incidental damages – Expenses saved + Consequential damages	Contract price + Incidental damages – Expenses saved + Consequential damages	Profits + Incidental damages – Salvage value + Consequential damages

---

[16] Revised UCC § 2-710.

[17] Revised UCC § 2-710; *Purina Mills, L.L.C. v Less,* 295 F Supp 2d 1017 (ND Iowa 2003).

[18] *In re Moltech Power Systems, Inc.,* 326 BR 178 (ND Fla 2005).

[19] UCC § 2-709(1)(a) and (b).

REMEDIES OF THE BUYER

When the seller breaches a sales contract, the buyer has a number of remedies under Article 2 of the UCC. Additional remedies based on contract or tort theories of product liability may also be available. (See Chapter 25.)

12. REJECTION OF IMPROPER TENDER

As discussed in Chapter 26, if the goods tendered by the seller do not conform to the contract in some way, the buyer may reject them. However, the rejection is the beginning of the buyer's remedies. Following rejection, the buyer can proceed to recover under the various formulas provided for buyers under the UCC.

13. REVOCATION OF ACCEPTANCE

The buyer may revoke acceptance of the goods when they do not conform to the contract, the defect substantially impairs the value of the contract to the buyer, and the buyer either could not discover the problem or kept the goods because of a seller's promise of repair (see Chapter 26). Again, following revocation of acceptance, the buyer has various remedies available under the UCC.

14. BUYER'S ACTION FOR DAMAGES FOR NONDELIVERY—MARKET PRICE RECOVERY

If the seller fails to deliver the goods as required by the contract or repudiates the contract, the buyer is entitled to collect from the seller damages for breach of contract. Under Revised Article 2, the buyer is entitled to recover the difference between the market price at the time of tender and the contract price; this is a change from the previous Article 2 that measured damages at the time the buyer learned of the breach.[20]

15. BUYER'S ACTION FOR DAMAGES FOR NONDELIVERY—COVER PRICE RECOVERY

A buyer may also choose, as a remedy for the seller's nondelivery of goods that conform to the contract, to purchase substitute goods or cover.[21] If the buyer acts in good faith, the measure of damages for the seller's nondelivery or repudiation is then the difference between the cost of cover and the contract price.[22]

The buyer need only make a reasonable cover purchase as a substitute for the contract goods. The goods purchased need not be identical to the contract goods. **For Example,** if the buyer could secure only 350 five-speed blenders when the contract called for 350 three-speed blenders, the buyer's cover would be reasonable despite the additional expense of the five-speed blenders.

---

[20] Revised UCC § 2-713.

[21] Revised UCC § 2-712; *Conagra, Inc. v Nierenberg,* 7 P3d 369 (Mont 2000). Buyers are also entitled to recover any deposits paid [*Selectouch Corp. v Perfect Starch, Inc.,*111 SW3d 830, 51 UCC Rep Serv 2d 1070 (Tex App 2004)].

[22] Revised UCC § 2-712(1) and (2). See *Conductores Monterrey, S.A. de C.V. v Remee Products Corp.,* 45 UCC Rep Serv 2d 111 (SDNY 2000).

CASE SUMMARY

Showdown over the Silverado Pickup

FACTS: Sonya Kaminski purchased from Billy Cain's Cornelia dealership a truck that was represented to her to be a 1989 Chevrolet Silverado pickup. However, subsequent incidents involving repair of the truck and its parts, as well as a title history, revealed that the truck was a GMC rather than a Chevrolet. Sales agents at the Cornelia dealership misrepresented the truck's character and sold the truck to Kaminski as a Chevrolet.

Kaminski filed suit for intentional fraud and deceit under the Georgia Fair Business Practices Act (FBPA) and for breach of express warranty. The jury awarded Kaminski $2,823.70 for breach of express warranty and $50,000 punitive (exemplary) damages. The judge added damages under the FBPA of $10,913.29 in actual damages and $9,295 in attorney fees and court costs. The dealership appealed.

DECISION: The judgment of the lower court is affirmed. A buyer can collect both incidental and consequential damages. Incidental expenses here included renting a vehicle to get to work. The buyer here was entitled to all forms of damages for the breach, including compensatory, consequential, and incidental damages. The punitive damages were for fraud because the evidence showed that the dealership knew that the truck's make and model were not correct. [**Billy Cain Ford Lincoln Mercury, Inc. v Kaminski, 496 SE2d 521 (Ga App 1998)**]

CPA

16. OTHER TYPES OF DAMAGES

The buyer is also entitled to collect incidental damages in situations in which he must find substitute goods. Those incidental damages could include additional shipping expenses or perhaps commissions paid to find the goods and purchase them. Buyers often also experience **consequential damages**, which are those damages the buyer experiences with respect to a third party as a result of the seller's breach. Revised UCC provides consequential damages for sellers and buyers. The seller's section provides, "Consequential damages resulting from the buyer's breach include any loss resulting from general or particular requirements and needs of which the buyer at the time of contracting had reason to know and which could not reasonably be prevented by resale or otherwise."[23] **For Example,** a seller's failure to deliver the goods may cause the buyer's production line to come to a halt. The buyer might then breach on its sales and delivery contracts with its buyers. In the case of a government contract, the buyer may have to pay a penalty for being late. These types of damages are consequential ones and can be recovered if the seller knew about the consequences or they were foreseeable. Under Revised Article 2, consequential damages cannot be recovered from a consumer.

consequential damages
damages the buyer experiences as a result of the seller's breach with respect to a third party.

17. ACTION FOR BREACH OF WARRANTY

A remedy available to a buyer when goods are delivered but fail to conform to warranties is an action for breach of warranty.

(a) NOTICE OF BREACH If the buyer has accepted goods that do not conform to the contract or there has been a breach of any warranties given, the buyer must notify

---

[23] Revised UCC § 2-710. Revised Article 2 redefines and broadens the availability of consequential damages. The revisions are expected to increase both the amounts and the recoverability of consequential damages.

the seller of the breach within a reasonable time after the breach is discovered or should have been discovered.[24]

(b) Measure of Damages   If the buyer has given the necessary notice of breach, the buyer may recover damages measured by the loss resulting in the normal course of events from the breach. If suit is brought for breach of warranty, the measure of damages is the difference between the value of the goods as they were at the time of tender and the value that they would have had if they had been as warranted. Under Revised Article 2, the buyer is also entitled to any of the other damage remedies necessary to make the buyer whole.

(c) Notice of Third-Party Action against Buyer   When a buyer elects the remedy of resale and sells the contract goods to a third party, that third party has the right of suit against the buyer for breach of warranty. In such a case, it is the buyer's option whether to give the seller notice of the action and request that the seller defend that action.

18. CANCELLATION BY BUYER

The buyer may cancel or rescind the contract if the seller fails to deliver the goods, if the seller has repudiated the contract, or if the goods have been rightfully rejected or their acceptance revoked.[25] A buyer who cancels the contract is entitled to recover as much of the purchase price as has been paid, including the value of any property given as a trade-in as part of the purchase price. The fact that the buyer cancels the contract does not destroy the buyer's cause of action against the seller for breach of that contract. The buyer may recover from the seller not only any payment made on the purchase price but also damages for the breach of the contract. The damages represent the difference between the contract price and the cost of cover.[26]

CASE SUMMARY

The Alpha Chi Omega Battle of the Sweaters

FACTS: Emily Lieberman and Amy Altomondo were members of the Alpha Chi Omega (AXO) sorority at Bowling Green State University. They negotiated with Johnathan James Furlong for the purchase of custom-designed sweaters for themselves and their sorority sisters for a total price of $3,612. Lieberman and Altomondo paid Furlong a $2,000 deposit.

When Lieberman and Altomondo saw the sweaters, they realized that Furlong had made color and design alterations in the lettering imprinted on the sweaters as part of their custom design. Altomondo, as president of AXO, called Furlong and told him that the sweaters were unacceptable and offered to return them. Furlong refused, stating that any changes were immaterial. Altomondo refused to pay the balance due and demanded the return of the $2,000 deposit. Furlong filed suit for breach of contract.

---

[24] *Dunleavey v Paris Ceramics, USA, Inc.,* 819 A2d 945 (Super Ct 2002); *Muehlbauer v General Motors Corp.,* 431 F Supp 2d 847 (ND Ill 2006).

[25] Revised UCC § 2-720.

[26] Revised UCC § 2-712(1), (2); *Valley Timber Sales, Inc. v Midway Forest Products, Inc.,* 563 So 2d 612 (Ala App 1990).

> ## CASE SUMMARY
>
> continued
>
> **DECISION:** The sorority rejected the sweaters within a reasonable time after delivery and notified the seller. The seller breached the contract. The sorority is entitled to cancel the contract, recover the amounts it paid, and hold the sweaters until recovery. The sweaters were altered without authorization and there is a breach of contract. Finally, and alternatively, Furlong should have entered into a contract that gave him discretion to make design changes without AXO's consent. These sweaters, as Furlong himself admits (and describes), were to be "custom-designed" for AXO. Thus, they were to be printed according to AXO's specifications, not according to Furlong's discretion.
>
> The sorority is entitled to a full refund of its deposit and any additional damages it experienced in defending this suit and seeking to collect the amounts it is due. [**Furlong v Alpha Chi Omega Sorority,** 657 NE2d 866 (Ohio Mun Ct 1993)]

The right of the buyer to cancel or rescind the sales contract may be lost by a delay in exercising the right. A buyer who, with full knowledge of the defects in the goods, makes partial payments or performs acts of ownership of the goods inconsistent with the decision to cancel may lose certain remedy provisions or be limited in recovery under Article 2.

19. BUYER'S RESALE OF GOODS

When the buyer has possession of the goods after rightfully rejecting them or after rightfully revoking acceptance, the buyer is treated as a seller in possession of goods after default by a buyer. When the seller has breached, the buyer has a security interest in the goods to protect the claim against the seller for breach and may proceed to resell the goods. From the proceeds of the sale, the aggrieved buyer is entitled to deduct any payments made to the seller and any expenses reasonably incurred in the inspection, receipt, transportation, care and custody, and resale of the goods.[27]

 ## 20. ACTION FOR SPECIFIC PERFORMANCE

Specific performance is available under both existing and Revised UCC. Revised UCC expands this remedy a bit.[28] Revised Article 2 does not limit specific performance to the buyer. Specific performance is available to both sellers and buyers, and it is enforceable as a contract provision in nonconsumer contracts.

Under Article 2, specific performance is a remedy available only to buyers in those circumstances in which the goods are specially manufactured, unique, or rare, such as antiques or goods with sentimental value for the buyer. For example, a buyer with a contract to buy a chair from Elvis Presley's home would be entitled to a specific performance remedy of delivery of the chair. Distributors have been granted specific performance against suppliers to deliver goods covered by supply contracts because of the unique dependence of the supply chain and the assumed continuous feeding of that chain.

---

[27] Revised UCC § 2-715(1); *Gordon v Gordon,* 929 So 2d 981 (Miss App 2006).
[28] Revised UCC § 2-716(1).

FIGURE 27-2   *Buyer's Remedies under Article 2*

REMEDY	SPECIFIC PERFORMANCE (REPLEVIN IDENTIFICATION)	COVER	MARKET PRICE
SECTION NUMBER	2–711	2–712 2–715	2–708 2–710
WHEN AVAILABLE	Rare or unique goods	Seller fails to deliver or goods are defective (rejection) or revocation of acceptance	Seller fails to deliver or goods are defective (rejection or revocation of acceptance)
NATURE OF REMEDY	Buyer gets goods + incidental damages + consequential damages	Cover price – Contract price + Incidental damages + Consequential damages – Expenses saved	Market price – Contract price + Incidental damages + Consequential damages – Expenses saved

Specific performance will not be granted, however, merely because the price of the goods purchased from the seller has gone up. In such a case, the buyer can still purchase the goods in the open market. The fact that it will cost more to cover can be compensated for by allowing the buyer to recover the cost increase from the seller.

21. NONSALE REMEDIES OF THE BUYER

In addition to the remedies given the buyer under UCC Article 2, the buyer may have remedies based on contract or tort theories of liability.

The pre-Code law on torts still applies in UCC Article 2 transactions. The seller may therefore be held liable to the buyer for any negligence, fraud, or strict tort liability that occurred in the transaction. (See Chapter 25.)

A defrauded buyer may both avoid the contract and recover damages. The buyer also has the choice of retaining the contract and recovering damages for the losses caused by the fraud.[29]

Figure 27-2 provides a summary of the remedies available to buyers under Article 2.

D   CONTRACT PROVISIONS ON REMEDIES

The parties to a sales contract may modify the remedies provided under Article 2 or limit those remedies.

---

[29] *Baker v Wade,* 949 SW2d 199 (Mo App 1997).

22. LIMITATION OF DAMAGES

CPA

liquidated damages
provision stipulating the amount of damages to be paid in the event of default or breach of contract.

(a) LIQUIDATED DAMAGES   The parties may specify the exact amount of damages that may be recovered in case of breach. A **liquidated damages** clause in a contract can be valid if it meets the standards of Article 2. Under Revised Article 2, the enforceability of a liquidated damages clause in a consumer contract is determined by comparing the amount of the liquidated damages specified with the anticipated or actual harm, the difficulties of proof of loss, and the availability of an otherwise adequate remedy. For nonconsumer contracts, the enforceability of a liquidated damages clause depends on whether the amount is reasonable in light of the anticipated or actual harm.

CASE SUMMARY

The Cost of Breaching a Jet-Set Contract

FACTS: On August 21, 1992, Miguel A. Diaz Rodriguez (Diaz) entered into a contract with Learjet to buy a model 60 jet aircraft for $3,000,000 with a $250,000 deposit made on execution of the contract; $750,000 payment on September 18, 1992; $1,000,000 180 days before delivery of the aircraft; and the balance due on delivery of the aircraft. Diaz paid the $250,000 deposit but made no other payments.

In September 1992, Diaz said he no longer wanted the aircraft and asked for the deposit to be returned. Learjet informed Diaz that the $250,000 deposit was being retained as liquidated damages because their contract provided as follows:

> *Learjet may terminate this Agreement as a result of the Buyer's failure to make any progress payment when due. If this Agreement is terminated by Learjet for any reason stipulated in the previous sentence, Learjet shall retain all payments theretofore made by the Buyer as liquidated damages and not as a penalty and the parties shall thenceforth be released from all further obligations hereunder. Such damages include, but are not limited to, loss of profit on this sale, direct and indirect costs incurred as a result of disruption in production, training expense advance and selling expenses in effecting resale of the Airplane.*

After Diaz breached the contract, Circus Circus Enterprises purchased the Learjet Diaz had ordered with some changes that cost $1,326. Learjet realized a $1,887,464 profit on the sale of the aircraft to Circus Circus, which was a larger profit than Learjet had originally budgeted for the sale to Diaz.

Diaz filed suit seeking to recover the $250,000 deposit. The district court granted summary judgment to Learjet, and Diaz appealed. The case was remanded for a determination of the reasonableness of the liquidated damages. The district court upheld the $250,000 as reasonable damages, and Diaz appealed.

DECISION: The lower court's judgment was affirmed. Diaz challenged the reasonableness of the liquidated damages clause. The $250,000 deposit as a liquidated damages clause in a contract in this price range was not unreasonable. Also, the seller was the one that lost its profits on a second sale that it would have made had Diaz not breached. The "lost volume" provision of the UCC permits nonbreaching sellers to recover the lost profits on a contract in which the other remedy sections do not compensate for the breach by the buyer. The evidence indicates that the lost profit from the Diaz contract would have been approximately $1.8 million. [**Rodriguez v Learjet, Inc., 946 P2d 1010 (Kan App 1997)**]

(b) EXCLUSION OF DAMAGES   The sales contract may provide that in case of breach, no damages may be recovered or no consequential damages may be recovered. When goods are sold for consumer use and personal injuries are sustained, such total exclusions are unconscionable and unenforceable. Such a contract limitation is not enforceable in other types of contracts (nonconsumer) unless the party seeking to enforce it is able to prove that the limitation of liability was commercially reasonable and fair rather than oppressive and surprising. As discussed in Chapter 25, limitations on damages for personal injuries resulting from breaches of warranty are not enforceable.

ETHICS & THE LAW

The Photo Finish on a Contract

Stock Solution is a "stock photo agency" that leases photographic transparencies produced by professional photographers for use in media advertising. Between October 1, 1994, and May 31, 1995, Stock Solution entered into four separate contracts with Axiom. Stock Solution delivered to Axiom, and Axiom took possession of 107 color transparencies to be used in Axiom's advertising. Each of the contracts between Stock Solution and Axiom contained identical provisions concerning the use and return of the leased transparencies. The contracts provided that in the event the transparencies were not returned by the specified "return date," Axiom would pay the following fees: (1) an initial "service charge" of $30; (2) "holding fee[s]" in the amount of "$5.00 per week per transparency"; (3) "service fees" at a rate of "one and one-half percent per month" on unpaid balances of invoices beginning 30 days after invoice; and (4) reimbursement for loss or damage of each "original transparency" in the amount of $1,500. Additionally, the contracts provided that if Stock Solution undertook the enforcement of the contracts, Axiom would "pay a reasonable attorney's fee ... together with all costs of court."

Axiom failed to return 37 of the 107 transparencies in breach of the contracts. Of the 37 missing transparencies, 36 were original color transparencies and 1 was a duplicate color transparency. Stock Solution filed suit seeking damages (1) for the 36 missing original transparencies, the agreed liquidated value of $54,000 plus sales tax of $3,294; (2) for the 1 missing duplicate color transparency, $1 plus sales tax of $0.06; (3) holding fees on the 37 missing transparencies in the amount of $23,914.83; (4) service fees and charges as provided for in the contracts; and (5) attorney fees.

Discuss whether the liquidated damage clause was enforceable under the law. Discuss the ethical issues in the collection of such large sums for damages on contracts with relatively low fees. Do you think this contract is governed by UCC or common law? [*Bair v Axiom Design, L.L.C.,* 20 P3d 388 (Utah 2001)]

23. DOWN PAYMENTS AND DEPOSITS

A buyer can make a deposit with the seller or an initial or down payment at the time of making the contract. If the contract contains a valid provision for liquidation of damages and the buyer defaults, the seller must return any part of the down payment or deposit in excess of the amount specified by the liquidated damages clause. In the absence of such a liquidated damages clause and in the absence of proof of greater damages, the seller's damages are computed as 20 percent of the purchase price or $500, whichever is smaller. Offsetting the $500 against actual damages has been eliminated under Revised Article 2.

24. LIMITATION OF REMEDIES

The parties may limit the remedies that are provided by the Code in the case of breach of contract. A seller may specify that the only remedy of the buyer for breach of warranty will be the repair or replacement of the goods or that the buyer will be limited to returning the goods and obtaining a refund of the purchase price, subject to the restrictions discussed in Chapter 25.

THINKING THINGS THROUGH

Software and Consequential Damages

The courts have been nearly universal in permitting software manufacturers to limit damages recoverable by buyers of software to replacement, return, or refund. Consequential damages have not been permitted as a part of a software purchaser's breach of contract against a manufacturer. Discuss the reasons the courts are willing to enforce these limitations that are limited to the price of software. [TAYLOR INVESTMENT CORP. V WEIL, 169 F Supp 2d 1046 (D Minn 2001)]

25. WAIVER OF DEFENSES

A buyer can be barred from claiming a breach of the contract by the seller if the sales contract expressly states that the buyer will not assert any defenses against the seller.

26. PRESERVATION OF DEFENSES

Consumer protection law prohibits the waiver of defenses in consumer contracts.

(a) PRESERVATION NOTICE Consumer defenses are preserved by a Federal Trade Commission (FTC) regulation. This regulation requires that the papers signed by a consumer contain a provision that expressly states that the consumer reserves any defense arising from the transaction.[30] A defense of the consumer arising from the original transaction may be asserted against any third person who acquires rights by assignment in the contract (see Chapter 33).

(b) PROHIBITION OF WAIVER When the FTC preservation notice is included in the contract that is obtained by, or transferred to, a third party, a waiver of defenses cannot be made. If the preservation notice is not included, the seller has committed an unfair trade practice.

---

[30] 316 CFR § 433.1: It is an unfair or deceptive trade practice to take or receive a consumer credit contract that fails to contain such a preservation notice.

REMEDIES IN THE INTERNATIONAL SALE OF GOODS

The United Nations Convention on Contracts for the International Sale of Goods (CISG) provides remedies for breach of a sales contract between parties from nations that have approved the CISG.

27. REMEDIES OF THE SELLER

Under the CISG, if the buyer fails to perform any obligations under the contract, the seller may require the buyer to pay the price, take delivery, and perform other obligations under the contract. The seller may also declare the contract void if the failure of the buyer to perform obligations under the contract amounts to a fundamental breach of contract.

E-COMMERCE AND CYBERLAW

Consequential Damages and Software

Computer systems and software often do not function as intended or have some glitches when installed at a company. For example, suppose that a software company sold to a utility a software package that was represented as one that would simplify the utility's billing processes. The program is installed and tested, and some changes are made as a result of trial runs. When the program was fully implemented and all customers and bills were run through the new system, there was a complete breakdown. The bills could not be produced or sent to customers, and the utility company was without cash flow. Without bills going out, no payments are coming in, and the utility must borrow from a high-interest line of credit at an interest cost of $400,000 per month. What damages could the utility collect? Could the software manufacturer limit its liability?

28. REMEDIES OF THE BUYER

Under the CISG, a buyer may reject goods only if the tender is a fundamental breach of the contract. This standard of materiality of rejection is in contrast to the UCC requirement of perfect tender. Under the CISG, a buyer may also reduce the price when nonconforming goods are delivered even though no notice of nonconformity is given. However, the buyer must have a reasonable cause for failure to give notice about the nonconformity.

 SUMMARY

The law provides a number of remedies for the breach of a sales contract. Remedies based on UCC theories generally are subject to a four-year statute of limitations, with Revised UCC adding an extension of one additional year (making it five years) in cases in which the breach is discovered in year four. If the remedy sought is based on a non-UCC theory, a tort or contract statute of limitations established by state statute will apply.

Remedies of the seller may include (1) a lien on the goods until the seller is paid, (2) the right to resell the goods, (3) the right to cancel the sales contract,

(4) the right to recover the goods from the carrier and the buyer, and (5) the right to bring an action for damages or, in some cases, for the purchase price. The seller may also have remedies because of secured transactions.

Remedies of the buyer may include (1) the rejection of nonconforming goods, (2) the revocation of acceptance, (3) an action for damages for nondelivery of conforming goods, (4) an action for breach of warranty, (5) the cancellation of the sales contract, (6) the right to resell the goods, (7) the right to bring an action for conversion, recovery of goods, or specific performance, and (8) the right to sue for damages and cancel if the seller has made a material breach of the contract.

The parties may modify their remedies by a contractual provision for liquidated damages, for limitations on statutory remedies, or for waiver of defenses. When consumers are involved, this freedom of contract is to some extent limited for their protection.

Under the CISG, the seller may require the buyer to pay the price, take delivery, and perform obligations under the contract, or the seller may avoid the contract if there is a fundamental breach.

A buyer may reject goods under the CISG only if there is a fundamental breach of contract. The buyer may also reduce the price of nonconforming goods.

> QUESTIONS AND CASE PROBLEMS

1. Firwood Manufacturing Co. had a contract to sell General Tire 55 model 1225 postcure inflators (PCIs). PCIs are $30,000 machines used by General Tire in its manufacturing process. The contract was entered into in 1989, and by April 1990 General Tire had purchased 22 PCIs from Firwood. However, General Tire then closed its Barrie, Michigan, plant. Firwood reminded General Tire that it still had the obligation to purchase the 33 remaining PCIs. General Tire communicated to Firwood that it would not be purchasing the remaining ones. Firwood then was able, over a period of three years, to sell the remaining PCIs. Some of the PCIs were sold as units, and others were broken down and sold to buyers who needed parts. Firwood's sales of the remaining 33 units brought in $187,513 less than the General Tire contract provided, and Firwood filed suit to collect the resale price difference plus interest. Can Firwood recover? Why or why not? [*Firwood Manufacturing Co., Inc. v General Tire, Inc.,* 96 F3d 163 (6th Cir)]

2. Soon after Gast purchased a used auto from a Chevrolet dealer, he experienced a series of mechanical problems with the car. Gast refused to make further payments on the bank note that had financed the purchase. The bank took possession of the automobile and sold it. Gast then brought an action against the dealer, alleging that he

had revoked his acceptance. Was Gast correct? Explain your answer. [*Gast v Rodgers-Dingus Chevrolet,* 585 So 2d 725 (Miss)]

3. Formetal Engineering submitted to Presto a sample and specifications for precut polyurethane pads to be used in making air-conditioning units. Formetal paid for the goods as soon as they were delivered but subsequently discovered that the pads did not conform to the sample and specifications in that there were incomplete cuts, color variances, and faulty adherence to the pad's paper backing. Formetal then informed Presto of the defects and notified Presto that it would reject the pads and return them to Presto, but they were not returned for 125 days. Presto argued that it was denied the right to cure because the goods were not returned until some 125 days after Formetal promised to do so. Was there a breach of the contract? Did the buyer (Formetal) do anything wrong in seeking its remedies? [*Presto Mfg. Co. v Formetal Engineering Co.,* 360 NE2d 510 (Ill App)]

4. Lam entered into contracts with Dallas Semiconductor to build six machines, referred to in its contracts as Tools A-F. The price and status of the tools were as follows:

Tool A priced at $3,629,298.10 had been tested, crated, and was ready to be shipped. Tool B priced at $4,121,049.30 had been tested and was ready to be shipped.

Tool C priced at $3,435,835.50—construction of the machine had begun but was not finished.

Tool D priced at $3,065,071.50—construction of the machine had never been started but materials had been ordered.

Tool E priced at $1,027,805—construction of the machine had never been started but materials had been ordered.

Tool F priced at $4,107,522.85—construction of the machine had never been started but materials had been ordered.

The contracts were entered into in 2000 and in 2001, but Maxim Integrated acquired Dallas Semiconductor in 2001. The employees at Dallas who were in charge of the contracts continued to assure Lam that everything was on track. Lam representatives also had meetings with Maxim representatives. However, those discussions broke down and after Lam issued a demand letter for which there was no response, he filed suit for breach of contract. Lam was able to sell the machines to other customers for an equal or greater price. Lam asked for total damages in the amount of $13,860,847, representing lost profits on all six tools, plus lost profits on the extended warranties and training packages for the tools. Is Lam entitled to such recovery? [*Lam Research Corp. v. Dallas Semiconductor Corp.,* Excerpt from 2006 WL 1000573 (Cal.App)]

5. McNeely entered into a contract with Wagner to pay $250,000 as a lump sum for all timber present in a given area that Wagner would remove for McNeely. The contract estimated that the volume in the area would be 780,000 board feet. Wagner also had provisions in the contract that made no warranties as to the amount of lumber and that he would keep whatever timber was not harvested if McNeely ended the contract before the harvesting was complete. The $250,000 was to be paid in three advances. McNeely paid two of the three advances but withheld the third payment and ended the contract because he said there was not enough timber. Wagner filed suit for the remaining one-third of the payment. McNeely said Wagner could not have the remaining one-third of the payment as well as the transfer; he had to choose between the two

remedies. Is he correct? [*Wagner v McNeely,* 38 UCC2d 1176 (Or)]

6. Brown Machine Company, a division of Kvaerner U.S., Inc., entered into a contract to supply a machine and tools to Hakim Plast, a food container–producing company based in Cairo, Egypt, to enable Hakim to meet its growing demand for plastic containers. The plastic containers were for customers to use in the ice cream distribution industry. It was understood that the equipment would be ready for delivery before the busy summer ice cream season. Brown Machine was not able to meet the twice extended deadline. It attempted to obtain another extension, but Hakim Plast refused without additional consideration. Brown refused to provide the requested consideration. Hakim Plast declared the contract breached on September 25, 1994. Brown then sold the equipment and brought suit for breach of contract, requesting damages for the loss of the sale. Hakim Plast countersued for Brown's breach seeking out-of-pocket expenses and consequential damages for loss of business. Discuss who breached the contract and determine what possible damages might be recovered. [*Kvaerner U.S., Inc. v Hakim Plast Co.,* 74 F Supp 2d 709 (ED Mich)]

7. When she was 17 years old, Cathy Bishop's parents signed a purchase contract for a new Hyundai automobile on which she made all payments. She was the primary driver of the vehicle, and while it was still under warranty, a manufacturing defect resulted in a fire that damaged it beyond reasonable repair. Although Hyundai was promptly notified and soon acknowledged responsibility for the fire, offers of replacement vehicles were rejected because they were not equivalent to the one destroyed, and monetary offers were rejected as being below its actual value. After Hyundai stated its final offer would expire on June 3, 1992 (some six months after negotiations began), Bishop sued for reimbursement of the vehicle's purchase price, as well as incidental and general damages, asking they be trebled by way of penalty for Hyundai's willful violation of the California "lemon law."

At trial, Bishop testified at length to her emotional distress resulting from the unavailability of her car upon which she had relied to attend college classes and from her inability to procure new transportation, due in part because of her obligation to make the car payments to the lender. The jury awarded Bishop the value of her car, or $8,312.18, plus damages for "loss of use" in the amount of $17,223, incidental damages of $1,444, and emotional distress damages of $5,000. The jury found Hyundai's lemon law violation to be willful, making its total award $95,937.54. Bishop was awarded more than $50,000 in costs and attorney fees. Discuss all of the damage awards other than the lemon law awards and determine whether they are proper damages under the UCC. [*Bishop v Hyundai Motor America,* 44 Cal App 4th 750, 52 Cal Rptr 2d 134]

8. Mrs. Kirby purchased a wheelchair from NMC/ Continue Care. The wheelchair was customized for her and her home. When the wheelchair arrived, it was too wide to fit through the doorways in her home. What options does Mrs. Kirby have? [*Kirby v NMC Continue Care,* 993 P2d 951 (Wyo)]

9. Wolosin purchased a vegetable and dairy refrigerator case from Evans Manufacturing Corp. When Evans sued Wolosin for the purchase price, Wolosin claimed damages for breach of warranty. The sales contract provided that Evans would replace defective parts free of charge for one year; it also stated, "This warranty is in lieu of any and all other warranties stated or inferred, and of all other obligations on the part of the manufacturer, which neither assumes nor authorizes anyone to assume for it any other obligations or liability in connection with the sale of its products." Evans claimed that it was liable only for replacement of parts. Wolosin claimed that the quoted clause was not sufficiently specific to satisfy the limitation-of-remedies requirement of UCC § 2-719. Provide some insight on this issue for the parties by discussing damage limitation clauses under the UCC. [*Evans Mfg. Corp. v Wolosin,* 47 Luzerne County Leg Reg 238 (Pa)]

10. McInnis purchased a tractor and scraper as new equipment of the current model year from Western Tractor & Equipment Co. The written contract stated that the seller disclaimed all warranties and that no warranties existed except those stated in the contract. Actually, the equipment was not the current model but that of the prior year. The equipment was not new but had been used for 68 hours as a demonstrator model, after which the hour meter had been reset to zero. The buyer sued the seller for damages. The seller's defense was based on the ground that all liability for warranties had been disclaimed. Was this defense valid? [*McInnis v Western Tractor & Equipment Co.,* 388 P2d 562 (Wash)]

11. Elmore purchased a car from Doenges Brothers Ford. The car had been placed with the dealership by a dealership employee as part of a consignment arrangement. Elmore was unable to obtain title to the car because the Environmental Protection Agency had issues with the car's compliance with emissions equipment requirements. Elmore was unable to drive the car. He brought suit because he was forced to sell the car for $10,300 less than he paid because of the title defect, and the fact that only a salvage dealer would purchase it. Because he lost his transportation, he was out of work for eight months and experienced a $20,000 decline in income. What damages could Elmore recover under the UCC? [*Elmore v Doenges Bros. Ford, Inc.,* 21 P3d 65 (Okla App)]

12. The day after Adventists Living Center declared bankruptcy, one of its creditors, who had sold food for the home, demanded the return of the food. Can you provide a legal right that the food vendor might have to reclaim the food? [*In re Adventist Living Centers, Inc.,* 52 F3d 159 (7th Cir)]

13. Ramtreat Metal Technology provided for a "double your money back" remedy in its contracts for the sale of its metal drilling assemblies. A buyer filed suit seeking consequential damages and cost of replacement. Ramtreat said that its clause was a limitation of remedies. Could Ramtreat limit its remedies to "double your money back"? [*Adcock v Ramtreat Metal Technology, Inc.,* 44 UCC Rep Serv 2d 1026 (Wash App)]

14. Joseph Perna purchased a 1981 Oldsmobile at a traffic auction conducted by Locascio. The car

had been seized pursuant to action taken by the New York City Parking Violation Bureau against Jose Cruz. Perna purchased the car for $1,800 plus tax and towing fees "subject to the terms and conditions of any and all chattel mortgages, rental agreements, liens, conditional bills of sale, and encumbrances that may be on the motor vehicle of the above judgment debtor." The Olds had 58,103 miles on it at the time of Perna's purchase. On May 7, 1993, Perna sold the car to Elio Marino, a coworker, for $1,200. The vehicle had about 65,000 miles on it at the time of this sale.

During his period of ownership, Marino replaced the radiator ($270), repaired the power steering and valve cover gasket ($117), and replaced a door lock ($97.45). He registered and insured the vehicle. In February 1994, Marino's son was stopped by the police and arrested for driving a stolen vehicle. The son was kept in jail until his arraignment, but the charges were eventually dropped. The Oldsmobile was never returned to Marino, who filed suit for breach of contract because he had been given a car with a defective title. He asked for damages that included the costs of getting his son out of jail and having the theft charges dropped. Is he entitled to those damages? [*Marino v Perna,* 629 NYS2d 669 (NY Cir)]

15. Stephan's Machine & Tool, Inc., purchased a boring mill from D&H Machinery Consultants. The mill was a specialized type of equipment and was essential to the operation of Stephan's plant. The purchase price was $96,000, and Stephan's had to borrow this amount from a bank to finance the sale. The loan exhausted Stephan's borrowing capacity. The mill was unfit, and D&H agreed to replace it with another one. D&H did not keep its promise, and Stephan's sued it for specific performance of the contract as modified by the replacement agreement. Is specific performance an appropriate remedy? Discuss. [*Stephan's Machine & Tool, Inc. v D&H Machinery Consultants, Inc.,* 417 NE2d 579 (Ohio App)]

> CPA QUESTIONS

1. On April 5, 1987, Anker, Inc., furnished Bold Corp. with Anker's financial statements dated March 31, 1987. The financial statements contained misrepresentations that indicated that Anker was solvent when in fact it was insolvent. Based on Anker's financial statements, Bold agreed to sell Anker 90 computers, "F.O.B.—Bold's loading dock." On April 14, Anker received 60 of the computers. The remaining 30 computers are in the possession of the common carrier and in transit to Anker. If, on April 28, Bold discovered that Anker was insolvent, then with respect to the computers delivered to Anker on April 14, Bold may:

a. Reclaim the computers upon making a demand

b. Reclaim the computers irrespective of the rights of any third party

c. Not reclaim the computers since 10 days have elapsed from their delivery

d. Not reclaim the computers since it is entitled to recover the price of the computers

2. February 15, Mazur Corp. contracted to sell 1,000 bushels of wheat to Good Bread, Inc., at $6.00 per bushel with delivery to be made on June 23. On June 1, Good advised Mazur that it would not accept or pay for the wheat. On June 2, Mazur sold the wheat to another customer at the market price of $5.00 per bushel. Mazur had advised Good that it intended to resell the wheat. Which of the following statements is correct?

a. Mazur can successfully sue Good for the difference between the resale price and the contract price.

b. Mazur can resell the wheat only after June 23.

c. Good can retract its anticipatory breach at any time before June 23.

d. Good can successfully sue Mazur for specific performance.

3. Lazur Corp. entered into a contract with Baker Suppliers, Inc., to purchase a used word processor from Baker. Lazur is engaged in the business of selling new and used word processors to the

general public. The contract required Baker to ship the goods to Lazur by common carrier pursuant to the following provision in the contract: "FOB Baker Suppliers, Inc., loading dock." Baker also represented in the contract that the word processor had been used for only 10 hours by its previous owner. The contract included the provision that the word processor was being sold "as is," and this provision was in a larger and different type style than the remainder of the contract. Assume that Lazur refused to accept the word processor even though it was in all respects conforming to the contract and that the contract is otherwise silent. Under the UCC Sales Article:

a. Baker can successfully sue for specific performance and make Lazur accept and pay for the word processor.
b. Baker may resell the word processor to another buyer.
c. Baker must sue for the difference between the market value of the word processor and the contract price plus its incidental damages.
d. Baker cannot successfully sue for consequential damages unless it attempts to resell the word processor.

NEGOTIABLE INSTRUMENTS

KINDS OF INSTRUMENTS, PARTIES, AND NEGOTIABILITY

 TYPES OF NEGOTIABLE INSTRUMENTS AND PARTIES
1. DEFINITION
2. KINDS OF INSTRUMENTS
3. PARTIES TO INSTRUMENTS

 NEGOTIABILITY
4. DEFINITION OF NEGOTIABILITY
5. REQUIREMENTS OF NEGOTIABILITY
6. FACTORS NOT AFFECTING NEGOTIABILITY
7. AMBIGUOUS LANGUAGE
8. STATUTE OF LIMITATIONS

LEARNING OBJECTIVES

After studying this chapter, you should be able to

LO.1 Explain the importance and function of negotiable instruments

LO.2 Name the parties to negotiable instruments

LO.3 Describe the concept of negotiability and distinguish it from assignability

LO.4 List the essential elements of a negotiable instrument

commercial paper written, transferable, signed promise or order to pay a specified sum of money; a negotiable instrument.

For convenience and as a way to facilitate transactions, businesses began to accept certain kinds of paper called **commercial paper** or negotiable instruments as substitutes for money or as a means of offering credit. Negotiable commercial paper is special paper created for the special purpose of facilitating transfer of funds and payment. In addition, the use of this special paper for special purposes can create additional rights in a special person status known as a *holder in due course.* Although the details on holders in due course are covered in Chapters 29 and 30, it is important to understand that one of the purposes of the use of special paper is to allow parties to achieve the special status of holder in due course and its protections and rights. Taking each component of negotiable instruments in step-by-step sequences, from their creation to the rights associated with each, and to their transfer, helps in understanding how commercial paper is used for special purposes in order to create rights for special persons.

TYPES OF NEGOTIABLE INSTRUMENTS AND PARTIES

Article 3 of the Uniform Commercial Code (UCC) defines the types of negotiable instruments and the parties for each.[1] Article 3 of the UCC was last amended in 2002 with those reforms adopted in some states and under consideration in others.[2] Those changes are explained in each of the relevant sections.

CPA

1. DEFINITION

negotiable instruments drafts, promissory notes, checks, and certificates of deposit that, in proper form, give special rights as "negotiable commercial paper."

Section 3-104(a)(1) and (2) of the UCC defines a **negotiable instrument** as "an unconditional promise or order to pay a fixed amount of money, . . . if it (1) is payable to bearer or order . . . ; (2) is payable on demand or at a definite time; and (3) does not state any other undertaking or instruction . . . to do any act in addition to the payment of money. . . ."[3] A *negotiable instrument* is a record of a signed promise or order to pay a specified sum of money.[4] The former requirement that the instrument be in writing to be valid has been changed to incorporate requirements of UETA (Uniform Electronic Transactions Act) and E-Sign (Electronic Signatures in Global and National Commerce Act of 2000). Many lenders now use electronic promissory notes.[5] In addition, we now have telephonic checks, or those withdrawals from your account that you authorize over the phone.

Instruments are negotiable when they contain certain elements required by the UCC. These elements are listed and explained in Section 5 of this chapter. However, even those instruments that do not meet the requirements for negotiability may still be referred to by their UCC names or classifications.

---

[1] The law covering negotiable instruments has been evolving and changing. The latest version of Article 3 was adopted in 1990. The 1990 version of Article 3 had been adopted in all 50 states by August 1999. States with variations are Alabama, Georgia, Montana, Ohio, South Dakota, and Wisconsin.

[2] As of June 2006, Arkansas, Minnesota, Nevada, and Texas had adopted the amendments to Article 3.

[3] UCC § 3-104(a)(1) and (2).

[4] See UCC § 3-104. Article 3 has also been adopted in the District of Columbia, Puerto Rico, and the Virgin Islands. The earlier version was called UCC-Commercial Paper, and the 1990 version is called UCC-Negotiable Instruments.

[5] Electronic Signatures in Global and National Commerce Act, 15 USCS § 7001 (Supp 2001); James A. Newell and Michael R. Gordon, "Electronic Commerce and Negotiable Instruments (Electronic Promissory Notes)," 31 *Idaho L. Rev.* 819, 826–834 (1995) (discussing the conversion of paper-based documentation to electronic form in commercial transactions).

FIGURE 28-1	*Promissory Note*

MARCH 31, 2007

Six months after date debtor undersigned hereby promises to pay to the order of Galactic Games, Inc., three thousand six hundred dollars with interest at the rate of 10.9%. This note is secured by the Video Arcade game purchased with its funds.

In the event of default, all sums due hereunder may be collected. Debtor agrees to pay all costs of collection including, but not limited to, attorney fees, costs of repossession, and costs of litigation.

JOHN R. HALDEHAND

VIDEO ARCADE, INC.

2. KINDS OF INSTRUMENTS

promissory note
unconditional promise in writing made by one person to another, signed by the maker engaging to pay on demand, or at a definite time, a sum certain in money to order or to bearer. (Parties—maker, payee)

certificate of deposit (CD) promise-to-pay instrument issued by a bank.

draft or bill of exchange an unconditional order in writing by one person upon another, signed by the person giving it, and ordering the person to whom it is directed to pay upon demand or at a definite time a sum certain in money to order or to bearer.

check order by a depositor on a bank to pay a sum of money to a payee; a bill of exchange drawn on a bank and payable on demand.

There are two categories of negotiable instruments: (1) promises to pay, which include promissory notes and certificates of deposit,[6] and (2) orders to pay, including drafts and checks.

(a) PROMISSORY NOTES   A **promissory note** is a written promise made and signed by the maker to pay a *sum certain* in money to the holder of the instrument.[7] (See Figure 28-1.)

(b) CERTIFICATES OF DEPOSIT   A **certificate of deposit (CD)** is a promise to pay issued by a bank.[8] Through a CD, a bank acknowledges the customer's deposit of a specific sum of money and promises to pay the customer that amount plus interest when the certificate is surrendered.

(c) DRAFTS   A **draft**, or **bill of exchange**, is an order by one party to pay a sum of money to a second party. (See Figure 28-2.) The party who gives the order is called the *drawer*, and the party on whom the order to pay is drawn is the *drawee*.[9] The party to whom payment is to be made is the *payee*. The drawer may also be named as the payee, as when a seller draws a draft naming a buyer as the drawee. The draft is then used as a means to obtain payment for goods delivered to that buyer. A drawee is not bound to pay a draft simply because the drawer has placed his name on it. However, the drawee may agree to pay the draft by accepting it, which then attaches the drawee's liability for payment.

(d) CHECKS   Under UCC § 3-104(f), *check* means "a draft, other than a documentary draft, payable on demand and drawn on a bank."[10] A **check** is an order by a depositor (the drawer) on a bank or credit union (the drawee) to pay a sum of money to the order of another party (the payee).[11]

---

[6] UCC § 3-104(j).

[7] *Apartment Inv. and Management Co. v National Loan Investors, L.P.*, 518 SE2d 627 (Va 1999).

[8] UCC § 3-104(j).

[9] UCC § 3-103(a)(2)–(3).

[10] UCC § 3-104(f).

[11] *Id.*

FIGURE 28-2 *Draft*

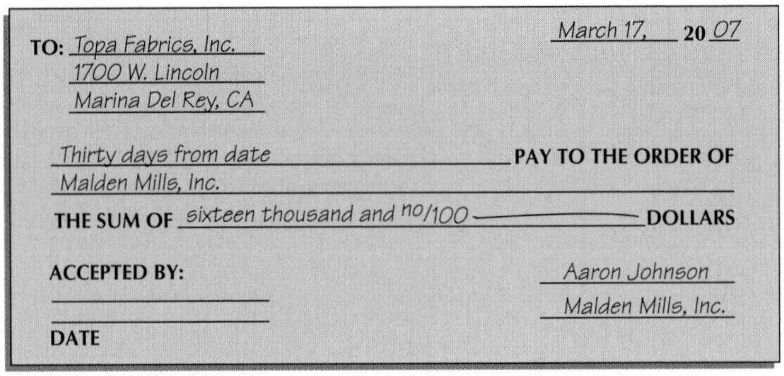

TO: *Topa Fabrics, Inc.*
      1700 W. Lincoln
      Marina Del Rey, CA

March 17, 20 *07*

Thirty days from date _____ PAY TO THE ORDER OF
Malden Mills, Inc. _____

THE SUM OF *sixteen thousand and ⁿᵒ/100* ——— DOLLARS

ACCEPTED BY:

                                                  Aaron Johnson
_____   *Malden Mills, Inc.*

DATE

cashier's check draft drawn by a bank on itself.

teller's check draft drawn by a bank on another bank in which it has an account.

traveler's check check that is payable on demand provided it is countersigned by the person whose specimen signature appears on the check.

money order draft issued by a bank or a nonbank.

party person involved in a legal transaction; may be a natural person, an artificial person (e.g., a corporation), or an unincorporated enterprise (e.g., a government agency).

maker party who writes or creates a promissory note.

    CPA

    CPA

    CPA

drawer person who writes out and creates a draft or bill of exchange, including a check.

drawee person to whom the draft is addressed and who is ordered to pay the amount of money specified in the draft.

In addition to the ordinary checks just described, there are also cashier's checks, teller's checks, traveler's checks, and bank money orders. A **cashier's check** is a draft drawn by a bank on itself. UCC § 3-104(g) defines a cashier's check as "a draft with respect to which the drawer and drawee are the same bank or branches of the same bank."[12] A **teller's check** is a draft drawn by a bank on another bank in which it has an account.[13] A **traveler's check** is a check that is payable on demand, provided it is countersigned by the person whose signature was placed on the check at the time the check was purchased.[14] Money orders are issued by both banks and nonbanks. A **money order** drawn by a bank is also a check.[15]

3. PARTIES TO INSTRUMENTS

A note has two original parties: the *maker* and the *payee*.[16] A draft or a check has three original parties: the *drawer*, the *drawee*, and the *payee*. The names given to the parties to these instruments are important because the liability of the parties varies depending on the parties' roles. The rights and liabilities of the various parties to negotiable instruments are covered in Chapters 29 and 30.

A **party** to an instrument may be a natural person, an artificial person such as a corporation, or an unincorporated enterprise such as a government agency.

(a) MAKER The **maker** is the party who writes or creates a promissory note, thereby promising to pay the amount specified in the note.

(b) DRAWER The **drawer** is the party who writes or creates a draft or check.

(c) DRAWEE The **drawee** is the party to whom the draft is addressed and who is ordered to pay the amount of money specified in the draft. The bank is the drawee

---

[12] UCC § 3-104(g).

[13] UCC § 3-104(h).

[14] UCC § 3-104(i).

[15] Some items are held to be checks for purposes other than Article 3 negotiability. For example, in *In re Armstrong* 291 F3d 517 (CA 8 2002), the court held that gambling markers were checks for purposes of the state's "bad check" law.

[16] UCC § 3-103(a)(5).

on a check, and the credit union is the drawee on a share draft. Again, a drawee on a draft has no responsibility under the draft until it has accepted that instrument.

(d) PAYEE   The **payee** is the person named in the instrument to receive payment. **For Example,** on a check with the words "Pay to the order of John Jones," the named person, John Jones, is the payee.

The payee has no rights in the instrument until the drawer or the maker has delivered it to the payee. Likewise, the payee is not liable on the instrument in any way until the payee transfers the instrument to someone else.

payee party to whom payment is to be made.

(e) ACCEPTOR   When the drawee of a draft has indicated by writing or record, a willingness to pay the amount specified in the draft, the drawee has accepted liability and is called the **acceptor.**[17]

acceptor drawee who has accepted the liability of paying the amount of money specified in a draft.

(f) SECONDARY OBLIGOR (ACCOMMODATION PARTY)   When a party who is not originally named in an instrument allows her name to be added to it for the benefit of another party in order to add strength to the collectability of the instrument, that party becomes a secondary obligor (formerly called an **accommodation party**) and assumes a liability role.[18] Revised Article 3 now refers to drawer, indorsers, and accommodation parties as "secondary obligors."[19]

accommodation party person who signs an instrument to lend credit to another party to the paper.

NEGOTIABILITY

An instrument is a form of contract that, if negotiable, affords certain rights and protections for the parties. **Negotiability** is the characteristic that distinguishes commercial paper and instruments from ordinary contracts or what makes such paper and instruments special paper.[20] That an instrument is negotiable means that certain rights and protections may be available to the parties to the instrument under Article 3. A **nonnegotiable instrument's** terms are enforceable, but the instrument is treated simply as a contract governed by contract law.[21]

negotiability quality of an instrument that affords special rights and standing.

nonnegotiable instrument contract, note, or draft that does not meet negotiability requirements of Article 3.

4. DEFINITION OF NEGOTIABILITY

If an instrument is negotiable, it is governed by Article 3 of the UCC, and it may be transferred by negotiation. This form of transfer permits the transferee to acquire rights greater than those afforded assignees of contracts under contract law. The quality of negotiability in instruments creates opportunities for transfers and financings that streamline payments in commerce. Transfers can be made with assurance of payment without the need for investigation of the underlying contract. The process of negotiation is covered in Chapter 29. For more information on the rights of assignees of contracts, refer to Chapter 18.

---

[17] UCC § 3-103(a)(1).

[18] UCC § 3-419; *In re TML, Inc.,* 291 BR 400, 50 UCC Rep Serv 2d 511 (WD Mich 2003); *Interbank of New York v Markou,* 649 NY Supp 2d 462 (1996).

[19] Revised Article 3, § 3-103(12), has the following definition of a secondary obligor on an instrument: "an indorser, a drawer, an accommodation party, or any other party to the instrument that has a right of recourse against another party to the instrument. . . ." This definition was changed to make the language of Revised Article 3 consistent with the Restatement of Surety.

[20] UCC § 3-104.

[21] A note payable when "lessee is granted possession of the premises" is not a negotiable instrument, but it is an enforceable contract. *Schiffer v United Grocers, Inc.,* 989 P2d 10 (Or 1999).

E-COMMERCE AND CYBERLAW

The Check Is in the Internet

The Check Clearing for the 21st Century Act ("Check 21") allows banks to use electronic images of checks as full and complete records of transactions, the same status formerly used only for paper checks that had been canceled.

CPA

5. REQUIREMENTS OF NEGOTIABILITY

To be negotiable, an instrument (1) must be evidenced by a record[22] and (2) must be signed (authenticated under Revised Article 3) by the maker or the drawer, (3) must contain an unconditional promise or order to pay, (4) must pay a sum certain, (5) must be payable in money, (6) must be payable on demand or at a definite time, and (7) must be payable to order or bearer, using what are known as words of negotiability.[23]

(a) A RECORD (WRITING) A negotiable instrument must be evidenced by a record. The requirement of a *record,* under Revised Article 3, is satisfied by handwriting, typing, printing, electronic record, and any other method of making a record. A negotiable instrument may be partly printed and partly typewritten. No particular form is required for an instrument to satisfy the record requirement, although customers of banks may agree to use the banks' forms as part of their contractual agreement with their banks. The telephonic check has become a widely used tool for consumers to pay bills. They simply contact their creditor, give the creditor the routing and account numbers for their checking accounts, and the creditor receives the payment electronically. At least one court has held that the telephonic check is a check, complete with a record, for purposes of Article 3 rights and obligations.

(b) AUTHENTICATED (SIGNED) BY THE MAKER OR DRAWER The instrument must be authenticated (signed under old Article 3) by the maker or the drawer. When a signature is used as authentication, it usually appears at the lower right-hand corner of the face of the instrument, but there is no requirement for where the signature must be placed on the instrument.[24]

The authentication may consist of the full name or of any symbol placed with the intent to authenticate the instrument. Other means of authentication that are valid as signatures include initials, figures, and marks. Electronic security devices

---

[22] This refers to Revised Article 3. Existing Article 3 requires a writing, but the revisions reflect electronic transactions and the federal mandate for recognizing electronic transactions as valid and on equal footing with paper transactions. The definition of a record is found in Revised UCC § 3-103(a)(14), which provides that *record* "means information that is inscribed on a tangible medium or which is stored in an electronic or other medium and is retrievable in perceivable form."

[23] UCC § 3-104.

[24] According to Revised UCC § 3-103, *authenticate* means (a) to sign or (b) to execute or otherwise adopt a symbol, or encrypt or similarly process a record in whole or in part, with the present intent of the authenticating person to identify the person and adopt or accept a record.

can be used as a means of authentication for electronic records. A person signing a trade name or an assumed name is liable just as if the signer's own name had been used.

(1) Agent. An authentication may be made by the drawer or the maker or by his or her authorized agent. **For Example,** Eileen Smith, the treasurer of Mills Company, could sign a note for her company as an agent. No particular form of authorization for an agent to authenticate an instrument is required. An authenticating agent should disclose on the instrument (1) the identity of the principal and (2) the fact that the authentication was done in a representative capacity. When this information appears on the face of the instrument, an authorized agent is not liable on it.

The representative capacity of an officer of an organization can be shown by the authentication of the officer along with the title of the office and the organization's name.[25] **For Example,** a signature of "James Shelton, Treasurer, NorWest Utilities, Inc.," or "NorWest Utilities, Inc., by James Shelton, Treasurer," on a note is enough to show Shelton's representative capacity. NorWest Utilities, not Shelton, would be liable on the note.

(2) Absence of Representative Capacity or Identification of Principal. If an instrument fails to show the **representative capacity** of the person who is authenticating or fails to identify the person, then the individual who authenticates the instrument is personally liable on the instrument to anyone who acquires superior rights, such as the rights of a holder in due course (see Chapter 30). Because the instrument is a final agreement, the parol evidence rule applies, and the party who authenticated is not permitted to introduce extrinsic evidence that might clarify his or her representative capacity. The party who authenticated, in order to avoid personal liability, must indicate on the face of the instrument his or her role in the principal, such as president or vice president. (For more information about the parol evidence rule, see Chapter 17.)

However, an agent is not personally liable on a check that is drawn on the bank account of the principal and authenticated by him or her, even though the agent failed to disclose his or her representative capacity on the check. **For Example,** a check that is already imprinted with the employer's name is not the check of the employee, regardless of whether the employee only authenticates with his or her name or also adds a title such as "Payroll Clerk" or "Treasurer" near the signature.

representative capacity
action taken by one on behalf of another, as the act of a personal representative on behalf of a decedent's estate, or action taken both on one's behalf and on behalf of others, as a shareholder bringing a representative action.

(c) Promise or Order to Pay A promissory note must contain a promise to pay money. A mere acknowledgment of a debt, such as a record stating "I.O.U.," is not a promise. A draft or check must contain an order or command to pay money.

(d) Unconditional Promise or Order For an instrument to be negotiable, the promise or order to pay must be unconditional.[26]

For Example, when an instrument makes the duty to pay dependent on the completion of the construction of a building, the promise is conditional and the instrument is nonnegotiable. The instrument is enforceable as a contract, but it is not a negotiable instrument given all the rights and protections afforded under Article 3.

---

[25] UCC § 3-402.
[26] UCC § 3-109(c).

CASE SUMMARY

The Sticky Note That Was a Reminder of Personal Liability

FACTS: Northwest Harvest Products, Inc., fell behind on payments on its account with Major Products Company, Inc. Major requested a note for the debt, and Northwest sent a $78,445.24 note. The Chief Executive Officer of Northwest at that time signed the note "Donald H. Eoll CEO," attached a Post-It fax transmittal memo indicating that the note came from Donald Eoll at Northwest, and sent the note via facsimile. The note was not paid, and Major sued both Eoll and Northwest for the debt. Only the facsimile copy of the note was presented at trial, and the trial court found that the writing on the Post-It note, coupled with the signature, identified Northwest as the principal on the note. The trial court held that Eoll was not personally liable for the debt because he signed the note as an agent for Northwest. Major appealed.

DECISION: The court held that Eoll was personally liable on the note. The Post-It note was separate from the document and anything that Eoll and Major wanted to be part of the promissory note should have been written on the promissory note. Without the Post-it, there is no indication of capacity on the promissory note, which leaves Eoll liable personally on that note. Reversed. [**Major Products Co., Inc. v Northwest Harvest Products, Inc. 979 P2d 905 (Wash App 1999)**]

THINKING THINGS THROUGH

Work through the following examples of signatures on negotiable instruments, capacity, and personal liability.

1. George S. Avery signed a letter regarding the unpaid balance on a $20,000 promissory note owed to Jim Whitworth in the form of a letter addressed to Whitworth stating: "This is your note for $45,000.00, secured individually and by our Company for your security, due February 7, 1984." The letter was signed: "Your friend, George S. Avery." It was typed on stationery with the name of Avery's employer, V & L Manufacturing Co., Inc., printed at the bottom and the words "George Avery, President" printed at the top. Avery says he is not personally liable on the note. The court granted summary judgment for Whitworth and Avery appealed. Who is liable? AVERY v WHITWORTH, 414 SE2d 725 (Ga App 1992)

2. A corporate guaranty was signed contemporaneously with the promissory note. The guaranty reads, "[f]or good and valuable consideration, The Producers Group of Florida, Inc. hereby guarantees the Tampa Bay Economic Development Corporation prompt and full payment of the following debt." The corporate guaranty was signed as follows:

   THE PRODUCERS GROUP OF FLA., INC. a Florida corporation, by

THINKING THINGS THROUGH

continued

the following officers solely on behalf of the corporation:

  /s/ Eddie Beverly, as its President

  CORPORATE PRESIDENT Eddie Beverly

  /s/ Stephen Edman, as its Secretary

  CORPORATE SECRETARY Steve Edman

  /s/ John Bauder, as its Treasurer

  CORPORATE TREASURER John Bauder

  Are the officers personally liable on the guaranty? TAMPA BAY ECONOMIC DEVELOPMENT CORP. V EDMAN, 598 So 2d 172 (Fla App 1992)

An order for the payment of money out of a particular fund is negotiable. The instrument can refer to a particular account or merely indicate a source of reimbursement for the drawee, such as "Charge my expense account." Nor is an instrument conditional when payment is to be made only from an identified fund if the issuer is a government or government unit or agency, or when payment is to be made from the assets of a partnership, unincorporated association, trust, or estate.[27] However, the fund noted must in fact exist because payment from a fund to be created by a future event would be conditional. **For Example,** making an instrument "payable from the account I'll establish when the sale of my house occurs" is conditional because the fund's creation is tied to an event whose time of occurrence is unknown.

The standards for negotiability do not require that the issuer of the instrument be personally obligated to pay it.[28] An instrument's negotiability is not destroyed by a reference to a related document. Section 3-106(b) provides, "A promise or order is not made conditional (i) by a reference to another writing for a statement of rights with respect to collateral, prepayment, or acceleration."[29] **For Example,** if a note includes the following phrase, "This note is secured by a mortgage on the property located at Hilding Lane," the note is still negotiable.[30]

money medium of exchange.

(e) PAYMENT IN MONEY   A negotiable instrument must be payable in money. **Money** is defined to include any medium of exchange adopted or authorized by the United States, a foreign government, or an intergovernmental organization. The parties to an instrument are free to decide which currency will be used for payment even though their transaction may occur in a different country.[31] **For Example,** two parties in the United States are free to agree that their note will be paid in pesos.

---

[27] *De Bry v Cascade Enterprises,* 879 P2d 1353 (Utah 1994).

[28] UCC § 3-110(c)(1)–(2) (1990); and *DH Cattle Holdings Co. v Smith,* 607 NYS2d 227 (1994).

[29] UCC § 3-106(b).

[30] Reference to a bill of lading does not affect negotiability. *Regent Corp., U.S.A. v Azmat Bangladesh, Ltd.,* 686 NYS2d 24 (1999).

[31] UCC § 3-107.

(**ETHICS & THE LAW**)

Hot Dog! He Has Liability!

Fred Dowie was the president and sole shareholder of Fred Dowie Enterprises, a catering business. Dowie learned that the Pope was coming to visit Des Moines, Iowa, and decided to operate a hot dog concession stand near the site of the Pope's speech. Dowie ordered 325,000 hot dog buns from Colonial Baking Company of Des Moines. He paid for them with a postdated check that had the name "Dowie Enterprises, Inc.," imprinted on it. Dowie signed the check "Frederick J. Dowie" in the appropriate place.

The demand for hot dogs during the Pope's visit to Des Moines was not what Dowie had anticipated. As a result, there was nothing left financially to Fred Dowie Enterprises. The check to Colonial did not clear the catering business account. Colonial then presented the check to Dowie for payment. Dowie has told Colonial he was not liable for the amount. Is he correct? What ethical issues do you see in one person running an undercapitalized corporation but enjoying the legal protection afforded this business entity? Apart from his legal obligation, does Dowie have an ethical obligation to pay for the buns? [*Colonial Baking Co. of Des Moines v Dowie,* 330 NW2d 279 (Iowa 1983)]

If the order or promise is not for money, the instrument is not negotiable. **For Example,** an instrument that requires the holder to take stock or goods in place of money is nonnegotiable. The instrument is enforceable as a contract, but it cannot qualify as a negotiable instrument for purposes of Article 3 rights.

CPA

sum certain amount due under an instrument that can be computed from its face with only reference to interest rates.

(f) Sum Certain Negotiable instruments must include a statement of a **sum certain,** or an exact amount of money. Without a definite statement as to how much is to be paid under the terms of the instrument, there is no way to determine how much the instrument is worth.

There are some minor variations from sum certain requirement. **For Example,** an instrument is not nonnegotiable because its interest rate provisions include changes in the rate at maturity or because it provides for certain costs and attorney fees to be recovered by the holder in the event of enforcement action or litigation.[32]

In most states, the sum payable under an instrument is certain even though it calls for the payment of a floating or variable interest rate.[33] An instrument is negotiable even though it provides for an interest rate of 1 percent above the prime rate of a named bank. It is immaterial that the exact amount of interest that will be paid cannot be determined at the time the paper is issued because the rate may later change. It is also immaterial that the amount due on the instrument cannot be determined without looking at records outside of the face of the instrument.[34]

---

[32] UCC § 3-106.

[33] *Means v Clardy,* 735 SW2d 6 (Mo App 1987); while revised Article 3 permits variable and market rates, notes entered into before the revised act was adopted will be governed under old Article 3; *YYY Corp. v Gazda,* 761 A2d 395 (NH 2000), *Barnsley v Empire Mortgage, Ltd. Partnership,* 720 A2d 63 (NH 1998).

[34] *SCADIF, S.A. v First Union Nat. Bank,* 208 F Supp 2d 1352 (SD Fla 2002), aff'd, 344 F3d 1123 (CA 11 2003). See also *Bankers Trust v 236 Beltway Investment,* 865 F Supp 1186 (ED Va 1994).

CPA

(g) Time of Payment A negotiable instrument must be payable on demand or at a definite time.[35] If an instrument is payable "when convenient," it is nonnegotiable because the day of payment may never arrive. An instrument payable only upon the happening of a particular event that may or may not happen is not negotiable. **For Example,** a provision in a note to pay the sum certain when a person marries is not payable at a definite time because that particular event may never occur. It is immaterial whether the contingency in fact has happened because from an examination of the instrument alone, it still appears to be subject to a condition that might not occur.

(1) Demand. An instrument is *payable on demand* when it expressly states that it is payable "on demand," at sight, or on presentation. UCC § 3-108(a) provides "A promise or order is 'payable on demand' if (i) it states that it is payable on demand or at sight, or otherwise indicates that it is payable at the will of the holder, or (ii) it does not state any time of payment."[36] Presentation occurs when a holder demands payment. Commercial paper is deemed to be payable on demand when no time for payment is stated in the instrument.[37]

definite time time of payment computable from the face of the instrument.

(2) Definite Time. The time of payment is a **definite time** if an exact time or times are specified or if the instrument is payable at a fixed time after sight or acceptance or at a time that is readily ascertainable. The time of payment is definite even though the instrument provides for prepayment, for acceleration, or for extensions at the option of a party or automatically on the occurrence of a specified contingency.

(3) Missing Date. An instrument that is not dated is deemed dated on the day it is issued to the payee. Any holder may add the correct date to the instrument.

(4) Effect of Date on a Demand Instrument. The date on a demand instrument controls the time of payment, and the paper is not due before its date. Consequently, a check that is postdated ceases to be demand paper and is not properly payable before the date on the check. A bank making earlier payment does not incur any liability for doing so unless the drawer has given the bank a postdated check notice.

CPA

payable to order term stating that a negotiable instrument is payable to the order of any person described in it or to a person or order.

bearer person in physical possession of commercial paper payable to bearer, a document of title directing delivery to bearer, or an investment security in bearer form.

(h) Words of Negotiability: Payable to Order or Bearer An instrument that is not a check must be **payable to order** or **bearer**.[38] This requirement is met by such phrases as "Pay to the order of John Jones," "Pay to John Jones or order," "Pay to bearer," and "Pay to John Jones or bearer." The use of the phrase "to the order of John Jones" or "to John Jones or order" shows that the person executing the instrument had no intention of restricting payment of the instrument to John Jones. These phrases indicate that there is no objection to paying anyone to whom John Jones orders the paper to be paid. Similarly, if the person executing the instrument originally wrote that it will be paid "to bearer" or "to John Jones or bearer," there is no restriction on the payment of the paper to the original payee. However, if the instrument is not a check and it is payable on its face "to John Jones," the instrument is not negotiable.[39] Whether an instrument is bearer or order paper is important because the two instruments are transferred in different ways and because the liability of the transferors can be different.

---

[35] UCC § 3-108.

[36] UCC § 3-108(a).

[37] UCC § 3-112; *Universal Premium Acceptance Corp. v York Bank's Trust Co.,* 69 F3d 695 (3d Cir 1995).

[38] *Smith v Haran,* 652 NE2d 1167 (Ill App 1995).

[39] UCC § 3-108.

CASE SUMMARY

The Pizza Note with No Definite Time for Delivery

FACTS: On September 30, 1987, Pefferoni Pizza agreed to purchase certain businesses from W. E. Peffer Enterprises. Duane J. Dowd, president of Pefferoni Pizza, signed a $125,000 promissory note payable to Peffer Enterprises. The note included the following provision:

The Maker hereof has certain rights under Purchase Agreement dated September 30, 1987, to negotiate a new loan for [Peffer Enterprises] to replace the Underlying Notes in an amount up to $125,000.00 at a lower rate of interest and for a term extending up to 84 months from and after the closing on the purchase. In the event that the Maker hereof negotiates such a loan, then as of the date that the Underlying Notes are paid in full or reduced with the proceeds of the new loan, the remaining principal balance due and owing under this Note shall be re-amortized over such term and at such rate of interest as may be negotiated for [Peffer Enterprises] by the Maker hereof on the new loan. When and if such events occurs [sic], a written amendment evidencing such modification shall be executed by the Maker and Holder hereof.

On January 14, 1988, Northern Bank loaned Walter Peffer, Jr., $35,000. As security for this $35,000 loan, Walter Peffer assigned the Pefferoni note to Northern. Northern advised Pefferoni of the assignment and that all payments should be made directly to Northern. Pefferoni had made all regular payments to Walter Peffer through July 1, 1988. However, Walter Peffer defaulted on his note and a judgment was entered against him on September 1, 1989. Northern filed suit to collect all payments from Pefferoni and the district court granted it summary judgment. The court of appeals held the note to be nonnegotiable, and Northern appealed.

DECISION: The Pefferoni note stipulated that it be paid in 60 equal monthly installments of $2,748.75 commencing on the first day of November 1987, and on the first of every month thereafter subject to the extension described. If Pefferoni Pizza were to negotiate a new loan for the underlying notes, the repayment schedule of the collateral note would be altered to match the repayment schedule of the renegotiated underlying notes. Although the renegotiation clause declares that the extension cannot exceed 84 months from and after the closing on the purchase, the note does not state the date of closing. The note is too ambiguous to compute the time for payment from the face of the note; it is not payable at a definite time and it is therefore not negotiable. [**Northern Bank v Pefferoni Pizza Co., 562 NW2d 374 (Neb 1997)**]

CPA

order paper instrument payable to the order of a party.

(1) Order Paper. An instrument is payable to order, or **order paper,** when by its terms it is payable to the order of any person described in it ("Pay to the order of K. Read") or to a person or order ("Pay to K. Read or order").

CPA

bearer paper instrument with no payee, payable to cash or payable to bearer.

(2) Bearer Paper. An instrument is payable to bearer, or **bearer paper,** when it is payable (1) to bearer or the order of bearer, (2) to a specified person or bearer, or (3) to "cash," "the order of cash," or any other designation that does not purport to identify a person or when (4) the last or only indorsement is a blank indorsement (an indorsement that does not name the person to whom the instrument is negotiated). An instrument that does not identify any payee is payable to bearer.[40]

---

[40] UCC § 3-104(d).

CASE SUMMARY

I May Be a Thief, But Under Article 3 Bearer Paper Rules, I Am Not A Forger

FACTS: Joshua Herrera found a purse in a dumpster near San Pedro and Kathryn Streets in Albuquerque. Herrera took the purse with him to a friend's house. Either Herrera or his friend called the owner of the purse and the owner retrieved the purse at some point. After the purse was returned to the owner, Herrera returned to the dumpster where he found a check and some other items. The check Herrera found was written out to "Cash" and he thought this meant that he "could get money for [the] check."

When he presented the check to the teller at a credit union to cash it, the teller instructed him to put his name on the payee line next to "Cash." Herrera added "to Joshua Herrera" next to the word "Cash" on the payee line of the check and indorsed the check.

Herrera had pleaded guilty to one count of forgery but moved to have the indictment dismissed on the grounds that adding his name to a bearer instrument was not forgery. He appealed the denial of the motion to dismiss the indictment.

DECISION: The court held that the instrument that Herrera originally found was bearer paper. By adding his named "to Joshua Herrera" to the "Pay to" line after "Cash" did not change the character of the instrument from bearer to order paper. At best, the addition of the words created an ambiguity and under the code interpretations should continue to be treated as bearer paper. Since he did not alter the nature of the instrument or convert it to a different instrument, he could not be charged with forgery. [**New Mexico v Herrera 20 P3d 810 (NM App 2001)**]

Whether an instrument is bearer or order paper is important for determining how the instrument is transferred (see Chapter 28) and what the liability of the parties under the instrument is. Review Figure 28-3 for more background.

CPA

6. FACTORS NOT AFFECTING NEGOTIABILITY

postdate to insert or place on an instrument a later date than the actual date on which it was executed.

Omitting a date of execution or antedating or **postdating** an instrument has no effect on its negotiability.

Provisions relating to **collateral**, such as specifying the collateral as security for the debt or a promise to maintain, protect, or give additional collateral, do not affect

collateral property pledged by a borrower as security for a debt.

FIGURE 28-3   *Bearer versus Order Paper*

"Pay to the order of ABC Corp."	ORDER
"Pay to the order of Bearer."	BEARER
"Pay to the order of ABC Corp. or Bearer"	BEARER
"Pay to the order of ABC Corp., Bearer"	ORDER
"Pay to the order of John Jones" (note)	NONNEGOTIABLE
"Pay to the order of John Jones" (check)	ORDER
"Pay to John Jones" (note)	NONNEGOTIABLE
"Pay to John Jones" (check)	NEGOTIABLE
"Pay to the order of John Jones or Bearer"	BEARER
"Pay to cash"	BEARER
"Pay to the order of cash"	BEARER

negotiability. **For Example,** the phrase "This note is secured by a first mortgage" does not affect negotiability.

7. AMBIGUOUS LANGUAGE

ambiguous having more than one reasonable interpretation.

The following rules are applied when **ambiguous** language exists in words or descriptions:

1. Words control figures where conflict exists.
2. Handwriting supersedes conflicting typewritten and printed terms.
3. Typewritten terms supersede preprinted terms.
4. If there is a failure to provide for the payment of interest or if there is a provision for the payment of interest but no rate is mentioned, the judgment rate at the place of payment applies from the date of the instrument.

8. STATUTE OF LIMITATIONS

Article 3 of the UCC establishes a three-year statute of limitations for most actions involving negotiable instruments. This limitation also applies to actions for the conversion of such instruments and for breach of warranty. There is a six-year statute of limitations for suits on certificates of deposit and accepted drafts.

> ## SUMMARY

An instrument or piece of commercial paper is a transferable, signed promise or order to pay a specified sum of money that is evidenced by a record. An instrument is negotiable when it contains the terms required by the UCC.

Negotiable instruments have two categories: (1) promises to pay and (2) orders to pay. Checks and drafts are orders to pay. Notes and certificates of deposits are promises to pay. In addition to ordinary checks, there are cashier's checks and teller's checks. A bank money order is a check even though it bears the words *money order.*

The original parties to a note are the maker and the payee. The original parties to a draft are the drawer, the drawee, and the payee. The term *party* may refer to a natural person or to an artificial person, such as a corporation. Indorsers and accommodation parties are considered secondary obligors.

The requirements of negotiability are that the instrument (1) be evidenced by a record, (2) be signed (authenticated) by the maker or the drawer, and (3) contain a promise or order (4) of an unconditional character (5) to pay in money (6) a sum certain (7) on demand or at a definite time (8) to order or bearer. A check may be negotiable without being payable to order or bearer.

If an instrument meets the requirements of negotiability, the parties have the rights and protections of Article 3. If it does not meet the requirements of negotiability, the rights of the parties are governed under contract law.

> ## QUESTIONS AND CASE PROBLEMS

1. Harold H. Heidingsfelder signed a credit agreement as vice president of J. O. H. Construction Co. for a line of credit with Pelican Plumbing Co. The credit agreement contained the following language:

   In consideration of an open account privilege, I hereby understand and agree to the above terms. Should it become necessary to place this account for collection I shall

   personally obligate myself and my corporation, if any, to pay the entire amount due including service charges (as outlined above terms) thirty-three and one-third (33⅓%) attorney's fees, and all costs of collection, including court costs.

   Signed [Harold H. Heidingsfelder]

   Company J. O. H. Construction Co., Inc.

When J. O. H. Construction failed to make payment, Pelican, claiming it was a holder of a negotiable instrument, sued Heidingsfelder to hold him personally liable for his failure to indicate a representative capacity on the credit agreement. He claims that a credit application is not a negotiable instrument and that he could not be held personally liable. Is he right? [*Pelican Plumbing Supply, Inc. v J. O. H. Construction Co., Inc.,* 653 So 2d 699 (La)]

2. East Penn Broadcasting Co. borrowed money from Hershey National Bank. The promissory note representing the loan was made payable "to the Hershey National Bank." It also contained a provision authorizing confession of judgment against the borrower at any time. This provision allowed a judgment to be entered against East Penn without giving the defendant the opportunity to make a defense or to oppose the entry of such judgment. The note was signed with the typewritten name of the borrowing corporation and the handwritten signature of three individuals including the defendant, Frank. The loan was not paid. The bank sued Frank and the others on the note; they raised defenses under the UCC. Who is liable on the note? [*Frank v Hershey National Bank,* 306 A2d 207 (Md Ct Spec App)]

3. Charter Bank of Gainesville had in its possession a note containing the following provision: "This note with interest is secured by a mortgage on real estate, of even date herewith, made by the maker hereof in favor of said payee. . . . The terms of said mortgage are by this reference made a part hereof." When the bank sued on the note, it said it was a holder of a negotiable instrument. Is this instrument negotiable? [*Holly Hill Acres, Ltd. v Charter Bank of Gainesville,* 314 So 2d 209 (Fla App)]

4. On October 14, 1980, United American Bank of Knoxville made a $1,700,000 loan to Frederic B. Ingram. William F. Earthman, the president of the bank and a beneficiary of the loan, had arranged for the loan and prepared the loan documents. Mr. Ingram and Mr. Earthman were old friends, and Mr. Ingram had loaned Mr. Earthman money in the past. Mr. Ingram was in jail at the time of this loan and was unable to complete the documents for the loan. Mr. Earthman says that Mr. Ingram authorized him to do the loan so long as it did not cost him anything to do it.

Also on October 14, 1980, Mr. Earthman prepared and executed a personal $1,700,000 note to Mr. Ingram, using a standard Commerce Union Bank note form. Mr. Earthman wrote "Frederic B. Ingram" in the space for identifying the lending bank and also filled in another blank stating that the note would be due "Eighteen Months after Date." With regard to the interest, Mr. Earthman checked a box signifying that the interest would be "At the Bank's 'Prime Rate' plus % per year." The standard form note defined the term "prime rate" as follows:

> *Prime Rate means the Bank's rate for loans to its most credit worthy customers for 90-day unsecured loans. At the time of this agreement, that rate is _____ % per year, although it will change from time to time. If a change in the Prime Rate occurs, the interest on my loan may be adjusted upward or downward.*

Mr. Earthman then sold both of the notes, which ended up in the hands of third parties (holders in due course) who demanded payment. Mr. Ingram raised the defense that he had not authorized Mr. Earthman to handle the transactions. The third parties said the notes were negotiable instruments and they were entitled to payment without listening to Mr. Ingram's defenses. Mr. Earthman says his note to Mr. Ingram as well as the bank note from Mr. Ingram are not negotiable and that they can both raise defenses to the third parties seeking payment.

Who is correct? What do you think of Mr. Earthman's banking processes and procedures? What ethical issues do you see in these loan transactions? [*Ingram v Earthman,* 993 SW2d 611 (Tenn)]

5. The state of Alaska was a tenant in a large office building owned by Univentures, a partnership. The state made a lease payment of $28,143.47 to Univentures with state treasury warrant No. 21045102. Charles LeViege, the managing partner of Univentures, assigned the warrant to Lee Garcia. A dispute then arose among the Univentures partners, and the company notified the state that it should no longer pay LeViege the rent. The state placed a stop payment order on the warrant. Garcia claimed that he was a holder of a negotiable instrument and that the state owed

him the money. The state claimed that a warrant did not qualify as a negotiable instrument. The warrant is in writing, is signed by the governor of the state, provides a definite sum of $28,143.47, and states that "it will be deemed paid unless redeemed within two years after the date of issue." The warrant states that it is "payable to the order of Univentures." Does the warrant meet the requirements for a negotiable instrument? [*National Bank v Univentures*, 824 P2d 1377 (Alaska)]

6. Nation-Wide Check Corp. sold money orders through local agents. A customer would purchase a money order by paying an agent the amount of the desired money order plus a fee. The customer would then sign the money order as the remitter or sender and would fill in the name of the person who was to receive the money following the printed words "Payable to." In a lawsuit between Nation-Wide and Banks, a payee on some of these orders, the question was raised whether these money orders were checks and could be negotiable even though not payable to order or to bearer. Are the money orders negotiable instruments? [*Nation-Wide Check Corp. v Banks*, 260 A2d 367 (DC)]

7. Nelson gave Buchert the following instrument, dated July 6, 1988:

> *One year after date I promise to pay to the order of Dale Buchert one thousand dollars in United States Savings Bonds payable at Last Mortgage Bank. (signed) Ronald K. Nelson*

Does this instrument qualify as a negotiable instrument?

8. Bellino made a promissory note that was payable in installments and contained the provision that on default of the payment of any installment, the holder had the option to declare the entire balance due and payable on demand. The note was negotiated to Cassiani, who sued Bellino for the full debt when there was a default on the installment. Is a note with an acceleration clause still negotiable? [*Cassiani v Bellino*, 157 NE2d 409 (Mass)]

9. A corporation borrowed money from a bank after the president negotiated the loan and signed the promissory note. On the first blank signature line of the note, the president wrote the name of the corporation. On the second such line, he signed his own name. The note was negotiated by the lending bank to the Federal Reserve Bank. The note was not paid when due, and the Federal Reserve Bank sued the corporation and its president. The president claimed that he was not bound on the note because he did not intend to bind himself and because the money obtained by the loan was used by the corporation. Is the president liable on the note? [*Talley v Blake*, 322 So 2d 877 (La App) (non-Code); *Geer v Farquhar*, 528 P2d 1335 (Or)]

10. Lloyd and Mario Spaulding entered into a contract to purchase property from Richard and Robert Krajcir. The two Spaulding brothers signed a promissory note to the Krajcir brothers with the following language: "The amount of $10,000 [is] to be paid sellers at the time of the initial closing [delivery of the deed]; plus, the principal amount payable to sellers at the time of the final indorsement of the subject H.U.D. loan." In litigation over the note, the Spauldings said it was not a negotiable instrument. The lower court found it to be a negotiable promissory note and the Spaulding partners appealed. Is the note negotiable? [*Krajcir v Egid*, 712 NE2d 917 (Ill App)]

11. Is the following instrument negotiable?

> *I, Richard Bell, hereby promise to pay to the order of Lorry Motors Ten Thousand Dollars ($10,000) upon the receipt of the final distribution from the estate of my deceased aunt, Rita Dorn. This negotiable instrument is given by me as the down payment on my purchase of a 1986 Buick to be delivered in three weeks.*
>
> *Richard Bell (signature).*

12. Smith has in his possession the following instrument:

> *September 1, 2003*
>
> *I, Selma Ray, hereby promise to pay Helen Savit One Thousand Dollars ($1,000) one year after date. This instrument was given for the purchase of Two Hundred (200) shares of Redding Mining Corporation, Interest 6%.*
>
> *Selma Ray (signature).*

What is this instrument? Is it negotiable?

13. Master Homecraft Co. received a promissory note with a stated face value from Sally and Tom

Zimmerman. The note was payment for remodeling their home and contained unused blanks for installment payments but contained no maturity date. When Master Homecraft sued the Zimmermans on the note, the couple argued that they should not be liable on the note because it is impossible to determine from its face the amount due or the date of maturity. Decide. [*Master Homecraft Co. v Zimmerman,* 22 A2d 440 (Pa)]

14. A note from Mark Johnson with HealthCo International as payee for $28,979.15 included the following language:

> [p]ayable in _____, *Successive Monthly Installments of $ Each, and in 11 Successive Monthly Installments of*

$2,414.92 Each thereafter, and in a final payment of $2,415.03 thereafter. The first installment being payable on the _____ day of _____ 20_____ , and the remaining install-ments on the same date of each month thereafter until paid.

Johnson signed the note. Is it negotiable? [*Barclays Bank, P.L.C. v Johnson,* 499 SE2d 769 (NC App)]

15. The text of text of a handwritten note stated simply that "'I Robert Harrison owe Peter Jacob $25,000 . . . ,' /s/ Robert Harrison." Peter Jacob sought to use the handwritten note as a negotiable promissory note. Can he? [*Jacob v Harrison,* 49 UCC Rep Serv 2d 554 (Del Super 2002)]

> CPA QUESTIONS

1. A company has in its possession the following instrument:

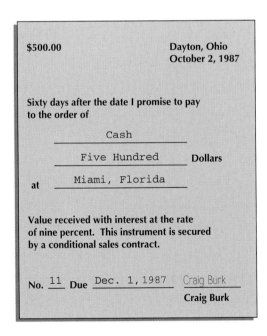

   This instrument is

   a. Not negotiable until December 1, 1987
   b. A negotiable bearer note
   c. A negotiable time draft
   d. A nonnegotiable note because it states that it is secured by a conditional sales contract

2. The instrument below is a

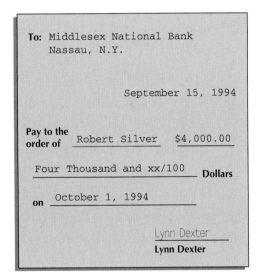

   a. Draft
   b. Postdated check
   c. Trade acceptance
   d. Promissory note

3. Under the commercial paper article of the UCC, for an instrument to be negotiable, it must

   a. Be payable to order or to bearer
   b. Be signed to the payee

c. Contain references to all agreements between the parties

d. Contain necessary conditions of payment

4. An instrument reads as follows:

$10,000	Ludlow, Vermont February 1, 1993

I promise to pay to the order of Custer Corp. $10,000 within 10 days after the sale of my two-carat diamond ring. I pledge the sale proceeds to secure my obligation hereunder.

R. Harris

R. Harris

Which of the following statements correctly describes this instrument?

a. The instrument is nonnegotiable because it is not payable at a definite time.

b. The instrument is nonnegotiable because it is secured by the proceeds of the sale of the ring.

c. The instrument is a negotiable promissory note.

d. The instrument is a negotiable sight draft payable on demand.

5. Which of the following instruments is subject to the provisions of the Negotiable Instruments Article of the UCC?

a. A bill of lading

b. A warehouse receipt

c. A certificate of deposit

d. An investment security

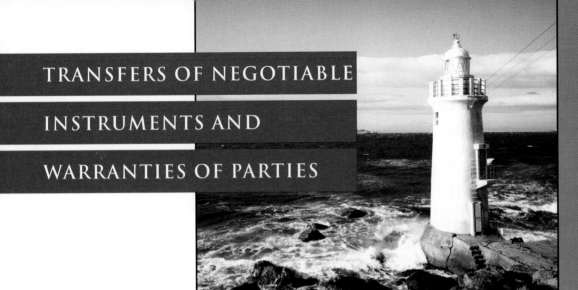

TRANSFERS OF NEGOTIABLE INSTRUMENTS AND WARRANTIES OF PARTIES

After studying this chapter, you should be able to

LO.1 Distinguish between an assignment and a negotiation

LO.2 Explain the difference between negotiation of order paper and negotiation of bearer paper

LO.3 List the types of indorsements and describe their uses

LO.4 Determine the legal effect of forged and unauthorized indorsements

LO.5 Be familiar with the forged payee impostor exceptions

LO.6 List the indorser's warranties and describe their significance

---

Much of the commercial importance of negotiable instruments lies in the ease with which they can be transferred. This chapter covers the requirements for, and issues in, the transfer or negotiation of negotiable instruments.

 TRANSFER OF NEGOTIABLE INSTRUMENTS

Negotiable instruments are transferred by a process known as *negotiation*.

1. EFFECT OF TRANSFER

When a contract is assigned, the transferee has the rights of the transferor. The transferee is entitled to enforce the contract but, as assignee, has no greater rights than the assignor. The assignee is in the same position as the original party to the contract and is subject to any defense that could be raised in a suit on an assigned contract.

When a negotiable instrument is transferred by negotiation, the transferee becomes the *holder of the paper*. A holder who meets certain additional requirements may also be a **holder in due course**. The status of holder in due course gives immunity from certain defenses that might have been asserted against the transferor (see Chapter 30 for a discussion of the rights and role of a holder in due course).

2. DEFINITION OF NEGOTIATION

Under UCC § 3-201(a), **negotiation** means "a transfer of possession . . . of an instrument by a person other than the issuer to a person who thereby becomes a holder."[1] Negotiation, then, is simply the transfer of a negotiable instrument in such a way that the transferee becomes a holder.[2] A **holder** is different from a possessor or an assignee of the paper. A holder is a transferee in possession of an instrument that runs to her. An instrument runs to a party if it is payable to her order, is indorsed to her, or is bearer paper.

holder in due course
a holder who has given value, taken in good faith without notice of dishonor, defenses, or that instrument is overdue, and who is afforded special rights or status.

negotiation the transfer of commercial paper by indorsement and delivery by the person to whom it is then payable in the case of order paper and by physical transfer in the case of bearer paper.

holder someone in possession of an instrument that runs to that person (i.e., is made payable to that person, is indorsed to that person, or is bearer paper).

---

[1] Revised UCC § 3-201(a).
[2] Revised UCC § 3-201; *Mandolfo v Chudy,* 564 NW2d 266 (Neb App 1997).

3. HOW NEGOTIATION OCCURS: THE ORDER OR BEARER CHARACTER OF AN INSTRUMENT

The order or bearer character of the paper determines how it may be negotiated. The order or bearer character of an instrument is determined according to the words of negotiability used (see Chapter 28 for a complete discussion of order and bearer words of negotiation and more examples of bearer versus order instruments). The types of instruments that qualify as bearer paper include those payable to bearer as well as those payable to the order of "Cash" or payable in blank. The character of an instrument is determined as of the time negotiation takes place even though its character originally or at the time of prior transfers may have been different.

HOW NEGOTIATION OCCURS: BEARER INSTRUMENTS

delivery constructive or actual possession.

UCC § 3-201(b) provides, "If an instrument is payable to bearer, it may be negotiated by transfer of possession alone."[3] If an instrument qualifies for bearer status, then it is negotiated by **delivery** to another.[4] Delivery can be accomplished by actual transfer of

> ## CASE SUMMARY
>
> ### Your Cheatin' Spouse, a Draft, and Delivery
>
> **FACTS:** Corey Brandon Bumgarner, who was separated from his wife, Crystal, had an accident caused by Donald Wood that resulted in $2,164.46 in damages to Corey's vehicle. Wood's insurance carrier mailed a draft in the amount of $2,164.46 drawn on Fleet Bank of Hartford, Connecticut, payable to Corey, to his box at P.O. Box 153, Hillsboro, North Carolina. The draft was negotiated at Community Bank and Trust, and the name, "Crystal Bumgarner," was written in handwriting on the back of the draft. Corey's name was written below Crystal Bumgarner's name. Crystal Bumgarner's driver's license number was hand-written on the front of the draft.
>
> Corey Bumgarner filed suit to have the insurer pay him the $2,164.46. The insurer indicated that it had sent order paper, that it had been delivered, and that there was, therefore, no claim against it or Wood. The trial court found that there had been no delivery and that Bumgarner was entitled to another check. Wood and his insurer appealed.
>
> **DECISION:** The Official Comment to § 3-420 states that delivery of an instrument occurs when it "comes into the payee's possession, as for example when it is put into the payee's mailbox." Constructive delivery had occurred with the delivery to the mailbox. While Corey may have a cause of action against his wife and her bank for cashing the draft, the delivery had been accomplished and the insurer and Wood had met their obligations. [**Bumgarner v Wood**, 563 SE2d 309, 47 UCC Rep Serv 2d 1099 (NC App 2002)]

---

[3] Revised UCC § 3-201(b).

[4] If no payee is named, the instrument is bearer paper and is negotiated by delivery. *Waldron v Delffs*, 998 SW2d 132 (Tenn App 1999).

CASE SUMMARY

Lost in the Shuffle: Delivery by Confusing Piles of Paperwork

FACTS: ABCO (Abbott Development Company) made a note payable to Western State Bank of Midland. The FDIC took over Western State's operations after it failed. ABCO had defaulted on the note, after which the FDIC permitted ABCO Homes to refinance the note, making its refinancing note payable to the FDIC. The FDIC indorsed its note to SMS Financial and inadvertently sent it to SMS as part of a large batch of documents. When litigation resulted on the note, SMS claimed it was the holder. Others challenged its status, saying that SMS never had the instrument delivered to it. The lower court held SMS was not a holder and SMS appealed.

DECISION: SMS is a holder of the note. Although the delivery was inadvertent, it was still delivery to the company the FDIC intended to have the instrument. SMS was the only one in possession of the instrument, it was intended to be transferred to SMS, and SMS had control of it, although it took awhile for it to find the note among the documents. [**SMS Financial, L.L.C. v ABCO Homes, Inc.**, 167 F3d 235 (5th Cir 1999)]

possession wherein the transferee has possession of the instrument, or constructive transfer, whereby the transferee has exclusive access. Bearer paper is negotiated to a person taking possession of it without regard to whether such possession is lawful. Because delivery of a bearer instrument is effective negotiation, it is possible for a thief or an embezzling officer to transfer title to an instrument. Such a person's presence in the chain of transfer does not affect the rights of those who have taken the bearer instrument in good faith.[5]

Even though a bearer instrument may be negotiated by a mere transfer of possession, the one to whom the instrument is delivered may require the bearer to indorse the instrument. This situation most commonly arises when a check payable to "Cash" is presented to a bank for payment. The reason a transferee of bearer paper would want an indorsement is to obtain the protection of an indorser's warranties from the bearer.[6] The bank wants an indorsement on a check made payable to "Cash" so that it can turn to the check casher in the event payment issues arise.

 ## HOW NEGOTIATION OCCURS: ORDER INSTRUMENTS

UCC § 3-201(b) provides, "if an instrument is payable to an identified person, negotiation requires transfer of possession of the instrument and its indorsement by the holder."[7] A negotiable instrument that is payable to the order of a specific party is

---

[5] Revised UCC §§ 3-202 and 3-204; *Midfirst Bank, SSB v C.W. Hayndi Co., Inc.*, 893 F Supp 1304 (DSC 1994).

[6] The Uniform Electronic Transactions Act (UETA), promulgated by the National Conference of Commissioners on Uniform State Laws in July 1999 and enacted in 38 states, provides that the transfer of a note by electronic record affords the transferee the same rights as a holder or holder in due course would have with regard to a tangible written note.

[7] Revised UCC § 3-201(b). Although the modern spelling is "endorsement," the UCC has retained the British spelling of "indorsement."

CASE SUMMARY

The Tax Man Cometh, but He Can't Provide Your Indorsement

FACTS: Thorton Ring was behind on his property taxes for his property in Freeport, Maine. When he received a check payable to his order from Advest, Inc., in the amount of $11,347.09, he wrote the following on the back of the check: "Payable to Town of Freeport Property Taxes 2 Main St."; he sent it along with a letter to the town offices. The letter included the following: "I have paid $11,347.09 of real estate taxes and request the appropriate action to redeem the corresponding property." Ring did nothing further and his property was then liened by the tax clerk. Ring objected because he had paid the taxes. The town argued that the check was not indorsed and Ring thus had not paid the taxes in time to avoid the lien. The lower court found for the town and Ring appealed.

DECISION: There was no indorsement. Ring's name must be signed for there to be negotiation of the instrument to the town. The check had only the first part of the necessary indorsement for order paper; Ring had to indorse the instrument for further negotiation. Indorsements vary according to the method of signing and the words used along with the signature. The nature of an indorsement also affects the future of the instrument in terms of its requirements for further negotiation. [**Town of Freeport v Ring, 727 A2d 901 (ME 1999)**]

---

order paper, which can be negotiated only through indorsement and transfer of possession of the paper.[8] **Indorsement** and transfer of possession can be made by the person to whom the instrument is then payable or by an authorized agent of that person.[9]

indorsement signature of the payee on an instrument.

4. BLANK INDORSEMENT

When the indorser merely signs a negotiable instrument, the indorsement is called a **blank indorsement** (see Figure 29-1). A blank indorsement does not indicate the person to whom the instrument is to be paid, that is, the transferee. A blank indorsement turns an order instrument into a bearer instrument. A person who possesses an instrument on which the last indorsement is blank is the holder.[10] **For Example,** if a check is payable to the order of Jill Barnes and Ms. Barnes indorses the check on the back "Jill Barnes," then the check that was originally an order instrument is now a bearer instrument. The check can now be transferred as bearer paper, which requires only delivery of possession. Once Jill Barnes's signature appears as a blank indorsement on the back, the check becomes transferrable simply by delivery of possession to another party.

blank indorsement an indorsement that does not name the person to whom the paper, document of title, or investment security is negotiated.

---

[8] Revised UCC § 3-204; *Knight Publishing Co., Inc. v Chase Manhattan Bank,* 479 SE2d 478 (NC App 1997).
[9] Revised UCC § 3-204.
[10] *Golden Years Nursing Home, Inc. v Gabbard,* 682 NE2d 731 (Ohio 1996).

FIGURE 29-1   *Blank Indorsement*

INDORSE HERE

x *Alan Parker*

DO NOT WRITE, STAMP, OR SIGN BELOW THIS LINE
RESERVED FOR FINANCIAL INSTITUTION USE

E-COMMERCE AND CYBERLAW

New Flexibility for Cyberspace Commercial Paper

The Check Clearing for the 21st Century Act (sometimes called "Check 21") allows banks to use images of checks as a substitute for paper checks. The substitute check is the legal equivalent of the paper check that has, for so long, dominated U.S. commerce. Federal Reserve Board regulations define the substitute check as follows: "A substitute check is a paper reproduction of an original check that contains an image of the front and back of the original check and is suitable for automated processing in the same manner as the original check." With Check 21, banks can sort items electronically and use images from automatic teller machine (ATM) transactions. All the new regulations on check substitutes are known as Regulation CC and can be found at Regulation CC, 12 CFR § 229.2(zz)(2).

5. SPECIAL INDORSEMENT

special indorsement an indorsement that specifies the person to whom the instrument is indorsed.

indorsee party to whom special indorsement is made.

A **special indorsement** consists of the signature of the indorser and words specifying the person to whom the indorser makes the instrument payable, that is, the **indorsee** (see Figure 29-2).[11] **For Example,** if Jill Barnes wrote on the back of the check payable to her "Pay to Jack Barnes, /s/ Jill Barnes," the check could be negotiated further only through the signature and possession of Jack Barnes. A special indorsement in this case continues an order instrument as an order instrument. If, after receiving the check, Jack Barnes simply signed it on the back, the check would become bearer paper and could be transferred through possession only.

Although words of negotiability are required on the front of negotiable instruments, it is not necessary that indorsements contain the word *order* or *bearer*. Consequently, the paper indorsed as shown in Figure 29-2 continues to be negotiable and may be negotiated further.[12]

An indorsement of "Pay to account [number]" is a special indorsement. In contrast, the inclusion of a notation indicating the debt to be paid is not a special indorsement.

---

[11] Revised UCC § 3-205; *Bolduc v Beal Bank,* 994 F Supp 2d 82 (DNH 1998).

[12] Only a check may use the phrase "Pay to" on its face and remain negotiable. All other instruments require words of negotiability on their face. Indorsements, however, are sufficient on all instruments with simply "Pay to." UCC § 3-110.

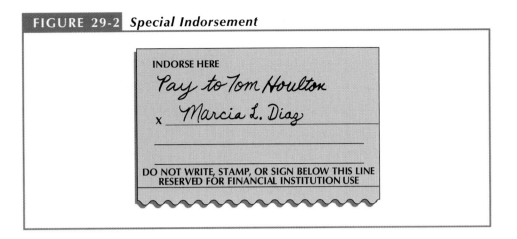

FIGURE 29-2 *Special Indorsement*

6. QUALIFIED INDORSEMENT

qualified indorsement an indorsement that includes words such as "without recourse" that disclaims certain liability of the indorser to a maker or a drawee.

A **qualified indorsement** is one that qualifies the effect of a blank or a special indorsement by disclaiming certain liability of the indorser to a maker or a drawee. This disclaimer is given by using the phrase "Without recourse" as part of the indorsement (see Figure 29-3). Any other words that indicate an intent to limit the indorser's secondary liability in the event the maker or the drawee does not pay on the instrument can also be used.[13]

The qualification of an indorsement does not affect the passage of title or the negotiable character of the instrument. It merely disclaims certain of the indorser's secondary liabilities for payment of the instrument in the event the original parties do not pay as the instrument provides.

This qualified form of indorsement is most commonly used when the indorser is a person who has no personal interest in the transaction. **For Example,** an agent or an attorney who is merely indorsing a check of a third person to a client might make a qualified indorsement because he is not actually a party to the transaction.

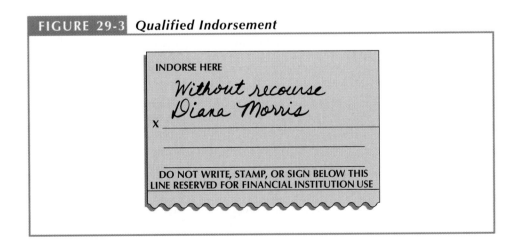

FIGURE 29-3 *Qualified Indorsement*

---

[13] *Florida Coast Bank v Monarch Dodge*, 430 So 2d 607 (Fla App 1983).

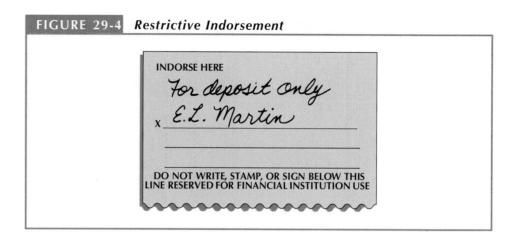

FIGURE 29-4 *Restrictive Indorsement*

> INDORSE HERE
>
> *For deposit only*
> x *E.L. Martin*
>
> _____
>
> _____
>
> DO NOT WRITE, STAMP, OR SIGN BELOW THIS
> LINE RESERVED FOR FINANCIAL INSTITUTION USE

CPA

7. RESTRICTIVE INDORSEMENT

restrictive indorsement an indorsement that restricts further transfer, such as in trust for or to the use of some other person, is conditional, or for collection or deposit.

A **restrictive indorsement** specifies the purpose of the indorsement or the use to be made of the instrument (see Figure 29-4).[14] An indorsement is restrictive when it includes words showing that the instrument is to be deposited (such as "For deposit only"), when it is negotiated for collection or to an agent or a trustee, or when the negotiation is conditional.[15]

A restrictive indorsement does not prevent transfer or negotiation of the instrument even when it expressly states that transfer or negotiation is prohibited. The indorsement "For deposit only" requires that the first party who receives the instrument after the restriction is placed on it comply with that restriction. The indorsement "For deposit only" makes an instrument a bearer instrument for any bank. If the indorser's account number is added to a "For deposit only" indorsement, then the only party who can take the instrument after this restrictive indorsement is a bank with that account number. A restrictive indorsement reduces the risk of theft or unauthorized transfer by eliminating the bearer quality of a blank indorsement.

8. CORRECTION OF NAME BY INDORSEMENT

Sometimes the name of the payee or the indorsee of an instrument is spelled improperly. **For Example,** H. A. Price may receive a paycheck that is payable to the order of "H. O. Price." If this error in Price's name was a clerical one and the check is indeed intended for H. A. Price, the employee may ask the employer to write a new check payable to the proper name. However, under Article 3, a much simpler solution allows the payee or indorsee whose name is misspelled to indorse the wrong name, the correct name, or both. The person giving or paying value or taking it for collection for the instrument may require both forms of the signature.[16]

This correction of name by indorsement may be used only when it was intended that the instrument should be payable to the person making the corrective indorsement. If there were in fact two employees, one named H. A. Price and the

---

[14] Revised UCC § 3-206.

[15] *Id.*

[16] Revised UCC § 3-204(d).

other H. O. Price, it would be forgery for one to take the check intended for the other and, by indorsing it, obtain the benefit of the proceeds of the check.[17]

A fictitious, assumed, or trade name is treated the same as a wrong name. The same procedure for correction of a misspelled name with indorsement of both names applies to these forms of payee identification as well.[18]

9. BANK INDORSEMENT

To simplify the transfer and collection of negotiable instruments from one bank to another, "any agreed method which identifies the transferor bank is sufficient for the item's further transfer to another bank."[19] A bank could simply indorse with its Federal Reserve System number instead of using its name.

Likewise, when a customer has deposited an instrument with a bank but has failed to indorse it, the bank may make an indorsement for the customer unless the instrument expressly requires the payee's personal indorsement. Furthermore, the mere stamping or marking on the item of any notation showing that it was deposited by the customer or credited to the customer's account is effective as an indorsement by the customer.

10. MULTIPLE PAYEES AND INDORSEMENTS

Ordinarily, one person is named as the payee in the instrument, but two or more payees may be named. In that case, the instrument may specify that it is payable to any one or more of them or that it is payable to all jointly. **For Example,** if the instrument is made payable "to the order of Ferns and Piercy," then Ferns and Piercy are joint payees. The indorsements of both Ferns and Piercy are required to negotiate the instrument.

If the instrument is payable to **alternative payees** or if it has been negotiated to alternative indorsees, such as "Stahl or Glass" or "Stahl/Glass," it may be indorsed and delivered by either of them.

Under old Article 3, if the instrument was not clear on the relationship or types of multiple payees or indorsees, they were to be considered joint, and the signatures of all parties were required. Under Revised Article 3, when a court is faced with two or more payees who are separated by a comma or other symbol, for example, "Pay to the order of Jeff Bridges–Susan Sarandon," the court must first determine whether the symbols or separating marks are sufficiently clear to make the instrument payable jointly. If the court concludes that the instrument is ambiguous, then the preference is for alternative payees, which means that either Jeff or Susan could negotiate the instrument with one signature; they would not have to have the other's indorsement for negotiation. Under Revised Article 3, if the instrument is ambiguous, the payees or indorsees are considered payees in the alternative.

alternative payees those persons to whom a negotiable instrument is made payable, any one of whom may indorse and take delivery of it.

11. AGENT OR OFFICER INDORSEMENT

An instrument may be made payable to the order of an officeholder. **For Example,** a check may read "Pay to the order of Receiver of Taxes." Such a check may be received

---

[17] If a check is made payable to an individual "as guardian" for another, it cannot be negotiated until that individual is actually appointed as guardian. *Citibank v Bank of Salem,* 35 UCC2d 173 (WDNY 1998).

[18] Revised UCC § 3-204(d).

[19] Revised UCC § 4-103.

CASE SUMMARY

Beautiful Palm Beach, A Mess of an Indorsement Issue

FACTS: J & D Financial Corporation is a factoring company. Skyscraper Building Maintenance, LLC, had a contract with Hyatt Corporation to perform maintenance work for various Hyatt hotels in South Florida. Skyscraper entered into a factoring agreement with J & D. As part of the factoring agreement, J & D requested Hyatt to make checks payable for maintenance services to Skyscraper and J & D. Of the many checks issued by Hyatt to Skyscraper and J & D, two were negotiated by the bank but indorsed only by Skyscraper. They were made payable as follows:

1. Check No. 1-78671 for $22,531 payable to:
   J & D Financial Corp. Skyscraper Building Maint P.O. Box 610250 North Miami, Florida 33261-0250
2. Check No. 1-75723 for $21,107 payable to:
   Skyscraper Building Maint J & D Financial Corp. P.O. Box 610250 North Miami, Florida 33261-0250

Only one of the payees, Skyscraper, endorsed these two checks. The bank cashed the checks. According to J & D, it did not receive the benefit of these two payments.

J & D filed a complaint against Skyscraper and Hyatt and the bank. J & D sought damages against Skyscraper under the factoring agreement and separately against Hyatt and the bank for negotiation of the two checks.

Hyatt's position was that the checks were not ambiguous, were payable jointly and not alternatively. The trial court granted summary judgment in favor of the bank. Hyatt appealed. J & D filed a cross-appeal.

DECISION: In 1990, Article 3 of the UCC was revised, and the language of UCC Section 3-116 was added to UCC section 3-110 and became subsection (d). Revised UCC Section 3-110(d), which added language to follow former 3-116(a) and (b), states, "If an instrument payable to two or more persons is ambiguous as to whether it is payable to the persons alternatively, the instrument is payable to the persons alternatively." The net effect of the amendment was to change the presumption. What was unambiguous before is now ambiguous.

With the statutory presumption removed, the same stacked payee designation that was unambiguous and payable jointly pre-1992 is now ambiguous and payable in the alternative. The bank could pay either party in these circumstances and need not have the signatures of both. The trial correct was correct in granting summary judgment. [**Hyatt Corp. v Palm Beach Nat. Bank, 840 So 2d 300 (Fla App 2003)**]

---

and negotiated by the person who at the time is the receiver of taxes. This general identification of a payee is a matter of convenience, and the drawer of the check is not required to find out the actual name of the receiver of taxes at that time.

If an instrument is drawn in favor of an officer of a named corporation, the instrument is payable to the corporation, the officer, or any successor to such officer. Any of these parties in possession of the instrument is the holder and may negotiate the instrument.[20]

---

[20] Revised UCC § 3-110(cc)(2)(li).

THINKING THINGS THROUGH

Dana Kaskel, a widow with five children, invested $250,000 of the proceeds of her late husband's life insurance policy with Martin, Livingston & Sterling, Ltd. (MLS) in the form of a loan that MLS was to repay at the end of six weeks with interest at an annual rate of 8 percent. She wrote a check for $250,000 to MLS, and an agent of MLS named Forrester mailed the check to a Dr. Steven Shook. He was supposed to use it to obtain a $25 million loan from a company of which he was a principal and to invest the proceeds of the loan, generating profits in which MLS would share over and above the amount necessary to repay Mrs. Kaskel's $250,000 loan with the agreed-upon interest. Shook deposited the check in his personal account at the Bank of America, which presented the check for payment to Northern Trust Company, that being the bank in which the insurance company had deposited the proceeds of Mr. Kaskel's life insurance policy in an account of which she was the beneficiary. Although MLS had not endorsed the check, Northern paid it and so

the $250,000 went into Shook's account. No one knows what happened to the money and Forrester remains a shadowy character, but he was authorized to send the check to Shook.

Mrs. Kaskel's loan to MLS has never been repaid, although over a period of slightly less than two years she did receive some $40,000 in dribs and drabs from Shook, MLS, and others. MLS still exists, and it acknowledges the debt, but whether the remaining balance of the loan will ever be repaid, with or without the mounting interest due on it, is uncertain. Mrs. Kaskel brought suit against Northern Trust because when Northern paid $250,000 from Mrs. Kaskel's account to Shook, it violated the terms of its contract with her by not requiring an indorsement. She was not aware there was no indorsement until she requested copies of the check from Northern. As permitted by law, Northern was not required to send copies of checks each month.

Is Mrs. Kaskel correct? Is Northern Trust responsible for her loss? KASKEL V NORTHERN TRUST CO., 328 F3d 358 (CA 7 2003)

ETHICS & THE LAW

Does it make a difference to you that Mrs. Kaskel accepted the loan payments? Is she raising the issue of the lack of indorsement too late? Is it fair to Northern Trust because it went on for two years without any objection? Why do you think Mrs. Kaskel was so taken in by MLS and Shook?

12. MISSING INDORSEMENT

When the parties intend to negotiate an order instrument but for some reason the holder fails to indorse it, there is no negotiation. The transfer without indorsement has only the effect of a contract assignment.[21] If the transferee gave value for the

---
[21] Revised UCC § 3-204(d).

instrument (see Chapter 30 for more information on what constitutes giving value), the transferee has the right to require that the transferor indorse the instrument unqualifiedly and thereby negotiate the instrument.

 PROBLEMS IN NEGOTIATION OF INSTRUMENTS

The issues of signatures and requirements for negotiation can become quite complex when issues such as forgery, employee misconduct, and embezzlement arise.

CPA

forged or unauthorized indorsement instrument indorsed by an agent for a principal without authorization or authority.

13. FORGED AND UNAUTHORIZED INDORSEMENTS

A **forged** or **unauthorized indorsement** is not a valid indorsement.[22] Accordingly, anyone who has possession of a forged instrument is not a holder because the indorsement of the person whose signature was forged was necessary for effective negotiation of the instrument to the possessor. However, proof of forgery requires expert testimony and a split from a pattern of payments is helpful.[23]

If payment of an instrument is made to one claiming under or through a forged indorsement, the payor ordinarily remains liable to the person who is the rightful owner of the paper. However, if the rightful owner has been negligent and contributed to the forgery or unauthorized signature problem, there are exceptions to these general rules on liability for forged indorsements (see Chapter 30 for more information on the rights and liabilities of the parties).

CPA

impostor rule an exception to the rules on liability for forgery that covers situations such as the embezzling payroll clerk.

14. QUASI FORGERIES: THE IMPOSTOR RULE

The **impostor rule** provides three exceptions to the rule that a forged indorsement is not effective to validly negotiate an instrument. If one of the three impostor exceptions applies, the instrument is still effectively negotiated, even though there may have been a forgery of an indorsement.

(a) WHEN THE IMPOSTOR RULE APPLIES   The impostor rule applies in cases where an indorser is impersonating a payee and in two cases where the indorser is a dummy payee.[24]

(1) Impersonating Payee.   The impersonation of a payee in the impostor rule exception includes impersonation of the agent of the person who is named as payee. **For Example,** if Jones pretends to be the agent of Brown Corporation and thereby obtains a check payable to the order of the corporation, the impostor exception applies.

(2) Dummy Payee.   Another impostor scenario arises when the preparer of the instrument intends that the named payee will never benefit from the instrument. Such a "dummy" payee may be an actual or a fictitious person. This situation arises when the owner of a checking account wishes to conceal the true purpose of taking money from the account at the bank. The account owner makes out a check purportedly in payment of a debt that in fact does not exist.[25]

---

[22] Revised UCC § 3-403(2); *Bloom v G.P.F.,* 588 So 2d 607 (Fla App 1991).

[23] *Wagner v Bank of America,* 51 UCC Rep Serv 2d (West) 781 (Cal App 2003).

[24] Revised UCC § 3-405; *Shearson Lehman Brothers, Inc. v Wasatch Bank,* 788 F Supp 1184 (D Utah 1992).

[25] *Texas Stadium Corp. v Savings of America,* 933 SW2d 616 (Tex 1996).

(3) Dummy Payee Supplied by Employee. The third impostor situation arises when an agent or employee of the maker or the drawer has supplied the name to be used for the payee, intending that the payee should not have any interest in the paper.[26] This last situation occurs when an employee fraudulently causes an employer to sign a check made to a customer or another person, whether existing or not. The employee does not intend to send it to that person but rather intends to forge the latter's indorsement, cash the check, and keep the money. This exception to the impostor rule imposes responsibility on employers to have adequate internal controls to prevent employees from taking advantage of an accounting system with loopholes so that others are not required to bear the cost of the employer's lack of appropriate precautions.

(b) Effect of Impostor Rule When the impostor rule is applicable, any person may indorse the name of the payee. This indorsement is treated as a genuine indorsement by the payee and cannot be attacked on the ground that it is a forgery. This recognition of the fictitious payee's signature as valid applies even though the dummy payee of the paper is a fictitious person.[27]

(c) Limitations on Impostor Rule The impostor rule does not apply when there is a valid check to an actual creditor for a correct amount owed by the drawer and someone later forges the payee's name. The impostor rule does not apply in this situation even if the forger is an employee of the drawer.

Even when the unauthorized indorsement of the payee's name is effective by virtue of the impostor rule, a person forging the payee's name is subject to civil and criminal liability for making such an indorsement.

For the impostor rule to apply, the holders or the takers of the instrument must show that they took the instrument (1) in good faith and (2) for payment or collection.

(d) Negligence of Drawee Not Required The impostor rule applies without regard to whether the drawee bank acted with reasonable care.

15. EFFECT OF INCAPACITY OR MISCONDUCT ON NEGOTIATION

A negotiation is effective even though (1) it was made by a minor or any other person lacking capacity; (2) it was an act beyond the powers of a corporation; (3) it was obtained by fraud, duress, or a mistake of any kind; or (4) the negotiation was part of an illegal transaction or was made in breach of duty. Under general principles of law apart from the UCC, the transferor in such cases may be able to set aside the negotiation or obtain some other form of legal relief.

However, rights of certain parties (holders in due course) may limit the ability to set aside the negotiation because of incapacity and other contract defenses (see Chapter 30).

16. LOST INSTRUMENTS

The liability on lost instruments depends on who is demanding payment from whom and on whether the instrument was order or bearer paper when it was lost.

---

[26] *Guardian Life Ins. Co. of America v Weisman*, 30 F Supp 3d 730 (DNJ 1998).
[27] *Bank of Glen Burnie v Elkridge Bank*, 707 A2d 438 (Md App 1988).

CASE SUMMARY

The Slick Oil Company Employee

FACTS: Getty Petroleum distributes gasoline through dealer-owned stations. Customers who buy gas at a Getty station can pay by cash or credit card. When a customer uses a credit card, Getty processes the transactions, receives payment from the credit card company, and then issues computer-generated checks payable to dealers to reimburse them for their credit card sales. Many checks, however, are not intended for negotiation and are never delivered to the payees. Instead, Getty uses these checks for bookkeeping purposes, voiding them and then crediting the check amount toward the dealer's future purchases of gasoline from Getty.

Lorna Lewis, a supervisor in Getty's credit processing department, stole over 130 checks, forged the indorsements of the payees by hand or rubber stamp, and then submitted the checks to American Express and other credit card companies to pay her own debts. The credit card companies then forwarded the checks through ordinary banking channels to Chemical Bank, where Getty had its checking account. Chemical Bank honored the checks Lewis had forged.

Getty, on discovering the larceny of Lewis, sought recovery of the amounts from the credit card companies. Getty sought payment on 31 of the checks from American Express (which had been paid by Chemical Bank). At trial, a judge held American Express liable to Getty for $58,841.60. The appeals court found that American Express was grossly negligent in taking and cashing the checks and also held it liable. American Express appealed.

DECISION: Losses caused by a forged instrument are allocated to the drawee bank because, as between that bank and its drawer, the drawee bank is in the better position to detect the forgery before payment. However, the risk of loss shifts to the drawer in situations where the drawer is the party best able to prevent the loss. Getty was in the best position to prevent the losses by its bookkeeping practices, by supervising its employees, by enforcing its rules, and by examining records relating to a fraud that had been in progress for a considerable time. The loss brought about by Lewis's misconduct falls to her employer, not the bank. [**Getty Petroleum Corp. v American Express Travel Related Services Co., Inc., 683 NE2d 311 (NY 1997)**]

(a) ORDER INSTRUMENTS If the lost instrument is order paper, the finder does not become the holder because the instrument has not been indorsed and delivered by the person to whom it was then payable. The former holder who lost it is still the rightful owner of the instrument.

(b) BEARER INSTRUMENTS If the lost instrument is in bearer form when it is lost, the finder, as the possessor of a bearer instrument, is the holder and is entitled to enforce payment.

 ## WARRANTIES IN NEGOTIATION

When a negotiable instrument is transferred by negotiation, the transferors give certain implied warranties.

17. WARRANTIES OF UNQUALIFIED INDORSER

When the transferor receives consideration for the indorsement and makes an unqualified indorsement, the warranties stated in this section are given by the transferor by implication. No distinction is made between an unqualified blank indorsement and an unqualified special indorsement.

(a) SCOPE OF WARRANTIES   The warranties of the unqualified indorser are found in § 3-416 of the Revised UCC as follows:

> *(1) the warrantor is a person entitled to enforce the instrument;*
> *(2) all signatures on the instrument are authentic and authorized;*
> *(3) the instrument has not been altered;*
> *(4) the instrument is not subject to a defense or claim in recoupment of any party which can be asserted against the warrantor;*
> *(4A) with respect to any item drawn on a consumer account, which does not bear a handwritten signature purporting to be the signature of the drawer, that the purported drawer of the draft has authorized the issuance of the item in the amount for which the item is drawn; and*
> *(5) the warrantor has no knowledge of any insolvency proceeding commenced with respect to the maker or acceptor or, in the case of an unaccepted draft, the drawer.[28]*

Those who present an instrument for payment (see Chapter 30), or the last party in line before the payor, make three warranties:

> *(1) the warrantor is, or was, at the time the warrantor transferred the draft, a person entitled to enforce the draft or authorized to obtain payment or acceptance of the draft on behalf of a person entitled to enforce the draft;*
> *(2) the draft has not been altered; and*
> *(3) the warrantor has no knowledge that the signature of the drawer of the draft is unauthorized.[29]*

If a forged indorsement has appeared during the transfer of the instrument, and there is a refusal to pay because of that problem, the last party who is a holder may turn to her transferor to recover on the basis of these implied warranties. These warranties give those who have transferred and held the instrument recourse against those parties who were involved in the transfer of the instrument, although they were not parties to the original instrument. This warranty section of Article 3 of the UCC attaches liability to those who transfer instruments.

(b) WHAT IS NOT WARRANTED   The implied warranties stated here do not guarantee that payment of the instrument will be made. Similarly, the holder's indorsement of a check does not give any warranty that the account of the drawer in the drawee bank contains funds sufficient to cover the check. However, implied warranties do, for example, promise that the signatures on the instrument are not forged. Likewise, they promise that no one has altered the amount on the

---

[28] Revised UCC § 3-416 (1990).

[29] Revised UCC § 3-417. These warranties are limited to consumer accounts and do not apply to commercial accounts.

instrument. The warranties are not warranties of payment or solvency. They are simply warranties about the nature of the instrument. A holder may not be paid the amount due on the instrument, but if the lack of payment results from a forgery, the holder has rights against those who transferred the instrument with a forged signature.

(c) Beneficiary of Implied Warranties The implied warranties of the unqualified indorser pass to the transferee and any subsequent transferees. There is no requirement that subsequent transferees take the instrument in good faith to be entitled to the warranties. Likewise, the transferee need not be a holder to enjoy warranty protections.

(d) Disclaimer of Warranties The unqualified indorser cannot disclaim any warranty when the instrument is a check. Warranties may be disclaimed when the instrument is not a check.

A disclaimer of warranties is ordinarily made by adding "Without warranties" to the indorsement.

(e) Notice of Breach of Warranty To enforce an implied warranty of an indorser, the party claiming under the warranty must give the indorser notice of the breach. This notice must be given within 30 days after the claimant learns or has reason to know of the breach and the identity of the indorser. If proper notice is not given, the warranty claim is reduced by the amount of the loss that could have been avoided had timely notice been given.

18. WARRANTIES OF OTHER PARTIES

Warranties are also made by the indorser who indorses "Without recourse" and by one who transfers by delivery only.

(a) Qualified Indorser The warranty liability of a qualified indorser is the same as that of an unqualified indorser.[30] A qualified indorsement means that the indorser does not assume liability for the payment of the instrument as written. (See § 3-416(4).) However, a qualified indorsement does not eliminate the implied warranties an indorser makes as a transferor of an instrument. The implied warranty that is waived by a qualified indorsement is the fourth warranty on defenses. A qualified indorser still makes the other warranties on signatures and alteration but waives the warranty on defenses.

(b) Transfer by Delivery When the negotiable instrument is negotiated by delivery without indorsement, the warranty liability of the transferor runs only to the immediate transferee. In all other respects, the warranty liability is the same as in the case of the unqualified indorser. **For Example,** Thomas, a minor, gives Craig his note payable to bearer. Craig transfers the note for value and by delivery only to Walsh, who negotiates it to Hall. Payment was refused by Thomas, who chose to disaffirm his contract. Hall cannot hold Craig liable. Craig, having negotiated the instrument by delivery only, is liable on his implied warranties only to his immediate transferee, Walsh. Likewise, because Craig did not indorse the note, he is not secondarily liable for payment of the note.

---

[30] Revised UCC § 3-416(a).

SUMMARY

Negotiation is the transferring of a negotiable instrument in such a way as to make the transferee the holder. When a negotiable instrument is transferred by negotiation, the transferee becomes the holder of the instrument. If such a holder becomes a holder in due course, the holder will be immune to certain defenses.

An *order instrument* is negotiated by an indorsement and delivery by the person to whom it is then payable. A bearer instrument is negotiated by delivery alone. The order or bearer character of an instrument is determined by the face of the instrument as long as the instrument is not indorsed. If the instrument has been indorsed, the character is determined by the last indorsement.

A number of different kinds of indorsements can be made on negotiable instruments. When an indorser merely authenticates the instrument, the indorsement is called a *blank indorsement*. If the last indorsement is a blank indorsement, the instrument is bearer paper, which may be negotiated by change of possession alone. A special indorsement consists of the authentication by the indorser and words specifying the person to whom the indorser makes the instrument payable. If the last indorsement is a special indorsement, the instrument is order paper and may be negotiated only by an indorsement and delivery. A qualified indorsement eliminates the liability of the indorser to answer for dishonor of the paper by the maker or the drawee. A restrictive indorsement specifies the purpose of the instrument or its use.

A forged or unauthorized indorsement is no indorsement, and the possessor of the instrument cannot be a holder. The impostor rule makes three exceptions to this rule: dummy payee; employee fraud; and impersonating a payee.

A negotiation is effective even though (1) it is made by a minor, (2) it is an act beyond the powers of a corporation, (3) it is obtained by fraud, or (4) the negotiation is part of an illegal transaction. However, the transferor may be able to set aside the negotiation under general legal principles apart from the UCC. The negotiation cannot be set aside if the instrument is held by a person paying it in good faith and without knowledge of the facts on which the rescission claim is based.

The warranties of the unqualified indorser are as follows: (1) the warrantor is a person entitled to enforce the instrument; (2) all signatures on the instrument are authentic and authorized; (3) the instrument has not been altered; (4) the instrument is not subject to a defense or claim in recoupment of any party that can be asserted against the warrantor; with respect to any item drawn on a consumer account, which does not bear a handwritten signature purporting to be the signature of the drawer, that the purported drawer of the draft has authorized the issuance of the item in the amount for which the item is drawn; and (5) the warrantor has no knowledge of any insolvency proceeding commenced with respect to the maker or acceptor or, in the case of an unaccepted draft, the drawer.

QUESTIONS AND CASE PROBLEMS

1. C&N and Alabama Siding perform construction work at job sites throughout the southeastern United States. On Wednesday of each week, the foreman at each job site telephoned Bivens and gave her the names of the employees working on the job and the number of hours they had worked. Bivens then conveyed this information to Automatic Data Processing (ADP). Under a contract with C&N and Alabama Siding, ADP prepared payroll checks for the two companies. After preparing the payroll checks based on the information given to it by Bivens, ADP sent the checks to the offices of C&N and Alabama Siding for authorized signatures. Bivens was not an authorized signer. After the checks were signed, Bivens sent the checks to the job site foreman to deliver to the employees.

Bivens soon began conveying false information and hours worked. On the basis of this false information, ADP prepared payroll checks payable to persons who were actually employees but had not worked the hours Bivens had indicated. After obtaining authorized signatures, Bivens intercepted the checks, forged the indorsements of the payees, and either cashed them at Community Bancshares or deposited them into her checking account at Community, often presenting numerous checks at one time. Bivens continued this practice for over a year, forging more than 100 indorsements.

The vice president of C&N discovered the embezzlement after noticing payroll checks payable to employees who had not recently performed services for the corporations. Bivens later admitted to forging the indorsements. C&N brought suit against the bank for paying on forged indorsements. Can C&N recover? [*C&N Contractors, Inc. v Community Bancshares, Inc.,* 646 So 2d 1357 (Ala)]

2. How could a check made out to "Joseph Klimas and his Attorney Fritzshall & Gleason & Blue Cross Blue Shield Company and Carpenters Welfare Fund" be negotiated further? What would be required? [*Chicago District Council of Carpenters Welfare Fund v Gleason's Fritzshall,* 693 NE2d 412 (Ill App)]

3. An insurer issued a settlement check on a claim brought by an injured minor that was payable to "Trudy Avants attorney for minor child Joseph Walton, mother Dolores Carpenter 11762 S. Harrells Ferry Road #E Baton Rouge LA 70816." The lawyer indorsed the check. Two unknown individuals forged indorsements for the other two names and obtained payment of the check. The insurer sued the payor bank claiming the instruments were not properly payable because of the forged indorsements. The court is unclear whether the indorsement required is one for an either/or payee or joint payee. What advice can you offer the court as it faces this issue? [*Coregis Insurance Co. v Fleet National Bank,* 793 A2d 254 (Conn App 2002)]

4. Higgins owes the Packard Appliance store $100. He mails a check to Packard. The check is drawn on First National Bank and states "Pay to the order of cash $100." This check is stapled to a letter stating that the $100 is in payment of the debt owed by Higgins. Edwards, who is employed by Packard in the mailroom, removes the letter from its envelope, detaches the check, and disappears. No one knows what has become of the check until a person identifying himself as Gene Howard presents it at First National Bank. The

bank pays this person $100 and debits that amount against the account of Higgins. Higgins protests that this cannot be done because the check was lost and never belonged to Howard. Is Higgins correct?

5. Jerry O. Peavy, Jr., who did not have a bank account of his own, received a draft from CNL Insurance America in the amount of $5,323.60. The draft was drawn on CNL's account at Bank South, N.A., and was "payable to the order of Jerry Peavy and Trust Company Bank." Jerry O. Peavy, Sr., allowed his son Peavy, Jr., to deposit the draft in his account at Bank South, N.A. Bank South accepted the draft and deposited it on December 29, 1992, with only the signature of Jerry Peavy, Jr. Both Mr. and Mrs. Peavy, Sr., then wrote checks on the amount of the draft using the full amount to benefit their son.

On March 30, 1993, Bank South realized that it had improperly deposited the draft because it was lacking an indorsement from Trust Company Bank and reversed the transaction by debiting Mr. and Mrs. Peavy's account for the full amount of the draft. A bank officer then called Mr. and Mrs. Peavy, told them what had happened with the draft, and "threatened to send them to jail if they did not immediately deposit the sum of $5,323.60." The Peavys deposited that amount from the sale of some stock they owned and then filed suit against Bank South for its conversion of their son's draft and funds. Do the Peavys have a case? [*Peavy v Bank South,* 474 SE2d 690 (Ga App)]

6. The Gasts owned a building that they contracted to sell to the Hannas. The building was insured against fire with American Casualty Co. Thereafter, when the building was damaged by fire, a settlement was reached with the insurance company through Sidney Rosenbaum, a public fire adjuster. In order to make payment for the loss, the insurance company drew a draft on itself payable to the Hannas, the Gasts, and Sidney Rosenbaum. Apparently the Hannas indorsed the draft, forged the names of the other payees as indorsers, cashed the draft by presenting it to American Casualty Co., and disappeared. Thereafter, the Gasts sued American Casualty. Decide. [*Gast v American Casualty Co.,* 240 A2d 682 (NJ Super)]

7. Snug Harbor Realty Co. had a checking account in First National Bank. When construction work was obtained by Snug Harbor, its superintendent, Magee, would examine the bills submitted for labor and materials. He would instruct the bookkeeper which bills were approved, and the bookkeeper then prepared the checks in accordance with his instructions. After the checks were signed by the proper official of Snug Harbor, Magee picked them up for delivery. Instead of delivering certain checks, he forged the signatures of the respective payees as indorsers and cashed the checks. The drawee bank then debited the Snug Harbor account with the amount of the checks. Snug Harbor claimed this was improper and sued the bank for the amount of the checks. The bank claimed it was protected by the impostor rule. Will the bank be successful? Explain. [*Snug Harbor Realty Co. v First National Bank,* 253 A2d 581 (NJ Super)]

8. Benton, as agent for Savidge, received an insurance settlement check from Metropolitan Life Insurance Co. He indorsed it "For deposit" and deposited it in Bryn Mawr Trust Co. in Savidge's account. What were the nature and effect of this indorsement? [*Savidge v Metropolitan Life Ins. Co.,* 110 A2d 730 (Pa)]

9. Allstate Insurance Company issued a check payable to "Chuk N. Tang & Rosa C. Tang HWJT" with "Bank of America" on the second line and the following explanation on the front of the check: "Settlement of our rental dwelling loss caused by fire on 11/21/93." The Tangs indorsed the check and forged the indorsement of Bank of America. When Bank of America objected, the Tangs claimed that only they needed to sign the instrument for further negotiations. The check was intended as a joint payment for Bank of America as the mortgagee on the Tangs' rental property because the insurance policy required that the mortgagee be paid first before any proceeds went to the property owners. Bank of America sued Allstate. Is Bank of America entitled to recover for the lack of its indorsement? Was its indorsement necessary for further negotiation? [*Bank of America Nat'l Trust & Savings Ass'n v Allstate Insurance Co.,* 29 F Supp 2d 1129 (CD Cal)]

10. When claims filed with an insurance company were approved for payment, they were given to the claims clerk, who would prepare checks to pay those claims and then give the checks to the treasurer to sign. The claims clerk of the insurance company made a number of checks payable to persons who did not have any claims and gave them to the treasurer with the checks for valid claims, and the treasurer signed all of the checks. The claims clerk then removed the false checks, indorsed them with the names of their respective payees, and cashed them at the bank where the insurance company had its account. The bank debited the account of the insurance company with the amount of these checks. The insurance company claimed that the bank could not do this because the indorsements on the checks were forgeries. Was the insurance company correct? [*General Accident Fire & Life Assur. Corp. v Citizens Fidelity Bank & Trust Co.,* 519 SW2d 817 (Ky)]

11. Eutsler forged his brother Richard's indorsement on certified checks and cashed them at First National Bank. When Richard sought to recover the funds from the bank, the bank stated that it would press criminal charges against Eutsler. Richard asked the bank to delay prosecution to give him time to collect directly from his brother. His brother promised to repay him the money but vanished some six months later without having paid any money. Richard sued the bank. What result? [*Eutsler v First Nat'l Bank, Pawhuska,* 639 P2d 1245 (Okla)]

12. Michael Sykes, the president of Sykes Corp., hired Richard Amelung to handle the company's bookkeeping and deal with all of its vendors. Amelung entered into an agreement with Eastern Metal Supply to help reduce Sykes's debt to Eastern. Whenever Sykes received a check, Amelung would sign it over to Eastern and allow it to keep 30 percent of the check amount. On 28 checks that totaled $200,000, Amelung indorsed the back as follows: "Sykes & Associates or Sykes Corporation, Richard Amelung." Amelung then turned the checks over to Eastern, and Eastern deposited them into its account at Barnett Bank. Eastern would then write one of its checks to Sykes Corp. for the 70 percent remaining from the checks. When Michael Sykes learned of the

arrangement, he demanded the return of the 30 percent from Barnett Bank, claiming that it had paid over an unauthorized signature and that the indorsement was restricted and had been violated by the deposit into Eastern's account. What type of indorsement did Amelung make? Did he have the authority to do so? Should Sykes be reimbursed by Barnett? [*Sykes Corp. v Eastern Metal Supply, Inc.,* 659 So 2d 475 (Fla App)]

13. In January 1998, Allied Capital Partners, L.P., and American Factors Corporation were in the business of factoring accounts receivable for third-party clients. Allied assigned its factoring contract with Complete Design, Inc., to American but retained an interest in the factoring of Complete Design's invoices. On January 25, 1998, in payment of invoices issued by Complete Design, Clark Wilson Homes, Inc., issued a check for $6,823.15. The check was payable to:

> Complete Design
> Allied Capital Partners, L.P.
> 2340 E. Trinity Mills Ste. 300
> Carrollton, Texas 75006

On February 10, 1998, Clark Wilson issued another check for $26,329.32 made payable to:

> Complete Design
> Allied Capital Partners, L.P.
> 2340 E. Trinity Mills Ste. 300
> Carrollton, Texas 75006

Complete Design deposited both checks in its account at Bank One. However, Allied and American received none of the proceeds of the checks.

Complete Design subsequently declared bankruptcy, and Allied and American made demand on Bank One for damages resulting from Bank One's conversion of the two checks. Bank One denied all liability for conversion of the checks. Allied and American subsequently sued Bank One, asserting conversion. Bank One filed a motion for summary judgment asserting that, because it was ambiguous to whom the checks at issue were payable, they were payable upon a single endorsement. The trial court granted Bank One's motion. Allied and American appealed. Who is correct here? Were both signatures necessary for a proper indorsement, or will one do? [*Allied Capital Partners, L.P. v Bank One, Texas, N.A.,* 68 SW3d 51 (Tex App)]

14. Would a bank be liable to a customer who indorsed a check "For deposit only into account #071698570" if that check were deposited into the wrong account? What if the customer's indorsement was "For deposit only"? Would any account qualify? Would any bank qualify? [*Qatar v First American Bank of Virginia,* 885 F Supp 849 (ED Va)]

15. Two employees of the state of New Mexico fraudulently procured and indorsed a warrant (a draft drawn against funds of the state) made out to the Greater Mesilla Valley Sanitation District. There was no such sanitation district. The employees obtained payment from Citizens Bank. Western Casualty, the state's insurer, reimbursed the state for its loss and then brought suit against the bank for negligently paying the warrant. Is the bank liable for its payment? Discuss your answer. [*Western Casualty & Surety Co. v Citizens Bank of Las Cruces,* 676 F2d 1344 (10th Cir)]

> CPA QUESTIONS

1. Hand executed and delivered to Rex a $1,000 negotiable note payable to Rex or bearer. Rex then negotiated it to Ford and endorsed it on the back by merely signing his name. Which of the following is a correct statement?

   a. Rex's endorsement was a special endorsement.
   b. Rex's endorsement was necessary to Ford's qualification as a holder.
   c. The instrument initially being bearer paper cannot be converted to order paper.
   d. The instrument is bearer paper, and Ford can convert it to order paper by writing "pay to the order of Ford" above Rex's signature.

2. Jane Lane, a sole proprietor, has in her possession several checks that she received from her

customers. Lane is concerned about the safety of the checks since she believes that many of them are bearer paper which may be cashed without endorsement. The checks in Lane's possession will be considered order paper rather than bearer paper if they were made payable (in the drawer's handwriting) to the order of

a. Cash

b. Ted Tint, and endorsed by Ted Tint in blank

c. Bearer, and endorsed by Ken Kent making them payable to Jane Lane

d. Bearer, and endorsed by Sam Sole in blank

3. West Corp. received a check that was originally made payable to the order of one of its customers, Ted Burns. The following endorsement was written on the back of the check:

   Ted Burns, without recourse, for collection only
   Which of the following describes the endorsement?

	Special	*Restrictive*
a.	Yes	Yes
b.	No	No
c.	No	Yes
d.	Yes	No

4. An instrument reads as follows:

$250.00 Chicago, Illinois   April 1, 1992

Thirty days after date I promise to pay to the

order of ___Cash_____

Two hundred and fifty_____**Dollars at**

New York City_____

Value received with interest at the rate of six percent per annum. This agreement arises out of a separate agreement.

No. 20 Due May 1, 1992   Robert Smith

Answer "Yes" or "No" for the following questions about the previous item.

a. The instrument is a draft.

b. The instrument is order paper.

c. This is a negotiable instrument.

d. Robert Smith is the maker.

e. The instrument may be negotiated without indorsement.

LIABILITY OF THE PARTIES UNDER NEGOTIABLE INSTRUMENTS

LEARNING OBJECTIVES

After studying this chapter, you should be able to

LO.1 Distinguish between an ordinary holder and a holder in due course

LO.2 List the requirements for becoming a holder in due course

LO.3 Explain the rights of a holder through a holder in due course

LO.4 List and explain the limited defenses not available against a holder in due course

LO.5 List and explain the universal defenses available against all holders

LO.6 Describe how the rights of a holder in due course have been limited by the Federal Trade Commission

Chapters 28 and 29 introduced the requirements for negotiable instruments and the methods for transfer of those instruments. However, the requirements of negotiability and transfer are simply preliminary steps for the discovery of the real benefit of using negotiable instruments in commerce, which is to streamline payment in commercial transactions. This chapter explains the streamlining special status and rights of the special parties to negotiable instruments. These special parties are protected from many underlying contract defenses that can arise between the original parties. The extent of the parties' rights and protections is covered in this chapter.

A   PARTIES TO NEGOTIABLE INSTRUMENTS: RIGHTS AND LIABILITIES

assignee third party to whom contract benefits are transferred.

The rights and defenses of the parties to negotiable instruments are determined by the types of parties involved.

holder someone in possession of an instrument that runs to that person (i.e., is made payable to that person, is indorsed to that person, or is bearer paper).

1. TYPES OF PARTIES

Parties with rights in a negotiable instrument can be **assignees** or **holders**. A holder may be an ordinary holder or a **holder in due course**. As noted in Chapter 28, a holder in due course is a special party to an instrument with special rights beyond those of the ordinary holder.

`CPA`

2. ORDINARY HOLDERS AND ASSIGNEES

holder in due course holder who has given value, taken in good faith without notice of dishonor, defenses, or that instrument is overdue, and who is afforded special rights or status.

A holder is a party in possession of an instrument that runs to him. An instrument "runs" to a party if it is payable to his order, is bearer paper, or is indorsed to him (see Chapter 29). Any holder has all of the rights given through and under the negotiable instrument. The holder may demand payment or bring suit for collection on the instrument. A holder can give a discharge or release from liability on the instrument.

A holder who seeks payment of the instrument is required only to produce the instrument and show that the signature of the maker, drawer, or indorser is genuine. If the party obligated to pay under the instrument has no valid defense (such as forgery, which was discussed in Chapter 29), the holder is entitled to payment of the instrument.

The holder can recover from any of the parties who are liable on the instrument, regardless of the order of the signatures on the instrument. A holder could recover from the first indorser on an instrument or from the last party to indorse the instrument.

The rights of a holder are no different from the rights of a contract assignee (see Chapter 18). The assignee of a contract is in the same position and has the same rights as an ordinary holder. **For Example,** if a farmer who signed a note to pay for his tractor has a warranty problem with the tractor, he has a defense to payment on the note. Anyone who is assigned that note as an assignee or holder is also subject to the farmer's defense. (See Figure 30-1 and also the provisions on consumer credit protection under the discussion of the Federal Trade Commission rule in Chapter 33 and later in this chapter.)

FIGURE 30-1 *Assignee, Holder, and Holder-in-Due-Course Rights*

Suppose that Farmer Fred signs an installment contract to purchase a tractor from John Deere for $153,000. John Deere assigns the contract to Finance Co.

Suppose that Farmer Fred signs a negotiable promissory note for $153,000 and John Deere then transfers it to Finance Co., a holder in due course.

Suppose that Farmer Fred has a roofing company replace the roof on his home, and he signs a negotiable promissory note for $5,000. Roofing Co. transfers the note to Finance Co.

3. THE HOLDER-IN-DUE-COURSE PROTECTIONS

The law gives certain holders of negotiable instruments special rights by protecting them from certain defenses. This protection makes negotiable instruments more attractive and allows greater ease of transfer. Holders in due course have an immunity from contract assignment defenses not enjoyed by ordinary holders or assignees. Figure 30-1 shows the different statuses of the parties as holders, assignees, and holders in due course.

(a) HOLDER IN DUE COURSE To obtain the preferred status of a holder in due course,[1] a person must first be a holder. However, the preferred status of holder in

---

[1] Revised UCC § 3-302; *Bolduc v Beal Bank, SSB,* 994 F Supp 82 (DNH 1998) aff'd and remanded on other grounds, 167 F3d 667 (1st Cir 1999).

due course requires these types of holder to meet additional standards. Those holders who do not meet the standards for holder in due course have all the rights of a holder. However, holders in due course enjoy additional protections beyond those basic holder rights. Under Uniform Commercial Code (UCC) § 3-302(a), there are four requirements for becoming a holder in due course.[2]

CPA

value consideration or antecedent debt or security given in exchange for the transfer of a negotiable instrument or creation of a security interest.

(1) Value.   **Value** is similar to consideration (see Chapter 15). **For Example,** a person who receives a negotiable note under a will does not give value because the note is a gift. An heir who receives her non–holder-in-due-course uncle's promissory notes under the provisions in his will is not a holder in due course because the notes were a gift, and she gave no value for the notes.[3]

A person takes an instrument for value when (1) the instrument is issued or transferred for a promised undertaking of performance, to the extent the promised undertaking has been performed; (2) the transferee acquires a security interest or other lien in the instrument, other than a lien obtained by judicial proceeding; (3) the instrument is issued or transferred as payment of, or as security for, an antecedent claim against any person, whether or not the claim is due; (4) the instrument is issued or transferred in exchange for a negotiable instrument; or (5) the instrument is issued or transferred in exchange for the incurring of an irrevocable obligation to a third party by the person taking the instrument.[4] As with consideration, the courts do not consider whether the value is enough; they determine only whether some value has been given.[5]

Under Revised Article 3, the original payee of a note is not a holder in due course unless that note is transferred to others and then back to the payee.[6]

A bank does not give value for a deposited check when it credits the depositor's account with the amount of the deposit. The bank gives value to the extent that the depositor is permitted to withdraw funds against that deposit.[7] **For Example,** if Janice deposits a $300 check into her account, which already has $400 in it, Janice's bank does not give value until Janice has written checks or withdrawn funds beyond the existing $400. The code follows FIFO (first in, first out) for drawing on funds. A bank that lets the customer draw on the funds deposited gives value.[8]

In a few special cases, a purchaser of a negotiable instrument is not considered a holder in due course. A holder who acquires a negotiable instrument by legal process or by purchase in an execution, bankruptcy, or creditor's sale or similar proceeding cannot be a holder in due course. A holder who acquires a negotiable instrument

---

[2] Revised UCC § 3-302(a).

[3] However, if the uncle were a holder in due course, it might be possible under a special Article 3 protection for the heir to also be a holder in due course despite the gift acquisition. UCC § 3-302(c)(iii). This protection for gift transfers by holders in due course is called the *shelter provision* (and is covered later in this chapter).

[4] Revised UCC § 3-303.

[5] Revised UCC § 3-303; *United Catholic Parish Schools of Beaver Dam Educational Ass'n v Card Services Center,* 636 NW2d 206 (Wis App 2001). *Agriliance, L.L.C. v Farmpro Services, Inc.,* 328 F Supp 2d 958 (SD Iowa 2003).

[6] Revised UCC § 3-302(c) provides "(c) A person does not become a holder in due course in a transaction in which the obligor issues or transfers the instrument directly to that party without the participation of a remitter or other intermediary."

[7] Revised UCC § 4-211 (1990).

[8] Allowing a deposit of a check with provisional credit does not make a bank a holder in due course, but on a cashier's check, when the bank becomes both the drawer and the drawee, the bank is obligated to pay on the instrument. *Flatiron Linen, Inc. v First American State Bank,* 23 P3d 1209 (Colo 2001). If the bank does not impose provisional credit and makes the funds available immediately for the customer, it gives value and qualifies as a holder in due course. *Maine Family Federal Credit Union v Sun Life Assur. Co. of Canada,* 727 A2d 335, 37 UCC2d 875 (Me 1999) but see *Travelers Cas. and Sur. Co. of America v Wells Fargo Bank N.A.,* 374 F3d 521, 53 UCC Rep Serv 2d 695 (CA 7 2004).

CASE SUMMARY

The Grain Checks as a Retainer: Planting the Seeds of Litigation

FACTS: Omni Trading issued two checks totaling $75,000 to Country Grain Elevators for grain it had purchased. Country Grain indorsed the checks over to the law firm of Carter & Grimsley as a retainer. Country Grain then collapsed as a business, and Omni stopped payment on the checks because all of its grain had not been delivered. Carter & Grimsley claimed it was a holder in due course and entitled to payment. However, the Department of Agriculture claimed its interest in the checks for liens and maintained that Carter & Grimsley was not a holder in due course because it had not given value. The trial court granted summary judgment for the Department of Agriculture because the checks were indorsed as a retainer for future legal work and Carter & Grimsley had not given value. Carter and Grimsley appealed.

DECISION: Carter & Grimsley was not a holder in due course. It had not given value with the promise of future services. There was no evidence of any work performed prior to the time of the check indorsement before or after the collapse of Country Grain. An executory promise to perform work is not giving value. [**Carter & Grimsley v Omni Trading, Inc., 716 NE2d 320 (Ill App 1999)**]

as part of a bulk transaction or as the successor in interest to an estate or other organization is also not a holder in due course.[9]

good faith absence of knowledge of any defects in or problems; "pure heart and an empty head."

(2) Good Faith.   The element of **good faith** for becoming a holder in due course requires that a holder of a negotiable instrument act honestly in acquiring the instrument. In addition, the taker must have observed reasonable standards of fair dealing.[10] Karl Llewellyn, one of the key drafters of the UCC, said that to comply with reasonable standards and good faith, the party must act with a "pure heart and an empty head."

Bad faith can sometimes exist just because the holder has given such a small amount as value. The transferee need not give value equal to the face of the negotiable instrument; however, a gross disparity between the value given and the value of the instrument may be evidence of bad faith. A steep discount on an instrument just before its due date should have been a signal that perhaps there were problems with the instrument. **For Example,** if a holder acquires a note at a 75 percent discount on the day before it is due, there is some indication that the note may have some issues because that close to its due date it should command a price close to its value.

close-connection doctrine circumstantial evidence, such as an ongoing or a close relationship, that can serve as notice of a problem with an instrument.

The **close-connection doctrine** applies in circumstances that indicate a problem with the instrument and put the party on notice. Under this doctrine, the holder has taken so many instruments from its transferor or is so closely connected with the transferor that any knowledge the transferor has is deemed transferred to the holder, preventing holder-in-due-course status. Examples include consumer transactions

---

[9] Revised UCC § 3-302(c).

[10] Revised UCC § 3-103(a)(4); *Choo Choo Tire Service, Inc. v Union Planters National Bank,* 498 SE2d 799 (Ga App 1998); issue of whether a party is a holder in due course is always an issue of fact, *In re SGE Mortgage Funding Corp.,* 278 BR 653 (MD Ga 2001).

where the holder in due course is a company that regularly does business with a company that has continual problems with consumer complaints.[11]

(3) Ignorance of the Instrument's Being Overdue or Dishonored. An instrument can be negotiated even though it has been dishonored, it is overdue,[12] or it is demand paper, such as a check, that has been outstanding for more than a reasonable time.[13] These instruments can still be transferred and the transferee is still a holder. However, the fact that the instrument is circulating at a late date or after it has been dishonored is a suspicious circumstance is notice that there may be some adverse claim or defense. A person who acquires title to the instrument under such circumstances can be a holder but cannot be a holder in due course. **For Example,** buying a discounted note after its due date is notice that something may be wrong with the instrument.

(4) Ignorance of Defenses and Adverse Claims. Prior parties on an instrument may have defenses that entitle them to withhold payment from a holder of an instrument. **For Example,** the drawer of a check, upon demand for payment by the payee, could assert as a defense to payment that the merchandise the payee delivered under the terms of their underlying contract was defective. A person who acquires an instrument with notice or knowledge that there is a defense that a party may have or that there is any adverse claim of ownership of the instrument cannot be a holder in due course. In general, transferees who are aware of facts that would make a reasonable person ask questions are deemed to know what they would have learned if they had asked questions.[14] Such knowledge and the failure to ask questions will cost them their special status of holder in due course; they remain simply holders.

Knowledge acquired by a holder after the instrument was acquired does not prevent the holder from being a holder in due course. Consequently, the fact that a holder, after acquiring the instrument, learns of a defense does not work retroactively to destroy the holder's character as a holder in due course.

CPA

holder through a holder in due course holder of an instrument who attains holder-in-due-course status because a holder in due course has held it previous to him or her.

(b) HOLDER THROUGH A HOLDER IN DUE COURSE Those persons who become holders of the instrument after a holder in due course has held it are given the same protection as the holder in due course, provided they are not parties to any fraud or illegality that affects the instrument. This status of **holder through a holder in due course** is given in these circumstances even if the transferee from a holder in due course does not satisfy the requirements for holder-in-due-course status. This elevated or protected status is called Article 3's "shelter rule," and it allows a person who is not a holder in due course to hide under the "umbrella" with a holder in due course and be sheltered from claims and defenses as if actually being a holder in due course. **For Example,** a person who acquires an instrument as an inheritance from an estate does not give value and is missing one of the requirements for being a holder in due course. However, if the estate was a holder in due course, that

---

[11] *Associates Home Equity Services, Inc. v Troup,* 778 A2d 529 (NJ Super AD 2001); *Gonzalez v Old Kent Mortgage Co.,* 2000 WL 1469313 (ED Pa 2000).

[12] *St. Bernard Savings & Loan Ass'n v Cella,* 826 F Supp 985 (ED La 1993); *Cadle Co. v DeVincent,* 57 Mass App Ct 13, 781 NE2d 817, 49 UCC Rep Serv 2d 1261 (Mass App 2003); *Federal Financial Co. v Gerard,* 949 P2d 412 (Wash App 1998).

[13] Revised UCC § 3-304.

[14] *Unr-Rohn, Inc. v Summit Bank,* 687 NE2d 235 (Ind App 1997); but see contra view, *Pero's Steak and Spaghetti House v Lee,* 90 SW3d 614 (Tenn 2002).

CASE SUMMARY

Any Kind of Check Won't Do

FACTS: In the 1990s, John G. Talcott, Jr., a 93-year-old Massachusetts resident, was sold an investment of $75,000 by D. J. Rivera, a "financial advisor" to Talcott, and Salvatore Guarino, a cohort of Rivera. The investment produced no returns.

On December 7, 1999, Guarino established check cashing privileges at Any Kind Checks Cashed, Inc. by filling out a customer card. On the card, Guarino listed himself as a broker.

On January 10, 2000, Rivera telephoned Talcott and talked him into sending him a check for $10,000 made out to Guarino, which was to be used for travel expenses to obtain a return on the original $75,000 investment. Rivera received the check on January 11.

Talcott spoke to Rivera on the morning of January 11. Rivera indicated that $10,000 was more than what was needed for travel. He said that $5,700 would meet the travel costs. Talcott called his bank and stopped payment on the $10,000 check.

Guarino went to Any Kind's Stuart, Florida, office on January 11 and presented the $10,000 check to Nancy Michael, a supervisor. Guarino showed Michael his driver's license and the Federal Express envelope from Talcott in which he received the check. Based on her experience, Michael believed the check was good; the Federal Express envelope was "very crucial" to her decision because it indicated that the maker of the check had sent it to the payee trying to cash the check. After deducting the 5 percent check cashing fee, Michael cashed the check and gave Guarino $9,500. The next day she deposited the check in the company's bank.

On January 15, 2000, Talcott sent a check for $5,700. On January 17, 2000, Guarino went into the Stuart Any Kind store and presented the $5,700 check to the teller, Joanne Kochakian. Kochakian noticed that Michael had previously approved the $10,000 check. She called Michael and told her about Guarino's check. Michael instructed the cashier not to cash the check until she contacted the maker, Talcott, to obtain approval. Talcott approved cashing the $5,700 check. There was no discussion of the $10,000 check. Any Kind cashed the second check for Guarino, from which it deducted a 3 percent fee.

On January 19, Rivera called Talcott to warn him that Guarino was a cheat and a thief. Talcott immediately called his bank and stopped payment on the $5,700 check. Talcott's daughter called Any Kind and told it of the stop payment on the $5,700 check.

Any Kind filed suit against Guarino and Talcott, claiming that it was a holder in due course. Talcott's defense was that Any Kind was not a holder in due course. The trial court entered judgment for Any Kind for only the $5,700 check. The court found that the circumstances surrounding the cashing of the $10,000 check were suspicious and should have put Any Kind on notice of a problem.

DECISION: The events and circumstances were sufficient to put Any Kind on notice of potential defenses. The circumstances of a person describing himself as a broker, receiving funds in the amount of $10,000, and negotiating the check for those funds at a $500 discount were sufficient to put Any Kind on inquiry notice that some confirmation or explanation should be obtained.

Any Kind should have approached the $10,000 check with some caution and should have verified it with the maker if it wanted to preserve its holder-in-due-course status. Affirmed. [**Any Kind Checks Cashed, Inc. v Talcott, 830 So 2d 160 (Fla App 2002)**]

status does transfer to the heir. Furthermore, suppose that Avery is a holder in due course of a $5,000 promissory note due May 31, 2007. Avery gives the note to his nephew Aaron for Aaron's birthday on June 1, 2007. Aaron did not give value because the note was a gift, and he has taken the note as a holder after it has

ETHICS & THE LAW

The Corner Check Cashing Company and Good Faith

Some public policy experts have argued that no check cashing company, defined as one that takes a portion of the amount of the check as a fee for cashing checks for individuals who cannot get them cashed at banks and credit unions, should ever be allowed holder in due course status. Do you agree with this argument? Are check cashing companies ethical in their behavior?

already become due. Nonetheless, because Avery was a holder in due course, Aaron assumes that status under Article 3's shelter provision.

B DEFENSES TO PAYMENT OF A NEGOTIABLE INSTRUMENT

One of the key reasons for attaining holder-in-due-course status is to be able to obtain payment on the negotiable instrument free of any underlying problems between the original parties to the instrument. A holder in due course takes an instrument free from certain types of defenses to payment. Whether a defense may be raised against a holder in due course claiming under a negotiable instrument depends on the nature of the defense.

CPA   ### 4. CLASSIFICATION OF DEFENSES

The importance of being a holder in due course or a holder through a holder in due course is that such holders are not subject to certain defenses called *limited defenses.* Another class of defenses, *universal defenses,* may be asserted against any party, whether an assignee, an ordinary holder, a holder in due course, or a holder through a holder in due course.[15]

5. DEFENSES AGAINST ASSIGNEE OR ORDINARY HOLDER

Assignees of negotiable instruments are subject to every defense raised. Similarly, a holder who does not become a holder in due course is subject to every payment defense just as though the instrument were not negotiable.

6. LIMITED DEFENSES NOT AVAILABLE AGAINST A HOLDER IN DUE COURSE

Holders in due course are not subject to any of the following defenses.

CPA   (a) ORDINARY CONTRACT DEFENSES   In general terms, the defenses that could be raised in a breach of contract claim cannot be raised against a holder in due course.

---

[15] Under the pre-Code law and under the 1952 Code, the universal defense was called a *real defense,* and the limited defense was called a *personal defense.* These terms have now been abandoned, but some licensing and CPA examinations may continue to use these pre-Code terms.

The defenses of lack, failure, or illegality of consideration with respect to the instrument's underlying transaction cannot be asserted against the holder in due course. Misrepresentation about the goods underlying the contract is also not a defense. **For Example,** a businessperson cannot refuse to pay a holder in due course on the note used to pay for her copy machine just because her copy machine does not have the speed she was promised.

(b) INCAPACITY OF MAKER OR DRAWER   Ordinarily, the maker's or drawer's lack of capacity (except minors) may not be raised as a defense to payment to a holder in due course. Such incapacity is a defense, however, if the incapacity is at a legal level that makes the instrument a nullity. **For Example,** a promissory note made by an insane person for whom a court has appointed a guardian is void. In the case of a claim on the note by a holder in due course, the incapacity of the maker would be a defense.

CPA

fraud in the inducement
fraud that occurs when a person is persuaded or induced to execute an instrument because of fraudulent statements.

(c) FRAUD IN THE INDUCEMENT   If a person is persuaded or induced to execute the instrument because of fraudulent statements, such **fraud in the inducement** cannot be raised against a party with holder-in-due-course status. **For Example,** suppose Mills is persuaded to purchase an automobile because of Pagan's statements that the car was a demonstrator for the dealership and in good mechanical condition with a certification from the dealership's head mechanic. Mills, a car dealer, gives Pagan a note, which is negotiated until it reaches Han, who is a holder in due course. Mills meanwhile learns that the car has been in an accident and has a cracked engine block, that the head mechanic was paid to sign the certification, and that Pagan's statements were fraudulent. When Han demands payment of the note, Mills cannot refuse to pay on the ground of Pagan's fraud. Mills must pay the note because Han, as a holder in due course, does not take the note subject to any fraud or misrepresentation in the underlying transaction. Mills is left with the remedy of recovering from Pagan for misrepresentation or fraud.

(d) MISCELLANEOUS DEFENSES[16]   The limited defenses listed in the preceding three subsections are those most commonly raised against demands by holders in due course for payment. In addition, the following limited defenses may be asserted: (1) prior payment or cancellation of the instrument, (2) nondelivery, (3) conditional or special-purpose delivery, (4) breach of warranty, (5) duress consisting of threats, (6) unauthorized completion, and (7) theft of a bearer instrument. These defenses, however, have a very limited effect in terms of defending against a holder in due course's demand for payment.

universal defenses defenses that are regarded as so basic that the social interest in preserving them outweighs the social interest of giving negotiable instruments the freely transferable qualities of money; accordingly, such defenses are given universal effect and may be raised against all holders.

7. UNIVERSAL DEFENSES AVAILABLE AGAINST ALL HOLDERS

Certain defenses are regarded as so basic that the social interest in preserving them outweighs the social interest of giving negotiable instruments the freely transferable qualities of money. Accordingly, such defenses are given universal effect and may be raised against all holders, whether ordinary holders, holders in due course, or holders through a holder in due course. These defenses are called **universal defenses.**[17]

---

[16] Revised UCC § 3-305.

[17] In previous versions of the Code, the universal defenses were referred to as *real* defenses.

CPA **(a) Fraud as to the Nature or Essential Terms of the Instrument** The fact that a person signs an instrument because the person is fraudulently deceived as to its nature or essential terms is a defense available against all holders.[18] When one person induces another to sign a note by falsely representing that, for example, it is a contract for repairs or that it is a character reference, the note is invalid, and the defense of the misrepresentation of the character of the instrument can be used against a holder in due course. This defense, however, cannot be raised when the defending party was negligent in examining and questioning the true nature and terms of the instrument. **For Example,** suppose that two homeowners are asked to sign a statement for a salesperson that he was in their home and did a demonstration of a new solar water heater. Just as the homeowners are about to sign the verification statement, the salesman distracts them and then switches the verification for a purchase contract and promissory note for a $5,000 solar water heating system that the owners declined to purchase. The owners would have a defense of fraud in factum against a holder in due course of this note. The difference between fraud in the inducement—a personal defense—and fraud in factum—a real defense—is that fraud in factum involves deception as to the documents themselves, not as to the underlying goods, services, or property.

CPA **(b) Forgery or Lack of Authority** The defense that a signature was forged or signed without authority can be raised by a drawer or maker against any holder unless the drawer or maker whose name was signed has ratified it or is estopped by conduct or negligence from denying it.[19] The fact that the negligence of the drawer helped the wrongdoer does not prevent the drawee from raising the defense of forgery. (See Chapters 29 and 31 for more discussion of the impact of forgery on liability.)

(c) Duress Depriving Control A party may execute or indorse a negotiable instrument in response to a force of such a nature that, under general principles of law, duress makes the transaction void rather than merely voidable. Duress of this type and level may be raised as a defense against any holder. Economic duress, in the form of a reluctance to enter into a financially demanding instrument, is not a universal defense.[20] Duress that is attempted murder is a universal defense.

(d) Incapacity The fact that the defendant is a minor who under general principles of contract law may avoid the obligation is a matter that may be raised against any kind of holder. Other kinds of incapacity may be raised as a defense if the effect of the incapacity is to make the instrument void, as when there has been a formal declaration of insanity.[21]

---

[18] Revised UCC § 3-305(a)(1)(iii).

[19] *Bank of Hoven v Rausch,* 382 NW2d 39 (SD 1986); for general discussion of estoppel and ratification, see *Ziegler Furniture and Funeral Home, Inc. v Cicmanec,* 709 NW2d 350, 2006 (SD 2006).

[20] *Miller v Calhoun/Johnson Co.,* 497 SE2d 397 (Ga App 1998); *Smith v Gordon, 598* SE2d 92 (Ga App 2004).

[21] Revised UCC § 3-305(a)(1)(ii).

(e) ILLEGALITY   If an instrument is void by law when executed in connection with certain conduct, such as a note for gambling or one that involves usury, such defenses may be raised against any holder.

alteration unauthorized change or completion of a negotiable instrument designed to modify the obligation of a party to the instrument.

(f) ALTERATION   An **alteration** is an unauthorized change or completion of a negotiable instrument designed to modify the obligation of a party to the instrument.[22] **For Example,** changing the amount of an instrument from $150 to $450 is an alteration.[23]

(1) Person Making Alteration.   By definition, an alteration is a change made by a party to the instrument. A change of the instrument made by a nonparty has no effect. Recovery on the instrument is still possible under the terms of the instrument as though the change had not been made, provided it can be proven how the instrument existed in its original form.

(2) Effect of Alteration.   If the alteration to the instrument was made fraudulently, the person whose obligations under the instrument are affected by that alteration is discharged from liability on the instrument. The instrument, however, can be enforced according to its original terms or its terms as completed. This right of enforcement is given to holders in due course who had no notice of such alteration.[24] While a holder in due course would come within the protected class on alteration, such status is not required for this recovery provision in the event of alteration. **For Example,** Ryan signed a negotiable demand note for $100 made payable to Long. A subsequent holder changed the amount from $100 to $700. A later holder in due course presented the note to Ryan for payment. Ryan would still be liable for the original amount of $100.

A summary of the universal and limited defenses is presented in Figure 30-2.

8. DENIAL OF HOLDER-IN-DUE-COURSE PROTECTION

In certain situations, the taker of a negotiable instrument is denied the status of a holder in due course or is denied the protection of a holder in due course.

(a) PARTICIPATING TRANSFEREE   The seller of goods on credit frequently assigns the sales contract and buyer's promissory note to the manufacturer who made the goods, to a finance company, or to a bank. In such a case, the assignee of the seller will be a holder in due course of the buyer's note if the note is properly negotiated and the transferee satisfies all of the elements of being a holder in due course. The transferee, however, may take such an active part in the sale to the seller's customer or may be so related to the seller that it is possible to conclude that the transferee was in fact a party to the original transaction. This close-connection doctrine (discussed earlier in this chapter as an issue in the good-faith requirement for

---

[22] Revised UCC § 3-407(a); *Stahl v St. Elizabeth Medical Center*, 948 SW2d 419 (Ky App 1997). A material alteration made based on the parties' negotiations (a 13 percent versus an 18 percent interest rate) is not fraudulent. *Darnall v Petersen*, 592 NW2d 505 (Neb App 1999); *Knoefler v Wojtalewicz*, 2003 WL 21496933 (Neb App 2003) (difference between bank interest rate and judgment interest rate is not material).

[23] However, if an instrument, such as a note, has been altered and the maker continues to pay without objection to the alteration, the alteration does not discharge the maker's liability. *Stahl v St. Elizabeth Medical Center*, 948 SW2d 419 (Ky App 1997); again, for a general discussion of continuing payment as estoppel, see *Ziegler Furniture and Funeral Home, Inc. v Cicmanec*, 709 NW2d 350, 2006 (SD 2006).

[24] Revised UCC § 3-407(b), (c).

FIGURE 30-2	*Defenses to Payment of Negotiable Instrument*

UNIVERSAL (AVAILABLE AGAINST ASSIGNEES, HOLDERS, AND HOLDERS IN DUE COURSE) (REAL)	LIMITED (AVAILABLE AGAINST ASSIGNEES AND HOLDERS BUT NOT AGAINST HOLDERS IN DUE COURSE) (PERSONAL)	MIXED (CIRCUMSTANCES VARY THE AVAILABILITY OF THESE DEFENSES)
FRAUD AS TO THE NATURE OF THE INSTRUMENT (FRAUD IN FACTUM)	FRAUD IN THE INDUCEMENT	DURESS
	MISREPRESENTATION	INCAPACITY
FORGERY	LACK OF CONSIDERATION	
UNAUTHORIZED SIGNATURE	BREACH OF WARRANTY	
INCAPACITY (DECLARATION)	CANCELLATION	
ILLEGALITY	FAILURE OF DELIVERY	
ALTERATION	UNAUTHORIZED COMPLETION	
CONSUMER CREDIT CONTRACTS WITH FTC NOTICE	ALL ORDINARY CONTRACT DEFENSES	

becoming a holder in due course) prevents a transferee with intimate knowledge of the transferor's business practices from becoming a holder in due course.[25]

(b) THE FEDERAL TRADE COMMISSION RULE In 1976, the Federal Trade Commission (FTC) adopted a rule that limits the rights of a holder in due course in a consumer credit transaction. The rule protects consumers who purchase goods or services for personal, family, or household use on credit.[26] When the note the buyer gave the seller as payment for the consumer goods is transferred to even a holder in due course, the consumer buyer may raise any defense that could have been raised against the seller. The FTC regulation requires that the following notice be included in boldface type at least 10 points in size in consumer credit contracts covered under the rule:

Notice
Any holder of this consumer credit contract is subject to all claims and defenses which the debtor could assert against the seller of goods or services obtained with the proceeds hereof. Recovery hereunder by the debtor shall not exceed amounts paid by the debtor hereunder.[27]

---

[25] *Midfirst Bank v C. W. Haynes & Co.*, 893 F Supp 1304 (DSC 1994), aff'd 87 F3d 1308 (4th Cir 1998); *AIG Global Securities Lending Corp. v Banc of America Securities LLC Slip Copy*, 2006 WL 1206333 (SDNY 2006).

[26] The regulation does not cover purchases of real estate, securities, or consumer goods or services for which the purchase price is more than $25,000. *Roosevelt Federal Savings & Loan Ass'n v Crider*, 722 SW2d 325 (Mo App 1986).

[27] One of the controversial changes to Article 3 is found in subsections 3-305(e) and (f). This change provides that if the Federal Trade Commission requires a notice to be included, but it is not, the instrument is deemed to have included it implicitly.

THINKING THINGS THROUGH

The Corner Check-Cashing Company and Thieves—Who Wins?

Now is an ideal time to bring together all of the concepts you have learned in Chapters 27, 28, and 29. Analyzing this problem will help you integrate your knowledge about negotiable instruments. Sid's Salmon has purchased salmon from Fred's Fisheries. Sid wrote a check for $22,000 to Fred's. A thief broke into Fred's offices and took the cash on hand as well as the unindorsed check from Sid's. The thief took the check to the Corner Check Cashing Company (CCCC) and received $22,000

less the cashing fee of $2,000. Fred notified Sid who then notified First Commerce Bank, the drawee of the check of the theft. CCCC has presented the check for payment, and First Commerce refuses to pay. CCCC says it is a holder in due course. Are you able to help First Commerce Bank develop its response to CCCC?

Suppose that Fred had already indorsed the check when the thief stole it. Would CCCC be a holder in due course?

When a notice preserving consumer defenses is included in a negotiable instrument, no subsequent person can be a holder in due course of the instrument.[28]

 ## LIABILITY ISSUES: HOW PAYMENT RIGHTS ARISE AND DEFENSES ARE USED

In this chapter and in Chapters 28 and 29, issues surrounding the types of instruments, transfers, holders, and holders in due course have been covered. However, there are procedures under Article 3 for bringing together all of the parties, instruments, and defenses so that ultimate liability and, hopefully, payment can be determined and achieved.

 9. THE ROLES OF PARTIES AND LIABILITY

primary party party to whom the holder or holder in due course must turn first to obtain payment.

maker party who writes or creates a promissory note.

drawee person to whom the draft is addressed and who is ordered to pay the amount of money specified in the draft.

Every instrument has primary and secondary parties. The **primary party** is the party to whom the holder or holder in due course must turn first to obtain payment. The primary party on a note or certificate of deposit is the **maker.** The primary party on a draft is the **drawee,** assuming that the drawee has accepted the draft. Although a check must first be presented to the drawee bank for payment, the bank is not primarily liable on the instrument because the bank has the right to refuse to pay the check (see following and Chapter 31). The drawee bank on a check is the party to whom a holder or holder in due course turns first for payment despite the lack of primary-party status on the part of that drawee bank. The maker of a note is the party to whom holders and holders in due course must turn first for payment.

---

[28] Revised UCC § 3-106(d). This goes beyond the scope of the FTC regulation. The latter merely preserves the defenses of the consumer but does not bar holder-in-due-course protection for other parties, such as an accommodation party to a consumer's note. Also, the FTC regulation does not change the common law and permits the maker to bring contract actions against the holder of the note for contract breaches committed by the maker's original contract party. The rule changes the status of the parties as holders in due course. It does not change contract rights. *LaBarre v Credit Acceptance Corp.,* 11 F Supp 2d 1071 (D Minn 1998); aff'd in part, reversed in part, 175 F3d 640 (8th Cir 1999).

secondary parties called *secondary obligors* under Revised Article 3; parties to an instrument to whom holders turn when the primary party, for whatever reason, fails to pay the instrument. `CPA`

indorser secondary party (or obligor) on a note.

drawer person who writes out and creates a draft or bill of exchange, including a check.

presentment formal request for payment on an instrument.

dishonor status when the primary party refuses to pay the instrument according to its terms.

notice of dishonor notice that an instrument has been dishonored; such notice can `CPA` be oral, written, or electronic but is subject to time limitations.

The **secondary parties** (or *secondary obligors,* as they are now called under Revised Article 3) to an instrument are those to whom holders turn when the primary party, for whatever reason, fails to pay the instrument. Secondary parties on notes are **indorsers**, and secondary parties on checks and drafts are **drawers** and *indorsers.*

10. ATTACHING LIABILITY OF THE PRIMARY PARTIES: PRESENTMENT

Presentment occurs when the holder or holder in due course of an instrument orally, in writing, or by electronic communication to the primary party requests that the instrument be paid according to its terms. The primary party has the right to require that the presentment be made in a "commercially reasonable manner," which would include reasonable times for presentment, such as during business hours. The primary party can also require identification, authorization, and even a signature of receipt of the funds due under the instrument. In addition, the primary party can demand a valid indorsement on the instrument prior to making payment. Upon presentment, the primary party is required to pay according to the terms of the instrument unless there are defenses such as forgery, any of the other universal defenses for holders in due course, or any defenses for holders.

If the primary party refuses to pay the instrument according to its terms, there has been a *dishonor,* and the holder is then left to turn to the secondary parties.

11. DISHONOR AND NOTICE OF DISHONOR

Dishonor occurs when the primary party refuses to pay the instrument according to its terms. The primary party is required to give **notice of dishonor.** The notice that the

E-COMMERCE AND CYBERLAW

Electronic Presentment: One Fell Swoop

The presentment of checks has evolved from the formal presentation of an original document to electronic check conversion (ECC), which Wal-Mart and other retailers used as a system of payment prior to the availability of debit cards. Under ECC, the check was run through an electronic system that read the magnetic encoding on the check and the check was presented to the bank for payment at the point of sale. The UCC permitted such electronic presentment. Now presentment occurs entirely electronically, and the only paper the consumer has at the point of sale is the receipt. The account is debited automatically at the time the transaction occurs. Likewise, the notion of electronic presentment allows electronic dishonor. The debit is honored only if the account has sufficient funds that are available at the time of the transaction. Some of the UCC Article 3 provisions are now unnecessary in these types of transactions, and the rights of the merchants and the buyers are covered under various federal and state laws on electronic funds transfers (covered in Chapter 31). Issues continue to evolve, such as what laws govern the popular PayPal system so closely affiliated with the millions of consumer transactions on eBay. Electronic technology requires that we change laws and grow into the new systems for commercial transactions and payments.

instrument has been dishonored can be oral, written, or electronic. That notice is subject to time limitations. **For Example,** a bank must give notice of dishonor by midnight of the next banking day. Nonbank primary parties must give notice of dishonor within 30 days following their receipt of notice of dishonor. Returning the dishonored check is sufficient notice of dishonor. (See Chapter 31 for more discussion of liability issues on dishonor of checks.) Upon dishonor, the holder must then turn to the secondary parties for payment.

limited defenses defenses available to secondary parties if the presenting party is a holder in due course.

The obligation of the secondary parties in these situations is to pay according to the terms of the instrument. These secondary parties will have **limited defenses** if the presenting party is a holder in due course. **For Example,** suppose that a check drawn on First Interstate Bank is written by Ben Paltrow to Julia Sutherland as payment for Julia's Bentley auto that Ben purchased. Julia deposits Ben's check into her account at AmeriBank, and AmeriBank sends the check to First Interstate to present it for payment. First Interstate finds that Ben's account has insufficient funds and dishonors the check. AmeriBank must notify First Interstate by midnight of the next banking day that the check has been dishonored, and then First Interstate must notify Julia by midnight of the next banking day that Ben's check was dishonored. Julia then has 30 days to notify Ben and turn to him as a drawer, or secondary party, for payment on the check.

> SUMMARY

A holder of a negotiable instrument can be either an ordinary holder or a holder in due course. The ordinary holder has the same rights that an assignee would have. Holders in due course and holders through a holder in due course are protected from certain defenses. To be a holder in due course, a person must first be a holder—that is, the person must have acquired the instrument by a proper negotiation. The holder must then also take for value, in good faith, without notice that the paper is overdue or dishonored, and without notice of defenses and adverse claims. Those persons who become holders of the instrument after a holder in due course are given the same protection as the holder in due course through the shelter provision, provided they are not parties to any fraud or illegality affecting the instrument.

The importance of being a holder in due course or a holder through a holder in due course is that those holders are not subject to certain defenses when they demand payment or bring suit on the instrument. These defenses are limited defenses and include ordinary contract defenses, incapacity unless it makes the instrument void, fraud in the inducement, prior payment or cancellation, nondelivery of an instrument, conditional delivery, duress consisting of threats, unauthorized completion, and theft of a bearer instrument. Universal defenses may be asserted against any plaintiff whether that party is an assignee, an ordinary holder, a holder in due course, or a holder through a holder in due course. Universal defenses include fraud as to the nature or essential terms of the paper, forgery or lack of authority, duress depriving control, incapacity, illegality that makes the instrument void, and alteration. Alteration is only a partial defense; the favored holder may enforce the instrument according to its original terms.

The Federal Trade Commission rule on consumer credit contracts limits the immunity of a holder in due course from defenses of consumer buyers against their sellers. Immunity is limited in consumer credit transactions if the notice specified by the FTC regulation is included in the sales contract. When a notice preserving consumer defenses is stated in a negotiable instrument, no subsequent person can be a holder in due course.

Holders and holders in due course are required to present instruments for payment to primary parties. Primary parties are makers and drawees. If the primary party refuses to pay, or dishonors, the instrument, it must give notice of dishonor in a timely fashion. The holder can then turn to secondary parties, drawers, and indorsers (secondary obligors) for payment.

> QUESTIONS AND CASE PROBLEMS

1. Randy Bocian had a bank account with First of America-Bank (FAB). On October 8, Bocian received a check for $28,800 from Eric Christenson as payment for constructing a pole barn on Christenson's property. Bocian deposited the check at FAB on October 9 and was permitted to draw on the funds through October 12. Bocian wrote checks totaling $12,334.21, which FAB cleared. On October 12, Christenson stopped payment on the check as the result of a contract dispute over the pole barn. Bocian's account was then overdrawn once the check was denied clearance by Christenson's bank. FAB brought suit against both Bocian and Christenson to collect its loss. Christenson counterclaimed against Bocian for his contract breach claims on the pole barn construction. FAB maintained that it had given value and was a holder in due course and that, as such, it was not required to be subject to the pole barn issues or the stop payment order. Is FAB right? [*First of America-Bank Northeast Illinois v Bocian,* 614 NE2d 890 (Ill App)]

2. Cronin, an employee of Epicycle, cashed his final paycheck at Money Mart Check Cashing Center. Epicycle had issued a stop payment order on the check. Money Mart deposited the check through normal banking channels. The check was returned to Money Mart marked "Payment Stopped." Money Mart brought an action against Epicycle, claiming that, as a holder in due course, it was entitled to recover against Epicycle. Epicycle argued that Money Mart could not be a holder in due course because it failed to verify the check as good prior to cashing it. Is Money Mart a holder in due course? [*Money Mart Check Cashing Center, Inc. v Epicycle Corp.,* 667 P2d 1372 (Colo)]

3. Halleck executed a promissory note payable to the order of Leopold. Halleck did not pay the note when due, and Leopold brought suit on the note, producing it in court. Halleck admitted that he had signed the note but claimed plaintiff Leopold was required to prove that the note had been issued for consideration and that the plaintiff was in fact the holder. Are these elements of proof required as part of the case? [*Leopold v Halleck,* 436 NE2d 29 (Ill App)]

4. Calhoun/Johnson Company d/b/a Williams Lumber Company (Williams) sold building materials to Donald Miller d/b/a Millercraft Construction Company (Millercraft) on credit. Miller had signed a personal guaranty for the materials. Miller requested lien waivers from Williams for four of his projects and asked for them from Fabian Boudreau, Williams's credit manager. Fabian refused to grant the waivers because Miller was $28,000 delinquent on his account. Miller agreed to bring his account current with the exception of $11,000 for which he signed a no-interest promissory note. Miller obtained the lien waivers and then defaulted on the note. Williams brought suit for payment, and Williams said there was lack of consideration and that the note was not valid. He said he must give value to be able to recover on the note. Was he correct? [*Miller v Calhoun/Johnson Co.,* 497 SE2d 397 (Ga App)]

5. Statham drew a check. The payee indorsed it to Kemp Motor Sales. Statham then stopped payment on the check on the grounds that there was a failure of consideration for the check. Kemp sued Statham on the check. When Statham raised the defense of failure of consideration, Kemp replied that he was a holder in due course. Statham claimed that Kemp could not recover because Statham learned of his defense before Kemp deposited the check in its bank account. Discuss the parties' arguments and rights in this situation. [*Kemp Motor Sales v Statham,* 171 SE2d 389 (Ga App)]

6. Can check cashing companies be holders in due course? What arguments can you make for and against their holder-in-due-course status? [*Dal-Tile Corp. v Cash N' Go,* 487 SE2d 529 (Ga App)]

7. Jones, wishing to retire from a business enterprise that he had been conducting for a number of years, sold all of the assets of the business to Jackson Corp. Included in the assets were a number of promissory notes payable to the order of Jones that he had taken from his customers. Upon the maturity of one of the notes, the maker refused to pay because there was a failure of consideration. Jackson Corp. sued the maker of the note. Who should succeed? Explain.

8. Elliot, an officer of Impact Marketing, drew six postdated checks on Impact's account. The checks were payable to Bell for legal services to be subsequently performed for Impact. Financial Associates purchased them from Bell and collected on four of the checks. Payment was stopped on the last two when Bell's services were terminated. Financial argued that it was a holder in due course and had the right to collect on the checks. Impact claimed that because the checks were postdated and issued for an executory promise, Financial could not be a holder in due course. Who was correct? Why? [*Financial Associates v Impact Marketing*, 394 NYS2d 814 (Misc)]

9. *D* drew a check to the order of *P*. *P* took the check postdated. *P* knew that *D* was having financial difficulties and that the particular checking account on which this check was drawn had been frequently overdrawn. Do these circumstances prevent *P* from being a holder in due course? [*Citizens Bank, Booneville v National Bank of Commerce*, 334 F2d 257 (10th Cir); *Franklin National Bank v Sidney Gotowner*, 4 UCC Rep Serv 953 (NY Supp)]

10. Daniel, Joel, and Claire Guerrette are the adult children of Elden Guerrette, who died on September 24, 1995. Before his death, Elden purchased a life insurance policy from Sun Life Assurance Company of Canada through a Sun Life agent, Steven Hall, and named his children as his beneficiaries. Upon his death, Sun Life issued three checks, each in the amount of $40,759.35, to each of Elden's children. The checks were drawn on Sun Life's account at Chase Manhattan Bank in Syracuse, New York. The checks were given to Hall for delivery to the Guerrettes. Hall and an associate, Paul Richard, then fraudulently induced the Guerrettes to indorse the checks in blank and to transfer them to Hall and Richard, purportedly to be invested in HER, Inc., a corporation formed by Hall and Richard. Hall took the checks from the Guerrettes and turned them over to Richard, who deposited them in his account at the Credit Union on October 26, 1995. The Credit Union immediately made the funds available to Richard.

The Guerrettes quickly regretted having negotiated their checks to Hall and Richard, and they contacted Sun Life the next day to request that Sun Life stop payment on the checks. Sun Life immediately ordered Chase Manhattan to stop payment on the checks. When the checks were ultimately presented to Chase Manhattan for payment, Chase refused to pay the checks, and they were returned to the Credit Union. The Credit Union received notice that the checks had been dishonored on November 3, 1995, the sixth business day following their deposit. By the time the Credit Union received notice, however, Richard had withdrawn from his account all of the funds represented by the three checks. The Credit Union was able to recover almost $80,000 from Richard, but there remained an unpaid balance of $42,366.56.

The Credit Union filed suit against Sun Life, and all of the parties became engulfed in litigation. The Credit Union indicated it was a holder in due course and was entitled to payment on the instrument. Sun Life alleged fraud. Is the Credit Union a holder in due course? Can the parties allege the fraud defense against it? [*Maine Family Federal Credit Union v Sun Life Assur. Co. of Canada*, 727 A2d 335 (Me)]

11. A bank customer purchased a bank money order and paid for it with a forged check. The money order was negotiable and was acquired by *N*, who was a holder in due course. When *N* sued the bank on the money order, the bank raised the defense that its customer had paid with a bad check. Could this defense be raised against *N*? Why or why not? [*Bank of Niles v American State Bank*, 303 NE2d 186 (Ill App)]

12. Sanders gave Clary a check but left the amount incomplete. The check was given as advance payment on the purchase of 100 LT speakers. The amount was left blank because Clary had the right to substitute other LT speakers if they became available and the substitution would change the price. It was agreed that in no event would the purchase price exceed $5,000. Desperate for cash, Clary wrongfully substituted much more expensive LT speakers, thereby increasing the price to $5,700. Clary then negotiated the check to Lawrence, one of his

suppliers. Clary filled in the $5,700 in Lawrence's presence, showing him the shipping order and the invoice applicable to the sale to Sanders. Lawrence accepted the check in payment of $5,000 worth of overdue debts and $700 in cash. Can Lawrence recover the full amount? Why or why not?

13. GRAS is a Michigan corporation engaged in the business of buying and selling cars. Between 1997 and 2000, Katrina Stewart was employed as a manager by GRAS. During that period, Stewart wrote checks, without authority, on GRAS's corporate account payable to MBNA and sent them to MBNA for payment of her husband's MBNA credit card account. MBNA accepted the checks and credited the proceeds to Stewart's husband's credit card debt. MBNA accepted and processed the GRAS checks in its normal manner through electronic processing. When MBNA receives a check for a credit card payment, the envelope containing the check and the payment slip is opened by machine and the check and the payment slip are electronically processed and credited to the cardholder's account balance. MBNA does not normally review checks for credit card payments. After crediting a payment check to the card holder's account, MBNA transfers it to the bank on which it is written for collection. Pursuant to its standard practice, MBNA did not review the checks it received from Stewart. GRAS did not have a customer relationship with MBNA during the relevant time period.

GRAS sought a refund of the amounts Stewart embezzled via the MBNA application of the checks to Stewart's husband's credit card account. MBNA said it was a holder in due course. Was MBNA a holder in due course? Was MBNA subject to GRAS's defense of unauthorized instruments? [*Grand Rapids Auto Sales, Inc. v MBNA America Bank,* 227 F Supp 2d 721 (WD Mich)]

14. Shade asked Dow to give him a check for $100 in return for Shade's delivery the next day of a television set. Dow gave the check, but Shade never delivered the television set. Does Dow have a defense if sued on the instrument (a) by Shade; (b) by Shade's brother, to whom Shade gave the unindorsed check as a gift; and (c) by a grocer to whom Shade's brother gave the instrument for value in the ordinary course of business the next day? (The grocer took the check without knowledge of the defense and while acting in good faith.) Explain your answers.

15. Dorsey was negligent in not determining that the paper he was signing was actually a promissory note. The note was negotiated by proper indorsement and delivery to New Jersey Mortgage & Investment Co., a holder in due course. Dorsey refused to pay, alleging fraud in the nature of essential terms. Decide. [*New Jersey Mortgage & Investment Co. v Dorsey,* 165 A2d 297 (NJ)]

> CPA QUESTIONS

1. Under the Commercial Paper Article of the UCC, which of the following requirements must be met for a person to be a holder in due course of a promissory note?

   a. The note must be payable to bearer.
   b. The note must be negotiable.
   c. All prior holders must have been holders in due course.
   d. The holder must be the payee of the note.

2. A maker of a note will have a real defense against a holder in due course as a result of any of the following conditions except

   a. Discharge in bankruptcy
   b. Forgery
   c. Fraud in the execution
   d. Lack of consideration

3. Under the commercial paper article of the UCC, in a nonconsumer transaction, which of the following are real (universal) defenses available against a holder in due course?

	Material Alteration	Discharge in Bankruptcy	Breach of Contract
a.	No	Yes	Yes
b.	Yes	Yes	No
c.	No	No	Yes
d.	Yes	No	No

4. A holder in due course will take free of which of the following defenses?

   a. Infancy, to the extent that it is a defense to a simple contract
   b. Discharge of the maker in bankruptcy
   c. A wrongful filling-in of the amount payable that was omitted from the instrument
   d. Duress of a nature that renders the obligation of the party a nullity

5. Mask stole one of Bloom's checks. The check was already signed by Bloom and made payable to Duval. The check was drawn on United Trust Company. Mask forged Duval's signature on the back of the check at the Corner Check Cashing Company, which in turn deposited it with its bank, Town National Bank of Toka. Town National proceeded to collect on the check from United. None of the parties mentioned were negligent. Who will bear the loss, assuming the amount cannot be recovered from Mask?

   a. Bloom
   b. Duval
   c. United Trust Company
   d. Corner Check Cashing Company

6. Robb stole one of Markum's blank checks, made it payable to himself, and forged Markum's signature to it. The check was drawn on the Unity Trust Company. Robb cashed the check at the Friendly Check Cashing Company, which in turn deposited it with its bank, Farmer's National. Farmer's National proceeded to collect on the check from Unity Trust. The theft and forgery were quickly discovered by Markum, who promptly notified Unity. None of the parties mentioned were negligent. Who will bear the loss, assuming the amount cannot be recovered from Robb?

   a. Markum
   b. Unity Trust Company
   c. Friendly Check Cashing Company
   d. Farmer's National

CHECKS AND FUNDS TRANSFERS

(A) CHECKS

1. NATURE OF A CHECK
2. CERTIFIED CHECKS
3. PRESENTMENT FOR OBTAINING PAYMENT ON A CHECK
4. DISHONOR OF A CHECK
5. THE CUSTOMER-BANK RELATIONSHIP
6. STOPPING PAYMENT OF A CHECK
7. WRONGFUL DISHONOR OF A CHECK
8. AGENCY STATUS OF COLLECTING BANK
9. BANK'S DUTY OF CARE

(B) LIABILITY OF A BANK

10. PREMATURE PAYMENT OF A POSTDATED CHECK
11. PAYMENT OVER A STOP PAYMENT ORDER
12. PAYMENT ON A FORGED SIGNATURE OF DRAWER
13. PAYMENT ON A FORGED OR MISSING INDORSEMENT
14. ALTERATION OF A CHECK
15. UNAUTHORIZED COLLECTION OF A CHECK
16. TIME LIMITATIONS

(C) CONSUMER FUNDS TRANSFERS

17. ELECTRONIC FUNDS TRANSFER ACT
18. TYPES OF ELECTRONIC FUNDS TRANSFER SYSTEMS
19. CONSUMER LIABILITY

(D) FUNDS TRANSFERS

20. WHAT LAW GOVERNS?
21. CHARACTERISTICS OF FUNDS TRANSFERS
22. PATTERN OF FUNDS TRANSFERS
23. SCOPE OF UCC ARTICLE 4A
24. DEFINITIONS
25. FORM OF PAYMENT ORDER
26. MANNER OF TRANSMITTING PAYMENT ORDER

27. SECURITY PROCEDURE
28. REGULATION BY AGREEMENT AND FUNDS
      TRANSFER SYSTEM RULES
29. ACCEPTANCE OF PAYMENT ORDER
30. REIMBURSEMENT OF THE BANK
31. REFUND ON NONCOMPLETION OF TRANSFER
32. ERROR IN FUNDS TRANSFER
33. LIABILITY FOR LOSS

LEARNING OBJECTIVES

After studying this chapter, you should be able to

LO.1 Discuss the significance of certification

LO.2 List and explain the duties of the drawee bank

LO.3 Explain the methods for, and legal effect of, stopping payment

LO.4 State when a check must be presented for payment to charge secondary parties

LO.5 Describe the liability of a bank for improper payment and collection

LO.6 Discuss the legal effect of forgeries and material alterations

LO.7 Specify the time limitations for reporting forgeries and alterations

LO.8 Describe the electronic transfer of funds and laws governing it

The three previous chapters have focused on the characteristics, parties, and transfer of all negotiable instruments. This chapter covers checks as negotiable instruments, the issues related to their transfer and payment because of the involvement of banks, and special rules applicable to banks as drawees. New technology has also enhanced the ability of banks and consumers to make rapid commercial transactions through the use of electronic funds transfers. Special rules and rights have been developed to govern these forms of payment that serve to facilitate everything from a consumer's withdrawing money from an automated teller machine to a buyer's wiring money to a seller whose business is located continents away.

 CHECKS

check order by a depositor on a bank to pay a sum of money to a payee; a bill of exchange drawn on a bank and payable on demand.

As discussed in Chapter 28, a **check** is a draft payable on demand that is drawn on a bank. Uniform Commercial Code (UCC) § 3-104(f) defines a check as "(i) a draft . . . payable on demand and drawn on a bank or (ii) a cashier's check or teller's check. An instrument may be a check even though it is described on its face by another term, such as 'money order.'"[1] Under Revised Article 4, the change in consumer payment patterns away from formal, signed checks is reflected with the addition of "remotely-created consumer item," which are items directing payment that are drawn on a consumer account but do not carry a handwritten signature of the drawer.[2] These

---

[1] Revised UCC § 3-104(f).
[2] Revised UCC § 3-104(16).

FIGURE 31-1	*Differences between a Check and a Draft*

Check	Draft
1. Drawee is always a bank.	1. Drawee is not necessarily a bank.
2. Check is drawn on assumption money is in bank to cover check.	2. No assumption drawee has any of drawer's money to pay instrument.
3. Check is payable on demand.	3. Draft may be payable on demand or at future date.
4. Drawee bank only accepts check through certification.	4. Acceptance is required for liability of drawee.

types of payments include PayPal authorizations to pay from consumer checking accounts and automatic bill payments that consumers direct remotely.

Consumer account is defined as a bank account used for household, family, or personal purposes.[3]

The distinguishing characteristics of checks[4] and drafts are summarized in Figure 31-1.

1. NATURE OF A CHECK

(a) SUFFICIENT FUNDS ON DEPOSIT   As a practical matter, a check is drawn on the assumption that the bank has on deposit in the drawer's account an amount sufficient to pay the check. In the case of other drafts, there is no assumption that the drawee has any of the drawer's money with which to pay the instrument. In international transactions, sellers may require buyers not only to accept a draft agreeing to pay but also to back up that draft with a line of credit from the buyer's bank. That line of credit is the backup should the funds for the draft not be forthcoming from the buyer.

If a draft is dishonored, the drawer is civilly liable. If a check is drawn with intent to defraud the person to whom it is delivered, the drawer is also subject to criminal prosecution in most states. The laws under which such drawers are prosecuted are known as **bad check laws.** Most states provide that if the check is not made good within a stated period, such as 10 days, there is a presumption that the drawer originally issued the check with the intent to defraud.

bad check laws laws making it a criminal offense to issue a bad check with intent to defraud.

---

[3] Revised UCC § 3-104(2).

[4] Checks are governed by both Article 3 of the UCC and Article 4 governing bank deposits and collections. The 2001 and 2002 versions of Article 4 are covered in this chapter, along with notations of the changes since the 1990 version. The new versions of Article 4 incorporate provisions in the American Bankers Association Bank Collection Code, enacted in 18 states, and followed in many other states. The purpose of the code was to introduce clarity into the processing of millions of electronic and paper transactions that banks must handle and to recognize the reality of electronic payments. The following states have adopted some of the 2001 version of Article 4 (including the definition changes in Article 1 of the UCC: Alabama, Arkansas, Connecticut, Delaware, Hawaii, Idaho, Minnesota, Montana, Nebraska, Nevada, New Mexico, Oklahoma, Texas, Virgin Islands, and Virginia. The following jurisdictions have adopted the 2002 amendments conforming to Revised Article 3 of the Code: Arkansas has adopted some portions; Minnesota with variations; Nevada with variations; and Texas with variations. There are significant state variations in the Articles 3 and 4 adoptions.

demand draft draft that is payable upon presentment.

postdate to insert or place on an instrument a later date than the actual date on which it was executed.

time draft bill of exchange payable at a stated time after sight or at a definite time.

(b) DEMAND PAPER A draft may be payable either on demand or at a future date. A check is a form of **demand draft.** The standard form of check does not specify when it is payable, and it is therefore automatically payable on demand.

One exception arises when a check is **postdated**—that is, when the check shows a date later than the actual date of execution. Postdating a check means that the check is not payable until the date arrives, and it changes the check from a demand draft to a **time draft.**[5] However, banks are not obligated to hold a postdated check until the time used on the check unless the drawer has filed the appropriate paperwork with the bank for such a delay. Because of electronic processing, banks are not required to examine each instrument and honor postdated instrument requests unless the hold is placed into the bank's processing system by the customer.

(c) FORM OF THE CHECK A check can be in any form of writing.[6] However, a bank customer may agree, as part of the contract with her bank, to use certain forms for check writing. A remotely created consumer item need only be evidenced by a *record,* not by a written document. Under Revised UCC § 3-104(a)(14), a *record* is defined as "information that is inscribed on a tangible medium or which is stored in an electronic or other medium and is retrievable in perceivable form."[7]

(d) DELIVERY NOT ASSIGNMENT The delivery of a check is not an assignment of the money on deposit, so it does not automatically transfer the rights of the depositor against the bank to the holder of the check. A check written by a drawer on his drawee bank does not result in a duty on the part of the drawee bank to the holder to pay the holder the amount of the check.[8] An ordinary check drawn on a customer's account is direction from a customer to the bank for payment, but it does not impose absolute primary liability on the bank at the time the check is written.

money order draft issued by a bank or a nonbank.

cashier's check draft drawn by a bank on itself.

teller's check draft drawn by a bank on another bank in which it has an account.

substitute check electronic image of a paper check that a bank can create and that has the same legal effect as the original instrument.

Banks assume more responsibility for some types of checks than for the ordinary customer's check. **For Example,** a bank **money order** payable to John Jones is a check and has the bank as both the drawer and the drawee.[9] UCC § 3-104(g) defines a cashier's check as "a draft with respect to which the drawer and drawee are the same bank or branches of the same bank."[10] In other words, a **cashier's check** is a check or draft drawn by a bank again on itself. If a cashier's check is drawn on another bank in which the drawer bank has an account, it is a **teller's check.** Although the drawer and drawee may be the same on a money order or a cashier's check, the instrument does not lose its three-party character or its status as a check.

Under new federal laws that Revised Article 4 recognizes, there is the new term **substitute check,** which is an electronic image or paper printout of an electronic image of a check. A substitute check has the same legal effect as a paper check. The bank that converts the paper check into electronic form, called

---

[5] *In re Channel Home Centers, Inc.,* 989 F2d 682 (3d Cir 1993), cert. denied, 510 U.S. 865 (1993). A bank is required to comply with a postdate on a check only if it is notified of the postdate in the same way the customer issues a stop payment order.

[6] Although not required for negotiation or presentment, a printed bank check, when the customer is using a written form, is preferable because it generally carries magnetic ink figures that facilitate sorting and posting.

[7] Revised UCC § 3-104(a)(14).

[8] *Roy Supply, Inc. v Wells Fargo Bank,* 46 Cal Rptr 2d 309 (1995); distinguished in an unpublished opinion, *Citibank v Shen,* 2003 WL 253962 (Cal App 2003).

[9] Revised UCC § 3-104(f) (2002).

[10] Revised UCC § 3-104(g).

E-COMMERCE AND CYBERLAW

A Pay Card in Lieu of a Paycheck

Some employees are using a new device known as the *payroll card*. Rather than issuing checks and running the risk of fictitious payees and other payroll scandals, employees are simply given a card that allows them access to their pay by using a personal identification number at the bank designated by the employer. The benefits of the system are that it is subject to greater controls and easier audits. The downside is that no one is quite sure how to handle the transactions under the law. Are they consumer electronic funds transfers? Are they governed by federal law, or would they be taken care of under state law and UCC provisions on electronic or substitute checks? The law once again has not quite caught up with the new means we have developed for commercial transactions.

the *reconverting bank*, has certain duties imposed by federal regulations to be certain that the electronic version or substitute check has all of the necessary legal information such as visible indorsements, magnetic bank code strip, payee, and signature of drawer.

2. CERTIFIED CHECKS

The drawee bank may *certify* or accept a check drawn on it. Under UCC § 3-409(d), a certified check is "a check accepted by the bank on which it is drawn."[11] While a bank is under no obligation to certify a check, if it does so, the certification has the effect of the bank accepting primary liability on the instrument. Check certification requires that the actual certification be written on the check and authenticated by the signature of an authorized representative of the bank.[12] Upon certification, the bank must set aside, in a special account maintained by the bank, the amount of the certified check taken from the drawer's account. The certification is a promise by the bank that when the check is presented for payment, the bank will make payment according to the terms of the check. Payment is made regardless of the status of the drawer's account at that time.

A holder or drawer may request that a check be certified by a bank. When certification is at the request of the holder, all prior indorsers and the drawer are released from liability. When certification is at the request of the drawer, the indorsers and drawer, as secondary parties, are not released. Unless otherwise agreed, the delivery of a certified check, a cashier's check, or a teller's check discharges the debt for which the check is given, up to the amount of that check.[13]

---

[11] Revised UCC § 3-409(d).

[12] Many courts treat cashier's checks and certified checks as the same because of their uniform commercial acceptability. See *Weldon v Trust Co. Bank of Columbus,* 499 SE2d 393 (Ga App 1998) (found later in the chapter). However, the rights of the parties are different because certification discharges all other parties to the instrument. A cashier's check does not result in the discharge of other parties on the instrument.

[13] Revised UCC § 3-104(h) defines a traveler's check as "a draft drawn by a bank (i) on another bank, or (ii) payable at or through a bank."

THINKING THINGS THROUGH

Writing Certified Checks for Psychics Means Trouble in the Future

Benito Dalessio was dating Jennifer Lopez. Ms. Lopez (no relation to Ben Affleck or Marc Anthony) introduced Dalessio to Linda Kressler, psychic. Kressler told Dalessio that Lopez would marry him if—and the future was contingent here—Dalessio gave Kressler money to pay her debts. Sadly, Dalessio believed Kressler and issued a check to her in the amount of $107,000, which Republic National Bank of New York certified at his request.

When Dalessio appeared at the bank the next day with another odd request, that of receiving $15,000 in cash, the teller asked the branch manager to step in. Dalessio then explained that Kressler and Lopez, unsatisfied, had been to his house and demanded the cash.

The branch manager then called Dalessio's sister, a co-signer on the bank account that had become the source of largesse for the psychic and her friend. The manager suggested legal help. The sister's lawyer went to court claiming fraud and naming the bank as a defendant in relation to the certified check. The judge entered a

temporary restraining order (TRO) stopping payment on the check. The TRO was served on the bank's assistant treasurer the next day. The same day, the bank paid the check, but no one was sure whether the bank paid the check before or after it received service of the TRO. There was also some confusion at the lower court on whether Kressler, as a psychic, could be a holder in due course.

The bank argued that it was powerless to stop payment on a certified check. Kressler argued that there was only fraud in the inducement and that she was still entitled to payment. UCC § 4-303 provides that knowledge, notice or stop orders, legal process served, or setoff exercised after certification of a check are too late to stop payment—but can a court injunction stop the payment of a certified check? What would happen if the payment of the check were permitted to stand as valid? What would happen if the payment on the certified check was set aside and the bank was held liable to Dalessio for its failure to honor the court order? [DALESSIO V KRESSLER, 773 NYS2D 434 (NY App Div 2004)]

3. PRESENTMENT FOR OBTAINING PAYMENT ON A CHECK

A holder of a check must take required steps to obtain payment. As discussed in Chapter 30, there are primary and secondary parties for every negotiable instrument. Primary parties are makers and drawees. Under Revised Article 3, secondary parties are referred to as *secondary obligors* and are defined to include "an indorser, a drawer, an accommodation party, or any other party to the instrument that has a right of recourse against another party to the instrument."[14]

The process for a holder to be paid on an instrument involves mandatory steps with time limitations. The holder must first seek payment from the drawee through **presentment**. No secondary obligor is liable on an instrument until presentment has been made. Presentment is required for checks, and presentment is made first to the drawee bank.[15]

presentment formal request for payment on an instrument.

---

[14] Revised UCC § 3-104(12).

[15] It is important to note that the bank is unique as a drawee because its contract as a primary party is limited by its right to dishonor a check and its right to give only provisional credit.

(a) PRESENTMENT REQUIREMENTS   Presentment occurs when the holder of a check or other consumer transaction authorization demands payment.[16] Under Revised Article 3, the party presents either the check or a record for payment. If the presentment is done in person, the party to whom presentment is made can require that the presenter exhibit identification. The holder who is presenting the instrument must present the check or record for payment in a commercially reasonable manner; banks can treat the transaction as having occurred the following day when presentment is made after *the close of the business day.*[17] In the case of electronic banking, banks are permitted to impose times after which posting will occur the next day. If a check is presented to the drawee bank for payment and paid, the drawer has no liability because payment has been made. (For more details on presentment, generally, of instruments, see Chapter 30.)

CPA   **(b) TIME FOR PRESENTMENT OF A CHECK FOR PAYMENT**[18]   Under the UCC, presentment must be made within a reasonable time after the drawers and indorsers have signed the check. What constitutes a reasonable time is determined by the nature of the instrument, by commercial usage, and by the facts of the particular case.

Failure to make timely presentment discharges all secondary obligors (prior indorsers) of the instrument. It also discharges the drawer to the extent that the drawer has lost, through the bank's failure, money that was on deposit at the bank to make the payment due under the check.[19]

The UCC establishes two presumptions as to what is a reasonable time for presentment of checks. If the check is not certified and is both drawn and payable within the United States, it is presumed that 90 days after the date of the check or the date of its issuance, whichever is later, is the reasonable period in which to make presentment for payment in order to attach secondary liability to the drawer.[20] With respect to attachment of the liability of an indorser, 30 days after indorsement is presumed to be a reasonable time.[21]

If a check is dated with the date of issue, it may be presented immediately for payment. If it is postdated, ordinarily it may not be presented until that date arrives. However, as noted earlier, the bank need not honor the date on the postdated instrument. If the holder delays in making presentment, the delay discharges the drawer if the bank itself fails during such delay.[22] If the holder of the check does not present it for payment or collection within 90 days after an indorsement was made, the secondary obligors (indorsers) are discharged from liability to the extent that the drawer has lost, through the bank's failure, money that was on deposit at the bank to meet the payment under the check.

Under Revised Articles 3 and 4, agreeing to honor an instrument beyond this time limit changes the obligation of the primary obligor and, as a result, changes the obligation of the secondary obligors. Such changes in the terms and conditions of payment serve to discharge the secondary obligors, a change that

---

[16] In addition to the UCC restrictions on times for presentment, banks must comply with federally imposed time constraints. Under the Expedited Funds Availability Act, USC § 401 *et seq.*, banks are required to lift provisional credits on customer accounts.

[17] Revised UCC § 4-107(1).

[18] Revised UCC § 3-501.

[19] Revised UCC § 3-605.

[20] Under the previous versions of Articles 3 and 4, the time was six months.

[21] Revised UCC § 3-304.

[22] Revised UCC § 4-208(c).

brings UCC Articles 3 and 4 in line with the principles of surety law
(see Chapter 33).

A bank may continue to honor checks presented for payment after the 90-day
period, but it does so with understanding of the discharge of liability for the
primary and secondary obligors. A bank honoring a check that is overdue subjects the
bank to questions about whether it exercised good faith and reasonable care in
honoring it.[23]

4. DISHONOR OF A CHECK

If the bank refuses to make payment, the drawer is then subject to the same secondary
liability as the drawer of an ordinary draft.[24] To be able to attach that secondary
liability, the holder of the instrument must notify the drawer of the dishonor by the
drawee. The notice of dishonor may be oral, written, or electronic.

CPA   **(a) Time for Notice of Dishonor**   Banks in the chain of collection for a check
must give notice of dishonor by midnight of the next banking day. Others, including the payee or holder of the check, must give notice of dishonor within 30 days
after learning that the instrument has been dishonored.[25] If proper notice of dishonor is not given to the drawer of the check, the drawer will be discharged from
liability to the same extent as the drawer of an ordinary draft.[26]

CPA   **(b) Overdraft**   If the bank pays the check but the funds in the account are not
sufficient to cover the amount, the excess of the payment over the amount on
deposit is an **overdraft.** This overdraft is treated as a loan from the bank to the
customer, and the customer must repay that amount to the bank.

overdraft negative balance
in a drawer's account.

If the bank account from which the check is drawn is one held by two or more
persons, the joint account holder who does not sign the check that creates an overdraft
is not liable for the amount of the overdraft if she received no benefit from the
proceeds of that check.[27] Additional issues on overdrafts and dishonor of checks are
covered in Section 5.

5. THE CUSTOMER-BANK RELATIONSHIP

The relationship between banks and customers is governed by Articles 3 and 4 of the
UCC as well as by several federal statutes. These laws impose duties and liabilities on
both banks and customers.

(a) Privacy   The bank owes its customer the duty of maintaining the privacy of the
information that the bank acquires in connection with its relationship with the customer. Law enforcement officers and administrative agencies cannot require the disclosure of information relating to a customer's account without first obtaining the

---

[23] Revised Article 3 changed the "negligence" of the bank to the "failure to exercise ordinary care" in § 3-406. A bank need
not pay a check that is presented to it after six months from the date of issue (except for certified checks), but it can honor
such a check and charge the customer's account if it does so in good faith.

[24] Revised UCC § 3-414.

[25] The former time frame for nonbanks was midnight of the third business day.

[26] Revised UCC § 4-213. Under Federal Reserve regulations, notice of dishonor may be given by telephone. *Security Bank and
Trust Co. v Federal Nat'l Bank,* 554 P2d 119 (Okla Ct App 1976). But see *General Motors Acceptance Corp. v Bank of
Richmondville,* 611 NYS2d 338 (App Div 1994) and *City Check Cashing, Inc. v Manufacturers Hanover Trust Co.,* 764 A2d
411, 43 UCC Rep Serv 2d 768 (NJ 2001).

[27] Revised UCC §§ 4-214 and 4-401(b).

USA Patriot Act federal law that, among other things, imposes reporting requirements on banks.

customer's consent or a search warrant or without following the statutory procedures designed to protect customers from unreasonable invasions of privacy.[28] The **USA Patriot Act** does impose certain reporting requirements on banks, financial institutions, and businesses with regard to deposits of cash and large cash payments. These reporting requirements were imposed to be able to track money laundering efforts as well as possible funding of terrorist activities.[29] For example, checks that involve amounts of more than $10,000 generally trigger the bank reporting systems under the USA Patriot Act.

With the advent of the Internet and other electronic exchanges of information, it has become much easier for businesses, including banks, to exchange information about customers. All businesses are subject to federal constraints on the use of customer information. (See Chapter 33 for more information.)

(b) PAYMENT   A bank is under a general contractual duty to its customers to pay on demand all checks to the extent of the funds in a depositor's account.

CPA

stale check a check whose date is longer than six months ago.

(1) Stale Checks.   A bank acting in good faith may pay a check presented more than six months after its date (commonly known as a **stale check**), but unless the check is certified, the bank is not required to do so.[30] The fact that a bank may refuse to pay a check that is more than six months old does not mean that it must pay a check that is less than six months old or that it is not required to exercise reasonable care in making payment on any check.

(2) Payment after Depositor's Death.   From the time of death, the bank can continue paying items until it actually knows of the customer's death.[31] The bank has the right to continue to pay items for 10 days unless, for example, an heir or a government tax agency steps in to stop the payments.[32]

CPA

6. STOPPING PAYMENT OF A CHECK

stop payment order order by a depositor to the bank to refuse to make payment of a check when presented for payment.

certified check check for which the bank has set aside in a special account sufficient funds to pay it; payment is made when check is presented regardless of amount in drawer's account at that time; discharges all parties except certifying bank when holder requests certification.

A drawer may stop payment of a check by notifying the drawee bank in the required manner.[33] **Stop payment orders** are often used when a check is lost or mislaid. The drawer can always write a duplicate check but wants assurance that the original lost or misplaced check will not then also be presented for payment. The drawer can stop payment on the first check to prevent double-dipping. A drawer can also use a stop payment order on a check if the payee has not kept his end of the contract or has failed to provide assurances (see Chapter 26). However, the drawer must keep in mind that if a holder in due course has the check, the holder in due course can demand payment because she would not be subject to the personal defenses of breach of contract or nonperformance of contract. (See Chapter 30 and the rights of holders in due course.)

Stop payment orders are invalid for some forms of checks even when properly executed. Neither the drawer nor a bank customer can stop payment of a **certified check.** A bank customer cannot stop payment of a cashier's check.

---

[28] Right to Financial Privacy Act of 1978, 12 USC § 3401 *et seq.*

[29] USC §§ 5311 *et seq.* 2001.

[30] Revised UCC §§ 3-304 and 4-404; *Leibling, P.C. v Mellon, PSFS (NJ) N.A.,* 710 A2d 1067, 35 UCC2d 590 (NJ 1998).

[31] Revised UCC § 4-405(2).

[32] Revised UCC § 4-405(b); *Hieber v Uptown Nat'l Bank of Chicago,* 557 NE2d 408 (Ill App 1990).

[33] Revised UCC § 4-403.

CASE SUMMARY

The Nine-Year-Old Check Racing through the System

FACTS: On July 15, 1986, IBP, Inc., issued and delivered to Meyer Land & Cattle Company a $135,234.18 check for the purchase of cattle. IBP wrote the check on its account at Mercantile Bank of Topeka.

In the fall of 1995, Meyer's president, Tim Meyer, found the 1986 undeposited check behind a desk drawer in his home. Meyer indorsed the check with the corporation's authorized and accepted indorsement stamp and deposited the check at Sylvan State Bank. Sylvan then forwarded the check through the Federal Reserve System for collection from Mercantile. Mercantile, on receipt of the check, checked its computers for any stop payment orders and, finding none, paid the check.

IBP issues thousands of checks on its account every month. For example, between July 1995 and December 1995, IBP drew 73,769 checks on its account at Mercantile. The amount of the Meyer check was not unusual; many checks issued by IBP exceed the Meyer check amount.

IBP claimed that Mercantile had improperly honored a stale check and demanded that its account be credited with the amount of the Meyer check. IBP also said that it had issued a stop payment order, although it did not provide evidence and there were no computer records of it at the bank. Mercantile moved for summary judgment.

DECISION: The bank used an automated check cashing system and acted in good faith by hand-checking for stop payment orders before cashing the check. Furthermore, the debt had not been satisfied and Meyer was entitled to payment, so there was no unjust enrichment. Stop payment orders last only six months, and it is the customer's obligation to renew such stop payment orders. [**IBP, Inc. v Mercantile Bank of Topeka,** 6 F Supp 2d 1258 (D Kan 1998)]

(a) FORM OF STOP PAYMENT ORDER The stop payment order may be either oral or by record (written or evidence of electronic order). If oral, however, the order is binding on the bank for only 14 calendar days unless confirmed in writing within that time. A record of the stop payment order or confirmation is effective for six months. A stop payment order can be renewed for an additional six months if the customer provides the bank a written extension.

(b) LIABILITY TO HOLDER FOR STOPPING PAYMENT The act of stopping payment may in some cases make the drawer liable to the holder of the check. If the drawer has no proper ground for stopping payment, the drawer is liable to the holder of the check. In any case, the drawer is liable for stopping payment with respect to any holder in due course or any other party having the rights of a holder in due course unless payment was stopped for a reason that may be asserted as a defense against a holder in due course (see Chapter 30). The fact that payment of a check has been stopped does not affect its negotiable character.[34]

7. WRONGFUL DISHONOR OF A CHECK

wrongfully dishonored error by a bank in refusing to pay a check.

A check is **wrongfully dishonored** by the drawee bank if the bank refuses to pay the amount of the check although (1) it is properly payable and (2) the account on which it is drawn is sufficient to pay the item.

---

[34] *Perini Corp. v First Nat'l Bank,* 553 F2d 398 (5th Cir 1977).

CASE SUMMARY

You Can Always Trust a Trust Company When It Comes to Stopping Payment

FACTS: Ann Weldon maintained an account at Trust Company Bank. James Weldon, her son and a garment broker, purchased textile goods from Sportswear Services for resale to another corporation known as Thicket Textiles. Sportswear demanded certified funds from James Weldon before it would ship the goods. When James Weldon requested a certified check from Trust Company, Trust Company officer Sweat informed James that if it issued a certified check, payment could not be stopped even if the merchandise delivered was not as promised under the terms of the contract.

Ann Weldon then obtained a $16,319.29 cashier's check drawn on her account and payable to Sportswear. James had deposited his funds into her account to cover the check. The check was delivered to Sportswear, and the goods were shipped the next day, but they were defective.

Ann Weldon went to Trust Company Bank to issue a stop payment order, and the bank, believing that the check had not yet been delivered to Sportswear, did so for $25. James Weldon then notified Sportswear of the stop payment order. After Trust Company dishonored the cashier's check, Sportswear's bank was in contact with the bank and informed it that the check had already been delivered to Sportswear. Trust Company honored the check and credited Ann Weldon's account with the $25 stop payment fee. Ann filed suit because Trust Company did not stop payment.

The trial court granted the bank's motion for summary judgment, and the Weldons appealed.

DECISION: There are two classes of checks. There are ordinary personal checks on which the drawee is not liable until they are accepted or paid. Cashier's checks, certified checks, and bank drafts are different; these checks operate more as assignments of funds. Stop payment orders are not valid after a bank has accepted or certified the item or paid the item in cash. The courts treat both cashier's checks and certified checks the same.

The UCC provides a special role for certified checks, but it does not accord cashier's checks a similar status; a cashier's check is nothing more than a negotiable instrument issued by a bank. The bank, as the drawer and drawee, can stop payment, as against a nonholder in due course. The rule is that once money is withdrawn from a bank customer's account and a cashier's check is issued in the payee's name, the check becomes the payee's property. The bank did nothing wrong, and there was no conversion of a customer's funds in honoring the check. [**Weldon v Trust Co. Bank of Columbus, 499 SE2d 393 (Ga App 1998)**]

Dishonor for lack of funds can be a breach of contract if the customer has an agreement with the bank that it will pay overdraft items.

 (a) BANK'S LIABILITY TO DRAWER OF CHECK The contract between the customer (drawer) and the bank (drawee) obligates the drawee bank to pay in accordance with the orders of its customer as long as sufficient money is on deposit to make such payment. If the bank improperly refuses to make payment, it is liable to the drawer for damages sustained by the drawer as a consequence of such dishonor.

(b) BANK'S LIABILITY TO HOLDER If a check has not been certified, the holder has no claim against the bank for the dishonor of the check regardless of the fact that the bank acted in breach of its contract with its customer. The bank that certifies a check is liable to the holder when it dishonors the check. The certification imposes primary liability on the bank and requires it to pay the face amount of the check.

(c) Holder's Notice of Dishonor of Check   When a check is dishonored by nonpayment, the holder must follow the procedure for notice to the secondary parties discussed earlier. Notice of dishonor need not be given to the drawer who has stopped payment on a check or to drawers and indorsers who are aware that there are insufficient funds on deposit to cover the check. In those circumstances, no party has reason to expect that the check will be paid by the bank.

8. AGENCY STATUS OF COLLECTING BANK

agent person or firm who is authorized by the principal or by operation of law to make contracts with third persons on behalf of the principal.

agency the relationship that exists between a person identified as a principal and another by virtue of which the latter may make contracts with third persons on behalf of the principal. (Parties–principal, agent, third person)

When a customer deposits negotiable instruments in a bank, the bank is regarded as being merely an **agent,** even though the customer may be given the right to make immediate withdrawals against the deposited item. Because of the bank's **agency** status, the customer remains the owner of the item and is subject to the risks of ownership involved in its collection.

When a bank cashes a check deposited by its customer or cashes a check drawn by its customer based on an amount from a deposited check, it is a holder of the check deposited by its customer. The bank may still collect from the parties on the check even though the bank is an agent for collection and has the right to charge back the amount of the deposited check if it cannot be collected.

9. BANK'S DUTY OF CARE

A bank is required to exercise ordinary care in the handling of items. The liability of a bank is determined by the law of the state where the bank, branch, or separate office involved is located.

CPA

(a) Modification of Bank Duties   The parties in the bank collection process may modify their rights and duties by agreement. However, a bank cannot disclaim liability for lack of good faith or failure to exercise ordinary care, nor can it limit the measure of damages for such lack of care.

When a bank handles checks by automated processes, the standard of ordinary care does not require the bank to make a physical examination of each item unless the bank's own procedures require such examination or general banking usage regards the absence of physical examination of the items as a lack of ordinary care.

encoding warranty warranty made by any party who encodes electronic information on an instrument; a warranty of accuracy.

(b) Encoding Warranty and Electronic Presentment   In addition to transfer and presentment warranties, an **encoding warranty** is also given by those who transfer instruments. Under this warranty, anyone placing information on an item or transmitting the information electronically warrants that the information is correct. When there is an agreement for electronic presentment, the presenter warrants that the transfer is made in accordance with the terms of the agreement for such transmissions.[35]

---

[35] Revised UCC §§ 4-207 to 4-209.

B **LIABILITY OF A BANK**

Banks can make mistakes in the payment and collection of items presented to them by their customers. **For Example,** a check may slip through and be cashed over a customer's properly executed stop payment order. The bank would be liable for this improper payment and may also be liable for improperly collecting, paying, or refusing to pay a check.

10. PREMATURE PAYMENT OF A POSTDATED CHECK

A check may be postdated, but the bank is not liable for making payments on the check before the date stated unless the drawer has given the bank prior notice. Such a notice is similar to a stop payment order; it must provide sufficient information so that the bank is moved to action by the trigger of the order the check as it flows through its electronic processing system.[36]

11. PAYMENT OVER A STOP PAYMENT ORDER

A bank must be given a reasonable time in which to put a stop payment order into effect. However, if the bank makes payment of a check after it has been properly notified to stop payment, and there has been sufficient time for the order to be put into the system, the bank is liable to the drawer (customer) for the loss the drawer sustains in the absence of a valid limitation of the bank's liability.[37] The burden of establishing losses that result from the bank's failure to stop payment rests with the customer. The bank must have complete information on a stop payment order, such as the payee, check number, and amount, to be held responsible for the failure to stop payment.

 ### 12. PAYMENT ON A FORGED SIGNATURE OF DRAWER

A forgery of the signature of the drawer occurs when the name of the drawer has been signed by another person without authority to do so with the intent to defraud by making it appear that the drawer signed the check. The bank is liable to the drawer if it pays a check on which the drawer's signature has been forged because a forgery ordinarily has no effect as a signature. The risk of loss caused by the forged signature of the drawer is placed on the bank without regard to whether the bank could have detected the forgery.[38] The reasoning behind the bank's liability for a forged drawer's signature is that the bank is presumed to know its own customers' signatures even if it does not regularly review checks for authenticity of the signature.

A bank's customer whose signature has been forged may be barred from holding the bank liable if the customer's negligence substantially contributed to the making of the forgery. This preclusion rule prevents or precludes the customer from making a forgery claim against the bank. However, to enjoy the protection of the preclusion rule, the bank, if negligent in its failure to detect the forgery or alteration, must have cashed the check in good faith or have taken it for value or collection.[39]

---

[36] Note that a "postdated check" is not a check but a time draft. UCC §§ 4-401 to 4-402.

[37] Revised UCC § 4-403(c); *Gornicki v M & T Bank,* 617 NYS2d 448 (1994).

[38] *Sun Bank v Merrill Lynch, Pierce, Fenner & Smith, Inc.,* 637 So 2d 279 (Fla App 1994).

[39] Revised UCC § 4-406(e); *Knight Pub. Co., Inc. v Chase Manhattan Bank, N.A.,* 479 SE2d 478 (NC App 1997), but see *American Airlines Employees Federal Credit Union v Martin,* 29 SW3d 86, 42 UCC Rep Serv 2d 359 (Tex 2000). For review (May 11, 1999).

The Double-Dipping Detective Agency: No Stopping Payment without Details

FACTS: Michael Rovell, a lawyer, wrote a check for $38,250 to the Pretty Eyes Detective Agency. After sending the check to Patricia O'Connor, the owner of Pretty Eyes, Rovell discovered that he had overpaid the invoice by more than $10,000. Rovell asked Lisa Fair, one of his employees and another lawyer, to contact American National Bank and make sure the check had not cleared.

Fair phoned Linda Williams, the law firm's account representative at the bank, and explained that if the check had not cleared, she wanted to stop payment and issue a new check for the correct amount. However, Fair did not know the check number, date of issue, the check amount, or the payee. Fair gave Williams check numbers 1084 and 1086 and, finding that they had not cleared, issued stop payment orders. Despite Williams's warning about waiting to issue a new check to Pretty Eyes, Fair issued a new check for $27,284.50. The original check had already cleared, and Pretty Eyes also cashed the second check. Rovell's account went into overdraft, and he sued for the bank's failure to honor a stop payment order.

DECISION: The bank has a duty to inform its customers of the requirements for a stop payment order. Once informed, the customer has the duty to provide the necessary information, including the check number. The customer did not provide the correct check number, the check in question had already cleared the day before, and the bank was not liable for both checks being paid. The customer here must bear the loss for the failure to provide all necessary information for a stop payment order. [**Rovell v American Nat'l Bank, 232 BR 381, 38 UCC2d 896 (ND Ill 1998)**]

Article 4 of the UCC extends forgery protections and rights to alterations and unauthorized signings (those made with no fraudulent intent). When an officer with authority limited to signing $5,000 checks signs a check for $7,500, the signature is unauthorized. If the principal for the drawer account is an organization and has a requirement that two or more designated persons sign negotiable instruments on its behalf, signatures by fewer than the specified number are also classified as unauthorized signatures.

 13. PAYMENT ON A FORGED OR MISSING INDORSEMENT

A drawee bank that honors a customer's check bearing a forged indorsement must recredit the customer's account upon the drawer's discovery of the forgery and notification to the bank. A drawee bank is liable for the loss when it pays a check that lacks an essential indorsement.[40] In such a case, the instrument is not properly payable. Without proper indorsements for an order instrument and special indorsements, the person presenting the check for payment is not the holder of the instrument and is not entitled to demand or receive payment. However, the bank can then turn to the indorsers and transferors of the instrument for breach of warranty liability in that all signatures were not genuine or authorized and they did not have title. All transferors can turn to their previous transferor until liability ultimately rests with the party who first accepted the forged indorsement. This party had face-to-face contact and could have verified signatures.

---

[40] *First Guaranty Bank v Northwest Georgia Bank*, 417 SE2d 348 (Ga App 1992).

When a customer deposits a check but does not indorse it, the customer's bank may make an indorsement on behalf of the depositor unless the check expressly requires the customer's indorsement. A bank cannot add the missing indorsement of a person who is not its customer when an item payable is deposited in a customer's bank account.[41]

14. ALTERATION OF A CHECK

If the face of a check has been altered so that the amount to be paid has been increased, the bank is liable to the drawer for the amount of the increase when it makes payment of the greater amount.

The drawer may be barred from claiming that there was an alteration if there was negligence in writing the check or reporting its alteration. A drawer is barred from claiming alteration if the check was written negligently, the negligence substantially contributed to the making of the material alteration, and the bank honored the check in good faith and observed reasonable commercial standards in doing so. **For Example,** the drawer is barred from claiming alteration when the check was written with blank spaces that readily permitted a change of "four" to "four hundred" and the drawee bank paid out the latter sum because the alteration was not obvious. A careful drawer will write figures and words close together and run a line through or cross out any blank spaces.

15. UNAUTHORIZED COLLECTION OF A CHECK

Although a bank acts as agent for its customer in obtaining payment of a check deposited with it by its customer, the bank may be liable to a third person when its customer's action toward that third person is unauthorized or unlawful. If a customer has no authority to deposit the check, some banks, in obtaining payment from the drawee of the check and later depositing the proceeds of the check in its customer's account, may be liable for conversion of the check to the person lawfully entitled to the check and its proceeds.

A collecting bank, or a bank simply collecting an item for a customer, is protected from liability when it follows its customer's instructions. It is not required to inquire or verify that the customer had the authority to give such instructions. In contrast, instructions do not protect a payor bank. It has an absolute duty to make proper payment. If it does not do so, it is liable unless it is protected by estoppel or by the preclusion rule. The person giving wrongful instructions is liable for the loss caused by those instructions.

16. TIME LIMITATIONS

The liability of the bank to its depositor is subject to certain time limitations.

CPA   **(a) Forgery and Alteration Reporting Time**   A customer must examine with reasonable care and promptness a bank statement and relevant checks that are paid in good faith and sent to the customer by the bank and must try to discover any unauthorized signature or alteration on the checks. The customer must notify the bank promptly after discovering either a forgery or an alteration. If the bank

---

[41] *Bursey v CFX Bank,* 756 A2d 1001, (NH 2000).

exercises ordinary care in paying a forged or an altered check and suffers a loss because the customer fails to discover and notify the bank of the forgery or alteration, the customer cannot assert the unauthorized signature or alteration against the bank.[42]

Under the Check Truncation Act (which is part of the Check 21 statute covered in Chapter 28), banks now have the right to substitute electronic images of checks for customer billing statements. The Check Truncation Act (CTA) became effective October 8, 2004. The CTA is largely implemented through Federal Reserve Board regulations found at 12 CFR § 229.2. Banks do not need to provide the original check to their customers and can simply send copies of electronic images so long as the image provides enough clarity for the customer to see payee, encoding, indorsements, and so on.

With the use of substituted checks and online banking, consumers now have additional rights and time limits with substituted checks. Under the Check 21 statute, consumers have a new right to an expedited recredit to their account if a substitute check was charged improperly to their account. They have the right to see the original check if they can explain why it is necessary and that they are suffering a loss as a result of the improper charge of a substitute check to their account. Consumers have 40 calendar days from whichever of the following is later: (1) the delivery of their monthly bank statements or (2) that date on which the substitute check was made available to them for examination and/or review. If a consumer has been traveling or been ill, the rules permit the extension of the deadline for purposes of challenging a substitute check. Consumers can even call their bank and challenge a payment, but they will not then get the benefit of all the rights and protections under Check 21 and its regulations if they choose to proceed without a written demand on a substitute check.[43] Once the demand is made, the bank must either recredit the consumer's account within one business day or explain why it believes the substitute check was charged properly to the consumer's account. The oral demand does not start this clock running for the consumer's protection. There are also fines and overdraft protections provided while the substitute check issue is in the dispute/investigation stage.

Some cases of forgery are the result of a customer's lack of care, such as when an employee is given too much authority and internal controls are lacking with the result that the employee is able to forge checks on a regular basis not easily detected by the bank. Referred to as the *fictitious payee and impostor exceptions*, this issue was covered in Chapter 29.

Customers are precluded from asserting unauthorized signatures or alterations if they do not report them within one year from the time the bank statement is received.[44] A forged indorsement must be reported within three years.

(b) Unauthorized Signature or Alteration by Same Wrongdoer If there is a series of improperly paid items and the same wrongdoer is involved, the customer is protected only as to those items that were paid by the bank before it received notification from the customer and during that reasonable amount of time that the customer has to examine items or statements and to notify the bank. The time limit on the customer's duty to examine the bank statement and report forgeries is 30 days. If the customer failed to exercise reasonable promptness and failed to notify the

---

[42] *Quilling v National City Bank of Michigan/Illinois.* Not reported in F Supp 2d, 2001 WL 1516732 (ND Ill), 46 UCC Rep Serv 2d 207 (ND Ill 2001).

[43] 12 CFR § 229.54(b)(1)(iii).

[44] Revised UCC § 4-406.

bank but the customer can show that the bank failed to exercise ordinary care in paying the items, the loss will be allocated between the customer and the bank.[45]

(c) Statute of Limitations   An action to enforce a liability imposed by Article 4 must be commenced within three years after the cause of action accrued.

CASE SUMMARY

Stealing Everything from Mom, Including What's Beneath the Kitchen Sink

FACTS: John G. Vowell and his wife, now deceased, had a checking account and a savings/money-market account with Mercantile Bank of Arkansas. They signed account agreements with a requirement that they examine them within 60 days.

In June 1997, Dr. Vowell and his wife allowed their daughter, Suzan Vowell, now also deceased, and her boyfriend to move in with them at their home. At that time, they knew that Suzan and her boyfriend had been involved with drugs, alcohol, writing bad checks, and stealing. They also knew that Suzan had stolen checks from them in the past and forged either Dr. Vowell's or his wife's signatures. They took precautions against future theft and forgeries by Suzan by hiding Mrs. Vowell's purse, which contained their checkbook, under the kitchen sink. Mrs. Vowell suffered from diabetes mellitus and alcoholism, conditions that forced her to stay in bed either all or most of the time. Mrs. Vowell reviewed the bank statements and balanced the checkbooks.

Beginning in June 1997, Suzan forged Mrs. Vowell's signature on 42 checks, drawn on both accounts, and committed nine unauthorized ATM withdrawals in the aggregate amount of $12,028.75. Suzan found her mother's purse hidden under the kitchen sink and stole the checkbooks and ATM card from the purse. She apparently had access to the personal identification number (PIN) for the accounts because the number was identical to the home security system code.

The Vowells received the following statements from the bank for the checking and savings accounts.

Statement Sent	Amount of forgery or ATM withdrawal	Dates of Transactions
July 9, 1997	$230.00	June 6–July 7, 1997
August 8, 1997	$1,235.25	July 8–August 6, 1997
August 23, 1997	$5,140.00	July 23–Aug 21, 1997
September 9, 1997	$1,423.50	Aug 7–Sept 7, 1997
September 26, 1997	$4,000.00	Aug 22–Sept 22, 1997

On September 15, 1997, Dr. Vowell discovered a receipt for an unauthorized credit-card transaction and notified Mercantile Bank about his discovery. Mercantile froze their accounts, alerted its tellers and computer system, and began investigating the alleged forgeries and other unauthorized transactions pursuant to its policy.

As a result of the alert on the account, Suzan was arrested on September 16, 1997, after she attempted to obtain an unauthorized cash advance at another branch. No more unauthorized transactions occurred after the alert was issued. There were 42 forged checks and nine unauthorized ATM withdrawals.

[45] Revised UCC § 4-406 (1990); but see *Tumlinson v First Victoria Nat'l Bank,* 865 SW2d 176 (Tex App 1993) and *Community Bank & Trust, S.S.B. v Fleck,* 21 SW3d 923 (Tex App 2000).

CASE SUMMARY

continued

The bank refused to credit the Vowells' account because it maintained that their negligence in handling their daughter caused the losses. The trial court found that the Vowells were not negligent, but they had failed to exercise reasonable promptness in the examination and reporting of the forged checks on the June checking account statement and the July checking account statement. The court found that the bank was liable for only $6,014.38, one-half of the entire sum of Suzan Vowell's unauthorized bank transactions and forgeries. The bank appealed.

DECISION: The appellate court found that neither the Vowells nor the bank were negligent in their behavior. However, the court noted that Vowells' could not recover for those items they could have prevented had they inspected their bank statements. Most of the losses could have been prevented just with a simple inspection of the checking and savings account statements. The amount that Dr. Vowell recovered was reduced to $1,725, the losses that were incurred during the time frame after the first notice was received and before the next losses occurred. [**Mercantile Bank of Arkansas v Vowell 117 SW3d 603 (Ark App 2003)**]

CONSUMER FUNDS TRANSFERS

Consumers are using electronic methods of payment at an increasing rate. From the swipe of the card at the grocery store checkout to the retrieval of funds from the local automated teller machine, *electronic funds transfers* represent a way of life for many consumers. A federal statute protects consumers making electronic funds transfers.

17. ELECTRONIC FUNDS TRANSFER ACT

Electronic Funds Transfer Act (EFTA) federal law that provides consumers with rights and protections in electronic funds transfers.

electronic funds transfer (EFT) any transfer of funds (other than a transaction originated by a check, draft, or similar paper instrument) that is initiated through an electronic terminal, telephone, computer, or magnetic tape so as to authorize a financial institution to debit or credit an account.

Congress passed the **Electronic Funds Transfer Act (EFTA)** to protect consumers making electronic transfers of funds.[46] **Electronic funds transfer (EFT)** means any transfer of funds (other than a transaction originated by check, draft, or similar paper instrument) that is initiated through an electronic terminal, telephone, computer, or magnetic tape that authorizes a financial institution to debit or credit an account. The service available from an automated teller machine is a common form of EFT.

18. TYPES OF ELECTRONIC FUNDS TRANSFER SYSTEMS

Currently, five common types of EFT systems are in use. In some of these systems, the consumer has a card to access a machine. The consumer usually has a private code that prevents others who wrongfully obtain the card from using it.

(a) AUTOMATED TELLER MACHINE The *automated teller machine (ATM)* performs many of the tasks once performed exclusively by bank employees. Once a user activates an ATM, he can deposit and withdraw funds from his account, transfer funds between accounts, make payments on loan accounts, and obtain cash advances from bank credit cards.[47]

---

[46] 15 USC § 1693 *et seq.*
[47] *Curde v Tri-City Bank & Trust Co.*, 826 SW2d 911 (Tenn App 1992).

(ETHICS & THE LAW)

Electronic funds transfer technology has made life very convenient. We can withdraw cash from teller machines at the bank, the university, the airport, or the mall. We can use our debit cards to pay for our groceries just by swiping our card through a machine at the checkout counter. The ease of credit card use finds us using such cards even for our fast-food purchases.

However, these electronic devices keep perfect records. Every cash withdrawal amount and location is recorded. Every grocery purchase can be traced. Your location can be determined by the last business where you used your credit card. The electronic age brings convenience, but it also brings a loss of privacy. With the information gained about you through the use of electronic funds transfers, a firm can put together a profile that estimates your income, outlines your budget and expenditures, specifies your shopping preferences, and provides an itemized list of grocery store purchases.

This extensive information is invaluable for effective marketing. Knowing when, where, and how much households and individual consumers spend can help companies target customers. Metromail is a consumer information firm that sells lists of customers to businesses. The lists are customized and are developed from Metromail's consumer database (which it says covers 90 percent of all U.S. households) following criteria established by the buyer. For example, Metromail sold a *Los Angeles Times* reporter a mailing list for children with 5,000 names. The reporter used the name of Richard Allen Davis, the convicted murderer of 12-year-old Polly Klaas, a young girl snatched from the bedroom of her home during a slumber party with her friends. Should there be restrictions on the use of EFT information? Do you think its use should be regulated? What policies would you implement to prevent misuse of information about customers?

(b) Pay-by-Phone System   This system facilitates paying telephone, mortgage, utility, and other bills without writing checks. The consumer calls the bank and directs the transfer of funds to a designated third party.

(c) Direct Deposit and Withdrawal   Employees may authorize their employers to deposit wages directly to their accounts. A consumer who has just purchased an automobile on credit may elect to have monthly payments withdrawn from a bank account to be paid directly to the seller.

(d) Point-of-Sale Terminal   The *point-of-sale terminal* allows a business with such a terminal to transfer funds from a consumer's account to the store's account. The consumer must be furnished in advance with the terms and conditions of all EFT services and must be given periodic statements covering account activity. Any automatic EFT from an individual's account must be authorized in writing in advance.

Financial institutions are liable to consumers for all damages proximately caused by the failure to make an EFT in accordance with the terms and conditions of an account. Exceptions exist if the consumer's account has insufficient funds, the funds are subject to legal process, the transfer would exceed an established credit limit, or insufficient cash is available in an ATM.

(e) INTERNET BANKING   Internet banking is the customer use of computer access to bank systems to pay bills, balance accounts, transfer funds, and even obtain loans. Increasing in popularity, this form of banking still suffers from concerns about privacy and security. However, the revisions to Articles 3 and 4 recognize electronic records as valid proof of payment.

19. CONSUMER LIABILITY

A consumer who notifies the issuer of an EFT card within two days after learning of a loss or theft of the card can be held to a maximum liability of $50 for unauthorized use of the card. Failure to notify within this time will increase the consumer's liability for losses to a maximum of $500.

Consumers have the responsibility to examine periodic statements provided by their financial institution. If a loss would not have occurred but for the failure of a consumer to report within 60 days of the transmittal of the statement any unauthorized transfer, then the loss is borne by the consumer.

D   FUNDS TRANSFERS

The funds transfers made by businesses are governed by the UCC and Federal Reserve regulations.

20. WHAT LAW GOVERNS?

In states that have adopted Article 4A of the Uniform Commercial Code, that article governs funds transfers.[48] In addition, whenever a Federal Reserve Bank is involved, the provisions of Article 4A apply by virtue of Federal Reserve regulations.

21. CHARACTERISTICS OF FUNDS TRANSFERS

The transfers regulated by Article 4A are characteristically made between highly sophisticated parties dealing with large sums of money. Speed of transfer is often an essential ingredient. An individual transfer may involve many millions of dollars, and the national total of such transfers on a business day can amount to trillions of dollars.

22. PATTERN OF FUNDS TRANSFERS

In the simplest form of funds transfer, both the debtor and the creditor have separate accounts in the same bank.[49] In this situation, the debtor can instruct the bank to pay the creditor a specified sum of money by subtracting that amount from the debtor's

---

[48] The following states have adopted the 1990 version of Article 4A: Alabama, Arizona, Arkansas, California, Colorado, Connecticut, Delaware, District of Columbia, Florida, Georgia, Hawaii, Idaho, Illinois, Indiana, Iowa, Kansas, Kentucky, Louisiana, Maine, Maryland, Massachusetts, Michigan, Minnesota, Mississippi, Missouri, Montana, Nebraska, Nevada, New Hampshire, New Jersey, New Mexico, New York, North Carolina, North Dakota, Ohio, Oklahoma, Oregon, Pennsylvania, Rhode Island, South Carolina, South Dakota, Tennessee, Texas, Utah, Vermont, Virginia, Washington, West Virginia, Wisconsin, and Wyoming. Article 4A has also been adopted in Puerto Rico.

[49] The text refers to *debtor* and *creditor* in the interest of simplicity and because that situation is the most common in the business world. However, a gift may be made by a funds transfer. Likewise, a person having separate accounts in two different banks may transfer funds from one bank to another.

account and adding it to the creditor's account. As a practical matter, the debtor merely instructs the bank to make the transfer, and the bank, upon making the transfer, debits the debtor's account.

A more complex situation is involved if each party has an account in a different bank. In that case, the funds transfer could involve only these two banks and no clearinghouse. The buyer can instruct the buyer's bank to direct the seller's bank to make payment to the seller. There is direct communication between the two banks. In a more complex situation, the buyer's bank may relay the payment order to another bank, called an **intermediary bank,** and that bank, in turn, transmits the payment order to the seller's bank. Such transactions become even more complex when two or more intermediary banks or a clearinghouse is involved.

intermediary bank bank between the originator and the beneficiary bank in the transfer of funds.

23. SCOPE OF UCC ARTICLE 4A

Article 4A applies to all funds transfers except as expressly excluded by its own terms, by federal preemption, or by agreement of the parties or clearinghouse rules. Some funds transfers are excluded from Article 4A because of their nature or because of the parties involved.

(a) EFTA AND CONSUMER TRANSACTIONS   Article 4A does not apply to consumer transaction payments to which the EFTA applies. If any part of the funds transfer is subject to the EFTA, the entire transfer is expressly excluded from the scope of UCC Article 4A.[50]

credit transfer transaction in which a person making payment, such as a buyer, requests payment be made to the beneficiary's bank.

debit transfer transaction in which a beneficiary entitled to money requests payment from a bank according to a prior agreement.

(b) CREDIT AND DEBIT TRANSFERS   When the person making payment, such as the buyer, requests that payment be made to the beneficiary's bank, the transaction is called a **credit transfer.** If the beneficiary entitled to money goes to the bank according to a prior agreement and requests payment, the transaction is called a **debit transfer.** The latter transfer type is not regulated by Article 4A. Article 4A applies only to transfers begun by the person authorizing payment to another.

(c) NONBANK TRANSFERS   For Article 4A to apply to a money transfer, it is necessary that once the transfer has begun, all communication be between banks. Thus, sending money by Western Union does not come under Article 4A because there is no bank-to-bank communication. Payment by check is also not covered because the drawer of the check sends the check directly to the payee. Banks have no involvement until the payee deposits the check or presents it for payment. Likewise, payment by credit card is excluded under Article 4A even when the transaction does not come within the scope of the EFTA.

funds transfer communication of instructions or requests to pay a specific sum of money to the credit of a specified account or person without an actual physical passing of money.

24. DEFINITIONS

Article 4A employs terms that are peculiar to that article or are used in a very different context from the contexts in which they appear elsewhere.

(a) FUNDS TRANSFER   A **funds transfer** is more accurately described as a communication of instructions or a request to pay a specific sum of money to, or to the

---

[50] UCC § 4A-108 (1990). This exclusion applies when any part of the transaction is subject to Regulation E adopted under the authority of that statute.

credit of, a specified account or person. There is no actual physical transfer or passing of money.

originator party who originates the funds transfer.

(b) ORIGINATOR The person starting the funds transfer is called the **originator** of the funds transfer.[51]

beneficiary person to whom the proceeds of a life insurance policy are payable, a person for whose benefit property is held in trust, or a person given property by a will; the ultimate recipient of the benefit of a funds transfer.

(c) BENEFICIARY The **beneficiary** is the ultimate recipient of the benefit of the funds transfer. Whether the recipient is the beneficiary personally, an account owned by the beneficiary, or a third person to whom the beneficiary owes money is determined by the payment order.

(d) BENEFICIARY'S BANK The **beneficiary's bank** is the final bank in the chain of transfer that carries out the transfer by making payment or application as directed by the payment order.

beneficiary's bank the final bank, which carries out the payment order, in the chain of a transfer of funds.

(e) PAYMENT ORDER The **payment order** is the direction the originator gives to the originator's bank or by any bank to a subsequent bank to make the specified funds transfer. Although called a *payment order*, it is in fact a request. No bank is required or obligated to accept a payment order unless it is so bound by a contract or a clearinghouse rule that operates independently of Article 4A.

payment order direction given by an originator to his or her bank or by any bank to a subsequent bank to make a specified funds transfer.

(f) ACCEPTANCE OF PAYMENT ORDER When a receiving bank other than the beneficiary's bank receives a payment order, it accepts or executes that order by issuing a payment order to the next bank in the transfer chain. When the beneficiary's bank agrees to, or actually makes, the application of funds as directed by the payment order, the order has been accepted by that bank.

25. FORM OF PAYMENT ORDER

The form of the payment order has no specific legal requirements. Funds transfer orders or documents are not required to be in writing. As a practical matter, there probably will be a written contract between an originator and the originator's bank. In addition, agreements between parties and banks as well as clearinghouse and funds transfer system rules may mandate a writing.

26. MANNER OF TRANSMITTING PAYMENT ORDER

Article 4A makes no provisions for the manner of transmitting a payment order. As a practical matter, most funds transfers under Article 4A are controlled by computers, and payment orders are electronically transmitted. Article 4A, however, applies to any funds transfer payment order even if made orally, such as by telephone, or in writing. Also, the agreement of the parties or the clearinghouse and funds transfer system rules may impose some restrictions on the methods for communicating orders.

27. SECURITY PROCEDURE

Because the typical electronic funds transfer involves no writing and no face-to-face contact, Article 4A contemplates that the banks in the transfer chain will agree on a

---

[51] UCC § 4A-201.

commercially reasonable security procedure. Reasonable commercial practice requires that a bank receiving a payment order be able to verify that the payment order was authorized by the purported sender and that it is free from error.[52] When a bank receives a payment order that passes the security procedure, it may act on the basis of the order. It is immaterial that the order was not authorized or was fraudulent.

28. REGULATION BY AGREEMENT AND FUNDS TRANSFER SYSTEM RULES

Article 4A, with minor limitations, permits the parties to make agreements that modify or change the provisions of Article 4A that would otherwise govern. Likewise, the rules of a clearinghouse or a funds transfer system through which the banks operate may change the provisions of the Code.

(a) CHOICE OF LAW   When the parties enter into an agreement for a funds transfer, they may designate the law that is to apply in interpreting the agreement. The parties are given a free hand to select a jurisdiction. Contrary to the rule applicable in other Code transactions, there is no requirement that the jurisdiction selected bear any relationship to the transaction.

(b) CLEARINGHOUSE RULES   The banks involved in a particular funds transfer may be members of the same clearinghouse. In such a case, they will be bound by the lawful rules and regulations of the house. The rights of the parties involved in a funds transfer may be determined by the rules of FedWire, a clearinghouse system operated by the Federal Reserve System, or by CHIPS, which is a similar system operated by the New York clearinghouse.

29. ACCEPTANCE OF PAYMENT ORDER

A bank receiving a payment order accepts the order when it complies with the order's terms. What acceptance means depends on whether the receiving bank is an intermediary bank or the beneficiary's bank.

(a) INTERMEDIARY BANK   An intermediary bank accepts a payment order when it carries out or executes the order by transmitting a similar payment order to the next bank in the transfer chain. Unlike a check sent through bank collection channels, the original payment order is not transferred, but a new payment order by the intermediary bank is dispatched.

(b) BENEFICIARY'S BANK   The beneficiary's bank accepts a payment order when it notifies the beneficiary that it holds the amount of the payment order at the disposal of the beneficiary. The payment order may require the beneficiary's bank to credit the amount to an account or to a named person. The person so named may be the beneficiary, as when a buyer uses a funds transfer to pay the purchase price to the seller. A beneficiary can also be a designated third person. **For Example,** a buyer could direct the crediting of the bank account of a manufacturer to discharge or reduce the debt of the seller to the manufacturer. The transfer to the

---

[52] UCC § 4A-201. But see *Credit Lyonnais–New York v Washington Strategic Consulting Group,* 886 F Supp 92 (DDC 1995). See also *Hedged Investment Partners, L.P. v Norwest Bank Minnesota,* 578 NW2d 765 (Minn 1998).

manufacturer would reduce or discharge the debt of the buyer to the seller by the amount transferred.

When the beneficiary's bank complies with the payment order, it accepts the order. When the bank does so, it takes the place of the originator as the debtor owing the beneficiary. In such a case, the originator no longer owes the beneficiary, and the debt to the beneficiary is discharged or reduced by the amount of the payment order.[53]

30. REIMBURSEMENT OF THE BANK

After the beneficiary's bank accepts the payment order, it and every bank ahead of it in the funds transfer chain is entitled to reimbursement of the amount paid to or for the beneficiary. This reimbursement is due from the preceding bank. By going back along the funds transfer chain, the originator's bank, and ultimately the originator, makes payment of this reimbursement amount.

31. REFUND ON NONCOMPLETION OF TRANSFER

If the funds transfer is not completed for any reason, the sender or originator is entitled to a refund of any payment that has been made in advance to the originator's bank. The sender or originator is not required to reimburse any bank for payment made by it.

32. ERROR IN FUNDS TRANSFER

There may be an error in a payment order. The effect of an error depends on its nature.

(a) Type of Error   The error in a payment order may consist of a wrong identification or a wrong amount.

(1) Wrong Beneficiary or Account Number.   The payment order received by the beneficiary's bank may contain an error in the designation of the beneficiary or in the account number. This error may result in payment being made to or for the wrong person or account.

(2) Excessive Amount.   The payment order may call for the payment of an amount that is larger than it should be. For example, the order may wrongly add an additional zero to the specified amount.

(3) Duplicating Amount.   The payment order may be issued after a similar payment order has already been transferred, so that the second order duplicates the first. This duplication would result in doubling the proper amount paid by the beneficiary's bank.

(4) Underpayment.   The payment order may call for the payment of a smaller sum than was ordered. For example, the order may drop off one of the zeros from the amount ordered by the originator.

(b) Effect of Error   When the error falls under one of the first three classes just discussed, the bank committing the error bears the loss because it will not be

---

[53] UCC § 4A-406.

reimbursed for any amount that it caused to be wrongfully paid. In contrast, when the error is merely underpayment, the bank making the mistake can cure the fault by making a supplementary order for the amount of the underpayment. If verification by the agreed-upon security procedure would disclose an error in the payment order, a bank is liable for any loss caused by the error if it failed to verify the payment order by such a procedure. In contrast, if the security procedure followed did not reveal any error, there is no liability for accepting the payment order.

When an error of any kind is made, there may be liability under a collateral agreement of the parties, a clearinghouse or funds transfer system rule, or general principles of contract law. However, the right of the originator to complain that there is an error may be lost in certain cases by failure to notify the involved bank that the mistake has been made.

33. LIABILITY FOR LOSS

Unless otherwise regulated by agreement or clearinghouse rule, very slight liability is imposed on a bank in the funds transfer chain that has followed the agreed-upon security procedure.

(a) UNAUTHORIZED ORDER If a bank executes or accepts an unauthorized payment order, it is liable to any prior party in the transfer chain for the loss caused. However, as a practical matter, such loss will rarely be imposed because the transfer is typically made under an agreement establishing a security procedure. If a bank acts on the basis of an unauthorized order that nevertheless is verified by the security procedure, the bank is not liable for the loss that is caused.

The customer, however, can avoid this effect of security procedure verification by proving that the security procedure was not commercially reasonable or that a total stranger initiated the payment order. The latter requires the customer to show that the initiator was not the customer's employee or agent having access to confidential security information or a person who obtained that information from a source controlled by the customer. However, it is immaterial whether the customer was at fault.

(b) FAILURE TO ACT A bank that fails to carry out a payment order is usually liable at the most for interest loss and expenses. There is no liability for the loss sustained by the originator or for consequential damages suffered because payment was not made to satisfy the originator's obligation to the beneficiary. A person seeking to exercise an option by forwarding money to the optionor cannot recover for the loss of the option when the failure of a bank to act results in the optionor's not receiving the money in time.

> SUMMARY

A *check* is a particular kind of draft; it is drawn on a bank and is payable on demand. A delivery of a check is not an assignment of money on deposit with the bank on which it is drawn. A check does not automatically transfer the rights of the depositor against the bank to the holder of the check, and there is no duty on the part of the drawee bank to the holder to pay the holder the amount of the check.

A check may be an *ordinary check, a cashier's check*, or a *teller's check.* The name on the paper is not controlling. Unless otherwise agreed, the delivery of a certified check, a cashier's check, or a teller's check discharges the debt for which it is given, up to the amount of the check.

Certification of a check by the bank is the acceptance of the check—the bank becomes the primary party. Certification may be at the request of the drawee or the holder. Certification by the holder releases all prior indorsers and the drawer from liability.

Notice of nonpayment of a check must be given to the drawer of a check. If no notice is given, the drawer is discharged from liability to the same extent as the drawer of an ordinary draft.

A depositor may stop payment on a check. However, the depositor is liable to a holder in due course unless the stop payment order was for a reason that may be raised against a holder in due course. The stop payment order may be made orally (binding for 14 calendar days) or with a record (effective for six months).

The depository bank is the agent of the depositor for the purpose of collecting a deposited item. The bank may become liable when it pays a check contrary to a stop payment order or when there has been a forgery or an alteration. The bank is not liable, however, if the drawer's negligence has substantially contributed to the forgery. A bank that pays on a forged instrument must recredit the drawer's account. A depositor is subject to certain time limitations to enforce liability of the bank. Banks are subject to reporting requirements under the Patriot Act.

A customer and a bank may agree that the bank should retain canceled checks and simply provide the customer with a list of paid items. The customer must examine canceled checks (or their electronic images) or paid items to see whether any were improperly paid.

An *electronic funds transfer (EFT)* is a transfer of funds (other than a transaction originated by check, draft, or other commercial paper) that is initiated through an electronic terminal, telephone, computer, or magnetic tape to authorize a financial institution to debit or credit an account. The Electronic Funds Transfer Act requires that a financial institution furnish consumers with specific information containing all the terms and conditions of all EFT services. Under certain conditions, the financial institution will bear the loss for unauthorized transfers. Under other circumstances, the consumer will bear the loss.

Funds transfers regulated by UCC Article 4A are those made between highly sophisticated parties that deal with large sums of money. If any part of the funds transfer is subject to the EFTA, such as consumer transactions, the entire transfer is expressly excluded from the scope of Article 4A. A funds transfer is simply a request or an instruction to pay a specific sum of money to, or to the credit of, a specified person. The person who originates the funds transfer is called the *funds transfer originator.* The beneficiary is the ultimate recipient of the funds transfer.

QUESTIONS AND CASE PROBLEMS

1. On August 24, 1989, Karrer and her son opened a joint checking account with Georgia State Bank. The signature card agreement contained a provision that Karrer should report any account problem to the bank within 60 days of her statement or lose her rights to assert the problem against the bank. On August 15, 1990, Karrer tendered a check signed by her in the amount of $1,510 to Casey Construction. At the time the check was tendered, Karrer knew there were insufficient funds in her account to cover the check. Casey, who had an account at the same bank, deposited the check to its account along with another check and received $965 in cash.

On Saturday, August 18, 1990, Karrer went to the main office of the bank and for the first time notified it that she wanted to stop payment on the check because of Casey's defective work. Her account did not have sufficient funds to honor the check, so the bank assured her that it would do everything to stop payment. The stop payment order was not implemented before the check was returned to Casey for insufficient funds. Casey's attorney notified Karrer on August

24 by registered mail that the check was dishonored and that if she failed to pay the full amount of the check, both civil and criminal actions would be filed against her. The letter was returned "Unclaimed." The letter was sent to the same address that Karrer and her son used when they opened the account.

Karrer was arrested on October 9 for the issuance of a bad check. She never tried to make the check good prior to her arrest or communicate to the bank any problems she had with the requested stop payment order or the return of the check for insufficient funds until June 4, 1991, almost eight months after her arrest. Even on closing her account in February 1991, she said nothing to the bank about its handling of the check or the stop payment order. In August 1991, Karrer filed suit against the bank, alleging that its return of the check for insufficient funds was wrongful, unlawful, and improper. She also alleged a breach of the agreement between herself and the bank and demanded damages for her arrest, imprisonment, and indictment on charges of issuing a bad check. Is she entitled to collect? [*Karrer v Georgia State Bank of Rome*, 452 SE2d 120 (Ga App)]

2. Helen was a very forgetful person, so she had placed her bank code (PIN number) on the back of her debit card. A thief stole Helen's card and was able to take $100 from an ATM on the day of the theft. That same day, Helen realized that the card was gone and phoned her bank. The following morning, the thief withdrew another $100. For how much, if anything, is Helen responsible? Why?

3. Shirley drew a check on her account at First Central Bank. She later telephoned the bank to stop payment on the check, and the bank agreed to do so. Sixteen days later, the check was presented to the bank for payment, and the bank paid it. Shirley sued the bank for violating the stop payment order. The bank claimed it was not liable. Is Shirley entitled to recover?

4. Arthur Odgers died, and his widow, Elizabeth Odgers (Elizabeth Salsman by remarriage), retained Breslow as the attorney for her husband's estate. She received a check payable to her drawn on First National City Bank. Breslow told her to deposit it in her husband's estate. She signed an indorsement "Pay to the order of Estate of Arthur J. Odgers." Breslow deposited this check in his trustee account in National Community Bank, which collected the amount of the check from the drawee, First City National Bank. Thereafter, Elizabeth, as administratrix of the estate of Arthur J. Odgers, sued National Community Bank for collecting this check and crediting Breslow's trustee account with the proceeds. Was National Community Bank liable? Explain. [*Salsman v National Community Bank*, 246 A2d 162 (NJ Super)]

5. Shipper was ill for 14 months. His wife did not take care of his affairs carefully, nor did she examine his bank statements as they arrived each month. One of Shipper's acquaintances had forged his name to a check in favor of himself for $10,000. The drawee bank paid the check and charged Shipper's account. Shipper's wife did not notify the bank for 13 months after she received the statement and the forged check. Can she compel the bank to reverse the charge? Why or why not?

6. Gloria maintains a checking account at First Bank. On the third day of January, the bank sent her a statement of her account for December accompanied by the checks that the bank had paid. One of the checks had her forged signature, which Gloria discovered on the 25th of the month when she prepared a bank reconciliation. On discovering this, Gloria immediately notified the bank. On January 21, the bank had paid another check forged by the same party who had forged the December item. Who must bear the loss on the forged January check?

7. Dean bought a car from Cannon. As payment, Dean gave him a check drawn on South Dorchester Bank of Eastern Shore Trust Co. Cannon cashed the check at the Cambridge Bank of Eastern Shore Trust Co. The drawee bank refused payment when the check was presented on the ground that Dean had stopped payment because of certain misrepresentations made by Cannon. Will Eastern Shore Trust Co. succeed in an action against Dean for payment? [*Dean v Eastern Shore Trust Co.*, 150 A 797 (Md)]

8. A depositor drew a check and delivered it to the payee. Fourteen months later, the check was presented to the drawee bank for payment. The bank had no knowledge that anything was wrong and paid the check. The depositor then sued the person receiving the money and the bank. The depositor claimed that the bank could not pay a stale check without asking the depositor whether payment should be made. Was the depositor correct? [*Advanced Alloys, Inc. v Sergeant Steel Corp.*, 340 NYS2d 266 (Queens Co Civ Ct)]

9. Siniscalchi drew a check on his account in Valley Bank of New York. About a week later, the holder cashed the check at the bank on a Saturday morning. The following Monday morning, Siniscalchi gave the bank a stop payment order on the check. The Saturday morning transaction had not yet been recorded, and neither the bank nor Siniscalchi knew that the check had been cashed. When that fact was learned, the bank debited Siniscalchi's account for the amount of the check. He claimed that the bank was liable because the stop payment order had been violated. Was the bank liable? [*Siniscalchi v Valley Bank of New York*, 359 NYS2d 173 (Nassau Co Dist Ct)]

10. Bogash drew a check on National Safety Bank and Trust Co. payable to the order of Fiss Corp. At the request of Fiss Corp., the bank certified the check. The bank later refused to make payment on the check because of a dispute between Bogash and the corporation over the amount due the corporation. The corporation sued the bank on the check. Can Fiss recover? [*Fiss Corp. v National Safety Bank and Trust Co.*, 77 So 2d 293 (NY City Ct)]

11. David Marx was a gentleman in his 90s and a longtime customer of Whitney National Bank. His account had been in his name only until April 24, 1995, when he added his son, Stanley Marx, and his daughter, Maxine Marx Goodman, as joint owners and signatories on the account. The account names read: "David Marx or Maxine M. Goodman or Stanley B. Marx." At that time, the bank began sending the statements to Stanley Marx.

    Joel Goodman, David Marx's grandson, visited his grandfather often and had access to his grandfather's checkbook. Joel forged 22 checks on his grandfather's account for a total of $22,834. The first ten checks went unnoticed because they were cleared and the bank statement David Marx received during this time was never reviewed. The last five checks, which appeared on the May 16, 1995, bank statement, were discovered when Stanley Marx reviewed the statement. David and Stanley notified the bank and completed the appropriate forms for the five checks, which totaled $10,000. Whitney National Bank refused to pay the $10,000, and David and Stanley filed suit. The trial court granted summary judgment for David and Stanley, and Whitney appealed. Who is liable on the checks? Did David and Stanley wait too long or are they protected by letting the bank know when they did?

12. Norris, who was ill in the hospital, was visited by his sister during his last days. Norris was very fond of his sister and wrote a check to her that she deposited in her bank account. Before the check cleared, Norris died. Could the sister collect on the check even though the bank knew of the depositor's death? Explain. [*In re Estate of Norris*, 532 P2d 981 (Colo)]

13. Scott D. Leibling gave his bank, Mellon Bank, an oral stop payment order. Nineteen months later, the check emerged and Mellon Bank honored it. Leibling has filed suit against Mellon Bank for acting unreasonably under the circumstances. Is Mellon Bank liable to Leibling for paying the 19-month-old check when there was an oral stop payment order? Discuss your reasons for your answer. [*Leibling, P.C. v Mellon, PSFS (NJ) N.A.*, 311 NJ Super 651, 710 A2d 1067, 35 UCC2d 590]

14. Hixson paid Galyen Petroleum Co. money he owed by issuing three checks to Galyen. The bank refused to cash the three checks because of insufficient funds in the Hixson account to pay all three. Galyen sued the bank. What was the result? Why? [*Galyen Petroleum Co. v Hixson*, 331 NW2d 1 (Neb)]

15. What is the maximum liability of a consumer who fails to notify the issuer of an EFT card after learning of the loss or theft of the card?

> CPA QUESTIONS

1. A check has the following endorsements on the back:

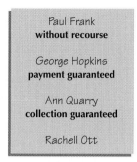

Paul Frank
without recourse

George Hopkins
payment guaranteed

Ann Quarry
collection guaranteed

Rachell Ott

Which of the following conditions occurring subsequent to the endorsements would discharge all of the endorsers?

a. Lack of notice of dishonor
b. Late presentment
c. Insolvency of the maker
d. Certification of the check

2. Blare bought a house and provided the required funds in the form of a certified check from a bank. Which of the following statements correctly describes the legal liability of Blare and the bank?

a. The bank has accepted; therefore, Blare is without liability.
b. The bank has not accepted; therefore, Blare has primary liability.
c. The bank has accepted, but Blare has secondary liability.
d. The bank has not accepted, but Blare has secondary liability.

3. In general, which of the following statements is correct concerning the priority among checks drawn on a particular account and presented to the drawee bank on a particular day?

a. The checks may be charged to the account in any order convenient to the bank.
b. The checks may be charged to the account in any order provided no charge creates an overdraft.
c. The checks must be charged to the account in the order in which the checks were dated.
d. The checks must be charged to the account in the order of lowest amount to highest amount to minimize the number of dishonored checks.

DEBTOR-CREDITOR RELATIONSHIPS

NATURE OF THE DEBTOR-CREDITOR RELATIONSHIP

(A) **CREATION OF THE CREDIT RELATIONSHIP**

(B) **SURETYSHIP AND GUARANTY**
1. **DEFINITIONS**
2. **INDEMNITY CONTRACT DISTINGUISHED**
3. **CREATION OF THE RELATIONSHIP**
4. **RIGHTS OF SURETIES**
5. **DEFENSES OF SURETIES**

(C) **LETTERS OF CREDIT**
6. **DEFINITION**
7. **PARTIES**
8. **DURATION**
9. **FORM**
10. **DUTY OF ISSUER**
11. **REIMBURSEMENT OF ISSUER**

LEARNING OBJECTIVES

After studying this chapter, you should be able to

LO.1 Distinguish a contract of suretyship from a contract of guaranty

LO.2 Define the parties to a contract of suretyship and a contract of guaranty

LO.3 List and explain the rights of sureties to protect themselves from loss

LO.4 Explain the defenses available to sureties

LO.5 Explain the nature of a letter of credit and the liabilities of the various parties to a letter of credit

LO.6 List the exceptions to the requirement of consideration

This section of the book deals with all aspects of debt: the creation of the debtor-creditor relationship, the statutory requirements for disclosure in those credit contracts, the means by which creditors can secure repayment of debt, and finally, what happens when debtors are unable to repay their debts. This chapter covers the creation of the debtor-creditor relationship, as well as two means of ensuring payment: the use of a surety or guarantor and the creation of a line of credit.

suretyship pledge or guarantee to pay the debt or be liable for the default of another.

CREATION OF THE CREDIT RELATIONSHIP

obligor promisor.

surety obligor of a suretyship; primarily liable for the debt or obligation of the principal debtor.

guaranty agreement or promise to answer for a debt; an undertaking to pay the debt of another if the creditor first sues the debtor.

A debtor-creditor relationship arises when the parties enter into a contract that provides for the creditor to advance funds to the debtor and requires the debtor to repay that principal amount with specified interest over an agreed-upon time. The credit contract, so long as it complies with all the requirements for formation and validity covered in Chapters 12 through 17, is enforceable just like any other contract. However, credit contracts often have additional statutory obligations and relationships that provide assurances on rights and collection for both the debtor and the creditor. Chapter 33 covers the rights of both debtors and creditors in consumer credit relationships. Chapter 34 covers the additional protection that creditors enjoy when debtors offer security interests in collateral. This chapter covers the additional relationships for securing repayment of debt known as *suretyships* and *lines of credit*.

SURETYSHIP AND GUARANTY

guarantor one who undertakes the obligation of guaranty.

principal person or firm who employs an agent; the person who, with respect to a surety, is primarily liable to the third person or creditor; property held in trust.

A debtor can make a separate contract with a third party that requires the third party to pay the debtor's creditor if the debtor does not pay or defaults in the performance of an obligation. This relationship, in which a third party agrees to be responsible for the debt or other obligation, is used most commonly to ensure that a debt will be paid or that a contractor will perform the work called for by a contract. **For Example,** a third-party arrangement occurs when a corporate officer agrees to be personally liable if his corporation does not repay funds received through a corporate note. Contractors are generally required to obtain a surety bond in which a third party agrees to pay damages or complete performance of the construction project in the event the contractor fails to perform in a timely manner or according to the contract terms.

1. DEFINITIONS

principal debtor original borrower or debtor.

debtor buyer on credit (i.e., a borrower).

obligee promisee who can claim the benefit of the obligation.

creditor person (seller or lender) who is owed money; also may be a secured party.

One type of agreement to answer for the debt or default of another is called a **suretyship.** The **obligor** or third party who makes good on a debtor's obligation is called a **surety.** The other kind of agreement is called a **guaranty,** and the obligor is called a **guarantor.** In both cases, the person who owes the money or is under the original obligation to pay or perform is called the **principal, principal debtor,** or **debtor.**[1] The person to whom the debt or obligation is owed is the **obligee** or **creditor.**

As discussed in Chapters 28 and 31, the revisions to Articles 3 and 4 put accommodation parties (now secondary obligors) in the same legal status as those in a surety/guarantor relationship. The revisions place secondary obligors in the position of a surety.

---

[1] Unless otherwise stated, *surety* as used in the text includes guarantor as well as surety. Often, the term *guarantee* is used for guaranty. In law, guarantee is actually one who benefits from the guaranty.

guaranty of collection form of guaranty in which creditor cannot proceed against guarantor until after proceeding against debtor.

absolute guaranty agreement that creates the same obligation for the guarantor as a suretyship does for the surety; a guaranty of payment creates an absolute guaranty.

CPA

guaranty of payment absolute promise to pay when a debtor defaults.

indemnity contract agreement by one person, for consideration, to pay another person a sum of money in the event that the other person sustains a specified loss.

Suretyship and guaranty undertakings have the common feature of a promise to answer for the debt or default of another. The terms are often used interchangeably. However, certain forms of guaranty are qualified by one distinction. A surety is liable from the moment the principal is in default. The creditor or obligee can demand performance or payment from the surety without first proceeding against the principal debtor. A **guaranty of collection** is one in which the creditor generally cannot proceed directly against the guarantor and must first attempt to collect from the principal debtor. An exception is an **absolute guaranty,** which creates the same obligation as a suretyship. A **guaranty of payment** creates an absolute guaranty and requires the guarantor to pay upon default by the principal debtor.

2. INDEMNITY CONTRACT DISTINGUISHED

Both suretyship and guaranty differ from an **indemnity contract.** An indemnity contract is an undertaking by one person, for a consideration, to pay another person a sum of money in the event that the other person sustains a specified loss. **For Example,** a fire insurance policy is an indemnity contract. The insurance you obtain when you use a rental car is also an example of an indemnity contract.

3. CREATION OF THE RELATIONSHIP

Suretyship, guaranty, and indemnity relationships are based on contract. The principles relating to capacity, formation, validity, and interpretation of contracts are applicable. Generally, the ordinary rules of offer and acceptance apply. Notice of acceptance usually must be given by the obligee to the guarantor.

In most states, the statute of frauds requires that contracts of suretyship and guaranty be in writing to be enforceable. No writing is required when the promise is made primarily for the promisor's benefit.

When the suretyship or guaranty is created at the same time as the original transaction, the consideration for the original promise that is covered by the guaranty is also consideration for the promise of the guarantor. When the suretyship or guaranty contract is entered into after and separate from the original transaction, there must be new consideration for the promise of the guarantor.

> ## CASE SUMMARY
>
> ### I'm Sure I'm not a Surety!
>
>
>
> **FACTS:** Charles Fontaine completed a form for Gordon Contractors in which he signed that portion of the form labeled "Name of Guarantor." His signature followed immediately after a paragraph beginning, "[I]n consideration of the extension of credit by Gordon Building Supply Inc. the undersigned customer hereby agrees that the terms and conditions of all sales are as follows." There was also a blank following this paragraph for "Customer Name," and it was signed by a Robert Schlaefli, although it is unclear whether he signed it individually or as an agent. At the beginning of the application, the blank for "Name of Individual Applying" was filled in with both Fontaine's and Schlaefli's names, and the blank for "Name of Company or Business" bore the words "McIntyre Development, Inc." Finally, the blank for "Names of People Authorized to Purchase" was filled in with Schlaefli's name and that of a Glen Bush.

CASE SUMMARY

continued

Upon default of the debtor (never clearly identified in the agreement), Gordon Contractors filed suit to collect from Fontaine as a guarantor. Fontaine moved for summary judgment because he was not identified on the contract as a guarantor. The trial court granted Gordon Contractors a summary judgment against Fontaine, and Fontaine appealed.

DECISION: Where a guaranty omits the name of the principal debtor, it is unenforceable as a matter of law. This is true even where the intent of the parties is obvious:

> *[W]here the name of the principal debtor is omitted from the document, the agreement is not enforceable because it fails to satisfy the statute of frauds. . . . [T]he contemporaneous writing rule, even if applicable, would not authorize a different result. Although the "Terms Agreement" and "Individual Personal Guaranty" appear on the same paper, the two sections do not incorporate each other by reference or use the same terms. The terms agreement refers to "seller" . . . and "purchaser." . . . In contrast, the individual personal guaranty refers to "company" (unidentified, unnamed) and seller. . . .*

The trial court correctly found that to determine the identity of the "company" debtor, it would have to make inferences and consider impermissible parol evidence. Judgment reversed. [**Fontaine v Gordon Contractors Building Supply, Inc., 567 SE2d 324 (Ga App 2002)**]

4. RIGHTS OF SURETIES

Sureties have a number of rights to protect them from loss, to obtain their discharge because of the conduct of others that would be harmful to them, or to recover money that they were required to pay because of the debtor's breach.

`CPA`

exoneration agreement or provision in an agreement that one party shall not be held liable for loss; the right of the surety to demand that those primarily liable pay the claim for which the surety is secondarily liable.

(a) EXONERATION   A surety can be exonerated from liability, a means of discharging or relieving liability, if the creditor could have taken steps to stop or limit the surety's exposure for the debt. For example, suppose that the surety learns that a debtor is about to leave the state, an act that makes it more difficult to collect debts. The surety may call on the creditor to take action against the debtor to provide a literal and figurative roadblock to the debtor's planned departure. If the creditor could proceed against the debtor who is about to leave and thereby protect the repayment and fails to do so, the surety is released or **exonerated** from liability to the extent that the surety has been harmed by such failure.

`CPA`

subrogation right of a party secondarily liable to stand in the place of the creditor after making payment to the creditor and to enforce the creditor's right against the party primarily liable to obtain indemnity from such primary party.

(b) SUBROGATION   When a surety pays a claim that it is obligated to pay, it automatically acquires the claim and the rights of the creditor. This stepping into the shoes or position of another is known as **subrogation**.[2] That is, once the creditor is paid in full, the surety stands in the same position as the creditor and may collect from the debtor or enforce any rights the creditor had against the debtor to recover the amount it has paid. The effect is the same as if the

---

[2] *Middlesex Mut. Assur. Co. v Vaszil*, 873 A2d 1030 (Conn App 2005); insurer had right of subrogation where guarantor had signed for tenant's liability for causing damage to the landlord's property once the insurer had paid the landlord.

indemnity right of a person secondarily liable to require that a person primarily liable pay for loss sustained when the secondary party discharges the obligation that the primary party should have CPA discharged; the right of an agent to be paid the amount of any loss or damage CPA sustained without fault because of obedience to the principal's instructions; an undertaking by one person for a consideration to pay another person a sum of money to indemnify that person when a specified loss is incurred.

contribution right of a co-obligor who has paid more than a proportionate share to demand that the other obligor pay the amount of the excess payment made. CPA

co-sureties sureties for the same debtor and obligator.

fraud act of making of a false statement of a past or existing fact, with knowledge of its falsity or with reckless indifference as to its truth, with the intent to cause another to rely thereon, and such person does rely thereon and is harmed thereby.

concealment failure to volunteer information not requested.

creditor, on being paid, made an express assignment of all rights to the surety. Likewise, the surety acquires any rights the debtor has against the creditor. **For Example,** if the creditor has not complied with statutory requirements, the surety can enforce those rights against the creditor just as the original debtor could.

(c) INDEMNITY   A surety that has made payment of a claim for which it was liable as surety is entitled to **indemnity** from the principal debtor; that is, it is entitled to demand from the principal reimbursement of the amount that it has paid.

(d) CONTRIBUTION   If there are two or more sureties (known as co-sureties), each is liable to the creditor or claimant for the full amount of the debt until the claim or debt has been paid in full. Between themselves, however, each co-surety is liable only for a proportionate share of the debt. Accordingly, if a surety has paid more than its share of the debt, it is entitled to demand **contribution** from its **co-sureties.** In the absence of a contrary agreement, co-sureties must share the debt repayment on a *pro rata* basis. **For Example,** Aaron and Bobette are co-sureties of $40,000 and $60,000, respectively, for Christi's $60,000 loan. If Christi defaults, Aaron owes $24,000 and Bobette owes $36,000.

5. DEFENSES OF SURETIES

The surety's defenses include those that may be raised by a party to any contract and special defenses that are peculiar to the suretyship relation.

(a) ORDINARY CONTRACT DEFENSES   Because the relationship of suretyship is based on a contract, the surety may raise any defense that a party to an ordinary contract may raise. For example, a surety may raise the defense of lack of capacity of parties, absence of consideration, fraud, or mistake.

Fraud and concealment are common defenses. Fraud on the part of the principal that is unknown to the creditor and in which the creditor has not taken part does not ordinarily release the surety.

Because the risk of the principal debtor's default is thrown on the surety, it is unfair for a creditor to conceal from the surety facts that are material to the surety's risk. Under common law, the creditor was not required to volunteer information to the surety and was not required to disclose that the principal was insolvent. A modern view that is receiving increased support is that the creditor should

THINKING THINGS THROUGH

Pro Rata Shares for Co-Sureties

AFC Corporation borrowed $90,000 from First Bank and demanded three sureties for the loan. Anna Flynn agreed to be a surety for $45,000 for AFC's debt. Frank Conlan agreed to be a surety for $60,000, and Charles Aspen agreed to be a surety for $75,000. When AFC owed $64,000, it defaulted on the loan and demanded payment from the co-sureties. However, Frank Conlan was in bankruptcy. How much would Anna and Charles have to pay to First Bank?

be required to inform the surety of matters material to the risk when the creditor has reason to believe that the surety does not possess such information.

(b) Suretyship Defenses Perhaps the most important thing for a surety to understand is the type of defense that does not result in a discharge of her obligation in the suretyship. The insolvency or bankruptcy of the principal debtor does not discharge the surety. The financial risk of the principal debtor is the reason that a surety was obtained from the outset. The lack of enforcement of the debt by the creditor is not a defense to the surety's obligation or a discharge. The creditor's failure to give the surety notice of default is not a defense. The creditor's right, without a specific guarantee of collection, is simply to turn to the surety for payment.[3]

pledge bailment given as security for the payment of a debt or the performance of an obligation owed to the pledgee. (Parties–pledgor, pledgee)

In some cases, the creditor may have also taken a **pledge** of collateral for the debt in addition to the commitment of a surety. It is the creditor's choice as to whether to proceed against the collateral or the surety. If, however, the creditor proceeds first against the surety, the surety then has the right of exoneration and can step into the shoes of the creditor and repossess that collateral.

Changes in the terms of the loan agreement do not discharge a compensated surety. A surety who is acting gratuitously, however, would be discharged in the event of such changes. Changes in the loan terms that would discharge a gratuitous surety's obligation include extension of the loan terms and acceptance of late payments.

A surety is discharged when the principal debtor performs his obligations under the original debt contract. If a creditor refuses to accept payment from a debtor, a surety is discharged.

A surety is also discharged, to the extent of the value of the collateral, if a creditor releases back to the debtor any collateral in the creditor's possession.

CASE SUMMARY

Damaged Diesels and Defenses of Sureties

FACTS: Tri County Truck & Diesel borrowed $165,000 from Security State Bank and pledged its inventory as security for the loan. In addition, Fred and Randelle Burk agreed to act as sureties for the loan. Tri County defaulted on the loan and Security Bank repossessed the collateral. The inventory was damaged while Security Bank held it, and as a result, the sale of the inventory brought only $5,257.50 at a public auction. The Burks raised the defense of the damages as a setoff to their surety amount for the remainder of the loan. Security Bank said the Burks could not raise the damages as a defense because the Burks were sureties and had guaranteed the full amount of the loan. The trial court granted summary judgment for Security Bank, and the Burks appealed.

DECISION: The Burks did not waive defenses in their suretyship agreement. Their rights were the same as the rights of Tri County, the original debtor. When a debtor defaults and there is an Article 9 security interest (see Chapter 33), the debtor has the right to require the creditor to sell the collateral in a commercially reasonable manner. Damages to the property represent an issue of commercial reasonableness, and because Tri County would have had the right to assert such damages as a defense, so also do the Burks. [**Security State Bank v Burk, 995 P2d 1272 (Wash App 2000)**]

---

[3] *Fleet National Bank v Phillips*, 2006 WL 2044655 (Mass App Div).

FIGURE 32-1   *No Release of Surety*

1. FRAUD BY DEBTOR
2. MISREPRESENTATION BY DEBTOR
3. CHANGES IN LOAN TERMS (E.G., EXTENSION OF PAYMENT)—COMPENSATED SURETY ONLY
4. RELEASE OF PRINCIPAL DEBTOR
5. BANKRUPTCY OF PRINCIPAL DEBTOR
6. INSOLVENCY OF PRINCIPAL DEBTOR
7. DEATH OF PRINCIPAL DEBTOR
8. INCAPACITY OF PRINCIPAL DEBTOR
9. LACK OF ENFORCEMENT BY CREDITOR
10. CREDITOR'S FAILURE TO GIVE NOTICE OF DEFAULT
11. FAILURE OF CREDITOR TO RESORT TO COLLATERAL

FIGURE 32-2   *Release of Surety*

1. PROPER PERFORMANCE BY DEBTOR
2. RELEASE, SURRENDER, OR DESTRUCTION OF COLLATERAL (TO EXTENT OF VALUE OF COLLATERAL)
3. SUBSTITUTION OF DEBTOR
4. FRAUD/MISREPRESENTATION BY CREDITOR
5. REFUSAL BY CREDITOR TO ACCEPT PAYMENT FROM DEBTOR
6. CHANGE IN LOAN TERMS—UNCOMPENSATED SURETY ONLY
7. STATUTE OF FRAUDS
8. STATUTE OF LIMITATIONS

For Example, suppose that Bank One has in its possession $10,000 in gold coins as collateral for a loan to Janice in the amount of $25,000. Albert has agreed to serve as a surety for the loan to Janice in the amount of $25,000. If a Bank One manager returns the $10,000 in coins to Janice, then Albert is discharged on his suretyship obligation to the extent of that $10,000. Following the release of the collateral, the most that Albert could be held liable for in the event of Janice's default is $15,000.

A surety is also discharged from her obligation if the creditor substitutes a different debtor. A surety and a guarantor make a promise that is personal to a specific debtor and do not agree to assume the risk of an assignment or a delegation of that responsibility to another debtor. A surety also enjoys the discharge rights afforded all parties to contracts, such as the statute of limitations. If the creditor does not enforce the suretyship agreement within the time limits provided for such contract enforcement in the surety's jurisdiction, the obligation is forever discharged.[4]

Figures 32-1 and 32-2 provide summaries of the defenses and release issues surrounding suretyship and guaranty relationships.

---

[4] *The Clark Const. Group, Inc. v Wentworth Plastering of Boca Raton, Inc.,* 840 So2d 357 (Fla App 2002).

> ## CASE SUMMARY
>
> ### It Was Greek to Me, But the Contract Was in English
>
> **FACTS:** Continental Airlines established an Air Travel Plan Account that permitted Regency Cruises to purchase air travel and other related services from Continental and charge those services to the Air Travel Plan Account. Regency Cruises is an owner and operator of a fleet of pleasure ships and a wholly owned subsidiary of Regency Holdings, which is incorporated in the Cayman Islands. Antonios Lelakis is the chairman of the board of Regency Holdings.
>
> Regency fell behind on its payments to Continental. Regency Holdings signed an addendum to the travel account agreement in which it agreed to be jointly and severally liable for any existing and future Regency Cruises debt. Regency Holdings also executed a promissory note payable to Continental in the amount of $10,476,992.23 to be paid by June 30, 1995. Lelakis signed an individual guarantee to Continental for the $10,476,992.23 note.
>
> Regency Holdings had made only two payments on the note and Continental declared Regency Holdings in default, accelerated the amount due, and demanded full payment of the note. Both Regency Holdings and Regency Cruises filed for Chapter 11 bankruptcy in November 1995. Continental demanded payment of the note from Lelakis as a surety. Lelakis refused on the grounds of misrepresentation, duress, and changes in the surety's obligations under the original agreement.
>
> **DECISION:** Lelakis remains liable as a surety for the obligation. He may not understand English, but Lelakis presented no facts to support that he was not negligent in signing the guaranty. The nature of the guaranty was never misrepresented, nor was Lelakis ever forced to sign without the chance to examine the documents and the nature of the obligation. Lelakis failed to take any steps either at the October 5, 1995, meeting or in the intervening days before he signed the guaranty on October 21, 1995, to ascertain the nature of the guaranty, as was his custom in business transactions. [**Continental Airlines, Inc. v Lelakis, 943 F Supp 300 (SDNY 1996); affirmed 129 F3d 113 (2nd Cir 1997)**]

 ## LETTERS OF CREDIT

letter of credit commercial device used to guarantee payment to a seller, primarily in an international business transaction.

issuer party who issues a document such as a letter of credit or a document of title such as a warehouse receipt or bill of lading.

standby letter letter of credit for a contractor ensuring he will complete the project as contracted.

A **letter of credit** is a three-party arrangement with a payor, a beneficiary, and a party on whom the letter of credit is drawn, or **issuer.** A letter of credit is an agreement that the issuer of the letter will pay drafts drawn by the beneficiary of the letter. Letters of credit are a form of advance arrangement for financing. Sellers of goods, for example, know in advance how much money may be obtained from the issuer of the letter. A letter of credit may also be used by a creditor as a security device because the creditor knows that the drafts that the creditor draws will be accepted or paid by the issuer of the letter.[5]

The use of letters of credit arose in international trade. While international trade continues to be the primary area of use, there is a growing use of letters in domestic sales and in transactions in which the letter of credit takes the place of a surety bond. A letter of credit has been used to ensure that a borrower would repay a loan, that a tenant would pay the rent due under a lease, and that a contractor would properly perform a construction contract. This kind of letter of credit is known as a **standby letter.**

---

[5] *U.S. Material Supply, Inc. v Korea Exchange Bank*, 417 F Supp 2d 652 (D NJ 2006), discussing the character and purpose of letters of credit.

FIGURE 32-3   *Letter of Credit*

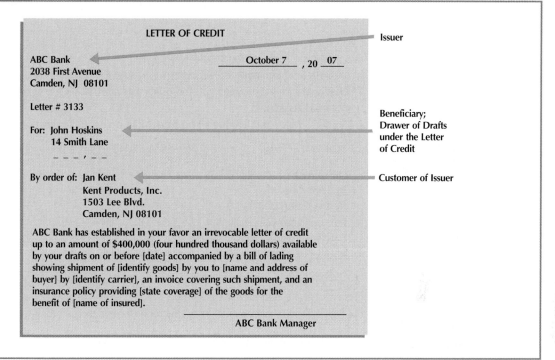

LETTER OF CREDIT   Issuer

ABC Bank   October 7 ____ , 20 __07__
2038 First Avenue
Camden, NJ 08101

Letter # 3133   Beneficiary;
                                                                                       Drawer of Drafts
For: John Hoskins   under the Letter
      14 Smith Lane   of Credit
      _ _ _ , _ _

By order of: Jan Kent   Customer of Issuer
              Kent Products, Inc.
              1503 Lee Blvd.
              Camden, NJ 08101

ABC Bank has established in your favor an irrevocable letter of credit
up to an amount of $400,000 (four hundred thousand dollars) available
by your drafts on or before [date] accompanied by a bill of lading
showing shipment of [identify goods] by you to [name and address of
buyer] by [identify carrier], an invoice covering such shipment, and an
insurance policy providing [state coverage] of the goods for the
benefit of [name of insured].
                                              _____
                                                    ABC Bank Manager

There are few formal requirements for creating a letter of credit. Although banks often use a standardized form for convenience, they may draw up individualized letters of credit for particular situations (see Figure 32-3).

In international letters of credit, there are several sources of recognized standards that businesses use for the creation and execution of letters of credit. Along with the UCC, there is the Uniform Customs and Practice for Documentary Credits (or UCP), something that reflects ordinary international banking operational practices on letters of credit. The UCP is revised, generally, about every ten years by the International Chamber of Commerce (ICC, see Chapter 7).

(ETHICS & THE LAW)

Getting Too Cozy with One's Debtor

Very often the creditors of a business can exercise a great deal of authority over the operation of the business when it has missed a payment on its debt or has experienced some business or market setbacks. Without owning any stock in a corporation, creditors will, in more than 50 percent of all cases in which they express concern about repayment, succeed in having both boards and officers replaced in part or in toto. **For Example,** Worlds of Wonder, Inc., a creative and innovative toy manufacturer

ETHICS & THE LAW

continued

that was responsible for the first talking toy, Teddy Ruxpin, was required by demands from its secured and unsecured creditors to obtain the resignation of its founder and CEO, Donald Kingsborough. Kingsborough was paid $212,500 at his departure for "emotional distress."*

Studies show** that creditors also have input on the following corporate actions:

Type of Decision	Percentage of Creditors with Vote
Declaration of dividends	48
Increased security	73
Restructuring of debt	55
Cap on borrowing	50
Cap on capital expenses	25
Restrictions on investment	23

Is it fair to have creditors control corporate governance? Will they always make the choices that are best for the shareholders? Is it unconscionable to have these control covenants in loan agreements? Why do creditors need them in their loan agreements?

---

* "Toymaker Has Financing Pact," *New York Times*, April 2, 1988, C1 (Reuters item).

** See Tim Reason, "Keeping Skin in the Game, *CFO Magazine*, February 1, 2005, **http://www.cfo.com**, for a discussion of why creditors are involved and what they can do to help manage a debtor.

6. DEFINITION

A letter of credit is an engagement by its issuer that it will pay or accept drafts when the conditions specified in the letter are satisfied. The issuer is usually a bank.

Three contracts are involved in letter-of-credit transactions: (1) the contract between the issuer and the customer of the issuer, (2) the letter of credit itself, and (3) the underlying agreement, often a contract of sale, between the beneficiary and the customer of the issuer of the letter of credit (see Figure 32-4). The letter of credit is completely independent from the other two contracts. Consideration is not required to establish or modify a letter of credit.

The issuer of the letter of credit is in effect the obligor on a third-party-beneficiary contract made for the benefit of the beneficiary of the letter. The key to the commercial success of letters of credit is their independence. **For Example,** a bank obligated to issue payment under a letter of credit "when the goods are delivered" must honor that obligation even if the buyer has complaints about the goods. It is the terms of the letter of credit that control the payment, not the relationship, contract, or problems of the beneficiary or issuer of the letter of credit.

The key to the commercial vitality and function of a letter of credit is that the issuing bank's promise is independent of the underlying contracts and the bank should not resort to them in interpreting a letter of credit. Sometimes called *the strict compliance rule,* banks must honor the letter of credit terms using strict interpretation. The respective parties are protected by a careful description of the documents that will trigger payment. The claim of a beneficiary of a letter of credit is not subject to

| **FIGURE 32-4** | *The Contracts Involved in Letter-of-Credit Transactions* |

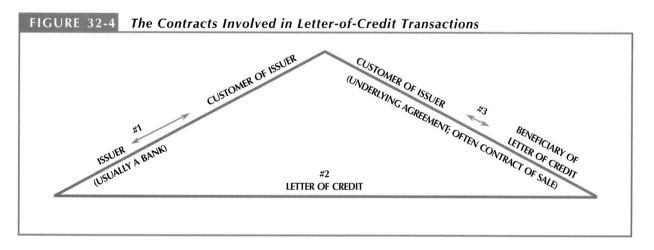

defenses normally applicable to third-party contracts. Known as the *independence rule,* banks cannot, except in limited circumstances, delve into the underlying contract issues; the focus of the bank is only on the terms of the letter of credit.

CASE SUMMARY

Give Me a Little Credit, Not Temporary Restraint

FACTS: In 1995, the Airport Authority of India (AAI) retained Transact International, Inc. (Transact), to build a cargo-handling facility at the Indira Gandhi International Airport in New Delhi, India. Webb-Stiles Company, Inc., a manufacturer of conveyor systems, was one of Transact's subcontractors on the airport project.

State Bank of India (SBI) agreed to guarantee Transact's performance to AAI. In return, SBI required that Transact obtain an irrevocable standby letter of credit in favor of SBI. Webb-Stiles helped Transact obtain the letter of credit from SouthTrust. On November 13, 1996, SouthTrust issued its letter of credit for $175,661. Transact signed the letter of credit as applicant, and Webb-Stiles signed as surety for Transact's obligation to reimburse SouthTrust for any payment made under the letter of credit. Although the letter of credit was originally to expire on September 30, 1998, the parties extended it to January 31, 2005.

Between 1999 and 2004, AAI and Transact had numerous disputes about their obligations under the contract. By late 2004, the parties were still unable to resolve their differences. On December 10, 2004, SBI notified SouthTrust that AAI had made a demand for the full amount of the performance guarantee ($175,661). In turn, SBI immediately made a demand on the letter of credit in the same amount. Under its terms, the letter of credit is payable by SouthTrust upon SouthTrust's receipt of a proper demand from SBI. SBI's demand conformed to the requirements of the letter of credit.

Webb-Stiles sued for an injunction to stop SouthTrust from honoring the letter of credit, claiming that AAI had fraudulently misrepresented its right to make demand against the SBI performance guarantee. The trial court granted Webb-Stiles a preliminary injunction preventing payment on the letter of credit. AAI appealed.

DECISION: The court held that the trial court should not have issued the temporary injunction because the circumstances in which a court should stop payment under a letter of credit are rare. The party asking for the injunction must be able to show that without it, it will have no remedies available. In this case, there are remedies, but they require litigation. The

CASE SUMMARY

continued

whole purpose of a letter of credit is that the parties negotiate a shift in risk. The letter of credit is there to ensure payment when there are disputes. While the parties can still litigate the issues in the underlying contract, those issues should not become part of the letter of credit terms. Issuing such injunctions would undermine all of the purposes of the commercial credit instruments and the clean means of payment and compensation. The grant of the injunction was reversed. [**SouthTrust Bank of Alabama, N.A. v Webb-Stiles Co., Inc.,** 2005 WL 2692482 (Ala), 58 UCC Rep Serv 2d 60 (Ala 2005)]

7. PARTIES

The parties to a letter of credit are (1) the issuer; (2) the customer who makes the arrangements with the issuer; and (3) the beneficiary, who will be the drawer of the drafts that will be drawn under the letter of credit. There may also be (4) an **advising bank**[6] if the local issuer of the letter of credit requests its **correspondent bank,** where the beneficiary is located, to notify or advise the beneficiary that the letter has been issued. **For Example,** a U.S. merchant may want to buy goods from a Spanish merchant. There may have been prior dealings between the parties so that the seller is willing to take the buyer's commercial paper as payment or to take trade acceptances drawn on the buyer. If the foreign seller is not willing to do this, the U.S. buyer, as customer, may go to a bank, the issuer, and obtain a letter of credit naming the Spanish seller as beneficiary. The U.S. bank's correspondent or advising bank in Spain will notify the Spanish seller that this has been done. The Spanish seller will then draw drafts on the U.S. buyer. Under the letter of credit, the issuer is required to accept or pay these drafts.

advising bank bank that tells beneficiary that letter of credit has been issued.

correspondent bank will honor the letter of credit from the domestic bank of the buyer.

8. DURATION

A letter of credit continues for any length of time it specifies. Generally, a maximum money amount is stated in the letter, so that the letter is exhausted or used up when the issuer has accepted or paid drafts aggregating that maximum. A letter of credit may be used in installments as the beneficiary chooses. The issuer or the customer cannot revoke or modify a letter of credit without the consent of the beneficiary unless that right is expressly reserved in the letter.

9. FORM

A letter of credit must be in writing and signed by the issuer. If the credit is issued by a bank and requires a documentary draft or a documentary demand for payment[7] or if

[6] See UCC § 5-107; *Sun Marine Terminals, Inc. v Artoc Bank and Trust, Ltd.,* 797 SW2d 7 (Tex 1990).

[7] A *documentary draft* or a *documentary demand for payment* is one for which honor is conditioned on the presentation of one or more documents. A document could be a document of title, security, invoice, certificate, notice of default, or other similar paper. UCC § 5-103(1)(b).

E-COMMERCE AND CYBERLAW

The E-Commerce Wallet

Internet transactions have provided new ways to guarantee payments. For example, there is now "digital cash," which is a virtual currency on the Web. Customers and retailers each have the software that permits them to transfer the digital cash and have it accepted. The Internet currency is purchased using real currency or a credit card. The software program simply dictates, as do letters of credit, when that Internet currency can be released to the retailer by the consumer.

Some Web customers are also setting up "digital wallets," which is a way of paying Web retailers through one source. Customers simply refer retailers to their digital wallet, set up through software programs, and provide the authorization necessary for the retailer to use the credit card(s) set up in the digital wallet for ease of payment.

the credit is issued by a nonbank and requires that the draft or demand for payment be accompanied by a document of title, the instrument is presumed to be a letter of credit (rather than a contract of guarantee). Otherwise, the instrument must conspicuously state that it is a letter of credit.

10. DUTY OF ISSUER

The issuer is obligated to honor drafts drawn under the letter of credit if the conditions specified in the letter have been satisfied. The issuer takes the risk that the papers submitted are the ones required by the letter. If they are not, the issuer cannot obtain reimbursement for payment made in reliance on such documents. The issuer has no duty to verify that the papers are properly supported by facts or that the underlying transaction has been performed. It is immaterial that the goods sold by the seller in fact do not conform to the contract so long as the seller tenders the documents specified by the letter of credit. If the issuer dishonors a draft without justification, it is liable to its customer for breach of contract.[8]

11. REIMBURSEMENT OF ISSUER

When the issuer of a letter of credit makes proper payment of drafts drawn under the letter of credit, it may obtain reimbursement from its customer for such payment. No reimbursement can be obtained if the payment was not proper. This will be the case if the payment is made after the letter has expired or if the payment is in an amount exceeding that authorized by the letter. Reimbursement cannot be obtained if the payment is made without the proper presentation of required documents or if the payment is made in violation of a court injunction against payment.

---

[8] *Amwest Sur. Ins. Co. v Concord Bank*, 248 F Supp 2d 867 (ED Mo 2003). In some cases, letters of credit are so poorly drafted that payment must be made despite evolving concerns by the parties. *Nissho Iwai Europe PLC v Korea First Bank*, 99 NY2d 115, 782 NE2d 55, 752 NYS2d 259, 49 UCC Rep Serv 2d 259 (NY 2002).

> SUMMARY

Suretyship and guaranty undertakings have the common feature of a promise to answer for the debt or default of another. The terms are used interchangeably, but a guarantor of collection is ordinarily only secondarily liable, which means that the guarantor does not pay until the creditor has exhausted all avenues of recovery. If the guarantor has made an absolute guarantee, then its status is the same as that of a surety, which means that both are liable for the debt in the event the debtor defaults, regardless of what avenues of collection, if any, the creditor has pursued.

Surety and guaranty relationships are based on contract. Sureties have a number of rights to protect them. They are exoneration, subrogation, indemnity, and contribution. In addition to those rights, sureties also have certain defenses. They include ordinary contract defenses as well as some defenses peculiar to the suretyship relationship, such as release of collateral, change in loan terms, substitution of debtor, and fraud by the creditor.

A letter of credit is an agreement that the issuer of the letter will pay drafts drawn on the issuer by the beneficiary of the letter. The issuer of the letter of credit is usually a bank. There are three contracts involved in letter-of-credit transactions: (1) the contract between the issuer and the customer of the issuer, (2) the letter of credit itself, and (3) the underlying agreement between the beneficiary and the customer of the issuer of the letter of credit.

The parties to a letter of credit are the issuer, the customer who makes the arrangement with the issuer, and the beneficiary who will be the drawer of the drafts to be drawn under the letter of credit. The letter of credit continues for any time it specifies. The letter of credit must be in writing and signed by the issuer. Consideration is not required to establish or modify a letter of credit. If the conditions in the letter of credit have been complied with, the issuer is obligated to honor drafts drawn under the letter of credit.

> QUESTIONS AND CASE PROBLEMS

1. First Interstate Bank issued a letter of credit in favor of Comdata Network. Comdata is engaged in money transfer services. It provides money to truckers on the road by way of cash advances through form checks written by truckers. When Comdata enters into a business relationship with a trucking company, it requires a letter of credit. This requirement is to secure advances made on behalf of the trucking company. One of the trucking companies defrauded the bank that issued the letter of credit. Comdata demanded that the bank make payment to it under the letter of credit for cash advances that the trucking company had not repaid. The bank, alleging fraud by the trucking company, refused. Comdata filed suit. Can Comdata force payment? [*Comdata Network, Inc. v First Interstate Bank of Fort Dodge*, 497 NW2d 807 (Iowa App)]

2. Kiernan Construction Co. entered into a contract with Jackson for Jackson to build a house for her. Century Surety Co. executed a bond to protect Jackson from loss if Kiernan failed to construct the house or pay labor and materials bills. Kiernan failed to build the house, and Jackson sued Century Surety, which claims that Jackson must first sue Kiernan. Is it correct?

3. On August 1, 1987, Dori Leeds signed a "guarantee of credit" with Sun Control Systems, which guaranteed "the prompt payment, when due, of every claim of [Sun Control Systems] against [Dori Leeds dba 'Blind Ambitions']." At the time she signed the guarantee of credit, Blind Ambitions was in the business of installing window treatments and installed only Faber brand blinds, which were purchased from Sun Control Systems. In 1991, Sun Control Systems sold and assigned all of its assets to Faber. Shortly thereafter, Dori assigned her interest in Blind Ambitions to David and Judith Leeds, who continued to do business as Blind Ambitions. In 1994 and 1995, Blind Ambitions made credit purchases from Faber and did not pay under the terms of those contracts. Faber brought suit against Dori Leeds as the guarantor of credit for Blind Ambitions. Dori refused to pay on the

grounds that she was acting as a personal guarantor for her business, not for Blind Ambitions. Is she correct? [*Faber Industries, Ltd. v Dori Leeds Witek*, 483 SE2d 443 (NC App)]

4. Fern Schimke's husband, Norbert, was obligated on two promissory notes in favor of Union National Bank. Some time prior to his death, Union National Bank prepared a guarantee contract that was given to Norbert for his wife to sign. She signed the guarantee at the request of her husband without any discussion with him about the provisions of the document she was signing. On Norbert's death, the bank brought suit against Fern on the basis of the guarantee. Fern argued that because there was no consideration for the guarantee, she could not be liable. Is Fern correct? Must there be consideration for a guarantor to be responsible for payment? [*Union Nat'l Bank v Fern Schimke*, 210 NW2d 176 (ND)]

5. In May 1989, Alma Equities Corp., owned by its sole shareholder and president, Lewis Futterman, purchased a hotel and restaurant in Vail, Colorado, from Alien for $3,900,000. Alma paid $600,000 in cash to Alien, and Alien provided a purchase money loan to Alma for the remaining amount of the sale price, with the loan secured by a deed of trust on the hotel and restaurant. The hotel and restaurant did not do well, and Futterman negotiated a friendly foreclosure on the property in 1991, whereby Alma would continue to operate the hotel and restaurant on a lease basis, with Futterman providing a personal guarantee for the lease. Alma failed to make the lease payments for the months of November and December 1991 and, following an unlawful detainer action filed by Alien for possession of the hotel and restaurant, was forced into bankruptcy. Alien turned to Futterman for satisfaction on the lease payments. Futterman said he should not have been forced to pay because Alien's unlawful detainer forced Alma into bankruptcy. Was Futterman correct? Did he have a defense? [*Alien, Inc. v Futterman*, 924 P2d 1063 (Colo)]

6. Eberstadt owed Terence $500 and gave his note for that amount to Terence. At the same time, an agreement signed by Reid and given to Terence was as follows: "I agree to be surety for the payment of Eberstadt's note for $500." On maturity of the note, Eberstadt paid $200 on account and gave a new note for $300 due in three months. Reid was not informed of this transaction. The new note was not paid at maturity. Terence sued Reid. Does Reid have any defense?

7. Gilbert signed a guarantee for the benefit of his son with Cobb Exchange Bank. The guarantee included all extensions and renewals of the son's obligation. Subsequently, a renewal of the note added an additional $600 to the original obligation. On the son's default, Cobb Bank brought suit on the guarantee. Who should win? Why? [*Gilbert v Cobb Exchange Bank*, 231 SE2d 508 (Ga App)]

8. In June 1995, Southern Energy and Gesellschaft Fur Bauen Und Wohnen Hannover (GBH) entered into a construction contract for the second of two housing projects known as "socialized housing" to be built in Hannover, Germany. The socialized housing contract called for a bank guarantee issued by a European bank as security for Southern Energy's performance of the contract. GBH wired to Southern Energy 555,117 deutsche marks, representing the first 30 percent due on the contract, less the 15 percent value-added tax. Deutsche Bank issued the performance guarantee to GBH on the condition that the guarantee would be secured by a standby letter of credit. To facilitate the performance guarantee in favor of GBH, AmSouth issued a letter of credit to Deutsche Bank for an amount not to exceed 1,276,770 deutsche marks relating to Southern Energy's performance under the socialized housing contract. The letter of credit served as Deutsche Bank's security for issuing the performance guarantee.

In January 1996, Southern Energy informed GBH that it would be unable to perform the contract at the agreed price without suffering a substantial financial loss. In February 1996, GBH responded by letter, stating that it would hold Southern Energy in default if Southern Energy failed to complete the project at the agreed time. GBH extended the deadline for performance from March 1, 1996, to March 15, 1996. GBH began rebidding the socialized housing project to other contractors. Southern Energy submitted another quote on the project, but GBH rejected its offer and awarded the contract to another builder. Meanwhile, the date of performance had passed on the initial contract. In June 1996, GBH requested that the advanced installment money on the contract, DM 555,117.39, be refunded. Southern Energy complied and transferred the money to GBH's account. Southern Energy asserted that because all of GBH's advanced monies had been returned, GBH no longer had any basis in fact to demand payment on the bank guarantee, and that Deutsche Bank had no legitimate basis to demand payment on the letter of credit. GBH, quoting the terms of the letter of credit itself, decided to "exercise its rights under the performance guarantee" by asserting its right to damages. The next day, Deutsche Bank presented a draft for payment. After AmSouth informed Southern Energy that it would honor the draft but before payment had been made, the Jefferson County Circuit Court granted Southern Energy's request for a temporary restraining order but later reversed itself. Southern Energy appealed. Should the temporary restraining order be reversed? Can a court halt the payment on a letter of credit? [*Southern Energy Homes, Inc. v AmSouth Bank of Alabama*, 709 So 2d 1180 (Ala)]

9. Ribaldgo Argo Consultores entered into a contract with R. M. Wade & Co. for the purchase of irrigation equipment. Ribaldgo obtained a letter of credit from Banco General, a bank with its principal place of business in Quito, Ecuador. The letter of credit required that Wade submit certain documents to obtain payment. The documents were submitted through Citibank as correspondent bank for Banco General. However, the documents were incomplete, and Citibank demanded additional information as required under the letter of credit. By the time Wade got the documents to Citibank, more than 15 days had expired, and the letter of credit required that Wade submit all documentation within 15 days of shipping the goods to obtain payment. Citibank refused to authorize the payment. Wade filed suit. Must Citibank pay? Why or why

not? [*Banco General Runinahui, S.A. v Citibank International*, 97 F3d 480 (11th Cir)]

10. Hugill agreed to deliver shingles to W. I. Carpenter Lumber Co. and furnished a surety bond to secure the faithful performance of the contract on his part. After a breach of the contract by Hugill, the lumber company brought an action to recover its loss from the surety, Fidelity & Deposit Co. of Maryland. The surety denied liability on the grounds that there was concealment of (a) the price to be paid for the shingles and (b) the fact that a material advance had been made to the contractor equal to the amount of the profit that he would make by performing the contract. Decide. [*W. I. Carpenter Lumber Co. v Hugill*, 270 P 94 (Wash)]

11. Donaldson sold plumbing supplies. The St. Paul-Mercury Indemnity Co., as surety for him, executed and delivered a bond to the state of California for the payment of all sales taxes. Donaldson failed to pay, and the surety paid the taxes that he owed and then sued him for the taxes. What was the result? [*St. Paul-Mercury Indemnity Co. v Donaldson*, 83 SE2d 159 (SC)]

12. Paul owed Charles a $1,000 debt due September 1. On August 15, George, for consideration, orally promised Charles to pay the debt if Paul did not. On September 1, Paul did not pay, so Charles demanded $1,000 from George. Is George liable? Why or why not?

13. First National Bank hired Longdon as a secretary and obtained a surety bond from Belton covering the bank against losses up to $100,000 resulting from Longdon's improper conduct in the performance of his duties. Both Longdon and the bank signed the application for the bond. After one year of service, Longdon was promoted to teller, and the original bond remained in effect. Shortly after Longdon's promotion, examination showed that Longdon had taken advantage of his new position and stolen $50,000. He was arrested and charged with embezzlement. Longdon had only $5,000 in assets at the time of his arrest. (a) If the bank demands a payment of $50,000 from Belton, what defense, if any, might Belton raise to deny any obligation to the bank? (b) If Belton fully reimburses the bank for its loss,

under what theory or theories, if any, may Belton attempt to recover from Longdon?

14. Jack Smith was required by his bank to obtain two sureties for his line of credit of $100,000. Ellen Weiss has agreed to act as a surety for $50,000, and Allen Fox has agreed to act as a surety for $75,000. Smith has used the full $100,000 in the line of credit and is now in bankruptcy. What is the maximum liability of Weiss and Fox if the bank chooses to collect from them for Smith's default? How should the $100,000 be allocated between Weiss and Fox?

15. Industrial Mechanical had a contract with Free Flow Cooling, Ltd., a British company. Free Flow owed Industrial $171,974.44 for work Industrial had performed on a construction project in Texas. Free Flow did not pay Industrial, and Industrial filed suit against Siemens Energy & Automation as a guarantor or surety on the debt. Industrial alleges that Siemens is a surety based on a fax it received from Siemens on January 27, 1994. The fax is handwritten and states: "We have received preliminary notices and we like [*sic*] to point out that the contract we have signed does not allow for such action to recourse [*sic*] with the customer. Please advise all subcontractors and suppliers that the only recourse that they will have is against Siemens." The fax was signed "kind regards" by Arnold Schultz, Siemens's senior project manager for the Texas construction project. Nowhere in the fax did Siemens guarantee the debt of any specified entity or state that Siemens was agreeing to indemnify anyone or pay the obligations on behalf of anyone else. The fax failed to identify the principal debtor whom Siemens purportedly agreed to indemnify and failed to state that Siemens agreed to answer for that entity's debt. Can Industrial collect the amount of Free Flow's debt from Siemens? Why or why not? [*Industrial Mechanical, Inc. v Siemens Energy & Automation, Inc.*, 495 SE2d 103 (Ga App)]

> CPA QUESTIONS

1. Marbury Surety, Inc., agreed to act as a guarantor of collection of Madison's trade accounts for one year beginning on April 30, 1980, and was compensated for same. Madison's trade debtors are in default in payment of $3,853 as of May 1, 1981. As a result,

   a. Marbury is liable to Madison without any action on Madison's part to collect the amounts due.

   b. Madison can enforce the guarantee even if it is not in writing because Marbury is a del credere agent.

   c. The relationship between the parties must be filed in the appropriate county office because it is a continuing security transaction.

   d. Marbury is liable for those debts for which a judgment is obtained and returned unsatisfied.

2. Queen paid Pax and Co. to become the surety on a loan that Queen obtained from Squire. The loan is due, and Pax wishes to compel Queen to pay Squire. Pax has not made any payments to Squire in its capacity as Queen's surety. Pax will be most successful if it exercises its right to

   a. Reimbursement (indemnification)

   b. Contribution

   c. Exoneration

   d. Subrogation

3. Which of the following defenses by a surety will be effective to avoid liability?

   a. Lack of consideration to support the surety undertaking

   b. Insolvency in the bankruptcy sense of the debtor

   c. Incompetency of the debtor to make the contract in question

   d. Fraudulent statements by the principal debtor that induced the surety to assume the obligation and that were unknown to the creditor

4. For each of the numbered words or phrases, select the one best phrase from the list a through j. Each response may be used only once.

   (1) Indemnity contract
   (2) Suretyship contract
   (3) Surety
   (4) Third-party beneficiary
   (5) Co-surety
   (6) Statute of Frauds
   (7) Right of contribution
   (8) Reimbursement
   (9) Subrogation
   (10) Exoneration

   a. Relationship whereby one person agrees to answer for the debt or default of another

   b. Requires certain contracts to be in writing to be enforceable
   c. Jointly and severally liable to creditor
   d. Promises to pay debt on default of principal debtor
   e. One party promises to reimburse debtor for payment of debt or loss if it arises
   f. Receives intended benefits of a contract
   g. Right of surety to require the debtor to pay before surety pays
   h. Upon payment of more than his/her proportionate share, each co-surety may compel other co-sureties to pay their shares
   i. Upon payment of debt, surety may recover payment from debtor
   j. Upon payment, surety obtains same rights against debtor that creditor had

CONSUMER PROTECTION

 GENERAL PRINCIPLES

 AREAS OF CONSUMER PROTECTION

LEARNING OBJECTIVES

After studying this chapter, you should be able to

LO.1 Discuss the purpose of consumer protection statutes

LO.2 Explain the areas of concern and regulation in consumer protection

LO.3 List the rights and protections that are available for consumer debtors under federal law

LO.4 Describe the role of the Federal Trade Commission in protecting consumer rights

LO.5 Give a description of the protections for consumers under the Truth-in-Lending laws, the Fair Credit Reporting Act, and the Fair Debt Collections Practices Act

LO.6 Explain the remedies available for consumers under protection laws

The consumer protection movement, which began in the 1960s, continues to expand with rights for consumers in everything from ads to credit collection. These statutory protections exist at both the state and federal level.

 GENERAL PRINCIPLES

Consumer protection began with the goal of protecting persons of limited means and limited knowledge. One writer described consumer protection statutes as laws that protect "the little guy."[1] Over the past 20 years, however, that protection has expanded considerably in both who is protected and the types of activities that are regulated or provide consumers with statutory remedies.

1. EXPANSION OF CONSUMER PROTECTION

Some statutes are worded so that consumer protections apply only to natural persons. Some statutes are interpreted to apply only to consumer transactions, not to commercial transactions. However, many consumer protection statutes, once limited to individuals, now include partnerships, corporations, banks, or government entities that use goods or services as consumers. The statutes thus go beyond providing protection only for the unsophisticated and uneducated.[2]

consumer any buyer afforded special protections by statute or regulation.

For Example, in defining **consumer**, courts have held that a collector paying nearly $100,000 for jade art objects, a glass manufacturer purchasing 3 million gallons of diesel oil fuel, and the city of Boston purchasing insurance are all consumers for purposes of statutory protections. Some states, such as Arizona, Arkansas, Delaware, Illinois, Iowa, Missouri, and New Jersey, even have two separate statutes, one for the protection of individual consumers and another for the protection of businesses. In addition, the protected consumer may be a firm of attorneys.[3]

---

[1] Olha N. M. Rybakoff, "An Overview of Consumer Protection and Fair Trade Regulation in Delaware," 8 *Delaware Law Review* 63 (2005). This article provides a good history and summary of consumer protection laws.

[2] *Boubelik v Liberty State Bank*, 527 NW2d 589 (Minn App 1995).

[3] *Catallo Associates, Inc. v MacDonald & Goren*, 465 NW2d 28 (Mich App 1990). Statutes that broaden the protected group to protect buyers of goods and services are often called *deceptive trade practices statutes* instead of being referred to by the earlier term, *consumer protection statutes.*

Today, all 50 states and the District of Columbia have some version of what are called "Little FTC Acts" (the Federal Trade Commission [FTC] discussed later in the chapter is the federal consumer protection statute that prohibits unfair or deceptive practices) or "unfair or deceptive acts or practices" ("UDAP") statutes. Although there are 51 versions of consumer protection statutes, they have several common threads. First, consumer protection statutes provide faster remedies for consumers. Statutory remedies under consumer protection statutes often mean that consumers need not establish that a tort has been committed or establish actual damage levels because the statute provides for both the elements for recovery and perhaps even a formula for recovery of damages. Second, the harms addressed by consumer statutes tend to affect the public generally and involve more than just one contract or even one seller. **For Example,** one area of consumer protection provides consumers control over both the release and content of their credit report information. The use of credit information, the granting of credit, and the use of credit to make purchases all have a profound impact on buyers, sellers, and national, state, and local economies. These protections provide a statutory formula for consumer damages when credit information is misused or is incorrect. Credit information on consumers is regulated because many consumers were affected by less-than-accurate information and unauthorized disclosures of their private credit information.

2. WHO IS A CONSUMER?

A consumer claiming a violation of the consumer protection statute has the burden of proving that the statutory definition of consumer has been satisfied. The business accused of unfair or deceptive trade practices then has the burden of showing that the statute does *not* apply, as well as establishing exceptions and exemptions. **For Example,** some consumer protection statutes do not apply when a buyer is purchasing goods for resale.

3. WHO IS LIABLE UNDER CONSUMER PROTECTION STATUTES?

Those who are liable for violations of consumer protection situations are persons or enterprises that regularly enter into the type of transaction in which the injured consumer was involved. **For Example,** the merchant seller, the finance company, the bank, the leasing company, the home contractor, and any others who regularly enter into transactions with consumers are subject to the statutes. Some consumer protection statutes apply only to specific types of merchants and service providers such as auto repair and sale statutes, funeral home disclosure statutes and regulations, and swimming pool contractors.

4. WHEN IS THERE LIABILITY UNDER CONSUMER PROTECTION STATUTES?

Consumer protection laws typically list the types of conduct or failures to act properly that are prohibited as harmful to consumers. For example, the failure to disclose all of the charges related to a consumer loan or a credit purchase made by a consumer would be an omission that carries rights for the consumers and penalties for the business. *Deceptive advertising* is an act that is prohibited by consumer protection statutes that provide remedies for consumers who were deceived or misled by the ads. Proof of these acts or omissions that are listed and described in detail in the consumer

CASE SUMMARY

The Client Who Was a Wreck Because of His Accident Lawyers

FACTS: Azar & Associates is a law firm specializing in personal injury lawsuits. In television advertisements that air throughout Colorado, the Azar firm represents itself as a firm that can recover money for its clients that other attorneys cannot. The commercials claim that the Azar firm will always "obtain as much as we can, as fast as we can" for its clients. One of the firm's commercials employs the slogan "In a wreck, get a check" while another portrays Franklin D. Azar, president of the Azar firm, as the "strong arm" who muscles insurance adjusters into paying up.

Richard E. Crowe saw the Azar firm's television commercials before and after he was injured in a multicar accident in Colorado Springs. He suffered numerous physical injuries, including mild traumatic brain injury with speech impairment, and his vehicle sustained heavy damages. According to the police report, a 17 year old driving a Dodge Ram truck caused the accident when he ran a stop sign and collided with Crowe's two-door Honda with an estimated impact speed of 45 mph. The 17 year old was charged with a traffic offense for failing to obey the stop sign.

Crowe retained Marc B. Tull and Franklin D. Azar to represent him in his personal injury claim. Crowe was offered $4,000 by the truck driver's insurer to settle the claim, and Tull advised him to accept the offer. Crowe relied on Tull's advice and accepted the $4,000 settlement offer.

Crowe later filed suit against Tull and Azar, claiming that the settlement was far below the real value of his claim given that he had already accumulated more than $17,000 in medical and rehabilitation costs and lost more than $7,000 in lost wages when Tull advised him to settle the case for $4,000. Crowe based his suit on professional negligence (legal malpractice), violation of the Colorado Consumer Protection Act (CCPA), and breach of fiduciary obligation. Crowe's CCPA and breach of fiduciary obligation claims were dismissed by the trial court. The court found that the "actual practice of law" was not a commercial activity regulated by the CCPA. Crowe appealed to the Colorado Supreme Court.

DECISION: The court held the CCPA did apply to attorney advertising. The court noted that the statute did not specifically exempt attorneys, but did not specifically include them and it was left to determine from the purpose of the statute whether this profession would be subject to consumer protection liability. The court discussed how pervasive legal advertising had become and how critical it is to those who lack information in making their decisions on choosing a lawyer. Furthermore, the court noted nothing inconsistent with existing attorney regulation and applying consumer protection because both have the same purpose of being certain that clients are treated fairly and given full information during the course of the attorney representation. The court noted that the ads and services and the unknowledgeable clients were the classic issues that underlie all consumer protection statutes and that attorneys were subject to the CCPA for deception in advertising. [**Crowe v Tull, 126 P3d 196 (Colo 2006)**]

protection statutes is often easier for consumers to prove than a common law case of fraud. Consumer protection statutes do not require proof of intent. An ad might not have seemed deceptive to the merchant selling computers when he reviewed the ad copy for the newspaper. However, a consumer without the merchant's sophistication could be misled. **For Example,** suppose that a consumer sees the ad for a 19-inch flat-screen computer monitor for $158 after rebate that reads, "Compare this price with any 19-inch flat-screen monitor, and you will see we cannot be matched." The average consumer might not understand that speakers are not included with such monitors. The computer store, on the other hand, might have assumed that everyone understands that flat-screen monitors with speakers are in a different price category. Adding "no speakers" or "speakers not included" would have allowed the consumer the information needed to shop and compare.

Consumers enjoy a great deal of protection when there are omissions or misleading information is given, but consumer protection does not protect consumers from their own negligence. If a consumer signs a contract without reading or understanding what it means, she is bound. Moreover, when the contract signed by the consumer clearly states one thing, the consumer cannot introduce evidence about statements the merchant made when the contract that was signed is clear. Consumers must exercise reasonable care and cannot blindly trust consumer protection law to rescue them from their own blunders.

5. WHAT REMEDIES DO CONSUMERS HAVE?

Although consumers have the theoretical right to bring suit for defenses to contracts or enforcement when the other party does not perform, the right to prove fraud, misrepresentation, duress, or breach is often of little practical value to consumers because both the costs of litigation and the burden of proof are high. The amount that the consumer has lost may be too small to be worth pursuing when compared with the cost of litigation. Consumer protection legislation provides special remedies for consumers so that pursuing their rights in court is cost beneficial. For example, some federal statutes permit debtors to bring class action suits, and their recovery is a statutory percentage of the net worth of the company that has violated their rights.

In addition, consumer statutes often provide initial or alternative means for consumers to enforce their rights. Consumer statutes provide procedural steps for consumers to use to try to resolve their problem and to document what has happened in their contract or relationship with a business. **For Example,** some statutes require consumers to give the business involved written notice of the consumer's complaint. Having this notice then provides the business an opportunity to examine the consumer's complaint or concerns and possibly work out a solution.[4]

In addition to procedural remedies other than litigation, consumer protection statutes provide other ways for consumers to seek their remedies, sometimes with the help of others who are more experienced in resolving consumer protection statutory violations.

(a) GOVERNMENT AGENCY ACTION At both the federal and state levels, administrative agencies that are responsible for the enforcement of laws and regulations also have the power to take steps to obtain relief for consumers. For example, the Federal Trade Commission (FTC) can file a complaint against a company for false advertising. In settling the complaint with the company that advertised, the FTC could require the company to refund to the consumers involved the money they spent on the product based on the ad claims.

(b) ACTION BY ATTORNEY GENERAL A number of states allow their state attorneys general to bring actions on behalf of consumers who are victims of fraud or other unfair conduct. In these actions, the attorney general can request that consumers' contracts be canceled and that they be given restitution of whatever they paid. These suits by attorneys general are not criminal actions; they are civil suits in

---

[4] *Fredericks v Rosenblatt*, 667 NE2d 287 (Mass App 1996).

which the standard of proof is a preponderance of the evidence, not proof beyond a reasonable doubt. For example, the litigation brought by state attorneys general for alleged deception by tobacco companies on the health harms of using tobacco resulted in settlements by those companies. The funds were used to compensate the states for health care costs for individuals with tobacco-related illnesses for whom the state was caring. The funds were also used to pay for educational programs and ads that caution young people not to smoke and warn them about the health hazards of using tobacco.

Many states also permit their attorneys general to bring actions for an injunction against violations of the consumer protection statute. These statutes commonly give the attorney general the authority to obtain a voluntary cease-and-desist consent decree (see Chapter 6) for improper practices before seeking an injunction from a court. The attorney general, like the agency, can impose a penalty for a violation.

(c) Action by Consumer   Consumer protection statutes can also provide that a consumer who has been harmed by a violation of the statutes may recover by his own suit against the business that acted improperly.[5] The consumer may either seek to recover a penalty provided for in the consumer protection statute or bring an action on behalf of consumers as a class. Consumer protection statutes are often designed to rely on private litigation as an aid to enforcement of the statutory provisions. The Consumer Product Safety Act of 1972 authorizes "any interested person" to bring a civil action to enforce a consumer product safety rule and certain orders of the Consumer Product Safety Commission.[6]

In other cases, however, the individual consumer cannot bring any action, and enforcement of the law is given exclusively to an administrative agency. However, consumer protection statutes are liberally construed to provide consumers with the maximum protection.[7]

(d) Replacement or Refund   Some state consumer protection statutes require that the consumer be made whole by the replacement of the good, the refund of the purchase price, or the repair of the item within a reasonable time.[8]

(e) Invalidation of Consumer's Contract   Other consumer protection statutes provide that when the contract made by a consumer violates the statute, the consumer's contract is void. In such a case, the seller cannot recover from the consumer buyer for any unpaid balance. Likewise, the seller cannot repossess the goods for nonpayment. The consumer keeps the goods without making any further payment.[9]

6. WHAT ARE THE CIVIL AND CRIMINAL PENALTIES UNDER CONSUMER PROTECTION STATUTES?

Only certain government agencies and attorneys general can seek criminal and civil penalties against those who violate consumer protection statutes. The agency or

---

[5] *Provident American Ins. Co. v Castaneda,* 914 SW2d 273 (Tex App 1996).

[6] 15 USC § 2051 *et seq.*

[7] *Equity Plus Consumer Finance & Mortgage Co. v Howes,* 861 P2d 214 (NM 1993).

[8] *Buford v General Motors Corp.,* 435 SE2d 782 (NC App 1993). Note that apart from these statutes, the buyer may have protection under a warranty to repair or replace. Likewise, a revocation of acceptance under the UCC would give the right to a refund of the purchase price.

[9] *Glouster Community Bank v Winchell,* 659 NE2d 330 (Ohio App 1995).

attorney general may use those penalties to provide compensation to consumers who have been victims of the violations. When consumers successfully bring individual or class action suits against those who violate their rights as consumers, they recover damages. Some consumer protection statutes authorize the recovery of **compensatory damages** to compensate the consumer for the loss. These types of statutes are designed to put the customer in as good a position as he would have been in had there not been a deception, breach, or violation of other requirements under the consumer protection statute. Other statutes authorize the recovery of **punitive damages,**[10] which are additional damages beyond compensatory damages and may be a percentage of the company's net worth. In the case of antitrust statutes that prohibit anticompetitive behavior, consumers could collect treble punitive damages for the violation. Although consumer protection statutes are interpreted in favor of the consumer, a consumer cannot claim both treble damages authorized by such a statute and punitive damages under the common law. Such double recovery would give the consumer duplicative remedies for the same wrong.

compensatory damages sum of money that will compensate an injured plaintiff for actual loss.

punitive damages damages, in excess of those required to compensate the plaintiff for the wrong done, that are imposed to punish the defendant because of the particularly wanton or willful character of wrongdoing; also called *exemplary damages.*

 AREAS OF CONSUMER PROTECTION

The following sections discuss important areas of consumer protection. Figure 33-1 provides an overview of these areas.

7. ADVERTISING

Statutes commonly prohibit fraudulent advertising. Most advertising regulations are entrusted to an administrative agency, such as the FTC, which is authorized to issue

FIGURE 33-1 *The Legal Environment of the Consumer*

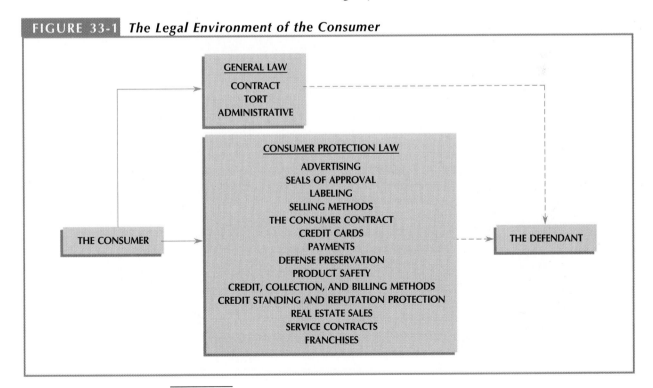

---
[10] *Maberry v Said,* 927 F Supp 1456 (D Kan 1996).

orders to stop false or misleading advertising. Statutes prohibiting false advertising are liberally interpreted.

A store is liable for false advertising when it advertises a reduced price sale of a particular item that is out of stock when the sale begins. It is no defense that the presale demand was greater than usual.

(a) DECEPTION   Under consumer protection statutes, *deception* rather than *fraud* is the significant element.[11] A breach of these statutes occurs even without proof that the wrongdoer intended to defraud or deceive anyone.

The deception statutes and regulations represent a shift in the law and public policy. These regulations are not laws based on fault; rather, they concern the problem of the buyer who is likely to be misled. The good faith of an advertiser or the absence of intent to deceive is immaterial. The purpose of false advertising regulation is to protect the *consumer* regardless of the advertiser's motives.

The FTC requires advertisers to maintain records of the data used as support for statements made in ads that deal with the safety, performance, efficacy, quality, or comparative price of an advertised product. The FTC can require the advertiser to produce these data and backup material. If it is in the interest of the consumer, the FTC can make this information public except to the extent that it contains trade secrets or privileged material.

(b) CORRECTIVE ADVERTISING   When an enterprise has made false and deceptive statements in advertising, the FTC may require new advertising to correct the former statements so that consumers are aware of the truth. This corrective advertising required by the FTC is also called *retractive advertising*.

CASE SUMMARY

Attacking the Maker of the Big Mac

FACTS: Ashley Pelman and others brought suit against McDonald's Corporation and several of its franchisees alleging that in making and selling their products, they engaged in deception and that this deception caused the minors who have consumed McDonald's products to injure their health because they have become overweight and have developed diabetes, coronary heart disease, high blood pressure, elevated cholesterol intake, and/or other detrimental and adverse health effects.

The district court dismissed the counts that alleged McDonald's had engaged in deceptive advertising, and the plaintiffs appealed.

DECISION: The appellate court held that the fact that there were questions of fact regarding how much they ate, how many times per day and what else they ate were not grounds for dismissing the complaint. The court held that the plaintiffs had raised enough questions and issues to raise the possibility that McDonald's had been deceptive in its ad claims and disclosures and that the case could go forward on the basis of the claims under the consumer protection statutes of New York. [**Pelman ex rel. Pelman v McDonald's Corp., 396 F3d 508 C.A.2 (NY 2005); and Pelman v McDonald's Corp., 237 F Supp 2d 512 (SDNY 2003)**]

---

[11] *Rucker v Huffman*, 392 SE2d 419 (NC App 1990).

SPORTS & ENTERTAINMENT LAW

No Dessert Until You Sign a Waiver

Seattle's Queen Ann Hill area has a popular restaurant, the 5 Spot, which features a dessert called The Bulge, a calorie-laden sugar-coated fried banana with ice cream, macadamia nuts, whipped cream, and two kinds of syrup. Before customers are permitted to have this dessert, they must first sign a liability waiver that states in part, "I release the 5 Spot from all liability of any weight gain that may result from ordering and devouring this sinfully fattening treat."* Is this waiver a response to cases such as the McDonald's case? Do you think the waiver would be legally binding?

---

*Sandy Coleman, "Drafting Manager's Duties," *Boston Globe*, September 25, 2003, 2; Shirleen Holt, "Go Ahead, Splurge on the Bulge, But Any Resulting Fat Is on You," *Seattle Times*, September 6, 2003, A1.

E-COMMERCE AND CYBERLAW

Undercover Buzz

Undercover marketing is all over the Internet. Sometimes called *buzz marketing* or *guerilla marketing,* this form of marketing on the Internet gets products and services noticed by Internet users because many of them are not aware that the companies are behind the informational type of approaches used. Sometimes also called *viral marketing,* this tactic uses a link, some news item, or an activity that makes the Internet consumers believe that they have come across a product or service as a function of serendipity from Internet surfing. They are not aware that the news, information, activity, or really cool Web page was created by the company in a stealth way (yet another name for this is *stealth marketing*) to grab their interest and sell a product or service. Lee Jeans used grainy video clips to attract attention on the Internet and from there built a campaign tied to a video game and secret codes found only on Lee products.

Buzz campaigns begin in chat rooms where experts in undercover marketing pretend to be chat room users who begin a conversation that leads to the company's product or service. They get the buzz going without identifying themselves as being associated with or working for the company. Personal blogs are also used for stealth marketing because the blogger does not always disclose affiliation with the company.

Internet users have objected to these practices, but others point out that companies have used "fake consumers" in coffee shops and as tourists to introduce products to consumers who believe they are simply talking with another patron or tourist about a camera or a car. While there is concern about the level of stealth marketing on the Internet, the ability to find out who and what is real can be difficult. State deceptive ad statutes may not cover these types of specific ad approaches, and the FTC faces the same investigative issues of finding out who is at the heart of the ads.

8. LABELING

Closely related to the regulation of advertising is the regulation of labeling and marking products. Various federal statutes are designed to give consumers accurate information about a product, whereas others require warnings about dangers of use or misuse. Consumer protection regulations prohibit labeling or marking products with such terms as *jumbo, giant,* and *full,* which tend to exaggerate and mislead. **For Example,** the health foods store Eating Well sold a number of foods with the label "Fat Free." This label was false, and Eating Well knew that the foods so labeled were ordinary foods not free of fat. Eating Well violated consumer protection statutes prohibiting false labeling. As for sales made with the false label, it also committed the tort of fraud and the crime of obtaining money by false pretenses.

THINKING THINGS THROUGH

Fruity Suit

On May 16, 2003, Sari Smith filed a class action lawsuit in Cook County, Illinois, against J.M. Smucker Co. on behalf of "[a]ll purchasers in the United States of America of spreadable fruit products labeled "Simply 100% Fruit" manufactured, produced, and sold by J.M. Smucker Co. excluding its directors, officers and employees" for consumer fraud, deceptive business practices, unjust enrichment, and breach of warranty, alleging that Smucker's Simply 100% Fruit products do not contain 100% fruit. The premium jam's label indicates that, for example, its Strawberry jam also contains "fruit syrup, lemon juice concentrate, fruit pectin, red grape juice concentrate and natural flavors."

Is the label a form of deceptive advertising? If you were a Smuckers executive, what would you argue in the case on deceptive ads? [J.M. SMUCKER CO. V RUDGE, 877 So 2d 820 (Fla App 2004)]

9. SELLING METHODS

In addition to regulating ads, consumer protection statutes regulate the methods used to sell goods and services.

(a) HOME-SOLICITED SALES A sale of goods or services for $25 or more made to a buyer at home may be set aside within three business days. This right of rescission may be exercised merely because the buyer does not want to go through with the contract. There is no requirement of proving any misconduct of the seller or any defect in the goods or services.[12]

When the buyer has made an oral agreement to purchase and the seller comes to the buyer's home to work out the details, the transaction is not a home-solicited sale and cannot be avoided under the federal regulation.[13] A sale was also not home-solicited when the seller phoned the consumer at his or her home for permission to mail the consumer a promotional brochure, and thereafter the consumer went to the seller's place of business where the contract was made.[14]

---

[12] Federal Trade Commission Regulation, 16 CFR § 429:1.

[13] *Cooper v Crow,* 574 So 2d 438 (La App 1991).

[14] *United Consumers Club v Griffin,* 619 NE2d 489 (Ohio App 1993).

(b) Referral Sales   The technique of giving the buyer a price reduction for referring customers to the seller is theoretically lawful. In effect, the seller is merely paying the buyer a commission for the promotion of other sales. In actual practice, however, this referral sales technique is often accompanied by fraud or exorbitant pricing, so consumer protection laws variously condemn referral selling. As a result, the referral system of selling has been condemned as unconscionable under the Uniforma Commercial Code (UCC) and is expressly prohibited by the UCC.

(c) Telemarketing Fraud   In recent years, high-pressure selling by telephone has produced a new kind of fraud that is estimated to rob U.S. citizens of some $40 billion a year. Following passage by Congress of a mandate on control of telemarketing, the Telephone Consumer Protection Act (TCPA), the FTC developed a series of rules on telemarketing restrictions.[15] The federal statute makes it unlawful for telemarketers to "make any call (other than a call made for emergency purposes or made with the prior express consent of the called party) using any automatic telephone dialing system or an artificial or prerecorded voice"; to "make any call to an emergency telephone line . . . the telephone line of any guest room or patient room of a hospital, health care facility, elderly home"; to "use any telephone facsimile machine, computer, or other device to send an unsolicited advertisement to a telephone facsimile machine"; or to make any calls "before 8 A.M. or after 9 P.M." There are additional state regulations on telemarketing, with some states requiring sellers who solicit orders by telephone to register with a particular government agency.[16]

In 2003, the FTC promulgated its rules for a National Do Not Call Registry.[17] Adding to its already extensive regulations on telemarketing, the FTC created a means whereby consumers could register to not be called as part of telephone solicitation campaigns by merchants and service providers.[18] As of the end of 2005, 100 million consumers had signed up for the Do Not Call Registry.

When a consumer registers with the do not call list, merchants and service providers cannot contact the consumer by telephone. Exceptions apply when the consumer has voluntarily given her telephone number to a company. Charitable organizations are also exempt from the rule. The constitutionality of the Do Not Call Registry was challenged in court but upheld.

10. THE CONSUMER CONTRACT

Consumer contracts are regulated in different ways.

(a) Form of Contract   Consumer protection laws commonly regulate the form of the contract, requiring that certain items be specifically listed, that payments under the contract be itemized, and that the allocation to such items as principal, interest, and insurance be indicated. Generally, certain portions of the contract or all of it must be printed in type of a certain size, and a copy must be furnished to the buyer. Such statutory requirements are more demanding than the statute of frauds section of the UCC. Often, the copy of the contract furnished to the consumer

---

[15] 47 USCA § 227.

[16] *Distributel, Inc. v Alaska,* 933 P2d 1137 (Alaska 1997).

[17] 16 CFR § 310.8.

[18] The national list supplements the law in 28 states that already had some form of do-not-call registers. However, constitutional issues (see Chapter 5) limited those protections across state lines so that the national regulation was necessary.

CASE SUMMARY

Put Us on Your No-Fax List!

FACTS: American Blast Fax, Inc., is a Texas corporation in the business of providing fax advertising services in the state of Missouri. Fax.com Inc. is a Delaware corporation doing business out of California. It transmits advertisements from California to telephone facsimile machines in Missouri. The Missouri attorney general brought suit against the two companies, alleging that they violated the Telephone Consumer Protection Act (TCPA) by sending fax advertisements when they had not received the express invitation or permission of persons to whom copies of advertisements were faxed. American and Fax.com filed motions to dismiss, arguing that the specific provision of the TCPA regarding unsolicited fax advertisements is unconstitutional.

DECISION: The TCPA makes it unlawful for any person "to use any telephone facsimile machine, computer, or other device to send an unsolicited advertisement to a telephone facsimile machine" [47 U.S.C. § 227(b)(1)(C)]. The term *unsolicited advertisement* is defined as "any material advertising the commercial availability or quality of any property, goods, or services which is transmitted to any person without that person's prior express invitation or permission" [§ 227(a)(4)].

The TCPA does not ban all unsolicited faxes, only advertisements. Fax recipients still bear the costs of printing others' messages, even if they strongly oppose the content of the messages.

There is no distinction between unsolicited advertisements and other unsolicited faxes. The recipient still must bear the cost, and the fax can still interfere with the use of his facsimile machine for business purposes. The court held that the (1) government demonstrated a substantial interest in preventing advertising cost shifting and interference with fax machines that such unwanted advertising places on the recipients, (2) the TCPA provision was reasonably related to substantial governmental interest, and (3) the provision was not more restrictive or extensive than necessary to accomplish that substantial governmental interest. The court held that 47 U.S.C. § 227(b)(1)(C) was constitutional because it represented reasonable regulation of one form of unsolicited speech. Those companies that advertised by fax had alternative means for advertising that did not force their messages upon all businesses and impose the burden of tying up their faxes and using their paper supplies for such ads. [**Missouri ex rel. Nixon v American Blast Fax, Inc., 323 F3d 649 (8th Cir 2003)**]

must be completely filled in. Back-page disclaimers are void if the front page of the contract does not call attention to the presence of such terms.

(b) Contracts Printed on Two Sides   To be sure that consumers see disclosures required by federal law, special provision is made when the terms of a transaction are printed on both the front and the back of a sheet or contract. In this case, (1) both sides of the sheet must carry the warning "NOTICE: see other side for important information," and (2) the page must be signed at the end of the second side. Conversely, the requirements of federal law are not satisfied if there is no warning of "see other side" and the parties sign the contract only on the face, or the first side, of the paper.

(c) Particular Sales and Leases   The Motor Vehicle Information and Cost Savings Act requires a dealer to disclose to the buyer various elements in the cost of an automobile. The act prohibits selling an automobile without informing the buyer that the odometer has been reset below the true mileage. A buyer who is caused actual loss by odometer fraud may recover from the seller three times the actual loss or $1,500, whichever amount is higher.[19] The federal statute is breached when the seller knows that the odometer has turned over at 100,000 miles but the seller states that the mileage is 20,073 miles instead of 120,073. The Consumer Leasing Act of 1976 requires that persons leasing automobiles and other durable goods make a full disclosure to consumers of the details of a transaction.[20]

Although the federal statute imposes liability only when the seller "knowingly" violates the statute, it is not necessary to prove actual knowledge. An experienced auto dealer cannot claim lack of knowledge that the odometer was false when that conclusion was reasonably apparent from the condition of the car.[21]

(d) CONTRACT TERMS Consumer protection legislation does not ordinarily affect the right of the parties to make a contract on whatever terms they choose. It is customary, however, to prohibit the use of certain clauses that are harsh on the debtor or that have too great a potential for exploitive abuse by a creditor, such as the UCCC prohibition against creditors entering a judgment against a debtor without giving the debtor any chance to make a defense.[22]

The federal Warranty Disclosure Act of 1974 establishes disclosure standards for consumer goods warranties to help consumers understand them.[23]

The parties to a credit transaction may agree that payment can be made in installments but that if there is a default on any installment, the creditor may accelerate the due date or declare the entire balance due at once. Such acceleration of the debt can cause the debtor great hardship. Some state statutes limit or prohibit the use of **acceleration clauses.**

(e) LIMITATIONS ON CREDIT Various laws may limit the ability to borrow money or purchase on credit. Some states prohibit **open-end mortgages** that secure a specified debt as well as additional loans that may be made later. Federal laws and regulations impose disclosure requirements on home equity loans.

An FTC regulation makes requiring a consumer borrowing or buying on credit to give the lender or seller a security interest in all of the consumer's household goods as collateral an unfair trade practice.[24]

Consumer debt in the United States had grown to more than $2 trillion dollars as of the end of 2005. Credit is available even to those who have bad credit histories through what has been called the **subprime lending market.** This credit market makes loans to consumers who have bankruptcies, no credit history, or a poor credit history. A subprime lender is one who offers credit to a high-risk consumer, often loaning money to pay off other debts the consumer is facing as due. The subprime market tripled in size, to $330 billion between 1997 and 2003. In addition to higher risk, the characteristics of a subprime market loan are lower loan amounts, higher origination costs, brokers' fees, credit insurance fees, high interest rates, significant collateral

acceleration clause
provision in a contract or any legal instrument that advances the time for the performance of specified obligations; for example, a provision making the balance due upon debtor's default.

open-end mortgage
mortgage given to secure additional loans to be made in the future as well as to secure the original loan.

subprime lending market
A credit market that makes loans to high-risk consumers (those who have bankruptcies, no credit history, or a poor credit history), often loaning money to pay off other debts the consumer has due.

---

[19] 15 USC § 1901 *et seq.,* as amended; recodified as 49 USC §§ 32701–32711.

[20] 15 USC § 1667.

[21] *Denmon v Nicks Auto Sales,* 537 So 2d 796 (La App 1989).

[22] UCCC §§ 2.415, 3.407.

[23] The act known as the *Magnuson Moss Act* is found at 15 USC § 2301.

[24] 16 CFR § 444.2(4)(1999).

pledges, large prepayment penalties so that the consumer debtor is locked into the high interest rate, faster repayment, and difficulty in determining all of the charges and fees from the documentation. The types of loans include title loans (when the loan is made in exchange for the title to the consumer's car or house, which will turn over to the lender upon default). Not all loans in the subprime market are unfair to consumers. Many of the terms of the loan are high to compensate the lender for the risk in loaning to a consumer with a poor credit history. However, part of the subprime lending market includes lenders who take advantage of less sophisticated consumers or even consumers who are just desperate for funds. These lenders use their superior bargaining positions to obtain credit terms that go well beyond compensating them for their risk. Sometimes called **predatory lending,** both states and the federal government have begun passing new statutes and regulations to cover predatory lending.[25] One of the issues in the regulation is defining what constitutes predatory lending that can be regulated and what may be ethical issues about lending practices to consumers in difficult financial situations.

predatory lending A practice on the part of the subprime lending market whereby lenders take advantage of less sophisticated consumers or those who are desperate for funds by using the lenders' superior bargaining positions to obtain credit terms that go well beyond compensating them for their risk.

(f) UNCONSCIONABILITY   To some extent, consumer protection has been provided under the UCC by those courts that hold that the "unconscionability" provision protects from "excessive" or "exorbitant" prices when goods are sold on credit.[26]

Some statutes are aimed at preventing price gouging on consumer goods or services for which the demand is abnormally greater than the supply. **For Example,** New York's statute provides: "During any abnormal disruption of the market for consumer goods and services vital and necessary for the health, safety, and welfare of consumers, resulting from stress of weather, convulsion of nature, failure or shortage of electric power or other source of energy . . . no merchant shall sell or offer to sell any such consumer goods or services for an amount which represents an unconscionably excessive price." *Consumer goods and services* are defined as "those used, bought, or rendered primarily for personal, family, or household purposes." Such a statute protects, for example, purchasers of electric generators for home use during a hurricane-caused blackout. During 2006, with the rise in gas prices, many attorneys general conducted investigations into price gouging on gas prices at the pump.

11. CREDIT DISCLOSURES

While general consumer statutes prohibit deception in ads and sales practices, specific federal laws require the disclosure of all interest charges, points, and fees for all types of loans and credit contracts. These laws require disclosure of an annual percentage rate (APR) so that the consumer can see just how much the transaction costs per year and can compare alternatives.[27] The Truth in Lending Act (TILA) provides the requirements for disclosures in credit contracts and consumer rights when full disclosure is not made. When a consumer sale or contract provides for payment in more than four installments, it is subject to the TILA. The application of the TILA is required even when there is no service or finance charge for the installment payments. There are additional obligations of disclosure under the

---

[25] NJ Stat Ann § 46:10B-22 (West 2006); 2003 Ark Acts 2598; Cal Fin Code §§ 4970-4979.7 (West 2006); Ga Code Ann § 7-6A-1-13 (2006); 2003 Ill Laws 93-561; 2003 NM Laws 436; 2001 NY Laws 11856; NC Gen Stat § 24-1.1e (2006); 2003 SC Acts 42; 2003 NC Sess Laws 24-10.2.

[26] UCC § 2-302(1).

[27] Consumer Credit Protection Act (CCPA), 15 USC §§ 1605, 1606, 1636; Regulation Z adopted by the Federal Reserve, 12 CFR § 226.5.

E-COMMERCE AND CYBERLAW

ID Theft

The largest identity theft ring in the history of the United States was broken up in December 2002 when federal authorities arrested those responsible for stealing the credit identities of at least 30,000 people. The total amount obtained through the identity theft is believed to have been about $3 million. In one example, the identity thieves opened a line of credit in another's name, using another's good credit. When the line of credit was funded for $35,000, the thief wrote a check for $34,000.

Ford Motor Credit was a key player in the arrests when it noticed that it was being billed for credit reports it did not order. The thieves used access codes to obtain credit reports and then had the companies billed. Other companies are now checking their bills and notifying those whose reports were ordered so that they can check for possible fraudulent charges and uses of their credit ratings to obtain credit cards and lines of credit.

USA Today offers the following insights on what identity thieves do:

- Change the mailing address on credit cards so cardholders do not notice the lack of bills or the charges.
- Purchase cell phones in another's name so they can give creditors a phone number.
- Open bank accounts with a line of credit, and write checks on the accounts.

The Department of Justice has information on its Web site for avoiding identity theft at **http://www.usdoj.gov/**.

Fair Credit and Charge Card Disclosure Act [28] and by the Home Equity Loan Consumer Protection Act.[29]

When consumer credit is advertised as repayable in more than four installments and no finance charge is expressly imposed, the advertisement must "clearly and conspicuously" state that "the cost of credit is included in the price" quoted for the goods and services.

If sellers advertise that they will sell or lease on credit, they cannot state merely the monthly installments that will be due. They must give the consumer additional information: (1) the total cash price, (2) the amount of the down payment required, (3) the number, amounts, and due dates of payments, and (4) the annual percentage rate of the credit charges.[30]

12. CREDIT CARDS

Credit cards permit cardholders to buy on credit. Credit cards and credit arrangements are so readily available that consumers tell of receiving credit cards when they apply in the name of their Labrador retrievers. Because of the extensive availability of credit cards and the ease with which they are issued, there are

---

[28] 15 USC § 1601, note, *et seq.*

[29] *Id.*

[30] Regulation Z, § 1210; Consumer Leasing Act of 1976, 15 USC § 1667.

extensive federal regulations of credit card use and the rights of consumers with credit cards.[31]

(a) Unsolicited Credit Cards   Federal regulations prohibit the unsolicited distribution of credit cards to persons who have not applied for them. The practice of simply sending credit cards through the mail to consumers is now illegal. The problems with rising identity theft have made this protection especially important to consumers because identity thieves were able to intercept the mail and seize the unsolicited credit cards.

(b) Surcharge Prohibited   Under some statutes, a seller cannot add any charge to the purchase price because the buyer uses a credit card instead of paying with cash or a check.[32]

(c) Unauthorized Use   A cardholder is not liable for more than $50 for the unauthorized use of a credit card. To even recover the $50 amount, the credit card issuer must show that (1) the credit card was an accepted card,[33] (2) the issuer gave the holder adequate notice of possible liability in such a case, (3) the issuer furnished the holder with notification means in the event of loss or theft of the credit card, (4) the issuer provided a method by which the user of the card could be identified as the person authorized to use it,[34] and (5) unauthorized use of the card had occurred or might occur as a result of loss, theft, or some other event.

The burden of proof is on the card issuer to show that the use of the card was authorized or that the holder is liable for its unauthorized use.[35]

(d) Unauthorized Purpose Distinguished   Unauthorized use of a credit card occurs only when it is used without the permission or approval of the cardholder. In contrast, the holder may authorize another person to use the card but only for a particular purpose, such as to buy a certain item. If the person uses the card for other than the purpose specified by the holder, this is still an authorized use of the card even though it is for an unauthorized purpose.[36] In such a case, the cardholder is liable for all charges made on the card even though they were not intended by the cardholder when the card was loaned. The same rule is applied when an employer has cards issued to employees for making employment-related purchases but an employee uses the card for personal purposes.

(e) Late Payment Fee   The contract between a credit card issuer and a holder may require the holder to pay a late payment fee computed as the rate of interest allowed by the law of the state where the bank is located. The federal Banking Deregulation Act cancels out any state consumer protection law that prohibits such a charge on bank credit cards.[37]

---

[31] Heidi Mandanis Schooner, "Consuming Debt: Structuring the Federal Response to Abuses in Consumer Credit," 18 *Loyola Consumer Law Review* 43 (2005).

[32] In contrast, the Truth in Lending Act Amendment of 1976, 15 USC § 1666f, permits a merchant to offer a discount to cash-paying customers but not to customers using a credit card.

[33] A credit card is accepted when the cardholder has requested and received or has signed, used, or authorized another to use the card for the purpose of obtaining money, property, labor, or services on credit.

[34] Regulation Z of the Board of Governors of the Federal Reserve, 12 CFR § 226.13(d), as amended, provides that the identification may be by signature, photograph, or fingerprint on the credit card or by electronic or mechanical confirmation.

[35] *Band v First Bankcard Center*, 644 So 2d 211 (La App 1994).

[36] *American Express Travel Related Services Co. v Web, Inc.*, 405 SE2d 652 (Ga 1991).

[37] *Stoorman v Greenwood Trust Co.*, 908 P2d 133 (Colo 1995).

13. PAYMENTS

Consumer legislation may provide that when a consumer makes a payment on an open charge account, the payment must be applied toward payment of the earliest charges. The result is that, should there be a default at a later date, any right of repossession of the creditor is limited to the later, unpaid items. This first-charged, first-payment-applied method outlaws contract provisions by which, on the default of the buyer, sellers could repossess all purchases that had been made at any prior time. Such a provision is outlawed by the UCCC and probably would be found unconscionable under the UCC. **For Example,** over the years, Jilda purchased many household articles from the Montparnasse Department Store by using her charge account. When Jilda made a payment on her account, Montparnasse applied a fraction of it to each item Jilda had purchased so that no item was ever paid for in full. Montparnasse claimed that it could do this because a creditor can decide how to apply payments when a debtor does not make any specification. Under the ordinary contract law rule, Montparnasse is correct, but consumer protection statutes in many states require the creditor to apply a payment to the oldest debt so that it is paid off in full and only the most recent remain unpaid. This means that Montparnasse would have no claim on Jilda's earlier purchases even though Jilda had not paid in full for the more recent ones.

14. PRESERVATION OF CONSUMER DEFENSES

Consumer protection laws generally prohibit a consumer from waiving or giving up any defense provided by law. In the ordinary contract situation, when goods or services purchased or leased by a consumer are not proper or are defective, the consumer is not required to pay the seller or lessor or is required to pay only a reduced amount. With the modern expansion of credit transactions, sellers and lessors have used several techniques for getting paid without regard to whether the consumer had any complaint against them. To prevent this, the FTC has adopted a regulation requiring that in every sale or lease of goods or services to a consumer, the contract contain a clause giving the consumer the right to assert defenses. This notice can be found in the discussion of negotiable instruments and the rights of the parties in Chapter 29.

15. PRODUCT SAFETY

A variety of statutes and rules of law, some of which antedate the modern consumer protection era, protects the health and well-being of consumers. Most states have laws governing the manufacture of various products and establishing product safety standards. The federal Consumer Product Safety Act provides for research and setting uniform standards for products to reduce health hazards. This act also establishes civil and criminal penalties for the distribution of unsafe products, recognizes the right of an aggrieved person to recover damages and to obtain an injunction against the distribution of unsafe products, and creates a Consumer Product Safety Commission to administer the act.[38]

A consumer, as well as various nonconsumers, may hold a seller or manufacturer liable for damages when a product causes harm. Liability may be based on guarantees, warranties, negligence, fraud, or strict tort liability (see Chapters 9 and 24).

---

[38] 15 USC §§ 2051–2081.

16. CREDIT, COLLECTION, AND BILLING METHODS

Various laws and regulations protect consumers from discriminatory and improper credit and collection practices.

(a) EQUAL CREDIT OPPORTUNITY ACT: CREDIT DISCRIMINATION   Under the Equal Credit Opportunity Act (ECOA), it is unlawful to discriminate against an applicant for credit on the basis of race, color, religion, national origin, gender, marital status, or age; because all or part of the applicant's income is obtained from a public assistance program; or because the applicant has in good faith exercised any right under the Consumer Credit Protection Act (CCPA). When a credit application is refused, the applicant must be furnished a written explanation. **For Example,** when Eloise applied for a loan from Tradesman Bank, she was told on the phone that the loan would not be made to her unless her husband, Robert, signed as cosigner. The bank violated antidiscrimination laws in two respects: (1) The bank was required to give Eloise a written explanation of why it would not make the loan to her and (2) it is unlawful to refuse to make a loan to a woman merely because she is married and her husband is not a cosigner.[39]

(b) FAIR CREDIT BILLING ACT: CORRECTION OF ERRORS   When a consumer believes that a credit card issuer has made a billing error, the consumer should send the creditor a written statement and explanation of the error. The creditor or card issuer must investigate and make a prompt written reply to the consumer.[40]

(c) IMPROPER COLLECTION METHODS   Unreasonable methods of debt collection are often expressly prohibited by statute or are held by courts to constitute an unreasonable invasion of privacy.[41] The Consumer Credit Protection Act (CCPA) prohibits the use of extortionate methods of loan collection. A creditor may be prohibited from informing a debtor's employer that the employee owes money.

A creditor is liable for unreasonably attempting to collect a bill that in fact has been paid. This liability can arise under general principles of tort law as well as under special consumer protection legislation.

(1) Fault of Agent or Employee.   When improper collection methods are used, it is no defense to the creditor that the improper acts were performed by an agent, an employee, or any other person acting on behalf of the creditor. Under general principles of agency law, a creditor hiring an individual or an agency to collect a debt is liable to the debtor for damages for unlawful conduct by the collector. It is no defense that the creditor did not intend, or have any knowledge of, this conduct.

(2) Fair Debt Collection Practices Act (FDCPA).   The federal FDCPA prohibits improper practices in the collection of debts incurred primarily for personal, family, or household purpose.[42]

---

[39] Richard A. Oppel, Jr., and Patrick McGeehan, "Citigroup Revamps Lending Unit to Avoid Abusive Practices," *New York Times,* November 6, 2000, C1, C2.
[40] Fair Credit Billing Act, 15 USC § 1601.
[41] Fair Debt Collection Practices Act, 15 USC § 1692 *et seq.;* Federal Trade Commission Regulation, 16 CFR pt. 237.
[42] *Bloom v I.C. System, Inc.,* 972 F2d 1067 (9th Cir 1992).

(i) Collection Letters. The act requires that the notice to a debtor state that the debtor has 30 days in which to dispute all or part of the debt.[43]

A debt collector who sends a form letter to debtors that uses the letterhead and the facsimile signature of a lawyer who is not actually representing the collector violates the FDCPA.[44] A letter from a collection agency to a consumer that gives the impression a lawsuit is about to be brought against the consumer when in fact it will not be brought is a violation of the FDCPA.[45]

A debt collection letter sent to the debtor's place of employment was a violation of the FDCPA when the words "final demand for payment" could be read through the envelope. The fact that it was likely that the debtor would be embarrassed by the delivery of such a letter to the employer's address affected the outcome of the case. In another case, a bank's threat to prosecute depositors if they did not return money that had been paid to them by mistake violated a state debt collection law. No criminal statute prohibited the depositors' conduct.

(ii) What Is Not a Defense. When a collection agency violates the FDCPA, it is liable to the debtor for damages. It is no defense that the debtor owed the money that the agency was seeking to collect. When a creditor uses improper collection methods, it is no defense that the improper acts were performed by an agent, employee, or any other person acting on behalf of the creditor.

CASE SUMMARY

High Priority: Collections and the Defaulting Drug Dealer

FACTS: Sometime in July 1999, Kenneth Luciano agreed with one "G" or "GC" of New York that Luciano would sell drugs for "G" in Great Barrington, Massachusetts. "G" (Michael Thompson) supplied Luciano with crack cocaine on the understanding that Luciano would sell the drugs and turn over to Thompson certain sale proceeds. Luciano did not do so; instead he consumed the drugs with his girlfriend.

On Labor Day in 1999, Michael Thompson and two others (a woman named Kelly McLennan and a man referred to as Dan) drove to Great Barrington for the purpose of collecting the money and having Thompson replace Luciano as the local drug distributor. After locating Luciano, the three people confronted him about the money he owed "G." Shortly thereafter, Thompson struck Luciano on the head with a hard plastic toy, and Dan stabbed Luciano with a knife that Thompson provided.

Among other things, Thompson was prosecuted for violation of Massachusetts Fair Debt Collections Practices Act for the use of force in collections. Thompson moved for dismissal of this particular charge on the grounds that he had not made a loan and that a drug deal could not be considered a credit transaction. The lower court upheld the charge and Thompson's conviction, and Thompson appealed.

DECISION: The appellate court upheld the charge and the conviction because the advance of funds or anything of value, regardless of the nature of the underlying transaction, is a loan. Any force used to collect the collateral or the money is a violation of the debt collection consumer protection statutes. [**Commonwealth v Thompson**, 780 NE2d 96 (Mass App 2002)]

---

[43] *Avila v Rubin*, 84 F3d 222 (7th Cir 1996).

[44] *Taylor v Perrin, Landry, duLauney & Durand*, 103 F3d 1232 (5th Cir 1996).

[45] *Bentley v Great Lakes Collection Bureau*, 6 F3d 60 (2d Cir 1993).

(iii) Applicability of Fair Debt Collection Practices Act.   The FDCPA applies not to original creditors but to third parties collecting for creditors. Lawyers who regularly engage in debt collection are also covered under the FDCPA.[46]

The FDCPA applies only to those who regularly engage in the business of collecting debts for others—primarily to collection agencies. The act does not apply when a bank attempts to collect debts owed to it by directly contacting the debtors.

ETHICS & THE LAW

Widowed, Broke, Sick, and in Debt to a Hospital with No Cash

Jeanette White was treated at Yale-New Haven Hospital for cancer. She died there in 1993 after almost 20 years of treatment. The hospital added interest of 10% per annum to the bill and the amount ultimately due was about $40,000. The hospital tried to collect the bill from her husband Quinton White, who was 77 and suffering from heart and kidney ailments.

Mr. White became a cause célèbre when the *Wall Street Journal* ran a top-fold B1 color-picture story on his plight. Yale-New Haven explained that while it was operating in the black, it had $52 million in bad debt and uncompensated care for 2002. The hospital itself does not charge interest, but when the debts are assigned to third parties, such as lawyers, for collection, they are permitted to charge interest.

Mr. White missed only 17 payments to the hospital since he began making payments for his wife's treatment in almost 20 years. However, the hospital was aggressive through its law firm in pursuing the Whites' assets whenever a payment was missed. The first suit resulted in a judgment for the hospital that was reduced to a lien on the White's house in 1982. If and when the house were sold, proceeds would go first to the mortgage company and then to the hospital. The Whites had offered to pay $25 per month on the bill, but the hospital declined and used the court proceedings. The judge ordered payments of $5 per week, which was tripled to $15 per week after Mrs. White died. Most of the 17 missed payments occurred during 2002 when Mr. White began experiencing his health problems. The hospital's law firm went back to court and received a judgment for Mr. White's bank account, a judgment that was halted when Mr. White established that all of the funds in the account were his Social Security payments.

When Mr. White's story was published, students at the free clinic at Yale Law School undertook representation of Mr. White. A plethora of stories about hospital bills, hospital collections, and excessive charges have followed along with class action suits challenging everything from hospital billing policies to collection practices.

What ethical issues arise for the hospitals on uncompensated care? What property does a judgment cover? Who has priority on the Whites' house? Why does a judgment last nearly 20 years?

Source: Lucette Lagnado, ''Twenty Years and Still Paying,'' *Wall Street Journal*, March 13, 2003, B1, B2; ''Dunned for Old Bills, Poor Find Some Hospitals Never Forget,'' *Wall Street Journal*, June 8, 2004, A1, A6; and ''Anatomy of a Hospital Bill,'' *Wall Street Journal*, Sept. 21, 2004, B1, B4.

---

[46]*Jenkins v Heintz*, 25 F3d 536 (7th Cir 1994), aff'd, 514 US 291 (1995).

(iv) Federal Preemption.   In a conflict between collection practices under federal law and a state consumer protection statute, federal law preempts or displaces state law.[47]

(d) Consumer Leases   In some states, the lease of goods to a consumer is treated as a consumer credit sale and is given the same statutory protection as transactions in which the consumer has the option to purchase at the end of the lease or becomes the owner after renting for a specified period of time.[48]

CPA   ## 17. PROTECTION OF CREDIT STANDING AND REPUTATION

When a person purchases on credit or applies for a loan, a job, or an insurance policy, those who will extend these benefits often wish to know more about the applicant. Credit reporting agencies gather such information on borrowers, buyers, and applicants and sell the information to interested persons.

The Fair Credit Reporting Act (FCRA)[49] protects consumers from various abuses that may arise as this information is recorded and revealed. This statute governs credit reporting agencies, sometimes called *credit bureaus.*

consumer credit credit for personal, family, and household use.

The FCRA applies only to **consumer credit,** which is defined as credit for "personal, family, and household" use; it does not apply to business or commercial transactions. The act does not apply to the investigation report made by an insurance company of a policy claim.[50]

(a) Privacy   A report on a person based on personal investigation and interviews is called an **investigative consumer report** and cannot be made without informing the subject of the right to discover the results of the investigation. Credit reporting agencies are not permitted to disclose information to persons not having a legitimate use for it. It is a federal crime to obtain or to furnish a credit report for an improper purpose.

investigative consumer report report on a person based on personal investigation and interviews.

On request, a credit reporting agency must tell a consumer the names and addresses of persons to whom it has made a credit report during the previous six months. It must also tell, when requested, which employers were given such a report during the previous two years.

A store may not publicly display a list of named customers from whom it will not accept checks; such action is an invasion of the privacy of those persons.

(b) Protection from False Information   Much of the information obtained by credit bureaus is based on statements made by persons, such as neighbors, when interviewed by the bureau's investigator. Sometimes the statements are incorrect. Quite often they are **hearsay evidence** and would not be admissible in a legal proceeding. Nevertheless, such statements may go on credit records without further verification and be furnished to a client of the agency, who will tend to regard them as accurate and true.

hearsay evidence statements made out of court that are offered in court as proof of the information contained in the statements and that, subject to many exceptions, are not admissible in evidence.

A person has a limited right to request that a credit bureau disclose the nature and substance of the information it possesses. The right to know, however, does not

---

[47] *Fischer v Unipac Service Corp.,* 519 NW2d 793 (Iowa 1994).

[48] *Muller v Colortyme, Inc.,* 518 NW2d 544 (Minn 1994); and *Rent-A-Center, Inc. v Hall,* 510 NW2d 789 (Wis App 1993), *reh'g denied,* 515 NW2d 715 (Wis 1994).

[49] 15 USC § 1681 *et seq.*

[50] *Reynolds v Hartford Financial Services Group, Inc.,* 416 F3d 1097 (CA 9 2005). The FCRA does apply, however, to insurers using credit reports to determine policy rates.

CASE SUMMARY

Trouble with the Future In-Laws and the FCRA

FACTS: Mary Grendahl's daughter Sarah became engaged to marry Lavon Phillips and moved in with him. Mary Grendahl became suspicious that Phillips was not telling the truth about his past, particularly about whether he was an attorney and whether he had done legal work in Washington, D.C. She also was confused about who his ex-wives and girlfriends were and where they lived. She contacted Kevin Fitzgerald, a family friend who worked for McDowell, a private investigation agency. She asked Fitzgerald to do a "background check" on Phillips, and she gave him the name of the woman Phillips had lived with before he began living with Sarah Grendahl.

Fitzgerald began his search by obtaining Phillips's Social Security number from a computer database. He searched public records in Minnesota and Alabama, where Phillips had lived earlier. He discovered one suit against Phillips for delinquent child support in Alabama, a suit to establish child support for two children in Minnesota, and one misdemeanor conviction for writing dishonored checks.

Fitzgerald then supplied the Social Security information to Econ Control and asked for "Finder's Reports" on Phillips and the former girlfriend. Econ Control was in the business of furnishing credit reports, Finder's Reports, and credit scoring for credit grantors and for private investigators. Econ Control did not ask why McDowell wanted the report, and McDowell did not tell them. Econ Control obtained a report from Computer Science Corporation on Phillips and passed it onto McDowell.

Fitzgerald met with Mary Grendahl and gave her the results of his investigation, including the Finder's Report. Phillips eventually found out about the background check and became angry, as did Sarah. Mary Grendahl then telephoned and left the following voicemail for Sarah: "Sarah, this is Mom. I didn't directly do a credit report. I hired a PI, and they have every right to do that." Phillips brought suit against Mary Grendahl, McDowell Agency, and Econ Control, alleging violations of the Fair Credit Reporting Act. Phillips appealed the lower court's summary judgment for Grendahl and the others on the grounds that what they had obtained was not a consumer report in violation of the FCRA.

DECISION: The court held that the information obtained was indeed a consumer report and that the reason the information was obtained was not one that was permitted under the statute. The background check was not done pursuant to a credit, security, or employment transaction and was not permitted under the law. The lower court's decision was reversed as to the summary judgment on the FCRA.* **[Phillips v Grendahl, 312 F3d 357 (8th Cir 2002)]**

---

*Apodaca v Discover Financial Services, 417 F Supp 2d 1220 (D NM 2006). There is disagreement among the federal circuits about whether violations by reporting agencies must be willful or simply negligent.

extend to medical information. The bureau is not required to identify the persons giving information to its investigators, nor is it required to give the applicant a copy of, or to permit the applicant to see, any file.

When a person claims that report information is erroneous, the credit bureau must take steps within a reasonable time to determine the accuracy of the disputed item.

Adverse information obtained by investigation cannot be given to a client after three months unless it is verified to determine that it is still valid. Most legal proceedings cannot be reported by a bureau after seven years, although a bankruptcy proceeding can be reported for ten years.

18. OTHER CONSUMER PROTECTIONS

Various laws aimed at protecting purchasers of real estate, buyers of services, and prospective franchisees have been adopted in the states and at the federal level.

(a) REAL ESTATE DEVELOPMENT SALES: INTERSTATE LAND SALES FULL DISCLOSURE ACT   Anyone promoting the sale of a real estate development that is divided into 50 or more parcels of less than 5 acres each must file a **development statement** with the secretary of Housing and Urban Development (HUD). This statement must set forth significant details of the development as required by the federal Interstate Land Sales Full Disclosure Act (ILSFDA).[51]

development statement statement that sets forth significant details of a real estate or property development as required by the federal Land Sales Act.

property report condensed version of a property development statement filed with the secretary of HUD and given to a prospective customer at least 48 hours before signing a contract to buy or lease property.

Anyone buying or renting one of the parcels in the subdivision must be given a **property report,** which is a condensed version of the development statement filed with the secretary of HUD. This report must be given to the prospective customer at least 48 hours before the signing of the contract to buy or lease.

If the development statement is not filed with HUD, the sale or rental of the real estate development may not be promoted through interstate commerce (telephones) or by the use of the mail.

If the property report is given to the prospective buyer or tenant less than 48 hours before the signing of a contract to buy or lease, or after it has been signed, the contract may be voided within 48 hours. If the property report is never received, the contract may be voided, and there is no statutory limitation on the time in which this may be done.

State statutes complement the ILSFDA and frequently require that particular enterprises selling property disclose certain information to prospective buyers. Some state statutes provide protection for sales of real property interests such as time-sharing condominiums that are not covered under the ILSFDA.[52]

(b) SERVICE CONTRACTS   The UCCC treats a consumer service contract the same as a consumer sale of goods if (1) payment is made in installments or a credit charge is made and (2) the amount financed does not exceed $25,000. The UCCC defines *services* broadly as embracing work, specified privileges, and insurance provided by a noninsurer. The inclusion of these privileges in service contracts makes the UCCC apply to contracts calling for payment on the installment plan or including a financing charge for transportation, hotel and restaurant accommodations, education, entertainment, recreation, physical culture (such as athletic clubs or bodybuilding schools), hospital accommodations, funerals, and cemetery accommodations.

In some states, it is unlawful for a repair shop to make unauthorized repairs to an automobile and then refuse to return the automobile to the customer until the customer has paid for the repairs. In some states, a consumer protection statute imposes multiple damages on a repair shop that delays unreasonably in performing a contract to repair property of the consumer.[53]

---

[51] 15 USC § 1701 *et seq.*

[52] *Becherer v Merrill Lynch, Pierce, Fenner & Smith, Inc.,* 127 F3d 479 (6th Cir 1997) (condominium units sold for 14-day time-sharing rights not covered under ILSFDA).

[53] *Crye v Smolak,* 674 NE2d 779 (Ohio App 1996).

franchisee person to whom franchise is granted.

franchisor party granting the franchise.

franchise (1) a privilege or authorization, generally exclusive, to engage in a particular activity within a particular geographic area, such as a government franchise to operate a taxi company within a specified city, or a private franchise as the grant by a manufacturer of a right to sell products within a particular territory or for a particular number of years; (2) the right to vote.

(c) FRANCHISES   To protect prospective **franchisees** from deception by **franchisors** that seek to sell interests, an FTC regulation requires that the franchisor give a prospective franchisee a disclosure statement 10 days before the franchisee signs a contract or pays any money for a **franchise.** The disclosure statement provides detailed information relating to the franchisor's finances, experience, size of operation, and involvement in litigation. The statement must set forth any restrictions imposed on the franchisee; any costs that must be paid initially or in the future; and the provisions for termination, cancellation, and renewal of the franchise. False statements regarding sales, income, or profits are prohibited. Violators of the regulation are subject to a fine of $10,000.

(d) AUTOMOBILE LEMON LAWS   All states have adopted special laws for the protection of consumers buying automobiles that develop numerous defects or defects that cannot be corrected. These statutes protect only persons buying automobiles for personal, family, or household use. They generally classify an automobile as a *lemon* if it cannot be put in proper or warranted condition within a specified period of time or after a specified number of repair attempts. In general, they give the buyer greater protection than is given to other buyers by the UCC or other consumer protection statutes (see Chapter 24). In some states, the seller of a car that turns out to be a lemon is required to give the buyer a brand-new replacement car. In some states, certain agencies may also bring an action to collect civil penalties from the seller of a lemon car.

Lemon laws in most states are designed to increase the prelitigation bargaining power of consumers and reduce the greater power of manufacturers to resist complaints or suits by consumers.[54] **For Example,** Abdul, who owned a paint store, purchased two automobiles from Prime Motors, one for delivering paint to his customers and the second for his wife to use for shopping and taking their children to school. Both cars were defective and in need of constant repair. Abdul claimed that he was entitled to remedies provided by the local automobile lemon law. He was wrong with respect to the store's delivery car because lemon laws do not cover cars purchased for commercial use, but the other car was protected by the lemon law because it was clearly a family car.

(LAWFLIX)

Matilda (1997) (PG)

This is a story of a brilliant little girl living with some unethical parents. Several scenes show Danny DeVito (the father and used car dealer) cheating. In one scene, he shows Matilda how to roll back odometers.

For movie clips that illustrate business law concepts, see LawFlix at **http://wdvl.westbuslaw.com.**

---

[54] *Church v Chrysler Corp.,* 585 NW2d 685 (Wis App 1998).

> SUMMARY

Modern methods of marketing, packaging, and financing have reduced the ordinary consumer to a subordinate position. To protect the consumer from the hardship, fraud, and oppression that could result from being in such an inferior position, consumer protection laws, at both the state and federal levels, afford rights to consumers and impose requirements on those who deal with consumers.

When a consumer protection statute is violated, an action may sometimes be brought by the consumer against the wrongdoer. More commonly, an action is brought by an administrative agency or by the state attorney general.

Consumer protection laws are directed at false and misleading advertising; misleading or false use of labels; the methods of selling, with specific requirements on the disclosure of terms, permitting consumer

cancellation of home-solicited sales, and types of credit arrangements. The consumer is protected in a contract agreement by regulation of its form, prohibition of unconscionable terms, and limitation of the credit that can be extended to a consumer. Credit card protections include prohibition of the unauthorized distribution of credit cards and limited liability of the cardholder for the unauthorized use of a credit card. Included in consumer protection laws are the application of payments; the preservation of consumer defenses as against a transferee of the consumer's contract; product safety; the protection of credit standing and reputation; and (to some extent) real estate development sales, franchises, and service contracts. Lemon laws provide special protection to buyers of automobiles for personal, household, or family use.

> QUESTIONS AND CASE PROBLEMS

1. The San Antonio Retail Merchants Association (SARMA) was a credit reporting agency. It was asked by one of its members to furnish information on William Douglas Thompson III. It supplied information from a file that contained data on William III and on William Daniel Thompson Jr. The agency had incorporated information related to William Jr. into the file relating to William III so that all information appeared to relate to William III. This was a negligent mistake because each William had a different Social Security number, which should have raised a suspicion that there was a mistake. In addition, SARMA should have used a number of checkpoints to ensure that incoming information would be put into the proper file. William Jr. had bad credit standing. Because of its mistake, SARMA gave a bad report on William III, who was denied credit by several enterprises. The federal Fair Credit Reporting Act makes a credit reporting agency liable to any consumer about whom it furnishes a consumer report without following reasonable procedures to ensure maximum possible accuracy of information. William III sued SARMA for its negligence in confusing him with William Jr. Is SARMA liable? [*Thompson v San*

Antonio Retail Merchants Ass'n, 682 F2d 509 (5th Cir Tex)]

2. Colgate-Palmolive Co. ran a television commercial to show that its shaving cream, Rapid Shave, could soften even the toughness of sandpaper. The commercial showed what was described as the sandpaper test. Actually, what was used was a sheet of Plexiglas on which sand had been sprinkled. The FTC claimed that this was a deceptive practice. The advertiser contended that actual sandpaper would merely look like ordinary colored paper and that Plexiglas had been used to give the viewer an accurate visual representation of the test. Could the FTC prohibit the use of this commercial? [*Federal Trade Commission v Colgate-Palmolive Co.,* 380 US 374]

3. Sharolyn Charles wrote a check for $17.93 to a Poncho's Restaurant on July 4, 1996, as payment for a meal she had there. The check was returned for insufficient funds. Poncho's forwarded the check to Check Rite for collection.

   On July 19, Check Rite sent a letter to Charles, stating that "[t]his is an attempt to collect a debt" and requesting total payment of $42.93—the amount of the check plus a service charge of $25. On August 7, Check Rite sent a second letter, requesting payment of $42.93 and advising Charles that failure to pay the total amount due might result in additional liability for damages and attorneys' fees, estimated at $242.93.

Check Rite subsequently referred the matter to the law firm of Lundgren & Associates for collection. On September 8, Lundgren sent a letter to Charles offering to settle within 10 days for a total amount of $127.93—the amount of the check plus a settlement amount of $110. Lundgren further advised that it had made no decision to file suit, that it could later decide to do so, and that Charles's potential liability was $317.93. Charles immediately sent to Lundgren a money order in the amount of $17.93. On September 13, Lundgren sent a second letter, repeating the settlement offer made in the September 8 letter. Lundgren then returned Charles's payment on September 14, declining to accept it as payment in full and repeating the settlement offer. On September 19, Lundgren sent a fourth letter to Charles, repeating the settlement offer.

On October 15, 1996, Charles filed suit in federal district court alleging violations of the Fair Debt Collections Practices Act (FDCPA). Lundgren & Associates moved to dismiss the case on the grounds that an attempt to collect on a check is not a "debt" governed by the FDCPA. The district court dismissed the case, and Charles appealed. Should Charles win? Is she protected under the FDCPA? [*Charles v Lundgren & Associates, P.C.,* 119 F3d 739 (9th Cir)]

4. On November 3, 1989, John York purchased a 1988 truck from Conway Ford for $5,350. York purchased the truck in reliance on representations from the Conway Ford sales staff that the truck was a "like-new" demonstrator and that it had never been titled to anyone other than the dealership. From the outset, the truck had problems that required its return to Conway for service. During one of his numerous visits to Conway, York was told by a mechanic that the truck had been in an accident and had a bent frame. York then returned the truck and asked for his money back. Conway refused. Conway stored the truck for a time and then sold it to satisfy

storage fees. York brought suit against Conway for breach of contract, fraud, and violation of South Carolina's Unfair Trade Practices Act (UTPA). Who wins? Why? [*York v Conway Ford, Inc.,* 480 SE2d 726 (SC)]

5. Thomas was sent a credit card through the mail by a company that had taken his name and address from the telephone book. Because he never requested the card, Thomas left the card lying on his desk. A thief stole the card and used it to purchase merchandise in several stores in Thomas's name. The issuer of the credit card claimed that Thomas was liable for the total amount of the purchases made by the thief. Thomas claimed that he was not liable for any amount. The court decided that Thomas was liable for $50. Who is correct? Why?

6. Wilke was contemplating retiring. In response to an advertisement, he purchased from Coinway 30 coin-operated testing machines because Coinway's representative stated that by placing these machines at different public places, Wilke could obtain supplemental income. This statement was made by the representative, although he had no experience with the cost of servicing the machines or their income-producing potential. Wilke's operational costs for the machines exceeded the income. Wilke sued Coinway to rescind the contract, alleging that it was fraudulent. Coinway argued that the statements made were merely matters of opinion and did not constitute deception. Does Wilke have any consumer protection remedies? [*Wilke v Coinway, Inc.,* 64 Cal Rptr 845 (Cal App)]

7. Iberlin and others subscribed to the services of TCI Cablevision of Wyoming, which imposed a $2 late charge on any bill not paid when due. Iberlin brought suit against the cable company, claiming that the late charge was for extending credit and thus did not comply with state and federal laws governing credit charges. Was Iberlin correct? [*Iberlin v TCI Cablevision of Wyoming,* 855 P2d 716 (Wyo)]

8. International Yogurt Co. (IYC) developed a unique mix for making frozen yogurt and related products. Morris and his wife purchased a franchise from the company but were not told that a franchise was not a requirement for

obtaining the mix—that the company would sell its yogurt mix to anyone. The Morrises' franchise business was a failure, and they sold it at a loss after three years. They then sued the company for fraud and for violation of the state Franchise Investment Protection Act and the state Consumer Protection Act for failing to inform them that the mix could be obtained without a franchise. IYC claimed that no liability could be imposed for failing to make the disclosure. Was it correct? [*Morris v International Yogurt Co.,* 729 P2d 33 (Wash)]

9. Lutz Appellate Services received unsolicited faxed messages from Curry & Taylor. The first of these messages read as follows:

CURRY & TAYLOR
IS NOW HIRING
ALL POSITIONS
CALL TODAY 1-800-222-8738

The second stated:

CURRY & TAYLOR
—APPELLATE SPECIALISTS NEEDED
—GENEROUS PAY STRUCTURE
—EXPERIENCE WELCOME BUT NOT
  NECESSARY
—CALL 1-800-409-0060 TODAY,
  ASK FOR BILL

Curry was a competitor of Lutz and was seeking to hire away employees. Lutz filed suit alleging that the unsolicited faxes were advertisements prohibited by the Telephone Consumer Protection Act. What do you think? Does the TCPA prohibit these faxes?

10. A suit was brought against General Foods on the grounds that it was violating the state law prohibiting false and deceptive advertising. Its defense was that the plaintiffs had failed to show that the public had been deceived by the advertising, that the public in fact had not relied on the advertising, and that there was no proof that anyone had sustained any damage because of the advertising. Were these valid defenses? [*Committee on Children's Television, Inc. v General Foods Corp.,* 673 P2d 660 (Cal)]

11. The town of Newport obtained a corporate MasterCard that was given to the town clerk for purchasing fuel for the town hall. The town clerk used the card for personal restaurant, hotel, and gift shop debts. The town refused to pay the card charges on the grounds that they were unauthorized. Was the town correct? [*MasterCard v Town of Newport,* 396 NW2d 345 (Wis App)]

12. Donnelly purchased a television set on credit from D.W.N. Advertising, Inc. He also contracted for service on the set. D.W.N. assigned the sales contract to Fairfield Credit Corp., D.W.N. went out of existence, and the service contract was never performed. Fairfield sued Donnelly for the balance due on the purchase price. Donnelly raised the defense that the service contract had never been performed. Fairfield claimed that this defense could not be asserted against it because the sales contract contained a waiver of defenses. Was Fairfield right? [*Fairfield Credit Corp. v Donnelly,* 264 A2d 547 (Conn)]

13. Stevens purchased a pair of softball shoes manufactured by Hyde Athletic Industries. Because of a defect in the shoes, she fell and broke an ankle. She sued Hyde under the state consumer protection act, which provided that "any person who is injured in . . . business or property . . . could sue for damages sustained." Hyde claimed that the act did not cover personal injuries. Stevens claimed that she was injured in her "property" because of the money that she had to spend for medical treatment and subsequent care. Decide. [*Stevens v Hyde Athletic Industries, Inc.,* 773 P2d 87 (Wash App)]

14. A consumer made a purchase on a credit card. The card issuer refused to accept the charge, and an attorney then sued the consumer for the amount due. In the complaint filed in the lawsuit, the attorney wrongly stated that interest was owed at 18 percent per annum. This statement was later corrected by an amendment of the complaint to 5 percent. The case against the consumer was ultimately settled, but the consumer then sued the attorney for penalties under the Fair Debt Collection Practices Act, claiming that the overstatement of the interest due in the original complaint was a violation of that act. The attorney defended on the ground

that the act did not apply. Did it? [*Green v Hocking*, 9 F3d 18 (6th Cir)]

15. Classify each of the following activities as proper or prohibited under the various consumer statutes you have studied.

   a. Calling a hospital room to talk to a debtor who is a patient there.

   b. Calling a hospital room to sell surgical stockings.

   c. Rolling back the odometer on one's car before selling it privately.

   d. No TILA disclosures on an instant tax refund program in which the lender takes 40 percent of the tax refund as a fee for advancing the money when the taxpayer files the tax return.

SECURED TRANSACTIONS IN PERSONAL PROPERTY

CHAPTER (34)

RIGHTS OF PARTIES AFTER DEFAULT
25. CREDITOR'S POSSESSION AND DISPOSITION OF COLLATERAL
26. CREDITOR'S RETENTION OF COLLATERAL
27. DEBTOR'S RIGHT OF REDEMPTION
28. DISPOSITION OF COLLATERAL
29. POSTDISPOSITION ACCOUNTING

LEARNING OBJECTIVES

After studying this chapter, you should be able to

LO.1 Describe a secured transaction in personal property

LO.2 Explain the requirements for creating a valid security interest

LO.3 List the major types of collateral

LO.4 Define perfection and explain its significance in secured transactions

LO.5 Discuss the priorities of parties with conflicting interests in collateral when default occurs

LO.6 State the rights of the parties on the debtor's default

To provide creditors additional assurance that money will be repaid, legal rights in property can be assigned to creditors so that if the person obligated to pay does not pay, the creditor can turn to the property as a means of satisfying the obligation.

A CREATION OF SECURED TRANSACTIONS

A *secured transaction* is one means by which personal property is used to provide a backup plan or security for the creditor in the event the borrower does not pay. Secured transactions are governed by Article 9 of the Uniform Commercial Code (UCC). Article 9 was revised in 2000, and the revisions to it have been adopted in all states and the District of Columbia.[1]

1. DEFINITIONS

secured transaction credit sale of goods or a secured loan that provides special protection for the creditor.

security interest property right that enables the creditor to take possession of the property if the debtor does not pay the amount owed.

A **secured transaction** in personal property is created by giving the creditor a security interest in that property. A **security interest** is like a lien in personal property; it is a property right that enables the creditor to take possession of the property if the debtor does not pay the amount owed. **For Example,** if you borrow money from a bank to buy a car, the bank takes a security interest in the car. If you do not repay the loan, the bank can repossess the car and sell it to recover the money the bank has loaned you. If you purchase a side-by-side refrigerator from Kelvin's Appliances on credit, Kelvin's takes a security interest in the refrigerator. If you do not repay Kelvin's, Kelvin's can repossess the refrigerator and sell it to cover the amount you still owe.

---

[1] All 50 states, including Louisiana, have some version of Article 9 as law. The latest version of Article 9 (Revised Article 9) was adopted in 1999 and took effect on July 1, 2001. This newest version, adopted as modified in 2000, is referred to as either "New Article 9" or "Revised Article 9." Contrasts between the previous Article 9 and Revised Article 9 are noted in footnotes throughout the chapter. Not all states, however, have adopted verbatim versions. For example, the application of Article 9 to governmental units varies significantly among the states.

collateral property pledged by a borrower as security for a debt.

The property that is subject to the security interest is called **collateral.** In the preceding examples, the car was the bank's collateral for the loan, and the refrigerator was Kelvin's collateral.

(a) PARTIES   The person to whom the money is owed, whether a seller or a lender, is called the **creditor** or **secured party.** The buyer on credit or the borrower is called the **debtor.**

creditor person (seller or lender) who is owed money; also may be a secured party.

secured party person owed the money, whether as a seller or a lender, in a secured transaction in personal property.

debtor buyer on credit (i.e., a borrower).

(b) NATURE OF CREDITOR'S INTEREST   The creditor does not own the collateral, but the security interest is a property right. That property right can ripen into possession and the right to transfer title by sale as the section on default in this chapter discusses. However, the creditor also has certain present property interests and rights even prior to default. **For Example,** having a security interest gives the creditor standing to sue a third person who damages, destroys, or improperly repossesses the collateral.

If the creditor has possession of the collateral, the UCC imposes a duty of care on the creditor. The UCC provides that reasonable care must be exercised in preserving the property. The creditor is liable for damage that results from failing to do so.

(c) NATURE OF DEBTOR'S INTEREST   A debtor who is a borrower ordinarily owns the collateral[2]; see Section 2(c) of this chapter. As such, the debtor has all rights of any property owner to recover damages for the loss or improper seizure of, or damage to, the collateral.[3]

CPA

2. CREATION OF A SECURITY INTEREST

An attachment, or the creation of a valid security interest, occurs when the following three conditions are satisfied: There is (1) a security agreement, (2) value has been given, and (3) the debtor has rights in the collateral. These three conditions can occur in any order. A security interest will attach when the last of these conditions has been met.[4] When the security interest attaches, it is then enforceable against the debtor and the collateral.

CPA

security agreement agreement of the creditor and the debtor that the creditor will have a security interest.

(a) AGREEMENT   The **security agreement** is the agreement of the creditor and the debtor that the creditor will have a security interest. This required agreement must identify the parties, contain a reasonable description of the collateral,[5] indicate the parties' intent that the creditor have a security interest in it, describe the debt or the performance that is secured thereby, and be authenticated by the debtor.

Revised Article 9 eliminated the signature requirement to permit electronic means of entering into security agreements. The standard is now not a signature

---

[2] *Gibson County Farm Bureau Co-op Ass'n v Greer,* 643 NE2d 313 (Ind App 1994); *Belke v M&I First Nat'l Bank,* 525 NW2d 737 (Wis App 1994).

[3] Article 9 does cover consignment arrangements. The consignor continues to own the goods, and the consignee is treated as a secured creditor with a purchase money security interest in the consigned goods.

[4] UCC § 9-203 (Revised Article 9, § 9-203); *Farm Credit Services of Midlands, PCA v First State Park of Newcastle, Wyoming,* 575 NW2d 250 (SD 1998). Because Revised Article 9 now includes bank accounts as a form of security, the security interest attaches when the creditor has "control" of the account (Revised Article 9, § 9-104) and there is a security agreement. *Control* is defined later in the chapter under *perfection by control.*

[5] UCC §§ 9-201 (Revised Article 9, § 9-203), 9-110 (Revised Article 9, § 9-108); *Color Leasing 3, L. P. v FDIC,* 975 F Supp 177 (D RI 1997). In *In re Cottage Grove Hospital,* 38 UCC2d 683 (Bankr Ct D Or 1999), the court held that "All Debtor's Income" was an insufficient description.

but an authenticated document; authentication can come from the debtor's actions that indicate an understanding of a credit and secured debt agreement.[6] Also under Revised Article 9, a description is valid if it "reasonably identifies what is described."[7] Examples of reasonable identification include a specific listing, category,[8] quantity, and computational or allocational formula. "Supergeneric descriptions"[9] such as "all the debtor's personal property" are insufficient,[10] but "livestock" is a sufficient description.[11] The requirement for description of consumer goods as collateral is more stringent than for other types of collateral.[12]

If the creditor has possession of the collateral, the security agreement may be oral regardless of the amount involved.[13] **For Example,** if you pledge your stereo system to a friend as security for the loan and the friend will keep it at his home until you have repaid him, your friend has possession of the collateral, and your oral security agreement is valid and enforceable by your friend. If the creditor does not have possession of the collateral, as in the case of credit sales and most secured loans, the

---

CASE SUMMARY

The Umbrella, the Saw, the Bracelet, the CD, the TV, the Luggage, and the Earrings as Collateral

FACTS: McLeod purchased several items from Sears, Roebuck on credit. The description of the items, in which Sears took a purchase money security interest, was as follows: "MITER SAW; LXITVRACDC [a television, videocassette recorder, and compact disc spinner]; 25" UPRIGHT, 28" UPRIGHT [two pieces of luggage]; BRACELET, DIA STUDS, RING; 14K EARR, P, EARRINGS, P [diamond bracelet, ring, and earrings]; and 9-INCH E-Z-LIFT [an outdoor umbrella]."

In a dispute over creditors' priorities in McLeod's bankruptcy, one creditor argued that the description of the goods was insufficient to give Sears a security interest.

DECISION: Because the security interest was a purchase money security interest in consumer goods, the brief descriptions were sufficient to identify the goods for purposes of the creditor's security interest. The words used made it sufficiently easy to identify the goods because they were distinctive from other goods that the debtor owned. [**McLeod v Sears, Roebuck & Co., 41 UCC2d 302 (Bankr ED Mich 2000)**]

---

[6] Revised Article 9, § 9-102(a)(69) defines *record,* the new substitute for *signed agreement* of old Article 9, as "information that is inscribed on a tangible medium and is retrievable in perceivable form." Authentication need not be a signature. One court held that a debtor using the proceeds from the loan that was the basis for the security interest constituted authentication, *Barlow Lane Holdings Ltd. v Applied Carbon Technology (America), Inc.,* 2004 WL 1792456 (WDNY 2004); see also 2004 WL 2110733 (WDNY 2004).

[7] UCC § 9-110.

[8] Commercial tort claims and consumer transactions cannot be sufficiently described by type of collateral. The security agreement must give more specifics. § 9-108(e)(1) and (2).

[9] UCC § 9-108(c).

[10] The comments to § 9-108 indicate that serial numbers are not necessarily required, but an outsider must be able to tell from the description what property is or is not included under the security agreement. Official Comment, § 9-108, 2.

[11] *Baldwin v Castro County Feeders I, Ltd.,* 678 NW2d 796 (SD 2004).

[12] Under § 9-108, in consumer transactions and goods, description by "type of collateral" is insufficient.

[13] UCC § 9-207 (Revised Article 9, § 9-207); *Myers v Fifth Third Bank,* 624 NE2d 748 (Ohio App 1993). If there is no written security agreement (*record* under Revised Article 9), the security interest itself is destroyed when the collateral is surrendered.

security agreement must be evidenced by a record and meet the other requirements stated earlier.

Field warehousing, covered in Chapter 22, is another form of possession of goods that permits an oral security agreement. Credit unions and banks can possess an account pledged as security if the funds cannot be used by the account holder without permission and clearance from a bank officer.

value consideration or antecedent debt or security given in exchange for the transfer of a negotiable instrument or creation of a security interest.

(b) VALUE The creditor gives **value** either by lending money to the debtor or by delivering goods on credit. The value may be part of a contemporaneous exchange or given previously as a loan. **For Example,** a debtor who already owes a creditor $5,000 could later pledge a water scooter as collateral for that loan and give the debtor a security interest in the scooter. In fact, creditors who become nervous about repayment often request collateral later during the course of performance of a previously unsecured loan.

(c) RIGHTS IN THE COLLATERAL The debtor must have rights in the collateral for a security interest to attach. These rights can include everything from title to the right to possession.[14]

CPA

3. PURCHASE MONEY SECURITY INTEREST

purchase money security interest (PMSI) the security interest in the goods a seller sells on credit that become the collateral for the creditor/seller.

When a seller sells on credit and is given a security interest in the goods sold, that interest is called a **purchase money security interest (PMSI)**. If the buyer borrows money from a third person so that the purchase can be made for cash, a security interest given the lender in the goods is also called a purchase money security interest.[15] Certain special priority rights are given in some circumstances to creditors who hold a PMSI.

CPA

4. THE NATURE AND CLASSIFICATION OF COLLATERAL

The nature of the collateral in a credit transaction, as well as its classification under Article 9, affect the procedural obligations and rights of creditors. Revised Article 9 contains an extensive list of the types of collateral, including the traditional types such as consumer goods, equipment, inventory, general intangibles, farm products, and fixtures,[16] but also accounts, accounts receivable, accounts receivable held because of credit card transactions or license fees, energy contracts, insurance policy proceeds, amounts due for services rendered, amounts earned from chartering a vessel, winnings in the state lottery, and health care insurance receivables. The general category of "account" does not include commercial tort claims, deposit accounts,[17] investment property, or letters of credit but does include insurance claims, lottery winnings, and property proceeds.[18] New Article 9 has also dropped prejudices against some potential forms of collateral. The result is that other issues with respect to these general categories of collateral arise, such as whether the security interest covers the collateral

---

[14] UCC § 9-112 (Revised Article 9, § 9-202).

[15] UCC § 9-107 (Revised Article 9, § 9-103); *First Nat'l Bank v Erb Equipment Co.,* 921 SW2d 57 (Mo App 1996).

[16] UCC §§ 9-106, 9-109. See Revised Article 9, § 9-102.

[17] Deposit accounts are not considered "general intangibles" under new Article 9 because of new, specific provisions on accounts. UCC §§ 9-102(a)(29), 9-104, 9-109(d)(13), 9-312(b)(1), and 9-314.

[18] UCC §§ 9-102(2)(a)(5), 9-102(72), and 9-109(a)(2).

when it changes form—for example, when the inventory is sold in exchange for a promissory note.

consumer goods goods used or bought primarily for personal, family, or household use.

(a) Consumer Goods Collateral that is classified as **consumer goods** can result in different rights and obligations under Article 9, regardless of the type of property it is. Collateral is considered consumer goods if it is "used or bought for use primarily for personal, family, or household purposes."[19] The use of the good, and not its properties, controls its classification. **For Example,** a computer purchased by an architect for her office is not a consumer good. That same computer purchased by the same architect for use by her children at their home is a consumer good. A refrigerator purchased for the kitchen near an office conference center is not a consumer good. That same model refrigerator purchased for a home is a consumer good. The use of the goods controls the label that is applied to the collateral.

CPA

after-acquired goods goods acquired after a security interest has attached.

floating lien claim in a changing or shifting stock of goods of the buyer.

(b) After-Acquired Collateral and Ongoing Credit A creditor's rights can be expanded to include coverage of all future loans and funds advances as well as future acquisitions of collateral. If the security agreement so provides, the security interest attaches to **after-acquired goods** and applies to all loans to the debtor.[20] **For Example,** a security interest can cover the current inventory of the debtor and any future replenishments if a clause in the security agreement adds "after-acquired property" to the description of the inventory. Referred to in lay terms as a **floating lien,** the creditor's interest attaches to the inventory regardless of its form or time of arrival in terms of the attached security interest.

There are restrictions on after-acquired clauses in consumer credit contracts. An after-acquired property clause in a consumer security agreement can cover only goods acquired by the debtor within 10 days after the creditor gave value to the debtor.

(c) Proceeds The UCC defines proceeds as "whatever is received upon the sale, exchange, collection, or other disposition of collateral."[21] Collateral may change its form and character during the course of the security agreement. **For Example,** a debtor who has pledged its inventory of cars as collateral will be selling those cars. However, the buyers will sign credit contracts for the purchase of those cars. Article 9 considers the credit contracts and the right to payment under those contracts as proceeds. If the collateral has been insured and is damaged or destroyed, the debtor will receive money from the insurance company. Proceeds are automatically subject to the creditor's security interest unless the contrary was stated in the security agreement. The proceeds may be in any form, such as cash, checks, promissory notes, or other property.

(d) Electronic Chattel Paper "Electronic chattel paper" is a record of a right to funds, payment, or property that is stored in an electronic medium. **For Example,** it is possible to pledge the funds you have available in your Internet shopping account as an Article 9 security interest.[22]

---

[19] UCC § 9-109(1).
[20] UCC § 9-109 (Revised Article 9, § 9-204).
[21] UCC § 9-306(1).
[22] UCC § 9-105.

PERFECTION OF SECURED TRANSACTIONS

The attachment of a security interest gives the creditor the important rights of enforcement of the debt through repossession of the collateral (see Section 25 for more discussion of enforcement and repossession). *Attachment* allows the secured party to resort to the collateral to collect the debt when the debtor defaults. However, more than one creditor may hold an attached security interest in the same collateral. A creditor who obtains a **perfected security interest** enjoys priority over unperfected interests and may in some cases enjoy priority over other perfected interests. A security interest is valid against the debtor even though it is not perfected. However, perfection provides creditors with rights superior to those of other creditors with unperfected interests. Attachment provides creditors with rights; perfection gives them priority.

A creditor can obtain perfection in collateral in several ways.

perfected security interest security interest with priority because of filing, possession, automatic or temporary priority status.

5. PERFECTION BY CREDITOR'S POSSESSION

If the collateral is in the possession of the creditor, the security interest in the possessed goods is perfected.[23] It remains perfected until that possession is surrendered. **For Example,** when a creditor has taken a security interest in 50 gold coins and has those gold coins in his vault, his possession of the coins is perfection.

A more complex example of possession as a means of perfection is found in the commercial tool of **field warehousing.** (See Chapter 22.) In this arrangement, a creditor actually has an agent on site at a buyer's place of business, and the creditor's agent controls the buyer's access to, use of, and transfer of the collateral. **For Example,** an aircraft manufacturer may have an agent on site at an aircraft dealership. That agent decides when the planes can be released to buyers and who will receive the buyers' payments or notes.[24]

field warehousing stored goods under the exclusive control of a warehouser but kept on the owner's premises rather than in a warehouse.

6. PERFECTION FOR CONSUMER GOODS

A purchase money security interest in consumer goods is perfected from the moment it attaches.[25] Known as **automatic perfection,** no other action is required for perfection as against other creditors. Because so many consumer purchases are made on credit, the UCC simplifies perfection so that creditors who are merchant sellers are not overly burdened with paperwork. However, as discussed later in this chapter in the section on priorities, the automatic perfection of a PMSI in consumer goods has some limitations. It may be destroyed by the debtor consumer's resale of the goods to a consumer who does not know of the security interest.

automatic perfection perfection given by statute without specific filing or possession requirements on the part of the creditor.

7. PERFECTION FOR HEALTH CARE INSURANCE RECEIVABLES

Revised Article 9 created a new form of collateral known as *health care insurance receivables.* This form of collateral has a unique method of perfection. When a consumer gives a creditor a security interest in health insurance proceeds that are forthcoming, the creditor need not make any filing or take any further steps to have a perfected security interest in those proceeds. The perfection is automatic.[26]

---

[23] UCC § 9-305; *Shurlow v Bonthuis,* 576 NW2d 159 (Mich 1998).

[24] Revised Article 9, § 9-312.

[25] UCC § 9-302 (Revised Article 9, §§ 9-301 and 9-304); *Heidelberg Eastern, Inc. v Weber Lithography, Inc.,* 631 NYS2d 370 (NY 1995).

[26] Revised Article 9, § 9-309.

8. AUTOMATIC PERFECTION

A creditor attains automatic perfection in certain circumstances under Article 9. **For Example,** a creditor has an automatic PMSI in software that is sold with a computer that is subject to a creditor's PMSI. If you buy an IBM ThinkPad® from CompUSA on credit and get Microsoft Office software as part of your package deal, CompUSA has an automatically perfected security interest not only in the consumer goods (your new computer) but also in the software sold with it.[27] The perfection for consumer purchase money security interests that occurs when the security interest attaches is also a form of automatic perfection.

9. TEMPORARY PERFECTION

temporary perfection
perfection given for a limited period of time to creditors.

Some creditors are given **temporary perfection** for the collateral.[28] **For Example,** a creditor is generally given four months to refile its financing statement in a state to which a debtor has relocated. During that four-month period, the interest of the creditor is temporarily perfected in the new state despite no filing of a financing statement in that state's public records. Most creditors' agreements provide that the failure of the debtor to notify the creditor of a move constitutes a default under the credit agreement. Creditors need to know of the move so that they can refile in the debtor's new state.[29] Creditors enjoy a 20-day temporary perfection in negotiable instruments taken as collateral. Following the expiration of the 20-day period, measured from the time their security interest attaches, creditors must perfect in another way, such as by filing a financing statement or by possession.

10. PERFECTION BY CONTROL

Control is a form of possession under Article 9;[30] it occurs when a bank or creditor is able to require the debtor account holder to clear all transactions in that account with the bank or creditor. The debtor cannot use the funds that have been pledged as collateral without permission from the party holding the control. **For Example,** a credit union member could secure a loan with the credit union by giving the credit union a security interest in her savings account. The credit union then has control of the account and is perfected by the ability to dictate what the credit union member can do with those funds.

11. PERFECTION FOR MOTOR VEHICLES

In most states, a non-Code statute provides that a security interest in a noninventory motor vehicle must be noted on the vehicle title registration. When so noted, the interest is perfected.[31] In states that do not have a separate motor vehicle perfection system, there must be a filing of a financing statement, as described in the next section.

---

[27] Revised Article 9, §§ 9-102 and 9-103.

[28] UCC § 9-304 (Revised Article 9, § 9-312).

[29] UCC § 9-316(a).

[30] UCC § 9-104.

[31] Revised Article 9 does not change this principle.

12. PERFECTION BY FILING A FINANCING STATEMENT

financing statement brief statement (record) that gives sufficient information to alert third persons that a particular creditor may have a security interest in the collateral described.

The **financing statement** (known as a *UCC-1*) is an authenticated record statement that gives sufficient information to alert third persons that a particular creditor may have a security interest in the collateral described (see Figure 34-1). Under previous Article 9, the financing statement had to be in writing and signed by the debtor. Under Revised Article 9, the creditor must simply be able to show that the documents filed were "authorized" and an "authenticated record."[32] In other words, the debtor's signature is not required for the financing statement to be valid. The notion of authorization by a debtor for financing statements is a critical one under Revised Article 9. Revised Article 9 gives three ways for the debtor to authorize a financing statement:

1. By authenticating a security agreement.[33]
2. By becoming bound under a security agreement, the debtor agrees to allow financing statements to be filed on the collateral in the security agreement.
3. By acquiring collateral subject to a security agreement.

An unauthorized financing statement filed without meeting one of these requirements does not provide the creditor perfected creditor status.[34]

(a) THE CONTENT OF THE FINANCING STATEMENT   A financing statement must provide "the name of the debtor . . . the name of the secured party or representative of the secured party . . . [and an indication of] the collateral covered by the financing statement."[35] The form provided by Revised Article 9 drafters (see Figure 34-1) includes much more information. Under § 9-516, additional requirements are imposed for initial financing statements that include "a mailing address for the debtor [and] . . . whether the debtor is an individual or organization."[36] Furthermore, § 9-511 requires that the secured party of record provide an address so that there is an address for mailing notices required under other sections. So, while a financing statement with simply the debtor's and secured party's name and a description of the collateral is sufficient for perfection, it may not provide all the rights and protections the parties need. The requirements are simply listed in different sections in revised Article 9 as opposed to a listing in one section in former Article 9.

Because the filings for Article 9 perfection became electronic in 2006, the precise identification of the debtor has become critical. With electronic filings, those who will be doing searches on debtors will not find matches when the name of the debtor has not been properly entered on the financing statement. Prior to the Article 9 revisions, the courts had some tolerance for human error in determining whether a financing statement identified the debtor sufficiently to provide notice of the security interest in the debtor's property. However, with computer technology, additional precision is necessary or the search is thwarted. The effect under the Revised Article 9 is to increase

---

[32] The sample financing form included with Revised Article 9, § 9-521 does not even have a place for the debtor's signature. While a signed security agreement and signed financing statement are valid for both the security agreement and financing statement, the revisions also make it clear that such formalities are no longer necessary.

[33] Revised Article 9, § 9-509 permits the debtor and creditor to agree otherwise. For example, a debtor can place a requirement in the security agreement that the creditor obtain his or her signature before filing a financing statement.

[34] Revised Article 9, § 9-510.

[35] UCC § 9-502(a).

[36] UCC § 9-516(b)(5).

FIGURE 34-1 *Sample Financial Statement*

UCC FINANCING STATEMENT
FOLLOW INSTRUCTIONS (front and back) CAREFULLY

A. NAME & PHONE OF CONTACT AT FILER [optional]

B. SEND ACKNOWLEDGEMENT TO: (Name and Address)

THE ABOVE SPACE IS FOR FILING OFFICE USE ONLY

1. DEBTOR'S EXACT FULL LEGAL NAME—Insert only <u>one</u> debtor name (1a or 1b)—do not abbreviate or combine

1a. ORGANIZATION'S NAME			

OR

1b. INDIVIDUAL'S LAST NAME	FIRST NAME	MIDDLE NAME	SUFFIX

1c. MAILING ADDRESS	CITY	STATE	POSTAL CODE	COUNTRY

1d. TAX ID# SSN OR EIN	ADD'L INFO RE ORGANIZATION DEBTOR	1e. TYPE OF ORGANIZATION	1f. JURISDICTION OF ORGANIZATION	1g. ORGANIZATION ID #, if any
				☐ NONE

2. ADDITIONAL DEBTOR'S EXACT FULL LEGAL NAME—Insert only <u>one</u> debtor name (2a or 2b)—do not abbreviate or combine names

2a. ORGANIZATION'S NAME			

OR

2b. INDIVIDUAL'S LAST NAME	FIRST NAME	MIDDLE NAME	SUFFIX

2c. MAILING ADDRESS	CITY	STATE	POSTAL CODE	COUNTRY

2d. TAX ID# SSN OR EIN	ADD'L INFO RE ORGANIZATION DEBTOR	2e. TYPE OF ORGANIZATION	2f. JURISDICTION OF ORGANIZATION	2g. ORGANIZATION ID #, If any
				☐ NONE

3. SECURED PARTY'S NAME (or NAME of TOTAL ASSIGNEE of ASSIGNOR S/P)—Insert only <u>one</u> secured party name (3a or 3b)

3a. ORGANIZATION'S NAME			

OR

3b. INDIVIDUAL'S LAST NAME	FIRST NAME	MIDDLE NAME	SUFFIX

3c. MAILING ADDRESS	CITY	STATE	POSTAL CODE	COUNTRY

4. This FINANCING STATEMENT covers the following collateral:

5. ALTERNATIVE DESIGNATION (if applicable) ☐ LESSEE/LEASOR ☐ CONSIGNEE/CONSIGNOR ☐ BAILEE/BAILOR ☐ SELLER/BUYER ☐ AG. LIEN ☐ NON-UCC FILING

6. ☐ This FINANCING STATEMENT is to be filed [for record](or recorded)in the REAL ESTATE RECORDS. Attach Addendum [if applicable]

7. Check to REQUEST SEARCH REPORT(s) on DEBTOR(s) [ADDITIONAL FEE] [optional] ☐ All Debtors ☐ Debtor 1 ☐ Debtor 2

8. OPTIONAL FILER REFERENCE DATA

NATIONAL UCC FINANCING STATEMENT (FORM UCC 1) (REV. 07/29/98)

CASE SUMMARY

"Net Work" vs. "Network": Just One Space Equals a World of Distance Under Article 9

FACTS: Dillard Smith hired Network Solutions, Inc., as a subcontractor on several projects. Network later assigned all rights that it had to payment for this work to Receivables Purchasing Company (Receivables) and R & R Drilling LLC (R & R). On April 2, 2001, Receivables filed a UCC-1 financing statement in Bartow County to perfect Receivables' security interest in these payments. The financing statement listed the debtor as "Net work Solutions, Inc." rather than the correct name "Network Solutions, Inc." R & R subsequently performed drilling services for Network, for which R & R was not paid. On May 23, 2002, R & R obtained a judgment against Network in the amount of $40,993.74. According to R & R's counsel, R & R performed a UCC search under the name "Network Solutions, Inc." to determine whether any individual or entity held a superior claim to the funds. When the search failed to reveal any debtor named Network Solutions, Inc., R & R filed a summons and affidavit of garnishment on July 12, 2002, against Network and Dillard Smith for the amount owed to R & R. Dillard Smith answered the summons, stating that it was holding a sum of $32,136.84 that was owed to Network but that these funds were also being claimed by Receivables. Dillard Smith requested the court to allow the $32,136.84 to be deposited with it. Receivables then filed a motion for withdrawal of the $32,136.84, contending that Receivables had a superior right to these funds by virtue of the UCC-1 financing statement it filed on April 2, 2001. R & R responded, arguing that Receivables' UCC-1 statement was not a perfected security interest that could defeat R & R's lien on the proceeds because Receivables failed to properly name Network Solutions, Inc., as the debtor on the financing statement. The trial court found in favor of R & R. Receivables appealed.

DECISION: The court held that the financing statement was not filed properly and was seriously misleading. The court found that the fact that not even those in charge of the filing system could pull up the name when they searched indicated that the financing statement was not properly filed and was seriously misleading. The court would not consider cases decided prior to Revised Article 9 because of the new standards under Article 9 that are geared toward the new electronic filing systems. [**Receivables Purchasing Co., Inc. v R & R Directional Drilling, L.L.C., 588 SE2d 831 (Ga App 2003)**]

---

the consequences for misspelling a consumer's name, which will be a loss of priority by perfection because the electronic search in the state did not uncover prior interests. Courts will be finding more variations in names to be "seriously misleading" because the nature of electronic filings has increased the need for precision.[37]

Like the security agreement changes under Revised Article 9, the requirements for description of the collateral in the financing statements are now more general.[38] The financing statement need not include the terms of the agreement between the parties. However, a security agreement can be filed as a financing statement if it contains all of the aforementioned required information.

Because the financing statement is intended as notice to third parties, it must be filed in a public place.[39] Revised Article 9 simplifies the formerly complex issues of filing location as a means of encouraging electronic systems that will be statewide,

---

[37] UCC § 9-506(a) (2000).

[38] However, the sample financing form included with Revised Article 9, § 9-521 includes boxes for all of the same information required under existing Article 9. The sample form in Figure 34-1 would meet the requirements for Revised Article 9.

[39] UCC § 9-401; *In re Pacific/West Communications Group, Inc.*, 301 F3d 1150, 48 UCC Rep Serv 2d 462 (9th Cir 2002).

E-COMMERCE AND CYBERLAW

Engines Are from Mars; Priorities Are from Financing Statements

In 2001, the International Association of Corporate Administrators promulgated Model Administrative Rules (MARS), a set of rules for the standards for search engines for court system, land, tax, and lien records. State and local governments will have different technology and standards that range from a liberal search engine to a strict search engine. A *liberal search engine* is similar to Google , which kicks back a corrected term and says, "Did you mean _____?" when you type in a name or word that is misspelled, A *strict search engine*, such as the simple one in Microsoft Word, will not find a word or phrase in a document unless you have spelled the search item exactly the way it appears in the document.

The MARS standards migrate toward the strict search engine. However, states have adopted different standards, and the result is that the electronic searches for debtors in various states can be very different. If there is a strict search engine in a state and the person doing the search types in "Ann Smythe," the correct spelling of the debtor's name, the financing statement against "Smythe" that was filed as "Ann Smith" will not be a match and the electronic system will kick out a "NO MATCH FOUND." Likewise, a creditor who files under the name "House, Roger" when the debtor's actual name is "Rodger House" has not perfected.* The same would be true of a financing statement filed under "Terry J. Kinderknecht" when the debtor's actual legal name is "Terrance Joseph Kinderknecht."**

Revised Article 9 created a standard rules for search logic that tend toward the "strict" end of the spectrum. The majority of states have now adopted some version of MARS, although many states have modified the rules in some respect (which has resulted in a great deal of inconsistency; furthermore, some states have not adopted any rule on search logic at all). In general, when a debtor's name has been modified by the applicable search logic, the search will produce a financing statement only if the names "exactly match." if there is no match, the security interest will be "seriously misleading," and therefore unperfected and susceptible to a "strong-arm" attack by a bankruptcy trustee or debtor-in-possession (see the following bankruptcy discussion).

---

* *Pankratz Implement Company v Citizens National Bank* 004 Kan App LEXIS 1173 (Nov. 19, 2004).

** These examples would result in a "NO MATCH FOUND" and emphasize the importance of using both the debtor's legal name and correct spelling. Furthermore, the courts in all three cases, which are Revised Article 9 cases, did not honor the financing statement as perfection because the names were misleading. The person doing the search is permitted to assume that the debtor has no other secured creditors. *In re Kinderknecht (Clark v Deere & Co.)*, 2004 Bankr LEXIS 477 (10th Cir BAP 2004).

---

accessible across state lines, and organized simply by name in any index. Revised Article 9's general rule is central filing for financing statements for all types of collateral. Filings for fixtures and other property-related interests have also been simplified with Revised Article 9, deferring to state laws on the proper filing location.[40]

---

[40] Revised Article 9, § 9-501.

THINKING THINGS THROUGH

You Say "Sang Woo Gu," I Put Down "Gu, Sang Woo"—Who Wins?

Creditor ABC filed a financing statement to protect its interest in the assets of debtor, Gu, who owed it $235,000. The financing statement filed in Dekalb County Superior Court listed the debtor's name as "Gu, Sang Woo" and stated the name of the business as "CCO Check Cashing-Buford." The debtor's name is actually "Sang Woo Gu," and the correct name of the business is "CCO Check Cashing." Gu sold his business (that included the assets described in the financing statement) to another party whose lawyer, Jim Choi, conducted a search to determine whether there were any liens or security interests in the property. When Choi ran the search on the correct name of Gu's business, the perfected security interests arose. Choi's client paid $197,000 for the business and ABC sought to foreclose on its interest in the assets so that it could sell them to satisfy the debt Gu owed. Choi claims his client is not subject to the security interest because the financing statement was seriously misleading. Who has priority here? Is the financing statement misleading? [ALL BUSINESS CORP. v CHOI, 2006 WL 1550710 (Ga App)]

Revised Article 9 also includes an option for filing financing statements for fixtures in the same way as for other forms of collateral. A typical central filing location in many states, both before and after Revised Article 9, is the office of the secretary of state.

(b) DEFECTIVE FILING   When the filing of the financing statement is defective either because the statement is so erroneous or incomplete that it is seriously misleading or the filing is made in a wrong county or office, the filing fails to perfect the security interest. The idea of perfection by filing is to give public notice of a creditor's interest. To the extent that the notice cannot be located or does not give sufficient information, the creditor then cannot rely on it to obtain the superior position of perfection.

Revised Article 9 has been referred to by commentators as "medium-neutral," which is their way of saying that the means the parties choose for filing, whether by fax or electronically, are to be treated as equals with formal writings for purposes of both the creation of a security interest and its perfection. A comment to Revised Article 9 reads, "data transmitted electronically to the filing office and reduced to tangible form constitute a financing statement or other filing under Article 9 if they provide all the information required under the applicable provision of Article 9." This sanctioning of electronic filing follows the Canadian lead where electronic filing was in place prior to the Article 9 changes here. Because of Revised Article 9, each state has developed its own system for such electronic filing (effective during 2006). While the electronic systems have created some additional issues that still require resolution, many of the issues and exceptions that caused confusion and complexity under old Article 9 have been eliminated with the fast, central, and efficient form of electronic filing.[41]

---

[41] For a discussion of the legal issues that have arisen in electronic filing, see Meghan M. Sercombe, "Good Technology and Bad Law: How Computerization Threatens Notice Filing Under Revised Article 9," 84 *Tex. L. Rev.* 1065 (2006).

13. LOSS OF PERFECTION

The perfection of the security interest can be lost if the creditor does not comply with the Article 9 requirements for continuing perfection.

(a) Possession of Collateral When perfection is obtained because the creditor takes possession of the collateral, that perfection is lost if the creditor voluntarily surrenders the collateral to the debtor without any restrictions.

(b) Consumer Goods The perfection obtained by the automatic status of a PMSI is lost in some cases by removal of the goods to another state. The security interest may also be destroyed by resale of the goods to a consumer. To protect against these types of losses of protection, the creditor needs to file a financing statement. In the case of a PMSI, the perfection is good against other creditors but is not superior when it comes to buyers of the goods.

(c) Lapse of Time The perfection obtained by filing a financing statement lasts five years. The perfection may be continued for successive five-year periods by filing a continuation statement within six months before the end of each five-year period.[42] Revised Article 9 permits a "manufactured home" exception allowing financing statements on mobile homes to be effective for 30 years.[43]

(d) Removal from State In most cases, the perfection of a security interest lapses when the collateral is taken by the debtor to another state unless, as noted earlier, the creditor makes a filing in that second state within the four-month period of temporary perfection.

(e) Motor Vehicles If the security interest is governed by a non-Code statute creating perfection by title certificate notation, the interest, if so noted, remains perfected without regard to lapse of time or removal to another state. The perfection is lost only if a state issues a new title without the security interest notation.

 ## RIGHTS OF PARTIES BEFORE DEFAULT

The rights of parties to a secured transaction are different in the time preceding the debtor's default from those in the time following the default.

14. STATUS OF CREDITOR BEFORE DEFAULT

The status of a creditor who has loaned money to a debtor is determined by ordinary principles of contract law. A creditor who is a seller of goods has the rights granted by Article 2, Sales, of the UCC. If the creditor is the lessor of goods, that status is determined by Article 2A, Leases, of the UCC.

---

[42] UCC § 9-403 (Revised Article 9, § 9-516). Failure to file with the secretary of state was fatal for a priority of secured creditor when a central filing was required, despite the filing at the county level. *In re Ferro*, 37 UCC2d 1175 (Bankr WD Mo 1999).

[43] Revised Article 9, § 9-515.

15. STATUS OF DEBTOR BEFORE DEFAULT

The status of the debtor before default depends on whether there is a loan, a sale, or a lease. The status of a debtor who has borrowed money from a creditor is determined by ordinary principles of contract law. If the debtor is a buyer or lessee of goods, the debtor's status is determined by Article 9, Secured Transactions, and by either Article 2 or 2A of the UCC.

16. STATEMENT OF ACCOUNT

To keep the record straight, the debtor may send the creditor a written statement of the amount the debtor thinks is due and an itemization of the collateral together with a request that the creditor approve the statement as submitted or correct and return the statement. Within two weeks after receiving the debtor's statement, the creditor must send the debtor a written approval or correction. If the secured creditor has assigned the secured claim, the creditor's reply must state the name and address of the assignee.

17. TERMINATION STATEMENTS

termination statement
document (record), which may be requested by a paid-up debtor, stating that a security interest is no longer claimed under the specified financing statement.

A debtor who has paid his debt in full may make a written demand on the secured creditor, or the latter's assignee if the security interest has been assigned, to send the debtor a **termination statement,**[44] which states that a security interest is no longer claimed under the specified financing statement. The debtor may present this statement to the filing officer, who marks the record terminated and returns the various papers that were filed to the secured party. The termination statement clears the debtor's record so subsequent buyers or lenders will not be subject to the now-satisfied security interest. The creditor has 20 days from receipt of a demand for a termination statement from a debtor to file a termination statement (one month for consumer goods).[45]

18. CORRECTION STATEMENTS

Because Revised Article 9 permits creditors and others to simply file "authorized" financing statements, debtors are given protection for abusive filings of Article 9 interests. Under Revised Article 9, debtors are permitted to protest filed financing statements with a filing of their own correction statements. While the security interest is not abolished by such a filing, its content does provide public notice of an underlying dispute. A debtor can also file a correction statement when a creditor fails to provide a termination statement.[46]

Ⓓ PRIORITIES

Two or more parties may have conflicting interests in the same collateral. This section discusses the rights of creditors and buyers with respect to each other and to collateral that carries a secured interest or perfected secured interest.

---

[44] UCC § 9-404 (Revised Article 9, § 9-513); *Kultura, Inc. v Southern Leasing Corp.,* 923 SW2d 536 (Tenn 1996), but see *Mac'Kie v Wal-Mart Stores, Inc.,* 127 F3d 1102 (6th Cir 1997).

[45] UCC § 9-513(b) and (c).

[46] Revised Article 9, § 9-518.

19. UNSECURED PARTY VERSUS UNSECURED PARTY

When creditors are unsecured, they have equal priority. In the event of insolvency or bankruptcy of the debtor, all the unsecured creditors stand at the end of the line in terms of repayment of their debts (see Chapter 35 for more details on bankruptcy priorities). If the assets of the debtor are insufficient to satisfy all unsecured debtors, the unsecured debtors simply receive a **pro rata** share of their debts.

pro rata proportionately, or divided according to a rate or standard.

20. SECURED PARTY VERSUS UNSECURED PARTY

A secured creditor has a right superior to that of an unsecured creditor because the secured creditor can take back the collateral from the debtor's assets, while an unsecured creditor simply waits for the leftovers once all secured creditors have taken back their collateral. If the collateral is insufficient to satisfy the secured creditor's debt, the secured debtor can still stand in line with the unsecured creditors and collect any additional amount not satisfied by the collateral or a pro rata share. **For Example,** suppose that Linens Galore has a security interest in Linens R Us's inventory. Linens Galore has the right to repossess the inventory and sell it to satisfy the debt Linens R Us owes. Suppose that Linens R Us owes Linens Galore $22,000, and the sale of the inventory brings $15,000. Linens Galore still has a claim as an unsecured creditor for the remaining $7,000 due.

21. SECURED PARTY VERSUS SECURED PARTY

If two creditors have a security interest in the same collateral, their priority is determined according to the **first-in-time provision;** that is, the creditor whose interest attached first has priority in the collateral.[47] The secured party whose interest was last to attach must then proceed against the debtor as an unsecured creditor because the collateral was given to the creditor whose interest attached first.
For Example, if Bob pledged his antique sign collection to Bill on January 15, 2007, with a signed security agreement in exchange for a $5,000 loan, and then pledged the same collection to Jane on February 20, 2007, with a signed security agreement, Bill has priority because his security agreement attached first.

first-in-time provision creditor whose interest attached first has priority in the collateral when two creditors have a secured interest.

22. PERFECTED SECURED PARTY VERSUS SECURED PARTY

The perfected secured creditor takes priority over the unperfected secured creditor and is entitled to take the collateral. The unperfected secured party is then left to seek remedies as an unsecured creditor because the collateral has been given to the perfected creditor. **For Example,** with respect to Bob's sign collection, if Jane filed a financing statement on February 21, 2007, she would have priority over Bill because her perfected interest would be superior to Bill's unperfected interest even though Bill's interest attached before Jane's.

The perfected secured party's interest as against other types of creditors, such as lienors, mortgagees, and judgment creditors, is also determined on a **first-to-perfect basis.** If the secured party perfects before a judgment lien or mortgage is recorded, the

first-to-perfect basis rule of priorities that holds that first in time in perfecting a security interest, mortgage, judgment, lien, or other property attachment right should have priority.

---

[47] UCC § 9-312 (Revised Article 9, § 9-313); *Melcher v Bank of Madison, Nebraska,* 529 NW2d 814 (Neb App 1995) and *Maryott v Oconto Cattle Co.,* 259 Neb 41, 607 NW2d 820, 41 UCC Rep Serv 2d 279 (Neb 2000).

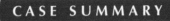

CASE SUMMARY

The Bank Does Not Win: When Secured Parties Take Priority over Overdrafts

FACTS: General Motors Acceptance Corporation (GMAC) financed the inventory of Donohue Ferrill Motor Company, Inc., which gave GMAC a security interest in its vehicle inventory and all of the proceeds of that inventory. The security agreement and financing statements were executed, and GMAC properly filed the financing statements.

Shortly before Donohue Ferrill's business failed, it sold six trucks and then deposited the proceeds of $124,610.80 from the sale of those trucks into its account at Lincoln National Bank. Lincoln took the deposited funds and applied them to Donohue Ferrill's account overdrafts. GMAC objected, saying that it had priority in those funds. The trial court and court of appeals found for the bank, and GMAC appealed.

DECISION: GMAC's security interest takes priority over the bank's right of setoff. The bank's interest is a statutory one, but an unsecured interest, and GMAC had a duly recorded security interest, which the bank knew of or should have known of at the time it took its offset rights. [**General Motors Acceptance Corp. v Lincoln Nat'l Bank, 18 SW3d 337 (Ky 2000)**]

---

perfected secured creditor has priority.[48] The perfected party takes priority over the secured party even when the perfected secured party is aware of the security interest prior to perfection.[49]

CPA   ## 23. PERFECTED SECURED PARTY VERSUS PERFECTED SECURED PARTY

The general rule for priority among two perfected secured creditors in the same collateral is also a first-in-time rule: The creditor who perfected first is given priority. **For Example,** again with respect to Bob's sign collection, if Bill filed a financing statement on February 22, 2007, Jane would still have priority because she perfected her interest first. If, however, Bill filed a financing statement on January 31, 2007, he would have priority over Jane. There are, however, three exceptions to this rule of first-in-time, first-in-right for perfected secured creditors.

CPA   **(a) THE PURCHASE MONEY SECURITY INTEREST IN INVENTORY[50]**   If the collateral is inventory, the purchase money secured creditor must do two things to prevail even over prior perfected secured creditors. The creditor must (1) perfect before the debtor receives possession of the goods that will be inventory and (2) give notice to any other secured party who has previously filed a financing statement with respect to that inventory.[51] The other secured parties must receive this notice before the debtor receives possession of the goods covered by the purchase money security interest. Compliance with these notice requirements gives the last creditor to

---

[48] *General Elec. Capital Corp. v Union Planters Bank*, N.A., 290 BR 676, 49 UCC Rep Serv 2d 1298 (ED *Mo* 2003)

[49] *St. Paul Mercury Insurance Company v Merchants & Marine Bank*, 882 So 2d 766 (Miss 2004).

[50] Revised Article 9, § 9-103 expands the definition of a PMSI in inventory. Consignments are treated as PMSIs in inventory.

[51] Revised Article 9, § 9-324.

extend credit for the inventory the priority position, which is a rule of law based on the practical notion that a debtor must be able to replenish its inventory to stay in business and keep creditors paid in a timely fashion. With this priority for subsequently perfected creditors, debtors have the opportunity to replenish inventory. **For Example,** suppose that First Bank has financed the inventory for Roberta's Exotic Pets, taken a security interest in the inventory, and filed a financing statement covering Roberta's inventory. Two months later, Animal Producers sells reptiles on credit to Roberta, taking a security interest in Roberta's inventory. To take priority over First Bank, Animal Producers would have to file the financing statement on the inventory before Roberta receives the reptiles and notify First Bank at the same time. The commercial rationale for this priority exception is to permit businesses to replenish their inventories by giving new suppliers a higher priority.

(b) PURCHASE MONEY SECURITY INTEREST—NONINVENTORY COLLATERAL   If the collateral is *noninventory collateral,* such as equipment, the purchase money secured creditor prevails over all others as to the same collateral if that creditor files a financing statement within 20 days after the debtor takes possession of the collateral. **For Example,** First Bank loans money to debtor Kwik Copy and properly files a financing statement covering all of Kwik Copy's present and subsequently acquired copying equipment. Second Bank then loans money to Kwik Copy for the purchase of a new copier. Second Bank's interest in the copier will be superior to First Bank's interest if Second Bank perfects its interest by filing either before the debtor receives the copier or within 20 days thereafter.

(c) STATUS OF REPAIR OR STORAGE LIEN   What happens when the debtor does not pay for the repair or storage of the collateral? In most states, a person repairing or storing goods has a lien or right to keep possession of the goods until paid for such services. The repairer or storer also has the right to sell the goods to obtain payment if the customer fails to pay and if proper notice is given.[52]

Article 9 makes a lien for repairs or storage superior to the perfected security interest in the collateral. The only exception to this rule makes the perfected security interest superior if the lien was created by statute rather than by common law and that statute expressly states that the lien is subordinate to a perfected security interest in the collateral.

Figure 34-2 provides a summary of the priorities of various parties with respect to secured and unsecured creditor interests.

---

24. SECURED PARTY VERSUS BUYER OF COLLATERAL FROM DEBTOR

The debtor may sell the collateral to a third person. How does this sale affect the secured creditor?

(a) SALES IN THE ORDINARY COURSE OF BUSINESS   A buyer who buys goods from the debtor in the ordinary course of business is not subject to any creditor's security interest regardless of whether the interest was perfected or unperfected and regardless of whether the buyer had actual knowledge of the security interest. The reason for this protection of buyers in the ordinary course of business is that subjecting

---

[52] UCC § 9-310 (Revised Article 9, § 9-333); *In re Northrup,* 220 BR 855, 35 UCCRS2d 711 (Bankr CED Pa 1998).

FIGURE 34-2   *Priority of Secured Interest under Article 9*

CONFLICT	PRIORITY
SECURED PARTY VERSUS SECURED PARTY	FIRST TO ATTACH
UNSECURED PARTY VERSUS SECURED PARTY	SECURED PARTY
PERFECTED SECURED PARTY VERSUS SECURED PARTY	PERFECTED SECURED PARTY
PERFECTED SECURED PARTY VERSUS PERFECTED SECURED PARTY	PARTY WHO IS FIRST TO PERFECT
PERFECTED SECURED PARTY VERSUS LIENOR	PARTY WHO FILED (FINANCING STATEMENT OR LIEN) FIRST [§ 9-307(2)] (REV. § 9-317)
EXCEPTIONS	
PMSI IN FIXTURES VERSUS PERFECTED SECURED PARTY	PMSI CREDITOR IF PERFECTED BEFORE ANNEXATION OR WITHIN 20 DAYS AFTER ANNEXATION (PMSI WILL HAVE PRIORITY EVEN OVER PRIOR PERFECTED SECURED PARTY) (§ 9-313, § 9-314) (REV. § 9-317)
PMSI IN EQUIPMENT VERSUS PERFECTED SECURED PARTY	PMSI IS PERFECTED WITHIN 20 DAYS AFTER DELIVERY [§ 9-301(2), § 9-312(4)] (REV. § 9-317)
PMSI IN INVENTORY VERSUS PERFECTED SECURED PARTY	PMSI IS PERFECTED BEFORE DELIVERY AND IF PERFECTED SECURED PARTY GIVEN NOTICE BEFORE DELIVERY [§ 9-312(3)] (REV. § 9-317)
PMSI IN CONSUMER GOODS VERSUS BUYER	BUYER UNLESS PERFECTION IS BY FILING BEFORE PURCHASE [§ 9-302(1)(D)] (REV. § 9-317)
PERFECTED SECURED PARTY VERSUS BUYER	BUYER IN ORDINARY COURSE WINS EVEN WITH KNOWLEDGE [§ 9-306(1)(D)] (REV. § 9-320)

buyers to a creditor's reclaim of goods would cause great delay and hesitation in commercial and consumer sales transactions.[53]

(b) SALES NOT IN THE ORDINARY COURSE OF BUSINESS: THE UNPERFECTED SECURITY INTEREST   A sale not in the ordinary course of business is one in which the seller is not usually a seller of such merchandise. **For Example,** if a buyer purchases a computer desk from an office supply store, the sale is in the ordinary course of business. If that same buyer purchases that same computer desk from a law firm

---

[53] Revised Article 9, § 9-320 covers the rights of buyers of goods.

The Motor Home That Traveled from Creditors to Debtors to Buyers in Ordinary Course

FACTS: In 1987, the Muirs bought a motor home. In 1988, the Muirs created and Bank of the West acquired and perfected a security interest in the motor home. In 1992, the Muirs entered into an agreement with Gateleys Fairway Motors by which Gateleys would sell the motor home by consignment. Gateleys was a motor home dealer and sold the motor home to Howard and Ann Schultz. The Schultzes did not know of the consignment arrangement or of the security interest of the bank. Gateleys failed to give the sales money to the Muirs and then filed for bankruptcy.

The Schultzes brought suit seeking a declaration that they owned the motor home free of the bank's security interest. The trial court granted the Schultzes summary judgment.

DECISION: The court of appeals reversed, noting that the UCC allows a buyer to qualify as a buyer in the ordinary course when the buyer purchases goods from a dealer who only possesses, but does not have legal title to, those goods. A buyer of consignment goods who purchases from a consignment dealer can be a buyer in ordinary course for the purposes of that statute. The Schultzes, as buyers, met the other requirements for being buyers in ordinary course and were such when they purchased the consigned motor home at Gateleys. [**Schultz v Bank of the West, C.B.C., 934 P2d 421 (Ore 1997)**]

that is going out of business, that buyer is not purchasing in the ordinary course of business. If a buyer is purchasing the collateral and the purchase is not in the ordinary course of business but the security interest is unperfected, such a security interest has no effect against a buyer who gives value and buys in good faith, that is, not knowing of the security interest. A buyer who does not satisfy these conditions is subject to the security interest.

CPA **(c) SALES NOT IN THE ORDINARY COURSE OF BUSINESS: THE PERFECTED SECURITY INTEREST**   If the security interest was perfected, the buyer of the collateral is ordinarily subject to the security interest unless the creditor consented to the sale.[54]

CPA **(d) SALES NOT IN THE ORDINARY COURSE OF BUSINESS: THE CONSUMER DEBTOR'S RESALE OF CONSUMER GOODS**   When the collateral constitutes consumer goods in the hands of the debtor, a resale of the goods to another consumer destroys the automatically perfected PMSI of the consumer debtor's creditor. Assuming that the buyer from the consumer debtor has no knowledge of a security interest, she will take the collateral free and clear from the creditor's security interest even though there was perfection by that creditor. Thus, the perfection without filing option afforded consumer PMSI creditors has a flaw in its coverage when it comes to a consumer debtor selling his refrigerator to a neighbor. Without a filed financing statement, the neighbor buyer takes the refrigerator free and clear of the creditor's security interest in it. However, consumer creditors can avoid the loss of this perfected interest by perfecting through filing. With filing, consumer PMSI creditors enjoy

---

[54] In Revised Article 9, § 1-201(9) adds that a purchase from a pawnbroker will not be considered a sale in the ordinary course of business.

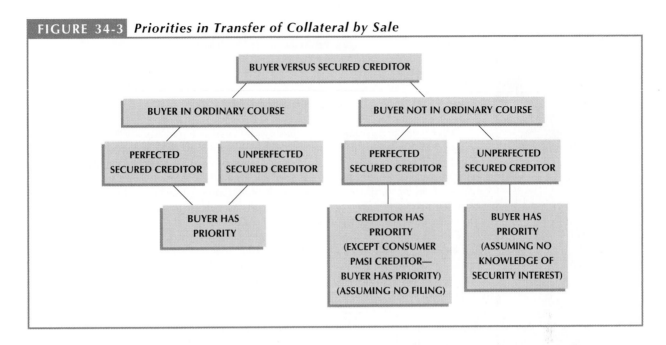

FIGURE 34-3 *Priorities in Transfer of Collateral by Sale*

continuation of their interests even when the neighbor has paid the consumer debtor for the refrigerator.

Figure 34-3 offers a summary of the rights of buyers of collateral with respect to the creditors who hold security interests in that collateral.

 RIGHTS OF PARTIES AFTER DEFAULT

When a debtor defaults on an obligation in a secured transaction, the secured creditor has the option to sue the debtor to enforce the debt or of proceeding against the collateral.

25. CREDITOR'S POSSESSION AND DISPOSITION OF COLLATERAL

Upon the debtor's default, the secured party is entitled to take the collateral from the debtor.[55] **Self-help repossession** is allowed if this can be done without causing a **breach of the peace.** If a breach of the peace might occur, the seller must use court action to obtain the collateral.

The secured creditor may sell, lease, or otherwise dispose of the collateral to pay the defaulted debt.[56] The sale may be private or public, at any time and place, and on any terms provided that the sale is done in a manner that is commercially reasonable. The creditor's sale eliminates all of the debtor's interest in the collateral.

self-help repossession
creditor's right to repossess the collateral without judicial proceedings.

breach of the peace
violation of the law in the repossession of the collateral.

---

[55] UCC § 9-503 (Revised Article 9, § 9-607). Repossession on private property where a creditor cut a lock was not a breach of the peace when security agreement authorized such trespass for repossession. *Wombles Charters, Inc. v Orix Credit Alliance, Inc.,* 39 UCC2d 599 (SDNY 1999).

[56] Revised Article 9, § 9-611 requires the secured party to notify all other secured parties and lienholders who have filed or recorded interests in the collateral of its intent to sell the collateral. This requirement was eliminated in the 1972 version of Article 9, but it is now once again a requirement.

CASE SUMMARY

I Was in My Driveway in My Underwear When They Repossessed My Car!

FACTS: Koontz entered into an agreement with Chrysler to purchase a 1988 Sundance in exchange for 60 monthly payments of $185.92. When Koontz defaulted on the contract in early 1991, Chrysler notified him that it would repossess the vehicle if he did not make up the missed payments. Koontz notified Chrysler that he would make every effort to catch up on the payments, that he did not want the vehicle to be repossessed, and that Chrysler was not to enter his private property to repossess the car. Chrysler repossessed the car, however, according to the self-help repossession statute of the UCC.

When Koontz heard the repossession in progress, he rushed outside in his underwear and hollered, "Don't take it," to the repossessor. The repossessor did not respond and proceeded to take the vehicle. Chrysler sold the car and filed a complaint against Koontz seeking a deficiency judgment for the balance due on the loan. Koontz alleged that the repossession was a breach of the peace. From a judgment in favor of Chrysler, Koontz appealed.

DECISION: There was no breach of the peace under Article 9 standards. Koontz only yelled, "Don't take it;" there was no verbal or physical response, no threat made at the repossessor, nor was there a breach of the peace. To find otherwise would be to invite the ridiculous situation whereby a debtor could avoid a deficiency judgment by merely stepping out of his house and yelling once at those sent to repossess the collateral. Such a narrow definition of the conduct necessary to breach the peace would render the self-help repossession statute useless. [**Chrysler Credit v Koontz, 661 NE2d 1171 (Ill App Ct 1996)**]

THINKING THINGS THROUGH

Breaking, Entering, and Dragging to Repossess

Christopher and Joy Callaway had purchased a 1993 Geo Tracker sport utility vehicle from Summerdale Budget Auto & Truck, Inc. Baldwin Finance, Inc., which financed the Callaways' purchase of the Tracker, held a lien on it. The Callaways fell behind on their payments, and the Tracker was repossessed once, but it was redeemed when the Callaways paid what was due. The Callaways fell behind in their payments again, and Baldwin sent Michael Whittenton to repossess the Tracker again. Joy heard noises outside their residence, and when she went outside to see what was happening, she saw Whittenton, who was repossessing the Tracker. Joy asked Whittenton to leave the property, but Whittenton continued with the repossession. Joy went back inside the house and told Christopher that Whittenton was taking the Tracker. Christopher told Whittenton to stop and told Whittenton that he needed to get some things out of the Tracker before Whittenton took it. Joy telephoned Budget to make sure that the due date for the October payment had been extended and,

THINKING THINGS THROUGH

continued

while she was on the telephone with Budget, she heard Christopher talking to Whittenton. Then she heard her husband scream.

The following events apparently preceded his scream. Whittenton had secured the Tracker to his truck, and Christopher saw Whittenton walk around to the driver's side of his truck and get in. Whittenton was not looking in Christopher's direction when Christopher walked outside. Christopher grabbed the roll bar on the Tracker as Whittenton began to drive away. Christopher banged on Whittenton's truck and yelled to get Whittenton's attention. Then, as Whittenton was driving down the driveway, the Tracker hit a pothole, and Christopher lost his balance. While he was trying to regain his balance, the rear tire on the driver's side of the Tracker ran over his foot. He then grabbed the roll bar on the Tracker again so that it would not run over him. Whittenton continued driving,

dragging Christopher down the driveway and 60 to 100 feet down Highway 10. One of the vehicles ran over the family's cat.

Whittenton's said that he did not have a conversation with Joy as he was hooking up the Tracker to tow it, and that he saw Christopher run through a ditch, run beside the Tracker, and jump onto the vehicle. Whittenton testified that he stopped his truck after turning onto Highway 10 because he saw Christopher jump between the truck towing the Tracker and the Tracker. Another witness, Ronnie Black, testified that he saw Christopher run through a ditch and jump onto the Tracker while it was on Highway 10.

The Callaways sued Whittenton, Budget, and Baldwin Finance, alleging assault and battery, negligence, wantonness, trespass, civil conspiracy, and wrongful repossession. Is this wrongful repossession? [CALLAWAY v WHITTENTON, 892 So 2d 852 (Ala 2003)]

26. CREDITOR'S RETENTION OF COLLATERAL

Instead of selling the collateral, the creditor may wish to keep it and cancel the debt owed.[57]

(a) NOTICE OF INTENTION   To retain the collateral in satisfaction of the debt, the creditor must send the debtor written notice of this intent.[58]

(b) COMPULSORY DISPOSITION OF COLLATERAL   In two situations, the creditor must dispose of the collateral. A creditor must sell the collateral if the debtor makes a written objection to retention within 21 days after the retention notice was sent. The creditor must also dispose of the collateral if it consists of consumer goods and the debtor has paid 60 percent or more of the cash price or of the loan secured by the security interest. The sale must be held within 90 days of the

---

[57] UCC § 9-505 (Revised Article 9, §§ 9-620, 9-621, 9-624).

[58] Revised Article 9, §§ 9-620 through 9-622.

ETHICS & THE LAW

Women, Children, and the Repo Guys

Repossessions of autos financed on credit are at an all-time high. Lenders explain that the growth period of the 1990s inspired many to overextend themselves with credit purchases, and now the repossessions are taking place.

According to the "repo industry," about 15 percent of debtors surrender their cars voluntarily. Confrontations occur about 10 percent of the time during repossession. Many debtors change the color of their cars, change the tires and rims, or cover the vehicle identification number to foil repossession companies' efforts. One auto dealer, trying to repossess a woman's car, had two male employees scale the fence of the Murfeesboro, Tennessee Domestic Violence Program Shelter. The shelter's security cameras spotted the men and after police were notified, they were ordered off the premises. The woman who owned the car left the shelter to make the necessary payments to bring her obligations current. The shelter director said that if the men had come through the proper administrative channels at the shelter, the shelter would have cooperated with them. The shelter director called the men's scaling of the fence at a shelter for women and children "irresponsible." Do you think it is ethical for the debtors to do these things? Should debtors surrender their cars voluntarily?

In two incidents in 2006, cars that were repossessed had children sleeping in them. The cars were hooked to the tow vehicle and the children were transported to the tow yards. An industry spokesman said that "repo guys" have to get in and hook the cars up as quickly as possible; they do not have time to check the inside of the vehicle.

Source: Rich Beattie, "Boom Times for Repo Guys," *New York Times*, April 18, 2003, D1, D8.

repossession. However, the debtor, after default, surrenders the right to require the resale.[59]

A creditor who fails to dispose of the collateral when required to do so is liable to the debtor for conversion of the collateral or for the penalty imposed by the Code for violation of Article 9.[60]

27. DEBTOR'S RIGHT OF REDEMPTION

The debtor may redeem the collateral at any time prior to the time the secured party has disposed of the collateral or entered into a binding contract for resale. To redeem, the debtor must tender the entire obligation that is owed plus any legal costs and expenses incurred by the secured party.[61]

---

[59] Revised Article 9, § 9-620.
[60] UCC § 9-507 (Revised Article 9, §§ 9-625 through 9-627).
[61] UCC § 9-506 (Revised Article 9, § 9-623).

28. DISPOSITION OF COLLATERAL

Upon the debtor's default, the creditor may sell the collateral at a public or private sale or may lease it to a third party. The creditor must give any required notice and act in a commercially reasonable manner. Revised Article 9 imposes specific notice requirements and provides a form that, if used by the creditor, is deemed adequate notice of sale. There are different notice forms for consumer and other transactions, but the basic information required is the day, time, location for the sale, and a contact number for questions the debtor and other secured parties might have. The notice must be sent to the debtor and any other creditors with an interest in the property.[62]

29. POSTDISPOSITION ACCOUNTING

When the creditor disposes of the collateral, the proceeds are applied in the following order. Proceeds are first used to pay the expenses of disposing of the collateral. Next, proceeds are applied to the debt owed the secured creditor making the disposition. Remaining proceeds are applied to any debts owed other creditors holding security interests in the same collateral that are subordinate to the interest of the disposing creditor.[63]

(a) DISTRIBUTION OF SURPLUS   If there is any money remaining, the surplus is paid to the debtor.[64]

(b) LIABILITY FOR DEFICIT   If the proceeds of the disposition are not sufficient to pay the costs and the debt of the disposing creditor, the debtor is liable for the deficiency. However, the disposition of the collateral must have been conducted in the manner required by the Code. This means that proper notice must have been given, if required, and that the disposition must have been made in a commercially reasonable manner.

LAWFLIX

Fun with Dick and Jane (1977) (PG)

Jane Fonda and George Segal play a married couple in financial distress. When Segal loses his job, creditors appear to reclaim purchases, including landscapers who repossess the lawn by rolling up the sod. What form of collateral is the sod? Is the repossession appropriate?

For movie clips that illustrate business law concepts, see LawFlix at **http://wdvl.westbuslaw.com.**

---

[62] UCC §§ 9-613 and 9-614.

[63] Revised Article 9, § 9-615.

[64] Revised Article 9, § 9-616. The distribution of proceeds remains substantially unchanged under Revised Article 9.

> SUMMARY

A security interest is an interest in personal property or fixtures that secures payment or performance of an obligation. The property that is subject to the interest is called the *collateral,* and the party holding the interest is called the *secured party. Attachment* is the creation of a security interest. To secure protection against third parties' claims to the collateral, the secured party must perfect the security interest. *Tangible collateral* is divided into classes: consumer goods, equipment, inventory, general intangibles, farm products, and fixtures. Under Revised Article 9, intangibles have been expanded to include bank accounts, checks, notes, and health care insurance receivables.

Perfection of a security interest is not required for its validity, but it does provide the creditor certain superior rights and priorities over other types of creditors and creditors with an interest in the same collateral. Perfection can be obtained through possession, filing, automatically (as in the case of a PMSI in consumer goods), by control for accounts under Revised Article 9, or temporarily when statutory protections are provided for creditors for limited periods of time.

Priority among creditors is determined according to their status. Unperfected, unsecured creditors simply wait to see whether there will be sufficient assets remaining after priority creditors are paid. Secured creditors have the right to take the collateral on a priority basis. As between secured creditors, the first creditor's interest to attach takes priority in the event the creditors hold security interests in the same collateral. A perfected secured creditor takes priority over an unperfected secured creditor. Perfected secured creditors with interests in the same collateral take priority generally on a first-to-perfect basis. Exceptions include PMSI inventory creditors who file a financing statement before delivery and notify all existing creditors, and equipment creditors who perfect within 20 days of attachment of their interests.

A buyer in the ordinary course of business always takes priority, even over perfected secured creditors who have knowledge of the creditor's interest. A buyer not in the ordinary course of business loses out to a perfected secured creditor but extinguishes the rights of a secured creditor unless the buyer had knowledge of the security interest. A buyer from a consumer debtor takes free and clear of the debtor's creditor's perfected security interest unless the creditor has filed a financing statement and perfected beyond just the automatic PMSI consumer goods perfection.

Upon default, a secured party may repossess the collateral from the buyer if this can be done without a breach of the peace. If a breach of the peace could occur, the secured party must use court action to regain the collateral. If the buyer has paid 60 percent or more of the cash price of the consumer goods, the seller must resell them within 90 days after repossession unless the buyer, after default, has waived this right in writing. Notice to the debtor of the sale of the collateral is usually required. A debtor may redeem the collateral prior to the time the secured party disposes of it or contracts to resell it.

> QUESTIONS AND CASE PROBLEMS

1. Charles Lakin, who did business as Sun Country Citrus, owned a citrus-packing plant in Yuma, Arizona. In 1985, the packing plant was leased to Sunco Partners. Under the terms of the lease, Sunco had the right to replace existing packing, sizing, and grading equipment with "state-of-the-art" equipment.

   In 1986, PKD, Inc., purchased Sunco. Sunco signed a bill of sale for all of its "personal property, including, but not limited to, packing equipment, boilers, compressors, and packinghouse-related supplies." The bill of sale was secured by an Article 9 security interest executed by PKD as the debtor and Lakin/Sunco as the creditors.

   In February 1987, PKD changed its name to Amcico and negotiated for the purchase and lease of citrus-sorting equipment from Pennwalt Corp., now Elf Atochem. The documents for the transaction specifically provided that title to the equipment would remain with Elf Atochem until all payments were made under the terms of the sale and lease agreement.

   In December 1987, Amcico defaulted on its payments to Lakin and Sunco. Lakin and

Sunco took possession of all of the equipment in the Yuma plant. Elf Atochem objected, claiming its title to the citrus-sorting equipment. Lakin and Sunco produced the security agreement giving them such equipment as collateral. Elf Atochem claimed that because it retained title in the citrus-sorting equipment, there was no interest in it on the part of Amcico, and the security interest of Sunco and Lakin never attached. Was Elf Atochem correct? [*Elf Atochem North America, Inc. v Celco, Inc.,* 927 P2d 355 (Ariz App)]

2. In 1983, Carpet Contracts owned a commercial lot and building, which it operated as a retail carpet outlet. In April of that year, Carpet Contracts entered into a credit sales agreement with Young Electric Sign Corp. (Yesco) for the purchase of a large electronic sign for the store. The total cost of the sign was $113,000, with a down payment of $25,000 and 60 monthly payments of $2,100 each.

In August 1985, Carpet Contracts agreed to sell the property to Interstate. As part of the sale, Carpet Contracts gave Interstate an itemized list showing that $64,522 of the proceeds from the sale would be used to pay for the "Electronic Sign." The property was transferred to Interstate, and the Carpet Contracts store continued to operate there, but now it paid rent to Interstate. In June 1986, Carpet Contracts asked Yesco to renegotiate the terms of the sign contract. Yesco reduced Carpet Contracts' monthly payments and filed a financing statement on the sign at the Utah Division of Corporations and Commercial Code.

In December 1986, Interstate agreed to sell the property and the sign to the Webbs, who conducted a title search on the property, which revealed no interest with respect to the electronic sign. Interstate conveyed the property to the Webbs. Carpet Contracts continued its operation but was struggling financially and had not made its payments to Yesco for some time. By 1989, Yesco declared the sign contract in default and contacted the Webbs, demanding the balance due of $26,100. The Webbs then filed suit, claiming Yesco had no priority as a creditor because its financing statement was not filed in the real property records where the Webbs had done their title search before purchasing the land. Was the financing statement filed properly for perfection? [*Webb v Interstate Land Corp.,* 920 P2d 1187 (Utah)]

3. Wayne Smith purchased a computer from Lee Sounds for personal use. Smith signed an installment purchase note and a security agreement. Under the terms of the note, Smith was to pay $100 down and $50 a month for 20 months. The security agreement included a description of the computer; however, Lee did not file a financing statement. Did Lee fulfill the requirements necessary for the attachment and perfection of its security interest in the computer? Why or why not?

4. When Johnson Hardware Shop borrowed $20,000 from First Bank, it used its inventory as collateral for the loan. First Bank perfected its security interest by filing a financing statement. The inventory was subsequently damaged by fire, and Flanders Insurance Co. paid Johnson Hardware $5,000 for the loss, but First Bank claimed the proceeds of the insurance. Was First Bank correct? Why or why not?

5. Consider the following cases and determine whether the financing statements as filed would be valid under Article 9. Be sure to consider the standard of "seriously misleading" under Revised Article 9.

   a. *In re Thriftway Auto Supply, Inc.,* 159 BR 948, 22 UCC Rep Serv 2d 605 (WD Okla). The creditor used the debtor's corporate trade name, "Thriftway Auto Stores," not its legal name, "Thriftway Auto Supply, Inc."

   b. *In re Mines Tire Co., Inc.,* 194 BR 23, 29 UCC2d 617 (Bankr WDNY). The creditor used the name "Mines Company Inc." instead of "Mines Tire Company, Inc."

   c. *Mountain Farm Credit Service, ACA v Purina Mills, Inc.,* 119 NC App 508, 459 SE2d 75, 27 UCC2d 1441. The creditor filed the financing statement under "Warren Killian and Robert Hetherington dba Grey Daw Farms" in a situation in which the two individuals were partners running Grey Daw Farms as a partnership.

   d. *B. T. Lazarus & Co. v Christofides,* 104 Ohio App 3d 335, 662 NE2d 41, 29 UCC2d 627.

The creditor filed a financing statement in the debtor's old name when, prior to filing, the debtor had changed its name from B.T.L., Inc., to Alma Manufacturing, Inc.

e. *In re SpecialCare, Inc.,* 209 BR 13, 34 UCC2d 857 (Bankr ND Ga). The creditor failed to refile an amended financing statement to reflect debtor's name change from "Davidson Therapeutic Services, Inc." to "SpecialCare, Inc."

f. *Industrial Machinery & Equipment Co. Inc. v Lapeer County Bank & Trust Co.,* 213 Mich App 676, 540 NW2d 781, 28 UCC2d 1033. The creditor filed the financing statement under the company's trade name, KMI, Inc., instead of its legal name, Koehler Machine, Inc.

g. *First Nat'l Bank of Lacon v Strong,* 278 Ill App 3d 762, 215 Ill Dec 421, 663 NE2d 432, 29 UCC2d 622. Creditor filed the financing statement using the trade name "Strong Oil Co." instead of the legal name "E. Strong Oil Company."

6. First Union Bank of Florida loaned money to Dale and Lynn Rix for their purchase of Ann's Hallmark, a Florida corporation. First Union took a security interest in the store's equipment, fixtures, and inventory and filed the financing statement under the names of Dale and Lynn Rix. Subsequently, the Rixes incorporated their newly acquired business as Michelle's Hallmark Cards & Gifts, Inc. When Michelle's went into bankruptcy, First Union claimed it had priority as a secured creditor because it had filed its financing statement first. Other creditors said First Union had priority against the Rixes but not against the corporation. Who was correct? What was the correct name for filing the financing statement? [*In re Michelle's Hallmark Cards & Gifts, Inc.,* 36 UCC2d 225 (Bankr MD Fla)]

7. Rawlings purchased a typewriter from Kroll Typewriter Co. for $600. At the time of the purchase, he made an initial payment of $75 and agreed to pay the balance in monthly installments. A security agreement that complied with the UCC was prepared, but no financing statement was ever filed for the transaction. Rawlings, at a time when he still owed a balance on the typewriter and without the consent of Kroll, sold the typewriter to a neighbor. The neighbor, who had no knowledge of the security interest, used the typewriter in her home. Could Kroll repossess the typewriter from the neighbor?

8. Kim purchased on credit a $1,000 freezer from Silas Household Appliance Store. After she had paid approximately $700, Kim missed the next monthly installment payment. Silas repossessed the freezer and billed Kim for the balance of the purchase price, $300. Kim claimed that the freezer, now in the possession of Silas, was worth much more than the balance due and requested that Silas sell the freezer to wipe out the balance of the debt and to leave something for her. Silas claimed that because Kim had broken her contract to pay the purchase price, she had no right to say what should be done with the freezer. Was Silas correct? Explain.

9. Benson purchased a new Ford Thunderbird automobile. She traded in her old car and used the Magnavox Employees Credit Union to finance the balance. The credit union took a security interest in the Ford. Subsequently, the Ford was involved in a number of accidents and was taken to a dealer for repairs. Benson was unable to pay for the work done. The dealer claimed a lien on the car for services and materials furnished. The Magnavox Employees Credit Union claimed priority. Which claim had priority? [*Magnavox Employees Credit Union v Benson,* 331 NE2d 46 (Ind App)]

10. Lockovich borrowed money from a bank to purchase a motorboat. The bank took a security interest in it but never filed a financing statement. A subsequent default on the loan occurred, and the debtor was declared bankrupt. The bank claimed priority in the boat, alleging that no financing statement had to be filed. Do you agree? Why? [*In re Lockovich,* 124 BR 660 (Bankr WD Pa)]

11. Hull-Dobbs sold an automobile to Mallicoat and then assigned the sales contract to Volunteer Finance & Loan Corp. Later Volunteer repossessed the automobile and sold it. When Volunteer sued Mallicoat for the deficiency between the contract price and the proceeds on resale, Mallicoat argued that he had not been properly notified of the resale. The loan manager

of the finance company testified that Mallicoat had been sent a registered letter stating that the car would be sold. He did not state, however, whether the letter merely declared in general terms that the car would be sold or specified a date for its resale. He admitted that the letter never was delivered to Mallicoat and was returned to the finance company "unclaimed." The loan manager also testified that the sale was advertised by posters, but on cross-examination, he admitted that he was not able to state when or where it was advertised. It was shown that Volunteer knew where Mallicoat and his father lived and where Mallicoat was employed. Mallicoat claimed that he had not been properly notified. Volunteer asserted that sufficient notice had been given. Was the notice of the resale sufficient? [*Mallicoat v Volunteer Finance & Loan Corp.,* 415 SW2d 347 (Tenn App)]

12. On April 18, 2000, Philip Purkett parked his car, on which he owed $213 in payments, in his garage and locked the garage. Later that night, TWAS, Inc., a vehicle repossession company, broke into the garage and repossessed the car without notice to Purkett. To get the car back, Purkett paid a $140 storage fee and signed a document stating that he would not hold TWAS liable for any damages. Did TWAS and Key Bank violate Article 9 requirements on repossession? [Purkett v Key Bank USA, Inc., 2001 WL 503050, 45 UCC Rep Serv 2d 1201 (ND Ill)]

13. *A* borrowed money from *B* and orally agreed that *B* had a security interest in certain equipment that was standing in *A*'s yard. Nothing was in writing, and no filing of any kind was made. Nine days later, *B* took possession of the equipment. What kind of interest did *B* have in the equipment after taking possession of it? [*Transport Equipment Co. v Guaranty State Bank,* 518 F2d 373 (10th Cir)]

14. Cook sold Martin a new tractor truck for approximately $13,000, with a down payment of approximately $3,000 and the balance to be paid in 30 monthly installments. The sales agreement provided that "on default in any payment, Cook [could] take immediate possession of the property . . . without notice or demand. For this purpose vendor may enter upon any premises

on which the property may be." Martin failed to pay the installments when due, and Cook notified him that the truck would be repossessed. Martin left the tractor truck attached to a loaded trailer and locked on the premises of a company in Memphis. Martin intended to drive to the West Coast with the trailer. When Cook located the tractor truck, no one was around. To disconnect the trailer from the truck (because he had no right to the trailer), Cook removed the wire screen over a ventilator hole by unscrewing it from the outside with his penknife. He next reached through the ventilator hole with a stick and unlocked the door of the tractor truck. He then disconnected the trailer and had the truck towed away. Martin sued Cook for unlawfully repossessing the truck by committing a breach of the peace. Decide. [*Martin v Cook,* 114 So 2d 669 (Miss)]

15. Muska borrowed money from the Bank of California and secured the loan by giving the bank a security interest in equipment and machinery at his place of business. To perfect the interest, the bank filed a financing statement that did not contain Muska's address. Muska later filed for bankruptcy. The trustee in bankruptcy claimed that the security interest of the bank was not perfected because the omission of the residence address from the financing statement made it defective. Was the financing statement valid? [*Lines v Bank of California,* 467 F2d 1274 (9th Cir)]

16. Kimbrell's Furniture Co. sold a new television set and tape player to Charlie O'Neil and his wife. Each purchase was on credit, and in each instance, a security agreement was executed. Later on the same day of purchase, O'Neil carried the items to Bonded Loan, a pawnbroker, and pledged the television and tape deck as security for a loan. Bonded Loan held possession of the television set and tape player as security for its loan and contended that its lien had priority over the unrecorded security interest of Kimbrell. Who had priority? [*Kimbrell's Furniture Co. v Sig Friedman, d/b/a Bonded Loan,* 198 SE2d 803 (SC)]

CPA QUESTIONS

1. On March 1, Green went to Easy Car Sales to buy a car. Green spoke to a salesperson and agreed to buy a car that Easy had in its showroom. On March 5, Green made a $500 down payment and signed a security agreement to secure the payment of the balance of the purchase price. On March 10, Green picked up the car. On March 15, Easy filed the security agreement. On what date did Easy's security interest attach?

   a. March 1
   b. March 5
   c. March 10
   d. March 15

2. Carr Corp. sells VCRs and videotapes to the public. Carr sold and delivered a VCR to Sutter on credit. Sutter executed and delivered to Carr a promissory note for the purchase price and a security agreement covering the VCR. Sutter purchased the VCR for personal use. Carr did not file a financing statement. Is Carr's security interest perfected?

   a. No, because the VCR was a consumer good
   b. No, because Carr failed to file a financing statement
   c. Yes, because Carr retained ownership of the VCR
   d. Yes, because it was perfected at the time of attachment

3. On July 8, Ace, a refrigerator wholesaler, purchased 50 refrigerators. This comprised Ace's entire inventory and was financed under an agreement with Rome Bank that gave Rome a security interest in all refrigerators on Ace's premises, all future-acquired refrigerators, and the proceeds of sales. On July 12, Rome filed a financing statement that adequately identified the collateral. On August 15, Ace sold one refrigerator to Cray for personal use and four refrigerators to Zone Co. for its business. Which of the following statements is correct?

   a. The refrigerators sold to Zone will be subject to Rome's security interest.
   b. The refrigerators sold to Zone will not be subject to Rome's security interest.
   c. The security interest does not include the proceeds from the sale of the refrigerators to Zone.
   d. The security interest may not cover after-acquired property even if the parties agree.

4. Fogel purchased a television set for $900 from Hamilton Appliance Store. Hamilton took a promissory note signed by Fogel and a security interest for the $800 balance due on the set. It was Hamilton's policy not to file a financing statement until the purchaser defaulted. Fogel obtained a loan of $500 from Reliable Finance, which took and recorded a security interest in the set. A month later, Fogel defaulted on several loans outstanding and one of his creditors, Harp, obtained a judgment against Fogel, which was properly recorded. After making several payments, Fogel defaulted on a payment due to Hamilton, who then recorded a financing statement subsequent to Reliable's filing and the entry of the Harp judgment. Subsequently, at a garage sale, Fogel sold the set for $300 to Mobray. Which of the parties has the priority claim to the set?

   a. Reliable
   b. Hamilton
   c. Harp
   d. Mobray

BANKRUPTCY

After studying this chapter, you should be able to

LO.1 List the requirements for the commencement of a voluntary bankruptcy case and an involuntary bankruptcy case

LO.2 Describe the rights of a trustee in bankruptcy

LO.3 Explain the procedure for the administration of a debtor's estate

LO.4 List a debtor's duties and exemptions

LO.5 Explain the significance of a discharge in bankruptcy

LO.6 Explain when a business reorganization and an extended-time payment plan might be used

What can a person or business do when overwhelmed by debts? Bankruptcy proceedings can provide temporary and sometimes permanent relief from those debts.

A BANKRUPTCY LAW

Bankruptcy is a statutory proceeding with detailed procedures and requirements.

1. THE FEDERAL LAW

Bankruptcy law is based on federal statutes that have been refined over the years. In October 2005, the Bankruptcy Abuse Prevention and Consumer Protection Act of 2005 (BAPCPA) took effect.[1] The BAPCPA was passed more than 10 years after the Bankruptcy Reform Commission was created, and the changes in bankruptcy law reflect an expressed congressional desire to curb a 15-year trend of increases in the number of bankruptcies.

> **bankruptcy courts** court of special jurisdiction to determine bankruptcy issues.

Jurisdiction over bankruptcy proceedings is vested in the federal district courts. The district courts have the authority to transfer such matters to courts of special jurisdiction called **bankruptcy courts.**

> **Chapter 7 bankruptcy** liquidation form of bankruptcy under federal law.

2. TYPES OF BANKRUPTCY PROCEEDINGS

The three types of bankruptcy proceedings that existed before the 2005 reforms are still available to individuals and businesses.

CPA

> **liquidation** process of converting property into money whether of particular items of property or of all the assets of a business or an estate.

(a) LIQUIDATION OR CHAPTER 7 BANKRUPTCY   A **Chapter 7 bankruptcy** is one in which all of the debtor's assets (with some exemptions) will be **liquidated** to pay debts. Those debts that remain unpaid or are paid only partially are discharged, with some exceptions. The debtor who declares Chapter 7 bankruptcy begins again with a nearly clean slate.

Chapter 7 bankruptcy is available to individuals, partnerships, and corporations. However, farmers, insurance companies, savings and loans, municipalities, Small

---

[1] Pub. L. No. 109-8, 119 Stat. 23 (2005); the act is codified at 11 USC § 101 *et. seq.*

ETHICS & THE LAW

Bankruptcy Records

According to **http://www.bankruptcydata.com**, the total bankruptcy filings in the United States from 2000 to 2005 were as follows:

Year	Total Business	Total Nonbusiness
2005	39,201	2,039,214
2004	34,317	1,563,145
2003	35,037	1,660,245
2002	38,540	1,566,358
2001	40,099	1,492,129
2000	35,472	1,217,972

According to **http://www.bankruptcydata.com**, the following are the largest bankruptcies in the history of the United States:

Company	Bankruptcy Date	Total Assets Prebankruptcy	Filing Court District
WorldCom, Inc.	7/21/2002	$103,914,000,000	NY-S
Enron Corp.	12/2/2001	63,392,000,000	NY-S
Conseco, Inc.	12/18/2002	61,392,000,000	IL-N
Texaco, Inc.	4/12/1987	35,892,000,000	NY-S
Financial Corp. of America	9/9/1988	33,864,000,000	CA-C
Refco	10/17/2005	33,333,172,000	NY-S
Global Crossing Ltd.	1/28/2002	30,185,000,000	NY-S
Pacific Gas and Electric Co.	4/6/2001	29,770,000,000	CA-N
Calpine	12/20/2005	27,216,088,000	NY-S
UAL Corp	12/9/2002	25,197,000,000	IL-N
Delta Air Lines	9/14/2005	21,801,000,000	NY-S
Adelphia Communications	6/25/2002	21,499,000,000	NY-S

Do you think, as many federal regulators and representatives and senators did in enacting the reforms, that the bankruptcy laws were being abused and that too many people were declaring bankruptcy just to avoid paying obligations? Is there an ethical component to declaring bankruptcy?

Business Administration companies, and railroads are not entitled to declare Chapter 7 bankruptcy because they are specifically governed by other statutes or specialized sections of the Bankruptcy Code.[2]

Under the BAPCPA, consumers will have difficulty filing immediately for Chapter 7 liquidation bankruptcy because the reforms require that the consumers demonstrate that they do not have the means to repay the debts before they are

---

[2] For example, the Small Business Investment Act governs the insolvency of small business investment companies, 11 USC § 109(b). Municipalities' bankruptcies are governed by Chapter 9 of the Bankruptcy Code, and farmers' bankruptcies are covered under Chapter 12.

permitted a Chapter 7 liquidation.[3] The means test, which is discussed later, considers the disposable income that is available after the bankruptcy court has deducted allowable expenses that are listed as part of the means section of the BAPCPA, including items such as health insurance and child support.

 CPA

Chapter 11 bankruptcy
reorganization form of
bankruptcy under federal
law.

(b) REORGANIZATION OR CHAPTER 11 BANKRUPTCY   **Chapter 11 bankruptcy** is a way for a debtor to reorganize and continue a business with protection from overwhelming debts and without the requirement of liquidation. Because the same credit counseling requirements apply to individuals who file for Chapter 7 liquidation and Chapter 11 protection, anyone who qualifies for one qualifies for the other. The same exemptions also apply with the exception of railroads, which may declare Chapter 11 bankruptcy. Stockbrokers, however, are not eligible for Chapter 11 bankruptcy.

CPA

Chapter 13 bankruptcy
proceeding of consumer
debt readjustment plan
bankruptcy.

(c) CHAPTER 13 BANKRUPTCY OR PAYMENT PLANS OR CONSUMER DEBT ADJUSTMENT PLANS   Chapter 13 of the federal Bankruptcy Code provides consumers an individual form of reorganization. Chapter 13 works with consumer debtors to develop a plan to repay debt. To be eligible for **Chapter 13 bankruptcy,** the individual must owe unsecured debts of less than $307,675 and secured debts of less than $922,975 and have regular income.[4] Under proposed reforms, Chapter 13 would play an expanded role in bankruptcy because reforms require debtors with the means to pay their debts to go first into Chapter 13 bankruptcy rather than automatically declaring Chapter 7 bankruptcy.

Ⓑ HOW BANKRUPTCY IS DECLARED

Bankruptcy can be declared in different ways. The federal Bankruptcy Code spells out in detail the exact requirements and process for declaration.

CPA

voluntary bankruptcy
proceeding in which the
debtor files the petition for
relief.

3. DECLARATION OF VOLUNTARY BANKRUPTCY

A **voluntary bankruptcy** is begun when the debtor files a petition with the bankruptcy court. A joint petition may be filed by a husband and wife. When a voluntary case is begun, the debtor must file a schedule of current income and current expenditures unless the court excuses this filing.

means test new standard
under the Reform Act that
requires that court to find
that the debtor does not have
the means to repay creditors;
goes beyond the past
requirement of petitions
being granting on the simple
assertion of the debtor
saying, "I have debts."

Under the 2005 reforms, a court can dismiss an individual debtor's (consumer's) petition for abuse if the debtor does not satisfy the **means test,** which measures the debtor's ability to pay by computing the debtor's disposable income. Only those debtors who fall below their state's median disposable income will be able to continue in a Chapter 7 proceeding. Individual debtors who meet the means test are required to go into Chapter 13 bankruptcy because they have not qualified for Chapter 7 bankruptcy. The formula for applying the means test is as follows:

Debtor's current monthly income less
Allowable expenses under the Bankruptcy Code = Disposable income
Disposable income × 60

[3] 11 USC §707(C)(2)(a). There are exceptions to the requirements of establishing no means, such as those who incurred their debts while on active military service.
[4] 11 USC §109(e).

The debtor is guilty of bankruptcy abuse if this number is not less than the lower of the following:

- 25 percent of the debtor's unsecured claims or $6,000, whichever is greater
- $10,000

A finding of abuse means that the debtor's Chapter 7 voluntary petition is dismissed. Previously, the law required the judge to find "substantial abuse" before dismissing the petition; now the standard reads only "abuse."[5]

Under the Reform Act, the bankruptcy judge also has the discretion to order the debtor's lawyer to reimburse the trustee for costs and attorney's fees and to assess a civil penalty against the lawyer if the court finds that the lawyer has not acted in good faith in filing the debtor's bankruptcy petition.[6] As part of this change, lawyers must declare themselves (in public ads as well as in an individual) to be "debt relief agencies" or state that they "help people file for relief under the Bankruptcy Code." The Code now requires those who help consumers deal with creditors to disclose that part of that assistance may include filing for bankruptcy. Lawyers who advertise their credit/bankruptcy expertise are subject to the laws and regulations that apply to debt relief agencies. If the agency/lawyer advises them to do something that causes the court to declare that there has been bankruptcy abuse, the lawyer/debt relief agency is responsible as well. As part of their role as a debt counselor, lawyers are prohibited under the changes in the law from advising clients to undertake more debt in contemplation of filing bankruptcy.[7]

SPORTS & ENTERTAINMENT LAW

Hip-Hop to the Top: Bankruptcy to the Bottom

TLC was an Atlanta rhythm, blues, and hip-hop band that performed at clubs in 1991. The three-woman group signed a recording contract with LaFace Records. The group's first album that LaFace produced, *Oooooooohhh on the TLC Tip*, sold almost 3 million albums in 1992. The group's second album, *Crazysexycool*, also produced by LaFace, sold 5 million albums through June 1996. The two albums together had six top-of-the-chart singles.

LaFace had the right to renew TLC's contract in 1996 following renegotiation of the contract terms. In the industry, royalty rates for unknown groups, as TLC was in 1991, are generally 7 percent of the revenues for the first 500,000 albums and 8 percent for sales on platinum albums (albums that sell over 1 million copies). The royalty rate increases to 9.5 percent for all sales on an eighth album. Established artists in the industry who renegotiate often have royalty rates of 13 percent, and artists with two platinum albums can command an even higher royalty.

The three women in TLC—Tionne Watkins (T-Boz), Lisa Lopes (Left-Eye, who has since died), and Romanda Thomas (Chili)—declared bankruptcy in July 1995. All three

---

[5] 11 USC § 707(b).
[6] 11 USC § 707(b)(4).
[7] 11 USC §§ 526–528.

SPORTS & ENTERTAINMENT LAW

continued

listed debts that exceeded their assets, which included sums owed to creditors for their cars and to Zale's and The Limited for credit purchases. Lopes was being sued by Lloyd's of London, which claimed she owed it $1.3 million it had paid on a policy held by her boyfriend on his home that was destroyed by fire. Lopes pleaded guilty to one count of arson in the destruction of the home but denied that she intended to destroy it. She was sentenced to five years probation and treatment at a halfway house.

Lopes asked that the Lloyd's claim be discharged in her bankruptcy. All three members of TLC asked that their contract with LaFace be discharged in bankruptcy because being bound to their old contract could impede their fresh financial starts.

Did the three women meet the standards for declaring bankruptcy? Evaluate whether Lopes's Lloyd's claim should be discharged. Determine whether the record contract should be discharged.

During 1996, the members of three music groups declared bankruptcy just before their contracts were due for renegotiation. One record company executive has noted that record company owners are frightened by the trend: "You invest all the money and time in making them stars. Then they leave for the bigger companies and a higher take on sales. It has all of us scared."

Is declaring bankruptcy by the members of these musical groups legal? Is it ethical? Are the musicians using bankruptcy as a way to avoid contract obligations? Are the musicians using bankruptcy as a way to maximize their income?

Pop singer Billy Joel also had a record contract with a small company during the initial stages of his career. When the company refused, during renegotiations, to increase his royalty rate, Joel did not produce another album during the period of the contract renewal option. Instead, he used a clause in the contract that limited him to nightclub and piano bar appearances in the event another album was not produced. For three years, Joel played small clubs and restaurants and did not produce an album. At the end of that period when his contract had expired, he negotiated a contract with Columbia. His first album with Columbia was *Piano Man,* a multiplatinum album. Did Joel take an ethical route? Is his solution more ethical than bankruptcy?

Debtors are required to undergo credit counseling (from an approved nonprofit credit counseling agency) within the 180 days prior to declaring a bankruptcy. In addition, the court applies the means test described earlier to determine whether the debtor qualifies for bankruptcy.[8]

---

[8] 11 USC § 109(h)(2) provides that "an individual may not be a debtor under this title unless such individual has, during the 180-day period preceding the date of filing the petition by such individual, received from an approved nonprofit budget and credit counseling agency . . . an individual or group briefing (including a briefing conducted by telephone or on the Internet) that outlined the opportunities for available credit counseling and assisted such individual in performing a related budget analysis." 11 USC § 106(e) lists the requirements for a counseling agency that are necessary before it can gain court approval for debtor counseling. There are exceptions to the counseling requirements such as active military duty, disability, and emergencies.

CASE SUMMARY

Disposable Income and Predisposed Not to Pay

FACTS: The Jasses filed for Chapter 13 bankruptcy relief. Their Form B22C indicated that their yearly household aggregate income was $143,403.96 based on income they received during the six-month period before filing. After deducting allowed expenses and deductions from their income, the Jasses' Statement of Current Monthly Income shows a "disposable income" of $3,625.63 per month.

The Jasses filed a Chapter 13 plan which proposed to return $790.00 to unsecured creditors. At the hearing, the Trustee objected to confirmation because the Jasses' "disposable income," as calculated on their Form B22C, is $3,625.63, and they proposed to pay only $790.00 to unsecured creditors. The Trustee argued that because the Jasses were not proposing to pay their full disposable income of $3,625.63 to unsecured creditors, their plan did not comply with this "disposable income test."

The Jasses argued that the word "projected" in the statute modifies the definition of "disposable income." Mrs. Jass testified that beginning in December 2005, her husband experienced serious medical problems involving injuries to his intestines. She testified that her family incurred $12,000 in medical expenses. In light of these expenses and medical problems, the Jasses argued that their income in the future will not be commensurate with the "disposable income" shown on Form B22C. They argued that the changes under the BAPCPA do not require them to pay unsecured creditors the amount resulting from their Form B22C, so long as they can show that the income and expenses reported on the Form are inadequate representations of their future budget.

DECISION: The court held that the word *projected* modifies *disposable income* and that the code intended that the disposable income figure be based on "projected income." The court acknowledged that the debtor will need to provide testimony regarding the change in circumstances that will result in a reduction of the income but also noted that without the word *projected* being used, the parties to a bankruptcy would be deprived of the fresh-start purpose the laws were intended to provide. They cannot pay more money to creditors than they will be earning and their change in health and financial circumstances means that they will simply not have the funds available to pay all that the form computes; the testimony on the future established the notion of *projected*. [***In re Jass,*** 40 BR 411 (Utah 2006)]

 CPA

4. DECLARATION OF INVOLUNTARY BANKRUPTCY

involuntary bankruptcy
proceeding in which a creditor or creditors file the petition for relief with the bankruptcy court.

(a) ELIGIBILITY   An **involuntary bankruptcy** is begun when creditors file a petition with the bankruptcy court. An involuntary case may be commenced against any individual, partnership, or corporation, except those excluded from filing voluntary petitions. Nonprofit corporations are also exempt from involuntary proceedings.[9]

 CPA

(b) NUMBER AND CLAIMS OF PETITIONING CREDITORS   If there are 12 or more creditors, at least 3 of those creditors whose unsecured and undisputed claims total $12,300 or more must sign the involuntary petition.[10] If there are fewer than 12 creditors,

---

[9] 11 USC § 303(a).

[10] 11 USC § 303. The term "undisputed" was added to this section and commentators are unclear as to whether this addition will make it easier for debtors to challenge involuntary bankruptcies.

THINKING THINGS THROUGH

Means Test Justifying the End of Debt

The following excerpt is a hypothetical case an experienced bankruptcy attorney worked through to illustrate the application of the means test because no bankruptcy means cases have made their way through to appellate decision.

The Brokes, a married couple in their early 40s, have two children in private schools. They are residents of Memphis, Shelby County, Tennessee; their annual gross income is $86,496. Like many debtors, the Brokes lost their home following an unsuccessful Chapter 13 case three years ago. They now rent a house for $2,000 a month. They owe back federal taxes in the amount of $9,000. They have secured debt on two cars with remaining balances of $10,000 and $6,000 and unsecured, consumer debt totaling $28,000. They desire to seek relief under Chapter 7 of the Bankruptcy Code.

The Brokes' gross monthly income is $7,208. After deducting taxes and other mandatory payroll deductions of $1,509, the couple has $5,699 in monthly income. The means test requires several additional deductions from the Brokes' gross monthly income. Section 707(b)(A)(2)(ii) provides a deduction for living and housing expenses using National Standards and Local Standards and additional Internal Revenue Service (IRS) figures. Allowable living expenses for a family of four in Ura and Ima Brokes' income bracket, based on national standards, total $1,564, while housing and utility figures for Shelby County, Tennessee, allow $1,354. In addition, there are allowable expenses for transportation. Based on IRS figures, the Brokes can subtract national ownership costs of $475 for the first car and $338 for the second, as well as regional operating and public transportation costs of

$242 and $336, respectively. They can also deduct their reasonably necessary health insurance costs, here the sum of $600, and $250 a month for private school tuition. Subtracting all of these figures from the Brokes' monthly income leaves $540.

Under § 707(b)(2)(A)(iii), the Brokes can subtract payments on secured debt. The amount contractually due on their two automobiles over the next 60 months is $16,000. After dividing this total by 60 and rounding to the nearest dollar, the monthly allowable deduction for secured debt is $267. Subtracting this amount from $540 leaves $273.

Next come priority claim deductions. The Brokes are not subject to any child support or alimony claims, but they do owe $9,000 in back taxes. Again, dividing this amount by 60 yields a deductible amount of $150. Subtracting this from $273 leaves $123 in disposable monthly income. This figure would be multiplied by 60, amounting to a total of $7,380 in disposable income over the five-year period. Abuse is thus statutorily presumed because the debtors' current monthly income reduced by allowable amounts is not less than either $7,000 (25 percent of their nonpriority unsecured claims of $28,000) or $6,000. The Brokes' Chapter 7 case will therefore be dismissed (or they will be allowed voluntarily to convert their Chapter 7 case to a case under Chapter 13).

Do you think that the use of the means test will make it more difficult for debtors to declare bankruptcy?*

---

* Robert J. Landry III and Nancy Hisey Mardis, "Consumer Bankruptcy Reform: Debtors' Prison without Bars or 'Just Desserts' for Deadbeats?" 36 *Golden Gate U. L. Rev.* 91 (2006).

ETHICS & THE LAW

The Nonprofit Credit Counselors with Ties to Profits

The credit counseling business is funded in one of two ways, the most common of which is that the agency works with debtors to develop a debt management plan (DMP) and then receives from the creditor a percentage of any payments the debtor makes to the creditor as part of the plan. A second way is that the debtor pays a fee to the agency for the service. For the most part, debtors had not been counseled on creditor relationships but had been convinced to develop a DMP. Under a DMP, the debtor pays one monthly payment to the credit counseling agency, the agency negotiates payments with the debtor's creditors (generally a reduced amount), and the agency keeps a percentage (generally 12 to 15 percent) of each payment made to each creditor.

The Federal Trade Commission (FTC) cited a third possible funding arrangement: Although it can collect a donation from the debtor, the agency is primarily funded through for-profit collection agencies that earn a percentage fee of the total amount collected from the debtor. In late 2003, the FTC had filed a complaint against AmeriDebt, alleging that the credit counseling agency duped new clients into making a "voluntary contribution" to enroll in the program, which allowed AmeriDebt to keep these "contributions" as fees without consumers' knowledge. Furthermore, the FTC alleged that AmeriDebt was not a charitable organization as it had advertised but was really a front organization for two for-profit agencies, DebtWorks and Andris Pukke, to which AmeriDebt funneled profits of approximately $170 million. By mid-2004, AmeriDebt had declared bankruptcy, and the FTC case was settled.

Discuss the ethics of AmeriDebt's operations. Was it fair to make these arrangements without telling the debtors of its ties to profit agencies? Do you think that the mandatory counseling requirement for bankruptcy will cause more problems such as AmeriDebt?*

---

* *In re AmeriDebt Inc.,* Case No. 04-23649-PM (D Md); *Federal Trade Commission v AmeriDebt, Inc., DebtWorks, Inc., Andris Pukke, and Pamela Pukke,* also known as Pamela Shuster, File No. 0223171 (D Md 2003); *In re AmeriDebt Inc.,* Case No. 04-23649-PM (D Md 2005).

---

excluding employees or insiders (that is, the debtor's relatives, partners, directors, and controlling persons), any creditor whose unsecured claim is at least $12,300 may sign the petition. In the case of involuntary consumer petitions, there is disagreement as to whether the debtor will still be required to complete the credit counseling requirement prior to the granting of the automatic stay.

bona fide in good faith; without any fraud or deceit.

If a creditor holds security for a claim, only the amount of the claim in excess of the value of the security is counted. The holder of a claim that is the subject of a **bona fide** dispute may not be counted as a petitioning creditor.[11] **For Example,** David, a CPA, is an unsecured creditor of Arco Company for $13,000. Arco has a total of 10 creditors, all of whom are unsecured. Arco has not paid any of the creditors for three months. The debtor has fewer than 12 creditors. Any one of the creditors may file the petition if the unsecured portion of the amount due that creditor is at least $12,300.[12] Because David is owed $13,000 in unsecured debts, he may file the petition alone.

---

[11] 11 USC § 303(b)(1).

[12] The amount was $10,000 originally, but the bankruptcy reforms had a built-in clause for increases in this figure. The amount $12,300 took effect on October 17, 2005.

CPA

(c) GROUNDS FOR RELIEF FOR INVOLUNTARY CASE   The mere filing of an involuntary case petition does not result in an order of relief. The debtor may contest the bankruptcy petition. If the debtor does not contest the petition, the court will enter an order of relief if at least one of the following grounds exists: (1) The debtor is generally not paying debts as they become due or (2) within 120 days before the filing of the petition, a custodian has been appointed for the debtor's property.

CPA

automatic stay order to prevent creditors from taking action such as filing suits or seeking foreclosure against the debtor.

5. AUTOMATIC STAY

Just the filing of either a voluntary or an involuntary petition operates as an **automatic stay,** which prevents creditors from taking action, such as filing suits or foreclosure actions, against the debtor.[13] The stay freezes all creditors in their filing date positions so that no one creditor gains an advantage over other creditors. This automatic stay ends when the bankruptcy case is closed or dismissed (for example, on a finding of abuse by the debtor who has failed to survive the means-to-pay test) or when the debtor is granted a discharge. An automatic stay means that all activity by creditors with respect to collection must stop, with some exceptions incorporated for child support and other family support issues under the 2005 reforms. All litigation with the debtor is halted, and any judgments in place cannot be executed.[14]

6. IF THE CREDITORS ARE WRONG: RIGHTS OF DEBTOR IN AN INVOLUNTARY BANKRUPTCY

If an involuntary petition is dismissed other than by consent of all petitioning creditors and the debtor, the court may award costs, reasonable attorney fees, or damages to the debtor. The damages are those that were caused by taking possession of the debtor's property. The debtor may also recover damages against any creditor who filed the petition in bad faith.[15]

Figure 35-1 provides a summary of the requirements for declaration of bankruptcy and the standards for relief.

 ADMINISTRATION OF THE BANKRUPTCY ESTATE

The administration of the bankruptcy estate varies according to the type of bankruptcy declared. This section of the chapter focuses on the process for liquidation or Chapter 7 bankruptcy. Figure 35-2 provides a flowchart view of the Chapter 7 liquidation process.

7. THE ORDER OF RELIEF

order of relief The order from the bankruptcy judge that starts the protection for the debtor; when the order of relief is entered by the court, the debtor's creditors must stop all proceedings and work through the bankruptcy court to recover debts (if possible). Court finding that creditors have met the standards for bankruptcy petitions.

The **order of relief** is granted by the bankruptcy court and is the procedural step required for the case to proceed in bankruptcy court.[16] An order of relief is entered automatically in a voluntary case and in an involuntary case when those filing the petition have established that the debtor is unable to pay his, her, or its debts as they become due. In consumer cases and Chapter 11 cases that involve an individual, the bankruptcy court must apply the means test to determine whether the individual is

---

[13] 11 USC § 362.

[14] The reforms exempt dissolution, custody, child support, and other related litigation from the stay.

[15] *Arizona Public Service v Apache County,* 847 P2d 1339 (Ariz App 1993).

[16] USC § 301.

FIGURE 35-1 *Declaration of Bankruptcy*

	CHAPTER 7	CHAPTER 11	CHAPTER 13
TRUSTEE	YES	NO	YES
ELIGIBLE PERSONS: INDIVIDUALS PARTNERSHIPS CORPORATIONS	YES (CONSUMER RESTRICTIONS) YES YES	YES (INDIVIDUAL RESTRICTIONS) YES YES	YES (CONSUMER RESTRICTIONS) NO NO
VOLUNTARY	YES	YES	YES
INVOLUNTARY	YES, EXCEPT FOR FARMERS AND NONPROFITS**	YES, EXCEPT FOR FARMERS AND NONPROFITS	NO
EXEMPTIONS	S & L's, CREDIT UNIONS, SBA, RAILROADS, MUNICIPALITIES	SAME AS CHAPTER 7 PLUS STOCKBROKERS*	ONLY INDIVIDUALS ALLOWED
REQUIREMENTS- VOLUNTARY	DEBTS; MEANS TEST APPLIES TO CONSUMERS	DEBTS; MEANS TEST APPLIES TO CONSUMERS	INCOME: <$307,675 UNSECURED; <$922,975 SECURED
REQUIREMENTS- INVOLUNTARY	<12 = 1/$12,300 ≥12 = 3/$12,300	<12 = 1/$12,300 ≥12 = 3/$12,300	N/A

*RAILROADS ARE ELIGIBLE
**CHAPTER 9 — MUNICIPALITIES; CHAPTER 12 — FARMERS

eligible for declaring bankruptcy or whether there has been an abuse of the bankruptcy court and system.

8. LIST OF CREDITORS

It is the debtor's responsibility to furnish the bankruptcy court a list of creditors. Although imposing the responsibility for disclosing debts on the debtor may not seem to be effective, the debtor has an incentive for full disclosure. Those debts not disclosed by the debtor will not be discharged in bankruptcy.

9. TRUSTEE IN BANKRUPTCY

trustee in bankruptcy
impartial person elected to administer the debtor's estate.

The **trustee in bankruptcy** is elected by the creditors. The court or the U.S. trustee will appoint an interim trustee if the creditors do not elect a trustee.

The trustee is the successor to the property rights of the debtor. By operation of law, the trustee automatically becomes the owner of all of the debtor's property in excess of the property to which the debtor is entitled under exemption laws. The trustee holds all of the rights formerly owned by the debtor.

 ## 10. THE BANKRUPT'S ESTATE

All of the debtor's property, with certain exceptions discussed later, is included in the *bankrupt's estate.* Property inherited by the debtor within six months after the filing of the petition also passes to the trustee.

In many cases, when a debtor knows that insolvency is a problem and bankruptcy is imminent, the debtor attempts to hang onto property or reputation by making

FIGURE 35-2 *Anatomy of Bankruptcy Case*

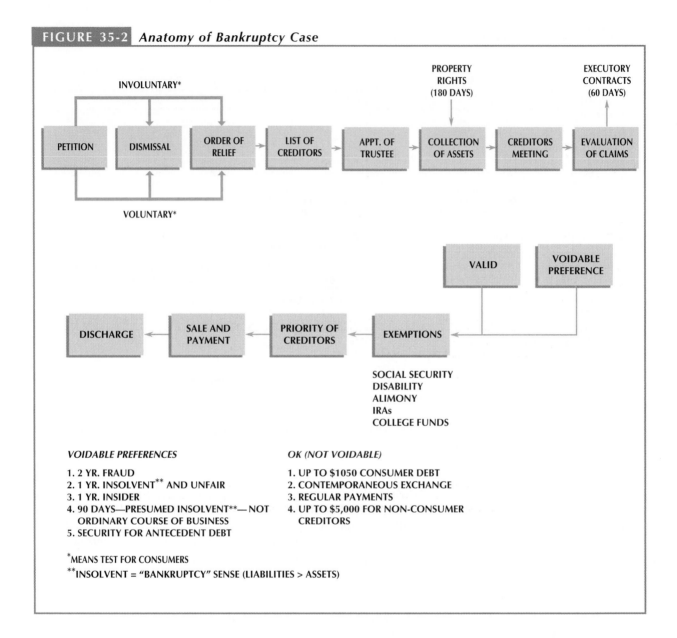

transfers of assets to friends, relatives, and creditors. However, trustees have the authority to set aside or void (1) transfers by the debtor that a creditor holding a valid claim under state law could have avoided at the commencement of the bankruptcy case, (2) **preferences,** that is, transfers of property by the debtor to a creditor, the effect of which is to enable the creditor to obtain payment of a higher percentage of the creditor's claim than the creditor would have received if the debtor's assets had been liquidated in bankruptcy, and (3) statutory liens that became effective against the debtor at the commencement of the bankruptcy.

preferences transfers of property by a debtor to one or more specific creditors to enable these creditors to obtain payment for debts owed.

11. VOIDABLE PREFERENCES

A debtor may not transfer property to prevent creditors from satisfying their legal claims. The trustee may void any such transfer, known as a *fraudulent transfer,* made or obligation incurred by the debtor within two years of bankruptcy when the debtor's actual intent was to hinder, delay, or defraud creditors by doing so.[17]

The trustee may also void certain transfers of property made by a debtor merely because their effect is to make the debtor insolvent or to reduce the debtor's assets to an unreasonably low amount.[18]

insolvency excess of debts and liabilities over assets, or inability to pay debts as they mature.

balance sheet test comparison of assets to liabilities made to determine solvency.

(a) THE INSOLVENT DEBTOR   A debtor is insolvent for purposes of determining voidable transfers when the total fair value of all of the debtor's assets does not exceed the debts owed by the debtor. This test for **insolvency** under voidable transfers is commonly called the **balance sheet test** because it is merely a comparison of assets to liabilities without considering whether the debtor will be able to meet future obligations as they become due. The debtor is presumed to be insolvent in the 90 days prior to declaration of bankruptcy.

preferential transfers certain transfers of money or security interests in the time frame just prior to bankruptcy that can be set aside if voidable.

(b) PREFERENTIAL TRANSFERS   A transfer of property by the debtor to a creditor may be set aside as **preferential transfers** and the property recovered by the debtor's trustee in bankruptcy if (1) the transfer was made to pay a debt incurred at some earlier time, (2) the transfer was made when the debtor was insolvent and within 90 days before the filing of the bankruptcy petition, and (3) the transfer resulted in the creditor receiving more than the creditor would have received in a liquidation of the debtor's estate. A debtor is presumed to be insolvent on and during the 90 days immediately preceding the date of the filing of the bankruptcy petition.[19]

insider full-time corporate employee or a director or their relatives.

Transfers made to **insiders** within the 12 months prior to the filing of the petition may be set aside.[20] **For Example,** if a building contractor transferred title to one of his model homes to the company accountant just six months before declaring bankruptcy, the transfer would be a preferential one that would be set aside. However, a transfer by an insider to a noninsider is not subject to recovery by the trustee. The sale of that same model home to a good faith buyer just three days before bankruptcy would be valid.

The trustee may not set aside certain transfers by a debtor as preferences. A transaction for a present consideration, such as a cash sale, is not set aside.[21] A payment by a debtor in the ordinary course of business, such as the payment of a utility bill, will not be set aside. Under the prior bankruptcy law, a payment was not a voidable preference if it was made in the ordinary course of business and it was made according to industry terms and practices. Under the 2005 reforms, the *and* is changed to *or,* and it is now easier for creditors to show that they were

---

[17] Prior to the reforms, the time period for fraudulent transfers was one year. However, the new two-year expanded scope takes effect only one year after the effective date of the 2005 amendments (October 2005).

[18] 11 USC § 548.

[19] 11 USC § 547(f).

[20] 11 USC § 547(b)(4)(B).

[21] *In re A. W. & Associates, Inc.,* 136 F3d 1439 (11th Cir 1998).

not the recipients of a voidable preference. Also under the 2005 reforms, non-consumer debt payments that have a value of less than $5,000 are not subject to the voidable preference standards. The expectation is that the time and effort spent by bankruptcy trustees and courts will be reduced because of the minimum amount required before a challenge can be made. In nonconsumer debts, transfers of less than $5,000 within the voidable preference period are not considered voidable preferences.

On consumer debts, a payment by an individual debtor is not subject to being set aside if the aggregate value of the transfer is less than $1,050. Child support and alimony payments are also not subject to the preferential provisions with some exceptions now provided for in the Reform Act.

(c) Self-Settled Trust   Under the Reform Act, the trustee has the ability to set aside the transfer of property into a "self-settled" (a self-created personal trust) any time within the past ten years if the trustee can establish that the trust was created with actual intent to hinder, delay, or defraud existing or future creditors.[22] This section was added to address the problem of the many assets of individuals being in personal trusts for which those individuals serve as trustees.

12. PROOF OF CLAIM

Bankruptcy law regulates the manner in which creditors present their claims and the way in which the debtor's assets are distributed in payment of these claims.

After the debtor has filed a list of creditors, the court then sends a notice of the bankruptcy proceedings to listed creditors. The creditors who wish to participate in the distribution of the proceeds of the liquidation of the debtor's estate must file a proof of claim. A **claim** is a right to payment, whether liquidated (certain and not disputed), unliquidated, contingent, unmatured, disputed, legal, or equitable. A **proof of claim** is a written statement, signed by the creditor or an authorized representative, setting forth any claim made against the debtor and the basis for it. It must ordinarily be filed within 90 days after the first meeting of creditors.[23] A creditor must file within that time even though the trustee in bankruptcy in fact knows of the existence of the creditor's claim.

claim creditor's right to payment.

proof of claim written statement, signed by the creditor or an authorized representative, setting forth any claim made against the debtor and the basis for it.

13. PRIORITY OF CLAIMS

Creditors who hold security for payment, such as a lien or a mortgage on the debtor's property, are not affected by the debtor's bankruptcy. Secured creditors may enforce their security interest to obtain payment of their claims up to the value of their security, the collateral in which they hold an interest. **For Example,** suppose that First Bank holds a mortgage on a company's office building. The mortgage amount is $750,000. The building is sold for $700,000. First Bank is entitled to the $700,000 from the sale. For the remaining portion of the debt, First Bank drops down in priority to wait with the other unsecured creditors for its remaining $50,000. Unsecured creditors with unsecured debts that have priority and their order of priority following the secured creditors' rights in their collateral are covered in the following

---

[22] 11 USC § 548(e).
[23] 11 USC § 302(c).

list.[24] Once the bottom of the priority list is reached, any remaining unsecured creditors share on a pro rata basis any remaining assets of the debtor. Any balance remaining after all creditors have been paid goes to the debtor. However, in 98 to 99 percent of all bankruptcies, no unsecured creditors receive any payments, so it is highly unlikely that the debtor would ever receive anything from the bankruptcy litigation of the debtor's property and funds.

The following is a list of the priorities for unsecured creditors following the payment to any secured creditors from the debtors' pledged property:[25]

1. Allowed claims for debts to a spouse, former spouse, or child of the debtor and for alimony to, maintenance for, or support of such spouse or child (that were obligations at the time of the filing of the bankruptcy petition).
2. Costs and expenses of administration of the bankruptcy case, including fees to trustees, attorneys, and accountants, and the reasonable expenses of creditors in recovering property transferred or concealed by the debtor.
3. Claims arising in the ordinary course of a debtor's business or financial affairs after the commencement of the case but before the order of relief (involuntary).
4. Claims for wages, salaries, or commissions, including vacation, severance, or sick leave pay earned within 180 days before the filing of the petition or the date of cessation of the debtor's business, whichever occurred first, limited, however, to $10,000 for each person.[26]
5. Claims arising for contributions to employee benefit plans, based on services rendered within 180 days before the filing of the petition or when the debtor ceased doing business, whichever occurred first; the maximum amount is $4,650. Under the 2005 reforms (especially in Chapter 11 reorganizations), payments of key-employee retention plans are not permitted unless the plans are"essential" to keeping the key employee at the company that is in bankruptcy. Proving that they are essential requires the key employee actually to have a "bona fide" offer of employment from another company. In addition, there are limits on how much can be paid under a key employee retention plans.
6. Farm producers (up to $10,000) and fishers against debtors who operate grain storage facilities or fish produce storage or processing facilities, up to $4,925 per claim.
7. Claims by consumer creditors, not to exceed $2,225 for each claimant, arising for the purchase of consumer goods or services when such property or services were not delivered or provided.
8. Certain taxes and penalties due government units, such as income and property taxes.
9. All other unsecured creditors.
10. Remainder (if any) to debtor.

Each claim must be paid in full before any lower claim is paid anything. If a class of claims cannot be paid in full, the claims in that case are paid on a pro rata basis. **For Example,** suppose that following the payment of all secured creditors, $10,000 is

---

[24] 11 USC § 507(1)–(6).

[25] 11 USCA § 507.

[26] Prior to the 2005 reforms, the amount limit was $4,650 and the time period was 90 days.

left to be distributed. The accountants who performed work on the bankruptcy are owed $15,000, and the lawyers who worked on it are owed $10,000. Because there is not enough to pay two parties in the same priority ranking, the $10,000 is split proportionately. The accountants will receive 15/25, or 3/5, of the $10,000, or $6,000, and the lawyers will receive 10/25, or 2/5, of the $10,000, or $4,000.

D   DEBTOR'S DUTIES AND EXEMPTIONS

Bankruptcy law imposes certain duties on the debtor and provides for specific exemptions of some of the debtor's estate from the claims of creditors.

14. DEBTOR'S DUTIES

A debtor must file with the court a list of creditors, a schedule of assets and liabilities, and a statement of her financial affairs. The debtor must also appear for examination under oath at the first meeting of creditors.

15. DEBTOR'S EXEMPTIONS

A debtor is permitted to claim certain property of the estate in the trustee's possession and keep it free from claims of creditors. Exemptions are provided under federal law, but state laws also provide for exemptions. In 14 states (examples are Massachusetts, New Jersey, Pennsylvania, and Connecticut), debtors can elect either federal or state exemption. In the other states (New York, California, Florida, and Delaware are examples), debtors are permitted to use only the state exemptions.[27] Examples of exempt property from the federal code include wedding rings, property used to earn a living, one VCR, and one car. New York exemptions include "all stoves in the home, one sewing machine, the family Bible, a pew in a public house of worship, enough food for sixty days, a wedding ring, and a watch not exceeding thirty-five dollars in value."[28] California exempts tools of the trade and the family cemetery plot.[29]

The principal exemptions provided by the Bankruptcy Code are the debtor's interest in real or personal property used as a residence. The Reform Act has greatly limited the homestead exemption and, in effect, preempts state law on this debtor exemption. Debtors are required to live in the home for two years prior to bankruptcy, and the amount of the homestead exemption would be limited to $125,000.[30] To be able to use a higher state homestead exemption, the debtor must have lived in the home for 1215 days (40 months).[31] Labeled as the most flagrant abuse of the existing bankruptcy system, debtors have used the homestead exemption to shift their assets into expensive homes to shield everything from bankruptcy. Known as the "mansion loophole," the changes in the reform act related to the homestead exemption were among the most debated and the most dramatic.[32] Florida's full exemption allows those declaring bankruptcy to shield an unlimited amount in their residences. **For Example,** actor Burt Reynolds declared bankruptcy in Florida and was relieved of millions in debt, but he was able to keep his $2.5 million Valhalla estate

---

[27] 11 USC § 522.

[28] NY CPLR § 5205 (McKinney 1997).

[29] Cal Civ Proc Code § 704.010-704.210 (West 1987).

[30] The time requirement is at 11 USC § 522(b)(3)(A), and the amount limitation is at 11 USC § 522(o)(1).

[31] 11 USC § 522(b)(2).

[32] 11 USC § 522(p).

ETHICS & THE LAW

The Skies Are Not So Friendly to Employee Pensions

As part of its Chapter 11 bankruptcy, United Airlines was relieved of its pension liabilities. Employees and unions wonder how a company can be permitted to renege on those benefits when so many protections were built into the law under ERISA. Congressional hearings now reveal that there were loopholes in the accounting processes for pension fund reporting that permitted United, and many others, to report pension numbers that made the pension funds look healthy when they really were not. The loopholes were Enronesque in nature. Companies could spin the pension obligations off the books so that the existing levels of obligations of the plan looked small and the assets very rich. Because of United's pension bailout, Congress will be examining and changing the accounting for pension plans to avoid the problem of the rosy picture when the funds really need further funding. One interesting approach to protecting pension plans is to require companies to fund the pension plans according to the numbers they have reported to the SEC in their financials. The numbers reported to the SEC for company pensions are accurate whereas the numbers reported for ERISA purposes are inflated. If United had funded its plans when its SEC numbers indicated it needed to (e.g., in 1998), the plan would have been sufficiently funded. Under ERISA guidelines, it was not required to kick in funds until 2002 when it was grossly underfunded.

Were companies acting ethically on their pension accounting? Were they acting legally?*

---

*Marry Williams Walsh, "Pension Law Loopholes Helped United Hide Its Troubles," *New York Times*, June 7, 2005, C1.

---

there. Corporate raider Paul Bilzerian, who was convicted of securities fraud, also declared bankruptcy in Florida but kept his mansion, the largest home in Hillsborough County, Florida. Wendy Gramm, who sat on Enron's board, purchased 200 acres of land in Texas and is constructing a large home with her husband, former senator Phil Gramm, to take advantage of homestead exemptions available in Texas. Former WorldCom CFO Scott Sullivan (who entered a guilty plea to fraud and other charges and is serving a five-year sentence) built a multimillion-dollar home in Florida to take advantage of Florida's protections for homeowners who declare bankruptcy. However, the Reform Act closed this corporate executive loophole by requiring that the $125,000 exemption apply to debtors who are convicted of securities fraud or bankruptcy fraud. These debtors cannot use the larger state exemptions.[33]

Other exemptions include payments under a life insurance contract, alimony and child support payments, and awards from personal injury litigation.[34] Under the Reform Act, college savings accounts and IRAs are exempt property under the federal exemptions and can be used even by those debtors who are using state exemptions. The IRA exemption is limited to $1,000,000.[35]

---

[33] 11 USC § 522(q).

[34] 11 USC § 522(d) (including automatic adjustments effective April 1, 1998); *Jost v Key Bank of Maine,* 136 F3d 1455 (11th Cir 1998).

[35] 11 USC § 522(n).

Businesses that declare bankruptcy would not have included in their bankruptcy estates employee pension plan contributions. Those contributions would be returned to the employees. The proposed changes are the result of the numerous large corporate bankruptcies, such as the one involving United Airlines and the pensions of its employees.[36]

16. DEBTOR'S PROTECTION AGAINST DISCRIMINATION

Federal, state, and local law may not discriminate against anyone on the basis of a discharge in bankruptcy. For example, a state cannot refuse to issue a new license to an individual if the license fees on a previous one have been discharged as a debt in the individual's declaration of bankruptcy.

 ## DISCHARGE IN BANKRUPTCY

discharge in bankruptcy
order of the bankruptcy court relieving the debtor from obligation to pay the unpaid balance of most claims.

The main objectives of a bankruptcy proceeding are to collect and distribute the debtor's assets and the subsequent **discharge in bankruptcy** of the debtor from obligations. The decree terminating the bankruptcy proceeding is generally a discharge that releases the debtor from most debts. Under the proposed reforms, a discharge would be available only once every eight years.

17. DENIAL OF DISCHARGE

The court will refuse to grant a discharge if the debtor has (1) within one year of the filing of the petition fraudulently transferred or concealed property with intent to hinder, delay, or defraud creditors, (2) failed to keep proper financial records, (3) made a false oath or account,[37] (4) failed to explain satisfactorily any loss of assets, (5) refused to obey any lawful order of the court or refused to testify after having been granted immunity, (6) obtained a discharge within the last eight years,[38] (7) filed a written waiver of discharge that is approved by the court,[39] or (8) in the case of a consumer debtor, has failed to complete a personal financial management instructional course.[40]

A discharge releases the debtor from the unpaid balance of most debts except for taxes, customs duties, child support obligations, and tax penalties.[41] Student loan obligations are not discharged in bankruptcy unless the loan first became due more than seven years before bankruptcy or unless not allowing a discharge would impose undue hardship on the debtor.

In addition, the following debts are not discharged by bankruptcy: (1) loans obtained by use of a false financial statement made with intent to deceive and on which the creditor reasonably relied, (2) debts not scheduled or listed with the court in time for allowance, (3) debts arising from fraud while the debtor was acting in a fiduciary capacity or by reason of embezzlement or larceny, (4) alimony and child

---

[36] 11 USC § 541(b).

[37] The debtor must actually make a false statement. In *In re Mercer*, 211 F3d 214 (5th Cir 2000), the debtor ran up $3,186.82 on a credit card she was given by AT&T with a $3,000 credit limit. The credit card was issued to the debtor on a preapproved basis, so there was no fraud, just a great deal of spending.

[38] 11 USC § 727(a)(8).

[39] 11 USC § 523; *Barax v Barax*, 667 NYS2d 733 (1998).

[40] 11 USC § 727(a)(11). The financial management course requirement applies to both Chapter 7 and Chapter 13 consumer bankruptcies.

[41] Child support obligations enjoy additional protections and priorities in bankruptcy. 11 USC § 507(a).

CASE SUMMARY

80 Grand Is Quite Enough for Making Good on Student Loans

FACTS: Jennifer Murphy (Murphy) filed an individual Chapter 7 petition. To finance her education at Virginia Polytechnic Institute and two years of medical school at Eastern Virginia Medical School, Murphy had taken out loans under various programs, including loans guaranteed by the United States through its Department of Education.

Murphy's oldest child, Kayla Murphy, was afflicted with Pfeiffer Syndrome. Because of her daughter's medical condition, Murphy discontinued medical school and is unable to work due to the daily requirements involved in caring for her daughter. Murphy owes approximately $58,000 in student loans.

Murphy last worked full-time from June to August 1991 as a laboratory intern at Virginia Polytechnic Institute. Murphy testified that she worked for Wal-Mart for a brief time after the birth of her daughter but was unable to continue working due to scheduling difficulties.

Mr. Murphy is a computer programmer and has been employed at BMH since December 1, 2003. Mr. Murphy's annual salary at BMH is $82,000. Prior to his employment at BMH, Mr. Murphy was a computer programmer for Net Decisions JAVA Business Solutions for four to five years. He earned $84,000 in 2001 and $83,500 in 2002.

The family expenses follow:

First mortgage	$891.00
Second mortgage	25.00
Utilities	125.00
Gas	80.00
Phone	40.00
Car payment	291.00
Groceries	700.00
Car repairs	150.00
Water	45.00
Sewer	15.00
Storm Water Management fee	5.00
AAA	5.83
Insect control	34.00
Tuition for daughter	507.00
Recreation	135.00
Sports fee	128.00
Insurance	363.00
Total	$3,539.83

These specific expenses, when deducted from her net family income, produce a monthly surplus of $1,360.17 available for student loan repayment. Murphy asked that her loans be discharged in bankruptcy.

DECISION: The court held that while Murphy's burden of caring for her disabled daughter is very difficult and her disappointment in not being able to complete her medical education immense, these tragic circumstances are not the basis for a student loan discharge. A discharge of a student loan must be founded on more than sympathy or fairness. Because of her husband's successful employment, Murphy and her dependents enjoy an income well in excess of nearly all who seek an undue hardship discharge and a substantially more comfortable lifestyle than the minimal one contemplated by the bankruptcy code and other decisions on discharge of student loans. While perhaps not entirely painless, Murphy can repay the remaining student loans of ECMC without inflicting serious financial burden on herself or her family. [**In re Murphy,** 305 BR 780 (ED Va 2004)]

FIGURE 35-3   *Nondischargeable Debts in Bankruptcy*

1. **TAXES WITHIN THREE YEARS OF FILING BANKRUPTCY PETITION**
2. **LIABILITY FOR OBTAINING MONEY OR PROPERTY BY FALSE PRETENSES**
3. **WILLFUL AND MALICIOUS INJURIES**
4. **DEBTS INCURRED BY DRIVING DWI***
5. **ALIMONY, MAINTENANCE, OR CHILD SUPPORT**
6. **UNSCHEDULED DEBTS (UNLESS ACTUAL NOTICE)**
7. **DEBTS RESULTING FROM FRAUD AS A FIDUCIARY (EMBEZZLEMENT)**
8. **GOVERNMENT FINES OR PENALTIES IMPOSED WITHIN THREE YEARS PRIOR**
9. **EDUCATIONAL LOANS DUE WITHIN SEVEN PRIOR YEARS (UNLESS HARDSHIP)**
10. **PRIOR BANKRUPTCY DEBTS IN WHICH DEBTOR WAIVED DISCHARGE**
11. **PRESUMPTION ON LUXURY GOODS: $1,150 GOODS; $1,150 CASH**
12. **REAFFIRMATION AGREEMENTS**
    - **WRITING**
    - **FILED WITH COURT**
    - **NOT RESCINDED PRIOR TO DISCHARGE**

***INCLUDES VESSELS AND AIRCRAFT**

support, (5) a judgment for willful and malicious injury, (6) a consumer debt to a single creditor totaling more than $500 for luxury goods or services (within 90 days of the order of relief) and cash advances exceeding $750 based on consumer open-end credit, such as a credit card (within 70 days of the order of relief),[42] (7) damages arising from drunk driving or the operation of vessels and aircrafts by people who are inebriated,[43] (8) loans used to pay taxes (including credit cards),[44] (9) taxes not paid as a result of a fraudulent return, although other unpaid taxes beyond the past three years can be discharged,[45] (10) prebankruptcy fees and assessments owed to homeowners associations, and (11) debts owed to tax-qualified retirement plans. **For Example,** in regard to (5), the finding of malice in *Goldman v O. J. Simpson* precluded the discharge by bankruptcy of the $8.5 million damage award from Simpson to the Goldmans and Browns. See Figure 35-3 for a listing of nondischargeable debts.

 ## REORGANIZATION PLANS UNDER CHAPTER 11

In addition to liquidation under Chapter 7, the Bankruptcy Code permits debtors to restructure the organization and finances of their businesses so that they may continue to operate. In these rehabilitation plans, the debtor keeps all of the assets (exempt and nonexempt), continues to operate the business, and makes a settlement that is acceptable to the majority of the creditors. This settlement is binding on the minority creditors.

---

[42] 11 USC § 523(a)(2)(c)(i).
[43] 11 USC § 523(a)(9).
[44] 11 USC § 523(a)(14A),(14B).
[45] 11 USC §§ 1129(a)(9)(c), (D), 1129(b)(2)(B), 1141(d)(6)(B).

Individuals, partnerships, and corporations in business may all be reorganized under the Bankruptcy Code. The first step is to file a plan for the debtor's reorganization. This plan may be filed by the debtor, any party in interest, or a committee of creditors. If the debtor wishes to move from a Chapter 11 proceeding (in the case of an individual debtor), the debtor must survive the means test that is now a requirement for determining eligibility for bankruptcy.

18. CONTENTS OF THE PLAN

The plan divides ownership interests and debts into those that will be affected by the adoption of the plan and those that will not be. It then specifies what will be done to those interests and claims that are affected. **For Example,** when mortgage payments are too high for the income of a corporation, a possible plan would be to reduce the mortgage payments and give the mortgage holder preferred stock to compensate for the loss sustained.

All creditors, shareholders, and other interest holders within a particular class must be treated the same way. **For Example,** the holders of first mortgage bonds must all be treated similarly.

A plan can also provide for the assumption, rejection, or assignment of executory contracts. The trustee or debtor can, under certain circumstances, suspend performance of a contract not yet fully performed. **For Example,** collective bargaining agreements may be rejected with the approval of the bankruptcy court.[46]

19. CONFIRMATION OF THE PLAN

After the plan is prepared, the court must approve or confirm it. A plan will be confirmed if it has been submitted in good faith and if its provisions are reasonable.[47] After the plan is confirmed, the owners and creditors of the enterprise have only the rights that are specified in the plan. They cannot go back to their original contract positions.

PAYMENT PLANS UNDER CHAPTER 13

The Bankruptcy Code also provides for the adoption of extended-time payment plans for individual debtors who have regular income. These debtors must owe unsecured debts of less than $307,675 and secured debts of less than $922,975.

An individual debtor who has a regular income may submit a plan for the installment payment of outstanding debts. If the court approves it, the debtor may then pay the debts in the installments specified by the plan even if the creditors had not originally agreed to such installment payments.

20. CONTENTS OF THE PLAN

The individual debtor plan is, in effect, a budget of the debtor's future income with respect to outstanding debts. The plan must provide for the eventual payment in full of all claims entitled to priority under the Bankruptcy Code. All creditors holding the same kind or class of claim must be treated the same way.

---

[46] 11 USC § 1113.
[47] 11 USC § 1129.

21. CONFIRMATION OF THE PLAN

The plan has no effect until the court approves or confirms it. A plan will be confirmed if it was submitted in good faith and is in the best interests of the creditors.[48] When the plan is confirmed, debts are payable in the manner specified in the plan.

22. DISCHARGE OF THE DEBTOR

After all of the payments called for by the plan have been made, the debtor is given a discharge. The discharge releases the debtor from liability for all debts except those that would not be discharged by an ordinary bankruptcy discharge.[49] Under the bankruptcy reforms, the court cannot grant a discharge until the debtor has completed an instructional course concerning personal financial management.[50] If the debtor does not perform under the plan, the creditors can move to transfer the debtor's case to a Chapter 7 proceeding, but they would still face the means test in qualifying for Chapter 7.

---

[48] 11 USC § 1325.

[49] 11 USC § 1328.

[50] 11 USC § 1328(g)(1).

> SUMMARY

Jurisdiction over bankruptcy cases is in U.S. district courts, which may refer all cases and related proceedings to adjunct bankruptcy courts.

Three bankruptcy proceedings are available: liquidation (Chapter 7), reorganization (Chapter 11), and extended-time payment (Chapter 13). A liquidation proceeding under Chapter 7 may be either voluntary or involuntary. A *voluntary case* is commenced by the debtor's filing a petition with the bankruptcy court. A voluntary petition is subject to the means test to determine if the debtor meets the standard for declaring bankruptcy. An involuntary case is commenced by the creditors' filing a petition with the bankruptcy court. If there are 12 or more creditors, at least 3 whose unsecured claims total $12,300 or more must sign the involuntary petition. If there are fewer than 12 creditors, any creditor whose unsecured claim is at least $12,300 may sign the petition. If the debtor contests the bankruptcy petition, it must be shown that the debtor is not paying debts as they become due. Eligibility for Chapters 7 and 11 bankruptcy excludes railroads, municipalities, and Small Business

Administration companies. Individual debtors are restricted on Chapter 7 and 11 filings by their ability to repay. If found to have the means to pay, they go into a Chapter 13 proceeding. Chapter 13 eligibility is limited to consumers with $307,675 in unsecured debt and $922,975 in secured debt.

An automatic stay prevents creditors from taking legal action against the debtor after a bankruptcy petition is filed. The trustee in bankruptcy is elected by the creditors and is the successor to, and acquires the rights of, the debtor. In certain cases, the trustee can avoid transfers of property to prevent creditors from satisfying their claims. Preferential transfers may be set aside. A transfer for a present consideration, such as a cash sale, is not a preference.

Bankruptcy law regulates the way creditors present their claims and how the assets of the debtor are to be distributed in payment of the claims. Some assets of the debtor are exempt from the bankruptcy estate, such as a portion of the value of the debtor's home.

Secured claims are not affected by the debtor's bankruptcy. Unsecured claims are paid in the following order of priority:

1. Support or maintenance for a spouse, former spouse, or child.
2. Costs and expenses of administration of the bankruptcy case.
3. Claims arising in the ordinary course of a debtor's business or financial affairs after the commencement of the case but before the order of relief (involuntary).
4. Claims for wages, salaries, or commissions, including vacation, severance, or sick leave pay earned within 180 days before the filing of the petition or the date of cessation of the debtor's business, limited to $10,000 for each person.
5. Claims arising for contributions (up to $4,650) to employee benefit plans based on services rendered within 180 days before the filing of the petition or when the debtor ceased doing business.
6. Farm producers (up to $10,000) and fishers against debtors who operate grain storage facilities or fish produce storage or processing facilities, up to $4,925 per claim.

7. Claims by consumer creditors, not to exceed $2,225 for each claimant.
8. Certain taxes and penalties due government units, such as income and property taxes.
9. All other unsecured creditors.
10. Remainder (if any) to debtor.

The decree terminating bankruptcy proceedings is generally a discharge that releases the debtor from most debts. Certain debts, such as income taxes, student loans, loans obtained by use of a false financial statement, alimony, and debts not listed by the debtor, are not discharged.

Under Chapter 11 bankruptcy, individuals, partnerships, and corporations in business may be reorganized so that the business can continue to operate. A plan for reorganization must be approved by the court. Under a Chapter 13 bankruptcy proceeding, individual debtors with a regular income may adopt extended-time payment plans for the payment of debts. A plan for extended-time payment must also be confirmed by the court. Federal, state, and local law may not discriminate against anyone on the basis of a discharge in bankruptcy.

> QUESTIONS AND CASE PROBLEMS

1. Hall-Mark regularly supplied electronic parts to Peter Lee. On September 11, 1992, Lee gave Hall-Mark a $100,000 check for parts it had received. Hall-Mark continued to ship parts to Lee. On September 23, 1992, Lee's check was dishonored by the bank. On September 25, 1992, Lee delivered to Hall-Mark a cashier's check for $100,000. Hall-Mark shipped nothing more to Lee after receipt of the cashier's check. On December 24, 1992, Lee filed a voluntary petition for bankruptcy. The trustee filed a complaint to have the $100,000 payment to Hall-Mark set aside as a voidable preference. Hall-Mark said it was entitled to the payment because it gave value to Lee. The trustee said that the payment was not actually made until the cashier's check was delivered on September 25, 1992, and that Hall-Mark gave no further value to Lee after that check was paid. Who was correct? [*In re Lee,* 108 F3d 239 (9th Cir)]

2. Orso, who had declared bankruptcy, received a structured tort settlement in a personal injury claim he had pending. The settlement would pay him an annuity each year for 30 years because the claim was the result of an auto accident that left him permanently and severely brain damaged with an IQ of about 70. His wife had a pending claim for $48,000 in arrearages on Orso's $1,000 per month child support payments. His wife wanted the annuity included in the bankruptcy estate. Would this property have been included in Orso's bankruptcy estate? [*In re Orso,* 214 F3d 637 (5th Cir)]

3. Harold McClellan sold ice-making machinery to Bobbie Cantrell's brother for $200,000 to be paid in installment payments. McClellan took a security interest in the ice machine but did not perfect it by filing a financing statement. The brother defaulted when he owed $100,000, and McClellan brought suit. With the suit

pending, the brother "sold" the ice machine to Bobbie Cantrell for $10. Bobbie then sold the machine to someone for $160,000 and refused to explain what happened to that money. McClellan added Bobbie as a defendant in his suit against her brother. Bobbie then declared bankruptcy. McClellan sought to have the various transfers set aside. The trial court refused to do so, and McClellan appealed. Should the transfers be set aside? Why or why not? [*McClellan v Cantrell*, 217 F3d 890 (7th Cir)]

4. Okamoto owed money to Hornblower & Weeks-Hemphill, Noyes (a law firm and hereafter Hornblower). Hornblower filed an involuntary bankruptcy petition against Okamoto, who moved to dismiss the petition on the ground that he had more than 12 creditors and the petition could not be filed by only one creditor. Hornblower replied that the other creditors' claims were too small to count and, therefore, the petition could be filed by one creditor. Decide. [*In re Okamoto*, 491 F2d 496 (9th Cir)]

5. Jane Leeves declared voluntary Chapter 7 bankruptcy. The trustee included the following property in her bankruptcy estate:

   - Jane's wedding ring
   - Jane's computer for her consulting business that she operated from her home
   - Jane's car
   - Payment from a client in the amount of $5,000 that was received 91 days after Jane filed bankruptcy

   After collecting all of Jane's assets, the bankruptcy trustee was trying to decide how to distribute the assets. Jane had the following creditors:

   - Mortgage company—owed $187,000 (the trustee sold Jane's house for $190,000)
   - Expenses of the bankruptcy—$3,000
   - Federal income taxes—$11,000
   - Utility bills—$1,000
   - Office supply store open account—$1,000

   The trustee had $11,500 in cash, including the $3,000 additional cash left from the sale of the house after the mortgage company was paid. How should the trustee distribute this money? What if the amount were $14,500; how should that be distributed?

6. Kentile sold goods over an extended period of time to Winham. The credit relationship began without Winham's being required to furnish a financial statement. After some time, payments were not made regularly, and Kentile requested a financial statement. Winham submitted a statement for the year that had just ended. After that, Kentile requested a second statement. The second statement was false. Kentile objected to Winham's discharge in bankruptcy because of the false financial statement. Should the discharge be granted? Why or why not?

7. Essex is in serious financial difficulty and is unable to meet current unsecured obligations of $40,000 to some 20 creditors, who are demanding immediate payment. Essex owes Stevens $5,000, and Stevens has decided to file an involuntary petition against Essex. Can Stevens file the petition?

8. Sonia, a retailer, has the following assets: a factory worth $1 million; accounts receivable amounting to $750,000, which fall due in four to six months; and $20,000 cash in the bank. Sonia's sole liability is a $200,000 note falling due today, which she is unable to pay. Can Sonia be forced into involuntary bankruptcy under the Bankruptcy Code?

9. Samson Industries ceased doing business and is in bankruptcy proceedings. Among the creditors are five employees seeking unpaid wages. Three of the employees are owed $3,500 each, and two are owed $1,500 each. These amounts became due within 90 days preceding the filing of the petition. Where, in the priority of claims, will the employees' wage claims fall?

10. Carol Cott, doing business as Carol Cott Fashions, is worried about an involuntary bankruptcy proceeding being filed by her creditors. Her net worth, using a balance sheet approach, is $8,000 ($108,000 in assets minus $100,000 in liabilities). However, her cash flow is negative, and she has been hard pressed to meet current obligations as they mature. She is in fact some $12,500 in arrears in payments to her creditors on bills submitted during the past two months. Will the fact that Cott is solvent in the balance sheet sense result in the court's dismissing the creditors' petition if Cott objects to the petition? Explain.

11. On July 1, Roger Walsh, a sole proprietor operating a grocery, was involuntarily petitioned into bankruptcy by his creditors. At that time, and for at least 90 days prior to that time, Walsh was unable to pay current obligations. On June 16, Walsh paid the May electric bill for his business. The trustee in bankruptcy claimed that this payment was a voidable preference. Was the trustee correct? Explain.

12. Steven and Teresa Hornsby are married and have three young children. On May 25, 1993, the Hornsbys filed a voluntary Chapter 7 petition. They had by that date accumulated more than $30,000 in debt, stemming almost entirely from student loans. They wanted a discharge of their student loans on grounds of undue hardship. The Hornsbys attended a succession of small Tennessee state colleges. Both studied business and computers, but neither graduated. Although they received several deferments and forbearances on the loans, they ultimately defaulted before making any payments. Interest had accumulated on the loans to the extent that Steven was indebted to the Tennessee Student Assistance Corporation (TSAC) for $15,058.52, and Teresa was indebted to TSAC for $18,329.15.

    Steven was working for AT&T in Dallas, Texas; he made $6.53 per hour, occasionally working limited overtime hours. Teresa was employed by KinderCare Learning Center. Although she had begun work in Tennessee, she had transferred to become the director of a child care facility in Dallas. Teresa was earning $17,500 per year with medical benefits at the time of the hearing. In monthly net income, Steven earned approximately $1,083.33, and Teresa earned $1,473.33, amounting to $2,556.66 of disposable income per month. The Hornsbys' reported monthly expenses came to $2,364.90. They operated with a monthly surplus of $191.76 to $280.43, depending on whether Steven earned overtime for a particular month. Under the federal bankruptcy laws, are the Hornsbys entitled to a discharge on their student loans? Explain your answer. [*In re Hornsby,* 144 F3d 433 (6th Cir)]

13. On March 19, 1997, Jairath, as seller, and Bletnitsky, as buyer, entered into a real estate contract for sale of an apartment building located at 930 Ontario in Oak Park, Illinois, for a price of $3.1 million. The contract closed on June 4, 1997. Jairath represented to Bletnitsky that the building contained 21 apartments. Jairath's real estate broker had told Bletnitsky that the building contained 21 units, and the real estate broker's package also stated that the building contained 21 units.

    While neither Jairath nor his realtor were shown to have stated expressly that all 21 units in the building were legally available to be converted to condos, Jairath's real estate broker represented that the building was suitable for conversion into condominiums. Also, the real estate broker's package provided "for condo developer, this opportunity provides an opportunity with substantial returns. See Real Estate Broker Package, Investment Property Description."

    The contract did not state the number of units in the building or warrant that the building was suitable for condominium use. In fact, the contract stated:

    It is understood and agreed that the Property is being sold as is; that Buyer has or will have prior to the closing date inspected the Property; and that neither the Seller nor Agent makes any representation or warranty as to the physical condition or value of the Property or its suitability for the Buyer's intended use.

    Prior to the closing on June 4, 1997, Bletnitsky received a copy of an inspection report prepared by an agency of the Village of Oak Park. The report stated that an inspection had taken place May 27, 1997, and that the apartment building contained only 20 units. On May 30, 1999, Bletnitsky wrote a letter to Jairath and indicated that he had received and read the Oak Park inspection report. In this letter, Bletnitsky stated that the inspection uncovered several violations, listed each violation, and estimated the repair costs at $88,595.

    In September 1997, Bletnitsky sought approval of Oak Park to convert all 21 units of the apartment building into condominiums. Oak Park informed Bletnitsky that 20 units could be converted but that unit 1E was an illegal apartment and must be demolished. Bletnitsky was unable to sell that unit as a condominium. Bletnitsky claims that he would not have paid $3.1 million dollars for the building had he known that it only contained 20 legal units. Bletnitsky claims that as a result of Jairath's representation that the building contained 21 units, he sustained a loss of $100,000. An arbitration proceeding awarded Bletnitsky damages for misrepresentation.

Jairath then filed for Chapter 7 bankruptcy. Bletnisky has filed to have the obligation on the damages from the arbitration not be discharged in the bankruptcy because there was fraud involved. Does Beltnisky have grounds for the obligation surviving Jairath's bankruptcy? [*In re Jairath,* 259 BR 308 (ND Ill)]

14. Place the following in order for a bankruptcy proceeding:

a. Order of relief
b. Collection of bankrupt's estate
c. List of creditors
d. Petition
e. Evaluation of claims
f. Voidable preferences
g. Discharge

15. Three general unsecured creditors are owed $45,000 as follows: *A,* $15,000; *B,* $5,000; and *C,* $25,000. After all other creditors were paid, the amount left for distribution to general unsecured creditors was $9,000. How will the $9,000 be distributed?

 ## CPA QUESTIONS

1. Which of the following statements is correct concerning the voluntary filing of a petition of bankruptcy?

a. If the debtor has 12 or more creditors, the unsecured claims must total at least $11,625.
b. The debtor must be solvent.
c. If the debtor has less than 12 creditors, the unsecured claims must total at least $11,625.
d. The petition may be filed jointly by spouses. (AICPA adapted)

2. On February 28, Master, Inc., had total assets with a fair market value of $1,200,000 and total liabilities of $990,000. On January 15, Master made a monthly installment note payment to Acme Distributors Corp., a creditor holding a properly perfected security interest in equipment having a fair market value greater than the balance due on the note. On March 15, Master voluntarily filed a petition in bankruptcy under the liquidation provisions of Chapter 7 of the federal Bankruptcy Code. One year later, the equipment was sold for less than the balance due on the note to Acme.

If a creditor challenged Master's right to file, the petition would be dismissed

a. if Master had less than 12 creditors at the time of filing.
b. unless Master can show that a reorganization under Chapter 11 of the federal Bankruptcy Code would have been unsuccessful.
c. unless Master can show that it is unable to pay its debts in the ordinary course of business or as they come due.
d. if Master is an insurance company.

3. A voluntary petition filed under the liquidation provisions of Chapter 7 of the federal Bankruptcy Code

a. is not available to a corporation unless it has previously filed a petition under the reorganization provisions of Chapter 11 of the federal Bankruptcy Code.
b. automatically stays collection actions against the debtor except by secured creditors for collateral only.

c. will be dismissed unless the debtor has 12 or more unsecured creditors whose claims total at least $11,625.

d. does not require the debtor to show that the debtor's liabilities exceed the fair market value of assets.

4. Which of the following conditions, if any, must a debtor meet to file a voluntary bankruptcy petition under Chapter 7 of the federal Bankruptcy Code?

	Insolvency	*Three or More Creditors*
a.	Yes	Yes
b.	Yes	No
c.	No	Yes
d.	No	No

5. On July 15, 1988, White, a sole proprietor, was involuntarily petitioned into bankruptcy under the liquidation provisions of the Bankruptcy Code. White's nonexempt property has been converted to $13,000 cash, which is available to satisfy the following claims:

Unsecured claim for 1986 state income tax	$10,000
Fee owed to Best & Co., CPAs, for services rendered from April 1, 1988, through June 30, 1988	$6,000
Unsecured claim by Stieb for wages earned as an employee of White during March 1988	$3,000

There are no other claims.

What is the maximum amount that will be distributed for the payment of the 1986 state income tax?

a. $4,000
b. $5,000
c. $7,000
d. $10,000

6. On May 1, 1997, two months after becoming insolvent, Quick Corp., an appliance wholesaler, filed a voluntary petition for bankruptcy under the provisions of Chapter 7 of the federal Bankruptcy Code. On October 15, 1996, Quick's board of directors had authorized and paid Erly $50,000 to repay Erly's April 1, 1996, loan to the corporation. Erly is a sibling of Quick's president. On March 15, 1996, Quick paid Kray $100,000 for inventory delivered that day. Which of the following is not relevant in determining whether the repayment of Erly's loan is a voidable preferential transfer?

a. Erly is an insider.
b. Quick's payment to Erly was made on account of an antecedent debt.
c. Quick's solvency when the loan was made by Erly.
d. Quick's payment to Erly was made within one year of the filing of the bankruptcy petition.

INSURANCE

 THE INSURANCE CONTRACT

1. THE PARTIES
2. INSURABLE INTEREST
3. THE CONTRACT
4. ANTILAPSE AND CANCELLATION STATUTES AND PROVISIONS
5. MODIFICATION OF CONTRACT
6. INTERPRETATION OF CONTRACT
7. BURDEN OF PROOF
8. INSURER BAD FAITH
9. TIME LIMITATIONS ON INSURED
10. SUBROGATION OF INSURER

 KINDS OF INSURANCE

11. BUSINESS LIABILITY INSURANCE
12. MARINE INSURANCE
13. FIRE AND HOMEOWNERS INSURANCE
14. AUTOMOBILE INSURANCE
15. LIFE INSURANCE

LEARNING OBJECTIVES

After studying this chapter, you should be able to

LO.1 Define *insurable interest*

LO.2 Compare contracts of insurance with ordinary contracts

LO.3 Explain the purpose of business liability insurance, marine insurance, fire and homeowners insurance, automobile insurance, and life insurance

LO.4 Explain the effect of an incontestability clause

By means of insurance, protection from loss and liability may be obtained.

 THE INSURANCE CONTRACT

insurance a plan of security against risks by charging the loss against a fund created by the payments made by policyholders.

Insurance is a contract by which one party for a stipulated consideration promises to pay another party a sum of money on the destruction of, loss of, or injury to something in which the other party has an interest or to indemnify that party for any loss or liability to which that party is subjected.

1. THE PARTIES

insurer promisor in an insurance contract.

underwriter insurer.

insured person to whom the promise in an insurance contract is made.

policy paper evidencing the contract of insurance.

insurance agent agent of an insurance company.

insurance broker independent contractor who is not employed by any one insurance company.

The promisor in an insurance contract is called the **insurer** or **underwriter.** The person to whom the promise is made is the **insured** or the policyholder. The promise of the insurer is generally set forth in a written contract called a **policy.**

Insurance contracts are ordinarily made through an agent or broker. The **insurance agent** is an agent of the insurance company, often working exclusively for one company. For the most part, the ordinary rules of agency law govern the dealings between this agent and the applicant for insurance.[1]

An **insurance broker** is generally an independent contractor who is not employed by any one insurance company. When a broker obtains a policy for a customer, the broker is the agent of the customer for the purpose of that transaction. Under some statutes, the broker is made an agent of the insurer with respect to transmitting the applicant's payments to the insurer.

2. INSURABLE INTEREST

A person obtaining insurance must have an insurable interest in the subject matter insured. If not, the insurance contract cannot be enforced.

(a) INSURABLE INTEREST IN PROPERTY   A person has an insurable interest in property whenever the destruction of the property will cause a direct pecuniary loss to that person.

It is immaterial whether the insured is the owner of the legal or equitable title, a lienholder, or merely a person in possession of the property.[2] **For Example,** Vin Harrington, a builder, maintained fire insurance on a building he was remodeling under a contract with its owner, Chestnut Hill Properties. The building was destroyed by fire before renovations were completed. Harrington had an insurable interest in the property to the extent of the amount owed him under the renovation contract.

To collect on property insurance, the insured must have an insurable interest at the time the loss occurs.

(b) INSURABLE INTEREST IN LIFE   A person who obtains life insurance can name anyone as beneficiary regardless of whether that beneficiary has an insurable interest in the life of the insured. A beneficiary who obtains a policy, however, must have an insurable interest in the life of the insured. Such an interest exists if the beneficiary can reasonably expect to receive pecuniary gain from the continued life of the other person and, conversely, would suffer financial loss from the latter's death. Thus, a

---

[1] *Tidelands Life Ins. Co. v France,* 711 So 2d 728 (Tex App 1986).

[2] *Gorman v Farm Bureau Town & Country Insurance Co.,* 977 SW2d 519 (Mo App 1998).

CASE SUMMARY

She Lost Interest When He Got the House

FACTS: While Dorothy and James Morgan were still married, Dorothy purchased insurance on their home from American Security Insurance Company. The policy was issued on November 3, 1981, listing the "insured" as Dorothy L. Morgan. Shortly thereafter the Morgans entered into a separation agreement under which Dorothy deeded her interest in the house to James. The Morgans were divorced on August 26, 1982. On November 28, 1982, the house was destroyed by fire. American Security refused to pay on the policy, claiming that Dorothy had no insurable interest in the property at the time of the loss. The Morgans sued the insurer, contending that they were entitled to payment under the policy issued to Dorothy.

DECISION: Judgment for American Security. In the case of property insurance, the insurable interest must exist at the time of the loss. If the insured parts with all interest in the property prior to the loss, that individual is not covered. Dorothy had conveyed her interest in the property prior to the loss. She did not have an insurable interest at the time of the loss and therefore could not recover on the policy. James Morgan was not insured under the policy. [**Morgan v American Security Ins. Co., 522 So 2d 454 (Fla App 1988)**]

creditor has an insurable interest in the life of the debtor because he may not be paid the amount owed upon the death of the debtor.

A partner or partnership has an insurable interest in the life of each of the partners because the death of any one of them will dissolve the firm and cause some degree of loss to the partnership. A business enterprise has an insurable interest in the life of an executive or a key employee because that person's death would inflict a financial loss on the business to the extent that a replacement might not be readily available or could not be found.

In the case of life insurance, the insurable interest must exist at the time the policy is obtained. It is immaterial that the interest no longer exists when the loss is actually sustained. Thus, the fact that a husband (insured) and wife (beneficiary) are divorced after the life insurance policy was procured does not affect the validity of the policy. Also, the fact that a partnership is terminated after a life insurance policy is obtained by one partner on another does not invalidate the policy.

CASE SUMMARY

Proceeds to the Surviving Partner or the Deceased Partner's Wife?

FACTS: Jewell Norred's husband, James Norred, was the business partner of Clyde Graves for ten years. On May 7, 1979, Graves and Norred took out life insurance policies, with Graves being the beneficiary of Norred's policy and Norred being the beneficiary of Graves's policy. Premiums were paid out of partnership funds. On February 28, 1983, Graves and Norred divided the partnership assets, but they did not perform the customary steps of dissolving and winding up the partnership. Graves became the sole owner of the business and

CASE SUMMARY

continued

continued to pay the premiums on both insurance policies until James Norred died on December 5, 1983. Jewell Norred sued Graves, seeking the proceeds of the insurance policy for herself, alleging that Graves had no insurable interest in the life of James Norred at the time of his death. From a judgment on behalf of the estate, Graves appealed.

DECISION: Judgment for Graves. A partner or partnership has an insurable interest in the life of one of the partners. This interest continues even if the partnership is discontinued prior to the death of one of the partners. Thus, Graves was entitled to the proceeds of the policy. [**Graves v Norred, 510 So 2d 816 (Ala 1987)**]

3. THE CONTRACT

The formation of a contract of insurance is governed by the general principles applicable to contracts. By statute, it is now commonly provided that an insurance policy must be written. To avoid deception, many statutes also specify the content of certain policies, in whole or in part. Some statutes specify the size and style of type to be used in printing the policies. Provisions in a policy that conflict with statutory requirements are generally void.

(a) THE APPLICATION AS PART OF THE CONTRACT   The application for insurance is generally attached to the policy when issued and is made part of the contract of insurance by express stipulation of the policy.

The insured is bound by all statements in the attached application.

(b) STATUTORY PROVISIONS AS PART OF THE CONTRACT   When a statute requires that insurance contracts contain certain provisions or cover certain specified losses, a contract of insurance that does not comply with the statute will be interpreted as though it contained all the provisions required by the statute. When a statute requires that all terms of the insurance contract be included in the written contract, the insurer cannot claim that a provision not stated in the written contract was binding on the insured.

4. ANTILAPSE AND CANCELLATION STATUTES AND PROVISIONS

If the premiums are not paid on time, the policy under ordinary contract law would lapse because of nonpayment. However, with life insurance policies, by either policy provision or statute, the insured is allowed a grace period of 30 or 31 days in which to make payment of the premium due. When there is a default in the payment of a premium by the insured, the insurer may be required by statute to (1) issue a paid-up policy in a smaller amount, (2) provide extended insurance for a period of time, or (3) pay the cash surrender value of the policy.

The contract of insurance may expressly declare that it may or may not be canceled by the insurer's unilateral act. By statute or policy provision, the insurer is commonly required to give a specific number of days' written notice of cancellation.[3]

---

[3] *Transamerican Ins. Co. v Tab Transportation,* 48 Cal Rptr 2d 159 (Sup Ct 1995).

(**E-COMMERCE AND CYBERLAW**)

Insurance Contracts and E-Sign

The Electronic Signatures in Global and National Commerce Act (E-Sign) applies broadly to the insurance business.* Thus, with consent of the consumer, contracts may be executed with electronic signatures and documents may be delivered by electronic means. E-Sign also provides protections for insurance agents against liability resulting from any deficiencies in the electronic procedures set forth in an electronic contract, provided the agent did not engage in tortious conduct and was not involved in the establishment of the electronic procedures.

Insurance providers are precluded from canceling health insurance or life insurance protection by means of electronic notices.

_____
* 15 USC § 7001(i).

5. MODIFICATION OF CONTRACT

As is the case with most contracts, a contract of insurance can be modified if both insurer and insured agree to the change. The insurer cannot modify the contract without the consent of the insured when the right to do so is not reserved in the insurance contract.

To make changes or corrections to the policy, it is not necessary to issue a new policy. An endorsement on the policy or the execution of a separate rider is effective for the purpose of changing the policy. When a provision of an endorsement conflicts with a provision of the policy, the endorsement controls because it is the later document.

6. INTERPRETATION OF CONTRACT

A contract of insurance is interpreted by the same rules that govern the interpretation of ordinary contracts. Words are to be given their plain and ordinary meaning and interpreted in light of the nature of the coverage intended. However, an insurance policy is construed strictly against the insurer, who chooses the language of the policy, and if a reasonable construction may be given that would justify recovery, a court will do so. **For Example,** Dr. Kolb consented to an elective surgical procedure on his right eye after which "something happened that caused the wound to start leaking" and resulted in loss of vision in his eye. This forced him to retire as an orthopedic surgeon. His Paul Revere Life Insurance disability income insurance policy provided income for life for a disability due to "accidental bodily injury." The policy provided benefits for a shorter duration if the disability was caused by "sickness." Dr. Kolb's vision loss was not expected and proceeded from an unidentified postsurgical cause. Applying the plain and ordinary meaning of "accidental" and "injury," the court decided that Dr. Kolb was entitled to income for life under the "injury" provision of the policy.[4]

The courts are increasingly recognizing the fact that most persons obtaining insurance are not specially trained. Therefore, the contract of insurance is to be read as

_____
[4] *Kolb v Paul Revere Life Insurance Co.,* 355 F3d 1132 (8th Cir 2004).

it would be understood by the average person or by the average person in business rather than by one with technical knowledge of the law or of insurance.[5]

If there is an ambiguity in the policy, the provision is interpreted against the insurer. **For Example,** on August 29, 2005, the Buentes' residence in Gulfport, Mississippi, was damaged during Hurricane Katrina. Allstate tendered a check for $2,600.35 net after the deductible, under its Deluxe Homeowner's Policy. The Buentes contend their covered losses are between $50,000 and $100,000. They brought suit against Allstate. The trial judge denied Allstate's motion to dismiss, finding the two provisions of the policy that purport to exclude coverage for wind and rain damage were ambiguous in light of other policy provisions granting coverage for wind and rain damage and in light of the inclusion of a "hurricane deductible" as part of the policy. The court found that because the policy was ambiguous, its weather exclusion was unenforceable in the context of loses attributable to wind and rain that occur in a hurricane.[6]

7. BURDEN OF PROOF

When an insurance claim is disputed by the insurer, the person bringing suit has the burden of proving that there was a loss, that it occurred while the policy was in force, and that the loss was of a kind that was within the coverage or scope of the policy.[7]

A policy will contain exceptions to the coverage. This means that the policy is not applicable when an exception applies to the situation. Exceptions to coverage are generally strictly interpreted against the insurer. The insurer has the burden of proving that the facts were such that there was no coverage because an exception applied.

Under state cancellation statutes, insurers must produce proof that each cancellation notice was mailed to the address of record.[8]

8. INSURER BAD FAITH

As is required in the case of all contracts, an insurer must act in good faith in processing and paying claims under its policy. In some states, laws have been enacted making an insurer liable for a statutory penalty and attorney fees in case of a bad-faith failure or delay in paying a valid claim within a specified period of time. A bad-faith refusal is generally considered to be any frivolous or unfounded refusal to comply with the demand of a policyholder to pay according to the policy.[9]

When it is a liability insurer's duty to defend the insured and the insurer wrongfully refuses to do so, the insurer is guilty of breach of contract and is liable for all consequential damages resulting from the breach. In some jurisdictions, an insured can recover for an excess judgment rendered against the insured when it is proven that the insurer was guilty of negligence or bad faith in failing to defend the action or settle the matter within policy limits.

If there is a reasonable basis for the insurer's belief that a claim is not covered by its policy, its refusal to pay the claim does not subject it to liability for a breach of good faith or for a statutory penalty.[10] This is so even though the court holds that the insurer is liable for the claim.

---

[5] *Bering Strait School District v RLT Ins. Co.*, 872 P2d 1292 (Alaska 1994).

[6] *Buente v Allstate Ins. Co.*, 422 F Supp 2d 690 (SD Miss 2006).

[7] *Koslik v Gulf Insurance Co.*, 673 NW2d 343 (Wis App 2003).

[8] *Ragan v Columbia Mutual Ins. Co.*, 701 NE2d 493 (Ill 1998).

[9] *Uberti v Lincoln National Life Ins. Co.*, 144 F Supp 2d 90 (D Conn 2001).

[10] *Shipes v Hanover Ins. Co.*, 884 F2d 1357 (11th Cir 1989).

For Example, the following illustrates an insurer's bad-faith failure to pay a claim, as opposed to an insurer's reasonable basis for failure to pay. Carmela Garza's home and possessions were destroyed in a fire set by an arsonist on August 19. Carmela's husband, Raul, who was no longer living at the home, had a criminal record. An investigator for the insurer stated that while he had no specific information to implicate the Garzas in the arson, Carmela may have wanted the proceeds to finance relocation to another city. By October, however, Aetna's investigators ruled out the possibility that Garza had the motive or the opportunity to set the fire. The insurer thus no longer had a reasonable basis to refuse to pay the claim after this date. Yet it took over a year and a half and court intervention for Aetna to allow Carmela to see a copy of her policy, which had been destroyed in the fire. Two years after the fire, Aetna paid only $28,624.55 for structural damage to the fire-gutted home, which was insured for $111,000. The court held that Aetna's actions constituted a bad-faith failure to pay by the insurer.[11]

In the case of a bad-faith breach of an insurance claim, the insurer not only is exposed to compensatory damages but also may be liable for exemplary or punitive damages. **For Example,** when State Farm intentionally and unreasonably denied payment on Cindy Robinson's personal injury auto accident claim and State Farm's position was found not to be "fairly debatable," the jury awarded $9.5 million in punitive damages. The state supreme court reviewing the case noted that the evidence showed that the insurer's claims-handling procedures were designed to increase profits by reducing costs using biased paper reviews and by inducing lower settlements through denial or delay of claims. Given State Farm's billions in profits, the court determined that the $9.5 million punitive damages award was not excessive and had a reasonable relation to an amount needed to stop similar conduct in the future.[12]

9. TIME LIMITATIONS ON INSURED

The insured must comply with a number of time limitations in making a claim. For example, the insured must promptly notify the insurer of any claim that may arise, submit a proof-of-loss statement within the time set forth in the policy, and bring any court action based on the policy within a specified time period.[13]

10. SUBROGATION OF INSURER

subrogation right of a party secondarily liable to stand in the place of the creditor after making payment to the creditor and to enforce the creditor's right against the party primarily liable in order to obtain indemnity from such primary party.

In some instances, the insured has a claim against a third person for the harm covered by the insurance policy. **For Example,** *A* sells an automobile insurance policy that provides collision coverage to *B*. *C* "rear-ends" *B*'s car at a traffic rotary in the city. *A* pays *B* the full amount of the property damage repair costs. *A* is then **subrogated** to *B*'s claim against *C*, the person who caused the harm. See Figure 36-1. When the insurer is subrogated to the insured's claim, the insurer may enforce that claim against the third person.[14]

---

[11] See *Aetna Casualty & Surety Co. v Garza,* 906 SW2d 543 (Tex App 1995).

[12] *Robinson v State Farm Mutual Automobile Ins. Co.,* 2000 Ida LEXIS 144. See *State Farm Mutual Automobile Co. v Campbell,* 123 S Ct 1513 (2003), where the U.S. Supreme Court set aside an award of $145 million in punitive damages against State Farm for its bad-faith failure to settle for the insured's policy limits; the compensatory damages were $1 million. The Court held that the due process clause of the Fourteenth Amendment prohibits the imposition of grossly excessive punitive damages.

[13] But see *Seeman v Sterling Ins. Co.,* 699 NYS2d 542 (App Div 1999), where the insured's four-month delay in notifying the insurer was excused because of his belief that only on-premises injuries were covered by his homeowners insurance policy and thus the policy would not cover an injury in which a paintball he fired at work struck his coworker in the eye.

[14] *Julson v Federated Mutual Ins. Co.,* 562 NW2d 117 (SD 1997).

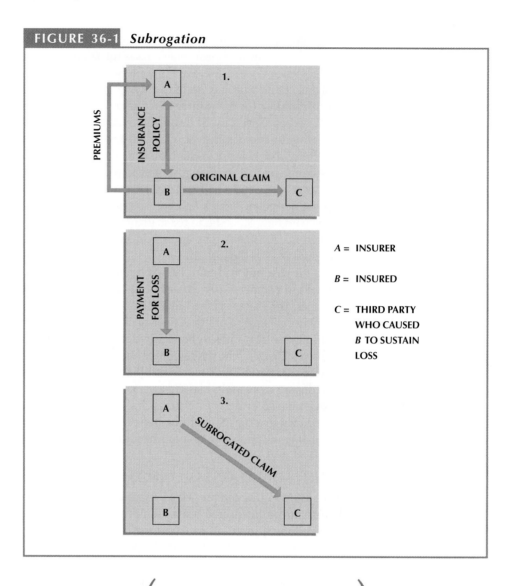

FIGURE 36-1 *Subrogation*

A = INSURER

B = INSURED

C = THIRD PARTY WHO CAUSED B TO SUSTAIN LOSS

ETHICS & THE LAW

On September 11, 2001, terrorist attacks killed 3,119 persons, devastated the U.S. airline industry, and had a severe impact on the U.S. insurance industry. In New York City, several office buildings, including One and Two World Trade Center, were destroyed, and other businesses in lower Manhattan were forced to shut down.

Business interruption insurance coverage is usually written as part of a company's commercial property insurance package. It not only covers policyholders for their lost profits and fixed charges and expenses for interruption to their business caused by physical damage or destruction to the insured's own property, but it may also cover "contingent business interruption" resulting from suspension of operations caused by damages to the property of a key supplier, distributor, or manufacturer. Such coverage,

ETHICS & THE LAW

continued

however, contains an exclusion for "war or military action." Are the September 11, 2001, terrorist attacks an "act of war" such that insurers are not responsible for business interruption claims? Can the president's words regarding war with al Qaeda be used to prove an "act of war" exclusion?

A court called upon to interpret an "act of war" exclusion will apply the plain and ordinary meaning of the policy's terms, and any ambiguity will be construed against the insurer. In *Pan American World Airways, Inc., v Aetna Casualty & Surety Co.,** the Second Circuit Court of Appeals held that an air carrier was entitled to recover for the destruction of its plane by terrorists in Cairo, Egypt, and the damage was not excluded under the policy's "act of war" exclusion. The court reasoned in part that there was no existing "war" between recognized sovereign states.

Pressured by historic losses, insurance companies in certain areas excluded perils resulting from "terrorism" in new commercial property insurance policies. The industry's framework for a definition of *terrorism* as a policy exclusion is an incident in which insured property damage exceeds $25 million and 50 or more individuals are seriously injured or die. Also excluded from coverage under the definition are losses due to nuclear, biological, or chemical weapons. Is it fair for insurers to exclude coverage altogether for losses due to acts of terrorism? Is it best to have the community absorb the losses? Is it best to have individuals and individual businesses cover the losses? See the Terrorism Risk Insurance Extension Act of 2005, by which Congress extended its temporary terrorism insurance program though December 31, 2007, providing a system of shared public private compensation for insured losses resulting from acts of terrorism. The Secretary of State in concurrence with the Attorney General of the United States has authority to certify an event as an act of terrorism, thereby initiating the provisions and benefits of the act.

*See *Pan American World Airways, Inc. v Aetna Casualty & Surety Co.,* 505 F2d 989 (2d Cir 1974).

B KINDS OF INSURANCE

> **risk** peril or contingency against which the insured is protected by the contract of insurance.

Businesses today have specialized **risk** managers who identify the risks to which individual businesses are exposed, measure those risks, and purchase insurance to cover those risks (or decide to self-insure in whole or in part).

Insurance policies can be grouped into certain categories. Five major categories of insurance are considered here: (1) business liability insurance, (2) marine and inland marine insurance, (3) fire and homeowners insurance, (4) automobile insurance, and (5) life insurance.

11. BUSINESS LIABILITY INSURANCE

Businesses may purchase Commercial General Liability (CGL) policies. This insurance is a broad, "all-risk" form of insurance providing coverage for all sums that the insured may become legally obligated to pay as damages because of "bodily injury" or "property damage" caused by an "occurrence." The insurer is obligated to defend the insured business and pay damages under CGL policies for product liability cases, actions for wrongful termination of employees, sexual harassment cases, damages caused by business advertising or employee dishonesty, and trademark infringement suits.[15] The insurer may also be obligated to pay for damages in the form of cleanup costs imposed for contamination of land, water, and air under environmental statutes.[16]

CASE SUMMARY

EPA's PRP Suits the Court Just Fine

FACTS: Anderson Development Company (ADC) manufactures and sells specialty organic materials in Adrian, Michigan. It built a lagoon to handle the occasional accidental discharge of Curene 442 process water, believing it to be insoluble in water. Curene 442, which it manufactured between 1970 and 1979, was a known animal carcinogen, and it turned out to be soluble. The lagoon's discharge piping was connected to the sewer system, and the Curene 442 found its way to the city's sewage treatment plant. In 1985, the Environmental Protection Agency (EPA) sent ADC a formal notification that it was considered a "potentially responsible party" (PRP) for the release of hazardous substances into the soil and groundwater. This notice was called a *PRP letter*. ADC notified Travelers Indemnity Company, its insurer, of the letter, and Travelers contended that it was not prepared to defend or cover ADC in the matter. ADC did a study that revealed contamination on its property. The EPA and ADC entered a consent decree wherein ADC agreed to the cleanup activities required by the EPA, spending more than $6 million on the cleanup. ADC brought an action against its insurer, seeking coverage under its general liability insurance policies for the cost of its defense and the cost of the cleanup. Travelers alleged that it was not liable under the policies.

DECISION: Judgment for insured. The state's highest court has held that a PRP letter issued by the EPA is the functional equivalent of a "suit" brought in a court of law because the EPA's extensive authority to determine and apportion liability allows it to essentially usurp the traditional role of a court. Thus, Travelers had an obligation to defend the insured under the contractual terms used in the policy: "defend any suit." Travelers is also liable for "damages" as that term is used in the insurance contract because state court decisions hold that EPA-mandated cleanup costs constitute damages. [**Anderson Development Co. v Travelers Indemnity Co., 49 F3d 1128 (6th Cir 1995)**]

The insurer must defend when coverage is a "close issue" regarding whether the policy would provide indemnity. It is common for the insurer to seek a declaratory judgment if it believes the policy does not call for either a defense or indemnity. **For Example,** Capital Associates sent unsolicited advertisements to the fax machines of a number of businesses that objected to them under the Telephone Consumer Protection Act, which resulted in a class action lawsuit on behalf of all recipients of those junk faxes. Capital Associates tendered the defense of the lawsuit to American States Insurance Co., its CGL insurer. In the declaratory judgment action brought by the insurer, the court determined that the CGL policy's intentional tort exclusion relieved the insurer of a need to defend or indemnify because Capital intended to send the faxes in violation of federal law.[17]

---

[15] *Charter Oak Fire Ins. Co. v Heedon & Cos.*, 280 F3d 730 (7th Cir 2002).

[16] *Chemical Leaman Tank Lines, Inc. v Aetna Casualty Co.*, 788 F Supp 846 (DNJ 1992); and *United States v Pepper's Steel, Inc.*, 823 F Supp 1574 (SD Fla 1993). But see *Northville Industries v National Union Fire and Ins. Co.*, 636 NYS2d 359 (Sup Ct App Div 1995); and *Aydin Corp. v First State Ins. Co.*, 62 Cal Rptr 2d 825 (Cal App 1997).

[17] *American States Insurance Co. v Capital Associates of Jackson County Inc.*, 392 F3d 939 (7th Cir 2004).

marine insurance policies that cover perils relating to the transportation of goods.

ocean marine policies that cover transportation of goods in vessels in international and coastal trade.

inland marine insurance that covers domestic shipments of goods over land and inland waterways.

hull insurance insurance that covers physical damage on a freight-moving vessel.

cargo insurance insurance that protects a cargo owner against financial loss if goods being shipped are lost or damaged at sea.

Businesses may purchase policies providing liability insurance for their directors and officers. Manufacturers and sellers may purchase product liability insurance. Professional persons, such as accountants, physicians, lawyers, architects, and engineers, may obtain liability insurance protection against malpractice suits. **For Example,** the architects of the MCI Center, a sports arena in Washington, D.C., were entitled under their professional liability insurance coverage to be defended by their insurer in a lawsuit seeking only injunctive relief for the firm's alleged failure to comply with the Americans with Disabilities Act's enhanced sightline requirements.[18]

12. MARINE INSURANCE

Marine insurance policies cover perils relating to the transportation of goods. **Ocean marine** insurance policies cover the transportation of goods in vessels in international and coastal trade. **Inland marine** insurance principally covers domestic shipments of goods over land and inland waterways.

(a) OCEAN MARINE   Ocean marine insurance is a form of insurance that covers ships and their cargoes against "perils of the sea." Four classes of ocean marine insurance are generally available: (1) hull, (2) cargo, (3) liability, and (4) freight. **Hull insurance** covers physical damage to the vessel.[19] **Cargo insurance** protects the cargo owner against financial loss if the goods being shipped are lost or damaged at sea.[20]

CASE SUMMARY

This Coverage Is Worth a Hill of Beans

FACTS: Commodities Reserve Company (CRC) contracted to sell 1,008 tons of beans and 50 tons of seed to purchasers in Venezuela. CRC purchased the beans and seeds in Turkey and chartered space on the ship *MV West Lion.* The cargo was insured under an ocean marine policy issued by St. Paul Fire & Marine Insurance Company. The Sue and Labor Clause in CRC's ocean marine policy with St. Paul provided: "In case of any loss or misfortune, it shall be lawful and necessary to and for the Assured . . . to sue, labor and travel for, in and about the defense, safeguard and recovery of the said goods and merchandise . . . to the charges whereof, the [insurer] will contribute according to the rate and quantity of the sum hereby insured." While the ship was sailing through Greek waters, Greek authorities seized the vessel for carrying munitions. CRC had to go to the expense of obtaining an order from a court in Crete to release the cargo. When St. Paul refused to pay the costs of the Cretan litigation to release the cargo, CRC brought suit against St. Paul.

DECISION: Judgment for CRC. The Sue and Labor Clause required CRC to sue for "recovery of the said goods and merchandise." The clause also requires the insurer to reimburse the insured for those expenses.. [**Commodities Reserve Co. v St. Paul Fire & Marine Ins. Co., 879 F2d 640 (9th Cir 1989)**]

Cargo insurance does not cover risks prior to the loading of the insured cargo on board the vessel. An additional warehouse coverage endorsement is needed to insure merchandise held in a warehouse prior to import or export voyages.

---

[18] *Washington Sports and Entertainment, Inc. v United Coastal Ins.,* 7 F Supp 2d 1 (DDC 1998).
[19] *Lloyd's v Labarca,* 260 F3d 3 (1st Cir 2001).
[20] *Kimta, A. S. v Royal Insurance Co., Inc.,* 9 P3d 239 (Wash App 2001).

liability insurance covers the shipowner's liability if the ship causes damage to another ship or its cargo.

freight insurance insures that shipowner will receive payment for transportation charges.

fire insurance policy a contract that indemnifies the insured for property destruction or damage caused by fire.

homeowners insurance policy combination of standard fire insurance and comprehensive personal liability insurance.

coinsurance clause clause requiring the insured to maintain insurance on property up to a stated amount and providing that to the extent that this is not done, the insured is to be deemed a coinsurer with the insurer, so that the latter is liable only for its proportionate share of the amount of insurance required to be carried.

Liability insurance covers the shipowner's liability if the ship causes damage to another ship or its cargo. **Freight insurance** ensures that the shipowner will receive payment for the transportation charges. "All-risk" policies consolidate coverage of all four classes of ocean marine insurance into one policy.[21]

(b) INLAND MARINE Inland marine insurance evolved from marine insurance. It protects goods in transit over land; by air; or on rivers, lakes, and coastal waters. Inland marine insurance can be used to insure property held by a bailee. Moreover, it is common for institutions financing automobile dealers' new car inventories to purchase inland marine insurance policies to insure against damage to the automobiles while in inventory.

13. FIRE AND HOMEOWNERS INSURANCE

A **fire insurance policy** is a contract to indemnify the insured for property destruction or damage caused by fire. In almost every state, the New York standard fire insurance form is the standard policy. A **homeowners insurance policy** is a combination of the standard fire insurance policy and comprehensive personal liability insurance. It thus provides fire, theft, and certain liability protection in a single insurance contract.

(a) FIRE INSURANCE For fire insurance to cover fire loss, there must be an actual hostile fire that is the immediate cause of the loss. A *hostile fire* is one that becomes uncontrollable, burns with excessive heat, or escapes from the place where it is intended to be. To illustrate, when soot is ignited and causes a fire in the chimney, the fire is hostile. On the other hand, if a loss is caused by the smoke or heat of a fire that has not broken out of its ordinary container or become uncontrollable, the loss results from a friendly fire. The policy does not cover damage from a friendly fire.

CASE SUMMARY

Excuse Me? The Fire Wasn't Hostile?

FACTS: Youse owned a ring that was insured with the Employers Fire Insurance Company against loss, including "all direct loss or damage by fire." Youse accidentally threw the ring into a trash burner, and it was damaged when the trash was burned. He sued the insurer.

DECISION: Judgment for insurer. A fire policy covers only loss caused by a hostile fire. The fire was not hostile because it burned in the area in which it was intended to burn. [**Youse v Employers Fire Ins. Co.**, 172 Kan 111, 238 P2d 472 (1951)]

By policy endorsement, however, the coverage may be extended to include loss by a friendly fire.

CPA **(1) Coinsurance.** The insurer is liable for the actual amount of the loss sustained up to the maximum amount stated in the policy. An exception exists when the policy contains a coinsurance clause. A **coinsurance clause** requires the insured to maintain insurance on the covered property up to a certain amount or a certain

---

[21] *Transamerican Leasing, Inc. v Institute of London Underwriters*, 7 F Supp 2d 1340 (SD Fla 1998).

percentage of the value (generally 80 percent). Under such a provision, if the policyholder insures the property for less than the required amount, the insurer is liable only for the proportionate share of the amount of insurance required to be carried. **For Example,** suppose that the owner of a building with a value of $400,000 insures it against loss to the extent of $240,000. The policy contains a coinsurance clause requiring that insurance of 80 percent of the value of the property be carried (in this case, $320,000). Assume that a $160,000 loss is then sustained. The insured would receive not $160,000 from the insurer but only three-fourths of that amount, which is $120,000, because the amount of the insurance carried ($240,000) is only three-fourths of the amount required ($360,000).

Some states prohibit the use of a coinsurance clause.

CPA *(2) Assignment.*   Fire insurance is a personal contract, and in the absence of statute or contractual authorization, it cannot be assigned without the consent of the insurer.

CPA *(3) Occupancy.*   Provisions in a policy of fire insurance relating to the use and occupancy of the property are generally strictly construed because they relate to the hazards involved.

(b) HOMEOWNERS INSURANCE   In addition to providing protection against losses resulting from fire, the homeowners policy provides liability coverage for accidents or injuries that occur on the premises of the insured. Moreover, the liability provisions provide coverage for unintentional injuries to others away from home for which the insured or any member of the resident family is held responsible, such as injuries caused to others by golfing, hunting, or fishing accidents.[22] Generally, motor vehicles, including mopeds and recreational vehicles, are excluded from such personal liability coverage.

A homeowners policy also provides protection from losses caused by theft. In addition, it provides protection for all permanent residents of the household, including all family members living with the insured. Thus, a child of the insured who lives at home is protected under the homeowners policy for the value of personal property lost when the home is destroyed by fire.

14. AUTOMOBILE INSURANCE

Associations of insurers, such as the National Bureau of Casualty Underwriters and the National Automobile Underwriters Association, have proposed standard forms of automobile insurance policies. These forms have been approved by the association members in virtually all states. The form used today by most insurers is the Personal Auto Policy (PAP).

(a) PERILS COVERED   Part A of the policy provides liability coverage that protects the insured driver or owner from the claims of others for bodily injuries or damage to their property. Part B of the policy provides coverage for medical expenses sustained by a covered person or persons in an accident. Part C of the PAP provides coverage for damages the insured is entitled to recover from an *uninsured motorist.*[23] Part D provides coverage for loss or damage to the covered automobile.

---

[22] *American Concept Ins. Co. v Lloyds of London,* 467 NW2d 480 (SD 1991).
[23] *Montano v Allstate Indemnity,* 2000 US App LEXIS (10th Cir 2002).

Coverage under Part D includes collision coverage and coverage of "other than collision" losses, such as fire and theft.

(b) COVERED PERSONS Covered persons include the named insured or any family member (a person related by blood, marriage, or adoption or a ward or foster child who is a resident of the household). If an individual is driving with the permission of the insured, that individual is also covered.

(c) USE AND OPERATION The coverage of the PAP policy is limited to claims arising from the "use and operation" of an automobile. The term *use and operation* does not require that the automobile be in motion. Thus, the term embraces loading and unloading as well as actual travel.[24]

(d) NOTICE AND COOPERATION The insured is under a duty to give notice of claims, to inform, and to cooperate with the insurer. Notice and cooperation are conditions precedent to the liability of the insurer.

CASE SUMMARY

Is Carrying a Transmission Down a Driveway "Loading or Unloading" a Truck? A Liberal Interpretation

FACTS: Gerhard Schillers was assisting his friend J. L. Loethen in removing a transmission from the bed of the Loethens' truck on the Loethens' property. While Schillers was carrying the transmission down a driveway, he fell and was seriously injured. J. L. was insured under his parents' automobile insurance policy with Shelter Mutual Insurance Company, which insured for liability, including "the loading and unloading" of the vehicle.

DECISION: Schillers's injuries were incidental to, and a consequence of, the unloading of the Loethens' pickup truck. The injuries would not have occurred if the men had not been unloading the truck. The unloading activity continued until the removed property was put in the place to which it was to be taken. Therefore, Schillers's injury was covered by the motor vehicle liability policy issued by Shelter Mutual. [**American Family Mutual Ins. Co. v Shelter Mutual Ins. Co.**, 747 SW2d 174 (Mo App 1988)]

(e) NO-FAULT INSURANCE Traditional tort law (negligence law) placed the economic losses resulting from an automobile accident on the one at fault. The purpose of automobile liability insurance is to relieve the wrongdoer from the consequences of a negligent act by paying defense costs and the damages assessed. Under no-fault laws, injured persons are barred from suing the party at fault for ordinary claims. When the insured is injured while using the insured automobile, the insurer will make a payment without regard to whose fault caused the harm. However, if the automobile collision results in a permanent serious disablement or disfigurement, or death, or if the medical bills and lost wages of the plaintiff exceed a specified amount, suit may be brought against the party who was at fault.

---

[24] *State Farm Ins. v Whitehead*, 711 SW2d 198 (Mo App 1986).

15. LIFE INSURANCE

There are three basic types of life insurance: term insurance, whole life insurance, and endowment insurance.

Term insurance is written for a specified number of years and terminates at the end of that period. If the insured dies within the time period covered by the policy, the face amount is paid to the beneficiary. If the insured is still alive at the end of the time period, the contract expires, and the insurer has no further obligation. Term policies have little or no cash surrender value.

Whole life insurance (or ordinary life insurance) provides lifetime insurance protection. It also has an investment element.

Part of every premium covers the cost of insurance, and the remainder of the premium builds up a **cash surrender value** of the policy.

An **endowment insurance** policy is one that pays the face amount of the policy if the insured dies within the policy period. If the insured lives to the end of the policy period, the face amount is paid to the insured at the end of the period.

Many life insurance companies pay double the amount of the policy, called **double indemnity,** if death is caused by an accident and death occurs within 90 days afterward. A comparatively small additional premium is charged for this special protection.

In consideration of an additional premium, many life insurance companies also provide insurance against total permanent disability of the insured. **Disability** is usually defined in a life insurance policy as any "incapacity resulting from bodily injury or disease to engage in any occupation for remuneration or profit."

(a) EXCLUSIONS   Life insurance policies frequently provide that death is not within the protection of the policy and that a double indemnity provision is not applicable when death is caused by (1) suicide,[25] (2) narcotics, (3) the intentional act of another, (4) execution for a crime, (5) war activities, or (6) operation of aircraft.

(b) THE BENEFICIARY   The recipient of life insurance policy proceeds that are payable upon the death of the insured is called the **beneficiary.** The beneficiary may be a third person or the estate of the insured, and there may be more than one beneficiary.

The beneficiary named in a policy may be barred from claiming the proceeds of the policy. It is generally provided by statute or stated by court decision that a beneficiary who has feloniously killed the insured is not entitled to receive the proceeds of the policy.

The customary policy provides that the insured reserves the right to change the beneficiary without the latter's consent. When the policy contains such a provision, the beneficiary cannot object to a change that destroys all of that beneficiary's rights under the policy and that names another person as beneficiary.

An insurance policy will ordinarily state that to change the beneficiary, the insurer must be so instructed in writing by the insured and the policy must then be endorsed by the company with the change of the beneficiary. These provisions are construed liberally. If the insured has notified the insurer but dies before the endorsement of the change by the company, the change of beneficiary is effective.[26] However, if the

---

term insurance policy written for a specified number of years that terminates at the end of that period.

whole life insurance ordinary life insurance providing lifetime insurance protection.

cash surrender value sum paid the insured upon the surrender of a policy to the insurer.

endowment insurance insurance that pays the face amount of the policy if the insured dies within the policy period.

double indemnity provision for payment of double the amount specified by the insurance contract if death is caused by an accident and occurs under specified circumstances.

disability any incapacity resulting from bodily injury or disease to engage in any occupation for remuneration or profit.

beneficiary person to whom the proceeds of a life insurance policy are payable, a person for whose benefit property is held in trust, or a person given property by a will; the ultimate recipient of the benefit of a funds transfer.

---

[25] *Mirza v Maccabees Life and Annuity Co.,* 466 NW2d 340 (Mich App 1991).
[26] *Zeigler v Cardona,* 830 F Supp 1395 (MD Ala 1993).

insured has not taken any steps to comply with the policy requirements, a change of beneficiary is not effective even though a change was intended.

(c) Incontestability Clause   Statutes commonly require the inclusion of an **incontestability clause** in life insurance policies. Ordinarily, this clause states that after the lapse of two years, the policy cannot be contested by the insurance company. The insurer is free to contest the validity of the policy at any time during the contestability period. Once the period has expired, the insurer must pay the stipulated sum upon the death of the insured and cannot claim that in obtaining the policy, the insured had been guilty of misrepresentation, fraud, or any other conduct that would entitle it to avoid the contract of insurance.[27]

incontestability clause
provision that after the lapse of a specified time the insurer cannot dispute the policy on the ground of misrepresentation or fraud of the insured or similar wrongful conduct.

CASE SUMMARY

The Impostor Defense: Dealing With Substitutes With Different Attributes

FACTS: The Allstate life insurance policy on which this case centers went into effect on September 20, 2000, insuring the life of John Miller. The policy stated that if the insured died while the policy was in force, Allstate would pay a death benefit to the policy beneficiaries upon receiving proof of death. As required by Fla. Stat. § 627.455, the policy further provided that it would become incontestable after remaining in force during the lifetime of the insured for a period of two years from its effective date. John Miller died on April 20, 2003—more than two years after the policy went into effect. The beneficiaries accordingly filed statements seeking to collect benefits under the policy. Rather than disburse the benefits, Allstate sought a declaratory judgment that the policy was void, alleging that the application was completed using fraudulent information and that an imposter had appeared at the medical exam in place of John Miller. The beneficiaries counterclaimed, alleging breach of contract based on Allstate's failure to pay benefits upon proof of death in accordance with the insurance policy's terms. Allstate appealed a judgment in favor of the beneficiaries.

DECISION: Judgment for the beneficiaries. The incontestability clause works to the mutual advantage of the insured, giving the insured a guarantee against expensive litigation to defeat the policy after it has been in effect during the lifetime of the insured for a period of two years from its date of issue and giving the company a reasonable time to ascertain whether the insurance contract should remain in force. Under Florida law where the insured's death occurred after the contestability period, Allstate could not void the policy on the ground that an imposter had undergone the precoverage physical examination in the insured's place. [**Allstate Life Ins. Co. v Miller, 424 F3d 1113 (11th Cir 2005)**]

Courts and legislatures have addressed the issue of "imposter fraud." In *Amex Life Assurance Co. v Superior Court,* the California Supreme Court concluded that after the contestability period had expired, an insurer may not assert the defense that an imposter took the medical examination. Jose Morales had applied for a life insurance policy from Amex. A paramedic working for Amex met a man claiming to be Morales and took blood and urine samples, listing him as 5′10″ and weighing 172 pounds. His blood sample was HIV negative. The individual did not provide identification. Some two years later, Morales died of AIDS–related causes. Morales had listed his height as 5′6″ and his weight as 142 on his insurance application. The California

---

[27] *Standard Insurance Co. v Carls,* 2000 U.S. Dist LEXIS 8401.

Supreme Court stated that Amex, which had done nothing to protect its interest but collect premiums, could not challenge coverage based on the imposter defense.[28] Subsequent to the court's decision, the California legislature amended state insurance law to provide for an "imposter defense" in that state. As set forth in the *Miller* case, Florida does not recognize an imposter defense to incontestability. The legislative purpose of such clauses is to protect beneficiaries from an insurer's refusal to honor policies by asserting pre-existing conditions, leaving beneficiaries in the untenable position of having to battle with powerful insurance companies in court.

LAWFLIX

Double Indemnity (1944)

In this Billy Wilder film, Fred MacMurray is an insurance salesman coerced into a murder plot. The movie provides good coverage of insurable interest in life.

For movie clips that illustrate business law concepts, see LawFlix at **http://wdvl.westbuslaw.com.**

---

[28] *Amex Life Assurance Co. v Superior Court,* 60 Cal Rptr 2d 898 (Sup Ct 1997).

SUMMARY

Insurance is a contract called a *policy.* Under an insurance policy, the insurer provides in consideration of premium payments, to pay the insured or beneficiary a sum of money if the insured sustains a specified loss or is subjected to a specified liability. These contracts are made through an insurance agent, who is an agent for the insurance company, or through an insurance broker, who is the agent of the insured when obtaining a policy for the latter.

The person purchasing an insurance contract must have an insurable interest in the insured's life or property. An insurable interest in property exists when the damage or destruction of the property will cause a direct monetary loss to the insured. In the case of property insurance, the insured must have an insurable interest at the time of loss. An insurable interest in the life of the insured exists if the purchaser would suffer a financial loss from the insured's death. This interest must exist as of the time the policy is obtained.

Ocean marine policies insure ships and their cargoes against the perils of the sea. Inland marine policies insure goods being transported by land, by air, or on inland and coastal waterways.

For fire insurance to cover a fire loss, there must be an actual hostile fire that is the immediate cause

of the loss. The insurer is liable for the actual amount of the loss sustained up to the maximum amount stated in the policy. An exception exists when the policy contains a coinsurance clause requiring the insured to maintain insurance up to a certain percentage of the value of the property. To the extent this is not done, the insured is deemed a coinsurer with the insurer, and the insurer is liable for only its proportional share of the amount of insurance required to be carried. A homeowners insurance policy provides fire, theft, and liability protection in a single contract.

Automobile insurance may provide protection for collision damage to the insured's property and injury to persons. It may also cover liability to third persons for injury and property damage as well as loss by fire or theft.

A life insurance policy requires the insurer to pay a stated sum of money to a named beneficiary upon the death of the insured. It may be a term insurance policy, a whole life policy, or an endowment policy. State law commonly requires the inclusion of an incontestability clause, whereby at the conclusion of the contestability period, the insurer cannot contest the validity of the policy.

QUESTIONS AND CASE PROBLEMS

1. Cecil Usher owned Belize NY, Inc. (Belize), a small construction company doing business in New York City. Belize purchased a commercial general liability insurance policy from Mount Vernon Fire Insurance Co. The policy's first page, entitled "Policy Declarations," describes the insured as "Belize N.Y., Inc.;" it classifies the "Form of Business" as "Corporation," the "Business Description" as "Carpentry," and indicates that Belize was afforded commercial liability insurance in the amount of $1,000,000 per occurrence and $2,000,000 in the aggregate for the period June 1, 1995, to June 1, 1996. Two classifications are listed under "Premium Computation" on the Declarations page: "Carpentry—Interior—001" and "Carpentry—001." The policy makes no further mention of these two terms. Belize performed some $60,000 of demolition work on the United House of Prayer's renovation project on 272 West 125th Street in New York City. Belize was thereafter hired to supervise subcontractors working on the job. During that period of time, a person entered the building, shot several people with a firearm, and started a fire. Seven people died and several others were injured. The estates of the victims sued Belize, Inc., for "negligence, carelessness and recklessness" regarding the fire, and Belize notified Mount Vernon of the lawsuit. Mount Vernon refused to defend or indemnify Belize because Belize was not engaging in its carpentry operations in the building at the time of the incident. It asserted that its risk is limited to carpentry operations in accordance with the classifications set forth in the policy. Belize contended that the language of the policy did not provide that the classification "Carpentry" defined covered risks, and exclusions should have been stated in the contract. Decide. [*Mount Vernon Fire Insurance Co. v Belize NY, Inc.*, 227 F3d 232 (2d Cir)]

2. Martin Carls, a San Francisco teacher and counselor, applied for disability insurance from Standard Insurance Co. on April 4, 1996. On the application and supplement, Carls ticked "no" in response to whether he suffered recurring headaches, heart disease, skin problems, a spinal condition, or immune system disorder. He also denied taking any prescription medicine, stated that he had visited doctors only for general checkups in the past five years, and stated that he was covered under one additional disability insurance policy. Standard issued a disability policy with an effective date of June 12, 1996. On February 2, 1999, Carls filed a claim for benefits under the policy, stating that he had become totally disabled by symptoms of AIDS. After investigating the claim, Standard denied coverage and filed a lawsuit seeking rescission of the insurance policy based on fraud. According to Standard, at the time Carls submitted his insurance application, he suffered from a variety of serious ailments, including recurrent migraines, heart disease, chronic back pain, and HIV-positive status. Also, Standard asserts that Carls willfully failed to disclose extensive medical treatments, prescription drugs, and four additional disability insurance policies. What defense will be raised on behalf of Carls? How would you decide this case? [*Standard Insurance Co. v Carls*, 2000 U.S. Dist LEXIS 8401].

3. On April 6, 1988, Luis Serrano purchased for $75,000 a 26′8″–long Carrera speedboat named *Hot Shot.* First Federal Savings Bank provided $65,000 financing for this purchase. Serrano obtained a marine yacht policy for hull insurance on the boat for $75,000 from El Fenix, with First Federal being named as payee under the policy.

   On May 2, 1988, Serrano sold the boat to Reinaldo Polito, and Serrano furnished First Federal with documents evidencing the sale. Polito assumed the obligation to pay off the balance due First Federal. On October 6, 1989, Serrano again applied to El Fenix for a new yacht policy, covering the period from October 6, 1989, through October 6, 1990, and the coverage extended to peril of confiscation by a governmental agency. Serrano did not have ownership or possession of the boat on October 6, 1989. First Federal, the named payee, had not perfected or recorded a mortgage on *Hot Shot* until July 5, 1990.

   On November 13, 1989, in the waters off Cooper Island in the British Virgin Islands (BVI), *Hot Shot* was found abandoned after a chase by governmental officials. A large shipment of cocaine was recovered, although no one was arrested. When Serrano and First Federal were informed that *Hot Shot* was subject to mandatory forfeiture under BVI law, they both filed claims under the October 6, 1989, insurance policy. What defenses would you raise on behalf of the insurer in this case? Decide. [*El Fenix v Serrano Gutierrez,* 786 F Supp 1065 (DPR)]

4. From the United Insurance Co., Rebecca Foster obtained a policy insuring the life of Lucille McClurkin and naming herself as beneficiary. McClurkin did not live with Foster, and Foster did not inform McClurkin of the existence of the policy. Foster paid the premiums on the policy and upon the death of McClurkin sued the United Insurance Co. for the amount of the insurance. At the trial, Foster testified vaguely that her father had told her that McClurkin was her second cousin on his side of the family. Was Foster entitled to recover on the policy? [*Foster v United Ins. Co.,* 158 SE2d 201 (SC)]

5. Dr. George Allard and his brother-in-law, Tom Rowland, did not get along after family land that was once used solely by Rowland was partitioned among family members after the death of Rowland's father. Rowland had a reputation in the community as a bully and a violent person. On December 17, Allard was moving cattle down a dirt road by "trolling" (leading the cattle with a bucket of feed, causing them to follow him). When he saw a forestry truck coming along the road, he led the cattle off the road onto Rowland's land to prevent frightening the cattle. When Rowland saw Allard, Rowland ran toward him screaming at him for being on his land. Allard, a small older man, retreated to his truck and obtained a 12-gauge shotgun. He pointed the gun toward the ground about an inch in front of Rowland's left foot and fired it. He stated that he fired the shot in this fashion to bring Rowland to his senses and that Rowland stepped forward into the line of fire. Allard claimed that if Rowland had not stepped forward, he would not have been hit and injured. Allard was insured by Farm Bureau homeowners and general liability policies, which did not cover liability resulting from intentional acts by the insured. Applying the policy exclusion to the facts of this case, was Farm Bureau obligated to pay the $100,000 judgment against Allard? [*Southern Farm Bureau Casualty Co. v Allard,* 611 So 2d 966 (Miss)]

6. Arthur Katz testified for the U.S. government in a stock manipulation case. He also pled guilty and testified against three of his law partners in an insurance fraud case. He received a six-month sentence in a halfway house and a $5,000 fine. Katz was placed in the Federal Witness Protection Program. He and his wife changed their names to Kane and moved to Florida under the program. Both he and his wife obtained new driver's licenses and Social Security numbers. Using his new identity, "Kane" obtained two life insurance policies totaling $1.5 million. He named his wife beneficiary. A routine criminal background check on Kane found no criminal history.

   From 1984 to 1987, Kane invested heavily in the stock market. On October 17, 1987, the day the stock market crashed, Kane shot and wounded his stockbroker, shot and killed the office manager, and then committed suicide. The insurers refused to pay on the policies, claiming that they never insure persons with criminal records. Mrs. Kane contended that the policies were incontestable after they had been in effect for two years. Decide. [*Bankers Security Life Ins. Society v Kane,* 885 F2d 820 (11th Cir)]

7. Linda Filasky held policies issued by Preferred Risk Mutual Insurance Co. Following an injury in an automobile accident and storm damage to the roof of her home, Filasky sustained loss of income, theft of property, and water damage to her home. These three kinds of losses were covered by the policies with Preferred, but the insurer delayed unreasonably in processing her claims and raised numerous groundless objections to them. Finally, the insurer paid the claims in full. Filasky then sued the insurer for the emotional distress caused by the bad-faith delay and obstructive tactics of the insurer. The insurer defended that it had paid the claims in full and that nothing was owed Filasky. Decide. [*Filasky v Preferred Risk Mut. Ins. Co.,* 734 P2d 76 (Ariz)]

8. Baurer purchased a White Freightliner tractor and agreed that his son-in-law, Britton, could use it in the trucking business. In return, Britton agreed to haul Baurer's hay and cattle, thus saving Baurer approximately $30,000 per year. Baurer insured the vehicle with Mountain West Farm

Bureau Insurance Company. The policy contained an exclusionary clause that provided: "We don't insure your [truck] while it is rented or leased to others. . . . This does not apply to the use of your [truck] on a share expense basis." When the vehicle was destroyed, Mountain West refused to pay on the policy, contending that the arrangement between Baurer and Britton was a lease of the vehicle, which was excluded under the policy. Baurer sued, contending that it was a "share expense basis" allowed under the policy. Is the insurance policy ambiguous? What rule of contract construction applies in this case? Decide. [*Baurer v Mountain West Farm Bureau Ins.,* 695 P2d 1307 (Mont)]

9. Collins obtained from South Carolina Insurance Co. a liability policy covering a Piper Colt airplane he owned. The policy provided that it did not cover loss sustained while the plane was being piloted by a person who did not have a valid pilot's certificate and a valid medical examination certificate. Collins held a valid pilot's certificate, but his medical examination certificate had expired three months before. Collins was piloting the plane when it crashed, and he was killed. The insurer denied liability because Collins did not have a valid medical certificate. It was stipulated by both parties that the crash was in no way caused by the absence of the medical certificate. Decide. [*South Carolina Ins. Co. v Collins,* 237 SE2d 358 (SC)]

10. Marshall Produce Co. had insured its milk- and egg-processing plant against fire. When smoke from a fire near its plant permeated the environment and was absorbed into the company's egg powder products, cans of powder delivered to the U.S. government were rejected as contaminated. Marshall Produce sued the insurance company for a total loss, but the insurer contended there had been no fire involving the insured property and no total loss. Decide. [*Marshall Produce Co. v St. Paul Fire & Marine Ins. Co.,* 98 NW2d 280 (Minn)]

11. Amador Pena, who had three insurance policies on his life, wrote a will in which he specified that the proceeds from the insurance policies should go to his children instead of to Leticia Pena Salinas and other beneficiaries named in the policies. He died the day after writing the will. The insurance companies paid the proceeds of the policies to the named beneficiaries. The executor of Pena's estate sued Salinas and the other beneficiaries for the insurance money. Decide. [*Pena v Salinas,* 536 SW2d 671 (Tex App)]

12. Spector owned a small automobile repair garage in rural Kansas that was valued at $40,000. He purchased fire insurance coverage against loss to the extent of $24,000. The policy contained an 80 percent coinsurance clause. A fire destroyed a portion of his parts room, causing a loss of $16,000. Spector believes he is entitled to be fully compensated for this loss, as it is less than the $24,000 of fire protection that he purchased and paid for. Is Spector correct?

13. Carman Tool & Abrasives, Inc., purchased two milling machines, FOB Taiwan, from the Dah Lih Machinery Co. Carman obtained ocean marine cargo insurance on the machines from St. Paul Fire and Marine Insurance Co. and authorized Dah Lih to arrange for the shipment of the two machines to Los Angeles, using the services of Evergreen Lines. Dah Lih booked the machinery for shipment on board Evergreen's container ship, the *M/V Ever Giant;* arranged for the delivery of the cargo to the ship; provided all of the shipping information for the bill of lading; and was the party to whom the bill was issued. Dah Lih then delivered the bill of lading to its bank, which in turn negotiated it to Carman's bank to authorize payment to Dah Lih. After the cargo was removed from the vessel in Los Angeles but before it was delivered to Carman, the milling machines were damaged to the extent of $115,000. Is the insurer liable to Carman? Can the insurer recover from Evergreen? [*Carman Tool & Abrasives, Inc. v Evergreen Lines,* 871 F2d 897 (9th Cir)]

14. Vallot was driving his farm tractor on the highway. It was struck from the rear by a truck, overturned, exploded, and burned. Vallot was killed, and a death claim was made against All American Insurance Co. The death of Vallot was covered by the company's policy if Vallot had died from "being struck or run over by" the truck. The insurance company claimed that the policy was not applicable because Vallot had not been struck; the farm tractor had been struck, and

Vallot's death occurred when the overturned tractor exploded and burned. The insurance company also claimed that it was necessary that the insured be both struck and run over by another vehicle. Decide. [*Vallot v All American Ins. Co.,* 302 So 2d 625 (La App)]

15. When Jorge de Guerrero applied for a $200,000 life insurance policy with John Hancock Mutual Life Insurance Co., he stated on the insurance application that he had not seen a physician within the past five years. In fact, he had had several consultations with his physician, who three weeks prior to the application had diagnosed him as overweight and suffering from goiter. His response to the question on drug and alcohol use was that he was not an alcoholic or user of drugs. In fact, he had been an active alcoholic since age 16 and was a marijuana user. De Guerrero died within the two-year contestability period included in the policy, and John Hancock refused to pay. The beneficiary contended that all premiums were fully paid on the policy and that any misstatements in the application were unintentional. John Hancock contended that if the deceased had given the facts, the policy would not have been issued. Decide. [*de Guerrero v John Hancock Mutual Life Ins. Co.,* 522 So 2d 1032 (Fla App)]

> CPA QUESTIONS

1. Beal occupies an office building as a tenant under a 25-year lease. Beal also has a mortgagee's (lender's) interest in an office building owned by Hill Corp. In which capacity does Beal have an insurable interest?

	Tenant	*Mortgagee*
a.	Yes	Yes
b.	Yes	No
c.	No	Yes
d.	No	No

2. With respect to property insurance, the insurable interest requirement

   a. Need only be satisfied at the time the policy is issued

   b. Must be satisfied both at the time the policy is issued and at the time of the loss

   c. Will be satisfied only if the insured owns the property in fee simple absolute

   d. Will be satisfied by an insured who possesses a leasehold interest in the property

3. Lawfo Corp. maintains a $200,000 standard fire insurance policy on one of its warehouses. The policy includes an 80 percent coinsurance clause. At the time the warehouse was originally insured, its value was $250,000. The warehouse now has a value of $300,000. If the warehouse sustains $30,000 of fire damage, Lawfo's insurance recovery will be a maximum of

   a. $20,000

   b. $24,000

   c. $25,000

   d. $30,000

4. In 1992, King bought a building for $250,000. At that time, King took out a $200,000 fire insurance policy with Omni Insurance Co. and a $50,000 fire insurance policy with Safe Insurance Corp. Each policy contained a standard 80 percent coinsurance clause. In 1996, when the building had a fair market value of $300,000, a fire caused $200,000 in damage. What dollar amount would King recover from Omni?

   a. $100,000

   b. $150,000

   c. $160,000

   d. $200,000

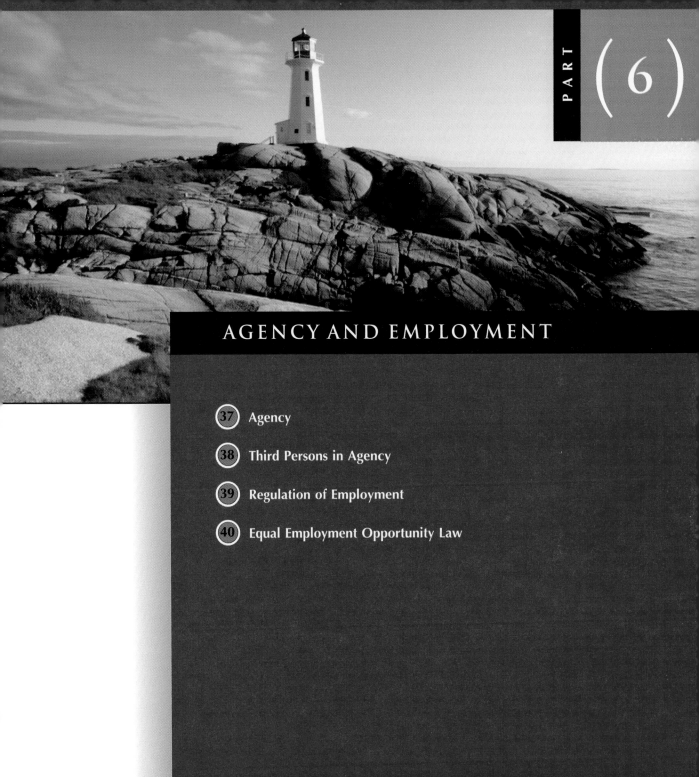

AGENCY AND EMPLOYMENT

AGENCY

CHAPTER (37)

LEARNING OBJECTIVES

*After studying
this chapter,
you should be
able to*

LO.1 Differentiate between an agent and an independent contractor

LO.2 Explain and illustrate who may be a principal and who may be an agent

LO.3 State the three classifications of agents

LO.4 Differentiate between express authority, incidental authority, customary authority, and apparent authority

LO.5 Explain the effect of the proper exercise of authority by an agent

LO.6 Describe the duty of a third person to determine the extent of an agent's authority

LO.7 List the four ways an agency relationship may be created

LO.8 List six ways an agency may be terminated by an act of one or both of the parties to the agency agreement

LO.9 List five ways an agency may be terminated by operation of law

---

One of the most common business relationships is that of agency.

By virtue of the agency device, one person can make contracts at numerous places with many different parties at the same time.

 NATURE OF THE AGENCY RELATIONSHIP

Agency is ordinarily based on the consent of the parties, and for that reason is called a *consensual relationship.* However, the law sometimes imposes an agency relationship. If consideration is present, the agency relationship is contractual.

---

1. DEFINITIONS AND DISTINCTIONS

agency relationship that exists between a person identified as a principal and another by virtue of which the latter may make contracts with third persons on behalf of the principal. (Parties—principal, agent, third person)

agent person or firm who is authorized by the principal or by operation of law to make contracts with third persons on behalf of the principal.

principal person or firm who employs an agent; person who, with respect to a surety, is primarily liable to the third person or creditor; property held in trust.

Agency is a relationship based on an express or implied agreement by which one person, the **agent**, is authorized to act under the control of and for another, the **principal**, in negotiating and making contracts with third persons.[1] The acts of the agent obligate the principal to third persons and give the principal rights against third persons. (See Figure 37-1.)

The term *agency* is frequently used with other meanings. It is sometimes used to denote the fact that one has the right to sell certain products, such as when a dealer is said to possess an automobile agency. In other instances, the term is used to mean an exclusive right to sell certain articles within a given territory. In these cases, however, the dealer is not an agent in the sense of representing the manufacturer.

It is important to be able to distinguish agencies from other relationships because certain rights and duties in agencies are not present in other relationships.

---

[1] Restatement (Second) of Agency § 1; *Union Miniere, S.A. v Parday Corp.*, 521 NE2d 700 (Ind App 1988).

FIGURE 37-1 | *Agency Relationships*

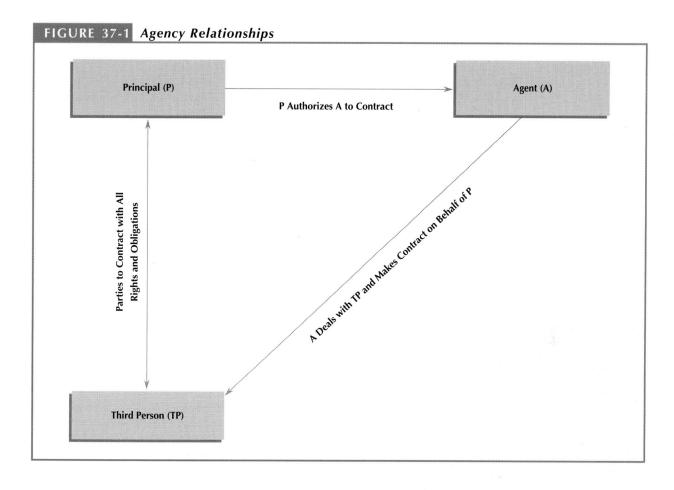

(a) EMPLOYEES AND INDEPENDENT CONTRACTORS   Control and authority are characteristics that distinguish ordinary employees and independent contractors from agents.

(1) Employees.   An agent is distinguished from an ordinary employee who is
not hired to represent the employer in making contracts with third persons.
It is possible, however, for the same person to be both an agent and an employee.
For Example, the driver for a spring water delivery service is an agent in making
contracts between the company and its customers but is an employee with respect
to the work of delivering products.

independent contractor
contractor who undertakes
to perform a specified task
according to the terms of a
contract but over whom the
other contracting party has
no control except as
provided for by the contract.

(2) Independent Contractors.   An **independent contractor** is bound by a contract
to produce a certain result—for example, to build a house. The actual performance
of the work is controlled by the contractor, not the owner. An agent or employee
differs from an independent contractor in that the principal or employer has the
right to control the agent or employee, but not the contractor, in the performance
of the work. **For Example,** Ned and Tracy Seizer contract with Fox Building
Company to build a new home on Hilton Head Island, South Carolina, according
to referenced plans and specifications. Individuals hired by Fox to work on the
home are subject to the authority and control of Fox, the independent contractor,
not the Seizers. However, Ned and Tracy could decide to build the home themselves, hiring two individuals from nearby Beaufort, Ted Chase and Marty
Bromley, to do the work the Seizers will direct each day. Because Ted and Marty

would be employees of the Seizers, the Seizers would be held responsible for any wrongs committed by these employees within the scope of their employment. As a general rule, on the other hand, the Seizers are not responsible for the torts of Fox, the independent contractor, and the contractor's employees. A "right to control" test determines whether an individual is an agent, an employee, or an independent contractor.[2]

CASE SUMMARY

Why Some Businesses Use Independent Agents Rather than Employees!

FACTS: Patricia Yelverton died from injuries sustained when an automobile owned and driven by Joseph Lamm crossed the center line of a roadway and struck the automobile driven by Yelverton. Yelverton's executor brought suit against Lamm and Lamm's alleged employer, Premier Industrial Products Inc. The relationship between Lamm and Premier was governed by a written contract entitled "Independent Agent Agreement," in which Lamm, as "Independent Agent," was given the right to sell Premier's products in a designated territory. The agreement provided that all orders were subject to acceptance by Premier and were not binding on Premier until so accepted. Lamm was paid by commission only. He was allowed to work on a self-determined schedule, retain assistants at his own expense, and sell the products of other companies not in competition with Premier. The executor claimed Lamm was an agent or employee of Premier. Premier stated Lamm was an independent contractor.

DECISION: Judgment for Premier. Lamm had no authority to make contracts for Premier but simply took orders. Therefore, he was not an agent. Lamm was not an employee of Premier. Premier had no right to control the way he performed his work and did not in fact do so. Lamm was an independent contractor. [**Yelverton v Lamm, 380 SE2d 621 (NC App 1989)**]

A person who appears to be an independent contractor may in fact be so controlled by the other party that the contractor is regarded as an agent of, or employee of, the controlling person. **For Example,** Pierce, who was under contract to Brookville Carriers, Inc., was involved in a tractor-trailer/car collision with Rich and others. Pierce owned the tractor involved in the accident on a lease from Brookville but could use it only to haul freight for Brookville; he had no authority to carry freight on his own, and all of his operating authority belonged to Brookville. The "owner/operator" was deemed an employee rather than independent contractor for purposes of assessing the liability of the employer.[3] The separate identity of an independent contractor may be concealed so that the public believes that it is dealing with the principal. When this situation occurs, the principal is liable as though the contractor were an agent or employee.

2. CLASSIFICATION OF AGENTS

special agent agent authorized to transact a specific transaction or to do a specific act.

A **special agent** is authorized by the principal to handle a definite business transaction or to do a specific act. One who is authorized by another to purchase a particular house is a special agent.

---

[2] *NE Ohio College of Massotherapy v Burek*, 759 NE2d 869 (Ohio App 2001).
[3] *Rich v Brookville Carriers, Inc.*, 256 F Supp 2d 26 (D Me 2003).

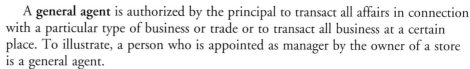

general agent agent authorized by the principal to transact all affairs in connection with a particular type of business or trade or to transact all business at a certain place.

universal agent agent authorized by the principal to do all acts that can lawfully be delegated to a representative.

interest in the authority form of agency in which an agent has been given or paid for the right to exercise authority.

interest in the subject matter form of agency in which an agent is given an interest in the property with which that agent is dealing.

A **general agent** is authorized by the principal to transact all affairs in connection with a particular type of business or trade or to transact all business at a certain place. To illustrate, a person who is appointed as manager by the owner of a store is a general agent.

A **universal agent** is authorized by the principal to do all acts that can be delegated lawfully to a representative. This form of agency arises when a person absent because of being in the military service gives another person a blanket power of attorney to do anything that must be done during such absence.

3. AGENCY COUPLED WITH AN INTEREST

An agent has an **interest in the authority** when consideration has been given or paid for the right to exercise the authority. To illustrate, when a lender, in return for making a loan of money, is given, as security, authority to collect rents due the borrower and to apply those rents to the payment of the debt, the lender becomes the borrower's agent with an interest in the authority given to collect the rents.

An agent has an **interest in the subject matter** when, for a consideration, she is given an interest in the property with which she is dealing. Hence, when the agent is authorized to sell property of the principal and is given a lien on such property as security for a debt owed to her by the principal, she has an interest in the subject matter.

B   CREATING THE AGENCY

An agency may arise by appointment, conduct, ratification, or operation of law.

4. AUTHORIZATION BY APPOINTMENT

express authorization authorization of an agent to perform a certain act.

power of attorney written authorization to an agent by the principal.

attorney in fact agent authorized to act for another under a power of attorney.

The usual method of creating an agency is by **express authorization;** that is, a person is appointed to act for, or on behalf of, another.

In most instances, the authorization of the agent may be oral. However, some appointments must be made in a particular way. A majority of the states, by statute, require the appointment of an agent to be in writing when the agency is created to acquire or dispose of any interest in land. A written authorization of agency is called a **power of attorney.** An agent acting under a power of attorney is referred to as an **attorney in fact.**[4]

5. AUTHORIZATION BY CONDUCT

Conduct consistent with the existence of an agency relationship may be sufficient to show authorization. The principal may have such dealing with third persons as to cause them to believe that the "agent" has authority. Thus, if the owner of a store places another person in charge, third persons may assume that the person in charge is the agent for the owner in that respect. The "agent" then appears to be authorized and is said to have *apparent authority*, and the principal is estopped from contradicting the appearance that has been created.[5]

The term *apparent authority* is used when there is only the appearance of authority but no actual authority, and that appearance of authority was created by the principal.

[4] *Lamb v Scott*, 643 So 2d 972 (Ala 1994).
[5] *Intersparex Leddin KG v AL-Haddad*, 852 SW2d 245 (Tenn App 1992).

The test for the existence of apparent authority is an objective test determined by the principal's outward manifestations through words or conduct that lead a third person reasonably to believe that the "agent" has authority. A principal's express restriction on authority not made known to a third person is no defense.

Apparent authority extends to all acts that a person of ordinary prudence, familiar with business usages and the particular business, would be justified in believing that the agent has authority to perform. It is essential to the concept of apparent authority that the third person reasonably believe that the agent has authority. The mere placing of property in the possession of another does not give that person either actual or apparent authority to sell the property.

6. AGENCY BY RATIFICATION

An agent may attempt, on behalf of the principal, to do an act that was not authorized, or a person who is not the agent of another may attempt to act as such an agent. Generally, in such cases, the principal for whom the agent claimed to act has the choice of ignoring the transaction or of ratifying it. Ordinarily, any unauthorized act may be ratified.

(a) INTENTION TO RATIFY   Initially, ratification is a question of intention. Just as in the case of authorization, when there is a question of whether the principal authorized the agent, there is a question of whether the principal intended to approve or ratify the action of the unauthorized agent.

The intention to ratify may be expressed in words, or it may be found in conduct indicating an intention to ratify.[6] **For Example**, James Reiner signed a five-year lease of commercial space on 320 West Main Street in Avon, Connecticut, because his father Calvin was away on vacation, and the owner, Robert Udolf, told James that if he did not come in and sign the lease, his father would lose the opportunity to rent the space in question. James was aware that his father had an interest in the space, and while telling Robert several times that he had no authority, James did sign his name to the lease. In fact, his father took occupancy of the space and paid rent for three years and then abandoned the space. James is not liable on the remainder of the lease because the owner knew at the time of signing that James did not have authority to act. Although he did not sign the lease, Calvin ratified the lease signed by James by his conduct of moving into the space and doing business there for three years with full knowledge of all material facts relating to the transaction. The owner, therefore, had to bring suit against Calvin, not James.[7]

(b) CONDITIONS FOR RATIFICATION   In addition to the intent to ratify, expressed in some instances with a certain formality, the following conditions must be satisfied for the intention to take effect as a ratification:

1. The agent must have purported to act on behalf of or as agent for the identified principal.
2. The principal must have been capable of authorizing the act both at the time of the act and at the time it was ratified.
3. The principal must have full knowledge of all material facts.

---

[6] *Streetscenes, LLC v ITC Entertainment Group, Inc.*, 126 Cal Rptr 2d 754 (Cal App 2002).
[7] *Udolf v Reiner*, 2000 Conn Super LEXIS 1252.

It is not always necessary, however, to show that the principal had actual knowledge. Knowledge will be imputed if a principal knows of other facts that would lead a prudent person to make inquiries or if that knowledge can be inferred from the knowledge of other facts or from a course of business. **For Example,** Stacey, without authorization but knowing that William needed money, contracted to sell one of William's paintings to Courtney for $298. Stacey told William about the contract that evening; William said nothing and helped her wrap the painting in a protective plastic wrap for delivery. A favorable newspaper article about William's art appeared the following morning and dramatically increased the value of all of his paintings. William cannot recover the painting from Courtney on the theory that he never authorized the sale because he ratified the unauthorized contract made by Stacey by his conduct in helping her wrap the painting with full knowledge of the terms of the sale. The effect is a legally binding contract between William and Courtney.

(c) EFFECT OF RATIFICATION   When an unauthorized act is ratified, the effect is the same as though the act had been originally authorized. Ordinarily, this means that the principal and the third party are bound by the contract made by the agent.[8] When the principal ratifies the act of the unauthorized person, such ratification releases that person from the liability that would otherwise be imposed for having acted without authority.

7. PROVING THE AGENCY RELATIONSHIP

The burden of proving the existence of an agency relationship rests on the person who seeks to benefit by such proof. The third person who desires to bind the principal because of the act of an alleged agent has the burden of proving that the latter person was in fact the authorized agent of the principal and possessed the authority to do the act in question.[9]

C   AGENT'S AUTHORITY

When there is an agent, it is necessary to determine the scope of the agent's authority.

8. SCOPE OF AGENT'S AUTHORITY

The scope of an agent's authority may be determined from the express words of the principal to the agent or it may be implied from the principal's words or conduct or from the customs of the trade or business.

(a) EXPRESS AUTHORITY   If the principal tells the agent to perform a certain act, the agent has express authority to do so. Express authority can be given orally or in writing.

incidental authority
authority of an agent that is reasonably necessary to execute express authority.

(b) INCIDENTAL AUTHORITY   An agent has implied **incidental authority** to perform any act reasonably necessary to execute the express authority given to the agent. **For Example,** if the principal authorizes the agent to purchase goods without

---

[8] *Bill McCurley Chevrolet v Rutz*, 808 P2d 1167 (Wash App 1991).
[9] *Cummings, Inc. v Nelson*, 115 P3d 536 (Alaska 2005).

furnishing funds to the agent to pay for them, the agent has the implied incidental authority to purchase the goods on credit.[10]

customary authority
authority of an agent to do any act that, according to the custom of the community, usually accompanies the transaction for which the agent is authorized to act.

apparent authority
appearance of authority created by the principal's words or conduct.

(c) Customary Authority An agent has implied **customary authority** to do any act that, according to the custom of the community, usually accompanies the transaction for which the agent is authorized to act. An agent who has express authority to receive payments from third persons, for example, has the implied customary authority to issue receipts.

(d) Apparent Authority A person has **apparent authority** as an agent when the principal's words or conduct leads a third person to reasonably believe that the person has that authority and the third person relies on that appearance.[11]

CASE SUMMARY

CSX Gets Railroaded by Albert Arillotta

FACTS: Recovery Express and Interstate Demolition (IDEC) are two separate corporations located at the same business address in Boston. On August 22, 2003, Albert Arillotta, a "partner" at IDEC, sent an e-mail to Len Whitehead, Jr. of CSX Transportation expressing an interest in buying "rail cars as scrap." Arillotta represented himself to be "from interstate demolition and recovery express" in the e-mail. The e-mail address from which he sent his inquiry was **albert@recoveryexpress.com**. Arillotta went to the CSX rail yard, disassembled the cars, and transported them away. Thereafter CSX sent invoices for the scrap rail cars totaling $115,757.36 addressed to IDEC at its Boston office shared with Recovery Express. Whitehead believed Arillotta was authorized to act for Recovery Express, based on the e-mail's domain name, recoveryexpress.com. Recovery claims that Arillotta never worked for it. Recovery's President Thomas Trafton allowed the "fledgling" company to use telephone, fax, and e-mail services at its offices but never shared anything—assets, funds, books of business, or financials with IDEC—CSX sued Recovery for the invoice amount on the doctrine of "apparent authority." IDEC is now defunct. Recovery claims that Arillotta never worked for it and that it is not liable.

DECISION: Judgment for Recovery. Issuance of an e-mail address with Recovery's domain name to an individual who shared office space with Recovery did not give the individual, Albert Arillotta, apparent authority to enter contracts on Recovery's behalf. No reasonable person could conclude that Arillotta had apparent authority on the basis of an e-mail domain name by itself. Given the anonymity of the Internet, the court warned businesses to take additional action to verify a purported agent's authority to make a deal. [**CSX Transportation, Inc. v Recovery Express, Inc.**, 415 F Supp 2d 6 (D Mass 2006)].

9. EFFECT OF PROPER EXERCISE OF AUTHORITY

When an agent with authority properly makes a contract with a third person that purports to bind the principal, there is by definition a binding contract between the principal and the third person. The agent is not a party to this contract. Consequently, when the owner of goods is the principal, the owner's agent is not liable for breach

[10] *Badger v Paulson Investment Co.*, 803 P2d 1178 (Ore 1991).
[11] *Alexander v Chandler*, 179 SW2d 385 (Mo App 2005).

E-COMMERCE AND CYBERLAW

Agency Law in Cyberspace

An *electronic agent* is a computer program or an electronic or other automated means used independently to initiate an action or respond to electronic records or performances in whole or in part without review or action by an individual at the time of the action or response.* An automated teller machine (ATM) is such an agent for the bank that owns the ATM, and the bank is the principal. Electronic agents are fabricated and do not have the human qualities attributable to human agents. Under the law of agency, agents themselves may be liable for their torts or for breach of contract when they exceed their authority. Of course, electronic agents, being nonhuman, are never liable for any action. It is the electronic agent's principal that may be liable. The law governing electronic agents is just beginning to develop because such agents are now an important part of e-commerce. Basic principles of agency, contract, and tort law along with judicial common sense will form the basis for the resolution of developing controversies.

Litigation has often arisen over the scope of a human agent's authority. The scope of an electronic agent's authority may well be an issue. Julie Frisoli placed an online order for a Taylor Made golf club with an Internet sporting goods supply company that serves both retail and wholesale customers. Because of a computer glitch that picked her up as a wholesale customer, the electronic agent listed the price for Julie as "$300 less a 20 percent discount," making the amount owed $240 plus shipping costs and tax, COD. Julie clicked her acceptance of the purchase online and was delighted that she had purchased it on sale. A half hour later, a supervisor discovered and "corrected" the mistaken discount intended for wholesale buyers only, raising the COD bill to the $300 retail price plus shipping and taxes. Julie insists she is legally entitled to the $240 price. Her position is correct. From an agency law perspective, electronic agents have authority to make contracts.** As to the third person, Julie, the principal sporting goods supply company held out the electronic agent as having authority to make the contract. Under contract law, the unilateral mistake of the agent is not a basis to set aside the contract when Julie did not know that a mistake was made.

---

*Electronic Signatures in Global and National Commerce Act, 15 USC § 7006(3).

**Uniform Electronic Transactions Act, § 14(1).

of warranty with respect to the goods "sold" by the agent. The owner-principal, not the agent, was the "seller" in the sales transaction.

 10. DUTY TO ASCERTAIN EXTENT OF AGENT'S AUTHORITY

A third person who deals with a person claiming to be an agent cannot rely on the statements made by the agent concerning the extent of authority.[12] If the agent is not authorized to perform the act or is not even the agent of the principal, the transaction between the alleged agent and the third person will have no legal effect between the principal and the third person.

---

[12] *Breed v Hughes Aircraft Col.*, 35 Fed App 864 (Fed Cir 2002).

Third persons who deal with an agent whose authority is limited to a special purpose are bound at their peril to find out the extent of the agent's authority. An attorney is such an agent. Unless the client holds the attorney out as having greater authority than usual, the attorney has no authority to settle a claim without approval from the client.

(a) AGENT'S ACTS ADVERSE TO PRINCIPAL The third person who deals with an agent is required to take notice of any acts that are clearly adverse to the interest of the principal. Thus, if the agent is obviously using funds of the principal for the agent's personal benefit, persons dealing with the agent should recognize that the agent may be acting without authority and that they are dealing with the agent at their peril.

The only certain way that third persons can protect themselves is to inquire of the principal whether the agent is in fact the agent of the principal and has the necessary authority. If the principal states that the agent has the authority, the principal cannot later deny this authorization unless the subject matter is such that an authorization must be in writing to be binding.

---

11. LIMITATIONS ON AGENT'S AUTHORITY

A person who has knowledge of a limitation on the agent's authority cannot ignore that limitation. When the third person knows that the authority of the agent depends on whether financing has been obtained, the principal is not bound by the act of the agent if the financing in fact was not obtained. If the authority of the agent is based on a writing and the third person knows that there is such a writing, the third person is charged with knowledge of limitations contained in it.

(a) "OBVIOUS" LIMITATIONS In some situations, it may be obvious to third persons that they are dealing with an agent whose authority is limited. When third persons know that they are dealing with a representative of a government agency, they should recognize that such a person will ordinarily have limited authority. Third persons should recognize that a contract made with such an officer or representative may not be binding unless ratified by the principal.

The federal government places the risk on any individual making arrangements with the government to accurately ascertain that the government agent is within the bounds of his or her authority.

CASE SUMMARY

Humlen Was Had

FACTS: The FBI approached Humlen for assistance in securing the conviction of a drug trafficker. Humlen executed an agreement with the FBI to formalize his status as an informant. The agreement he signed contained compensation figures significantly less than those he had been promised by the FBI agents with whom he was dealing. Humlen claims that five agents repeatedly assured him that he would receive the extra compensation they had discussed with him, despite the wording of the contract. It was explained that the agreement had to be "couched" in that way because it was a discoverable document in any future criminal prosecution

> ## CASE SUMMARY
>
> *continued*
>
> and thus could be used to destroy his credibility. Based on the information provided by Humlen, an arrest was made, and Humlen sought the remainder of his promised monetary reward from the FBI. The FBI refused to pay him any more than the contract stipulated. When no additional payment was forthcoming, Humlen sued the U.S. government.
>
> **DECISION:** Judgment for the United States. The government, unlike private parties, cannot be bound by the apparent authority of its agents. When an agent exceeds his or her authority, the government can disavow the agent's words and is not bound by an implied contract. As a general rule, FBI agents lack the requisite actual authority—either express or implied—to contractually bind the United States to remit rewards to confidential informants. Moreover, Humlen's claims directly collide with the plain language of the agreement. [**Humlen v United States, 49 Fed Cl 497 (2001)**]

(b) SECRET LIMITATIONS   If the principal has clothed an agent with authority to perform certain acts but the principal gives secret instructions that limit the agent's authority, the third person is allowed to take the authority of the agent at its face value. The third person is not bound by the secret limitations of which the third person has no knowledge.

 ## DUTIES AND LIABILITIES OF PRINCIPAL AND AGENT

The creation of the principal-agent relationship gives rise to duties and liabilities.

12. DUTIES AND LIABILITIES OF AGENT DURING AGENCY

While the agency relationship exists, the agent owes certain duties to the principal.

(a) LOYALTY   An agent must be loyal or faithful to the principal. The agent must not obtain any secret benefit from the agency. If the principal is seeking to buy or rent property, the agent cannot secretly obtain the property and then sell or lease it to the principal at a profit.

An agent who owns property cannot sell it to the principal without disclosing that ownership to the principal. If disclosure is not made, the principal may avoid the contract even if the agent's conduct did not cause the principal any financial loss. Alternatively, the principal can approve the transaction and sue the agent for any secret profit obtained by the agent.

A contract is voidable by the principal if the agent who was employed to sell the property purchases the property, either directly or indirectly, without full disclosure to the principal.

An agent cannot act as agent for both parties to a transaction unless both know of the dual capacity and agree to it. If the agent does act in this capacity without the consent of both parties, any principal who did not know of the agent's double status can avoid the transaction.

An agent must not accept secret gifts or commissions from third persons in connection with the agency. If the agent does so, the principal may sue the agent for those gifts or commissions. Such practices are condemned because the judgment of the agent may be influenced by the receipt of gifts or commissions.

It is a violation of an agent's duty of loyalty to make and retain secret profits.

CASE SUMMARY

Was Grappolini a "Bad Boy"?

FACTS: Arthur Frigo, an adjunct professor at the Kellogg Graduate School of Management, formed Lucini Italia Co. (Lucini) to import and sell premium extra virgin olive oil and other products from Italy. Lucini's officers hired Guiseppe Grappolini as their olive oil supplier. They also hired him as their consultant, Grappolini signed an exclusivity agreement and a confidentiality agreement acknowledging the confidential nature of Lucini's product development, plans, and strategies. Grappolini was "branded" as a "master cultivator" in Lucini's literature and commercials.

In 1998, Lucini and Grappolini, as his consultant, discussed adding a line of extra virgin olive oils blended with "essential oils," for example, natural extracts such as lemon and garlic. It spent more than $800,000 developing the market information, testing flavors, designing labels and packaging, creating recipes, and generating trade secrets for the new products. Vegetal-Progress s.r.l. (Vegetal) was identified as the only company in Italy that was capable of producing the superior products Lucini sought, and Grappolini was assigned responsibility to obtain an exclusive supply contract with Vegetal.

In direct contravention of his representations to Lucini, Grappolini secretly negotiated an exclusive supply contract for the Grappolini Co., not for Lucini. Moreover, Grappolini Co. began to sell flavored olive oils in the United States, which coincided with Lucini's market research and recipe development that had been disclosed to Grappolini. When Lucini officers contacted Vegetal, they acknowledged that Grappolini was a "bad boy" in procuring the contract for his own company rather than for Lucini, but they would not renege on the contract. Lucini sued Grappolini.

DECISION: Judgment for Lucini. Grappolini was Lucini's agent and owed Lucini a duty to advance Lucini's interests, not his own. When he obtained an exclusive supply agreement with Vegetal for the Grappolini Co. instead of Lucini, he was disloyal and breached his fiduciary duties. As a result, Lucini suffered lost profits and damages of $4.17 million. In addition to these damages, Grappolini was ordered to pay $1,000,000 in punitive damages to deter similar acts in the future. Additionally, a permanent injunction was issued prohibiting Grappolini from using Lucini's trade secrets. [**Lucini Italia Co. v Grappolini, 2003 WL 1989605 (ND Ill 2003)**]

An agent is, of course, prohibited from aiding the competitors of a principal or disclosing to them information relating to the business of the principal. It is also a breach of duty for the agent to knowingly deceive a principal.[13]

(b) OBEDIENCE AND PERFORMANCE   An agent is under a duty to obey all lawful instructions.[14] The agent is required to perform the services specified for the period and in the way specified. An agent who does not do so is liable to the principal for any harm caused. For example, if an agent is instructed to take cash payments only but accepts a check in payment, the agent is liable for the loss caused the principal if a check is dishonored by nonpayment.

---

[13] *Koontz v Rosener*, 787 P2d 192 (Colo App 1990).
[14] *Stanford v Neiderer*, 341 SE2d 892 (Ga App 1986).

(c) Reasonable Care   It is the duty of an agent to act with the care that a reasonable person would exercise under the circumstances. **For Example,** Ethel Wilson applied for fire insurance for her house with St. Paul Reinsurance Co., Ltd., through her agent Club Services Corp. She thought she was fully covered. Unbeknown to her, however, St. Paul had refused coverage and returned her premium to Club Services, who did not refund it to Ms. Wilson or inform her that coverage had been denied. Fire destroyed her garage and St. Paul denied coverage. Litigation resulted, and St. Paul ended up expending $305,406 to settle the Wilson matter. Thereafter, St. Paul successfully sued Club Services Corp. under basic agency law principles that an agent (Club Services) is liable to its principal for all damages resulting from the agent's failure to discharge its duties.[15] In addition, if the agent possesses a special skill, as in the case of a broker or an attorney, the agent must exercise that skill.

(d) Accounting   An agent must account to the principal for all property or money belonging to the principal that comes into the agent's possession. The agent must, within a reasonable time, give notice of collections made and render an accurate account of all receipts and expenditures. The agency agreement may state at what intervals or on what dates such accountings are to be made. An agent must keep the principal's property and money separate and distinct from that of the agent.

(e) Information   It is the duty of an agent to keep the principal informed of all facts relating to the agency that are relevant to protecting the principal's interests.[16]

13. DUTIES AND LIABILITIES OF AGENT AFTER TERMINATION OF AGENCY

When the agency relationship ends, the duties of the agent continue only to the extent necessary to perform prior obligations. For example, the agent must return to the former principal any property that had been entrusted to the agent for the purpose of the agency. With the exception of such "winding-up" duties, the agency relationship is terminated, and the former agent can deal with the principal as freely as with a stranger.[17]

14. DUTIES AND LIABILITIES OF PRINCIPAL TO AGENT

The principal must perform the contract, compensate the agent for services, make reimbursement for proper expenditures and, under certain circumstances, must indemnify the agent for loss.

(a) Employment According to Terms of Contract   When the contract is for a specified time, the principal is obligated to permit the agent to act as agent for the term of the contract. Exceptions are made for just cause or contract provisions that permit the principal to terminate the agency sooner. If the principal gives the agent an exclusive right to act in that capacity, the principal cannot give anyone else the authority to act as agent, nor may the principal do the act to which the exclusive agent's authority relates. **For Example,** if Jill Baker gives Brett Stamos the exclusive

---

[15] *St. Paul Reinsurance Co., Ltd. v Club Services Corp.,* 2002 US App LEXIS 2277.

[16] Restatement (Second) of Agency § 381; *Lumberman's Mutual Ins. Co. v Franey Muha Alliant Ins.,* 388 F Supp 2d 292 (SDNY 2005).

[17] *Corron & Black of Illinois, Inc. v Magner,* 494 NE2d 785 (Ill App 1986).

right for six months to sell her house, she cannot give another real estate agent the right to sell it during the six-month period or undertake to sell the house herself. If the principal or another agent sells the house, the exclusive agent is entitled to full compensation just as though the act had been performed by the exclusive agent.

CASE SUMMARY

Would You Ever Sign an Exclusive Listing Agreement after Reading This Case?

FACTS: The Holzmans signed an exclusive listing agreement with the Blum real estate brokerage firm. The contract provided that the Holzmans had an obligation to pay a commission "if they enter into a written agreement to sell the property to any person during the term of this exclusive listing agreement." The Holzmans entered into a written agreement to sell their three-story brick house, containing eight bedrooms and nine full baths and located on several acres of land in Baltimore County, for $715,000 to the Noravians. On the advice of their attorney, the Holzmans included a default provision in this contract that stated in the event of default by the Holzmans, the Noravians' only remedy would be a refund of their deposit. Subsequently, Gil and Ellen Stern offered $850,000 for the property, and the Holzmans canceled their contract with the Noravians and returned the deposit. After the exclusive listing period expired, the Holzmans executed a contract to sell their property to the Sterns at the offered price of $850,000, with the contract calling for the Holzmans to pay half of the real estate fee to Blum and half to a cooperating broker. Blum was in fact paid this fee of $21,500. Thereafter, Blum brought suit against Holzman seeking the full commission for the Noravian contract under the exclusive listing agreement. From a judgment for Blum for the full amount of the commission, less an offset for the commission paid Blum in the subsequent sale to the Sterns, plus attorney fees, both parties appealed, with Blum objecting to the offset.

DECISION: Judgment of the trial court was affirmed. In his testimony, Mr. Blum acknowledged that when the Holzmans decided to pursue the Sterns' offer, he did not advise them about their obligation to pay the full commission under the Noravian contract. Indeed, Mr. Blum testified that he was "advised by . . . [counsel] not to say anything to the Holzmans." However, the exclusive listing agreement clearly addressed the terms and conditions under which the Holzmans would owe the broker a fee, and Blum had no *legal* duty to remind them of the terms of the agreement that they had signed.

In a footnote, the court pointed out that given Mr. Blum's testimony as to "his desire to do the best" for the clients, "it is somewhat surprising that the Broker, in effect, opposed its client's desire to obtain the highest possible purchase prices for the Property. Similarly, in pursuing its contract claim against the Sellers, we assume the Broker fully considered the impact such a suit might have on its reputation as an advocate for its customers." [**Holzman v Blum, 726 A2d 818 (Md App 1999)**]

(b) COMPENSATION   The principal must pay the agent the agreed compensation.[18] If the parties have not fixed the amount of the compensation by their agreement but intended that the agent should be paid, the agent may recover the customary compensation for such services. If there is no established compensation, the agent may recover the reasonable value of the services rendered.

---

[18] *American Chocolates, Inc. v Mascot Pecan Co., Inc.*, 592 So 2d 93 (Miss 1992).

(1) Repeating Transactions.   In certain industries, third persons make repeated transactions with the principal. In these cases, the agent who made the original contract with the third person commonly receives a certain compensation or percentage of commissions on all subsequent renewal or additional contracts. In the insurance business, for example, the insurance agent obtaining the policyholder for the insurer receives a substantial portion of the first year's premiums and then receives a smaller percentage of the premiums paid by the policyholder in subsequent years.

(2) Postagency Transactions.   An agent is not ordinarily entitled to compensation in connection with transactions, such as sales or renewals of insurance policies, occurring after the termination of the agency even if the postagency transactions are the result of the agent's former activities. However, if the parties' employment contract calls for such compensation, it must be paid. **For Example,** real estate agent Laura McLane's contract called for her to receive $1.50 for every square foot the Atlanta Committee for the Olympic Games, Inc. (ACOG), leased at an Atlanta building; and even though she had been terminated at the time ACOG executed a lease amendment for 164,412 additional square feet, she was contractually entitled to a $246,618 commission.[19]

 ## TERMINATION OF AGENCY

An agency may be terminated by the act of one or both of the parties to the agency agreement or by operation of law. When the authority of an agent is terminated, the agent loses all right to act for the principal.

15. TERMINATION BY ACT OF PARTIES

The duration of the agency relationship is commonly stated in the contract creating the relationship. In most cases, either party has the power to terminate the agency relationship at any time. However, the terminating party may be liable for damages to the other if the termination is in violation of the agency contract.

When a principal terminates an agent's authority, it is not effective until the agent receives the notice. Because a known agent will have the appearance of still being an agent, notice must be given to third persons of the termination, and the agent may have the power to bind the principal and third persons until this notice 'is given.

16. TERMINATION BY OPERATION OF LAW

The agency relationship is a personal one, and anything that renders one of the parties incapable of performing will result in the termination of the relationship by operation of law. The death of either the principal or the agent ordinarily terminates the authority of an agent automatically even if the death is unknown to the other.[20]

An agency is also terminated by operation of law on the (1) insanity of the principal or agent, (2) bankruptcy of the principal or agent, (3) impossibility of performance, such as the destruction of the subject matter, or (4) when the country of the principal is at war with that of the agent.

---

[19] *McLane v Atlanta Market Center Management Co.,* 486 SE2d 30 (Ga App 1997).
[20] *New York Life Ins. Co. v Estate of Haelen,* 521 NYS2d 970 (Sup Ct AD 1987).

CASE SUMMARY

Missing Out by Minutes

FACTS: William Moore, a fire chief for the city of San Francisco, suffered severe head injuries in a fall while fighting a fire. Moore sued the building owner, Lera, for negligence. The attorneys for the parties held a conference and reached a settlement at 5:15 P.M. Unknown to them, Moore had died at 4:50 P.M. on that day. Was the settlement agreement binding?

DECISION: No. The death of either the principal or the agent terminates the agency. Thus, the death of a client terminates the authority of his agent to act on his behalf. Because Moore died at 4:50 P.M., his attorney no longer had authority to act on his behalf, and the settlement was not enforceable. [**Moore v Lera Development Inc., 274 Cal Rptr 658 (Cal App 1990)**]

17. DISABILITY OF THE PRINCIPAL UNDER THE UDPAA

The Uniform Durable Power of Attorney Act (UDPAA) permits the creation of an agency by specifying that "this power of attorney shall not be affected by subsequent disability or incapacity of the principal." Alternatively, the UDPAA permits the agency to come into existence upon the disability or incapacity of the principal. For this to be effective, the principal must designate the attorney in fact in writing. The writing must contain words showing the intent of the principal that the authority conferred shall continue notwithstanding the disability or incapacity of the principal. The UDPAA, which has been adopted by most states,[21] changes the common law and the general rule that insanity of the principal terminates the agent's authority to act for the principal. Society today recognizes that it may be in the best interest of a principal and good for the business environment for a principal to designate another as an attorney in fact to act for the principal when the principal becomes incapacitated.[22] It may be prudent to grant durable powers of attorney to different persons for property matters and for health care decisions.

Durable powers of attorney grant only those powers that are specified in the instrument. A durable power of attorney may be terminated by revocation by a competent principal and by the death of the principal.

CASE SUMMARY

Broad Powers . . . But There is a Limit, Lucille

FACTS: On May 31, 2000, Thomas Graham made his niece Lucille Morrison his attorney in fact by executing a durable power of attorney. It was notarized and filed at the Registry of Deeds. The power of attorney granted Lucille broad powers and discretion in Graham's

---

[21] The Uniform Durable Power of Attorney Act has been adopted in some fashion in all states except Connecticut, Florida, Georgia, Illinois, Indiana, Louisiana, and Missouri.

[22] The Uniform Probate Code and the Uniform Durable Power of Attorney Act provide for the coexistence of durable powers and guardians or conservators. These acts allow the attorney in fact to continue to manage the principal's financial affairs while the court-appointed fiduciary takes the place of the principal in overseeing the actions of the attorney in fact. See *Rice v Flood*, 768 SW2d 57 (Ky 1989).

CASE SUMMARY

continued

affairs. However, it did not contain express authority to make gifts. On October 26, 2000, Lucille conveyed 11.92 acres of property valued at between $400,000 and $700,000 to herself based on consideration of services rendered to the principal, Thomas Graham. On June 5, 2001, Lucille, as attorney in fact for Graham, conveyed Graham's house in Charlotte to her son Ladd Morrison. On June 20, 2001, she conveyed Graham's Oakview Terrace property to her brother John Hallman for $3,000 to pay for an attorney to defend Graham in a competency proceeding. Thomas Graham died on August 7, 2001, and his estate sued to set aside the deeds, alleging Lucille's breach of fiduciary duties. After a judgment for the defendants, the estate appealed.

DECISION: Judgment for the estate regarding the 11.92 acre parcel of land Lucille conveyed to herself. When an attorney in fact conveys property to herself based on consideration of services rendered to the principal, the consideration must reflect a fair and reasonable price when compared to the market value of the property. There was no testimony regarding the value of Lucille's services compared to the value of the real property. The deed must be set aside. The conveyance of Graham's home to Ladd Morrison was a gift that was not authorized by her power of attorney and must be set aside. Lucille had authority to sell the principal's property to John Hallman to obtain funds to pay an attorney to represent the principal. The estate's claim of conversion regarding this sale was denied. [**Estate of Graham v Morrison, 607 SE2d 295 (NC App 2005)**]

18. TERMINATION OF AGENCY COUPLED WITH AN INTEREST

An agency coupled with an interest is an exception to the general rule as to the termination of an agency. Such an agency cannot be revoked by the principal before the expiration of the interest. It is not terminated by the death or insanity of either the principal or the agent.

19. PROTECTION OF AGENT FROM TERMINATION OF AUTHORITY

The modern world of business has developed several methods of protecting an agent from the termination of authority for any reason.[23]

These methods include the use of an exclusive agency contract, a secured transaction, an escrow deposit, a standby letter of agreement, or a guarantee agreement.

20. EFFECT OF TERMINATION OF AUTHORITY

If the principal revokes the agency, the authority to act for the principal is not terminated until the agent receives notice of revocation. As between the principal and the agent, the right of the agent to bind the principal to third persons generally ends immediately upon the termination of the agent's authority. This termination is effective without giving notice to third persons.

When the agency is terminated by the act of the principal, notice must be given to third persons. If this notice is not given, the agent may have the power to make contracts that will bind the principal and third persons. This rule is predicated on the theory that a known agent will have the appearance of still being the agent unless

---

[23] These methods generally replace the concept of an agency coupled with an interest because of the greater protection given to the agent. Typically, the rights of the agent under these modern devices cannot be defeated by the principal, by operation of law, or by claims of other creditors.

notice to the contrary is given to third persons. **For Example,** Seltzer owns property in Boca Raton that he uses for the month of February and leases the remainder of the year. O'Neil has been Seltzer's rental agent for the past seven years, renting to individuals like Ed Tucker under a power of attorney that gives him authority to lease the property for set seasonal and off-season rates. O'Neil's right to bind Seltzer on a rental agreement ended when Seltzer faxed O'Neil a revocation of the power of attorney on March 1. A rental contract with Ed Tucker signed by O'Neil on behalf of Seltzer on March 2 will bind Seltzer, however, because O'Neil still appeared to be Seltzer's agent and Tucker had no notice to the contrary.

When the law requires giving notice in order to end the power of the agent to bind the principal, individual notice must be given or mailed to all persons who had prior dealings with the agent. In addition, notice to the general public can be given by publishing in a newspaper of general circulation in the affected geographic area a statement that the agency has been terminated.

If a notice is actually received, the power of the agent is terminated without regard to whether the method of giving notice was proper. Conversely, if proper notice is given, it is immaterial that it does not actually come to the attention of the party notified. Thus, a member of the general public cannot claim that the principal is bound on the ground that the third person did not see the newspaper notice stating that the agent's authority had been terminated.

> SUMMARY

An agency relationship is created by an express or implied agreement by which one person, the agent, is authorized to make contracts with third persons on behalf of, and subject to, the control of another person, the principal. An agent differs from an independent contractor in that the principal, who controls the acts of an agent, does not have control over the details of performance of work by the independent contractor. Likewise, an independent contractor does not have authority to act on behalf of the other contracting party.

A special agent is authorized by the principal to handle a specific business transaction. A general agent is authorized by the principal to transact all business affairs of the principal at a certain place. A universal agent is authorized to perform all acts that can be lawfully delegated to a representative.

The usual method of creating an agency is by express authorization. However, an agency relationship may be found to exist when the principal causes or permits a third person to reasonably believe that an agency relationship exists. In such a case, the "agent" appears to be authorized and is said to have apparent authority.

An unauthorized transaction by an agent for a principal may be ratified by the principal.

An agent acting with authority has the power to bind the principal. The scope of an agent's authority may be determined from the express words of the principal to the agent; this is called *express authority.* An agent has incidental authority to perform any act reasonably necessary to execute the authority given the agent. An agent's authority may be implied so as to enable the agent to perform any act in accordance with the general customs or usages in a business or an industry. This authority is often referred to as customary authority.

The effect of a proper exercise of authority by an agent is to bind the principal and third person to a contract. The agent, not being a party to the contract, is not liable in any respect under the contract. A third person dealing with a person claiming to be an agent has a duty to ascertain the extent of the agent's authority and a duty to take notice of any acts that are clearly adverse to the principal's interests. The third person cannot claim that apparent authority existed when that person has notice that the agent's conduct is adverse to the interests of the principal. A third person who has knowledge of limitations on an agent's authority is bound by those limitations. A third person is not bound by secret limitations.

While the agency relationship exists, the agent owes the principal the duties of (1) being loyal, (2) obeying all lawful instructions, (3) exercising reasonable care, (4) accounting for all property or money belonging to the principal, and (5) informing the principal of all facts relating to the agency that are relevant to the principal's interests. An agency relationship can be terminated by act of either the principal or the agent. However, the terminating party may be liable for damages to the other if the termination is in violation of the agency contract.

Because a known agent will have the appearance of still being an agent, notice must be given to third persons of the termination, and the agent may have the power to bind the principal and third persons until this notice is given.

An agency is terminated by operation of law upon (1) the death of the principal or agent, (2) insanity of the principal or agent, (3) bankruptcy of the principal or agent, (4) impossibility of performance, caused, for example, by the destruction of the subject matter, or (5) war.

In states that have adopted the Uniform Durable Power of Attorney Act (UDPAA), an agency may be created that is not affected by subsequent disability or incapacity of the principal. In UDPAA states, the agency may also come into existence upon the "disability or incapacity of the principal." The designation of an attorney in fact under the UDPAA must be in writing.

> QUESTIONS AND CASE PROBLEMS

1. How does an agent differ from an independent contractor?
2. Compare authorization of an agent by (a) appointment and (b) ratification.
3. Ernest A. Kotsch executed a durable power of attorney when he was 85 years old, giving his son, Ernie, the power to manage and sell his real estate and personal property "and to do all acts necessary for maintaining and caring for [the father] during his lifetime." Thereafter, Kotsch began "keeping company" with a widow, Margaret Gradl. Ernie believed that the widow was attempting to alienate his father from him, and he observed that she was exerting a great deal of influence over his father. Acting under the durable power of attorney and without informing his father, Ernie created the "Kotsch Family Irrevocable Trust," to which he transferred $700,000, the bulk of his father's liquid assets, with the father as grantor and initial beneficiary and Ernie's three children as additional beneficiaries. Ernie named himself trustee. His father sued to avoid the trust. Ernie defended his action on the ground that he had authority to create the trust under the durable power of attorney. Decide. [*Kotsch v Kotsch*, 608 So 2d 879 (Fla App)]
4. Ken Jones, the number-one-ranked prizefighter in his weight class, signed a two-year contract with Howard Stayword. The contract obligated Stayword to represent and promote Jones in all business and professional matters, including the arrangement of fights. For these services, Jones was to pay Stayword 10 percent of gross earnings. After a year, when Stayword proved unsuccessful in arranging a title match with the champion, Jones fired Stayword. During the following year, Jones earned $4 million. Stayword sued Jones for $400,000. Jones defended himself on the basis that a principal has the absolute power at any time to terminate an agency relationship by discharging the agent, so he was not liable to Stayword. Was Jones correct?
5. Paul Strich did business as an optician in Duluth, Minnesota. Paul used only the products of the Plymouth Optical Co., a national manufacturer of optical products and supplies with numerous retail outlets and some franchise arrangements in areas other than Duluth. To increase business, Paul renovated his office and changed the sign on it to read "Plymouth Optical Co." Paul did business this way for more than three years—advertised under that name, paid bills with checks bearing the name of Plymouth Optical Co., and

listed himself in the telephone and city directories by that name. Plymouth immediately became aware of what Paul was doing. However, because Paul used only Plymouth products and Plymouth did not have a franchise in Duluth, it saw no advantage at that time in prohibiting Paul from using the name and losing him as a customer. Paul contracted with the *Duluth Tribune* for advertising, making the contract in the name of Plymouth Optical Co. When the advertising bill was not paid, the *Duluth Tribune* sued Plymouth Optical Co. for payment. Plymouth's defense was that it had never authorized Paul to do business under the name, nor had it authorized him to make a contract with the newspaper. Decide.

6. Record owned a farm that was managed by his agent, Berry, who lived on the farm. Berry hired Wagner to bale the hay and told him to bill Record for this work. Wagner did so and was paid by Record. By the summer of the following year, the agency had been terminated by Record, but Berry remained in possession as tenant of the farm and nothing appeared changed. Late in the summer, Berry asked Wagner to bale the hay as he had done the previous year and bill Record for the work. He did so, but Record refused to pay on the ground that Berry was not then his agent. Wagner sued him. Decide. [*Record v Wagner*, 100 NH 419]

7. Gilbert Church owned Church Farms, Inc., in Manteno, Illinois. Church advertised its well-bred stallion Imperial Guard for breeding rights at $50,000, directing all inquiries to "Herb Bagley, Manager." Herb Bagley lived at Church Farms and was the only person available to visitors. Vern Lundberg answered the ad, and after discussions in which Bagley stated that Imperial Guard would remain in Illinois for at least a two-year period, Lundberg and Bagley executed a two-year breeding rights contract. The contract was signed by Lundberg and by Bagley as "Church Farms, Inc., H. Bagley, Mgr." When Gil Church moved Imperial Guard to Oklahoma prior to the second year of the contract, Lundberg brought suit for breach of contract. Church testified that Bagley had no authority to sign contracts for Church Farms. Decide. [*Lundberg v Church Farms, Inc.*, 502 NE2d 806 (Ill)]

8. Although a woman of means, Bird was living in deplorable conditions. Neighbors contacted her cousin, Logan Ledbetter, who, in turn, had Bird examined by Dr. Phillips, a psychiatrist. Dr. Phillips determined that Bird was suffering from "an organic brain syndrome, chronic," that "her mental function was very impaired," and that, in his opinion, Bird was "mentally incompetent at the time of the examination." Ledbetter planned to deal with the situation by selling off a number of valuable real estate holdings owned by Bird and using the proceeds to pay for proper care for her.

Soon thereafter, Bird executed a power of attorney designating Logan Ledbetter as her attorney in fact, and Ledbetter entered into a contract to sell a large parcel of Bird's land to Andleman Associates. Bird's niece, Barbara, who disliked Ledbetter, filed a petition to have Bird declared incompetent and herself named guardian of her estate. The court appointed Barbara as guardian, and Barbara refused to allow the sale of the land to Andleman. In the lawsuit that resulted, Ledbetter and Andleman contended that Ledbetter acted in good faith and had a properly executed power of attorney; therefore, his signing the sales contract with Andleman was binding on Bird (the principal). Atkins (the real estate agent who had produced the ready, willing, and able buyer) sought his 10 percent commission under the listing agreement signed by Ledbetter as agent for Bird. Barbara contended that the power of attorney was void and that Ledbetter owed the real estate commission because he breached his implied warranty that he had a principal with capacity. Decide.

9. Tillie Flinn properly executed a durable power of attorney designating her nephew James C. Flanders and/or Martha E. Flanders, his wife, as her attorney in fact. Seven months later, Martha Flanders went to the Capitol Federal Savings and Loan Association office. She had the durable power of attorney instrument, five certificates of deposit, and a hand-printed letter identifying Martha as an attorney in fact and stating that Tillie wished to cash her five CDs that Martha had with her. At approximately 10:31 A.M., five checks were given to Martha in the aggregate

amount of $135,791.34, representing the funds in the five CDs less penalties for early withdrawal. Some of the checks were drawn to the order of Martha individually and some to the order of James and Martha, as individuals. Tillie was found dead of heart disease later that day. The time of death stated on her death certificate was 11:30 A.M. The Flanderses spent the money on themselves. Bank IV, as administrator of Tillie's estate, sued Capitol Federal to recover the amount of the funds paid to the Flanderses. It contended that Capitol Federal breached its duty to investigate before issuing the checks. Capitol Federal contended that it did all that it had a duty to do. Decide. [*Bank IV v Capitol Federal Savings and Loan Ass'n*, 828 P2d 355 (Kan)]

10. Lew owns a store on Canal Street in New Orleans. He paid a person named Mike and other individuals commissions for customers brought into the store. Lew testified that he had known Mike for less than a week. Boulos and Durso, partners in a wholesale jewelry business, were visiting New Orleans on a business trip when Mike brought them into the store to buy a stereo. While Durso finalized the stereo transaction with the store's manager, Boulos and Mike negotiated to buy 2 cameras, 3 videos, and 20 gold Dupont lighters. Unknown to the store's manager, Mike was given $8,250 in cash and was to deliver the merchandise later that evening to the Marriott Hotel, where Boulos and Durso were staying. Mike gave a receipt for the cash, but it showed no sales tax or indication that the goods were to be delivered. Boulos testified that he believed Mike was the store owner. Mike never delivered the merchandise and disappeared. Boulos and Durso contended that Lew is liable for the acts of his agent, Mike. Lew denied that Mike was his agent, and the testimony showed that Mike had no actual authority to make a sale, to use a cash register, or even to go behind a sales counter. What ethical principle applies to the conduct of Boulos and Durso? Decide. [*Boulos v Morrison*, 503 So 2d 1(La)]

11. Martha Christiansen owns women's apparel stores bearing her name in New Seabury, Massachusetts; Lake Placid, New York; Palm Beach, Florida; and Palm Springs, California. At a meeting with her four store managers, she discussed styles she thought appropriate for the forthcoming season, advised them as always to use their best judgment in the goods they purchased for each of their respective stores, and cautioned "but no blue jeans." Later, Jane Farley, the manager of the Lake Placid store, purchased a line of high-quality blue denim outfits (designer jeans with jacket and vest options) from Women's Wear, Inc., for the summer season. The outfits did not sell. Martha refused to pay for them, contending that she told all of her managers "no blue jeans" and that if it came to a lawsuit, she would fly in three managers to testify that Jane Farley had absolutely no authority to purchase denim outfits and was, in fact, expressly forbidden to do so. Women's Wear sued Martha, and the three managers testified for her. Is the fact that Martha had explicitly forbidden Farley to purchase the outfits in question sufficient to protect her from liability for the purchases made by Farley?

12. Fred Schilling, the president and administrator of Florence General Hospital, made a contract, dated August 16, 1989, on behalf of the hospital with CMK Associates to transfer the capacity to utilize 25 beds from the hospital to the Faith Nursing Home. Schilling, on behalf of the hospital, had previously made a contract with CMK Associates on May 4, 1987. Schilling had been specifically authorized by the hospital board to make the 1987 contract. The hospital refused to honor the 1989 contract because the board had not authorized it. CMK contended that Schilling had apparent authority to bind the hospital because he was president and administrator of the hospital and he had been the person who negotiated and signed a contract with CMK in 1987. Thus, according to CMK, the hospital had held out Schilling as having apparent authority to make the contract. The hospital disagreed. Decide. [*Pee Dee Nursing Home v Florence General Hospital*, 419 SE2d 843 (SC Ct App)]

13. Barbara Fox was the agent of Burt Hollander, a well-known athlete. She discovered that Tom Lanceford owned a 1957 Chevrolet convertible,

which had been stored in a garage for the past 15 years. After demonstrating to Lanceford that she was the authorized agent of Hollander, she made a contract with Lanceford on behalf of Hollander to purchase the Chevrolet. Lanceford later discovered that the car was much more valuable than he originally believed, and he refused to deliver the car to Fox. Fox sued Lanceford for breach of contract. Can she recover?

14. Francis Gagnon, an elderly gentleman, signed a power of attorney authorizing his daughter, Joan, "to sell any of my real estate and to execute any document needed to carry out the sale . . . and to add property to a trust of which I am grantor or beneficiary." This power was given in case Gagnon was not available to take care of matters personally because he was traveling. When Joan learned that Gagnon intended to sell his Shelburne property to Cosby for $750,000, she created an irrevocable trust naming Gagnon as beneficiary and herself as trustee. Acting then on the basis of the authority set forth in the power of attorney, she conveyed the Shelburne property to herself as trustee of the irrevocable trust, thus blocking the sale to Cosby. When Gagnon learned of this, he demanded that Joan return the Shelburne property to him, but she refused, saying she had acted within the authority set forth

in the power of attorney. Did Joan violate any duty owed to Gagnon? Must she reconvey the property to Gagnon? [*Gagnon v Coombs*, 654 NE2d 54 (Mass App)]

15. Daniels and Julian were employed by the Marriott Hotel in New Orleans and were close personal friends. One day after work, Daniels and Julian went to Werlein's music store to open a credit account. Julian, with Daniels's authorization and in her presence, applied for credit using Daniels's name and credit history. Later, Julian went to Werlein's without Daniels and charged the purchase of a television set to Daniels's account, executing a retail installment contract by signing Daniels's name. Daniels saw the new television in Julian's home and was informed that it was charged to the Werlein's account. Daniels told Julian to continue making payments. When Werlein's credit manager first contacted Daniels and informed her that her account was delinquent, she claimed that a money order for the television was in the mail. On the second call, she asked for a "payment balance." Some four months after the purchase, she informed Werlein's that she had not authorized the purchase of the television nor had she ratified the purchase. Werlein's sued Daniels for the unpaid balance. Decide. [*Philip Werlein, Ltd. v Daniels*, 536 So 2d 722 (La App)]

> CPA QUESTIONS

1. Generally, an agency relationship is terminated by operation of law in all of the following situations except the

   a. Principal's death
   b. Principal's incapacity
   c. Agent's renunciation of the agency
   d. Agent's failure to acquire a necessary business license

2. Able, on behalf of Pix Corp., entered into a contract with Sky Corp., by which Sky agreed to sell computer equipment to Pix. Able disclosed to Sky that she was acting on behalf of Pix. However, Able had exceeded her actual authority by entering into the contract with Sky. If Pix

wishes to ratify the contract with Sky, which of the following statements is correct?

   a. Pix must notify Sky that Pix intends to ratify the contract.
   b. Able must have acted reasonably and in Pix's best interest.
   c. Able must be a general agent of Pix.
   d. Pix must have knowledge of all material facts relating to the contract at the time it is ratified.

3. Which of the following actions requires an agent for a corporation to have a written agency agreement?

a. Purchasing office supplies for the principal's business
b. Purchasing an interest in undeveloped land for the principal
c. Hiring an independent general contractor to renovate the principal's office building
d. Retaining an attorney to collect a business debt owed the principal

4. Simmons, an agent for Jensen, has the express authority to sell Jensen's goods. Simmons also has the express authority to grant discounts of up to 5 percent of list price. Simmons sold Hemple a 10 percent discount. Hemple had not previously dealt with either Simmons or Jensen. Which of the following courses of action may Jensen properly take?

a. Seek to void the sale to Hemple
b. Seek recovery of $50 from Hemple only
c. Seek recovery of $50 from Simmons only
d. Seek recovery of $50 from either Hemple or Simmons

5. Ogden Corp. hired Thorp as a sales representative for nine months at a salary of $3,000 per month plus 4 percent of sales. Which of the following statements is correct?

a. Thorp is obligated to act solely in Ogden's interest in matters concerning Ogden's business.
b. The agreement between Ogden and Thorp formed an agency coupled with an interest.
c. Ogden does not have the power to dismiss Thorp during the nine-month period without cause.
d. The agreement between Ogden and Thorp is not enforceable unless it is in writing and signed by Thorp.

6. Frost's accountant and business manager has the authority to

a. Mortgage Frost's business property
b. Obtain bank loans for Frost
c. Insure Frost's property against fire loss
d. Sell Frost's business

THIRD PERSONS IN AGENCY

CHAPTER

(38)

 A LIABILITY OF AGENT TO THIRD PERSON
1. ACTION OF AUTHORIZED AGENT OF DISCLOSED PRINCIPAL
2. UNAUTHORIZED ACTION
3. DISCLOSURE OF PRINCIPAL
4. ASSUMPTION OF LIABILITY
5. EXECUTION OF CONTRACT
6. TORTS AND CRIMES

 B LIABILITY OF PRINCIPAL TO THIRD PERSON
7. AGENT'S CONTRACTS
8. PAYMENT TO AGENT
9. AGENT'S STATEMENTS
10. AGENT'S KNOWLEDGE

 C LIABILITY OF PRINCIPAL FOR TORTS AND CRIMES OF AGENT
11. VICARIOUS LIABILITY FOR TORTS AND CRIMES
12. NEGLIGENT HIRING AND RETENTION OF EMPLOYEES
13. NEGLIGENT SUPERVISION AND TRAINING
14. AGENT'S CRIMES
15. OWNER'S LIABILITY FOR ACTS OF AN INDEPENDENT CONTRACTOR
16. ENFORCEMENT OF CLAIM BY THIRD PERSON

 D TRANSACTIONS WITH SALES PERSONNEL
17. SOLICITING AND CONTRACTING AGENTS

LEARNING OBJECTIVES

After studying this chapter, you should be able to

LO.1 Describe how to execute a contract as an agent on behalf of a principal

LO.2 Identify when an agent is liable to a third person on a contract

LO.3 State the effect of a payment made by a third person to an authorized agent

LO.4 Explain and illustrate the doctrine of *respondeat superior*

LO.5 Contrast the liability of an owner for a tort committed by an independent contractor with the liability of an employer for a tort committed by an employee

LO.6 Distinguish between the authority of a soliciting agent and that of a contracting agent

The rights and liabilities of the principal, the agent, and the third person with whom the agent deals are generally determined by contract law. In some cases, tort or criminal law may be applicable.

(A) LIABILITY OF AGENT TO THIRD PERSON

The liability of the agent to the third person depends on the existence of authority and the manner of executing the contract.

1. ACTION OF AUTHORIZED AGENT OF DISCLOSED PRINCIPAL

If an agent makes a contract with a third person on behalf of a disclosed principal and has proper authority to do so and if the contract is executed properly, the agent has no personal liability on the contract. Whether the principal performs the contract or not, the agent cannot be held liable by the third party.

In speaking of an agent's action as authorized or unauthorized, it must be remembered that *authorized* includes action that, though originally *unauthorized*, was subsequently ratified by the principal. Once there is an effective ratification, the original action of the agent is no longer treated as unauthorized.

2. UNAUTHORIZED ACTION

If a person makes a contract as agent for another but lacks authority to do so, the contract does not bind the principal. When a person purports to act as agent for a principal, an implied warranty arises that that person has authority to do so.[1] If the agent lacks authority, there is a breach of this warranty.

If the agent's act causes loss to the third person, that third person may generally hold the agent liable for the loss.

---

[1] *Walz v Todd & Honeywell, Inc.,* 599 NYS2d 638 (App Div 1993).

CASE SUMMARY

The Company President Was Personally Liable When the Charcoal Plant Deal Did Not Ignite

FACTS: Craig Industries was in the business of manufacturing charcoal. Craig, the corporation's president, contracted in the name of the corporation to sell the company's plants to Husky Industries. Craig did not have authority from the board of directors to make the contract, and later the board of directors voted not to accept it. Husky Industries sued Craig on the theory that he, as agent for the corporation, exceeded his authority and should be held personally liable for damages.

DECISION: Judgment for Husky Industries. An agent who purports to contract in the name of a principal without, or in excess of, authority to do so is personally liable to the other contracting party for the agent's breach of implied warranty of authority. This liability is implied unless the agent manifests that no warranty of authority is made or the other contracting party knows the agent is not authorized. There was no discussion by the contracting parties concerning a limitation of Craig's warranty of authority to contract for the corporation, and Husky Industries was not aware that Craig was not authorized to make the contract. [**Husky Industries v Craig, 618 SW2d 458 (Mo App 1981)**]

It is no defense for the agent in such a case that she acted in good faith or misunderstood the scope of authority. The purported agent is not liable for conduct in excess of authority when the third person knows that she is acting beyond the authority given by the principal.

An agent with a written authorization may avoid liability on the implied warranty of authority by showing the written authorization to the third person and permitting the third person to determine the scope of the agent's authority.

3. DISCLOSURE OF PRINCIPAL

There are three degrees to which the existence and identity of the principal may be disclosed or not disclosed. An agent's liability as a party to a contract with a third person is affected by the degree of disclosure.

(a) DISCLOSED PRINCIPAL When the agent makes known the identity of the principal and the fact that the agent is acting on behalf of that principal, the principal is called a **disclosed principal**. The third person dealing with an agent of a disclosed principal ordinarily intends to make a contract with the principal, not the agent. Consequently, the agent is not a party to, and is not bound by, the contract that is made.[2]

(b) PARTIALLY DISCLOSED PRINCIPAL When the agent makes known the existence of a principal but not the principal's identity, the principal is a **partially disclosed principal**. Because the third party does not know the identity of the principal, the third person is making the contract with the agent, and the agent is therefore a party to the contract.

(c) UNDISCLOSED PRINCIPAL When the third person is not told or does not know that the agent is acting as an agent for anyone else, the unknown principal is called an **undisclosed principal**.[3] In this case, the third person is making the contract with the agent, and the agent is a party to that contract.

disclosed principal principal whose identity is made known by the agent as well as the fact that the agent is acting on the principal's behalf.

partially disclosed principal principal whose existence is made known but whose identity is not.

undisclosed principal principal on whose behalf an agent acts without disclosing to the third person the fact of agency or the identity of the principal.

---

[2] *Stinchfield v Weinreb*, 797 NYS2d 521 (App Div 2005).
[3] *Brunswick Leasing Corp. v Wisconsin Central, Ltd.*, 136 F3d 521 (7th Cir 1998).

CASE SUMMARY

You've Got to Tell Them You're Contracting on Behalf of the Named Principal, Silly

FACTS: Lowell Shoemaker, an architect, was hired by Affhouse to work on a land development project. In September 1999, Shoemaker contacted Central Missouri Professional Services about providing engineering and surveying services for the project. Central submitted a written proposal to Shoemaker in October 1999. About a week later, Shoemaker orally agreed that Central should proceed with the work outlined in the proposal. The first phase of the work was completed in late 1999. Billing for phase one in the amount of $5,864 was sent to Shoemaker on January 5, 2000. On February 15, 2000, Shoemaker called Central and requested that all bills be sent directly to the owner/developer, Affhouse. When the bills were not paid, Central sued Shoemaker and Affhouse. The trial court entered a judgment against Shoemaker for $5,864, and he appealed. Shoemaker acknowledged that he failed to disclose the identity of the principal to Central at the time the transaction was conducted.

Q. You never told Mike Bates or Central Missouri Professional Services that you were an agent for Affhouse or any other undisclosed principal?
A. That's correct. I never did.
Q. Another note I wrote down was that the subject of Affhouse came up in your conversations with Mike Bates of Central Missouri Professional Services after he sent the bill to you in the year 2000?
A. The early part of the year, yes.
Q. All right. I think it was January 2000.

Shoemaker contends that since he made clear to Central that he was an architect and not the developer, there was no binding oral contract between Central and him.

DECISION: Judgment for Central. It is the agent's duty to inform the third party at the time of the making of the contract that not only that he or she is acting as an agent but also the identity of the principal to protect the agent from personal liability on the transaction. Shoemaker failed to disclose to Central that he was acting as an agent and failed to disclose the identity of the principal, Affhouse, to Central at the time of the transaction. The fact that Central knew Shoemaker was an architect, not a developer, is immaterial. [**Central Missouri Professional Services v Shoemaker, 108 SW3d 6 (Mo App 2003)**]

4. ASSUMPTION OF LIABILITY

Agents may intentionally make themselves liable on contracts with third persons.[4] This situation frequently occurs when the agent is a well-established local brokerage house or other agency and when the principal is located out of town and is not known locally.

In some situations, the agent makes a contract that will be personally binding. If the principal is not disclosed, the agent is necessarily the other contracting party and is bound by the contract. Even when the principal is disclosed, the agent may be personally bound if it was the intention of the parties that the agent assume a personal obligation even though this was done to further the principal's business. To illustrate,

---

[4] *Fairchild Publications v Rosston*, 584 NYS2d 389 (NY County Sup 1992).

an attorney who hires an expert witness to testify on behalf of a client is an agent acting on behalf of a disclosed principal and is not personally liable for an expert witness fee.

However, when an expert witness asks the attorney about payment and the attorney states, "Don't worry, I will take care of it," the attorney (agent) has assumed a personal obligation and is liable for the fee.[5]

5. EXECUTION OF CONTRACT

A simple contract that would appear to be the contract of the agent can be shown by other evidence, if believed, to have been intended as a contract between the principal and the third party.

CASE SUMMARY

If You Sign as an Agent, You Don't Have to Pay

FACTS: Audrey Walton was transferred from a hospital to Mariner Health Nursing Home on January 26, 2001. Her daughter Patricia Walton signed a 30-page document, "Resident's Agent Financial Agreement." Patricia indicated in that agreement that the only method of payment would be Medicare or Medical Assistance. Medicare assistance stopped in February 2001. On January 10, 2003, Mariner Health sued both Audrey and Patricia for unpaid monthly bills amounting to $86,235. From a judgment for Mariner Health against both the patient and her daughter, Patricia appealed.

DECISION: Judgment for Patricia. As an agent, Patricia entered into the contract only for the benefit of Audrey and is personally insulated from liability by virtue of her status as an agent. *Note:* A state Nursing Home Bill of Rights did not authorize a nursing home to bring a private cause of action against a patient's agent for breach of contract unless the agent voluntarily and knowingly agreed to pay for the care with her or his own funds. [**Walton v Mariner Health, 894 A2d 584 (Md 2006)**]

To avoid any question of interpretation, an agent should execute an instrument by signing the principal's name and either *by* or *per* and the agent's name. **For Example,** if Jane R. Craig is an agent for B. G. Gray, Craig should execute instruments by signing either "B. G. Gray, by Jane R. Craig" or "B. G. Gray, per Jane R. Craig." Such a signing is in law a signing by Gray, and the agent is therefore not a party to the contract. The signing of the principal's name by an authorized agent without indicating the agent's name or identity is likewise in law the signature of the principal.

If the instrument is ambiguous as to whether the agent has signed in a representative or an individual capacity, parol evidence is admissible as between the original parties to the transaction for establishing the character in which the agent was acting.

6. TORTS AND CRIMES

Agents are liable for harm caused third persons by the agents' fraudulent, intentional, or negligent acts.[6] The fact that persons were acting as agents at the time or that they acted in good faith under the directions of a principal does not relieve them of liability if their conduct would impose liability on them when acting for themselves.

---

[5] *Boros v Carter*, 537 So 2d 1134 (Fla App 1989).
[6] *Mannish v Lacayo*, 496 So 2d 242 (Fla App 1986).

CASE SUMMARY

Employees Are Not Personally Liable for Roadway Accidents While at Work, Are They?

FACTS: Ralls was an employee of the Arkansas State Highway Department. While repairing a state highway, he negligently backed a state truck onto the highway, causing a collision with Mittlesteadt's car. Mittlesteadt sued Ralls, who raised the defense that, because he was acting on behalf of the state, he was not liable for his negligence.

DECISION: The fact that an employee or agent is acting on behalf of someone else does not excuse or exonerate the agent or employee from liability for torts committed by the agent or employee. Ralls was therefore liable for his negligence even though it occurred within the scope of his employment by the state. [**Ralls v Mittlesteadt, 596 SW2d 349 (Ark 1980)**]

ETHICS & THE LAW

Some time ago, dairy farmers owned large tracts of land in south Tempe, Arizona. The farmers used the land for grazing animals. Economic growth in this suburb of Phoenix was limited because of the state's inability at that time to attract large businesses to the area for relocation or location of new facilities.

In 1973, three farmers who owned adjoining parcels of land in the south Tempe area were approached by a local real estate agent with an offer for the purchase of their property. The amount of the offer was approximately 10 percent above the property's appraised value. The three farmers discussed the offer and concluded that with their need to retire, it was best to accept the offer and sell the land. All three signed contracts for the sale of their land.

After the contracts were entered into but before the transactions had closed, the three farmers learned that the land was being purchased by a real estate development firm from southern California. The development firm had planned, and would be proposing to the Tempe City Council, a residential community, the Lakes. The Lakes would consist of upper-end homes in a community laced with parks, lakes, and ponds, with each house in the developed area backing up to its own dock and water recreation. The development firm had begun the project because it had learned of the plans of American Express, Rubbermaid, and Dial to locate major facilities in the Phoenix area.

The three farmers objected to the sale of their land when they learned the identity of the buyer. "If we had known who was coming in here and why, we never would have sold for such a low price." Were the farmers' contracts binding?

Is it ethical to use the strategy of an undisclosed principal? What is the role of an agent in a situation in which the third party is making a decision not as beneficial to him or her as it could or should be? Can the agent say anything?

If an agent commits a crime, such as stealing from a third person or shooting a third person, the agent is liable for the crime without regard to the fact of acting as an agent. The agent is liable without regard to whether the agent acted in self-interest or sought to advance the interest of the principal.

B LIABILITY OF PRINCIPAL TO THIRD PERSON

The principal is liable to the third person for the properly authorized and executed contracts of the agent and, in certain circumstances, for the agent's unauthorized contracts.

7. AGENT'S CONTRACTS

The liability of a principal to a third person on a contract made by an agent depends on the extent of disclosure of the principal and the form of the contract that is executed.

(a) Simple Contract with Principal Disclosed When a disclosed principal with contractual capacity authorizes or ratifies an agent's transaction with a third person and when the agent properly executes a contract with the third person, a binding contract exists between the principal and the third person. The principal and the third person may each sue the other in the event of a breach of the contract. The agent is not a party to the contract, is not liable for its performance, and cannot sue for its breach.[7]

The liability of a disclosed principal to a third person is not discharged by the fact that the principal gives the agent money with which to pay the third person. Consequently, the liability of a buyer for the purchase price of goods is not terminated by the fact that the buyer gave the buyer's agent the purchase price to remit to the seller.

(b) Simple Contract with Principal Partially Disclosed A partially disclosed principal is liable for a simple contract made by an authorized agent. The third person may recover from either the agent or the principal.

(c) Simple Contract with Principal Undisclosed An undisclosed principal is liable for a simple contract made by an authorized agent. Although the third person initially contracted with the agent alone, the third person, on learning of the existence of the undisclosed principal, may sue that principal.[8] In most jurisdictions, third persons can sue and collect judgments from the agent, the principal, or both until the judgment is fully satisfied (joint and several liability).[9]

8. PAYMENT TO AGENT

When the third person makes payment to an authorized agent, the payment is deemed made to the principal. Even if the agent never remits or delivers the payment to the principal, the principal must give the third person full credit for the payment so

---

[7] *Levy v Gold & Co., Inc.*, 529 NYS2d 133 (App Div 1988).
[8] *McDaniel v Hensons, Inc.*, 493 SE2d 529 (Ga App 1997).
[9] *Crown Controls, Inc. v Smiley*, 756 P2d 717 (Wash 1988).

long as the third person made the payment in good faith and had no reason to know that the agent would be guilty of misconduct.[10]

CASE SUMMARY

But We Already Paid!

FACTS: E.I. duPont de Nemours & Company licensed Enjay Chemical Company (now Exxon) and Johnson & Johnson to use certain chemical processes in return for which royalty payments by check were to be made to duPont. By agreement between the companies, the royalty payments to be made to duPont were to be by check sent to a specified duPont employee, C.H.D., in its Control Division. These checks were sent during the next nine years. C.H.D. altered some of them so that he was named thereon as the payee. He then cashed them and used the money for his own purposes. Liberty Mutual Insurance Company, which insured the fidelity of duPont's employees, and duPont sued Enjay and Johnson & Johnson on the basis that they still owed the amounts embezzled by C.H.D.

DECISION: Judgment for Enjay and Johnson & Johnson. Payment to an authorized agent has the legal effect of payment to the principal regardless of whether the agent remits the payment to the principal or embezzles it. C.H.D. was the agent authorized to receive the royalty checks. Therefore, the defendants had effectively paid the royalties when they sent C.H.D. the checks. His misconduct did not revive the debts that were paid by sending him the checks. [**Liberty Mutual Ins. Co. v Enjay Chemical Co.**, 316 A2d 219 (Del Super 1974)]

Because apparent authority has the same legal effect as actual authority, a payment made to a person with apparent authority to receive the payment is deemed a payment to the apparent principal.

When a debtor makes payment to a person who is not the actual or apparent agent of the creditor, such a payment does not discharge the debt unless that person in fact pays the money to the creditor.

9. AGENT'S STATEMENTS

A principal is bound by a statement made by an agent while transacting business within the scope of authority. This means that the principal cannot later contradict the statement of the agent and show that it is not true. Statements or declarations of an agent, in order to bind the principal, must be made at the time of performing the act to which they relate or shortly thereafter.

10. AGENT'S KNOWLEDGE

The principal is bound by knowledge or notice of any fact that is acquired by an agent while acting within the scope of actual or apparent authority. When a fact is known to the agent of the seller, the sale is deemed made by the seller with knowledge of that fact.

The rule that the agent's knowledge is imputed to the principal is extended in some cases to knowledge gained prior to the creation of the agency relationship. The notice

---

[10] This general rule of law is restated in some states by Section 2 of the Uniform Fiduciaries Act, which is expressly extended by Section 1 of the act to agents, partners, and corporate officers. Similar statutory provisions are found in a number of other states.

and knowledge in any case must be based on reliable information. Thus, when the agent hears only rumors, the principal is not charged with notice.

If the subject matter is outside the scope of the agent's authority, the agent is under no duty to inform the principal of the knowledge, and the principal is not bound by it. The principal is not charged with knowledge of an agent when (1) the agent is acting adversely to the principal's interest or (2) the third party acts in collusion with the agent for the purpose of cheating the principal.

LIABILITY OF PRINCIPAL FOR TORTS AND CRIMES OF AGENT

Under certain circumstances, the principal may be liable for the torts or crimes of the agent or the employee.

11. VICARIOUS LIABILITY FOR TORTS AND CRIMES

Assume that an agent or an employee causes harm to a third person. Is the principal or the employer liable for this conduct? If the conduct constitutes a crime, can the principal or the employer be criminally prosecuted? The answer is that in many instances, the principal or the employer is liable civilly and may also be prosecuted criminally. That is, the principal or the employer is liable although personally free from fault and not guilty of any wrong. This concept of imposing liability for the fault of another is known as **vicarious liability.**

vicarious liability imposing liability for the fault of another.

This situation arises both when an employer's employee or a principal's agent commits the wrong. The rules of law governing the vicarious liability of the principal and the employer are the same. In the interest of simplicity, this section is stated in terms of employees acting in the course of employment. Remember that these rules are equally applicable to agents acting within the scope of their authority. As a practical matter, some situations will arise only with agents. **For Example,** the vicarious liability of a seller for the misrepresentations made by a salesperson arise only when the seller appointed an agent to sell. In contrast, both the employee hired to drive a truck and an agent driving to visit a customer could negligently injure a third person with their vehicles. In many situations, a person employed by another is both an employee and an agent, and the tort is committed within the phase of "employee work."

respondeat superior doctrine that the principal or employer is vicariously liable for the unauthorized torts committed by an agent or employee while acting within the scope of the agency or the course of the employment, respectively.

The rule of law imposing vicarious liability on an innocent employer for the wrong of an employee is also known as the doctrine of ***respondeat superior.*** In modern times, this doctrine can be justified on the grounds that the business should pay for the harm caused in the doing of the business, that the employer will be more careful in the selection of employees if made responsible for their actions, and that the employer may obtain liability insurance to protect against claims of third persons.

(a) Nature of Act   The wrongful act committed by an employee may be a negligent act, an intentional act, a fraudulent act, or a violation of a government regulation. It may give rise only to civil liability of the employer, or it may also subject the employer to prosecution for crime.

(1) Negligent Act.   Historically, the act for which liability would be imposed under the doctrine of *respondeat superior* was a negligent act committed within the scope of employment.

(2) Intentional Act.   Under the common law, a master was not liable for an intentional tort committed by a servant. The modern law holds that an employer is liable for an intentional tort committed by an employee for the purpose of furthering the employer's business.[11] **For Example,** Crane Brothers, Inc., drilled a well for Stephen May. When May did not pay his bill, two Crane Brothers' employees went to May's workplace, and an altercation ensued in which May was injured. Crane Brothers, Inc., was held vicariously liable for the torts of the employees, not because the employer itself committed the wrongful acts but because it was answerable for the manner in which its agents, the two employees, conducted themselves in doing the business of the employer.[12]

(3) Fraud.   Modern decisions hold the employer liable for fraudulent acts or misrepresentations. The rule is commonly applied to a principal-agent relationship. To illustrate, when an agent makes fraudulent statements in selling stock, the principal is liable for the buyer's loss. In states that follow the common law rule of no liability for intentional torts, the principal is not liable for the agent's fraud when the principal did not authorize or know of the agent's fraud.

(4) Government Regulation.   The employer may be liable because of the employee's violation of a government regulation. These regulations are most common in the areas of business and of protection of the environment. In such cases, the employer may be held liable for a penalty imposed by the government. In some cases, the breach of the regulation will impose liability on the employer in favor of a third person who is injured as a consequence of the violation.

(b) COURSE OF EMPLOYMENT   The mere fact that a tort or crime is committed by an employee does not necessarily impose vicarious liability on the employer. It must also be shown that the individual was acting within the scope of authority if an agent or in the course of employment if an employee. If an employee was not acting within the scope of employment, there is no vicarious liability.[13] **For Example,** after Rev. Joel Thomford accidentally shot and killed his parishioner during a deer hunting trip, the parishioner's wife brought a wrongful death action against the pastor and the church. Because the accident occurred on the pastor's day off and the trip was not sponsored by the church, the pastor was not acting within the course of his employment at the time of the accident, and the church was not liable.[14]

CASE SUMMARY

He Was Back to Nettie's Business When He Hit the Studebaker

FACTS: Judith Studebaker was injured when a van owned and driven by James Ferry collided with her vehicle. On the morning of the incident, Ferry made his usual runs for the florist for whom he delivered flowers, Nettie's Flower Garden. Studebaker brought an action against Nettie's on a *respondeat superior* theory on the belief that Ferry was Nettie's employee

---

[11] *Restatement (Second) of Agency* § 231.

[12] *Crane Brothers, Inc. v May,* 556 SE2d 865 (Ga App 2001).

[13] *Young v Taylor-White LLC,* 181 SW2d 324 (Tenn 2005).

[14] *Hentges v Thomford,* 569 NW2d 424 (Minn App 1997).

CASE SUMMARY

continued

at the time of the accident. Nettie's defended that Ferry was an independent contractor, not an employee. From a judgment in favor of Studebaker for $125,000, Nettie's appealed.

DECISION: Judgment against Nettie's. Applying a "right to control" test, it is clear that Nettie's controlled or had the right to control Ferry at the time of the collision. Nettie's set standards for Ferry's dress and conduct, determined his territory, and set standards for his van. Although Ferry made a slight detour prior to the accident to conduct personal business at a pawnshop, this did not relieve the employer from liability because he was clearly back to Nettie's business at the time of the accident. [**Studebaker v Nettie's Flower Garden Inc., 842 SW2d 227 (Mo App 1992)**]

(c) EMPLOYEE OF THE UNITED STATES   The Federal Tort Claims Act (FTCA) declares that the United States shall be liable vicariously whenever a federal employee driving a motor vehicle in the course of employment causes harm under such circumstances that a private employer would be liable. Contrary to the general rule, the statute exempts the employee driver from liability.[15]

12. NEGLIGENT HIRING AND RETENTION OF EMPLOYEES

In addition to a complaint against the employer based on the doctrine of *respondeat superior,* a lawsuit may often raise a second theory, that of negligent hiring or retention of an employee.[16] Unlike the *respondeat superior* theory by which the employer may be vicariously liable for the tort of an employee, the negligent hiring theory is based on the negligence of the employer in the hiring process. Under the *respondeat superior* rule, the employer is liable only for those torts committed within the scope of employment or in the furtherance of the employer's interests. The negligent hiring theory has been used to impose liability in cases when an employee commits an intentional tort, almost invariably outside the scope of employment, against a customer or the general public, and the employer knew or should have known that the employee was incompetent, violent, dangerous, or criminal.[17]

(a) NEED FOR DUE CARE IN HIRING   An employer may be liable on a theory of negligent hiring when it is shown that the employer knew, or in the exercise of ordinary care should have known, that the job applicant would create an undue risk of harm to others in carrying out job responsibilities. Moreover, it must also be shown that the employer could have reasonably foreseen injury to the third party. Thus, an employer who knows of an employee's preemployment drinking problems and violent behavior may be liable to customers assaulted by that employee.

Employers might protect themselves from liability in a negligent hiring case by having each prospective employee fill out an employment application form and then checking into the applicant's work experience, background, character, and qualifications. This would be evidence of due care in hiring. Generally, the scope of a

---

[15] Claims of negligent hiring are not permissible under the FTCA. See *Tonelli v United States,* 60 F3d 492 (8th Cir 1995).

[16] *Medina v Graham's Cowboys, Inc.,* 827 P2d 859 (NM App 1992).

[17] *Rockwell v Sun Harbor Budget Suites,* 925 P2d 1175 (Nev 1996).

preemployment investigation should correlate to the degree of opportunity the prospective employee would have to do harm to third persons. A minimum investigation consisting of filling out an application form and conducting a personal interview would be satisfactory for hiring an outside maintenance person, but a full background inquiry would be necessary for hiring a security guard. However, such inquiry does not bar *respondeat superior* liability.

(b) EMPLOYEES WITH CRIMINAL RECORDS The hiring of an individual with a criminal record does not by itself establish the tort of negligent hiring.[18] An employer who knows that an applicant has a criminal record has a duty to investigate to determine whether the nature of the conviction in relationship to the job to be performed creates an unacceptable risk to third persons.

(c) NEGLIGENT RETENTION Courts assign liability under negligent retention on a basis similar to that of negligent hiring. That is, the employer knew, or should have known, that the employee would create an undue risk of harm to others in carrying out job responsibilities.

A hospital is liable for negligent retention when it continues the staff privileges of a physician that it knew or should have known had sexually assaulted a female patient in the past.[19]

CASE SUMMARY

(1) Alcohol, (2) Battery, and (3) Negligent Retention: Three Strikes and You're Out!

FACTS: Mark Livigni was manager of the National Super Markets store in Cahokia, Illinois. After drinking alcoholic beverages one evening, he stopped by the store to check the premises when he observed a ten-year-old boy's unacceptable behavior outside the store. Livigni chased the boy to a car, where he pulled another child, a four-year-old named Farris Bryant, from the car and threw him through the air. A multicount lawsuit was brought against National and Livigni. The evidence revealed that some eight years before the incident with Farris Bryant, Livigni had thrown an empty milk crate at a subordinate employee, striking him on the arm and necessitating medical treatment, and that some two years before the incident, he threw his 13-year-old son onto a bed while disciplining him, causing the boy to sustain a broken collarbone. Livigni was promoted to store manager subsequent to the milk crate incident, and he pled guilty to aggravated battery to his child and was sentenced to two years' probation. A verdict was rendered against National for $20,000 under a *respondeat superior* theory for the battery of Farris Bryant. A verdict was also rendered against National for $15,000 for negligent retention of Livigni and for $115,000 in punitive damages for willful and wanton retention. National appealed the trial court's denial of its motions for directed verdicts on these counts.

DECISION: Judgment for Bryant. Employers that wrongfully hire or retain unfit employees expose the public to the acts of these employees, and it is not unreasonable to hold the employer accountable when the employee causes injury to another. The principle is not

---

[18] *Connes v Molalla Transportation Systems*, 831 P2d 1316 (Colo 1992).

[19] *Capithorne v Framingham Union Hospital*, 520 NE2d 139 (Mass 1988); see also *Sparks Regional Medical Center v Smith*, 976 SW2d 396 (Ark App 1998), in which the hospital was found negligent in supervising an employee following a report that the employee had abused other psychiatric patients.

CASE SUMMARY

continued

respondeat superior; rather, it is premised on the wrongful conduct of the employer itself. In addition, the employer in this case is responsible under *respondeat superior* because Livigni was prompted to act, in part, to protect store property. A dissenting opinion stated that the decision would send the wrong message to employers on the negligent retention issue and cause them to terminate any employee who has ever had an altercation on or off company premises, which is contrary to the state's public policy of rehabilitating criminal offenders. [Bryant v Livigni, 619 NE2d 550 (Ill App 1993)]

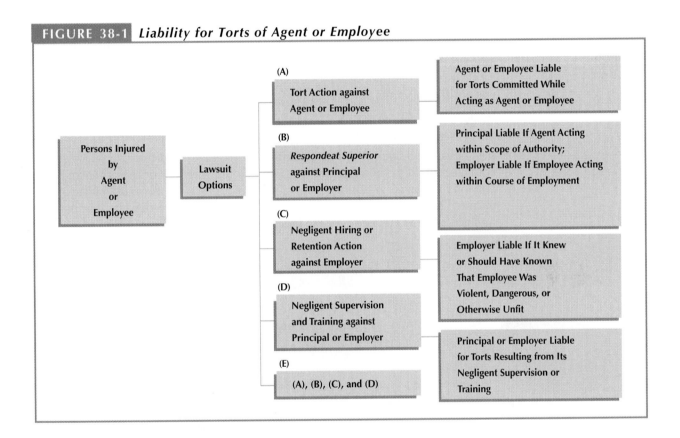

FIGURE 38-1 *Liability for Torts of Agent or Employee*

13. NEGLIGENT SUPERVISION AND TRAINING

A separate theory of liability in addition to the doctrine of *respondeat superior* is that of negligent supervision and training, that holds the principal directly liable for its negligence in regard to training and supervision of its employees and agents. **For Example,** Monadnock Training Council, Inc., certified Robert Hebert as an "authorized Monadnock instructor" and granted him actual authority to market and promote its PR-24 police baton. In a training session run by Hebert at the Chesire County House of Corrections in New Hampshire, Charles Herman suffered severe head trauma when training with Hebert without protective headgear in a room with unpadded cement walls. Monadnock was held directly liable for Herman's injuries based on its negligent supervision and training of Hebert.[20]

14. AGENT'S CRIMES

A principal is liable for the crimes of an agent committed at the principal's direction. When not authorized, however, the principal is ordinarily not liable for an agent's crime merely because it was committed while the agent was otherwise acting within the scope of the latter's authority or employment. **For Example,** the owner of the Main Tower Cafe in Hartford, Connecticut, was not vicariously liable for injuries sustained by a patron who was shot by a bouncer while attempting to enter the bar because the bouncer's intentional and willful act was motivated by his own spleen and malevolence against the victim in clear departure from his employment.[21] As an exception to the rule of nonliability just stated, courts now hold an employer criminally liable when the employee has in the course of employment violated environmental protection laws, liquor sales laws, pure food laws, or laws regulating prices or prohibiting false weights. **For Example,** an employer may be held criminally responsible for an employee's sale of liquor to a minor in violation of the liquor law even though the sale was not known to the employer and violated instructions given to the employee.

15. OWNER'S LIABILITY FOR ACTS OF AN INDEPENDENT CONTRACTOR

If work is done by an independent contractor rather than by an employee, the owner is not liable for harm caused by the contractor to third persons or their property. Likewise, the owner is not bound by the contracts made by the independent contractor. The owner is ordinarily not liable for harm caused to third persons by the negligence of the employees of the independent contractor.[22]

> ## CASE SUMMARY
>
>
>
> ### Retaining Control Led to Liability
>
> FACTS: Leo Bongers died intestate on October 8, 1992. Alfred Bongers and Delores Kuhl, Leo's nephew and niece, were appointed personal representatives of his estate. Leo left substantial real and personal property, including farms and more than 120 antique cars, trucks, and motorcycles. The estate hired Bauer-Moravec to sell the vehicles at auction. Auctioneer Russ Moravec suggested that the vehicles be sold at an airstrip auction in May, June, or July 1993. The estate rejected this recommendation and insisted that the sale be conducted on a farm owned by the estate in January 1993. On January 30, 1993, the auction took place beginning at 9:30 A.M. with temperatures below freezing and some 800 people jammed into the bid barn. One auctioneer had purchased Putnam hitch balls to be used with mylar-type ropes so that small farm tractors could tow vehicles into and out of the bid barn. Doug Reznicek assisted the auctioneer in making arrangements to move vehicles. One hour

---

[20] *Herman v Monadnock PR-24 Training Council, Inc.,* 2002 NH LEXIS 78.

[21] *Pruitt v Main & Tower, Inc.,* 2002 WL 532467 (Conn Super 2002); see also *Tanks v Lockheed Martin Corp.,* 417 F3d 456 (5th Cir 2005).

[22] *King v Lens Creek, Ltd., Partnership,* 483 SE2d 265 (W Va 1996).

continued

into the auction, Joseph Haag was seriously injured when a hitch ball came loose from the drawbar of the tractor towing an antique Studebaker truck. Haag brought a multiple-count suit, including an action against the estate, claiming that Bauer-Moravec was acting as agent for the estate and that its negligence in not properly attaching the hitch ball as well as using mylar-type tow rope rather than chains should be imputed to the estate under the doctrine of *respondeat superior.* From a judgment for Haag, the estate appealed.

DECISION: Generally, the employer of an independent contractor is not liable for physical harm caused to another by the acts or omissions of the contractor or its servants. However, an exception exists if the employer retains control over the contractor's work. The auctioneers served as independent contractors. However, the estate exercised sufficient control over the auction and auctioneers to subject it to liability. It approved the use of tractors to tow the vehicles at the auction. It approved the use of assistants and paid them. The estate insisted that the auction be heavily advertised, resulting in a shoulder-to-shoulder crowd through which the vehicles were to be towed. Bongers was present at the auction at the time of the accident. [**Haag v Bongers, 589 NW2d 318 (Neb 1999)**]

(a) EXCEPTIONS TO OWNER'S IMMUNITY   There is a trend toward imposing liability on the owner when work undertaken by an independent contractor is inherently dangerous.[23] That is, the law is taking the position that if the owner wishes to engage in a particular activity, the owner must be responsible for the harm it causes. The owner cannot be insulated from such liability by the device of hiring an independent contractor to do the work.

Regardless of the nature of the activity, the owner may be liable for the torts and contracts of the independent contractor when the owner controls the conduct of the independent contractor.

In certain circumstances, such as providing security for a business, collecting bills, and repossessing collateral, there is an increased risk that torts may be committed by the individuals performing such duties. The trend of the law is to refuse to allow the use of an independent contractor for such work to insulate the employer.

(b) UNDISCLOSED INDEPENDENT CONTRACTOR   In some situations, the owner appears to be doing the act in question because the existence of the independent contractor is not disclosed or apparent. This situation occurs most commonly when a franchisee does business under the name of the franchisor; when a concessionaire, such as a restaurant in a hotel, appears to be the hotel restaurant, although in fact it is operated by an independent concessionaire; or when the buyer of a business continues to run the business in the seller's name. In such cases of an undisclosed independent contractor, it is generally held that the apparent owner (that is, the franchisor, the grantor of the concession, or the seller) is liable for the torts and contracts of the undisclosed independent contractor.

16. ENFORCEMENT OF CLAIM BY THIRD PERSON

A lawsuit may be brought by a third person against the agent or the principal if each is liable. In most states and in the federal courts, the plaintiff may sue either or both in

[23] *Hinger v Parker & Parsley Petroleum Co.,* 902 P2d 1033 (NM App 1995).

one action when both are liable. If both are sued, the plaintiff may obtain a judgment against both, although the plaintiff is allowed to collect the full amount of the judgment only once.

 ## TRANSACTIONS WITH SALES PERSONNEL

Many transactions with sales personnel do not result in a contract with the third person with whom the salesperson deals.

17. SOLICITING AND CONTRACTING AGENTS

soliciting agent salesperson.

Giving an order to a salesperson often does not give rise to a contract. Ordinarily, a salesperson is a **soliciting agent,** whose authority is limited to soliciting offers from third persons and transmitting them to the principal for acceptance or rejection. Such an agent does not have authority to make a contract that will bind the principal to the third person. The employer of the salesperson is not bound by a contract until the employer accepts the order, and the third person (customer) may withdraw the offer at any time prior to acceptance.

contracting agent agent with authority to make contracts; person with whom the buyer deals.

In contrast, if the person with whom the buyer deals is a **contracting agent** with authority to make contracts, by definition a binding contract exists between the principal and the customer from the moment that the agent agrees with the customer. In other words, the contract arises when the agent accepts the customer's order.

> SUMMARY

An agent of a disclosed principal who makes a contract with a third person within the scope of authority has no personal liability on the contract. It is the principal and the third person who may each sue the other in the event of a breach. A person purporting to act as an agent for a principal warrants by implication that there is an existing principal with legal capacity and that the principal has authorized the agent to act. The person acting as an agent is liable for any loss caused the third person for breach of these warranties. An agent of a partially disclosed or an undisclosed principal is a party to the contract with the third person. The agent may enforce the contract against the third person and is liable for its breach. To avoid problems of interpretation, an agent should execute a contract "Principal, by Agent." Agents are liable for harm caused third persons by their fraudulent, malicious, or negligent acts.

An undisclosed or a partially disclosed principal is liable to a third person on a simple contract made by an authorized agent. When a third person makes payment to an authorized agent, it is deemed paid to the principal.

A principal or an employer is vicariously liable under the doctrine of *respondeat superior* for the torts of an agent or an employee committed within the scope of authority or the course of employment. The principal or the employer may also be liable for some crimes committed in the course of employment. An owner is not liable for torts caused by an independent contractor to third persons or their property unless the work given to the independent contractor is inherently hazardous.

A salesperson is ordinarily an agent whose authority is limited to soliciting offers (orders) from third persons and transmitting them to the principal. The principal is not bound until he or she accepts the order. The customer may withdraw an offer at any time prior to acceptance.

QUESTIONS AND CASE PROBLEMS

1. Richard Pawlus was an owner of Dutch City Wood Products, Inc., which did business as "Dutch City Marketing." Pawlus purchased merchandise from Rothschild Sunsystems from April 24 to June 24 using the designation "Richard Pawlus Dutch City Marketing" on orders and correspondence. In October, Rothschild was notified that Pawlus was acting on behalf of the corporation when the merchandise was purchased. Rothschild sued Pawlus for payment for the merchandise. Pawlus contended that he was an agent of the corporation and was thus not personally liable. Decide. [*Rothschild Sunsystems, Inc. v Pawlus,* 514 NYS2d 572 (App Div)]

2. Myles Murphy was appointed by Cy Sinden, a famous developer, to purchase land for a shopping center near the intersection of I-95 and Route 1. Mary Mason, the property owner, contracted with Murphy for the sale of the property. Because of an economic downturn, Sinden was unable to provide the planned behind-the-scenes financing for the venture, and the contract was not performed. Mason's real estate experts determined that she lost $2 million because of the breach of contract. Mason also discovered that Sinden was "behind the deal." If Mason elects to sue Sinden, who turns out to be unable to pay the judgment because of the collapse of his business "empire," can she later bring suit against Murphy?

3. What is the justification for the doctrine of *respondeat superior?*

4. Beverly Baumann accompanied her mother to Memorial Hospital, where her mother was placed in intensive care for heart problems. A nurse asked Baumann to sign various documents, including one that authorized the hospital to release medical information and to receive the mother's insurance benefits directly. This form stated: "I understand I am financially responsible to the hospital for charges not covered by this authorization." Baumann's mother died during the course of her hospitalization. The hospital later sued Baumann to recover $19,013.42 in unpaid hospital charges based on the form she signed, which the hospital called a "guarantee of payment." Baumann contended that she signed the document as an agent for her mother and was thus not personally liable. Decide. [*Memorial Hospital v Baumann,* 474 NYS2d 636]

5. Mills Electric Co. signed a contract with S&S Horticulture Architects, a two-person landscaping partnership operated by Sullivan and Smyth, to maintain the grounds and flowers at the Mills Electric Co. plant in Jacksonville, Florida. Mills checked references of S&S and found the company to be highly reputable. The contract set forth that S&S would select the flowers for each season and would determine when to maintain the lawns so long as they were properly maintained. The contract called for payments to be made to S&S on the first workday of each month, and the contract stipulated that "nothing herein shall make S&S an agent of the company." The contract also required that S&S personnel wear uniforms identifying them as employees of S&S. S&S had other accounts, but the large Mills Electric plant took up most of its time. While working on a terraced area near the visitors' entrance to the plant, Sullivan lost control of his large commercial mower, and the mower struck Gillespie, a plant visitor, causing her serious injury. A witness heard Sullivan apologizing to Gillespie and saying that "running that mower on the terrace is a two-person job." Gillespie brought suit against Mills Electric Co., contending Mills should be held vicariously liable. Decide.

6. A. D. McLeod contacted Thompson's agent and agreed that certain property would be leased for a period of two years at a rental rate of $700 per month for the first year and $800 per month for the second year. McLeod's personal check paid the first month's rent. McLeod and his associates manufactured mattresses on the premises under the trademark Sleep, and the business was incorporated as Sleep System, Inc. After some six months of operation during which the rent was paid by the corporation, McLeod informed Thompson that he had been "kicked out" of the company. When the subsequent rent was not

paid, Thompson sued McLeod for the back rent. McLeod alleged that Thompson knew or should have known that McLeod was acting as an agent of Sleep System, Inc., and that after he was "kicked out" of the company, it should have been very clear that he would no longer be responsible for rent. Thompson responded that if McLeod were an agent, he had an obligation to disclose that he was acting in a representative capacity when the lease was made, not six months later. Decide. [*McLeod v Thompson*, 615 So 2d 90 (Ala Civ App)]

7. On July 11, 1984, José Padilla was working as a vacation-relief route salesperson for Frito-Lay. He testified that he made a route stop at Sal's Beverage Shop, where he was told by Mrs. Ramos that she was dissatisfied with Frito-Lay service and no longer wanted its products in the store. He asked if there was anything he could do to change her mind. She said no and told him to pick up his merchandise. He took one company-owned merchandise rack to his van and was about to pick up another rack when Mr. Ramos said that the rack had been given to him by the regular route salesperson. Padilla said the route salesperson had no authority to give away Frito-Lay racks. A confrontation occurred over the rack, and Padilla pushed Mr. Ramos against the cash register, injuring Ramos's back. Frito-Lay has a company policy, clearly communicated to all employees, that prohibits them from getting involved in any type of physical confrontation with a customer. Frito-Lay contended that Padilla was not acting within the course and scope of his employment when the pushing incident took place and that the company was therefore not liable to Ramos. Ramos contended that Frito-Lay was responsible for the acts of its employee Padilla. [*Frito-Lay, Inc. v Ramos*, 770 SW2d 887 (Tex App)]

8. Jason Lasseigne, a Little League baseball player, was seriously injured at a practice session when he was struck on the head by a poorly thrown baseball from a team member, Todd Landry. The league was organized by American Legion Post 38. Claude Cassel and Billy Johnson were the volunteer coaches of the practice session. The Lasseignes brought suit on behalf of Jason against Post 38, claiming that the coaching was negligent and that Post 38 was vicariously liable for the harm caused by such negligence. Post 38 contended that it had no right to control the work of the volunteer coaches or the manner in which practices were conducted and as a result should not be held vicariously liable for the actions of the coaches. Decide. [*Lasseigne v American Legion Post 38*, 543 So 2d 1111 (La App)]

9. Moritz, a guest at Pines Hotel, was sitting in the lobby when Brown, a hotel employee, dropped a heavy vacuum cleaner on her knee. When Moritz complained, the employee insulted her and hit her with his fist, knocking her unconscious. She sued the hotel for damages. Was the hotel liable? [*Moritz v Pines Hotel, Inc.*, 383 NYS2d 704 (App Div)]

10. Steve Diezel, an employee of Island City Flying Service in Key West, Florida, stole a General Electric Credit Corp. (GECC) aircraft and crashed the plane while attempting to take off. GECC brought suit against Island City on the theory that it had negligently hired Diezel as an employee and was therefore legally responsible for Diezel's act of theft. Diezel had a military prison record as a result of a drug offense and had been fired by Island City twice previously but had been immediately reinstated each time. Island City claimed that the evidence was insufficient to establish that it had been negligent in employing Diezel. Decide. [*Island City Flying Service v General Electric*, 585 So 2d 274 (Fla)]

11. The Bay State Harness Horse Racing and Breeding Association conducted horse races at a track where music for patrons was supplied by an independent contractor hired by the association. Some of the music played was subject to a copyright held by Famous Music Corp. The playing of that music was a violation of the copyright unless royalties were paid to Famous Music. No royalties were paid, and Famous Music sued the association, which raised the defense that the violation had been committed by an independent contractor specifically instructed not to play Famous Music's copyrighted material. Decide. [*Famous Music Corp. v*

Bay State Harness Horse Racing and Breeding Association, Inc., 554 F2d 1213 (1st Cir)]

12. Steven Trujillo, told by the assistant door manager of Cowboys Bar "to show up to work tonight in case we need you as a doorman," came to the bar that evening wearing a jacket with the bar logo on it. Trujillo "attacked" Rocky Medina in the parking lot of the bar, causing him serious injury. Prior to working for Cowboys, Trujillo was involved in several fights at that bar and in its parking lot, and Cowboys knew of these matters. Medina sued Cowboys on two theories of liability: (1) *respondeat superior* and (2) negligent hiring of Trujillo. Cowboys's defense was that *respondeat superior* theory should be dismissed because the assault was clearly not within the course of Trujillo's employment. Concerning the negligent hiring theory, Cowboys asserted that Trujillo was not on duty that night as a doorman. Decide. [*Medina v Graham's Cowboys, Inc.,* 827 P2d 859 (NM App)]

13. Neal Rubin, while driving his car in Chicago, inadvertently blocked the path of a Yellow Cab Co. taxi driven by Robert Ball, causing the taxi to swerve and hit Rubin's car. Angered by Rubin's driving, Ball got out of his cab and hit Rubin on the head and shoulders with a metal pipe. Rubin sued Yellow Cab Co. for the damages caused by this beating, contending that the employer was vicariously liable for the beating under the doctrine of *respondeat superior* because the beating occurred in furtherance of the employer's business, which was to obtain fares without delay. The company argued that Ball's beating of Rubin was not an act undertaken to further the employer's business. Is the employer liable under *respondeat superior*? [*Rubin v Yellow Cab Co.,* 507 NE2d 114 (Ill App)]

14. Brazilian & Colombian Co. (B&C), a food broker, ordered 40 barrels of olives from Mawer-Gulden-Annis (MGA). MGA's shipping clerk was later told to make out the bill of lading to B&C's customer Pantry Queen; the olives were shipped directly to Pantry Queen. Eight days after delivery, the president of B&C wrote MGA to give it the name of its principal, Pantry Queen, and advised MGA to bill the principal directly. Pantry Queen was unable to pay for the olives, and MGA sued B&C for payment. B&C contended that it was well known to MGA that B&C was a food broker (agent) and the olives were shipped directly to the principal by MGA. It stated that as an agent, it was not a party to the contract and was thus not liable. Decide. [*Mawer-Gulden-Annis, Inc. v Brazilian & Colombian Coffee Co.,* 199 NE2d 222 (Ill App)]

⟩ CPA QUESTIONS

1. Frey entered into a contract with Cara Corp. to purchase televisions on behalf of Lux, Inc. Lux authorized Frey to enter into the contract in Frey's name without disclosing that Frey was acting on behalf of Lux. If Cara repudiates the contract, which of the following statements concerning liability on the contract is *not* correct?

   a. Frey may not hold Cara liable and obtain money damages.
   b. Frey may hold Cara liable and obtain specific performance.
   c. Lux may hold Cara liable upon disclosing the agency relationship with Frey.
   d. Cara will be free from liability to Lux if Frey fraudulently stated that he was acting on his own behalf.

2. A principal will *not* be liable to a third party for a tort committed by an agent

   a. Unless the principal instructed the agent to commit the tort
   b. Unless the tort was committed within the scope of the agency relationship
   c. If the agency agreement limits the principal's liability for the agent's tort
   d. If the tort is also regarded as a criminal act

3. Cox engaged Datz as her agent. It was mutually agreed that Datz would *not* disclose that he was acting as Cox's agent. Instead, he was to deal with prospective customers as if he were a principal acting on his own behalf. This he did and made several contracts for Cox. Assuming Cox, Datz, or

the customer seeks to avoid liability on one of the contracts involved, which of the following statements is correct?

a. Cox must ratify the Datz contracts in order to be held liable.
b. Datz has *no* liability once he discloses that Cox was the real principal.
c. The third party can avoid liability because he believed he was dealing with Datz as a principal.
d. The third party may choose to hold either Datz or Cox liable.

4. Which of the following statements is (are) correct regarding the relationship between an agent and a nondisclosed principal?

   I. The principal is required to indemnify the agent for any contract entered into by the agent within the scope of the agency agreement.
   II. The agent has the same actual authority as if the principal had been disclosed.

a. I only
b. II only
c. Both I and II
d. Neither I nor II

REGULATION
OF EMPLOYMENT

LEARNING OBJECTIVES

After studying this chapter, you should be able to

LO.1 Explain the contractual nature of the employment relationship

LO.2 Identify the five employer unfair labor practices

LO.3 Identify the nine union unfair labor practices

LO.4 State the four ways in which ERISA provides protection for the pension interests of employees

LO.5 Set forth the eligibility requirements for unemployment compensation

LO.6 Explain how the Occupational Safety and Health Act is designed to reach the goal of ensuring safe and healthful working conditions

LO.7 List the three types of benefits provided by workers' compensation statutes

Employment law involves the law of contracts and the law established by lawmakers, courts, and administrative agencies.

THE EMPLOYMENT RELATIONSHIP

The relationship of an employer and an employee exists when, pursuant to an express or implied agreement of the parties, one person, the employee, undertakes to perform services or to do work under the direction and control of another, the employer, for compensation. In older cases, this relationship was called the *master-servant relationship.*

1. CHARACTERISTICS OF RELATIONSHIP

An employee is hired to work under the control of the employer. An employee differs from an agent, who is to negotiate or make contracts with third persons on behalf of, and under the control of, a principal. However, a person may be both an employee and an agent for the other party. An employee also differs from an independent contractor, who is to perform a contract independent of, or free from, control by the other party.[1]

---

[1] *Ost v West Suburban Travelers Limousine, Inc.,* 88 F3d 435 (7th Cir 1996).

2. CREATION OF EMPLOYMENT RELATIONSHIP

The relationship of employer and employee can be created only with the consent of both parties. Generally, the agreement of the parties is a contract. It is therefore subject to all of the principles applicable to contracts. The contract will ordinarily be express, but it may be implied, such as when the employer accepts the rendering of services that a reasonable person would recognize as being rendered with the expectation of receiving compensation.

(a) INDIVIDUAL EMPLOYMENT CONTRACTS   As in contracts generally, both parties must assent to the terms of an employment contract. Subject to statutory restrictions, the parties are free to make a contract on any terms they wish.

(b) COLLECTIVE BARGAINING CONTRACTS   Collective bargaining contracts govern the rights and obligations of employers and employees in many private and public areas of employment. Under collective bargaining, representatives of the employees bargain with a single employer or a group of employers for an agreement on wages, hours, and working conditions. The agreement worked out by the representatives of the employees, usually union officials, is generally subject to a ratification vote by the employees. Terms usually found in collective bargaining contracts are (1) identification of the work belonging exclusively to designated classes of employees, (2) wage and benefits clauses, (3) promotion and layoff clauses, which are generally tied in part to seniority, (4) a management's rights clause, and (5) a grievance procedure. A grievance procedure provides a means by which persons claiming that the contract was violated or that they were disciplined or discharged without just cause may have their cases decided by impartial labor arbitrators.

3. DURATION AND TERMINATION OF EMPLOYMENT CONTRACT

In many instances, the employment contract does not state any time or duration. In such a case, it may be terminated at any time by either party. In contrast, the employment contract may expressly state that it shall last for a specified period of time; an example would be an individual's contract to work as general manager for five years. In some instances, a definite duration may be implied by the circumstances.

(a) EMPLOYMENT-AT-WILL DOCTRINE AND DEVELOPING EXCEPTIONS   Ordinarily, a contract of employment may be terminated in the same manner as any other contract. If it is to run for a definite period of time, the employer cannot terminate the contract at an earlier date without justification. If the employment contract does not have a definite duration, it is terminable at will. Under the **employment-at-will doctrine,** the employer has historically been allowed to terminate the employment contract at any time for any reason or for no reason.[2] Recent court decisions—and in some instances, statutes—have changed the rule in most states by limiting the power of the employer to discharge the employee. Some courts have carved out exceptions to the employment-at-will doctrine when the discharge violated an established public policy.

employment-at-will doctrine doctrine in which the employer has historically been allowed to terminate the employment contract at any time for any reason or for no reason.

---

[2] *Brown v Hammond*, 810 F Supp 644 (ED Pa 1993).

Public policy exceptions are often made to the employment-at-will doctrine when an employee is discharged in retaliation for insisting that the employer comply with the state's food and drug act or for filing a workers' compensation claim.[3] In some states, so-called whistle-blower laws have been enacted to protect employees who disclose employer practices that endanger public health or safety. Also, a statutory right exists for at-will employees who are terminated in retaliation for cooperating with a federal criminal prosecution or are terminated in violation of the public policy to provide truthful testimony.[4]

CASE SUMMARY

Pretext at the Pizzeria

FACTS: While working his nighttime cooking shift at Pizzeria Uno, Gerald Adams noticed that the restaurant's kitchen floor was saturated with a foul-smelling liquid coming from the drains. Adams left work, complaining of illness, and contacted the Department of Health about the drainage problem in the restaurant's kitchen. Upon returning to the restaurant a few days later, Adams was ordered into his manager's office. He was accused of stealing a softball shirt and taking home a work schedule. A shouting match ensued, and Adams was later arraigned on a criminal charge of disorderly conduct. The charges were eventually dropped and have since been expunged from his record. Adams contends that he was unlawfully terminated in violation of the state's whistle-blower act because he notified the Board of Health regarding the unsanitary kitchen conditions. Uno contends he was fired for threatening the supervisor, which is an untenable act.

DECISION: Judgment for Adams in the amount of $7,500. The confrontation between Adams and his employer was calculated by the employer to provoke a reaction from Adams that would serve as an excuse to fire him, a pretext for the real reason—Adam's phone call to the Board of Health. The wrongful termination and criminal charges that ensued from the verbal altercation were sufficient to establish damages for emotional distress. Adams's loss of security clearance in the National Guard, which prevented him from participating in an overseas mission in Germany, also supported the jury's finding of compensable emotional distress. [**Adams v Uno Restaurants, Inc., 18 IER Cases 998 (RI 2002)**]

The contract of employment may be construed to bar a discharge of the employee except for cause. If so construed, good cause would then be required for the discharge of an at-will employee. Written personnel policies used as guidelines for supervisors have also been interpreted as being part of the employment contract. These policies have thus been held to restrict the employer's right to discharge at-will employees without proof of good or just cause. Moreover, employee handbooks that provide for "proper notice and investigation" before termination may bar employers from terminating employees without providing such notice and an investigation.[5]

---

[3] *Brigham v Dillon Companies, Inc.,* 935 P2d 1054 (Kan 1997).

[4] *Fitzgerald v Salsbury Chemical, Inc.,* 613 NW2d 275 (Iowa 2000). In *Garcetti v Ceballos,* 126 SCt 1951 (2006), the U.S. Supreme Court held that when public employees make statements pursuant to their official duties, the First Amendment of the Constitution does not insulate their communications from employer discipline because the employees are not speaking as citizens for First Amendment purposes. In his dissent, Justice Souter argued that a public employee should have constitutional protection when the employee acts as a whistle-blower, pointing out the limitations of protections afforded public employee whistle-blowers (at pages 1970 and 1971).

[5] *Carlson v Lake Chelan Community Hospital,* 66 P3d 1080 (Wash App 2003); but see *Trabing v Kinko's, Inc.,* 57 P3d 1248 (Wyo 2002) and *Williams v First Tennessee National Corp.,* 97 SW3d 798 (Tex App 2003).

Other courts still follow the common law at-will rule because they believe that a court should not rewrite the contract of the parties to provide employee protection that was never intended.[6]

(b) JUSTIFIABLE DISCHARGE An employer may be justified in discharging an employee because of the employee's (1) nonperformance of duties, (2) misrepresentation or fraud in obtaining the employment, (3) disobedience of proper directions, (4) disloyalty, (5) theft or other dishonesty, (6) possession or use of drugs or intoxicants, (7) misconduct, or (8) incompetence.

Employers generally have the right to lay off employees because of economic conditions, including a lack of work. Such actions are sometimes referred to as *reductions in force (RIFs)*.

Employers, however, must be very careful not to make layoffs based on age, for that is a violation of the Age Discrimination in Employment Act.

In some states, a "service letter" statute requires an employer on request to furnish to a discharged employee a letter stating the reason for the discharge.

4. WHISTLE-BLOWER PROTECTION UNDER THE SARBANES-OXLEY ACT

The Sarbanes-Oxley Act (SOA or SOX Act) of 2002 was enacted to restore investor confidence in financial markets following the exposure in 2001–2002 of widespread misconduct by directors and officers of publicly held companies. The SOA contains reforms regarding corporate accountability, enhanced disclosure requirements, and enforcement and liability provisions. Title VIII of the act contains protections for corporate whistle-blowers.[7]

(a) PROTECTION PROVIDED The SOA prohibits a publicly traded company or any agent of it from taking an adverse employment action against an employee who provides information, testifies, or "otherwise assists" in proceedings regarding (1) mail, wire, bank, or securities fraud, (2) any violation of an SEC rule or regulation, or (3) any federal law protecting shareholders against fraud. The act sets forth the types of adverse employment actions that qualify for protection, specifically protecting employees from discharge, demotion, suspension, threats, harassment, failure to hire or rehire, blacklisting, or action otherwise discriminatory against employees in their terms and conditions of employment.

An employee who provides information to the SEC may be incorrect in the belief that an activity is illegal. Nevertheless, the employee is considered involved in a protected activity so long as the employee had an objectively "reasonable belief" that the reported activity was in violation of a federal law protecting shareholders from fraud. **For Example,** when an employee reported to the SEC what he believed to be a financial impropriety regarding delays in payments owed by the company to a subsequent quarter and an SEC investigation exonerated the employer, an administrative law judge found the whistle-blower to have been engaged in "protected activities" because he had a reasonable belief that the company action was illegal.[8]

(b) PROCEDURES An individual who believes that she has been subject to an adverse employment action because of whistle-blowing activities must file a complaint with

---

[6] See *Texas Farm Bureau Mutual Insurance Co. v Sears*, 84 SW3d 604 (Tex 2002).

[7] 18 USC § 1514A (2005).

[8] *Halloum v Intel Corp.*, 2003-SOX-7 (ALJ Mar. 4, 2004).

the Department of Labor's Occupational Safety and Health Administration (OSHA) within 90 days after the asserted adverse employment action. OSHA administers 13 other federal whistle-blower laws and has experienced investigators to facilitate its responsibilities under the SOA.[9]

The burden of proof is on the complainant to demonstrate that the complainant's protected activity was a "contributing factor" in the adverse employment action. If this is established, the burden shifts to the employer to prove by "clear and convincing evidence"—a heavy burden of proof—that it would have taken the same adverse action in the absence of the protected activity.[10]

Whistle-blowers are entitled to make whole relief including reinstatement with all rights unimpaired and compensatory damages, including back pay with interest, and "special damages" such as reasonable attorneys' fees and expert witness fees.

CASE SUMMARY

Welch Likes the SOX—Sarbanes-Oxley

FACTS: On January 28, 2004, the first recommended decision by an administrative law judge that an employer, a rural Virginia bank, Cardinal Bankshares Corp., had violated the SOA was issued. The administrative law judge found that the bank's chief financial officer (CFO) David Welch had been terminated for engaging in protected whistle-blower activity under the SOA. Welch sought to be reinstated to his CFO position with back pay. The bank contended that Welch is unfit to be CFO because of the hostility engendered by the litigation, leaving Welch to work closely with employees, officers, and directors who have critized him since the litigation began.

DECISION: Judgment for Welch. Although Welch will be required to report to a CEO and board of directors who have been openly critical of him since this litigation was initiated, that circumstance is not sufficiently unusual in the context of a Sarbanes-Oxley whistle-blower case to warrant denying him reinstatement. Indeed, doing so would send a clear message to other corporate officers that the act, which Congress passed for the express purpose of encouraging employees to disclose conduct that they reasonably believe to be unlawful, does not apply to them. The recommended order includes reinstatement, back pay, benefits, and attorney's fees. [**Welch v Cardinal Bankshares Corp., 2003-SOX-15 (ALJ Feb 15, 2005)**]

Criminal penalties may be imposed against the employer or its agents for retaliating against an informant who has provided truthful information relating to a federal offense.[11]

5. DUTIES OF THE EMPLOYEE

The duties of an employee are determined primarily by the contract of employment with the employer. The law also implies certain obligations.

(a) SERVICES   Employees are under the duty to perform such services as may be required by the contract of employment.

---

[9] An investigator has authority to order reinstatement of an employee claiming protection of the SOA at the investigatory stage. See *Bechtel v Competitive Technologies, Inc.,* 205-SOX-33 (Oct. 5, 2005).

[10] 18 USC § 1514A(b)(2)(C), and 29 CFR § 1980.104.

[11] 18 USC § 1513(e) (2005).

(b) Trade Secrets An employee may be given confidential trade secrets by the employer but must not disclose this knowledge to others. An agreement by the employee to refrain from disclosing trade secrets is binding. If the employee violates this obligation, the employer may enjoin the use of the information by the employee and by any person to whom it has been disclosed by the employee.

Former employees who are competing with their former employer may be enjoined from using information about suppliers and customers that they obtained while employees when this information is of vital importance to the employer's business. Injunctive relief is denied, however, if the information is not important or not secret.

(c) Inventions Employment contracts commonly provide that an employer will own any invention or discovery made by an employee, whether during work hours, after work hours, or for a period of one or two years after leaving the employment. In the absence of an express or implied agreement to the contrary, the inventions of an employee usually belong to the employee. This is true even though the employee used the time and property of the employer in the discovery. In this case, however, the employer has what is known as a **shop right** to use the invention without cost in its operations.

> **shop right** right of an employer to use in business without charge an invention discovered by an employee during working hours and with the employer's material and equipment.

6. RIGHTS OF THE EMPLOYEE

The rights of an employee are determined by the contract of employment and by the law as declared by courts, lawmakers, and administrative agencies.

(a) Compensation The rights of an employee with respect to compensation are governed in general by the same principles that apply to the compensation of an agent. In the absence of an agreement to the contrary, when an employee is discharged, whether for cause or not, the employer must pay wages to the expiration of the last pay period. State statutes commonly authorize employees to sue employers for wages improperly withheld and to recover penalties and attorney fees. In addition to hourly wages, payments due for vacations and certain bonuses are considered "wages" under state statutes.[12] **For Example,** Diane Beard worked for Summit Institute as a licensed practical nurse for 13 months when she walked off the job and terminated her employment. She requested her accrued vacation pay of $432, but Summit refused to pay her, claiming she had abandoned her job and thus forfeited her right to vacation pay under company policy. Accrued vacation qualifies as "wages," and she was entitled to the $432 vacation pay plus a penalty equal to 90 days' wages at the employee's rate of pay or $9,720, plus $2,400 in attorneys' fees for the trial and an additional $2,600 in attorneys' fees for the appeal. These statutes with their penalty provisions are designed as a coercive means to compel employers to promptly pay their employees.[13]

CPA **(b) Federal Wage and Hour Law** Workers at enterprises engaged in interstate commerce are covered by the Fair Labor Standards Act (FLSA),[14] popularly known

---

[12] *Knutson v Snyder Industries, Inc.*, 436 NW2d 496 (Neb 1989).

[13] *Beard v Summit Institute of Pulmonary Medicine and Rehabilitation, Inc.*, 707 So 2d 1233 (La 1998); see also *Beckman v Kansas Dep't. of Human Resources*, 43 P3d 891 (Kan App 2002).

[14] PL 75-718, 52 Stat 1060, 29 USC § 201 *et seq.*

as the Wage and Hour Act. These workers cannot be paid less than a specified minimum wage.

CASE SUMMARY

What Is a "Willful" Violation?

FACTS: An action against an employer for violating the Fair Labor Standards Act must be brought within two years unless the violation was willful, in which case it may be brought within three years. McLaughlin, the secretary of labor, brought suit against Richland Shoe Company for failing to pay the minimum wage. Richland claimed that the suit was barred because more than two years had elapsed. McLaughlin claimed that the violation was willful, in which case the action was properly brought because three years had not expired. The parties disagreed as to what proof was required to establish that the violation was "willful."

DECISION: To be "willful" within the statute, the violation must be intentional or made with reckless indifference to whether the statute has been satisfied. Because the case had not been tried on the basis of this standard, the case was remanded to the lower court to determine the matter in the light of the new definition of *willful.* [**McLaughlin v Richland Shoe Co., 486 US 128 (1988)**]

The FLSA has been amended to cover domestic service workers, including housekeepers, cooks, and full-time babysitters. Executive, administrative, and professional employees and outside salespersons are exempt from both the minimum wage and overtime provisions of the law.

(1) Subminimum Wage Provisions.   The FLSA allows for the employment of full-time students at institutions of higher education at wage rates below the statutory minimum. Also, individuals whose productive capacity is impaired by age, physical or mental deficiency, or injury may be employed at less than the minimum wage to prevent the curtailment of work opportunities for these individuals. In these cases, however, a special certificate is needed by the employer from the Department of Labor's (DOL) Wage and Hour Division, which has offices throughout the United States.

(2) Wage Issues.   Deductions made from wages as a result of cash or merchandise shortages and deductions for tools of the trade are not legal if they reduce wages below the minimum wage. An employer's requirement that employees provide uniforms or tools of their own is a violation of the law to the extent that the expenses for these items reduce wages below the minimum wage.

Job-related training generally is compensable under the FLSA. However, an exception exists for voluntary training not directly related to an employee's job when the employee does not perform productive work. **For Example,** Hogar, Inc., operates a nursing home and required new employees to undergo two days of unpaid training before assuming paid duties as nurses' aides, maintenance/laundry workers, and kitchen workers. Little or no instruction was offered to these "trainees," and each individual would perform the regular duties of the position for the two-day period. Hogar's practices did not fall within the training exception because the trainees performed productive work with little or no actual training during a regular shift. In a lawsuit brought by the Secretary of Labor, Hogar was ordered by the court to pay

14 hours' pay (two days' pay) for each employee so "trained," plus liquidated damages of an additional 14 hours pay.[15]

(3) Overtime Pay.   Overtime must be paid at a rate of one and a half times the employee's regular rate of pay for each hour worked in excess of 40 hours in a workweek.[16]

(4) Child Labor Provisions.   The FLSA child labor provisions are designed to protect educational opportunities for minors and prohibit their employment in occupations detrimental to their health and well-being. The FLSA restricts hours of work for minors under 16 and lists hazardous occupations too dangerous for minors to perform.

B   LABOR RELATIONS LAWS

Even if employers are not presently unionized, they are subject to certain obligations under federal labor relations law. It is important to both unionized and nonunionized employers to know their rights and obligations under the National Labor Relations Act (NLRA).[17] Employee rights and obligations are also set forth in this act. The Labor-Management Reporting and Disclosure Act regulates internal union affairs.[18]

7. THE NATIONAL LABOR RELATIONS ACT

The National Labor Relations Act (NLRA), passed in 1935, was based on the federal government's power to regulate interstate commerce granted in Article 1, Section 8, of the Constitution. Congress, in enacting this law, explained that its purpose was to remove obstructions to commerce caused by employers who denied their employees the right to join unions and refused to accept collective bargaining.[19] Congress stated that these obstructions resulted in depression of wages, poor working conditions, and diminution of purchasing power.

Section 7 of the amended NLRA is the heart of the act, stating in part that "[e]mployees shall have the right to self-organization . . . to bargain collectively through representatives of their own choosing and to engage in other concerted activities for the purpose of collective bargaining or other mutual aid or protection . . . and shall have the right to refrain from such activities. . . ."

Section 8 of the NLRA contains employer and union unfair labor practices, set forth in Figure 39-1, and authorizes the National Labor Relations Board to conduct proceedings to stop such practices.

The act applies to private-sector employers with gross incomes of $500,000 or more. The Railway Labor Act applies to employees of railroad and air carriers.

---

[15] *Herman v Hogar Praderas De Amor, Inc.,* 130 F Supp 2d 257 (SD PR 2001).

[16] New DOL regulations, referred to as the *white collar exemptions* from the overtime requirements of the FLSA took effect on August 23, 2004. Generally, executive, administrative, professional, outside sales, computer professional, and certain "highly compensated employees" are exempt from the overtime requirements if they meet the "tests" set forth in the new regulations. The U.S. Department of Labor's fact sheets on the new rule are available at **http://www.dol.gov/regs/compliance/whd/fairpay/main.htm**.

[17] 29 USC §§ 141–169. Note that in the *Lechmere* and *Transportation Management* cases presented in this section, the employers were not unionized.

[18] 29 USC §§ 401–531.

[19] NLRA § 1; 29 USC § 141.

FIGURE 39-1   *Employer and Union Unfair Labor Practices Charge*

UNFAIR LABOR PRACTICES CHARGES AGAINST EMPLOYERS	SECTION OF THE NLRA*
1. Restrain or coerce employees in the exercise of their rights under section 7; threat of reprisals or promise of benefits	8(a)(1); 8(c)
2. Dominate or interfere with the formation or administration of a labor organization or contribute financial or other support to it	8(a)(2)
3. Discriminate in regard to hire or tenure of employment or any term or condition of employment in order to encourage or discourage membership in any labor organization	8(a)(3)
4. Discharge or otherwise discriminate against employees because they have given testimony under the act	8(a)(4)
5. Refuse to bargain collectively with representatives of its employees	8(a)(5)

UNFAIR LABOR PRACTICES CHARGES AGAINST UNIONS	SECTION OF THE NLRA
1. Restrain or coerce employees in the exercise of their rights under section 7	8(b)(1)(A)
2. Restrain or coerce an employer in the selection of its representatives	8(b)(1)(B)
3. Cause or attempt to cause an employer to discriminate against an employee	8(b)(2)
4. Refuse to bargain collectively with the employer	8(b)(3)
5. Require employees to pay excessive fees for membership	8(b)(5)
6. Engage in "featherbed practices" of seeking pay for services not performed	8(b)(6)
7. Use secondary boycotts (banned, except for publicity proviso)	8(b)(4)
8. Allow recognitional and organizational picketing by an uncertified union	8(b)(7)
9. Enter into "hot cargo" agreements, except for construction and garment industries	8(e)

* 29 USC § 151.

8. NATIONAL LABOR RELATIONS BOARD

Administration of the NLRA is entrusted to the five-member National Labor Relations Board (NLRB, or Board) and the general counsel of the Board. The general counsel is responsible for investigating and prosecuting all unfair labor practice cases. The five-member Board's major function is to decide unfair labor practice cases brought before it by the general counsel.

The Board is also responsible for conducting representation and decertification elections. This responsibility is delegated to the regional directors of the 32 regional offices located throughout the United States who (1) determine the appropriateness of each proposed bargaining unit for the purpose of collective bargaining, (2) investigate petitions for the certification or decertification of unions, and (3) conduct elections to determine the choice of the majority of those employees voting in the election. Should a majority of the employees voting select a union, the NLRB will certify that union as the exclusive representative of all employees within the unit for the purpose of bargaining with the employer to obtain a contract with respect to wages, hours, and other conditions of employment.

9. ELECTION CONDUCT

The Board of the NLRB has promulgated preelection rules restricting electioneering activities so that the election will express the true desire of employees. The NLRA prohibits employer interference or coercion during the preelection period. The act also prohibits during this period employer statements that contain threats of reprisal or promises of benefits. **For Example,** it is a violation of section 8(c) of the NLRA for a Southern California manufacturer to make implied threats to relocate its plant to Mexico if the employees choose union representation. Furthermore, when the company announced its intent to move to Mexico one day after the union won a representation election, the Labor Board obtained an injunction against the move.[20]

The Board prohibits all electioneering activities at polling places and has formulated a "24-hour rule," which prohibits both unions and employers from making speeches to captive audiences within 24 hours of an election. The rationale is to preserve free elections and prevent any party from obtaining undue advantage.

10. UNION ACTIVITY ON PRIVATE PROPERTY

Although section 7 of the NLRA gives employees the statutory right to self-organization, employers have the undisputed right to make rules to maintain discipline in their establishments. Generally speaking, employers may prohibit union solicitation by employees during work periods. During nonworking time, employers may prohibit activity and communications only for legitimate efficiency and safety reasons and only if the prohibitions are not manifestly intended to impede employees' exercise of their rights under the law. Nonunion employers, moreover, may not refuse to interview or retain union members because of their union membership. And even if a union pays an individual working for a nonunion employer to help organize the company, that individual is still protected under the NLRA.[21]

---

[20] See *Quadrtech Corp.*, NLRB, No 21–CA–33997 (settlement Dec. 11, 2000).
[21] *NLRB v Town & Country Electric, Inc.*, 516 US 85 (1995).

An employer may validly post its property against all nonemployee solicitations, including distribution of union literature, if reasonable efforts by the union through other available channels of communication would enable it to reach the employees with its message.

CASE SUMMARY

The Supreme Court Is Always Right

FACTS: Lechmere, Inc., owned and operated a retail store located in a shopping plaza in Newington, a suburb of Hartford, Connecticut. Lechmere was also part owner of the plaza's parking lot, which was separated from a public highway by a 46-foot-wide grassy strip. Almost all of the strip was public property. In a campaign to organize Lechmere employees, nonemployee union organizers from Local 919 of the United Food and Commercial Workers placed handbills on the windshields of cars parked in the employees' part of the parking lot. After Lechmere denied the organizers access to the lot, they picketed from the grassy strip. In addition, they were able to contact directly some 20 percent of the employees. The union filed an unfair labor practice charge with the Board, alleging that Lechmere had violated the NLRA by barring the organizers from its property. An administrative law judge ruled in the union's favor. The Board affirmed, and the court of appeals enforced the Board's order. The matter was heard by the Supreme Court.

DECISION: Judgment for Lechmere. A two-stage test is used in evaluating the accommodation between the employees' right to learn of the advantages of unionization from outside union organizers and an employer's property rights. Stage 1 considers whether the outsiders have reasonable access to employees off the employer's property. Stage 2 applies if the access is infeasible. In such a case, the employer's property rights must yield to the extent needed to communicate information on organizational rights. The Court majority determined that the outsiders had reasonable access from the grassy strip. The dissent believed that holding up signs from the grassy strip was not sufficient to learn of advantages of unionization. [**Lechmere, Inc. v NLRB, 502 US 527 (1992)**]

ETHICS & THE LAW

May a "Salt" Lie His Way into a Job?

"Salting" is a practice whereby a union inserts paid organizers into a workforce in the hope of organizing it. Starnes stated on his job application for work at Hartman Brothers, Inc., that he had been "laid off" by a previous employer from a job paying $11 an hour when in truth he had taken a leave of absence to participate in a union's organizing efforts at Hartman Brothers. Hartman Brothers paid $8.50 per hour, so had Starnes disclosed that he had taken a leave of absence from a higher-paying job, Hartman might have "smelled a rat," for why would someone take a leave of absence to earn less pay unless he were a "salt"? When Mr. Hartman was informed Starnes was a union organizer, Starnes was sent home. State law makes it a crime for a person to "knowingly or intentionally make a false or misleading written statement with the intent to obtain . . . employment." A lie related solely to one's union affiliation or unionizing intentions, rather than one's fitness for the

ETHICS & THE LAW

continued

job, cannot be material to a hiring decision under the U.S. Supreme Court's *Town & Country* decision. Can an employer turn down an applicant for a job on the basis of a lie about salt status? Will state law prevail over the *Town & Country* precedent? Is an employer entitled to infer that a salt will not be a bona fide employee? Is it ethical for an employee to lie about salt status when he knows that if he tells the truth, he will not be hired? [See *Hartman Brothers Heating & Air Conditioning, Inc. v NLRB*, 280 F3d 1110 (7th Cir 2002); and *Fluor Daniel Inc., v NLRB*, 332 F3d 961 (6th Cir 2003), *cert denied* 125 SCt 964 (2005)]

E-COMMERCE AND CYBERLAW

Union Organizing and Other Management Challenges Through Electronic Communications

E-mail and the Internet are efficient and effective means of communicating information about employment-related matters. Section 7 of the National Labor Relations Act permits "employees" to engage in "concerted activities for the purposes of collective bargaining or other mutual aid or protection." The term *employee* is broadly defined to include job applicants and all current nonsupervisory employees, either union or nonunion. Many labor unions maintain Web sites that assist individuals in forming labor unions.* And many employees with access to computers at work can readily communicate with one another about the benefits of unionization or otherwise challenge certain management policies.

In the National Labor Relations Board's Timekeeping Systems Inc.** decision, the Board ordered the reinstatement with back pay of a nonunion software employee, Lawrence Leinweber, who was fired for sending an e-mail to fellow employees critical of the company's new mandatory vacation policy that would close the business December 23 and reopen it on January 2 each year. The company memo announcing the policy asserted that employees would "actually get more days off each year." Leinweber demonstrated in his e-mail that the company's assertion was false. The Board found that the e-mail message to other employees in opposition to the company's proposal was "concerted activity" protected under section 7 of the NLRA even though the company was a nonunion employer.

The Timekeeping Systems case indicates that the NLRB will apply traditional labor law precedents to electronic communications.

---

*For example, the United Auto Workers's Web site is **http://www.uaw.org;** the United Food and Commercial Workers's Web site is **http://www.ufcw.org;** and the Teamsters Union's Web site is **http://www.teamsters.org.**

**323 NLRB No. 30 (1997).

11. FIRING EMPLOYEES FOR UNION ACTIVITY

Although employers and supervisors often feel betrayed by individual employees who take leadership roles in forming organizations, the NLRA prohibits discrimination against such employees because of their union activity.

The NLRB has found evidence of discrimination against active union supporters when the employer

1. Discharges on the strength of past misdeeds that were condoned;
2. Neglects to give customary warnings prior to discharge;
3. Discharges for a rule generally unenforced;
4. Applies disproportionately severe punishment to union supporters; or
5. Effects layoffs in violation of seniority status with disproportionate impact on union supporters.

The NLRA preserves the right of the employer to maintain control over the workforce in the interest of discipline, efficiency, and pleasant and safe customer relations. Employees, on the other hand, have the right to be free from coercive discrimination resulting from union activity.

At times these two rights may collide. For example, an employee may be discharged for apparently two reasons: (1) violation of a valid company rule and (2) union activity. The employer gives the former as the reason for termination; the latter remains unstated on the employer's part, causing the filing of a section 8(a)(3) unfair labor practice charge against the employer. These are known as *dual motive cases.* The general counsel must present on behalf of the dismissed employee a prima facie case that such protected conduct as union activity was a motivating factor in the dismissal. After this showing, the burden shifts to the employer, who must prove that the employee would have been dismissed for legitimate business reasons even absent the protected conduct.

CASE SUMMARY

The Sam Santillo Story

FACTS: Prior to his discharge, Sam Santillo was a bus driver for Transportation Management Corporation. On March 19, Santillo talked to officials of the Teamsters Union about organizing the drivers who worked with him. Over the next four days, Santillo discussed with his fellow drivers the possibility of joining the Teamsters and distributed authorization cards. On the night of March 23, George Patterson, who supervised Santillo and the other drivers, told one of the drivers that he had heard of Santillo's activities. Patterson referred to Santillo as two-faced and promised to get even with him. Later that evening, Patterson talked to Ed West, who was also a bus driver. Patterson asked, "What's with Sam and the Union?" Patterson said that he took Santillo's actions personally, recounted several favors he had done for Santillo, and added that he would remember Santillo's activities when Santillo again asked for a favor. On Monday, March 26, Santillo was discharged. Patterson told Santillo that he was being fired for leaving his keys in the bus and taking unauthorized breaks. Santillo filed charges with the Board, and the general counsel issued a complaint, contending that Santillo was discharged because of his union activities in distributing authorization cards to fellow

employees. The evidence revealed that the practice of leaving keys in buses was commonplace among company employees and the company tolerated the practice of taking coffee breaks. The company had never taken disciplinary action against an employee for the behavior in question.

DECISION: Judgment for Santillo and the NLRB. The general counsel established a prima facie case by showing that Santillo was involved in union-organizing activities just prior to his discharge. The employer did not meet its burden of proving that Santillo was fired for a legitimate business reason. The infractions involved were commonplace, and no discipline had ever been issued to any employee previously. The reasons given by the company were pretextual. Santillo would not have been fired had the employer not considered his effort to establish a union. [**NLRB v Transportation Management Corp.**, 462 US 393 (1983)]

12. DUTY OF EMPLOYER TO BARGAIN COLLECTIVELY

Once a union wins a representative election, the Board certifies the union as the exclusive bargaining representative of the employees. The employer then has the obligation under the NLRA to bargain with the union in good faith over wages, hours, and working conditions. These matters are *mandatory subjects of bargaining* and include seniority provisions, promotions, layoff and recall provisions, no-strike no-lockout clauses, and grievance procedures. Employers also have an obligation to bargain about the "effects" of the shutdown of a part of a business[22] and may have an obligation to bargain over the decision to relocate bargaining unit work to other plants.[23]

Permissive subjects of bargaining are those over which an employer's refusal to bargain is not a section 8(a)(5) unfair labor practice. Examples are the required use of union labels, internal union affairs, union recognition clauses, and benefits for already retired workers.

13. RIGHT TO WORK

right-to-work laws laws restricting unions and employees from negotiating clauses in their collective bargaining agreements that make union membership compulsory.

The NLRA allows states to enact **right-to-work laws.** These laws restrict unions and employers from negotiating clauses in their collective bargaining agreements that make union membership compulsory.[24]

Advocates of such laws contend that compulsory union membership is contrary to the First Amendment right of freedom of association. Unions have attacked these laws as unfair because unions must represent all employees, and in right-to-work states where a majority of employees vote for union representation, nonunion employees receive all of the benefits of collective bargaining contracts without paying union dues.

---

[22] *First National Maintenance v NLRB,* 452 US 666 (1981).

[23] *Dubuque Packing Co. and UFCWIU, Local 150A,* 303 NLRB 66 (1991).

[24] Right-to-work statutes declare unlawful any agreement that denies persons the right to work because of nonmembership in a union or the failure to pay dues to a union as a condition of employment. These laws have been adopted in Alabama, Arizona, Arkansas, Florida, Georgia, Idaho, Iowa, Kansas, Louisiana, Mississippi, Nebraska, Nevada, North Carolina, North Dakota, Oklahoma, South Carolina, South Dakota, Tennessee, Texas, Utah, Virginia, and Wyoming.

14. STRIKE AND PICKETING ACTIVITY

If the parties reach an impasse in the negotiation process for a collective bargaining agreement, a union may call a strike and undertake picketing activity to enforce its bargaining demands. Strikers in such a situation are called **economic strikers.** Although the strike activity is legal, the employers may respond by hiring temporary or permanent replacement workers.

economic strikers union strikers trying to enforce bargaining demands when an impasse has been reached in the negotiation process for a collective bargaining agreement.

(a) RIGHTS OF STRIKERS   Economic strikers who unconditionally apply for reinstatement when their positions are filled by permanent replacements are not entitled to return to work at the end of the economic strike. They are, however, entitled to full reinstatement when positions become available.

CASE SUMMARY

Avoiding the Sack—The Pilots Returned Before Their Positions Were Filled

FACTS: Striking pilots of Eastern Airlines made an unconditional offer to return to work on November 22, 1989. As of that date, some 227 new-hire replacement pilots were in training but had not obtained certificates from the Federal Aviation Administration permitting them to fly revenue flights. The striking pilots contended that the trainees were not permanent replacement pilots on the date they offered to go back to work because the trainees could not lawfully fly revenue flights. Eastern contended that the new-hire pilots were permanent employees and as such should not be displaced.

DECISION: The pilots' positions were not filled by permanent replacements at the time the striking pilots unconditionally applied to return to work. The new-hire replacement pilots were not qualified to fill the positions at that time. Giving preference to trainees over returning strikers would discourage employees from exercising their right to strike. [**Eastern Airlines Inc. v Airline Pilots Association Int'l, 970 F2d 722 (11th Cir 1990)**]

primary picketing legal presentations in front of a business notifying the public of a labor dispute.

mass picketing illegal tactic of employees massing together in great numbers to effectively shut down entrances of the employer's facility.

secondary picketing picketing an employer with which a union has no dispute to persuade the employer to stop doing business with a party to the dispute; generally illegal under the NLRA.

Strikers responsible for misconduct while out on strike may be refused reemployment by the employer.

When employees strike to protest an employer's unfair labor practice, such as firing an employee for union-organizing activity, these unfair labor practice strikers have a right to return to their jobs immediately at the end of the strike. This right exists even if the employer has hired permanent replacements.[25]

(b) PICKETING   Placing persons outside a business at the site of a labor dispute so that they may, by signs or banners, inform the public of the existence of a labor dispute is called **primary picketing** and is legal. Should the picketing employees mass together in great numbers in front of the gates of the employer's facility to effectively shut down the entrances, such coercion is called **mass picketing**; it is illegal. **Secondary picketing** is picketing an employer with whom a union has no dispute to persuade the employer to stop doing business with a party to the

<hr>

[25] *Poly America, Inc. v NLRB,* 260 F3d 465 (5th Cir 2001).

dispute. Secondary picketing is generally illegal under the NLRA. An exception exists for certain product picketing at supermarkets or other multiproduct retail stores provided that it is limited to asking customers not to purchase the struck product at the neutral employer's store.[26]

15. REGULATION OF INTERNAL UNION AFFAIRS

To ensure the honest and democratic administration of unions, Congress passed the Labor-Management Reporting and Disclosure Act (LMRDA).[27] Title IV of the LMRDA establishes democratic standards for all elections for union offices, including

1. Secret ballots in local union elections;
2. Opportunity for members to nominate candidates;
3. Advance notice of elections;
4. Observers at polling and at ballot-counting stations for all candidates;
5. Publication of results and preservation of records for one year;
6. Prohibition of any income from dues or assessments to support candidates for union office; and
7. Advance opportunity for each candidate to inspect the membership name and address lists.

PENSION PLANS AND FEDERAL REGULATION

The Employee Retirement Income Security Act (ERISA)[28] was adopted in 1974 to protect employee pensions.

16. ERISA

The act sets forth fiduciary standards and requirements for administration, vesting, funding, and termination insurance.

(a) ADMINISTRATION   Commonly a "benefits claims committee" is set up under the plan to make determinations about coverage issues, and courts will not disturb the finding of a benefits committee unless the determinations are "arbitrary and capricious." **For Example,** Joe Gustafson, who provided chauffeur services for senior executives at NYNEX for a number of years while classified as an independent contractor, sought benefits under ERISA because he asserted he was a common law employee of NYNEX. While the court determined he was in fact an employee entitled to overtime compensation under the Fair Labor Standards Act, the court was compelled to defer to the benefits committee's determination that Gustafson was not an employee under the NYNEX plan because he was not "on the payroll" as required by the plan guidelines. The court found that such a determination was not arbitrary or capricious.[29]

(b) FIDUCIARY STANDARDS AND REPORTING   Persons administering a pension fund must handle it to protect the interest of employees.[30]

---

[26] *NLRB v Fruit and Vegetable Packers, Local 760 (Tree Fruits, Inc.),* 377 US 58 (1964); but see *NLRB v Retail Clerks, Local 1001 (Safeco Title Ins. Co.),* 477 US 607 (1980).

[27] 29 USC §§ 401–531.

[28] PL 93-406, 88 Stat 829, 29 USC §§ 1001–1381.

[29] *Gustafson v Bell Atlantic Corp.,* 171 F Supp 2d 311 (SDNY 2001).

[30] *John Hancock Mutual Life Ins. Co. v Harris Trust,* 510 US 86 (1993).

CASE SUMMARY

Placing a Conglomerate's Money-Losing Eggs in One Financially Rickety Basket

FACTS: Charles Howe and others worked for Massey-Ferguson, a wholly owned subsidiary of Varity Corporation. These employees were beneficiaries of Massey-Ferguson's self-funded employee welfare benefit plan, an ERISA-protected plan that Massey-Ferguson itself administered. In the mid-1980s, Varity became concerned that some of Massey-Ferguson's money-losing divisions were losing too much money, and it developed a business plan to deal with the problem that amounted to placing many of Varity's money-losing eggs in one financially rickety basket. It called for a transfer of Massey-Ferguson's money-losing divisions, along with other debts, to a newly created, separately incorporated subsidiary called Massey Combines. The plan foresaw the possibility that Massey Combines would fail, but it viewed such a failure, from Varity's business perspective, as closer to a victory than to a defeat because failure would eliminate several poorly performing divisions and eradicate various debts that Varity would transfer to Massey Combines. Among the obligations that Varity hoped the reorganization would eliminate were those arising from the benefits plan's promises to pay medical and other nonpension benefits to employees of Massey-Ferguson's money-losing divisions. To persuade the employees of the failing divisions to accept the change of employer and benefits, Varity called them together at a special meeting and talked to them about its likely financial viability and the security of their employee benefits. The thrust of Varity's remarks was that the employees' benefits would remain secure if they voluntarily transferred to Massey Combines. As Varity knew, however, the reality was very different. The evidence showed that Massey Combines was insolvent from the day of its creation and that it hid its $46 million negative net worth by overvaluing its assets and underestimating its liabilities. After Massey Combines went into receivership, the employees lost their benefits, and Howe and others sued for reinstatement of the old plan. Varity's defense was that individuals did not have a right to bring an ERISA lawsuit for individual relief. It also contended that when its managers talked to employees at the special meeting, they did so in their capacity as employer and not as plan administrators.

DECISION: Judgment for Howe and the other employees restoring plan benefits. When an employer runs a benefits plan and its managers or agents, regardless of their job titles, talk about those benefits to employees, painting a false picture of security to induce them to transfer to a new company by saying "your benefits are secure," they are fiduciaries, and their breach of fiduciary duties in making false and misleading statements is binding on the employer. ERISA § 502(a)(3) authorizes lawsuits for individual equitable relief for breach of fiduciary duties. [**Varity Corp. v Howe, 516 US 489 (1996)**]

The fact that an employer contributed all or part of the money to the pension fund does not entitle it to use the fund as though the employer still owned it. Persons administering pension plans must make detailed reports to the Secretary of Labor.

CPA (C) **VESTING** *Vesting* is the right of an employee to pension benefits paid into a pension plan in the employee's name by the employer. Prior to ERISA, many pension plans did not vest accrued benefits until an employee had 20 to 25 years of service. Thus, an employee who was forced to terminate service after 18 years would have no pension rights or benefits. Under ERISA, employees' rights must be fully vested within five or seven years in accordance with the two vesting options available under the law.

In the past, it had been common for pension plans to contain break-in-service clauses, whereby employees who left their employment for a period longer than one year for any reason other than an on-the-job injury lost pension eligibility rights. Under the Retirement Equity Act of 1984,[31] an individual can leave the workforce for up to five consecutive years and still retain eligibility for pension benefits.

CPA   **(d)** FUNDING   ERISA requires that employers make contributions to their pension funds on a basis that is actuarially determined so that the pension fund will be large enough to make the payments that will be required of it.

(e) TERMINATION INSURANCE   ERISA established an insurance plan to protect employees when an employer goes out of business. To provide this protection, the statute created a Pension Benefit Guaranty Corporation (PBGC). In effect, this corporation guarantees that employees will receive benefits in much the same way as the Federal Deposit Insurance Corporation protects bank depositors. The PBGC is financed by small payments made by employers for every employee covered by a pension plan.

(f) ENFORCEMENT   ERISA authorizes the Secretary of Labor and employees to bring court actions to compel the observance of statutory requirements.

Ⓓ UNEMPLOYMENT BENEFITS, FAMILY LEAVES, AND SOCIAL SECURITY

Generally, when employees are without work through no fault of their own, they are eligible for unemployment compensation benefits. Twelve-week maternity, paternity, or adoption leaves and family and medical leaves are available for qualifying employees. Social Security provides certain benefits, including retirement and disability benefits.

17. UNEMPLOYMENT COMPENSATION

Unemployment compensation today is provided primarily through a federal-state system under the unemployment insurance provisions of the Social Security Act of 1935.[32] All states have laws that provide similar benefits, and the state agencies are loosely coordinated under the federal act. Agricultural employees, domestic employees, and state and local government employees are not covered by this federal-state system. Federal programs of unemployment compensation exist for federal civilian workers and former military service personnel. A separate federal unemployment program applies to railroad workers.

(a) ELIGIBILITY   In most states, an unemployed person must be available for placement in a similar job and willing to take such employment at a comparable rate of pay. Full-time students generally have difficulty proving that they are available for work while they are still going to school.

---

[31] PL 98-397, 29 USC § 1001.
[32] 42 USC §§ 301–1397e.

CASE SUMMARY

Priority of Necessity: Work Comes Before School

FACTS: Robert Evjen was a full-time employee of Boise Cascade. At the same time, he was a full-time student at Chemata Community College. He was laid off as part of a general economy move by the employer. He applied for unemployment compensation. His claim was opposed on the ground that he was not available for work because he was going to school. The referee found that Evjen never missed work to go to classes, that he could not afford to go to school without working, and that, in case of any conflict between work and school, work came first.

DECISION: Judgment for Evjen. To obtain unemployment benefits, an unemployed individual must prove, among other things, that she or he is "available for work" and is unable to obtain suitable work. A student's unavailability for work during school hours is contrary to the concept of "available for work," which requires availability for all shifts of suitable work. However, Evjen's uncontroverted testimony that his education was secondary to his employment was sufficient to overcome either an inference or a presumption of nonavailability. He was available for work and therefore entitled to unemployment compensation. [**Evjen v Employment Agency, 539 P2d 662 (Or App 1975)**]

If an employee quits a job without cause or is fired for misconduct, the employee is ordinarily disqualified from receiving unemployment compensation benefits. **For Example,** stealing property from an employer constitutes misconduct for which benefits will be denied. Moreover, an employee's refusal to complete the aftercare portion of an alcohol treatment program has been found to be misconduct connected with work, disqualifying the employee from receiving benefits.

(b) Funding Employers are taxed for unemployment benefits based on each employer's "experience rating" account. Thus, employers with a stable workforce with no layoffs, who therefore do not draw on the state unemployment insurance fund, pay lower tax rates. Employers whose experience ratings are higher pay higher rates. Motivated by the desire to avoid higher unemployment taxes, employers commonly challenge the state's payment of unemployment benefits to individuals who they believe are not properly entitled to benefits.

18. FAMILY AND MEDICAL LEAVES OF ABSENCE

The Family and Medical Leave Act of 1993 (FMLA)[33] entitles an eligible employee, whether male or female, to a total of 12 workweeks of unpaid leave during any 12-month period (1) because of the birth or adoption of the employee's son or daughter, (2) to care for the employee's spouse, son, daughter, or parent with a serious health condition, or (3) because of a serious health condition that makes the employee unable to perform the functions of his or her position. Notice should be given by the employer to an employee that the leave he or she is taking will count against FMLA entitlement in order to comply with the Secretary of Labor's regulations.[34] In the case of an employee's serious health condition or that of a covered family member, an employer may require the employee to use any accrued paid vacation, personal,

---

[33] 29 USC §§ 2601–2654.
[34] See *Ragsdale v Volverine World Wide, Inc.*, 122 S Ct 1155 (2002).

medical, or sick leave toward any part of the 12-week leave provided by the act. When an employee requests leave because of the birth or adoption of a child, the employer may require the employee to use all available paid personal, vacation, and medical leave, but not sick leave, toward any FMLA leave.

To be eligible for FMLA leave, an employee must have been employed by a covered employer for at least 12 months and have worked at least 1,250 hours during the 12-month period preceding the leave. Covered employers are those that employ 50 or more employees.[35] Upon return from FMLA leave, the employee is entitled to be restored to the same or an equivalent position with equivalent pay and benefits. **For Example,** when Magda Brenlla returned to her position at LaSorsa Buick in the Bronx, New York, after quadruple bypass surgery, she was terminated by the owner who told her he had decided to consolidate the positions of office manager and controller, even though he had no business plan for restructuring, and soon thereafter had to hire additional help in the office. The judge upheld a jury verdict of $320,000, finding that the jury had ample evidence to conclude that the real reason for her termination was her FMLA leave.[36]

The FMLA provides specific statutory relief for violations of the provisions of the act, including pay to the employee for damages equal to lost wages and benefits or any actual monetary losses, plus interest, plus an equal amount in liquidated damages.[37]

19. LEAVES FOR MILITARY SERVICE UNDER USERRA

The Uniformed Services Employment and Re-Employment Rights Act (USERRA) was enacted in 1994 to encourage noncareer service in the armed services, minimize the disruption experienced in the civilian careers of reservists, and promote prompt reemployment of reservists upon return from military leave.[38] In the context of mobilizing more than 500,000 reservists between September 11, 2001, and the summer of 2006, the USERRA has and will have a broad impact on U.S. employers as it provides reemployment and benefit protection rights for returning military personnel and prohibits discrimination against individuals because of their application for or performance of military service.[39]

(a) PROTECTIONS   Section 4312 of the USERRA generally requires returning reservists to be "promptly reemployed" and returned to the same or comparable positions of like seniority, status, and pay they would have had if they had not been activated. Moreover, Section 4316(c) provides that persons reemployed under the act shall not be discharged from employment within a year of their reemployment if their period of service was more than 180 days. For service of more than 30 days, the protective period is 180 days. However, the employer may terminate an individual for cause regardless of the duration of service.

Sections 4312(a)(3) and (4) provide protection for those disabled while in the service and requires employers to make reasonable efforts to accommodate each

---

[35] *Bellum v PCE Constructors Inc.*, 407 F3d 734 (5th Cir 2005).

[36] *Brenlla v LaSorsa Buick*, 2002 WL 1059117 (SDNY 2002).

[37] See *Arban v West Publishing Co.*, 345 F3d 390 (6th Cir 2003), in which the U.S. Court of Appeals required the doubling of a jury verdict of $130,000 under the FMLA provision providing for liquidated damages unless the employer is able to prove that it acted "in good faith. . ." and had reasonable grounds to believe it was not in violation of the FMLA. 29 USC § 2617(a)(iii).

[38] 38 USC.§ 4301 (2005).

[39] 38 USC § 4312, 4316, and 4317 (2005).

employee's disability so that each individual may return to the same or comparable positions or, if no longer qualified for the position, allow for the transfer to a position the disabled individual can perform closest to the prior position in terms of seniority, status, and pay.

Section 4323 of the act provides a full range of remedies, including back pay for loss of wages and benefits as well as liquidated damages in an amount equal to the actual damages when the employer's failure to comply with the act was willful. The Department of Labor has issued USERRA regulations.[40] The act's enforcement is performed by the U.S. Justice Department's Division of Civil Rights.

(b) Defenses In addition to an employer's right to terminate a reemployed service-person for cause, employers may be excused from reemploying or continuing employment of persons under § 4312(d)(1) of the act when the employer's circumstances have so changed as to make reemployment impossible, unreasonable, or an undue hardship. The burden of proof on the matter is on the employer. **For Example,** Joseph Duarte was called to active duty in the Marine Corps Reserve from November 2002 to July 2003. On his return, he was given his same pay but diminished status by being assigned a temporary assignment rather than acting as a primary consultant to one of the employer's business groups. Faced with financial need to reduce its payroll, the employer eliminated Duarte's temporary assignment and terminated him in November 2003 for what it believed was economic "cause." Duarte believed that his termination violated the USERRA. The court disagreed with the employer and determined that Duarte was within the act's one-year protective period and had been returned to work in the diminished status of a temporary assignment that was a direct result of his military service. Duarte was awarded back pay of $114,500 and front pay of $324,000, less $55,000 in severance benefits already paid him, for a total of $384,000 in damages.[41] Liquidated damages equal to $384,000 were declined because the employer's actions were not deemed willful.

(c) Discrimination and Retaliation Protection As opposed to the protections contained in Section 4312, the act's Section 4311 provides separate and distinct statutory protection against discrimination of employees on the basis of military service and retaliation against individuals, whether military or not, who give testimony or statements on behalf of a USERRA claimant. **For Example,** a Section 4311 descrimination violation is made out that bakery driver Robert Mills was terminated by Multigrain Baking Co. because of his need to have time off for reserve duty training after the personnel director, Marsha Coyle, testified on cross-examination, "If we knew Bobby Mills was in the Guard, we would not have hired him. These drivers have to be available to protect their territories or we lose business."

20. SOCIAL SECURITY

Employees and employers are required to pay Social Security taxes, which provide employees with four types of insurance protection: retirement benefits, disability benefits, life insurance benefits, and health insurance (Medicare). The federal Social

---

[40] 30 Federal Register Vol. 70 No. 242 (Dec. 19, 2005).

[41] *Duarte v Agilent Technologies, Inc.*, 366 F Supp 2d 1039 (D Colo 2005).

Security Act established a federal program of aid for the aged, the blind, and the disabled. This is called the Supplemental Security Income (SSI) program. Payments are administered directly by the Social Security Administration, which became an independent government agency in 1995.

 ## EMPLOYEES' HEALTH AND SAFETY

The Occupational Safety and Health Act of 1970 (OSHA) was passed to assure every worker, so far as possible, safe and healthful working conditions and to preserve the country's human resources.[42] OSHA provides for (1) the establishment of safety and health standards and (2) effective enforcement of these standards and the other employer duties required by OSHA.

21. STANDARDS

The Secretary of Labor has broad authority under OSHA to promulgate occupational safety and health standards.[43] Except in emergency situations, public hearings and publication in the *Federal Register* are required before the secretary can issue a new standard. Any person adversely affected may then challenge the validity of the standard in a U.S. court of appeals. The secretary's standards will be upheld if they are reasonable and supported by substantial evidence. The secretary must demonstrate a need for a new standard by showing that it is reasonably necessary to protect employees against a "significant risk" of material health impairment. The cost of compliance with new standards may run into billions of dollars. The secretary is not required to do a cost-benefit analysis for a new standard but must show that the standard is economically feasible.

22. EMPLOYER DUTIES

Employers have a "general duty" to furnish each employee a place of employment that is free from hazards that are likely to cause death or serious physical injuries.

OSHA requires employers to maintain records of occupational illness and injuries if they result in death, loss of consciousness, or one or more lost workdays or if they require medical treatment other than first aid. Such records have proven to be a valuable aid in recognizing areas of risk. They have been especially helpful in identifying the presence of occupational illnesses.

23. ENFORCEMENT

The Occupational Safety and Health Administration (also identified as OSHA) is the agency within the Department of Labor that administers the act. OSHA has authority to conduct inspections and to seek enforcement action when noncompliance has occurred. Worksite inspections are conducted when employer records indicate incidents involving fatalities or serious injuries.[44] These inspections may also result from employee complaints. The act protects employees making complaints from employer retaliation. Employers have the right to require an OSHA inspector to secure a warrant before inspecting the employer's plant.

---

[42] 29 USC § 651 *et seq.*

[43] *Martin v OSHRC*, 499 US 144 (1991).

[44] *Chao v Mallard Bay Drilling Co.*, 122 S Ct 738 (2002).

If OSHA issues a citation for a violation of workplace health or safety standards, the employer may challenge the citation before the Occupational Safety and Health Review Commission (OSHRC). Judicial review of a commission ruling is obtained before a U.S. court of appeals. **For Example,** after an accident at Staley Manufacturing Company's Decatur, Illinois, plant in which an employee was fatally asphyxiated, OSHA inspectors issued citations for multiple violations of the OSH Act. The employer challenged the citations before the OSHRC. Upon review by the U.S. Court of Appeals, the court affirmed OSHRC's decision, finding that the company's "plain indifference" to act on the hazards at the workplace and train employees how to handle the hazards was a willful violation of the act, allowing for civil penalty of no more than $70,000 for each violation.[45]

The Occupational Safety and Health Act provides that no employer shall discharge or in any manner discriminate against employees because they filed a complaint with OSHA, testified in any OSHA proceeding, or exercised any right afforded by the act. A regulation issued by the Secretary of Labor under the act provides that if employees with no reasonable alternative refuse in good faith to expose themselves to a dangerous condition, they will be protected against subsequent discrimination. The Secretary of Labor may obtain injunctive and other appropriate relief in a U.S. district court against an employer who discriminates against employees for testifying or exercising any right under the act.

CASE SUMMARY

To Work or Not to Work? Empowering Employees to Refuse to Expose Themselves to Dangerous Duties

FACTS: Virgil Deemer and Thomas Cornwell, employees at a Whirlpool Corporation plant, refused to comply with a supervisor's order that they perform maintenance work on certain mesh screens located some 20 feet above the plant floor. Twelve days before this incident, a fellow employee had fallen to his death from the screens. After their refusal to work on the screens, the men were ordered to stop work and leave the plant. They were not paid for the remaining six hours of their shift, and written reprimands for insubordination were placed in their employment files. The Secretary of Labor filed suit against Whirlpool, contending that Whirlpool's actions against Deemer and Cornwell constituted "discrimination" under the secretary's regulation and Section 11(C)(1) of the act. Whirlpool contended that the regulation encouraged workers to engage in "self-help" and unlawfully permitted a "strike with pay."

DECISION: Judgment against Whirlpool. The Occupational Safety and Health Act's "general duty" clause requires an employer to furnish a workplace free from hazards that are likely to cause death or serious injury to employees. OSHA inspectors cannot be present around the clock in every workplace to enforce this clause. Thus, each worker has the power to make a good-faith decision that there is danger. In the unusual circumstances that Deemer and Cornwell faced, when in good faith and without reasonable alternatives they refused to expose themselves to the dangerous work on the mesh screens, the secretary's regulation protects them against subsequent discrimination by the employer for the refusal. The secretary's regulation is consistent with the act's "general duty" clause, and the employer violated this regulation when it placed reprimands in the personnel files of Deemer and Cornwell. [**Whirpool v Marshall,** 445 US 1 (1980)]

---

[45] *A. E. Staley Manufacturing Co. v Chao,* 295 F3d 1341 (DC Cir 2002).

24. STATE "RIGHT-TO-KNOW" LEGISLATION

Laws that guarantee individual workers the "right to know" if there are hazardous substances in their workplaces have been enacted by many states in recent years. These laws commonly require an employer to make known to an employee's physician the chemical composition of certain workplace substances in connection with the employee's diagnosis and treatment by the physician. Furthermore, local fire and public health officials, as well as local neighborhood residents, are given the right to know if local employers are working with hazardous substances that could pose health or safety problems.

 COMPENSATION FOR EMPLOYEES' INJURIES

For most kinds of employment, workers' compensation statutes govern compensation for injuries. These statutes provide that an injured employee is entitled to compensation for accidents occurring in the course of employment from a risk involved in that employment.

 ## 25. COMMON LAW STATUS OF EMPLOYER

In some employment situations, common law principles apply. Workers' compensation statutes commonly do not apply to employers with fewer than a prescribed minimum number of employees or to agricultural, domestic, or casual employment. When an exempted area of employment is involved, it is necessary to consider the duties and defenses of employers apart from workers' compensation statutes.

(a) Duties   The employer is under the common law duty to furnish an employee with a reasonably safe place in which to work, reasonably safe tools and appliances, and a sufficient number of competent fellow employees for the work involved. The employer is also under the common law duty to warn the employee of any unusual dangers particular to the employer's business.

(b) Defenses   At common law, the employer is not liable to an injured employee if the employee is harmed by the act of a fellow employee. Similarly, an employer is not liable at common law to an employee harmed by an ordinary hazard of the work because the employee assumed such risks. If the employee is guilty of contributory negligence, regardless of the employer's negligence, the employer is not liable at common law to an injured employee.

26. STATUTORY CHANGES

The rising incidence of industrial accidents resulting from the increasing use of more powerful machinery and the growth of the industrial labor population led to a demand for statutory modification of common law rules relating to the liability of employers for industrial accidents.

(a) Modification of Employer's Common Law Defenses   One type of change by statute was to modify the defenses that an employer could assert when sued by an employee for damages. **For Example,** under the Federal Employer's Liability Act (FELA), which covers railroad workers, the injured employee must still bring an action in court and prove the negligence of the employer or other employees. However, the burden of proving the case is made lighter by limitations on employers' defenses. Under FELA, contributory negligence is a defense only in mitigation of damages; assumption of the risk is not a defense.[46]

(b) Workers' Compensation   A more sweeping development was made by the adoption of workers' compensation statutes in every state. In addition, civil employees of the U.S. government are covered by the Federal Employees' Compensation Act. When an employee is covered by a workers' compensation statute and the injury is job connected, the employee's remedy is limited to that provided in the workers' compensation statute.[47]

Workers' compensation proceedings are brought before a special administrative agency or workers' compensation board. In contrast, a common law action for damages or an action for damages under an employer's liability statute is brought in a court of law.

CASE SUMMARY

Locked In

FACTS: Bryant is the administrator of the estate of the deceased and the guardian of the deceased's minor child. Bryant sued Wal-Mart for damages following the death of the deceased based on the theory of false imprisonment. While working on the night restocking crew, the deceased suffered a stroke. Medical personnel arrived six minutes later but could not enter the store because management had locked all doors of the store for security reasons and no manager was present to open a door. By the time the medical crew entered the store to assist her, they were unable to revive her, and she died 15 hours later. Bryant contended that the false imprisonment occurred between the time the deceased became ill and the time the medical team was unable to enter the store. Wal-Mart contended that Bryant's exclusive remedy is the Workers' Compensation Act.

DECISION: Judgment for Wal-Mart. It is well settled that a claim under the Workers' Compensation Act is the sole and exclusive remedy for injury or occupational disease incurred in the course of employment. In exchange for the right to recover scheduled compensation without proof of negligence on the part of the employer, employees forgo other rights and remedies they once had. Injuries to an employee's peace, happiness, and feelings are not compensable under the act. [**Bryant v Wal-Mart Stores, Inc., 417 SE2d 688 (Ga App 1992)**]

For injuries arising within the course of the employee's work from a risk involved in that work, workers' compensation statutes usually provide (1) immediate medical benefits, (2) prompt periodic wage replacement, often computed as a percentage of weekly wages (ranging from 50 percent to 80 percent of the injured employee's wage) for a specified number of weeks, and (3) a death benefit of a limited amount.[48] In such cases, compensation is paid without regard to whether the employer or the

---

[46] 45 USC § 1 *et seq.*

[47] Immunity from a tort action based on workers' compensation law applies only to the injured employee's employer, not the owner of the work location. See *Peronto v Case Corp.,* 693 NW2d 133 (Wisc App 2005).

[48] *Union Light & Power Co. v DC Department of Employment Services,* 796 A2d 665 (DC App 2002).

employee was negligent. However, no compensation is generally allowed for a willful, self-inflicted injury or one sustained while intoxicated.

There has been a gradual widening of the workers' compensation statutes, so compensation today is generally recoverable for both accident-inflicted injuries and occupational diseases.

 ## EMPLOYEE PRIVACY

Employers may want to monitor employee telephone conversations in the ordinary course of their business to evaluate employee performance and customer service; to document business transactions between employees and customers; or to meet special security, efficiency, or other needs. Employers may likewise want to monitor e-mail for what they perceive to be sound business reasons. Employers also may seek to test employees for drug use or search employee lockers for illicit drugs. Litigation may result because employees may believe that such activities violate their right to privacy.

27. SOURCE OF PRIVACY RIGHTS

The Bill of Rights contained in the U.S. Constitution, including the Fourth Amendment, which protects against unreasonable search and seizure, provides a philosophical and legal basis for individual privacy rights for federal employees. The Fourteenth Amendment applies this privacy protection to actions taken by state and local governments that affect their employees. The privacy rights of individuals working in the private sector are not directly controlled by the Bill of Rights, however, because challenged employer actions are not government actions. Limited employee privacy rights in the private sector are provided by statute, case law, and collective bargaining agreements.

28. MONITORING EMPLOYEE TELEPHONE CONVERSATIONS

The Federal Wiretapping Act[49] makes it unlawful to intercept oral and electronic communications and provides for both criminal liability and civil damages against the violator. There are two major exceptions, however. The first allows an employer to monitor a firm's telephones in the "ordinary course of business" through the use of extension telephones; a second exception applies when there is prior employee consent to the interception. If employer monitoring results in the interception of a business call, it is within the ordinary-course-of-business exception. Personal calls can be monitored, however, only to the extent necessary to determine that the call is personal, and the employer must then cease listening. **For Example,** Newell Spears taped all phone conversations at his store in trying to find out if an employee was connected to a store theft. He listened to virtually all 22 hours of intercepted and recorded telephone conversations between his employee Sibbie Deal and her boyfriend Calvin Lucas without regard to the conversations' relation to Spears's business interest. While Spears might well have legitimately monitored Deal's calls to the extent necessary to determine that the calls were personal and made or received in violation of store policy, the scope of the interception in this case was well

---

[49] Title III of the Omnibus Crime Control and Safe Streets Act of 1968, 28 USC §§ 2510–2520.

beyond the boundaries of the ordinary-course-of-business exception and in violation of the act.[50]

Employer monitoring of employee phone calls can be accomplished without fear of violating the act if consent is established. Consent may be established by prior written notice to employees of the employer's monitoring policy. It is prudent, as well, for the employer to give customers notice of the policy through a recorded message as part of the employer's phone-answering system.

29. E-MAIL MONITORING

Electronic mail (e-mail) is a primary means of communication in many of today's businesses, serving for some employers as an alternative to faxes, telephones, or the U.S. Postal Service. Employers may want to monitor employees' e-mail messages to evaluate the efficiency and effectiveness of their employees or for corporate security purposes, including the protection of trade secrets and other intangible property interests. When employees are disciplined or terminated for alleged wrongful activities discovered as a result of e-mail searches, however, the issue of privacy may be raised. (See Chapter 2 for a discussion of use of e-mail in litigation and discovery.)

The Electronic Communications Privacy Act of 1986 (ECPA)[51] amended the federal wiretap statute and was intended in part to apply to e-mail. However, ordinary-course-of-business and consent exceptions apply to e-mail, and it would appear that employers have broad latitude to monitor employee e-mail use. **For Example,** Alana Shoars, an e-mail administrator for Epson America, was fired after complaining about her supervisor's reading of employee e-mail messages. Her state court invasion of privacy case was unsuccessful.[52] Very few cases involving e-mail and Web site issues have been adjudicated so far under the ECPA. It has been held that for an employee's secure Web site to be "intercepted" in violation of the wiretap act, the electronic documents acquired must be acquired during transmission, not while in electronic storage.[53]

An employer can place itself within the consent exception of the act by issuing a policy statement to all employees that informs them of the monitoring program and its purposes and justification.

30. PROPERTY SEARCHES

Protected by the Fourth Amendment, public-sector employees have a reasonable expectation of privacy with respect to their desks and file cabinets. However, depending on the fact-specific purpose, justification, and scope of the search, the balance of interest should favor the public employer because its interests in supervision, control, and the efficient operation of the workplace outweigh a public employee's privacy interests.[54] Search of a postal service employee's locker was held not to be a Fourth Amendment violation because well-publicized regulations informed employees that their lockers were subject to search to combat pilferage and stealing. However, the warrantless search of the desk and files of a psychiatrist

[50] *Deal v Spears*, 580 F2d 1153 (8th Cir 1992); *Arias v Mutual Central Alarm Services, Inc.,* 182 FRD 407 (SDNY 1998).

[51] 18 USC §§ 2510–2520.

[52] See *Shoars v Epson America, Inc.,* 1994 Cal LEXIS 3670 (June 29, 1994).

[53] *Konop v Hawaiian Airlines, Inc.,* 302 F3d 868 (9th Cir 2002); *Fraser v Nationwide Mutual Insurance Co.,* 352 F3d 107 (3rd Cir 2003) (court held that the wiretaps act was not violated because the employer did not "intercept" the e-mail but retrieved it after it had been sent and received).

[54] *O'Connor v Ortega,* 480 US 709 (1987).

employed by a state hospital was found to be a Fourth Amendment violation, exceeding the scope of a reasonable work-related search when the search examined his private possessions, including purely personal belongings, and management sought to justify the search on false grounds.[55]

In the private sector, employers may create a reasonable expectation of privacy by providing an employee a locker and allowing the employee to provide his or her own lock. A search of that locker could be an invasion of privacy.[56] If, however, the employer provides a locker and lock but retains a master key and this is known to employees, the lockers may be subject to legitimate reasonable searches by the employer. If a private-sector employer notifies all employees of its policy on lockers, desks, and office searches and the employer complies with its own policy, employees will have no actionable invasion of privacy case.

Many businesses use overt or hidden video cameras as a security method in the workplace to enhance worker safety and to prevent and/or detect theft or other criminal conduct. To avoid state constitutional or statutory claims for invasion of privacy, employers should not set up video cameras in areas where employees have a reasonable expectation of privacy.[57] Utilizing signs to notify employees and members of the public that certain areas are under video surveillance is a common business practice not likely to initiate privacy claims. Additionally, employers should disseminate their written policy on surveillance and obtain a consent form from employees acknowledging that they received this notice to preserve their consent defense.

31. DRUG AND ALCOHOL TESTING

Drug and alcohol testing is an additional source of privacy concerns for employees. Public-sector employees may see drug and alcohol testing as potentially infringing on their Fourth and Fifth Amendment rights, although they may be subject to this testing on the basis of reasonable suspicion. In ordinary circumstances, however, random drug testing is not permissible in the public sector except for mass transit workers and some safety-sensitive positions. The Federal Omnibus Transportation Employee Testing Act,[58] which covers certain classes of employees working in the airline, railroad, and trucking industries, makes covered employees subject to random drug and alcohol testing. Random drug and alcohol testing of employees working in safety-sensitive positions in the private sector also is permissible, as is the testing of private-sector employees on the basis of reasonable suspicion.

EMPLOYER-RELATED IMMIGRATION LAWS

The Immigration and Naturalization Act (INA), the Immigration Reform and Control Act of 1986 (IRCA), and the Immigration Act of 1990[59] are the principal employer-related immigration laws.

---

[55] *Ortega v O'Connor,* 146 F3d 1149 (9th Cir 1998).

[56] *Kmart Corp. v Trotti,* 677 SW2d 632 (Tex App 1984).

[57] See *Kline v Security Guards, Inc.,* 386 F3d 246 (3rd Cir 2004). Some 370 employees of Dana Corporation's Reading, Pennsylvania, facility sued the corporation and its security guard company after employees learned that a new audio and video surveillance system at the entrance of the facility allowed what was said in the area where employees "punch in" for work to be observed and heard in the guard booth. The Third Circuit Court of Appeals rejected the employer's preemption claims and remanded the matter to the state court to handle the invasion of privacy and other tort claims.

[58] PL 102-143, 105 Stat 952, 49 USC § 1301 nt.

[59] PL 101-649, 8 USC § 1101.

32. EMPLOYER LIABILITY

The IRCA sets criminal and civil penalties against employers who knowingly hire aliens who have illegally entered the United States. The IRCA was designed to stop illegal immigration by eliminating job opportunities for these aliens.

33. EMPLOYER VERIFICATION AND SPECIAL HIRING PROGRAMS

Upon hiring a new employee, an employer must verify that the employee is legally entitled to work in the United States. Both the employer and the employee must fill out portions of Form I-9. Verification documents include a U.S. passport, a certificate of U.S. citizenship, or an Alien Registration Card ("green card"). In lieu of these documents, a state driver's license and a Social Security card are sufficient to prove eligibility to work. The 1990 act prohibits employers from demanding other documentation. Thus, if a prospective employee with a "foreign accent" offers a driver's license and Social Security card and the employer seeks a certificate of U.S. citizenship or a green card, the employer has committed an unfair immigration practice. The employer will be ordered to hire the individual and provide back pay.

H-1 classification visas allow aliens of "distinguished merit and ability" to enter and work in the United States on a temporary basis. These persons include architects, engineers, lawyers, physicians, and teachers. Temporary, foreign, high-tech, "highly skilled" workers are classified as H-1B visa employees. The H-1B Visa Reform Act of 2004 exempts 20,000 individuals from the annual cap applied to the H-1B visa classification of 65,000 visas if the applicants involved have a master's or doctoral degree from a U.S. college or university.[60]

The hiring employer must attest that it will not lay off a U.S. employee 90 days before or after filing a petition to employ a foreign worker regarding any position to be filled by the foreign worker. H-1B professionals must be paid the higher of the actual or prevailing wage for each position to eliminate economic incentives to use this foreign workers program. H-1B professionals may work in the United States for up to six years.

(THINKING THINGS THROUGH)

Unemployed U.S. information technology workers are upset that U.S. high-tech companies are utilizing the H-1B visa program to hire foreign workers in a period of economic decline; they are also upset that U.S. companies are moving computer jobs overseas to countries where labor costs are a fraction of the living wages paid in the United States. For example, General Electric has its computer programming work performed for its worldwide operations in India, employing some 10,000 workers there. Are H-1B foreign professionals taking jobs from qualified U.S. workers? What is the rationale for the H1-B program? Should laws exist restricting the transfer of U.S. technology jobs to countries paying very low wages?

---

[60] PL 108-447, 8 USC § 1101 (2005).

> SUMMARY

The relationship of employer and employee is created by the agreement of the parties and is subject to the principles applicable to contracts. If the employment contract sets forth a specific duration, the employer cannot terminate the contract at an earlier date unless just cause exists. If no definite time period is set forth, the individual is an at-will employee. Under the employment-at-will doctrine, an employer can terminate the contract of an at-will employee at any time for any reason or for no reason. Courts in many jurisdictions, however, have carved out exceptions to this doctrine when the discharge violates public policy or is contrary to good faith and fair dealing in the employment relationship. The Fair Labor Standards Act regulates minimum wages, overtime hours, and child labor.

Under the National Labor Relations Act, employees have the right to form a union to obtain a collective bargaining contract or to refrain from organizational activities. The National Labor Relations Board conducts elections to determine whether employees in an appropriate bargaining unit desire to be represented by a union. The NLRA prohibits employers' and unions' unfair labor practices and authorizes the NLRB to conduct proceedings to stop such practices. Economic strikes have limited reinstatement rights. Federal law sets forth democratic standards for the election of union offices.

The Employees Retirement Income Security Act (ERISA) protects employees' pensions by requiring (1) high standards of those administering the funds, (2) reasonable vesting of benefits, (3) adequate funding, and (4) an insurance program to guarantee payments of earned benefits.

Unemployment compensation benefits are paid to persons for a limited period of time if they are out of work through no fault of their own. Persons receiving unemployment compensation must be available for placement in a job similar in duties and comparable in rate of pay to the job they lost. Twelve-week maternity, paternity, and adoption leaves are available under the Family and Medical Leave Act. Employers and employees pay Social Security taxes to provide retirement benefits, disability benefits, life insurance benefits, and Medicare.

The Occupational Safety and Health Act provides for the (1) establishment of safety and health standards and (2) effective enforcement of these standards. Many states have enacted "right-to-know" laws, which require employers to inform their employees of any hazardous substances present in the workplace.

Workers' compensation laws provide for the prompt payment of compensation and medical benefits to persons injured in the course of employment without regard to fault. An injured employee's remedy is generally limited to the remedy provided by the workers' compensation statute. Most states also provide compensation to workers for occupational diseases.

The Bill of Rights is the source of public-sector employees' privacy rights. Private-sector employees may obtain limited privacy rights from statutes, case law, and collective bargaining agreements. Employers may monitor employee telephone calls, although once it is determined that the call is personal, the employer must stop listening or be in violation of the federal wiretap statute. The ordinary-course-of-business and consent exceptions to the Electronic Communications Privacy Act of 1986 (ECPA) give private employers a great deal of latitude to monitor employee e-mail. Notification to employees of employers' policies on searching lockers, desks, and offices reduces employees' expectations of privacy, and a search conducted in conformity with a known policy is generally not an invasion of privacy. Drug and alcohol testing is generally permissible if it is based on reasonable suspicion; random drug and alcohol testing may also be permissible in safety-sensitive positions.

Immigration laws prohibit the employment of aliens who have illegally entered the United States.

> QUESTIONS AND CASE PROBLEMS

1. What remedies does an employee who has been wrongfully discharged have against an employer?
2. Michael Smyth was an operations manager at Pillsbury Co., and his employment status was that of an employee at will. Smyth received certain e-mail messages at home, and he replied to his supervisor by e-mail. His messages contained some provocative language including the phrase

"kill the backstabbing bastards" and a reference to an upcoming company party as the "Jim Jones Koolaid affair." Later, Smyth was given two weeks' notice of his termination, and he was told that his e-mail remarks were inappropriate and unprofessional. Smyth believes that he is the victim of invasion of privacy because the e-mail messages caused his termination, and the company had promised that e-mail communications would not be intercepted and used as a basis for discipline or discharge. The company denies that it intercepted the e-mail messages and points out that Smyth himself sent the unprofessional comments to his supervisor. Is Smyth entitled to reinstatement and back pay because of the invasion of privacy? [*Smyth v Pillsbury Co.*, 914 F Supp 97 (ED Pa)]

3. Michael Hauck claimed that he was discharged by his employer, Sabine Pilot Service, because he refused its direction to perform the illegal act of pumping the bilges of the employer's vessel into the waterways. Hauck was an employee at will, and Sabine contends that it therefore had the right to discharge him without having to show cause. Hauck brought a wrongful discharge action against Sabine. Decide. [*Sabine Pilot Service, Inc., v Hauck*, 687 SW2d 733 (Tex)]

4. Jeanne Eenkhoorn worked as a supervisor at a business office for the New York Telephone Co. While at work, she invented a process for terminating the telephone services of delinquent subscribers. The telephone company used the process but refused to compensate her for it, claiming a shop right. Eenkhoorn then sued for damages on a quasi-contract theory. Decide. [*Eenkhoorn v New York Telephone Co.*, 568 NYS2d 677]

5. One Monday, a labor organization affiliated with the International Ladies Garment Workers Union began an organizational drive among the employees of Whittal & Son. On the following Monday, six of the employees who were participating in the union drive were discharged. Immediately after the firings, the head of the company gave a speech to the remaining workers in which he made a variety of antiunion statements and threats. The union filed a complaint with the NLRB, alleging that the six employees were fired because they were engaging in organizational activity and were thus discharged in violation of the NLRA. The employer defended its position, arguing that it had a business to run and that it was barely able to survive in the global economy against cheap labor from third-world countries. It asserted that the last thing it needed was "union baloney." Was the NLRA violated?

6. David Stark submitted an application to the maintenance department of Wyman-Gordon Co. Stark was a journeyman millwright with nine years' experience at a neighboring company at the time of his application to Wyman-Gordon. Stark was vice president of the local industrial workers' union. In his preliminary interview with the company, Ms. Peevler asked if Stark was involved in union activity, and Stark detailed his involvement to her. She informed Stark that Wyman-Gordon was a nonunion shop and asked how he felt about this. Peevler's notes from the interview characterize Stark's response to this question as "seems to lean toward third-party intervention." Company officials testified that Stark's qualifications were "exactly what we were looking for," but he was not hired. Stark claimed that he was discriminated against. Wyman-Gordon denied that any discrimination had occurred. Is a job applicant (as opposed to an employee) entitled to protection from antiunion discrimination? On the facts of this case, has any discrimination taken place? [*Wyman-Gordon Co. v NLRB*, 108 LRRM 2085 (1st Cir)]

7. Michael Paolella was employed as sales manager for Browning-Ferris, Inc. (BFI), with responsibility for a district in Delaware. When the state's Solid Waste Authority announced plans to raise disposal rates 25 percent, the district manager, Ronald Hanley, devised a scheme to increase BFI's revenues by leading customers to believe that increased fees were the result of the 25 percent increase in disposal rates when, in fact, a significant portion of the increased charges to customers was based on an artificially inflated average weight per cubic yard. Paolella admitted that he did not object to the plan when it was proposed by Hanley. He testified that later he raised concern with Hanley at least twice weekly but nevertheless complied with instructions to

send a letter to customers advising them of the 25 percent increase in June 1992. He also negotiated contracts with customers based on these rates.

In late 1993, Paolella sent BFI a letter warning BFI to "cease all illegal activities." He was fired at 51 years of age, on January 17, 1994, for "poor performance." He sued BFI for wrongful discharge under the public policy exception to the employment-at-will doctrine based on the public policy set forth in the state law against theft by false pretenses. The jury returned a verdict of $732,000, representing $135,000 of back pay and $597,000 in front pay. The judge reduced the damages by $132,000 because of Paolella's participation. BFI appealed, contending that Paolella's participation should preclude him from relying on the public policy exception, and it contended that the front pay was excessive. Is BFI correct? Decide. [*Paolella v Browning-Ferris, Inc.*, 158 F3d 195 (3d Cir)]

8. Armenda Malone and Stephen Krantz were induced to leave other employment and join ABI's CD-Rom division as national account managers in part because of a favorable commission agreement at ABI. Their employment relationship with ABI had no set duration, and as such they were employees at will. For the first two quarters of their employment, their commission reports were approved by the president of the division and paid without incident. Thereafter, a new management team took over the division. When the mid-level manager presented third quarter commission reports based on the prior practice to the new vice president, Bruce Lowry, for approval, he was told, "You got to learn how to f— these people." Lowry then utilized severable variables—some of which the mid-level manager found "ridiculous"—to reduce the commission figures. After much discourse that carried on well into the fourth quarter, Lowry announced that a new model for determining commissions would be implemented. Commissions for both the third and fourth quarters, ending in December, were then calculated based on this model. ABI asserts that because Malone and Krantz were employees at will, the employer had the right to interpret or alter how it pays employees as it sees fit. Krantz

and Malone left ABI and have sued for what they believe are the full commissions earned in the third and fourth quarters. Present a legal theory on behalf of Malone and Krantz for the payment of back commissions. Assess the strengths and weaknesses of Lowry's approach to employee relations. How would you decide this case? [*Malone v American Business Information, Inc.*, 647 NW2d 569 (Neb)]

9. Jane Richards was employed as the sole crane operator of Gale Corp. and held the part-time union position of shop steward for the plant. On May 15, Richards complained to OSHA concerning what she contended were seven existing violations of the Occupational Safety and Health Act that were brought to her attention by members of the bargaining unit. On May 21, she stated to the company's general manager at a negotiating session: "If we don't have a new contract by the time the present one expires on June 15, we will strike." On May 22, an OSHA inspector arrived at the plant, and Richards told her supervisor, "I blew the whistle." On May 23, the company rented and later purchased two large electric forklifts that were used to do the work previously performed by the crane, and the crane operator's job was abolished. Under the existing collective bargaining contract, the company had the right to lay off for lack of work. The contract also provided for arbitration, and it prohibited discipline or discharge without "just cause." On May 23, Richards was notified that she was being laid off "for lack of work" within her classification of crane operator. She was also advised that the company was not planning on using the crane in the future and that, if she were smart, she would get another job. Richards claimed that her layoff violated the National Labor Relations Act, the Occupational Safety and Health Act, and the collective bargaining agreement. Was she correct?

10. Samuel Sullivan, president of the Truck Drivers and Helpers International Union, also holds the position of president of the union's pension fund. The fund consists of both employer and employee contributions, which are forwarded quarterly to the fund's offices in New York City. Sullivan ordered Mark Gilbert, the treasurer of the fund, not to give out any information to

anyone at any time concerning the fund because it was union money and because the union was entitled to take care of its own internal affairs. Was Sullivan correct?

11. In May, the nurses union at Waterbury Hospital went on strike, and the hospital was shut down. In mid-June, the hospital began hiring replacements and gradually opened many units. To induce nurses to take employment during the strike, the hospital guaranteed replacement nurses their choice of positions and shifts. If a preferred position was in a unit that was not open at that time, the hospital guaranteed that the individual would be placed in that position at the end of the strike. The strike ended in October and as the striking workers returned to work, the hospital began opening units that had been closed during the strike. It staffed many of these positions with replacement nurses. The nurses who had the positions prior to the strike and were waiting to return to work believed that they should have been called to fill these positions rather than the junior replacements who had held other positions during the strike. Decide. [*Waterbury Hospital v NLRB,* 950 F2d 849 (2d Cir)]

12. Buffo was employed by the Baltimore & Ohio Railroad. Along with a number of other workers, he was removing old brakes from railroad cars and replacing them with new brakes. In the course of the work, rivet heads and scrap from the brakes accumulated on the tracks under the cars. This debris was removed only occasionally when the workers had time. Buffo, while holding an air hammer in both arms, was crawling under a car when his foot slipped on scrap on the ground, causing him to strike and injure his knee. He sued the railroad for damages under the Federal Employers Liability Act. Decide. [*Buffo v Baltimore & Ohio Railroad Co.,* 72 A2d 593 (Pa)]

13. Mark Phipps was employed as a cashier at a Clark gas station. A customer drove into the station and asked him to pump leaded gasoline into her 1976 Chevrolet, an automobile equipped to receive only unleaded gasoline. The station manager told Phipps to comply with the request, but he refused, believing that his dispensing leaded gasoline into the gas tank was a violation of law. Phipps stated that he was willing to pump unleaded gas into the tank, but the manager immediately fired him. Phipps sued Clark for wrongful termination. Clark contended that it was free to terminate Phipps, an employee at will, for any reason or no reason. Decide. [*Phipps v Clark Oil & Refining Corp.,* 396 NW2d 588 (Minn App)]

14. Reno, Nevada, police officers John Bohach and Jon Catalano communicated with each other on the Alphapage computer system, typing messages on a keyboard and sending them to each other by use of a "send" key. The computer dials a commercial paging company, which receives the message by modem, and the message is then sent to the person paged by radio broadcast. When the system was installed, the police chief warned that every Alphapage message was logged on the network, and he barred messages that were critical of department policy or discriminatory. The two police officers sought to block a department investigation into their messages and prevent disclosure of the messages' content. They claimed that the messages should be treated the same as telephone calls under federal wiretap law. The department contended that the system was essentially a form of e-mail whose messages are by definition stored in a computer, and the storage was itself not part of the communication. Was the federal wiretap law violated? [*Bohach v City of Reno,* No. 96-403-ECR (DC Nev)]

15. Michael Kittell was employed at Vermont Weatherboard. While operating a saw at the plant, Kittell was seriously injured when a splinter flew into his eye and penetrated his head. Kittell sued Vermont Weatherboard, seeking damages under a common law theory. His complaint alleged that he suffered severe injuries solely because of the employer's wanton and willful acts and omissions. The complaint stated that he was an inexperienced worker, put to work without instructions or warning on a saw from which the employer had stripped away all safety devices. Vermont Weatherboard made a motion to dismiss the complaint on the ground that the Workers' Compensation Act provided the exclusive remedy for his injury. Decide. [*Kittell v Vermont Weatherboard, Inc.,* 417 A2d 926 (Vt)]

EQUAL EMPLOYMENT OPPORTUNITY LAW

CHAPTER

(40)

LEARNING OBJECTIVES

*After studying
this chapter,
you should be
able to*

LO.1 Explain and illustrate the difference between disparate treatment employment discrimination and disparate impact employment discrimination

LO.2 Recognize and remedy sexual harassment problems in the workplace

LO.3 Evaluate the legality of voluntary affirmative action programs by applying five court-approved principles

LO.4 State the consequences of discriminating against employees and job applicants because of their age

LO.5 State and illustrate an employer's legal obligation to make reasonable accommodations for individuals with disabilities

Laws of the United States reflect our society's concern that all Americans, including minorities, women, and persons with disabilities, have equal employment opportunities and that the workplace is free from discrimination and harassment. Title VII of the Civil Rights Act of 1964, as amended in 1972, 1978, and 1991, is the principal law regulating equal employment opportunities in the United States. Other federal laws require equal pay for men and women doing substantially the same work and forbid discrimination because of age or disability.

TITLE VII OF THE CIVIL RIGHTS ACT OF 1964, AS AMENDED

Title VII of the Civil Rights Act of 1964[1] seeks to eliminate employer and union practices that discriminate against employees and job applicants on the basis of race, color, religion, sex, or national origin. The law applies to the hiring process and to discipline, discharge, promotion, and benefits.

1. THEORIES OF DISCRIMINATION

The Supreme Court has created, and the Civil Rights Act of 1991 has codified, two principal legal theories under which a plaintiff may prove a case of unlawful employment discrimination: disparate treatment and disparate impact.

A *disparate treatment* claim exists where an employer treats some individuals less favorably than others because of their race, color, religion, sex, or national origin. Proof of the employer's discriminatory motive is essential in a disparate treatment case.[2]

Disparate impact exists when an employer's facially neutral employment practices, such as hiring or promotion examinations, although neutrally applied and making no adverse reference to race, color, religion, sex, or national origin, have a significantly

---

[1] 42 USC § 2000(e) *et seq.*

[2] *Woodson v Scott Paper Co.,* 109 F3d 913 (3d Cir 1997).

adverse or disparate impact on a protected group. In addition, the employment practice in question is not shown by the employer to be job related and consistent with business necessity. Under the disparate impact theory, it is not a defense for an employer to demonstrate that it did not intend to discriminate.

For Example, if plant manager Jones is heard telling the personnel director that the vacant welder's position should be filled by a male because "this is man's work," a qualified female applicant turned down for the job would prevail in a *disparate treatment* theory case against the employer because she was not hired because of her gender. Necessary evidence of the employer's discriminatory motive would be satisfied by testimony about the manager's "this is man's work" statement.

If the policy for hiring new pilots at Generic Airlines, Inc., required a minimum height of 5 feet 7 inches, and no adverse reference to gender was stated in this employment policy, nevertheless, the 5-feet-7-inch minimum height policy has an adverse or disparate impact on women because far fewer women than men reach this height. Such an employment policy would be set aside on a *disparate impact* theory, and a minimum height for the position would be established by the court based on evidence of job-relatedness and business necessity. A 5-feet-5-inch height requirement was set by one court for pilots.

CASE SUMMARY

Number I on the Charts! The Case That Created the Disparate Impact Theory

FACTS: Griggs and other black employees of the Duke Power Company's Dan River Station challenged Duke Power's requirement of a high school diploma and passing standardized general intelligence tests for transfer to more desirable "inside" jobs. The district court and court of appeals found no violation of Title VII because the employer did not adopt the diploma and test requirements with the purpose of intentionally discriminating against black employees. The Supreme Court granted certiorari.

DECISION: Judgment for Griggs. The absence of any intent on the part of the employer to discriminate was not a defense. Title VII prohibits not only overt discrimination but also practices that are fair in form but discriminatory in operation. If any employment practice, such as a diploma or testing requirement, that operates to exclude minorities at a substantially higher rate than white applicants cannot be shown to be "job-related" and consistent with "business necessity," the practice is prohibited. [**Griggs v Duke Power Co., 401 US 424 (1971)**]

2. THE EQUAL EMPLOYMENT OPPORTUNITY COMMISSION

The Equal Employment Opportunity Commission (EEOC) is a five-member body appointed by the president to establish equal employment opportunity policy under the laws it administers. The EEOC supervises the agency's conciliation and enforcement efforts.

The EEOC administers Title VII of the Civil Rights Act, the Equal Pay Act (EPA), the Age Discrimination in Employment Act (ADEA), section 501 of the Rehabilitation Act (which prohibits federal-sector discrimination against persons with disabilities), and Title I (the employment provisions) of the Americans with Disabilities Act (ADA).

(a) Procedure   Where a state or local EEO agency with the power to act on claims of discriminatory practices exists, the charging party must file a complaint with that agency. The charging party must wait 60 days or until the termination of the state proceedings, whichever occurs first, before filing a charge with the EEOC. If no state or local agency exists, a charge may be filed directly with the EEOC so long as it is filed within 180 days of the occurrence of the discriminatory act. The commission conducts an investigation to determine whether reasonable cause exists to believe that the charge is true. If such cause is found to exist, the EEOC attempts to remedy the unlawful practice through conciliation. If the EEOC does not resolve the matter to the satisfaction of the parties, it may decide to litigate the case when unusual circumstances exist, including a "pattern or practice of discrimination." In most instances, however, the EEOC issues the charging party a *right-to-sue letter.* Thereafter, the individual claiming a violation of EEO law has 90 days to file a lawsuit in a federal district court.[3]

(b) Damages   Title VII sets damages available to victims of discrimination (see Figure 40-1).

(c) The Arbitration Option   With the exception of transportation employees, employers can craft arbitration agreements that require employees to arbitrate any employment dispute, including statutory discrimination claims, and these mandatory arbitration clauses can be enforced in federal courts under the Federal Arbitration Act.[4] Courts do, however, require that the arbitration clauses be "fair." Moreover, a party agreeing to arbitration does not forgo substantive rights afforded by Title VII or alter federal antidiscrimination statutes. A fair arbitration clause requires adequate discovery, mandates that the arbitrator have authority to apply the same types of relief available from a court, and should not preclude an employee from vindicating statutory rights because of arbitration costs.[5]

 ## PROTECTED CLASSES AND EXCEPTIONS

To successfully pursue a Title VII lawsuit, an individual must belong to a protected class and meet the appropriate burden of proof. Exceptions exist for certain employment practices.

3. RACE AND COLOR

The legislative history of Title VII of the Civil Rights Act demonstrates that a primary purpose of the act is to provide fair employment opportunities for black Americans. The protections of the act are applied to blacks based on race or color.

---

[3] An individual who misses the filing deadline of Title VII may be able to bring a race discrimination case under the two-year time limit allowed under section 1981 of the Civil Rights Act of 1964, codified at 42 USC § 1981, and sometimes called a *section 1981 lawsuit.* In the *Edelman v Lynchburg College decision,* 152 L Ed 2d 188 (2002), the U.S. Supreme Court approved an EEOC regulation that allows certain defective charges to be cured, with the cured charge relating back to the date the EEOC first received the initial charge, which was within the 300-day filing period.

[4] *Circuit City Stores, Inc. v Adams,* 121 S Ct 1302 (2001).

[5] See *Circuit City II,* 279 F3d 889 (9th Cir 2002).

FIGURE 40-1   *Unlawful Discrimination under Title VII of the Civil Rights Act of 1964 as Amended by the Civil Rights Act of 1991*

DISCRIMINATORY TREATMENT IN EMPLOYMENT DECISIONS ON THE BASIS OF RACE, COLOR, RELIGION, SEX, OR NATIONAL ORIGIN

DISPARATE TREATMENT THEORY	DISPARATE IMPACT THEORY
NONNEUTRAL PRACTICE OR NONNEUTRAL APPLICATION	FACIALLY NEUTRAL PRACTICE AND NEUTRAL APPLICATION
REQUIRES PROOF OF DISCRIMINATORY INTENT	DOES NOT REQUIRE PROOF OF DISCRIMINATORY INTENT REQUIRES PROOF OF ADVERSE EFFECT ON PROTECTED GROUP AND EMPLOYER IS UNABLE TO SHOW THAT THE CHALLENGED PRACTICE IS JOB-RELATED FOR THE POSITION IN QUESTION AND IS CONSISTENT WITH BUSINESS NECESSITY
EITHER PARTY HAS A RIGHT TO REQUIRE A JURY TRIAL WHEN SEEKING COMPENSATORY OR PUNITIVE DAMAGES	NO RIGHT TO A JURY TRIAL
REMEDY REINSTATEMENT, HIRING, OR PROMOTION BACK PAY LESS INTERIM EARNINGS RETROACTIVE SENIORITY ATTORNEY AND EXPERT WITNESS FEES PLUS COMPENSATORY* AND PUNITIVE DAMAGES DAMAGES CAPPED FOR CASES OF SEX AND RELIGIOUS DISCRIMINATION DEPENDING ON SIZE OF EMPLOYER:	**REMEDY** REINSTATEMENT, HIRING, OR PROMOTION BACK PAY LESS INTERIM EARNINGS RETROACTIVE SENIORITY ATTORNEY AND EXPERT WITNESS FEES

NUMBER OF EMPLOYEES	DAMAGES CAP
100 OR FEWER	$ 50,000
101 TO 200	100,000
201 TO 500	200,000
OVER 500	300,000
NO CAP ON DAMAGES FOR RACE CASES	

* COMPENSATORY DAMAGES INCLUDE FUTURE PECUNIARY LOSSES AND NONPECUNIARY LOSSES SUCH AS EMOTIONAL PAIN AND SUFFERING.

The word *race* as used in the act applies to all members of the four major racial groupings: white, black, Native American, and Asian-Pacific. Native Americans can file charges and receive the protection of the act on the basis of national origin, race, or, in some instances, color. Individuals of Asian-Pacific origin may file discrimination charges based on race, color, or, in some instances, national origin. Whites are also protected against discrimination because of race and color.

For Example, two white professors at a predominately black university were successful in discrimination suits against the university when it was held that the university had discriminated against them on the basis of race and color in tenure decisions.[6]

---

4. RELIGION

Title VII requires employers to accommodate their employees' or prospective employees' religious practices. Most cases involving allegations of religious discrimination revolve around the determination of whether an employer has made reasonable efforts to accommodate religious beliefs.

If an employee's religious beliefs prohibit working on Saturday, an employer's obligation under Title VII is to try to find a volunteer to cover for the employee on Saturdays. The employer would not have an obligation to violate a seniority provision of a collective bargaining agreement or call in a substitute worker if such accommodation would require more than a *de minimis* or very small cost.

Many employers have work rules or grooming policies for employees who provide service to customers on behalf of the employers. Employees have challenged employer bans on body art as religious discrimination, asserting that the employers have not made reasonable efforts to accommodate religious beliefs. EEOC's 1980 Guidelines broadly define religion "to include moral or ethical beliefs as to what is right and wrong which are sincerely held with the strength of traditional religious views."[7] The Guidelines do not limit religion to theistic practices or to beliefs professed by organized religions. **For Example,** Kimberly Cloutier was a member of the Church of Body Modification. Costco's grooming policy prohibited any "visible facial or tongue jewelry" in order to present a professional image to its customers. Ms. Cloutier wore an eyebrow ring as a religious practice. Ms. Cloutier rejected Costco's offer to return her to work if she wore a band-aid or plastic retainer over the jewelry because it would violate her religious beliefs. The U.S. Court of Appeals determined that her refusal to accept an accommodation short of an exemption was an undue hardship for the employer because an exemption would negatively impact the company's policy of professionalism.[8]

Some courts, however, look for actual proof of harm to the employer in assessing whether undue hardship exists for an employer. **For Example,** the EEOC brought an action against Red Robin Gourmet Burgers, Inc., for failure to provide an exemption from its grooming policy for an employee's religious tattoos surrounding his wrists. The federal district court looked for actual proof of the restaurant's assertion that the tattoos contravened the company's "family-oriented image," such as customer complaints or other evidence, as opposed to the mere assertion. The court concluded that the employer failed to provide sufficient evidence of undue hardship in accommodating an exemption for the employee.[9]

Title VII permits religious societies to grant hiring preferences in favor of members of their religion. It also provides an exemption for educational institutions to hire

---

[6] *Turgeon v Howard University,* 571 F Supp 679 (DDC 1983).

[7] 29 CFR § 1605.1 (1980). The EEOC's definition of religion was derived from early Selective Service cases that moved beyond institutional religions and theistic belief structures in handling exemptions to the draft and military service. See *Welsh v U.S.,* 398 U.S. 333, 343-44 (1970), which allows for expansion of belief systems to include nonreligious ethical or moral codes.

[8] *Cloutier v Costco,* 390 F3d 126 (1st Cir 2004).

[9] *EEOC v Red Robin Gourmet Burger, Inc.,* 2005 US Dist LEXIS 36219.

employees of a particular religion if the institution is owned, controlled, or managed by a particular religious society. The exemption is a broad one and is not restricted to the religious activities of the institution.

5. SEX

Employers who discriminate against female or male employees because of their sex are held to be in violation of Title VII. The EEOC and the courts have determined that the word *sex* as used in Title VII means a person's gender, not the person's sexual orientation. State and local legislation, however, may provide specific protection against discrimination based on sexual orientation.

(a) HEIGHT, WEIGHT, AND PHYSICAL ABILITY REQUIREMENTS   Under the *Griggs v Duke Power* precedent, an employer must be able to show that criteria used to make an employment decision that has a disparate impact on women, such as minimum height and weight requirements, are in fact job related. All candidates for a position requiring physical strength must be given an opportunity to demonstrate their capability to perform the work. Women cannot be precluded from consideration just because they have not traditionally performed such work.

(b) PREGNANCY-RELATED BENEFITS   Title VII was amended by the Pregnancy Discrimination Act (PDA) in 1978. The amendment prevents employers from treating pregnancy, childbirth, and related medical conditions in a manner different from the manner in which other medical conditions are treated. Thus, women unable to work as a result of pregnancy, childbirth, or related medical conditions must be provided the same benefits as all other workers. These include temporary and long-term disability insurance, sick leave, and other forms of employee benefit programs. An employer who does not provide disability benefits or paid sick leave to other employees is not required to provide them for pregnant workers.

6. SEXUAL HARASSMENT

Tangible employment action and hostile work environment are two classifications of sexual harassment.

(a) TANGIBLE EMPLOYMENT ACTION   Sexual harassment classified as *tangible employment action* involves situations in which a supervisor performs an "official act" of the enterprise, such as discharge, demotion, or undesirable reassignment, against a subordinate employee because of the employee's refusal to submit to the supervisor's demand for sexual favors. The employer is always vicariously liable for this harassment by a supervisor under the so-called aided-in-the-agency-relation standard. That is, the supervisor is aided in accomplishing the wrongful objective by the existence of the agency relationship. The employer empowered the supervisor as a distinct class of agent to make economic decisions affecting other employees under the supervisor's control. The employer can raise no affirmative defense based on the presence of an employer's antiharassment policy in such a case.

(b) HOSTILE WORK ENVIRONMENT   A second type of sexual harassment classified as *hostile work environment* occurs when a supervisor's conduct does not affect an employee's economic benefits but causes anxiety and "poisons" the work environment for the employee. Such conduct may include unwelcome sexual flirtation, propositions, or other abuses of a sexual nature, including the use of degrading words or the display of sexually explicit pictures.[10] This type of sexual harassment applies to all cases involving supervisors in which the enterprise takes no official act, including constructive discharge cases. The plaintiff must prove severe and pervasive conduct on the supervisor's part to meet the plaintiff's burden of proof.[11] The employer may raise an affirmative defense to liability for damages by proving that (1) it exercised reasonable care to prevent and promptly correct any sexually harassing behavior at its workplace and (2) the plaintiff employee unreasonably failed to take advantage of corrective opportunities provided by the employer. The existence of an employer's sexual harassment policy and notification procedures (see Figure 40-2) will aid the employer in proving the affirmative defense in hostile working environment cases.

(c) RATIONALE The "primary objective of Title VII, like that of any statute meant to influence primary conduct, is not to provide redress but to avoid harm."[12] When there is no "official act" of the employer, the employer may raise an affirmative defense. This approach fosters the preventative aspect of Title VII, encouraging employers to exercise reasonable care to prevent and correct sexual harassment while providing damages only when the conduct is clearly attributed to an official action of the enterprise or when the employer has not exercised reasonable care to prevent and correct misconduct. **For Example,** Kim Ellerth alleged that she was subject to constant sexual harassment by her supervisor, Ted Slowik, at Burlington Industries. Slowik made comments about her breasts, told her to "loosen up," and warned, "You know, Kim, I could make your life very hard or very easy at Burlington." When Kim was being considered for promotion, Slowik expressed reservations that she was not "loose enough" and then reached over and rubbed her knee. She received the promotion, however. After other such incidents, she quit and filed charges alleging that she was constructively discharged because of the unendurable working conditions resulting from the hostile work environment created by Slowik. She did not use Burlington's sexual harassment internal complaint procedures. Because she was not a victim of a tangible employment action involving an official act of the enterprise, because she received the promotion sought, the employer will be able to raise an affirmative defense. She will be able to prove severe and pervasive conduct on the part of a supervisor under a hostile work environment theory. However, the employer may defeat liability by proving both that it exercised reasonable care to prevent and correct sexual

---

[10] According to EEOC Guidelines § 1604.11(f), unwelcome sexual advances, requests for sexual favors, and other verbal or physical conduct of a sexual nature constitute sexual harassment when (1) submission to or rejection of such conduct has the purpose or effect of unreasonably interfering with an individual's work performance or creating an intimidating, hostile, or offensive working environment.

[11] *Oncale v Sundowner Offshore Services, Inc.,* 523 US 75 (1998). The Supreme Court stated in *Oncale* that it did not intend to turn Title VII into a civility code, and the Court set forth the standard for judging whether the conduct in question amounted to sexual harassment requiring that the conduct be judged from the perspective of a reasonable person in the plaintiff's position, considering all circumstances. The Court warned that "common sense" and "context" must apply in determining whether the conduct was hostile or abusive.

[12] *Faragher v City of Boca Raton,* 524 US 775 at 805 (citing *Albemale Paper Co. v Moody,* 422 US 405, 418 (1975).

FIGURE 40-2 *Employer Procedure—Sexual Harassment*

A. DEVELOP AND IMPLEMENT AN EQUAL EMPLOYMENT POLICY THAT SPECIFICALLY PROHIBITS SEXUAL HARASSMENT AND IMPOSES DISCIPLINE UP TO AND INCLUDING DISCHARGE. SET FORTH SPECIFIC EXAMPLES OF CONDUCT THAT WILL NOT BE TOLERATED SUCH AS

- UNWELCOME SEXUAL ADVANCES, WHETHER OR NOT THEY INVOLVE PHYSICAL TOUCHING

- SEXUAL EPITHETS AND JOKES; WRITTEN OR ORAL REFERENCES TO SEXUAL CONDUCT; GOSSIP REGARDING ONE'S SEX LIFE; COMMENTS ON AN INDIVIDUAL'S BODY; AND COMMENTS ABOUT AN INDIVIDUAL'S SEXUAL ACTIVITY, DEFICIENCIES, OR PROWESS

- DISPLAY OF SEXUALLY SUGGESTIVE OBJECTS, PICTURES, AND CARTOONS

- UNWELCOME LEERING, WHISTLING, BRUSHING AGAINST THE BODY, SEXUAL GESTURES, AND SUGGESTIVE OR INSULTING COMMENTS

- INQUIRIES INTO ONE'S SEXUAL EXPERIENCES

- DISCUSSION OF ONE'S SEXUAL ACTIVITIES

B. ESTABLISH ONGOING EDUCATIONAL PROGRAMS, INCLUDING ROLE PLAYING AND FILMS TO DEMONSTRATE UNACCEPTABLE BEHAVIOR.

C. DESIGNATE A RESPONSIBLE SENIOR OFFICIAL TO WHOM COMPLAINTS OF SEXUAL HARASSMENT CAN BE MADE. AVOID ANY PROCEDURE THAT REQUIRES AN EMPLOYEE TO FIRST COMPLAIN TO THE EMPLOYEE'S SUPERVISOR, BECAUSE THAT INDIVIDUAL MAY BE THE OFFENDING PERSON. MAKE CERTAIN COMPLAINANTS KNOW THAT THERE WILL BE NO RETALIATION FOR FILING A COMPLAINT.

D. INVESTIGATE ALL COMPLAINTS PROMPTLY AND THOROUGHLY.

E. KEEP COMPLAINTS AND INVESTIGATIONS AS CONFIDENTIAL AS POSSIBLE AND LIMIT ALL INFORMATION TO ONLY THOSE WHO NEED TO KNOW.

F. IF A COMPLAINT HAS MERIT, IMPOSE APPROPRIATE AND CONSISTENT DISCIPLINE.

harassing behavior through its internal company complaint policies and that Kim unreasonably failed to take advantage of the company procedures.[13]

(d) NONSUPERVISORS An employer is liable for the sexual harassment caused its employees by coworkers or customers only when it knew or should have known of the misconduct and failed to take prompt remedial action.

[13] *Burlington Industries, Inc. v Ellerth,* 524 US 742 (1998); see also *Faragher v City of Boca Raton,* 524 US 775 (1998). In *Pennsylvania v Suders,* 542 U.S. 129 (2004), the U.S. Supreme Court reviewed a decision of the Third Circuit Court of Appeals that held that a "constructive discharge," if proved, constituted a "tangible employment action" that renders the employer liable for damages and precludes an affirmative defense. The Supreme Court disagreed with the Third Circuit's reading of its *Ellerth/Faragher* decisions, and made it very clear that "an official act of the enterprise" is necessary for the plaintiff to defeat the employer's right to raise an affirmative defense.

7. PROTECTION AGAINST RETALIATION

Section 704(a) of Title VII prohibits retaliation against an employee "because he [or she] has made a charge, testified, assisted or participated in any manner in an investigation, proceeding hearing under this subchapter." This antiretaliation provision prohibits employer actions that are "materially adverse" to a reasonable employee or applicant. The reference to "material adversity" is to separate significant harms that are prohibited by the act as opposed to trivial harms that are not actionable. A retaliation plaintiff must show that the challenged employer action "well might have dissuaded a reasonable worker from making or supporting a charge of discrimination."[14]

The EEOC takes the position that claims can be filed for retaliation not only under Title VII but also under the Americans with Disabilities Act, the Age Discrimination in Employment Act, and the Equal Pay Act.

CASE SUMMARY

New Traction for the Antiretaliation Provisions Thanks to Track Laborer White

FACTS: BNSF Railway hired Shelia White as a track laborer at its Tennessee Yard. She was the only woman in the track department. When hired, she was given the job of forklift operator as opposed to ordinary track labor tasks. Three months after being hired, she complained to the roadmaster that her foreman treated her differently than male employees and had twice made inappropriate remarks. The foreman was suspended without pay for ten days and ordered to attend training on sexual harassment. Also at that time, the roadmaster reassigned the forklift duties to the former operator who was "senior" to White and assigned White to track labor duties. Six months into her employment, White refused to ride in a truck as directed by a different foreman, and she was suspended for insubordination. Thirty-seven days later, she was reinstated with full back pay, and the discipline was removed from her record. She filed a complaint with the EEOC, claiming that the reassignment to track laborer duties was unlawful gender discrimination and retaliation for her complaint about her treatment by the foreman. The 37-day suspension led to a second retaliation charge. A jury rejected her gender discrimination claim and awarded her compensatory damages for her retaliation claims. BNSF appealed, contending that Ms. White was hired as a track laborer and it was not retaliatory to assign her to do the work she was hired to do. It also asserted that the 37-days suspension had been corrected and she had been made whole for her loss.

DECISION: Judgment for White. The Supreme Court held that the jury could reasonably conclude that the reassignment from forklift operator to track laborer duties would have been materially adverse to a reasonable employee, thus constituting retaliatory discrimination. Moreover, the Court held that an indefinite suspension without pay for a month, even if the employee later received back pay, could well act as a deterrent to filing a discrimination complaint. [**Burlington Northern Santa Fe Railway Co. v White, 126 SCt 2405 (2006)**]

---

14 *Burlington Northern Sante Fe Railway Co. v White, 126 SCt 2405 (2006).*

8. NATIONAL ORIGIN

Title VII protects members of all nationalities from discrimination. The judicial principles that have emerged from cases involving race, color, and gender employment discrimination are generally applicable to cases involving allegations of discrimination related to national origin. Thus, physical standards, such as minimum height requirements, that tend to exclude persons of a particular national origin because of the physical stature of the group have been found unlawful when these standards cannot be justified by business necessity.

Adverse employment action based on an individual's lack of English language skills violates Title VII when the language requirement bears no demonstrable relationship to the successful performance of the job to which it is applied.

CASE SUMMARY

A Close Call

FACTS: Manuel Fragante applied for a clerk's job with the city and county of Honolulu. Although he placed high enough on a civil service eligibility list to be chosen for the position, he was not selected because of a perceived deficiency in oral communication skills caused by his "heavy Filipino accent." Fragante brought suit, alleging that the defendants discriminated against him on the basis of his national origin in violation of Title VII of the Civil Rights Act.

DECISION: Judgment for the city and county of Honolulu. Accents and national origin are inextricably intertwined in many cases. Courts look carefully at nonselection decisions based on foreign accents because an employer may unlawfully discriminate against someone based on national origin by falsely stating that it was the individual's inability to measure up to the communication skills demanded of the job. Because the record showed that the ability to speak clearly was one of the most important skills required for the clerk's position and because the judge confirmed that Fragante was difficult to understand, the court dismissed his complaint. [**Fragante v City and County of Honolulu, 888 F2d 591 (9th Cir 1989)**]

9. TITLE VII EXCEPTIONS

Section 703 of Title VII defines which employment activities are unlawful. This same section, however, also exempts several key practices from the scope of Title VII enforcement. The most important are the bona fide occupational qualification exception, the testing and educational requirement exception, and the seniority system exception.

(a) BONA FIDE OCCUPATIONAL QUALIFICATION EXCEPTION   It is not an unlawful employment practice for an employer to hire employees on the basis of religion, sex, or national origin in those certain instances where religion, sex, or national origin is a bona fide occupational qualification (BFOQ) reasonably necessary to the normal operation of a particular enterprise. **For Example,** a valid BFOQ is a men's clothing store's policy of hiring only males to do measurements for suit alterations. An airline's policy of hiring only female flight attendants is not a valid BFOQ because such a policy is not reasonably necessary to safely operate an airline. Note that there is no BFOQ for race or color.

CASE SUMMARY

It's a Woman's Choice

FACTS: Johnson Controls, Inc. (JCI), manufactures batteries. A primary ingredient in the battery-manufacturing process is lead. Occupational exposure to lead entails health risks, including the risk of harm to any fetus carried by a female employee. After eight of its employees became pregnant while maintaining blood lead levels exceeding those set by the Centers for Disease Control as dangerous for a worker planning to have a family, respondent JCI announced a policy barring all women, except those whose infertility was medically documented, from jobs involving lead exposure exceeding the OSHA standard. The United Auto Workers (UAW) brought a class action in the district court, claiming that the policy constituted sex discrimination violative of Title VII of the Civil Rights Act of 1964, as amended. The court granted summary judgment for JCI based on its BFOQ defense, and the court of appeals affirmed. The Supreme Court granted certiorari.

DECISION: Judgment for the UAW. JCI's fetal protection policy discriminated against women because the policy applied only to women and did not deal with the harmful effect of lead exposure on the male reproductive system. JCI's concerns about the welfare of the next generation do not suffice to establish a BFOQ of female sterility. Title VII, as amended, mandates that decisions about the welfare of future children be left to the parents who conceive, bear, support, and raise them rather than to the employers who hire those parents or to the courts. Moreover, an employer's tort liability for potential fetal injuries does not require a different result. If, under general tort principles, Title VII bans sex-specific fetal-protection policies, the employer fully informs the woman of the risk, and the employer has not acted negligently, the basis for holding an employer liable seems remote at best. [**UAW v Johnson Controls, Inc., 499 US 187 (1991)**]

(b) TESTING AND EDUCATIONAL REQUIREMENTS   Section 703(h) of the act authorizes the use of "any professionally developed ability test [that is not] designed, intended, or used to discriminate." Employment testing and educational requirements must be "job related"; that is, the employers must prove that the tests and educational requirements bear a relationship to job performance.

Courts will accept prior court-approved validation studies developed for a different employer in a different state or region so long as it is demonstrated that the job for which the test was initially validated is essentially the same job function for which the test is currently being used. **For Example,** a firefighters' test that has been validated in a study in California will be accepted as valid when later used in Virginia. Such application is called *validity generalization.*

The Civil Rights Act of 1991 makes it an unlawful employment practice for an employer to adjust scores or use different cutoff scores or otherwise alter the results of employment tests to favor any race, color, religion, sex, or national origin. This provision addresses the so-called race-norming issue, whereby the results of hiring and promotion tests are adjusted to ensure that a minimum number of minorities are included in application pools.

(c) SENIORITY SYSTEM   Section 703(h) provides that differences in employment terms based on a bona fide seniority system are sanctioned so long as the differences do not stem from an intention to discriminate. The term *seniority system is* generally understood to mean a set of rules that ensures that workers with longer years of continuous service for an employer will have a priority claim to a job over others with fewer years of service. Because such rules provide workers with considerable job security, organized labor has continually and successfully fought to secure seniority provisions in collective bargaining agreements.

10. AFFIRMATIVE ACTION AND REVERSE DISCRIMINATION

affirmative action plan (AAP) plan to have a diverse and representative workforce.

Employers have an interest in *affirmative action* because it is fundamentally fair to have a diverse and representative workforce. Employers, under **affirmative action plans** (AAPs), may undertake special recruiting and other efforts to hire and train minorities and women and help them advance within the company. The plan may also provide job preferences for minorities and women. Such aspects of affirmative action plans have resulted in numerous lawsuits contending that Title VII, the Fifth and Fourteenth Amendments, or collective bargaining contracts have been violated.[15]

(a) PERMISSIBLE AAPs   A permissible AAP should conform to the following criteria:

1. The affirmative action must be in connection with a "plan."
2. There must be a showing that affirmative action is justified as a remedial measure.
3. The plan must be voluntary.
4. The plan must not unnecessarily trammel the interests of whites.
5. The plan must be temporary.[16]

(b) REVERSE DISCRIMINATION   When an employer's AAP is not shown to be justified or "unnecessarily trammels" the interests of nonminority employees, it is often called *reverse discrimination.* **For Example,** a city's decision to rescore police promotional tests to achieve specific racial and gender percentages unnecessarily trammeled the interests of nonminority police officers.[17]

(c) EXECUTIVE ORDER   Presidential Executive Order 11246 regulates contractors and subcontractors doing business with the federal government. This order forbids discrimination against minorities and women and in certain situations requires affirmative action to be taken to offer better employment opportunities to minorities and women. The Secretary of Labor has established the Office of Federal Contract Compliance Programs (OFCCP) to administer the order.

---

[15] In *Adarand Constructors, Inc. v Pena,* 115 S Ct 2097 (1995), the U.S. Supreme Court held that a subcontractor had standing to receive relief where a federal program provided financial incentives to prime contractors to hire "disadvantaged" subcontractors, and race-based presumptions were used to identify such individuals. The program was found to violate the equal protection component of the Fifth Amendment's due process clause. After this decision, the EEOC issued a statement on affirmative action, stating in part, "Affirmative action is lawful only when it is designed to respond to a demonstrated and serious imbalance in the workforce, is flexible, time-limited, applies only to qualified workers, and respects the rights of non-minorities and men." Daily Lab Rep (BNA) No. 147, at S-47 (August 1, 1995).

[16] *Steelworkers v Weber,* 443 US 193 (1979); *Johnson v Santa Clara County Transportation Agency,* 480 US 616 (1987).

[17] *San Francisco Police Officers Ass'n v San Francisco,* 812 F2d 1125 (9th Cir 1987).

(**ETHICS & THE LAW**)

T. J. Rodgers was the founder and CEO of Cypress Semiconductors. Some time ago, Mr. Rodgers received a letter from Sister Doris Gromley, the director of corporate social responsibility for the Sisters of St. Francis of Philadelphia, stating that her order would use its shareholder votes against the Cypress board (including Mr. Rodgers) to attempt to remove them because of a lack of women and minorities on the Cypress board. Mr. Rodgers responded with a detailed letter to Sister Gromley. Part of the letter follows:

Thank you for your letter criticizing the lack of racial and gender diversity of Cypress's Board of Directors. I received the same letter from you last year. I will reiterate the management arguments opposing your position. Then I will provide the philosophical basis behind our rejection of the operating principles espoused in your letter, which we believe to be not only unsound, but even immoral. . . .

The semiconductor business is a tough one with significant competition from the Japanese, Taiwanese, and Koreans. There have been more corporate casualties than survivors. For that reason, our Board of Directors is not a ceremonial watchdog, but a critical management function. The essential criteria for Cypress board member-ship are as follows:

— Experience as a CEO of an important technology company
— Direct expertise in the semiconductor business based on education and management experience
— Direct experience in the management of a company that buys from the semi-conductor industry

A search based on these criteria usually yields a male who is 50-plus years old, has a Master's degree in engineering science, and has moved up the managerial ladder to the top spot in one or more corporations. Unfortunately, there are currently few minorities and almost no women who chose to be engineering graduate students 30 years ago (this picture will be dramatically different in 10 years, due to the greater diversification of graduate students in the 80s). Bluntly stated, a "woman's view" on how to run our semiconductor company does not help us, unless that woman has an advanced technical degree and experience as a CEO. I do realize there are other industries in which the last statement does not hold true. We would quickly embrace the opportunity to include any woman or minority person who could help us as a director, because we pursue talent and we don't care in what package that talent comes.

I believe that placing arbitrary racial or gender quotas on corporate boards is fundamentally wrong.

Explain to Mr. Rodgers the advantages of having women and minorities on the board. Do you believe that Cypress, if it wanted to, could find highly qualified women and minorities who could help it as directors? Suggest such a person or persons (for example, Anne Mulcahy, CEO of Xerox, or Patricia Russo, CEO of Lucent Technologies). Has Mr. Rodgers violated any laws with his posture? Is the board an appropriate place for affirmative action?

OTHER EQUAL EMPLOYMENT OPPORTUNITY (EEO) LAWS

Major federal laws require equal pay for men and women doing equal work and forbid discrimination against older people and those with disabilities.

---

11. EQUAL PAY

The Equal Pay Act prohibits employers from paying employees of one gender a lower wage rate than the rate paid employees of the other gender for equal work, or substantially equal work, in the same establishment for jobs that require substantially equal skill, effort, and responsibility and that are performed under similar working conditions.[18] The Equal Pay Act does not prohibit all variations in wage rates paid men and women but only those variations based solely on gender. The act sets forth four exceptions. Variances in wages are allowed where there is (1) a seniority system, (2) a merit system, (3) a system that measures earnings by quantity or quality of production, or (4) a differential based on any factor other than gender.

---

12. AGE DISCRIMINATION

The Age Discrimination in Employment Act (ADEA) forbids discrimination by employers, unions, and employment agencies against persons over 40 years of age.[19] Section 4(a) of the ADEA sets forth the employment practices that are unlawful under the act, including the failure to hire because of age and the discharge of employees because of age. Section 7(b) of the ADEA allows for doubling the damages in cases of willful violations of the act. Consequently, an employer who willfully violates the ADEA is liable not only for back wages and benefits but also for an additional amount as liquidated damages.[20]

> ## CASE SUMMARY
>
> ### Miffed at Being RIF-ed
>
>
>
> **FACTS:** Calvin Rhodes began his employment with Dresser Industries in 1955 as an oil industry salesman. In the throes of a severe economic downturn, Rhodes took a job selling oil field equipment at another Dresser company that became Guiberson Oil Tools. After seven months, he was discharged and told that the reason was a reduction in force (RIF) but that he would be eligible for rehiring. At that time, he was 56 years old. Within two months, Guiberson hired a 42-year-old salesperson to do the same job. Rhodes sued Guiberson for violating the ADEA. At the trial, Lee Snyder, the supervisor who terminated Rhodes, testified in part that Jack Givens, Snyder's boss who instructed Snyder to fire Rhodes, once said that he could hire two young salesmen for what some of the older salesmen were costing.

---

[18] 29 USC § 206 (d)(1).

[19] 29 USC § 623.

[20] In *Reeves v Sanderson Plumbing Products Co., Inc.,* 120 S Ct 2097 (2000), the Supreme Court reinstated a $98,490 judgment for Roger Reeves, which included $35,000 in back pay, $35,000 in liquidated damages, and $28,490.80 in front pay, and held that the plaintiff's evidence establishing a prima facie case and showing that the employer's stated reason for the termination was false was sufficient to prove that age was the motivation for the discharge.

CASE SUMMARY

continued

DECISION: Judgment for Rhodes. The official reason given Rhodes, that he was being terminated under a RIF, was false. Every other reason given by the employer was countered with evidence that Rhodes was an excellent salesman. Based on all of the evidence, including the statement about hiring two young salesmen for what some of the older salesmen were costing, a reasonable jury could find that Guiberson Oil discriminated against Rhodes on the basis of age. [**Rhodes v Guiberson Oil Tools, 75 F3d 989 (5th Cir 1996)**]

The Older Workers Benefit Protection Act (OWBPA) of 1990[21] amends the ADEA by prohibiting age discrimination in employee benefits and establishing minimum standards for determining the validity of waivers of age claims. The OWBPA amends the ADEA by adopting an "equal benefit or equal cost" standard, providing that older workers must be given benefits at least equal to those provided for younger workers unless the employer can prove that the cost of providing an equal benefit would be more for an older worker than for a younger one.

Employers commonly require that employees electing to take early retirement packages waive all claims against their employers, including their rights or claims under the ADEA. The OWBPA requires that employees be given a specific period of time to evaluate a proposed package.

Enforcement of the ADEA is the responsibility of the EEOC. Procedures and time limitations for filing and processing ADEA charges are the same as those under Title VII.[22]

13. DISCRIMINATION AGAINST PERSONS WITH DISABILITIES

The right of persons with disabilities to enjoy equal employment opportunities was established on the federal level with the enactment of the Rehabilitation Act of 1973.[23]

Although not specifically designed as an employment discrimination measure but as a comprehensive plan to meet many of the needs of persons with disabilities, the act contains three sections that provide guarantees against discrimination in employment. Section 501 is applicable to the federal government itself, section 503 applies to federal contractors, and section 504 applies to the recipients of federal funds.

Title I of the Americans with Disabilities Act[24] extends protection in employment-related cases beyond the federal level. This complex statute prohibits all private

---

[21] 29 USC § 623. This law reverses the Supreme Court's 1989 ruling in *Public Employees Retirement System of Ohio v Betts,* 492 US 158 (1989), which had the effect of exempting employee benefit programs from the ADEA.

[22] In *Smith v City of Jackson, Mississippi,* 544 US 228 (2005), the U.S. Supreme Court determined that disparate impact claims of age discrimination are permitted under the ADEA. The Court relied on its Title VII *Griggs v Duke Power Co.* precedent, which interpreted text identical to that in the ADEA, with the substitution of the word "age" for the words "race, color, religion, sex or national origin," the narrowing of the coverage of the ADEA, which permits employers to take actions that would otherwise be prohibited based on "reasonable factors other than age" (called the *RFOA provision*) and the EEOC regulations permitting disparate impact claims. The dissenting justices asserted that in the nearly four decades since the law's enactment, the Court had never read it to impose liability on an employer without proof of discriminatory intent. The *Smith v City of Jackson* court decided the disparate impact case before it against the petitioning police officers, finding that the City's larger pay raises to younger employees were based on a RFOA that responded to the City's legitimate goal of retaining its new police officers.

[23] 42 USC §§ 701–794.

[24] Id. §§ 12101–12117.

employers with 15 or more employees from discriminating against individuals with disabilities who, with or without reasonable accommodations, are qualified to perform the essential functions of the job. Enforcement of Title I of the ADA is the responsibility of the EEOC.

Title III of the ADA forbids discrimination against disabled "clients and customers" in areas of "public accommodation," and its application may have employment implications. **For Example,** professional golfer Casey Martin, who paid the Professional Golf Association $3,000 for an opportunity to compete in qualifying tournaments, was thus a "client or customer" of the PGA and because of his circulatory disorder that makes walking an 18-hole golf course painfully difficult, using a golf cart was found to be a "reasonable accommodation" to the PGA rule requiring golfers to walk the course during professional rounds. The court determined that the accommodation did not fundamentally alter the nature of the golf competition.[25]

Under Title I of the ADA, an employer may make preemployment inquiries into the ability of a job applicant to perform job-related functions. Under new "user-friendly" EEOC guidelines on preemployment inquiries under the ADA, an employer may ask applicants whether they will need reasonable accommodations for the hiring process. If the answer is yes, the employer may ask for reasonable documentation of the disability. In general, the employer may not ask questions about whether an applicant will need reasonable accommodations to do the job. However, the employer may make preemployment inquiries regarding job applicant's ability to perform job-related functions.

After making a job offer contingent on passing a medical examination, an offer may be rescinded when the position in question poses a direct threat to the worker's health or safety. **For Example,** Mario Echazabal was initially offered a job at Chevron's El Segundo, California, oil refinery, but the offer was rescinded when company doctors determined that exposure to chemicals on the job would further damage his already reduced liver functions due to his hepatitis C and might potentially kill him. An affirmative defense then exists for employers not only when hiring an individual poses a direct threat to the health or safety of other employees in the workplace but also when there is a direct threat to self. However, the employer must make an individualized medical risk assessment of the employee's condition.[26]

(a) Proving a Case   The plaintiff must prove that she or he is "disabled," which ordinarily involves proving that she or he suffers from a physical or mental impairment that substantially limits a major life activity.[27] The focus is not solely on workplace limitations. When addressing each major life activity, the central inquiry must be whether the individual is substantially limited or unable to perform the tasks central to most people's daily lives, not just the tasks of a particular job.[28] Major life activities include seeing, hearing, speaking, walking, breathing, performing manual tasks, learning, and working.

---

[25] *PGA Tour, Inc. v Martin,* 121 S Ct 1879 (2001).

[26] *Chevron v Echazabal,* 122 S Ct 2045 (2002).

[27] 42 USC § 12111(8).

[28] *Toyota Motor Manufacturing, Inc., v Williams,* 122 S Ct 681 (2002).

> # CASE SUMMARY
>
> ## Disabled within the Meaning of the ADA
>
> **FACTS:** Ella Williams contended that she was disabled because she was substantially limited in the major life activity of "manual tasks." She could not do the tasks associated with certain types of assembly line jobs at Toyota Kentucky including doing repetitive work with hands and arms extended at or above her shoulder for extended periods of time due to her carpal tunnel syndrome. The Sixth Circuit determined that she was "disabled" under the ADA, and the decision was appealed to the U.S. Supreme Court.
>
> **DECISION:** Judgment for Toyota. The Sixth Circuit failed to uphold the central tenet of *Sutton* that an inquiry into disability cannot be focused simply on the plaintiff's own job. Rather than focus on the tasks of a single job, the disability inquiry must focus on the individual's ability to perform the tasks central to most people's daily lives. The Sixth Circuit should have focused on Williams's own testimony that she could perform household chores, bathe, tend to her flower garden, do laundry, fix breakfast, and pick up around the house—which are manual tasks of central importance to people's daily lives—and this should have been part of the assessment of whether she was substantially limited in performing manual tasks. [**Toyota Motor Manufacturing Kentucky, Inc, v Williams, 534 YS 184 (2002)**]

Impairments are evaluated in their corrected state to determine whether they are disabilities covered under Title I of the ADA.

(b) INDIVIDUALIZED ASSESSMENTS   The assessment of a disability must be made on a case-by-case basis. **For Example,** persons with monocular vision "ordinarily" will meet the ADA's definition of disabled, but they must prove their disability by offering evidence in terms of their own experience concerning loss of depth perception and visual field, thus showing that their major life activity of seeing is substantially limited.[29] Concerning individuals with contagious diseases protected under the ADA, individualized medical judgments are utilized in each case to determine whether such an individual can work. This approach reconciles competing interests in prohibiting discrimination and preventing the spread of disease. Persons with an HIV infection, even when the disease has not progressed to the symptomatic phase, are protected under the ADA.[30]

(c) REASONABLE ACCOMMODATIONS UNDER THE ADA   Section 101(9) of the ADA defines an employer's obligation to make "reasonable accommodations" for individuals with disabilities to include (1) making existing facilities accessible to and usable by individuals with disabilities and (2) restructuring jobs, providing modified work schedules, and acquiring or modifying equipment or devices. An employer is not obligated under the ADA to make accommodations that would be an "undue hardship" on the employer.

---

[29] See *Albertson, Inc., v Kirkingburg*, 119 S Ct 2162 (1999).
[30] *Bragdon v Abbott*, 118 S Ct 2196 (1998).

For Example, before passage of the ADA, a supermarket meatcutter unable to carry meat from a refrigerator to a processing area might have been refused clearance to return to work after a back injury until he was able to perform all job functions. Today, under the ADA, it would be the employer's obligation to provide that worker with a cart to assist him in performing the job even if the cart cost $500. However, if the meatcutter was employed by a small business with limited financial resources, an "accommodation" costing $500 might be an undue hardship that the employer could lawfully refuse to make.

Seniority systems provide for a fair and uniform method of treating employees whereby employees with more years of service have a priority over employees with less years of service when it comes to layoffs, job selection, and other benefits such as days off and vacation periods. Seniority rules apply not only under collective bargaining agreements but also to many nonunion job classifications and to nonunion settings. An employer's showing that a requested accommodation conflicts with seniority rules is ordinarily sufficient to show that the requested "accommodation" is not "reasonable." **For Example,** Robert Barnett, a cargo handler for U.S. Airways, Inc., sought a less physically demanding job in the mailroom due to a back injury. Because a senior employee bid the job, U.S. Airways refused Barnett's request to accommodate his disability by allowing him to work the mailroom position. Barnett filed suit under the ADA, and the case progressed to the U.S. Supreme Court, which determined that ordinarily such a requested accommodation is not "reasonable." On remand to the trial court, Barnett was given the opportunity to show that the company allowed exceptions to the seniority rules and he fit within such exceptions.[31]

(d) Exclusions from Coverage of the ADA   The act excludes from its coverage employees or applicants who are "currently engaging in the illegal use of drugs." The exclusion does not include an individual who has been successfully rehabilitated from such use or is participating in or has completed supervised drug rehabilitation and is no longer engaging in the illegal use of drugs.

Title V of the act states that behaviors such as transvestitism, transsexualism, pedophilia, exhibitionism, compulsive gambling, kleptomania, pyromania, and psychoactive substance use disorders resulting from current illegal use of drugs are not in and of themselves considered disabilities.

 EXTRATERRITORIAL EMPLOYMENT

The Civil Rights Act of 1991 amended both Title VII and the ADA to protect U.S. citizens employed in foreign countries by American-owned or American-controlled companies against discrimination based on race, color, religion, national origin, sex, or disability.[32] The 1991 act contains an exemption if compliance with Title VII or the ADA would cause a company to violate the law of the foreign country in which it is located.

---

[31] *U.S. Airways v Barnett,* 122 S Ct 1516 (2002).

[32] Section 109 of the Civil Rights Act of 1991, PL 102-166, 105 Stat 1071.

Disclosure (1996) (R)

Michael Douglas and Demi Moore portray corporate climbers involved in a power struggle. The movie also depicts the sticky issue of sexual harassment. Several scenes during the course of the arbitration hearing offer definitions of sexual harassment and background as to why this problem exists and is prohibited in the workplace.

For movie clips that illustrate business law concepts, see LawFlix at **http://wdvl.westbuslaw.com.**

> SUMMARY

Title VII of the Civil Rights Act of 1964, as amended, forbids discrimination on the basis of race, color, religion, sex, or national origin. The EEOC administers the act. Intentional discrimination is unlawful when there is disparate treatment of individuals because of their race, color, religion, gender, or national origin. Also, employment practices that make no reference to race, color, religion, sex, or national origin, but that nevertheless have an adverse or disparate impact on the protected group, are unlawful. In disparate impact cases, the fact that an employer did not intend to discriminate is no defense. The employer must show that there is a job-related business necessity for the disparate impact practice in question. Employers have several defenses they may raise in a Title VII case to explain differences in employment conditions: (1) bona fide occupational qualifications reasonably necessary to the normal operation of the business, (2) job-related professionally developed ability tests, and (3) bona fide seniority systems. If a state EEO agency or the EEOC is not able to resolve the case, the EEOC issues a right-to-sue letter that enables the person claiming a Title VII violation to sue in a federal district court. An affirmative action plan is legal under Title VII provided there is a voluntary "plan" justified as a remedial measure and provided it does not unnecessarily trammel the interests of whites.

Under the Equal Pay Act (EPA), employers must not pay employees of one gender a lower wage rate than the rate paid to employees of the other gender for substantially equal work. Workers over 40 years old are protected from discrimination by the Age Discrimination in Employment Act (ADEA). Employment discrimination against persons with disabilities is prohibited by the Americans with Disabilities Act (ADA). Under the ADA, employers must make reasonable accommodations without undue hardship on them to enable individuals with disabilities to work.

> QUESTIONS AND CASE PROBLEMS

1. List the major federal statutes dealing with the regulation of equal rights in employment.
2. Casey Martin, a professional golfer with a circulatory disorder that makes walking an 18-hole golf course painfully difficult, was successful in his Title III of the Americans with Disabilities Act lawsuit against the PGA, and he was allowed to use a golf cart as a reasonable accommodation to the PGA rule requiring golfers on the professional tour to walk the course during professional rounds. Subsequently, Stephan Kuketz, a world-class wheelchair racquetball player, sued the Brockton Athletic Club under the ADA when the club refused to allow him to participate in nonhandicapped tournaments, with the only adjustment to the rules being that he be allowed

two bounces rather than one, before he hit the ball from his wheelchair. Did the Casey Martin accommodation fundamentally alter the golf competition? Did the Kuketz proposed accommondation fundamentally alter the racquetball competition? Decide. [*Kuketz v Brockton Athletic Club, Boston Globe,* August 30, 2001, B-1]

3. Dial Corp. implemented a "work tolerance test," which all new employees were required to pass to obtain employment in its Armour Star brand sausage-making department. Of the applicants who passed the test, 97 percent were male and 38 percent were female. The EEOC "demonstrated" that the facially neutral work tolerance test "caused" a disparate impact on women. The defending employer did not deny that the employment practice in question caused the disparate impact. Rather, the employer responded that the test was "job related" and "necessary" to reduce job-related injuries at the plant and submitted evidence that the number of job injuries had been reduced after implementation of the testing program. The evidence showed that the company had initiated numerous other safety initiatives that had an impact on reducing injuries at the plant. After they failed the test, 52 women were denied jobs. Decide this case. [*EEOC v Dial Corp.,* 2005 WL 2839977]

4. Continental Photo, Inc., is a portrait photography company. Alex Riley, a black man, applied for a position as a photographer with Continental. Riley submitted an application and was interviewed. In response to a question on a written application, Riley indicated that he had been convicted for forgery (a felony) six years before the interview, had received a suspended sentence, and was placed on five-year probation. He also stated that he would discuss the matter with his interviewer if necessary. The subject of the forgery conviction was subsequently not mentioned by Continental's personnel director in his interview with Riley. Riley's application for employment was eventually rejected. Riley inquired about the reason for his rejection. The personnel director, Geuther, explained to him that the prior felony conviction on his application was a reason for his rejection. Riley contended that the refusal to hire him because of his conviction record was actually discrimination against him because of his race in violation of Title VII. Riley felt that his successful completion of a five-year probation without incident and his steady work over the years qualified him for the job. Continental maintained that because its photographers handle approximately $10,000 in cash per year, its policy of not hiring applicants whose honesty was questionable was justified. Continental's policy excluded all applicants with felony convictions. Decide. Would the result have been different if Riley had been a convicted murderer? [*Continental Photo, Inc.,* 26 Fair Empl Prac Cas (BNA) 1799 (EEOC)]

5. Beth Faragher worked part-time and summers as an ocean lifeguard for the Marine Safety Section of the city of Boca Raton, Florida. Bill Terry and David Silverman were her supervisors over the five-year period of her employment. During this period, Terry repeatedly touched the bodies of female employees without invitation and would put his arm around Faragher, with his hand on her buttocks. He made crudely demeaning references to women generally. Silverman once told Faragher, "Date me or clean the toilets for a year." She was not so assigned, however. The city adopted a sexual harassment policy addressed to all employees. The policy was not disseminated to the Marine Safety Section at the beach, however. Faragher resigned and later brought action against the city, claiming a violation of Title VII and seeking nominal damages, costs, and attorney fees. The city defended that Terry and Silverman were not acting within the scope of their employment when they engaged in harassing conduct, and the city should not be held liable for their actions. Are part-time employees covered by Title VII? Was Silverman's threat, "Date me or clean toilets for a year," a basis for *quid pro quo* vicarious liability against the city? Decide this case. [*Faragher v City of Boca Raton,* 118 S Ct 2275]

6. Mohen is a member of the Sikh religion whose practice forbids cutting or shaving facial hair and requires wearing a turban that covers the head. In accordance with the dictates of his religion, Mohen wore a long beard. He applied for a position as breakfast cook at the Island Manor Restaurant. He was told that the restaurant's

policy was to forbid cooks to wear facial hair for sanitary and good grooming reasons and that he would have to shave his beard or be denied a position. Mohen contended that the restaurant had an obligation to make a reasonable accommodation to his religious beliefs and let him keep his beard. Is he correct?

7. Sylvia Hayes worked as a staff technician in the radiology department of Shelby Memorial Hospital. On October 1, Hayes was told by her physician that she was pregnant. When Hayes informed the doctor of her occupation as an X-ray technician, the doctor advised Hayes that she could continue working until the end of April so long as she followed standard safety precautions. On October 8, Hayes told Gail Nell, the director of radiology at Shelby, that she had discovered she was two months pregnant. On October 14, Hayes was discharged by the hospital. The hospital's reason for terminating Hayes was its concern for the safety of her fetus given the X-ray exposure that occurs during employment as an X-ray technician. Hayes brought an action under Title VII, claiming that her discharge was unlawfully based on her condition of pregnancy. She cited scientific evidence and the practice of other hospitals where pregnant women were allowed to remain in their jobs as X-ray technicians. The hospital claimed that Hayes's discharge was based on business necessity. Moreover, the hospital claimed that the potential for future liability existed if an employee's fetus was damaged by radiation encountered at the workplace. Decide. [*Hayes v Shelby Memorial Hospital,* 546 F Supp 259 (ND Ala)]

8. Overton suffered from depression and was made sleepy at work by medication taken for this condition. Also, because of his medical condition, Overton needed a work area away from public access and substantial supervision to complete his tasks. His employer terminated him because of his routinely sleeping on the job, his inability to maintain contact with the public, and his need for supervision. Overton argued that he is a person with a disability under the ADA and the Rehabilitation Act, fully qualified to perform the essential functions of the job, and that the employer had an obligation to make reasonable accommodations, such as allowing some catnaps as needed and providing some extra supervision. Decide. [*Overton v Reilly,* 977 F2d 1190 (7th Cir)]

9. A teenage female high school student named Salazar was employed part-time at Church's Fried Chicken Restaurant. Salazar was hired and supervised by Simon Garza, the assistant manager of the restaurant. Garza had complete supervisory powers when the restaurant's manager, Garza's roommate, was absent. Salazar claimed that while she worked at the restaurant, Garza would refer to her and all other females by a Spanish term that she found objectionable. According to Salazar, Garza once made an offensive comment about her body and repeatedly asked her about her personal life. On another occasion, Garza allegedly physically removed eye shadow from Salazar's face because he claimed it was unattractive. Salazar also claimed that one night she was restrained in a back room of the restaurant while Garza and another employee fondled her. Later that night, when Salazar told a customer what had happened, she was fired. Salazar brought suit under Title VII against Garza and Church's Fried Chicken, alleging sexual harassment. Church's, the corporate defendant, maintained that it should not be held liable under Title VII for Garza's harassment. Church's based its argument on the existence of a published fair treatment policy. Decide. [*Salazar v Church's Fried Chicken, Inc.,* 44 Fair Empl Prac Cas (BNA) 472 (SD Tex)]

10. John Chadbourne was hired by Raytheon on February 4, 1980. His job performance reviews were uniformly high. In December 1983, Chadbourne was hospitalized and diagnosed with AIDS. In January 1984, his physician informed Raytheon that Chadbourne was able to return to work. On January 20, 1984, Chadbourne took a return-to-work physical examination required by Raytheon. The company's doctor wrote the County Communicable Disease Control Director, Dr. Juels, seeking a determination of the appropriateness of Chadbourne's returning to work. Dr. Juels informed the company that "contact of employees to an AIDS patient appears to pose no risk from all evidence accumulated to date." Dr. Juels also visited the plant and advised

the company doctor that there was no medical risk to other employees at the plant if Chadbourne returned to work. Raytheon refused to reinstate Chadbourne to his position until July 19, 1984. Its basis for denying reinstatement was that coworkers might be at risk of contracting AIDS. Was Raytheon entitled to bar Chadbourne from work during the six-month period of January through July? [*Raytheon v Fair Employment and Housing Commission*, 261 Cal Rptr 197 (Ct App)]

11. Connie Cunico, a white woman, was employed by the Pueblo, Colorado, School District as a social worker. She and other social workers were laid off in seniority order because of the district's poor financial situation. However, the school board thereafter decided to retain Wayne Hunter, a black social worker with less seniority than Cunico because he was the only black on the administrative staff. No racial imbalance existed in the relevant workforce with black persons constituting 2 percent. Cunico, who was rehired over two years later, claimed that she was the victim of reverse discrimination. She stated that she lost $110,361 in back wages plus $76,000 in attorney fees and costs. The school district replied that it was correct in protecting with special consideration the only black administrator in the district under the general principles it set forth in its AAP. Did the employer show that its affirmative action in retaining Hunter was justified as a remedial measure? Decide. [*Cunico v Pueblo School District No. 6*, 917 F2d 431 (10th Cir)]

12. Della Janich was employed as a matron at the Yellowstone County Jail in Montana. The duties of the position of matron resemble those of a parallel male position of jailer. Both employees have the responsibility for booking prisoners, showering and dressing them, and placing them in the appropriate section of the jail depending on the offender's sex. Because 95 percent of the prisoners at the jail were men and 5 percent were women, the matron was assigned more book-keeping duties than the jailer. At all times during Janich's employment at the jail, her male counterparts received $125 more per month as jailers. Janich brought an action under the Equal Pay Act, alleging discrimination against her in her wages because of her sex. The county sheriff denied the charge. Decide. [*Janich v Sheriff*, 29 Fair Empl Prac Cas (BNA) 1195 (D Mont)]

13. Following a decline in cigarette sales, L & M, Inc., hired J. Gfeller as vice president of sales and charged him to turn around the sales decline. After receiving an analysis of the ages of sales personnel and first-line management, Gfeller and his assistant, T. McMorrow, instituted an intensive program of personnel changes that led to the termination of many older managers and sales representatives. A top manager who sought to justify keeping an older manager was informed that he was "not getting the message." Gfeller and McMorrow emphasized that they wanted young and aggressive people and that the older people were not able to conform or adapt to new procedures. R. E. Moran, who had been rated a first-rate division manager, was terminated and replaced by a 27-year-old employee. Gfeller and McMorrow made statements about employees with many years' experience: "It was not 20 years' experience, but rather 1 year's experience 20 times." The EEOC brought suit on behalf of the terminated managers and sales representatives. The company vigorously denied any discriminatory attitude in regard to age. Decide. [*EEOC v Liggett and Meyers, Inc.*, 29 FEP 1611 (EDNC)]

14. Mazir Coleman had driven a school bus for the Casey County, Kentucky, Board of Education for four years. After that time, Coleman's left leg had to be amputated. Coleman was fitted with an artificial leg and underwent extensive rehabilitation to relearn driving skills. When his driving skills had been sufficiently relearned over the course of four years, Coleman applied to the county board of education for a job as a school bus driver. The board refused to accept Coleman's application, saying that it had no alternative but to deny Coleman a bus-driving job because of a Kentucky administrative regulation. That regulation stated in part: "No person shall drive a school bus who does not possess both of these natural bodily parts: feet, legs, hands, arms, eyes, and ears. The driver shall have normal use of the above named body parts." Coleman

brought an action under the Rehabilitation act, claiming discrimination based on his physical handicap. The county board of education denied this charge, claiming that the reason they rejected Coleman was because of the requirement of the state regulation. Could Coleman have maintained an action for employment discrimination in light of the state regulation on natural body parts? Decide. [*Coleman v Casey County Board of Education,* 510 F Supp 301 (ND Ky)]

15. Marcia Saxton worked for Jerry Richardson, a supervisor at AT&T's International Division. Richardson made advances to Saxton on two occasions over a three-week period. Each time Saxton told him she did not appreciate his advances. No further advances were made, but thereafter Saxton felt that Richardson treated her condescendingly and stopped speaking to her on a social basis at work. Four months later, Saxton filed a formal internal complaint, asserting sexual harassment, and went on "paid leave." AT&T found inconclusive evidence of sexual harassment but determined that the two employees should be separated. Saxton declined a transfer to another department, so AT&T transferred Richardson instead. Saxton still refused to return to work. Thereafter, AT&T terminated Saxton for refusal to return to work. Saxton contended she was a victim of hostile working environment sexual harassment. AT&T argued that while the supervisor's conduct was inappropriate and unprofessional, it fell short of the type of action necessary for sexual harassment under federal law (the *Harris* case). Decide. [*Saxton v AT&T Co.,* 10 F3d 526 (7th Cir)]

HOW TO FIND THE LAW

In order to determine what the law on a particular question or issue is, it may be necessary to examine (1) compilations of constitutions, treaties, statutes, executive orders, proclamations, and administrative regulations; (2) reports of state and federal court decisions; (3) digests of opinions; (4) treatises on the law; and (5) loose-leaf services. These sources can be either researched traditionally or using fee- and/or non-fee-based computerized legal research accessed through the World Wide Web.

 ## COMPILATIONS

In the consideration of a legal problem in business it is necessary to determine whether the matter is affected or controlled by a constitution, national or state; by a national treaty; by an Act of Congress or a state legislature, or by a city ordinance; by a decree or proclamation of the President of the United States, a governor, or a mayor; or by a regulation of a federal, state, or local administrative agency.

Each body or person that makes laws, regulations, or ordinances usually compiles and publishes at the end of each year or session all of the matter that it has adopted. In addition to the periodical or annual volumes, it is common to compile all the treaties, statutes, regulations, or ordinances in separate volumes. To illustrate, the federal Anti-Injunction Act may be cited as the Act of March 23, 1932, 47 Stat 70, 29 USC Sections 101 et seq. This means that this law was enacted on March 23, 1932, and that it can be found at page 70 in Volume 47 of the reports that contain all of the statutes adopted by the Congress.

The second part of the citation, 29 USC Sections 101 et seq., means that in the collection of all of the federal statutes, which is known as the United States Code, the full text of the statute can be found in the sections of the 29th title beginning with Section 101.

 ## COURT DECISIONS

For complicated or important legal cases or when an appeal is to be taken, a court will generally write an opinion, which explains why the court made the decision. Appellate courts as a rule write opinions. The great majority of these decisions, particularly in the case of the appellate courts, are collected and printed. In order to avoid confusion, the opinions of each court are ordinarily printed in a separate set of reports, either by official reporters or private publishers.

In the reference "Pennoyer v Neff, 95 US 714, 24 LEd 565," the first part states the names of the parties. It does not necessarily tell who was the plaintiff and who was the defendant. When an action is begun in a lower court, the first name is that of the plaintiff and the second name that of the defendant. When the case is appealed, generally the name of the person taking the appeal appears on the records of the higher court as the first one and that of the adverse party as the second. Sometimes, therefore, the original order of the names of the parties is reversed.

The balance of the reference consists of two citations. The first citation, 95 US 714, means that the opinion which the court filed in the case of Pennoyer v Neff may be found on page 714 of the 95th volume of a series of books in which are printed officially the opinions of the United States Supreme Court. Sometimes the same opinion is printed in two different sets of volumes. In the example, 24 LEd 565 means that in the 24th volume of another set of books, called Lawyer's Edition, of the United States Supreme Court Reports, the same opinion begins on page 565.

In opinions by a state court there may also be two citations, as in the case of "Morrow v Corbin, 122 Tex 553, 62 SW2d 641." This means that the opinion in the lawsuit between Morrow and Corbin may be found in the 122d volume of the reports of the highest court of Texas, beginning on page 553; and also in Volume 62 of the Southwestern Reporter, Second Series, at page 641.

The West Publishing Company publishes a set of sectional reporters covering the entire United States. They are called "sectional" because each reporter, instead of being limited to a particular court or a particular state, covers the decisions of the courts of a particular section of the country. Thus the decisions of the courts of Arkansas, Kentucky, Missouri, Tennessee, and Texas are printed by the West Publishing company as a group in a sectional reporter called the Southwestern Reporter.[1] Because of the large number of decisions involved, generally only the opinions of the state appellate courts are printed. A number of states[2] have discontinued publication of the opinions of their courts, and those opinions are now found only in the West reporters.

The reason for the "Second Series" in the Southwestern citation is that when there were 300 volumes in the original series, instead of calling the next volume 301, the publisher called it Volume 1, Second Series. Thus 62 SW2d Series really means the 362d volume of the Southwestern Reporter. Six to eight volumes appear in a year for each geographic section.

In addition to these state reporters, the West Publishing Company publishes a Federal Supplement, which primarily reports the opinions of the Federal District Courts; the Federal Reporter, which primarily reports the decisions of the United States Courts of Appeals; and the Supreme Court Reporter, which reports the decisions of the United States Supreme Court. The Supreme Court decisions are also reported in a separate set called the Lawyers' Edition, published by the Lawyers Cooperative Publishing Company.

The reports published by the West Publishing Company and Lawyers Cooperative Publishing Company are unofficial reports, while those bearing the name or abbreviation of the United States or of a state, such as "95 US 714" or "122 Tex 553" are official reports. This means that in the case of the latter, the particular court, such as the United States Supreme Court, has officially authorized that its decisions be printed and that by federal statute such official printing is made. In the case of the unofficial reporters, the publisher prints the decisions of a court on its own initiative. Such opinions are part of the public domain and not subject to any copyright or similar restriction.

 ## DIGESTS OF OPINIONS

The reports of court decisions are useful only if one has the citation, that is, the name and volume number of the book and the page number of the opinion one is seeking. For this reason, digests of the decisions have been prepared. These digests organize the entire field of law under major headings, which are then arranged in alphabetical order. Under each heading, such as "Contracts," the subject is divided into the different questions that can arise with respect to that field. A master outline is thus created on the subject. This outline includes short paragraphs describing what each case holds and giving its citation.

 ## TREATISES AND RESTATEMENTS

Very helpful in finding a case or a statute are the treatises on the law. These may be special books, each written by an author on a particular subject, such as Williston on Contracts, Bogert on Trusts, Fletcher on Corporations, or they may be general encyclopedias, as in the case of American Jurisprudence, American Jurisprudence, Second, and Corpus Juris Secundum.

Another type of treatise is found in the restatements of the law prepared by the American Law Institute. Each restatement consists of one or more volumes devoted to a particular phase of the law, such as the Restatement of the Law of Contracts, Restatement of the Law of Agency, and Restatement of the Law of Property. In each restatement, the American Law Institute, acting through special committees of judges, lawyers, and professors of law, has set forth what the law is; and in many areas where there is no law or the present rule is regarded as unsatisfactory, the restatement specifies what the Institute deems to be the desirable rule.

 ## LOOSE-LEAF SERVICES

A number of private publishers, notably Commerce Clearing House and Prentice-Hall, publish loose-leaf books devoted to particular branches of the law. Periodically, the publisher sends to the purchaser a number of pages that set forth any decision, regulation, or statute made or adopted since the prior set of pages was prepared. Such services are unofficial.

COMPUTERIZED LEGAL RESEARCH

National and local computer services are providing constantly widening assistance for legal research. The database in such a system may be opinions, statutes, or administrative regulations stored word for word; or the later history of a particular case giving its full citation and showing whether the case has been followed by other courts; or the text of forms and documents. By means of a terminal connected to the system, the user can retrieve the above information at a great saving of time and with the assurance that it is up-to-date.

There are two leading, fee-based systems for computer-aided research. Listed alphabetically, they are LEXIS and WESTLAW.

A specialized service of legal forms for business is provided by Shepard's BUSINESS LAW CASE MANAGEMENT SYSTEM. A monthly fee is required for usage.

---

[1]The sectional reporters are: Atlantic—A. (Connecticut, Delaware, District of Columbia, Maine, Maryland, New Hampshire, New Jersey, Pennsylvania, Rhode Island, Vermont); Northeastern—N.E. (Illinois, Indiana, Massachusetts, New York, Ohio); N.W. (Iowa, Michigan, Minnesota, Nebraska, North Dakota, South Dakota, Wisconsin); Pacific—P. (Alaska, Arizona, California, Colorado, Hawaii, Idaho, Kansas, Montana, Nevada, New Mexico, Oklahoma, Oregon, Utah, Washington, Wyoming); Southeastern—S.E. (Georgia, North Carolina, South Carolina, Virginia, West Virginia); Southwestern—S.W. (Arkansas, Kentucky, Missouri, Tennessee, Texas); and Southern—So. (Alabama, Florida, Louisiana, Mississippi). There is also a special New York State reporter known as the New York Supplement and a special California State reporter known as the California Reporter.

[2]See, for example, Alaska, Florida, Iowa, Kentucky, Louisiana, Maine, Mississippi, Missouri, North Dakota, Oklahoma, Texas, and Wyoming.

Numerous free, private sites offer a lot of legal resources. The federal government offers a variety of case law, regulations, and code enactments, either pending or newly promulgated. To find the most comprehensive source of government-maintained legal information, go to **http://www.law.house.gov/**.

Increasingly, some states offer their regulations and codes online. As an example, go to the State of California's site, **http://www.leginfo.ca.gov/**, as an example of a government-based legal information provider. For a complete listing of state homepages, go to **http://www.law.house.gov/17.htm**.

For sources of all types of law, and legal resources, a new internet site, Hieros Gamos, **http://www.hg.org** claims that "virtually all online and offline (published) legal information is accessible within three levels." It is important to note, however, that non-fee-based services do not guarantee the integrity of the information provided. Therefore, when accessing free information over the Internet, one should be careful to double-check the authority of the provider and the accuracy of the data obtained. This caution extends to sites maintained by federal and state governments as well.

The computer field has expanded to such an extent that there is now a Legal Software Review of over 500 pages prepared by Lawyers Library, 12761 New Hall Ferry, Florissant, MO 63033.

THE CONSTITUTION
OF THE UNITED STATES

We the people of the United States of America, in order to form a more perfect union, establish justice, insure domestic tranquility, provide for the common defense, promote the general welfare, and secure the blessings of liberty to ourselves and our posterity, do ordain and establish this Constitution for the United States of America.

ARTICLE I

Section 1. All legislative powers herein granted shall be vested in a Congress of the United States, which shall consist of a Senate and House of Representatives.

Section 2. 1. The House of Representatives shall be composed of members chosen every second year by the people of the several States, and the electors in each State shall have the qualifications requisite for electors of the most numerous branch of the State legislature.

2. No person shall be a representative who shall not have attained to the age of twenty-five years, and been seven years a citizen of the United States, and who shall not, when elected, be an inhabitant of that State in which he shall be chosen.

3. Representatives and direct taxes shall be apportioned among the several States which may be included within this Union, according to their respective numbers, which shall be determined by adding to the whole number of free persons, including those bound to service for a term of years, and excluding Indians not taxed, three fifths of all other persons.[1] The actual enumeration shall be made within three years after the first meeting of the Congress of the United States, and within every subsequent term of ten years, in such manner as they shall by law direct. The number of representatives shall not exceed one for every thirty thousand, but each State shall have at least one representative; and until such enumeration shall be made, the State of New Hampshire shall be entitled to choose three, Massachusetts eight, Rhode Island and Providence Plantations one, Connecticut five, New York six, New Jersey four, Pennsylvania eight, Delaware one, Maryland six, Virginia ten, North Carolina five, South Carolina five, and Georgia three.

4. When vacancies happen in the representation from any State, the executive authority thereof shall issue writs of election to fill such vacancies.

5. The House of Representatives shall choose their speaker and other officers; and shall have the sole power of impeachment.

Section 3. 1. The Senate of the United States shall be composed of two senators from each State, chosen by the legislature thereof, for six years; and each senator shall have one vote.

2. Immediately after they shall be assembled in consequence of the first election, they shall be divided as equally as may be into three classes. The seats of the senators of the first class shall be vacated at the expiration of the second year, of the second class at the expiration of the fourth year, and of the third class at the expiration of the sixth year, so that one third may be chosen every second year; and if vacancies happen by resignation, or otherwise, during the recess of the legislature of any State, the executive thereof may make temporary appointments until the next meeting of the legislature, which shall then fill such vacancies.[2]

3. No person shall be a senator who shall not have attained to the age of thirty years, and been nine years a citizen of the United States, and who shall not, when elected, be an inhabitant of that State for which he shall be chosen.

4. The Vice President of the United States shall be President of the Senate, but shall have no vote, unless they be equally divided.

5. The Senate shall choose their other officers, and also a president pro tempore, in the absence of the Vice President, or when he shall exercise the office of the President of the United States.

[1]See the 14th Amendment.

[2]See the 17th Amendment.

6. The Senate shall have the sole power to try all impeachments. When sitting for that purpose, they shall be on oath or affirmation. When the President of the United States is tried, the chief justice shall preside: and no person shall be convicted without the concurrence of two thirds of the members present.

7. Judgment in cases of impeachment shall not extend further than to removal from office, and disqualification to hold and enjoy any office of honor, trust or profit under the United States: but the party convicted shall nevertheless be liable and subject to indictment, trial, judgment and punishment, according to law.

Section 4. 1. The times, places, and manner of holding elections for senators and representatives, shall be prescribed in each State by the legislature thereof; but the Congress may at any time by law make or alter such regulations, except as to the places of choosing senators.

2. The Congress shall assemble at least once in every year, and such meeting shall be on the first Monday in December, unless they shall by law appoint a different day.

Section 5. 1. Each House shall be the judge of the elections, returns and qualifications of its own members, and a majority of each shall constitute a quorum to do business; but a smaller number may adjourn from day to day, and may be authorized to compel the attendance of absent members, in such manner, and under such penalties as each House may provide.

2. Each House may determine the rules of its proceedings, punish its members for disorderly behavior, and, with the concurrence of two thirds, expel a member.

3. Each House shall keep a journal of its proceedings, and from time to time publish the same, excepting such parts as may in their judgment require secrecy; and the yeas and nays of the members of either House on any question shall, at the desire of one fifth of those present, be entered on the journal.

4. Neither House, during the session of Congress, shall, without the consent of the other, adjourn for more than three days, nor to any other place than that in which the two Houses shall be sitting.

Section 6. 1. The senators and representatives shall receive a compensation for their services, to be ascertained by law, and paid out of the Treasury of the United States. They shall in all cases, except treason, felony, and breach of the peace, be privileged from arrest during their attendance at the session of their respective Houses, and in going to and returning from the same; and for any speech or debate in either House, they shall not be questioned in any other place.

2. No senator or representative shall, during the time for which he was elected, be appointed to any civil office under the authority of the United States, which shall have been created, or the emoluments whereof shall have been increased during such time; and no person holding any office under the United States shall be a member of either House during his continuance in office.

Section 7. 1. All bills for raising revenue shall originate in the House of Representatives; but the Senate may propose or concur with amendments as on other bills.

2. Every bill which shall have passed the House of Representatives and the Senate, shall, before it becomes a law, be presented to the President of the United States; if he approves he shall sign it, but if not he shall return it, with his objections to that House in which it shall have originated, who shall enter the objections at large on their journal, and proceed to reconsider it. If after such reconsideration two thirds of that House shall agree to pass the bill, it shall be sent, together with the objections, to the other House, by which it shall likewise be reconsidered, and if approved by two thirds of that House, it shall become a law. But in all such cases the votes of both Houses shall be determined by yeas and nays, and the names of the persons voting for and against the bill shall be entered on the journal of each House respectively. If any bill shall not be returned by the President within ten days (Sundays excepted) after it shall have been presented to him, the same shall be a law, in like manner as if he had signed it, unless the Congress by their adjournment prevent its return, in which case it shall not be a law.

3. Every order, resolution, or vote to which the concurrence of the Senate and the House of Representatives may be necessary (except on a question of adjournment) shall be presented to the President of the United States; and before the same shall take effect, shall be approved by him, or being disapproved by him, shall be repassed by two thirds of the Senate and House of Representatives, according to the rules and limitations prescribed in the case of a bill.

Section 8. The Congress shall have the power

1. To lay and collect taxes, duties, imposts, and excises, to pay the debts and provide for the common defense and general welfare of the United States; but all duties, imposts, and excises shall be uniform throughout the United States;

2. To borrow money on the credit of the United States;

3. To regulate commerce with foreign nations, and among the several States, and with the Indian tribes;

4. To establish a uniform rule of naturalization, and uniform laws on the subject of bankruptcies throughout the United States;

5. To coin money, regulate the value thereof, and of foreign coin, and fix the standard of weights and measures;

6. To provide for the punishment of counterfeiting the securities and current coin of the United States;

7. To establish post offices and post roads;

8. To promote the progress of science and useful arts, by securing for limited times to authors and inventors the exclusive rights to their respective writings and discoveries;

9. To constitute tribunals inferior to the Supreme Court;

10. To define and punish piracies and felonies committed on the high seas, and offenses against the law of nations;

11. To declare war, grant letters of marque and reprisal, and make rules concerning captures on land and water;

12. To raise and support armies, but no appropriation of money to that use shall be for a longer term than two years;

13. To provide and maintain a navy;

14. To make rules for the government and regulation of the land and naval forces;

15. To provide for calling forth the militia to execute the laws of the Union, suppress insurrections and repel invasions;

16. To provide for organizing, arming, and disciplining the militia, and for governing such part of them as may be employed in the service of the United States, reserving to the States respectively, the appointment of the officers, and the authority of training the militia according to the discipline prescribed by Congress;

17. To exercise exclusive legislation in all cases whatsoever, over such district (not exceeding ten miles square) as may, by cession of particular States, and the acceptance of Congress, become the seat of the government of the United States, and to exercise like authority over all places purchased by the consent of the legislature of the State in which the same shall be, for the erection of forts, magazines, arsenals, dockyards, and other needful buildings; and

18. To make all laws which shall be necessary and proper for carrying into execution the foregoing powers, and all other powers vested by this Constitution in the government of the United States, or in any department or officer thereof.

Section 9. 1. The migration or importation of such persons as any of the States now existing shall think proper to admit, shall not be prohibited by the Congress prior to the year one thousand eight hundred and eight, but a tax or duty may be imposed on such importation, not exceeding ten dollars for each person.

2. The privilege of the writ of habeas corpus shall not be suspended, unless when in cases of rebellion or invasion the public safety may require it.

3. No bill of attainder or ex post facto law shall be passed.

4. No capitation, or other direct, tax shall be laid, unless in proportion to the census or enumeration hereinbefore directed to be taken.[3]

5. No tax or duty shall be laid on articles exported from any State.

6. No preference shall be given by any regulation of commerce or revenue to the ports of one State over those of another: nor shall vessels bound to, or from, one State be obliged to enter, clear, or pay duties in another.

7. No money shall be drawn from the treasury, but in consequence of appropriations made by law; and a regular statement and account of the receipts and expenditures of all public money shall be published from time to time.

8. No title of nobility shall be granted by the United States: and no person holding any office of profit or trust under them, shall, without the consent of the Congress, accept of any present, emolument, office, or title, of any kind whatever, from any king, prince, or foreign State.

Section 10. 1. No State shall enter into any treaty, alliance, or confederation; grant letters of marque and reprisal; coin money; emit bills of credit; make anything but gold and silver coin a tender in payment of debts; pass any bill of attainder, ex post facto law, or law impairing the obligation of contracts, or grant any title of nobility.

2. No State shall, without the consent of the Congress, lay any imposts or duties on imports or exports, except what may be absolutely necessary for executing its inspection laws: and the net produce of all duties and imposts laid by any State on imports or exports, shall be for the use of the treasury of the United States; and all such laws shall be subject to the revision and control of the Congress.

3. No State shall, without the consent of the Congress, lay any duty of tonnage, keep troops, or ships of war in time of peace, enter into any agreement or compact with another State, or with a foreign power, or engage in war, unless actually invaded, or in such imminent danger as will not admit of delay.

ARTICLE II

Section 1. 1. The executive power shall be vested in a President of the United States of America. He shall hold his office during the term of four years, and, together with the Vice President, chosen for the same term, be elected as follows:

2. Each State shall appoint, in such manner as the legislature thereof may direct, a number of electors, equal to the whole number of senators and representatives to which the State may be entitled in the Congress: but no senator or representative, or person holding an office of trust or profit under the United States, shall be appointed an elector.

The electors shall meet in their respective States, and vote by ballot for two persons, of whom one at least shall not be an inhabitant of the same State with themselves. And they shall make a list of all the persons voted for, and of the number of votes for each; which list they shall sign and certify, and transmit sealed to the seat of the government of the United States, directed to the president of the Senate. The president of the Senate shall, in the presence of the Senate and House of Representatives, open all the certificates,

[3]See the 16th Amendment.

and the votes shall then be counted. The person having the greatest number of votes shall be the President, if such number be a majority of the whole number of electors appointed; and if there be more than one who have such majority, and have an equal number of votes, then the House of Representatives shall immediately choose by ballot one of them for President; and if no person have a majority, then from the five highest on the list the said House shall in like manner choose the President. But in choosing the President, the votes shall be taken by States, the representation from each State having one vote; a quorum for this purpose shall consist of a member or members from two thirds of the States, and a majority of all the States shall be necessary to a choice. In every case, after the choice of the President, the person having the greatest number of votes of the electors shall be the Vice President. But if there should remain two or more who have equal votes, the Senate shall choose from them by ballot the Vice President.[4]

3. The Congress may determine the time of choosing the electors, and the day on which they shall give their votes; which day shall be the same throughout the United States.

4. No person except a natural born citizen, or a citizen of the United States, at the time of the adoption of this Constitution, shall be eligible to the office of President; neither shall any person be eligible to that office who shall not have attained to the age of thirty-five years, and been fourteen years a resident within the United States.

5. In the case of removal of the President from office, or of his death, resignation, or inability to discharge the powers and duties of the said office, the same shall devolve on the Vice President, and the Congress may by law provide for the case of removal, death, resignation, or inability, both of the President and Vice President, declaring what officer shall then act as President, and such officer shall act accordingly, until the disability be removed, or a President shall be elected.

6. The President shall, at stated times, receive for his services a compensation, which shall neither be increased nor diminished during the period for which he shall have been elected, and he shall not receive within that period any other emolument from the United States, or any of them.

7. Before he enter on the execution of his office, he shall take the following oath or affirmation:—"I do solemnly swear (or affirm) that I will faithfully execute the office of President of the United States, and will to the best of my ability, preserve, protect and defend the Constitution of the United States."

Section 2.   1. The President shall be commander in chief of the army and navy of the United States, and of the militia of the several States, when called into the actual service of the United States; he may require the opinion, in writing, of the principal officer in each of the executive departments, upon any subject relating to the duties of their respective office, and he shall have power to grant reprieves and pardons for offenses against the United States, except in cases of impeachment.

2. He shall have power, by and with the advice and consent of the Senate, to make treaties, provided two thirds of the senators present concur; and he shall nominate, and by and with the advice and consent of the Senate, shall appoint ambassadors, other public ministers and consuls, judges of the Supreme Court, and all other officers of the United States, whose appointments are not herein otherwise provided for, and which shall be established by law: but the Congress may by law vest the appointment of such inferior officers, as they think proper, in the President alone, in the courts of law, or in the heads of departments.

3. The President shall have power to fill up all vacancies that may happen during the recess of the Senate, by granting commissions which shall expire at the end of their next session.

Section 3.   He shall from time to time give to the Congress information of the state of the Union, and recommend to their consideration such measures as he shall judge necessary and expedient; he may, on extraordinary occasions, convene both Houses, or either of them, and in case of disagreement between them with respect to the time of adjournment, he may adjourn them to such time as he shall think proper; he shall receive ambassadors and other public ministers; he shall take care that the laws be faithfully executed, and shall commission all the officers of the United States.

Section 4.   The President, Vice President, and all civil officers of the United States, shall be removed from office on impeachment for, and conviction of, treason, bribery, or other high crimes and misdemeanors.

ARTICLE III

Section 1.   The judicial power of the United States shall be vested in one Supreme Court, and in such inferior courts as the Congress may from time to time ordain and establish. The judges, both of the Supreme and inferior courts, shall hold their offices during good behavior, and shall, at stated times, receive for their services, a compensation, which shall not be diminished during their continuance in office.

Section 2.   1. The judicial power shall extend to all cases, in law and equity, arising under this Constitution, the laws of the United States, and treaties made, or which shall be made, under their authority;—to all cases affecting ambassadors, other public ministers and consuls;—to all cases of admiralty and maritime jurisdiction;—to controversies to which the United States shall be a party;—to controversies

---

[4]Superseded by the 12th Amendment.

between two or more States; between a State and citizens of another State;[5]—between citizens of different States;—between citizens of the same State claiming lands under grants of different States, and between a State, or the citizens thereof, and foreign States, citizens or subjects.

2. In all cases affecting ambassadors, other public ministers and consuls, and those in which a State shall be party, the Supreme Court shall have original jurisdiction. In all the other cases before mentioned, the Supreme Court shall have appellate jurisdiction, both as to law and to fact, with such exceptions, and under such regulations as the Congress shall make.

3. The trial of all crimes, except in cases of impeachment, shall be by jury; and such trial shall be held in the State where the said crimes shall have been committed; but when not committed within any State, the trial shall be at such place or places as the Congress may by law have directed.

Section 3. 1. Treason against the United States shall consist only in levying war against them, or in adhering to their enemies, giving them aid and comfort. No person shall be convicted of treason unless on the testimony of two witnesses to the same overt act, or on confession in open court.

2. The Congress shall have power to declare the punishment of treason, but no attainder of treason shall work corruption of blood, or forfeiture except during the life of the person attainted.

ARTICLE IV

Section 1. Full faith and credit shall be given in each State to the public acts, records, and judicial proceedings of every other State. And the Congress may by general laws prescribe the manner in which such acts, records and proceedings shall be proved, and the effect thereof.

Section 2. 1. The citizens of each State shall be entitled to all privileges and immunities of citizens in the several States.[6]

2. A person charged in any State with treason, felony, or other crime, who shall flee from justice, and be found in another State, shall on demand of the executive authority of the State from which he fled, be delivered up to be removed to the State having jurisdiction of the crime.

3. No person held to service or labor in one State under the laws thereof, escaping into another, shall in consequence of any law or regulation therein, be discharged from such service or labor, but shall be delivered up on claim of the party to whom such service or labor may be due.[7]

Section 3. 1. New States may be admitted by the Congress into this Union; but no new State shall be formed or erected within the jurisdiction of any other State, nor any

State be formed by the junction of two or more States, or parts of States, without the consent of the legislatures of the States concerned as well as of the Congress.

2. The Congress shall have power to dispose of and make all needful rules and regulations respecting the territory or other property belonging to the United States; and nothing in this Constitution shall be so construed as to prejudice any claims of the United States, or of any particular State.

Section 4. The United States shall guarantee to every State in this Union a republican form of government, and shall protect each of them against invasion; and on application of the legislature, or of the executive (when the legislature cannot be convened) against domestic violence.

ARTICLE V

The Congress, whenever two thirds of both Houses shall deem it necessary, shall propose amendments to this Constitution, or, on the application of the legislature of two thirds of the several States, shall call a convention for proposing amendments, which in either case, shall be valid to all intents and purposes, as part of this Constitution when ratified by the legislatures of three fourths of the several States, or by conventions in three fourths thereof, as the one or the other mode of ratification may be proposed by the Congress; provided that no amendment which may be made prior to the year one thousand eight hundred and eight shall in any manner affect the first and fourth clauses in the ninth section of the first article; and that no State, without its consent, shall be deprived of its equal suffrage in the Senate.

ARTICLE VI

1. All debts contracted and engagements entered into, before the adoption of this Constitution, shall be as valid against the United States under this Constitution, as under the Confederation.[8]

2. This Constitution, and the laws of the United States which shall be made in pursuance thereof; and all treaties made, or which shall be made, under the authority of the United States, shall be the supreme law of the land; and the judges in every State shall be bound thereby, anything in the Constitution or laws of any State to the contrary notwithstanding.

3. The senators and representatives before mentioned, and the members of the several State legislatures, and all executive and judicial officers, both of the United States and of the several States, shall be bound by oath or affirmation to support this Constitution; but no religious test shall ever be required as a qualification to any office or public trust under the United States.

---

[5]See the 11th Amendment.
[6]See the 14th Amendment, Sec. 1.
[7]See the 13th Amendment.

[8]See the 14th Amendment, Sec. 4.

ARTICLE VII

The ratification of the conventions of nine States shall be sufficient for the establishment of this Constitution between the States so ratifying the same.

Done in Convention by the unanimous consent of the States present the seventeenth day of September in the year of our Lord one thousand seven hundred and eighty-seven, and of the independence of the United States of America the twelfth. In witness whereof we have hereunto subscribed our names.

AMENDMENTS

First Ten Amendments passed by Congress Sept. 25, 1789. Ratified by three-fourths of the States December 15, 1791.

AMENDMENT I

Congress shall make no law respecting an establishment of religion, or prohibiting the free exercise thereof; or abridging the freedom of speech, or of the press; or the right of the people peaceably to assemble, and to petition the government for a redress of grievances.

AMENDMENT II

A well regulated militia, being necessary to the security of a free State, the right of the people to keep and bear arms, shall not be infringed.

AMENDMENT III

No soldier shall, in time of peace be quartered in any house, without the consent of the owner, nor in time of war, but in a manner to be prescribed by law.

AMENDMENT IV

The right of the people to be secure in their persons, houses, papers, and effects, against unreasonable searches and seizures, shall not be violated, and no warrants shall issue, but upon probable cause, supported by oath or affirmation, and particularly describing the place to be searched, and the person or things to be seized.

AMENDMENT V

No person shall be held to answer for a capital, or otherwise infamous crime, unless on a presentment or indictment of a grand jury, except in cases arising in the land or naval forces, or in the militia, when in actual service in time of war or public danger; nor shall any person be subject for the same offense to be twice put in jeopardy of life or limb; nor shall be compelled in any criminal case to be a witness against himself, nor be deprived of life, liberty, or property, without due process of law; nor shall private property be taken for public use without just compensation.

AMENDMENT VI

In all criminal prosecutions, the accused shall enjoy the right to a speedy and public trial, by an impartial jury of the State and district wherein the crime shall have been committed, which district shall have been previously ascertained by law, and to be informed of the nature and cause of the accusation; to be confronted with the witnesses against him; to have compulsory process for obtaining witnesses in his favor, and to have the assistance of counsel for his defense.

AMENDMENT VII

In suits at common law, where the value in controversy shall exceed twenty dollars, the right of trial by jury shall be preserved, and no fact tried by a jury shall be otherwise reexamined in any court of the United States, then according to the rules of the common law.

AMENDMENT VIII

Excessive bail shall not be required, nor excessive fines imposed, nor cruel and unusual punishments inflicted.

AMENDMENT IX

The enumeration in the Constitution of certain rights shall not be construed to deny or disparage others retained by the people.

AMENDMENT X

The powers not delegated to the United States by the Constitution, nor prohibited by it to the States, are reserved to the States respectively, or to the people.

AMENDMENT XI

Passed by Congress March 5, 1794. Ratified January 8, 1798.

The judicial power of the United States shall not be construed to extend to any suit in law or equity, commenced or prosecuted against one of the United States by citizens of another State, or by citizens or subjects of any foreign State.

AMENDMENT XII

Passed by Congress December 12, 1803. Ratified September 25, 1804.

The electors shall meet in their respective States, and vote by ballot for President and Vice President, one of whom, at least, shall not be an inhabitant of the same State with themselves; they shall name in their ballots the person voted for as President, and in distinct ballots, the person voted for as Vice President, and they shall make distinct lists of all persons voted for as President and of all persons voted for as Vice President, and of the number of votes for each, which lists they shall sign and certify, and transmit sealed to the seat of the government of the United States, directed to the President of the Senate;—The President of the Senate shall, in the presence of the Senate and House of Representatives, open all the certificates and the votes shall then be counted;—The person having the greatest number of votes for President, shall be the President, if such number be a majority of the whole number of electors appointed; and if no person have such majority, then from the persons having the highest numbers not exceeding three on the list of those voted for as President, the House of Representatives shall choose immediately, by ballot, the President. But in choosing the President, the votes shall be taken by States, the representation from each State having one vote; a quorum for this purpose shall consist of a member or members from two thirds of the States, and a majority of all the States shall be necessary to a choice. And if the House of Representatives shall not choose a President whenever the right of choice shall devolve upon them, before the fourth day of March next following, then the Vice President shall act as President, as in the case of the death or other constitutional disability of the President. The person having the greatest number of votes as Vice President shall be the Vice President, if such number be a majority of the whole number of electors appointed, and if no person have a majority, then from the two highest numbers on the list, the Senate shall choose the Vice President; a quorum for the purpose shall consist of two thirds of the whole number of Senators, and a majority of the whole number shall be necessary to a choice. But no person constitutionally ineligible to the office of President shall be eligible to that of Vice President of the United States.

AMENDMENT XIII

Passed by Congress February 1, 1865. Ratified December 18, 1865.

Section 1. Neither slavery nor involuntary servitude, except as punishment for crime whereof the party shall have been duly convicted, shall exist within the United States, or any place subject to their jurisdiction.

Section 2. Congress shall have power to enforce this article by appropriate legislation.

AMENDMENT XIV

Passed by Congress June 16, 1866. Ratified July 23, 1868.

Section 1. All persons born or naturalized in the United States, and subject to the jurisdiction thereof, are citizens of the United States and of the State wherein they reside. No State shall make or enforce any law which shall abridge the privileges or immunities of citizens of the United States; nor shall any State deprive any person of life, liberty, or property, without due process of law; nor deny to any person within its jurisdiction the equal protection of the laws.

Section 2. Representatives shall be apportioned among the several States according to their respective numbers, counting the whole number of persons in each State, excluding Indians not taxed. But when the right to vote at any election for the choice of electors for President and Vice President of the United States, representatives in Congress, the executive and judicial officers of a State, or the members of the legislature thereof, is denied to any of the male inhabitants of such State, being twenty-one years of age, and citizens of the United States, or in any way abridged, except for participation in rebellion, or other crime, the basis of representation therein shall be reduced in the proportion which the number of such male citizens shall bear to the whole number of male citizens twenty-one years of age in such State.

Section 3. No person shall be a senator or representative in Congress, or elector of President and Vice President, or hold any office, civil or military, under the United States, or under any State, who having previously taken an oath, as a member of Congress, or as an officer of the United States, or as a member of any State legislature, or as an executive or judicial officer of any State, to support the Constitution of the United States, shall have engaged in insurrection or rebellion against the same, or given aid or comfort to the enemies thereof. But Congress may by a vote of two thirds of each House, remove such disability.

Section 4. The validity of the public debt of the United States, authorized by law, including debts incurred for payment of pensions and bounties for services in suppressing insurrection or rebellion, shall not be questioned. But neither the United States nor any State shall assume or pay any debt or obligation incurred in aid of insurrection or rebellion against the United States, or any claim for the loss or emancipation of any slave; but all such debts, obligations, and claims shall be held illegal and void.

Section 5. The Congress shall have power to enforce, by appropriate legislation, the provisions of this article.

AMENDMENT XV

Passed by Congress February 27, 1869. Ratified March 30, 1870.

Section 1. The right of citizens of the United States to vote shall not be denied or abridged by the United States or by any State on account of race, color, or previous condition of servitude.

Section 2. The Congress shall have power to enforce this article by appropriate legislation.

AMENDMENT XVI

Passed by Congress July 12, 1909. Ratified February 25, 1913.

The Congress shall have power to lay and collect taxes on incomes, from whatever source derived, without apportionment among the several States, and without regard to any census or enumeration.

AMENDMENT XVII

Passed by Congress May 16, 1912. Ratified May 31, 1913.

The Senate of the United States shall be composed of two senators from each State, elected by the people thereof, for six years; and each senator shall have one vote. The electors in each State shall have the qualifications requisite for electors of the most numerous branch of the State legislature.

When vacancies happen in the representation of any State in the Senate, the executive authority of such State shall issue writs of election to fill such vacancies: Provided, That the legislature of any State may empower the executive thereof to make temporary appointments until the people fill the vacancies by election as the legislature may direct.

This amendment shall not be so construed as to affect the election or term of any senator chosen before it becomes valid as part of the Constitution.

AMENDMENT XVIII

Passed by Congress December 17, 1917. Ratified January 29, 1919.

After one year from the ratification of this article, the manufacture, sale, or transportation of intoxicating liquors within, the importation thereof into, or the exportation thereof from the United States and all territory subject to the jurisdiction thereof for beverage purposes is hereby prohibited.

The Congress and the several States shall have concurrent power to enforce this article by appropriate legislation.

This article shall be inoperative unless it shall have been ratified as an amendment to the Constitution by the legislatures of the several States, as provided in the Constitution, within seven years from the date of the submission hereof to the States by Congress.

AMENDMENT XIX

Passed by Congress June 5, 1919. Ratified August 26, 1920.

The right of citizens of the United States to vote shall not be denied or abridged by the United States or by any State on account of sex.

The Congress shall have power by appropriate legislation to enforce the provisions of this article.

AMENDMENT XX

Passed by Congress March 3, 1932. Ratified January 23, 1933.

Section 1. The terms of the President and Vice President shall end at noon on the 20th day of January, and the terms of Senators and Representatives at noon on the 3d day of January, of the years in which such terms would have ended if this article had not been ratified; and the terms of their successors shall then begin.

Section 2. The Congress shall assemble at least once in every year, and such meeting shall begin at noon on the 3d day of January, unless they shall by law appoint a different day.

Section 3. If, at the time fixed for the beginning of the term of the President, the President-elect shall have died, the Vice President-elect shall become President. If a President shall not have been chosen before the time fixed for the beginning of his term, or if the President-elect shall have failed to qualify, then the Vice President-elect shall act as President until a President shall have qualified; and the Congress may by law provide for the case wherein neither a President-elect nor a Vice President-elect shall have qualified, declaring who shall then act as President, or the manner in which one who is to act shall be selected, and such person shall act accordingly until a President or Vice President shall have qualified.

Section 4. The Congress may by law provide for the case of the death of any of the persons from whom the House of Representatives may choose a President whenever the right of choice shall have devolved upon them, and for the case of the death of any of the persons from whom the Senate may choose a Vice President whenever the right of choice shall have devolved upon them.

Section 5. Sections 1 and 2 shall take effect on the 15th day of October following the ratification of this article.

Section 6. This article shall be inoperative unless it shall have been ratified as an amendment to the Constitution by the legislatures of three-fourths of the several States within seven years from the date of its submission.

AMENDMENT XXI

Passed by Congress February 20, 1933. Ratified December 5, 1933.

Section 1. The eighteenth article of amendment to the Constitution of the United States is hereby repealed.

Section 2. The transportation or importation into any State, Territory, or possession of the United States for delivery or use therein of intoxicating liquors in violation of the laws thereof, is hereby prohibited.

Section 3. This article shall be inoperative unless it shall have been ratified as an amendment to the Constitution by conventions in the several States, as provided in the Constitution, within seven years from the date of the submission thereof to the States by the Congress.

AMENDMENT XXII

Passed by Congress March 24, 1947. Ratified February 26, 1951.

Section 1. No person shall be elected to the office of the President more than twice, and no person who has held the office of President, or acted as President, for more than two years of a term to which some other person was elected President shall be elected to the office of the President more than once. But this article shall not apply to any person holding the office of President when this article was proposed by the Congress, and shall not prevent any person who may be holding the office of President, or acting as President, during the term within which this article becomes operative from holding the office of President or acting as President during the remainder of such term.

Section 2. This article shall be inoperative unless it shall have been ratified as an amendment to the Constitution by the legislatures of three-fourths of the several States within seven years from the date of its submission to the States by the Congress.

AMENDMENT XXIII

Passed by Congress June 16, 1960. Ratified April 3, 1961.

Section 1. The District constituting the seat of Government of the United States shall appoint in such manner as the Congress may direct:

A number of electors of President and Vice President equal to the whole number of Senators and Representatives in Congress to which the District would be entitled if it were a State, but in no event more than the least populous State; they shall be in addition to those appointed by the States, but they shall be considered, for the purposes of the election of President and Vice President, to be electors appointed by a State; and they shall meet in the District and perform such duties as provided by the twelfth article of amendment.

Section 2. The Congress shall have power to enforce this article by appropriate legislation.

AMENDMENT XXIV

Passed by Congress August 27, 1962. Ratified February 4, 1964.

Section 1. The right of citizens of the United States to vote in any primary or other election for President or Vice President, for electors for President or Vice President, or for Senator or Representative in Congress, shall not be denied or abridged by the United States or any State by reason of failure to pay any poll tax or other tax.

Section 2. The Congress shall have power to enforce this article by appropriate legislation.

AMENDMENT XXV

Passed by Congress July 6, 1965. Ratified February 23, 1967.

Section 1. In case of the removal of the President from office or of his death or resignation, the Vice President shall become President.

Section 2. Whenever there is a vacancy in the office of the Vice President, the President shall nominate a Vice President who shall take office upon confirmation by a majority vote of both Houses of Congress.

Section 3. Whenever the President transmits to the President pro tempore of the Senate and the Speaker of the House of Representatives his written declaration that he is unable to discharge the powers and duties of his office, and until he transmits to them a written declaration to the contrary, such powers and duties shall be discharged by the Vice President as Acting President.

Section 4. Whenever the Vice President and a majority of either the principal officers of the executive departments or of such other body as Congress may by law provide, transmit to the President pro tempore of the Senate and the Speaker of the House of Representatives their written declaration that the President is unable to discharge the powers and duties of his office, the Vice President shall immediately assume the powers and duties of the office as Acting President.

Thereafter, when the President transmits to the President pro tempore of the Senate and the Speaker of the House of Representatives his written declaration that no inability exists, he shall resume the powers and duties of his office unless the Vice President and a majority of either the principal officers of the executive department or of such other body as Congress may by law provide, transmit within four days to the President pro tempore of the Senate and the Speaker of the House of Representatives their written declaration that the President is unable to discharge the powers and duties of his office. Thereupon Congress shall decide the issue, assembling within forty-eight hours for that purpose if not in session. If the Congress, within twenty-one days after receipt of the latter written declaration, or, if Congress is not in session, within twenty-one days after Congress is required to assemble, determines by two-thirds vote of both Houses that the President is unable to discharge the powers and duties of his office, the Vice President shall continue to discharge the same as Acting President; otherwise, the President shall resume the powers and duties of his office.

AMENDMENT XXVI

Passed by Congress March 23, 1971. Ratified July 5, 1971.

Section 1. The right of citizens of the United States, who are eighteen years of age or older, to vote shall not be denied or abridged by the United States or by any State on account of age.

AMENDMENT XXVII

Passed by Congress September 25, 1789. Ratified May 18, 1992.

No law, varying the compensation for the services of the Senators and Representatives, shall take effect, until an election of Representatives shall have intervened.

UNIFORM COMMERCIAL CODE

(Adopted in fifty-two jurisdictions; all fifty States, although Louisiana has adopted only Articles 1, 3, 4, 7, 8, and 9; the District of Columbia; and the Virgin Islands.)

The Code consists of the following articles:

Art.

> ARTICLE 1 GENERAL PROVISIONS

PART 1 SHORT TITLE, CONSTRUCTION, APPLICATION AND SUBJECT MATTER OF THE ACT

§1—101. Short Title. This Act shall be known and may be cited as Uniform Commercial Code.

§1—102. Purposes; Rules of Construction; Variation by Agreement.

(1) This Act shall be liberally construed and applied to promote its underlying purposes and policies.

(2) Underlying purposes and policies of this Act are

(a) to simplify, clarify and modernize the law governing commercial transactions;

(b) to permit the continued expansion of commercial practices through custom, usage and agreement of the parties;

(c) to make uniform the law among the various jurisdictions.

(3) The effect of provisions of this Act may be varied by agreement, except as otherwise provided in this Act and except that the obligations of good faith, diligence, reasonableness and care prescribed by this Act may not be disclaimed by agreement but the parties may by agreement determine the standards by which the performance of such obligations is to be measured if such standards are not manifestly unreasonable.

(4) The presence in certain provisions of this Act of the words "unless otherwise agreed" or words of similar import does not imply that the effect of other provisions may not be varied by agreement under subsection (3).

(5) In this Act unless the context otherwise requires

(a) words in the singular number include the plural, and in the plural include the singular;

(b) words of the masculine gender include the feminine and the neuter, and when the sense so indicates words of the neuter gender may refer to any gender.

§1—103. Supplementary General Principles of Law Applicable. Unless displaced by the particular provisions of this Act, the principles of law and equity, including the law merchant and the law relative to capacity to contract, principal and agent, estoppel, fraud, misrepresentation, duress, coercion, mistake, bankruptcy, or other validating or invalidating cause shall supplement its provisions.

§1—104. Construction Against Implicit Repeal. This Act being a general act intended as a unified coverage of its subject matter, no part of it shall be deemed to be impliedly repealed by subsequent legislation if such construction can reasonably be avoided.

§1—105. *Territorial Application of the Act; Parties' Power to Choose Applicable Law.*

(1) Except as provided hereafter in this section, when a transaction bears a reasonable relation to this state and also to another state or nation the parties may agree that the law either of this state or of such other state or nation shall govern their rights and duties. Failing such agreement this Act applies to transactions bearing an appropriate relation to this state.

(2) Where one of the following provisions of this Act specifies the applicable law, that provision governs and a contrary agreement is effective only to the extent permitted by the law (including the conflict of laws rules) so specified:

Rights of creditors against sold goods. Section 2—402.

Applicability of the Article on Leases. Sections 2A—105 and 2A—106.

Applicability of the Article on Bank Deposits and Collections. Section 4—102.

Governing law in the Article on Funds Transfers. Section 4A—507.

Letters of Credit, Section 5—116.

Bulk sales subject to the Article on Bulk Sales. Section 6—103.

Applicability of the Article on Investment Securities. Section 8—106.

Law governing perfection, the effect of perfection or non-perfection, and the priority of security interests and agricultural liens. Sections 9—301 through 9—307.

As amended in 1972, 1987, 1988, 1989, 1994, 1995, and 1999.

§1—106. *Remedies to Be Liberally Administered.*

(1) The remedies provided by this Act shall be liberally administered to the end that the aggrieved party may be put in as good a position as if the other party had fully performed but neither consequential or special nor penal damages may be had except as specifically provided in this Act or by other rule of law.

(2) Any right or obligation declared by this Act is enforceable by action unless the provision declaring it specifies a different and limited effect.

§1—107. *Waiver or Renunciation of Claim or Right After Breach.*   Any claim or right arising out of an alleged breach can be discharged in whole or in part without consideration by a written waiver or renunciation signed and delivered by the aggrieved party.

§1—108. *Severability.*   If any provision or clause of this Act or application thereof to any person or circumstances is held invalid, such invalidity shall not affect other provisions or applications of the Act which can be given effect without the invalid provision or application, and to this end the provisions of this Act are declared to be severable.

§1—109. *Section Captions.*   Section captions are parts of this Act.

PART 2 GENERAL DEFINITIONS AND PRINCIPLES OF INTERPRETATION

§1—201. *General Definitions.*   Subject to additional definitions contained in the subsequent Articles of this Act which are applicable to specific Articles or Parts thereof, and unless the context otherwise requires, in this Act:

(1) "Action" in the sense of a judicial proceeding includes recoupment, counterclaim, set-off, suit in equity and any other proceedings in which rights are determined.

(2) "Aggrieved party" means a party entitled to resort to a remedy.

(3) "Agreement" means the bargain of the parties in fact as found in their language or by implication from other circumstances including course of dealing or usage of trade or course of performance as provided in this Act (Sections 1—205 and 2—208). Whether an agreement has legal consequences is determined by the provisions of this Act, if applicable; otherwise by the law of contracts (Section 1—103). (Compare "Contract".)

(4) "Bank" means any person engaged in the business of banking.

(5) "Bearer" means the person in possession of an instrument, document of title, or certificated security payable to bearer or indorsed in blank.

(6) "Bill of lading" means a document evidencing the receipt of goods for shipment issued by a person engaged in the business of transporting or forwarding goods, and includes an airbill. "Airbill" means a document serving for air transportation as a bill of lading does for marine or rail transportation, and includes an air consignment note or air waybill.

(7) "Branch" includes a separately incorporated foreign branch of a bank.

(8) "Burden of establishing" a fact means the burden of persuading the triers of fact that the existence of the fact is more probable than its non-existence.

(9) "Buyer in ordinary course of business" means a person that buys goods in good faith, without knowledge that the sale violates the rights of another person in the goods, and in the ordinary course from a person, other than a pawnbroker, in the business of selling goods of that kind. A person buys goods in the ordinary course if the sale to the person comports with the usual or customary practices in the kind of business in which the seller is engaged or with the seller's own usual or customary practices. A person that sells oil, gas, or other minerals at the wellhead or minehead is a person in the business of selling goods of that kind. A

buyer in ordinary course of business may buy for cash, by exchange of other property, or on secured or unsecured credit, and may acquire goods or documents of title under a pre-existing contract for sale. Only a buyer that takes possession of the goods or has a right to recover the goods from the seller under Article 2 may be a buyer in ordinary course of business. A person that acquires goods in a transfer in bulk or as security for or in total or partial satisfaction of a money debt is not a buyer in ordinary course of business.

(10) "Conspicuous": A term or clause is conspicuous when it is so written that a reasonable person against whom it is to operate ought to have noticed it. A printed heading in capitals (as: NON-NEGOTIABLE BILL OF LADING) is conspicuous. Language in the body of a form is "conspicuous" if it is in larger or other contrasting type or color. But in a telegram any stated term is "conspicuous". Whether a term or clause is "conspicuous" or not is for decision by the court.

(11) "Contract" means the total legal obligation which results from the parties' agreement as affected by this Act and any other applicable rules of law. (Compare "Agreement".)

(12) "Creditor" includes a general creditor, a secured creditor, a lien creditor and any representative of creditors, including an assignee for the benefit of creditors, a trustee in bankruptcy, a receiver in equity and an executor or administrator of an insolvent debtor's or assignor's estate.

(13) "Defendant" includes a person in the position of defendant in a cross-action or counterclaim.

(14) "Delivery" with respect to instruments, documents of title, chattel paper, or certificated securities means voluntary transfer of possession.

(15) "Document of title" includes bill of lading, dock warrant, dock receipt, warehouse receipt or order for the delivery of goods, and also any other document which in the regular course of business or financing is treated as adequately evidencing that the person in possession of it is entitled to receive, hold and dispose of the document and the goods it covers. To be a document of title a document must purport to be issued by or addressed to a bailee and purport to cover goods in the bailee's possession which are either identified or are fungible portions of an identified mass.

(16) "Fault" means wrongful act, omission or breach.

(17) "Fungible" with respect to goods or securities means goods or securities of which any unit is, by nature or usage of trade, the equivalent of any other like unit. Goods which are not fungible shall be deemed fungible for the purposes of this Act to the extent that under a particular agreement or document unlike units are treated as equivalents.

(18) "Genuine" means free of forgery or counterfeiting.

(19) "Good faith" means honesty in fact in the conduct or transaction concerned.

(20) "Holder" with respect to a negotiable instrument, means the person in possession if the instrument is payable to bearer or, in the cases of an instrument payable to an identified person, if the identified person is in possession. "Holder" with respect to a document of title means the person in possession if the goods are deliverable to bearer or to the order of the person in possession.

(21) To "honor" is to pay or to accept and pay, or where a credit so engages to purchase or discount a draft complying with the terms of the credit.

(22) "Insolvency proceedings" includes any assignment for the benefit of creditors or other proceedings intended to liquidate or rehabilitate the estate of the person involved.

(23) A person is "insolvent" who either has ceased to pay his debts in the ordinary course of business or cannot pay his debts as they become due or is insolvent within the meaning of the federal bankruptcy law.

(24) "Money" means a medium of exchange authorized or adopted by a domestic or foreign government and includes a monetary unit of account established by an intergovernmental organization or by agreement between two or more nations.

(25) A person has "notice" of a fact when

    (a) he has actual knowledge of it; or

    (b) he has received a notice or notification of it; or

    (c) from all the facts and circumstances known to him at the time in question he has reason to know that it exists.

A person "knows" or has "knowledge" of a fact when he has actual knowledge of it. "Discover" or "learn" or a word or phrase of similar import refers to knowledge rather than to reason to know. The time and circumstances under which a notice or notification may cease to be effective are not determined by this Act.

(26) A person "notifies" or "gives" a notice or notification to another by taking such steps as may be reasonably required to inform the other in ordinary course whether or not such other actually comes to know of it. A person "receives" a notice or notification when

    (a) it comes to his attention; or

    (b) it is duly delivered at the place of business through which the contract was made or at any other place held out by him as the place for receipt of such communications.

(27) Notice, knowledge or a notice or notification received by an organization is effective for a particular transaction from the time when it is brought to the attention of the individual conducting that transaction, and in any event from the time when it would have been brought to his attention if the organization had exercised due diligence. An organization exercises due diligence if it maintains reasonable routines for communicating significant information to the person conducting the transaction and there is reasonable compliance with the routines. Due diligence does not require an individual acting for the organization to communicate information unless such communication is part of his regular duties or unless he has reason to know of the

transaction and that the transaction would be materially affected by the information.

(28) "Organization" includes a corporation, government or governmental subdivision or agency, business trust, estate, trust, partnership or association, two or more persons having a joint or common interest, or any other legal or commercial entity.

(29) "Party", as distinct from "third party", means a person who has engaged in a transaction or made an agreement within this Act.

(30) "Person" includes an individual or an organization (See Section 1—102).

(31) "Presumption" or "presumed" means that the trier of fact must find the existence of the fact presumed unless and until evidence is introduced which would support a finding of its non-existence.

(32) "Purchase" includes taking by sale, discount, negotiation, mortgage, pledge, lien, issue or re-issue, gift or any other voluntary transaction creating an interest in property.

(33) "Purchaser" means a person who takes by purchase.

(34) "Remedy" means any remedial right to which an aggrieved party is entitled with or without resort to a tribunal.

(35) "Representative" includes an agent, an officer of a corporation or association, and a trustee, executor or administrator of an estate, or any other person empowered to act for another.

(36) "Rights" includes remedies.

(37) "Security interest" means an interest in personal property or fixtures which secures payment or performance of an obligation. The term also includes any interest of a consignor and a buyer of accounts, chattel paper, a payment intangible, or a promissory note in a transaction that is subject to Article 9. The special property interest of a buyer of goods on identification of those goods to a contract for sale under Section 2—401 is not a "security interest", but a buyer may also acquire a "security interest" by complying with Article 9. Except as otherwise provided in Section 2—505, the right of a seller or lessor of goods under Article 2 or 2A to retain or acquire possession of the goods is not a "security interest", but a seller or lessor may also acquire a "security interest" by complying with Article 9. The retention or reservation of title by a seller of goods notwithstanding shipment or delivery to the buyer (Section 2—401) is limited in effect to a reservation of a "security interest".

Whether a transaction creates a lease or security interest is determined by the facts of each case; however, a transaction creates a security interest if the consideration the lessee is to pay the lessor for the right to possession and use of the goods is an obligation for the term of the lease not subject to termination by the lessee, and

(a) the original term of the lease is equal to or greater than the remaining economic life of the goods,

(b) the lessee is bound to renew the lease for the remaining economic life of the goods or is bound to become the owner of the goods,

(c) the lessee has an option to renew the lease for the remaining economic life of the goods for no additional consideration or nominal additional consideration upon compliance with the lease agreement, or

(d) the lessee has an option to become the owner of the goods for no additional consideration or nominal additional consideration upon compliance with the lease agreement.

A transaction does not create a security interest merely because it provides that

(a) the present value of the consideration the lessee is obligated to pay the lessor for the right to possession and use of the goods is substantially equal to or is greater than the fair market value of the goods at the time the lease is entered into,

(b) the lessee assumes risk of loss of the goods, or agrees to pay taxes, insurance, filing, recording, or registration fees, or service or maintenance costs with respect to the goods,

(c) the lessee has an option to renew the lease or to become the owner of the goods,

(d) the lessee has an option to renew the lease for a fixed rent that is equal to or greater than the reasonably predictable fair market rent for the use of the goods for the term of the renewal at the time the option is to be performed, or

(e) the lessee has an option to become the owner of the goods for a fixed price that is equal to or greater than the reasonably predictable fair market value of the goods at the time the option is to be performed.

For purposes of this subsection (37):

(x) Additional consideration is not nominal if (i) when the option to renew the lease is granted to the lessee the rent is stated to be the fair market rent for the use of the goods for the term of the renewal determined at the time the option is to be performed, or (ii) when the option to become the owner of the goods is granted to the lessee the price is stated to be the fair market value of the goods determined at the time the option is to be performed. Additional consideration is nominal if it is less than the lessee's reasonably predictable cost of performing under the lease agreement if the option is not exercised;

(y) "Reasonably predictable" and "remaining economic life of the goods" are to be determined with reference to the facts and circumstances at the time the transaction is entered into; and

(z) "Present value" means the amount as of a date certain of one or more sums payable in the future, discounted to the date certain. The discount is determined by the interest rate specified by the parties if the rate is not manifestly unreasonable at the time the transaction is entered into; otherwise, the discount is determined by a commercially reasonable rate that takes into account the facts and circumstances of each case at the time the transaction was entered into.

(38) "Send" in connection with any writing or notice means to deposit in the mail or deliver for transmission by any other usual means of communication with postage or cost of transmission provided for and properly addressed and in the case of an instrument to an address specified thereon or otherwise agreed, or if there be none to any address reasonable under the circumstances. The receipt of any writing or notice within the time at which it would have arrived if properly sent has the effect of a proper sending.

(39) "Signed" includes any symbol executed or adopted by a party with present intention to authenticate a writing.

(40) "Surety" includes guarantor.

(41) "Telegram" includes a message transmitted by radio, teletype, cable, any mechanical method of transmission, or the like.

(42) "Term" means that portion of an agreement which relates to a particular matter.

(43) "Unauthorized" signature means one made without actual, implied or apparent authority and includes a forgery.

(44) "Value". Except as otherwise provided with respect to negotiable instruments and bank collections (Sections 3—303, 4—210 and 4—211) a person gives "value" for rights if he acquires them

    (a) in return for a binding commitment to extend credit or for the extension of immediately available credit whether or not drawn upon and whether or not a chargeback is provided for in the event of difficulties in collection; or

    (b) as security for or in total or partial satisfaction of a pre-existing claim; or

    (c) by accepting delivery pursuant to a preexisting contract for purchase; or

    (d) generally, in return for any consideration sufficient to support a simple contract.

(45) "Warehouse receipt" means a receipt issued by a person engaged in the business of storing goods for hire.

(46) "Written" or "writing" includes printing, typewriting or any other intentional reduction to tangible form.

§1—202. Prima Facie Evidence by Third Party Documents.
A document in due form purporting to be a bill of lading, policy or certificate of insurance, official weigher's or inspector's certificate, consular invoice, or any other document authorized or required by the contract to be issued by a third party shall be prima facie evidence of its own authenticity and genuineness and of the facts stated in the document by the third party.

§1—203. Obligation of Good Faith.
Every contract or duty within this Act imposes an obligation of good faith in its performance or enforcement.

§1—204. Time; Reasonable Time; "Seasonably".

(1) Whenever this Act requires any action to be taken within a reasonable time, any time which is not manifestly unreasonable may be fixed by agreement.

(2) What is a reasonable time for taking any action depends on the nature, purpose and circumstances of such action.

(3) An action is taken "seasonably" when it is taken at or within the time agreed or if no time is agreed at or within a reasonable time.

§1—205. Course of Dealing and Usage of Trade.

(1) A course of dealing is a sequence of previous conduct between the parties to a particular transaction which is fairly to be regarded as establishing a common basis of understanding for interpreting their expressions and other conduct.

(2) A usage of trade is any practice or method of dealing having such regularity of observance in a place, vocation or trade as to justify an expectation that it will be observed with respect to the transaction in question. The existence and scope of such a usage are to be proved as facts. If it is established that such a usage is embodied in a written trade code or similar writing the interpretation of the writing is for the court.

(3) A course of dealing between parties and any usage of trade in the vocation or trade in which they are engaged or of which they are or should be aware give particular meaning to and supplement or qualify terms of an agreement.

(4) The express terms of an agreement and an applicable course of dealing or usage of trade shall be construed wherever reasonable as consistent with each other; but when such construction is unreasonable express terms control both course of dealing and usage of trade and course of dealing controls usage trade.

(5) An applicable usage of trade in the place where any part of performance is to occur shall be used in interpreting the agreement as to that part of the performance.

(6) Evidence of a relevant usage of trade offered by one party is not admissible unless and until he has given the other party such notice as the court finds sufficient to prevent unfair surprise to the latter.

§1—206. Statute of Frauds for Kinds of Personal Property Not Otherwise Covered.

(1) Except in the cases described in subsection (2) of this section a contract for the sale of personal property is not enforceable by way of action or defense beyond five thousand dollars in amount or value of remedy unless there is some writing which indicates that a contract for sale has been made between the parties at a defined or stated price, reasonably identifies the subject matter, and is signed by the party against whom enforcement is sought or by his authorized agent.

(2) Subsection (1) of this section does not apply to contracts for the sale of goods (Section 2—201) nor of securities (Section 8—113) nor to security agreements (Section 9—203). As amended in 1994.

§1—207. Performance or Acceptance Under Reservation of Rights.

(1) A party who with explicit reservation of rights performs or promises performance or assents to performance in a manner demanded or offered by the other party does not thereby prejudice the rights reserved. Such words as "without prejudice", "under protest" or the like are sufficient.

(2) Subsection (1) does not apply to an accord and satisfaction. As amended in 1990.

§1—208. Option to Accelerate at Will.

A term providing that one party or his successor in interest may accelerate payment or performance or require collateral or additional collateral "at will" or "when he deems himself insecure" or in words of similar import shall be construed to mean that he shall have power to do so only if he in good faith believes that the prospect of payment or performance is impaired. The burden of establishing lack of good faith is on the party against whom the power has been exercised.

§1—209. Subordinated Obligations.

An obligation may be issued as subordinated to payment of another obligation of the person obligated, or a creditor may subordinate his right to payment of an obligation by agreement with either the person obligated or another creditor of the person obligated. Such a subordination does not create a security interest as against either the common debtor or a subordinated creditor. This section shall be construed as declaring the law as it existed prior to the enactment of this section and not as modifying it. Added 1966.

Note: *This new section is proposed as an optional provision to make it clear that a subordination agreement does not create a security interest unless so intended.*

 # ARTICLE 2 SALES

PART 1 SHORT TITLE, GENERAL CONSTRUCTION AND SUBJECT MATTER

§2—101. Short Title.

This Article shall be known and may be cited as Uniform Commercial Code—Sales.

§2—102. Scope; Certain Security and Other Transactions Excluded From This Article.

Unless the context otherwise requires, this Article applies to transactions in goods; it does not apply to any transaction which although in the form of an unconditional contract to sell or present sale is intended to operate only as a security transaction nor does this Article impair or repeal any statute regulating sales to consumers, farmers or other specified classes of buyers.

§2—103. Definitions and Index of Definitions.

(1) In this Article unless the context otherwise requires

(a) "Buyer" means a person who buys or contracts to buy goods.

(b) "Good faith" in the case of a merchant means honesty in fact and the observance of reasonable commercial standards of fair dealing in the trade.

(c) "Receipt" of goods means taking physical possession of them.

(d) "Seller" means a person who sells or contracts to sell goods.

(2) Other definitions applying to this Article or to specified Parts thereof, and the sections in which they appear are:

"Acceptance". Section 2—606.
"Banker's credit". Section 2—325.
"Between merchants". Section 2—104.
"Cancellation". Section 2—106(4).
"Commercial unit". Section 2—105.
"Confirmed credit". Section 2—325.
"Conforming to contract". Section 2—106.
"Contract for sale". Section 2—106.
"Cover". Section 2—712.
"Entrusting". Section 2—403.
"Financing agency". Section 2—104.
"Future goods". Section 2—105.
"Goods". Section 2—105.
"Identification". Section 2—501.
"Installment contract". Section 2—612.
"Letter of Credit". Section 2—325.
"Lot". Section 2—105.
"Merchant". Section 2—104.
"Overseas". Section 2—323.
"Person in position of seller". Section 2—707.
"Present sale". Section 2—106.
"Sale". Section 2—106.
"Sale on approval". Section 2—326.
"Sale or return". Section 2—326.
"Termination". Section 2—106.

(3) The following definitions in other Articles apply to this Article:

"Check". Section 3—104.
"Consignee". Section 7—102.
"Consignor". Section 7—102.
"Consumer goods". Section 9—109.
"Dishonor". Section 3—507.
"Draft". Section 3—104.

(4) In addition Article 1 contains general definitions and principles of construction and interpretation applicable throughout this Article. As amended in 1994 and 1999.

§2—104. Definitions: "Merchant"; "Between Merchants"; "Financing Agency".

(1) "Merchant" means a person who deals in goods of the kind or otherwise by his occupation holds himself out as having knowledge or skill peculiar to the practices or goods involved in the transaction or to whom such knowledge or skill may be attributed by his employment of an agent or broker or other intermediary who by his occupation holds himself out as having such knowledge or skill.

(2) "Financing agency" means a bank, finance company or other person who in the ordinary course of business makes advances against goods or documents of title or who by arrangement with either the seller or the buyer intervenes in ordinary course to make or collect payment due or claimed under the contract for sale, as by purchasing or paying the seller's draft or making advances against it or by merely taking it for collection whether or not documents of title accompany the draft. "Financing agency" includes also a bank or other person who similarly intervenes between persons who are in the position of seller and buyer in respect to the goods (Section 2—707).

(3) "Between merchants" means in any transaction with respect to which both parties are chargeable with the knowledge or skill of merchants.

§2—105. Definitions: Transferability; "Goods"; "Future" Goods; "Lot"; "Commercial Unit".

(1) "Goods" means all things (including specially manufactured goods) which are movable at the time of identification to the contract for sale other than the money in which the price is to be paid, investment securities (Article 8) and things in action. "Goods" also includes the unborn young of animals and growing crops and other identified things attached to realty as described in the section on goods to be severed from realty (Section 2—107).

(2) Goods must be both existing and identified before any interest in them can pass. Goods which are not both existing and identified are "future" goods. A purported present sale of future goods or of any interest therein operates as a contract to sell.

(3) There may be a sale of a part interest in existing identified goods.

(4) An undivided share in an identified bulk of fungible goods is sufficiently identified to be sold although the quantity of the bulk is not determined. Any agreed proportion of such a bulk or any quantity thereof agreed upon by number, weight or other measure may to the extent of the seller's interest in the bulk be sold to the buyer who then becomes an owner in common.

(5) "Lot" means a parcel or a single article which is the subject matter of a separate sale or delivery, whether or not it is sufficient to perform the contract.

(6) "Commercial unit" means such a unit of goods as by commercial usage is a single whole for purposes of sale and division of which materially impairs its character or value on the market or in use. A commercial unit may be a single article (as a machine) or a set of articles (as a suite of furniture or an assortment of sizes) or a quantity (as a bale, gross, or carload) or any other unit treated in use or in the relevant market as a single whole.

§2—106. Definitions: "Contract"; "Agreement"; "Contract for Sale"; "Sale"; "Present Sale"; "Conforming" to Contract; "Termination"; "Cancellation".

(1) In this Article unless the context otherwise requires "contract" and "agreement" are limited to those relating to the present or future sale of goods. "Contract for sale" includes both a present sale of goods and a contract to sell goods at a future time. A "sale" consists in the passing of title from the seller to the buyer for a price (Section 2—401). A "present sale" means a sale which is accomplished by the making of the contract.

(2) Goods or conduct including any part of a performance are "conforming" or conform to the contract when they are in accordance with the obligations under the contract.

(3) "Termination" occurs when either party pursuant to a power created by agreement or law puts an end to the contract otherwise than for its breach. On "termination" all obligations which are still executory on both sides are discharged but any right based on prior breach or performance survives.

(4) "Cancellation" occurs when either party puts an end to the contract for breach by the other and its effect is the same as that of "termination" except that the cancelling party also retains any remedy for breach of the whole contract or any unperformed balance.

§2—107. Goods to Be Severed From Realty: Recording.

(1) A contract for the sale of minerals or the like (including oil and gas) or a structure or its materials to be removed from realty is a contract for the sale of goods within this Article if they are to be severed by the seller but until severance a purported present sale thereof which is not effective as a transfer of an interest in land is effective only as a contract to sell.

(2) A contract for the sale apart from the land of growing crops or other things attached to realty and capable of severance without material harm thereto but not described in subsection (1) or of timber to be cut is a contract for the sale of goods within this Article whether the subject matter is to be severed by the buyer or by the seller even though it forms part of the realty at the time of contracting, and the parties can by identification effect a present sale before severance.

(3) The provisions of this section are subject to any third party rights provided by the law relating to realty records, and the contract for sale may be executed and recorded as a document transferring an interest in land and shall then

constitute notice to third parties of the buyer's rights under the contract for sale.
As amended in 1972.

PART 2 FORM, FORMATION AND READJUSTMENT OF CONTRACT

§2—201. Formal Requirements; Statute of Frauds.

(1) Except as otherwise provided in this section a contract for the sale of goods for the price of $500 or more is not enforceable by way of action or defense unless there is some writing sufficient to indicate that a contract for sale has been made between the parties and signed by the party against whom enforcement is sought or by his authorized agent or broker. A writing is not insufficient because it omits or incorrectly states a term agreed upon but the contract is not enforceable under this paragraph beyond the quantity of goods shown in such writing.

(2) Between merchants if within a reasonable time a writing in confirmation of the contract and sufficient against the sender is received and the party receiving it has reason to know its contents, its satisfies the requirements of subsection (1) against such party unless written notice of objection to its contents is given within ten days after it is received.

(3) A contract which does not satisfy the requirements of subsection (1) but which is valid in other respects is enforceable

   (a) if the goods are to be specially manufactured for the buyer and are not suitable for sale to others in the ordinary course of the seller's business and the seller, before notice of repudiation is received and under circumstances which reasonably indicate that the goods are for the buyer, has made either a substantial beginning of their manufacture or commitments for their procurement; or

   (b) if the party against whom enforcement is sought admits in his pleading, testimony or otherwise in court that a contract for sale was made, but the contract is not enforceable under this provision beyond the quantity of goods admitted; or

   (c) with respect to goods for which payment has been made and accepted or which have been received and accepted (Sec. 2—606).

§2—202. Final Written Expression: Parol or Extrinsic Evidence.
Terms with respect to which the confirmatory memoranda of the parties agree or which are otherwise set forth in a writing intended by the parties as a final expression of their agreement with respect to such terms as are included therein may not be contradicted by evidence of any prior agreement or of a contemporaneous oral agreement but may be explained or supplemented

   (a) by course of dealing or usage of trade (Section 1—205) or by course of performance (Section 2—208); and

   (b) by evidence of consistent additional terms unless the court finds the writing to have been intended also as a complete and exclusive statement of the terms of the agreement.

§2—203. Seals Inoperative.
The affixing of a seal to a writing evidencing a contract for sale or an offer to buy or sell goods does not constitute the writing a sealed instrument and the law with respect to sealed instruments does not apply to such a contract or offer.

§2—204. Formation in General.

(1) A contract for sale of goods may be made in any manner sufficient to show agreement, including conduct by both parties which recognizes the existence of such a contract.

(2) An agreement sufficient to constitute a contract for sale may be found even though the moment of its making is undetermined.

(3) Even though one or more terms are left open a contract for sale does not fail for indefiniteness if the parties have intended to make a contract and there is a reasonably certain basis for giving an appropriate remedy.

§2—205. Firm Offers.
An offer by a merchant to buy or sell goods in a signed writing which by its terms gives assurance that it will be held open is not revocable, for lack of consideration, during the time stated or if no time is stated for a reasonable time, but in no event may such period of irrevocability exceed three months; but any such term of assurance on a form supplied by the offeree must be separately signed by the offeror.

§2—206. Offer and Acceptance in Formation of Contract.

(1) Unless other unambiguously indicated by the language or circumstances

   (a) an offer to make a contract shall be construed as inviting acceptance in any manner and by any medium reasonable in the circumstances;

   (b) an order or other offer to buy goods for prompt or current shipment shall be construed as inviting acceptance either by a prompt promise to ship or by the prompt or current shipment of conforming or nonconforming goods, but such a shipment of non-conforming goods does not constitute an acceptance if the seller seasonably notifies the buyer that the shipment is offered only as an accommodation to the buyer.

(2) Where the beginning of a requested performance is a reasonable mode of acceptance an offeror who is not notified of acceptance within a reasonable time may treat the offer as having lapsed before acceptance.

§2—207. Additional Terms in Acceptance or Confirmation.

(1) A definite and seasonable expression of acceptance or a written confirmation which is sent within a reasonable time operates as an acceptance even though it states terms additional to or different from those offered or agreed upon, unless acceptance is expressly made conditional on assent to the additional or different terms.

(2) The additional terms are to be construed as proposals for addition to the contract. Between merchants such terms become part of the contract unless:

    (a) the offer expressly limits acceptance to the terms of the offer;

    (b) they materially alter it; or

    (c) notification of objection to them has already been given or is given within a reasonable time after notice of them is received.

(3) Conduct by both parties which recognizes the existence of a contract is sufficient to establish a contract for sale although the writings of the parties do not otherwise establish a contract. In such case the terms of the particular contract consist of those terms on which the writings of the parties agree, together with any supplementary terms incorporated under any other provisions of this Act.

§2—208. Course of Performance or Practical Construction.

(1) Where the contract for sale involves repeated occasions for performance by either party with knowledge of the nature of the performance and opportunity for objection to it by the other, any course of performance accepted or acquiesced in without objection shall be relevant to determine the meaning of the agreement.

(2) The express terms of the agreement and any such course of performance, as well as any course of dealing and usage of trade, shall be construed whenever reasonable as consistent with each other; but when such construction is unreasonable, express terms shall control course of performance and course of performance shall control both course of dealing and usage of trade (Section 1—205).

(3) Subject to the provisions of the next section on modification and waiver, such course of performance shall be relevant to show a waiver or modification of any term inconsistent with such course of performance.

§2—209. Modification, Rescission and Waiver.

(1) An agreement modifying a contract within this Article needs no consideration to be binding.

(2) A signed agreement which excludes modification or rescission except by a signed writing cannot be otherwise modified or rescinded, but except as between merchants such a requirement on a form supplied by the merchant must be separately signed by the other party.

(3) The requirements of the statute of frauds section of this Article (Section 2—201) must be satisfied if the contract as modified is within its provisions.

(4) Although an attempt at modification or rescission does not satisfy the requirements of subsection (2) or (3) it can operate as a waiver.

(5) A party who has made a waiver affecting an executory portion of the contract may retract the waiver by reasonable notification received by the other party that strict performance will be required of any term waived, unless the retraction would be unjust in view of a material change of position in reliance on the waiver.

§2—210. Delegation of Performance; Assignment of Rights.

(1) A party may perform his duty through a delegate unless otherwise agreed or unless the other party has a substantial interest in having his original promisor perform or control the acts required by the contract. No delegation of performance relieves the party delegating of any duty to perform or any liability for breach.

(2) Except as otherwise provided in Section 9—406, unless otherwise agreed, all rights of either seller or buyer can be assigned except where the assignment would materially change the duty of the other party, or increase materially the burden or risk imposed on him by his contract, or impair materially his chance of obtaining return performance. A right to damages for breach of the whole contract or a right arising out of the assignor's due performance of his entire obligation can be assigned despite agreement otherwise.

(3) The creation, attachment, perfection, or enforcement of a security interest in the seller's interest under a contract is not a transfer that materially changes the duty of or increases materially the burden or risk imposed on the buyer or impairs materially the buyer's chance of obtaining return performance within the purview of subsection (2) unless, and then only to the extent that, enforcement actually results in a delegation of material performance of the seller. Even in that event, the creation, attachment, perfection, and enforcement of the security interest remain effective, but (i) the seller is liable to the buyer for damages caused by the delegation to the extent that the damages could not reasonably by prevented by the buyer, and (ii) a court having jurisdiction may grant other appropriate relief, including cancellation of the contract for sale or an injunction against enforcement of the security interest or consummation of the enforcement.

(4) Unless the circumstnaces indicate the contrary a prohibition of assignment of "the contract" is to be construed as barring only the delegation to the assignes of the assignor's performance.

(5) An assignment of "the contract" or of "all my rights under the contract" or an assignment in similar general terms is an assignment of rights and unless the language or

the circumstances (as in an assignment for security) indicate the contrary, it is a delegation of performance of the duties of the assignor and its acceptance by the assignee constitutes a promise by him to perform those duties. This promise is enforceable by either the assignor or the other party to the original contract.

(6) The other party may treat any assignment which delegates performance as creating reasonable grounds for insecurity and may without prejudice to his rights against the assignor demand assurances from the assignee (Section 2—609). As amended in 1999.

PART 3 GENERAL OBLIGATION AND CONSTRUCTION OF CONTRACT

§2—301. General Obligations of Parties.   The obligation of the seller is to transfer and deliver and that of the buyer is to accept and pay in accordance with the contract.

§2—302. Unconscionable Contract or Clause.

(1) If the court as a matter of law finds the contract or any clause of the contract to have been unconscionable at the time it was made the court may refuse to enforce the contract, or it may enforce the remainder of the contract without the unconscionable clause, or it may so limit the application of any unconscionable clause as to avoid any unconscionable result.

(2) When it is claimed or appears to the court that the contract or any clause thereof may be unconscionable the parties shall be afforded a reasonable opportunity to present evidence as to its commercial setting, purpose and effect to aid the court in making the determination.

§2—303. Allocations or Division of Risks.   Where this Article allocates a risk or a burden as between the parties "unless otherwise agreed", the agreement may not only shift the allocation but may also divide the risk or burden.

§2—304. Price Payable in Money, Goods, Realty, or Otherwise.

(1) The price can be made payable in money or otherwise. If it is payable in whole or in part in goods each party is a seller of the goods which he is to transfer.

(2) Even though all or part of the price is payable in an interest in realty the transfer of the goods and the seller's obligations with reference to them are subject to this Article, but not the transfer of the interest in realty or the transferor's obligations in connection therewith.

§2—305. Open Price Term.

(1) The parties if they so intend can conclude a contract for sale even though the price is not settled. In such a case the price is a reasonable price at the time for delivery if
   (a) nothing is said as to price; or
   (b) the price is left to be agreed by the parties and they fail to agree; or

   (c) the price is to be fixed in terms of some agreed market or other standard as set or recorded by a third person or agency and it is not so set or recorded.

(2) A price to be fixed by the seller or by the buyer means a price for him to fix in good faith.

(3) When a price left to be fixed otherwise than by agreement of the parties fails to be fixed through fault of one party the other may at his option treat the contract as cancelled or himself fix a reasonable price.

(4) Where, however, the parties intend not to be bound unless the price be fixed or agreed and it is not fixed or agreed there is no contract. In such a case the buyer must return any goods already received or if unable so to do must pay their reasonable value at the time of delivery and the seller must return any portion of the price paid on account.

§2—306. Output, Requirements and Exclusive Dealings.

(1) A term which measures the quantity by the output of the seller or the requirements of the buyer means such actual output or requirements as may occur in good faith, except that no quantity unreasonably disproportionate to any stated estimate or in the absence of a stated estimate to any normal or otherwise comparable prior output or requirements may be tendered or demanded.

(2) A lawful agreement by either the seller or the buyer for exclusive dealing in the kind of goods concerned imposes unless otherwise agreed an obligation by the seller to use best efforts to supply the goods and by the buyer to use best efforts to promote their sale.

§2—307. Delivery in Single Lot or Several Lots.   Unless otherwise agreed all goods called for by a contract for sale must be tendered in a single delivery and payment is due only on such tender but where the circumstances give either party the right to make or demand delivery in lots the price if it can be apportioned may be demanded for each lot.

§2—308. Absence of Specified Place for Delivery.   Unless otherwise agreed
   (a) the place for delivery of goods is the seller's place of business or if he has none his residence; but
   (b) in a contract for sale of identified goods which to the knowledge of the parties at the time of contracting are in some other place, that place is the place for their delivery; and
   (c) documents of title may be delivered through customary banking channels.

§2—309. Absence of Specific Time Provisions; Notice of Termination.

(1) The time for shipment or delivery or any other action under a contract if not provided in this Article or agreed upon shall be a reasonable time.

(2) Where the contract provides for successive performances but is indefinite in duration it is valid for a reasonable time but unless otherwise agreed may be terminated at any time by either party.

(3) Termination of a contract by one party except on the happening of an agreed event requires that reasonable notification be received by the other party and an agreement dispensing with notification is invalid if its operation would be unconscionable.

§2—310. Open Time for Payment or Running of Credit; Authority to Ship Under Reservation. Unless otherwise agreed

(a) payment is due at the time and place at which the buyer is to receive the goods even though the place of shipment is the place of delivery; and

(b) if the seller is authorized to send the goods he may ship them under reservation, and may tender the documents of title, but the buyer may inspect the goods after their arrival before payment is due unless such inspection is inconsistent with the terms of the contract (Section 2—513); and

(c) if delivery is authorized and made by way of documents of title otherwise than by subsection (b) then payment is due at the time and place at which the buyer is to receive the documents regardless of where the goods are to be received; and

(d) where the seller is required or authorized to ship the goods on credit the credit period runs from the time of shipment but post-dating the invoice or delaying its dispatch will correspondingly delay the starting of the credit period.

§2—311. Options and Cooperation Respecting Performance.

(1) An agreement for sale which is otherwise sufficiently definite (subsection (3) of Section 2—204) to be a contract is not made invalid by the fact that it leaves particulars of performance to be specified by one of the parties. Any such specification must be made in good faith and within limits set by commercial reasonableness.

(2) Unless otherwise agreed specifications relating to assortment of the goods are at the buyer's option and except as otherwise provided in subsections (1)(c) and (3) of Section 2—319 specifications or arrangements relating to shipment are at the seller's option.

(3) Where such specification would materially affect the other party's performance but is not seasonably made or where one party's cooperation is necessary to the agreed performance of the other but is not seasonably forthcoming, the other party in addition to all other remedies

(a) is excused for any resulting delay in his own performance; and

(b) may also either proceed to perform in any reasonable manner or after the time for a material part of his own performance treat the failure to specify or to cooperate as a breach by failure to deliver or accept the goods.

§2—312. Warranty of Title and Against Infringement; Buyer's Obligation Against Infringement.

(1) Subject to subsection (2) there is in a contract for sale a warranty by the seller that

(a) the title conveyed shall be good, and its transfer rightful; and

(b) the goods shall be delivered free from any security interest or other lien or encumbrance of which the buyer at the time of contracting has no knowledge.

(2) A warranty under subsection (1) will be excluded or modified only by specific language or by circumstances which give the buyer reason to know that the person selling does not claim title in himself or that he is purporting to sell only such right or title as he or a third person may have.

(3) Unless otherwise agreed a seller who is a merchant regularly dealing in goods of the kind warrants that the goods shall be delivered free of the rightful claim of any third person by way of infringement or the like but a buyer who furnishes specifications to the seller must hold the seller harmless against any such claim which arises out of compliance with the specifications.

§2—313. Express Warranties by Affirmation, Promise, Description, Sample.

(1) Express warranties by the seller are created as follows:

(a) Any affirmation of fact or promise made by the seller to the buyer which relates to the goods and becomes part of the basis of the bargain creates an express warranty that the goods shall conform to the affirmation or promise.

(b) Any description of the goods which is made part of the basis of the bargain creates an express warranty that the goods shall conform to the description.

(c) Any sample or model which is made part of the basis of the bargain creates an express warranty that the whole of the goods shall conform to the sample or model.

(2) It is not necessary to the creation of an express warranty that the seller use formal words such as "warrant" or "guarantee" or that he have a specific intention to make a warranty, but an affirmation merely of the value of the goods or a statement purporting to be merely the seller's opinion or commendation of the goods does not create a warranty.

§2—314. Implied Warranty: Merchantability; Usage of Trade.

(1) Unless excluded or modified (Section 2—316), a warranty that the goods shall be merchantable is implied in a contract for their sale if the seller is a merchant with respect to goods of that kind. Under this section the serving for value of food or drink to be consumed either on the premises or elsewhere is a sale.

(2) Goods to be merchantable must be at least such as

(a) pass without objection in the trade under the contract description; and

(b) in the case of fungible goods, are of fair average quality within the description; and

(c) are fit for the ordinary purposes for which such goods are used; and

(d) run, within the variations permitted by the agreement, of even kind, quality and quantity within each unit and among all units involved; and

(e) are adequately contained, packaged, and labeled as the agreement may require; and

(f) conform to the promises or affirmations of fact made on the container or label if any.

(3) Unless excluded or modified (Section 2—316) other implied warranties may arise from course of dealing or usage of trade.

§2—315. Implied Warranty: Fitness for Particular Purpose.

Where the seller at the time of contracting has reason to know any particular purpose for which the goods are required and that the buyer is relying on the seller's skill or judgment to select or furnish suitable goods, there is unless excluded or modified under the next section an implied warranty that the goods shall be fit for such purpose.

§2—316. Exclusion or Modification of Warranties.

(1) Words or conduct relevant to the creation of an express warranty and words or conduct tending to negate or limit warranty shall be construed wherever reasonable as consistent with each other; but subject to the provisions of this Article on parol or extrinsic evidence (Section 2—202) negation or limitation is inoperative to the extent that such construction is unreasonable.

(2) Subject to subsection (3), to exclude or modify the implied warranty of merchantability or any part of it the language must mention merchantability and in case of a writing must be conspicuous, and to exclude or modify any implied warranty of fitness the exclusion must be by a writing and conspicuous. Language to exclude all implied warranties of fitness is sufficient if it states, for example, that "There are no warranties which extend beyond the description on the face hereof."

(3) Notwithstanding subsection (2)

(a) unless the circumstances indicate otherwise, all implied warranties are excluded by expressions like "as is", "with all faults" or other language which in common understanding calls the buyer's attention to the exclusion of warranties and makes plain that there is no implied warranty; and

(b) when the buyer before entering into the contract has examined the goods or the sample or model as fully as he desired or has refused to examine the goods there is no implied warranty with regard to defects which an examination ought in the circumstances to have revealed to him; and

(c) an implied warranty can also be excluded or modified by course of dealing or course of performance or usage of trade.

(4) Remedies for breach of warranty can be limited in accordance with the provisions of this Article on liquidation or limitation of damages and on contractual modification of remedy (Sections 2—718 and 2—719).

§2—317. Cumulation and Conflict of Warranties Express or Implied.

Warranties whether express or implied shall be construed as consistent with each other and as cumulative, but if such construction is unreasonable the intention of the parties shall determine which warranty is dominant. In ascertaining that intention the following rules apply:

(a) Exact or technical specifications displace an inconsistent sample or model or general language of description.

(b) A sample from an existing bulk displaces inconsistent general language of description.

(c) Express warranties displace inconsistent implied warranties other than an implied warranty of fitness for a particular purpose.

§2—318. Third Party Beneficiaries of Warranties Express or Implied.

Note: If this Act is introduced in the Congress of the United States this section should be omitted. (States to select one alternative.)

ALTERNATIVE A

A seller's warranty whether express or implied extends to any natural person who is in the family or household of his buyer or who is a guest in his home if it is reasonable to expect that such person may use, consume or be affected by the goods and who is injured in person by breach of the warranty. A seller may not exclude or limit the operation of this section.

ALTERNATIVE B

A seller's warranty whether express or implied extends to any natural person who may reasonably be expected to use, consume or be affected by the goods and who is injured in person by breach of the warranty. A seller may not exclude or limit the operation of this section.

ALTERNATIVE C

A seller's warranty whether express or implied extends to any person who may reasonably be expected to use, consume or be affected by the goods and who is injured by breach of the warranty. A seller may not exclude or limit the

operation of this section with respect to injury to the person of an individual to whom the warranty extends.
As amended 1966.

§2—319. F.O.B. and F.A.S. Terms.

(1) Unless otherwise agreed the term F.O.B. (which means "free on board") at a named place, even though used only in connection with the stated price, is a delivery term under which

(a) when the term is F.O.B. the place of shipment, the seller must at that place ship the goods in the manner provided in this Article (Section 2—504) and bear the expense and risk of putting them into the possession of the carrier; or

(b) when the term is F.O.B. the place of destination, the seller must at his own expense and risk transport the goods to that place and there tender delivery of them in the manner provided in this Article (Section 2—503);

(c) when under either (a) or (b) the term is also F.O.B. vessel, car or other vehicle, the seller must in addition at his own expense and risk load the goods on board. If the term is F.O.B. vessel the buyer must name the vessel and in an appropriate case the seller must comply with the provisions of this Article on the form of bill of lading (Section 2—323).

(2) Unless otherwise agreed the term F.A.S. vessel (which means "free alongside") at a named port, even though used only in connection with the stated price, is a delivery term under which the seller must

(a) at his own expense and risk deliver the goods alongside the vessel in the manner usual in that port or on a dock designated and provided by the buyer; and

(b) obtain and tender a receipt for the goods in exchange for which the carrier is under a duty to issue a bill of lading.

(3) Unless otherwise agreed in any case falling within subsection (1)(a) or (c) or subsection (2) the buyer must seasonably give any needed instructions for making delivery, including when the term is F.A.S. or F.O.B. the loading berth of the vessel and in an appropriate case its name and sailing date. The seller may treat the failure of needed instructions as a failure of cooperation under this Article (Section 2—311). He may also at his option move the goods in any reasonable manner preparatory to delivery or shipment.

(4) Under the term F.O.B. vessel or F.A.S. unless otherwise agreed the buyer must make payment against tender of the required documents and the seller may not tender nor the buyer demand delivery of the goods in substitution for the documents.

§2—320. C.I.F. and C. & F. Terms.

(1) The term C.I.F. means that the price includes in a lump sum the cost of the goods and the insurance and freight to the named destination. The term C. & F. or C.F. means that the price so includes cost and freight to the named destination.

(2) Unless otherwise agreed and even though used only in connection with the stated price and destination, the term C.I.F. destination or its equivalent requires the seller at his own expense and risk to

(a) put the goods into the possession of a carrier at the port for shipment and obtain a negotiable bill or bills of lading covering the entire transportation to the named destination; and

(b) load the goods and obtain a receipt from the carrier (which may be contained in the bill of lading) showing that the freight has been paid or provided for; and

(c) obtain a policy or certificate of insurance, including any war risk insurance, of a kind and on terms then current at the port of shipment in the usual amount, in the currency of the contract, shown to cover the same goods covered by the bill of lading and providing for payment of loss to the order of the buyer or for the account of whom it may concern; but the seller may add to the price the amount of the premium for any such war risk insurance; and

(d) prepare an invoice of the goods and procure any other documents required to effect shipment or to comply with the contract; and

(e) forward and tender with commercial promptness all the documents in due form and with any indorsement necessary to perfect the buyer's rights.

(3) Unless otherwise agreed the term C. & F. or its equivalent has the same effect and imposes upon the seller the same obligations and risks as a C.I.F. term except the obligation as to insurance.

(4) Under the term C.I.F. or C. & F. unless otherwise agreed the buyer must make payment against tender of the required documents and the seller may not tender nor the buyer demand delivery of the goods in substitution for the documents.

§2—321. C.I.F. or C. & F.: "Net Landed Weights"; "Payment on Arrival"; Warranty of Condition on Arrival. Under a contract containing a term C.I.F. or C. & F.

(1) Where the price is based on or is to be adjusted according to "net landed weights", "delivered weights", "out turn" quantity or quality or the like, unless otherwise agreed the seller must reasonably estimate the price. The payment due on tender of the documents called for by the contract is the amount so estimated, but after final adjustment of the price a settlement must be made with commercial promptness.

(2) An agreement described in subsection (1) or any warranty of quality or condition of the goods on arrival places upon the seller the risk of ordinary deterioration, shrinkage and the like in transportation but has no effect on the place or time of identification to the contract for sale or delivery or on the passing of the risk of loss.

(3) Unless otherwise agreed where the contract provides for payment on or after arrival of the goods the seller must

before payment allow such preliminary inspection as is feasible; but if the goods are lost delivery of the documents and payment are due when the goods should have arrived.

§2—322. Delivery "Ex-Ship".

(1) Unless otherwise agreed a term for delivery of goods "ex-ship" (which means from the carrying vessel) or in equivalent language is not restricted to a particular ship and requires delivery from a ship which has reached a place at the named port of destination where goods of the kind are usually discharged.

(2) Under such a term unless otherwise agreed

    (a) the seller must discharge all liens arising out of the carriage and furnish the buyer with a direction which puts the carrier under a duty to deliver the goods; and

    (b) the risk of loss does not pass to the buyer until the goods leave the ship's tackle or are otherwise properly unloaded.

§2—323. Form of Bill of Lading Required in Overseas Shipment; "Overseas".

(1) Where the contract contemplates overseas shipment and contains a term C.I.F. or C. & F. or F.O.B. vessel, the seller unless otherwise agreed must obtain a negotiable bill of lading stating that the goods have been loaded on board or, in the case of a term C.I.F. or C. & F., received for shipment.

(2) Where in a case within subsection (1) a bill of lading has been issued in a set of parts, unless otherwise agreed if the documents are not to be sent from abroad the buyer may demand tender of the full set; otherwise only one part of the bill of lading need be tendered. Even if the agreement expressly requires a full set

    (a) due tender of a single part is acceptable within the provisions of this Article on cure of improper delivery (subsection (1) of Section 2—508); and

    (b) even though the full set is demanded, if the documents are sent from abroad the person tendering an incomplete set may nevertheless require payment upon furnishing an indemnity which the buyer in good faith deems adequate.

(3) A shipment by water or by air or a contract contemplating such shipment is "overseas" insofar as by usage of trade or agreement it is subject to the commercial, financing or shipping practices characteristic of international deep water commerce.

§2—324. "No Arrival, No Sale" Term.

Under a term "no arrival, no sale" or terms of like meaning, unless otherwise agreed,

    (a) the seller must properly ship conforming goods and if they arrive by any means he must tender them on arrival but he assumes no obligation that the goods will arrive unless he has caused the non-arrival; and

    (b) where without fault of the seller the goods are in part lost or have so deteriorated as no longer to conform to the contract or arrive after the contract time, the buyer may proceed as if there had been casualty to identified goods (Section 2—613).

§2—325. "Letter of Credit" Term; "Confirmed Credit".

(1) Failure of the buyer seasonably to furnish an agreed letter of credit is a breach of the contract for sale.

(2) The delivery to seller of a proper letter of credit suspends the buyer's obligation to pay. If the letter of credit is dishonored, the seller may on seasonable notification to the buyer require payment directly from him.

(3) Unless otherwise agreed the term "letter of credit" or "banker's credit" in a contract for sale means an irrevocable credit issued by a financing agency of good repute and, where the shipment is overseas, of good international repute. The term "confirmed credit" means that the credit must also carry the direct obligation of such an agency which does business in the seller's financial market.

§2—326. Sale on Approval and Sale or Return; Rights of Creditors.

(1) Unless otherwise agreed, if delivered goods may be returned by the buyer even though they conform to the contract, the transaction is

    (a) a "sale on approval" if the goods are delivered primarily for use, and

    (b) a "sale or return" if the goods are delivered primarily for resale.

(2) Goods held on approval are not subject to the claims of the buyer's creditors until acceptance; goods held on sale or return are subject to such claims while in the buyer's possession.

(3) Any "or return" term of a contract for sale is to be treated as a separate contract for sale within the statute of frauds section of this Article (Section 2—201) and as contradicting the sale aspect of the contract within the provisions of this Article or on parol or extrinsic evidence (Section 2—202).

As amended in 1999.

§2—327. Special Incidents of Sale on Approval and Sale or Return.

(1) Under a sale on approval unless otherwise agreed

    (a) although the goods are identified to the contract the risk of loss and the title do not pass to the buyer until acceptance; and

    (b) use of the goods consistent with the purpose of trial is not acceptance but failure seasonably to notify the seller of election to return the goods is acceptance, and if the goods conform to the contract acceptance of any part is acceptance of the whole; and

(c) after due notification of election to return, the return is at the seller's risk and expense but a merchant buyer must follow any reasonable instructions.

(2) Under a sale or return unless otherwise agreed

(a) the option to return extends to the whole or any commercial unit of the goods while in substantially their original condition, but must be exercised seasonably; and

(b) the return is at the buyer's risk and expense.

§2—328. Sale by Auction.

(1) In a sale by auction if goods are put up in lots each lot is the subject of a separate sale.

(2) A sale by auction is complete when the auctioneer so announces by the fall of the hammer or in other customary manner. Where a bid is made while the hammer is falling in acceptance of a prior bid the auctioneer may in his discretion reopen the bidding or declare the goods sold under the bid on which the hammer was falling.

(3) Such a sale is with reserve unless the goods are in explicit terms put up without reserve. In an auction with reserve the auctioneer may withdraw the goods at any time until he announces completion of the sale. In an auction without reserve, after the auctioneer calls for bids on an article or lot, that article or lot cannot be withdrawn unless no bid is made within a reasonable time. In either case a bidder may retract his bid until the auctioneer's announcement of completion of the sale, but a bidder's retraction does not revive any previous bid.

(4) If the auctioneer knowingly receives a bid on the seller's behalf or the seller makes or procures such as bid, and notice has not been given that liberty for such bidding is reserved, the buyer may at his option avoid the sale or take the goods at the price of the last good faith bid prior to the completion of the sale. This subsection shall not apply to any bid at a forced sale.

PART 4 TITLE, CREDITORS AND GOOD FAITH PURCHASERS

§2—401. Passing of Title; Reservation for Security; Limited Application of This Section.

Each provision of this Article with regard to the rights, obligations and remedies of the seller, the buyer, purchasers or other third parties applies irrespective of title to the goods except where the provision refers to such title. Insofar as situations are not covered by the other provisions of this Article and matters concerning title became material the following rules apply:

(1) Title to goods cannot pass under a contract for sale prior to their identification to the contract (Section 2—501), and unless otherwise explicitly agreed the buyer acquires by their identification a special property as limited by this Act. Any retention or reservation by the seller of the title (property) in goods shipped or delivered to the buyer is limited in effect to a reservation of a security interest. Subject to these provisions and to the provisions of the Article on Secured Transactions (Article 9), title to goods passes from the seller to the buyer in any manner and on any conditions explicitly agreed on by the parties.

(2) Unless otherwise explicitly agreed title passes to the buyer at the time and place at which the seller completes his performance with reference to the physical delivery of the goods, despite any reservation of a security interest and even though a document of title is to be delivered at a different time or place; and in particular and despite any reservation of a security interest by the bill of lading

(a) if the contract requires or authorizes the seller to send the goods to the buyer but does not require him to deliver them at destination, title passes to the buyer at the time and place of shipment; but

(b) if the contract requires delivery at destination, title passes on tender there.

(3) Unless otherwise explicitly agreed where delivery is to be made without moving the goods,

(a) if the seller is to deliver a document of title, title passes at the time when and the place where he delivers such documents; or

(b) if the goods are at the time of contracting already identified and no documents are to be delivered, title passes at the time and place of contracting.

(4) A rejection or other refusal by the buyer to receive or retain the goods, whether or not justified, or a justified revocation of acceptance revests title to the goods in the seller. Such revesting occurs by operation of law and is not a "sale".

§2—402. Rights of Seller's Creditors Against Sold Goods.

(1) Except as provided in subsections (2) and (3), rights of unsecured creditors of the seller with respect to goods which have been identified to a contract for sale are subject to the buyer's rights to recover the goods under this Article (Sections 2—502 and 2—716).

(2) A creditor of the seller may treat a sale or an identification of goods to a contract for sale as void if as against him a retention of possession by the seller is fraudulent under any rule of law of the state where the goods are situated, except that retention of possession in good faith and current course of trade by a merchant-seller for a commercially reasonable time after a sale or identification is not fraudulent.

(3) Nothing in this Article shall be deemed to impair the rights of creditors of the seller

(a) under the provisions of the Article on Secured Transactions (Article 9); or

(b) where identification to the contract or delivery is made not in current course of trade but in satisfaction of or as security for a pre-existing claim for money, security or the like and is made under circumstances which under any rule of law of the state where the goods are situated would apart from this Article constitute the transaction a fraudulent transfer or voidable preference.

§2—403. Power to Transfer; Good Faith Purchase of Goods; "Entrusting".

(1) A purchaser of goods acquires all title which his transferor had or had power to transfer except that a purchaser of a limited interest acquires rights only to the extent of the interest purchased. A person with voidable title has power to transfer a good title to a good faith purchaser for value. When goods have been delivered under a transaction of purchase the purchaser has such power even though

   (a) the transferor was deceived as to the identity of the purchaser, or

   (b) the delivery was in exchange for a check which is later dishonored, or

   (c) it was agreed that the transaction was to be a "cash sale", or

   (d) the delivery was procured through fraud punishable as larcenous under the criminal law.

(2) Any entrusting of possession of goods to a merchant who deals in goods of that kind gives him power to transfer all rights of the entruster to a buyer in ordinary course of business.

(3) "Entrusting" includes any delivery and any acquiescence in retention of possession regardless of any condition expressed between the parties to the delivery or acquiescence and regardless of whether the procurement of the entrusting or the possessor's disposition of the goods have been such as to be larcenous under the criminal law.

(4) The rights of other purchasers of goods and of lien creditors are governed by the Articles on Secured Transactions (Article 9), Bulk Transfers (Article 6) and Documents of Title (Article 7).

As amended in 1988.

PART 5 PERFORMANCE

§2—501. Insurable Interest in Goods; Manner of Identification of Goods.

(1) The buyer obtains a special property and an insurable interest in goods by identification of existing goods as goods to which the contract refers even though the goods so identified are non-conforming and he has an option to return or reject them. Such identification can be made at any time and in any manner explicitly agreed to by the parties. In the absence of explicit agreement identification occurs

   (a) when the contract is made if it is for the sale of goods already existing and identified;

   (b) if the contract is for the sale of future goods other than those described in paragraph (c), when goods are

shipped, marked or otherwise designated by the seller as goods to which the contract refers;

   (c) when the crops are planted or otherwise become growing crops or the young are conceived if the contract is for the sale of unborn young to be born within twelve months after contracting or for the sale of crops to be harvested within twelve months or the next normal harvest season after contracting whichever is longer.

(2) The seller retains an insurable interest in goods so long as title to or any security interest in the goods remains in him and where the identification is by the seller alone he may until default or insolvency or notification to the buyer that the identification is final substitute other goods for those identified.

(3) Nothing in this section impairs any insurable interest recognized under any other statute or rule of law.

§2—502. Buyer's Right to Goods on Seller's Insolvency.

(1) Subject to subsections (2) and (3) and even though the goods have not been shipped a buyer who has paid a part or all of the price of goods in which he has a special property under the provisions of the immediately preceding section may on making and keeping good a tender of any unpaid portion of their price recover them from the seller if:

   (a) in the case of goods bought for personal, family, or household purposes, the seller repudiates or fails to deliver as required by the contract; or

   (b) in all cases, the seller becomes insolvent within ten days after receipt of the first installment on their price.

(2) The buyer's right to recover the goods under subsection (1)(a) vests upon acquisition of a special property, even if the seller had not then repudiated or failed to deliver.

(3) If the identification creating his special property has been made by the buyer he acquires the right to recover the goods only if they conform to the contract for sale.

As amended in 1999.

§2—503. Manner of Seller's Tender of Delivery.

(1) Tender of delivery requires that the seller put and hold conforming goods at the buyer's disposition and give the buyer any notification reasonably necessary to enable him to take delivery. The manner, time and place for tender are determined by the agreement and this Article, and in particular

   (a) tender must be at a reasonable hour, and if it is of goods they must be kept available for the period reasonably necessary to enable the buyer to take possession; but

   (b) unless otherwise agreed the buyer must furnish facilities reasonably suited to the receipt of the goods.

(2) Where the case is within the next section respecting shipment tender requires that the seller comply with its provisions.

(3) Where the seller is required to deliver at a particular destination tender requires that he comply with subsection (1) and also in any appropriate case tender documents as described in subsections (4) and (5) of this section.

(4) Where goods are in the possession of a bailee and are to be delivered without being moved

(a) tender requires that the seller either tender a negotiable document of title covering such goods or procure acknowledgment by the bailee of the buyer's right to possession of the goods; but

(b) tender to the buyer of a non-negotiable document of title or of a written direction to the bailee to deliver is sufficient tender unless the buyer seasonably objects, and receipt by the bailee of notification of the buyer's rights fixes those rights as against the bailee and all third persons; but risk of loss of the goods and of any failure by the bailee to honor the non-negotiable document of title or to obey the direction remains on the seller until the buyer has had a reasonable time to present the document or direction, and a refusal by the bailee to honor the document or to obey the direction defeats the tender.

(5) Where the contract requires the seller to deliver documents

(a) he must tender all such documents in correct form, except as provided in this Article with respect to bills of lading in a set (subsection (2) of Section 2—323); and

(b) tender through customary banking channels is sufficient and dishonor of a draft accompanying the documents constitutes non-acceptance or rejection.

§2—504. *Shipment by Seller.*

Where the seller is required or authorized to send the goods to the buyer and the contract does not require him to deliver them at a particular destination, then unless otherwise agreed he must

(a) put the goods in the possession of such a carrier and make such a contract for their transportation as may be reasonable having regard to the nature of the goods and other circumstances of the case; and

(b) obtain and promptly deliver or tender in due form any document necessary to enable the buyer to obtain possession of the goods or otherwise required by the agreement or by usage of trade; and

(c) promptly notify the buyer of the shipment.

Failure to notify the buyer under paragraph (c) or to make a proper contract under paragraph (a) is a ground for rejection only if material delay or loss ensues.

§2—505. *Seller's Shipment under Reservation.*

(1) Where the seller has identified goods to the contract by or before shipment:

(a) his procurement of a negotiable bill of lading to his own order or otherwise reserves in him a security interest in the goods. His procurement of the bill to the order of a financing agency or of the buyer indicates in addition only the seller's expectation of transferring that interest to the person named.

(b) a non-negotiable bill of lading to himself or his nominee reserves possession of the goods as security but except in a case of conditional delivery (subsection (2) of Section 2—507) a non-negotiable bill of lading naming the buyer as consignee reserves no security interest even though the seller retains possession of the bill of lading.

(2) When shipment by the seller with reservation of a security interest is in violation of the contract for sale it constitutes an improper contract for transportation within the preceding section but impairs neither the rights given to the buyer by shipment and identification of the goods to the contract nor the seller's powers as a holder of a negotiable document.

§2—506. *Rights of Financing Agency.*

(1) A financing agency by paying or purchasing for value a draft which relates to a shipment of goods acquires to the extent of the payment or purchase and in addition to its own rights under the draft and any document of title securing it any rights of the shipper in the goods including the right to stop delivery and the shipper's right to have the draft honored by the buyer.

(2) The right to reimbursement of a financing agency which has in good faith honored or purchased the draft under commitment to or authority from the buyer is not impaired by subsequent discovery of defects with reference to any relevant document which was apparently regular on its face.

§2—507. *Effect of Seller's Tender; Delivery on Condition.*

(1) Tender of delivery is a condition to the buyer's duty to accept the goods and, unless otherwise agreed, to his duty to pay for them. Tender entitles the seller to acceptance of the goods and to payment according to the contract.

(2) Where payment is due and demanded on the delivery to the buyer of goods or documents of title, his right as against the seller to retain or dispose of them is conditional upon his making the payment due.

§2—508. *Cure by Seller of Improper Tender or Delivery; Replacement.*

(1) Where any tender or delivery by the seller is rejected because non-conforming and the time for performance has not yet expired, the seller may seasonably notify the buyer of his intention to cure and may then within the contract time make a conforming delivery.

(2) Where the buyer rejects a non-conforming tender which the seller had reasonable grounds to believe would be acceptable with or without money allowance the seller may if he seasonably notifies the buyer have a further reasonable time to substitute a conforming tender.

§2—509. Risk of Loss in the Absence of Breach.

(1) Where the contract requires or authorizes the seller to ship the goods by carrier

(a) if it does not require him to deliver them at a particular destination, the risk of loss passes to the buyer when the goods are duly delivered to the carrier even though the shipment is under reservation (Section 2—505); but

(b) if it does require him to deliver them at a particular destination and the goods are there duly tendered while in the possession of the carrier, the risk of loss passes to the buyer when the goods are there duly so tendered as to enable the buyer to take delivery.

(2) Where the goods are held by a bailee to be delivered without being moved, the risk of loss passes to the buyer

(a) on his receipt of a negotiable document of title covering the goods; or

(b) on acknowledgment by the bailee of the buyer's right to possession of the goods; or

(c) after his receipt of a non-negotiable document of title or other written direction to deliver, as provided in subsection (4)(b) of Section 2—503.

(3) In any case not within subsection (1) or (2), the risk of loss passes to the buyer on his receipt of the goods if the seller is a merchant; otherwise the risk passes to the buyer on tender of delivery.

(4) The provisions of this section are subject to contrary agreement of the parties and to the provisions of this Article on sale on approval (Section 2—327) and on effect of breach on risk of loss (Section 2—510).

§2—510. Effect of Breach on Risk of Loss.

(1) Where a tender or delivery of goods so fails to conform to the contract as to give a right of rejection the risk of their loss remains on the seller until cure or acceptance.

(2) Where the buyer rightfully revokes acceptance he may to the extent of any deficiency in his effective insurance coverage treat the risk of loss as having rested on the seller from the beginning.

(3) Where the buyer as to conforming goods already identified to the contract for sale repudiates or is otherwise in breach before risk of their loss has passed to him, the seller may to the extent of any deficiency in his effective insurance coverage treat the risk of loss as resting on the buyer for a commercially reasonable time.

§2—511. Tender of Payment by Buyer; Payment by Check.

(1) Unless otherwise agreed tender of payment is a condition to the seller's duty to tender and complete any delivery.

(2) Tender of payment is sufficient when made by any means or in any manner current in the ordinary course of business unless the seller demands payment in legal tender and gives any extension of time reasonably necessary to procure it.

(3) Subject to the provisions of this Act on the effect of an instrument on an obligation (Section 3—310), payment by check is conditional and is defeated as between the parties by dishonor of the check on due presentment.

As amended in 1994.

§2—512. Payment by Buyer Before Inspection.

(1) Where the contract requires payment before inspection non-conformity of the goods does not excuse the buyer from so making payment unless

(a) the non-conformity appears without inspection; or

(b) despite tender of the required documents the circumstances would justify injunction against honor under this Act (Section 5—109(b)).

(2) Payment pursuant to subsection (1) does not constitute an acceptance of goods or impair the buyer's right to inspect or any of his remedies.

As amended in 1995.

§2—513. Buyer's Right to Inspection of Goods.

(1) Unless otherwise agreed and subject to subsection (3), where goods are tendered or delivered or identified to the contract for sale, the buyer has a right before payment or acceptance to inspect them at any reasonable place and time and in any reasonable manner. When the seller is required or authorized to send the goods to the buyer, the inspection may be after their arrival.

(2) Expenses of inspection must be borne by the buyer but may be recovered from the seller if the goods do not conform and are rejected.

(3) Unless otherwise agreed and subject to the provisions of this Article on C.I.F. contracts (subsection (3) of Section 2—321), the buyer is not entitled to inspect the goods before payment of the price when the contract provides

(a) for delivery "C.O.D." or on other like terms; or

(b) for payment against documents of title, except where such payment is due only after the goods are to become available for inspection.

(4) A place or method of inspection fixed by the parties is presumed to be exclusive but unless otherwise expressly agreed it does not postpone identification or shift the place for delivery or for passing the risk of loss. If compliance becomes impossible, inspection shall be as provided in this section unless the place or method fixed was clearly intended as an indispensable condition failure of which avoids the contract.

§2—514. When Documents Deliverable on Acceptance; When on Payment.
Unless otherwise agreed documents against which a draft is drawn are to be delivered to the

drawee on acceptance of the draft if it is payable more than three days after presentment; otherwise, only on payment.

§2—515. *Preserving Evidence of Goods in Dispute.* In furtherance of the adjustment of any claim or dispute

(a) either party on reasonable notification to the other and for the purpose of ascertaining the facts and preserving evidence has the right to inspect, test and sample the goods including such of them as may be in the possession or control of the other; and

(b) the parties may agree to a third party inspection or survey to determine the conformity or condition of the goods and may agree that the findings shall be binding upon them in any subsequent litigation or adjustment.

PART 6 BREACH, REPUDIATION AND EXCUSE

§2—601. *Buyer's Rights on Improper Delivery.* Subject to the provisions of this Article on breach in installment contracts (Section 2—612) and unless otherwise agreed under the sections on contractual limitations of remedy (Sections 2—718 and 2—719), if the goods or the tender of delivery fail in any respect to conform to the contract, the buyer may

(a) reject the whole; or

(b) accept the whole; or

(c) accept any commercial unit or units and reject the rest.

§2—602. *Manner and Effect of Rightful Rejection.*

(1) Rejection of goods must be within a reasonable time after their delivery or tender. It is ineffective unless the buyer seasonably notifies the seller.

(2) Subject to the provisions of the two following sections on rejected goods (Sections 2—603 and 2—604),

(a) after rejection any exercise of ownership by the buyer with respect to any commercial unit is wrongful as against the seller; and

(b) if the buyer has before rejection taken physical possession of goods in which he does not have a security interest under the provisions of this Article (subsection (3) of Section 2—711), he is under a duty after rejection to hold them with reasonable care at the seller's disposition for a time sufficient to permit the seller to remove them; but

(c) the buyer has no further obligations with regard to goods rightfully rejected.

(3) The seller's rights with respect to goods wrongfully rejected are governed by the provisions of this Article on Seller's remedies in general (Section 2—703).

§2—603. *Merchant Buyer's Duties as to Rightfully Rejected Goods.*

(1) Subject to any security interest in the buyer (subsection (3) of Section 2—711), when the seller has no agent or place of business at the market of rejection a merchant buyer is under a duty after rejection of goods in his possession or control to follow any reasonable instructions received from the seller with respect to the goods and in the absence of such instructions to make reasonable efforts to sell them for the seller's account if they are perishable or threaten to decline in value speedily. Instructions are not reasonable if on demand indemnity for expenses is not forthcoming.

(2) When the buyer sells goods under subsection (1), he is entitled to reimbursement from the seller or out of the proceeds for reasonable expenses of caring for and selling them, and if the expenses include no selling commission then to such commission as is usual in the trade or if there is none to a reasonable sum not exceeding ten per cent on the gross proceeds.

(3) In complying with this section the buyer is held only to good faith and good faith conduct hereunder is neither acceptance nor conversion nor the basis of an action for damages.

§2—604. *Buyer's Options as to Salvage of Rightfully Rejected Goods.* Subject to the provisions of the immediately preceding section on perishables if the seller gives no instructions within a reasonable time after notification of rejection the buyer may store the rejected goods for the seller's account or reship them to him or resell them for the seller's account with reimbursement as provided in the preceding section. Such action is not acceptance or conversion.

§2—605. *Waiver of Buyer's Objections by Failure to Particularize.*

(1) The buyer's failure to state in connection with rejection a particular defect which is ascertainable by reasonable inspection precludes him from relying on the unstated defect to justify rejection or to establish breach

(a) where the seller could have cured it if stated seasonably; or

(b) between merchants when the seller has after rejection made a request in writing for a full and final written statement of all defects on which the buyer proposes to rely.

(2) Payment against documents made without reservation of rights precludes recovery of the payment for defects apparent on the face of the documents.

§2—606. *What Constitutes Acceptance of Goods.*

(1) Acceptance of goods occurs when the buyer

(a) after a reasonable opportunity to inspect the goods signifies to the seller that the goods are conforming or that he will take or retain them in spite of their nonconformity; or

(b) fails to make an effective rejection (subsection (1) of Section 2—602), but such acceptance does not occur until the buyer has had a reasonable opportunity to inspect them; or

(c) does any act inconsistent with the seller's ownership; but if such act is wrongful as against the seller it is an acceptance only if ratified by him.

(2) Acceptance of a part of any commercial unit is acceptance of that entire unit.

§2−607. Effect of Acceptance; Notice of Breach; Burden of Establishing Breach After Acceptance; Notice of Claim or Litigation to Person Answerable Over.

(1) The buyer must pay at the contract rate for any goods accepted.

(2) Acceptance of goods by the buyer precludes rejection of the goods accepted and if made with knowledge of a non-conformity cannot be revoked because of it unless the acceptance was on the reasonable assumption that the non-conformity would be seasonably cured but acceptance does not of itself impair any other remedy provided by this Article for non-conformity.

(3) Where a tender has been accepted

(a) the buyer must within a reasonable time after he discovers or should have discovered any breach notify the seller of breach or be barred from any remedy; and

(b) if the claim is one for infringement or the like (subsection (3) of Section 2—312) and the buyer is sued as a result of such a breach he must so notify the seller within a reasonable time after he receives notice of the litigation or be barred from any remedy over for liability established by the litigation.

(4) The burden is on the buyer to establish any breach with respect to the goods accepted.

(5) Where the buyer is sued for breach of a warranty or other obligation for which his seller is answerable over

(a) he may give his seller written notice of the litigation. If the notice states that the seller may come in and defend and that if the seller does not do so he will be bound in any action against him by his buyer by any determination of fact common to the two litigations, then unless the seller after seasonable receipt of the notice does come in and defend he is so bound.

(b) if the claim is one for infringement or the like (subsection (3) of Section 2—312) the original seller may demand in writing that his buyer turn over to him control of the litigation including settlement or else be barred from any remedy over and if he also agrees to bear all expense and to satisfy any adverse judgment, then unless the buyer after seasonable receipt of the demand does turn over control the buyer is so barred.

(6) The provisions of subsections (3), (4) and (5) apply to any obligation of a buyer to hold the seller harmless against infringement or the like (subsection (3) of Section 2—312).

§2−608. Revocation of Acceptance in Whole or in Part.

(1) The buyer may revoke his acceptance of a lot or commercial unit whose non-conformity substantially impairs its value to him if he has accepted it

(a) on the reasonable assumption that its nonconformity would be cured and it has not been seasonably cured; or

(b) without discovery of such non-conformity if his acceptance was reasonably induced either by the difficulty of discovery before acceptance or by the seller's assurances.

(2) Revocation of acceptance must occur within a reasonable time after the buyer discovers or should have discovered the ground for it and before any substantial change in condition of the goods which is not caused by their own defects. It is not effective until the buyer notifies the seller of it.

(3) A buyer who so revokes has the same rights and duties with regard to the goods involved as if he had rejected them.

§2−609. Right to Adequate Assurance of Performance.

(1) A contract for sale imposes an obligation on each party that the other's expectation of receiving due performance will not be impaired. When reasonable grounds for insecurity arise with respect to the performance of either party the other may in writing demand adequate assurance of due performance and until he receives such assurance may if commercially reasonable suspend any performance for which he has not already received the agreed return.

(2) Between merchants the reasonableness of grounds for insecurity and the adequacy of any assurance offered shall be determined according to commercial standards.

(3) Acceptance of any improper delivery or payment does not prejudice the party's right to demand adequate assurance of future performance.

(4) After receipt of a justified demand failure to provide within a reasonable time not exceeding thirty days such assurance of due performance as is adequate under the circumstances of the particular case is a repudiation of the contract.

§2−610. Anticipatory Repudiation. When either party repudiates the contract with respect to a performance not yet due the loss of which will substantially impair the value of the contract to the other, the aggrieved party may

(a) for a commercially reasonable time await performance by the repudiating party; or

(b) resort to any remedy for breach (Section 2—703 or Section 2—711), even though he has notified the repudiating party that he would await the latter's performance and has urged retraction; and

(c) in either case suspend his own performance or proceed in accordance with the provisions of this Article on the seller's right to identify goods to the contract notwithstanding breach or to salvage unfinished goods (Section 2—704).

§2—611. Retraction of Anticipatory Repudiation.

(1) Until the repudiating party's next performance is due he can retract his repudiation unless the aggrieved party has since the repudiation cancelled or materially changed his position or otherwise indicated that he considers the repudiation final.

(2) Retraction may be by any method which clearly indicates to the aggrieved party that the repudiating party intends to perform, but must include any assurance justifiably demanded under the provisions of this Article (Section 2—609).

(3) Retraction reinstates the repudiating party's rights under the contract with due excuse and allowance to the aggrieved party for any delay occasioned by the repudiation.

§2—612. "Installment Contract"; Breach.

(1) An "installment contract" is one which requires or authorizes the delivery of goods in separate lots to be separately accepted, even though the contract contains a clause "each delivery is a separate contract" or its equivalent.

(2) The buyer may reject any installment which is nonconforming if the non-conformity substantially impairs the value of that installment and cannot be cured or if the non-conformity is a defect in the required documents; but if the non-conformity does not fall within subsection (3) and the seller gives adequate assurance of its cure the buyer must accept that installment.

(3) Whenever non-conformity or default with respect to one or more installments substantially impairs the value of the whole contract there is a breach of the whole. But the aggrieved party reinstates the contract if he accepts a non-conforming installment without seasonably notifying of cancellation or if he brings an action with respect only to past installments or demands performance as to future installments.

§2—613. Casualty to Identified Goods.

Where the contract requires for its performance goods identified when the contract is made, and the goods suffer casualty without fault of either party before the risk of loss passes to the buyer, or in a proper case under a "no arrival, no sale" term (Section 2—324) then

(a) if the loss is total the contract is avoided; and

(b) if the loss is partial or the goods have so deteriorated as no longer to conform to the contract the buyer may nevertheless demand inspection and at his option either treat the contract as voided or accept the goods with due allowance from the contract price for the deterioration or the deficiency in quantity but without further right against the seller.

§2—614. Substituted Performance.

(1) Where without fault of either party the agreed berthing, loading, or unloading facilities fail or an agreed type of carrier becomes unavailable or the agreed manner of delivery otherwise becomes commercially impracticable but a commercially reasonable substitute is available, such substitute performance must be tendered and accepted.

(2) If the agreed means or manner of payment fails because of domestic or foreign governmental regulation, the seller may withhold or stop delivery unless the buyer provides a means or manner of payment which is commercially a substantial equivalent. If delivery has already been taken, payment by the means or in the manner provided by the regulation discharges the buyer's obligation unless the regulation is discriminatory, oppressive or predatory.

§2—615. Excuse by Failure of Presupposed Conditions.

Except so far as a seller may have assumed a greater obligation and subject to the preceding section on substituted performance:

(a) Delay in delivery or non-delivery in whole or in part by a seller who complies with paragraphs (b) and (c) is not a breach of his duty under a contract for sale if performance as agreed has been made impracticable by the occurrence of a contingency the nonoccurrence of which was a basic assumption on which the contract was made or by compliance in good faith with any applicable foreign or domestic governmental regulation or order whether or not it later proves to be invalid.

(b) Where the causes mentioned in paragraph (a) affect only a part of the seller's capacity to perform, he must allocate production and deliveries among his customers but may at his option include regular customers not then under contract as well as his own requirements for further manufacture. He may so allocate in any manner which is fair and reasonable.

(c) The seller must notify the buyer seasonably that there will be delay or non-delivery and, when allocation is required under paragraph (b), of the estimated quota thus made available for the buyer.

§2—616. Procedure on Notice Claiming Excuse.

(1) Where the buyer receives notification of a material or indefinite delay or an allocation justified under the preceding section he may by written notification to the seller as to any delivery concerned, and where the prospective deficiency substantially impairs the value of the whole contract under the provisions of this Article relating to breach of installment contracts (Section 2—612), then also as to the whole,

(a) terminate and thereby discharge any unexecuted portion of the contract; or

(b) modify the contract by agreeing to take his available quota in substitution.

(2) If after receipt of such notification from the seller the buyer fails so to modify the contract within a reasonable time not exceeding thirty days the contract lapses with respect to any deliveries affected.

(3) The provisions of this section may not be negated by agreement except in so far as the seller has assumed a greater obligation under the preceding section.

PART 7 REMEDIES

§2—701. Remedies for Breach of Collateral Contracts Not Impaired.
Remedies for breach of any obligation or promise collateral or ancillary to a contract for sale are not impaired by the provisions of this Article.

§2—702. Seller's Remedies on Discovery of Buyer's Insolvency.

(1) Where the seller discovers the buyer to be insolvent he may refuse delivery except for cash including payment for all goods theretofore delivered under the contract, and stop delivery under this Article (Section 2—705).

(2) Where the seller discovers that the buyer has received goods on credit while insolvent he may reclaim the goods upon demand made within ten days after the receipt, but if misrepresentation of solvency has been made to the particular seller in writing within three months before delivery the ten day limitation does not apply. Except as provided in this subsection the seller may not base a right to reclaim goods on the buyer's fraudulent or innocent misrepresentation of solvency or of intent to pay.

(3) The seller's right to reclaim under subsection (2) is subject to the rights of a buyer in ordinary course or other good faith purchaser under this Article (Section 2—403). Successful reclamation of goods excludes all other remedies with respect to them.

§2—703. Seller's Remedies in General.
Where the buyer wrongfully rejects or revokes acceptance of goods or fails to make a payment due on or before delivery or repudiates with respect to a part or the whole, then with respect to any goods directly affected and, if the breach is of the whole contract (Section 2—612), then also with respect to the whole undelivered balance, the aggrieved seller may

    (a) withhold delivery of such goods;

    (b) stop delivery by any bailee as hereafter provided (Section 2—705);

    (c) proceed under the next section respecting goods still unidentified to the contract;

    (d) resell and recover damages as hereafter provided (Section 2—706);

    (e) recover damages for non-acceptance (Section 2—708) or in a proper case the price (Section 2—709);

    (f) cancel.

§2—704. Seller's Right to Identify Goods to the Contract Notwithstanding Breach or to Salvage Unfinished Goods.

(1) An aggrieved seller under the preceding section may

    (a) identify to the contract conforming goods not already identified if at the time he learned of the breach they are in his possession or control;

    (b) treat as the subject of resale goods which have demonstrably been intended for the particular contract even though those goods are unfinished.

(2) Where the goods are unfinished an aggrieved seller may in the exercise of reasonable commercial judgment for the purposes of avoiding loss and of effective realization either complete the manufacture and wholly identify the goods to the contract or cease manufacture and resell for scrap or salvage value or proceed in any other reasonable manner.

§2—705. Seller's Stoppage of Delivery in Transit or Otherwise.

(1) The seller may stop delivery of goods in the possession of a carrier or other bailee when he discovers the buyer to be insolvent (Section 2—702) and may stop delivery of carload, truckload, planeload or larger shipments of express or freight when the buyer repudiates or fails to make a payment due before delivery or if for any other reason the seller has a right to withhold or reclaim the goods.

(2) As against such buyer the seller may stop delivery until

    (a) receipt of the goods by the buyer; or

    (b) acknowledgment to the buyer by any bailee of the goods except a carrier that the bailee holds the goods for the buyer; or

    (c) such acknowledgment to the buyer by a carrier by reshipment or as warehouseman; or

    (d) negotiation to the buyer of any negotiable document of title covering the goods.

(3) (a) To stop delivery the seller must so notify as to enable the bailee by reasonable diligence to prevent delivery of the goods.

    (b) After such notification the bailee must hold and deliver the goods according to the directions of the seller but the seller is liable to the bailee for any ensuing charges or damages.

    (c) If a negotiable document of title has been issued for goods the bailee is not obliged to obey a notification to stop until surrender of the document.

    (d) A carrier who has issued a non-negotiable bill of lading is not obliged to obey a notification to stop received from a person other than the consignor.

§2—706. Seller's Resale Including Contract for Resale.

(1) Under the conditions stated in Section 2—703 on seller's remedies, the seller may resell the goods concerned or the undelivered balance thereof. Where the resale is made

in good faith and in a commercially reasonable manner the seller may recover the difference between the resale price and the contract price together with any incidental damages allowed under the provisions of this Article (Section 2—710), but less expenses saved in consequence of the buyer's breach.

(2) Except as otherwise provided in subsection (3) or unless otherwise agreed resale may be at public or private sale including sale by way of one or more contracts to sell or of identification to an existing contract of the seller. Sale may be as a unit or in parcels and at any time and place and on any terms but every aspect of the sale including the method, manner, time, place and terms must be commercially reasonable. The resale must be reasonably identified as referring to the broken contract, but it is not necessary that the goods be in existence or that any or all of them have been identified to the contract before the breach.

(3) Where the resale is at private sale the seller must give the buyer reasonable notification of his intention to resell.

(4) Where the resale is at public sale

(a) only identified goods can be sold except where there is a recognized market for a public sale of futures in goods of the kind; and

(b) it must be made at a usual place or market for public sale if one is reasonably available and except in the case of goods which are perishable or threaten to decline in value speedily the seller must give the buyer reasonable notice of the time and place of the resale; and

(c) if the goods are not to be within the view of those attending the sale the notification of sale must state the place where the goods are located and provide for their reasonable inspection by prospective bidders; and

(d) the seller may buy.

(5) A purchaser who buys in good faith at a resale takes the goods free of any rights of the original buyer even though the seller fails to comply with one or more of the requirements of this section.

(6) The seller is not accountable to the buyer for any profit made on any resale. A person in the position of a seller (Section 2—707) or a buyer who has rightfully rejected or justifiably revoked acceptance must account for any excess over the amount of his security interest, as hereinafter defined (subsection (3) of Section 2—711).

§2—707. "Person in the Position of a Seller".

(1) A "person in the position of a seller" includes as against a principal an agent who has paid or become responsible for the price of goods on behalf of his principal or anyone who otherwise holds a security interest or other right in goods similar to that of a seller.

(2) A person in the position of a seller may as provided in this Article withhold or stop delivery (Section 2—705) and resell (Section 2—706) and recover incidental damages (Section 2—710).

§2—708. Seller's Damages for Non-Acceptance or Repudiation.

(1) Subject to subsection (2) and to the provisions of this Article with respect to proof of market price (Section 2—723), the measure of damages for non-acceptance or repudiation by the buyer is the difference between the market price at the time and place for tender and the unpaid contract price together with any incidental damages provided in this Article (Section 2—710), but less expenses saved in consequence of the buyer's breach.

(2) If the measure of damages provided in subsection (1) is inadequate to put the seller in as good a position as performance would have done then the measure of damages is the profit (including reasonable overhead) which the seller would have made from full performance by the buyer, together with any incidental damages provided in this Article (Section 2—710), due allowance for costs reasonably incurred and due credit for payments or proceeds of resale.

§2—709. Action for the Price.

(1) When the buyer fails to pay the price as it becomes due the seller may recover, together with any incidental damages under the next section, the price

(a) of goods accepted or of conforming goods lost or damaged within a commercially reasonable time after risk of their loss has passed to the buyer; and

(b) of goods identified to the contract if the seller is unable after reasonable effort to resell them at a reasonable price or the circumstances reasonably indicate that such effort will be unavailing.

(2) Where the seller sues for the price he must hold for the buyer any goods which have been identified to the contract and are still in his control except that if resale becomes possible he may resell them at any time prior to the collection of the judgment. The net proceeds of any such resale must be credited to the buyer and payment of the judgment entitles him to any goods not resold.

(3) After the buyer has wrongfully rejected or revoked acceptance of the goods or has failed to make a payment due or has repudiated (Section 2—610), a seller who is held not entitled to the price under this section shall nevertheless be awarded damages for non-acceptance under the preceding section.

§2—710. Seller's Incidental Damages. Incidental damages to an aggrieved seller include any commercially reasonable charges, expenses or commissions incurred in stopping delivery, in the transportation, care and custody of goods after the buyer's breach, in connection with return or resale of the goods or otherwise resulting from the breach.

§2—711. Buyer's Remedies in General; Buyer's Security Interest in Rejected Goods.

(1) Where the seller fails to make delivery or repudiates or the buyer rightfully rejects or justifiably revokes acceptance

then with respect to any goods involved, and with respect to the whole if the breach goes to the whole contract (Section 2—612), the buyer may cancel and whether or not he has done so may in addition to recovering so much of the price as has been paid

(a) "cover" and have damages under the next section as to all the goods affected whether or not they have been identified to the contract; or

(b) recover damages for non-delivery as provided in this Article (Section 2—713).

(2) Where the seller fails to deliver or repudiates the buyer may also

(a) if the goods have been identified recover them as provided in this Article (Section 2—502); or

(b) in a proper case obtain specific performance or replevy the goods as provided in this Article (Section 2—716).

(3) On rightful rejection or justifiable revocation of acceptance a buyer has a security interest in goods in his possession or control for any payments made on their price and any expenses reasonably incurred in their inspection, receipt, transportation, care and custody and may hold such goods and resell them in like manner as an aggrieved seller (Section 2—706).

§2—712. "Cover"; Buyer's Procurement of Substitute Goods.

(1) After a breach within the preceding section the buyer may "cover" by making in good faith and without unreasonable delay any reasonable purchase of or contract to purchase goods in substitution for those due from the seller.

(2) The buyer may recover from the seller as damages the difference between the cost of cover and the contract price together with any incidental or consequential damages as hereinafter defined (Section 2—715), but less expenses saved in consequence of the seller's breach.

(3) Failure of the buyer to effect cover within this section does not bar him from any other remedy.

§2—713. Buyer's Damages for Non-Delivery or Repudiation.

(1) Subject to the provisions of this Article with respect to proof of market price (Section 2—723), the measure of damages for non-delivery or repudiation by the seller is the difference between the market price at the time when the buyer learned of the breach and the contract price together with any incidental and consequential damages provided in this Article (Section 2—715), but less expenses saved in consequence of the seller's breach.

(2) Market price is to be determined as of the place for tender or, in cases of rejection after arrival or revocation of acceptance, as of the place of arrival.

§2—714. Buyer's Damages for Breach in Regard to Accepted Goods.

(1) Where the buyer has accepted goods and given notification (subsection (3) of Section 2—607) he may recover as damages for any non-conformity of tender the loss resulting in the ordinary course of events from the seller's breach as determined in any manner which is reasonable.

(2) The measure of damages for breach of warranty is the difference at the time and place of acceptance between the value of the goods accepted and the value they would have had if they had been as warranted, unless special circumstances show proximate damages of a different amount.

(3) In a proper case any incidental and consequential damages under the next section may also be recovered.

§2—715. Buyer's Incidental and Consequential Damages.

(1) Incidental damages resulting from the seller's breach include expenses reasonably incurred in inspection, receipt, transportation and care and custody of goods rightfully rejected, any commercially reasonable charges, expenses or commissions in connection with effecting cover and any other reasonable expense incident to the delay or other breach.

(2) Consequential damages resulting from the seller's breach include

(a) any loss resulting from general or particular requirements and needs of which the seller at the time of contracting had reason to know and which could not reasonably be prevented by cover or otherwise; and

(b) injury to person or property proximately resulting from any breach of warranty.

§2—716. Buyer's Right to Specific Performance or Replevin.

(1) Specific performance may be decreed where the goods are unique or in other proper circumstances.

(2) The decree for specific performance may include such terms and conditions as to payment of the price, damages, or other relief as the court may deem just.

(3) The buyer has a right of replevin for goods identified to the contract if after reasonable effort he is unable to effect cover for such goods or the circumstances reasonably indicate that such effort will be unavailing or if the goods have been shipped under reservation and satisfaction of the security interest in them has been made or tendered. In the case of goods bought for personal, family, or household purposes, the buyer's right of replevin vests upon acquisition of a special property, even if the seller had not then repudiated or failed to deliver.

As amended in 1999.

§2—717. Deduction of Damages From the Price.   The

buyer on notifying the seller of his intention to do so may

deduct all or any part of the damages resulting from any breach of the contract from any part of the price still due under the same contract.

§2—718. Liquidation or Limitation of Damages; Deposits.

(1) Damages for breach by either party may be liquidated in the agreement but only at an amount which is reasonable in the light of the anticipated or actual harm caused by the breach, the difficulties of proof of loss, and the inconvenience or nonfeasibility of otherwise obtaining an adequate remedy. A term fixing unreasonably large liquidated damages is void as a penalty.

(2) Where the seller justifiably withholds delivery of goods because of the buyer's breach, the buyer is entitled to restitution of any amount by which the sum of his payments exceeds

    (a) the amount to which the seller is entitled by virtue of terms liquidating the seller's damages in accordance with subsection (1), or

    (b) in the absence of such terms, twenty per cent of the value of the total performance for which the buyer is obligated under the contract or $500, whichever is smaller.

(3) The buyer's right to restitution under subsection (2) is subject to offset to the extent that the seller establishes

    (a) a right to recover damages under the provisions of this Article other than subsection (1), and

    (b) the amount or value of any benefits received by the buyer directly or indirectly by reason of the contract.

(4) Where a seller has received payment in goods their reasonable value or the proceeds of their resale shall be treated as payments for the purposes of subsection (2); but if the seller has notice of the buyer's breach before reselling goods received in part performance, his resale is subject to the conditions laid down in this Article on resale by an aggrieved seller (Section 2—706).

§2—719. Contractual Modification or Limitation of Remedy.

(1) Subject to the provisions of subsections (2) and (3) of this section and of the preceding section on liquidation and limitation of damages,

    (a) the agreement may provide for remedies in addition to or in substitution for those provided in this Article and may limit or alter the measure of damages recoverable under this Article, as by limiting the buyer's remedies to return of the goods and repayment of the price or to repair and replacement of nonconforming goods or parts; and

    (b) resort to a remedy as provided is optional unless the remedy is expressly agreed to be exclusive, in which case it is the sole remedy.

(2) Where circumstances cause an exclusive or limited remedy to fail of its essential purpose, remedy may be had as provided in this Act.

(3) Consequential damages may be limited or excluded unless the limitation or exclusion is unconscionable. Limitation of consequential damages for injury to the person in the case of consumer goods is prima facie unconscionable but limitation of damages where the loss is commercial is not.

§2—720. Effect of "Cancellation" or "Rescission" on Claims for Antecedent Breach.
Unless the contrary intention clearly appears, expressions of "cancellation" or "rescission" of the contract or the like shall not be construed as a renunciation or discharge of any claim in damages for an antecedent breach.

§2—721. Remedies for Fraud.
Remedies for material misrepresentation or fraud include all remedies available under this Article for non-fraudulent breach. Neither rescission or a claim for rescission of the contract for sale nor rejection or return of the goods shall bar or be deemed inconsistent with a claim for damages or other remedy.

§2—722. Who Can Sue Third Parties for Injury to Goods.
Where a third party so deals with goods which have been identified to a contract for sale as to cause actionable injury to a party to that contract

(a) a right of action against the third party is in either party to the contract for sale who has title to or a security interest or a special property or an insurable interest in the goods; and if the goods have been destroyed or converted a right of action is also in the party who either bore the risk of loss under the contract for sale or has since the injury assumed that risk as against the other;

(b) if at the time of the injury the party plaintiff did not bear the risk of loss as against the other party to the contract for sale and there is no arrangement between them for disposition of the recovery, his suit or settlement is, subject to his own interest, as a fiduciary for the other party to the contract;

(c) either party may with the consent of the other sue for the benefit of whom it may concern.

§2—723. Proof of Market Price: Time and Place.

(1) If an action based on anticipatory repudiation comes to trial before the time for performance with respect to some or all of the goods, any damages based on market price (Section 2—708 or Section 2—713) shall be determined according to the price of such goods prevailing at the time when the aggrieved party learned of the repudiation.

(2) If evidence of a price prevailing at the times or places described in this Article is not readily available the price prevailing within any reasonable time before or after the time described or at any other place which in commercial judgment or under usage of trade would serve as a reasonable substitute for the one described may be used, making any

proper allowance for the cost of transporting the goods to or from such other place.

(3) Evidence of a relevant price prevailing at a time or place other than the one described in this Article offered by one party is not admissible unless and until he has given the other party such notice as the court finds sufficient to prevent unfair surprise.

§2—724. Admissibility of Market Quotations.

Whenever the prevailing price or value of any goods regularly bought and sold in any established commodity market is in issue, reports in official publications or trade journals or in newspapers or periodicals of general circulation published as the reports of such market shall be admissible in evidence. The circumstances of the preparation of such a report may be shown to affect its weight but not its admissibility.

§2—725. Statute of Limitations in Contracts for Sale.

(1) An action for breach of any contract for sale must be commenced within four years after the cause of action has accrued. By the original agreement the parties may reduce the period of limitation to not less than one year but may not extend it.

(2) A cause of action accrues when the breach occurs, regardless of the aggrieved party's lack of knowledge of the breach. A breach of warranty occurs when tender of delivery is made, except that where a warranty explicitly extends to future performance of the goods and discovery of the breach must await the time of such performance the cause of action accrues when the breach is or should have been discovered.

(3) Where an action commenced within the time limited by subsection (1) is so terminated as to leave available a remedy by another action for the same breach such other action may be commenced after the expiration of the time limited and within six months after the termination of the first action unless the termination resulted from voluntary discontinuance or from dismissal for failure or neglect to prosecute.

(4) This section does not alter the law on tolling of the statute of limitations nor does it apply to causes of action which have accrued before this Act becomes effective.

 ## ARTICLE 2 AMENDMENTS (EXCERPTS)

PART 1 SHORT TITLE, GENERAL CONSTRUCTION AND SUBJECT MATTER

* * * *

§2—103. Definitions and Index of Definitions.

(1) In this article unless the context otherwise requires

* * * *

(b) "Conspicuous", with reference to a term, means so written, displayed, or presented that a reasonable person against which it is to operate ought to have noticed it.

A term in an electronic record intended to evoke a response by an electronic agent is conspicuous if it is presented in a form that would enable a reasonably configured electronic agent to take it into account or react to it without review of the record by an individual. Whether a term is "conspicuous" or not is a decision for the court. Conspicuous terms include the following:

(i) for a person:

(A) a heading in capitals equal to or greater in size than the surrounding text, or in contrasting type, font, or color to the surrounding text of the same or lesser size;

(B) language in the body of a record or display in larger type than the surrounding text, or in contrasting type, font, or color to the surrounding text of the same size, or set off from surrounding text of the same size by symbols or other marks that call attention to the language; and

(ii) for a person or an electronic agent, a term that is so placed in a record or display that the person or electronic agent cannot proceed without taking action with respect to the particular term.

(c) "Consumer" means an individual who buys or contracts to buy goods that, at the time of contracting, are intended by the individual to be used primarily for personal, family, or household purposes.

(d) "Consumer contract" means a contract between a merchant seller and a consumer.

* * * *

(j) "Good faith" means honesty in fact and the observance of reasonable commercial standards of fair dealing.

(k) "Goods" means all things that are movable at the time of identification to a contract for sale. The term includes future goods, specially manufactured goods, the unborn young of animals, growing crops, and other identified things attached to realty as described in Section 2—107. The term does not include information, the money in which the price is to be paid, investment securities under Article 8, the subject matter of foreign exchange transactions, and choses in action.

* * * *

(m) "Record" means information that is inscribed on a tangible medium or that is stored in an electronic or other medium and is retrievable in perceivable form.

(n) "Remedial promise" means a promise by the seller to repair or replace the goods or to refund all or part of the price upon the happening of a specified event.

* * * *

(p) "Sign" means, with present intent to authenticate or adopt a record,

(i) to execute or adopt a tangible symbol; or
(ii) to attach to or logically associate with the record an electronic sound, symbol, or process.

* * * *

PART 2 FORM, FORMATION, TERMS AND READJUSTMENT OF CONTRACT; ELECTRONIC CONTRACTING

§2—201. Formal Requirements; Statute of Frauds.

(1) A contract for the sale of goods for the price of $5,000 or more is not enforceable by way of action or defense unless there is some record sufficient to indicate that a contract for sale has been made between the parties and signed by the party against whom which enforcement is sought or by the party's authorized agent or broker. A record is not insufficient because it omits or incorrectly states a term agreed upon but the contract is not enforceable under this subsection beyond the quantity of goods shown in the record.

(2) Between merchants if within a reasonable time a record in confirmation of the contract and sufficient against the sender is received and the party receiving it has reason to know its contents, it satisfies the requirements of subsection (1) against such party the recipient unless notice of objection to its contents is given in a record within 10 days after it is received.

(3) A contract which does not satisfy the requirements of subsection (1) but which is valid in other respects is enforceable

(a) if the goods are to be specially manufactured for the buyer and are not suitable for sale to others in the ordinary course of the seller's business and the seller, before notice of repudiation is received and under circumstances which reasonably indicate that the goods are for the buyer, has made either a substantial beginning of their manufacture or commitments for their procurement; or

(b) if the party against whom which enforcement is sought admits in the party's pleading, or in the party's testimony or otherwise under oath that a contract for sale was made, but the contract is not enforceable under this paragraph beyond the quantity of goods admitted; or

(c) with respect to goods for which payment has been made and accepted or which have been received and accepted (Sec. 2—606).

(4) A contract that is enforceable under this section is not rendered unenforceable merely because it is not capable of being performed within one year or any other applicable period after its making.

* * * *

§2—207. Terms of Contract; Effect of Confirmation.
If (i) conduct by both parties recognizes the existence of a contract although their records do not otherwise establish a contract, (ii) a contract is formed by an offer and acceptance, or (iii) a contract formed in any manner is confirmed by a record that contains terms additional to or different from those in the contract being confirmed, the terms of the contract, subject to Section 2—202, are:

(a) terms that appear in the records of both parties;

(b) terms, whether in a record or not, to which both parties agree; and

(c) terms supplied or incorporated under any provision of this Act.

* * * *

PART 3 GENERAL OBLIGATION AND CONSTRUCTION OF CONTRACT
* * * *

§2—312. Warranty of Title and Against Infringement; Buyer's Obligation Against Infringement.

(1) Subject to subsection (2) there is in a contract for sale a warranty by the seller that

(a) the title conveyed shall be good, good and its transfer rightful and shall not, because of any colorable claim to or interest in the goods, unreasonably expose the buyer to litigation; and

(b) the goods shall be delivered free from any security interest or other lien or encumbrance of which the buyer at the time of contracting has no knowledge.

(2) Unless otherwise agreed a seller that is a merchant regularly dealing in goods of the kind warrants that the goods shall be delivered free of the rightful claim of any third person by way of infringement or the like but a buyer that furnishes specifications to the seller must hold the seller harmless against any such claim that arises out of compliance with the specifications.

(3) A warranty under this section may be disclaimed or modified only by specific language or by circumstances that give the buyer reason to know that the seller does not claim title, that the seller is purporting to sell only the right or title as the seller or a third person may have, or that the seller is selling subject to any claims of infringement or the like.

§2—313. Express Warranties by Affirmation, Promise, Description, Sample; Remedial Promise.

(1) In this section, "immediate buyer" means a buyer that enters into a contract with the seller.
* * * *

(4) Any remedial promise made by the seller to the immediate buyer creates an obligation that the promise will be performed upon the happening of the specified event.

§2—313A. Obligation to Remote Purchaser Created by Record Packaged with or Accompanying Goods.

(1) This section applies only to new goods and goods sold or leased as new goods in a transaction of purchase in the normal chain of distribution. In this section:

(a) "Immediate buyer" means a buyer that enters into a contract with the seller.

(b) "Remote purchaser" means a person that buys or leases goods from an immediate buyer or other person in the normal chain of distribution.

(2) If a seller in a record packaged with or accompanying the goods makes an affirmation of fact or promise that relates to the goods, provides a description that relates to the goods, or makes a remedial promise, and the seller reasonably expects the record to be, and the record is, furnished to the remote purchaser, the seller has an obligation to the remote purchaser that:

(a) the goods will conform to the affirmation of fact, promise or description unless a reasonable person in the position of the remote purchaser would not believe that the affirmation of fact, promise or description created an obligation; and

(b) the seller will perform the remedial promise.

(3) It is not necessary to the creation of an obligation under this section that the seller use formal words such as "warrant" or "guarantee" or that the seller have a specific intention to undertake an obligation, but an affirmation merely of the value of the goods or a statement purporting to be merely the seller's opinion or commendation of the goods does not create an obligation.

(4) The following rules apply to the remedies for breach of an obligation created under this section:

(a) The seller may modify or limit the remedies available to the remote purchaser if the modification or limitation is furnished to the remote purchaser no later than the time of purchase or if the modification or limitation is contained in the record that contains the affirmation of fact, promise or description.

(b) Subject to a modification or limitation of remedy, a seller in breach is liable for incidental or consequential damages under Section 2—715, but the seller is not liable for lost profits.

(c) The remote purchaser may recover as damages for breach of a seller's obligation arising under subsection (2) the loss resulting in the ordinary course of events as determined in any manner that is reasonable.

(5) An obligation that is not a remedial promise is breached if the goods did not conform to the affirmation of fact, promise or description creating the obligation when the goods left the seller's control.

§2—313B. Obligation to Remote Purchaser Created by Communication to the Public.

(1) This section applies only to new goods and goods sold or leased as new goods in a transaction of purchase in the normal chain of distribution. In this section:

(a) "Immediate buyer" means a buyer that enters into a contract with the seller.

(b) "Remote purchaser" means a person that buys or leases goods from an immediate buyer or other person in the normal chain of distribution.

(2) If a seller in advertising or a similar communication to the public makes an affirmation of fact or promise that relates to the goods, provides a description that relates to the goods, or makes a remedial promise, and the remote purchaser enters into a transaction of purchase with knowledge of and with the expectation that the goods will conform to the affirmation of fact, promise, or description, or that the seller will perform the remedial promise, the seller has an obligation to the remote purchaser that:

(a) the goods will conform to the affirmation of fact, promise or description unless a reasonable person in the position of the remote purchaser would not believe that the affirmation of fact, promise or description created an obligation; and

(b) the seller will perform the remedial promise.

(3) It is not necessary to the creation of an obligation under this section that the seller use formal words such as "warrant" or "guarantee" or that the seller have a specific intention to undertake an obligation, but an affirmation merely of the value of the goods or a statement purporting to be merely the seller's opinion or commendation of the goods does not create an obligation.

(4) The following rules apply to the remedies for breach of an obligation created under this section:

(a) The seller may modify or limit the remedies available to the remote purchaser if the modification or limitation is furnished to the remote purchaser no later than the time of purchase. The modification or limitation may be furnished as part of the communication that contains the affirmation of fact, promise or description.

(b) Subject to a modification or limitation of remedy, a seller in breach is liable for incidental or consequential damages under Section 2—715, but the seller is not liable for lost profits.

(c) The remote purchaser may recover as damages for breach of a seller's obligation arising under subsection (2) the loss resulting in the ordinary course of events as determined in any manner that is reasonable.

(5) An obligation that is not a remedial promise is breached if the goods did not conform to the affirmation of fact, promise or description creating the obligation when the goods left the seller's control.

* * * *

§2—316. Exclusion or Modification of Warranties.
* * * *

(2) Subject to subsection (3), to exclude or modify the implied warranty of merchantability or any part of it in a consumer contract the language must be in a record, be conspicuous and state "The seller undertakes no responsibility for the quality of the goods except as otherwise provided in this contract," and in any other contract the language must mention merchantability and in case of a record must be conspicuous. Subject to subsection (3), to exclude or modify

the implied warranty of fitness the exclusion must be in a record and be conspicuous. Language to exclude all implied warranties of fitness in a consumer contract must state "The seller assumes no responsibility that the goods will be fit for any particular purpose for which you may be buying these goods, except as otherwise provided in the contract," and in any other contract the language is sufficient if it states, for example, that "There are no warranties which extend beyond the description on the face hereof." Language that satisfies the requirements of this subsection for the exclusion and modification of a warranty in a consumer contract also satisfies the requirements for any other contract.

(3) Notwithstanding subsection (2):

(a) unless the circumstances indicate otherwise, all implied warranties are excluded by expressions like "as is", "with all faults" or other language which in common understanding calls the buyer's attention to the exclusion of warranties, makes plain that there is no implied warranty, and in a consumer contract evidenced by a record is set forth conspicuously in the record; and

(b) when the buyer before entering into the contract has examined the goods or the sample or model as fully as desired or has refused to examine the goods after a demand by the seller there is no implied warranty with regard to defects which an examination ought in the circumstances to have revealed to the buyer; and

(c) an implied warranty can also be excluded or modified by course of dealing or course of performance or usage of trade.

* * * *

§2—318. Third Party Beneficiaries of Warranties Express or Implied.

(1) In this section:

(a) "Immediate buyer" means a buyer that enters into a contract with the seller.

(b) "Remote purchaser" means a person that buys or leases goods from an immediate buyer or other person in the normal chain of distribution.

ALTERNATIVE A TO SUBSECTION (2)

(2) A seller's warranty whether express or implied to an immediate buyer, a seller's remedial promise to an immediate buyer, or a seller's obligation to a remote purchaser under Section 2—313A or 2—313B extends to any natural person who is in the family or household of the immediate buyer or the remote purchaser or who is a guest in the home of either if it is reasonable to expect that the person may use, consume or be affected by the goods and who is injured in person by breach of the warranty, remedial promise or obligation. A seller may not exclude or limit the operation of this section.

ALTERNATIVE B TO SUBSECTION (2)

(2) A seller's warranty whether express or implied to an immediate buyer, a seller's remedial promise to an immediate buyer, or a seller's obligation to a remote purchaser under Section 2—313A or 2—313B extends to any natural person who may reasonably be expected to use, consume or be affected by the goods and who is injured in person by breach of the warranty, remedial promise or obligation. A seller may not exclude or limit the operation of this section.

ALTERNATIVE C TO SUBSECTION (2)

(2) A seller's warranty whether express or implied to an immediate buyer, a seller's remedial promise to an immediate buyer, or a seller's obligation to a remote purchaser under Section 2—313A or 2—313B extends to any person that may reasonably be expected to use, consume or be affected by the goods and that is injured by breach of the warranty, remedial promise or obligation. A seller may not exclude or limit the operation of this section with respect to injury to the person of an individual to whom the warranty, remedial promise or obligation extends.

* * * *

PART 5 PERFORMANCE
* * * *

§2—502. Buyer's Right to Goods on Seller's Insolvency.

(1) Subject to subsections (2) and (3) and even though the goods have not been shipped a buyer who that has paid a part or all of the price of goods in which the buyer has a special property under the provisions of the immediately preceding section may on making and keeping good a tender of any unpaid portion of their price recover them from the seller if:

(a) in the case of goods bought by a consumer, the seller repudiates or fails to deliver as required by the contract; or

(b) in all cases, the seller becomes insolvent within ten days after receipt of the first installment on their price.

(2) The buyer's right to recover the goods under subsection (1) vests upon acquisition of a special property, even if the seller had not then repudiated or failed to deliver.

(3) If the identification creating the special property has been made by the buyer, the buyer acquires the right to recover the goods only if they conform to the contract for sale.

* * * *

§2—508. Cure by Seller of Improper Tender or Delivery; Replacement.

(1) Where the buyer rejects goods or a tender of delivery under Section 2—601 or 2—612 or except in a consumer

contract justifiably revokes acceptance under Section 2—608(1)(b) and the agreed time for performance has not expired, a seller that has performed in good faith, upon seasonable notice to the buyer and at the seller's own expense, may cure the breach of contract by making a conforming tender of delivery within the agreed time. The seller shall compensate the buyer for all of the buyer's reasonable expenses caused by the seller's breach of contract and subsequent cure.

(2) Where the buyer rejects goods or a tender of delivery under Section 2—601 or 2—612 or except in a consumer contract justifiably revokes acceptance under Section 2—608(1)(b) and the agreed time for performance has expired, a seller that has performed in good faith, upon seasonable notice to the buyer and at the seller's own expense, may cure the breach of contract, if the cure is appropriate and timely under the circumstances, by making a tender of conforming goods. The seller shall compensate the buyer for all of the buyer's reasonable expenses caused by the seller's breach of contract and subsequent cure.

§2—509. Risk of Loss in the Absence of Breach.

(1) Where the contract requires or authorizes the seller to ship the goods by carrier

(a) if it does not require the seller to deliver them at a particular destination, the risk of loss passes to the buyer when the goods are delivered to the carrier even though the shipment is under reservation (Section 2—505); but

(b) if it does require the seller to deliver them at a particular destination and the goods are there tendered while in the possession of the carrier, the risk of loss passes to the buyer when the goods are there so tendered as to enable the buyer to take delivery.

(2) Where the goods are held by a bailee to be delivered without being moved, the risk of loss passes to the buyer

(a) on the buyer's receipt of a negotiable document of title covering the goods; or

(b) on acknowledgment by the bailee to the buyer of the buyer's right to possession of the goods; or

(c) after the buyer's receipt of a non-negotiable document of title or other direction to deliver in a record, as provided in subsection (4)(b) of Section 2—503.

(3) In any case not within subsection (1) or (2), the risk of loss passes to the buyer on the buyer's receipt of the goods.
* * * *

§2—513. Buyer's Right to Inspection of Goods.
* * * *

(3) Unless otherwise agreed, the buyer is not entitled to inspect the goods before payment of the price when the contract provides

(a) for delivery on terms that under applicable course of performance, course of dealing, or usage of trade are interpreted to preclude inspection before payment; or

(b) for payment against documents of title, except where such payment is due only after the goods are to become available for inspection.
* * * *

PART 6 BREACH, REPUDIATION AND EXCUSE
* * * *

§2—605. Waiver of Buyer's Objections by Failure to Particularize.

(1) The buyer's failure to state in connection with rejection a particular defect or in connection with revocation of acceptance a defect that justifies revocation precludes the buyer from relying on the unstated defect to justify rejection or revocation of acceptance if the defect is ascertainable by reasonable inspection

(a) where the seller had a right to cure the defect and could have cured it if stated seasonably; or

(b) between merchants when the seller has after rejection made a request in a record for a full and final statement in record form of all defects on which the buyer proposes to rely.

(2) A buyer's payment against documents tendered to the buyer made without reservation of rights precludes recovery of the payment for defects apparent on the face of the documents.
* * * *

§2—607. Effect of Acceptance; Notice of Breach; Burden of Establishing Breach After Acceptance; Notice of Claim or Litigation to Person Answerable Over.
* * * *

(3) Where a tender has been accepted

(a) the buyer must within a reasonable time after the buyer discovers or should have discovered any breach notify the seller; however, failure to give timely notice bars the buyer from a remedy only to the extent that the seller is prejudiced by the failure and

(b) if the claim is one for infringement or the like (subsection (3) of Section 2—312) and the buyer is sued as a result of such a breach the buyer must so notify the seller within a reasonable time after the buyer receives notice of the litigation or be barred from any remedy over for liability established by the litigation.
* * * *

§2—608. Revocation of Acceptance in Whole or in Part.
* * * *

(4) If a buyer uses the goods after a rightful rejection or justifiable revocation of acceptance, the following rules apply:

(a) Any use by the buyer that is unreasonable under the circumstances is wrongful as against the seller and is an acceptance only if ratified by the seller.

(b) Any use of the goods that is reasonable under the circumstances is not wrongful as against the seller and is not an acceptance, but in an appropriate case the buyer shall be obligated to the seller for the value of the use to the buyer.

* * * *

§2—612. "Installment Contract"; Breach.
* * * *

(2) The buyer may reject any installment which is non-conforming if the non-conformity substantially impairs the value of that installment to the buyer or if the non-conformity is a defect in the required documents; but if the non-conformity does not fall within subsection (3) and the seller gives adequate assurance of its cure the buyer must accept that installment.

(3) Whenever non-conformity or default with respect to one or more installments substantially impairs the value of the whole contract there is a breach of the whole. But the aggrieved party reinstates the contract if the party accepts a non-conforming installment without seasonably notifying of cancellation or if the party brings an action with respect only to past installments or demands performance as to future installments.

* * * *

PART 7 REMEDIES

§2—702. Seller's Remedies on Discovery of Buyer's Insolvency.
* * * *

(2) Where the seller discovers that the buyer has received goods on credit while insolvent the seller may reclaim the goods upon demand made within a reasonable time after the buyer's receipt of the goods. Except as provided in this subsection the seller may not base a right to reclaim goods on the buyer's fraudulent or innocent misrepresentation of solvency or of intent to pay.

* * * *

§2—705. Seller's Stoppage of Delivery in Transit or Otherwise.

(1) The seller may stop delivery of goods in the possession of a carrier or other bailee when the seller discovers the buyer to be insolvent (Section 2—702) or when the buyer repudiates or fails to make a payment due before delivery or if for any other reason the seller has a right to withhold or reclaim the goods.

* * * *

§2—706. Seller's Resale Including Contract for Resale.

(1) In an appropriate case involving breach by the buyer, the seller may resell the goods concerned or the undelivered balance thereof. Where the resale is made in good faith and in a commercially reasonable manner the seller may recover the difference between the contract price and the resale price together with any incidental or consequential damages allowed under the provisions of this Article (Section 2—710), but less expenses saved in consequence of the buyer's breach.

* * * *

§2—708. Seller's Damages for Non-Acceptance or Repudiation.

(1) Subject to subsection (2) and to the provisions of this Article with respect to proof of market price (Section 2—723)

    (a) the measure of damages for non-acceptance by the buyer is the difference between the contract price and the market price at the time and place for tender together with any incidental or consequential damages provided in this Article (Section 2—710), but less expenses saved in consequence of the buyer's breach; and

    (b) the measure of damages for repudiation by the buyer is the difference between the contract price and the market price at the place for tender at the expiration of a commercially reasonable time after the seller learned of the repudiation, but no later than the time stated in paragraph (a), together with any incidental or consequential damages provided in this Article (Section 2—710), but less expenses saved in consequence of the buyer's breach.

(2) If the measure of damages provided in subsection (1) or in Section 2—706 is inadequate to put the seller in as good a position as performance would have done then the measure of damages is the profit (including reasonable overhead) which the seller would have made from full performance by the buyer, together with any incidental or consequential damages provided in this Article (Section 2—710).

§2—709. Action for the Price.

(1) When the buyer fails to pay the price as it becomes due the seller may recover, together with any incidental or consequential damages under the next section, the price

    (a) of goods accepted or of conforming goods lost or damaged within a commercially reasonable time after risk of their loss has passed to the buyer; and

    (b) of goods identified to the contract if the seller is unable after reasonable effort to resell them at a reasonable price or the circumstances reasonably indicate that such effort will be unavailing.

* * * *

§2—710. Seller's Incidental and Consequential Damages.

(1) Incidental damages to an aggrieved seller include any commercially reasonable charges, expenses or commissions incurred in stopping delivery, in the transportation, care and custody of goods after the buyer's breach, in connection with return or resale of the goods or otherwise resulting from the breach.

(2) Consequential damages resulting from the buyer's breach include any loss resulting from general or particular requirements and needs of which the buyer at the time of contracting had reason to know and which could not reasonably be prevented by resale or otherwise.

(3) In a consumer contract, a seller may not recover consequential damages from a consumer.

* * * *

§2—713. Buyer's Damages for Non-Delivery or Repudiation.

(1) Subject to the provisions of this Article with respect to proof of market price (Section 2—723), if the seller wrongfully fails to deliver or repudiates or the buyer rightfully rejects or justifiably revokes acceptance

(a) the measure of damages in the case of wrongful failure to deliver by the seller or rightful rejection or justifiable revocation of acceptance by the buyer is the difference between the market price at the time for tender under the contract and the contract price together with any incidental or consequential damages provided in this Article (Section 2—715), but less expenses saved in consequence of the seller's breach; and

(b) the measure of damages for repudiation by the seller is the difference between the market price at the expiration of a commercially reasonable time after the buyer learned of the repudiation, but no later than the time stated in paragraph (a), and the contract price together with any incidental or consequential damages provided in this Article (Section 2—715), but less expenses saved in consequence of the seller's breach.

* * * *

§2—725. Statute of Limitations in Contracts for Sale.

(1) Except as otherwise provided in this section, an action for breach of any contract for sale must be commenced within the later of four years after the right of action has accrued under subsection (2) or (3) or one year after the breach was or should have been discovered, but no longer than five years after the right of action accrued. By the original agreement the parties may reduce the period of limitation to not less than one year but may not extend it; however, in a consumer contract, the period of limitation may not be reduced.

(2) Except as otherwise provided in subsection (3), the following rules apply:

(a) Except as otherwise provided in this subsection, a right of action for breach of a contract accrues when the breach occurs, even if the aggrieved party did not have knowledge of the breach.

(b) For breach of a contract by repudiation, a right of action accrues at the earlier of when the aggrieved party elects to treat the repudiation as a breach or when a commercially reasonable time for awaiting performance has expired.

(c) For breach of a remedial promise, a right of action accrues when the remedial promise is not performed when due.

(d) In an action by a buyer against a person that is answerable over to the buyer for a claim asserted against the buyer, the buyer's right of action against the person answerable over accrues at the time the claim was originally asserted against the buyer.

(3) If a breach of a warranty arising under Section 2—312, 2—313(2), 2—314, or 2—315, or a breach of an obligation other than a remedial promise arising under Section 2—313A or 2—313B, is claimed the following rules apply:

(a) Except as otherwise provided in paragraph (c), a right of action for breach of a warranty arising under Section 2—313(2), 2—314 or 2—315 accrues when the seller has tendered delivery to the immediate buyer, as defined in Section 2—313, and has completed performance of any agreed installation or assembly of the goods.

(b) Except as otherwise provided in paragraph (c), a right of action for breach of an obligation other than a remedial promise arising under Section 2—313A or 2—313B accrues when the remote purchaser, as defined in sections 2—313A and 2—313B, receives the goods.

(c) Where a warranty arising under Section 2—313(2) or an obligation other than a remedial promise arising under 2—313A or 2—313B explicitly extends to future performance of the goods and discovery of the breach must await the time for performance the right of action accrues when the immediate buyer as defined in Section 2—313 or the remote purchaser as defined in Sections 2—313A and 2—313B discovers or should have discovered the breach.

(d) A right of action for breach of warranty arising under Section 2—312 accrues when the aggrieved party discovers or should have discovered the breach. However, an action for breach of the warranty of noninfringement may not be commenced more than six years after tender of delivery of the goods to the aggrieved party.

* * * *

> ARTICLE 2A LEASES

PART 1 GENERAL PROVISIONS

§2A—101. Short Title.   This Article shall be known and may be cited as the Uniform Commercial Code—Leases.

§2A—102. Scope.   This Article applies to any transaction, regardless of form, that creates a lease.

§2A—103. Definitions and Index of Definitions.

(1) In this Article unless the context otherwise requires:

(a) "Buyer in ordinary course of business" means a person who in good faith and without knowledge that the sale to him [or her] is in violation of the ownership rights or security interest or leasehold interest of a third party in the goods buys in ordinary course from a person in the business of selling goods of that kind but does not include a pawnbroker. "Buying" may be for cash or by exchange of other property or on secured or unsecured credit and includes receiving goods or documents of title under a pre-existing contract for sale but does not include a transfer in bulk or as security for or in total or partial satisfaction of a money debt.

(b) "Cancellation" occurs when either party puts an end to the lease contract for default by the other party.

(c) "Commercial unit" means such a unit of goods as by commercial usage is a single whole for purposes of lease and division of which materially impairs its character or value on the market or in use. A commercial unit may be a single article, as a machine, or a set of articles, as a suite of furniture or a line of machinery, or a quantity, as a gross or carload, or any other unit treated in use or in the relevant market as a single whole.

(d) "Conforming" goods or performance under a lease contract means goods or performance that are in accordance with the obligations under the lease contract.

(e) "Consumer lease" means a lease that a lessor regularly engaged in the business of leasing or selling makes to a lessee who is an individual and who takes under the lease primarily for a personal, family, or household purpose [, if the total payments to be made under the lease contract, excluding payments for options to renew or buy, do not exceed $_____].

(f) "Fault" means wrongful act, omission, breach, or default.

(g) "Finance lease" means a lease with respect to which:

(i) the lessor does not select, manufacture or supply the goods;

(ii) the lessor acquires the goods or the right to possession and use of the goods in connection with the lease; and

(iii) one of the following occurs:

(A) the lessee receives a copy of the contract by which the lessor acquired the goods or the right to possession and use of the goods before signing the lease contract;

(B) the lessee's approval of the contract by which the lessor acquired the goods or the right to possession and use of the goods is a condition to effectiveness of the lease contract;

(C) the lessee, before signing the lease contract, receives an accurate and complete statement designating the promises and warranties, and any disclaimers of warranties, limitations or modifications of remedies, or liquidated damages, including those of a third party, such as the manufacturer of the goods, provided to the lessor by the person supplying the goods in connection with or as part of the contract by which the lessor acquired the goods or the right to possession and use of the goods; or

(D) if the lease is not a consumer lease, the lessor, before the lessee signs the lease contract, informs the lessee in writing (a) of the identity of the person supplying the goods to the lessor, unless the lessee has selected that person and directed the lessor to acquire the goods or the right to possession and use of the goods from that person, (b) that the lessee is entitled under this Article to any promises and warranties, including those of any third party, provided to the lessor by the person supplying the goods in connection with or as part of the contract by which the lessor acquired the goods or the right to possession and use of the goods, and (c) that the lessee may communicate with the person supplying the goods to the lessor and receive an accurate and complete statement of those promises and warranties, including any disclaimers and limitations of them or of remedies.

(h) "Goods" means all things that are movable at the time of identification to the lease contract, or are fixtures (Section 2A—309), but the term does not include money, documents, instruments, accounts, chattel paper, general intangibles, or minerals or the like, including oil and gas, before extraction. The term also includes the unborn young of animals.

(i) "Installment lease contract" means a lease contract that authorizes or requires the delivery of goods in separate lots to be separately accepted, even though the lease contract contains a clause "each delivery is a separate lease" or its equivalent.

(j) "Lease" means a transfer of the right to possession and use of goods for a term in return for consideration, but a sale, including a sale on approval or a sale or return, or retention or creation of a security interest is not a lease. Unless the context clearly indicates otherwise, the term includes a sublease.

(k) "Lease agreement" means the bargain, with respect to the lease, of the lessor and the lessee in fact as found in their language or by implication from other circumstances including course of dealing or usage of trade or course of performance as provided in this Article. Unless the context clearly indicates otherwise, the term includes a sublease agreement.

(l) "Lease contract" means the total legal obligation that results from the lease agreement as affected by this Article and any other applicable rules of law. Unless the context clearly indicates otherwise, the term includes a sublease contract.

(m) "Leasehold interest" means the interest of the lessor or the lessee under a lease contract.

(n) "Lessee" means a person who acquires the right to possession and use of goods under a lease. Unless the context clearly indicates otherwise, the term includes a sublessee.

(o) "Lessee in ordinary course of business" means a person who in good faith and without knowledge that the lease to him [or her] is in violation of the ownership rights or security interest or leasehold interest of a third party in the goods, leases in ordinary course from a person in the business of selling or leasing goods of that kind but does not include a pawnbroker. "Leasing" may be for cash or by exchange of other property or on secured or unsecured credit and includes receiving goods or documents of title under a pre-existing lease contract but does not include a transfer in bulk or as security for or in total or partial satisfaction of a money debt.

(p) "Lessor" means a person who transfers the right to possession and use of goods under a lease. Unless the context clearly indicates otherwise, the term includes a sublessor.

(q) "Lessor's residual interest" means the lessor's interest in the goods after expiration, termination, or cancellation of the lease contract.

(r) "Lien" means a charge against or interest in goods to secure payment of a debt or performance of an obligation, but the term does not include a security interest.

(s) "Lot" means a parcel or a single article that is the subject matter of a separate lease or delivery, whether or not it is sufficient to perform the lease contract.

(t) "Merchant lessee" means a lessee that is a merchant with respect to goods of the kind subject to the lease.

(u) "Present value" means the amount as of a date certain of one or more sums payable in the future, discounted to the date certain. The discount is determined by the interest rate specified by the parties if the rate was not manifestly unreasonable at the time the transaction was entered into; otherwise, the discount is determined by a commercially reasonable rate that takes into account the facts and circumstances of each case at the time the transaction was entered into.

(v) "Purchase" includes taking by sale, lease, mortgage, security interest, pledge, gift, or any other voluntary transaction creating an interest in goods.

(w) "Sublease" means a lease of goods the right to possession and use of which was acquired by the lessor as a lessee under an existing lease.

(x) "Supplier" means a person from whom a lessor buys or leases goods to be leased under a finance lease.

(y) "Supply contract" means a contract under which a lessor buys or leases goods to be leased.

(z) "Termination" occurs when either party pursuant to a power created by agreement or law puts an end to the lease contract otherwise than for default.

(2) Other definitions applying to this Article and the sections in which they appear are:

"Accessions". Section 2A—310(1).
"Construction mortgage". Section 2A—309(1)(d).
"Encumbrance". Section 2A—309(1)(e).
"Fixtures". Section 2A—309(1)(a).
"Fixture filing". Section 2A—309(1)(b).
"Purchase money lease". Section 2A—309(1)(c).

(3) The following definitions in other Articles apply to this Article:

"Accounts". Section 9—106.
"Between merchants". Section 2—104(3).
"Buyer". Section 2—103(1)(a).
"Chattel paper". Section 9—105(1)(b).
"Consumer goods". Section 9—109(1).
"Document". Section 9—105(1)(f).
"Entrusting". Section 2—403(3).
"General intangibles". Section 9—106.
"Good faith". Section 2—103(1)(b).
"Instrument". Section 9—105(1)(i).
"Merchant". Section 2—104(1).
"Mortgage". Section 9—105(1)(j).
"Pursuant to commitment". Section 9—105(1)(k).
"Receipt". Section 2—103(1)(c).
"Sale". Section 2—106(1).
"Sale on approval". Section 2—326.
"Sale or return". Section 2—326.
"Seller". Section 2—103(1)(d).

(4) In addition Article 1 contains general definitions and principles of construction and interpretation applicable throughout this Article.

As amended in 1990 and 1999.

§2A—104. Leases Subject to Other Law.

(1) A lease, although subject to this Article, is also subject to any applicable:

(a) certificate of title statute of this State: (list any certificate of title statutes covering automobiles, trailers, mobile homes, boats, farm tractors, and the like);

(b) certificate of title statute of another jurisdiction (Section 2A—105); or

(c) consumer protection statute of this State, or final consumer protection decision of a court of this State existing on the effective date of this Article.

(2) In case of conflict between this Article, other than Sections 2A—105, 2A—304(3), and 2A—305(3), and a statute or decision referred to in subsection (1), the statute or decision controls.

(3) Failure to comply with an applicable law has only the effect specified therein.

As amended in 1990.

§2A—105. *Territorial Application of Article to Goods Covered by Certificate of Title.*

Subject to the provisions of Sections 2A—304(3) and 2A—305(3), with respect to goods covered by a certificate of title issued under a statute of this State or of another jurisdiction, compliance and the effect of compliance or noncompliance with a certificate of title statute are governed by the law (including the conflict of laws rules) of the jurisdiction issuing the certificate until the earlier of (a) surrender of the certificate, or (b) four months after the goods are removed from that jurisdiction and thereafter until a new certificate of title is issued by another jurisdiction.

§2A—106. *Limitation on Power of Parties to Consumer Lease to Choose Applicable Law and Judicial Forum.*

(1) If the law chosen by the parties to a consumer lease is that of a jurisdiction other than a jurisdiction in which the lessee resides at the time the lease agreement becomes enforceable or within 30 days thereafter or in which the goods are to be used, the choice is not enforceable.

(2) If the judicial forum chosen by the parties to a consumer lease is a forum that would not otherwise have jurisdiction over the lessee, the choice is not enforceable.

§2A—107. *Waiver or Renunciation of Claim or Right After Default.*

Any claim or right arising out of an alleged default or breach of warranty may be discharged in whole or in part without consideration by a written waiver or renunciation signed and delivered by the aggrieved party.

§2A—108. *Unconscionability.*

(1) If the court as a matter of law finds a lease contract or any clause of a lease contract to have been unconscionable at the time it was made the court may refuse to enforce the lease contract, or it may enforce the remainder of the lease contract without the unconscionable clause, or it may so limit the application of any unconscionable clause as to avoid any unconscionable result.

(2) With respect to a consumer lease, if the court as a matter of law finds that a lease contract or any clause of a lease contract has been induced by unconscionable conduct or that unconscionable conduct has occurred in the collection of a claim arising from a lease contract, the court may grant appropriate relief.

(3) Before making a finding of unconscionability under subsection (1) or (2), the court, on its own motion or that of a party, shall afford the parties a reasonable opportunity to present evidence as to the setting, purpose, and effect of the lease contract or clause thereof, or of the conduct.

(4) In an action in which the lessee claims unconscionability with respect to a consumer lease:

(a) If the court finds unconscionability under subsection (1) or (2), the court shall award reasonable attorney's fees to the lessee.

(b) If the court does not find unconscionability and the lessee claiming unconscionability has brought or maintained an action he [or she] knew to be groundless, the court shall award reasonable attorney's fees to the party against whom the claim is made.

(c) In determining attorney's fees, the amount of the recovery on behalf of the claimant under subsections (1) and (2) is not controlling.

§2A—109. *Option to Accelerate at Will.*

(1) A term providing that one party or his [or her] successor in interest may accelerate payment or performance or require collateral or additional collateral "at will" or "when he [or she] deems himself [or herself] insecure" or in words of similar import must be construed to mean that he [or she] has power to do so only if he [or she] in good faith believes that the prospect of payment or performance is impaired.

(2) With respect to a consumer lease, the burden of establishing good faith under subsection (1) is on the party who exercised the power; otherwise the burden of establishing lack of good faith is on the party against whom the power has been exercised.

PART 2 FORMATION AND CONSTRUCTION OF LEASE CONTRACT

§2A—201. *Statute of Frauds.*

(1) A lease contract is not enforceable by way of action or defense unless:

(a) the total payments to be made under the lease contract, excluding payments for options to renew or buy, are less than $1,000; or

(b) there is a writing, signed by the party against whom enforcement is sought or by that party's authorized agent, sufficient to indicate that a lease contract has been made between the parties and to describe the goods leased and the lease term.

(2) Any description of leased goods or of the lease term is sufficient and satisfies subsection (1)(b), whether or not it is specific, if it reasonably identifies what is described.

(3) A writing is not insufficient because it omits or incorrectly states a term agreed upon, but the lease contract is not enforceable under subsection (1)(b) beyond the lease term and the quantity of goods shown in the writing.

(4) A lease contract that does not satisfy the requirements of subsection (1), but which is valid in other respects, is enforceable:

(a) if the goods are to be specially manufactured or obtained for the lessee and are not suitable for lease or sale to others in the ordinary course of the lessor's business, and the lessor, before notice of repudiation is received and under circumstances that reasonably indicate that the goods are for the lessee, has made either a substantial beginning of their manufacture or commitments for their procurement;

(b) if the party against whom enforcement is sought admits in that party's pleading, testimony or otherwise in court that a lease contract was made, but the lease contract is not enforceable under this provision beyond the quantity of goods admitted; or

(c) with respect to goods that have been received and accepted by the lessee.

(5) The lease term under a lease contract referred to in subsection (4) is:

(a) if there is a writing signed by the party against whom enforcement is sought or by that party's authorized agent specifying the lease term, the term so specified;

(b) if the party against whom enforcement is sought admits in that party's pleading, testimony, or otherwise in court a lease term, the term so admitted; or

(c) a reasonable lease term.

§2A—202. Final Written Expression: Parol or Extrinsic Evidence.

Terms with respect to which the confirmatory memoranda of the parties agree or which are otherwise set forth in a writing intended by the parties as a final expression of their agreement with respect to such terms as are included therein may not be contradicted by evidence of any prior agreement or of a contemporaneous oral agreement but may be explained or supplemented:

(a) by course of dealing or usage of trade or by course of performance; and

(b) by evidence of consistent additional terms unless the court finds the writing to have been intended also as a complete and exclusive statement of the terms of the agreement.

§2A—203. Seals Inoperative.

The affixing of a seal to a writing evidencing a lease contract or an offer to enter into a lease contract does not render the writing a sealed instrument and the law with respect to sealed instruments does not apply to the lease contract or offer.

§2A—204. Formation in General.

(1) A lease contract may be made in any manner sufficient to show agreement, including conduct by both parties which recognizes the existence of a lease contract.

(2) An agreement sufficient to constitute a lease contract may be found although the moment of its making is undetermined.

(3) Although one or more terms are left open, a lease contract does not fail for indefiniteness if the parties have intended to make a lease contract and there is a reasonably certain basis for giving an appropriate remedy.

§2A—205. Firm Offers.

An offer by a merchant to lease goods to or from another person in a signed writing that by its terms gives assurance it will be held open is not revocable, for lack of consideration, during the time stated or, if no time is stated, for a reasonable time, but in no event may the period of irrevocability exceed 3 months. Any such term of assurance on a form supplied by the offeree must be separately signed by the offeror.

§2A—206. Offer and Acceptance in Formation of Lease Contract.

(1) Unless otherwise unambiguously indicated by the language or circumstances, an offer to make a lease contract must be construed as inviting acceptance in any manner and by any medium reasonable in the circumstances.

(2) If the beginning of a requested performance is a reasonable mode of acceptance, an offeror who is not notified of acceptance within a reasonable time may treat the offer as having lapsed before acceptance.

§2A—207. Course of Performance or Practical Construction.

(1) If a lease contract involves repeated occasions for performance by either party with knowledge of the nature of the performance and opportunity for objection to it by the other, any course of performance accepted or acquiesced in without objection is relevant to determine the meaning of the lease agreement.

(2) The express terms of a lease agreement and any course of performance, as well as any course of dealing and usage of trade, must be construed whenever reasonable as consistent with each other; but if that construction is unreasonable, express terms control course of performance, course of performance controls both course of dealing and usage of trade, and course of dealing controls usage of trade.

(3) Subject to the provisions of Section 2A—208 on modification and waiver, course of performance is relevant to show a waiver or modification of any term inconsistent with the course of performance.

§2A—208. Modification, Rescission and Waiver.

(1) An agreement modifying a lease contract needs no consideration to be binding.

(2) A signed lease agreement that excludes modification or rescission except by a signed writing may not be otherwise modified or rescinded, but, except as between merchants, such a requirement on a form supplied by a merchant must be separately signed by the other party.

(3) Although an attempt at modification or rescission does not satisfy the requirements of subsection (2), it may operate as a waiver.

(4) A party who has made a waiver affecting an executory portion of a lease contract may retract the waiver by reasonable notification received by the other party that strict performance will be required of any term waived, unless the retraction would be unjust in view of a material change of position in reliance on the waiver.

§2A—209. Lessee under Finance Lease as Beneficiary of Supply Contract.

(1) The benefit of the supplier's promises to the lessor under the supply contract and of all warranties, whether express or implied, including those of any third party provided in connection with or as part of the supply contract, extends to the lessee to the extent of the lessee's leasehold interest under a finance lease related to the supply contract, but is subject to the terms warranty and of the supply contract and all defenses or claims arising therefrom.

(2) The extension of the benefit of supplier's promises and of warranties to the lessee (Section 2A—209(1)) does not: (i) modify the rights and obligations of the parties to the supply contract, whether arising therefrom or otherwise, or (ii) impose any duty or liability under the supply contract on the lessee.

(3) Any modification or rescission of the supply contract by the supplier and the lessor is effective between the supplier and the lessee unless, before the modification or rescission, the supplier has received notice that the lessee has entered into a finance lease related to the supply contract. If the modification or rescission is effective between the supplier and the lessee, the lessor is deemed to have assumed, in addition to the obligations of the lessor to the lessee under the lease contract, promises of the supplier to the lessor and warranties that were so modified or rescinded as they existed and were available to the lessee before modification or rescission.

(4) In addition to the extension of the benefit of the supplier's promises and of warranties to the lessee under subsection (1), the lessee retains all rights that the lessee may have against the supplier which arise from an agreement between the lessee and the supplier or under other law.
As amended in 1990.

§2A—210. Express Warranties.

(1) Express warranties by the lessor are created as follows:
(a) Any affirmation of fact or promise made by the lessor to the lessee which relates to the goods and becomes part of the basis of the bargain creates an express warranty that the goods will conform to the affirmation or promise.
(b) Any description of the goods which is made part of the basis of the bargain creates an express warranty that the goods will conform to the description.
(c) Any sample or model that is made part of the basis of the bargain creates an express warranty that the whole of the goods will conform to the sample or model.

(2) It is not necessary to the creation of an express warranty that the lessor use formal words, such as "warrant" or "guarantee," or that the lessor have a specific intention to make a warranty, but an affirmation merely of the value of the goods or a statement purporting to be merely the lessor's opinion or commendation of the goods does not create a warranty.

§2A—211. Warranties Against Interference and Against Infringement; Lessee's Obligation Against Infringement.

(1) There is in a lease contract a warranty that for the lease term no person holds a claim to or interest in the goods that arose from an act or omission of the lessor, other than a claim by way of infringement or the like, which will interfere with the lessee's enjoyment of its leasehold interest.

(2) Except in a finance lease there is in a lease contract by a lessor who is a merchant regularly dealing in goods of the kind a warranty that the goods are delivered free of the rightful claim of any person by way of infringement or the like.

(3) A lessee who furnishes specifications to a lessor or a supplier shall hold the lessor and the supplier harmless against any claim by way of infringement or the like that arises out of compliance with the specifications.

§2A—212. Implied Warranty of Merchantability.

(1) Except in a finance lease, a warranty that the goods will be merchantable is implied in a lease contract if the lessor is a merchant with respect to goods of that kind.

(2) Goods to be merchantable must be at least such as
(a) pass without objection in the trade under the description in the lease agreement;
(b) in the case of fungible goods, are of fair average quality within the description;
(c) are fit for the ordinary purposes for which goods of that type are used;
(d) run, within the variation permitted by the lease agreement, of even kind, quality, and quantity within each unit and among all units involved;
(e) are adequately contained, packaged, and labeled as the lease agreement may require; and
(f) conform to any promises or affirmations of fact made on the container or label.

(3) Other implied warranties may arise from course of dealing or usage of trade.

§2A—213. Implied Warranty of Fitness for Particular Purpose.
Except in a finance of lease, if the lessor at the time the lease contract is made has reason to know of any particular purpose for which the goods are required and that the lessee is relying on the lessor's skill or judgment to select or furnish suitable goods, there is in the lease contract an implied warranty that the goods will be fit for that purpose.

§2A—214. Exclusion or Modification of Warranties.

(1) Words or conduct relevant to the creation of an express warranty and words or conduct tending to negate or limit a warranty must be construed wherever reasonable as consistent with each other; but, subject to the provisions of Section 2A—202 on parol or extrinsic evidence, negation or limitation is inoperative to the extent that the construction is unreasonable.

(2) Subject to subsection (3), to exclude or modify the implied warranty of merchantability or any part of it the language must mention "merchantability", be by a writing, and be conspicuous. Subject to subsection (3), to exclude or modify any implied warranty of fitness the exclusion must be by a writing and be conspicuous. Language to exclude all implied warranties of fitness is sufficient if it is in writing, is conspicuous and states, for example, "There is no warranty that the goods will be fit for a particular purpose".

(3) Notwithstanding subsection (2), but subject to subsection (4),

    (a) unless the circumstances indicate otherwise, all implied warranties are excluded by expressions like "as is" or "with all faults" or by other language that in common understanding calls the lessee's attention to the exclusion of warranties and makes plain that there is no implied warranty, if in writing and conspicuous;

    (b) if the lessee before entering into the lease contract has examined the goods or the sample or model as fully as desired or has refused to examine the goods, there is no implied warranty with regard to defects that an examination ought in the circumstances to have revealed; and

    (c) an implied warranty may also be excluded or modified by course of dealing, course of performance, or usage of trade.

(4) To exclude or modify a warranty against interference or against infringement (Section 2A—211) or any part of it, the language must be specific, be by a writing, and be conspicuous, unless the circumstances, including course of performance, course of dealing, or usage of trade, give the lessee reason to know that the goods are being leased subject to a claim or interest of any person.

§2A—215. Cumulation and Conflict of Warranties Express or Implied.

Warranties, whether express or implied, must be construed as consistent with each other and as cumulative, but if that construction is unreasonable, the intention of the parties determines which warranty is dominant. In ascertaining that intention the following rules apply:

    (a) Exact or technical specifications displace an inconsistent sample or model or general language of description.

    (b) A sample from an existing bulk displaces inconsistent general language of description.

(c) Express warranties displace inconsistent implied warranties other than an implied warranty of fitness for a particular purpose.

§2A—216. Third-Party Beneficiaries of Express and Implied Warranties.

ALTERNATIVE A

A warranty to or for the benefit of a lessee under this Article, whether express or implied, extends to any natural person who is in the family or household of the lessee or who is a guest in the lessee's home if it is reasonable to expect that such person may use, consume, or be affected by the goods and who is injured in person by breach of the warranty. This section does not displace principles of law and equity that extend a warranty to or for the benefit of a lessee to other persons. The operation of this section may not be excluded, modified, or limited, but an exclusion, modification, or limitation of the warranty, including any with respect to rights and remedies, effective against the lessee is also effective against any beneficiary designated under this section.

ALTERNATIVE B

A warranty to or for the benefit of a lessee under this Article, whether express or implied, extends to any natural person who may reasonably be expected to use, consume, or be affected by the goods and who is injured in person by breach of the warranty. This section does not displace principles of law and equity that extend a warranty to or for the benefit of a lessee to other persons. The operation of this section may not be excluded, modified, or limited, but an exclusion, modification, or limitation of the warranty, including any with respect to rights and remedies, effective against the lessee is also effective against the beneficiary designated under this section.

ALTERNATIVE C

A warranty to or for the benefit of a lessee under this Article, whether express or implied, extends to any person who may reasonably be expected to use, consume, or be affected by the goods and who is injured by breach of the warranty. The operation of this section may not be excluded, modified, or limited with respect to injury to the person of an individual to whom the warranty extends, but an exclusion, modification, or limitation of the warranty, including any with respect to rights and remedies, effective against the lessee is also effective against the beneficiary designated under this section.

§2A—217. Identification.

Identification of goods as goods to which a lease contract refers may be made at any time and in any manner explicitly agreed to by the parties. In the absence of explicit agreement, identification occurs:

(a) when the lease contract is made if the lease contract is for a lease of goods that are existing and identified;

(b) when the goods are shipped, marked, or otherwise designated by the lessor as goods to which the lease contract refers, if the lease contract is for a lease of goods that are not existing and identified; or

(c) when the young are conceived, if the lease contract is for a lease of unborn young of animals.

§2A—218. Insurance and Proceeds.

(1) A lessee obtains an insurable interest when existing goods are identified to the lease contract even though the goods identified are nonconforming and the lessee has an option to reject them.

(2) If a lessee has an insurable interest only by reason of the lessor's identification of the goods, the lessor, until default or insolvency or notification to the lessee that identification is final, may substitute other goods for those identified.

(3) Notwithstanding a lessee's insurable interest under subsections (1) and (2), the lessor retains an insurable interest until an option to buy has been exercised by the lessee and risk of loss has passed to the lessee.

(4) Nothing in this section impairs any insurable interest recognized under any other statute or rule of law.

(5) The parties by agreement may determine that one or more parties have an obligation to obtain and pay for insurance covering the goods and by agreement may determine the beneficiary of the proceeds of the insurance.

§2A—219. Risk of Loss.

(1) Except in the case of a finance lease, risk of loss is retained by the lessor and does not pass to the lessee. In the case of a finance lease, risk of loss passes to the lessee.

(2) Subject to the provisions of this Article on the effect of default on risk of loss (Section 2A—220), if risk of loss is to pass to the lessee and the time of passage is not stated, the following rules apply:

(a) If the lease contract requires or authorizes the goods to be shipped by carrier

(i) and it does not require delivery at a particular destination, the risk of loss passes to the lessee when the goods are duly delivered to the carrier; but

(ii) if it does require delivery at a particular destination and the goods are there duly tendered while in the possession of the carrier, the risk of loss passes to the lessee when the goods are there duly so tendered as to enable the lessee to take delivery.

(b) If the goods are held by a bailee to be delivered without being moved, the risk of loss passes to the lessee on acknowledgment by the bailee of the lessee's right to possession of the goods.

(c) In any case not within subsection (a) or (b), the risk of loss passes to the lessee on the lessee's receipt of the goods if the lessor, or, in the case of a finance lease, the supplier, is a merchant; otherwise the risk passes to the lessee on tender of delivery.

§2A—220. Effect of Default on Risk of Loss.

(1) Where risk of loss is to pass to the lessee and the time of passage is not stated:

(a) If a tender or delivery of goods so fails to conform to the lease contract as to give a right of rejection, the risk of their loss remains with the lessor, or, in the case of a finance lease, the supplier, until cure or acceptance.

(b) If the lessee rightfully revokes acceptance, he [or she], to the extent of any deficiency in his [or her] effective insurance coverage, may treat the risk of loss as having remained with the lessor from the beginning.

(2) Whether or not risk of loss is to pass to the lessee, if the lessee as to conforming goods already identified to a lease contract repudiates or is otherwise in default under the lease contract, the lessor, or, in the case of a finance lease, the supplier, to the extent of any deficiency in his [or her] effective insurance coverage may treat the risk of loss as resting on the lessee for a commercially reasonable time.

§2A—221. Casualty to Identified Goods. If a lease contract requires goods identified when the lease contract is made, and the goods suffer casualty without fault of the lessee, the lessor or the supplier before delivery, or the goods suffer casualty before risk of loss passes to the lessee pursuant to the lease agreement or Section 2A—219, then:

(a) if the loss is total, the lease contract is avoided; and

(b) if the loss is partial or the goods have so deteriorated as to no longer conform to the lease contract, the lessee may nevertheless demand inspection and at his [or her] option either treat the lease contract as avoided or, except in a finance lease that is not a consumer lease, accept the goods with due allowance from the rent payable for the balance of the lease term for the deterioration or the deficiency in quantity but without further right against the lessor.

PART 3 EFFECT OF LEASE CONTRACT

§2A—301. Enforceability of Lease Contract. Except as otherwise provided in this Article, a lease contract is effective and enforceable according to its terms between the parties, against purchasers of the goods and against creditors of the parties.

§2A—302. Title to and Possession of Goods. Except as otherwise provided in this Article, each provision of this

Article applies whether the lessor or a third party has title to the goods, and whether the lessor, the lessee, or a third party has possession of the goods, notwithstanding any statute or rule of law that possession or the absence of possession is fraudulent.

§2A—303. Alienability of Party's Interest Under Lease Contract or of Lessor's Residual Interest in Goods; Delegation of Performance; Transfer of Rights.

(1) As used in this section, "creation of a security interest" includes the sale of a lease contract that is subject to Article 9, Secured Transactions, by reason of Section 9—109(a)(3).

(2) Except as provided in subsections (3) and Section 9—407, a provision in a lease agreement which (i) prohibits the voluntary or involuntary transfer, including a transfer by sale, sublease, creation or enforcement of a security interest, or attachment, levy, or other judicial process, of an interest of a party under the lease contract or of the lessor's residual interest in the goods, or (ii) makes such a transfer an event of default, gives rise to the rights and remedies provided in subsection (4), but a transfer that is prohibited or is an event of default under the lease agreement is otherwise effective.

(3) A provision in a lease agreement which (i) prohibits a transfer of a right to damages for default with respect to the whole lease contract or of a right to payment arising out of the transferor's due performance of the transferor's entire obligation, or (ii) makes such a transfer an event of default, is not enforceable, and such a transfer is not a transfer that materially impairs the propsect of obtaining return performance by, materially changes the duty of, or materially increases the burden or risk imposed on, the other party to the lease contract within the purview of subsection (4).

(4) Subject to subsection (3) and Section 9—407:

(a) if a transfer is made which is made an event of default under a lease agreement, the party to the lease contract not making the transfer, unless that party waives the default or otherwise agrees, has the rights and remedies described in Section 2A—501(2);

(b) if paragraph (a) is not applicable and if a transfer is made that (i) is prohibited under a lease agreement or (ii) materially impairs the prospect of obtaining return performance by, materially changes the duty of, or materially increases the burden or risk imposed on, the other party to the lease contract, unless the party not making the transfer agrees at any time to the transfer in the lease contract or otherwise, then, except as limited by contract, (i) the transferor is liable to the party not making the transfer for damages caused by the transfer to the extent that the damages could not reasonably be prevented by the party not making the transfer and (ii) a court having jurisdiction may grant other appropriate relief, including cancellation of the lease contract or an injunction against the transfer.

(5) A transfer of "the lease" or of "all my rights under the lease", or a transfer in similar general terms, is a transfer of rights and, unless the language or the circumstances, as in a transfer for security, indicate the contrary, the transfer is a delegation of duties by the transferor to the transferee. Acceptance by the transferee constitutes a promise by the transferee to perform those duties. The promise is enforceable by either the transferor or the other party to the lease contract.

(6) Unless otherwise agreed by the lessor and the lessee, a delegation of performance does not relieve the transferor as against the other party of any duty to perform or of any liability for default.

(7) In a consumer lease, to prohibit the transfer of an interest of a party under the lease contract or to make a transfer an event of default, the language must be specific, by a writing, and conspicuous.

As amended in 1990 and 1999.

§2A—304. Subsequent Lease of Goods by Lessor.

(1) Subject to Section 2A—303, a subsequent lessee from a lessor of goods under an existing lease contract obtains, to the extent of the leasehold interest transferred, the leasehold interest in the goods that the lessor had or had power to transfer, and except as provided in subsection (2) and Section 2A—527(4), takes subject to the existing lease contract. A lessor with voidable title has power to transfer a good leasehold interest to a good faith subsequent lessee for value, but only to the extent set forth in the preceding sentence. If goods have been delivered under a transaction of purchase the lessor has that power even though:

(a) the lessor's transferor was deceived as to the identity of the lessor;

(b) the delivery was in exchange for a check which is later dishonored;

(c) it was agreed that the transaction was to be a "cash sale"; or

(d) the delivery was procured through fraud punishable as larcenous under the criminal law.

(2) A subsequent lessee in the ordinary course of business from a lessor who is a merchant dealing in goods of that kind to whom the goods were entrusted by the existing lessee of that lessor before the interest of the subsequent lessee became enforceable against that lessor obtains, to the extent of the leasehold interest transferred, all of that lessor's and the existing lessee's rights to the goods, and takes free of the existing lease contract.

(3) A subsequent lessee from the lessor of goods that are subject to an existing lease contract and are covered by a certificate of title issued under a statute of this State or of another jurisdiction takes no greater rights than those provided both by this section and by the certificate of title statute.

As amended in 1990.

§2A—305. Sale or Sublease of Goods by Lessee.

(1) Subject to the provisions of Section 2A—303, a buyer or sublessee from the lessee of goods under an existing lease

contract obtains, to the extent of the interest transferred, the leasehold interest in the goods that the lessee had or had power to transfer, and except as provided in subsection (2) and Section 2A—511(4), takes subject to the existing lease contract. A lessee with a voidable leasehold interest has power to transfer a good leasehold interest to a good faith buyer for value or a good faith sublessee for value, but only to the extent set forth in the preceding sentence. When goods have been delivered under a transaction of lease the lessee has that power even though:

   (a) the lessor was deceived as to the identity of the lessee;

   (b) the delivery was in exchange for a check which is later dishonored; or

   (c) the delivery was procured through fraud punishable as larcenous under the criminal law.

(2) A buyer in the ordinary course of business or a sublessee in the ordinary course of business from a lessee who is a merchant dealing in goods of that kind to whom the goods were entrusted by the lessor obtains, to the extent of the interest transferred, all of the lessor's and lessee's rights to the goods, and takes free of the existing lease contract.

(3) A buyer or sublessee from the lessee of goods that are subject to an existing lease contract and are covered by a certificate of title issued under a statute of this State or of another jurisdiction takes no greater rights than those provided both by this section and by the certificate of title statute.

§2A—306. Priority of Certain Liens Arising by Operation of Law.

If a person in the ordinary course of his [or her] business furnishes services or materials with respect to goods subject to a lease contract, a lien upon those goods in the possession of that person given by statute or rule of law for those materials or services takes priority over any interest of the lessor or lessee under the lease contract or this Article unless the lien is created by statute and the statute provides otherwise or unless the lien is created by rule of law and the rule of law provides otherwise.

§2A—307. Priority of Liens Arising by Attachment or Levy on, Security Interests in, and Other Claims to Goods.

(1) Except as otherwise provided in Section 2A—306, a creditor of a lessee takes subject to the lease contract.

(2) Except as otherwise provided in subsection (3) and in Sections 2A—306 and 2A—308, a creditor of a lessor takes subject to the lease contract unless the creditor holds a lien that attached to the goods before the lease contract became enforceable.

(3) Except as otherwise provided in Sections 9—317, 9—321, and 9—323, a lessee takes a leasehold interest subject to a security interest held by a creditor of the lessor.
As amended in 1990 and 1999.

§2A—308. Special Rights of Creditors.

(1) A creditor of a lessor in possession of goods subject to a lease contract may treat the lease contract as void if as against the creditor retention of possession by the lessor is fraudulent under any statute or rule of law, but retention of possession in good faith and current course of trade by the lessor for a commercially reasonable time after the lease contract becomes enforceable is not fraudulent.

(2) Nothing in this Article impairs the rights of creditors of a lessor if the lease contract (a) becomes enforceable, not in current course of trade but in satisfaction of or as security for a pre-existing claim for money, security, or the like, and (b) is made under circumstances which under any statute or rule of law apart from this Article would constitute the transaction a fraudulent transfer or voidable preference.

(3) A creditor of a seller may treat a sale or an identification of goods to a contract for sale as void if as against the creditor retention of possession by the seller is fraudulent under any statute or rule of law, but retention of possession of the goods pursuant to a lease contract entered into by the seller as lessee and the buyer as lessor in connection with the sale or identification of the goods is not fraudulent if the buyer bought for value and in good faith.

§2A—309. Lessor's and Lessee's Rights When Goods Become Fixtures.

(1) In this section:

   (a) goods are "fixtures" when they become so related to particular real estate that an interest in them arises under real estate law;

   (b) a "fixture filing" is the filing, in the office where a mortgage on the real estate would be filed or recorded, of a financing statement covering goods that are or are to become fixtures and conforming to the requirements of Section 9—502(a) and (b);

   (c) a lease is a "purchase money lease" unless the lessee has possession or use of the goods or the right to possession or use of the goods before the lease agreement is enforceable;

   (d) a mortgage is a "construction mortgage" to the extent it secures an obligation incurred for the construction of an improvement on land including the acquisition cost of the land, if the recorded writing so indicates; and

   (e) "encumbrance" includes real estate mortgages and other liens on real estate and all other rights in real estate that are not ownership interests.

(2) Under this Article a lease may be of goods that are fixtures or may continue in goods that become fixtures, but no lease exists under this Article of ordinary building materials incorporated into an improvement on land.

(3) This Article does not prevent creation of a lease of fixtures pursuant to real estate law.

(4) The perfected interest of a lessor of fixtures has priority over a conflicting interest of an encumbrancer or owner of the real estate if:

(a) the lease is a purchase money lease, the conflicting interest of the encumbrancer or owner arises before the goods become fixtures, the interest of the lessor is perfected by a fixture filing before the goods become fixtures or within ten days thereafter, and the lessee has an interest of record in the real estate or is in possession of the real estate; or

(b) the interest of the lessor is perfected by a fixture filing before the interest of the encumbrancer or owner is of record, the lessor's interest has priority over any conflicting interest of a predecessor in title of the encumbrancer or owner, and the lessee has an interest of record in the real estate or is in possession of the real estate.

(5) The interest of a lessor of fixtures, whether or not perfected, has priority over the conflicting interest of an encumbrancer or owner of the real estate if:

(a) the fixtures are readily removable factory or office machines, readily removable equipment that is not primarily used or leased for use in the operation of the real estate, or readily removable replacements of domestic appliances that are goods subject to a consumer lease, and before the goods become fixtures the lease contract is enforceable; or

(b) the conflicting interest is a lien on the real estate obtained by legal or equitable proceedings after the lease contract is enforceable; or

(c) the encumbrancer or owner has consented in writing to the lease or has disclaimed an interest in the goods as fixtures; or

(d) the lessee has a right to remove the goods as against the encumbrancer or owner. If the lessee's right to remove terminates, the priority of the interest of the lessor continues for a reasonable time.

(6) Notwithstanding paragraph (4)(a) but otherwise subject to subsections (4) and (5), the interest of a lessor of fixtures, including the lessor's residual interest, is subordinate to the conflicting interest of an encumbrancer of the real estate under a construction mortgage recorded before the goods become fixtures if the goods become fixtures before the completion of the construction. To the extent given to refinance a construction mortgage, the conflicting interest of an encumbrancer of the real estate under a mortgage has this priority to the same extent as the encumbrancer of the real estate under the construction mortgage.

(7) In cases not within the preceding subsections, priority between the interest of a lessor of fixtures, including the lessor's residual interest, and the conflicting interest of an encumbrancer or owner of the real estate who is not the lessee is determined by the priority rules governing conflicting interests in real estate.

(8) If the interest of a lessor of fixtures, including the lessor's residual interest, has priority over all conflicting interests of all owners and encumbrancers of the real estate, the lessor or the lessee may (i) on default, expiration, termination, or cancellation of the lease agreement but subject to the agreement and this Article, or (ii) if necessary to enforce other rights and remedies of the lessor or lessee under this Article, remove the goods from the real estate, free and clear of all conflicting interests of all owners and encumbrancers of the real estate, but the lessor or lessee must reimburse any encumbrancer or owner of the real estate who is not the lessee and who has not otherwise agreed for the cost of repair of any physical injury, but not for any diminution in value of the real estate caused by the absence of the goods removed or by any necessity of replacing them. A person entitled to reimbursement may refuse permission to remove until the party seeking removal gives adequate security for the performance of this obligation.

(9) Even though the lease agreement does not create a security interest, the interest of a lessor of fixtures, including the lessor's residual interest, is perfected by filing a financing statement as a fixture filing for leased goods that are or are to become fixtures in accordance with the relevant provisions of the Article on Secured Transactions (Article 9).
As amended in 1990 and 1999.

§2A—310. Lessor's and Lessee's Rights When Goods Become Accessions.

(1) Goods are "accessions" when they are installed in or affixed to other goods.

(2) The interest of a lessor or a lessee under a lease contract entered into before the goods became accessions is superior to all interests in the whole except as stated in subsection (4).

(3) The interest of a lessor or a lessee under a lease contract entered into at the time or after the goods became accessions is superior to all subsequently acquired interests in the whole except as stated in subsection (4) but is subordinate to interests in the whole existing at the time the lease contract was made unless the holders of such interests in the whole have in writing consented to the lease or disclaimed an interest in the goods as part of the whole.

(4) The interest of a lessor or a lessee under a lease contract described in subsection (2) or (3) is subordinate to the interest of

(a) a buyer in the ordinary course of business or a lessee in the ordinary course of business of any interest in the whole acquired after the goods became accessions; or

(b) a creditor with a security interest in the whole perfected before the lease contract was made to the extent that the creditor makes subsequent advances without knowledge of the lease contract.

(5) When under subsections (2) or (3) and (4) a lessor or a lessee of accessions holds an interest that is superior to all interests in the whole, the lessor or the lessee may (a) on

default, expiration, termination, or cancellation of the lease contract by the other party but subject to the provisions of the lease contract and this Article, or (b) if necessary to enforce his [or her] other rights and remedies under this Article, remove the goods from the whole, free and clear of all interests in the whole, but he [or she] must reimburse any holder of an interest in the whole who is not the lessee and who has not otherwise agreed for the cost of repair of any physical injury but not for any diminution in value of the whole caused by the absence of the goods removed or by any necessity for replacing them. A person entitled to reimbursement may refuse permission to remove until the party seeking removal gives adequate security for the performance of this obligation.

§2A—311. Priority Subject to Subordination. Nothing in this Article prevents subordination by agreement by any person entitled to priority.

As added in 1990.

PART 4 PERFORMANCE OF LEASE CONTRACT: REPUDIATED, SUBSTITUTED AND EXCUSED

§2A—401. Insecurity: Adequate Assurance of Performance.

(1) A lease contract imposes an obligation on each party that the other's expectation of receiving due performance will not be impaired.

(2) If reasonable grounds for insecurity arise with respect to the performance of either party, the insecure party may demand in writing adequate assurance of due performance. Until the insecure party receives that assurance, if commercially reasonable the insecure party may suspend any performance for which he [or she] has not already received the agreed return.

(3) A repudiation of the lease contract occurs if assurance of due performance adequate under the circumstances of the particular case is not provided to the insecure party within a reasonable time, not to exceed 30 days after receipt of a demand by the other party.

(4) Between merchants, the reasonableness of grounds for insecurity and the adequacy of any assurance offered must be determined according to commercial standards.

(5) Acceptance of any nonconforming delivery or payment does not prejudice the aggrieved party's right to demand adequate assurance of future performance.

§2A—402. Anticipatory Repudiation. If either party repudiates a lease contract with respect to a performance not yet due under the lease contract, the loss of which performance will substantially impair the value of the lease contract to the other, the aggrieved party may:

    (a) for a commercially reasonable time, await retraction of repudiation and performance by the repudiating party;

    (b) make demand pursuant to Section 2A—401 and await assurance of future performance adequate under the circumstances of the particular case; or

    (c) resort to any right or remedy upon default under the lease contract or this Article, even though the aggrieved party has notified the repudiating party that the aggrieved party would await the repudiating party's performance and assurance and has urged retraction. In addition, whether or not the aggrieved party is pursuing one of the foregoing remedies, the aggrieved party may suspend performance or, if the aggrieved party is the lessor, proceed in accordance with the provisions of this Article on the lessor's right to identify goods to the lease contract notwithstanding default or to salvage unfinished goods (Section 2A—524).

§2A—403. Retraction of Anticipatory Repudiation.

(1) Until the repudiating party's next performance is due, the repudiating party can retract the repudiation unless, since the repudiation, the aggrieved party has cancelled the lease contract or materially changed the aggrieved party's position or otherwise indicated that the aggrieved party considers the repudiation final.

(2) Retraction may be by any method that clearly indicates to the aggrieved party that the repudiating party intends to perform under the lease contract and includes any assurance demanded under Section 2A—401.

(3) Retraction reinstates a repudiating party's rights under a lease contract with due excuse and allowance to the aggrieved party for any delay occasioned by the repudiation.

§2A—404. Substituted Performance.

(1) If without fault of the lessee, the lessor and the supplier, the agreed berthing, loading, or unloading facilities fail or the agreed type of carrier becomes unavailable or the agreed manner of delivery otherwise becomes commercially impracticable, but a commercially reasonable substitute is available, the substitute performance must be tendered and accepted.

(2) If the agreed means or manner of payment fails because of domestic or foreign governmental regulation:

    (a) the lessor may withhold or stop delivery or cause the supplier to withhold or stop delivery unless the lessee provides a means or manner of payment that is commercially a substantial equivalent; and

    (b) if delivery has already been taken, payment by the means or in the manner provided by the regulation discharges the lessee's obligation unless the regulation is discriminatory, oppressive, or predatory.

§2A—405. Excused Performance. Subject to Section 2A—404 on substituted performance, the following rules apply:

    (a) Delay in delivery or nondelivery in whole or in part by a lessor or a supplier who complies with paragraphs (b) and (c) is not a default under the lease contract if performance as agreed has been made impracticable by the occurrence of a contingency the nonoccurrence of which was a basic assumption on which the lease contract was made or by compliance in good faith with any applicable foreign or domestic governmental regulation or order, whether or not the regulation or order later proves to be invalid.

(b) If the causes mentioned in paragraph (a) affect only part of the lessor's or the supplier's capacity to perform, he [or she] shall allocate production and deliveries among his [or her] customers but at his [or her] option may include regular customers not then under contract for sale or lease as well as his [or her] own requirements for further manufacture. He [or she] may so allocate in any manner that is fair and reasonable.

(c) The lessor seasonably shall notify the lessee and in the case of a finance lease the supplier seasonably shall notify the lessor and the lessee, if known, that there will be delay or nondelivery and, if allocation is required under paragraph (b), of the estimated quota thus made available for the lessee.

§2A—406. Procedure on Excused Performance.

(1) If the lessee receives notification of a material or indefinite delay or an allocation justified under Section 2A—405, the lessee may by written notification to the lessor as to any goods involved, and with respect to all of the goods if under an installment lease contract the value of the whole lease contract is substantially impaired (Section 2A—510):

(a) terminate the lease contract (Section 2A—505(2)); or

(b) except in a finance lease that is not a consumer lease, modify the lease contract by accepting the available quota in substitution, with due allowance from the rent payable for the balance of the lease term for the deficiency but without further right against the lessor.

(2) If, after receipt of a notification from the lessor under Section 2A—405, the lessee fails so to modify the lease agreement within a reasonable time not exceeding 30 days, the lease contract lapses with respect to any deliveries affected.

§2A—407. Irrevocable Promises: Finance Leases.

(1) In the case of a finance lease that is not a consumer lease the lessee's promises under the lease contract become irrevocable and independent upon the lessee's acceptance of the goods.

(2) A promise that has become irrevocable and independent under subsection (1):

(a) is effective and enforceable between the parties, and by or against third parties including assignees of the parties, and

(b) is not subject to cancellation, termination, modification, repudiation, excuse, or substitution without the consent of the party to whom the promise runs.

(3) This section does not affect the validity under any other law of a covenant in any lease contract making the lessee's promises irrevocable and independent upon the lessee's acceptance of the goods.
As amended in 1990.

PART 5 DEFAULT A. IN GENERAL

§2A—501. Default: Procedure.

(1) Whether the lessor or the lessee is in default under a lease contract is determined by the lease agreement and this Article.

(2) If the lessor or the lessee is in default under the lease contract, the party seeking enforcement has rights and remedies as provided in this Article and, except as limited by this Article, as provided in the lease agreement.

(3) If the lessor or the lessee is in default under the lease contract, the party seeking enforcement may reduce the party's claim to judgment, or otherwise enforce the lease contract by self-help or any available judicial procedure or nonjudicial procedure, including administrative proceeding, arbitration, or the like, in accordance with this Article.

(4) Except as otherwise provided in Section 1—106(1) or this Article or the lease agreement, the rights and remedies referred to in subsections (2) and (3) are cumulative.

(5) If the lease agreement covers both real property and goods, the party seeking enforcement may proceed under this Part as to the goods, or under other applicable law as to both the real property and the goods in accordance with that party's rights and remedies in respect of the real property, in which case this Part does not apply.
As amended in 1990.

§2A—502. Notice After Default.
Except as otherwise provided in this Article or the lease agreement, the lessor or lessee in default under the lease contract is not entitled to notice of default or notice of enforcement from the other party to the lease agreement.

§2A—503. Modification or Impairment of Rights and Remedies.

(1) Except as otherwise provided in this Article, the lease agreement may include rights and remedies for default in addition to or in substitution for those provided in this Article and may limit or alter the measure of damages recoverable under this Article.

(2) Resort to a remedy provided under this Article or in the lease agreement is optional unless the remedy is expressly agreed to be exclusive. If circumstances cause an exclusive or limited remedy to fail of its essential purpose, or provision for an exclusive remedy is unconscionable, remedy may be had as provided in this Article.

(3) Consequential damages may be liquidated under Section 2A—504, or may otherwise be limited, altered, or excluded unless the limitation, alteration, or exclusion is unconscionable. Limitation, alteration, or exclusion of consequential damages for injury to the person in the case of

consumer goods is prima facie unconscionable but limitation, alteration, or exclusion of damages where the loss is commercial is not prima facie unconscionable.

(4) Rights and remedies on default by the lessor or the lessee with respect to any obligation or promise collateral or ancillary to the lease contract are not impaired by this Article. As amended in 1990.

§2A—504. Liquidation of Damages.

(1) Damages payable by either party for default, or any other act or omission, including indemnity for loss or diminution of anticipated tax benefits or loss or damage to lessor's residual interest, may be liquidated in the lease agreement but only at an amount or by a formula that is reasonable in light of the then anticipated harm caused by the default or other act or omission.

(2) If the lease agreement provides for liquidation of damages, and such provision does not comply with subsection (1), or such provision is an exclusive or limited remedy that circumstances cause to fail of its essential purpose, remedy may be had as provided in this Article.

(3) If the lessor justifiably withholds or stops delivery of goods because of the lessee's default or insolvency (Section 2A—525 or 2A—526), the lessee is entitled to restitution of any amount by which the sum of his [or her] payments exceeds:

(a) the amount to which the lessor is entitled by virtue of terms liquidating the lessor's damages in accordance with subsection (1); or

(b) in the absence of those terms, 20 percent of the then present value of the total rent the lessee was obligated to pay for the balance of the lease term, or, in the case of a consumer lease, the lesser of such amount or $500.

(4) A lessee's right to restitution under subsection (3) is subject to offset to the extent the lessor establishes:

(a) a right to recover damages under the provisions of this Article other than subsection (1); and

(b) the amount or value of any benefits received by the lessee directly or indirectly by reason of the lease contract.

§2A—505. Cancellation and Termination and Effect of Cancellation, Termination, Rescission, or Fraud on Rights and Remedies.

(1) On cancellation of the lease contract, all obligations that are still executory on both sides are discharged, but any right based on prior default or performance survives, and the cancelling party also retains any remedy for default of the whole lease contract or any unperformed balance.

(2) On termination of the lease contract, all obligations that are still executory on both sides are discharged but any right based on prior default or performance survives.

(3) Unless the contrary intention clearly appears, expressions of "cancellation," "rescission," or the like of the lease

contract may not be construed as a renunciation or discharge of any claim in damages for an antecedent default.

(4) Rights and remedies for material misrepresentation or fraud include all rights and remedies available under this Article for default.

(5) Neither rescission nor a claim for rescission of the lease contract nor rejection or return of the goods may bar or be deemed inconsistent with a claim for damages or other right or remedy.

§2A—506. Statute of Limitations.

(1) An action for default under a lease contract, including breach of warranty or indemnity, must be commenced within 4 years after the cause of action accrued. By the original lease contract the parties may reduce the period of limitation to not less than one year.

(2) A cause of action for default accrues when the act or omission on which the default or breach of warranty is based is or should have been discovered by the aggrieved party, or when the default occurs, whichever is later. A cause of action for indemnity accrues when the act or omission on which the claim for indemnity is based is or should have been discovered by the indemnified party, whichever is later.

(3) If an action commenced within the time limited by subsection (1) is so terminated as to leave available a remedy by another action for the same default or breach of warranty or indemnity, the other action may be commenced after the expiration of the time limited and within 6 months after the termination of the first action unless the termination resulted from voluntary discontinuance or from dismissal for failure or neglect to prosecute.

(4) This section does not alter the law on tolling of the statute of limitations nor does it apply to causes of action that have accrued before this Article becomes effective.

§2A—507. Proof of Market Rent: Time and Place.

(1) Damages based on market rent (Section 2A—519 or 2A—528) are determined according to the rent for the use of the goods concerned for a lease term identical to the remaining lease term of the original lease agreement and prevailing at the times specified in Sections 2A—519 and 2A—528.

(2) If evidence of rent for the use of the goods concerned for a lease term identical to the remaining lease term of the original lease agreement and prevailing at the times or places described in this Article is not readily available, the rent prevailing within any reasonable time before or after the time described or at any other place or for a different lease term which in commercial judgment or under usage of trade would serve as a reasonable substitute for the one described may be used, making any proper allowance for the difference, including the cost of transporting the goods to or from the other place.

(3) Evidence of a relevant rent prevailing at a time or place or for a lease term other than the one described in this

Article offered by one party is not admissible unless and until he [or she] has given the other party notice the court finds sufficient to prevent unfair surprise.

(4) If the prevailing rent or value of any goods regularly leased in any established market is in issue, reports in official publications or trade journals or in newspapers or periodicals of general circulation published as the reports of that market are admissible in evidence. The circumstances of the preparation of the report may be shown to affect its weight but not its admissibility.

As amended in 1990.

B. DEFAULT BY LESSOR

§2A—508. Lessee's Remedies.

(1) If a lessor fails to deliver the goods in conformity to the lease contract (Section 2A—509) or repudiates the lease contract (Section 2A—402), or a lessee rightfully rejects the goods (Section 2A—509) or justifiably revokes acceptance of the goods (Section 2A—517), then with respect to any goods involved, and with respect to all of the goods if under an installment lease contract the value of the whole lease contract is substantially impaired (Section 2A—510), the lessor is in default under the lease contract and the lessee may:

(a) cancel the lease contract (Section 2A—505(1));

(b) recover so much of the rent and security as has been paid and is just under the circumstances;

(c) cover and recover damages as to all goods affected whether or not they have been identified to the lease contract (Sections 2A—518 and 2A—520), or recover damages for nondelivery (Sections 2A—519 and 2A—520);

(d) exercise any other rights or pursue any other remedies provided in the lease contract.

(2) If a lessor fails to deliver the goods in conformity to the lease contract or repudiates the lease contract, the lessee may also:

(a) if the goods have been identified, recover them (Section 2A—522); or

(b) in a proper case, obtain specific performance or replevy the goods (Section 2A—521).

(3) If a lessor is otherwise in default under a lease contract, the lessee may exercise the rights and pursue the remedies provided in the lease contract, which may include a right to cancel the lease, and in Section 2A—519(3).

(4) If a lessor has breached a warranty, whether express or implied, the lessee may recover damages (Section 2A—519(4)).

(5) On rightful rejection or justifiable revocation of acceptance, a lessee has a security interest in goods in the lessee's possession or control for any rent and security that has been paid and any expenses reasonably incurred in their inspection, receipt, transportation, and care and custody and may

hold those goods and dispose of them in good faith and in a commercially reasonable manner, subject to Section 2A—527(5).

(6) Subject to the provisions of Section 2A—407, a lessee, on notifying the lessor of the lessee's intention to do so, may deduct all or any part of the damages resulting from any default under the lease contract from any part of the rent still due under the same lease contract.

As amended in 1990.

§2A—509. Lessee's Rights on Improper Delivery; Rightful Rejection.

(1) Subject to the provisions of Section 2A—510 on default in installment lease contracts, if the goods or the tender or delivery fail in any respect to conform to the lease contract, the lessee may reject or accept the goods or accept any commercial unit or units and reject the rest of the goods.

(2) Rejection of goods is ineffective unless it is within a reasonable time after tender or delivery of the goods and the lessee seasonably notifies the lessor.

§2A—510. Installment Lease Contracts: Rejection and Default.

(1) Under an installment lease contract a lessee may reject any delivery that is nonconforming if the nonconformity substantially impairs the value of that delivery and cannot be cured or the nonconformity is a defect in the required documents; but if the nonconformity does not fall within subsection (2) and the lessor or the supplier gives adequate assurance of its cure, the lessee must accept that delivery.

(2) Whenever nonconformity or default with respect to one or more deliveries substantially impairs the value of the installment lease contract as a whole there is a default with respect to the whole. But, the aggrieved party reinstates the installment lease contract as a whole if the aggrieved party accepts a nonconforming delivery without seasonably notifying of cancellation or brings an action with respect only to past deliveries or demands performance as to future deliveries.

§2A—511. Merchant Lessee's Duties as to Rightfully Rejected Goods.

(1) Subject to any security interest of a lessee (Section 2A—508(5)), if a lessor or a supplier has no agent or place of business at the market of rejection, a merchant lessee, after rejection of goods in his [or her] possession or control, shall follow any reasonable instructions received from the lessor or the supplier with respect to the goods. In the absence of those instructions, a merchant lessee shall make reasonable efforts to sell, lease, or otherwise dispose of the goods for the lessor's account if they threaten to decline in value speedily. Instructions are not reasonable if on demand indemnity for expenses is not forthcoming.

(2) If a merchant lessee (subsection (1)) or any other lessee (Section 2A—512) disposes of goods, he [or she] is entitled to reimbursement either from the lessor or the supplier or out of the proceeds for reasonable expenses of caring for and disposing of the goods and, if the expenses include no disposition commission, to such commission as is usual in the trade, or if there is none, to a reasonable sum not exceeding 10 percent of the gross proceeds.

(3) In complying with this section or Section 2A—512, the lessee is held only to good faith. Good faith conduct hereunder is neither acceptance or conversion nor the basis of an action for damages.

(4) A purchaser who purchases in good faith from a lessee pursuant to this section or Section 2A—512 takes the goods free of any rights of the lessor and the supplier even though the lessee fails to comply with one or more of the requirements of this Article.

§2A—512. Lessee's Duties as to Rightfully Rejected Goods.

(1) Except as otherwise provided with respect to goods that threaten to decline in value speedily (Section 2A—511) and subject to any security interest of a lessee (Section 2A—508(5)):

(a) the lessee, after rejection of goods in the lessee's possession, shall hold them with reasonable care at the lessor's or the supplier's disposition for a reasonable time after the lessee's seasonable notification of rejection;

(b) if the lessor or the supplier gives no instructions within a reasonable time after notification of rejection, the lessee may store the rejected goods for the lessor's or the supplier's account or ship them to the lessor or the supplier or dispose of them for the lessor's or the supplier's account with reimbursement in the manner provided in Section 2A—511; but

(c) the lessee has no further obligations with regard to goods rightfully rejected.

(2) Action by the lessee pursuant to subsection (1) is not acceptance or conversion.

§2A—513. Cure by Lessor of Improper Tender or Delivery; Replacement.

(1) If any tender or delivery by the lessor or the supplier is rejected because nonconforming and the time for performance has not yet expired, the lessor or the supplier may seasonably notify the lessee of the lessor's or the supplier's intention to cure and may then make a conforming delivery within the time provided in the lease contract.

(2) If the lessee rejects a nonconforming tender that the lessor or the supplier had reasonable grounds to believe would be acceptable with or without money allowance, the lessor or the supplier may have a further reasonable time to substitute a conforming tender if he [or she] seasonably notifies the lessee.

§2A—514. Waiver of Lessee's Objections.

(1) In rejecting goods, a lessee's failure to state a particular defect that is ascertainable by reasonable inspection precludes the lessee from relying on the defect to justify rejection or to establish default:

(a) if, stated seasonably, the lessor or the supplier could have cured it (Section 2A—513); or

(b) between merchants if the lessor or the supplier after rejection has made a request in writing for a full and final written statement of all defects on which the lessee proposes to rely.

(2) A lessee's failure to reserve rights when paying rent or other consideration against documents precludes recovery of the payment for defects apparent on the face of the documents.

§2A—515. Acceptance of Goods.

(1) Acceptance of goods occurs after the lessee has had a reasonable opportunity to inspect the goods and

(a) the lessee signifies or acts with respect to the goods in a manner that signifies to the lessor or the supplier that the goods are conforming or that the lessee will take or retain them in spite of their nonconformity; or

(b) the lessee fails to make an effective rejection of the goods (Section 2A—509(2)).

(2) Acceptance of a part of any commercial unit is acceptance of that entire unit.

§2A—516. Effect of Acceptance of Goods; Notice of Default; Burden of Establishing Default after Acceptance; Notice of Claim or Litigation to Person Answerable Over.

(1) A lessee must pay rent for any goods accepted in accordance with the lease contract, with due allowance for goods rightfully rejected or not delivered.

(2) A lessee's acceptance of goods precludes rejection of the goods accepted. In the case of a finance lease, if made with knowledge of a nonconformity, acceptance cannot be revoked because of it. In any other case, if made with knowledge of a nonconformity, acceptance cannot be revoked because of it unless the acceptance was on the reasonable assumption that the nonconformity would be seasonably cured. Acceptance does not of itself impair any other remedy provided by this Article or the lease agreement for nonconformity.

(3) If a tender has been accepted:

(a) within a reasonable time after the lessee discovers or should have discovered any default, the lessee shall notify the lessor and the supplier, if any, or be barred from any remedy against the party notified;

(b) except in the case of a consumer lease, within a reasonable time after the lessee receives notice of litigation for infringement or the like (Section 2A—211) the lessee shall notify the lessor or be barred from any remedy over for liability established by the litigation; and

(c) the burden is on the lessee to establish any default.

(4) If a lessee is sued for breach of a warranty or other obligation for which a lessor or a supplier is answerable over the following apply:

(a) The lessee may give the lessor or the supplier, or both, written notice of the litigation. If the notice states that the person notified may come in and defend and that if the person notified does not do so that person will be bound in any action against that person by the lessee by any determination of fact common to the two litigations, then unless the person notified after seasonable receipt of the notice does come in and defend that person is so bound.

(b) The lessor or the supplier may demand in writing that the lessee turn over control of the litigation including settlement if the claim is one for infringement or the like (Section 2A—211) or else be barred from any remedy over. If the demand states that the lessor or the supplier agrees to bear all expense and to satisfy any adverse judgment, then unless the lessee after seasonable receipt of the demand does turn over control the lessee is so barred.

(5) Subsections (3) and (4) apply to any obligation of a lessee to hold the lessor or the supplier harmless against infringement or the like (Section 2A—211).

As amended in 1990.

§2A—517. *Revocation of Acceptance of Goods.*

(1) A lessee may revoke acceptance of a lot or commercial unit whose nonconformity substantially impairs its value to the lessee if the lessee has accepted it:

(a) except in the case of a finance lease, on the reasonable assumption that its nonconformity would be cured and it has not been seasonably cured; or

(b) without discovery of the nonconformity if the lessee's acceptance was reasonably induced either by the lessor's assurances or, except in the case of a finance lease, by the difficulty of discovery before acceptance.

(2) Except in the case of a finance lease that is not a consumer lease, a lessee may revoke acceptance of a lot or commercial unit if the lessor defaults under the lease contract and the default substantially impairs the value of that lot or commercial unit to the lessee.

(3) If the lease agreement so provides, the lessee may revoke acceptance of a lot or commercial unit because of other defaults by the lessor.

(4) Revocation of acceptance must occur within a reasonable time after the lessee discovers or should have discovered the ground for it and before any substantial change in condition of the goods which is not caused by the nonconformity. Revocation is not effective until the lessee notifies the lessor.

(5) A lessee who so revokes has the same rights and duties with regard to the goods involved as if the lessee had rejected them.

As amended in 1990.

§2A—518. *Cover; Substitute Goods.*

(1) After a default by a lessor under the lease contract of the type described in Section 2A—508(1), or, if agreed, after other default by the lessor, the lessee may cover by making any purchase or lease of or contract to purchase or lease goods in substitution for those due from the lessor.

(2) Except as otherwise provided with respect to damages liquidated in the lease agreement (Section 2A—504) or otherwise determined pursuant to agreement of the parties (Sections 1—102(3) and 2A—503), if a lessee's cover is by lease agreement substantially similar to the original lease agreement and the new lease agreement is made in good faith and in a commercially reasonable manner, the lessee may recover from the lessor as damages (i) the present value, as of the date of the commencement of the term of the new lease agreement, of the rent under the new lease agreement applicable to that period of the new lease term which is comparable to the then remaining term of the original lease agreement minus the present value as of the same date of the total rent for the then remaining lease term of the original lease agreement, and (ii) any incidental or consequential damages, less expenses saved in consequence of the lessor's default.

(3) If a lessee's cover is by lease agreement that for any reason does not qualify for treatment under subsection (2), or is by purchase or otherwise, the lessee may recover from the lessor as if the lessee had elected not to cover and Section 2A—519 governs.

As amended in 1990.

§2A—519. *Lessee's Damages for Non-Delivery, Repudiation, Default, and Breach of Warranty in Regard to Accepted Goods.*

(1) Except as otherwise provided with respect to damages liquidated in the lease agreement (Section 2A—504) or otherwise determined pursuant to agreement of the parties (Sections 1—102(3) and 2A—503), if a lessee elects not to cover or a lessee elects to cover and the cover is by lease agreement that for any reason does not qualify for treatment under Section 2A—518(2), or is by purchase or otherwise, the measure of damages for non-delivery or repudiation by the lessor or for rejection or revocation of acceptance by the lessee is the present value, as of the date of the default, of the then market rent minus the present value as of the same date of the original rent, computed for the remaining lease term of the original lease agreement, together with incidental

and consequential damages, less expenses saved in consequence of the lessor's default.

(2) Market rent is to be determined as of the place for tender or, in cases of rejection after arrival or revocation of acceptance, as of the place of arrival.

(3) Except as otherwise agreed, if the lessee has accepted goods and given notification (Section 2A—516(3)), the measure of damages for non-conforming tender or delivery or other default by a lessor is the loss resulting in the ordinary course of events from the lessor's default as determined in any manner that is reasonable together with incidental and consequential damages, less expenses saved in consequence of the lessor's default.

(4) Except as otherwise agreed, the measure of damages for breach of warranty is the present value at the time and place of acceptance of the difference between the value of the use of the goods accepted and the value if they had been as warranted for the lease term, unless special circumstances show proximate damages of a different amount, together with incidental and consequential damages, less expenses saved in consequence of the lessor's default or breach of warranty.
As amended in 1990.

§2A—520. Lessee's Incidental and Consequential Damages.

(1) Incidental damages resulting from a lessor's default include expenses reasonably incurred in inspection, receipt, transportation, and care and custody of goods rightfully rejected or goods the acceptance of which is justifiably revoked, any commercially reasonable charges, expenses or commissions in connection with effecting cover, and any other reasonable expense incident to the default.

(2) Consequential damages resulting from a lessor's default include:

   (a) any loss resulting from general or particular requirements and needs of which the lessor at the time of contracting had reason to know and which could not reasonably be prevented by cover or otherwise; and

   (b) injury to person or property proximately resulting from any breach of warranty.

§2A—521. Lessee's Right to Specific Performance or Replevin.

(1) Specific performance may be decreed if the goods are unique or in other proper circumstances.

(2) A decree for specific performance may include any terms and conditions as to payment of the rent, damages, or other relief that the court deems just.

(3) A lessee has a right of replevin, detinue, sequestration, claim and delivery, or the like for goods identified to the lease contract if after reasonable effort the lessee is unable to effect cover for those goods or the circumstances reasonably indicate that the effort will be unavailing.

§2A—522. Lessee's Right to Goods on Lessor's Insolvency.

(1) Subject to subsection (2) and even though the goods have not been shipped, a lessee who has paid a part or all of the rent and security for goods identified to a lease contract (Section 2A—217) on making and keeping good a tender of any unpaid portion of the rent and security due under the lease contract may recover the goods identified from the lessor if the lessor becomes insolvent within 10 days after receipt of the first installment of rent and security.

(2) A lessee acquires the right to recover goods identified to a lease contract only if they conform to the lease contract.

C. DEFAULT BY LESSEE

§2A—523. Lessor's Remedies.

(1) If a lessee wrongfully rejects or revokes acceptance of goods or fails to make a payment when due or repudiates with respect to a part or the whole, then, with respect to any goods involved, and with respect to all of the goods if under an installment lease contract the value of the whole lease contract is substantially impaired (Section 2A—510), the lessee is in default under the lease contract and the lessor may:

   (a) cancel the lease contract (Section 2A—505(1));

   (b) proceed respecting goods not identified to the lease contract (Section 2A—524);

   (c) withhold delivery of the goods and take possession of goods previously delivered (Section 2A—525);

   (d) stop delivery of the goods by any bailee (Section 2A—526);

   (e) dispose of the goods and recover damages (Section 2A—527), or retain the goods and recover damages (Section 2A—528), or in a proper case recover rent (Section 2A—529)

   (f) exercise any other rights or pursue any other remedies provided in the lease contract.

(2) If a lessor does not fully exercise a right or obtain a remedy to which the lessor is entitled under subsection (1), the lessor may recover the loss resulting in the ordinary course of events from the lessee's default as determined in any reasonable manner, together with incidental damages, less expenses saved in consequence of the lessee's default.

(3) If a lessee is otherwise in default under a lease contract, the lessor may exercise the rights and pursue the remedies provided in the lease contract, which may include a right to cancel the lease. In addition, unless otherwise provided in the lease contract:

   (a) if the default substantially impairs the value of the lease contract to the lessor, the lessor may exercise the rights and pursue the remedies provided in subsections (1) or (2); or

(b) if the default does not substantially impair the value of the lease contract to the lessor, the lessor may recover as provided in subsection (2).

As amended in 1990.

§2A—524. Lessor's Right to Identify Goods to Lease Contract.

(1) After default by the lessee under the lease contract of the type described in Section 2A—523(1) or 2A—523(3)(a) or, if agreed, after other default by the lessee, the lessor may:

(a) identify to the lease contract conforming goods not already identified if at the time the lessor learned of the default they were in the lessor's or the supplier's possession or control; and

(b) dispose of goods (Section 2A—527(1)) that demonstrably have been intended for the particular lease contract even though those goods are unfinished.

(2) If the goods are unfinished, in the exercise of reasonable commercial judgment for the purposes of avoiding loss and of effective realization, an aggrieved lessor or the supplier may either complete manufacture and wholly identify the goods to the lease contract or cease manufacture and lease, sell, or otherwise dispose of the goods for scrap or salvage value or proceed in any other reasonable manner.

As amended in 1990.

§2A—525. Lessor's Right to Possession of Goods.

(1) If a lessor discovers the lessee to be insolvent, the lessor may refuse to deliver the goods.

(2) After a default by the lessee under the lease contract of the type described in Section 2A—523(1) or 2A—523(3)(a) or, if agreed, after other default by the lessee, the lessor has the right to take possession of the goods. If the lease contract so provides, the lessor may require the lessee to assemble the goods and make them available to the lessor at a place to be designated by the lessor which is reasonably convenient to both parties. Without removal, the lessor may render unusable any goods employed in trade or business, and may dispose of goods on the lessee's premises (Section 2A—527).

(3) The lessor may proceed under subsection (2) without judicial process if that can be done without breach of the peace or the lessor may proceed by action.

As amended in 1990.

§2A—526. Lessor's Stoppage of Delivery in Transit or Otherwise.

(1) A lessor may stop delivery of goods in the possession of a carrier or other bailee if the lessor discovers the lessee to be insolvent and may stop delivery of carload, truckload, planeload, or larger shipments of express or freight if the lessee repudiates or fails to make a payment due before delivery, whether for rent, security or otherwise under the lease contract, or for any other reason the lessor has a right to withhold or take possession of the goods.

(2) In pursuing its remedies under subsection (1), the lessor may stop delivery until

(a) receipt of the goods by the lessee;

(b) acknowledgment to the lessee by any bailee of the goods, except a carrier, that the bailee holds the goods for the lessee; or

(c) such an acknowledgment to the lessee by a carrier via reshipment or as warehouseman.

(3) (a) To stop delivery, a lessor shall so notify as to enable the bailee by reasonable diligence to prevent delivery of the goods.

(b) After notification, the bailee shall hold and deliver the goods according to the directions of the lessor, but the lessor is liable to the bailee for any ensuing charges or damages.

(c) A carrier who has issued a nonnegotiable bill of lading is not obliged to obey a notification to stop received from a person other than the consignor.

§2A—527. Lessor's Rights to Dispose of Goods.

(1) After a default by a lessee under the lease contract of the type described in Section 2A—523(1) or 2A—523(3)(a) or after the lessor refuses to deliver or takes possession of goods (Section 2A—525 or 2A—526), or, if agreed, after other default by a lessee, the lessor may dispose of the goods concerned or the undelivered balance thereof by lease, sale, or otherwise.

(2) Except as otherwise provided with respect to damages liquidated in the lease agreement (Section 2A—504) or otherwise determined pursuant to agreement of the parties (Sections 1—102(3) and 2A—503), if the disposition is by lease agreement substantially similar to the original lease agreement and the new lease agreement is made in good faith and in a commercially reasonable manner, the lessor may recover from the lessee as damages (i) accrued and unpaid rent as of the date of the commencement of the term of the new lease agreement, (ii) the present value, as of the same date, of the total rent for the then remaining lease term of the original lease agreement minus the present value, as of the same date, of the rent under the new lease agreement applicable to that period of the new lease term which is comparable to the then remaining term of the original lease agreement, and (iii) any incidental damages allowed under Section 2A—530, less expenses saved in consequence of the lessee's default.

(3) If the lessor's disposition is by lease agreement that for any reason does not qualify for treatment under subsection (2), or is by sale or otherwise, the lessor may recover from the lessee as if the lessor had elected not to dispose of the goods and Section 2A—528 governs.

(4) A subsequent buyer or lessee who buys or leases from the lessor in good faith for value as a result of a disposition under this section takes the goods free of the original lease contract and any rights of the original lessee even though

the lessor fails to comply with one or more of the requirements of this Article.

(5) The lessor is not accountable to the lessee for any profit made on any disposition. A lessee who has rightfully rejected or justifiably revoked acceptance shall account to the lessor for any excess over the amount of the lessee's security interest (Section 2A—508(5)).

As amended in 1990.

§2A—528. Lessor's Damages for Non-acceptance, Failure to Pay, Repudiation, or Other Default.

(1) Except as otherwise provided with respect to damages liquidated in the lease agreement (Section 2A—504) or otherwise determined pursuant to agreement of the parties (Section 1—102(3) and 2A—503), if a lessor elects to retain the goods or a lessor elects to dispose of the goods and the disposition is by lease agreement that for any reason does not qualify for treatment under Section 2A—527(2), or is by sale or otherwise, the lessor may recover from the lessee as damages for a default of the type described in Section 2A—523(1) or 2A—523(3)(a), or if agreed, for other default of the lessee, (i) accrued and unpaid rent as of the date of the default if the lessee has never taken possession of the goods, or, if the lessee has taken possession of the goods, as of the date the lessor repossesses the goods or an earlier date on which the lessee makes a tender of the goods to the lessor, (ii) the present value as of the date determined under clause (i) of the total rent for the then remaining lease term of the original lease agreement minus the present value as of the same date of the market rent as the place where the goods are located computed for the same lease term, and (iii) any incidental damages allowed under Section 2A—530, less expenses saved in consequence of the lessee's default.

(2) If the measure of damages provided in subsection (1) is inadequate to put a lessor in as good a position as performance would have, the measure of damages is the present value of the profit, including reasonable overhead, the lessor would have made from full performance by the lessee, together with any incidental damages allowed under Section 2A—530, due allowance for costs reasonably incurred and due credit for payments or proceeds of disposition.

As amended in 1990.

§2A—529. Lessor's Action for the Rent.

(1) After default by the lessee under the lease contract of the type described in Section 2A—523(1) or 2A—523(3)(a) or, if agreed, after other default by the lessee, if the lessor complies with subsection (2), the lessor may recover from the lessee as damages:

    (a) for goods accepted by the lessee and not repossessed by or tendered to the lessor, and for conforming goods lost or damaged within a commercially reasonable time after risk of loss passes to the lessee (Section 2A—219),

(i) accrued and unpaid rent as of the date of entry of judgment in favor of the lessor (ii) the present value as of the same date of the rent for the then remaining lease term of the lease agreement, and (iii) any incidental damages allowed under Section 2A—530, less expenses saved in consequence of the lessee's default; and

    (b) for goods identified to the lease contract if the lessor is unable after reasonable effort to dispose of them at a reasonable price or the circumstances reasonably indicate that effort will be unavailing, (i) accrued and unpaid rent as of the date of entry of judgment in favor of the lessor, (ii) the present value as of the same date of the rent for the then remaining lease term of the lease agreement, and (iii) any incidental damages allowed under Section 2A—530, less expenses saved in consequence of the lessee's default.

(2) Except as provided in subsection (3), the lessor shall hold for the lessee for the remaining lease term of the lease agreement any goods that have been identified to the lease contract and are in the lessor's control.

(3) The lessor may dispose of the goods at any time before collection of the judgment for damages obtained pursuant to subsection (1). If the disposition is before the end of the remaining lease term of the lease agreement, the lessor's recovery against the lessee for damages is governed by Section 2A—527 or Section 2A—528, and the lessor will cause an appropriate credit to be provided against a judgment for damages to the extent that the amount of the judgment exceeds the recovery available pursuant to Section 2A—527 or 2A—528.

(4) Payment of the judgment for damages obtained pursuant to subsection (1) entitles the lessee to the use and possession of the goods not then disposed of for the remaining lease term of and in accordance with the lease agreement.

(5) After default by the lessee under the lease contract of the type described in Section 2A—523(1) or Section 2A—523(3)(a) or, if agreed, after other default by the lessee, a lessor who is held not entitled to rent under this section must nevertheless be awarded damages for non-acceptance under Sections 2A—527 and 2A—528.

As amended in 1990.

§2A—530. Lessor's Incidental Damages.
Incidental damages to an aggrieved lessor include any commercially reasonable charges, expenses, or commissions incurred in stopping delivery, in the transportation, care and custody of goods after the lessee's default, in connection with return or disposition of the goods, or otherwise resulting from the default.

§2A—531. Standing to Sue Third Parties for Injury to Goods.

(1) If a third party so deals with goods that have been identified to a lease contract as to cause actionable injury to a

party to the lease contract (a) the lessor has a right of action against the third party, and (b) the lessee also has a right of action against the third party if the lessee:

(i)   has a security interest in the goods;

(ii)   has an insurable interest in the goods; or

(iii)   bears the risk of loss under the lease contract or has since the injury assumed that risk as against the lessor and the goods have been converted or destroyed.

(2) If at the time of the injury the party plaintiff did not bear the risk of loss as against the other party to the lease contract and there is no arrangement between them for disposition of the recovery, his [or her] suit or settlement, subject to his [or her] own interest, is as a fiduciary for the other party to the lease contract.

(3) Either party with the consent of the other may sue for the benefit of whom it may concern.

§2A—532. Lessor's Rights to Residual Interest.   In addition to any other recovery permitted by this Article or other law, the lessor may recover from the lessee an amount that will fully compensate the lessor for any loss of or damage to the lessor's residual interest in the goods caused by the default of the lessee.

As added in 1990.

> REVISED ARTICLE 3
NEGOTIABLE INSTRUMENTS

PART 1 GENERAL PROVISIONS AND DEFINITIONS

§3—101. Short Title.   This Article may be cited as Uniform Commercial Code—Negotiable Instruments.

§3—102. Subject Matter.

(a)   This Article applies to negotiable instruments. It does not apply to money, to payment orders governed by Article 4A, or to securities governed by Article 8.

(b)   If there is conflict between this Article and Article 4 or 9, Articles 4 and 9 govern.

(c)   Regulations of the Board of Governors of the Federal Reserve System and operating circulars of the Federal Reserve Banks supersede any inconsistent provision of this Article to the extent of the inconsistency.

§3—103. Definitions.

(a)   In this Article:

(1)   "Acceptor" means a drawee who has accepted a draft.

(2)   "Drawee" means a person ordered in a draft to make payment.

(3)   "Drawer" means a person who signs or is identified in a draft as a person ordering payment.

(4)   "Good faith" means honesty in fact and the observance of reasonable commercial standards of fair dealing.

(5)   "Maker" means a person who signs or is identified in a note as a person undertaking to pay.

(6)   "Order" means a written instruction to pay money signed by the person giving the instruction. The instruction may be addressed to any person, including the person giving the instruction, or to one or more persons jointly or in the alternative but not in succession. An authorization to pay is not an order unless the person authorized to pay is also instructed to pay.

(7)   "Ordinary care" in the case of a person engaged in business means observance of reasonable commercial standards, prevailing in the area in which the person is located, with respect to the business in which the person is engaged. In the case of a bank that takes an instrument for processing for collection or payment by automated means, reasonable commercial standards do not require the bank to examine the instrument if the failure to examine does not violate the bank's prescribed procedures and the bank's procedures do not vary unreasonably from general banking usage not disapproved by this Article or Article 4.

(8)   "Party" means a party to an instrument.

(9)   "Promise" means a written undertaking to pay money signed by the person undertaking to pay. An acknowledgment of an obligation by the obligor is not a promise unless the obligor also undertakes to pay the obligation.

(10)   "Prove" with respect to a fact means to meet the burden of establishing the fact (Section 1—201(8)).

(11)   "Remitter" means a person who purchases an instrument from its issuer if the instrument is payable to an identified person other than the purchaser.

(b)   [Other definitions' section references deleted.]

(c)   [Other definitions' section references deleted.]

(d)   In addition, Article 1 contains general definitions and principles of construction and interpretation applicable throughout this Article.

§3—104. Negotiable Instrument.

(a)   Except as provided in subsections (c) and (d), "negotiable instrument" means an unconditional promise or order to pay a fixed amount of money, with or without interest or other charges described in the promise or order, if it:

(1)   is payable to bearer or to order at the time it is issued or first comes into possession of a holder;

(2)   is payable on demand or at a definite time; and

(3)   does not state any other undertaking or instruction by the person promising or ordering payment to do any act in addition to the payment of money, but the

promise or order may contain (i) an undertaking or power to give, maintain, or protect collateral to secure payment, (ii) an authorization or power to the holder to confess judgment or realize on or dispose of collateral, or (iii) a waiver of the benefit of any law intended for the advantage or protection of an obligor.

(b) "Instrument" means a negotiable instrument.

(c) An order that meets all of the requirements of subsection (a), except paragraph (1), and otherwise falls within the definition of "check" in subsection (f) is a negotiable instrument and a check.

(d) A promise or order other than a check is not an instrument if, at the time it is issued or first comes into possession of a holder, it contains a conspicuous statement, however expressed, to the effect that the promise or order is not negotiable or is not an instrument governed by this Article.

(e) An instrument is a "note" if it is a promise and is a "draft" if it is an order. If an instrument falls within the definition of both "note" and "draft," a person entitled to enforce the instrument may treat it as either.

(f) "Check" means (i) a draft, other than a documentary draft, payable on demand and drawn on a bank or (ii) a cashier's check or teller's check. An instrument may be a check even though it is described on its face by another term, such as "money order."

(g) "Cashier's check" means a draft with respect to which the drawer and drawee are the same bank or branches of the same bank.

(h) "Teller's check" means a draft drawn by a bank (i) on another bank, or (ii) payable at or through a bank.

(i) "Traveler's check" means an instrument that (i) is payable on demand, (ii) is drawn on or payable at or through a bank, (iii) is designated by the term "traveler's check" or by a substantially similar term, and (iv) requires, as a condition to payment, a countersignature by a person whose specimen signature appears on the instrument.

(j) "Certificate of deposit" means an instrument containing an acknowledgment by a bank that a sum of money has been received by the bank and a promise by the bank to repay the sum of money. A certificate of deposit is a note of the bank.

§3—105. Issue of Instrument.

(a) "Issue" means the first delivery of an instrument by the maker or drawer, whether to a holder or nonholder, for the purpose of giving rights on the instrument to any person.

(b) An unissued instrument, or an unissued incomplete instrument that is completed, is binding on the maker or drawer, but nonissuance is a defense. An instrument that is conditionally issued or is issued for a special purpose is binding on the maker or drawer, but failure of the condition or special purpose to be fulfilled is a defense.

(c) "Issuer" applies to issued and unissued instruments and means a maker or drawer of an instrument.

§3—106. Unconditional Promise or Order.

(a) Except as provided in this section, for the purposes of Section 3—104(a), a promise or order is unconditional unless it states (i) an express condition to payment, (ii) that the promise or order is subject to or governed by another writing, or (iii) that rights or obligations with respect to the promise or order are stated in another writing. A reference to another writing does not of itself make the promise or order conditional.

(b) A promise or order is not made conditional (i) by a reference to another writing for a statement of rights with respect to collateral, prepayment, or acceleration, or (ii) because payment is limited to resort to a particular fund or source.

(c) If a promise or order requires, as a condition to payment, a countersignature by a person whose specimen signature appears on the promise or order, the condition does not make the promise or order conditional for the purposes of Section 3—104(a). If the person whose specimen signature appears on an instrument fails to countersign the instrument, the failure to countersign is a defense to the obligation of the issuer, but the failure does not prevent a transferee of the instrument from becoming a holder of the instrument.

(d) If a promise or order at the time it is issued or first comes into possession of a holder contains a statement, required by applicable statutory or administrative law, to the effect that the rights of a holder or transferee are subject to claims or defenses that the issuer could assert against the original payee, the promise or order is not thereby made conditional for the purposes of Section 3—104(a); but if the promise or order is an instrument, there cannot be a holder in due course of the instrument.

§3—107. Instrument Payable in Foreign Money.
Unless the instrument otherwise provides, an instrument that states the amount payable in foreign money may be paid in the foreign money or in an equivalent amount in dollars calculated by using the current bank-offered spot rate at the place of payment for the purchase of dollars on the day on which the instrument is paid.

§3—108. Payable on Demand or at Definite Time.

(a) A promise or order is "payable on demand" if it (i) states that it is payable on demand or at sight, or otherwise indicates that it is payable at the will of the holder, or (ii) does not state any time of payment.

(b) A promise or order is "payable at a definite time" if it is payable on elapse of a definite period of time after sight or acceptance or at a fixed date or dates or at a time or times readily ascertainable at the time the promise or order is issued, subject to rights of (i) prepayment, (ii) acceleration, (iii) extension at the option of the holder, or (iv) extension to a further definite time at the option of the maker or acceptor or automatically upon or after a specified act or event.

(c) If an instrument, payable at a fixed date, is also payable upon demand made before the fixed date, the instrument is payable on demand until the fixed date and, if demand for payment is not made before that date, becomes payable at a definite time on the fixed date.

§3—109. Payable to Bearer or to Order.

(a) A promise or order is payable to bearer if it:

(1) states that it is payable to bearer or to the order of bearer or otherwise indicates that the person in possession of the promise or order is entitled to payment;

(2) does not state a payee; or

(3) states that it is payable to or to the order of cash or otherwise indicates that it is not payable to an identified person.

(b) A promise or order that is not payable to bearer is payable to order if it is payable (i) to the order of an identified person or (ii) to an identified person or order. A promise or order that is payable to order is payable to the identified person.

(c) An instrument payable to bearer may become payable to an identified person if it is specially indorsed pursuant to Section 3—205(a). An instrument payable to an identified person may become payable to bearer if it is indorsed in blank pursuant to Section 3—205(b).

§3—110. Identification of Person to Whom Instrument Is Payable.

(a) The person to whom an instrument is initially payable is determined by the intent of the person, whether or not authorized, signing as, or in the name or behalf of, the issuer of the instrument. The instrument is payable to the person intended by the signer even if that person is identified in the instrument by a name or other identification that is not that of the intended person. If more than one person signs in the name or behalf of the issuer of an instrument and all the signers do not intend the same person as payee, the instrument is payable to any person intended by one or more of the signers.

(b) If the signature of the issuer of an instrument is made by automated means, such as a check-writing machine, the payee of the instrument is determined by the intent of the person who supplied the name or identification of the payee, whether or not authorized to do so.

(c) A person to whom an instrument is payable may be identified in any way, including by name, identifying number, office, or account number. For the purpose of determining the holder of an instrument, the following rules apply:

(1) If an instrument is payable to an account and the account is identified only by number, the instrument is payable to the person to whom the account is payable.

If an instrument is payable to an account identified by number and by the name of a person, the instrument is payable to the named person, whether or not that person is the owner of the account identified by number.

(2) If an instrument is payable to:

(i) a trust, an estate, or a person described as trustee or representative of a trust or estate, the instrument is payable to the trustee, the representative, or a successor of either, whether or not the beneficiary or estate is also named;

(ii) a person described as agent or similar representative of a named or identified person, the instrument is payable to the represented person, the representative, or a successor of the representative;

(iii) a fund or organization that is not a legal entity, the instrument is payable to a representative of the members of the fund or organization; or

(iv) an office or to a person described as holding an office, the instrument is payable to the named person, the incumbent of the office, or a successor to the incumbent.

(d) If an instrument is payable to two or more persons alternatively, it is payable to any of them and may be negotiated, discharged, or enforced by any or all of them in possession of the instrument. If an instrument is payable to two or more persons not alternatively, it is payable to all of them and may be negotiated, discharged, or enforced only by all of them. If an instrument payable to two or more persons is ambiguous as to whether it is payable to the persons alternatively, the instrument is payable to the persons alternatively.

§3—111. Place of Payment.
Except as otherwise provided for items in Article 4, an instrument is payable at the place of payment stated in the instrument. If no place of payment is stated, an instrument is payable at the address of the drawee or maker stated in the instrument. If no address is stated, the place of payment is the place of business of the drawee or maker. If a drawee or maker has more than one place of business, the place of payment is any place of business of the drawee or maker chosen by the person entitled to enforce the instrument. If the drawee or maker has no place of business, the place of payment is the residence of the drawee or maker.

§3—112. Interest.

(a) Unless otherwise provided in the instrument, (i) an instrument is not payable with interest, and (ii) interest on an interest-bearing instrument is payable from the date of the instrument.

(b) Interest may be stated in an instrument as a fixed or variable amount of money or it may be expressed as a fixed or variable rate or rates. The amount or rate of interest may be stated or described in the instrument in any manner and may require reference to information not contained in the instrument. If an instrument provides for interest, but the amount of interest payable cannot be ascertained from the description, interest is payable at the judgment rate in effect at the place of payment of the instrument and at the time interest first accrues.

§3—113. Date of Instrument.

(a) An instrument may be antedated or postdated. The date stated determines the time of payment if the instrument is payable at a fixed period after date. Except as provided in Section 4—401(c), an instrument payable on demand is not payable before the date of the instrument.

(b) If an instrument is undated, its date is the date of its issue or, in the case of an unissued instrument, the date it first comes into possession of a holder.

§3—114. Contradictory Terms of Instrument. If an instrument contains contradictory terms, typewritten terms prevail over printed terms, handwritten terms prevail over both, and words prevail over numbers.

§3—115. Incomplete Instrument.

(a) "Incomplete instrument" means a signed writing, whether or not issued by the signer, the contents of which show at the time of signing that it is incomplete but that the signer intended it to be completed by the addition of words or numbers.

(b) Subject to subsection (c), if an incomplete instrument is an instrument under Section 3—104, it may be enforced according to its terms if it is not completed, or according to its terms as augmented by completion. If an incomplete instrument is not an instrument under Section 3—104, but, after completion, the requirements of Section 3—104 are met, the instrument may be enforced according to its terms as augmented by completion.

(c) If words or numbers are added to an incomplete instrument without authority of the signer, there is an alteration of the incomplete instrument under Section 3—407.

(d) The burden of establishing that words or numbers were added to an incomplete instrument without authority of the signer is on the person asserting the lack of authority.

§3—116. Joint and Several Liability; Contribution.

(a) Except as otherwise provided in the instrument, two or more persons who have the same liability on an instrument as makers, drawers, acceptors, indorsers who indorse as joint payees, or anomalous indorsers are jointly and severally liable in the capacity in which they sign.

(b) Except as provided in Section 3—419(e) or by agreement of the affected parties, a party having joint and several liability who pays the instrument is entitled to receive from any party having the same joint and several liability contribution in accordance with applicable law.

(c) Discharge of one party having joint and several liability by a person entitled to enforce the instrument does not affect the right under subsection (b) of a party having the same joint and several liability to receive contribution from the party discharged.

§3—117. Other Agreements Affecting Instrument. Subject to applicable law regarding exclusion of proof of contemporaneous or previous agreements, the obligation of a party to an instrument to pay the instrument may be modified, supplemented, or nullified by a separate agreement of the obligor and a person entitled to enforce the instrument, if the instrument is issued or the obligation is incurred in reliance on the agreement or as part of the same transaction giving rise to the agreement. To the extent an obligation is modified, supplemented, or nullified by an agreement under this section, the agreement is a defense to the obligation.

§3—118. Statute of Limitations.

(a) Except as provided in subsection (e), an action to enforce the obligation of a party to pay a note payable at a definite time must be commenced within six years after the due date or dates stated in the note or, if a due date is accelerated, within six years after the accelerated due date.

(b) Except as provided in subsection (d) or (e), if demand for payment is made to the maker of a note payable on demand, an action to enforce the obligation of a party to pay the note must be commenced within six years after the demand. If no demand for payment is made to the maker, an action to enforce the note is barred if neither principal nor interest on the note has been paid for a continuous period of 10 years.

(c) Except as provided in subsection (d), an action to enforce the obligation of a party to an unaccepted draft to pay the draft must be commenced within three years after dishonor of the draft or 10 years after the date of the draft, whichever period expires first.

(d) An action to enforce the obligation of the acceptor of a certified check or the issuer of a teller's check, cashier's check, or traveler's check must be commenced within three years after demand for payment is made to the acceptor or issuer, as the case may be.

(e) An action to enforce the obligation of a party to a certificate of deposit to pay the instrument must be commenced within six years after demand for payment is made to the maker, but if the instrument states a due date and the maker is not required to pay before that date, the six-year period begins when a demand for payment is in effect and the due date has passed.

(f) An action to enforce the obligation of a party to pay an accepted draft, other than a certified check, must be commenced (i) within six years after the due date or dates stated in the draft or acceptance if the obligation of the acceptor is payable at a definite time, or (ii) within six years after the date of the acceptance if the obligation of the acceptor is payable on demand.

(g) Unless governed by other law regarding claims for indemnity or contribution, an action (i) for conversion of an instrument, for money had and received, or like action based on conversion, (ii) for breach of warranty, or (iii) to enforce an obligation, duty, or right arising under this Article and not governed by this section must be commenced within three years after the [cause of action] accrues.

§3—119. Notice of Right to Defend Action. In an action for breach of an obligation for which a third person is answerable over pursuant to this Article or Article 4, the defendant may give the third person written notice of the litigation, and the person notified may then give similar notice to any other person who is answerable over. If the notice states (i) that the person notified may come in and defend and (ii) that failure to do so will bind the person notified in an action later brought by the person giving the notice as to any determination of fact common to the two litigations, the person notified is so bound unless after seasonable receipt of the notice the person notified does come in and defend.

PART 2 NEGOTIATION, TRANSFER, AND INDORSEMENT

§3—201. Negotiation.

(a) "Negotiation" means a transfer of possession, whether voluntary or involuntary, of an instrument by a person other than the issuer to a person who thereby becomes its holder.

(b) Except for negotiation by a remitter, if an instrument is payable to an identified person, negotiation requires transfer of possession of the instrument and its indorsement by the holder. If an instrument is payable to bearer, it may be negotiated by transfer of possession alone.

§3—202. Negotiation Subject to Rescission.

(a) Negotiation is effective even if obtained (i) from an infant, a corporation exceeding its powers, or a person without capacity, (ii) by fraud, duress, or mistake, or (iii) in breach of duty or as part of an illegal transaction.

(b) To the extent permitted by other law, negotiation may be rescinded or may be subject to other remedies, but those remedies may not be asserted against a subsequent holder in due course or a person paying the instrument in good faith and without knowledge of facts that are a basis for rescission or other remedy.

§3—203. Transfer of Instrument; Rights Acquired by Transfer.

(a) An instrument is transferred when it is delivered by a person other than its issuer for the purpose of giving to the person receiving delivery the right to enforce the instrument.

(b) Transfer of an instrument, whether or not the transfer is a negotiation, vests in the transferee any right of the transferor to enforce the instrument, including any right as a holder in due course, but the transferee cannot acquire rights of a holder in due course by a transfer, directly or indirectly, from a holder in due course if the transferee engaged in fraud or illegality affecting the instrument.

(c) Unless otherwise agreed, if an instrument is transferred for value and the transferee does not become a holder because of lack of indorsement by the transferor, the transferee has a specifically enforceable right to the unqualified indorsement of the transferor, but negotiation of the instrument does not occur until the indorsement is made.

(d) If a transferor purports to transfer less than the entire instrument, negotiation of the instrument does not occur. The transferee obtains no rights under this Article and has only the rights of a partial assignee.

§3—204. Indorsement.

(a) "Indorsement" means a signature, other than that of a signer as maker, drawer, or acceptor, that alone or accompanied by other words is made on an instrument for the purpose of (i) negotiating the instrument, (ii) restricting payment of the instrument, or (iii) incurring indorser's liability on the instrument, but regardless of the intent of the signer, a signature and its accompanying words is an indorsement unless the accompanying words, terms of the instrument, place of the signature, or other circumstances unambiguously indicate that the signature was made for a purpose other than indorsement. For the purpose of determining whether a signature is made on an instrument, a paper affixed to the instrument is a part of the instrument.

(b) "Indorser" means a person who makes an indorsement.

(c) For the purpose of determining whether the transferee of an instrument is a holder, an indorsement that transfers a security interest in the instrument is effective as an unqualified indorsement of the instrument.

(d) If an instrument is payable to a holder under a name that is not the name of the holder, indorsement may be made by the holder in the name stated in the instrument or in the holder's name or both, but signature in both names may be required by a person paying or taking the instrument for value or collection.

§3—205. Special Indorsement; Blank Indorsement; Anomalous Indorsement.

(a) If an indorsement is made by the holder of an instrument, whether payable to an identified person or payable to bearer, and the indorsement identifies a person to whom it makes the instrument payable, it is a "special indorsement." When specially indorsed, an instrument becomes payable to the identified person and may be negotiated only by the indorsement of that person. The principles stated in Section 3—110 apply to special indorsements.

(b) If an indorsement is made by the holder of an instrument and it is not a special indorsement, it is a "blank indorsement." When indorsed in blank, an instrument becomes payable to bearer and may be negotiated by transfer of possession alone until specially indorsed.

(c) The holder may convert a blank indorsement that consists only of a signature into a special indorsement by writing, above the signature of the indorser, words identifying the person to whom the instrument is made payable.

(d) "Anomalous indorsement" means an indorsement made by a person who is not the holder of the instrument. An anomalous indorsement does not affect the manner in which the instrument may be negotiated.

§3—206. Restrictive Indorsement.

(a) An indorsement limiting payment to a particular person or otherwise prohibiting further transfer or negotiation of the instrument is not effective to prevent further transfer or negotiation of the instrument.

(b) An indorsement stating a condition to the right of the indorsee to receive payment does not affect the right of the indorsee to enforce the instrument. A person paying the instrument or taking it for value or collection may disregard the condition, and the rights and liabilities of that person are not affected by whether the condition has been fulfilled.

(c) If an instrument bears an indorsement (i) described in Section 4—201(b), or (ii) in blank or to a particular bank using the words "for deposit," "for collection," or other words indicating a purpose of having the instrument collected by a bank for the indorser or for a particular account, the following rules apply:

(1) A person, other than a bank, who purchases the instrument when so indorsed converts the instrument unless the amount paid for the instrument is received by the indorser or applied consistently with the indorsement.

(2) A depositary bank that purchases the instrument or takes it for collection when so indorsed converts the instrument unless the amount paid by the bank with respect to the instrument is received by the indorser or applied consistently with the indorsement.

(3) A payor bank that is also the depositary bank or that takes the instrument for immediate payment over the counter from a person other than a collecting bank converts the instrument unless the proceeds of the instrument are received by the indorser or applied consistently with the indorsement.

(4) Except as otherwise provided in paragraph (3), a payor bank or intermediary bank may disregard the indorsement and is not liable if the proceeds of the instrument are not received by the indorser or applied consistently with the indorsement.

(d) Except for an indorsement covered by subsection (c), if an instrument bears an indorsement using words to the effect that payment is to be made to the indorsee as agent, trustee, or other fiduciary for the benefit of the indorser or another person, the following rules apply:

(1) Unless there is notice of breach of fiduciary duty as provided in Section 3—307, a person who purchases the instrument from the indorsee or takes the instrument from the indorsee for collection or payment may pay the proceeds of payment or the value given for the instrument to the indorsee without regard to whether the indorsee violates a fiduciary duty to the indorser.

(2) A subsequent transferee of the instrument or person who pays the instrument is neither given notice nor otherwise affected by the restriction in the indorsement unless the transferee or payor knows that the fiduciary dealt with the instrument or its proceeds in breach of fiduciary duty.

(e) The presence on an instrument of an indorsement to which this section applies does not prevent a purchaser of the instrument from becoming a holder in due course of the instrument unless the purchaser is a converter under subsection (c) or has notice or knowledge of breach of fiduciary duty as stated in subsection (d).

(f) In an action to enforce the obligation of a party to pay the instrument, the obligor has a defense if payment would violate an indorsement to which this section applies and the payment is not permitted by this section.

§3—207. Reacquisition.
Reacquisition of an instrument occurs if it is transferred to a former holder, by negotiation or otherwise. A former holder who reacquires the instrument may cancel indorsements made after the reacquirer first became a holder of the instrument. If the cancellation causes the instrument to be payable to the reacquirer or to bearer, the reacquirer may negotiate the instrument. An indorser whose indorsement is canceled is discharged, and the discharge is effective against any subsequent holder.

PART 3 ENFORCEMENT OF INSTRUMENTS

§3—301. Person Entitled to Enforce Instrument.
"Person entitled to enforce" an instrument means (i) the holder of the instrument, (ii) a nonholder in possession of the instrument who has the rights of a holder, or (iii) a person not in possession of the instrument who is entitled to enforce the instrument pursuant to Section 3—309 or 3—418(d). A person may be a person entitled to enforce the instrument even though the person is not the owner of the instrument or is in wrongful possession of the instrument.

§3—302. Holder in Due Course.

(a) Subject to subsection (c) and Section 3—106(d), "holder in due course" means the holder of an instrument if:

(1) the instrument when issued or negotiated to the holder does not bear such apparent evidence of forgery or alteration or is not otherwise so irregular or incomplete as to call into question its authenticity; and

(2) the holder took the instrument (i) for value, (ii) in good faith, (iii) without notice that the instrument is overdue or has been dishonored or that there is an

uncured default with respect to payment of another instrument issued as part of the same series, (iv) without notice that the instrument contains an unauthorized signature or has been altered, (v) without notice of any claim to the instrument described in Section 3—306, and (vi) without notice that any party has a defense or claim in recoupment described in Section 3—305(a).

(b) Notice of discharge of a party, other than discharge in an insolvency proceeding, is not notice of a defense under subsection (a), but discharge is effective against a person who became a holder in due course with notice of the discharge. Public filing or recording of a document does not of itself constitute notice of a defense, claim in recoupment, or claim to the instrument.

(c) Except to the extent a transferor or predecessor in interest has rights as a holder in due course, a person does not acquire rights of a holder in due course of an instrument taken (i) by legal process or by purchase in an execution, bankruptcy, or creditor's sale or similar proceeding, (ii) by purchase as part of a bulk transaction not in ordinary course of business of the transferor, or (iii) as the successor in interest to an estate or other organization.

(d) If, under Section 3—303(a)(1), the promise of performance that is the consideration for an instrument has been partially performed, the holder may assert rights as a holder in due course of the instrument only to the fraction of the amount payable under the instrument equal to the value of the partial performance divided by the value of the promised performance.

(e) If (i) the person entitled to enforce an instrument has only a security interest in the instrument and (ii) the person obliged to pay the instrument has a defense, claim in recoupment, or claim to the instrument that may be asserted against the person who granted the security interest, the person entitled to enforce the instrument may assert rights as a holder in due course only to an amount payable under the instrument which, at the time of enforcement of the instrument, does not exceed the amount of the unpaid obligation secured.

(f) To be effective, notice must be received at a time and in a manner that gives a reasonable opportunity to act on it.

(g) This section is subject to any law limiting status as a holder in due course in particular classes of transactions.

§3—303. Value and Consideration.

(a) An instrument is issued or transferred for value if:
   (1) the instrument is issued or transferred for a promise of performance, to the extent the promise has been performed;
   (2) the transferee acquires a security interest or other lien in the instrument other than a lien obtained by judicial proceeding;
   (3) the instrument is issued or transferred as payment of, or as security for, an antecedent claim against any person, whether or not the claim is due;

   (4) the instrument is issued or transferred in exchange for a negotiable instrument; or
   (5) the instrument is issued or transferred in exchange for the incurring of an irrevocable obligation to a third party by the person taking the instrument.

(b) "Consideration" means any consideration sufficient to support a simple contract. The drawer or maker of an instrument has a defense if the instrument is issued without consideration. If an instrument is issued for a promise of performance, the issuer has a defense to the extent performance of the promise is due and the promise has not been performed. If an instrument is issued for value as stated in subsection (a), the instrument is also issued for consideration.

§3—304. Overdue Instrument.

(a) An instrument payable on demand becomes overdue at the earliest of the following times:
   (1) on the day after the day demand for payment is duly made;
   (2) if the instrument is a check, 90 days after its date; or
   (3) if the instrument is not a check, when the instrument has been outstanding for a period of time after its date which is unreasonably long under the circumstances of the particular case in light of the nature of the instrument and usage of the trade.

(b) With respect to an instrument payable at a definite time the following rules apply:
   (1) If the principal is payable in installments and a due date has not been accelerated, the instrument becomes overdue upon default under the instrument for nonpayment of an installment, and the instrument remains overdue until the default is cured.
   (2) If the principal is not payable in installments and the due date has not been accelerated, the instrument becomes overdue on the day after the due date.
   (3) If a due date with respect to principal has been accelerated, the instrument becomes overdue on the day after the accelerated due date.

(c) Unless the due date of principal has been accelerated, an instrument does not become overdue if there is default in payment of interest but no default in payment of principal.

§3—305. Defenses and Claims in Recoupment.

(a) Except as stated in subsection (b), the right to enforce the obligation of a party to pay an instrument is subject to the following:
   (1) a defense of the obligor based on (i) infancy of the obligor to the extent it is a defense to a simple contract, (ii) duress, lack of legal capacity, or illegality of the transaction which, under other law, nullifies the obligation of the obligor, (iii) fraud that induced the obligor to sign the instrument with neither knowledge nor reasonable opportunity to learn of its character or its

essential terms, or (iv) discharge of the obligor in insolvency proceedings;

(2) a defense of the obligor stated in another section of this Article or a defense of the obligor that would be available if the person entitled to enforce the instrument were enforcing a right to payment under a simple contract; and

(3) a claim in recoupment of the obligor against the original payee of the instrument if the claim arose from the transaction that gave rise to the instrument; but the claim of the obligor may be asserted against a transferee of the instrument only to reduce the amount owing on the instrument at the time the action is brought.

(b) The right of a holder in due course to enforce the obligation of a party to pay the instrument is subject to defenses of the obligor stated in subsection (a)(1), but is not subject to defenses of the obligor stated in subsection (a)(2) or claims in recoupment stated in subsection (a)(3) against a person other than the holder.

(c) Except as stated in subsection (d), in an action to enforce the obligation of a party to pay the instrument, the obligor may not assert against the person entitled to enforce the instrument a defense, claim in recoupment, or claim to the instrument (Section 3—306) of another person, but the other person's claim to the instrument may be asserted by the obligor if the other person is joined in the action and personally asserts the claim against the person entitled to enforce the instrument. An obligor is not obliged to pay the instrument if the person seeking enforcement of the instrument does not have rights of a holder in due course and the obligor proves that the instrument is a lost or stolen instrument.

(d) In an action to enforce the obligation of an accommodation party to pay an instrument, the accommodation party may assert against the person entitled to enforce the instrument any defense or claim in recoupment under subsection (a) that the accommodated party could assert against the person entitled to enforce the instrument, except the defenses of discharge in insolvency proceedings, infancy, and lack of legal capacity.

§3—306. Claims to an Instrument.

A person taking an instrument, other than a person having rights of a holder in due course, is subject to a claim of a property or possessory right in the instrument or its proceeds, including a claim to rescind a negotiation and to recover the instrument or its proceeds. A person having rights of a holder in due course takes free of the claim to the instrument.

§3—307. Notice of Breach of Fiduciary Duty.

(a) In this section:

(1) "Fiduciary" means an agent, trustee, partner, corporate officer or director, or other representative owing a fiduciary duty with respect to an instrument.

(2) "Represented person" means the principal, beneficiary, partnership, corporation, or other person to whom the duty stated in paragraph (1) is owed.

(b) If (i) an instrument is taken from a fiduciary for payment or collection or for value, (ii) the taker has knowledge of the fiduciary status of the fiduciary, and (iii) the represented person makes a claim to the instrument or its proceeds on the basis that the transaction of the fiduciary is a breach of fiduciary duty, the following rules apply:

(1) Notice of breach of fiduciary duty by the fiduciary is notice of the claim of the represented person.

(2) In the case of an instrument payable to the represented person or the fiduciary as such, the taker has notice of the breach of fiduciary duty if the instrument is (i) taken in payment of or as security for a debt known by the taker to be the personal debt of the fiduciary, (ii) taken in a transaction known by the taker to be for the personal benefit of the fiduciary, or (iii) deposited to an account other than an account of the fiduciary, as such, or an account of the represented person.

(3) If an instrument is issued by the represented person or the fiduciary as such, and made payable to the fiduciary personally, the taker does not have notice of the breach of fiduciary duty unless the taker knows of the breach of fiduciary duty.

(4) If an instrument is issued by the represented person or the fiduciary as such, to the taker as payee, the taker has notice of the breach of fiduciary duty if the instrument is (i) taken in payment of or as security for a debt known by the taker to be the personal debt of the fiduciary, (ii) taken in a transaction known by the taker to be for the personal benefit of the fiduciary, or (iii) deposited to an account other than an account of the fiduciary, as such, or an account of the represented person.

§3—308. Proof of Signatures and Status as Holder in Due Course.

(a) In an action with respect to an instrument, the authenticity of, and authority to make, each signature on the instrument is admitted unless specifically denied in the pleadings. If the validity of a signature is denied in the pleadings, the burden of establishing validity is on the person claiming validity, but the signature is presumed to be authentic and authorized unless the action is to enforce the liability of the purported signer and the signer is dead or incompetent at the time of trial of the issue of validity of the signature. If an action to enforce the instrument is brought against a person as the undisclosed principal of a person who signed the instrument as a party to the instrument, the plaintiff has the burden of establishing that the defendant is liable on the instrument as a represented person under Section 3—402(a).

(b) If the validity of signatures is admitted or proved and there is compliance with subsection (a), a plaintiff producing the instrument is entitled to payment if the plaintiff proves entitlement to enforce the instrument under Section 3—301, unless the defendant proves a defense or claim in recoupment. If a defense or claim in recoupment is proved, the right to payment of the plaintiff is subject to the defense or claim, except to the extent the plaintiff proves that the plaintiff has rights of a holder in due course which are not subject to the defense or claim.

§3—309. Enforcement of Lost, Destroyed, or Stolen Instrument.

(a) A person not in possession of an instrument is entitled to enforce the instrument if (i) the person was in possession of the instrument and entitled to enforce it when loss of possession occurred, (ii) the loss of possession was not the result of a transfer by the person or a lawful seizure, and (iii) the person cannot reasonably obtain possession of the instrument because the instrument was destroyed, its whereabouts cannot be determined, or it is in the wrongful possession of an unknown person or a person that cannot be found or is not amenable to service of process.

(b) A person seeking enforcement of an instrument under subsection (a) must prove the terms of the instrument and the person's right to enforce the instrument. If that proof is made, Section 3—308 applies to the case as if the person seeking enforcement had produced the instrument. The court may not enter judgment in favor of the person seeking enforcement unless it finds that the person required to pay the instrument is adequately protected against loss that might occur by reason of a claim by another person to enforce the instrument. Adequate protection may be provided by any reasonable means.

§3—310. Effect of Instrument on Obligation for Which Taken.

(a) Unless otherwise agreed, if a certified check, cashier's check, or teller's check is taken for an obligation, the obligation is discharged to the same extent discharge would result if an amount of money equal to the amount of the instrument were taken in payment of the obligation. Discharge of the obligation does not affect any liability that the obligor may have as an indorser of the instrument.

(b) Unless otherwise agreed and except as provided in subsection (a), if a note or an uncertified check is taken for an obligation, the obligation is suspended to the same extent the obligation would be discharged if an amount of money equal to the amount of the instrument were taken, and the following rules apply:

(1) In the case of an uncertified check, suspension of the obligation continues until dishonor of the check or until it is paid or certified. Payment or certification of the check results in discharge of the obligation to the extent of the amount of the check.

(2) In the case of a note, suspension of the obligation continues until dishonor of the note or until it is paid. Payment of the note results in discharge of the obligation to the extent of the payment.

(3) Except as provided in paragraph (4), if the check or note is dishonored and the obligee of the obligation for

which the instrument was taken is the person entitled to enforce the instrument, the obligee may enforce either the instrument or the obligation. In the case of an instrument of a third person which is negotiated to the obligee by the obligor, discharge of the obligor on the instrument also discharges the obligation.

(4) If the person entitled to enforce the instrument taken for an obligation is a person other than the obligee, the obligee may not enforce the obligation to the extent the obligation is suspended. If the obligee is the person entitled to enforce the instrument but no longer has possession of it because it was lost, stolen, or destroyed, the obligation may not be enforced to the extent of the amount payable on the instrument, and to that extent the obligee's rights against the obligor are limited to enforcement of the instrument.

(c) If an instrument other than one described in subsection (a) or (b) is taken for an obligation, the effect is (i) that stated in subsection (a) if the instrument is one on which a bank is liable as maker or acceptor, or (ii) that stated in subsection (b) in any other case.

§3—311. Accord and Satisfaction by Use of Instrument.

(a) If a person against whom a claim is asserted proves that (i) that person in good faith tendered an instrument to the claimant as full satisfaction of the claim, (ii) the amount of the claim was unliquidated or subject to a bona fide dispute, and (iii) the claimant obtained payment of the instrument, the following subsections apply.

(b) Unless subsection (c) applies, the claim is discharged if the person against whom the claim is asserted proves that the instrument or an accompanying written communication contained a conspicuous statement to the effect that the instrument was tendered as full satisfaction of the claim.

(c) Subject to subsection (d), a claim is not discharged under subsection (b) if either of the following applies:

(1) The claimant, if an organization, proves that (i) within a reasonable time before the tender, the claimant sent a conspicuous statement to the person against whom the claim is asserted that communications concerning disputed debts, including an instrument tendered as full satisfaction of a debt, are to be sent to a designated person, office, or place, and (ii) the instrument or accompanying communication was not received by that designated person, office, or place.

(2) The claimant, whether or not an organization, proves that within 90 days after payment of the instrument, the claimant tendered repayment of the amount of the instrument to the person against whom the claim is asserted. This paragraph does not apply if the claimant is an organization that sent a statement complying with paragraph (1)(i).

(d) A claim is discharged if the person against whom the claim is asserted proves that within a reasonable time before collection of the instrument was initiated, the claimant, or an agent of the claimant having direct responsibility with respect to the disputed obligation, knew that the instrument was tendered in full satisfaction of the claim.

§3—312. Lost, Destroyed, or Stolen Cashier's Check, Teller's Check, or Certified Check.*

(a) In this section:

(1) "Check" means a cashier's check, teller's check, or certified check.

(2) "Claimant" means a person who claims the right to receive the amount of a cashier's check, teller's check, or certified check that was lost, destroyed, or stolen.

(3) "Declaration of loss" means a written statement, made under penalty of perjury, to the effect that (i) the declarer lost possession of a check, (ii) the declarer is the drawer or payee of the check, in the case of a certified check, or the remitter or payee of the check, in the case of a cashier's check or teller's check, (iii) the loss of possession was not the result of a transfer by the declarer or a lawful seizure, and (iv) the declarer cannot reasonably obtain possession of the check because the check was destroyed, its whereabouts cannot be determined, or it is in the wrongful possession of an unknown person or a person that cannot be found or is not amenable to service of process.

(4) "Obligated bank" means the issuer of a cashier's check or teller's check or the acceptor of a certified check.

(b) A claimant may assert a claim to the amount of a check by a communication to the obligated bank describing the check with reasonable certainty and requesting payment of the amount of the check, if (i) the claimant is the drawer or payee of a certified check or the remitter or payee of a cashier's check or teller's check, (ii) the communication contains or is accompanied by a declaration of loss of the claimant with respect to the check, (iii) the communication is received at a time and in a manner affording the bank a reasonable time to act on it before the check is paid, and (iv) the claimant provides reasonable identification if requested by the obligated bank. Delivery of a declaration of loss is a warranty of the truth of the statements made in the declaration. If a claim is asserted in compliance with this subsection, the following rules apply:

(1) The claim becomes enforceable at the later of (i) the time the claim is asserted, or (ii) the 90th day following the date of the check, in the case of a cashier's check or teller's check, or the 90th day following the date of the acceptance, in the case of a certified check.

(2) Until the claim becomes enforceable, it has no legal effect and the obligated bank may pay the check or, in the case of a teller's check, may permit the drawee to pay the check. Payment to a person entitled to enforce the check discharges all liability of the obligated bank with respect to the check.

(3) If the claim becomes enforceable before the check is presented for payment, the obligated bank is not obliged to pay the check.

(4) When the claim becomes enforceable, the obligated bank becomes obliged to pay the amount of the check to the claimant if payment of the check has not been made to a person entitled to enforce the check. Subject to Section 4—302(a)(1), payment to the claimant discharges all liability of the obligated bank with respect to the check.

(c) If the obligated bank pays the amount of a check to a claimant under subsection (b)(4) and the check is presented for payment by a person having rights of a holder in due course, the claimant is obliged to (i) refund the payment to the obligated bank if the check is paid, or (ii) pay the amount of the check to the person having rights of a holder in due course if the check is dishonored.

(d) If a claimant has the right to assert a claim under subsection (b) and is also a person entitled to enforce a cashier's check, teller's check, or certified check which is lost, destroyed, or stolen, the claimant may assert rights with respect to the check either under this section or Section 3—309.

Added in 1991.

PART 4 LIABILITY OF PARTIES

§3—401. Signature.

(a) A person is not liable on an instrument unless (i) the person signed the instrument, or (ii) the person is represented by an agent or representative who signed the instrument and the signature is binding on the represented person under Section 3—402.

(b) A signature may be made (i) manually or by means of a device or machine, and (ii) by the use of any name, including a trade or assumed name, or by a word, mark, or symbol executed or adopted by a person with present intention to authenticate a writing.

§3—402. Signature by Representative.

(a) If a person acting, or purporting to act, as a representative signs an instrument by signing either the name of the represented person or the name of the signer, the

---

*[Section 3—312 was not adopted as part of the 1990 Official Text of Revised Article 3. It was officially approved and recommended for enactment in all states in August 1991 by the National Conference of Commissioners on Uniform State Laws.]

represented person is bound by the signature to the same extent the represented person would be bound if the signature were on a simple contract. If the represented person is bound, the signature of the representative is the "authorized signature of the represented person" and the represented person is liable on the instrument, whether or not identified in the instrument.

(b) If a representative signs the name of the representative to an instrument and the signature is an authorized signature of the represented person, the following rules apply:

(1) If the form of the signature shows unambiguously that the signature is made on behalf of the represented person who is identified in the instrument, the representative is not liable on the instrument.

(2) Subject to subsection (c), if (i) the form of the signature does not show unambiguously that the signature is made in a representative capacity or (ii) the represented person is not identified in the instrument, the representative is liable on the instrument to a holder in due course that took the instrument without notice that the representative was not intended to be liable on the instrument. With respect to any other person, the representative is liable on the instrument unless the representative proves that the original parties did not intend the representative to be liable on the instrument.

(c) If a representative signs the name of the representative as drawer of a check without indication of the representative status and the check is payable from an account of the represented person who is identified on the check, the signer is not liable on the check if the signature is an authorized signature of the represented person.

§3−403. Unauthorized Signature.

(a) Unless otherwise provided in this Article or Article 4, an unauthorized signature is ineffective except as the signature of the unauthorized signer in favor of a person who in good faith pays the instrument or takes it for value. An unauthorized signature may be ratified for all purposes of this Article.

(b) If the signature of more than one person is required to constitute the authorized signature of an organization, the signature of the organization is unauthorized if one of the required signatures is lacking.

(c) The civil or criminal liability of a person who makes an unauthorized signature is not affected by any provision of this Article which makes the unauthorized signature effective for the purposes of this Article.

§3−404. Impostors; Fictitious Payees.

(a) If an impostor, by use of the mails or otherwise, induces the issuer of an instrument to issue the instrument to the impostor, or to a person acting in concert with the impostor, by impersonating the payee of the instrument or a person authorized to act for the payee, an indorsement of the instrument by any person in the name of the payee is effective as the indorsement of the payee in favor of a person who, in good faith, pays the instrument or takes it for value or for collection.

(b) If (i) a person whose intent determines to whom an instrument is payable (Section 3—110(a) or (b)) does not intend the person identified as payee to have any interest in the instrument, or (ii) the person identified as payee of an instrument is a fictitious person, the following rules apply until the instrument is negotiated by special indorsement:

(1) Any person in possession of the instrument is its holder.

(2) An indorsement by any person in the name of the payee stated in the instrument is effective as the indorsement of the payee in favor of a person who, in good faith, pays the instrument or takes it for value or for collection.

(c) Under subsection (a) or (b), an indorsement is made in the name of a payee if (i) it is made in a name substantially similar to that of the payee or (ii) the instrument, whether or not indorsed, is deposited in a depositary bank to an account in a name substantially similar to that of the payee.

(d) With respect to an instrument to which subsection (a) or (b) applies, if a person paying the instrument or taking it for value or for collection fails to exercise ordinary care in paying or taking the instrument and that failure substantially contributes to loss resulting from payment of the instrument, the person bearing the loss may recover from the person failing to exercise ordinary care to the extent the failure to exercise ordinary care contributed to the loss.

§3−405. Employer's Responsibility for Fraudulent Indorsement by Employee.

(a) In this section:

(1) "Employee" includes an independent contractor and employee of an independent contractor retained by the employer.

(2) "Fraudulent indorsement" means (i) in the case of an instrument payable to the employer, a forged indorsement purporting to be that of the employer, or (ii) in the case of an instrument with respect to which the employer is the issuer, a forged indorsement purporting to be that of the person identified as payee.

(3) "Responsibility" with respect to instruments means authority (i) to sign or indorse instruments on behalf of the employer, (ii) to process instruments received by the employer for bookkeeping purposes, for deposit to an account, or for other disposition, (iii) to prepare or process instruments for issue in the name of the employer, (iv) to supply information determining the names or addresses of payees of instruments to be issued in the name of the employer, (v) to control the disposition of instruments to be issued in the name of the employer, or (vi) to act otherwise with respect to instruments in a responsible capacity. "Responsibility" does not include authority that merely allows an employee to have access to instruments or blank or incomplete instrument forms

that are being stored or transported or are part of incoming or outgoing mail, or similar access.

(b) For the purpose of determining the rights and liabilities of a person who, in good faith, pays an instrument or takes it for value or for collection, if an employer entrusted an employee with responsibility with respect to the instrument and the employee or a person acting in concert with the employee makes a fraudulent indorsement of the instrument, the indorsement is effective as the indorsement of the person to whom the instrument is payable if it is made in the name of that person. If the person paying the instrument or taking it for value or for collection fails to exercise ordinary care in paying or taking the instrument and that failure substantially contributes to loss resulting from the fraud, the person bearing the loss may recover from the person failing to exercise ordinary care to the extent the failure to exercise ordinary care contributed to the loss.

(c) Under subsection (b), an indorsement is made in the name of the person to whom an instrument is payable if (i) it is made in a name substantially similar to the name of that person or (ii) the instrument, whether or not indorsed, is deposited in a depositary bank to an account in a name substantially similar to the name of that person.

§3—406. Negligence Contributing to Forged Signature or Alteration of Instrument.

(a) A person whose failure to exercise ordinary care substantially contributes to an alteration of an instrument or to the making of a forged signature on an instrument is precluded from asserting the alteration or the forgery against a person who, in good faith, pays the instrument or takes it for value or for collection.

(b) Under subsection (a), if the person asserting the preclusion fails to exercise ordinary care in paying or taking the instrument and that failure substantially contributes to loss, the loss is allocated between the person precluded and the person asserting the preclusion according to the extent to which the failure of each to exercise ordinary care contributed to the loss.

(c) Under subsection (a), the burden of proving failure to exercise ordinary care is on the person asserting the preclusion. Under subsection (b), the burden of proving failure to exercise ordinary care is on the person precluded.

§3—407. Alteration.

(a) "Alteration" means (i) an unauthorized change in an instrument that purports to modify in any respect the obligation of a party, or (ii) an unauthorized addition of words or numbers or other change to an incomplete instrument relating to the obligation of a party.

(b) Except as provided in subsection (c), an alteration fraudulently made discharges a party whose obligation is affected by the alteration unless that party assents or is precluded from asserting the alteration. No other alteration discharges a party, and the instrument may be enforced according to its original terms.

(c) A payor bank or drawee paying a fraudulently altered instrument or a person taking it for value, in good faith and without notice of the alteration, may enforce rights with respect to the instrument (i) according to its original terms, or (ii) in the case of an incomplete instrument altered by unauthorized completion, according to its terms as completed.

§3—408. Drawee Not Liable on Unaccepted Draft.
A check or other draft does not of itself operate as an assignment of funds in the hands of the drawee available for its payment, and the drawee is not liable on the instrument until the drawee accepts it.

§3—409. Acceptance of Draft; Certified Check.

(a) "Acceptance" means the drawee's signed agreement to pay a draft as presented. It must be written on the draft and may consist of the drawee's signature alone. Acceptance may be made at any time and becomes effective when notification pursuant to instructions is given or the accepted draft is delivered for the purpose of giving rights on the acceptance to any person.

(b) A draft may be accepted although it has not been signed by the drawer, is otherwise incomplete, is overdue, or has been dishonored.

(c) If a draft is payable at a fixed period after sight and the acceptor fails to date the acceptance, the holder may complete the acceptance by supplying a date in good faith.

(d) "Certified check" means a check accepted by the bank on which it is drawn. Acceptance may be made as stated in subsection (a) or by a writing on the check which indicates that the check is certified. The drawee of a check has no obligation to certify the check, and refusal to certify is not dishonor of the check.

§3—410. Acceptance Varying Draft.

(a) If the terms of a drawee's acceptance vary from the terms of the draft as presented, the holder may refuse the acceptance and treat the draft as dishonored. In that case, the drawee may cancel the acceptance.

(b) The terms of a draft are not varied by an acceptance to pay at a particular bank or place in the United States, unless the acceptance states that the draft is to be paid only at that bank or place.

(c) If the holder assents to an acceptance varying the terms of a draft, the obligation of each drawer and indorser that does not expressly assent to the acceptance is discharged.

§3—411. Refusal to Pay Cashier's Checks, Teller's Checks, and Certified Checks.

(a) In this section, "obligated bank" means the acceptor of a certified check or the issuer of a cashier's check or teller's check bought from the issuer.

(b) If the obligated bank wrongfully (i) refuses to pay a cashier's check or certified check, (ii) stops payment of a teller's check, or (iii) refuses to pay a dishonored teller's check, the person asserting the right to enforce the check is entitled to compensation for expenses and loss of interest resulting from the nonpayment and may recover consequential damages if the obligated bank refuses to pay after receiving notice of particular circumstances giving rise to the damages.

(c) Expenses or consequential damages under subsection (b) are not recoverable if the refusal of the obligated bank to pay occurs because (i) the bank suspends payments, (ii) the obligated bank asserts a claim or defense of the bank that it has reasonable grounds to believe is available against the person entitled to enforce the instrument, (iii) the obligated bank has a reasonable doubt whether the person demanding payment is the person entitled to enforce the instrument, or (iv) payment is prohibited by law.

§3—412. Obligation of Issuer of Note or Cashier's Check.

The issuer of a note or cashier's check or other draft drawn on the drawer is obliged to pay the instrument (i) according to its terms at the time it was issued or, if not issued, at the time it first came into possession of a holder, or (ii) if the issuer signed an incomplete instrument, according to its terms when completed, to the extent stated in Sections 3—115 and 3—407. The obligation is owed to a person entitled to enforce the instrument or to an indorser who paid the instrument under Section 3—415.

§3—413. Obligation of Acceptor.

(a) The acceptor of a draft is obliged to pay the draft (i) according to its terms at the time it was accepted, even though the acceptance states that the draft is payable "as originally drawn" or equivalent terms, (ii) if the acceptance varies the terms of the draft, according to the terms of the draft as varied, or (iii) if the acceptance is of a draft that is an incomplete instrument, according to its terms when completed, to the extent stated in Sections 3—115 and 3—407. The obligation is owed to a person entitled to enforce the draft or to the drawer or an indorser who paid the draft under Section 3—414 or 3—415.

(b) If the certification of a check or other acceptance of a draft states the amount certified or accepted, the obligation of the acceptor is that amount. If (i) the certification or acceptance does not state an amount, (ii) the amount of the instrument is subsequently raised, and (iii) the instrument is then negotiated to a holder in due course, the obligation of the acceptor is the amount of the instrument at the time it was taken by the holder in due course.

§3—414. Obligation of Drawer.

(a) This section does not apply to cashier's checks or other drafts drawn on the drawer.

(b) If an unaccepted draft is dishonored, the drawer is obliged to pay the draft (i) according to its terms at the time it was issued or, if not issued, at the time it first came into possession of a holder, or (ii) if the drawer signed an incomplete instrument, according to its terms when completed, to the

extent stated in Sections 3—115 and 3—407. The obligation is owed to a person entitled to enforce the draft or to an indorser who paid the draft under Section 3—415.

(c) If a draft is accepted by a bank, the drawer is discharged, regardless of when or by whom acceptance was obtained.

(d) If a draft is accepted and the acceptor is not a bank, the obligation of the drawer to pay the draft if the draft is dishonored by the acceptor is the same as the obligation of an indorser under Section 3—415(a) and (c).

(e) If a draft states that it is drawn "without recourse" or otherwise disclaims liability of the drawer to pay the draft, the drawer is not liable under subsection (b) to pay the draft if the draft is not a check. A disclaimer of the liability stated in subsection (b) is not effective if the draft is a check.

(f) If (i) a check is not presented for payment or given to a depositary bank for collection within 30 days after its date, (ii) the drawee suspends payments after expiration of the 30-day period without paying the check, and (iii) because of the suspension of payments, the drawer is deprived of funds maintained with the drawee to cover payment of the check, the drawer to the extent deprived of funds may discharge its obligation to pay the check by assigning to the person entitled to enforce the check the rights of the drawer against the drawee with respect to the funds.

§3—415. Obligation of Indorser.

(a) Subject to subsections (b), (c), and (d) and to Section 3—419(d), if an instrument is dishonored, an indorser is obliged to pay the amount due on the instrument (i) according to the terms of the instrument at the time it was indorsed, or (ii) if the indorser indorsed an incomplete instrument, according to its terms when completed, to the extent stated in Sections 3—115 and 3—407. The obligation of the indorser is owed to a person entitled to enforce the instrument or to a subsequent indorser who paid the instrument under this section.

(b) If an indorsement states that it is made "without recourse" or otherwise disclaims liability of the indorser, the indorser is not liable under subsection (a) to pay the instrument.

(c) If notice of dishonor of an instrument is required by Section 3—503 and notice of dishonor complying with that section is not given to an indorser, the liability of the indorser under subsection (a) is discharged.

(d) If a draft is accepted by a bank after an indorsement is made, the liability of the indorser under subsection (a) is discharged.

(e) If an indorser of a check is liable under subsection (a) and the check is not presented for payment, or given to a depositary bank for collection, within 30 days after the day the indorsement was made, the liability of the indorser under subsection (a) is discharged.

As amended in 1993.

§3—416. Transfer Warranties.

(a) A person who transfers an instrument for consideration warrants to the transferee and, if the transfer is by indorsement, to any subsequent transferee that:

(1) the warrantor is a person entitled to enforce the instrument;

(2) all signatures on the instrument are authentic and authorized;

(3) the instrument has not been altered;

(4) the instrument is not subject to a defense or claim in recoupment of any party which can be asserted against the warrantor; and

(5) the warrantor has no knowledge of any insolvency proceeding commenced with respect to the maker or acceptor or, in the case of an unaccepted draft, the drawer.

(b) A person to whom the warranties under subsection (a) are made and who took the instrument in good faith may recover from the warrantor as damages for breach of warranty an amount equal to the loss suffered as a result of the breach, but not more than the amount of the instrument plus expenses and loss of interest incurred as a result of the breach.

(c) The warranties stated in subsection (a) cannot be disclaimed with respect to checks. Unless notice of a claim for breach of warranty is given to the warrantor within 30 days after the claimant has reason to know of the breach and the identity of the warrantor, the liability of the warrantor under subsection (b) is discharged to the extent of any loss caused by the delay in giving notice of the claim.

(d) A [cause of action] for breach of warranty under this section accrues when the claimant has reason to know of the breach.

§3—417. Presentment Warranties.

(a) If an unaccepted draft is presented to the drawee for payment or acceptance and the drawee pays or accepts the draft, (i) the person obtaining payment or acceptance, at the time of presentment, and (ii) a previous transferor of the draft, at the time of transfer, warrant to the drawee making payment or accepting the draft in good faith that:

(1) the warrantor is, or was, at the time the warrantor transferred the draft, a person entitled to enforce the draft or authorized to obtain payment or acceptance of the draft on behalf of a person entitled to enforce the draft;

(2) the draft has not been altered; and

(3) the warrantor has no knowledge that the signature of the drawer of the draft is unauthorized.

(b) A drawee making payment may recover from any warrantor damages for breach of warranty equal to the amount paid by the drawee less the amount the drawee received or is entitled to receive from the drawer because of the payment.

In addition, the drawee is entitled to compensation for expenses and loss of interest resulting from the breach. The right of the drawee to recover damages under this subsection is not affected by any failure of the drawee to exercise ordinary care in making payment. If the drawee accepts the draft, breach of warranty is a defense to the obligation of the acceptor. If the acceptor makes payment with respect to the draft, the acceptor is entitled to recover from any warrantor for breach of warranty the amounts stated in this subsection.

(c) If a drawee asserts a claim for breach of warranty under subsection (a) based on an unauthorized indorsement of the draft or an alteration of the draft, the warrantor may defend by proving that the indorsement is effective under Section 3—404 or 3—405 or the drawer is precluded under Section 3—406 or 4—406 from asserting against the drawee the unauthorized indorsement or alteration.

(d) If (i) a dishonored draft is presented for payment to the drawer or an indorser or (ii) any other instrument is presented for payment to a party obliged to pay the instrument, and (iii) payment is received, the following rules apply:

(1) The person obtaining payment and a prior transferor of the instrument warrant to the person making payment in good faith that the warrantor is, or was, at the time the warrantor transferred the instrument, a person entitled to enforce the instrument or authorized to obtain payment on behalf of a person entitled to enforce the instrument.

(2) The person making payment may recover from any warrantor for breach of warranty an amount equal to the amount paid plus expenses and loss of interest resulting from the breach.

(e) The warranties stated in subsections (a) and (d) cannot be disclaimed with respect to checks. Unless notice of a claim for breach of warranty is given to the warrantor within 30 days after the claimant has reason to know of the breach and the identity of the warrantor, the liability of the warrantor under subsection (b) or (d) is discharged to the extent of any loss caused by the delay in giving notice of the claim.

(f) A [cause of action] for breach of warranty under this section accrues when the claimant has reason to know of the breach.

§3—418. Payment or Acceptance by Mistake.

(a) Except as provided in subsection (c), if the drawee of a draft pays or accepts the draft and the drawee acted on the mistaken belief that (i) payment of the draft had not been stopped pursuant to Section 4—403 or (ii) the signature of the drawer of the draft was authorized, the drawee may recover the amount of the draft from the person to whom or for whose benefit payment was made or, in the case of acceptance, may revoke the acceptance. Rights of the drawee under this subsection are not affected by failure of the drawee to exercise ordinary care in paying or accepting the draft.

(b) Except as provided in subsection (c), if an instrument has been paid or accepted by mistake and the case is not covered by subsection (a), the person paying or accepting may, to the extent permitted by the law governing mistake and restitution, (i) recover the payment from the person to whom or for whose benefit payment was made or (ii) in the case of acceptance, may revoke the acceptance.

(c) The remedies provided by subsection (a) or (b) may not be asserted against a person who took the instrument in good faith and for value or who in good faith changed position in reliance on the payment or acceptance. This subsection does not limit remedies provided by Section 3—417 or 4—407.

(d) Notwithstanding Section 4—215, if an instrument is paid or accepted by mistake and the payor or acceptor recovers payment or revokes acceptance under subsection (a) or (b), the instrument is deemed not to have been paid or accepted and is treated as dishonored, and the person from whom payment is recovered has rights as a person entitled to enforce the dishonored instrument.

§3—419. Instruments Signed for Accommodation.

(a) If an instrument is issued for value given for the benefit of a party to the instrument ("accommodated party") and another party to the instrument ("accommodation party") signs the instrument for the purpose of incurring liability on the instrument without being a direct beneficiary of the value given for the instrument, the instrument is signed by the accommodation party "for accommodation."

(b) An accommodation party may sign the instrument as maker, drawer, acceptor, or indorser and, subject to subsection (d), is obliged to pay the instrument in the capacity in which the accommodation party signs. The obligation of an accommodation party may be enforced notwithstanding any statute of frauds and whether or not the accommodation party receives consideration for the accommodation.

(c) A person signing an instrument is presumed to be an accommodation party and there is notice that the instrument is signed for accommodation if the signature is an anomalous indorsement or is accompanied by words indicating that the signer is acting as surety or guarantor with respect to the obligation of another party to the instrument. Except as provided in Section 3—605, the obligation of an accommodation party to pay the instrument is not affected by the fact that the person enforcing the obligation had notice when the instrument was taken by that person that the accommodation party signed the instrument for accommodation.

(d) If the signature of a party to an instrument is accompanied by words indicating unambiguously that the party is guaranteeing collection rather than payment of the obligation of another party to the instrument, the signer is obliged to pay the amount due on the instrument to a person entitled to enforce the instrument only if (i) execution of judgment against the other party has been returned unsatisfied,

(ii) the other party is insolvent or in an insolvency proceeding, (iii) the other party cannot be served with process, or (iv) it is otherwise apparent that payment cannot be obtained from the other party.

(e) An accommodation party who pays the instrument is entitled to reimbursement from the accommodated party and is entitled to enforce the instrument against the accommodated party. An accommodated party who pays the instrument has no right of recourse against, and is not entitled to contribution from, an accommodation party.

§3—420. Conversion of Instrument.

(a) The law applicable to conversion of personal property applies to instruments. An instrument is also converted if it is taken by transfer, other than a negotiation, from a person not entitled to enforce the instrument or a bank makes or obtains payment with respect to the instrument for a person not entitled to enforce the instrument or receive payment. An action for conversion of an instrument may not be brought by (i) the issuer or acceptor of the instrument or (ii) a payee or indorsee who did not receive delivery of the instrument either directly or through delivery to an agent or a co-payee.

(b) In an action under subsection (a), the measure of liability is presumed to be the amount payable on the instrument, but recovery may not exceed the amount of the plaintiff's interest in the instrument.

(c) A representative, other than a depositary bank, who has in good faith dealt with an instrument or its proceeds on behalf of one who was not the person entitled to enforce the instrument is not liable in conversion to that person beyond the amount of any proceeds that it has not paid out.

PART 5 DISHONOR

§3—501. Presentment.

(a) "Presentment" means a demand made by or on behalf of a person entitled to enforce an instrument (i) to pay the instrument made to the drawee or a party obliged to pay the instrument or, in the case of a note or accepted draft payable at a bank, to the bank, or (ii) to accept a draft made to the drawee.

(b) The following rules are subject to Article 4, agreement of the parties, and clearing-house rules and the like:

> (1) Presentment may be made at the place of payment of the instrument and must be made at the place of payment if the instrument is payable at a bank in the United States; may be made by any commercially reasonable means, including an oral, written, or electronic communication; is effective when the demand for payment or acceptance is received by the person to whom presentment is made; and is effective if made to any one of two or more makers, acceptors, drawees, or other payors.

(2) Upon demand of the person to whom presentment is made, the person making presentment must (i) exhibit the instrument, (ii) give reasonable identification and, if presentment is made on behalf of another person, reasonable evidence of authority to do so, and (. . .) sign a receipt on the instrument for any payment made or surrender the instrument if full payment is made.

(3) Without dishonoring the instrument, the party to whom presentment is made may (i) return the instrument for lack of a necessary indorsement, or (ii) refuse payment or acceptance for failure of the presentment to comply with the terms of the instrument, an agreement of the parties, or other applicable law or rule.

(4) The party to whom presentment is made may treat presentment as occurring on the next business day after the day of presentment if the party to whom presentment is made has established a cut-off hour not earlier than 2 P.M. for the receipt and processing of instruments presented for payment or acceptance and presentment is made after the cut-off hour.

§3—502. Dishonor.

(a) Dishonor of a note is governed by the following rules:
(1) If the note is payable on demand, the note is dishonored if presentment is duly made to the maker and the note is not paid on the day of presentment.
(2) If the note is not payable on demand and is payable at or through a bank or the terms of the note require presentment, the note is dishonored if presentment is duly made and the note is not paid on the day it becomes payable or the day of presentment, whichever is later.
(3) If the note is not payable on demand and paragraph (2) does not apply, the note is dishonored if it is not paid on the day it becomes payable.

(b) Dishonor of an unaccepted draft other than a documentary draft is governed by the following rules:
(1) If a check is duly presented for payment to the payor bank otherwise than for immediate payment over the counter, the check is dishonored if the payor bank makes timely return of the check or sends timely notice of dishonor or nonpayment under Section 4—301 or 4—302, or becomes accountable for the amount of the check under Section 4—302.
(2) If a draft is payable on demand and paragraph (1) does not apply, the draft is dishonored if presentment for payment is duly made to the drawee and the draft is not paid on the day of presentment.
(3) If a draft is payable on a date stated in the draft, the draft is dishonored if (i) presentment for payment is duly made to the drawee and payment is not made on the day the draft becomes payable or the day of presentment, whichever is later, or (ii) presentment for acceptance is duly made before the day the draft becomes

payable and the draft is not accepted on the day of presentment.
(4) If a draft is payable on elapse of a period of time after sight or acceptance, the draft is dishonored if presentment for acceptance is duly made and the draft is not accepted on the day of presentment.

(c) Dishonor of an unaccepted documentary draft occurs according to the rules stated in subsection (b)(2), (3), and (4), except that payment or acceptance may be delayed without dishonor until no later than the close of the third business day of the drawee following the day on which payment or acceptance is required by those paragraphs.

(d) Dishonor of an accepted draft is governed by the following rules:
(1) If the draft is payable on demand, the draft is dishonored if presentment for payment is duly made to the acceptor and the draft is not paid on the day of presentment.
(2) If the draft is not payable on demand, the draft is dishonored if presentment for payment is duly made to the acceptor and payment is not made on the day it becomes payable or the day of presentment, whichever is later.

(e) In any case in which presentment is otherwise required for dishonor under this section and presentment is excused under Section 3—504, dishonor occurs without presentment if the instrument is not duly accepted or paid.

(f) If a draft is dishonored because timely acceptance of the draft was not made and the person entitled to demand acceptance consents to a late acceptance, from the time of acceptance the draft is treated as never having been dishonored.

§3—503. Notice of Dishonor.

(a) The obligation of an indorser stated in Section 3—415(a) and the obligation of a drawer stated in Section 3—414(d) may not be enforced unless (i) the indorser or drawer is given notice of dishonor of the instrument complying with this section or (ii) notice of dishonor is excused under Section 3—504(b).

(b) Notice of dishonor may be given by any person; may be given by any commercially reasonable means, including an oral, written, or electronic communication; and is sufficient if it reasonably identifies the instrument and indicates that the instrument has been dishonored or has not been paid or accepted. Return of an instrument given to a bank for collection is sufficient notice of dishonor.

(c) Subject to Section 3—504(c), with respect to an instrument taken for collection by a collecting bank, notice of dishonor must be given (i) by the bank before midnight of the next banking day following the banking day on which the bank receives notice of dishonor of the instrument, or (ii) by any other person within 30 days following the day on which the person receives notice of dishonor. With respect to any other instrument, notice of dishonor must be given within 30 days following the day on which dishonor occurs.

§3—504. Excused Presentment and Notice of Dishonor.

(a) Presentment for payment or acceptance of an instrument is excused if (i) the person entitled to present the instrument cannot with reasonable diligence make presentment, (ii) the maker or acceptor has repudiated an obligation to pay the instrument or is dead or in insolvency proceedings, (iii) by the terms of the instrument presentment is not necessary to enforce the obligation of indorsers or the drawer, (iv) the drawer or indorser whose obligation is being enforced has waived presentment or otherwise has no reason to expect or right to require that the instrument be paid or accepted, or (v) the drawer instructed the drawee not to pay or accept the draft or the drawee was not obligated to the drawer to pay the draft.

(b) Notice of dishonor is excused if (i) by the terms of the instrument notice of dishonor is not necessary to enforce the obligation of a party to pay the instrument, or (ii) the party whose obligation is being enforced waived notice of dishonor. A waiver of presentment is also a waiver of notice of dishonor.

(c) Delay in giving notice of dishonor is excused if the delay was caused by circumstances beyond the control of the person giving the notice and the person giving the notice exercised reasonable diligence after the cause of the delay ceased to operate.

§3—505. Evidence of Dishonor.

(a) The following are admissible as evidence and create a presumption of dishonor and of any notice of dishonor stated:

    (1) a document regular in form as provided in subsection (b) which purports to be a protest;

    (2) a purported stamp or writing of the drawee, payor bank, or presenting bank on or accompanying the instrument stating that acceptance or payment has been refused unless reasons for the refusal are stated and the reasons are not consistent with dishonor;

    (3) a book or record of the drawee, payor bank, or collecting bank, kept in the usual course of business which shows dishonor, even if there is no evidence of who made the entry.

(b) A protest is a certificate of dishonor made by a United States consul or vice consul, or a notary public or other person authorized to administer oaths by the law of the place where dishonor occurs. It may be made upon information satisfactory to that person. The protest must identify the instrument and certify either that presentment has been made or, if not made, the reason why it was not made, and that the instrument has been dishonored by nonacceptance

or nonpayment. The protest may also certify that notice of dishonor has been given to some or all parties.

PART 6 DISCHARGE AND PAYMENT

§3—601. Discharge and Effect of Discharge.

(a) The obligation of a party to pay the instrument is discharged as stated in this Article or by an act or agreement with the party which would discharge an obligation to pay money under a simple contract.

(b) Discharge of the obligation of a party is not effective against a person acquiring rights of a holder in due course of the instrument without notice of the discharge.

§3—602. Payment.

(a) Subject to subsection (b), an instrument is paid to the extent payment is made (i) by or on behalf of a party obliged to pay the instrument, and (ii) to a person entitled to enforce the instrument. To the extent of the payment, the obligation of the party obliged to pay the instrument is discharged even though payment is made with knowledge of a claim to the instrument under Section 3—306 by another person.

(b) The obligation of a party to pay the instrument is not discharged under subsection (a) if:

    (1) a claim to the instrument under Section 3—306 is enforceable against the party receiving payment and (i) payment is made with knowledge by the payor that payment is prohibited by injunction or similar process of a court of competent jurisdiction, or (ii) in the case of an instrument other than a cashier's check, teller's check, or certified check, the party making payment accepted, from the person having a claim to the instrument, indemnity against loss resulting from refusal to pay the person entitled to enforce the instrument; or

    (2) the person making payment knows that the instrument is a stolen instrument and pays a person it knows is in wrongful possession of the instrument.

§3—603. Tender of Payment.

(a) If tender of payment of an obligation to pay an instrument is made to a person entitled to enforce the instrument, the effect of tender is governed by principles of law applicable to tender of payment under a simple contract.

(b) If tender of payment of an obligation to pay an instrument is made to a person entitled to enforce the instrument and the tender is refused, there is discharge, to the extent of the amount of the tender, of the obligation of an indorser or accommodation party having a right of recourse with respect to the obligation to which the tender relates.

(c) If tender of payment of an amount due on an instrument is made to a person entitled to enforce the instrument, the obligation of the obligor to pay interest after the due date on the amount tendered is discharged. If presentment is required with respect to an instrument and the obligor is able and ready to pay on the due date at every place of payment stated in the instrument, the obligor is deemed to have made tender of payment on the due date to the person entitled to enforce the instrument.

§3—604. Discharge by Cancellation or Renunciation.

(a) A person entitled to enforce an instrument, with or without consideration, may discharge the obligation of a party to pay the instrument (i) by an intentional voluntary act, such as surrender of the instrument to the party, destruction, mutilation, or cancellation of the instrument, cancellation or striking out of the party's signature, or the addition of words to the instrument indicating discharge, or (ii) by agreeing not to sue or otherwise renouncing rights against the party by a signed writing.

(b) Cancellation or striking out of an indorsement pursuant to subsection (a) does not affect the status and rights of a party derived from the indorsement.

§3—605. Discharge of Indorsers and Accommodation Parties.

(a) In this section, the term "indorser" includes a drawer having the obligation described in Section 3—414(d).

(b) Discharge, under Section 3—604, of the obligation of a party to pay an instrument does not discharge the obligation of an indorser or accommodation party having a right of recourse against the discharged party.

(c) If a person entitled to enforce an instrument agrees, with or without consideration, to an extension of the due date of the obligation of a party to pay the instrument, the extension discharges an indorser or accommodation party having a right of recourse against the party whose obligation is extended to the extent the indorser or accommodation party proves that the extension caused loss to the indorser or accommodation party with respect to the right of recourse.

(d) If a person entitled to enforce an instrument agrees, with or without consideration, to a material modification of the obligation of a party other than an extension of the due date, the modification discharges the obligation of an indorser or accommodation party having a right of recourse against the person whose obligation is modified to the extent the modification causes loss to the indorser or accommodation party with respect to the right of recourse. The loss suffered by the indorser or accommodation party as a result of the modification is equal to the amount of the right of recourse unless the person enforcing the instrument proves that no loss was caused by the modification or that the loss caused by the modification was an amount less than the amount of the right of recourse.

(e) If the obligation of a party to pay an instrument is secured by an interest in collateral and a person entitled to enforce the instrument impairs the value of the interest in collateral, the obligation of an indorser or accommodation party having a right of recourse against the obligor is discharged to the extent of the impairment. The value of an interest in collateral is impaired to the extent (i) the value of the interest is reduced to an amount less than the amount of the right of recourse of the party asserting discharge, or (ii) the reduction in value of the interest causes an increase in the amount by which the amount of the right of recourse exceeds the value of the interest. The burden of proving impairment is on the party asserting discharge.

(f) If the obligation of a party is secured by an interest in collateral not provided by an accommodation party and a person entitled to enforce the instrument impairs the value of the interest in collateral, the obligation of any party who is jointly and severally liable with respect to the secured obligation is discharged to the extent the impairment causes the party asserting discharge to pay more than that party would have been obliged to pay, taking into account rights of contribution, if impairment had not occurred. If the party asserting discharge is an accommodation party not entitled to discharge under subsection (e), the party is deemed to have a right to contribution based on joint and several liability rather than a right to reimbursement. The burden of proving impairment is on the party asserting discharge.

(g) Under subsection (e) or (f), impairing value of an interest in collateral includes (i) failure to obtain or maintain perfection or recordation of the interest in collateral, (ii) release of collateral without substitution of collateral of equal value, (iii) failure to perform a duty to preserve the value of collateral owed, under Article 9 or other law, to a debtor or surety or other person secondarily liable, or (iv) failure to comply with applicable law in disposing of collateral.

(h) An accommodation party is not discharged under subsection (c), (d), or (e) unless the person entitled to enforce the instrument knows of the accommodation or has notice under Section 3—419(c) that the instrument was signed for accommodation.

(i) A party is not discharged under this section if (i) the party asserting discharge consents to the event or conduct that is the basis of the discharge, or (ii) the instrument or a separate agreement of the party provides for waiver of discharge under this section either specifically or by general language indicating that parties waive defenses based on suretyship or impairment of collateral.

> ADDENDUM TO REVISED ARTICLE 3 NOTES TO LEGISLATIVE COUNSEL

1. If revised Article 3 is adopted in your state, the reference in Section 2—511 to Section 3—802 should be changed to Section 3—310.

2. If revised Article 3 is adopted in your state and the Uniform Fiduciaries Act is also in effect in your state, you may want to consider amending Uniform Fiduciaries Act @3:§9 to conform to Section 3—307(b)(2)(iii) and (4)(iii). See Official Comment 3 to Section 3—307.

> REVISED ARTICLE 4 BANK DEPOSITS AND COLLECTIONS

PART 1 GENERAL PROVISIONS AND DEFINITIONS

§4—101. Short Title. This Article may be cited as Uniform Commercial Code—Bank Deposits and Collections. As amended in 1990.

§4—102. Applicability.

(a) To the extent that items within this Article are also within Articles 3 and 8, they are subject to those Articles. If there is conflict, this Article governs Article 3, but Article 8 governs this Article.

(b) The liability of a bank for action or non-action with respect to an item handled by it for purposes of presentment, payment, or collection is governed by the law of the place where the bank is located. In the case of action or non-action by or at a branch or separate office of a bank, its liability is governed by the law of the place where the branch or separate office is located.

§4—103. Variation by Agreement; Measure of Damages; Action Constituting Ordinary Care.

(a) The effect of the provisions of this Article may be varied by agreement, but the parties to the agreement cannot disclaim a bank's responsibility for its lack of good faith or failure to exercise ordinary care or limit the measure of damages for the lack or failure. However, the parties may determine by agreement the standards by which the bank's responsibility is to be measured if those standards are not manifestly unreasonable.

(b) Federal Reserve regulations and operating circulars, clearing-house rules, and the like have the effect of agreements under subsection (a), whether or not specifically assented to by all parties interested in items handled.

(c) Action or non-action approved by this Article or pursuant to Federal Reserve regulations or operating circulars is the exercise of ordinary care and, in the absence of special instructions, action or non-action consistent with clearing-house rules and the like or with a general banking usage not disapproved by this Article, is prima facie the exercise of ordinary care.

(d) The specification or approval of certain procedures by this Article is not disapproval of other procedures that may be reasonable under the circumstances.

(e) The measure of damages for failure to exercise ordinary care in handling an item is the amount of the item reduced by an amount that could not have been realized by the exercise of ordinary care. If there is also bad faith it includes any other damages the party suffered as a proximate consequence.
As amended in 1990.

§4—104. Definitions and Index of Definitions.

(a) In this Article, unless the context otherwise requires:
(1) "Account" means any deposit or credit account with a bank, including a demand, time, savings, passbook, share draft, or like account, other than an account evidenced by a certificate of deposit;
(2) "Afternoon" means the period of a day between noon and midnight;
(3) "Banking day" means the part of a day on which a bank is open to the public for carrying on substantially all of its banking functions;
(4) "Clearing house" means an association of banks or other payors regularly clearing items;
(5) "Customer" means a person having an account with a bank or for whom a bank has agreed to collect items, including a bank that maintains an account at another bank;
(6) "Documentary draft" means a draft to be presented for acceptance or payment if specified documents, certificated securities (Section 8—102) or instructions for uncertificated securities (Section 8—102), or other certificates, statements, or the like are to be received by the drawee or other payor before acceptance or payment of the draft;
(7) "Draft" means a draft as defined in Section 3—104 or an item, other than an instrument, that is an order;
(8) "Drawee" means a person ordered in a draft to make payment;
(9) "Item" means an instrument or a promise or order to pay money handled by a bank for collection or payment. The term does not include a payment order governed by Article 4A or a credit or debit card slip;
(10) "Midnight deadline" with respect to a bank is midnight on its next banking day following the banking day on which it receives the relevant item or notice or from which the time for taking action commences to run, whichever is later;
(11) "Settle" means to pay in cash, by clearing-house settlement, in a charge or credit or by remittance, or otherwise as agreed. A settlement may be either provisional or final;
(12) "Suspends payments" with respect to a bank means that it has been closed by order of the supervisory authorities, that a public officer has been appointed to take it over, or that it ceases or refuses to make payments in the ordinary course of business.

(b) [Other definitions' section references deleted.]

(c) [Other definitions' section references deleted.]

(d) In addition, Article 1 contains general definitions and principles of construction and interpretation applicable throughout this Article.

§4—105. "Bank"; "Depositary Bank"; "Payor Bank"; "Intermediary Bank"; "Collecting Bank"; "Presenting Bank". In this Article:

(1) "Bank" means a person engaged in the business of banking, including a savings bank, savings and loan association, credit union, or trust company;

(2) "Depositary bank" means the first bank to take an item even though it is also the payor bank, unless the item is presented for immediate payment over the counter;

(3) "Payor bank" means a bank that is the drawee of a draft;

(4) "Intermediary bank" means a bank to which an item is transferred in course of collection except the depositary or payor bank;

(5) "Collecting bank" means a bank handling an item for collection except the payor bank;

(6) "Presenting bank" means a bank presenting an item except a payor bank.

§4—106. Payable Through or Payable at Bank: Collecting Bank.

(a) If an item states that it is "payable through" a bank identified in the item, (i) the item designates the bank as a collecting bank and does not by itself authorize the bank to pay the item, and (ii) the item may be presented for payment only by or through the bank.

ALTERNATIVE A

(b) If an item states that it is "payable at" a bank identified in the item, the item is equivalent to a draft drawn on the bank.

ALTERNATIVE B

(b) If an item states that it is "payable at" a bank identified in the item, (i) the item designates the bank as a collecting bank and does not by itself authorize the bank to pay the item, and (ii) the item may be presented for payment only by or through the bank.

(c) If a draft names a nonbank drawee and it is unclear whether a bank named in the draft is a co-drawee or a collecting bank, the bank is a collecting bank.

As added in 1990.

§4—107. Separate Office of Bank. A branch or separate office of a bank is a separate bank for the purpose of computing the time within which and determining the place at

or to which action may be taken or notices or orders shall be given under this Article and under Article 3.

As amended in 1962 and 1990.

§4—108. Time of Receipt of Items.

(a) For the purpose of allowing time to process items, prove balances, and make the necessary entries on its books to determine its position for the day, a bank may fix an afternoon hour of 2 P.M. or later as a cutoff hour for the handling of money and items and the making of entries on its books.

(b) An item or deposit of money received on any day after a cutoff hour so fixed or after the close of the banking day may be treated as being received at the opening of the next banking day.

As amended in 1990.

§4—109. Delays.

(a) Unless otherwise instructed, a collecting bank in a good faith effort to secure payment of a specific item drawn on a payor other than a bank, and with or without the approval of any person involved, may waive, modify, or extend time limits imposed or permitted by this [act] for a period not exceeding two additional banking days without discharge of drawers or indorsers or liability to its transferor or a prior party.

(b) Delay by a collecting bank or payor bank beyond time limits prescribed or permitted by this [act] or by instructions is excused if (i) the delay is caused by interruption of communication or computer facilities, suspension of payments by another bank, war, emergency conditions, failure of equipment, or other circumstances beyond the control of the bank, and (ii) the bank exercises such diligence as the circumstances require.

§4—110. Electronic Presentment.

(a) "Agreement for electronic presentment" means an agreement, clearing-house rule, or Federal Reserve regulation or operating circular, providing that presentment of an item may be made by transmission of an image of an item or information describing the item ("presentment notice") rather than delivery of the item itself. The agreement may provide for procedures governing retention, presentment, payment, dishonor, and other matters concerning items subject to the agreement.

(b) Presentment of an item pursuant to an agreement for presentment is made when the presentment notice is received.

(c) If presentment is made by presentment notice, a reference to "item" or "check" in this Article means the presentment notice unless the context otherwise indicates.

As added in 1990.

§4—111. Statute of Limitations. An action to enforce an obligation, duty, or right arising under this Article must be

commenced within three years after the [cause of action] accrues.

As added in 1990.

PART 2 COLLECTION OF ITEMS: DEPOSITARY AND COLLECTING BANKS

§4—201. Status of Collecting Bank as Agent and Provisional Status of Credits; Applicability of Article; Item Indorsed "Pay Any Bank".

(a) Unless a contrary intent clearly appears and before the time that a settlement given by a collecting bank for an item is or becomes final, the bank, with respect to an item, is an agent or sub-agent of the owner of the item and any settlement given for the item is provisional. This provision applies regardless of the form of indorsement or lack of indorsement and even though credit given for the item is subject to immediate withdrawal as of right or is in fact withdrawn; but the continuance of ownership of an item by its owner and any rights of the owner to proceeds of the item are subject to rights of a collecting bank, such as those resulting from outstanding advances on the item and rights of recoupment or setoff. If an item is handled by banks for purposes of presentment, payment, collection, or return, the relevant provisions of this Article apply even though action of the parties clearly establishes that a particular bank has purchased the item and is the owner of it.

(b) After an item has been indorsed with the words "pay any bank" or the like, only a bank may acquire the rights of a holder until the item has been:

(1) returned to the customer initiating collection; or

(2) specially indorsed by a bank to a person who is not a bank.

As amended in 1990.

§4—202. Responsibility for Collection or Return; When Action Timely.

(a) A collecting bank must exercise ordinary care in:

(1) presenting an item or sending it for presentment;

(2) sending notice of dishonor or nonpayment or returning an item other than a documentary draft to the bank's transferor after learning that the item has not been paid or accepted, as the case may be;

(3) settling for an item when the bank receives final settlement; and

(4) notifying its transferor of any loss or delay in transit within a reasonable time after discovery thereof.

(b) A collecting bank exercises ordinary care under subsection (a) by taking proper action before its midnight deadline following receipt of an item, notice, or settlement. Taking proper action within a reasonably longer time may constitute the exercise of ordinary care, but the bank has the burden of establishing timeliness.

(c) Subject to subsection (a)(1), a bank is not liable for the insolvency, neglect, misconduct, mistake, or default of another bank or person or for loss or destruction of an item in the possession of others or in transit.

As amended in 1990.

§4—203. Effect of Instructions.

Subject to Article 3 concerning conversion of instruments (Section 3—420) and restrictive indorsements (Section 3—206), only a collecting bank's transferor can give instructions that affect the bank or constitute notice to it, and a collecting bank is not liable to prior parties for any action taken pursuant to the instructions or in accordance with any agreement with its transferor.

§4—204. Methods of Sending and Presenting; Sending Directly to Payor Bank.

(a) A collecting bank shall send items by a reasonably prompt method, taking into consideration relevant instructions, the nature of the item, the number of those items on hand, the cost of collection involved, and the method generally used by it or others to present those items.

(b) A collecting bank may send:

(1) an item directly to the payor bank;

(2) an item to a nonbank payor if authorized by its transferor; and

(3) an item other than documentary drafts to a nonbank payor, if authorized by Federal Reserve regulation or operating circular, clearing-house rule, or the like.

(c) Presentment may be made by a presenting bank at a place where the payor bank or other payor has requested that presentment be made.

As amended in 1990.

§4—205. Depositary Bank Holder of Unindorsed Item.

If a customer delivers an item to a depositary bank for collection:

(1) the depositary bank becomes a holder of the item at the time it receives the item for collection if the customer at the time of delivery was a holder of the item, whether or not the customer indorses the item, and, if the bank satisfies the other requirements of Section 3—302, it is a holder in due course; and

(2) the depositary bank warrants to collecting banks, the payor bank or other payor, and the drawer that the amount of the item was paid to the customer or deposited to the customer's account.

As amended in 1990.

§4—206. Transfer Between Banks.

Any agreed method that identifies the transferor bank is sufficient for the item's further transfer to another bank.

As amended in 1990.

§4—207. Transfer Warranties.

(a) A customer or collecting bank that transfers an item and receives a settlement or other consideration warrants to the transferee and to any subsequent collecting bank that:

(1) the warrantor is a person entitled to enforce the item;

(2) all signatures on the item are authentic andauthorized;

(3) the item has not been altered;

(4) the item is not subject to a defense or claim in recoupment (Section 3—305(a)) of any party that can be asserted against the warrantor; and

(5) the warrantor has no knowledge of any insolvency proceeding commenced with respect to the maker or acceptor or, in the case of an unaccepted draft, the drawer.

(b) If an item is dishonored, a customer or collecting bank transferring the item and receiving settlement or other consideration is obliged to pay the amount due on the item (i) according to the terms of the item at the time it was transferred, or (ii) if the transfer was of an incomplete item, according to its terms when completed as stated in Sections 3—115 and 3—407. The obligation of a transferor is owed to the transferee and to any subsequent collecting bank that takes the item in good faith. A transferor cannot disclaim its obligation under this subsection by an indorsement stating that it is made "without recourse" or otherwise disclaiming liability.

(c) A person to whom the warranties under subsection (a) are made and who took the item in good faith may recover from the warrantor as damages for breach of warranty an amount equal to the loss suffered as a result of the breach, but not more than the amount of the item plus expenses and loss of interest incurred as a result of the breach.

(d) The warranties stated in subsection (a) cannot be disclaimed with respect to checks. Unless notice of a claim for breach of warranty is given to the warrantor within 30 days after the claimant has reason to know of the breach and the identity of the warrantor, the warrantor is discharged to the extent of any loss caused by the delay in giving notice of the claim.

(e) A cause of action for breach of warranty under this section accrues when the claimant has reason to know of the breach.

As amended in 1990.

§4—208. Presentment Warranties.

(a) If an unaccepted draft is presented to the drawee for payment or acceptance and the drawee pays or accepts the draft, (i) the person obtaining payment or acceptance, at the time of presentment, and (ii) a previous transferor of the draft, at the time of transfer, warrant to the drawee that pays or accepts the draft in good faith that:

(1) the warrantor is, or was, at the time the warrantor transferred the draft, a person entitled to enforce the draft or authorized to obtain payment or acceptance of the draft on behalf of a person entitled to enforce the draft;

(2) the draft has not been altered; and

(3) the warrantor has no knowledge that the signature of the purported drawer of the draft is unauthorized.

(b) A drawee making payment may recover from a warrantor damages for breach of warranty equal to the amount paid by the drawee less the amount the drawee received or is entitled to receive from the drawer because of the payment. In addition, the drawee is entitled to compensation for expenses and loss of interest resulting from the breach. The right of the drawee to recover damages under this subsection is not affected by any failure of the drawee to exercise ordinary care in making payment. If the drawee accepts the draft (i) breach of warranty is a defense to the obligation of the acceptor, and (ii) if the acceptor makes payment with respect to the draft, the acceptor is entitled to recover from a warrantor for breach of warranty the amounts stated in this subsection.

(c) If a drawee asserts a claim for breach of warranty under subsection (a) based on an unauthorized indorsement of the draft or an alteration of the draft, the warrantor may defend by proving that the indorsement is effective under Section 3—404 or 3—405 or the drawer is precluded under Section 3—406 or 4—406 from asserting against the drawee the unauthorized indorsement or alteration.

(d) If (i) a dishonored draft is presented for payment to the drawer or an indorser or (ii) any other item is presented for payment to a party obliged to pay the item, and the item is paid, the person obtaining payment and a prior transferor of the item warrant to the person making payment in good faith that the warrantor is, or was, at the time the warrantor transferred the item, a person entitled to enforce the item or authorized to obtain payment on behalf of a person entitled to enforce the item. The person making payment may recover from any warrantor for breach of warranty an amount equal to the amount paid plus expenses and loss of interest resulting from the breach.

(e) The warranties stated in subsections (a) and (d) cannot be disclaimed with respect to checks. Unless notice of a claim for breach of warranty is given to the warrantor within 30 days after the claimant has reason to know of the breach and the identity of the warrantor, the warrantor is discharged to the extent of any loss caused by the delay in giving notice of the claim.

(f) A cause of action for breach of warranty under this section accrues when the claimant has reason to know of the breach.

As amended in 1990.

§4—209. Encoding and Retention Warranties.

(a) A person who encodes information on or with respect to an item after issue warrants to any subsequent collecting bank and to the payor bank or other payor that the information is correctly encoded. If the customer of a depositary bank encodes, that bank also makes the warranty.

(b) A person who undertakes to retain an item pursuant to an agreement for electronic presentment warrants to any subsequent collecting bank and to the payor bank or other payor that retention and presentment of the item comply with the agreement. If a customer of a depositary bank undertakes to retain an item, that bank also makes this warranty.

(c) A person to whom warranties are made under this section and who took the item in good faith may recover from the warrantor as damages for breach of warranty an amount equal to the loss suffered as a result of the breach, plus expenses and loss of interest incurred as a result of the breach. As added in 1990.

§4—210. Security Interest of Collecting Bank in Items, Accompanying Documents and Proceeds.

(a) A collecting bank has a security interest in an item and any accompanying documents or the proceeds of either:

(1) in case of an item deposited in an account, to the extent to which credit given for the item has been withdrawn or applied;

(2) in case of an item for which it has given credit available for withdrawal as of right, to the extent of the credit given, whether or not the credit is drawn upon or there is a right of charge-back; or

(3) if it makes an advance on or against the item.

(b) If credit given for several items received at one time or pursuant to a single agreement is withdrawn or applied in part, the security interest remains upon all the items, any accompanying documents or the proceeds of either. For the purpose of this section, credits first given are first withdrawn.

(c) Receipt by a collecting bank of a final settlement for an item is a realization on its security interest in the item, accompanying documents, and proceeds. So long as the bank does not receive final settlement for the item or give up possession of the item or accompanying documents for purposes other than collection, the security interest continues to that extent and is subject to Article 9, but:

(1) no security agreement is necessary to make the security interest enforceable (Section 9—203(1)(a));

(2) no filing is required to perfect the security interest; and

(3) the security interest has priority over conflicting perfected security interests in the item, accompanying documents, or proceeds.

As amended in 1990 and 1999.

§4—211. When Bank Gives Value for Purposes of Holder in Due Course.
For purposes of determining its status as a holder in due course, a bank has given value to the extent it has a security interest in an item, if the bank otherwise complies with the requirements of Section 3—302 on what constitutes a holder in due course.

As amended in 1990.

§4—212. Presentment by Notice of Item Not Payable by, Through, or at Bank; Liability of Drawer or Indorser.

(a) Unless otherwise instructed, a collecting bank may present an item not payable by, through, or at a bank by sending to the party to accept or pay a written notice that the bank holds the item for acceptance or payment. The notice must be sent in time to be received on or before the day when presentment is due and the bank must meet any requirement of the party to accept or pay under Section 3—501 by the close of the bank's next banking day after it knows of the requirement.

(b) If presentment is made by notice and payment, acceptance, or request for compliance with a requirement under Section 3—501 is not received by the close of business on the day after maturity or, in the case of demand items, by the close of business on the third banking day after notice was sent, the presenting bank may treat the item as dishonored and charge any drawer or indorser by sending it notice of the facts.

As amended in 1990.

§4—213. Medium and Time of Settlement by Bank.

(a) With respect to settlement by a bank, the medium and time of settlement may be prescribed by Federal Reserve regulations or circulars, clearing-house rules, and the like, or agreement. In the absence of such prescription:

(1) the medium of settlement is cash or credit to an account in a Federal Reserve bank of or specified by the person to receive settlement; and

(2) the time of settlement is:

(i) with respect to tender of settlement by cash, a cashier's check, or teller's check, when the cash or check is sent or delivered;

(ii) with respect to tender of settlement by credit in an account in a Federal Reserve Bank, when the credit is made;

(iii) with respect to tender of settlement by a credit or debit to an account in a bank, when the credit or debit is made or, in the case of tender of settlement by authority to charge an account, when the authority is sent or delivered; or

(iv) with respect to tender of settlement by a funds transfer, when payment is made pursuant to Section 4A—406(a) to the person receiving settlement.

(b) If the tender of settlement is not by a medium authorized by subsection (a) or the time of settlement is not fixed by subsection (a), no settlement occurs until the tender of settlement is accepted by the person receiving settlement.

(c) If settlement for an item is made by cashier's check or teller's check and the person receiving settlement, before its midnight deadline:

(1) presents or forwards the check for collection, settlement is final when the check is finally paid; or

(2) fails to present or forward the check for collection, settlement is final at the midnight deadline of the person receiving settlement.

(d) If settlement for an item is made by giving authority to charge the account of the bank giving settlement in the bank receiving settlement, settlement is final when the charge is made by the bank receiving settlement if there are funds available in the account for the amount of the item.

As amended in 1990.

§4—214. Right of Charge-Back or Refund; Liability of Collecting Bank: Return of Item.

(a) If a collecting bank has made provisional settlement with its customer for an item and fails by reason of dishonor, suspension of payments by a bank, or otherwise to receive settlement for the item which is or becomes final, the bank may revoke the settlement given by it, charge back the amount of any credit given for the item to its customer's account, or obtain refund from its customer, whether or not it is able to return the item, if by its midnight deadline or within a longer reasonable time after it learns the facts it returns the item or sends notification of the facts. If the return or notice is delayed beyond the bank's midnight deadline or a longer reasonable time after it learns the facts, the bank may revoke the settlement, charge back the credit, or obtain refund from its customer, but it is liable for any loss resulting from the delay. These rights to revoke, charge back, and obtain refund terminate if and when a settlement for the item received by the bank is or becomes final.

(b) A collecting bank returns an item when it is sent or delivered to the bank's customer or transferor or pursuant to its instructions.

(c) A depositary bank that is also the payor may charge back the amount of an item to its customer's account or obtain refund in accordance with the section governing return of an item received by a payor bank for credit on its books (Section 4—301).

(d) The right to charge back is not affected by:
(1) previous use of a credit given for the item; or
(2) failure by any bank to exercise ordinary care with respect to the item, but a bank so failing remains liable.

(e) A failure to charge back or claim refund does not affect other rights of the bank against the customer or any other party.

(f) If credit is given in dollars as the equivalent of the value of an item payable in foreign money, the dollar amount of any charge-back or refund must be calculated on the basis of the bank-offered spot rate for the foreign money prevailing on the day when the person entitled to the charge-back or refund learns that it will not receive payment in ordinary course.

As amended in 1990.

§4—215. Final Payment of Item by Payor Bank; When Provisional Debits and Credits Become Final; When Certain Credits Become Available for Withdrawal.

(a) An item is finally paid by a payor bank when the bank has first done any of the following:
(1) paid the item in cash;
(2) settled for the item without having a right to revoke the settlement under statute, clearing-house rule, or agreement; or
(3) made a provisional settlement for the item and failed to revoke the settlement in the time and manner permitted by statute, clearing-house rule, or agreement.

(b) If provisional settlement for an item does not become final, the item is not finally paid.

(c) If provisional settlement for an item between the presenting and payor banks is made through a clearing house or by debits or credits in an account between them, then to the extent that provisional debits or credits for the item are entered in accounts between the presenting and payor banks or between the presenting and successive prior collecting banks seriatim, they become final upon final payment of the item by the payor bank.

(d) If a collecting bank receives a settlement for an item which is or becomes final, the bank is accountable to its customer for the amount of the item and any provisional credit given for the item in an account with its customer becomes final.

(e) Subject to (i) applicable law stating a time for availability of funds and (ii) any right of the bank to apply the credit to an obligation of the customer, credit given by a bank for an item in a customer's account becomes available for withdrawal as of right:
(1) if the bank has received a provisional settlement for the item, when the settlement becomes final and the bank has had a reasonable time to receive return of the item and the item has not been received within that time;
(2) if the bank is both the depositary bank and the payor bank, and the item is finally paid, at the opening of the bank's second banking day following receipt of the item.

(f) Subject to applicable law stating a time for availability of funds and any right of a bank to apply a deposit to an obligation of the depositor, a deposit of money becomes available for withdrawal as of right at the opening of the bank's next banking day after receipt of the deposit.

As amended in 1990.

§4—216. Insolvency and Preference.

(a) If an item is in or comes into the possession of a payor or collecting bank that suspends payment and the item has not been finally paid, the item must be returned by the receiver, trustee, or agent in charge of the closed bank to the presenting bank or the closed bank's customer.

(b) If a payor bank finally pays an item and suspends payments without making a settlement for the item with its customer or the presenting bank which settlement is or becomes final, the owner of the item has a preferred claim against the payor bank.

(c) If a payor bank gives or a collecting bank gives or receives a provisional settlement for an item and thereafter suspends payments, the suspension does not prevent or interfere with the settlement's becoming final if the finality occurs automatically upon the lapse of certain time or the happening of certain events.

(d) If a collecting bank receives from subsequent parties settlement for an item, which settlement is or becomes final and the bank suspends payments without making a settlement for the item with its customer which settlement is or becomes final, the owner of the item has a preferred claim against the collecting bank.

As amended in 1990.

PART 3 COLLECTION OF ITEMS: PAYOR BANKS

§4—301. Deferred Posting; Recovery of Payment by Return of Items; Time of Dishonor; Return of Items by Payor Bank.

(a) If a payor bank settles for a demand item other than a documentary draft presented otherwise than for immediate payment over the counter before midnight of the banking day of receipt, the payor bank may revoke the settlement and recover the settlement if, before it has made final payment and before its midnight deadline, it

(1) returns the item; or

(2) sends written notice of dishonor or nonpayment if the item is unavailable for return.

(b) If a demand item is received by a payor bank for credit on its books, it may return the item or send notice of dishonor and may revoke any credit given or recover the amount thereof withdrawn by its customer, if it acts within the time limit and in the manner specified in subsection (a).

(c) Unless previous notice of dishonor has been sent, an item is dishonored at the time when for purposes of dishonor it is returned or notice sent in accordance with this section.

(d) An item is returned:

(1) as to an item presented through a clearing house, when it is delivered to the presenting or last collecting bank or to the clearing house or is sent or delivered in accordance with clearing-house rules; or

(2) in all other cases, when it is sent or delivered to the bank's customer or transferor or pursuant to instructions.

As amended in 1990.

§4—302. Payor Bank's Responsibility for Late Return of Item.

(a) If an item is presented to and received by a payor bank, the bank is accountable for the amount of:

(1) a demand item, other than a documentary draft, whether properly payable or not, if the bank, in any case in which it is not also the depositary bank, retains the item beyond midnight of the banking day of receipt without settling for it or, whether or not it is also the depositary bank, does not pay or return the item or send notice of dishonor until after its midnight deadline; or

(2) any other properly payable item unless, within the time allowed for acceptance or payment of that item, the bank either accepts or pays the item or returns it and accompanying documents.

(b) The liability of a payor bank to pay an item pursuant to subsection (a) is subject to defenses based on breach of a presentment warranty (Section 4—208) or proof that the person seeking enforcement of the liability presented or transferred the item for the purpose of defrauding the payor bank.

As amended in 1990.

§4—303. When Items Subject to Notice, Stop-Payment Order, Legal Process, or Setoff; Order in Which Items May Be Charged or Certified.

(a) Any knowledge, notice, or stop-payment order received by, legal process served upon, or setoff exercised by a payor bank comes too late to terminate, suspend, or modify the bank's right or duty to pay an item or to charge its customer's account for the item if the knowledge, notice, stop-payment order, or legal process is received or served and a reasonable time for the bank to act thereon expires or the setoff is exercised after the earliest of the following:

(1) the bank accepts or certifies the item;

(2) the bank pays the item in cash;

(3) the bank settles for the item without having a right to revoke the settlement under statute, clearing-house rule, or agreement;

(4) the bank becomes accountable for the amount of the item under Section 4—302 dealing with the payor bank's responsibility for late return of items; or

(5) with respect to checks, a cutoff hour no earlier than one hour after the opening of the next banking day after the banking day on which the bank received the check and no later than the close of that next banking day or, if no cutoff hour is fixed, the close of the next banking day after the banking day on which the bank received the check.

(b) Subject to subsection (a), items may be accepted, paid, certified, or charged to the indicated account of its customer in any order.

As amended in 1990.

PART 4 RELATIONSHIP BETWEEN PAYOR BANK AND ITS CUSTOMER

§4—401. *When Bank May Charge Customer's Account.*

(a) A bank may charge against the account of a customer an item that is properly payable from the account even though the charge creates an overdraft. An item is properly payable if it is authorized by the customer and is in accordance with any agreement between the customer and bank.

(b) A customer is not liable for the amount of an overdraft if the customer neither signed the item nor benefited from the proceeds of the item.

(c) A bank may charge against the account of a customer a check that is otherwise properly payable from the account, even though payment was made before the date of the check, unless the customer has given notice to the bank of the postdating describing the check with reasonable certainty. The notice is effective for the period stated in Section 4—403(b) for stop-payment orders, and must be received at such time and in such manner as to afford the bank a reasonable opportunity to act on it before the bank takes any action with respect to the check described in Section 4—303. If a bank charges against the account of a customer a check before the date stated in the notice of postdating, the bank is liable for damages for the loss resulting from its act. The loss may include damages for dishonor of subsequent items under Section 4—402.

(d) A bank that in good faith makes payment to a holder may charge the indicated account of its customer according to:

    (1) the original terms of the altered item; or

    (2) the terms of the completed item, even though the bank knows the item has been completed unless the bank has notice that the completion was improper.

As amended in 1990.

§4—402. *Bank's Liability to Customer for Wrongful Dishonor; Time of Determining Insufficiency of Account.*

(a) Except as otherwise provided in this Article, a payor bank wrongfully dishonors an item if it dishonors an item that is properly payable, but a bank may dishonor an item that would create an overdraft unless it has agreed to pay the overdraft.

(b) A payor bank is liable to its customer for damages proximately caused by the wrongful dishonor of an item. Liability is limited to actual damages proved and may include damages for an arrest or prosecution of the customer or other consequential damages. Whether any consequential damages are proximately caused by the wrongful dishonor is a question of fact to be determined in each case.

(c) A payor bank's determination of the customer's account balance on which a decision to dishonor for insufficiency of available funds is based may be made at any time between the time the item is received by the payor bank and the time that the payor bank returns the item or gives notice in lieu of return, and no more than one determination need be made. If, at the election of the payor bank, a subsequent balance determination is made for the purpose of reevaluating the bank's decision to dishonor the item, the account balance at that time is determinative of whether a dishonor for insufficiency of available funds is wrongful.

As amended in 1990.

§4—403. *Customer's Right to Stop Payment; Burden of Proof of Loss.*

(a) A customer or any person authorized to draw on the account if there is more than one person may stop payment of any item drawn on the customer's account or close the account by an order to the bank describing the item or account with reasonable certainty received at a time and in a manner that affords the bank a reasonable opportunity to act on it before any action by the bank with respect to the item described in Section 4—303. If the signature of more than one person is required to draw on an account, any of these persons may stop payment or close the account.

(b) A stop-payment order is effective for six months, but it lapses after 14 calendar days if the original order was oral and was not confirmed in writing within that period. A stop-payment order may be renewed for additional six-month periods by a writing given to the bank within a period during which the stop-payment order is effective.

(c) The burden of establishing the fact and amount of loss resulting from the payment of an item contrary to a stop-payment order or order to close an account is on the customer. The loss from payment of an item contrary to a stop-payment order may include damages for dishonor of subsequent items under Section 4—402.

As amended in 1990.

§4—404. *Bank Not Obliged to Pay Check More Than Six Months Old.* A bank is under no obligation to a customer having a checking account to pay a check, other than a certified check, which is presented more than six months after its date, but it may charge its customer's account for a payment made thereafter in good faith.

§4—405. *Death or Incompetence of Customer.*

(a) A payor or collecting bank's authority to accept, pay, or collect an item or to account for proceeds of its collection, if otherwise effective, is not rendered ineffective by incompetence of a customer of either bank existing at the time the item is issued or its collection is undertaken if the bank does not know of an adjudication of incompetence. Neither death nor incompetence of a customer revokes the authority to accept, pay, collect, or account until the bank knows of the fact of death or of an adjudication of incompetence and has reasonable opportunity to act on it.

(b) Even with knowledge, a bank may for 10 days after the date of death pay or certify checks drawn on or before the date unless ordered to stop payment by a person claiming an interest in the account.

As amended in 1990.

§4—406. Customer's Duty to Discover and Report Unauthorized Signature or Alteration.

(a) A bank that sends or makes available to a customer a statement of account showing payment of items for the account shall either return or make available to the customer the items paid or provide information in the statement of account sufficient to allow the customer reasonably to identify the items paid. The statement of account provides sufficient information if the item is described by item number, amount, and date of payment.

(b) If the items are not returned to the customer, the person retaining the items shall either retain the items or, if the items are destroyed, maintain the capacity to furnish legible copies of the items until the expiration of seven years after receipt of the items. A customer may request an item from the bank that paid the item, and that bank must provide in a reasonable time either the item or, if the item has been destroyed or is not otherwise obtainable, a legible copy of the item.

(c) If a bank sends or makes available a statement of account or items pursuant to subsection (a), the customer must exercise reasonable promptness in examining the statement or the items to determine whether any payment was not authorized because of an alteration of an item or because a purported signature by or on behalf of the customer was not authorized. If, based on the statement or items provided, the customer should reasonably have discovered the unauthorized payment, the customer must promptly notify the bank of the relevant facts.

(d) If the bank proves that the customer failed, with respect to an item, to comply with the duties imposed on the customer by subsection (c), the customer is precluded from asserting against the bank:

   (1) the customer's unauthorized signature or any alteration on the item, if the bank also proves that it suffered a loss by reason of the failure; and

   (2) the customer's unauthorized signature or alteration by the same wrongdoer on any other item paid in good faith by the bank if the payment was made before the bank received notice from the customer of the unauthorized signature or alteration and after the customer had been afforded a reasonable period of time, not exceeding 30 days, in which to examine the item or statement of account and notify the bank.

(e) If subsection (d) applies and the customer proves that the bank failed to exercise ordinary care in paying the item and that the failure substantially contributed to loss, the loss is allocated between the customer precluded and the bank asserting the preclusion according to the extent to which the failure of the customer to comply with subsection (c) and the failure of the bank to exercise ordinary care contributed to the loss. If the customer proves that the bank did not pay the item in good faith, the preclusion under subsection (d) does not apply.

(f) Without regard to care or lack of care of either the customer or the bank, a customer who does not within one year after the statement or items are made available to the customer (subsection (a)) discover and report the customer's unauthorized signature on or any alteration on the item is precluded from asserting against the bank the unauthorized signature or alteration. If there is a preclusion under this subsection, the payor bank may not recover for breach or warranty under Section 4—208 with respect to the unauthorized signature or alteration to which the preclusion applies.

As amended in 1990.

§4—407. Payor Bank's Right to Subrogation on Improper Payment.
If a payor has paid an item over the order of the drawer or maker to stop payment, or after an account has been closed, or otherwise under circumstances giving a basis for objection by the drawer or maker, to prevent unjust enrichment and only to the extent necessary to prevent loss to the bank by reason of its payment of the item, the payor bank is subrogated to the rights

   (1) of any holder in due course on the item against the drawer or maker;

   (2) of the payee or any other holder of the item against the drawer or maker either on the item or under the transaction out of which the item arose; and

   (3) of the drawer or maker against the payee or any other holder of the item with respect to the transaction out of which the item arose.

As amended in 1990.

PART 5 COLLECTION OF DOCUMENTARY DRAFTS

§4—501. Handling of Documentary Drafts; Duty to Send for Presentment and to Notify Customer of Dishonor.
A bank that takes a documentary draft for collection shall present or send the draft and accompanying documents for presentment and, upon learning that the draft has not been paid or accepted in due course, shall seasonably notify its customer of the fact even though it may have discounted or bought the draft or extended credit available for withdrawal as of right.

As amended in 1990.

§4—502. Presentment of "On Arrival" Drafts.
If a draft or the relevant instructions require presentment "on arrival", "when goods arrive" or the like, the collecting bank need not present until in its judgment a reasonable time for arrival of the goods has expired. Refusal to pay or accept

because the goods have not arrived is not dishonor; the bank must notify its transferor of the refusal but need not present the draft again until it is instructed to do so or learns of the arrival of the goods.

§4—503. Responsibility of Presenting Bank for Documents and Goods; Report of Reasons for Dishonor; Referee in Case of Need.
Unless otherwise instructed and except as provided in Article 5, a bank presenting a documentary draft:

(1) must deliver the documents to the drawee on acceptance of the draft if it is payable more than three days after presentment, otherwise, only on payment; and

(2) upon dishonor, either in the case of presentment for acceptance or presentment for payment, may seek and follow instructions from any referee in case of need designated in the draft or, if the presenting bank does not choose to utilize the referee's services, it must use diligence and good faith to ascertain the reason for dishonor, must notify its transferor of the dishonor and of the results of its effort to ascertain the reasons therefor, and must request instructions. However, the presenting bank is under no obligation with respect to goods represented by the documents except to follow any reasonable instructions seasonably received; it has a right to reimbursement for any expense incurred in following instructions and to prepayment of or indemnity for those expenses.

As amended in 1990.

§4—504. Privilege of Presenting Bank to Deal With Goods; Security Interest for Expenses.

(a) A presenting bank that, following the dishonor of a documentary draft, has seasonably requested instructions but does not receive them within a reasonable time may store, sell, or otherwise deal with the goods in any reasonable manner.

(b) For its reasonable expenses incurred by action under subsection (a) the presenting bank has a lien upon the goods or their proceeds, which may be foreclosed in the same manner as an unpaid seller's lien.

As amended in 1990.

 ## ARTICLE 4A FUNDS TRANSFERS

PART 1 SUBJECT MATTER AND DEFINITIONS

§4A—101. Short Title.
This Article may be cited as Uniform Commercial Code-Funds Transfers.

§4A—102. Subject Matter.
Except as otherwise provided in Section 4A—108, this Article applies to funds transfers defined in Section 4A—104.

§4A—103. Payment Order—Definitions.

(a) In this Article:

(1) "Payment order" means an instruction of a sender to a receiving bank, transmitted orally, electronically, or in writing, to pay, or to cause another bank to pay, a fixed or determinable amount of money to a beneficiary if:

   (i) the instruction does not state a condition to payment to the beneficiary other than time of payment,

   (ii) the receiving bank is to be reimbursed by debiting an account of, or otherwise receiving payment from, the sender, and

   (iii) the instruction is transmitted by the sender directly to the receiving bank or to an agent, funds-transfer system, or communication system for transmittal to the receiving bank.

(2) "Beneficiary" means the person to be paid by the beneficiary's bank.

(3) "Beneficiary's bank" means the bank identified in a payment order in which an account of the beneficiary is to be credited pursuant to the order or which otherwise is to make payment to the beneficiary if the order does not provide for payment to an account.

(4) "Receiving bank" means the bank to which the sender's instruction is addressed.

(5) "Sender" means the person giving the instruction to the receiving bank.

(b) If an instruction complying with subsection (a)(1) is to make more than one payment to a beneficiary, the instruction is a separate payment order with respect to each payment.

(c) A payment order is issued when it is sent to the receiving bank.

§4A—104. Funds Transfer—Definitions.
In this Article:

(a) "Funds transfer" means the series of transactions, beginning with the originator's payment order, made for the purpose of making payment to the beneficiary of the order. The term includes any payment order issued by the originator's bank or an intermediary bank intended to carry out the originator's payment order. A funds transfer is completed by acceptance by the beneficiary's bank of a payment order for the benefit of the beneficiary of the originator's payment order.

(b) "Intermediary bank" means a receiving bank other than the originator's bank or the beneficiary's bank.

(c) "Originator" means the sender of the first payment order in a funds transfer.

(d) "Originator's bank" means (i) the receiving bank to which the payment order of the originator is issued if the originator is not a bank, or (ii) the originator if the originator is a bank.

§4A—105. Other Definitions.

(a) In this Article:

(1) "Authorized account" means a deposit account of a customer in a bank designated by the customer as a source of payment of payment orders issued by the customer to the bank. If a customer does not so designate an account, any account of the customer is an authorized account if payment of a payment order from that account is not inconsistent with a restriction on the use of that account.

(2) "Bank" means a person engaged in the business of banking and includes a savings bank, savings and loan association, credit union, and trust company. A branch or separate office of a bank is a separate bank for purposes of this Article.

(3) "Customer" means a person, including a bank, having an account with a bank or from whom a bank has agreed to receive payment orders.

(4) "Funds-transfer business day" of a receiving bank means the part of a day during which the receiving bank is open for the receipt, processing, and transmittal of payment orders and cancellations and amendments of payment orders.

(5) "Funds-transfer system" means a wire transfer network, automated clearing house, or other communication system of a clearing house or other association of banks through which a payment order by a bank may be transmitted to the bank to which the order is addressed.

(6) "Good faith" means honesty in fact and the observance of reasonable commercial standards of fair dealing.

(7) "Prove" with respect to a fact means to meet the burden of establishing the fact (Section 1—201(8)).

(b) Other definitions applying to this Article and the sections in which they appear are:

"Acceptance"	Section 4A—209
"Beneficiary"	Section 4A—103
"Beneficiary's bank"	Section 4A—103
"Executed"	Section 4A—301
"Execution date"	Section 4A—301
"Funds transfer"	Section 4A—104
"Funds-transfer system rule"	Section 4A—501
"Intermediary bank"	Section 4A—104
"Originator"	Section 4A—104
"Originator's bank"	Section 4A—104
"Payment by beneficiary's bank to beneficiary"	Section 4A—405
"Payment by originator to beneficiary"	Section 4A—406
"Payment by sender to receiving bank"	Section 4A—403
"Payment date"	Section 4A—401

"Payment order"	Section 4A—103
"Receiving bank"	Section 4A—103
"Security procedure"	Section 4A—201
"Sender"	Section 4A—103

(c) The following definitions in Article 4 apply to this Article:

"Clearing house"	Section 4—104
"Item"	Section 4—104
"Suspends payments"	Section 4—104

(d) In addition, Article 1 contains general definitions and principles of construction and interpretation applicable throughout this Article.

§4A—106. Time Payment Order Is Received.

(a) The time of receipt of a payment order or communication cancelling or amending a payment order is determined by the rules applicable to receipt of a notice stated in Section 1—201(27). A receiving bank may fix a cut-off time or times on a funds-transfer business day for the receipt and processing of payment orders and communications cancelling or amending payment orders. Different cut-off times may apply to payment orders, cancellations, or amendments, or to different categories of payment orders, cancellations, or amendments. A cut-off time may apply to senders generally or different cut-off times may apply to different senders or categories of payment orders. If a payment order or communication cancelling or amending a payment order is received after the close of a funds-transfer business day or after the appropriate cut-off time on a funds-transfer business day, the receiving bank may treat the payment order or communication as received at the opening of the next funds-transfer business day.

(b) If this Article refers to an execution date or payment date or states a day on which a receiving bank is required to take action, and the date or day does not fall on a funds-transfer business day, the next day that is a funds-transfer business day is treated as the date or day stated, unless the contrary is stated in this Article.

§4A—107. Federal Reserve Regulations and Operating Circulars.
Regulations of the Board of Governors of the Federal Reserve System and operating circulars of the Federal Reserve Banks supersede any inconsistent provision of this Article to the extent of the inconsistency.

§4A—108. Exclusion of Consumer Transactions Governed by Federal Law.
This Article does not apply to a funds transfer any part of which is governed by the Electronic Fund Transfer Act of 1978 (Title XX, Public Law 95—630, 92 Stat. 3728, 15 U.S.C. §1693 et seq.) as amended from time to time.

PART 2 ISSUE AND ACCEPTANCE OF PAYMENT ORDER

§4A—201. Security Procedure. "Security procedure" means a procedure established by agreement of a customer and a receiving bank for the purpose of (i) verifying that a payment order or communication amending or cancelling a payment order is that of the customer, or (ii) detecting error in the transmission or the content of the payment order or communication. A security procedure may require the use of algorithms or other codes, identifying words or numbers, encryption, callback procedures, or similar security devices. Comparison of a signature on a payment order or communication with an authorized specimen signature of the customer is not by itself a security procedure.

§4A—202. Authorized and Verified Payment Orders.

(a) A payment order received by the receiving bank is the authorized order of the person identified as sender if that person authorized the order or is otherwise bound by it under the law of agency.

(b) If a bank and its customer have agreed that the authenticity of payment orders issued to the bank in the name of the customer as sender will be verified pursuant to a security procedure, a payment order received by the receiving bank is effective as the order of the customer, whether or not authorized, if (i) the security procedure is a commercially reasonable method of providing security against unauthorized payment orders, and (ii) the bank proves that it accepted the payment order in good faith and in compliance with the security procedure and any written agreement or instruction of the customer restricting acceptance of payment orders issued in the name of the customer. The bank is not required to follow an instruction that violates a written agreement with the customer or notice of which is not received at a time and in a manner affording the bank a reasonable opportunity to act on it before the payment order is accepted.

(c) Commercial reasonableness of a security procedure is a question of law to be determined by considering the wishes of the customer expressed to the bank, the circumstances of the customer known to the bank, including the size, type, and frequency of payment orders normally issued by the customer to the bank, alternative security procedures offered to the customer, and security procedures in general use by customers and receiving banks similarly situated. A security procedure is deemed to be commercially reasonable if (i) the security procedure was chosen by the customer after the bank offered, and the customer refused, a security procedure that was commercially reasonable for that customer, and (ii) the customer expressly agreed in writing to be bound by any payment order, whether or not authorized, issued in its name and accepted by the bank in compliance with the security procedure chosen by the customer.

(d) The term "sender" in this Article includes the customer in whose name a payment order is issued if the order is the authorized order of the customer under subsection (a), or it is effective as the order of the customer under subsection (b).

(e) This section applies to amendments and cancellations of payment orders to the same extent it applies to payment orders.

(f) Except as provided in this section and in Section 4A—203(a)(1), rights and obligations arising under this section or Section 4A—203 may not be varied by agreement.

§4A—203. Unenforceability of Certain Verified Payment Orders.

(a) If an accepted payment order is not, under Section 4A—202(a), an authorized order of a customer identified as sender, but is effective as an order of the customer pursuant to Section 4A—202(b), the following rules apply:

(1) By express written agreement, the receiving bank may limit the extent to which it is entitled to enforce or retain payment of the payment order.

(2) The receiving bank is not entitled to enforce or retain payment of the payment order if the customer proves that the order was not caused, directly or indirectly, by a person (i) entrusted at any time with duties to act for the customer with respect to payment orders or the security procedure, or (ii) who obtained access to transmitting facilities of the customer or who obtained, from a source controlled by the customer and without authority of the receiving bank, information facilitating breach of the security procedure, regardless of how the information was obtained or whether the customer was at fault. Information includes any access device, computer software, or the like.

(b) This section applies to amendments of payment orders to the same extent it applies to payment orders.

§4A—204. Refund of Payment and Duty of Customer to Report with Respect to Unauthorized Payment Order.

(a) If a receiving bank accepts a payment order issued in the name of its customer as sender which is (i) not authorized and not effective as the order of the customer under Section 4A—202, or (ii) not enforceable, in whole or in part, against the customer under Section 4A—203, the bank shall refund any payment of the payment order received from the customer to the extent the bank is not entitled to enforce payment and shall pay interest on the refundable amount calculated from the date the bank received payment to the date of the refund. However, the customer is not entitled to interest from the bank on the amount to be refunded if the customer fails to exercise ordinary care to determine that the order was not authorized by the customer and to notify the bank of the relevant facts within a reasonable time not exceeding 90 days after the date the customer received notification from the bank that the order was accepted or that the customer's account was debited with respect to the order. The bank is not entitled to any recovery from the customer on account of a failure by the customer to give notification as stated in this section.

(b) Reasonable time under subsection (a) may be fixed by agreement as stated in Section 1—204(1), but the obligation of a receiving bank to refund payment as stated in subsection (a) may not otherwise be varied by agreement.

§4A—205. Erroneous Payment Orders.

(a) If an accepted payment order was transmitted pursuant to a security procedure for the detection of error and the payment order (i) erroneously instructed payment to a beneficiary not intended by the sender, (ii) erroneously instructed payment in an amount greater than the amount intended by the sender, or (iii) was an erroneously transmitted duplicate of a payment order previously sent by the sender, the following rules apply:

(1) If the sender proves that the sender or a person acting on behalf of the sender pursuant to Section 4A—206 complied with the security procedure and that the error would have been detected if the receiving bank had also complied, the sender is not obliged to pay the order to the extent stated in paragraphs (2) and (3).

(2) If the funds transfer is completed on the basis of an erroneous payment order described in clause (i) or (iii) of subsection (a), the sender is not obliged to pay the order and the receiving bank is entitled to recover from the beneficiary any amount paid to the beneficiary to the extent allowed by the law governing mistake and restitution.

(3) If the funds transfer is completed on the basis of a payment order described in clause (ii) of subsection (a), the sender is not obliged to pay the order to the extent the amount received by the beneficiary is greater than the amount intended by the sender. In that case, the receiving bank is entitled to recover from the beneficiary the excess amount received to the extent allowed by the law governing mistake and restitution.

(b) If (i) the sender of an erroneous payment order described in subsection (a) is not obliged to pay all or part of the order, and (ii) the sender receives notification from the receiving bank that the order was accepted by the bank or that the sender's account was debited with respect to the order, the sender has a duty to exercise ordinary care, on the basis of information available to the sender, to discover the error with respect to the order and to advise the bank of the relevant facts within a reasonable time, not exceeding 90 days, after the bank's notification was received by the sender. If the bank proves that the sender failed to perform that duty, the sender is liable to the bank for the loss the bank proves it incurred as a result of the failure, but the liability of the sender may not exceed the amount of the sender's order.

(c) This section applies to amendments to payment orders to the same extent it applies to payment orders.

§4A—206. Transmission of Payment Order through Funds-Transfer or Other Communication System.

(a) If a payment order addressed to a receiving bank is transmitted to a funds-transfer system or other third party communication system for transmittal to the bank, the system is deemed to be an agent of the sender for the purpose of transmitting the payment order to the bank. If there is a discrepancy between the terms of the payment order transmitted to the system and the terms of the payment order transmitted by the system to the bank, the terms of the payment order of the sender are those transmitted by the system. This section does not apply to a funds-transfer system of the Federal Reserve Banks.

(b) This section applies to cancellations and amendments to payment orders to the same extent it applies to payment orders.

§4A—207. Misdescription of Beneficiary.

(a) Subject to subsection (b), if, in a payment order received by the beneficiary's bank, the name, bank account number, or other identification of the beneficiary refers to a nonexistent or unidentifiable person or account, no person has rights as a beneficiary of the order and acceptance of the order cannot occur.

(b) If a payment order received by the beneficiary's bank identifies the beneficiary both by name and by an identifying or bank account number and the name and number identify different persons, the following rules apply:

(1) Except as otherwise provided in subsection (c), if the beneficiary's bank does not know that the name and number refer to different persons, it may rely on the number as the proper identification of the beneficiary of the order. The beneficiary's bank need not determine whether the name and number refer to the same person.

(2) If the beneficiary's bank pays the person identified by name or knows that the name and number identify different persons, no person has rights as beneficiary except the person paid by the beneficiary's bank if that person was entitled to receive payment from the originator of the funds transfer. If no person has rights as beneficiary, acceptance of the order cannot occur.

(c) If (i) a payment order described in subsection (b) is accepted, (ii) the originator's payment order described the beneficiary inconsistently by name and number, and (iii) the beneficiary's bank pays the person identified by number as permitted by subsection (b)(1), the following rules apply:

(1) If the originator is a bank, the originator is obliged to pay its order.

(2) If the originator is not a bank and proves that the person identified by number was not entitled to receive payment from the originator, the originator is not

obliged to pay its order unless the originator's bank proves that the originator, before acceptance of the originator's order, had notice that payment of a payment order issued by the originator might be made by the beneficiary's bank on the basis of an identifying or bank account number even if it identifies a person different from the named beneficiary. Proof of notice may be made by any admissible evidence. The originator's bank satisfies the burden of proof if it proves that the originator, before the payment order was accepted, signed a writing stating the information to which the notice relates.

(d) In a case governed by subsection (b)(1), if the beneficiary's bank rightfully pays the person identified by number and that person was not entitled to receive payment from the originator, the amount paid may be recovered from that person to the extent allowed by the law governing mistake and restitution as follows:

(1) If the originator is obliged to pay its payment order as stated in subsection (c), the originator has the right to recover.

(2) If the originator is not a bank and is not obliged to pay its payment order, the originator's bank has the right to recover.

§4A—208. Misdescription of Intermediary Bank or Beneficiary's Bank.

(a) This subsection applies to a payment order identifying an intermediary bank or the beneficiary's bank only by an identifying number.

(1) The receiving bank may rely on the number as the proper identification of the intermediary or beneficiary's bank and need not determine whether the number identifies a bank.

(2) The sender is obliged to compensate the receiving bank for any loss and expenses incurred by the receiving bank as a result of its reliance on the number in executing or attempting to execute the order.

(b) This subsection applies to a payment order identifying an intermediary bank or the beneficiary's bank both by name and an identifying number if the name and number identify different persons.

(1) If the sender is a bank, the receiving bank may rely on the number as the proper identification of the intermediary or beneficiary's bank if the receiving bank, when it executes the sender's order, does not know that the name and number identify different persons. The receiving bank need not determine whether the name and number refer to the same person or whether the number refers to a bank. The sender is obliged to compensate the receiving bank for any loss and expenses incurred by the receiving bank as a result of its reliance on the number in executing or attempting to execute the order.

(2) If the sender is not a bank and the receiving bank proves that the sender, before the payment order was accepted, had notice that the receiving bank might rely on the number as the proper identification of the intermediary or beneficiary's bank even if it identifies a person different from the bank identified by name, the rights and obligations of the sender and the receiving bank are governed by subsection (b)(1), as though the sender were a bank. Proof of notice may be made by any admissible evidence. The receiving bank satisfies the burden of proof if it proves that the sender, before the payment order was accepted, signed a writing stating the information to which the notice relates.

(3) Regardless of whether the sender is a bank, the receiving bank may rely on the name as the proper identification of the intermediary or beneficiary's bank if the receiving bank, at the time it executes the sender's order, does not know that the name and number identify different persons. The receiving bank need not determine whether the name and number refer to the same person.

(4) If the receiving bank knows that the name and number identify different persons, reliance on either the name or the number in executing the sender's payment order is a breach of the obligation stated in Section 4A—302(a)(1).

§4A—209. Acceptance of Payment Order.

(a) Subject to subsection (d), a receiving bank other than the beneficiary's bank accepts a payment order when it executes the order.

(b) Subject to subsections (c) and (d), a beneficiary's bank accepts a payment order at the earliest of the following times:

(1) When the bank (i) pays the beneficiary as stated in Section 4A—405(a) or 4A—405(b), or (ii) notifies the beneficiary of receipt of the order or that the account of the beneficiary has been credited with respect to the order unless the notice indicates that the bank is rejecting the order or that funds with respect to the order may not be withdrawn or used until receipt of payment from the sender of the order;

(2) When the bank receives payment of the entire amount of the sender's order pursuant to Section 4A—403(a)(1) or 4A—403(a)(2); or

(3) The opening of the next funds-transfer business day of the bank following the payment date of the order if, at that time, the amount of the sender's order is fully covered by a withdrawable credit balance in an authorized account of the sender or the bank has otherwise received full payment from the sender, unless the order was rejected before that time or is rejected within (i) one hour after that time, or (ii) one hour after the opening of the next business day of the sender following the payment date if that time is later. If notice of rejection is received by the sender after the payment date and the

authorized account of the sender does not bear interest, the bank is obliged to pay interest to the sender on the amount of the order for the number of days elapsing after the payment date to the day the sender receives notice or learns that the order was not accepted, counting that day as an elapsed day. If the withdrawable credit balance during that period falls below the amount of the order, the amount of interest payable is reduced accordingly.

(c) Acceptance of a payment order cannot occur before the order is received by the receiving bank. Acceptance does not occur under subsection (b)(2) or (b)(3) if the beneficiary of the payment order does not have an account with the receiving bank, the account has been closed, or the receiving bank is not permitted by law to receive credits for the beneficiary's account.

(d) A payment order issued to the originator's bank cannot be accepted until the payment date if the bank is the beneficiary's bank, or the execution date if the bank is not the beneficiary's bank. If the originator's bank executes the originator's payment order before the execution date or pays the beneficiary of the originator's payment order before the payment date and the payment order is subsequently cancelled pursuant to Section 4A—211(b), the bank may recover from the beneficiary any payment received to the extent allowed by the law governing mistake and restitution.

§4A—210. Rejection of Payment Order.

(a) A payment order is rejected by the receiving bank by a notice of rejection transmitted to the sender orally, electronically, or in writing. A notice of rejection need not use any particular words and is sufficient if it indicates that the receiving bank is rejecting the order or will not execute or pay the order. Rejection is effective when the notice is given if transmission is by a means that is reasonable in the circumstances. If notice of rejection is given by a means that is not reasonable, rejection is effective when the notice is received. If an agreement of the sender and receiving bank establishes the means to be used to reject a payment order, (i) any means complying with the agreement is reasonable and (ii) any means not complying is not reasonable unless no significant delay in receipt of the notice resulted from the use of the noncomplying means.

(b) This subsection applies if a receiving bank other than the beneficiary's bank fails to execute a payment order despite the existence on the execution date of a withdrawable credit balance in an authorized account of the sender sufficient to cover the order. If the sender does not receive notice of rejection of the order on the execution date and the authorized account of the sender does not bear interest, the bank is obliged to pay interest to the sender on the amount of the order for the number of days elapsing after the execution date to the earlier of the day the order is cancelled pursuant to Section 4A—211(d) or the day the sender receives notice or learns that the order was not executed,

counting the final day of the period as an elapsed day. If the withdrawable credit balance during that period falls below the amount of the order, the amount of interest is reduced accordingly.

(c) If a receiving bank suspends payments, all unaccepted payment orders issued to it are are deemed rejected at the time the bank suspends payments.

(d) Acceptance of a payment order precludes a later rejection of the order. Rejection of a payment order precludes a later acceptance of the order.

§4A—211. Cancellation and Amendment of Payment Order.

(a) A communication of the sender of a payment order cancelling or amending the order may be transmitted to the receiving bank orally, electronically, or in writing. If a security procedure is in effect between the sender and the receiving bank, the communication is not effective to cancel or amend the order unless the communication is verified pursuant to the security procedure or the bank agrees to the cancellation or amendment.

(b) Subject to subsection (a), a communication by the sender cancelling or amending a payment order is effective to cancel or amend the order if notice of the communication is received at a time and in a manner affording the receiving bank a reasonable opportunity to act on the communication before the bank accepts the payment order.

(c) After a payment order has been accepted, cancellation or amendment of the order is not effective unless the receiving bank agrees or a funds-transfer system rule allows cancellation or amendment without agreement of the bank.

(1) With respect to a payment order accepted by a receiving bank other than the beneficiary's bank, cancellation or amendment is not effective unless a conforming cancellation or amendment of the payment order issued by the receiving bank is also made.

(2) With respect to a payment order accepted by the beneficiary's bank, cancellation or amendment is not effective unless the order was issued in execution of an unauthorized payment order, or because of a mistake by a sender in the funds transfer which resulted in the issuance of a payment order (i) that is a duplicate of a payment order previously issued by the sender, (ii) that orders payment to a beneficiary not entitled to receive payment from the originator, or (iii) that orders payment in an amount greater than the amount the beneficiary was entitled to receive from the originator. If the payment order is cancelled or amended, the beneficiary's bank is entitled to recover from the beneficiary any amount paid to the beneficiary to the extent allowed by the law governing mistake and restitution.

(d) An unaccepted payment order is cancelled by operation of law at the close of the fifth funds-transfer business day of the receiving bank after the execution date or payment date of the order.

(e) A cancelled payment order cannot be accepted. If an accepted payment order is cancelled, the acceptance is nullified and no person has any right or obligation based on the acceptance. Amendment of a payment order is deemed to be cancellation of the original order at the time of amendment and issue of a new payment order in the amended form at the same time.

(f) Unless otherwise provided in an agreement of the parties or in a funds-transfer system rule, if the receiving bank, after accepting a payment order, agrees to cancellation or amendment of the order by the sender or is bound by a funds-transfer system rule allowing cancellation or amendment without the bank's agreement, the sender, whether or not cancellation or amendment is effective, is liable to the bank for any loss and expenses, including reasonable attorney's fees, incurred by the bank as a result of the cancellation or amendment or attempted cancellation or amendment.

(g) A payment order is not revoked by the death or legal incapacity of the sender unless the receiving bank knows of the death or of an adjudication of incapacity by a court of competent jurisdiction and has reasonable opportunity to act before acceptance of the order.

(h) A funds-transfer system rule is not effective to the extent it conflicts with subsection (c)(2).

§4A—212. Liability and Duty of Receiving Bank Regarding Unaccepted Payment Order.

If a receiving bank fails to accept a payment order that it is obliged by express agreement to accept, the bank is liable for breach of the agreement to the extent provided in the agreement or in this Article, but does not otherwise have any duty to accept a payment order or, before acceptance, to take any action, or refrain from taking action, with respect to the order except as provided in this Article or by express agreement. Liability based on acceptance arises only when acceptance occurs as stated in Section 4A—209, and liability is limited to that provided in this Article. A receiving bank is not the agent of the sender or beneficiary of the payment order it accepts, or of any other party to the funds transfer, and the bank owes no duty to any party to the funds transfer except as provided in this Article or by express agreement.

PART 3 EXECUTION OF SENDER'S PAYMENT ORDER BY RECEIVING BANK

§4A—301. Execution and Execution Date.

(a) A payment order is "executed" by the receiving bank when it issues a payment order intended to carry out the payment order received by the bank. A payment order received by the beneficiary's bank can be accepted but cannot be executed.

(b) "Execution date" of a payment order means the day on which the receiving bank may properly issue a payment order in execution of the sender's order. The execution date may be determined by instruction of the sender but cannot be earlier than the day the order is received and, unless otherwise determined, is the day the order is received. If the sender's instruction states a payment date, the execution date is the payment date or an earlier date on which execution is reasonably necessary to allow payment to the beneficiary on the payment date.

§4A—302. Obligations of Receiving Bank in Execution of Payment Order.

(a) Except as provided in subsections (b) through (d), if the receiving bank accepts a payment order pursuant to Section 4A—209(a), the bank has the following obligations in executing the order:

(1) The receiving bank is obliged to issue, on the execution date, a payment order complying with the sender's order and to follow the sender's instructions concerning (i) any intermediary bank or funds-transfer system to be used in carrying out the funds transfer, or (ii) the means by which payment orders are to be transmitted in the funds transfer. If the originator's bank issues a payment order to an intermediary bank, the originator's bank is obliged to instruct the intermediary bank according to the instruction of the originator. An intermediary bank in the funds transfer is similarly bound by an instruction given to it by the sender of the payment order it accepts.

(2) If the sender's instruction states that the funds transfer is to be carried out telephonically or by wire transfer or otherwise indicates that the funds transfer is to be carried out by the most expeditious means, the receiving bank is obliged to transmit its payment order by the most expeditious available means, and to instruct any intermediary bank accordingly. If a sender's instruction states a payment date, the receiving bank is obliged to transmit its payment order at a time and by means reasonably necessary to allow payment to the beneficiary on the payment date or as soon thereafter as is feasible.

(b) Unless otherwise instructed, a receiving bank executing a payment order may (i) use any funds-transfer system if use of that system is reasonable in the circumstances, and (ii) issue a payment order to the beneficiary's bank or to an intermediary bank through which a payment order conforming to the sender's order can expeditiously be issued to the beneficiary's bank if the receiving bank exercises ordinary care in the selection of the intermediary bank. A receiving bank is not required to follow an instruction of the sender designating a funds-transfer system to be used in carrying out the funds transfer if the receiving bank, in good faith, determines that it is not feasible to follow the instruction or that following the instruction would unduly delay completion of the funds transfer.

(c) Unless subsection (a)(2) applies or the receiving bank is otherwise instructed, the bank may execute a payment order by transmitting its payment order by first class mail or by any means reasonable in the circumstances. If the receiving bank is instructed to execute the sender's order by transmitting its payment order by a particular means, the receiving bank may issue its payment order by the means stated or by any means as expeditious as the means stated.

(d) Unless instructed by the sender, (i) the receiving bank may not obtain payment of its charges for services and expenses in connection with the execution of the sender's order by issuing a payment order in an amount equal to the amount of the sender's order less the amount of the charges, and (ii) may not instruct a subsequent receiving bank to obtain payment of its charges in the same manner.

§4A—303. Erroneous Execution of Payment Order.

(a) A receiving bank that (i) executes the payment order of the sender by issuing a payment order in an amount greater than the amount of the sender's order, or (ii) issues a payment order in execution of the sender's order and then issues a duplicate order, is entitled to payment of the amount of the sender's order under Section 4A—402(c) if that subsection is otherwise satisfied. The bank is entitled to recover from the beneficiary of the erroneous order the excess payment received to the extent allowed by the law governing mistake and restitution.

(b) A receiving bank that executes the payment order of the sender by issuing a payment order in an amount less than the amount of the sender's order is entitled to payment of the amount of the sender's order under Section 4A—402(c) if (i) that subsection is otherwise satisfied and (ii) the bank corrects its mistake by issuing an additional payment order for the benefit of the beneficiary of the sender's order. If the error is not corrected, the issuer of the erroneous order is entitled to receive or retain payment from the sender of the order it accepted only to the extent of the amount of the erroneous order. This subsection does not apply if the receiving bank executes the sender's payment order by issuing a payment order in an amount less than the amount of the sender's order for the purpose of obtaining payment of its charges for services and expenses pursuant to instruction of the sender.

(c) If a receiving bank executes the payment order of the sender by issuing a payment order to a beneficiary different from the beneficiary of the sender's order and the funds transfer is completed on the basis of that error, the sender of the payment order that was erroneously executed and all previous senders in the funds transfer are not obliged to pay the payment orders they issued. The issuer of the erroneous order is entitled to recover from the beneficiary of the order the payment received to the extent allowed by the law governing mistake and restitution.

§4A—304. Duty of Sender to Report Erroneously Executed Payment Order.
If the sender of a payment order that is erroneously executed as stated in Section 4A—303

receives notification from the receiving bank that the order was executed or that the sender's account was debited with respect to the order, the sender has a duty to exercise ordinary care to determine, on the basis of information available to the sender, that the order was erroneously executed and to notify the bank of the relevant facts within a reasonable time not exceeding 90 days after the notification from the bank was received by the sender. If the sender fails to perform that duty, the bank is not obliged to pay interest on any amount refundable to the sender under Section 4A—402(d) for the period before the bank learns of the execution error. The bank is not entitled to any recovery from the sender on account of a failure by the sender to perform the duty stated in this section.

§4A—305. Liability for Late or Improper Execution or Failure to Execute Payment Order.

(a) If a funds transfer is completed but execution of a payment order by the receiving bank in breach of Section 4A—302 results in delay in payment to the beneficiary, the bank is obliged to pay interest to either the originator or the beneficiary of the funds transfer for the period of delay caused by the improper execution. Except as provided in subsection (c), additional damages are not recoverable.

(b) If execution of a payment order by a receiving bank in breach of Section 4A—302 results in (i) noncompletion of the funds transfer, (ii) failure to use an intermediary bank designated by the originator, or (iii) issuance of a payment order that does not comply with the terms of the payment order of the originator, the bank is liable to the originator for its expenses in the funds transfer and for incidental expenses and interest losses, to the extent not covered by subsection (a), resulting from the improper execution. Except as provided in subsection (c), additional damages are not recoverable.

(c) In addition to the amounts payable under subsections (a) and (b), damages, including consequential damages, are recoverable to the extent provided in an express written agreement of the receiving bank.

(d) If a receiving bank fails to execute a payment order it was obliged by express agreement to execute, the receiving bank is liable to the sender for its expenses in the transaction and for incidental expenses and interest losses resulting from the failure to execute. Additional damages, including consequential damages, are recoverable to the extent provided in an express written agreement of the receiving bank, but are not otherwise recoverable.

(e) Reasonable attorney's fees are recoverable if demand for compensation under subsection (a) or (b) is made and refused before an action is brought on the claim. If a claim is made for breach of an agreement under subsection (d) and the agreement does not provide for damages, reasonable attorney's fees are recoverable if demand for compensation under subsection (d) is made and refused before an action is brought on the claim.

(f) Except as stated in this section, the liability of a receiving bank under subsections (a) and (b) may not be varied by agreement.

PART 4 PAYMENT

§4A—401. Payment Date.
"Payment date" of a payment order means the day on which the amount of the order is payable to the beneficiary by the beneficiary's bank. The payment date may be determined by instruction of the sender but cannot be earlier than the day the order is received by the beneficiary's bank and, unless otherwise determined, is the day the order is received by the beneficiary's bank.

§4A—402. Obligation of Sender to Pay Receiving Bank.

(a) This section is subject to Sections 4A—205 and 4A—207.

(b) With respect to a payment order issued to the beneficiary's bank, acceptance of the order by the bank obliges the sender to pay the bank the amount of the order, but payment is not due until the payment date of the order.

(c) This subsection is subject to subsection (e) and to Section 4A—303. With respect to a payment order issued to a receiving bank other than the beneficiary's bank, acceptance of the order by the receiving bank obliges the sender to pay the bank the amount of the sender's order. Payment by the sender is not due until the execution date of the sender's order. The obligation of that sender to pay its payment order is excused if the funds transfer is not completed by acceptance by the beneficiary's bank of a payment order instructing payment to the beneficiary of that sender's payment order.

(d) If the sender of a payment order pays the order and was not obliged to pay all or part of the amount paid, the bank receiving payment is obliged to refund payment to the extent the sender was not obliged to pay. Except as provided in Sections 4A—204 and 4A—304, interest is payable on the refundable amount from the date of payment.

(e) If a funds transfer is not completed as stated in subsection (c) and an intermediary bank is obliged to refund payment as stated in subsection (d) but is unable to do so because not permitted by applicable law or because the bank suspends payments, a sender in the funds transfer that executed a payment order in compliance with an instruction, as stated in Section 4A—302(a)(1), to route the funds transfer through that intermediary bank is entitled to receive or retain payment from the sender of the payment order that it accepted. The first sender in the funds transfer that issued an instruction requiring routing through that intermediary bank is subrogated to the right of the bank that paid the intermediary bank to refund as stated in subsection (d).

(f) The right of the sender of a payment order to be excused from the obligation to pay the order as stated in subsection (c) or to receive refund under subsection (d) may not be varied by agreement.

§4A—403. Payment by Sender to Receiving Bank.

(a) Payment of the sender's obligation under Section 4A—402 to pay the receiving bank occurs as follows:

(1) If the sender is a bank, payment occurs when the receiving bank receives final settlement of the obligation through a Federal Reserve Bank or through a funds-transfer system.

(2) If the sender is a bank and the sender (i) credited an account of the receiving bank with the sender, or (ii) caused an account of the receiving bank in another bank to be credited, payment occurs when the credit is withdrawn or, if not withdrawn, at midnight of the day on which the credit is withdrawable and the receiving bank learns of that fact.

(3) If the receiving bank debits an account of the sender with the receiving bank, payment occurs when the debit is made to the extent the debit is covered by a withdrawable credit balance in the account.

(b) If the sender and receiving bank are members of a funds-transfer system that nets obligations multilaterally among participants, the receiving bank receives final settlement when settlement is complete in accordance with the rules of the system. The obligation of the sender to pay the amount of a payment order transmitted through the funds-transfer system may be satisfied, to the extent permitted by the rules of the system, by setting off and applying against the sender's obligation the right of the sender to receive payment from the receiving bank of the amount of any other payment order transmitted to the sender by the receiving bank through the funds-transfer system. The aggregate balance of obligations owed by each sender to each receiving bank in the funds-transfer system may be satisfied, to the extent permitted by the rules of the system, by setting off and applying against that balance the aggregate balance of obligations owed to the sender by other members of the system. The aggregate balance is determined after the right of setoff stated in the second sentence of this subsection has been exercised.

(c) If two banks transmit payment orders to each other under an agreement that settlement of the obligations of each bank to the other under Section 4A—402 will be made at the end of the day or other period, the total amount owed with respect to all orders transmitted by one bank shall be set off against the total amount owed with respect to all orders transmitted by the other bank. To the extent of the setoff, each bank has made payment to the other.

(d) In a case not covered by subsection (a), the time when payment of the sender's obligation under Section 4A—402(b) or 4A—402(c) occurs is governed by applicable principles of law that determine when an obligation is satisfied.

§4A—404. Obligation of Beneficiary's Bank to Pay and Give Notice to Beneficiary.

(a) Subject to Sections 4A—211(e), 4A—405(d), and 4A—405(e), if a beneficiary's bank accepts a payment order, the bank is obliged to pay the amount of the order to the beneficiary of the order. Payment is due on the payment date of the order, but if acceptance occurs on the payment date after the close of the funds-transfer business day of the bank, payment is due on the next funds-transfer business day. If the bank refuses to pay after demand by the beneficiary and receipt of notice of particular circumstances that will give rise to consequential damages as a result of nonpayment, the beneficiary may recover damages resulting from the refusal to pay to the extent the bank had notice of the damages, unless the bank proves that it did not pay because of a reasonable doubt concerning the right of the beneficiary to payment.

(b) If a payment order accepted by the beneficiary's bank instructs payment to an account of the beneficiary, the bank is obliged to notify the beneficiary of receipt of the order before midnight of the next funds-transfer business day following the payment date. If the payment order does not instruct payment to an account of the beneficiary, the bank is required to notify the beneficiary only if notice is required by the order. Notice may be given by first class mail or any other means reasonable in the circumstances. If the bank fails to give the required notice, the bank is obliged to pay interest to the beneficiary on the amount of the payment order from the day notice should have been given until the day the beneficiary learned of receipt of the payment order by the bank. No other damages are recoverable. Reasonable attorney's fees are also recoverable if demand for interest is made and refused before an action is brought on the claim.

(c) The right of a beneficiary to receive payment and damages as stated in subsection (a) may not be varied by agreement or a funds-transfer system rule. The right of a beneficiary to be notified as stated in subsection (b) may be varied by agreement of the beneficiary or by a funds-transfer system rule if the beneficiary is notified of the rule before initiation of the funds transfer.

§4A—405. Payment by Beneficiary's Bank to Beneficiary.

(a) If the beneficiary's bank credits an account of the beneficiary of a payment order, payment of the bank's obligation under Section 4A—404(a) occurs when and to the extent (i) the beneficiary is notified of the right to withdraw the credit, (ii) the bank lawfully applies the credit to a debt of the beneficiary, or (iii) funds with respect to the order are otherwise made available to the beneficiary by the bank.

(b) If the beneficiary's bank does not credit an account of the beneficiary of a payment order, the time when payment of the bank's obligation under Section 4A—404(a) occurs is governed by principles of law that determine when an obligation is satisfied.

(c) Except as stated in subsections (d) and (e), if the beneficiary's bank pays the beneficiary of a payment order under a condition to payment or agreement of the beneficiary giving the bank the right to recover payment from the beneficiary if the bank does not receive payment of the order, the condition to payment or agreement is not enforceable.

(d) A funds-transfer system rule may provide that payments made to beneficiaries of funds transfers made through the system are provisional until receipt of payment by the beneficiary's bank of the payment order it accepted. A beneficiary's bank that makes a payment that is provisional under the rule is entitled to refund from the beneficiary if (i) the rule requires that both the beneficiary and the originator be given notice of the provisional nature of the payment before the funds transfer is initiated, (ii) the beneficiary, the beneficiary's bank, and the originator's bank agreed to be bound by the rule, and (iii) the beneficiary's bank did not receive payment of the payment order that it accepted. If the beneficiary is obliged to refund payment to the beneficiary's bank, acceptance of the payment order by the beneficiary's bank is nullified and no payment by the originator of the funds transfer to the beneficiary occurs under Section 4A—406.

(e) This subsection applies to a funds transfer that includes a payment order transmitted over a funds-transfer system that (i) nets obligations multilaterally among participants, and (ii) has in effect a loss-sharing agreement among participants for the purpose of providing funds necessary to complete settlement of the obligations of one or more participants that do not meet their settlement obligations. If the beneficiary's bank in the funds transfer accepts a payment order and the system fails to complete settlement pursuant to its rules with respect to any payment order in the funds transfer, (i) the acceptance by the beneficiary's bank is nullified and no person has any right or obligation based on the acceptance, (ii) the beneficiary's bank is entitled to recover payment from the beneficiary, (iii) no payment by the originator to the beneficiary occurs under Section 4A—406, and (iv) subject to Section 4A—402(e), each sender in the funds transfer is excused from its obligation to pay its payment order under Section 4A—402(c) because the funds transfer has not been completed.

§4A—406. Payment by Originator to Beneficiary; Discharge of Underlying Obligation.

(a) Subject to Sections 4A—211(e), 4A—405(d), and 4A—405(e), the originator of a funds transfer pays the beneficiary of the originator's payment order (i) at the time a payment order for the benefit of the beneficiary is accepted by the beneficiary's bank in the funds transfer and (ii) in an amount equal to the amount of the order accepted by the beneficiary's bank, but not more than the amount of the originator's order.

(b) If payment under subsection (a) is made to satisfy an obligation, the obligation is discharged to the same extent discharge would result from payment to the beneficiary of the same amount in money, unless (i) the payment under subsection (a) was made by a means prohibited by the contract of the beneficiary with respect to the obligation, (ii) the beneficiary, within a reasonable time after receiving notice of receipt of the order by the beneficiary's bank, notified the originator of the beneficiary's refusal of the payment, (iii) funds with respect to the order were not withdrawn by the beneficiary or applied to a debt of the beneficiary, and (iv) the beneficiary would suffer a loss that could reasonably have been avoided if payment had been made by a means complying with the contract. If payment by the originator does not result in discharge under this section, the originator is subrogated to the rights of the beneficiary to receive payment from the beneficiary's bank under Section 4A—404(a).

(c) For the purpose of determining whether discharge of an obligation occurs under subsection (b), if the beneficiary's bank accepts a payment order in an amount equal to the amount of the originator's payment order less charges of one or more receiving banks in the funds transfer, payment to the beneficiary is deemed to be in the amount of the originator's order unless upon demand by the beneficiary the originator does not pay the beneficiary the amount of the deducted charges.

(d) Rights of the originator or of the beneficiary of a funds transfer under this section may be varied only by agreement of the originator and the beneficiary.

PART 5 MISCELLANEOUS PROVISIONS

§4A—501. Variation by Agreement and Effect of Funds-Transfer System Rule.

(a) Except as otherwise provided in this Article, the rights and obligations of a party to a funds transfer may be varied by agreement of the affected party.

(b) "Funds-transfer system rule" means a rule of an association of banks (i) governing transmission of payment orders by means of a funds-transfer system of the association or rights and obligations with respect to those orders, or (ii) to the extent the rule governs rights and obligations between banks that are parties to a funds transfer in which a Federal Reserve Bank, acting as an intermediary bank, sends a payment order to the beneficiary's bank. Except as otherwise provided in this Article, a funds-transfer system rule governing rights and obligations between participating banks using the system may be effective even if the rule conflicts with this Article and indirectly affects another party to the funds transfer who does not consent to the rule. A funds-transfer system rule may also govern rights and obligations of parties other than participating banks using the system to the extent stated in Sections 4A—404(c), 4A—405(d), and 4A—507(c).

§4A—502. Creditor Process Served on Receiving Bank; Setoff by Beneficiary's Bank.

(a) As used in this section, "creditor process" means levy, attachment, garnishment, notice of lien, sequestration, or similar process issued by or on behalf of a creditor or other claimant with respect to an account.

(b) This subsection applies to creditor process with respect to an authorized account of the sender of a payment order if the creditor process is served on the receiving bank. For the purpose of determining rights with respect to the creditor process, if the receiving bank accepts the payment order the balance in the authorized account is deemed to be reduced by the amount of the payment order to the extent the bank did not otherwise receive payment of the order, unless the creditor process is served at a time and in a manner affording the bank a reasonable opportunity to act on it before the bank accepts the payment order.

(c) If a beneficiary's bank has received a payment order for payment to the beneficiary's account in the bank, the following rules apply:

(1) The bank may credit the beneficiary's account. The amount credited may be set off against an obligation owed by the beneficiary to the bank or may be applied to satisfy creditor process served on the bank with respect to the account.

(2) The bank may credit the beneficiary's account and allow withdrawal of the amount credited unless creditor process with respect to the account is served at a time and in a manner affording the bank a reasonable opportunity to act to prevent withdrawal.

(3) If creditor process with respect to the beneficiary's account has been served and the bank has had a reasonable opportunity to act on it, the bank may not reject the payment order except for a reason unrelated to the service of process.

(d) Creditor process with respect to a payment by the originator to the beneficiary pursuant to a funds transfer may be served only on the beneficiary's bank with respect to the debt owed by that bank to the beneficiary. Any other bank served with the creditor process is not obliged to act with respect to the process.

§4A—503. Injunction or Restraining Order with Respect to Funds Transfer.
For proper cause and in compliance with applicable law, a court may restrain (i) a person from issuing a payment order to initiate a funds transfer, (ii) an originator's bank from executing the payment order of the originator, or (iii) the beneficiary's bank from releasing funds to the beneficiary or the beneficiary from withdrawing the funds. A court may not otherwise restrain a person from issuing a payment order, paying or receiving payment of a payment order, or otherwise acting with respect to a funds transfer.

§4A—504. Order in Which Items and Payment Orders May Be Charged to Account; Order of Withdrawals from Account.

(a) If a receiving bank has received more than one payment order of the sender or one or more payment orders and other items that are payable from the sender's account, the bank may charge the sender's account with respect to the various orders and items in any sequence.

(b) In determining whether a credit to an account has been withdrawn by the holder of the account or applied to a debt of the holder of the account, credits first made to the account are first withdrawn or applied.

§4A—505. Preclusion of Objection to Debit of Customer's Account.

If a receiving bank has received payment from its customer with respect to a payment order issued in the name of the customer as sender and accepted by the bank, and the customer received notification reasonably identifying the order, the customer is precluded from asserting that the bank is not entitled to retain the payment unless the customer notifies the bank of the customer's objection to the payment within one year after the notification was received by the customer.

§4A—506. Rate of Interest.

(a) If, under this Article, a receiving bank is obliged to pay interest with respect to a payment order issued to the bank, the amount payable may be determined (i) by agreement of the sender and receiving bank, or (ii) by a funds-transfer system rule if the payment order is transmitted through a funds-transfer system.

(b) If the amount of interest is not determined by an agreement or rule as stated in subsection (a), the amount is calculated by multiplying the applicable Federal Funds rate by the amount on which interest is payable, and then multiplying the product by the number of days for which interest is payable. The applicable Federal Funds rate is the average of the Federal Funds rates published by the Federal Reserve Bank of New York for each of the days for which interest is payable divided by 360. The Federal Funds rate for any day on which a published rate is not available is the same as the published rate for the next preceding day for which there is a published rate. If a receiving bank that accepted a payment order is required to refund payment to the sender of the order because the funds transfer was not completed, but the failure to complete was not due to any fault by the bank, the interest payable is reduced by a percentage equal to the reserve requirement on deposits of the receiving bank.

§4A—507. Choice of Law.

(a) The following rules apply unless the affected parties otherwise agree or subsection (c) applies:

    (1) The rights and obligations between the sender of a payment order and the receiving bank are governed by the law of the jurisdiction in which the receiving bank is located.

    (2) The rights and obligations between the beneficiary's bank and the beneficiary are governed by the law of the jurisdiction in which the beneficiary's bank is located.

    (3) The issue of when payment is made pursuant to a funds transfer by the originator to the beneficiary is governed by the law of the jurisdiction in which the beneficiary's bank is located.

(b) If the parties described in each paragraph of subsection (a) have made an agreement selecting the law of a particular jurisdiction to govern rights and obligations between each other, the law of that jurisdiction governs those rights and obligations, whether or not the payment order or the funds transfer bears a reasonable relation to that jurisdiction.

(c) A funds-transfer system rule may select the law of a particular jurisdiction to govern (i) rights and obligations between participating banks with respect to payment orders transmitted or processed through the system, or (ii) the rights and obligations of some or all parties to a funds transfer any part of which is carried out by means of the system. A choice of law made pursuant to clause (i) is binding on participating banks. A choice of law made pursuant to clause (ii) is binding on the originator, other sender, or a receiving bank having notice that the funds-transfer system might be used in the funds transfer and of the choice of law by the system when the originator, other sender, or receiving bank issued or accepted a payment order. The beneficiary of a funds transfer is bound by the choice of law if, when the funds transfer is initiated, the beneficiary has notice that the funds-transfer system might be used in the funds transfer and of the choice of law by the system. The law of a jurisdiction selected pursuant to this subsection may govern, whether or not that law bears a reasonable relation to the matter in issue.

(d) In the event of inconsistency between an agreement under subsection (b) and a choice-of-law rule under subsection (c), the agreement under subsection (b) prevails.

(e) If a funds transfer is made by use of more than one funds-transfer system and there is inconsistency between choice-of-law rules of the systems, the matter in issue is governed by the law of the selected jurisdiction that has the most significant relationship to the matter in issue.

* * * *

 REVISED ARTICLE 9
SECURED TRANSACTIONS

PART 1 GENERAL PROVISIONS
[SUBPART 1. SHORT TITLE, DEFINITIONS, AND GENERAL CONCEPTS]

§9—101. Short Title.
This article may be cited as Uniform Commercial Code—Secured Transactions.

§9—102. Definitions and Index of Definitions.

(a) In this article:

    (1) "Accession" means goods that are physically united with other goods in such a manner that the identity of the original goods is not lost.

(2) "Account", except as used in "account for", means a right to payment of a monetary obligation, whether or not earned by performance, (i) for property that has been or is to be sold, leased, licensed, assigned, or otherwise disposed of, (ii) for services rendered or to be rendered, (iii) for a policy of insurance issued or to be issued, (iv) for a secondary obligation incurred or to be incurred, (v) for energy provided or to be provided, (vi) for the use or hire of a vessel under a charter or other contract, (vii) arising out of the use of a credit or charge card or information contained on or for use with the card, or (viii) as winnings in a lottery or other game of chance operated or sponsored by a State, governmental unit of a State, or person licensed or authorized to operate the game by a State or governmental unit of a State. The term includes health-care insurance receivables. The term does not include (i) rights to payment evidenced by chattel paper or an instrument, (ii) commercial tort claims, (iii) deposit accounts, (iv) investment property, (v) letter-of-credit rights or letters of credit, or (vi) rights to payment for money or funds advanced or sold, other than rights arising out of the use of a credit or charge card or information contained on or for use with the card.

(3) "Account debtor" means a person obligated on an account, chattel paper, or general intangible. The term does not include persons obligated to pay a negotiable instrument, even if the instrument constitutes part of chattel paper.

(4) "Accounting", except as used in "accounting for", means a record:

(A) authenticated by a secured party;

(B) indicating the aggregate unpaid secured obligations as of a date not more than 35 days earlier or 35 days later than the date of the record; and

(C) identifying the components of the obligations in reasonable detail.

(5) "Agricultural lien" means an interest, other than a security interest, in farm products:

(A) which secures payment or performance of an obligation for:

(i) goods or services furnished in connection with a debtor's farming operation; or

(ii) rent on real property leased by a debtor in connection with its farming operation;

(B) which is created by statute in favor of a person that:

(i) in the ordinary course of its business furnished goods or services to a debtor in connection with a debtor's farming operation; or

(ii) leased real property to a debtor in connection with the debtor's farming operation; and

(C) whose effectiveness does not depend on the person's possession of the personal property.

(6) "As-extracted collateral" means:

(A) oil, gas, or other minerals that are subject to a security interest that:

(i) is created by a debtor having an interest in the minerals before extraction; and

(ii) attaches to the minerals as extracted; or

(B) accounts arising out of the sale at the wellhead or minehead of oil, gas, or other minerals in which the debtor had an interest before extraction.

(7) "Authenticate" means:

(A) to sign; or

(B) to execute or otherwise adopt a symbol, or encrypt or similarly process a record in whole or in part, with the present intent of the authenticating person to identify the person and adopt or accept a record.

(8) "Bank" means an organization that is engaged in the business of banking. The term includes savings banks, savings and loan associations, credit unions, and trust companies.

(9) "Cash proceeds" means proceeds that are money, checks, deposit accounts, or the like.

(10) "Certificate of title" means a certificate of title with respect to which a statute provides for the security interest in question to be indicated on the certificate as a condition or result of the security interest's obtaining priority over the rights of a lien creditor with respect to the collateral.

(11) "Chattel paper" means a record or records that evidence both a monetary obligation and a security interest in specific goods, a security interest in specific goods and software used in the goods, a security interest in specific goods and license of software used in the goods, a lease of specific goods, or a lease of specific goods and license of software used in the goods. In this paragraph, "monetary obligation" means a monetary obligation secured by the goods or owed under a lease of the goods and includes a monetary obligation with respect to software used in the goods. The term does not include (i) charters or other contracts involving the use or hire of a vessel or (ii) records that evidence a right to payment arising out of the use of a credit or charge card or information contained on or for use with the card. If a transaction is evidenced by records that include an instrument or series of instruments, the group of records taken together constitutes chattel paper.

(12) "Collateral" means the property subject to a security interest or agricultural lien. The term includes:

(A) proceeds to which a security interest attaches;

(B) accounts, chattel paper, payment intangibles, and promissory notes that have been sold; and

(C) goods that are the subject of a consignment.

(13) "Commercial tort claim" means a claim arising in tort with respect to which:

(A) the claimant is an organization; or

(B) the claimant is an individual and the claim:

(i) arose in the course of the claimant's business or profession; and

(ii) does not include damages arising out of personal injury to or the death of an individual.

(14) "Commodity account" means an account maintained by a commodity intermediary in which a commodity contract is carried for a commodity customer.

(15) "Commodity contract" means a commodity futures contract, an option on a commodity futures contract, a commodity option, or another contract if the contract or option is:

(A) traded on or subject to the rules of a board of trade that has been designated as a contract market for such a contract pursuant to federal commodities laws; or

(B) traded on a foreign commodity board of trade, exchange, or market, and is carried on the books of a commodity intermediary for a commodity customer.

(16) "Commodity customer" means a person for which a commodity intermediary carries a commodity contract on its books.

(17) "Commodity intermediary" means a person that:

(A) is registered as a futures commission merchant under federal commodities law; or

(B) in the ordinary course of its business provides clearance or settlement services for a board of trade that has been designated as a contract market pursuant to federal commodities law.

(18) "Communicate" means:

(A) to send a written or other tangible record;

(B) to transmit a record by any means agreed upon by the persons sending and receiving the record; or

(C) in the case of transmission of a record to or by a filing office, to transmit a record by any means prescribed by filing-office rule.

(19) "Consignee" means a merchant to which goods are delivered in a consignment.

(20) "Consignment" means a transaction, regardless of its form, in which a person delivers goods to a merchant for the purpose of sale and:

(A) the merchant:

(i) deals in goods of that kind under a name other than the name of the person making delivery;

(ii) is not an auctioneer; and

(iii) is not generally known by its creditors to be substantially engaged in selling the goods of others;

(B) with respect to each delivery, the aggregate value of the goods is $1,000 or more at the time of delivery;

(C) the goods are not consumer goods immediately before delivery; and

(D) the transaction does not create a security interest that secures an obligation.

(21) "Consignor" means a person that delivers goods to a consignee in a consignment.

(22) "Consumer debtor" means a debtor in a consumer transaction.

(23) "Consumer goods" means goods that are used or bought for use primarily for personal, family, or household purposes.

(24) "Consumer-goods transaction" means a consumer transaction in which:

(A) an individual incurs an obligation primarily for personal, family, or household purposes; and

(B) a security interest in consumer goods secures the obligation.

(25) "Consumer obligor" means an obligor who is an individual and who incurred the obligation as part of a transaction entered into primarily for personal, family, or household purposes.

(26) "Consumer transaction" means a transaction in which (i) an individual incurs an obligation primarily for personal, family, or household purposes, (ii) a security interest secures the obligation, and (iii) the collateral is held or acquired primarily for personal, family, or household purposes. The term includes consumer-goods transactions.

(27) "Continuation statement" means an amendment of a financing statement which:

(A) identifies, by its file number, the initial financing statement to which it relates; and

(B) indicates that it is a continuation statement for, or that it is filed to continue the effectiveness of, the identified financing statement.

(28) "Debtor" means:

(A) a person having an interest, other than a security interest or other lien, in the collateral, whether or not the person is an obligor;

(B) a seller of accounts, chattel paper, payment intangibles, or promissory notes; or

(C) a consignee.

(29) "Deposit account" means a demand, time, savings, passbook, or similar account maintained with a bank. The term does not include investment property or accounts evidenced by an instrument.

(30) "Document" means a document of title or a receipt of the type described in Section 7—201(2).

(31) "Electronic chattel paper" means chattel paper evidenced by a record or records consisting of information stored in an electronic medium.

(32) "Encumbrance" means a right, other than an ownership interest, in real property. The term includes mortgages and other liens on real property.

(33) "Equipment" means goods other than inventory, farm products, or consumer goods.

(34) "Farm products" means goods, other than standing timber, with respect to which the debtor is engaged in a farming operation and which are:

(A) crops grown, growing, or to be grown, including:

(i) crops produced on trees, vines, and bushes; and

(ii) aquatic goods produced in aquacultural operations;

(B) livestock, born or unborn, including aquatic goods produced in aquacultural operations;

(C) supplies used or produced in a farming operation; or

(D) products of crops or livestock in their unmanufactured states.

(35) "Farming operation" means raising, cultivating, propagating, fattening, grazing, or any other farming, livestock, or aquacultural operation.

(36) "File number" means the number assigned to an initial financing statement pursuant to Section 9—519(a).

(37) "Filing office" means an office designated in Section 9—501 as the place to file a financing statement.

(38) "Filing-office rule" means a rule adopted pursuant to Section 9—526.

(39) "Financing statement" means a record or records composed of an initial financing statement and any filed record relating to the initial financing statement.

(40) "Fixture filing" means the filing of a financing statement covering goods that are or are to become fixtures and satisfying Section 9—502(a) and (b). The term includes the filing of a financing statement covering goods of a transmitting utility which are or are to become fixtures.

(41) "Fixtures" means goods that have become so related to particular real property that an interest in them arises under real property law.

(42) "General intangible" means any personal property, including things in action, other than accounts, chattel paper, commercial tort claims, deposit accounts, documents, goods, instruments, investment property, letter-of-credit rights, letters of credit, money, and oil, gas, or other minerals before extraction. The term includes payment intangibles and software.

(43) "Good faith" means honesty in fact and the observance of reasonable commercial standards of fair dealing.

(44) "Goods" means all things that are movable when a security interest attaches. The term includes (i) fixtures, (ii) standing timber that is to be cut and removed under a conveyance or contract for sale, (iii) the unborn young of animals, (iv) crops grown, growing, or to be grown, even if the crops are produced on trees, vines, or bushes, and (v) manufactured homes. The term also includes a computer program embedded in goods and any supporting information provided in connection with a transaction relating to the program if (i) the program is associated with the goods in such a manner that it customarily is considered part of the goods, or (ii) by becoming the owner of the goods, a person acquires a right to use the program in connection with the goods. The term does not include a computer program embedded in goods that consist solely of the medium in which the program is embedded. The term also does not include accounts, chattel paper, commercial tort claims, deposit accounts, documents, general intangibles, instruments, investment property, letter-of-credit rights, letters of credit, money, or oil, gas, or other minerals before extraction.

(45) "Governmental unit" means a subdivision, agency, department, county, parish, municipality, or other unit of the government of the United States, a State, or a foreign country. The term includes an organization having a separate corporate existence if the organization is eligible to issue debt on which interest is exempt from income taxation under the laws of the United States.

(46) "Health-care-insurance receivable" means an interest in or claim under a policy of insurance which is a right to payment of a monetary obligation for health-care goods or services provided.

(47) "Instrument" means a negotiable instrument or any other writing that evidences a right to the payment of a monetary obligation, is not itself a security agreement or lease, and is of a type that in ordinary course of business is transferred by delivery with any necessary indorsement or assignment. The term does not include (i) investment property, (ii) letters of credit, or (iii) writings that evidence a right to payment arising out of the use of a credit or charge card or information contained on or for use with the card.

(48) "Inventory" means goods, other than farm products, which:

(A) are leased by a person as lessor;

(B) are held by a person for sale or lease or to be furnished under a contract of service;

(C) are furnished by a person under a contract of service; or

(D) consist of raw materials, work in process, or materials used or consumed in a business.

(49) "Investment property" means a security, whether certificated or uncertificated, security entitlement, securities account, commodity contract, or commodity account.

(50) "Jurisdiction of organization", with respect to a registered organization, means the jurisdiction under whose law the organization is organized.

(51) "Letter-of-credit right" means a right to payment or performance under a letter of credit, whether or not the beneficiary has demanded or is at the time entitled

to demand payment or performance. The term does not include the right of a beneficiary to demand payment or performance under a letter of credit.

(52) "Lien creditor" means:

(A) a creditor that has acquired a lien on the property involved by attachment, levy, or the like;

(B) an assignee for benefit of creditors from the time of assignment;

(C) a trustee in bankruptcy from the date of the filing of the petition; or

(D) a receiver in equity from the time of appointment.

(53) "Manufactured home" means a structure, transportable in one or more sections, which, in the traveling mode, is eight body feet or more in width or 40 body feet or more in length, or, when erected on site, is 320 or more square feet, and which is built on a permanent chassis and designed to be used as a dwelling with or without a permanent foundation when connected to the required utilities, and includes the plumbing, heating, air-conditioning, and electrical systems contained therein. The term includes any structure that meets all of the requirements of this paragraph except the size requirements and with respect to which the manufacturer voluntarily files a certification required by the United States Secretary of Housing and Urban Development and complies with the standards established under Title 42 of the United States Code.

(54) "Manufactured-home transaction" means a secured transaction:

(A) that creates a purchase-money security interest in a manufactured home, other than a manufactured home held as inventory; or

(B) in which a manufactured home, other than a manufactured home held as inventory, is the primary collateral.

(55) "Mortgage" means a consensual interest in real property, including fixtures, which secures payment or performance of an obligation.

(56) "New debtor" means a person that becomes bound as debtor under Section 9—203(d) by a security agreement previously entered into by another person.

(57) "New value" means (i) money, (ii) money's worth in property, services, or new credit, or (iii) release by a transferee of an interest in property previously transferred to the transferee. The term does not include an obligation substituted for another obligation.

(58) "Noncash proceeds" means proceeds other than cash proceeds.

(59) "Obligor" means a person that, with respect to an obligation secured by a security interest in or an agricultural lien on the collateral, (i) owes payment or other performance of the obligation, (ii) has provided property

other than the collateral to secure payment or other performance of the obligation, or (iii) is otherwise accountable in whole or in part for payment or other performance of the obligation. The term does not include issuers or nominated persons under a letter of credit.

(60) "Original debtor", except as used in Section 9—310(c), means a person that, as debtor, entered into a security agreement to which a new debtor has become bound under Section 9—203(d).

(61) "Payment intangible" means a general intangible under which the account debtor's principal obligation is a monetary obligation.

(62) "Person related to", with respect to an individual, means:

(A) the spouse of the individual;

(B) a brother, brother-in-law, sister, or sister-in-law of the individual;

(C) an ancestor or lineal descendant of the individual or the individual's spouse; or

(D) any other relative, by blood or marriage, of the individual or the individual's spouse who shares the same home with the individual.

(63) "Person related to", with respect to an organization, means:

(A) a person directly or indirectly controlling, controlled by, or under common control with the organization;

(B) an officer or director of, or a person performing similar functions with respect to, the organization;

(C) an officer or director of, or a person performing similar functions with respect to, a person described in subparagraph (A);

(D) the spouse of an individual described in subparagraph (A), (B), or (C); or

(E) an individual who is related by blood or marriage to an individual described in subparagraph (A), (B), (C), or (D) and shares the same home with the individual.

(64) "Proceeds", except as used in Section 9—609(b), means the following property:

(A) whatever is acquired upon the sale, lease, license, exchange, or other disposition of collateral;

(B) whatever is collected on, or distributed on account of, collateral;

(C) rights arising out of collateral;

(D) to the extent of the value of collateral, claims arising out of the loss, nonconformity, or interference with the use of, defects or infringement of rights in, or damage to, the collateral; or

(E) to the extent of the value of collateral and to the extent payable to the debtor or the secured party, insurance payable by reason of the loss or nonconformity of, defects or infringement of rights in, or damage to, the collateral.

(65) "Promissory note" means an instrument that evidences a promise to pay a monetary obligation, does not evidence an order to pay, and does not contain an acknowledgment by a bank that the bank has received for deposit a sum of money or funds.

(66) "Proposal" means a record authenticated by a secured party which includes the terms on which the secured party is willing to accept collateral in full or partial satisfaction of the obligation it secures pursuant to Sections 9—620, 9—621, and 9—622.

(67) "Public-finance transaction" means a secured transaction in connection with which:

(A) debt securities are issued;

(B) all or a portion of the securities issued have an initial stated maturity of at least 20 years; and

(C) the debtor, obligor, secured party, account debtor or other person obligated on collateral, assignor or assignee of a secured obligation, or assignor or assignee of a security interest is a State or a governmental unit of a State.

(68) "Pursuant to commitment", with respect to an advance made or other value given by a secured party, means pursuant to the secured party's obligation, whether or not a subsequent event of default or other event not within the secured party's control has relieved or may relieve the secured party from its obligation.

(69) "Record", except as used in "for record", "of record", "record or legal title", and "record owner", means information that is inscribed on a tangible medium or which is stored in an electronic or other medium and is retrievable in perceivable form.

(70) "Registered organization" means an organization organized solely under the law of a single State or the United States and as to which the State or the United States must maintain a public record showing the organization to have been organized.

(71) "Secondary obligor" means an obligor to the extent that:

(A) the obligor's obligation is secondary; or

(B) the obligor has a right of recourse with respect to an obligation secured by collateral against the debtor, another obligor, or property of either.

(72) "Secured party" means:

(A) a person in whose favor a security interest is created or provided for under a security agreement, whether or not any obligation to be secured is outstanding;

(B) a person that holds an agricultural lien;

(C) a consignor;

(D) a person to which accounts, chattel paper, payment intangibles, or promissory notes have been sold;

(E) a trustee, indenture trustee, agent, collateral agent, or other representative in whose favor a security interest or agricultural lien is created or provided for; or

(F) a person that holds a security interest arising under Section 2—401, 2—505, 2—711(3), 2A—508(5), 4—210, or 5—118.

(73) "Security agreement" means an agreement that creates or provides for a security interest.

(74) "Send", in connection with a record or notification, means:

(A) to deposit in the mail, deliver for transmission, or transmit by any other usual means of communication, with postage or cost of transmission provided for, addressed to any address reasonable under the circumstances; or

(B) to cause the record or notification to be received within the time that it would have been received if properly sent under subparagraph (A).

(75) "Software" means a computer program and any supporting information provided in connection with a transaction relating to the program. The term does not include a computer program that is included in the definition of goods.

(76) "State" means a State of the United States, the District of Columbia, Puerto Rico, the United States Virgin Islands, or any territory or insular possession subject to the jurisdiction of the United States.

(77) "Supporting obligation" means a letter-of-credit right or secondary obligation that supports the payment or performance of an account, chattel paper, a document, a general intangible, an instrument, or investment property.

(78) "Tangible chattel paper" means chattel paper evidenced by a record or records consisting of information that is inscribed on a tangible medium.

(79) "Termination statement" means an amendment of a financing statement which:

(A) identifies, by its file number, the initial financing statement to which it relates; and

(B) indicates either that it is a termination statement or that the identified financing statement is no longer effective.

(80) "Transmitting utility" means a person primarily engaged in the business of:

(A) operating a railroad, subway, street railway, or trolley bus;

(B) transmitting communications electrically, electromagnetically, or by light;

(C) transmitting goods by pipeline or sewer; or

(D) transmitting or producing and transmitting electricity, steam, gas, or water.

(b) The following definitions in other articles apply to this article:

"Applicant."	Section 5—102
"Beneficiary."	Section 5—102
"Broker."	Section 8—102
"Certificated security."	Section 8—102
"Check."	Section 3—104
"Clearing corporation."	Section 8—102
"Contract for sale."	Section 2—106
"Customer."	Section 4—104
"Entitlement holder."	Section 8—102
"Financial asset."	Section 8—102
"Holder in due course."	Section 3—302
"Issuer" (with respect to a letter of credit or letter-of-credit right).	Section 5—102
"Issuer" (with respect to a security).	Section 8—201
"Lease."	Section 2A—103
"Lease agreement."	Section 2A—103
"Lease contract."	Section 2A—103
"Leasehold interest."	Section 2A—103
"Lessee."	Section 2A—103
"Lessee in ordinary course of business."	Section 2A—103
"Lessor."	Section 2A—103
"Lessor's residual interest."	Section 2A—103
"Letter of credit."	Section 5—102
"Merchant."	Section 2—104
"Negotiable instrument."	Section 3—104
"Nominated person."	Section 5—102
"Note."	Section 3—104
"Proceeds of a letter of credit."	Section 5—114
"Prove."	Section 3—103
"Sale."	Section 2—106
"Securities account."	Section 8—501
"Securities intermediary."	Section 8—102
"Security."	Section 8—102
"Security certificate."	Section 8—102
"Security entitlement."	Section 8—102
"Uncertificated security."	Section 8—102

(c) Article 1 contains general definitions and principles of construction and interpretation applicable throughout this article.

Amended in 1999 and 2000.

§9—103. Purchase-Money Security Interest; Application of Payments; Burden of Establishing.

(a) In this section:

(1) "purchase-money collateral" means goods or software that secures a purchase-money obligation incurred with respect to that collateral; and

(2) "purchase-money obligation" means an obligation of an obligor incurred as all or part of the price of the collateral or for value given to enable the debtor to acquire rights in or the use of the collateral if the value is in fact so used.

(b) A security interest in goods is a purchase-money security interest:

(1) to the extent that the goods are purchase-money collateral with respect to that security interest;

(2) if the security interest is in inventory that is or was purchase-money collateral, also to the extent that the security interest secures a purchase-money obligation incurred with respect to other inventory in which the secured party holds or held a purchase-money security interest; and

(3) also to the extent that the security interest secures a purchase-money obligation incurred with respect to software in which the secured party holds or held a purchase-money security interest.

(c) A security interest in software is a purchase-money security interest to the extent that the security interest also secures a purchase-money obligation incurred with respect to goods in which the secured party holds or held a purchase-money security interest if:

(1) the debtor acquired its interest in the software in an integrated transaction in which it acquired an interest in the goods; and

(2) the debtor acquired its interest in the software for the principal purpose of using the software in the goods.

(d) The security interest of a consignor in goods that are the subject of a consignment is a purchase-money security interest in inventory.

(e) In a transaction other than a consumer-goods transaction, if the extent to which a security interest is a purchase-money security interest depends on the application of a payment to a particular obligation, the payment must be applied:

(1) in accordance with any reasonable method of application to which the parties agree;

(2) in the absence of the parties' agreement to a reasonable method, in accordance with any intention of the obligor manifested at or before the time of payment; or

(3) in the absence of an agreement to a reasonable method and a timely manifestation of the obligor's intention, in the following order:

(A) to obligations that are not secured; and

(B) if more than one obligation is secured, to obligations secured by purchase-money security interests in the order in which those obligations were incurred.

(f) In a transaction other than a consumer-goods transaction, a purchase-money security interest does not lose its status as such, even if:

(1) the purchase-money collateral also secures an obligation that is not a purchase-money obligation;

(2) collateral that is not purchase-money collateral also secures the purchase-money obligation; or

(3) the purchase-money obligation has been renewed, refinanced, consolidated, or restructured.

(g) In a transaction other than a consumer-goods transaction, a secured party claiming a purchase-money security interest has the burden of establishing the extent to which the security interest is a purchase-money security interest.

(h) The limitation of the rules in subsections (e), (f), and (g) to transactions other than consumer-goods transactions is intended to leave to the court the determination of the proper rules in consumer-goods transactions. The court may not infer from that limitation the nature of the proper rule in consumer-goods transactions and may continue to apply established approaches.

§9—104. *Control of Deposit Account.*

(a) A secured party has control of a deposit account if:
(1) the secured party is the bank with which the deposit account is maintained;
(2) the debtor, secured party, and bank have agreed in an authenticated record that the bank will comply with instructions originated by the secured party directing disposition of the funds in the deposit account without further consent by the debtor; or
(3) the secured party becomes the bank's customer with respect to the deposit account.

(b) A secured party that has satisfied subsection (a) has control, even if the debtor retains the right to direct the disposition of funds from the deposit account.

§9—105. *Control of Electronic Chattel Paper.*

A secured party has control of electronic chattel paper if the record or records comprising the chattel paper are created, stored, and assigned in such a manner that:
(1) a single authoritative copy of the record or records exists which is unique, identifiable and, except as otherwise provided in paragraphs (4), (5), and (6), unalterable;
(2) the authoritative copy identifies the secured party as the assignee of the record or records;
(3) the authoritative copy is communicated to and maintained by the secured party or its designated custodian;
(4) copies or revisions that add or change an identified assignee of the authoritative copy can be made only with the participation of the secured party;
(5) each copy of the authoritative copy and any copy of a copy is readily identifiable as a copy that is not the authoritative copy; and
(6) any revision of the authoritative copy is readily identifiable as an authorized or unauthorized revision.

§9—106. *Control of Investment Property.*

(a) A person has control of a certificated security, uncertificated security, or security entitlement as provided in Section 8—106.

(b) A secured party has control of a commodity contract if:
(1) the secured party is the commodity intermediary with which the commodity contract is carried; or
(2) the commodity customer, secured party, and commodity intermediary have agreed that the commodity intermediary will apply any value distributed on account of the commodity contract as directed by the secured party without further consent by the commodity customer.

(c) A secured party having control of all security entitlements or commodity contracts carried in a securities account or commodity account has control over the securities account or commodity account.

§9—107. *Control of Letter-of-Credit Right.*

A secured party has control of a letter-of-credit right to the extent of any right to payment or performance by the issuer or any nominated person if the issuer or nominated person has consented to an assignment of proceeds of the letter of credit under Section 5—114(c) or otherwise applicable law or practice.

§9—108. *Sufficiency of Description.*

(a) Except as otherwise provided in subsections (c), (d), and (e), a description of personal or real property is sufficient, whether or not it is specific, if it reasonably identifies what is described.

(b) Except as otherwise provided in subsection (d), a description of collateral reasonably identifies the collateral if it identifies the collateral by:
(1) specific listing;
(2) category;
(3) except as otherwise provided in subsection (e), a type of collateral defined in [the Uniform Commercial Code];
(4) quantity;
(5) computational or allocational formula or procedure; or
(6) except as otherwise provided in subsection (c), any other method, if the identity of the collateral is objectively determinable.

(c) A description of collateral as "all the debtor's assets" or "all the debtor's personal property" or using words of similar import does not reasonably identify the collateral.

(d) Except as otherwise provided in subsection (e), a description of a security entitlement, securities account, or commodity account is sufficient if it describes:
(1) the collateral by those terms or as investment property; or
(2) the underlying financial asset or commodity contract.

(e) A description only by type of collateral defined in [the Uniform Commercial Code] is an insufficient description of:
(1) a commercial tort claim; or
(2) in a consumer transaction, consumer goods, a security entitlement, a securities account, or a commodity account.

[SUBPART 2. APPLICABILITY OF ARTICLE]

§9—109. Scope.

(a) Except as otherwise provided in subsections (c) and (d), this article applies to:

(1) a transaction, regardless of its form, that creates a security interest in personal property or fixtures by contract;

(2) an agricultural lien;

(3) a sale of accounts, chattel paper, payment intangibles, or promissory notes;

(4) a consignment;

(5) a security interest arising under Section 2—401, 2—505, 2—711(3), or 2A—508(5), as provided in Section 9—110; and

(6) a security interest arising under Section 4—210 or 5—118.

(b) The application of this article to a security interest in a secured obligation is not affected by the fact that the obligation is itself secured by a transaction or interest to which this article does not apply.

(c) This article does not apply to the extent that:

(1) a statute, regulation, or treaty of the United States preempts this article;

(2) another statute of this State expressly governs the creation, perfection, priority, or enforcement of a security interest created by this State or a governmental unit of this State;

(3) a statute of another State, a foreign country, or a governmental unit of another State or a foreign country, other than a statute generally applicable to security interests, expressly governs creation, perfection, priority, or enforcement of a security interest created by the State, country, or governmental unit; or

(4) the rights of a transferee beneficiary or nominated person under a letter of credit are independent and superior under Section 5—114.

(d) This article does not apply to:

(1) a landlord's lien, other than an agricultural lien;

(2) a lien, other than an agricultural lien, given by statute or other rule of law for services or materials, but Section 9—333 applies with respect to priority of the lien;

(3) an assignment of a claim for wages, salary, or other compensation of an employee;

(4) a sale of accounts, chattel paper, payment intangibles, or promissory notes as part of a sale of the business out of which they arose;

(5) an assignment of accounts, chattel paper, payment intangibles, or promissory notes which is for the purpose of collection only;

(6) an assignment of a right to payment under a contract to an assignee that is also obligated to perform under the contract;

(7) an assignment of a single account, payment intangible, or promissory note to an assignee in full or partial satisfaction of a preexisting indebtedness;

(8) a transfer of an interest in or an assignment of a claim under a policy of insurance, other than an assignment by or to a health-care provider of a health-care-insurance receivable and any subsequent assignment of the right to payment, but Sections 9—315 and 9—322 apply with respect to proceeds and priorities in proceeds;

(9) an assignment of a right represented by a judgment, other than a judgment taken on a right to payment that was collateral;

(10) a right of recoupment or set-off, but:

(A) Section 9—340 applies with respect to the effectiveness of rights of recoupment or set-off against deposit accounts; and

(B) Section 9—404 applies with respect to defenses or claims of an account debtor;

(11) the creation or transfer of an interest in or lien on real property, including a lease or rents thereunder, except to the extent that provision is made for:

(A) liens on real property in Sections 9—203 and 9—308;

(B) fixtures in Section 9—334;

(C) fixture filings in Sections 9—501, 9—502, 9—512, 9—516, and 9—519; and

(D) security agreements covering personal and real property in Section 9—604;

(12) an assignment of a claim arising in tort, other than a commercial tort claim, but Sections 9—315 and 9—322 apply with respect to proceeds and priorities in proceeds; or

(13) an assignment of a deposit account in a consumer transaction, but Sections 9—315 and 9—322 apply with respect to proceeds and priorities in proceeds.

§9—110. Security Interests Arising under Article 2 or 2A.

A security interest arising under Section 2—401, 2—505, 2—711(3), or 2A—508(5) is subject to this article. However, until the debtor obtains possession of the goods:

(1) the security interest is enforceable, even if Section 9—203(b)(3) has not been satisfied;

(2) filing is not required to perfect the security interest;

(3) the rights of the secured party after default by the debtor are governed by Article 2 or 2A; and

(4) the security interest has priority over a conflicting security interest created by the debtor.

PART 2 EFFECTIVENESS OF SECURITY AGREEMENT; ATTACHMENT OF SECURITY INTEREST; RIGHTS OF PARTIES TO SECURITY AGREEMENT [SUBPART 1. EFFECTIVENESS AND ATTACHMENT]

§9—201. General Effectiveness of Security Agreement.

(a) Except as otherwise provided in [the Uniform Commercial Code], a security agreement is effective according to its terms between the parties, against purchasers of the collateral, and against creditors.

(b) A transaction subject to this article is subject to any applicable rule of law which establishes a different rule for consumers and [insert reference to (i) any other statute or regulation that regulates the rates, charges, agreements, and practices for loans, credit sales, or other extensions of credit and (ii) any consumer-protection statute or regulation].

(c) In case of conflict between this article and a rule of law, statute, or regulation described in subsection (b), the rule of law, statute, or regulation controls. Failure to comply with a statute or regulation described in subsection (b) has only the effect the statute or regulation specifies.

(d) This article does not:

(1) validate any rate, charge, agreement, or practice that violates a rule of law, statute, or regulation described in subsection (b); or

(2) extend the application of the rule of law, statute, or regulation to a transaction not otherwise subject to it.

§9—202. Title to Collateral Immaterial.

Except as otherwise provided with respect to consignments or sales of accounts, chattel paper, payment intangibles, or promissory notes, the provisions of this article with regard to rights and obligations apply whether title to collateral is in the secured party or the debtor.

§9—203. Attachment and Enforceability of Security Interest; Proceeds; Supporting Obligations; Formal Requisites.

(a) A security interest attaches to collateral when it becomes enforceable against the debtor with respect to the collateral, unless an agreement expressly postpones the time of attachment.

(b) Except as otherwise provided in subsections (c) through (i), a security interest is enforceable against the debtor and third parties with respect to the collateral only if:

(1) value has been given;

(2) the debtor has rights in the collateral or the power to transfer rights in the collateral to a secured party; and

(3) one of the following conditions is met:

(A) the debtor has authenticated a security agreement that provides a description of the collateral and, if the security interest covers timber to be cut, a description of the land concerned;

(B) the collateral is not a certificated security and is in the possession of the secured party under Section 9—313 pursuant to the debtor's security agreement;

(C) the collateral is a certificated security in registered form and the security certificate has been delivered to the secured party under Section 8—301 pursuant to the debtor's security agreement; or

(D) the collateral is deposit accounts, electronic chattel paper, investment property, or letter-of-credit rights, and the secured party has control under Section 9—104, 9—105, 9—106, or 9—107 pursuant to the debtor's security agreement.

(c) Subsection (b) is subject to Section 4—210 on the security interest of a collecting bank, Section 5—118 on the security interest of a letter-of-credit issuer or nominated person, Section 9—110 on a security interest arising under Article 2 or 2A, and Section 9—206 on security interests in investment property.

(d) A person becomes bound as debtor by a security agreement entered into by another person if, by operation of law other than this article or by contract:

(1) the security agreement becomes effective to create a security interest in the person's property; or

(2) the person becomes generally obligated for the obligations of the other person, including the obligation secured under the security agreement, and acquires or succeeds to all or substantially all of the assets of the other person.

(e) If a new debtor becomes bound as debtor by a security agreement entered into by another person:

(1) the agreement satisfies subsection (b)(3) with respect to existing or after-acquired property of the new debtor to the extent the property is described in the agreement; and

(2) another agreement is not necessary to make a security interest in the property enforceable.

(f) The attachment of a security interest in collateral gives the secured party the rights to proceeds provided by Section 9—315 and is also attachment of a security interest in a supporting obligation for the collateral.

(g) The attachment of a security interest in a right to payment or performance secured by a security interest or other lien on personal or real property is also attachment of a security interest in the security interest, mortgage, or other lien.

(h) The attachment of a security interest in a securities account is also attachment of a security interest in the security entitlements carried in the securities account.

(i) The attachment of a security interest in a commodity account is also attachment of a security interest in the commodity contracts carried in the commodity account.

§9—204. After-Acquired Property; Future Advances.

(a) Except as otherwise provided in subsection (b), a security agreement may create or provide for a security interest in after-acquired collateral.

(b) A security interest does not attach under a term constituting an after-acquired property clause to:

(1) consumer goods, other than an accession when given as additional security, unless the debtor acquires rights in them within 10 days after the secured party gives value; or

(2) a commercial tort claim.

(c) A security agreement may provide that collateral secures, or that accounts, chattel paper, payment intangibles, or promissory notes are sold in connection with, future advances or other value, whether or not the advances or value are given pursuant to commitment.

§9—205. Use or Disposition of Collateral Permissible.

(a) A security interest is not invalid or fraudulent against creditors solely because:

(1) the debtor has the right or ability to:

(A) use, commingle, or dispose of all or part of the collateral, including returned or repossessed goods;

(B) collect, compromise, enforce, or otherwise deal with collateral;

(C) accept the return of collateral or make repossessions; or

(D) use, commingle, or dispose of proceeds; or

(2) the secured party fails to require the debtor to account for proceeds or replace collateral.

(b) This section does not relax the requirements of possession if attachment, perfection, or enforcement of a security interest depends upon possession of the collateral by the secured party.

§9—206. Security Interest Arising in Purchase or Delivery of Financial Asset.

(a) A security interest in favor of a securities intermediary attaches to a person's security entitlement if:

(1) the person buys a financial asset through the securities intermediary in a transaction in which the person is obligated to pay the purchase price to the securities intermediary at the time of the purchase; and

(2) the securities intermediary credits the financial asset to the buyer's securities account before the buyer pays the securities intermediary.

(b) The security interest described in subsection (a) secures the person's obligation to pay for the financial asset.

(c) A security interest in favor of a person that delivers a certificated security or other financial asset represented by a writing attaches to the security or other financial asset if:

(1) the security or other financial asset:

(A) in the ordinary course of business is transferred by delivery with any necessary indorsement or assignment; and

(B) is delivered under an agreement between persons in the business of dealing with such securities or financial assets; and

(2) the agreement calls for delivery against payment.

(d) The security interest described in subsection (c) secures the obligation to make payment for the delivery.

[SUBPART 2. RIGHTS AND DUTIES]

§9—207. Rights and Duties of Secured Party Having Possession or Control of Collateral.

(a) Except as otherwise provided in subsection (d), a secured party shall use reasonable care in the custody and preservation of collateral in the secured party's possession. In the case of chattel paper or an instrument, reasonable care includes taking necessary steps to preserve rights against prior parties unless otherwise agreed.

(b) Except as otherwise provided in subsection (d), if a secured party has possession of collateral:

(1) reasonable expenses, including the cost of insurance and payment of taxes or other charges, incurred in the custody, preservation, use, or operation of the collateral are chargeable to the debtor and are secured by the collateral;

(2) the risk of accidental loss or damage is on the debtor to the extent of a deficiency in any effective insurance coverage;

(3) the secured party shall keep the collateral identifiable, but fungible collateral may be commingled; and

(4) the secured party may use or operate the collateral:

(A) for the purpose of preserving the collateral or its value;

(B) as permitted by an order of a court having competent jurisdiction; or

(C) except in the case of consumer goods, in the manner and to the extent agreed by the debtor.

(c) Except as otherwise provided in subsection (d), a secured party having possession of collateral or control of collateral under Section 9—104, 9—105, 9—106, or 9—107:

(1) may hold as additional security any proceeds, except money or funds, received from the collateral;

(2) shall apply money or funds received from the collateral to reduce the secured obligation, unless remitted to the debtor; and

(3) may create a security interest in the collateral.

(d) If the secured party is a buyer of accounts, chattel paper, payment intangibles, or promissory notes or a consignor:

(1) subsection (a) does not apply unless the secured party is entitled under an agreement:

(A) to charge back uncollected collateral; or

(B) otherwise to full or limited recourse against the debtor or a secondary obligor based on the nonpayment or other default of an account debtor or other obligor on the collateral; and

(2) subsections (b) and (c) do not apply.

particular jurisdiction, that jurisdiction is the bank's jurisdiction.

(4) If none of the preceding paragraphs applies, the bank's jurisdiction is the jurisdiction in which the office identified in an account statement as the office serving the customer's account is located.

(5) If none of the preceding paragraphs applies, the bank's jurisdiction is the jurisdiction in which the chief executive office of the bank is located.

§9—305. Law Governing Perfection and Priority of Security Interests in Investment Property.

(a) Except as otherwise provided in subsection (c), the following rules apply:

(1) While a security certificate is located in a jurisdiction, the local law of that jurisdiction governs perfection, the effect of perfection or nonperfection, and the priority of a security interest in the certificated security represented thereby.

(2) The local law of the issuer's jurisdiction as specified in Section 8—110(d) governs perfection, the effect of perfection or nonperfection, and the priority of a security interest in an uncertificated security.

(3) The local law of the securities intermediary's jurisdiction as specified in Section 8—110(e) governs perfection, the effect of perfection or nonperfection, and the priority of a security interest in a security entitlement or securities account.

(4) The local law of the commodity intermediary's jurisdiction governs perfection, the effect of perfection or nonperfection, and the priority of a security interest in a commodity contract or commodity account.

(b) The following rules determine a commodity intermediary's jurisdiction for purposes of this part:

(1) If an agreement between the commodity intermediary and commodity customer governing the commodity account expressly provides that a particular jurisdiction is the commodity intermediary's jurisdiction for purposes of this part, this article, or [the Uniform Commercial Code], that jurisdiction is the commodity intermediary's jurisdiction.

(2) If paragraph (1) does not apply and an agreement between the commodity intermediary and commodity customer governing the commodity account expressly provides that the agreement is governed by the law of a particular jurisdiction, that jurisdiction is the commodity intermediary's jurisdiction.

(3) If neither paragraph (1) nor paragraph (2) applies and an agreement between the commodity intermediary and commodity customer governing the commodity account expressly provides that the commodity account is maintained at an office in a particular jurisdiction, that jurisdiction is the commodity intermediary's jurisdiction.

(4) If none of the preceding paragraphs applies, the commodity intermediary's jurisdiction is the jurisdiction in which the office identified in an account statement as the office serving the commodity customer's account is located.

(5) If none of the preceding paragraphs applies, the commodity intermediary's jurisdiction is the jurisdiction in which the chief executive office of the commodity intermediary is located.

(c) The local law of the jurisdiction in which the debtor is located governs:

(1) perfection of a security interest in investment property by filing;

(2) automatic perfection of a security interest in investment property created by a broker or securities intermediary; and

(3) automatic perfection of a security interest in a commodity contract or commodity account created by a commodity intermediary.

§9—306. Law Governing Perfection and Priority of Security Interests in Letter-of-Credit Rights.

(a) Subject to subsection (c), the local law of the issuer's jurisdiction or a nominated person's jurisdiction governs perfection, the effect of perfection or nonperfection, and the priority of a security interest in a letter-of-credit right if the issuer's jurisdiction or nominated person's jurisdiction is a State.

(b) For purposes of this part, an issuer's jurisdiction or nominated person's jurisdiction is the jurisdiction whose law governs the liability of the issuer or nominated person with respect to the letter-of-credit right as provided in Section 5—116.

(c) This section does not apply to a security interest that is perfected only under Section 9—308(d).

§9—307. Location of Debtor.

(a) In this section, "place of business" means a place where a debtor conducts its affairs.

(b) Except as otherwise provided in this section, the following rules determine a debtor's location:

(1) A debtor who is an individual is located at the individual's principal residence.

(2) A debtor that is an organization and has only one place of business is located at its place of business.

(3) A debtor that is an organization and has more than one place of business is located at its chief executive office.

(c) Subsection (b) applies only if a debtor's residence, place of business, or chief executive office, as applicable, is located in a jurisdiction whose law generally requires information concerning the existence of a nonpossessory security interest to be made generally available in a filing, recording, or registration system as a condition or result of the security interest's obtaining priority over the rights of a lien creditor with respect to the collateral. If subsection (b) does not apply, the debtor is located in the District of Columbia.

(d) A person that ceases to exist, have a residence, or have a place of business continues to be located in the jurisdiction specified by subsections (b) and (c).

(e) A registered organization that is organized under the law of a State is located in that State.

(f) Except as otherwise provided in subsection (i), a registered organization that is organized under the law of the United States and a branch or agency of a bank that is not organized under the law of the United States or a State are located:

(1) in the State that the law of the United States designates, if the law designates a State of location;

(2) in the State that the registered organization, branch, or agency designates, if the law of the United States authorizes the registered organization, branch, or agency to designate its State of location; or

(3) in the District of Columbia, if neither paragraph (1) nor paragraph (2) applies.

(g) A registered organization continues to be located in the jurisdiction specified by subsection (e) or (f) notwithstanding:

(1) the suspension, revocation, forfeiture, or lapse of the registered organization's status as such in its jurisdiction of organization; or

(2) the dissolution, winding up, or cancellation of the existence of the registered organization.

(h) The United States is located in the District of Columbia.

(i) A branch or agency of a bank that is not organized under the law of the United States or a State is located in the State in which the branch or agency is licensed, if all branches and agencies of the bank are licensed in only one State.

(j) A foreign air carrier under the Federal Aviation Act of 1958, as amended, is located at the designated office of the agent upon which service of process may be made on behalf of the carrier.

(k) This section applies only for purposes of this part.

[SUBPART 2. PERFECTION]

§9—308. When Security Interest or Agricultural Lien Is Perfected; Continuity of Perfection.

(a) Except as otherwise provided in this section and Section 9—309, a security interest is perfected if it has attached and all of the applicable requirements for perfection in Sections 9—310 through 9—316 have been satisfied. A security interest is perfected when it attaches if the applicable requirements are satisfied before the security interest attaches.

(b) An agricultural lien is perfected if it has become effective and all of the applicable requirements for perfection in Section 9—310 have been satisfied. An agricultural lien is perfected when it becomes effective if the applicable requirements are satisfied before the agricultural lien becomes effective.

(c) A security interest or agricultural lien is perfected continuously if it is originally perfected by one method under this article and is later perfected by another method under this article, without an intermediate period when it was unperfected.

(d) Perfection of a security interest in collateral also perfects a security interest in a supporting obligation for the collateral.

(e) Perfection of a security interest in a right to payment or performance also perfects a security interest in a security interest, mortgage, or other lien on personal or real property securing the right.

(f) Perfection of a security interest in a securities account also perfects a security interest in the security entitlements carried in the securities account.

(g) Perfection of a security interest in a commodity account also perfects a security interest in the commodity contracts carried in the commodity account.

Legislative Note: Any statute conflicting with subsection (e) must be made expressly subject to that subsection.

§9—309. Security Interest Perfected upon Attachment. The following security interests are perfected when they attach:

(1) a purchase-money security interest in consumer goods, except as otherwise provided in Section 9—311(b) with respect to consumer goods that are subject to a statute or treaty described in Section 9—311(a);

(2) an assignment of accounts or payment intangibles which does not by itself or in conjunction with other assignments to the same assignee transfer a significant part of the assignor's outstanding accounts or payment intangibles;

(3) a sale of a payment intangible;

(4) a sale of a promissory note;

(5) a security interest created by the assignment of a health-care-insurance receivable to the provider of the health-care goods or services;

(6) a security interest arising under Section 2—401, 2—505, 2—711(3), or 2A—508(5), until the debtor obtains possession of the collateral;

(7) a security interest of a collecting bank arising under Section 4—210;

(8) a security interest of an issuer or nominated person arising under Section 5—118;

(9) a security interest arising in the delivery of a financial asset under Section 9—206(c);

(10) a security interest in investment property created by a broker or securities intermediary;

(11) a security interest in a commodity contract or a commodity account created by a commodity intermediary;

(12) an assignment for the benefit of all creditors of the transferor and subsequent transfers by the assignee thereunder; and

(13) a security interest created by an assignment of a beneficial interest in a decedent's estate; and

(14) a sale by an individual of an account that is a right to payment of winnings in a lottery or other game of chance.

§9—310. When Filing Required to Perfect Security Interest or Agricultural Lien; Security Interests and Agricultural Liens to Which Filing Provisions Do Not Apply.

(a) Except as otherwise provided in subsection (b) and Section 9—312(b), a financing statement must be filed to perfect all security interests and agricultural liens.

(b) The filing of a financing statement is not necessary to perfect a security interest:

(1) that is perfected under Section 9—308(d), (e), (f), or (g);

(2) that is perfected under Section 9—309 when it attaches;

(3) in property subject to a statute, regulation, or treaty described in Section 9—311(a);

(4) in goods in possession of a bailee which is perfected under Section 9—312(d)(1) or (2);

(5) in certificated securities, documents, goods, or instruments which is perfected without filing or possession under Section 9—312(e), (f), or (g);

(6) in collateral in the secured party's possession under Section 9—313;

(7) in a certificated security which is perfected by delivery of the security certificate to the secured party under Section 9—313;

(8) in deposit accounts, electronic chattel paper, investment property, or letter-of-credit rights which is perfected by control under Section 9—314;

(9) in proceeds which is perfected under Section 9—315; or

(10) that is perfected under Section 9—316.

(c) If a secured party assigns a perfected security interest or agricultural lien, a filing under this article is not required to continue the perfected status of the security interest against creditors of and transferees from the original debtor.

§9—311. Perfection of Security Interests in Property Subject to Certain Statutes, Regulations, and Treaties.

(a) Except as otherwise provided in subsection (d), the filing of a financing statement is not necessary or effective to perfect a security interest in property subject to:

(1) a statute, regulation, or treaty of the United States whose requirements for a security interest's obtaining priority over the rights of a lien creditor with respect to the property preempt Section 9—310(a);

(2) [list any certificate-of-title statute covering automobiles, trailers, mobile homes, boats, farm tractors, or the like, which provides for a security interest to be indicated on the certificate as a condition or result of

perfection, and any non-Uniform Commercial Code central filing statute]; or

(3) a certificate-of-title statute of another jurisdiction which provides for a security interest to be indicated on the certificate as a condition or result of the security interest's obtaining priority over the rights of a lien creditor with respect to the property.

(b) Compliance with the requirements of a statute, regulation, or treaty described in subsection (a) for obtaining priority over the rights of a lien creditor is equivalent to the filing of a financing statement under this article. Except as otherwise provided in subsection (d) and Sections 9—313 and 9—316(d) and (e) for goods covered by a certificate of title, a security interest in property subject to a statute, regulation, or treaty described in subsection (a) may be perfected only by compliance with those requirements, and a security interest so perfected remains perfected notwithstanding a change in the use or transfer of possession of the collateral.

(c) Except as otherwise provided in subsection (d) and Section 9—316(d) and (e), duration and renewal of perfection of a security interest perfected by compliance with the requirements prescribed by a statute, regulation, or treaty described in subsection (a) are governed by the statute, regulation, or treaty. In other respects, the security interest is subject to this article.

(d) During any period in which collateral subject to a statute specified in subsection (a)(2) is inventory held for sale or lease by a person or leased by that person as lessor and that person is in the business of selling goods of that kind, this section does not apply to a security interest in that collateral created by that person.

Legislative Note: This Article contemplates that perfection of a security interest in goods covered by a certificate of title occurs upon receipt by appropriate State officials of a properly tendered application for a certificate of title on which the security interest is to be indicated, without a relation back to an earlier time. States whose certificate-of-title statutes provide for perfection at a different time or contain a relation-back provision should amend the statutes accordingly.

§9—312. Perfection of Security Interests in Chattel Paper, Deposit Accounts, Documents, Goods Covered by Documents, Instruments, Investment Property, Letter-of-Credit Rights, and Money; Perfection by Permissive Filing; Temporary Perfection without Filing or Transfer of Possession.

(a) A security interest in chattel paper, negotiable documents, instruments, or investment property may be perfected by filing.

(b) Except as otherwise provided in Section 9—315(c) and (d) for proceeds:

(1) a security interest in a deposit account may be perfected only by control under Section 9—314;

(2) and except as otherwise provided in Section 9—308(d), a security interest in a letter-of-credit right may be perfected only by control under Section 9—314; and

(3) a security interest in money may be perfected only by the secured party's taking possession under Section 9—313.

(c) While goods are in the possession of a bailee that has issued a negotiable document covering the goods:

(1) a security interest in the goods may be perfected by perfecting a security interest in the document; and

(2) a security interest perfected in the document has priority over any security interest that becomes perfected in the goods by another method during that time.

(d) While goods are in the possession of a bailee that has issued a nonnegotiable document covering the goods, a security interest in the goods may be perfected by:

(1) issuance of a document in the name of the secured party;

(2) the bailee's receipt of notification of the secured party's interest; or

(3) filing as to the goods.

(e) A security interest in certificated securities, negotiable documents, or instruments is perfected without filing or the taking of possession for a period of 20 days from the time it attaches to the extent that it arises for new value given under an authenticated security agreement.

(f) A perfected security interest in a negotiable document or goods in possession of a bailee, other than one that has issued a negotiable document for the goods, remains perfected for 20 days without filing if the secured party makes available to the debtor the goods or documents representing the goods for the purpose of:

(1) ultimate sale or exchange; or

(2) loading, unloading, storing, shipping, transshipping, manufacturing, processing, or otherwise dealing with them in a manner preliminary to their sale or exchange.

(g) A perfected security interest in a certificated security or instrument remains perfected for 20 days without filing if the secured party delivers the security certificate or instrument to the debtor for the purpose of:

(1) ultimate sale or exchange; or

(2) presentation, collection, enforcement, renewal, or registration of transfer.

(h) After the 20-day period specified in subsection (e), (f), or (g) expires, perfection depends upon compliance with this article.

§9—313. When Possession by or Delivery to Secured Party Perfects Security Interest without Filing.

(a) Except as otherwise provided in subsection (b), a secured party may perfect a security interest in negotiable documents, goods, instruments, money, or tangible chattel paper by taking possession of the collateral. A secured party may perfect a security interest in certificated securities by taking delivery of the certificated securities under Section 8—301.

(b) With respect to goods covered by a certificate of title issued by this State, a secured party may perfect a security interest in the goods by taking possession of the goods only in the circumstances described in Section 9—316(d).

(c) With respect to collateral other than certificated securities and goods covered by a document, a secured party takes possession of collateral in the possession of a person other than the debtor, the secured party, or a lessee of the collateral from the debtor in the ordinary course of the debtor's business, when:

(1) the person in possession authenticates a record acknowledging that it holds possession of the collateral for the secured party's benefit; or

(2) the person takes possession of the collateral after having authenticated a record acknowledging that it will hold possession of collateral for the secured party's benefit.

(d) If perfection of a security interest depends upon possession of the collateral by a secured party, perfection occurs no earlier than the time the secured party takes possession and continues only while the secured party retains possession.

(e) A security interest in a certificated security in registered form is perfected by delivery when delivery of the certificated security occurs under Section 8—301 and remains perfected by delivery until the debtor obtains possession of the security certificate.

(f) A person in possession of collateral is not required to acknowledge that it holds possession for a secured party's benefit.

(g) If a person acknowledges that it holds possession for the secured party's benefit:

(1) the acknowledgment is effective under subsection (c) or Section 8—301(a), even if the acknowledgment violates the rights of a debtor; and

(2) unless the person otherwise agrees or law other than this article otherwise provides, the person does not owe any duty to the secured party and is not required to confirm the acknowledgment to another person.

(h) A secured party having possession of collateral does not relinquish possession by delivering the collateral to a person other than the debtor or a lessee of the collateral from the debtor in the ordinary course of the debtor's business if the person was instructed before the delivery or is instructed contemporaneously with the delivery:

(1) to hold possession of the collateral for the secured party's benefit; or

(2) to redeliver the collateral to the secured party.

(i) A secured party does not relinquish possession, even if a delivery under subsection (h) violates the rights of a debtor. A person to which collateral is delivered under subsection (h) does not owe any duty to the secured party and is not required to confirm the delivery to another person unless the person otherwise agrees or law other than this article otherwise provides.

§9—314. Perfection by Control.

(a) A security interest in investment property, deposit accounts, letter-of-credit rights, or electronic chattel paper may be perfected by control of the collateral under Section 9—104, 9—105, 9—106, or 9—107.

(b) A security interest in deposit accounts, electronic chattel paper, or letter-of-credit rights is perfected by control under Section 9—104, 9—105, or 9—107 when the secured party obtains control and remains perfected by control only while the secured party retains control.

(c) A security interest in investment property is perfected by control under Section 9—106 from the time the secured party obtains control and remains perfected by control until:

(1) the secured party does not have control; and

(2) one of the following occurs:

(A) if the collateral is a certificated security, the debtor has or acquires possession of the security certificate;

(B) if the collateral is an uncertificated security, the issuer has registered or registers the debtor as the registered owner; or

(C) if the collateral is a security entitlement, the debtor is or becomes the entitlement holder.

§9—315. Secured Party's Rights on Disposition of Collateral and in Proceeds.

(a) Except as otherwise provided in this article and in Section 2—403(2):

(1) a security interest or agricultural lien continues in collateral notwithstanding sale, lease, license, exchange, or other disposition thereof unless the secured party authorized the disposition free of the security interest or agricultural lien; and

(2) a security interest attaches to any identifiable proceeds of collateral.

(b) Proceeds that are commingled with other property are identifiable proceeds:

(1) if the proceeds are goods, to the extent provided by Section 9—336; and

(2) if the proceeds are not goods, to the extent that the secured party identifies the proceeds by a method of tracing, including application of equitable principles, that is permitted under law other than this article with respect to commingled property of the type involved.

(c) A security interest in proceeds is a perfected security interest if the security interest in the original collateral was perfected.

(d) A perfected security interest in proceeds becomes unperfected on the 21st day after the security interest attaches to the proceeds unless:

(1) the following conditions are satisfied:

(A) a filed financing statement covers the original collateral;

(B) the proceeds are collateral in which a security interest may be perfected by filing in the office in which the financing statement has been filed; and

(C) the proceeds are not acquired with cash proceeds;

(2) the proceeds are identifiable cash proceeds; or

(3) the security interest in the proceeds is perfected other than under subsection (c) when the security interest attaches to the proceeds or within 20 days thereafter.

(e) If a filed financing statement covers the original collateral, a security interest in proceeds which remains perfected under subsection (d)(1) becomes unperfected at the later of:

(1) when the effectiveness of the filed financing statement lapses under Section 9—515 or is terminated under Section 9—513; or

(2) the 21st day after the security interest attaches to the proceeds.

§9—316. Continued Perfection of Security Interest Following Change in Governing Law.

(a) A security interest perfected pursuant to the law of the jurisdiction designated in Section 9—301(1) or 9—305(c) remains perfected until the earliest of:

(1) the time perfection would have ceased under the law of that jurisdiction;

(2) the expiration of four months after a change of the debtor's location to another jurisdiction; or

(3) the expiration of one year after a transfer of collateral to a person that thereby becomes a debtor and is located in another jurisdiction.

(b) If a security interest described in subsection (a) becomes perfected under the law of the other jurisdiction before the earliest time or event described in that subsection, it remains perfected thereafter. If the security interest does not become perfected under the law of the other jurisdiction before the earliest time or event, it becomes unperfected and is deemed never to have been perfected as against a purchaser of the collateral for value.

(c) A possessory security interest in collateral, other than goods covered by a certificate of title and as-extracted collateral consisting of goods, remains continuously perfected if:

(1) the collateral is located in one jurisdiction and subject to a security interest perfected under the law of that jurisdiction;

(2) thereafter the collateral is brought into another jurisdiction; and

(3) upon entry into the other jurisdiction, the security interest is perfected under the law of the other jurisdiction.

(d) Except as otherwise provided in subsection (e), a security interest in goods covered by a certificate of title which is perfected by any method under the law of another jurisdiction when the goods become covered by a certificate of title from this State remains perfected until the security interest would have become unperfected under the law of the other jurisdiction had the goods not become so covered.

(e) A security interest described in subsection (d) becomes unperfected as against a purchaser of the goods for value and is deemed never to have been perfected as against a purchaser of the goods for value if the applicable requirements for perfection under Section 9—311(b) or 9—313 are not satisfied before the earlier of:

(1) the time the security interest would have become unperfected under the law of the other jurisdiction had the goods not become covered by a certificate of title from this State; or

(2) the expiration of four months after the goods had become so covered.

(f) A security interest in deposit accounts, letter-of-credit rights, or investment property which is perfected under the law of the bank's jurisdiction, the issuer's jurisdiction, a nominated person's jurisdiction, the securities intermediary's jurisdiction, or the commodity intermediary's jurisdiction, as applicable, remains perfected until the earlier of:

(1) the time the security interest would have become unperfected under the law of that jurisdiction; or

(2) the expiration of four months after a change of the applicable jurisdiction to another jurisdiction.

(g) If a security interest described in subsection (f) becomes perfected under the law of the other jurisdiction before the earlier of the time or the end of the period described in that subsection, it remains perfected thereafter. If the security interest does not become perfected under the law of the other jurisdiction before the earlier of that time or the end of that period, it becomes unperfected and is deemed never to have been perfected as against a purchaser of the collateral for value.

[SUBPART 3. PRIORITY]

§9—317. Interests That Take Priority over or Take Free of Security Interest or Agricultural Lien.

(a) A security interest or agricultural lien is subordinate to the rights of:

(1) a person entitled to priority under Section 9—322; and

(2) except as otherwise provided in subsection (e), a person that becomes a lien creditor before the earlier of the time:

(A) the security interest or agricultural lien is perfected; or

(B) one of the conditions specified in Section 9—203(b)(3) is met and a financing statement covering the collateral is filed.

(b) Except as otherwise provided in subsection (e), a buyer, other than a secured party, of tangible chattel paper, documents, goods, instruments, or a security certificate takes free of a security interest or agricultural lien if the buyer gives value and receives delivery of the collateral without knowledge of the security interest or agricultural lien and before it is perfected.

(c) Except as otherwise provided in subsection (e), a lessee of goods takes free of a security interest or agricultural lien if the lessee gives value and receives delivery of the collateral without knowledge of the security interest or agricultural lien and before it is perfected.

(d) A licensee of a general intangible or a buyer, other than a secured party, of accounts, electronic chattel paper, general intangibles, or investment property other than a certificated security takes free of a security interest if the licensee or buyer gives value without knowledge of the security interest and before it is perfected.

(e) Except as otherwise provided in Sections 9—320 and 9—321, if a person files a financing statement with respect to a purchase-money security interest before or within 20 days after the debtor receives delivery of the collateral, the security interest takes priority over the rights of a buyer, lessee, or lien creditor which arise between the time the security interest attaches and the time of filing.

As amended in 2000.

§9—318. No Interest Retained in Right to Payment That Is Sold; Rights and Title of Seller of Account or Chattel Paper with Respect to Creditors and Purchasers.

(a) A debtor that has sold an account, chattel paper, payment intangible, or promissory note does not retain a legal or equitable interest in the collateral sold.

(b) For purposes of determining the rights of creditors of, and purchasers for value of an account or chattel paper from, a debtor that has sold an account or chattel paper, while the buyer's security interest is unperfected, the debtor is deemed to have rights and title to the account or chattel paper identical to those the debtor sold.

§9—319. Rights and Title of Consignee with Respect to Creditors and Purchasers.

(a) Except as otherwise provided in subsection (b), for purposes of determining the rights of creditors of, and purchasers for value of goods from, a consignee, while the goods are in the possession of the consignee, the consignee is deemed to have rights and title to the goods identical to those the consignor had or had power to transfer.

(b) For purposes of determining the rights of a creditor of a consignee, law other than this article determines the rights and title of a consignee while goods are in the consignee's possession if, under this part, a perfected security interest held by the consignor would have priority over the rights of the creditor.

§9—320. Buyer of Goods.

(a) Except as otherwise provided in subsection (e), a buyer in ordinary course of business, other than a person buying farm products from a person engaged in farming operations, takes free of a security interest created by the buyer's seller, even if the security interest is perfected and the buyer knows of its existence.

(b) Except as otherwise provided in subsection (e), a buyer of goods from a person who used or bought the goods for use primarily for personal, family, or household purposes takes free of a security interest, even if perfected, if the buyer buys:

> (1) without knowledge of the security interest;
>
> (2) for value;
>
> (3) primarily for the buyer's personal, family, or household purposes; and
>
> (4) before the filing of a financing statement covering the goods.

(c) To the extent that it affects the priority of a security interest over a buyer of goods under subsection (b), the period of effectiveness of a filing made in the jurisdiction in which the seller is located is governed by Section 9—316(a) and (b).

(d) A buyer in ordinary course of business buying oil, gas, or other minerals at the wellhead or minehead or after extraction takes free of an interest arising out of an encumbrance.

(e) Subsections (a) and (b) do not affect a security interest in goods in the possession of the secured party under Section 9—313.

§9—321. Licensee of General Intangible and Lessee of Goods in Ordinary Course of Business.

(a) In this section, "licensee in ordinary course of business" means a person that becomes a licensee of a general intangible in good faith, without knowledge that the license violates the rights of another person in the general intangible, and in the ordinary course from a person in the business of licensing general intangibles of that kind. A person becomes a licensee in the ordinary course if the license to the person comports with the usual or customary practices in the kind of business in which the licensor is engaged or with the licensor's own usual or customary practices.

(b) A licensee in ordinary course of business takes its rights under a nonexclusive license free of a security interest in the general intangible created by the licensor, even if the security interest is perfected and the licensee knows of its existence.

(c) A lessee in ordinary course of business takes its leasehold interest free of a security interest in the goods created by the lessor, even if the security interest is perfected and the lessee knows of its existence.

§9—322. Priorities among Conflicting Security Interests in and Agricultural Liens on Same Collateral.

(a) Except as otherwise provided in this section, priority among conflicting security interests and agricultural liens in the same collateral is determined according to the following rules:

> (1) Conflicting perfected security interests and agricultural liens rank according to priority in time of filing or perfection. Priority dates from the earlier of the time a filing covering the collateral is first made or the security

interest or agricultural lien is first perfected, if there is no period thereafter when there is neither filing nor perfection.

> (2) A perfected security interest or agricultural lien has priority over a conflicting unperfected security interest or agricultural lien.
>
> (3) The first security interest or agricultural lien to attach or become effective has priority if conflicting security interests and agricultural liens are unperfected.

(b) For the purposes of subsection (a)(1):

> (1) the time of filing or perfection as to a security interest in collateral is also the time of filing or perfection as to a security interest in proceeds; and
>
> (2) the time of filing or perfection as to a security interest in collateral supported by a supporting obligation is also the time of filing or perfection as to a security interest in the supporting obligation.

(c) Except as otherwise provided in subsection (f), a security interest in collateral which qualifies for priority over a conflicting security interest under Section 9—327, 9—328, 9—329, 9—330, or 9—331 also has priority over a conflicting security interest in:

> (1) any supporting obligation for the collateral; and
>
> (2) proceeds of the collateral if:
>
>> (A) the security interest in proceeds is perfected;
>>
>> (B) the proceeds are cash proceeds or of the same type as the collateral; and
>>
>> (C) in the case of proceeds that are proceeds of proceeds, all intervening proceeds are cash proceeds, proceeds of the same type as the collateral, or an account relating to the collateral.

(d) Subject to subsection (e) and except as otherwise provided in subsection (f), if a security interest in chattel paper, deposit accounts, negotiable documents, instruments, investment property, or letter-of-credit rights is perfected by a method other than filing, conflicting perfected security interests in proceeds of the collateral rank according to priority in time of filing.

(e) Subsection (d) applies only if the proceeds of the collateral are not cash proceeds, chattel paper, negotiable documents, instruments, investment property, or letter-of-credit rights.

(f) Subsections (a) through (e) are subject to:

> (1) subsection (g) and the other provisions of this part;
>
> (2) Section 4—210 with respect to a security interest of a collecting bank;
>
> (3) Section 5—118 with respect to a security interest of an issuer or nominated person; and
>
> (4) Section 9—110 with respect to a security interest arising under Article 2 or 2A.

(g) A perfected agricultural lien on collateral has priority over a conflicting security interest in or agricultural lien on the same collateral if the statute creating the agricultural lien so provides.

§9—323. *Future Advances.*

(a) Except as otherwise provided in subsection (c), for purposes of determining the priority of a perfected security interest under Section 9—322(a)(1), perfection of the security interest dates from the time an advance is made to the extent that the security interest secures an advance that:

> (1) is made while the security interest is perfected only:
>
> > (A) under Section 9—309 when it attaches; or
> >
> > (B) temporarily under Section 9—312(e), (f), or (g); and
>
> (2) is not made pursuant to a commitment entered into before or while the security interest is perfected by a method other than under Section 9—309 or 9—312(e), (f), or (g).

(b) Except as otherwise provided in subsection (c), a security interest is subordinate to the rights of a person that becomes a lien creditor to the extent that the security interest secures an advance made more than 45 days after the person becomes a lien creditor unless the advance is made:

> (1) without knowledge of the lien; or
>
> (2) pursuant to a commitment entered into without knowledge of the lien.

(c) Subsections (a) and (b) do not apply to a security interest held by a secured party that is a buyer of accounts, chattel paper, payment intangibles, or promissory notes or a consignor.

(d) Except as otherwise provided in subsection (e), a buyer of goods other than a buyer in ordinary course of business takes free of a security interest to the extent that it secures advances made after the earlier of:

> (1) the time the secured party acquires knowledge of the buyer's purchase; or
>
> (2) 45 days after the purchase.

(e) Subsection (d) does not apply if the advance is made pursuant to a commitment entered into without knowledge of the buyer's purchase and before the expiration of the 45-day period.

(f) Except as otherwise provided in subsection (g), a lessee of goods, other than a lessee in ordinary course of business, takes the leasehold interest free of a security interest to the extent that it secures advances made after the earlier of:

> (1) the time the secured party acquires knowledge of the lease; or
>
> (2) 45 days after the lease contract becomes enforceable.

(g) Subsection (f) does not apply if the advance is made pursuant to a commitment entered into without knowledge of the lease and before the expiration of the 45-day period.
As amended in 1999.

§9—324. *Priority of Purchase-Money Security Interests.*

(a) Except as otherwise provided in subsection (g), a perfected purchase-money security interest in goods other than inventory or livestock has priority over a conflicting security interest in the same goods, and, except as otherwise provided in Section 9—327, a perfected security interest in its identifiable proceeds also has priority, if the purchase-money security interest is perfected when the debtor receives possession of the collateral or within 20 days thereafter.

(b) Subject to subsection (c) and except as otherwise provided in subsection (g), a perfected purchase-money security interest in inventory has priority over a conflicting security interest in the same inventory, has priority over a conflicting security interest in chattel paper or an instrument constituting proceeds of the inventory and in proceeds of the chattel paper, if so provided in Section 9—330, and, except as otherwise provided in Section 9—327, also has priority in identifiable cash proceeds of the inventory to the extent the identifiable cash proceeds are received on or before the delivery of the inventory to a buyer, if:

> (1) the purchase-money security interest is perfected when the debtor receives possession of the inventory;
>
> (2) the purchase-money secured party sends an authenticated notification to the holder of the conflicting security interest;
>
> (3) the holder of the conflicting security interest receives the notification within five years before the debtor receives possession of the inventory; and
>
> (4) the notification states that the person sending the notification has or expects to acquire a purchase-money security interest in inventory of the debtor and describes the inventory.

(c) Subsections (b)(2) through (4) apply only if the holder of the conflicting security interest had filed a financing statement covering the same types of inventory:

> (1) if the purchase-money security interest is perfected by filing, before the date of the filing; or
>
> (2) if the purchase-money security interest is temporarily perfected without filing or possession under Section 9—312(f), before the beginning of the 20-day period thereunder.

(d) Subject to subsection (e) and except as otherwise provided in subsection (g), a perfected purchase-money security interest in livestock that are farm products has priority over a conflicting security interest in the same livestock, and, except as otherwise provided in Section 9—327, a perfected security interest in their identifiable proceeds and identifiable products in their unmanufactured states also has priority, if:

> (1) the purchase-money security interest is perfected when the debtor receives possession of the livestock;
>
> (2) the purchase-money secured party sends an authenticated notification to the holder of the conflicting security interest;
>
> (3) the holder of the conflicting security interest receives the notification within six months before the debtor receives possession of the livestock; and

(4) the notification states that the person sending the notification has or expects to acquire a purchase-money security interest in livestock of the debtor and describes the livestock.

(e) Subsections (d)(2) through (4) apply only if the holder of the conflicting security interest had filed a financing statement covering the same types of livestock:

(1) if the purchase-money security interest is perfected by filing, before the date of the filing; or

(2) if the purchase-money security interest is temporarily perfected without filing or possession under Section 9—312(f), before the beginning of the 20-day period thereunder.

(f) Except as otherwise provided in subsection (g), a perfected purchase-money security interest in software has priority over a conflicting security interest in the same collateral, and, except as otherwise provided in Section 9—327, a perfected security interest in its identifiable proceeds also has priority, to the extent that the purchase-money security interest in the goods in which the software was acquired for use has priority in the goods and proceeds of the goods under this section.

(g) If more than one security interest qualifies for priority in the same collateral under subsection (a), (b), (d), or (f):

(1) a security interest securing an obligation incurred as all or part of the price of the collateral has priority over a security interest securing an obligation incurred for value given to enable the debtor to acquire rights in or the use of collateral; and

(2) in all other cases, Section 9—322(a) applies to the qualifying security interests.

§9—325. Priority of Security Interests in Transferred Collateral.

(a) Except as otherwise provided in subsection (b), a security interest created by a debtor is subordinate to a security interest in the same collateral created by another person if:

(1) the debtor acquired the collateral subject to the security interest created by the other person;

(2) the security interest created by the other person was perfected when the debtor acquired the collateral; and

(3) there is no period thereafter when the security interest is unperfected.

(b) Subsection (a) subordinates a security interest only if the security interest:

(1) otherwise would have priority solely under Section 9—322(a) or 9—324; or

(2) arose solely under Section 2—711(3) or 2A—508(5).

§9—326. Priority of Security Interests Created by New Debtor.

(a) Subject to subsection (b), a security interest created by a new debtor which is perfected by a filed financing statement that is effective solely under Section 9—508 in collateral in which a new debtor has or acquires rights is subordinate to a security interest in the same collateral which is perfected other than by a filed financing statement that is effective solely under Section 9—508.

(b) The other provisions of this part determine the priority among conflicting security interests in the same collateral perfected by filed financing statements that are effective solely under Section 9—508. However, if the security agreements to which a new debtor became bound as debtor were not entered into by the same original debtor, the conflicting security interests rank according to priority in time of the new debtor's having become bound.

§9—327. Priority of Security Interests in Deposit Account.

The following rules govern priority among conflicting security interests in the same deposit account:

(1) A security interest held by a secured party having control of the deposit account under Section 9—104 has priority over a conflicting security interest held by a secured party that does not have control.

(2) Except as otherwise provided in paragraphs (3) and (4), security interests perfected by control under Section 9—314 rank according to priority in time of obtaining control.

(3) Except as otherwise provided in paragraph (4), a security interest held by the bank with which the deposit account is maintained has priority over a conflicting security interest held by another secured party.

(4) A security interest perfected by control under Section 9—104(a)(3) has priority over a security interest held by the bank with which the deposit account is maintained.

§9—328. Priority of Security Interests in Investment Property.

The following rules govern priority among conflicting security interests in the same investment property:

(1) A security interest held by a secured party having control of investment property under Section 9—106 has priority over a security interest held by a secured party that does not have control of the investment property.

(2) Except as otherwise provided in paragraphs (3) and (4), conflicting security interests held by secured parties each of which has control under Section 9—106 rank according to priority in time of:

(A) if the collateral is a security, obtaining control;

(B) if the collateral is a security entitlement carried in a securities account and:

(i) if the secured party obtained control under Section 8—106(d)(1), the secured party's becoming the person for which the securities account is maintained;

(ii) if the secured party obtained control under Section 8—106(d)(2), the securities intermediary's agreement to comply with the secured party's entitlement orders with respect to security entitlements carried or to be carried in the securities account; or

(iii) if the secured party obtained control through another person under Section 8—106(d)(3), the time on which priority would be based under this paragraph if the other person were the secured party; or

(C) if the collateral is a commodity contract carried with a commodity intermediary, the satisfaction of the requirement for control specified in Section 9—106(b)(2) with respect to commodity contracts carried or to be carried with the commodity intermediary.

(3) A security interest held by a securities intermediary in a security entitlement or a securities account maintained with the securities intermediary has priority over a conflicting security interest held by another secured party.

(4) A security interest held by a commodity intermediary in a commodity contract or a commodity account maintained with the commodity intermediary has priority over a conflicting security interest held by another secured party.

(5) A security interest in a certificated security in registered form which is perfected by taking delivery under Section 9—313(a) and not by control under Section 9—314 has priority over a conflicting security interest perfected by a method other than control.

(6) Conflicting security interests created by a broker, securities intermediary, or commodity intermediary which are perfected without control under Section 9—106 rank equally.

(7) In all other cases, priority among conflicting security interests in investment property is governed by Sections 9—322 and 9—323.

§9—329. Priority of Security Interests in Letter-of-Credit Right.

The following rules govern priority among conflicting security interests in the same letter-of-credit right:

(1) A security interest held by a secured party having control of the letter-of-credit right under Section 9—107 has priority to the extent of its control over a conflicting security interest held by a secured party that does not have control.

(2) Security interests perfected by control under Section 9—314 rank according to priority in time of obtaining control.

§9—330. Priority of Purchaser of Chattel Paper or Instrument.

(a) A purchaser of chattel paper has priority over a security interest in the chattel paper which is claimed merely as proceeds of inventory subject to a security interest if:

(1) in good faith and in the ordinary course of the purchaser's business, the purchaser gives new value and takes possession of the chattel paper or obtains control of the chattel paper under Section 9—105; and

(2) the chattel paper does not indicate that it has been assigned to an identified assignee other than the purchaser.

(b) A purchaser of chattel paper has priority over a security interest in the chattel paper which is claimed other than merely as proceeds of inventory subject to a security interest if the purchaser gives new value and takes possession of the chattel paper or obtains control of the chattel paper under Section 9—105 in good faith, in the ordinary course of the purchaser's business, and without knowledge that the purchase violates the rights of the secured party.

(c) Except as otherwise provided in Section 9—327, a purchaser having priority in chattel paper under subsection (a) or (b) also has priority in proceeds of the chattel paper to the extent that:

(1) Section 9—322 provides for priority in the proceeds; or

(2) the proceeds consist of the specific goods covered by the chattel paper or cash proceeds of the specific goods, even if the purchaser's security interest in the proceeds is unperfected.

(d) Except as otherwise provided in Section 9—331(a), a purchaser of an instrument has priority over a security interest in the instrument perfected by a method other than possession if the purchaser gives value and takes possession of the instrument in good faith and without knowledge that the purchase violates the rights of the secured party.

(e) For purposes of subsections (a) and (b), the holder of a purchase-money security interest in inventory gives new value for chattel paper constituting proceeds of the inventory.

(f) For purposes of subsections (b) and (d), if chattel paper or an instrument indicates that it has been assigned to an identified secured party other than the purchaser, a purchaser of the chattel paper or instrument has knowledge that the purchase violates the rights of the secured party.

§9—331. Priority of Rights of Purchasers of Instruments, Documents, and Securities under Other Articles; Priority of Interests in Financial Assets and Security Entitlements under Article 8.

(a) This article does not limit the rights of a holder in due course of a negotiable instrument, a holder to which a negotiable document of title has been duly negotiated, or a protected purchaser of a security. These holders or purchasers take priority over an earlier security interest, even if perfected, to the extent provided in Articles 3, 7, and 8.

(b) This article does not limit the rights of or impose liability on a person to the extent that the person is protected against the assertion of a claim under Article 8.

(c) Filing under this article does not constitute notice of a claim or defense to the holders, or purchasers, or persons described in subsections (a) and (b).

§9—332. Transfer of Money; Transfer of Funds from Deposit Account.

(a) A transferee of money takes the money free of a security interest unless the transferee acts in collusion with the debtor in violating the rights of the secured party.

(b) A transferee of funds from a deposit account takes the funds free of a security interest in the deposit account unless the transferee acts in collusion with the debtor in violating the rights of the secured party.

§9—333. Priority of Certain Liens Arising by Operation of Law.

(a) In this section, "possessory lien" means an interest, other than a security interest or an agricultural lien:

(1) which secures payment or performance of an obligation for services or materials furnished with respect to goods by a person in the ordinary course of the person's business;

(2) which is created by statute or rule of law in favor of the person; and

(3) whose effectiveness depends on the person's possession of the goods.

(b) A possessory lien on goods has priority over a security interest in the goods unless the lien is created by a statute that expressly provides otherwise.

§9—334. Priority of Security Interests in Fixtures and Crops.

(a) A security interest under this article may be created in goods that are fixtures or may continue in goods that become fixtures. A security interest does not exist under this article in ordinary building materials incorporated into an improvement on land.

(b) This article does not prevent creation of an encumbrance upon fixtures under real property law.

(c) In cases not governed by subsections (d) through (h), a security interest in fixtures is subordinate to a conflicting interest of an encumbrancer or owner of the related real property other than the debtor.

(d) Except as otherwise provided in subsection (h), a perfected security interest in fixtures has priority over a conflicting interest of an encumbrancer or owner of the real property if the debtor has an interest of record in or is in possession of the real property and:

(1) the security interest is a purchase-money security interest;

(2) the interest of the encumbrancer or owner arises before the goods become fixtures; and

(3) the security interest is perfected by a fixture filing before the goods become fixtures or within 20 days thereafter.

(e) A perfected security interest in fixtures has priority over a conflicting interest of an encumbrancer or owner of the real property if:

(1) the debtor has an interest of record in the real property or is in possession of the real property and the security interest:

(A) is perfected by a fixture filing before the interest of the encumbrancer or owner is of record; and

(B) has priority over any conflicting interest of a predecessor in title of the encumbrancer or owner;

(2) before the goods become fixtures, the security interest is perfected by any method permitted by this article and the fixtures are readily removable:

(A) factory or office machines;

(B) equipment that is not primarily used or leased for use in the operation of the real property; or

(C) replacements of domestic appliances that are consumer goods;

(3) the conflicting interest is a lien on the real property obtained by legal or equitable proceedings after the security interest was perfected by any method permitted by this article; or

(4) the security interest is:

(A) created in a manufactured home in a manufactured-home transaction; and

(B) perfected pursuant to a statute described in Section 9—311(a)(2).

(f) A security interest in fixtures, whether or not perfected, has priority over a conflicting interest of an encumbrancer or owner of the real property if:

(1) the encumbrancer or owner has, in an authenticated record, consented to the security interest or disclaimed an interest in the goods as fixtures; or

(2) the debtor has a right to remove the goods as against the encumbrancer or owner.

(g) The priority of the security interest under paragraph (f)(2) continues for a reasonable time if the debtor's right to remove the goods as against the encumbrancer or owner terminates.

(h) A mortgage is a construction mortgage to the extent that it secures an obligation incurred for the construction of an improvement on land, including the acquisition cost of the land, if a recorded record of the mortgage so indicates. Except as otherwise provided in subsections (e) and (f), a security interest in fixtures is subordinate to a construction mortgage if a record of the mortgage is recorded before the goods become fixtures and the goods become fixtures before the completion of the construction. A mortgage has this priority to the same extent as a construction mortgage to the extent that it is given to refinance a construction mortgage.

(i) A perfected security interest in crops growing on real property has priority over a conflicting interest of an encumbrancer or owner of the real property if the debtor has an interest of record in or is in possession of the real property.

(j) Subsection (i) prevails over any inconsistent provisions of the following statutes:

[List here any statutes containing provisions inconsistent with subsection (i).]

Legislative Note: States that amend statutes to remove provisions inconsistent with subsection (i) need not enact subsection (j).

§9—335. Accessions.

(a) A security interest may be created in an accession and continues in collateral that becomes an accession.

(b) If a security interest is perfected when the collateral becomes an accession, the security interest remains perfected in the collateral.

(c) Except as otherwise provided in subsection (d), the other provisions of this part determine the priority of a security interest in an accession.

(d) A security interest in an accession is subordinate to a security interest in the whole which is perfected by compliance with the requirements of a certificate-of-title statute under Section 9—311(b).

(e) After default, subject to Part 6, a secured party may remove an accession from other goods if the security interest in the accession has priority over the claims of every person having an interest in the whole.

(f) A secured party that removes an accession from other goods under subsection (e) shall promptly reimburse any holder of a security interest or other lien on, or owner of, the whole or of the other goods, other than the debtor, for the cost of repair of any physical injury to the whole or the other goods. The secured party need not reimburse the holder or owner for any diminution in value of the whole or the other goods caused by the absence of the accession removed or by any necessity for replacing it. A person entitled to reimbursement may refuse permission to remove until the secured party gives adequate assurance for the performance of the obligation to reimburse.

§9—336. Commingled Goods.

(a) In this section, "commingled goods" means goods that are physically united with other goods in such a manner that their identity is lost in a product or mass.

(b) A security interest does not exist in commingled goods as such. However, a security interest may attach to a product or mass that results when goods become commingled goods.

(c) If collateral becomes commingled goods, a security interest attaches to the product or mass.

(d) If a security interest in collateral is perfected before the collateral becomes commingled goods, the security interest that attaches to the product or mass under subsection (c) is perfected.

(e) Except as otherwise provided in subsection (f), the other provisions of this part determine the priority of a security interest that attaches to the product or mass under subsection (c).

(f) If more than one security interest attaches to the product or mass under subsection (c), the following rules determine priority:

    (1) A security interest that is perfected under subsection (d) has priority over a security interest that is unperfected at the time the collateral becomes commingled goods.

    (2) If more than one security interest is perfected under subsection (d), the security interests rank equally in proportion to the value of the collateral at the time it became commingled goods.

§9—337. Priority of Security Interests in Goods Covered by Certificate of Title.

If, while a security interest in goods is perfected by any method under the law of another jurisdiction, this State issues a certificate of title that does not show that the goods are subject to the security interest or contain a statement that they may be subject to security interests not shown on the certificate:

    (1) a buyer of the goods, other than a person in the business of selling goods of that kind, takes free of the security interest if the buyer gives value and receives delivery of the goods after issuance of the certificate and without knowledge of the security interest; and

    (2) the security interest is subordinate to a conflicting security interest in the goods that attaches, and is perfected under Section 9—311(b), after issuance of the certificate and without the conflicting secured party's knowledge of the security interest.

§9—338. Priority of Security Interest or Agricultural Lien Perfected by Filed Financing Statement Providing Certain Incorrect Information.

If a security interest or agricultural lien is perfected by a filed financing statement providing information described in Section 9—516(b)(5) which is incorrect at the time the financing statement is filed:

    (1) the security interest or agricultural lien is subordinate to a conflicting perfected security interest in the collateral to the extent that the holder of the conflicting security interest gives value in reasonable reliance upon the incorrect information; and

    (2) a purchaser, other than a secured party, of the collateral takes free of the security interest or agricultural lien to the extent that, in reasonable reliance upon the incorrect information, the purchaser gives value and, in the case of chattel paper, documents, goods, instruments, or a security certificate, receives delivery of the collateral.

§9—339. Priority Subject to Subordination.

This article does not preclude subordination by agreement by a person entitled to priority.

[SUBPART 4. RIGHTS OF BANK]

§9—340. Effectiveness of Right of Recoupment or Set-Off against Deposit Account.

(a) Except as otherwise provided in subsection (c), a bank with which a deposit account is maintained may exercise any right of recoupment or set-off against a secured party that holds a security interest in the deposit account.

(b) Except as otherwise provided in subsection (c), the application of this article to a security interest in a deposit account does not affect a right of recoupment or set-off of the secured party as to a deposit account maintained with the secured party.

(c) The exercise by a bank of a set-off against a deposit account is ineffective against a secured party that holds a security interest in the deposit account which is perfected by control under Section 9—104(a)(3), if the set-off is based on a claim against the debtor.

§9—341. Bank's Rights and Duties with Respect to Deposit Account. Except as otherwise provided in Section 9—340(c), and unless the bank otherwise agrees in an authenticated record, a bank's rights and duties with respect to a deposit account maintained with the bank are not terminated, suspended, or modified by:

(1) the creation, attachment, or perfection of a security interest in the deposit account;

(2) the bank's knowledge of the security interest; or

(3) the bank's receipt of instructions from the secured party.

§9—342. Bank's Right to Refuse to Enter into or Disclose Existence of Control Agreement. This article does not require a bank to enter into an agreement of the kind described in Section 9—104(a)(2), even if its customer so requests or directs. A bank that has entered into such an agreement is not required to confirm the existence of the agreement to another person unless requested to do so by its customer.

PART 4 RIGHTS OF THIRD PARTIES

§9—401. Alienability of Debtor's Rights.

(a) Except as otherwise provided in subsection (b) and Sections 9—406, 9—407, 9—408, and 9—409, whether a debtor's rights in collateral may be voluntarily or involuntarily transferred is governed by law other than this article.

(b) An agreement between the debtor and secured party which prohibits a transfer of the debtor's rights in collateral or makes the transfer a default does not prevent the transfer from taking effect.

§9—402. Secured Party Not Obligated on Contract of Debtor or in Tort.

The existence of a security interest, agricultural lien, or authority given to a debtor to dispose of or use collateral, without more, does not subject a secured party to liability in contract or tort for the debtor's acts or omissions.

§9—403. Agreement Not to Assert Defenses against Assignee.

(a) In this section, "value" has the meaning provided in Section 3—303(a).

(b) Except as otherwise provided in this section, an agreement between an account debtor and an assignor not to assert against an assignee any claim or defense that the account debtor may have against the assignor is enforceable by an assignee that takes an assignment:

(1) for value;

(2) in good faith;

(3) without notice of a claim of a property or possessory right to the property assigned; and

(4) without notice of a defense or claim in recoupment of the type that may be asserted against a person entitled to enforce a negotiable instrument under Section 3—305(a).

(c) Subsection (b) does not apply to defenses of a type that may be asserted against a holder in due course of a negotiable instrument under Section 3—305(b).

(d) In a consumer transaction, if a record evidences the account debtor's obligation, law other than this article requires that the record include a statement to the effect that the rights of an assignee are subject to claims or defenses that the account debtor could assert against the original obligee, and the record does not include such a statement:

(1) the record has the same effect as if the record included such a statement; and

(2) the account debtor may assert against an assignee those claims and defenses that would have been available if the record included such a statement.

(e) This section is subject to law other than this article which establishes a different rule for an account debtor who is an individual and who incurred the obligation primarily for personal, family, or household purposes.

(f) Except as otherwise provided in subsection (d), this section does not displace law other than this article which gives effect to an agreement by an account debtor not to assert a claim or defense against an assignee.

§9—404. Rights Acquired by Assignee; Claims and Defenses against Assignee.

(a) Unless an account debtor has made an enforceable agreement not to assert defenses or claims, and subject to subsections (b) through (e), the rights of an assignee are subject to:

(1) all terms of the agreement between the account debtor and assignor and any defense or claim in recoupment arising from the transaction that gave rise to the contract; and

(2) any other defense or claim of the account debtor against the assignor which accrues before the account debtor receives a notification of the assignment authenticated by the assignor or the assignee.

(b) Subject to subsection (c) and except as otherwise provided in subsection (d), the claim of an account debtor against an assignor may be asserted against an assignee under subsection (a) only to reduce the amount the account debtor owes.

(c) This section is subject to law other than this article which establishes a different rule for an account debtor who is an individual and who incurred the obligation primarily for personal, family, or household purposes.

(d) In a consumer transaction, if a record evidences the account debtor's obligation, law other than this article requires that the record include a statement to the effect that the account debtor's recovery against an assignee with respect to claims and defenses against the assignor may not exceed amounts paid by the account debtor under the record, and the record does not include such a statement, the extent to which a claim of an account debtor against the assignor may be asserted against an assignee is determined as if the record included such a statement.

(e) This section does not apply to an assignment of a health-care-insurance receivable.

§9—405. Modification of Assigned Contract.

(a) A modification of or substitution for an assigned contract is effective against an assignee if made in good faith. The assignee acquires corresponding rights under the modified or substituted contract. The assignment may provide that the modification or substitution is a breach of contract by the assignor. This subsection is subject to subsections (b) through (d).

(b) Subsection (a) applies to the extent that:

(1) the right to payment or a part thereof under an assigned contract has not been fully earned by performance; or

(2) the right to payment or a part thereof has been fully earned by performance and the account debtor has not received notification of the assignment under Section 9—406(a).

(c) This section is subject to law other than this article which establishes a different rule for an account debtor who is an individual and who incurred the obligation primarily for personal, family, or household purposes.

(d) This section does not apply to an assignment of a health-care-insurance receivable.

§9—406. Discharge of Account Debtor; Notification of Assignment; Identification and Proof of Assignment; Restrictions on Assignment of Accounts, Chattel Paper, Payment Intangibles, and Promissory Notes Ineffective.

(a) Subject to subsections (b) through (i), an account debtor on an account, chattel paper, or a payment intangible may discharge its obligation by paying the assignor until, but not after, the account debtor receives a notification, authenticated by the assignor or the assignee, that the amount due or to become due has been assigned and that payment is to be made to the assignee. After receipt of the notification, the account debtor may discharge its obligation by paying the assignee and may not discharge the obligation by paying the assignor.

(b) Subject to subsection (h), notification is ineffective under subsection (a):

(1) if it does not reasonably identify the rights assigned;

(2) to the extent that an agreement between an account debtor and a seller of a payment intangible limits the account debtor's duty to pay a person other than the seller and the limitation is effective under law other than this article; or

(3) at the option of an account debtor, if the notification notifies the account debtor to make less than the full amount of any installment or other periodic payment to the assignee, even if:

(A) only a portion of the account, chattel paper, or payment intangible has been assigned to that assignee;

(B) a portion has been assigned to another assignee; or

(C) the account debtor knows that the assignment to that assignee is limited.

(c) Subject to subsection (h), if requested by the account debtor, an assignee shall seasonably furnish reasonable proof that the assignment has been made. Unless the assignee complies, the account debtor may discharge its obligation by paying the assignor, even if the account debtor has received a notification under subsection (a).

(d) Except as otherwise provided in subsection (e) and Sections 2A—303 and 9—407, and subject to subsection (h), a term in an agreement between an account debtor and an assignor or in a promissory note is ineffective to the extent that it:

(1) prohibits, restricts, or requires the consent of the account debtor or person obligated on the promissory note to the assignment or transfer of, or the creation, attachment, perfection, or enforcement of a security interest in, the account, chattel paper, payment intangible, or promissory note; or

(2) provides that the assignment or transfer or the creation, attachment, perfection, or enforcement of the security interest may give rise to a default, breach, right of recoupment, claim, defense, termination, right of termination, or remedy under the account, chattel paper, payment intangible, or promissory note.

(e) Subsection (d) does not apply to the sale of a payment intangible or promissory note.

(f) Except as otherwise provided in Sections 2A—303 and 9—407 and subject to subsections (h) and (i), a rule of law, statute, or regulation that prohibits, restricts, or requires the consent of a government, governmental body or official, or account debtor to the assignment or transfer of, or creation of a security interest in, an account or chattel paper is ineffective to the extent that the rule of law, statute, or regulation:

(1) prohibits, restricts, or requires the consent of the government, governmental body or official, or account debtor to the assignment or transfer of, or the creation, attachment, perfection, or enforcement of a security interest in the account or chattel paper; or

(2) provides that the assignment or transfer or the creation, attachment, perfection, or enforcement of the security interest may give rise to a default, breach, right of recoupment, claim, defense, termination, right of

termination, or remedy under the account or chattel paper.

(g) Subject to subsection (h), an account debtor may not waive or vary its option under subsection (b)(3).

(h) This section is subject to law other than this article which establishes a different rule for an account debtor who is an individual and who incurred the obligation primarily for personal, family, or household purposes.

(i) This section does not apply to an assignment of a health-care-insurance receivable.

(j) This section prevails over any inconsistent provisions of the following statutes, rules, and regulations:

[List here any statutes, rules, and regulations containing provisions inconsistent with this section.]

Legislative Note: States that amend statutes, rules, and regulations to remove provisions inconsistent with this section need not enact subsection (j).

As amended in 1999 and 2000.

§9—407. Restrictions on Creation or Enforcement of Security Interest in Leasehold Interest or in Lessor's Residual Interest.

(a) Except as otherwise provided in subsection (b), a term in a lease agreement is ineffective to the extent that it:

(1) prohibits, restricts, or requires the consent of a party to the lease to the assignment or transfer of, or the creation, attachment, perfection, or enforcement of a security interest in an interest of a party under the lease contract or in the lessor's residual interest in the goods; or

(2) provides that the assignment or transfer or the creation, attachment, perfection, or enforcement of the security interest may give rise to a default, breach, right of recoupment, claim, defense, termination, right of termination, or remedy under the lease.

(b) Except as otherwise provided in Section 2A—303(7), a term described in subsection (a)(2) is effective to the extent that there is:

(1) a transfer by the lessee of the lessee's right of possession or use of the goods in violation of the term; or

(2) a delegation of a material performance of either party to the lease contract in violation of the term.

(c) The creation, attachment, perfection, or enforcement of a security interest in the lessor's interest under the lease contract or the lessor's residual interest in the goods is not a transfer that materially impairs the lessee's prospect of obtaining return performance or materially changes the duty of or materially increases the burden or risk imposed on the lessee within the purview of Section 2A—303(4) unless, and then only to the extent that, enforcement actually results in a delegation of material performance of the lessor.

As amended in 1999.

§9—408. Restrictions on Assignment of Promissory Notes, Health-Care-Insurance Receivables, and Certain General Intangibles Ineffective.

(a) Except as otherwise provided in subsection (b), a term in a promissory note or in an agreement between an account debtor and a debtor which relates to a health-care-insurance receivable or a general intangible, including a contract, permit, license, or franchise, and which term prohibits, restricts, or requires the consent of the person obligated on the promissory note or the account debtor to, the assignment or transfer of, or creation, attachment, or perfection of a security interest in, the promissory note, health-care-insurance receivable, or general intangible, is ineffective to the extent that the term:

(1) would impair the creation, attachment, or perfection of a security interest; or

(2) provides that the assignment or transfer or the creation, attachment, or perfection of the security interest may give rise to a default, breach, right of recoupment, claim, defense, termination, right of termination, or remedy under the promissory note, health-care-insurance receivable, or general intangible.

(b) Subsection (a) applies to a security interest in a payment intangible or promissory note only if the security interest arises out of a sale of the payment intangible or promissory note.

(c) A rule of law, statute, or regulation that prohibits, restricts, or requires the consent of a government, governmental body or official, person obligated on a promissory note, or account debtor to the assignment or transfer of, or creation of a security interest in, a promissory note, health-care-insurance receivable, or general intangible, including a contract, permit, license, or franchise between an account debtor and a debtor, is ineffective to the extent that the rule of law, statute, or regulation:

(1) would impair the creation, attachment, or perfection of a security interest; or

(2) provides that the assignment or transfer or the creation, attachment, or perfection of the security interest may give rise to a default, breach, right of recoupment, claim, defense, termination, right of termination, or remedy under the promissory note, health-care-insurance receivable, or general intangible.

(d) To the extent that a term in a promissory note or in an agreement between an account debtor and a debtor which relates to a health-care-insurance receivable or general intangible or a rule of law, statute, or regulation described in subsection (c) would be effective under law other than this article but is ineffective under subsection (a) or (c), the creation, attachment, or perfection of a security interest in the promissory note, health-care-insurance receivable, or general intangible:

(1) is not enforceable against the person obligated on the promissory note or the account debtor;

(2) does not impose a duty or obligation on the person obligated on the promissory note or the account debtor;

(3) does not require the person obligated on the promissory note or the account debtor to recognize the security interest, pay or render performance to the secured party, or accept payment or performance from the secured party;

(4) does not entitle the secured party to use or assign the debtor's rights under the promissory note, health-care-insurance receivable, or general intangible, including any related information or materials furnished to the debtor in the transaction giving rise to the promissory note, health-care-insurance receivable, or general intangible;

(5) does not entitle the secured party to use, assign, possess, or have access to any trade secrets or confidential information of the person obligated on the promissory note or the account debtor; and

(6) does not entitle the secured party to enforce the security interest in the promissory note, health-care-insurance receivable, or general intangible.

(e) This section prevails over any inconsistent provisions of the following statutes, rules, and regulations:

[List here any statutes, rules, and regulations containing provisions inconsistent with this section.]

Legislative Note: States that amend statutes, rules, and regulations to remove provisions inconsistent with this section need not enact subsection (e).

As amended in 1999.

§9—409. Restrictions on Assignment of Letter-of-Credit Rights Ineffective.

(a) A term in a letter of credit or a rule of law, statute, regulation, custom, or practice applicable to the letter of credit which prohibits, restricts, or requires the consent of an applicant, issuer, or nominated person to a beneficiary's assignment of or creation of a security interest in a letter-of-credit right is ineffective to the extent that the term or rule of law, statute, regulation, custom, or practice:

(1) would impair the creation, attachment, or perfection of a security interest in the letter-of-credit right; or

(2) provides that the assignment or the creation, attachment, or perfection of the security interest may give rise to a default, breach, right of recoupment, claim, defense, termination, right of termination, or remedy under the letter-of-credit right.

(b) To the extent that a term in a letter of credit is ineffective under subsection (a) but would be effective under law other than this article or a custom or practice applicable to the letter of credit, to the transfer of a right to draw or otherwise demand performance under the letter of credit, or to the assignment of a right to proceeds of the letter of credit, the creation, attachment, or perfection of a security interest in the letter-of-credit right:

(1) is not enforceable against the applicant, issuer, nominated person, or transferee beneficiary;

(2) imposes no duties or obligations on the applicant, issuer, nominated person, or transferee beneficiary; and

(3) does not require the applicant, issuer, nominated person, or transferee beneficiary to recognize the security interest, pay or render performance to the secured party, or accept payment or other performance from the secured party.

As amended in 1999.

PART 5 FILING
[SUBPART 1. FILING OFFICE; CONTENTS AND EFFECTIVENESS OF FINANCING STATEMENT]

§9—501. Filing Office.

(a) Except as otherwise provided in subsection (b), if the local law of this State governs perfection of a security interest or agricultural lien, the office in which to file a financing statement to perfect the security interest or agricultural lien is:

(1) the office designated for the filing or recording of a record of a mortgage on the related real property, if:

(A) the collateral is as-extracted collateral or timber to be cut; or

(B) the financing statement is filed as a fixture filing and the collateral is goods that are or are to become fixtures; or

(2) the office of [ ] [or any office duly authorized by [ ]], in all other cases, including a case in which the collateral is goods that are or are to become fixtures and the financing statement is not filed as a fixture filing.

(b) The office in which to file a financing statement to perfect a security interest in collateral, including fixtures, of a transmitting utility is the office of [ ]. The financing statement also constitutes a fixture filing as to the collateral indicated in the financing statement which is or is to become fixtures.

Legislative Note: The State should designate the filing office where the brackets appear. The filing office may be that of a governmental official (e.g., the Secretary of State) or a private party that maintains the State's filing system.

§9—502. Contents of Financing Statement; Record of Mortgage as Financing Statement; Time of Filing Financing Statement.

(a) Subject to subsection (b), a financing statement is sufficient only if it:

(1) provides the name of the debtor;

(2) provides the name of the secured party or a representative of the secured party; and

(3) indicates the collateral covered by the financing statement.

(b) Except as otherwise provided in Section 9—501(b), to be sufficient, a financing statement that covers as-extracted collateral or timber to be cut, or which is filed as a fixture filing and covers goods that are or are to become fixtures, must satisfy subsection (a) and also:

(1) indicate that it covers this type of collateral;

(2) indicate that it is to be filed [for record] in the real property records;

(3) provide a description of the real property to which the collateral is related [sufficient to give constructive notice of a mortgage under the law of this State if the description were contained in a record of the mortgage of the real property]; and

(4) if the debtor does not have an interest of record in the real property, provide the name of a record owner.

(c) A record of a mortgage is effective, from the date of recording, as a financing statement filed as a fixture filing or as a financing statement covering as-extracted collateral or timber to be cut only if:

(1) the record indicates the goods or accounts that it covers;

(2) the goods are or are to become fixtures related to the real property described in the record or the collateral is related to the real property described in the record and is as-extracted collateral or timber to be cut;

(3) the record satisfies the requirements for a financing statement in this section other than an indication that it is to be filed in the real property records; and

(4) the record is [duly] recorded.

(d) A financing statement may be filed before a security agreement is made or a security interest otherwise attaches.

Legislative Note: Language in brackets is optional. Where the State has any special recording system for real property other than the usual grantor-grantee index (as, for instance, a tract system or a title registration or Torrens system) local adaptations of subsection (b) and Section 9—519(d) and (e) may be necessary. See, e.g., Mass. Gen. Laws Chapter 106, Section 9—410.

§9—503. Name of Debtor and Secured Party.

(a) A financing statement sufficiently provides the name of the debtor:

(1) if the debtor is a registered organization, only if the financing statement provides the name of the debtor indicated on the public record of the debtor's jurisdiction of organization which shows the debtor to have been organized;

(2) if the debtor is a decedent's estate, only if the financing statement provides the name of the decedent and indicates that the debtor is an estate;

(3) if the debtor is a trust or a trustee acting with respect to property held in trust, only if the financing statement:

(A) provides the name specified for the trust in its organic documents or, if no name is specified, provides the name of the settlor and additional information sufficient to distinguish the debtor from other trusts having one or more of the same settlors; and

(B) indicates, in the debtor's name or otherwise, that the debtor is a trust or is a trustee acting with respect to property held in trust; and

(4) in other cases:

(A) if the debtor has a name, only if it provides the individual or organizational name of the debtor; and

(B) if the debtor does not have a name, only if it provides the names of the partners, members, associates, or other persons comprising the debtor.

(b) A financing statement that provides the name of the debtor in accordance with subsection (a) is not rendered ineffective by the absence of:

(1) a trade name or other name of the debtor; or

(2) unless required under subsection (a)(4)(B), names of partners, members, associates, or other persons comprising the debtor.

(c) A financing statement that provides only the debtor's trade name does not sufficiently provide the name of the debtor.

(d) Failure to indicate the representative capacity of a secured party or representative of a secured party does not affect the sufficiency of a financing statement.

(e) A financing statement may provide the name of more than one debtor and the name of more than one secured party.

§9—504. Indication of Collateral. A financing statement sufficiently indicates the collateral that it covers if the financing statement provides:

(1) a description of the collateral pursuant to Section 9—108; or

(2) an indication that the financing statement covers all assets or all personal property.

As amended in 1999.

§9—505. Filing and Compliance with Other Statutes and Treaties for Consignments, Leases, Other Bailments, and Other Transactions.

(a) A consignor, lessor, or other bailor of goods, a licensor, or a buyer of a payment intangible or promissory note may file a financing statement, or may comply with a statute or treaty described in Section 9—311(a), using the terms "consignor", "consignee", "lessor", "lessee", "bailor", "bailee", "licensor", "licensee", "owner", "registered owner", "buyer", "seller", or words of similar import, instead of the terms "secured party" and "debtor".

(b) This part applies to the filing of a financing statement under subsection (a) and, as appropriate, to compliance that is equivalent to filing a financing statement under Section 9—311(b), but the filing or compliance is not of itself a factor in determining whether the collateral secures an obligation. If it is determined for another reason that the collateral secures an obligation, a security interest held by the consignor, lessor, bailor, licensor, owner, or buyer which attaches to the collateral is perfected by the filing or compliance.

§9—506. Effect of Errors or Omissions.

(a) A financing statement substantially satisfying the requirements of this part is effective, even if it has minor errors or omissions, unless the errors or omissions make the financing statement seriously misleading.

(b) Except as otherwise provided in subsection (c), a financing statement that fails sufficiently to provide the name of the debtor in accordance with Section 9—503(a) is seriously misleading.

(c) If a search of the records of the filing office under the debtor's correct name, using the filing office's standard search logic, if any, would disclose a financing statement that fails sufficiently to provide the name of the debtor in accordance with Section 9—503(a), the name provided does not make the financing statement seriously misleading.

(d) For purposes of Section 9—508(b), the "debtor's correct name" in subsection (c) means the correct name of the new debtor.

§9—507. Effect of Certain Events on Effectiveness of Financing Statement.

(a) A filed financing statement remains effective with respect to collateral that is sold, exchanged, leased, licensed, or otherwise disposed of and in which a security interest or agricultural lien continues, even if the secured party knows of or consents to the disposition.

(b) Except as otherwise provided in subsection (c) and Section 9—508, a financing statement is not rendered ineffective if, after the financing statement is filed, the information provided in the financing statement becomes seriously misleading under Section 9—506.

(c) If a debtor so changes its name that a filed financing statement becomes seriously misleading under Section 9—506:

    (1) the financing statement is effective to perfect a security interest in collateral acquired by the debtor before, or within four months after, the change; and

    (2) the financing statement is not effective to perfect a security interest in collateral acquired by the debtor more than four months after the change, unless an amendment to the financing statement which renders the financing statement not seriously misleading is filed within four months after the change.

§9—508. Effectiveness of Financing Statement If New Debtor Becomes Bound by Security Agreement.

(a) Except as otherwise provided in this section, a filed financing statement naming an original debtor is effective to perfect a security interest in collateral in which a new debtor has or acquires rights to the extent that the financing statement would have been effective had the original debtor acquired rights in the collateral.

(b) If the difference between the name of the original debtor and that of the new debtor causes a filed financing statement that is effective under subsection (a) to be seriously misleading under Section 9—506:

    (1) the financing statement is effective to perfect a security interest in collateral acquired by the new debtor before, and within four months after, the new debtor becomes bound under Section 9B—203(d); and

    (2) the financing statement is not effective to perfect a security interest in collateral acquired by the new debtor more than four months after the new debtor becomes bound under Section 9—203(d) unless an initial financing statement providing the name of the new debtor is filed before the expiration of that time.

(c) This section does not apply to collateral as to which a filed financing statement remains effective against the new debtor under Section 9—507(a).

§9—509. Persons Entitled to File a Record.

(a) A person may file an initial financing statement, amendment that adds collateral covered by a financing statement, or amendment that adds a debtor to a financing statement only if:

    (1) the debtor authorizes the filing in an authenticated record or pursuant to subsection (b) or (c); or

    (2) the person holds an agricultural lien that has become effective at the time of filing and the financing statement covers only collateral in which the person holds an agricultural lien.

(b) By authenticating or becoming bound as debtor by a security agreement, a debtor or new debtor authorizes the filing of an initial financing statement, and an amendment, covering:

    (1) the collateral described in the security agreement; and

    (2) property that becomes collateral under Section 9—315(a)(2), whether or not the security agreement expressly covers proceeds.

(c) By acquiring collateral in which a security interest or agricultural lien continues under Section 9—315(a)(1), a debtor authorizes the filing of an initial financing statement, and an amendment, covering the collateral and property that becomes collateral under Section 9—315(a)(2).

(d) A person may file an amendment other than an amendment that adds collateral covered by a financing statement or an amendment that adds a debtor to a financing statement only if:

    (1) the secured party of record authorizes the filing; or

    (2) the amendment is a termination statement for a financing statement as to which the secured party of record has failed to file or send a termination statement as required by Section 9—513(a) or (c), the debtor authorizes the filing, and the termination statement indicates that the debtor authorized it to be filed.

(e) If there is more than one secured party of record for a financing statement, each secured party of record may authorize the filing of an amendment under subsection (d). As amended in 2000.

§9—510. Effectiveness of Filed Record.

(a) A filed record is effective only to the extent that it was filed by a person that may file it under Section 9—509.

(b) A record authorized by one secured party of record does not affect the financing statement with respect to another secured party of record.

(c) A continuation statement that is not filed within the six-month period prescribed by Section 9—515(d) is ineffective.

§9—511. Secured Party of Record.

(a) A secured party of record with respect to a financing statement is a person whose name is provided as the name of the secured party or a representative of the secured party in an initial financing statement that has been filed. If an initial financing statement is filed under Section 9—514(a), the assignee named in the initial financing statement is the secured party of record with respect to the financing statement.

(b) If an amendment of a financing statement which provides the name of a person as a secured party or a representative of a secured party is filed, the person named in the amendment is a secured party of record. If an amendment is filed under Section 9—514(b), the assignee named in the amendment is a secured party of record.

(c) A person remains a secured party of record until the filing of an amendment of the financing statement which deletes the person.

§9—512. Amendment of Financing Statement.

[ALTERNATIVE A]

(a) Subject to Section 9—509, a person may add or delete collateral covered by, continue or terminate the effectiveness of, or, subject to subsection (e), otherwise amend the information provided in, a financing statement by filing an amendment that:

(1) identifies, by its file number, the initial financing statement to which the amendment relates; and

(2) if the amendment relates to an initial financing statement filed [or recorded] in a filing office described in Section 9—501(a)(1), provides the information specified in Section 9—502(b).

[ALTERNATIVE B]

(a) Subject to Section 9—509, a person may add or delete collateral covered by, continue or terminate the effectiveness of, or, subject to subsection (e), otherwise amend the information provided in, a financing statement by filing an amendment that:

(1) identifies, by its file number, the initial financing statement to which the amendment relates; and

(2) if the amendment relates to an initial financing statement filed [or recorded] in a filing office described in Section 9—501(a)(1), provides the date [and time] that the initial financing statement was filed [or recorded] and the information specified in Section 9—502(b).

[END OF ALTERNATIVES]

(b) Except as otherwise provided in Section 9—515, the filing of an amendment does not extend the period of effectiveness of the financing statement.

(c) A financing statement that is amended by an amendment that adds collateral is effective as to the added collateral only from the date of the filing of the amendment.

(d) A financing statement that is amended by an amendment that adds a debtor is effective as to the added debtor only from the date of the filing of the amendment.

(e) An amendment is ineffective to the extent it:

(1) purports to delete all debtors and fails to provide the name of a debtor to be covered by the financing statement; or

(2) purports to delete all secured parties of record and fails to provide the name of a new secured party of record.

Legislative Note: States whose real-estate filing offices require additional information in amendments and cannot search their records by both the name of the debtor and the file number should enact Alternative B to Sections 9—512(a), 9—518(b), 9—519(f), and 9—522(a).

§9—513. Termination Statement.

(a) A secured party shall cause the secured party of record for a financing statement to file a termination statement for the financing statement if the financing statement covers consumer goods and:

(1) there is no obligation secured by the collateral covered by the financing statement and no commitment to make an advance, incur an obligation, or otherwise give value; or

(2) the debtor did not authorize the filing of the initial financing statement.

(b) To comply with subsection (a), a secured party shall cause the secured party of record to file the termination statement:

(1) within one month after there is no obligation secured by the collateral covered by the financing statement and no commitment to make an advance, incur an obligation, or otherwise give value; or

(2) if earlier, within 20 days after the secured party receives an authenticated demand from a debtor.

(c) In cases not governed by subsection (a), within 20 days after a secured party receives an authenticated demand from a debtor, the secured party shall cause the secured party of record for a financing statement to send to the debtor a termination statement for the financing statement or file the termination statement in the filing office if:

(1) except in the case of a financing statement covering accounts or chattel paper that has been sold or goods that are the subject of a consignment, there is no obligation secured by the collateral covered by the financing statement and no commitment to make an advance, incur an obligation, or otherwise give value;

(2) the financing statement covers accounts or chattel paper that has been sold but as to which the account debtor or other person obligated has discharged its obligation;

(3) the financing statement covers goods that were the subject of a consignment to the debtor but are not in the debtor's possession; or

(4) the debtor did not authorize the filing of the initial financing statement.

(d) Except as otherwise provided in Section 9—510, upon the filing of a termination statement with the filing office, the financing statement to which the termination statement relates ceases to be effective. Except as otherwise provided in Section 9—510, for purposes of Sections 9—519(g), 9—522(a), and 9—523(c), the filing with the filing office of a termination statement relating to a financing statement that indicates that the debtor is a transmitting utility also causes the effectiveness of the financing statement to lapse.
As amended in 2000.

§9—514. Assignment of Powers of Secured Party of Record.

(a) Except as otherwise provided in subsection (c), an initial financing statement may reflect an assignment of all of the secured party's power to authorize an amendment to the financing statement by providing the name and mailing address of the assignee as the name and address of the secured party.

(b) Except as otherwise provided in subsection (c), a secured party of record may assign of record all or part of its power to authorize an amendment to a financing statement by filing in the filing office an amendment of the financing statement which:

(1) identifies, by its file number, the initial financing statement to which it relates;

(2) provides the name of the assignor; and

(3) provides the name and mailing address of the assignee.

(c) An assignment of record of a security interest in a fixture covered by a record of a mortgage which is effective as a financing statement filed as a fixture filing under Section 9—502(c) may be made only by an assignment of record of the mortgage in the manner provided by law of this State other than [the Uniform Commercial Code].

§9—515. Duration and Effectiveness of Financing Statement; Effect of Lapsed Financing Statement.

(a) Except as otherwise provided in subsections (b), (e), (f), and (g), a filed financing statement is effective for a period of five years after the date of filing.

(b) Except as otherwise provided in subsections (e), (f), and (g), an initial financing statement filed in connection with a public-finance transaction or manufactured-home transaction is effective for a period of 30 years after the date of filing if it indicates that it is filed in connection with a public-finance transaction or manufactured-home transaction.

(c) The effectiveness of a filed financing statement lapses on the expiration of the period of its effectiveness unless before the lapse a continuation statement is filed pursuant to subsection (d). Upon lapse, a financing statement ceases to be effective and any security interest or agricultural lien that was perfected by the financing statement becomes unperfected, unless the security interest is perfected otherwise. If the security interest or agricultural lien becomes unperfected upon lapse, it is deemed never to have been perfected as against a purchaser of the collateral for value.

(d) A continuation statement may be filed only within six months before the expiration of the five-year period specified in subsection (a) or the 30-year period specified in subsection (b), whichever is applicable.

(e) Except as otherwise provided in Section 9—510, upon timely filing of a continuation statement, the effectiveness of the initial financing statement continues for a period of five years commencing on the day on which the financing statement would have become ineffective in the absence of the filing. Upon the expiration of the five-year period, the financing statement lapses in the same manner as provided in subsection (c), unless, before the lapse, another continuation statement is filed pursuant to subsection (d). Succeeding continuation statements may be filed in the same manner to continue the effectiveness of the initial financing statement.

(f) If a debtor is a transmitting utility and a filed financing statement so indicates, the financing statement is effective until a termination statement is filed.

(g) A record of a mortgage that is effective as a financing statement filed as a fixture filing under Section 9—502(c) remains effective as a financing statement filed as a fixture filing until the mortgage is released or satisfied of record or its effectiveness otherwise terminates as to the real property.

§9—516. What Constitutes Filing; Effectiveness of Filing.

(a) Except as otherwise provided in subsection (b), communication of a record to a filing office and tender of the filing fee or acceptance of the record by the filing office constitutes filing.

(b) Filing does not occur with respect to a record that a filing office refuses to accept because:

(1) the record is not communicated by a method or medium of communication authorized by the filing office;

(2) an amount equal to or greater than the applicable filing fee is not tendered;

(3) the filing office is unable to index the record because:

(A) in the case of an initial financing statement, the record does not provide a name for the debtor;

(B) in the case of an amendment or correction statement, the record:

(i) does not identify the initial financing statement as required by Section 9—512 or 9—518, as applicable; or

(ii) identifies an initial financing statement whose effectiveness has lapsed under Section 9—515;

(C) in the case of an initial financing statement that provides the name of a debtor identified as an individual or an amendment that provides a name of a debtor identified as an individual which was not previously provided in the financing statement to which the record relates, the record does not identify the debtor's last name; or

(D) in the case of a record filed [or recorded] in the filing office described in Section 9—501(a)(1), the record does not provide a sufficient description of the real property to which it relates;

(4) in the case of an initial financing statement or an amendment that adds a secured party of record, the record does not provide a name and mailing address for the secured party of record;

(5) in the case of an initial financing statement or an amendment that provides a name of a debtor which was not previously provided in the financing statement to which the amendment relates, the record does not:

(A) provide a mailing address for the debtor;

(B) indicate whether the debtor is an individual or an organization; or

(C) if the financing statement indicates that the debtor is an organization, provide:

(i) a type of organization for the debtor;

(ii) a jurisdiction of organization for the debtor; or

(iii) an organizational identification number for the debtor or indicate that the debtor has none;

(6) in the case of an assignment reflected in an initial financing statement under Section 9—514(a) or an amendment filed under Section 9—514(b), the record does not provide a name and mailing address for the assignee; or

(7) in the case of a continuation statement, the record is not filed within the six-month period prescribed by Section 9—515(d).

(c) For purposes of subsection (b):

(1) a record does not provide information if the filing office is unable to read or decipher the information; and

(2) a record that does not indicate that it is an amendment or identify an initial financing statement to which it relates, as required by Section 9—512, 9—514, or 9—518, is an initial financing statement.

(d) A record that is communicated to the filing office with tender of the filing fee, but which the filing office refuses to accept for a reason other than one set forth in subsection (b), is effective as a filed record except as against a purchaser of the collateral which gives value in reasonable reliance upon the absence of the record from the files.

§9—517. Effect of Indexing Errors.

The failure of the filing office to index a record correctly does not affect the effectiveness of the filed record.

§9—518. Claim Concerning Inaccurate or Wrongfully Filed Record.

(a) A person may file in the filing office a correction statement with respect to a record indexed there under the person's name if the person believes that the record is inaccurate or was wrongfully filed.

[ALTERNATIVE A]

(b) A correction statement must:

(1) identify the record to which it relates by the file number assigned to the initial financing statement to which the record relates;

(2) indicate that it is a correction statement; and

(3) provide the basis for the person's belief that the record is inaccurate and indicate the manner in which the person believes the record should be amended to cure any inaccuracy or provide the basis for the person's belief that the record was wrongfully filed.

[ALTERNATIVE B]

(b) A correction statement must:

(1) identify the record to which it relates by:

(A) the file number assigned to the initial financing statement to which the record relates; and

(B) if the correction statement relates to a record filed [or recorded] in a filing office described in Section 9—501(a)(1), the date [and time] that the initial financing statement was filed [or recorded] and the information specified in Section 9—502(b);

(2) indicate that it is a correction statement; and

(3) provide the basis for the person's belief that the record is inaccurate and indicate the manner in which the person believes the record should be amended to cure any inaccuracy or provide the basis for the person's belief that the record was wrongfully filed.

[END OF ALTERNATIVES]

(c) The filing of a correction statement does not affect the effectiveness of an initial financing statement or other filed record.

Legislative Note: States whose real-estate filing offices require additional information in amendments and cannot search their records by both the name of the debtor and the file number should enact Alternative B to Sections 9—512(a), 9—518(b), 9—519(f), and 9—522(a).

[SUBPART 2. DUTIES AND OPERATION OF FILING OFFICE]

§9—519. Numbering, Maintaining, and Indexing Records; Communicating Information Provided in Records.

(a) For each record filed in a filing office, the filing office shall:

(1) assign a unique number to the filed record;

(2) create a record that bears the number assigned to the filed record and the date and time of filing;

(3) maintain the filed record for public inspection; and

(4) index the filed record in accordance with subsections (c), (d), and (e).

(b) A file number [assigned after January 1, 2002,] must include a digit that:

(1) is mathematically derived from or related to the other digits of the file number; and

(2) aids the filing office in determining whether a number communicated as the file number includes a single-digit or transpositional error.

(c) Except as otherwise provided in subsections (d) and (e), the filing office shall:

(1) index an initial financing statement according to the name of the debtor and index all filed records relating to the initial financing statement in a manner that associates with one another an initial financing statement and all filed records relating to the initial financing statement; and

(2) index a record that provides a name of a debtor which was not previously provided in the financing statement to which the record relates also according to the name that was not previously provided.

(d) If a financing statement is filed as a fixture filing or covers as-extracted collateral or timber to be cut, [it must be filed for record and] the filing office shall index it:

(1) under the names of the debtor and of each owner of record shown on the financing statement as if they were the mortgagors under a mortgage of the real property described; and

(2) to the extent that the law of this State provides for indexing of records of mortgages under the name of the mortgagee, under the name of the secured party as if the secured party were the mortgagee thereunder, or, if indexing is by description, as if the financing statement were a record of a mortgage of the real property described.

(e) If a financing statement is filed as a fixture filing or covers as-extracted collateral or timber to be cut, the filing office shall index an assignment filed under Section 9—514(a) or an amendment filed under Section 9—514(b):

(1) under the name of the assignor as grantor; and

(2) to the extent that the law of this State provides for indexing a record of the assignment of a mortgage under the name of the assignee, under the name of the assignee.

[ALTERNATIVE A]

(f) The filing office shall maintain a capability:

(1) to retrieve a record by the name of the debtor and by the file number assigned to the initial financing statement to which the record relates; and

(2) to associate and retrieve with one another an initial financing statement and each filed record relating to the initial financing statement.

[ALTERNATIVE B]

(f) The filing office shall maintain a capability:

(1) to retrieve a record by the name of the debtor and:

(A) if the filing office is described in Section 9—501(a)(1), by the file number assigned to the initial financing statement to which the record relates and the date [and time] that the record was filed [or recorded]; or

(B) if the filing office is described in Section 9—501(a)(2), by the file number assigned to the initial financing statement to which the record relates; and

(2) to associate and retrieve with one another an initial financing statement and each filed record relating to the initial financing statement.

[END OF ALTERNATIVES]

(g) The filing office may not remove a debtor's name from the index until one year after the effectiveness of a financing statement naming the debtor lapses under Section 9—515 with respect to all secured parties of record.

(h) The filing office shall perform the acts required by subsections (a) through (e) at the time and in the manner prescribed by filing-office rule, but not later than two business days after the filing office receives the record in question.

[(i) Subsection[s] [(b)] [and] [(h)] do[es] not apply to a filing office described in Section 9—501(a)(1).]

Legislative Notes:

1. States whose filing offices currently assign file numbers that include a verification number, commonly known as a "check digit," or can implement this requirement before the effective date of this Article should omit the bracketed language in subsection (b).

2. In States in which writings will not appear in the real property records and indices unless actually recorded the bracketed language in subsection (d) should be used.

3. States whose real-estate filing offices require additional information in amendments and cannot search their records by both the name of the debtor and the file number should enact Alternative B to Sections 9—512(a), 9—518(b), 9—519(f), and 9—522(a).

4. A State that elects not to require real-estate filing offices to comply with either or both of subsections (b) and (h) may adopt an applicable variation of subsection (i) and add "Except as otherwise provided in subsection (i)," to the appropriate subsection or subsections.

§9—520. Acceptance and Refusal to Accept Record.

(a) A filing office shall refuse to accept a record for filing for a reason set forth in Section 9—516(b) and may refuse to accept a record for filing only for a reason set forth in Section 9—516(b).

(b) If a filing office refuses to accept a record for filing, it shall communicate to the person that presented the record the fact of and reason for the refusal and the date and time the record would have been filed had the filing office accepted it. The communication must be made at the time and in the manner prescribed by filing-office rule but [, in the case of a filing office described in Section 9—501(a)(2),] in no event more than two business days after the filing office receives the record.

(c) A filed financing statement satisfying Section 9—502(a) and (b) is effective, even if the filing office is required to refuse to accept it for filing under subsection (a). However, Section 9—338 applies to a filed financing statement providing information described in Section 9—516(b)(5) which is incorrect at the time the financing statement is filed.

(d) If a record communicated to a filing office provides information that relates to more than one debtor, this part applies as to each debtor separately.

Legislative Note: A State that elects not to require real-property filing offices to comply with subsection (b) should include the bracketed language.

§9—521. Uniform Form of Written Financing Statement and Amendment.

(a) A filing office that accepts written records may not refuse to accept a written initial financing statement in the following form and format except for a reason set forth in Section 9—516(b):

[NATIONAL UCC FINANCING STATEMENT (FORM UCC1)(REV. 7/29/98)]

[NATIONAL UCC FINANCING STATEMENT ADDENDUM (FORM UCC1Ad)(REV. 07/29/98)]

(b) A filing office that accepts written records may not refuse to accept a written record in the following form and format except for a reason set forth in Section 9—516(b):

[NATIONAL UCC FINANCING STATEMENT AMENDMENT (FORM UCC3)(REV. 07/29/98)]

[NATIONAL UCC FINANCING STATEMENT AMENDMENT ADDENDUM (FORM UCC3Ad)(REV. 07/29/98)]

§9—522. Maintenance and Destruction of Records.

[ALTERNATIVE A]

(a) The filing office shall maintain a record of the information provided in a filed financing statement for at least one year after the effectiveness of the financing statement has lapsed under Section 9—515 with respect to all secured parties of record. The record must be retrievable by using the name of the debtor and by using the file number assigned to the initial financing statement to which the record relates.

[ALTERNATIVE B]

(a) The filing office shall maintain a record of the information provided in a filed financing statement for at least one year after the effectiveness of the financing statement has lapsed under Section 9—515 with respect to all secured parties of record. The record must be retrievable by using the name of the debtor and:

(1) if the record was filed [or recorded] in the filing office described in Section 9—501(a)(1), by using the file number assigned to the initial financing statement to which the record relates and the date [and time] that the record was filed [or recorded]; or

(2) if the record was filed in the filing office described in Section 9—501(a)(2), by using the file number assigned to the initial financing statement to which the record relates.

[END OF ALTERNATIVES]

(b) Except to the extent that a statute governing disposition of public records provides otherwise, the filing office immediately may destroy any written record evidencing a financing statement. However, if the filing office destroys a written record, it shall maintain another record of the financing statement which complies with subsection (a).

Legislative Note: States whose real-estate filing offices require additional information in amendments and cannot search their records by both the name of the debtor and the file number should enact Alternative B to Sections 9—512(a), 9—518(b), 9—519(f), and 9—522(a).

§9—523. Information from Filing Office; Sale or License of Records.

(a) If a person that files a written record requests an acknowledgment of the filing, the filing office shall send to the person an image of the record showing the number assigned to the record pursuant to Section 9—519(a)(1) and the date and time of the filing of the record. However, if the person furnishes a copy of the record to the filing office, the filing office may instead:

(1) note upon the copy the number assigned to the record pursuant to Section 9—519(a)(1) and the date and time of the filing of the record; and

(2) send the copy to the person.

(b) If a person files a record other than a written record, the filing office shall communicate to the person an acknowledgment that provides:

(1) the information in the record;

(2) the number assigned to the record pursuant to Section 9—519(a)(1); and

(3) the date and time of the filing of the record.

(c) The filing office shall communicate or otherwise make available in a record the following information to any person that requests it:

(1) whether there is on file on a date and time specified by the filing office, but not a date earlier than three business days before the filing office receives the request, any financing statement that:

(A) designates a particular debtor [or, if the request so states, designates a particular debtor at the address specified in the request];

(B) has not lapsed under Section 9—515 with respect to all secured parties of record; and

(C) if the request so states, has lapsed under Section 9—515 and a record of which is maintained by the filing office under Section 9—522(a);

(2) the date and time of filing of each financing statement; and

(3) the information provided in each financing statement.

(d) In complying with its duty under subsection (c), the filing office may communicate information in any medium. However, if requested, the filing office shall communicate information by issuing [its written certificate] [a record that can be admitted into evidence in the courts of this State without extrinsic evidence of its authenticity].

(e) The filing office shall perform the acts required by subsections (a) through (d) at the time and in the manner prescribed by filing-office rule, but not later than two business days after the filing office receives the request.

(f) At least weekly, the [insert appropriate official or governmental agency] [filing office] shall offer to sell or license to the public on a nonexclusive basis, in bulk, copies of all records filed in it under this part, in every medium from time to time available to the filing office.

Legislative Notes:

1. States whose filing office does not offer the additional service of responding to search requests limited to a particular address should omit the bracketed language in subsection (c)(1)(A).

2. A State that elects not to require real-estate filing offices to comply with either or both of subsections (e) and (f) should specify in the appropriate subsection(s) only the filing office described in Section 9—501(a)(2).

§9—524. Delay by Filing Office.
Delay by the filing office beyond a time limit prescribed by this part is excused if:

(1) the delay is caused by interruption of communication or computer facilities, war, emergency conditions, failure of equipment, or other circumstances beyond control of the filing office; and

(2) the filing office exercises reasonable diligence under the circumstances.

§9—525. Fees.

(a) Except as otherwise provided in subsection (e), the fee for filing and indexing a record under this part, other than an initial financing statement of the kind described in subsection (b), is [the amount specified in subsection (c), if applicable, plus]:

(1) $[X] if the record is communicated in writing and consists of one or two pages;

(2) $[2X] if the record is communicated in writing and consists of more than two pages; and

(3) $[1/2X] if the record is communicated by another medium authorized by filing-office rule.

(b) Except as otherwise provided in subsection (e), the fee for filing and indexing an initial financing statement of the following kind is [the amount specified in subsection (c), if applicable, plus]:

(1) $——————— if the financing statement indicates that it is filed in connection with a public-finance transaction;

(2) $——————— if the financing statement indicates that it is filed in connection with a manufactured-home transaction.

[ALTERNATIVE A]

(c) The number of names required to be indexed does not affect the amount of the fee in subsections (a) and (b).

[ALTERNATIVE B]

(c) Except as otherwise provided in subsection (e), if a record is communicated in writing, the fee for each name more than two required to be indexed is $————————.

[END OF ALTERNATIVES]

(d) The fee for responding to a request for information from the filing office, including for [issuing a certificate showing] [communicating] whether there is on file any financing statement naming a particular debtor, is:

 (1) $———————— if the request is communicated in writing; and

 (2) $———————— if the request is communicated by another medium authorized by filing-office rule.

(e) This section does not require a fee with respect to a record of a mortgage which is effective as a financing statement filed as a fixture filing or as a financing statement covering as-extracted collateral or timber to be cut under Section 9—502(c). However, the recording and satisfaction fees that otherwise would be applicable to the record of the mortgage apply.

Legislative Notes:

1. To preserve uniformity, a State that places the provisions of this section together with statutes setting fees for other services should do so without modification.

2. A State should enact subsection (c), Alternative A, and omit the bracketed language in subsections (a) and (b) unless its indexing system entails a substantial additional cost when indexing additional names.

As amended in 2000.

§9—526. *Filing-Office Rules.*

(a) The [insert appropriate governmental official or agency] shall adopt and publish rules to implement this article. The filing-office rules must be[:

 (1)] consistent with this article[; and

 (2) adopted and published in accordance with the [insert any applicable state administrative procedure act]].

(b) To keep the filing-office rules and practices of the filing office in harmony with the rules and practices of filing offices in other jurisdictions that enact substantially this part, and to keep the technology used by the filing office compatible with the technology used by filing offices in other jurisdictions that enact substantially this part, the [insert appropriate governmental official or agency], so far as is consistent with the purposes, policies, and provisions of this article, in adopting, amending, and repealing filing-office rules, shall:

 (1) consult with filing offices in other jurisdictions that enact substantially this part; and

 (2) consult the most recent version of the Model Rules promulgated by the International Association of Corporate Administrators or any successor organization; and

 (3) take into consideration the rules and practices of, and the technology used by, filing offices in other jurisdictions that enact substantially this part.

§9—527. *Duty to Report.*

The [insert appropriate governmental official or agency] shall report [annually on or before ————————] to the [Governor and Legislature] on the operation of the filing office. The report must contain a statement of the extent to which:

 (1) the filing-office rules are not in harmony with the rules of filing offices in other jurisdictions that enact substantially this part and the reasons for these variations; and

 (2) the filing-office rules are not in harmony with the most recent version of the Model Rules promulgated by the International Association of Corporate Administrators, or any successor organization, and the reasons for these variations.

PART 6 DEFAULT
[SUBPART 1. DEFAULT AND ENFORCEMENT OF SECURITY INTEREST]

§9—601. *Rights after Default; Judicial Enforcement; Consignor or Buyer of Accounts, Chattel Paper, Payment Intangibles, or Promissory Notes.*

(a) After default, a secured party has the rights provided in this part and, except as otherwise provided in Section 9—602, those provided by agreement of the parties. A secured party:

 (1) may reduce a claim to judgment, foreclose, or otherwise enforce the claim, security interest, or agricultural lien by any available judicial procedure; and

 (2) if the collateral is documents, may proceed either as to the documents or as to the goods they cover.

(b) A secured party in possession of collateral or control of collateral under Section 9—104, 9—105, 9—106, or 9—107 has the rights and duties provided in Section 9—207.

(c) The rights under subsections (a) and (b) are cumulative and may be exercised simultaneously.

(d) Except as otherwise provided in subsection (g) and Section 9—605, after default, a debtor and an obligor have the rights provided in this part and by agreement of the parties.

(e) If a secured party has reduced its claim to judgment, the lien of any levy that may be made upon the collateral by virtue of an execution based upon the judgment relates back to the earliest of:

 (1) the date of perfection of the security interest or agricultural lien in the collateral;

 (2) the date of filing a financing statement covering the collateral; or

(3) any date specified in a statute under which the agricultural lien was created.

(f) A sale pursuant to an execution is a foreclosure of the security interest or agricultural lien by judicial procedure within the meaning of this section. A secured party may purchase at the sale and thereafter hold the collateral free of any other requirements of this article.

(g) Except as otherwise provided in Section 9—607(c), this part imposes no duties upon a secured party that is a consignor or is a buyer of accounts, chattel paper, payment intangibles, or promissory notes.

§9—602. Waiver and Variance of Rights and Duties.
Except as otherwise provided in Section 9—624, to the extent that they give rights to a debtor or obligor and impose duties on a secured party, the debtor or obligor may not waive or vary the rules stated in the following listed sections:

(1) Section 9—207(b)(4)(C), which deals with use and operation of the collateral by the secured party;

(2) Section 9—210, which deals with requests for an accounting and requests concerning a list of collateral and statement of account;

(3) Section 9—607(c), which deals with collection and enforcement of collateral;

(4) Sections 9—608(a) and 9—615(c) to the extent that they deal with application or payment of noncash proceeds of collection, enforcement, or disposition;

(5) Sections 9—608(a) and 9—615(d) to the extent that they require accounting for or payment of surplus proceeds of collateral;

(6) Section 9—609 to the extent that it imposes upon a secured party that takes possession of collateral without judicial process the duty to do so without breach of the peace;

(7) Sections 9—610(b), 9—611, 9—613, and 9—614, which deal with disposition of collateral;

(8) Section 9—615(f), which deals with calculation of a deficiency or surplus when a disposition is made to the secured party, a person related to the secured party, or a secondary obligor;

(9) Section 9—616, which deals with explanation of the calculation of a surplus or deficiency;

(10) Sections 9—620, 9—621, and 9—622, which deal with acceptance of collateral in satisfaction of obligation;

(11) Section 9—623, which deals with redemption of collateral;

(12) Section 9—624, which deals with permissible waivers; and

(13) Sections 9—625 and 9—626, which deal with the secured party's liability for failure to comply with this article.

§9—603. Agreement on Standards Concerning Rights and Duties.

(a) The parties may determine by agreement the standards measuring the fulfillment of the rights of a debtor or obligor and the duties of a secured party under a rule stated in Section 9—602 if the standards are not manifestly unreasonable.

(b) Subsection (a) does not apply to the duty under Section 9—609 to refrain from breaching the peace.

§9—604. Procedure If Security Agreement Covers Real Property or Fixtures.

(a) If a security agreement covers both personal and real property, a secured party may proceed:

(1) under this part as to the personal property without prejudicing any rights with respect to the real property; or

(2) as to both the personal property and the real property in accordance with the rights with respect to the real property, in which case the other provisions of this part do not apply.

(b) Subject to subsection (c), if a security agreement covers goods that are or become fixtures, a secured party may proceed:

(1) under this part; or

(2) in accordance with the rights with respect to real property, in which case the other provisions of this part do not apply.

(c) Subject to the other provisions of this part, if a secured party holding a security interest in fixtures has priority over all owners and encumbrancers of the real property, the secured party, after default, may remove the collateral from the real property.

(d) A secured party that removes collateral shall promptly reimburse any encumbrancer or owner of the real property, other than the debtor, for the cost of repair of any physical injury caused by the removal. The secured party need not reimburse the encumbrancer or owner for any diminution in value of the real property caused by the absence of the goods removed or by any necessity of replacing them. A person entitled to reimbursement may refuse permission to remove until the secured party gives adequate assurance for the performance of the obligation to reimburse.

§9—605. Unknown Debtor or Secondary Obligor.
A secured party does not owe a duty based on its status as secured party:

(1) to a person that is a debtor or obligor, unless the secured party knows:

(A) that the person is a debtor or obligor;

(B) the identity of the person; and

(C) how to communicate with the person; or

(2) to a secured party or lienholder that has filed a financing statement against a person, unless the secured party knows:

(A) that the person is a debtor; and

(B) the identity of the person.

§9—606. Time of Default for Agricultural Lien.

For purposes of this part, a default occurs in connection with an agricultural lien at the time the secured party becomes entitled to enforce the lien in accordance with the statute under which it was created.

§9—607. Collection and Enforcement by Secured Party.

(a) If so agreed, and in any event after default, a secured party:

(1) may notify an account debtor or other person obligated on collateral to make payment or otherwise render performance to or for the benefit of the secured party;

(2) may take any proceeds to which the secured party is entitled under Section 9—315;

(3) may enforce the obligations of an account debtor or other person obligated on collateral and exercise the rights of the debtor with respect to the obligation of the account debtor or other person obligated on collateral to make payment or otherwise render performance to the debtor, and with respect to any property that secures the obligations of the account debtor or other person obligated on the collateral;

(4) if it holds a security interest in a deposit account perfected by control under Section 9—104(a)(1), may apply the balance of the deposit account to the obligation secured by the deposit account; and

(5) if it holds a security interest in a deposit account perfected by control under Section 9—104(a)(2) or (3), may instruct the bank to pay the balance of the deposit account to or for the benefit of the secured party.

(b) If necessary to enable a secured party to exercise under subsection (a)(3) the right of a debtor to enforce a mortgage nonjudicially, the secured party may record in the office in which a record of the mortgage is recorded:

(1) a copy of the security agreement that creates or provides for a security interest in the obligation secured by the mortgage; and

(2) the secured party's sworn affidavit in recordable form stating that:

(A) a default has occurred; and

(B) the secured party is entitled to enforce the mortgage nonjudicially.

(c) A secured party shall proceed in a commercially reasonable manner if the secured party:

(1) undertakes to collect from or enforce an obligation of an account debtor or other person obligated on collateral; and

(2) is entitled to charge back uncollected collateral or otherwise to full or limited recourse against the debtor or a secondary obligor.

(d) A secured party may deduct from the collections made pursuant to subsection (c) reasonable expenses of collection and enforcement, including reasonable attorney's fees and legal expenses incurred by the secured party.

(e) This section does not determine whether an account debtor, bank, or other person obligated on collateral owes a duty to a secured party.

As amended in 2000.

§9—608. Application of Proceeds of Collection or Enforcement; Liability for Deficiency and Right to Surplus.

(a) If a security interest or agricultural lien secures payment or performance of an obligation, the following rules apply:

(1) A secured party shall apply or pay over for application the cash proceeds of collection or enforcement under Section 9—607 in the following order to:

(A) the reasonable expenses of collection and enforcement and, to the extent provided for by agreement and not prohibited by law, reasonable attorney's fees and legal expenses incurred by the secured party;

(B) the satisfaction of obligations secured by the security interest or agricultural lien under which the collection or enforcement is made; and

(C) the satisfaction of obligations secured by any subordinate security interest in or other lien on the collateral subject to the security interest or agricultural lien under which the collection or enforcement is made if the secured party receives an authenticated demand for proceeds before distribution of the proceeds is completed.

(2) If requested by a secured party, a holder of a subordinate security interest or other lien shall furnish reasonable proof of the interest or lien within a reasonable time. Unless the holder complies, the secured party need not comply with the holder's demand under paragraph (1)(C).

(3) A secured party need not apply or pay over for application noncash proceeds of collection and enforcement under Section 9—607 unless the failure to do so would be commercially unreasonable. A secured party that applies or pays over for application noncash proceeds shall do so in a commercially reasonable manner.

(4) A secured party shall account to and pay a debtor for any surplus, and the obligor is liable for any deficiency.

(b) If the underlying transaction is a sale of accounts, chattel paper, payment intangibles, or promissory notes, the debtor is not entitled to any surplus, and the obligor is not liable for any deficiency.

As amended in 2000.

§9—609. Secured Party's Right to Take Possession after Default.

(a) After default, a secured party:

(1) may take possession of the collateral; and

(2) without removal, may render equipment unusable and dispose of collateral on a debtor's premises under Section 9—610.

(b) A secured party may proceed under subsection (a):

(1) pursuant to judicial process; or

(2) without judicial process, if it proceeds without breach of the peace.

(c) If so agreed, and in any event after default, a secured party may require the debtor to assemble the collateral and make it available to the secured party at a place to be designated by the secured party which is reasonably convenient to both parties.

§9—610. Disposition of Collateral after Default.

(a) After default, a secured party may sell, lease, license, or otherwise dispose of any or all of the collateral in its present condition or following any commercially reasonable preparation or processing.

(b) Every aspect of a disposition of collateral, including the method, manner, time, place, and other terms, must be commercially reasonable. If commercially reasonable, a secured party may dispose of collateral by public or private proceedings, by one or more contracts, as a unit or in parcels, and at any time and place and on any terms.

(c) A secured party may purchase collateral:

(1) at a public disposition; or

(2) at a private disposition only if the collateral is of a kind that is customarily sold on a recognized market or the subject of widely distributed standard price quotations.

(d) A contract for sale, lease, license, or other disposition includes the warranties relating to title, possession, quiet enjoyment, and the like which by operation of law accompany a voluntary disposition of property of the kind subject to the contract.

(e) A secured party may disclaim or modify warranties under subsection (d):

(1) in a manner that would be effective to disclaim or modify the warranties in a voluntary disposition of property of the kind subject to the contract of disposition; or

(2) by communicating to the purchaser a record evidencing the contract for disposition and including an express disclaimer or modification of the warranties.

(f) A record is sufficient to disclaim warranties under subsection (e) if it indicates "There is no warranty relating to title, possession, quiet enjoyment, or the like in this disposition" or uses words of similar import.

§9—611. Notification before Disposition of Collateral.

(a) In this section, "notification date" means the earlier of the date on which:

(1) a secured party sends to the debtor and any secondary obligor an authenticated notification of disposition; or

(2) the debtor and any secondary obligor waive the right to notification.

(b) Except as otherwise provided in subsection (d), a secured party that disposes of collateral under Section 9—610 shall send to the persons specified in subsection (c) a reasonable authenticated notification of disposition.

(c) To comply with subsection (b), the secured party shall send an authenticated notification of disposition to:

(1) the debtor;

(2) any secondary obligor; and

(3) if the collateral is other than consumer goods:

(A) any other person from which the secured party has received, before the notification date, an authenticated notification of a claim of an interest in the collateral;

(B) any other secured party or lienholder that, 10 days before the notification date, held a security interest in or other lien on the collateral perfected by the filing of a financing statement that:

(i) identified the collateral;

(ii) was indexed under the debtor's name as of that date; and

(iii) was filed in the office in which to file a financing statement against the debtor covering the collateral as of that date; and

(C) any other secured party that, 10 days before the notification date, held a security interest in the collateral perfected by compliance with a statute, regulation, or treaty described in Section 9—311(a).

(d) Subsection (b) does not apply if the collateral is perishable or threatens to decline speedily in value or is of a type customarily sold on a recognized market.

(e) A secured party complies with the requirement for notification prescribed by subsection (c)(3)(B) if:

(1) not later than 20 days or earlier than 30 days before the notification date, the secured party requests, in a commercially reasonable manner, information concerning financing statements indexed under the debtor's name in the office indicated in subsection (c)(3)(B); and

(2) before the notification date, the secured party:

(A) did not receive a response to the request for information; or

(B) received a response to the request for information and sent an authenticated notification of disposition to each secured party or other lienholder named in that response whose financing statement covered the collateral.

§9—612. *Timeliness of Notification before Disposition of Collateral.*

(a) Except as otherwise provided in subsection (b), whether a notification is sent within a reasonable time is a question of fact.

(b) In a transaction other than a consumer transaction, a notification of disposition sent after default and 10 days or more before the earliest time of disposition set forth in the notification is sent within a reasonable time before the disposition.

§9—613. *Contents and Form of Notification before Disposition of Collateral: General.* Except in a consumer-goods transaction, the following rules apply:

(1) The contents of a notification of disposition are sufficient if the notification:

(A) describes the debtor and the secured party;

(B) describes the collateral that is the subject of the intended disposition;

(C) states the method of intended disposition;

(D) states that the debtor is entitled to an accounting of the unpaid indebtedness and states the charge, if any, for an accounting; and

(E) states the time and place of a public disposition or the time after which any other disposition is to be made.

(2) Whether the contents of a notification that lacks any of the information specified in paragraph (1) are nevertheless sufficient is a question of fact.

(3) The contents of a notification providing substantially the information specified in paragraph (1) are sufficient, even if the notification includes:

(A) information not specified by that paragraph; or

(B) minor errors that are not seriously misleading.

(4) A particular phrasing of the notification is not required.

(5) The following form of notification and the form appearing in Section 9—614(3), when completed, each provides sufficient information:

NOTIFICATION OF DISPOSITION OF COLLATERAL

To: *[Name of debtor, obligor, or other person to which the notification is sent]*

From: *[Name, address, and telephone number of secured party]*

Name of Debtor(s): *[Include only if debtor(s) are not an addressee]*

[For a public disposition:]

We will sell [or lease or license, *as applicable*] the *[describe collateral]* [to the highest qualified bidder] in public as follows:

Day and Date: ——————————

Time: ——————————

Place: ——————————

[For a private disposition:]

We will sell [or lease or license, *as applicable*] the *[describe collateral]* privately sometime after *[day and date]*.

You are entitled to an accounting of the unpaid indebtedness secured by the property that we intend to sell [or lease or license, *as applicable*] [for a charge of $——————————]. You may request an accounting by calling us at *[telephone number]*.

[End of Form]

As amended in 2000.

§9—614. *Contents and Form of Notification before Disposition of Collateral: Consumer-Goods Transaction.* In a consumer-goods transaction, the following rules apply:

(1) A notification of disposition must provide the following information:

(A) the information specified in Section 9—613(1);

(B) a description of any liability for a deficiency of the person to which the notification is sent;

(C) a telephone number from which the amount that must be paid to the secured party to redeem the collateral under Section 9—623 is available; and

(D) a telephone number or mailing address from which additional information concerning the disposition and the obligation secured is available.

(2) A particular phrasing of the notification is not required.

(3) The following form of notification, when completed, provides sufficient information:

[Name and address of secured party]

[Date]

NOTICE OF OUR PLAN TO SELL PROPERTY

[Name and address of any obligor who is also a debtor]

Subject: *[Identification of Transaction]*

We have your [describe collateral], because you broke promises in our agreement.

[For a public disposition:]

We will sell *[describe collateral]* at public sale. A sale could include a lease or license. The sale will be held as follows:

Date: ——————————

Time: ——————————

Place: ——————————

You may attend the sale and bring bidders if you want.

[For a private disposition:]

We will sell *[describe collateral]* at private sale sometime after *[date]*. A sale could include a lease or license.

The money that we get from the sale (after paying our costs) will reduce the amount you owe. If we get less money than you owe, you *[will or will not, as applicable]* still owe us the difference. If we get more money than you owe, you will get the extra money, unless we must pay it to someone else.

You can get the property back at any time before we sell it by paying us the full amount you owe (not just the past due payments), including our expenses. To learn the exact amount you must pay, call us at *[telephone number]*.

If you want us to explain to you in writing how we have figured the amount that you owe us, you may call us at *[telephone number]* [or write us at *[secured party's address]*] and request a written explanation. [We will charge you $——————— for the explanation if we sent you another written explanation of the amount you owe us within the last six months.]

If you need more information about the sale call us at *[telephone number]* [or write us at *[secured party's address]*].

We are sending this notice to the following other people who have an interest in [describe collateral] or who owe money under your agreement:

[Names of all other debtors and obligors, if any]

[End of Form]

(4) A notification in the form of paragraph (3) is sufficient, even if additional information appears at the end of the form.

(5) A notification in the form of paragraph (3) is sufficient, even if it includes errors in information not required by paragraph (1), unless the error is misleading with respect to rights arising under this article.

(6) If a notification under this section is not in the form of paragraph (3), law other than this article determines the effect of including information not required by paragraph (1).

§9—615. Application of Proceeds of Disposition; Liability for Deficiency and Right to Surplus.

(a) A secured party shall apply or pay over for application the cash proceeds of disposition under Section 9—610 in the following order to:

(1) the reasonable expenses of retaking, holding, preparing for disposition, processing, and disposing, and, to the extent provided for by agreement and not prohibited by law, reasonable attorney's fees and legal expenses incurred by the secured party;

(2) the satisfaction of obligations secured by the security interest or agricultural lien under which the disposition is made;

(3) the satisfaction of obligations secured by any subordinate security interest in or other subordinate lien on the collateral if:

(A) the secured party receives from the holder of the subordinate security interest or other lien an authenticated demand for proceeds before distribution of the proceeds is completed; and

(B) in a case in which a consignor has an interest in the collateral, the subordinate security interest or other lien is senior to the interest of the consignor; and

(4) a secured party that is a consignor of the collateral if the secured party receives from the consignor an authenticated demand for proceeds before distribution of the proceeds is completed.

(b) If requested by a secured party, a holder of a subordinate security interest or other lien shall furnish reasonable proof of the interest or lien within a reasonable time. Unless the holder does so, the secured party need not comply with the holder's demand under subsection (a)(3).

(c) A secured party need not apply or pay over for application noncash proceeds of disposition under Section 9—610 unless the failure to do so would be commercially unreasonable. A secured party that applies or pays over for application noncash proceeds shall do so in a commercially reasonable manner.

(d) If the security interest under which a disposition is made secures payment or performance of an obligation, after making the payments and applications required by subsection (a) and permitted by subsection (c):

(1) unless subsection (a)(4) requires the secured party to apply or pay over cash proceeds to a consignor, the secured party shall account to and pay a debtor for any surplus; and

(2) the obligor is liable for any deficiency.

(e) If the underlying transaction is a sale of accounts, chattel paper, payment intangibles, or promissory notes:

(1) the debtor is not entitled to any surplus; and

(2) the obligor is not liable for any deficiency.

(f) The surplus or deficiency following a disposition is calculated based on the amount of proceeds that would have been realized in a disposition complying with this part to a transferee other than the secured party, a person related to the secured party, or a secondary obligor if:

(1) the transferee in the disposition is the secured party, a person related to the secured party, or a secondary obligor; and

(2) the amount of proceeds of the disposition is significantly below the range of proceeds that a complying disposition to a person other than the secured party, a person related to the secured party, or a secondary obligor would have brought.

(g) A secured party that receives cash proceeds of a disposition in good faith and without knowledge that the receipt violates the rights of the holder of a security interest or other lien that is not subordinate to the security interest or agricultural lien under which the disposition is made:

(1) takes the cash proceeds free of the security interest or other lien;

(2) is not obligated to apply the proceeds of the disposition to the satisfaction of obligations secured by the security interest or other lien; and

(3) is not obligated to account to or pay the holder of the security interest or other lien for any surplus.

As amended in 2000.

§9—616. *Explanation of Calculation of Surplus or Deficiency.*

(a) In this section:

    (1) "Explanation" means a writing that:

        (A) states the amount of the surplus or deficiency;

        (B) provides an explanation in accordance with subsection (c) of how the secured party calculated the surplus or deficiency;

        (C) states, if applicable, that future debits, credits, charges, including additional credit service charges or interest, rebates, and expenses may affect the amount of the surplus or deficiency; and

        (D) provides a telephone number or mailing address from which additional information concerning the transaction is available.

    (2) "Request" means a record:

        (A) authenticated by a debtor or consumer obligor;

        (B) requesting that the recipient provide an explanation; and

        (C) sent after disposition of the collateral under Section 9—610.

(b) In a consumer-goods transaction in which the debtor is entitled to a surplus or a consumer obligor is liable for a deficiency under Section 9—615, the secured party shall:

    (1) send an explanation to the debtor or consumer obligor, as applicable, after the disposition and:

        (A) before or when the secured party accounts to the debtor and pays any surplus or first makes written demand on the consumer obligor after the disposition for payment of the deficiency; and

        (B) within 14 days after receipt of a request; or

    (2) in the case of a consumer obligor who is liable for a deficiency, within 14 days after receipt of a request, send to the consumer obligor a record waiving the secured party's right to a deficiency.

(c) To comply with subsection (a)(1)(B), a writing must provide the following information in the following order:

    (1) the aggregate amount of obligations secured by the security interest under which the disposition was made, and, if the amount reflects a rebate of unearned interest or credit service charge, an indication of that fact, calculated as of a specified date:

        (A) if the secured party takes or receives possession of the collateral after default, not more than 35 days before the secured party takes or receives possession; or

        (B) if the secured party takes or receives possession of the collateral before default or does not take possession of the collateral, not more than 35 days before the disposition;

    (2) the amount of proceeds of the disposition;

    (3) the aggregate amount of the obligations after deducting the amount of proceeds;

    (4) the amount, in the aggregate or by type, and types of expenses, including expenses of retaking, holding, preparing for disposition, processing, and disposing of the collateral, and attorney's fees secured by the collateral which are known to the secured party and relate to the current disposition;

    (5) the amount, in the aggregate or by type, and types of credits, including rebates of interest or credit service charges, to which the obligor is known to be entitled and which are not reflected in the amount in paragraph (1); and

    (6) the amount of the surplus or deficiency.

(d) A particular phrasing of the explanation is not required. An explanation complying substantially with the requirements of subsection (a) is sufficient, even if it includes minor errors that are not seriously misleading.

(e) A debtor or consumer obligor is entitled without charge to one response to a request under this section during any six-month period in which the secured party did not send to the debtor or consumer obligor an explanation pursuant to subsection (b)(1). The secured party may require payment of a charge not exceeding $25 for each additional response.

§9—617. *Rights of Transferee of Collateral.*

(a) A secured party's disposition of collateral after default:

    (1) transfers to a transferee for value all of the debtor's rights in the collateral;

    (2) discharges the security interest under which the disposition is made; and

    (3) discharges any subordinate security interest or other subordinate lien [other than liens created under [cite acts or statutes providing for liens, if any, that are not to be discharged]].

(b) A transferee that acts in good faith takes free of the rights and interests described in subsection (a), even if the secured party fails to comply with this article or the requirements of any judicial proceeding.

(c) If a transferee does not take free of the rights and interests described in subsection (a), the transferee takes the collateral subject to:

    (1) the debtor's rights in the collateral;

    (2) the security interest or agricultural lien under which the disposition is made; and

    (3) any other security interest or other lien.

§9—618. *Rights and Duties of Certain Secondary Obligors.*

(a) A secondary obligor acquires the rights and becomes obligated to perform the duties of the secured party after the secondary obligor:

    (1) receives an assignment of a secured obligation from the secured party;

(2) receives a transfer of collateral from the secured party and agrees to accept the rights and assume the duties of the secured party; or

(3) is subrogated to the rights of a secured party with respect to collateral.

(b) An assignment, transfer, or subrogation described in subsection (a):

(1) is not a disposition of collateral under Section 9—610; and

(2) relieves the secured party of further duties under this article.

§9—619. Transfer of Record or Legal Title.

(a) In this section, "transfer statement" means a record authenticated by a secured party stating:

(1) that the debtor has defaulted in connection with an obligation secured by specified collateral;

(2) that the secured party has exercised its post-default remedies with respect to the collateral;

(3) that, by reason of the exercise, a transferee has acquired the rights of the debtor in the collateral; and

(4) the name and mailing address of the secured party, debtor, and transferee.

(b) A transfer statement entitles the transferee to the transfer of record of all rights of the debtor in the collateral specified in the statement in any official filing, recording, registration, or certificate-of-title system covering the collateral. If a transfer statement is presented with the applicable fee and request form to the official or office responsible for maintaining the system, the official or office shall:

(1) accept the transfer statement;

(2) promptly amend its records to reflect the transfer; and

(3) if applicable, issue a new appropriate certificate of title in the name of the transferee.

(c) A transfer of the record or legal title to collateral to a secured party under subsection (b) or otherwise is not of itself a disposition of collateral under this article and does not of itself relieve the secured party of its duties under this article.

§9—620. Acceptance of Collateral in Full or Partial Satisfaction of Obligation; Compulsory Disposition of Collateral.

(a) Except as otherwise provided in subsection (g), a secured party may accept collateral in full or partial satisfaction of the obligation it secures only if:

(1) the debtor consents to the acceptance under subsection (c);

(2) the secured party does not receive, within the time set forth in subsection (d), a notification of objection to the proposal authenticated by:

(A) a person to which the secured party was required to send a proposal under Section 9—621; or

(B) any other person, other than the debtor, holding an interest in the collateral subordinate to the security interest that is the subject of the proposal;

(3) if the collateral is consumer goods, the collateral is not in the possession of the debtor when the debtor consents to the acceptance; and

(4) subsection (e) does not require the secured party to dispose of the collateral or the debtor waives the requirement pursuant to Section 9—624.

(b) A purported or apparent acceptance of collateral under this section is ineffective unless:

(1) the secured party consents to the acceptance in an authenticated record or sends a proposal to the debtor; and

(2) the conditions of subsection (a) are met.

(c) For purposes of this section:

(1) a debtor consents to an acceptance of collateral in partial satisfaction of the obligation it secures only if the debtor agrees to the terms of the acceptance in a record authenticated after default; and

(2) a debtor consents to an acceptance of collateral in full satisfaction of the obligation it secures only if the debtor agrees to the terms of the acceptance in a record authenticated after default or the secured party:

(A) sends to the debtor after default a proposal that is unconditional or subject only to a condition that collateral not in the possession of the secured party be preserved or maintained;

(B) in the proposal, proposes to accept collateral in full satisfaction of the obligation it secures; and

(C) does not receive a notification of objection authenticated by the debtor within 20 days after the proposal is sent.

(d) To be effective under subsection (a)(2), a notification of objection must be received by the secured party:

(1) in the case of a person to which the proposal was sent pursuant to Section 9—621, within 20 days after notification was sent to that person; and

(2) in other cases:

(A) within 20 days after the last notification was sent pursuant to Section 9—621; or

(B) if a notification was not sent, before the debtor consents to the acceptance under subsection (c).

(e) A secured party that has taken possession of collateral shall dispose of the collateral pursuant to Section 9—610 within the time specified in subsection (f) if:

(1) 60 percent of the cash price has been paid in the case of a purchase-money security interest in consumer goods; or

(2) 60 percent of the principal amount of the obligation secured has been paid in the case of a non-purchase-money security interest in consumer goods.

(f) To comply with subsection (e), the secured party shall dispose of the collateral:

(1) within 90 days after taking possession; or

(2) within any longer period to which the debtor and all secondary obligors have agreed in an agreement to that effect entered into and authenticated after default.

(g) In a consumer transaction, a secured party may not accept collateral in partial satisfaction of the obligation it secures.

§9—621. Notification of Proposal to Accept Collateral.

(a) A secured party that desires to accept collateral in full or partial satisfaction of the obligation it secures shall send its proposal to:

(1) any person from which the secured party has received, before the debtor consented to the acceptance, an authenticated notification of a claim of an interest in the collateral;

(2) any other secured party or lienholder that, 10 days before the debtor consented to the acceptance, held a security interest in or other lien on the collateral perfected by the filing of a financing statement that:

(A) identified the collateral;

(B) was indexed under the debtor's name as of that date; and

(C) was filed in the office or offices in which to file a financing statement against the debtor covering the collateral as of that date; and

(3) any other secured party that, 10 days before the debtor consented to the acceptance, held a security interest in the collateral perfected by compliance with a statute, regulation, or treaty described in Section 9—311(a).

(b) A secured party that desires to accept collateral in partial satisfaction of the obligation it secures shall send its proposal to any secondary obligor in addition to the persons described in subsection (a).

§9—622. Effect of Acceptance of Collateral.

(a) A secured party's acceptance of collateral in full or partial satisfaction of the obligation it secures:

(1) discharges the obligation to the extent consented to by the debtor;

(2) transfers to the secured party all of a debtor's rights in the collateral;

(3) discharges the security interest or agricultural lien that is the subject of the debtor's consent and any subordinate security interest or other subordinate lien; and

(4) terminates any other subordinate interest.

(b) A subordinate interest is discharged or terminated under subsection (a), even if the secured party fails to comply with this article.

§9—623. Right to Redeem Collateral.

(a) A debtor, any secondary obligor, or any other secured party or lienholder may redeem collateral.

(b) To redeem collateral, a person shall tender:

(1) fulfillment of all obligations secured by the collateral; and

(2) the reasonable expenses and attorney's fees described in Section 9—615(a)(1).

(c) A redemption may occur at any time before a secured party:

(1) has collected collateral under Section 9—607;

(2) has disposed of collateral or entered into a contract for its disposition under Section 9—610; or

(3) has accepted collateral in full or partial satisfaction of the obligation it secures under Section 9—622.

§9—624. Waiver.

(a) A debtor or secondary obligor may waive the right to notification of disposition of collateral under Section 9—611 only by an agreement to that effect entered into and authenticated after default.

(b) A debtor may waive the right to require disposition of collateral under Section 9—620(e) only by an agreement to that effect entered into and authenticated after default.

(c) Except in a consumer-goods transaction, a debtor or secondary obligor may waive the right to redeem collateral under Section 9—623 only by an agreement to that effect entered into and authenticated after default.

[SUBPART 2. NONCOMPLIANCE WITH ARTICLE]

§9—625. Remedies for Secured Party's Failure to Comply with Article.

(a) If it is established that a secured party is not proceeding in accordance with this article, a court may order or restrain collection, enforcement, or disposition of collateral on appropriate terms and conditions.

(b) Subject to subsections (c), (d), and (f), a person is liable for damages in the amount of any loss caused by a failure to comply with this article. Loss caused by a failure to comply may include loss resulting from the debtor's inability to obtain, or increased costs of, alternative financing.

(c) Except as otherwise provided in Section 9—628:

(1) a person that, at the time of the failure, was a debtor, was an obligor, or held a security interest in or other lien on the collateral may recover damages under subsection (b) for its loss; and

(2) if the collateral is consumer goods, a person that was a debtor or a secondary obligor at the time a secured party failed to comply with this part may recover for that failure in any event an amount not less than the credit service charge plus 10 percent of the principal amount of the obligation or the time-price differential plus 10 percent of the cash price.

(d) A debtor whose deficiency is eliminated under Section 9—626 may recover damages for the loss of any surplus. However, a debtor or secondary obligor whose deficiency is eliminated or reduced under Section 9—626 may not otherwise recover under subsection (b) for noncompliance with the provisions of this part relating to collection, enforcement, disposition, or acceptance.

(e) In addition to any damages recoverable under subsection (b), the debtor, consumer obligor, or person named as a debtor in a filed record, as applicable, may recover $500 in each case from a person that:

(1) fails to comply with Section 9—208;

(2) fails to comply with Section 9—209;

(3) files a record that the person is not entitled to file under Section 9—509(a);

(4) fails to cause the secured party of record to file or send a termination statement as required by Section 9—513(a) or (c);

(5) fails to comply with Section 9—616(b)(1) and whose failure is part of a pattern, or consistent with a practice, of noncompliance; or

(6) fails to comply with Section 9—616(b)(2).

(f) A debtor or consumer obligor may recover damages under subsection (b) and, in addition, $500 in each case from a person that, without reasonable cause, fails to comply with a request under Section 9—210. A recipient of a request under Section 9—210 which never claimed an interest in the collateral or obligations that are the subject of a request under that section has a reasonable excuse for failure to comply with the request within the meaning of this subsection.

(g) If a secured party fails to comply with a request regarding a list of collateral or a statement of account under Section 9—210, the secured party may claim a security interest only as shown in the list or statement included in the request as against a person that is reasonably misled by the failure. As amended in 2000.

§9—626. Action in Which Deficiency or Surplus Is in Issue.

(a) In an action arising from a transaction, other than a consumer transaction, in which the amount of a deficiency or surplus is in issue, the following rules apply:

(1) A secured party need not prove compliance with the provisions of this part relating to collection, enforcement, disposition, or acceptance unless the debtor or a secondary obligor places the secured party's compliance in issue.

(2) If the secured party's compliance is placed in issue, the secured party has the burden of establishing that the collection, enforcement, disposition, or acceptance was conducted in accordance with this part.

(3) Except as otherwise provided in Section 9—628, if a secured party fails to prove that the collection, enforcement, disposition, or acceptance was conducted in accordance with the provisions of this part relating to collection, enforcement, disposition, or acceptance, the liability of a debtor or a secondary obligor for a deficiency is limited to an amount by which the sum of the secured obligation, expenses, and attorney's fees exceeds the greater of:

(A) the proceeds of the collection, enforcement, disposition, or acceptance; or

(B) the amount of proceeds that would have been realized had the noncomplying secured party proceeded in accordance with the provisions of this part relating to collection, enforcement, disposition, or acceptance.

(4) For purposes of paragraph (3)(B), the amount of proceeds that would have been realized is equal to the sum of the secured obligation, expenses, and attorney's fees unless the secured party proves that the amount is less than that sum.

(5) If a deficiency or surplus is calculated under Section 9—615(f), the debtor or obligor has the burden of establishing that the amount of proceeds of the disposition is significantly below the range of prices that a complying disposition to a person other than the secured party, a person related to the secured party, or a secondary obligor would have brought.

(b) The limitation of the rules in subsection (a) to transactions other than consumer transactions is intended to leave to the court the determination of the proper rules in consumer transactions. The court may not infer from that limitation the nature of the proper rule in consumer transactions and may continue to apply established approaches.

§9—627. Determination of Whether Conduct Was Commercially Reasonable.

(a) The fact that a greater amount could have been obtained by a collection, enforcement, disposition, or acceptance at a different time or in a different method from that selected by the secured party is not of itself sufficient to preclude the secured party from establishing that the collection, enforcement, disposition, or acceptance was made in a commercially reasonable manner.

(b) A disposition of collateral is made in a commercially reasonable manner if the disposition is made:

(1) in the usual manner on any recognized market;

(2) at the price current in any recognized market at the time of the disposition; or

(3) otherwise in conformity with reasonable commercial practices among dealers in the type of property that was the subject of the disposition.

(c) A collection, enforcement, disposition, or acceptance is commercially reasonable if it has been approved:

(1) in a judicial proceeding;

(2) by a bona fide creditors' committee;

(3) by a representative of creditors; or

(4) by an assignee for the benefit of creditors.

(d) Approval under subsection (c) need not be obtained, and lack of approval does not mean that the collection, enforcement, disposition, or acceptance is not commercially reasonable.

§9—628. Nonliability and Limitation on Liability of Secured Party; Liability of Secondary Obligor.

(a) Unless a secured party knows that a person is a debtor or obligor, knows the identity of the person, and knows how to communicate with the person:

(1) the secured party is not liable to the person, or to a secured party or lienholder that has filed a financing statement against the person, for failure to comply with this article; and

(2) the secured party's failure to comply with this article does not affect the liability of the person for a deficiency.

(b) A secured party is not liable because of its status as secured party:

(1) to a person that is a debtor or obligor, unless the secured party knows:

(A) that the person is a debtor or obligor;

(B) the identity of the person; and

(C) how to communicate with the person; or

(2) to a secured party or lienholder that has filed a financing statement against a person, unless the secured party knows:

(A) that the person is a debtor; and

(B) the identity of the person.

(c) A secured party is not liable to any person, and a person's liability for a deficiency is not affected, because of any act or omission arising out of the secured party's reasonable belief that a transaction is not a consumer-goods transaction or a consumer transaction or that goods are not consumer goods, if the secured party's belief is based on its reasonable reliance on:

(1) a debtor's representation concerning the purpose for which collateral was to be used, acquired, or held; or

(2) an obligor's representation concerning the purpose for which a secured obligation was incurred.

(d) A secured party is not liable to any person under Section 9—625(c)(2) for its failure to comply with Section 9—616.

(e) A secured party is not liable under Section 9—625(c)(2) more than once with respect to any one secured obligation.

PART 7 TRANSITION

§9—701. Effective Date.   This [Act] takes effect on July 1, 2001.

§9—702. Savings Clause.

(a) Except as otherwise provided in this part, this [Act] applies to a transaction or lien within its scope, even if the transaction or lien was entered into or created before this [Act] takes effect.

(b) Except as otherwise provided in subsection (c) and Sections 9—703 through 9—709:

(1) transactions and liens that were not governed by [former Article 9], were validly entered into or created before this [Act] takes effect, and would be subject to this [Act] if they had been entered into or created after this [Act] takes effect, and the rights, duties, and interests flowing from those transactions and liens remain valid after this [Act] takes effect; and

(2) the transactions and liens may be terminated, completed, consummated, and enforced as required or permitted by this [Act] or by the law that otherwise would apply if this [Act] had not taken effect.

(c) This [Act] does not affect an action, case, or proceeding commenced before this [Act] takes effect.

As amended in 2000.

§9—703. Security Interest Perfected before Effective Date.

(a) A security interest that is enforceable immediately before this [Act] takes effect and would have priority over the rights of a person that becomes a lien creditor at that time is a perfected security interest under this [Act] if, when this [Act] takes effect, the applicable requirements for enforceability and perfection under this [Act] are satisfied without further action.

(b) Except as otherwise provided in Section 9—705, if, immediately before this [Act] takes effect, a security interest is enforceable and would have priority over the rights of a person that becomes a lien creditor at that time, but the applicable requirements for enforceability or perfection under this [Act] are not satisfied when this [Act] takes effect, the security interest:

(1) is a perfected security interest for one year after this [Act] takes effect;

(2) remains enforceable thereafter only if the security interest becomes enforceable under Section 9—203 before the year expires; and

(3) remains perfected thereafter only if the applicable requirements for perfection under this [Act] are satisfied before the year expires.

§9—704. Security Interest Unperfected before Effective Date.   A security interest that is enforceable immediately before this [Act] takes effect but which would be subordinate to the rights of a person that becomes a lien creditor at that time:

(1) remains an enforceable security interest for one year after this [Act] takes effect;

(2) remains enforceable thereafter if the security interest becomes enforceable under Section 9—203 when this [Act] takes effect or within one year thereafter; and

(3) becomes perfected:

(A) without further action, when this [Act] takes effect if the applicable requirements for perfection under this [Act] are satisfied before or at that time; or

(B) when the applicable requirements for perfection are satisfied if the requirements are satisfied after that time.

§9—705. Effectiveness of Action Taken before Effective Date.

(a) If action, other than the filing of a financing statement, is taken before this [Act] takes effect and the action would have resulted in priority of a security interest over the rights of a person that becomes a lien creditor had the security interest become enforceable before this [Act] takes effect, the action is effective to perfect a security interest that attaches under this [Act] within one year after this [Act] takes effect. An attached security interest becomes unperfected one year after this [Act] takes effect unless the security interest becomes a perfected security interest under this [Act] before the expiration of that period.

(b) The filing of a financing statement before this [Act] takes effect is effective to perfect a security interest to the extent the filing would satisfy the applicable requirements for perfection under this [Act].

(c) This [Act] does not render ineffective an effective financing statement that, before this [Act] takes effect, is filed and satisfies the applicable requirements for perfection under the law of the jurisdiction governing perfection as provided in [former Section 9—103]. However, except as otherwise provided in subsections (d) and (e) and Section 9—706, the financing statement ceases to be effective at the earlier of:

(1) the time the financing statement would have ceased to be effective under the law of the jurisdiction in which it is filed; or

(2) June 30, 2006.

(d) The filing of a continuation statement after this [Act] takes effect does not continue the effectiveness of the financing statement filed before this [Act] takes effect. However, upon the timely filing of a continuation statement after this [Act] takes effect and in accordance with the law of the jurisdiction governing perfection as provided in Part 3, the effectiveness of a financing statement filed in the same office in that jurisdiction before this [Act] takes effect continues for the period provided by the law of that jurisdiction.

(e) Subsection (c)(2) applies to a financing statement that, before this [Act] takes effect, is filed against a transmitting utility and satisfies the applicable requirements for perfection under the law of the jurisdiction governing perfection as provided in [former Section 9—103] only to the extent that

Part 3 provides that the law of a jurisdiction other than the jurisdiction in which the financing statement is filed governs perfection of a security interest in collateral covered by the financing statement.

(f) A financing statement that includes a financing statement filed before this [Act] takes effect and a continuation statement filed after this [Act] takes effect is effective only to the extent that it satisfies the requirements of Part 5 for an initial financing statement.

§9—706. When Initial Financing Statement Suffices to Continue Effectiveness of Financing Statement.

(a) The filing of an initial financing statement in the office specified in Section 9—501 continues the effectiveness of a financing statement filed before this [Act] takes effect if:

(1) the filing of an initial financing statement in that office would be effective to perfect a security interest under this [Act];

(2) the pre-effective-date financing statement was filed in an office in another State or another office in this State; and

(3) the initial financing statement satisfies subsection (c).

(b) The filing of an initial financing statement under subsection (a) continues the effectiveness of the pre-effective-date financing statement:

(1) if the initial financing statement is filed before this [Act] takes effect, for the period provided in [former Section 9—403] with respect to a financing statement; and

(2) if the initial financing statement is filed after this [Act] takes effect, for the period provided in Section 9—515 with respect to an initial financing statement.

(c) To be effective for purposes of subsection (a), an initial financing statement must:

(1) satisfy the requirements of Part 5 for an initial financing statement;

(2) identify the pre-effective-date financing statement by indicating the office in which the financing statement was filed and providing the dates of filing and file numbers, if any, of the financing statement and of the most recent continuation statement filed with respect to the financing statement; and

(3) indicate that the pre-effective-date financing statement remains effective.

§9—707. Amendment of Pre-Effective-Date Financing Statement.

(a) In this section, "Pre-effective-date financing statement" means a financing statement filed before this [Act] takes effect.

(b) After this [Act] takes effect, a person may add or delete collateral covered by, continue or terminate the effectiveness of, or otherwise amend the information provided in, a pre-effective-date financing statement only in accordance with the law of the jurisdiction governing perfection as provided in Part 3. However, the effectiveness of a pre-effective-date financing statement also may be terminated in accordance with the law of the jurisdiction in which the financing statement is filed.

(c) Except as otherwise provided in subsection (d), if the law of this State governs perfection of a security interest, the information in a pre-effective-date financing statement may be amended after this [Act] takes effect only if:

(1) the pre-effective-date financing statement and an amendment are filed in the office specified in Section 9—501;

(2) an amendment is filed in the office specified in Section 9—501 concurrently with, or after the filing in that office of, an initial financing statement that satisfies Section 9—706(c); or

(3) an initial financing statement that provides the information as amended and satisfies Section 9—706(c) is filed in the office specified in Section 9—501.

(d) If the law of this State governs perfection of a security interest, the effectiveness of a pre-effective-date financing statement may be continued only under Section 9—705(d) and (f) or 9—706.

(e) Whether or not the law of this State governs perfection of a security interest, the effectiveness of a pre-effective-date financing statement filed in this State may be terminated after this [Act] takes effect by filing a termination statement in the office in which the pre-effective-date financing statement is filed, unless an initial financing statement that satisfies Section 9—706(c) has been filed in the office specified by the law of the jurisdiction governing perfection as provided in Part 3 as the office in which to file a financing statement.

As amended in 2000.

§9—708. Persons Entitled to File Initial Financing Statement or Continuation Statement. A person may file an initial financing statement or a continuation statement under this part if:

(1) the secured party of record authorizes the filing; and

(2) the filing is necessary under this part:

(A) to continue the effectiveness of a financing statement filed before this [Act] takes effect; or

(B) to perfect or continue the perfection of a security interest.

As amended in 2000.

§9—709. Priority.

(a) This [Act] determines the priority of conflicting claims to collateral. However, if the relative priorities of the claims were established before this [Act] takes effect, [former Article 9] determines priority.

(b) For purposes of Section 9—322(a), the priority of a security interest that becomes enforceable under Section 9—203 of this [Act] dates from the time this [Act] takes effect if the security interest is perfected under this [Act] by the filing of a financing statement before this [Act] takes effect which would not have been effective to perfect the security interest under [former Article 9]. This subsection does not apply to conflicting security interests each of which is perfected by the filing of such a financing statement.

As amended in 2000.

GLOSSARY

(A)

absolute guaranty—agreement that creates the same obligation for the guarantor as a suretyship does for the surety; a guaranty of payment creates an absolute guaranty.

absolute privilege—complete defense against the tort of defamation, as in the speeches of members of Congress on the floor and witnesses in a trial.

acceleration clause—provision in a contract or any legal instrument that advances the time for the performance of specified obligations; for example, a provision making the balance due upon debtor's default.

acceptance—unqualified assent to the act or proposal of another; as the acceptance of a draft (bill of exchange), of an offer to make a contract, of goods delivered by the seller, or of a gift or deed.

acceptance—unqualified assent to the act or proposal of another; as the acceptance of an offer to make a contract.

acceptor—drawee who has accepted the liability of paying the amount of money specified in a draft.

accommodation party—person who signs an instrument to lend credit to another party to the paper.

accord and satisfaction—agreement to substitute for an existing debt some alternative form of discharging that debt, coupled with the actual discharge of the debt by the substituted performance.

act-of-state doctrine—doctrine whereby every sovereign state is bound to respect the independence of every other sovereign state, and the courts of one country will not sit in judgment of another government's acts done within its own territory.

administrative agency—government body charged with administering and implementing legislation.

administrative law—law governing administrative agencies.

Administrative Procedure Act—federal law that establishes the operating rules for administrative agencies.

administrative regulations—rules made by state and federal administrative agencies.

administrator, administratrix—person (man, woman) appointed to wind up and settle the estate of a person who has died without a will.

admissibility—the quality of the evidence in a case that allows it to be presented to the jury.

advising bank—bank that tells beneficiary that letter of credit has been issued.

affirm—action taken by an appellate court that approves the decision of the court below.

affirmative action plan (AAP)—plan to have a diverse and representative workforce.

after-acquired goods—goods acquired after a security interest has attached.

agency—the relationship that exists between a person identified as a principal and another by virtue of which the latter may make contracts with third persons on behalf of the principal. (Parties–principal, agent, third person)

agent—person or firm who is authorized by the principal or by operation of law to make contracts with third persons on behalf of the principal.

airbill—document of title issued to a shipper whose goods are being sent via air.

alteration—unauthorized change or completion of a negotiable instrument designed to modify the obligation of a party to the instrument.

alternative payees—those persons to whom a negotiable instrument is made payable, any one of whom may indorse and take delivery of it.

ambiguous—having more than one reasonable interpretation.

answer—what a defendant must file to admit or deny facts asserted by the plaintiff.

anticipatory breach—promisor's repudiation of the contract prior to the time that performance is required when such repudiation is accepted by the promisee as a breach of the contract.

anticipatory repudiation—repudiation made in advance of the time for performance of the contract obligations.

apparent authority—appearance of authority created by the principal's words or conduct.

appeal—taking a case to a reviewing court to determine whether the judgment of the lower court or administrative agency was correct. (Parties–appellant, appellee)

appellate jurisdiction—the power of a court to hear and decide a given class of cases on appeal from another court or administrative agency.

appropriation—taking of an image, likeness, or name for commercial advantage.

arbitration—the settlement of disputed questions, whether of law or fact, by one or more arbitrators by whose decision the parties agree to be bound.

Article 2—section of Uniform Commercial Code that governs contracts for the sale of goods.

assignee—third party to whom contract benefits are transferred.

assignment—transfer of a right; generally used in connection with personal property rights, as rights under a contract, commercial paper, an insurance policy, a mortgage, or a lease. (Parties–assignor, assignee.)

assignor—party who assigns contract rights to a third party.

association tribunal—a court created by a trade association or group for the resolution of disputes among its members.

attorney in fact—agent authorized to act for another under a power of attorney.

automatic perfection—perfection given by statute without specific filing or possession requirements on the part of the creditor.

automatic stay—order to prevent creditors from taking action such as filing suits or seeking foreclosure against the debtor.

(B)

bad check laws—laws making it a criminal offense to issue a bad check with intent to defraud.

bailee—person who accepts possession of a property.

bailee's lien—specific, possessory lien of the bailee upon the goods for work done to them. Commonly extended by statute to any bailee's claim for compensation, eliminating the necessity of retention of possession.

bailment—relationship that exists when personal property is delivered into the possession of another under an agreement, express or implied, that the identical property will be returned or will be delivered in accordance with the agreement. (Parties–bailor, bailee)

bailment for mutual benefit—bailment in which the bailor and bailee derive a benefit from the bailment.

bailor—person who turns over the possession of a property.

balance sheet test—comparison of assets to liabilities made to determine solvency.

bankruptcy—procedure by which one unable to pay debts may surrender all assets in excess of any exemption claim to the court for administration and distribution to creditors, and the debtor is given a discharge that releases him from the unpaid balance due on most debts.

bankruptcy courts—court of special jurisdiction to determine bankruptcy issues.

battle of the forms—merchants' exchanges of invoices and purchase orders with differing boilerplate terms.

bearer—person in physical possession of commercial paper payable to bearer, a document of title directing delivery to bearer, or an investment security in bearer form.

bearer paper—instrument with no payee, payable to cash or payable to bearer.

bedrock view—a strict constructionist interpretation of a constitution.

beneficiary—person to whom the proceeds of a life insurance policy are payable, a person for whose benefit property is held in trust, or a person given property by a will; the ultimate recipient of the benefit of a funds transfer.

beneficiary's bank—the final bank, which carries out the payment order, in the chain of a transfer of funds.

bicameral—a two-house form of the legislative branch of government.

bilateral contract—agreement under which one promise is given in exchange for another.

bill of lading—document issued by a carrier acknowledging the receipt of goods and the terms of the contract of transportation.

bill of sale—writing signed by the seller reciting that the personal property therein described has been sold to the buyer.

blackmail—extortion demands made by a nonpublic official.

blank indorsement—an indorsement that does not name the person to whom the paper, document of title, or investment security is negotiated.

blocking laws—laws that prohibit the disclosure, copying, inspection, or removal of documents located in the enacting country in compliance with orders from foreign authorities.

bona fide—in good faith; without any fraud or deceit.

breach—failure to act or perform in the manner called for in a contract.

breach of the peace—violation of the law in the repossession of the collateral.

business ethics—balancing the goal of profits with values of individuals and society.

(C)

cancellation provision—crossing out of a part of an instrument or a destruction of all legal effect of the instrument, whether by act of party, upon breach by the other party, or pursuant to agreement or decree of court.

cargo insurance—insurance that protects a cargo owner against financial loss if goods being shipped are lost or damaged at sea.

carrier—individual or organization undertaking the transportation of goods.

case law—law that includes principles that are expressed for the first time in court decisions.

cash surrender value—sum paid the insured upon the surrender of a policy to the insurer.

cashier's check—draft drawn by a bank on itself.

cause of action—right to damages or other judicial relief when a legally protected right of the plaintiff is violated by an unlawful act of the defendant.

cease-and-desist order—order issued by a court or administrative agency to stop a practice that it decides is improper.

certificate of deposit (CD)—promise-to-pay instrument issued by a bank.

certified check—check for which the bank has set aside in a special account sufficient funds to pay it; payment is made when check is presented regardless of amount in drawer's account at that time; discharges all parties except certifying bank when holder requests certification.

CF—cost and freight.

Chapter 11 bankruptcy—reorganization form of bankruptcy under federal law.

Chapter 7 bankruptcy—liquidation form of bankruptcy under federal law.

Chapter 13 bankruptcy—proceeding of consumer debt readjustment plan bankruptcy.

check—order by a depositor on a bank to pay a sum of money to a payee; a bill of exchange drawn on a bank and payable on demand.

choice-of-law clause—clause in an agreement that specifies which law will govern should a dispute arise.

chose in action—intangible personal property in the nature of claims against another, such as a claim for accounts receivable or wages.

CIF—cost, insurance, and freight.

civil disobedience—the term used when natural law proponents violate positive law.

claim—creditor's right to payment.

Clayton Act—a federal law that prohibits price discrimination.

close-connection doctrine—circumstantial evidence, such as an

ongoing or a close relationship, that can serve as notice of a problem with an instrument.

COD—cash on delivery.

coinsurance clause—clause requiring the insured to maintain insurance on property up to a stated amount and providing that to the extent that this is not done, the insured is to be deemed a coinsurer with the insurer, so that the latter is liable only for its proportionate share of the amount of insurance required to be carried.

collateral—property pledged by a borrower as security for a debt.

comity—principle of international and national law that the laws of all nations and states deserve the respect legitimately demanded by equal participants.

commerce clause—that section of the U.S. Constitution allocating business regulation.

commercial impracticability—situation that occurs when costs of performance rise suddenly and performance of a contract will result in a substantial loss.

commercial lease—any nonconsumer lease.

commercial paper—written, transferable, signed promise or order to pay a specified sum of money; a negotiable instrument.

commercial unit—standard of the trade for shipment or packaging of a good.

commission merchant—bailee to whom goods are consigned for sale.

commission or **factorage**—consignee's compensation.

common carrier—carrier that holds out its facilities to serve the general public for compensation without discrimination.

common law—the body of unwritten principles originally based upon the usages and customs of the community that were recognized and enforced by the courts.

community property—cotenancy held by husband and wife in property acquired during their marriage under the law of some of the states, principally in the southwestern United States.

compensatory damages—sum of money that will compensate an injured plaintiff for actual loss.

complaint—the initial pleading filed by the plaintiff in many actions, which in many states may be served as original process to acquire jurisdiction over the defendant.

composition of creditors—agreement among creditors that each shall accept a partial payment as full payment in consideration of the other creditors doing the same.

computer crimes—wrongs committed using a computer or with knowledge of computers.

concealment—failure to volunteer information not requested.

condition—stipulation or prerequisite in a contract, will, or other instrument.

condition precedent—event that if unsatisfied would mean that no rights would arise under a contract.

condition subsequent—event whose occurrence or lack thereof terminates a contract.

confidential relationship—relationship in which, because of the legal status of the parties or their respective physical or mental conditions or knowledge, one party places full confidence and trust in the other.

conflict of interest—conduct that compromises an employee's allegiance to that company.

consent decrees—informal settlements of enforcement actions brought by agencies.

consequential damages—damages the buyer experiences as a result of the seller's breach with respect to a third party; also called *special damages.*

consideration—promise or performance that the promisor demands as the price of the promise.

consignee—(1) person to whom goods are shipped, (2) dealer who sells goods for others.

consignment—bailment made for the purpose of sale by the bailee. (Parties–consignor, consignee)

consignor—(1) person who delivers goods to the carrier for shipment, (2) party with title who turns goods over to another for sale.

conspiracy—agreement between two or more persons to commit an unlawful act.

constitution—a body of principles that establishes the structure of a government and the relationship of the government to the people who are governed.

constructive bailment—bailment imposed by law as opposed to one created by contract, whereby the bailee must preserve the property and redeliver it to the owner.

constructive delivery—see "symbolic delivery."

consumer—any buyer afforded special protections by statute or regulation.

consumer credit—credit for personal, family, and household use.

consumer goods—goods used or bought primarily for personal, family, or household use.

consumer lease—lease of goods by a natural person for personal, family, or household use.

contract—a binding agreement based on the genuine assent of the parties, made for a lawful object, between competent parties, in the form required by law, and generally supported by consideration.

contract carrier—carrier that transports on the basis of individual contracts that it makes with each shipper.

contract interference—tort in which a third party interferes with others' freedom to contract.

contract of adhesion—contract offered by a dominant party to a party with inferior bargaining power on a take-it-or-leave-it basis.

contract under seal—contract executed by affixing a seal or making an impression on the paper or on some adhering substance such as wax attached to the document.

contracting agent—agent with authority to make contracts; person with whom the buyer deals.

Contracts for the International Sale of Goods (CISG)—uniform international contract code contracts for international sale of goods.

contractual capacity—ability to understand that a contract is being made and to understand its general meaning.

contribution—right of a co-obligor who has paid more than a proportionate share to demand that the other obligor pay the amount of the excess payment made.

contributory negligence—negligence of the plaintiff that contributes to injury and at common law bars from recovery from the defendant although the defendant may have been more negligent than the plaintiff.

conversion—act of taking personal property by a person not entitled to it and keeping it from its true owner or prior possessor without consent.

copyright—exclusive right given by federal statute to the creator of a literary or an artistic work to use, reproduce, and display the work.

correspondent bank—will honor the letter of credit from the domestic bank of the buyer.

cost plus—method of determining the purchase price or contract price equal to the seller's or contractor's costs plus a stated percentage as the profit.

co-sureties—sureties for the same debtor and obligor.

cotenancy—when two or more persons hold concurrent rights and interests in the same property.

counterclaim—a claim that the defendant in an action may make against the plaintiff.

counteroffer—proposal by an offeree to the offeror that changes the terms of, and thus rejects, the original offer.

course of dealing—pattern of performance between two parties to a contract.

court—a tribunal established by government to hear and decide matters properly brought to it.

credit transfer—transaction in which a person making payment, such as a buyer, requests payment be made to the beneficiary's bank.

creditor—person (seller or lender) who is owed money; also may be a secured party.

crime—violation of the law that is punished as an offense against the state or government.

cross-examination—the examination made of a witness by the attorney for the adverse party.

customary authority—authority of an agent to do any act that, according to the custom of the community, usually accompanies the transaction for which the agent is authorized to act.

cybercrime—crimes committed via the Internet.

cyberlaw—laws and precedent applicable to Internet transactions and communications.

cyberspace—World Wide Web and Internet communication.

cybersquatters—term for those who register and set up domain names on the Internet for resale to the famous users of the names in question.

(D)

debit transfer—transaction in which a beneficiary entitled to money requests payment from a bank according to a prior agreement.

debtor—buyer on credit (i.e., a borrower).

decedent—person whose estate is being administered.

defamation—untrue statement by one party about another to a third party.

defendant—party charged with a violation of civil or criminal law in a proceeding.

definite time—time of payment computable from the face of the instrument.

delegated powers—powers expressly granted the national government by the Constitution.

delegation—transfer to another of the right and power to do an act.

delegation of duties—transfer of duties by a contracting party to another person who is to perform them.

delivery—constructive or actual possession.

demand draft—draft that is payable upon presentment.

demurrer—a pleading to dismiss the adverse party's pleading for not stating a cause of action or a defense.

deposition—the testimony of a witness taken out of court before a person authorized to administer oaths.

depositor—person, or bailor, who gives property for storage.

development statement—statement that sets forth significant details of a real estate or property development as required by the federal Land Sales Act.

direct damages—losses that are caused by breach of a contract.

direct examination—examination of a witness by his or her attorney.

directed verdict—a direction by the trial judge to the jury to return a verdict in favor of a specified party to the action.

disability—any incapacity resulting from bodily injury or disease to engage in any occupation for remuneration or profit.

discharge in bankruptcy—order of the bankruptcy court relieving the debtor from obligation to pay the unpaid balance of most claims.

disclosed principal—principal whose identity is made known by the agent as well as the fact that the agent is acting on the principal's behalf.

discovery—procedures for ascertaining facts prior to the time of trial in order to eliminate the element of surprise in litigation.

dishonor—status when the primary party refuses to pay the instrument according to its terms.

Dispute Settlement Body—means, provided by the World Trade Organization, for member countries to resolve trade disputes rather than engage in unilateral trade sanctions or a trade war.

distributor—entity that takes title to goods and bears the financial and commercial risks for the subsequent sale of the goods.

divestiture order—a court order to dispose of interests that could lead to a monopoly.

divisible contract—agreement consisting of two or more parts, each calling for corresponding performances of each part by the parties.

document of title—document treated as evidence that a person is entitled to receive, hold, and dispose of the document and the goods it covers.

donee—recipient of a gift.

donor—person making a gift.

double indemnity—provision for payment of double the amount specified by the insurance contract if death is caused by an accident and occurs under specified circumstances.

downsizing—a reduction in workforce.

draft or bill of exchange—an unconditional order in writing by one person upon another, signed by the person giving it, and ordering the person to whom it is directed to pay upon demand or at a definite time a sum certain in money to order or to bearer.

drawee—person to whom the draft is addressed and who is ordered to pay the amount of money specified in the draft.

drawer—person who writes out and creates a draft or bill of exchange, including a check.

due process—the constitutional right to be heard, question witnesses, and present evidence.

due process clause—in the Fifth and Fourteenth Amendments, a guarantee of protection from unreasonable procedures and unreasonable laws.

dumping—selling goods in another country at less than their fair value.

duress—conduct that deprives the victim of free will and that generally gives the victim the right to set aside any transaction entered into under such circumstances.

duty—an obligation of law imposed on a person to perform or refrain from performing a certain act.

(E)

economic duress—threat of financial loss.

Economic Espionage Act (EEA)—federal law that makes it a felony to copy, download, transmit, or in any way transfer proprietary files, documents, and information from a computer to an unauthorized person.

economic strikers—union strikers trying to enforce bargaining demands when an impasse has been reached in the negotiation process for a collective bargaining agreement.

effects doctrine—doctrine that states that U.S. courts will assume jurisdiction and will apply antitrust laws to conduct outside of the United States when the activity of business firms has direct and substantial effect on U.S. commerce; the rule has been modified to require that the effect on U.S. commerce also be foreseeable.

electronic funds transfer (EFT)—any transfer of funds (other than a transaction originated by a check, draft, or similar paper instrument) that is initiated through an electronic terminal, telephone, computer, or magnetic tape so as to authorize a financial institution to debit or credit an account.

Electronic Funds Transfer Act (EFTA)—federal law that provides consumers with rights and protections in electronic funds transfers.

embezzlement—statutory offense consisting of the unlawful conversion of property entrusted to the wrongdoer.

employment-at-will doctrine—doctrine in which the employer has historically been allowed to terminate the employment contract at any time for any reason or for no reason.

en banc—the term used when the full panel of judges on the appellate court hears a case.

encoding warranty—warranty made by any party who encodes electronic information on an instrument; a warranty of accuracy.

endowment insurance—insurance that pays the face amount of the policy if the insured dies within the policy period.

equity—the body of principles that originally developed because of the inadequacy of the rules then applied by the common law courts of England.

escheat—transfer to the state of the title to a decedent's property when the owner of the property dies intestate and is not survived by anyone capable of taking the property as heir.

E-sign—signature over the Internet.

estoppel—principle by which a person is barred from pursuing a certain course of action or of disputing the truth of certain matters.

ethics—a branch of philosophy dealing with values that relate to the nature of human conduct and values associated with that conduct.

ex post facto law—a law making criminal an act that was lawful when done or that increases the penalty when done. Such laws are generally prohibited by constitutional provisions.

exculpatory clause—provision in a contract stating that one of the parties shall not be liable for damages in case of breach; also called a *limitation-of-liability clause.*

executed contract—agreement that has been completely performed.

execution—the carrying out of a judgment of a court, generally directing that property owned by the defendant be sold and the proceeds first be used to pay the execution or judgment creditor.

executive branch—the branch of government (e.g., the president) formed to execute the laws.

executor, executrix—person (man, woman) named in a will to administer the estate of the decedent.

executory contract—agreement by which something remains to be done by one or both parties.

exhaustion of administrative remedies—requirement that an agency make its final decision before the parties can go to court.

existing goods—goods that physically exist and are owned by the seller at the time of a transaction.

exoneration—agreement or provision in an agreement that one party shall not be held liable for loss; the right of the surety to demand that those primarily liable pay the claim for which the surety is secondarily liable.

expert witness—one who has acquired special knowledge in a particular field as through practical experience or study, or both, whose opinion is admissible as an aid to the trier of fact.

export sale—direct sale to customers in a foreign country.

express authorization—authorization of an agent to perform a certain act.

express contract—agreement of the parties manifested by their words, whether spoken or written.

express warranty—statement by the defendant relating to the goods, which statement is part of the basis of the bargain.

extortion—illegal demand by a public officer acting with apparent authority.

(F)

facilitation payments—(grease payments) legal payments to speed up or ensure performance of normal government duties.

factor—bailee to whom goods are consigned for sale.

fair use—principle that allows the limited use of copyrighted material for teaching, research, and news reporting.

false imprisonment—intentional detention of a person without that person's consent; called the *shopkeeper's tort when shoplifters are unlawfully detained.*

FAS—free alongside the named vessel.

federal district court—a general trial court of the federal system.

Federal Register—government publication issued five days a week that lists all administrative regulations, all presidential proclamations and executive orders, and other documents and classes of documents that the president or Congress direct to be published.

Federal Register Act—federal law requiring agencies to make public disclosure of proposed rules, passed rules, and activities.

Federal Sentencing Guidelines—federal standards used by judges in determining mandatory sentence terms for those convicted of federal crimes.

federal system—the system of government in which a central government is given power to administer to national concerns while individual states retain the power to administer to local concerns.

felony—criminal offense that is punishable by confinement in prison for more than one year or by death, or that is expressly stated by statute to be a felony.

field warehousing—stored goods under the exclusive control of a warehouse but kept on the owner's premises rather than in a warehouse.

Fifth Amendment—constitutional protection against self-incrimination; also guarantees due process.

finance lease—three-party lease agreement in which there is a lessor, a lessee, and a financier.

financing statement—brief statement (record) that gives sufficient information to alert third persons that a particular creditor may have a security interest in the collateral described.

fire insurance policy—a contract that indemnifies the insured for property destruction or damage caused by fire.

firm offer—offer stated to be held open for a specified time, which must be so held in some states even in the absence of an option contract, or under the UCC, with respect to merchants.

first-in-time provision—creditor whose interest attached first has priority in the collateral when two creditors have a secured interest.

first-to-perfect basis—rule of priorities that holds that first in time in perfecting a security interest, mortgage, judgment, lien, or other property attachment right should have priority.

floating lien—claim in a changing or shifting stock of goods of the buyer.

FOB place of destination—general commercial language for delivery to the buyer.

FOB place of shipment—"ship to" contract.

forbearance—refraining from doing an act.

Foreign Corrupt Practices Act (FCPA)—federal law that makes it a felony to influence decision makers in other countries for the purpose of obtaining business, such as contracts for sales and services; also imposes financial reporting requirements on certain U.S. corporations.

forged or unauthorized indorsement—instrument indorsed by an agent for a principal without authorization or authority.

forgery—fraudulently making or altering an instrument that apparently creates or alters a legal liability of another.

formal contracts—written contracts or agreements whose formality signifies the parties' intention to abide by the terms.

Fourth Amendment—privacy protection in the U.S. Constitution; prohibits unauthorized searches and seizures.

franchise—(1) a privilege or authorization, generally exclusive, to engage in a particular activity within a particular geographic area, such as a government franchise to operate a taxi company within a specified city, or a private franchise as the grant by a manufacturer of a right to sell products within a particular territory or for a particular number of years; (2) the right to vote.

franchisee—person to whom franchise is granted.

franchising—granting of permission to use a trademark, trade name, or copyright under specified conditions; a form of licensing.

franchisor—party granting the franchise.

fraud—making of a false statement of a past or existing fact, with knowledge of its falsity or with reckless indifference as to its truth, with the intent to cause another to rely thereon, and such person does rely thereon and is harmed thereby.

fraud in factum—fraud committed through deception on documents or the nature of the transaction as opposed to the subject matter or parties in the transaction (fraud in the inducement).

fraud in the inducement—fraud that occurs when a person is persuaded or induced to execute an instrument because of fraudulent statements.

Freedom of Information Act—federal law permitting citizens to request documents and records from administrative agencies.

freight forwarder—one who contracts to have goods transported and, in turn, contracts with carriers for such transportation.

freight insurance—insures that shipowner will receive payment for transportation charges.

full warranty—obligation of a seller to fix or replace a defective product within a reasonable time without cost to the buyer.

funds transfer—communication of instructions or requests to pay a specific sum of money to the credit of a specified account or person without an actual physical passing of money.

fungible goods—homogeneous goods of which any unit is the equivalent of any other unit.

future goods—goods that exist physically but are not owned by the seller and goods that have not yet been produced.

(G)

garnishment—the name given in some states to attachment proceedings.

general agent—agent authorized by the principal to transact all affairs in connection with a particular type of business or trade or to transact all business at a certain place.

general jurisdiction—the power to hear and decide most controversies involving legal rights and duties.

gift—title to an owner's personal property voluntarily transferred by a party not receiving anything in exchange.

gift causa mortis—gift, made by the donor in the belief that death was immediate and impending, that is revoked or is revocable under certain circumstances.

good faith—absence of knowledge of any defects or problems.

good faith—absence of knowledge of any defects in or problems; "pure heart and an empty head."

goods—anything movable at the time it is identified as the subject of a transaction.

gratuitous bailment—bailment in which the bailee does not receive any compensation or advantage.

gray market goods—foreign-made goods with U.S. trademarks brought into the United States by a third party without the consent of the trademark owners to compete with these owners.

grease payments—(facilitation payments) legal payments to speed up or ensure performance of normal government duties.

guarantor—one who undertakes the obligation of guaranty.

guaranty—agreement or promise to answer for a debt; an undertaking to pay the debt of another if the creditor first sues the debtor.

guaranty of collection—form of guaranty in which creditor cannot proceed against guarantor until after proceeding against debtor.

guaranty of payment—absolute promise to pay when a debtor defaults.

guest—transient who contracts for a room or site at a hotel.

(H)

hearsay evidence—statements made out of court that are offered in court as proof of the information contained in the statements and that, subject to many exceptions, are not admissible in evidence.

"hell or high water" clause—lease agreement clause that requires the lessee to continue paying regardless of any problems with the lease.

holder—someone in possession of an instrument that runs to that person (i.e., is made payable to that person, is indorsed to that person, or is bearer paper).

holder in due course—a holder who has given value, taken in good faith without notice of dishonor, defenses, or that instrument is overdue, and who is afforded special rights or status.

holder through a holder in due course—holder of an instrument who attains holder-in-due-course status because a holder in due course has held it previous to him or her.

homeowners insurance policy—combination of standard fire insurance and comprehensive personal liability insurance.

hotelkeeper—one regularly engaged in the business of offering living accommodations to all transient persons.

hull insurance—insurance that covers physical damage on a freight-moving vessel.

(I)

identification—point in the transaction when the buyer acquires an interest in the goods subject to the contract.

identified—term applied to particular goods selected by either the buyer or the seller as the goods called for by the sales contract.

identity theft—use of another's credit tools, social security number, or other IDs to obtain cash, goods, or credit without permission.

illusory promise—promise that in fact does not impose any obligation on the promisor.

impeach—using prior inconsistent evidence to challenge the credibility of a witness.

implied contract—contract expressed by conduct or implied or deduced from the facts.

implied warranty—warranty that was not made but is implied by law.

implied warranty of merchantability—group of promises made by the seller, the most important of which is that the goods are fit for the ordinary purposes for which they are sold.

impostor rule—an exception to the rules on liability for forgery that covers situations such as the embezzling payroll clerk.

in pari delicto—equally guilty; used in reference to a transaction as to which relief will not be granted to either party because both are equally guilty of wrongdoing.

incidental authority—authority of an agent that is reasonably necessary to execute express authority.

incidental damages—incurred by the nonbreaching party as part of the process of trying to cover (buy substitute goods) or sell (selling subject matter of contract to another); includes storage fees, commissions, and the like.

incontestability clause—provision that after the lapse of a specified time the insurer cannot dispute the policy on the ground of misrepresentation or fraud of the insured or similar wrongful conduct.

incorporation by reference—contract consisting of both the original or skeleton document and the detailed statement that is incorporated in it.

indemnity—right of a person secondarily liable to require that a person primarily liable pay for loss sustained when the secondary party discharges the obligation that the primary party should have discharged; the right of an agent to be paid the amount of any loss or damage sustained without fault because of obedience to the principal's instructions; an undertaking by one person for a consideration to pay another person a sum of money to indemnify that person when a specified loss is incurred.

indemnity contract—agreement by one person, for consideration, to pay another person a sum of money in the event that the other person sustains a specified loss.

independent contractor—contractor who undertakes to perform a specified task according to the terms of a contract but over whom the other contracting party has no control except as provided for by the contract.

indorsee—party to whom special indorsement is made.

indorsement—signature of the payee on an instrument.

indorser—secondary party (or obligor) on a note.

informal contract—simple oral or written contract.

informal settlements—negotiated disposition of a matter before an administrative agency, generally without public sanctions.

infringement—violation of trademarks, patents, or copyrights by copying or using material without permission.

injunction—order of a court of equity to refrain from doing (negative injunction) or to do (affirmative or mandatory injunction) a specified act.

inland marine—insurance that covers domestic shipments of goods over land and inland waterways.

insider—full-time corporate employee or a director or their relatives.

insolvency—excess of debts and liabilities over assets, or inability to pay debts as they mature.

instruction—summary of the law given to jurors by the judge before deliberation begins.

insurable interest—the right to hold a valid insurance policy on a person or property.

insurance—a plan of security against risks by charging the loss against a fund created by the payments made by policyholders.

insurance agent—agent of an insurance company.

insurance broker—independent contractor who is not employed by any one insurance company.

insured—person to whom the promise in an insurance contract is made.

insurer—promisor in an insurance contract.

integrity—the adherence to one's values and principles despite the costs and consequences.

intellectual property rights—trademark, copyright, and patent rights protected by law.

intended beneficiary—third person of a contract whom the contract is intended to benefit.

intentional infliction of emotional distress—tort that produces mental anguish caused by conduct that exceeds all bounds of decency.

intentional torts—civil wrong that results from intentional conduct.

inter vivos gift—any transaction that takes place between living persons and creates rights prior to the death of any of them.

interest in the authority—form of agency in which an agent has been given or paid for the right to exercise authority.

interest in the subject matter—form of agency in which an agent is given an interest in the property with which that agent is dealing.

intermediary bank—bank between the originator and the beneficiary bank in the transfer of funds.

interrogatories—written questions used as a discovery tool that must be answered under oath.

invasion of privacy—tort of intentional intrusion into the private affairs of another.

investigative consumer report—report on a person based on personal investigation and interviews.

involuntary bankruptcy—proceeding in which a creditor or creditors file the petition for relief with the bankruptcy court.

issuer—party who issues a document such as a letter of credit or a document of title such as a warehouse receipt or bill of lading.

(J)

joint tenancy—estate held jointly by two or more with the right of survivorship as between them, unless modified by statute.

joint venture—relationship in which two or more persons or firms combine their labor or property for a single undertaking and share profits and losses equally unless otherwise agreed.

judge—primary officer of the court.

judgment n.o.v.,—or *non obstante veredicto* (notwithstanding the verdict), a judgment entered after verdict upon the motion of the losing party on the ground that the verdict is so wrong that a judgment should be entered the opposite of the verdict.

judicial branch—the branch of government (courts) formed to interpret the laws.

judicial triage—court management tool used by judges to expedite certain cases in which time is of the essence, such as asbestos cases in which the plaintiffs are gravely ill.

jurisdiction—the power of a court to hear and determine a given class of cases; the power to act over a particular defendant.

jurisdictional rule of reason—rule that balances the vital interests, including laws and policies, of the United States with those of a foreign country.

jury—a body of citizens sworn by a court to determine by verdict the issues of fact submitted to them.

(L)

law—the order or pattern of rules that society establishes to govern the conduct of individuals and the relationships among them.

lease—agreement between the owner of property and a tenant by which the former agrees to give possession of the property to the latter for payment of rent. (Parties–landlord or lessor, tenant or lessee)

legislative branch—the branch of government (e.g., Congress) formed to make the laws.

letter of credit—commercial device used to guarantee payment to a seller, primarily in an international business transaction.

liability insurance—covers the shipowner's liability if the ship causes damage to another ship or its cargo.

libel—written or visual defamation without legal justification.

licensing—transfer of technology rights to a product so that it may be produced by a different business organization in a foreign country in exchange for royalties and other payments as agreed.

limitation-of-liability clause—provision in a contract stating that one of the parties shall not be liable for damages in case of breach; also called an *exculpatory clause.*

limited defenses—defenses available to secondary parties if the presenting party is a holder in due course.

limited (special) jurisdiction—the authority to hear only particular kinds of cases.

limited warranty—any warranty that does not provide the complete protection of a full warranty.

liquidated damages—damages established in advance of breach as an alternative to establishing compensatory damages at the time of the breach.

liquidated damages clause—specification of exact compensation in case of a breach of contract.

liquidation—process of converting property into money whether of particular items of property or of all the assets of a business or an estate.

living-document view—the term used when a constitution is interpreted according to changes in conditions.

lottery—any plan by which a consideration is given for a chance to win a prize; it consists of three elements: (1) there must be a payment of money or something of value for an opportunity to win, (2) a prize must be available, and (3) the prize must be offered by lot or chance.

(M)

mailbox rule—timing for acceptance tied to proper acceptance.

maker—party who writes or creates a promissory note.

malpractice—when services are not properly rendered in accordance with commonly accepted standards; negligence by a professional in performing his or her skill.

marine insurance—policies that cover perils relating to the transportation of goods.

market power—the ability to control price and exclude competitors.

mask work—specific form of expression embodied in a chip design, including the stencils used in manufacturing semiconductor chip products.

mass picketing—illegal tactic of employees massing together in great numbers to effectively shut down entrances of the employer's facility.

means test—new standard under the Reform Act that requires the court to find that the debtor does not have the means to repay creditors; goes beyond the past requirement of petitions being granted on the simple assertion of the debtor saying, "I have debts."

mediation—the settlement of a dispute through the use of a messenger who carries to each side of the dispute the issues and offers in the case.

merchant—seller who deals in specific goods classified by the UCC.

minitrial—a trial held on portions of the case or certain issues in the case.

***Miranda* warnings**—warnings required to prevent self-incrimination in a criminal matter.

mirror image rule—common law contract rule on acceptance that requires language to be absolutely the same as the offer, unequivocal and unconditional.

misdemeanor—criminal offense with a sentence of less than one year that is neither treason nor a felony.

misrepresentation—false statement of fact, although made innocently without any intent to deceive.

mistrial—a court's declaration that terminates a trial and postpones it to a later date; commonly entered when evidence has been of a highly prejudicial character or when a juror has been guilty of misconduct.

money—medium of exchange.

money order—draft issued by a bank or a nonbank.

moral relativism—takes into account motivation and circumstance to determine whether an act was ethical.

most-favored-nation clause—clause in treaties between countries whereby any privilege subsequently granted to a third country in relation to a given treaty subject is extended to the other party to the treaty.

motion for summary judgment—request that the court decide a case on basis of law only because there are no material issues disputed by the parties.

motion to dismiss—a pleading that may be filed to attack the adverse party's pleading as not stating a cause of action or a defense.

(N)

natural law—a system of principles to guide human conduct independent of, and sometimes contrary to, enacted law and discovered by man's rational intelligence.

necessaries—things indispensable or absolutely necessary for the sustenance of human life.

negligence—failure to exercise due care under the circumstances in consequence of which harm is proximately caused to one to whom the defendant owed a duty to exercise due care.

negligence—failure to exercise due care under the circumstances that results in harm proximately caused to one owed a duty to exercise due care.

negotiability—quality of an instrument that affords special rights and standing.

negotiable bill of lading—document of title that by its terms calls for goods to be delivered "to the bearer" or "to the order of" a named person.

negotiable instruments—drafts, promissory notes, checks, and certificates of deposit that, in proper form, give special rights as "negotiable commercial paper."

negotiable warehouse receipt—receipt that states the covered goods will be delivered "to the bearer" or "to the order of."

negotiation—the transfer of commercial paper by indorsement and delivery by the person to whom it is then payable in the case of order paper and by physical transfer in the case of bearer paper.

nominal damages—nominal sum awarded the plaintiff in order to establish that legal rights have been violated although the plaintiff in fact has not sustained any actual loss or damages.

nonconsumer lease—lease that does not satisfy the definition of a consumer lease; also known as a *commercial lease.*

nonnegotiable bill of lading—see *straight bill of lading.*

nonnegotiable instrument—contract, note, or draft that does not meet negotiability requirements of Article 3.

nonnegotiable warehouse receipt—receipt that states the covered goods received will be delivered to a specific person.

notice of dishonor—notice that an instrument has been dishonored; such notice can be oral, written, or electronic but is subject to time limitations.

novation—substitution for an old contract with a new one that either replaces an existing obligation with a new obligation or replaces an original party with a new party.

(O)

obligee—promisee who can claim the benefit of the obligation.

obligor—promisor.

ocean marine—policies that cover transportation of goods in vessels in international and coastal trade.

offer—expression of an offeror's willingness to enter into a contractual agreement.

offeree—person to whom an offer is made.

offeror—person who makes an offer.

ombudsman—a government official designated by a statute to examine citizen complaints.

open-end mortgage—mortgage given to secure additional loans to be made in the future as well as to secure the original loan.

open meeting law—law that requires advance notice of agency meeting and public access.

opening statements—statements by opposing attorneys that tell the jury what their cases will prove.

operation of law—attaching of certain consequences to certain facts because of legal principles that operate automatically as contrasted with consequences that arise because of the voluntary action of a party designed to create those consequences.

option contract—contract to hold an offer to make a contract open for a fixed period of time.

order of relief—The order from the bankruptcy judge that starts the protection for the debtor; when the order of relief is entered by the court, the debtor's creditors must stop all proceedings and work through the bankruptcy court to recover debts (if possible). Court finding that creditors have met the standards for bankruptcy petitions.

order paper—instrument payable to the order of a party.

original jurisdiction—the authority to hear a controversy when it is first brought to court.

originator—party who originates the funds transfer.

output contract—contract of a producer to sell its entire production or output to a buyer.

overdraft—negative balance in a drawer's account.

(P)

parol evidence rule—rule that prohibits the introduction into evidence of oral or written statements made prior to or contemporaneously with the execution of a complete written contract, deed, or instrument, in the absence of clear proof of fraud, accident, or mistake causing the omission of the statement in question.

partially disclosed principal—principal whose existence is made known but whose identity is not.

party—person involved in a legal transaction; may be a natural person, an artificial person (e.g., a corporation), or an unincorporated enterprise (e.g., a government agency).

past consideration—something that has been performed in the past and which, therefore, cannot be consideration for a promise made in the present.

payable to order—term stating that a negotiable instrument is payable to the order of any person described in it or to a person or order.

payee—party to whom payment is to be made.

payment order—direction given by an originator to his or her bank or by any bank to a subsequent bank to make a specified funds transfer.

perfected security interest—security interest with priority because of filing, possession, automatic or temporary priority status.

personal property—property that is movable or intangible, or rights in such things.

personal representative—administrator or executor who represents decedents under UPC.

physical duress—threat of physical harm to person or property.

plaintiff—the party who initiates a lawsuit.

pleadings—the papers filed by the parties in an action in order to set forth the facts and frame the issues to be tried, although, under some systems, the pleadings merely give notice or a general indication of the nature of the issues.

pledge—bailment given as security for the payment of a debt or the performance of an obligation owed to the pledgee. (Parties– pledgor, pledgee)

police power—the power to govern; the power to adopt laws for the protection of the public health, welfare, safety, and morals.

policy—paper evidencing the contract of insurance.

positive law—law enacted and codified by governmental authority.

postdate—to insert or place on an instrument a later date than the actual date on which it was executed.

power of attorney—written authorization to an agent by the principal.

precedent—a decision of a court that stands as the law for a particular problem in the future.

predatory lending—A practice on the part of the subprime lending market whereby lenders take advantage of less sophisticated consumers or those who are desperate for funds by using the lenders' superior bargaining positions to obtain credit terms that go well beyond compensating them for their risk.

predicate act—qualifying underlying offense for RICO liability.

preemption—the federal government's superior regulatory position over state laws on the same subject area.

preferences—transfers of property by a debtor to one or more specific creditors to enable these creditors to obtain payment for debts owed.

preferential transfers—certain transfers of money or security interests in the time frame just prior to bankruptcy that can be set aside if voidable.

presentment—formal request for payment on an instrument.

price discrimination—the charging practice by a seller of different prices to different buyers for commodities of similar grade and quality, resulting in reduced competition or a tendency to create a monopoly.

prima facie—evidence that, if believed, is sufficient by itself to lead to a particular conclusion.

primary party—party to whom the holder or holder in due course must turn first to obtain payment.

primary picketing—legal presentations in front of a business notifying the public of a labor dispute.

primum non nocere—above all do no harm.

principal—person or firm who employs an agent; person who, with respect to a surety, is primarily liable to the third person or creditor; property held in trust.

principal debtor—original borrower or debtor.

private carrier—carrier owned by the shipper, such as a company's own fleet of trucks.

private law—the rules and regulations parties agree to as part of their contractual relationships.

privileges and immunities clause—a clause that entitles a person going into another state to make contracts, own property, and engage in business to the same extent as citizens of that state.

privity—succession or chain of relationship to the same thing or right, such as privity of contract, privity of estate, privity of possession.

privity of contract—relationship between a promisor and the promisee.

pro rata—proportionately, or divided according to a rate or standard.

procedural law—the law that must be followed in enforcing rights and liabilities.

process—paperwork served personally on a defendant in a civil case.

product disparagement—false statements made about a product or business.

promisee—person to whom a promise is made.

promisor—person who makes a promise.

promissory estoppel—doctrine that a promise will be enforced although it is not supported by consideration when the promisor should have reasonably expected that the promise would induce action or forbearance of a definite and substantial character on the part of the promised and injustice can be avoided only by enforcement of the promise.

promissory note—unconditional promise in writing made by one person to another, signed by the maker engaging to pay on demand, or at a definite time, a sum certain in money to order or to bearer. (Parties—maker, payee)

proof of claim—written statement, signed by the creditor or an authorized representative, setting forth any claim made against the debtor and the basis for it.

property report—condensed version of a property development statement filed with the secretary of HUD and given to a prospective customer at least 48 hours before signing a contract to buy or lease property.

prosecutor—party who originates a criminal proceeding.

public policy—certain objectives relating to health, morals, and integrity of government that the law seeks to advance by declaring invalid any contract that conflicts with those objectives even though there is no statute expressly declaring such a contract illegal.

public warehouses—entities that serve the public generally without discrimination.

pump-and-dump—self-touting a stock to drive its price up and then selling it.

punitive damages—damages, in excess of those required to compensate the plaintiff for the wrong done, that are imposed in order to punish the defendant because of the particularly wanton or willful character of wrongdoing; also called *exemplary damages*.

purchase money security interest (PMSI)—the security interest in the goods a seller sells on credit that become the collateral for the creditor/seller.

Q

qualified indorsement—an indorsement that includes words such as "without recourse" that disclaims certain liability of the indorser to a maker or a drawee.

qualified privilege—media privilege to print inaccurate information without liability for defamation, so long as a retraction is printed and there was no malice.

quantum meruit—as much as deserved; an action brought for the value of the services rendered the defendant when there was no express contract as to the purchase price.

quasi contract—court-imposed obligation to prevent unjust enrichment in the absence of a contract.

quasi-judicial proceedings—forms of hearings in which the rules of evidence and procedure are more relaxed but each side still has a chance to be heard.

(R)

Racketeer Influenced and Corrupt Organizations (RICO) Act—federal law, initially targeting organized crime, that has expanded in scope and provides penalties and civil recovery for multiple criminal offenses, or a pattern of racketeering.

real property—land and all rights in land.

recognizance—obligation entered into before a court to do some act, such as to appear at a later date for a hearing. Also called a *contract of record*.

recross-examination—an examination by the other side's attorney that follows the redirect examination.

redirect examination—questioning after cross-examination, in which the attorney for the witness testifying may ask the same witness other questions to overcome effects of the cross-examination.

reference to a third person—settlement that allows a nonparty to resolve the dispute.

reformation—remedy by which a written instrument is corrected when it fails to express the actual intent of both parties because of fraud, accident, or mistake.

remand—term used when an appellate court sends a case back to trial court for additional hearings or a new trial.

remedy—action or procedure that is followed in order to enforce a right or to obtain damages for injury to a right.

rent-a-judge plan—dispute resolution through private courts with judges paid to be referees for the cases.

representative capacity—action taken by one on behalf of another, as the act of a personal representative on behalf of a decedent's estate, or action taken both on one's behalf and on behalf of others, as a shareholder bringing a representative action.

repudiation—result of a buyer or seller refusing to perform the contract as stated.

request for production of documents—discovery tool for uncovering paper evidence in a case.

requirements contract—contract in which the buyer buys its needs (requirements) from the seller.

rescission—action of one party to a contract to set the contract aside when the other party is guilty of a breach of the contract.

reservation of rights—assertion by a party to a contract that even though a tendered performance (e.g., a defective product) is accepted, the right to damages for nonconformity to the contract is reserved.

respondeat superior—doctrine that the principal or employer is vicariously liable for the unauthorized torts committed by an agent or employee while acting within the scope of the agency or the course of the employment, respectively.

restrictive indorsement—an indorsement that restricts further transfer, such as in trust for or to the use of some other person, is conditional, or for collection or deposit.

reverse—the term used when the appellate court sets aside the verdict or judgment of a lower court.

reversible error—an error or defect in court proceedings of so serious a nature that on appeal the appellate court will set aside the proceedings of the lower court.

right—legal capacity to require another person to perform or refrain from an action.

right of first refusal—right of a party to meet the terms of a proposed contract before it is executed, such as a real estate purchase agreement.

right of privacy—the right to be free from unreasonable intrusion by others.

right to cure—second chance for a seller to make a proper tender of conforming goods.

right-to-work laws—laws restricting unions and employees from negotiating clauses in their collective bargaining agreements that make union membership compulsory.

risk—peril or contingency against which the insured is protected by the contract of insurance.

risk of loss—in contract performance, the cost of damage or injury to the goods contracted for.

Robinson-Patman Act—a federal statute designed to eliminate price discrimination in interstate commerce.

(S)

sale on approval—term indicating that no sale takes place until the buyer approves or accepts the goods.

sale or return—sale in which the title to the property passes to the buyer at the time of the transaction but the buyer is given the option of returning the property and restoring the title to the seller.

search engine—Internet service used to locate Web sites.

search warrant—judicial authorization for a search of property where there is the expectation of privacy.

seasonable—timely.

secondary parties—called *secondary obligors* under Revised Article 3; parties to an instrument to whom holders turn when the primary party, for whatever reason, fails to pay the instrument.

secondary picketing—picketing an employer with which a union has no dispute to persuade the employer to stop doing business with a party to the dispute; generally illegal under the NLRA.

secrecy laws—confidentiality laws applied to home-country banks.

secured party—person owed the money, whether as a seller or a lender, in a secured transaction in personal property.

secured transaction—credit sale of goods or a secured loan that provides special protection for the creditor.

security agreement—agreement of the creditor and the debtor that the creditor will have a security interest.

security interest—property right that enables the creditor to take possession of the property if the debtor does not pay the amount owed.

self-help repossession—creditor's right to repossess the collateral without judicial proceedings.

selling on consignment—entrusting a person with possession of property for the purpose of sale.

semiconductor chip product—product placed on a piece of semiconductor material in accordance with a predetermined pattern that is intended to perform electronic circuitry functions.

service mark—mark that identifies a service.

severalty—ownership of property by one person.

shared powers—powers that are held by both state and national governments.

Sherman Antitrust Act—a federal statute prohibiting combinations and contracts in restraint of interstate trade, now generally inapplicable to labor union activity.

shop right—right of an employer to use in business without charge an invention discovered by an employee during working hours and with the employer's material and equipment.

shopkeeper's privilege—right of a store owner to detain a suspected shoplifter based on reasonable cause and for a reasonable time without resulting liability for false imprisonment.

situational ethics—a flexible standard of ethics that permits an examination of circumstances and motivation before attaching the label of right or wrong to conduct.

Sixth Amendment—the U.S. constitutional amendment that guarantees a speedy trial.

slander—defamation of character by spoken words or gestures.

slander of title—malicious making of false statements as to a seller's title.

small claims courts—courts that resolve disputes between parties when those disputes do not exceed a minimal level; no lawyers are permitted; the parties represent themselves.

soliciting agent—salesperson.

sovereign compliance doctrine—doctrine that allows a defendant to raise as an affirmative defense to an antitrust action the fact that the defendant's actions were compelled by a foreign state.

sovereign immunity doctrine—doctrine that states that a foreign sovereign generally cannot be sued unless an exception to the Foreign Sovereign Immunities Act of 1976 applies.

special agent—agent authorized to transact a specific transaction or to do a specific act.

special drawing rights (SDRs)—rights that allow a country to borrow enough money from other International Money Fund (IMF) members to permit that country to maintain the stability of its currency's relationship to other world currencies.

special indorsement—an indorsement that specifies the person to whom the instrument is indorsed.

specific lien—right of a creditor to hold particular property or assert a lien on particular property of the debtor because of the creditor's having done work on or having some other association with the property, as distinguished from having a lien generally against the assets of the debtor merely because the debtor is indebted to the lien holder.

specific performance—action brought to compel the adverse party to perform a contract on the theory that merely suing for damages for its breach will not be an adequate remedy.

stakeholder analysis—the term used when a decision maker views a problem from different perspectives and measures the impact of a decision on various groups.

stakeholders—those who have a stake, or interest, in the activities of a corporation; stakeholders include employees, members of the community in which the corporation operates, vendors, customers, and any others who are affected by the actions and decisions of the corporation.

stale check—a check whose date is longer than six months ago.

standby letter—letter of credit for a contractor ensuring he will complete the project as contracted.

stare decisis—"let the decision stand"; the principle that the decision of a court should serve as a guide or precedent and control the decision of a similar case in the future.

status quo ante—original positions of the parties.

statute of frauds—statute that, in order to prevent fraud through the use of perjured testimony, requires that certain kinds of transactions be evidenced in writing in order to be binding or enforceable.

statute of limitations—statute that restricts the period of time within which an action may be brought.

statutory law—legislative acts declaring, commanding, or prohibiting something.

stop payment order—order by a depositor to the bank to refuse to make payment of a check when presented for payment.

straight (or nonnegotiable) bill of lading—document of title that consigns transported goods to a named person.

strict liability—civil wrong for which there is absolute liability because of the inherent danger in the underlying activity, for example, the use of explosives.

strict tort liability—product liability theory that imposes liability upon the manufacturer, seller, or distributor of goods for harm caused by defective goods.

subject matter jurisdiction—judicial authority to hear a particular type of case.

subprime lending market—A credit market that makes loans to high-risk consumers (those who have bankruptcies, no credit history, or a poor credit history), often loaning money to pay off other debts the consumer has due.

subrogation—right of a party secondarily liable to stand in the place of the creditor after making payment to the creditor and to enforce the creditor's right against the party primarily liable in order to obtain indemnity from such primary party.

substantial impairment—material defect in a good.

substantial performance—equitable rule that if a good-faith attempt to perform does not precisely meet the terms of the agreement, the agreement will still be considered complete if the essential purpose of the contract is accomplished.

substantive law—the law that defines rights and liabilities.

substitute check—electronic image of a paper check that a bank can create and that has the same legal effect as the original instrument.

substitution—substitution of a new contract between the same parties.

sum certain—amount due under an instrument that can be computed from its face with only reference to interest rates.

summary jury trial—a mock or dry-run trial for parties to get a feel for how their cases will play to a jury.

summation—the attorney address that follows all the evidence presented in court and sums up a case and recommends a particular verdict be returned by the jury.

surety—obligor of a suretyship; primarily liable for the debt or obligation of the principal debtor.

suretyship—pledge or guarantee to pay the debt or be liable for the default of another.

symbolic delivery—delivery of goods by delivery of the means of control, such as a key or a relevant document of title, such as a negotiable bill of lading; also called *constructive delivery*.

(T)

takeover laws—laws that guard against unfairness in corporate takeover situations.

tariff—(1) domestically—government-approved schedule of charges that may be made by a regulated business, such as a common carrier or warehouser; (2) internationally—tax imposed by a country on goods crossing its borders, without regard to whether the purpose is to raise revenue or to discourage the traffic in the taxed goods.

teller's check—draft drawn by a bank on another bank in which it has an account.

temporary perfection—perfection given for a limited period of time to creditors.

tenancy by entirety or **tenancy by entireties**—transfer of property to both husband and wife.

tenancy in common—relationship that exists when two or more persons own undivided interests in property.

tender—goods have arrived, are available for pickup, and buyer is notified.

term insurance—policy written for a specified number of years that terminates at the end of that period.

termination statement—document (record), which may be requested by a paid-up debtor, stating that a security interest is no longer claimed under the specified financing statement.

third-party beneficiary—third person whom the parties to a contract intend to benefit by the making of the contract and to confer upon such person the right to sue for breach of contract.

time draft—bill of exchange payable at a stated time after sight or at a definite time.

tort—civil wrong that interferes with one's property or person.

trade dress—product's total image including its overall packaging look.

trade libel—written defamation about a product or service.

trade secret—any formula, device, or compilation of information that is used in one's business and is of such a nature that it provides an advantage over competitors who do not have the information.

trademark—mark that identifies a product.

traveler's check—check that is payable on demand provided it is countersigned by the person whose specimen signature appears on the check.

treble damages—three times the damages actually sustained.

trespass—unauthorized action with respect to person or property.

trial *de novo*—a trial required to preserve the constitutional right to a jury trial by allowing an appeal to proceed as though there never had been any prior hearing or decision.

tripartite—three-part division (of government).

trustee in bankruptcy—impartial person elected to administer the debtor's estate.

tying—the anticompetitive practice of requiring buyers to purchase one product in order to get another.

U

unconscionable—unreasonable, not guided or restrained by conscience and often referring to a contract grossly unfair to one party because of the superior bargaining powers of the other party.

underwriter—insurer.

undisclosed principal—principal on whose behalf an agent acts without disclosing to the third person the fact of agency or the identity of the principal.

undue influence—influence that is asserted upon another person by one who dominates that person.

unilateral contract—contract under which only one party makes a promise.

universal agent—agent authorized by the principal to do all acts that can lawfully be delegated to a representative.

universal defenses—defenses that are regarded as so basic that the social interest in preserving them outweighs the social interest of giving negotiable instruments the freely transferable qualities of money; accordingly, such defenses are given universal effect and may be raised against all holders.

USA Patriot Act—federal law that, among other things, imposes reporting requirements on banks.

usage of trade—language and customs of an industry.

usury—lending money at an interest rate that is higher than the maximum rate allowed by law.

uttering—crime of issuing or delivering a forged instrument to another person.

V

valid—legal.

valid contract—agreement that is binding and enforceable.

value—consideration or antecedent debt or security given in exchange for the transfer of a negotiable instrument or creation of a security interest.

vicarious liability—imposing liability for the fault of another.

void agreement—agreement that cannot be enforced.

voidable contract—agreement that is otherwise binding and enforceable but may be rejected at the option of one of the parties as the result of specific circumstances.

voidable title—title of goods that carries with it the contingency of an underlying problem.

voir dire examination—the preliminary examination of a juror or a witness to ascertain fitness to act as such.

voluntary bankruptcy—proceeding in which the debtor files the petition for relief.

waiver—release or relinquishment of a known right or objection.

warehouse—entity engaged in the business of storing the goods of others for compensation.

warehouse receipt—receipt issued by the warehouse for stored goods. Regulated by the UCC, which clothes the receipt with some degree of negotiability.

warrant—authorization via court order to search private property for tools or evidence of a crime.

warranty—promise either express or implied about the nature, quality, or performance of the goods.

warranty against encumbrances—warranty that there are no liens or other encumbrances to goods except those noted by seller.

warranty of title—implied warranty that title to the goods is good and transfer is proper.

White-Collar Crime Penalty Enhancement Act of 2002—federal reforms passed as a result of the collapses of companies such as Enron; provides for longer sentences and higher fines for both executives and companies.

white-collar crimes—crimes that do not use nor threaten to use force or violence or do not cause injury to persons or property.

whole life insurance—ordinary life insurance providing lifetime insurance protection.

writ of *certiorari*—order by the U.S. Supreme Court granting a right of review by the court of a lower court decision.

wrongfully dishonored—error by a bank in refusing to pay a check.

CASE INDEX

New cases to this edition are in red boldface. Opinion cases are in boldface type: cited cases are in Roman type.